ENGLISH HISTORICAL DOCUMENTS

General Editor
DAVID C. DOUGLAS
M.A., F.B.A.

ENGLISH HISTORICAL DOCUMENTS

General Editor: DAVID C. DOUGLAS, M.A., F.B.A.

*The following is a complete list of volumes in preparation; those marked * are already published*

Vol. I. *c.* 500–1042. DOROTHY WHITELOCK, M.A., LITT.D, F.S.A.

*Vol. II. 1042–1189. DAVID DOUGLAS, M.A., F.B.A., and G. W. GREENAWAY, M.A.

Vol. III. 1189–1327. HARRY ROTHWELL, M.A., PH.D.

Vol. IV. 1327–1485. A. HAMILTON THOMPSON, C.B.E., M.A., D.LITT., LL.D., F.B.A.

Vol. V. 1485–1558. C. H. WILLIAMS, M.A.

Vol. VI. 1558–1603. DOUGLAS PRICE, M.A., B.LITT., F.S.A.

Vol. VII. 1603–1660. MARY COATE, M.A.

Vol. VIII. 1660–1714. ANDREW BROWNING, M.A., D.LITT.

Vol. IX. 1714–1783. D. B. HORN, M.A., D.LITT.

VOL. X. 1783–1832. A. ASPINALL, M.A., LITT.D.

Vol. XI. 1833–1874. G. M. YOUNG, M.A., and W. D. HANDCOCK, M.A., B.LITT.

Vol. XII. 1874–1914. G. M. YOUNG, M.A., and W. D. HANDCOCK, M.A., B.LITT.

Vol. XIII. American Colonial Documents to 1776. MERRILL JENSEN, M.A., PH.D.

GENERAL PREFACE

ENGLISH HISTORICAL DOCUMENTS is a work designed to meet a present need. Its purpose is to make generally accessible a wide selection of the fundamental sources of English history.

During the past half-century there has been an immense accumulation of historical material, but only a fraction of this has been made readily available to the majority of those who teach or who study history. The transcendent importance of the original authorities is recognized, but direct approach to them remains difficult, and even some of the basic texts (which are frequently quoted) are hard to consult. A gulf has thus opened between the work of the specialist scholar and those students, both at schools and universities, who best can profit by his labours. Historical studies tend too often today to consist of a commentary on documents which are not included in the available books; and, in the absence of any representative and accessible collection of the sources, the formation of opinion proceeds without that direct study of the evidence which alone can give validity to historical judgment. Correspondingly, the reading public outside schools and universities, has no adequate means of checking, by reference to the evidence itself, tendentious or partial interpretations of the past.

The editors of these volumes consider that this situation now calls for a remedy. They have striven to supply one by providing what they hope can be regarded as an authoritative work in primary reference.

An enterprise of this nature could only be effective if planned on a large scale. In scope and content, therefore, these volumes differ materially from the conventional "source-books" which usually contain only a restricted number of selected extracts. Here, within much wider limits, each editor has sought to produce a comprehensive *corpus* of evidence relating generally to the period with which he deals. His aim, in each case, has been to present the material with scholarly accuracy, and without bias. Editorial comment has thus been directed in the main towards making the evidence intelligible, and not to drawing conclusions from it. Full account has been taken of modern textual criticism to compile a reliable collection of authentic testimony, but the reader has in general been left to pass his own judgment upon this, and to appraise for himself the value of current historical verdicts. For this reason, everything in this work has been presented in such a manner as to be comprehensible by readers of English, and critical bibliographies have been added to assist further investigation.

The decision to display the texts (where necessary) in an English translation was thus dictated by the general purpose of this work. A translated text can, of course, never be a complete substitute for the original. But those who, today, can utilize a document in Anglo-Saxon, Latin or Old French are few, and are decreasing in number. This is certainly to be regretted. Nevertheless, there seems no adequate reason why the majority of those interested in English history should be arbitrarily deprived of the opportunity to consult the basic sources of their study. In this work, therefore, there is nothing that cannot be used by those who can only read English. At the same time, in every case where a translation appears, a reference is given to the place where the text in its original language may be found. In like manner, spelling and punctuation have been adapted to modern usage in all texts prior to 1714. After that date, all documents are in their original form.

The editors of these volumes are fully aware of the magnitude of the undertaking to which they have addressed themselves. They are conscious of the hazards of selecting from the inexhaustible store of historical material. They realize also the difficulties involved in editing so large a mass of very varied texts in accordance with the exigent demands of modern scholarship. They believe, however, that the essential prerequisite for the healthy development of English historical studies is wider acquaintance with the original authorities for English history. And they are content that their work should be judged by the degree to which they have succeeded in promoting this object.

DAVID DOUGLAS

VOLUME II

ENGLISH HISTORICAL DOCUMENTS

1042–1189

ENGLISH HISTORICAL DOCUMENTS

1042–1189

Edited by
DAVID C. DOUGLAS, M.A.
Fellow of the British Academy, and Professor of History in the University of Bristol

and

GEORGE W. GREENAWAY, M.A.
Lecturer on Medieval History, University College, Exeter

New York
OXFORD UNIVERSITY PRESS
1953

Printed in Great Britain

ACKNOWLEDGEMENTS

THE chief obligation incurred by the editors of this volume is to Miss S. I. Tucker, Senior Lecturer in English to the University of Bristol. Miss Tucker's translation of the Anglo-Saxon Chronicle has given a distinction to this book which it would not otherwise have possessed, and it has supplied a sound text which alone has permitted the arrangement and presentation of that source to be undertaken with confidence. Miss Tucker's contributions to this volume have not, however, been confined to the work for which she made herself directly responsible, for she has always been ready to place her expert linguistic knowledge at the disposal of the editors in connexion with any Anglo-Saxon document. They wish to record their lively gratitude for what she has done.

The editors have been permitted, in certain cases, to make use of translations which have previously been printed. They wish in particular to thank Sir Frank Stenton in respect of Nos. 205, 245, 257, 262, and 263; Miss Dorothy Whitelock in respect of Nos. 181, 183, 187, 188, and 189; and Miss A. J. Robertson in respect of Nos. 61, 173, 174, 175, 185, and 278. Nor could advantage have been taken of the kindness of these scholars, had not permission to do so been given by the publishers of their books. The titles of these are given at the head of the relevant documents, but the editors desire in this place to make grateful acknowledgment to the Clarendon Press in connexion with the work of Sir Frank Stenton cited above, and to the Cambridge University Press in connexion with the work of Miss Whitelock and Miss Robertson. With equal kindness the proprietors of the Victoria County History accorded permission (in connexion with Nos. 180, 205, 206, 208, 210, and 212) for use to be made of translations appearing in that work. Like permission was kindly given, in connexion with No. 211, by the Council of the Lincoln Record Society. Thanks are due to the Comptroller of H.M. Stationery Office for permission to include in this book translations of documents the originals of which have been printed by that office.

The debt of the Editors is not, however, to be discharged even by the grateful recognition of these specific obligations. Sir Frank Stenton has stood friend to this volume, and to the series of which it forms a part, ever since work was first begun upon it. Miss Whitelock has always been ready to answer the numerous questions which have been addressed to her. Mr. Douglas Jerrold has been fruitful in practical advice. And Mr. H. P. R. Finberg has made many valuable suggestions both as to the setting out of the texts and as to their matter. These are, moreover, only a few among those who have most generously assisted this protracted undertaking by their encouragement and counsel. To all of them the editors now tender their sincere thanks.

DAVID DOUGLAS
G. W. GREENAWAY

CONTENTS

Part II. GOVERNMENT AND ADMINISTRATION

A. SELECT DOCUMENTS OF A GENERAL NATURE RELATING TO THE ROYAL ADMINISTRATION

B. THE KING'S COURT AND HOUSEHOLD

C. THE SHERIFF AND LOCAL GOVERNMENT

D. JUDICIAL ORGANIZATION

(*a*) *Reports of trials*

(*b*) *Legal treatises and statements of procedure*

E. ROYAL FINANCE

(a) *Evidence relating to the Anglo-Saxon fiscal system*

(b) *Evidence relating to the origin of the Exchequer*

(c) *Evidence relating to the work of the Exchequer in the time of Henry II and before*

(d) *Select passages from the Pipe Rolls*

PART III. THE CHURCH

A. THE CHURCH IN ENGLAND, 1042–1089

(a) *Miscellaneous documents relating to the Church in England* (1042–1089)

B. THE CHURCH IN ENGLAND, 1089-1154

(a) *Material relating to the life and policy of Archbishop Anselm*

(b) *Church and State in the reign of Stephen*

(c) *Material relating to the establishment of the Cistercian Order in England*

C. THE CHURCH IN ENGLAND, 1154-1189

(a) *Thomas Becket and Henry II*

(i) Thomas Becket as chancellor and archbishop

(ii) The disputes between Henry II and Thomas Becket (1162–November 1164)

PAGE

(iii) Material relating to the dispute between Henry II and Thomas Becket during the period of the archbishop's exile (November 1164–November 1170)

(iv) The murder of Thomas Becket and its sequel (December 1170–February 1173)

PART IV. LAND AND PEOPLE

A. ENGLISH AGRARIAN SOCIETY, 1042–1189

(a) *Surveys and statements of services*

(b) *Select charters and 'wills' illustrating English agrarian society between 1042 and 1189*

B. THE DOMESDAY SURVEY

(*a*) *Evidence relating to the making of Domesday Book*

(*b*) *Domesday Book*

(*c*) *Surveys connected with Domesday Book*

C. ANGLO-NORMAN FEUDALISM

(a) The introduction of tenure by knight-service into England during the reign of William the Conqueror

(b) The Cartae Baronum *of 1166, being the returns made by his tenants-in-chief to King Henry II in respect of an inquiry instituted by him as to the knights enfeoffed on their honours*

(c) Select feudal charters

APPENDICES

INDEX TO TEXTS

INTRODUCTION

INTRODUCTION

(i) THE PERIOD

THE subject of this book is the history of England between 1042 and 1189. Its object is to display the evidence for that history, and to indicate the main texts on which must be based our knowledge of English development at that time. The general purpose of this volume thus calls for no comment, nor even (as may be hoped) for any justification. But the particular delimitation of the period with which it deals may none the less demand an explanation. The isolation of any historical epoch must always, to some extent, mask the essential flux in human affairs, and since all periods are ages of transition, to set up barriers between them can hardly fail, in one sense, to be misleading. Nevertheless, expediency demands the device, and it is not solely for reasons of convenience that it may, with proper qualifications, be defended. To say, for example, that a break in English growth occurred either in 1042 or 1189 would be manifestly untrue, but on the other hand it would be reasonable to assert that between these dates there took place changes in English society, and in English politics, so fundamental as to warrant their separate consideration. The period which is the subject of this book derives its unity from the working out of a single complex process. During the reign of Edward the Confessor there were posed those problems whose resolution entailed the Norman Conquest. In the reigns of William I and Henry I that Conquest was successfully concluded. With Henry II there were brought to completion many of the consequential developments which the Norman Conquest involved. Indeed, so notable was this transition and so spectacular were the events which brought it about that there is even a danger of forgetting the thread of continuity linking the England of Edward the Confessor with the England of Henry II. English history did not begin in 1066. Nor in any sense did it then end.

Partly because of its intrinsic importance and partly because of its dramatic character, this period has received perhaps more attention from historians than any other epoch in English medieval history, and the modern literature relating to the Norman Conquest covers almost the whole span of English prose.[1] As early as 1613 John Hayward produced what may be described as the first text-book of English history at this time, and the interest has never flagged. Thus in 1623 John Selden published his remarkable edition of Eadmer's *Historia Novorum*,

[1] For information about the secondary authorities for this period the reader is referred to the various bibliographies contained in this volume, and especially to that which immediately follows this essay. No particular reference is therefore made in the course of this introduction to the many modern works which have been gratefully used in its compilation. The footnotes to this introductory essay refer exclusively to texts subsequently printed in this book.

and six years later Sir Henry Spelman inaugurated the study of Anglo-Norman feudalism with his great essay on *Feuds and Tenures by Knight Service*. The legal antiquities of the eleventh century were likewise investigated in detail by Sir Robert Brady, Physician-in-Ordinary to Charles II, whilst Sir Matthew Hale, Lord Chief Justice of the King's Bench under the same king, devoted to the theme no less than forty pages of his notable *History of the Common Law*. Similarly, when Sir William Temple issued in 1695 his *Introduction to the History of England* it was found that five-sixths of that book were devoted to the Norman Conquest; the subject was treated again with great fullness in the standard Whig histories of Echard and Tyrell; and in the eighteenth century Abraham Farley devoted fifty years of his laborious life to produce in 1783 what is still the best edition of Domesday Book. Meanwhile Lord Lyttelton had cast a backward glance over the whole period in his long and comprehensive *Life of King Henry II*, and in the nineteenth century the work was fully sustained. Lingard's account of the period in his *History of England* was in many respects a notable performance, and Sir Francis Palgrave treated the theme in detail in his *Normandy and England*. Finally (to cite no other names), between 1867 and 1879 Edward Freeman, summing up in himself a long tradition, produced in five large octavo volumes the most elaborate history of the Norman Conquest which has ever been compiled.

This extensive production was, moreover, no less remarkable for its character than for its bulk. It was perhaps natural that a turning-point in English history should have provoked a mass of erudition which is staggering in its weight, but it is more surprising that a political crisis of the eleventh century should for generations have led statesmen and lawyers, pamphleteers and scribblers into a war of words. Yet so it was. Again and again, during centuries, the history of this remote age elicited from the most unlikely quarters a torrent of ink which exhibited both profound scholarship and ebullient polemic, and the most notable feature of the literature devoted to this theme is to be found in the manner in which it was inspired by current controversies or present political stress. Thus the exuberant nationalism of the seventeenth century was easily transferred to the age of William the Conqueror. John Hayward could praise the earliest Norman kings as men "who laid the foundations of this English Empire", and Sir William Temple could dilate on "the happy circumstances of this famous Conquest". Aristocratic prejudice tended in the same direction, and to assert descent from one who fought for William at Hastings came very early to be almost a matter of course in any noble family. Although the names of less than forty of King William's followers at Hastings can be vouched by express testimony, and although direct descent in the male line from any one of these would be very hard to establish, "to have come over with the Conqueror" is a boast not entirely unknown today.

In such manner has the Norman Conquest been treated as a matter for patriotic pride. But the same preoccupation with nationalism led to an equally strained interpretation in the opposite sense, and by many writers the Norman Conquest has been represented as a national tragedy. Thus Winston Churchill, father of the first duke of Marlborough, paid tribute to those who fought against William at Hastings as men "who bravely strove to save their country from the calamity of foreign servitude", and this conception has been endlessly reiterated. It also has entailed curious consequences. First propagated at a time when Puritanism was in the ascendant, it supplied the obvious occasion for a moral judgment. A famous passage in the chronicle of William of Malmesbury[1] thus gave the opportunity to John Milton to depict the Conquest as a punishment for the sins of England, and this view also has been frequently reproduced. Sir Francis Palgrave found an explanation of the Norman Conquest in a degeneracy in the Anglo-Saxon character, and Thomas Carlyle in the same sense re-echoed Milton with ringing emphasis.

> Without the Normans [he cried] what had it ever been? A gluttonous race of Jutes and Angles capable of no grand combinations; lumbering about in pot-bellied equanimity; not dreaming of heroic toil and silence and endurance such as leads to the high places of this universe and the golden mountain tops where dwell the spirits of the dawn.

It was a strange judgment strangely expressed, but it derived easily out of certain earlier notions of the Conquest. Moreover, certain writers, impressed with this sense of the Norman Conquest as a national humiliation, were strongly tempted to explain it away, and from the seventeenth century onwards there has been a continued effort in certain quarters to regard the period of Norman and Angevin rule in England as a kind of interruption – as an unprofitable interlude – in our national story. "For nearly two centuries after the Norman Conquest", asserts the writer of a deservedly popular manual, "there is no history of the English people." Only after the influence of the Conquest had passed away was it possible for the waking life of the nation to be resumed once more.

Whatever truth there may be in all, or any, of these diverse interpretations of eleventh-century history, it will be seen how easily they could be adapted to English political controversies. Despite a half-hearted attempt by certain writers such as Temple and Toland to draw an analogy between the first William and the third, it may broadly be said that the Conqueror was always regarded as in a special sense an enemy by the Whigs. The controversies of the Oxford Parliament in 1681 were thus embellished by a documented diatribe against the first Norman king which quoted Coke that it was neither "ingenious or prudent for Englishmen to deprave their birthright", and concluded that "the true honour of our worthy Saxon ancestors" should be supported. "Should we allow our

[1] No. 8 (pp. 290-291).

laws to have an uncertain original," added another writer in 1714, "I fear some people would of themselves fix their Original from William the First and . . . I don't know what ill use the Champions of Absolute monarchy may be inclined to make of such a concession."

It was a useful theory, and it could be profitably developed. William might be depicted as a tyrant, but, if proper advantage were to be taken of the story, it was necessary to assume that the people he subdued were imbued with Protestant sympathies, and possessed of democratic or at least Whig institutions. The attempt was made. As early as the time of Elizabeth, Matthew Parker had sponsored a great movement in Anglo-Saxon scholarship in the hope that he might find in the Old English Church a prototype of the reformed Establishment over which he was called to preside, and in 1709 another scholar called attention to "the Agreement of the reformed and the ancient Saxon church". But for the analogy to be made effective for propaganda it had to be pressed more particularly on the secular side, and in this manner there was prepared the still familiar picture of Anglo-Saxon society, not only anti-papal in sentiment, but also consisting of communities of freemen legislating for themselves in democratic communities which in the last resort could elect and depose their kings. The wheel had at last turned full circle. William the Conqueror was no longer the founder of British greatness: he had become the subverter of the English constitution. The Anglo-Saxons whom he overthrew were no longer a race of drink-sodden degenerates but the fit forebears of the Glorious Revolution.

The vast literature which has been so strangely devoted to this period is in no sense to be derided as merely an antiquarian curiosity, since it comprised work of magisterial learning, and the names of Selden and Spelman, of Brady, Wanley and Farley (to name no others) are themselves sufficient to redeem it from oblivion. Nevertheless, the topical controversies which Anglo-Norman history has provoked in the past have exercised an unhappy influence even upon some more recent work on eleventh-century England. Thus it is customary to regard the modern study of this period as beginning with the publication of Freeman's great book, and certainly it is those who have most knowledge of the age who are most conscious of its value. But in a real sense Freeman belonged in this respect to the earlier tradition. He too, like so many of his predecessors, treated the eleventh-century struggle almost as a matter of present politics, and judged it accordingly. He declared he would gladly have fought at Hastings as one of the supporters of the "patriotic leaders" of the "national party". Indeed, in one respect he carried these preconceptions a stage further. Many previous writers had compiled as history a political polemic against the Conqueror, but usually they had done this, not in the interests of Godwine and Harold, earls of Wessex, but in those of Edgar Atheling. For William Temple, Harold was "perfidious and insolent"; for Matthew Hale a "usurper". William's title, according to Blackstone was "altogether as good as Harold's". But to Freeman, Harold and Godwine were the true champions of English nationalism, they were the enemies of priestcraft; and, most strangely of all, they were to be numbered among the friends of constitutional government.

It was particularly unfortunate that Freeman's fine erudition, and his exhaustive knowledge of the chronicles of the age, should have been coloured by such partisanship, for, as a result, his book, though magisterial, was not definitive; and very much Anglo-Norman scholarship since his day has been marked, not so much by a development of his ideas, as by a reaction from them. The savage criticism supplied by John Horace Round thus influenced these studies for a generation and gave a new start to the investigation of feudalism in England, and also to the study of Domesday Book. At the same time a revulsion against the nationalistic treatment of the Norman Conquest has been stimulated by the impact upon English historical scholarship of a new assessment of the Scandinavian factor in English history. The agrarian investigations associated with the names of Maitland and Vinogradoff contributed to this, and Sir Frank Stenton, reinforcing his conclusions by the systematic study of English place-names, has brought this Scandinavian learning into direct relation with eleventh-century England. The Scandinavian sympathies of large regions of eleventh-century England are today appreciated better than ever before, and the crisis of 1066 is visualized less as a struggle between 'English' and 'Normans' than as a triangular contest between a Norman duke, a Norwegian king, and a West-Saxon earl, as a result of which it would be determined whether for the remainder of the Middle Ages the development of England would be linked up with Latin Europe or the Scandinavian north.

Finally, the interpretation of the period has in recent years been vitally affected by the development of Anglo-Saxon studies. The real weakness of Freeman's treatment of his theme was not that he overpraised Anglo-Saxon culture but that he championed the Old English State for the least admirable of its features; and an appreciation of what the Normans accomplished in England should involve no disparagement of the Anglo-Saxon achievement. In agrarian organization, in the courts of shire and hundred, in the connexion of these with the monarchy, and in many other ways, the work of the older order was, as will be seen, to survive into the new. Moreover, it would be possible in acknowledging what the Normans created in England to forget what they destroyed. Judged by the standards of art and literature England in the middle of the eleventh century was one of the most civilized states of Europe. Her metal work was famous, and her coinage was beautiful. English embroidery was particularly esteemed, and English book-production, particularly that of the Winchester school, was of great beauty. Similarly, in the eleventh century, England was continuing to produce with unabated vigour a vernacular literature not to be paralleled in contemporary Europe. The homilies of Ælfric, who was not to find a worthy successor as a translator of the Bible until the days of William Tyndale, were matched by the eloquence of Wulfstan and by the historical prose of the Anglo-Saxon Chronicles. If England can be judged as politically decadent in 1066, it is by no means so certain that this decadence had then as yet seriously affected the civilization which the Saxons had created but which they were no longer able to defend.

This vernacular culture was by the Norman Conquest brought to an untimely end, and after an interval its place was to be taken in England by a more cosmopolitan civilization which drew its inspiration from the general movements of Latin Europe. Henceforth for more than a century, with rare exceptions, whatever was thought or written by Englishmen was thought and written in Latin; and the place of Ælfric as an English scholar was to be taken by men like John of Salisbury, a humanist equally at home in France and in England. Lanfranc and Anselm were to make their highly individual contributions to theology as part of continental controversies, and the same tendency was at length to appear in education. The history of English universities falls in the main outside this period, but the obscure origins of Oxford may probably be referred to the reign of Henry II and connected with a migration of scholars from Paris in or about 1167. The very idea of a university was itself a reflexion of the new type of culture which England began to absorb in the twelfth century, for to it scholars came from all parts, and the learning which was there taught was in the main stream of Western European development. To this civilization, ecumenical, ecclesiastical, non-national, the older vernacular culture which had been the glory of pre-Conquest England could only with difficulty conform. England in the time of Henry II was a country distinguished in art and letters, in architecture and scholarship, but something of the individual quality of the earlier indigenous endeavour had to some extent departed. Great was the calamity, but great also was the part which by political events England had been brought to play in the renaissance of the twelfth century, a renaissance which may be justly described as marking one of the brightest epochs in the history of European civilization.

A final appraisal of the loss and gain involved in these events has yet to be made, but the extent to which recent studies in Anglo-Saxon antiquities have affected the interpretation of this age can be seen in the work of its greatest living historian. In 1908 Professor Stenton published his *William the Conqueror*: in 1943 he issued his definitive study of *Anglo-Saxon England*, wherein, by carrying the story down to 1086, he included the best short account of the Norman Conquest which has ever been written. No one who benefits by both these remarkable books will fail to observe in the latter a greater insistence on the value and persistence of Anglo-Saxon tradition.

Perhaps the two greatest achievements of medieval England were Anglo-Saxon vernacular culture and Anglo-Norman executive administration, and it is the unique interest of this period to record the conclusion of the one and the climax of the other. The historian has now the opportunity to essay a judgment between them, and to do justice to both without denaturalizing the critical decades which divided them. In this attempt he will find himself placed in a quite special relation to his predecessors. He will be faced with astonishing variations of polemic which have distorted the age he studies, but he will also be gratefully conscious of the accumulated erudition he has inherited. The long sustained interest, which this subject has excited in generations of writers, has not only tended to create legends of this remote age: it has also, by stimulating a productive research, helped to preserve the evidence by which those legends may be corrected. In respect of no period therefore is it more necessary to check current theories by reference to the evidence upon which they purport to be based, to separate from the bare testimony the interpretations which have been put upon it, and, by discarding more modern notions of politics as extraneous to the eleventh century, to seek to enter through the minds of contemporaries into the authentic atmosphere they breathed. The task is in very truth not easy. But it is hoped that some opportunity for its performance may haply be provided by the material printed in this book.

(ii) THE SOURCES

The materials for the study of English history between 1042 and 1189 are, considering the remote period from which they derive, remarkably copious. In the Anglo-Saxon Chronicle[1] and in Domesday Book[2] the student is presented with two sources to which it would be hard to find any contemporary parallel; the Bayeux Tapestry[3] stands by itself as a pictorial representation of the most decisive event in English medieval history; and the *Dialogus de Scaccario*[4] is unique as a detailed description of the working of a great governmental department in the twelfth century. These famous texts are, moreover, but outstanding examples of a mass of testimony notable both for its interest and its extent. Eleventh-century charters, for instance, are nowhere common, but they are probably less rare in England than elsewhere;[5] and although a conscious interest in history was more prevalent in the Middle Ages than is sometimes supposed, its study in the twelfth century was prosecuted nowhere more successfully than in the England of William of Malmesbury[6] and William of Newburgh.[7] Students of the Anglo-Norman Church have reason to be grateful that Lanfranc was an indefatigable correspondent,[8] and it is to this period that must be assigned

[1] No. 1. [2] Nos. 205–213. [3] No. 5. [4] No. 70.
[5] Cf. Nos. 31–41; 77–80; 238–241; 269–274. [6] No. 8. [7] No. 12. [8] Nos. 91–106.

the earliest of English 'Public Records'.[1] Without exaggeration it may be said that from no other country in the world has there been preserved from this distant age a collection of historical evidence comparable to that which illustrates the history of England during these years.

The relative abundance of material relating to England at this period is itself a fact of some historical significance, and one which demands some explanation. The assiduity with which at least three of the versions of the Anglo-Saxon Chronicle were being continued in different monasteries between 1042 and 1066[2] testifies in some measure to the literary interests of the late Old English Church, and the numerous royal writs surviving from the reign of Edward the Confessor are evidence of the administrative activity of that king. Much of the material relating to the last period of the Anglo-Saxon State derives, however, from the policy of a Conqueror who strove to be a conservative. The early writs and charters of William I do not differ appreciably in form from those of the Confessor,[3] and they were evidently the product of a chancery which retained many of the traditions of the English royal writing-office. The numerous pleas of the Conqueror's reign[4] frequently referred to earlier conditions, and in them judgment was often based upon the testimony of men to whom those conditions were familiar. Domesday Book is a description of the England of Edward the Confessor almost as much as of the England of William I. The historical student indeed owes very much to the efficient central administration which the Norman monarchy was able to create. The fact that the Domesday Survey was ever undertaken is scarcely less wonderful than the book which it produced, and if the *Dialogus de Scaccario*[5] is a unique account of royal finance in the twelfth century, its compilation would not have been possible apart from the contemporary development of the Exchequer it describes.

Hardly less remarkable than this lavish production of contemporary evidence in England between 1042 and 1189 is the extent to which it has been preserved. This must be partly attributed to that continuous reverence for the past, which foreign observers, not always with approval, have noted as characteristically English. During the later Middle Ages a productive interest in history was sustained in many English monasteries, and most of them carefully cherished their title deeds. In secular affairs the royal practice of enrolment[6] preserved many early documents that might otherwise have been lost. The destruction which occurred during the earlier half of the sixteenth century was undoubtedly considerable, but it was mitigated by the efforts of many who in an age of change never lost their concern with the past, and during the seventeenth century most of the controversial problems which vexed contemporary society were debated by reference to precedent. Such a temper, prevailing almost to

[1] No. 61.
[2] Cf. pp. 107, 108.
[3] Nos. 31–40.
[4] Nos. 50, 51, 52.
[5] No. 70.
[6] Nos. 62–64, 71–73.

our own days, undoubtedly stimulated research [illegible] English medieval history and safeguarded their survival. [illegible]

If, however, the evidence for this period o[illegible]ous, it is far from complete. The past bequeathes no [illegible]her a few fragments of a picture which in its totality w[illegible]nd in the case of a remote period, Time takes his reve[illegible]mains. All items of enduring testimony possess, therefo[illegible] of exceptional survival, and any selection from amo[illegible] here been attempted thus entails additional hazard. No[illegible]aterial, here assembled, being the product of men separated f[illegible] of centuries, reflects habits of mind no longer easily comprehensible, [illegible] evidence is thus not only fragmentary but difficult to interpret. Too much may easily be expected from it, and it deserves the fullest emphasis that no medieval chronicle or document was compiled in order to answer the questions of modern scholars. They were produced to satisfy the intellectual curiosity, or to serve the practical needs, of the men who made them. The first essential, therefore, in studying any original source is to comprehend the reasons for which it was created. Only after this has been done does it become safe to approach the larger question as to what further information it may fortuitously provide. And only thus may it, on rare occasions, become possible to penetrate through the immediate preoccupations which produced the evidence into a comprehension of its particular application to those permanent problems of human life which are common to all ages in the human struggle.

To define what constitutes an historical source is scarcely necessary. Anything that a past age has left offers material to the historian – the language men used, the arts they enjoyed, the fortifications they erected, the temples in which they worshipped, the narratives they composed, the documents they produced – anything and everything they bequeathed to their posterity may be utilized to depict the life they lived. To insist thus upon the obvious may be otiose, but at least it serves to direct attention to the fact that it is with but one category of historical evidence that this book is concerned – the written material relating to the history of one country in a particular age.

Thus delimited, the evidence set out in this book may be seen to be of two types. Firstly there are what, for want of a better term, may be called the *narrative sources* of which the most important are annals and chronicles, and with these must be included such compilations as biographies, treatises and sermons. Secondly, there are the *record sources*, official acts of government and texts of legal import, such as charters, writs and 'wills', together with the records of administration issued by the king or by his magnates, lay and ecclesiastical. The distinction between these two types of written sources is fundamental, and broadly speaking it may be said that modern scholarship has tended to stress the tr… of 'records'. They provide (it is rightly urged) more … y of fact; they are less coloured by personal prejudic… ore precisely dated; and almost always, having been pro… ediate practical need, they convey a contemporary ac… y otherwise be attained. They are in fact the essential b…

The pr… h is now accorded to the record sources of medieval E… vever have led to some neglect of the chronicles which durir… ntury were so admirably, but too exclusively, studied. For … mething of his own to contribute to an understanding of the past. … e record is stark; it is sometimes arid. The chronicle was written to be read with interest; and often it is interesting. It conveys what might be called the personal touch, and when it is written by a man of intellectual distinction, such as was William of Newburgh,[1] the critical comments of the author will be of the highest value, especially when he is dealing with events of which he was an eyewitness, or of which he had gained his information from reliable sources. For these reasons it has seemed that this is a case when a balance should be struck even at the risk of incurring a charge of reaction. An attempt, therefore, has here been made to make a thorough use of record evidence to elucidate each major topic of English history during these years, and at the same time to cover the whole period with the writings of representative chroniclers.

To arrange all this material in a manner which may be easily comprehensible has involved (as may be surmised) problems of considerable magnitude. In this volume the evidence has been arranged with appropriate subdivisions under four general headings. The first[2] contains a representative selection of the annals and chronicles which, ranging from the Anglo-Saxon Chronicle to the work of William of Newburgh, comprise a collection of general historical narratives that are outstanding both in their quality and their extent. The second part of this volume[3] contains evidence relating to government and administration, and includes not only the cardinal texts of English constitutional history in this period but also testimony relating to the financial administration of the monarchy, and the development in theory and practice of the royal justice. Thirdly,[4] there is the material which more specifically relates to the ecclesiastical life of the time and to the influence of the Church upon secular politics. Finally, in the fourth part of this book[5] will be found material illustrating social and economic affairs, having particular reference to Domesday Book, to feudal society, to agrarian and municipal life, in short to the condition of the people of England in this age.

Such a scheme may, it is hoped, be justified on grounds of logic as well as of

[1] No. 12. [2] pp. 107–390. [3] pp. 399–583. [4] pp. 599–796. [5] pp. 813–974.

convenience, but the hazards of this, or indeed of any, arbitrary classification of historical material deserve emphasis. A text may legitimately be placed as illustrating the historical problem to which it most particularly relates, but it will most probably also serve as testimony to other aspects of contemporary life. Few of the documents here printed have thus exclusive reference to the sections in which they will be found. The great political narratives of the age are indispensable also to the elucidation of constitutional and social development; the secular history of this period was influenced at every turn by the Church; and there is no feature of the history of feudal England which is not reflected in some measure in the feudal charter. The widespread implications of the documents here printed can thus only partially be suggested by means of cross-references, and whilst in each case the special significance of a text printed in this book is indicated by the introductory note which precedes it, immediate attention must be called to their close interrelation. To discover new implications in the evidence is indeed one of the major objectives of research, and by so doing the student will become ever more conscious how fallacious it is to separate history into the familiar divisions of 'political', 'economic', 'constitutional' and the like. The texts by their very nature cry out against such divisions. Being themselves the urgent emanations of sentient men, they display of necessity the many-sided nature of humanity, enforcing the lesson that institutions cannot be understood apart from the men who worked them, and that though man lives by bread, he does not live by bread alone.

The most cursory survey of the sources of English history between 1042 and 1189 may at least serve to display their variety and extent. It is not to be supposed that they can provide easy answers to all the questions relating to English affairs at this time, or that the material itself is ever easy to interpret. The greater texts such as Domesday Book,[1] or the *Dialogus de Scaccario*,[2] the Pipe Rolls[3] or the *Cartae Baronum*[4] all need separate criticism before their testimony can be utilized or assessed; the Anglo-Saxon Chronicle is not to be appreciated apart from the special circumstances which attended the composition of its several surviving versions;[4] and even the chroniclers of Henry I and Henry II demand the particular attention due to men of strong individuality.[5] And if all the historical material bequeathed to posterity from this remote age must be used with care, so also must it be regarded even in its totality as incomplete. Much has perished; much more perhaps remains to be discovered. There is no finality in historical research. Nevertheless the evidence which is at present available is already sufficient to justify the hope that most of the major problems respecting English history between 1042 and 1189 may in time admit solution, and that even now a general estimate may be justifiably made of the significance of this critical epoch in England's growth.

[1] Nos. 205–213. [2] No. 70. [3] Nos. 71–73. [4] Nos. 224–234. [5] Nos. 8, 10, 11, 12–16, 107.

(iii) THE CONQUEST

In 1042 a new king was called to rule in England over a distracted realm, and the significance of the important reign of Edward the Confessor is best to be studied in the three versions of the Anglo-Saxon Chronicle which record it.[1] It was to no easy inheritance that he succeeded. England had very recently been part of the Scandinavian empire of Cnut the Great, and retained many social and political filiations with the northern lands. Edward therefore from the start had to face the imminent threat of an invasion from Scandinavia which would certainly receive support from many regions of England. Nor was his position at home wholly secure. The great earldoms established by Cnut had produced their local dynasties: that of Siward in Northumbria, that of Leofric in Mercia, and that of Godwine in Wessex. It was in fact practically as the nominee of Earl Godwine that Edward the Confessor became king, and his marriage with Godwine's daughter, Edith,[2] symbolized the close connexion between them. The task confronting the new king was thus not only to ward off an attack from the Baltic lands, but also to maintain peace among his greater subjects and to emancipate the monarchy from control by any one of them.

No interpretation of this age can be adequate which fails to appreciate the provincial differences existing in the late Old English State. It is true that the West-Saxon royal dynasty, strong in its traditional prestige, enjoyed great respect even in the north. It is true also that in the various versions of the Anglo-Saxon Chronicle there are to be found passages indicating the existence of political sentiments common to the whole of England.[3] Such statements must be accorded full weight. But these sentiments seem to have found but rare expression in the politics of the time. The social structure of eleventh-century England was marked by cleavages separating one region from another, Northumbria from Kent,[4] East Anglia[5] from the western Midlands; and over all, there appears in Domesday Book the abiding division between the Danelaw and the rest of England.[6] Northumbria ever preserved a strong tradition of particularism, and English political history during the reign of Edward the Confessor was dominated by the rivalries of the three great earldoms. Among these the comital dynasty of Wessex was the most important, and its policy was in this respect hardly to be distinguished in quality from that of its rivals. Godwine and Harold, it would seem, normally acted in the interests of their family, and the latter could never be regarded as a national king. The careers and influence of these great earls of Wessex have, it is true, been very diversely judged by historians, and the reader must be left to pass his own judgment upon them. But in 1042 it could hardly have been supposed that English national

[1] No. 1, pp. 110–141.
[2] See Table 7.
[3] No. 1, pp. 122, 123, 127.
[4] No. 206.
[5] No. 212.
[6] Cf. Nos. 205, 211.

unity could ever be brought about by the comital dynasty of Wessex which then held the balance of political power in its hands.

Faced by these formidable threats from within and without his realm, Edward essayed his task of kingship. His character was perhaps little suited to his obligations, but he was never a negligible factor in the politics of his age. An attempt to estimate his merits and defects should take some account of his posthumous fame, of his numerous writs[1] which indicate a consistent attempt at administration, and of the fact, for instance, that he imposed by his own will an unpopular earl on the north for ten years.[2] He added something of his own to the prestige of the family to which he belonged, and if it is arguable that his acts were frequently unwise and ineffective, his aims at least were well defined. He would if possible emancipate the monarchy from the control of the magnates, and as a means to this end he would enlist the support of the Norman duchy in which as an exile he had spent his youth. Here he hoped to find a counterbalancing influence alike to the Scandinavian threat and to the formidable coalition which Earl Godwine was building up to control the English monarchy.

In the middle of the eleventh century the Norman province was entering on its greatness. The product of a Scandinavian settlement comparable to that which had created the English Danelaw, it had since the tenth century developed upon original lines. The Scandinavian impress remained to distinguish it from its neighbours in Gaul, and perhaps in some respects it was still nearer than they to the barbarian past. Nevertheless it had already become deeply subject to extraneous influences, some of which had been welcomed within its borders with an especial fervour. Already before 1042 it had been remarked that Romance speech was already again current in Rouen, though the Scandinavian language was still predominant in Bayeux; and by the fourth decade of the eleventh century Normandy had become Latin in its speech, in its sentiments and in its political ideas. The influence of Rouen, the Latin and ecclesiastical capital, had spread throughout the province, and in particular the whole of Normandy had been conditioned afresh as a social unit by the operation of three forces. The Church had been re-established mainly through the influence of Cluniac monasticism backed by the secular powers within the duchy; a new aristocracy, composed of families which for the most part did not rise to eminence before the eleventh century, had been established; and the ducal house had risen to such power that not even the disastrous anarchy which in 1035 followed the accession of a boy could destroy its authority. The dominant theme of early Norman history had been the modification of a Scandinavian inheritance through the consolidation of a dynasty, the revival of a Church, and the formation of an aristocracy; and the direct impact of Normandy upon England, long prepared, occurred when, after the battle of Val-ès-Dunes in 1047,[3] these

[1] See, for instance, Nos. 31, 32, 34, 182, 186. [2] No. 1, pp. 133–140. [3] No, 1, p. 115.

three movements, which were never unrelated, began to be fused together by the constructive genius of Duke William to provide the exceptional energy of a province unique in Christendom.[1]

In the early years of the reign of Edward the Confessor the parties in England were thus becoming defined with momentous consequences for the future. It was still uncertain whether England would achieve a uniform system of political order which could absorb the great men of the land, bring them into legal relations with each other, and subordinate them to the directing control of the king. It was equally uncertain whether England would, so to speak, become part and parcel of the Scandinavian north with a vernacular culture of her own linked to that of the Baltic lands, or whether, losing much of that vernacular culture, she would for the remainder of the Middle Ages become an integral part of a Latin Europe that was beginning itself to be dominated by the rising political power of the papacy and to be impregnated by the ideas associated with the renaissance of the twelfth century. Before this period had closed, an answer had been given to all these questions through the agency of men of an alien race, and herein is the unity of this epoch revealed.

Such are some of the considerations which make significant the remarkable account given of the reign of Edward the Confessor in the Anglo-Saxon Chronicles. Between 1042 and 1051 the Scandinavian threat is constant, and a Scandinavian invasion is only postponed by civil wars in the Baltic lands. At the same time the king is intruding into the higher places of Church and State a number of Norman counsellors. Norman colonies are planted, for instance, in Sussex[2] and Herefordshire;[3] Norman prelates are introduced into the English Church. The king's nephew, Ralph the Timid, son of Dreux, count of Mantes,[4] becomes a leader of this movement on its lay side, whilst Robert, formerly abbot of Jumièges, made bishop of London in 1044 and archbishop of Canterbury in 1051,[5] heads the Norman movement in the Church. This process was naturally resisted, and in particular Godwine and his sons raised up against it any opposition they could organize. At the same time they strove to concentrate even more power in their own hands, at the expense both of the king and of their rivals, the earls of Mercia and Northumbria. To a degree they succeeded, but before 1051 the advantage lay mainly with the king, and in that year he enjoyed his triumph by crushing a formidable rebellion which Godwine had raised against him.[6] The earl of Wessex and his sons were sent into exile, the Norman party already dominant in the Church and powerful in the State was further strengthened, and most significant of all, William, the duke of Normandy, came, as it seems at this time, on a formal visit to England,[7] where, as seems probable, he received from the king a solemn promise of the succession.

[1] Nos. 6, 7. [2] No. 52. [3] Nos. 1, 2, pp. 133, 208, 210 [4] See Table 1.
[5] Nos. 1, 2, p. 209. [6] Nos. 1, pp. 120–125, 2. [7] No. 1, p. 124.

If the conditions prevailing at the close of 1051 had been allowed to continue, it is even possible that the change of dynasty might in due course have been peaceably achieved. But the royal triumph of that year was followed by a reaction. Godwine and his sons effected their return by force, and had the king at their mercy.[1] The Norman party was suppressed and most of its members expelled. The family of the West-Saxon earldom became supreme in England, and in 1053 with the death of Godwine the leadership of the house passed to his greater son, Harold.[2] From then on to 1066 this family was in fact to remain the most powerful force in English politics, and its chief preoccupation was to maintain its superiority over the rival comital houses. The moment of its greatest power arrived in 1055 when even the earldom of Northumbria passed into the hands of Tosti, Harold's brother.[3] The crisis of 1051–1052, so far from ensuring a peaceful solution to the English problem, had in fact brought the two rival forces into a more direct opposition. Soon too the issue was to be made yet clearer. In 1057 there came to England from exile in Hungary, Edward, the son of Edmund Ironside, who by heredity might be considered as the next in line of succession to the throne.[4] Shortly after landing he died in mysterious circumstances,[5] and Earl Harold, who was already the most powerful man in England, must from this time forth have begun to think of the succession for himself. Across the sea Duke William, who claimed already to have had the promise of the king, was biding his time. Thus all the large issues confronting England at last became narrowed down to the personal rivalry of two remarkable men.

Such was the situation when, on 5 January 1066, Edward the Confessor died childless,[6] and a succession question of the first importance opened for England. By heredity the legitimate successor was now Edgar, the son of that Edward who had died in 1057, but he was only a boy and at this stage his claims seem hardly to have been considered. The new king, it would seem, must be sought in one of three places. The first was Scandinavia, for it was highly probable that some prince of the north, such as Harold Hardraada, king of Norway, would seize this opportunity to re-establish a Scandinavian dynasty in a country where many districts were strongly Scandinavian in sympathy. Secondly, there was Harold, son of Godwine, who from 1053 had been the most powerful man in England, who since 1057 had entertained hopes of the succession for himself, and who perhaps, as may be suggested by the Bayeux Tapestry,[7] had been designated as king by Edward the Confessor on his death-bed. Finally, there was William, duke of Normandy, who also asserted, and most probably with truth, that he had the promise of the late king,[8] and who represented a social and ecclesiastical culture which between 1042 and 1051 the

[1] No. 1, p. 129. [2] No. 1, 2, pp. 130, 209–212. [3] No. 1, p. 133. [4] See Table 1.
[5] No. 1, pp. 135–136. [6] Nos. 1, p. 141, 3. [7] No. 5, Plate XXXII. [8] Nos. 3, 4.

Confessor had successfully propagated in England. He had already shown himself to be a prince of outstanding ability,[1] and he felt it as a personal challenge when on the very day of Edward's funeral the earl of Wessex had himself crowned king of England in the presence of a small group of magnates and of London citizens.[2]

This *coup d'état* rendered inevitable the triangular struggle which filled up the ensuing nine months. It is described in the Anglo-Saxon Chronicles[3] and in the Norman narrative of William of Poitiers,[4] and it has been made part of the English consciousness through the famous pictures of the Bayeux Tapestry.[5] Harold, the new king, was strong in his own West-Saxon earldom, but he was received with scant enthusiasm elsewhere, and his power had recently been weakened by two events. In the previous year, Tosti, Harold's brother, had been expelled from his Northumbrian earldom, and his place in the north had been taken by Morcar, brother of Edwin, earl of Mercia, and grandson of Earl Leofric, the old rival of Godwine.[6] Tosti thereupon had taken refuge with the king of Norway and was already urging him to attempt a large-scale invasion of England. Shortly before this, moreover, Harold had compromised himself with the Norman duke. At some uncertain date, but probably in 1064, Harold, when voyaging in the Channel, had been wrecked on the French coast, and had been rescued by William from the count of Ponthieu, who had captured him.[7] He had then sworn an oath to William, the terms of which are best described in the narrative of William of Poitiers,[8] and which was regarded as pledging the earl of Wessex to assist the duke to the throne of England, or at all events not to oppose him. Harold was thus made to appear by Norman writers not only as a usurper but as a perjured vassal, and this view, widely accepted on the continent of Europe, inflicted much damage to his prestige.

During the spring of 1066 active preparations to invade England were made both in Norway and in Normandy. Each of the claimants was well placed. The king of Norway had achieved a transitory pre-eminence in the Baltic lands, and William, owing to the deaths in 1060 of King Henry I of France and of Count Geoffrey Martel of Anjou, had been rid of his two chief opponents in northern Gaul. By August, therefore, the king of England was expecting an attack, and it was clearly essential to his defence that he should decide correctly from which quarter it would first come. He decided that the danger from Normandy was the more imminent, and he had good reason for so doing, since a large Norman fleet had already assembled at the mouth of the Dives. He therefore took up his position in Sussex.[9] Early in September, however, two events occurred to modify the situation. The strain of providing for Harold's troops proved too much for the countryside and he had to disband many of them,[10] and then on

[1] No. 7. [2] No. 1, p. 142. [3] No. 1, pp. 142–146; cf. No. 2. [4] No. 4; cf. No. 3.
[5] No. 5. [6] No. 1, p. 140. [7] Nos. 3, 4, 5. [8] No. 4; and cf. No. 5.
[9] Nos. 1, 2, 3. [10] Nos. 1, pp. 143, 144; 2, p. 213.

12 September the first of the equinoctial gales blew up the Channel and drove William's fleet to take refuge at the port of St. Valery at the mouth of the Somme.[1] It was this delay which enabled the king of Norway to strike first. The Viking fleet put to sea and by 18 September a Scandinavian host led by Harold Hardraada, and supported not only by Tosti but by many of the inhabitants of northern England, had landed at the mouth of the Humber. An army raised from the Midland shires under Edwin, earl of Mercia, was ready to meet it and bar its way to York.[2] On 20 September, therefore, the first of the three great battles of 1066 took place at Fulford.[3] There the Scandinavian host was completely victorious; the Mercian levies were cut to pieces; and on 24 September York, the northern capital, surrendered to the Norwegian king.[4]

The problem for King Harold, who was still in the south, was thus clearly posed. Was it possible for him to march north to cope with the Norwegian host and to get back to the south before the wind in the Channel permitted William to sail? He essayed the task and his conduct of the campaign is conclusive testimony to his high ability as a general. Forced marches brought him to Tadcaster within four days of the battle of Fulford, and on the very next day he advanced to meet the Scandinavian host at Stamford Bridge. He achieved surprise and immediately attacked with tired troops. By nightfall he had gained one of the most complete victories of the Middle Ages.[5] Tosti and Harold Hardraada were killed and the king was supreme in the north. It was a magnificent achievement, but it failed in its ultimate purpose through the Channel wind. William, waiting at St. Valery is described as offering prayers to the local saint for a favourable wind and looking anxiously at the weather-vane on the church tower.[6] The event was to justify his concern. Three days after Stamford Bridge a favourable wind began to blow. With the utmost haste the duke put to sea, and on 28 or 29 September he crossed the Channel and landed at Pevensey. At that time he could hardly have heard the result of Stamford Bridge, or have known which of the two Harolds would eventually oppose him–a king of Norway backed by a Scandinavian host with its supporters from northern England, or the king of England at the head of troops recruited from southern England. He took his risk and by so doing he overcame one of the greatest obstacles to his plan through securing an unopposed landing on an unguarded coast.[7]

The new king at York did not delay in meeting the fresh threat. By 5 October he was in London where he tarried for a week hoping for reinforcements, and then on 12 October he moved to the south and encamped on the Sussex Downs near Hastings. There on the morning of 14 October the battle was joined. No

[1] No. 4. [2] Nos. 1, 2. [3] No. 2, p. 213. [4] No. 1, p. 145
[5] No. 1, pp. 143–145, and No. 2. [6] No. 4 and No. 5. [7] No. 4.

adequate contemporary description of it exists in an English source,[1] but the account given by William of Poitiers[2] is admirable and may be regarded as reliable. It appears that the engagement resolved itself into a prolonged attack by Norman horsemen charging up the hill and seeking to dislodge the English infantry massed in very close order on the summit. At first the issue was doubtful, but by means of repeated assaults, by the device of feigned flights to tempt the defenders to pursuit, and at last by the employment of archers who rained down their arrows on the defenders, the hill was captured. The defeat then became a rout, and the rout a slaughter. Harold and his brothers were among those slain during the battle, and the Norman triumph was complete. The whole account of the battle as given by William of Poitiers and depicted in the Bayeux Tapestry[3] deserves to be studied in detail, for many modern writers, such as Freeman, have introduced into their description details taken from the unreliable evidence of Wace, the twelfth-century Norman poet. Here only two general points need be made respecting the battle and the campaign which preceded it. The Norman triumph could not have been obtained without command of the Channel by the invaders for at least a number of hours, and an appraisal of the campaign must therefore take into account the reductions in the royal fleet recorded in the Anglo-Saxon Chronicles as having occurred in 1049 and 1050.[4] Again, the Norman victory of Hastings was won by the employment of a new technique of warfare which England had refused to perfect. The specially armed and mounted knight achieved his first and most spectacular triumph on the hill at Hastings, and so important did William regard the equipment of his knights that these brought their horses with them in their little ships.[5] It does not seem unreasonable to conclude that the English defeat at Hastings was due in large measure, firstly to their having lost command of the Narrow Seas, and secondly to their failure to keep abreast with the latest developments in military science. At all events, Hastings was perhaps the most decisive battle ever waged on English soil.

William's victory at Hastings was final. His skilled conduct of affairs in the following autumn was but a preface to the inevitable culmination when the Norman duke, having been presented to his followers by Geoffrey, bishop of Coutances, and to the English by Aldred, archbishop of York, was crowned with traditional ceremony as king of the English on Christmas Day, 1066, in the church of St. Peter at Westminster.[6] Thenceforth, he was enabled to subdue his new realm province by province, suppressing local risings, for example at Exeter in 1068,[7] and two years later the revolt of Hereward in the Fens.[8] His main difficulties were in the north, and the Northumbrian risings of 1069 and 1070, inspired largely by Scandinavian sentiment, were formidable, but with

[1] But see No. 1, p. 144. [2] No. 4, end of No. 3 and No. 5. [3] No. 5, Plates LXV–LXXIX.
[4] No. 1, p. 119. [5] See No. 5, Plates XLI–XLVI, and cf. No. 2, p. 213. [6] Nos. 1, 2, 3, 4.
[7] Nos. 1, 4, 7. [8] No. 1.

the terrible harrying of the north they were suppressed.[1] William in fact had always possessed his own party in England. Respected English prelates such as Wulfstan of Worcester and Aldred of York supported his régime almost from the start, and there were already English soldiers in his army when he marched against Exeter in 1068. Englishmen were also soon to serve under him in his continental wars. In 1073 many of them followed him to Maine,[2] and it was to an Englishman that he owed his life at the siege of Gerberoi in 1079.[3] Such conditions undoubtedly facilitated the task of the new king in England. Within five years of the battle of Hastings the full work of the Norman settlement of England could proceed unchecked, and before the Conqueror's death the results of that settlement were to be recorded in Domesday Book. The climax of the spectacular drama whose first acts were played before the eyes of Europe during the reign of Edward the Confessor had been reached and passed in 1066. Henceforth the far-reaching consequences of the Norman Conquest were to be inexorably disclosed.

(iv) THE ARISTOCRACY

The immediate consequence of the Norman Conquest was to establish a new aristocracy in England, and the redistribution of land which this entailed, the results of which were recorded in Domesday Book, constituted nothing less than a tenurial revolution. The fate of the Old English nobility after 1066 was catastrophic. Domesday Book records all the greater landowners in England in 1086 and it is rare to find an English name among them.[4] The king's thegns who formed the nucleus of the aristocracy in the time of the Confessor had all but disappeared, and the survivors were in shire after shire relegated to a kind of appendix where they took their place among the king's Norman servants or among people of depressed condition.[5] The three great battles of 1066 had undoubtedly taken a heavy toll from this class. Fulford was a long and sanguinary engagement in which the bulk of the Mercian army was destroyed. The victory of Stamford Bridge cannot have been achieved without loss, and the defeat of Hastings was followed by a wholesale slaughter. It was, moreover, precisely the thegnly class which suffered most from the suppression of the various risings between 1066 and 1070, and those who remained found themselves in a precarious position depending upon such terms as they could individually make with the new masters of England.[6] It is little wonder that many went into exile. Most of the surviving notables in the north departed to Scotland where, establishing themselves under the protection of Margaret, the sister of Edgar Atheling, who married Malcolm Canmore,[7] they made their own contribution to Scottish history. Others went to Flanders, the traditional refuge of English exiles in the

[1] Nos. 1, 7. [2] No. 1. [3] No. 1. [4] Cf. No. 205.
[5] Cf. No. 205, pp. 861–862. [6] No. 238. [7] No. 1, p. 148.

time of the Confessor, and yet more travelled to Byzantium to form part of the Varangian bodyguard of the Eastern emperors. By death, by exile, by misfortune, the Anglo-Saxon aristocracy was so suppressed as a result of the Norman Conquest as to cease after 1070 to be an integral part of English society. By 1086 only about eight per cent of the land of England remained in the possession of surviving members of this class.

Its place was taken by a new aristocracy recruited from overseas and richly endowed with English land. Of all the land of England surveyed in Domesday Book, about a fifth was held directly by the king, about a quarter by the Church, and nearly half by the greater followers of the king. These figures are impressive, and their significance is enhanced if they be further analysed. The new aristocracy was not only powerful: it was also small. The immediate tenants of the king as recorded in Domesday Book are a large and miscellaneous class but those among them who were important were few. Less than one hundred and eighty persons will there be found holding estates whose annual value is more than £100 a year. Moreover, about half the land held by lay tenure from the king had after the Conquest been granted to only ten men. Their names deserve record: Odo, bishop of Bayeux and earl of Kent;[1] Robert, count of Mortain;[1] William fitz Osbern;[2] Roger of Montgomery;[3] William of Warenne; Hugh of Avranches;[4] Eustace, count of Boulogne; Richard fitz Gilbert;[5] Geoffrey, bishop of Coutances; and Geoffrey of Manneville in the Bessin. These between them received nearly a quarter of the land of England, and their establishment indicates the degree to which, after the destruction of the older nobility, the territorial wealth of England was concentrated into a few powerful hands.

Small in number the new aristocracy was also remarkably homogeneous in character. The men who accompanied Duke William on his great enterprise had, it is true, been drawn widely from north-western Europe, and some of those from outside Normandy, such as Eustace, count of Boulogne, and Arnulf of Hesdins, were to receive lands in England. A considerable contingent came from Brittany such as Brian and Alan the counts, the latter of whom was to receive the great lordship of Richmond in Yorkshire. But the bulk of the new aristocracy came from Normandy, and in it was represented the flower of the new Norman nobility. From the ducal house, for instance, came not only the duke's half-brothers, Odo, bishop of Bayeux, and Robert, count of Mortain,[6] but also, among others, Robert, count of Eu, Richard, count of Evreux, and Richard fitz Gilbert,[7] all of whom were grandsons of Duke Richard the Fearless. William fitz Osbern,[8] Robert of Beaumont,[9] Hugh of Grantmesnil, William Malet and Ralph of Tosny (to name no others) were among the most

[1] See Table 2. [2] See Table 10. [3] See Table 13. [4] See Table 14. [5] See Table 11.
[6] See Table 2. [7] See Table 11. [8] See Table 10. [9] See Table 12.

powerful magnates of the duchy, and they all received large estates in England. They brought with them their own followers, whose territorial names, scattered over England, indicate their original connexion in Normandy with their lords.

The Anglo-Norman aristocracy was also knit together by intermarriage, and in many cases bound by kinship to the ducal house. The half-brothers and cousins of the Conqueror who came with him to England took a prominent part in the settlement, and William fitz Osbern, perhaps the greatest lay magnate of the period of the Conquest, could claim a double descent from the ducal family.[1] Similarly, the feudal families of Anglo-Norman England were mostly interconnected by marriage or common descent. The wife of Richard fitz Gilbert was, for instance, a daughter of the elder Walter Giffard, and a daughter of William fitz Osbern married Ralph of Gael, earl of Norfolk.[2] The widow of Robert of Beaumont, first earl of Leicester,[3] married William of Warenne, first earl of Surrey; and Roger Bigot, one of the largest landowners in Norfolk at the time of Domesday, married a daughter of Ralph of Tosny whose family was powerful not only in central Normandy but also in the English Midlands. These connexions were, moreover, but typical of the whole structure of Anglo-Norman aristocracy, and such alliances, like that between the daughter of Roger, earl of Warwick, and Geoffrey Clinton, chamberlain of King Henry I,[4] might affect the political fortunes of whole counties. They illustrate from a fresh angle the solidarity of the aristocratic group in which they took place. The Norman settlement of England was to be effected very largely by inter-related great families. Ties of kinship knit them together in their common enterprise, and inspired such co-operation among them as enabled them to survive as a small constructive minority in an alien land.

This aristocracy received its lands out of the spoils of conquest, and it is one of the strongest indications of the overriding genius of the Conqueror that the enrichment of the members of a competitive nobility in a country which they had recently subdued took place without general anarchy. William dominated his followers by the strength of his personality, and his claim to rule as the legitimate successor of the Confessor was reflected in his will that his magnates should take up from their English predecessors such rights and obligations as had been established by tradition. It was therefore usual for a Norman lord to find himself endowed (within each shire) not with a miscellaneous bundle of manors, but rather with all the estates which had previously belonged to one or more pre-Conquest landowners. Disputes – and there were many – were, if possible, to be settled by legal process, and in the great pleas which are characteristic of the reign, appeal was regularly made to Anglo-Saxon precedent.[5] It was thus under the cloak of an astute conservatism that the territory of England was

[1] See Table 10.
[2] No. 1, p. 156.
[3] See Table 12.
[4] No. 256.
[5] Nos. 50, 51, 52.

redistributed. Broadly speaking, the grants may be said to have taken two forms. In some cases a large compact block of territory was bestowed as, for instance, on William fitz Osbern, Hugh of Avranches, and Roger of Montgomery, later to become respectively earls of Hereford, Chester and Shrewsbury. Similarly the 'rapes' of Sussex were allocated severally to individual magnates, among whom were Robert, count of Eu, William of Warenne and the king's half-brother, Robert, count of Mortain. The regions where grants of this kind were made–the Welsh border, the 'invasion coast', Sussex, Cornwall, Holderness, Durham and so forth–suggest the desire of the king to place specially trusted followers at vulnerable points in his realm. For the bulk of the grants made after the Conquest were of a very different nature. The estates of a great Norman baron were normally scattered about over a wide area. It has frequently been suggested that this distribution was made according to a definite plan whereby the king designed to prevent any one man from having too great a local influence, but it is perhaps more probable that, just as the Conquest proceeded province by province, so also were grants made piecemeal as different regions came under the Conqueror's control. And it is notable that in many cases the Norman barons received entire the estates of one or more of the earlier English landholders.

The terms on which these grants were made were scarcely less important than their extent. Broadly speaking, they involved the establishment of English feudalism. The evidence relating to the inception and development of this military system, which entailed such widespread social consequences, is set out and discussed in some detail below,[1] so that here it is necessary merely to recall that the arrangements thus made shortly after the Norman Conquest between the king and his greater followers owed very little to Old English precedent. If English rural society in 1086 was essentially the same as it had been in 1042, the conditions of aristocracy had been transformed by the wholesale application to the greatest men in the land of the principle of dependent tenure in return for definite service. Homage and dependency had of course existed in Anglo-Saxon England. But a new phase in social organization opened when every great lord received his land in return for an obligation to provide a specified number of trained and equipped knights in the king's service. The amount of this *servitium debitum*, as it was called, was fixed by means of an individual arrangement with the king and bore no definite relation to the amount or value of the lord's lands. Nor did it necessarily correspond to the number of knights whom the lord had in fact endowed with land on his own estates. Originally the assessments were the result of private bargains between the king and his tenants-in-chief, and for the most part they are unrecorded. Only by means of the returns made in 1166 to Henry II[2] is it possible to ascertain the amount of knight-service owed in

[1] Nos. 218-234. [2] Nos. 224–234.

return for their lands by the Anglo-Norman magnates of England during the century which followed the Norman Conquest.

The imposition of tenure by service on his greater followers is yet another indication of the overmastering purpose of the Conqueror. The Normandy over which he was duke knew feudal tenure,[1] and it knew the *servitium debitum*, but the scheme of service was as yet applied to Normandy with no such uniformity as was now imposed upon England, and the assessments were, and always remained, much lower in the duchy than in the kingdom. It was William's triumph and perhaps the condition of the survival of his dynasty in England, that not only did he firmly establish his followers as a new aristocracy on English soil, but he made their endowment subserve the military needs of his new realm.[2] The conditions upon which the new magnates received the lands of the Old English nobility ensured the king the service of at least four thousand trained soldiers and provided him with a fighting force which could show itself a match for any that might be brought against it. The very fact that the provision of these troops rested in the hands of a comparatively few men closely attached to the king by kinship or association made these arrangements yet more efficient. The Norman polity in England was from its inception an aristocracy, organized for war, and thus did it endure.

The military success of this organization depended upon the fact that it was not merely soldiers who were thus to be provided, but expert warriors specially trained and specially equipped. It was by the service specifically of *knights* that the Norman aristocracy held their lands, and the knight in England was himself a product of the Norman Conquest. Before 1066 the typical English warrior had been the thegn,[3] whose military service derived from his rank, who had an assured personal status characterized by a high wergild or blood-payment, and who fought, when he fought, on foot. Within twenty years of the battle of Hastings he had been replaced in England by the knight[4] who underwent apprenticeship in mounted warfare as a condition of his status, and who if he held land did so on condition of performing military service. The Norman victory had been won by men trained in a new technique of warfare, and by the simplest definition the Norman knight was a man who had mastered this technique. He was distinguished from his fellows, not by wealth or birth or social position, but by his proficiency in arms: he was a soldier trained to fight in a specialized manner, and possessed of the weapons and equipment for so doing. He need not even hold land. Landless knights forming part of the household of a lord are a constant feature of early Norman society.[5] Such, for instance, were the armed and mounted men who rioted outside Westminster Abbey during the Conqueror's coronation, or the French retainers of Abbot Thurstan,

[1] No. 235. [2] Cf. Nos. 218, 223. [3] Cf. Nos. 188, 189.
[4] Cf. Nos. 222, 223. [5] No. 224.

who, "fully weaponed", outraged the monks of Glastonbury in the abbey church in 1083.[1] They were a dangerous class, and William in fact dismissed many of them from his own service in 1067. The knightly retinue of the abbot of Ely shortly after the Conquest caused havoc on the abbey lands, and it was the misbehaviour of the household knights of Walcher, bishop of Durham, which precipitated the northern rebellion of 1080. The household knight belongs in fact essentially to a society that is imperfectly stabilized. When it was no longer necessary for lords to have equipped knights ready for instant defence, the number of household knights began rapidly to diminish.

From the earliest days of Anglo-Norman feudalism it was the custom for the tenants-in-chief of the king to make provision for at least some of their knights on their own estates. Early charters of enfeoffment are rare and not always unambiguous, but some survive from the eleventh century,[2] and the enfeoffed knight is already a characteristic figure in feudal society by the time of Domesday Book.[3] By far the greater number of the enfeoffments recorded in the *cartae* of 1166 were originally made before 1135,[4] and by the middle of the twelfth century the typical knight in England was a man holding land by hereditary tenure in return for the performance of specialized military service for his lord. Knighthood, in short, was beginning to be recognized as the badge not, as heretofore, merely of military aptitude, but of a social class, and the way was prepared for the evolution of a minor aristocracy distinguished by a particular form of land tenure, by special privileges, and by its liability to those feudal incidents which before 1189 were described and defined by Glanville.[5] Already before the death of Henry II the knight as a landowner of position in his shire is seen to have many judicial and other duties to perform as distinct from his military service.[6] The evolution of a knightly class was, however, very gradual, and in the Norman period the knights of England formed a very miscellaneous company. Alongside of humble retainers, there were classed as knights, important men possessed of large estates who were socially the equals of their lord and who might even hold in chief elsewhere. Such were probably the land-holding men of account who attended the famous Salisbury moot of 1086,[7] and they are very often described as the *barons* of the honours to which they belonged.[8]

The honour of the tenant-in-chief, created in most cases by grants made shortly after the Conquest and normally comprising land and men in many shires, was the fundamental unit in feudal society. It was self-conscious and self-administered.[9] It had its *caput*, which was the lord's chief residence and which might be a castle. It had its court, to which the military tenants of the honour owed suit as in feudal duty bound. It was highly organized. A great

[1] No. 1, p. 160. [2] Nos. 219–222. [3] No. 206. [4] Nos. 224–234. [5] No. 268.
[6] No. 58. [7] No. 1, pp. 161–162. [8] Nos. 243, 246, 249, 253. [9] No. 249.

Anglo-Norman lord might well have a *corps* of officials comparable even to those of the king himself:[1] he might have his stewards, butlers, chamberlains and so forth; he might have his justices and sheriffs; he might even, it seems, have his own exchequer.[2] His household, smaller and less differentiated, might well be of the same pattern as that of the king.[3] His chief military tenants, such as those who in 1093–1096 were listed as belonging to the honour of the archbishop of Canterbury,[4] will sometimes call themselves "peers" of the honour,[5] and in their lord's court they will take their full share in shaping the policy of their lord, in helping to adjudicate disputes among themselves, in witnessing the lord's charters,[6] and generally in supplying their lord with counsel and support. Just as liege homage–the homage owed by a man to the lord from whom he held his chief tenement–was the strongest bond in the feudal world,[7] and incidentally the bond which bound all the tenants-in-chief to the king, so also was the honour in a sense a microcosm of the feudal State. The court of the king–the *curia regis*–was in the first instance the court of the greatest honour in the land.[8] The revenues of the king derived like that of the great lord primarily from the feudal incidents, and in both cases these were regulated by custom,[9] and sometimes, as by the 'Coronation Charter' of Henry I,[10] modified by specific enactment.

The connexion in principle between the organization of the feudal honour and the organization of the feudal kingdom was a fundamental factor in the history of England during this period. It is a fallacy to postulate as the dominant theme in that history an inherent opposition between crown and baronage. There is of course a certain balance and tension to be observed in the operation of all political systems, and there was always a danger of baronial revolts such as occurred in 1075 or in 1102. Henry I strove to raise up a new nobility "out of the dust" to counter-balance the personal influence of some of the older Norman families, and after his death a disputed succession provoked a disastrous civil war. But neither king nor barons had anything to gain from a permanent opposition between them, and thus while the kings were content in general to support baronial authority in the shires, so also were the magnates normally ready to assist the royal administration in the interests of order. The treaty between the earls of Chester and Leicester[11] was one of the factors which brought to an end the anarchy of Stephen's reign, and when Henry II came to initiate a new development of the royal power, he found among the great men of the land many who were ready to work in his service. In this way the older Anglo-Norman nobility was, though not without friction, to produce in time from itself a new aristocracy of the court who, as ministers of the king, would operate the expanding royal administration.

[1] Nos. 241, 249. [2] No. 69. [3] No. 30. [4] No. 222. [5] Nos. 249, 253; cf. No. 57.
[6] Nos. 235–267. [7] No. 57. [8] Cf. No. 52. [9] No. 268. [10] No. 19. [11] No. 257.

The Anglo-Norman baronage is not to be regarded as a collection of barbarians loving violence for its own sake and pillage for its transitory reward. It produced its ruffians in full measure such as Geoffrey 'de Mandeville', earl of Essex, in the reign of Stephen,[1] but the activities of men of this type were a menace to their fellows almost as much as to the king. The magnates of Anglo-Norman England were in the last resort dependent for their position upon a social order which they or their immediate ancestors had helped to establish, and in the maintenance of this order they shared an interest common with their kings. Nor would it be wise to underrate the ability of these men. This was probably the most remarkable aristocracy existing in contemporary Europe, and many of its members were men of responsibility and high ability who well deserved the panegyric which William of Poitiers lavished upon them.[2] Knit together by kinship, strong in their newly won possessions they speedily advanced to dominance, and if too many of them abused their power, many more used it with sagacity and strength. They were stained with the worst vices of a violent age but, although unamenable to control, they yet contrived to co-operate in large measure with their kings. Secular and rapacious in their habits, they came at last in some degree to foster the Church in England. The superabundant virility which was apparent in their private lives brought them to supremacy, and many of them were well fitted to work under kings of outstanding ability to provide ordered government for a conquered land.

The establishment of this nobility after the Norman Conquest dominated the social and constitutional history of England during the ensuing century. The feudal organization introduced by the Conqueror was to be modified in detail, but in all essentials it remained unchanged until the time of Henry II, providing at once a structure for aristocracy and a means for the defence of the realm. Owing little to Anglo-Saxon precedent, it may be regarded as perhaps the outstanding product of the Conquest. It conditioned the developing administration of great kings who exalted the royal power. It conditioned likewise the operation of local government which was at every turn affected by the fortunes and interrelations of great families.[3] To term the Anglo-Norman baronage anti-monarchical in influence, or to dub the Anglo-Norman monarchy as anti-feudal in policy is to intrude into the twelfth century ideas imported from Locke and Burke. The truth was at once more simple and more revealing. These men inhabited a feudal world of their own creation, and they no more challenged its modes than they questioned the pattern of their hills and fields. They believed that it was to the advantage of everyone in this feudal world, including the king, to hold fast to his proper rights, and not to encroach upon the rights of others. Such in twelfth-century England was the basis of secular politics. The definition of feudal rights and obligations might cause dispute, but

[1] Nos. 45, 255. [2] No. 4, p. 230. [3] Nos. 244, 245.

their ultimate sanction was undisputed. It was through a common acceptance of feudal principle by both king and magnates that, within a century of the Norman Conquest, England was made by their joint efforts into what was probably the best governed, and the strongest, kingdom in Western Europe.

(v) THE MONARCHY

Over the Anglo-Norman aristocracy there presided the Anglo-Norman king, and it was the great good fortune of England to acquire between 1066 and 1189 three kings who were among the most notable figures of their age. Individual character is a stronger factor in historical development than is always allowed, and it was of especial importance at a time when monarchy was regarded as being personal in nature. Medieval monarchy was not conceived as absolute: it was considered to be an office held for the well-being of the governed;[1] and the sharpest distinction was made on these lines between the king and the tyrant, the former being regarded as in a sense the divinely appointed agent of secular government, and the latter as one who, having committed treason against God, was worthy of such eternal punishment as was imagined in the river of boiling blood which Dante prepared for his reception and immersion. "It is meet and just", remarked John of Salisbury, "to kill a tyrant", and if this was an extreme statement, it served to emphasize the medieval opinion that the king had a specific duty to perform to society. Above all he should be a "lion of justice" and the protector of the weak against the strong. If he fulfilled this task in the interests of social order, much else would be forgiven him: if he failed, no other quality would compensate for the deficiency. After relating the harshness of the Conqueror in England, the Anglo-Saxon chronicler pays tribute to the "good security which he made in this country",[2] and the worst accusation which the same chronicler can bring against Stephen is that "he was a mild man and gentle and good and did not exact the full penalties of the law".[3]

It is against this background of opinion that the great kings of England in this period must be judged, for a man's place in history depends not only on his abstract qualities, but on the manner in which he conforms to, and moulds, the needs of his time. In respect of the Conqueror himself it is thus particularly fortunate that there survive three excellent and early accounts: one written by an Englishman who frequented his court;[4] the second by a monk of Caen;[5] and the third written at a later date by the gifted pen of Ordericus Vitalis.[6] To them little need here be added, and he who reads them, after making full allowance for the diversity of more modern judgments, will probably find it

[1] No. 170. [2] No. 1, p. 164. [3] No. 1, p. 199.
[4] No. 1, pp. 163–165. [5] No. 6. [6] No. 7.

difficult not to share the admiration evidently felt by contemporaries for one who so signally bestrode his generation. Succeeding as a bastard child to a province racked by anarchy, brought up in constant perils in the midst of a corrupt and bloodstained court, this man by his own unflinching purpose rose to dominance. His character was bitterly annealed by violence and treachery into an efficient ruthlessness which enabled him between 1047 and 1054, while still in his early twenties, to wage successfully against heavy odds an almost continuous war for the survival of his power. "No man dared do anything against his will", but there must have been a wonderful strength of personality in this young man which enabled him to elicit the support which alone made possible such an exhibition of power. Perhaps the quality of his leadership can best be appreciated in some of the minor incidents of his life: his grim joke to the abbot of Holy Trinity, Rouen;[1] his care for the Norman countryside on which his army was quartered;[2] the secret burial of his sailors drowned at sea;[3] and his calculated courage on that fateful night in 1066 when, having lost touch with his ships, he found himself alone in mid-Channel, with all his fortunes in the balance, and thereupon feasted "as if at home" to restore the courage of his men.[4]

Such was the man who was enabled to make a lasting impress upon England. Strong in body and a mighty warrior, he was a commander of talent and a skilled diplomatist. His negotiations in 1066 were, for instance, remarkable, and made his expedition to England appear to Europe in the light of a crusade. Having become master of England by force of arms, he yet succeeded in some measure in imposing himself upon his new subjects as the legitimate successor of the Confessor. His greatness was indeed never more manifest than in the early period of his English rule, when at the moment of his triumph he attempted to associate in his government those whom he had subdued. His writs during this period are often couched in the vernacular,[5] and frequently addressed to English officials, while English magnates are to be found at his court.[6] The plan failed after the Northumbrian rising of 1069–1070; and the harrying of the north, perhaps the most inexcusable act of the Conqueror, may probably be regarded as a measure of his disappointment. But his early conciliation undoubtedly helped him to bridge four most critical years, and stamped the whole of his government of England with a peculiar quality. Between 1070 and 1085 the new Norman aristocracy was established in England, and even as the redistribution of English land was effected without anarchy, so also was the new nobility linked straitly to the monarchy by the king. Thus the Norman régime which William set up in England was made competent to deal with the last crisis of the reign, when in 1085 external invasion and internal disorder menaced the

[1] No. 239.
[2] No. 4, p. 219.
[3] No. 4, p. 221.
[4] No. 4, p. 221.
[5] Nos. 33, 35, 238, 269.
[6] See No. 77.

continuance of Norman rule. The decisions of the Gloucester court in that year,[1] the Domesday Survey and the Salisbury moot of 1086[2] were the concluding achievements of the Conqueror's rule.

This was a strong and pitiless ruler, a man to fear rather than to love. He was stained with blood, and not all the victims of his purpose deserved their fate. But he was no tyrant, nor was he accounted as such by his contemporaries. The harshness of his rule they had felt for themselves, but, having experienced also the 'good security' which he maintained, they left it to God to judge his ruthless suppression of disorder. William had the kingly virtues in an age, and in two countries, which stood in sore need of them. And it was further noted that he could be "gentle to the good men who loved God".[3] His ecclesiastical appointments were good;[4] his co-operation with Lanfranc was a credit to them both; and the pope whom he opposed commended his zeal for religion.[5] He was regarded with justice as a benefactor to the Church, and there is no need to question the sincerity of his personal devotion.[6] He was abstemious in food and drink, and his continence was regarded as exceptional.[7] His private character was, however, always subordinate to his public prestige. Norman writers inevitably extolled the glory of their victorious duke, but he also made Englishmen take pride in a conqueror who was "a very wise man and very powerful and more worshipful and stronger than were any of his predecessors".[8] As a constructive genius he dominated his age, and his achievement is best to be judged in relation to the permanence of what he wrought. He gave a new orientation to English history.

A hush fell over regality at his death. Several of his greater followers left the world to retire into monasteries, and a great fear spread among humbler folk who foretold the disturbance which would follow his passing.[9] Their apprehension was justified. His eldest son, Robert, replete with those boyish qualities of feckless turbulence which gave him a facile popularity, speedily allowed the Norman duchy to sink back into an anarchy which was a misery to its inhabitants. In England, the Conqueror's second surviving son, William Rufus, ruled with violence rather than strength, seeking in his own interest to distort the careful institutions established by his father. To maintain the royal authority he imposed illegal burdens on his followers: to safeguard the secular power of the monarchy he infringed the rights claimed by the Church.[10] He not only satisfied, he also displayed, his lust for dominion, and he lacked that overt moderation which had supplied sinews to his father's power. Nevertheless, Rufus himself is not a negligible figure. He was no weakling, and he did something to justify that significant popular clamour which at his accession welcomed him as his father's successor. He was at least an expert in the technicalities of

[1] No. 1, p. 151. [2] No. 1, p. 161. [3] No. 1, p. 163. [4] No. 7. [5] Nos. 93, 94, 96, 99, 105.
[6] Nos. 6–7. [7] No. 6. [8] No. 1, p. 163 [9] No. 7. [10] Nos. 8, 107.

feudal obligations.[1] Perhaps, indeed, the unattractive simplicity of his character may itself be somewhat illusory. Prodigal, violent, passionate, and utterly illiterate, he was yet, it seems, involved in some of the subtler meshes of politics, and if his wickedness was blatant, his vices lacked the excuse of crudity. He has been accused of participation in Catharism, and his court was a notorious centre of homosexuality. His own name was never associated with that of any woman. There is in short something unexpectedly enigmatic about this man who has posed so successfully to posterity as a barbarian warrior devoid of sophistication, and his mysterious death in the New Forest[2] was a fit conclusion to a life whose inner intricacies have never been wholly explained. His public importance rests upon the fact that during the thirteen years through which he ruled England there was, despite upheavals for which he was partly responsible, no breakdown in the new social order which his father had established.

To William Rufus there succeeded as king of England a swart man of middle height, aged thirty-four, but already somewhat bald, squat, strong and fleshy,[3] and it might have seemed that with the advent of Henry I an abrupt change had occurred in the personal history of the monarchy. In place of violence and prodigality, there was now affability and parsimony; in place of physical prowess a preference for diplomacy over war; in place of homosexuality, a ruler who begat more bastards than any other king who ever reigned over England.[4] Nor was the contrast apparent merely in the sphere of private conduct. The coronation of the new king was marked by the issue of a charter[5] which proclaimed afresh the feudal basis of society, and with a backward glance at Rufus insisted that feudal rights should henceforward be exercised in a just and legitimate manner. Further, the new reign was signalized by a politic marriage whereby the king allied himself to the old West-Saxon dynasty by wedding Maud, niece of Edgar Atheling.[6] It is probable, however, that these acts were less significant than they were deliberately made to appear. The marriage was in keeping with the theory of the Conqueror's English rule, and with its overt practice between 1066 and 1070; and Henry's bid for English popularity must be judged in connexion with the English acclaim which in 1087 had greeted Rufus on his accession. Nor was there much in the 'Coronation Charter' that was new, even if it had not before been so clearly expressed. It would, in short, be unwise to regard the reign of Rufus too much as an interlude in Anglo-Norman government, or that of Henry I as marking too great a breach with tradition. The aims of the third Anglo-Norman king were the same as those of his predecessors. His methods were his own.

The genius of the Conqueror continued in the twelfth century to control the purpose of the English monarchy, and the work of Henry I would have been

[1] No. 84. [2] No. 8. [3] No. 8. [4] See Table 4. [5] No. 19. [6] No. 1, p. 176.

impossible apart from the regal inheritance bequeathed him by his father. It was natural therefore for William of Malmesbury when summarizing his achievement to hark back almost to the words of the Anglo-Saxon panegyric on William I.[1] Henry I in his turn is praised above all in that "he so restrained the rebellious that peace prevailed in England". Of less commanding stature than his father, of greater subtlety than his brother, Henry I succeeded in developing the power the one had created and the other had with difficulty preserved. His ways were tortuous, lacking at once the nobility of the Conqueror's dominance, and the crudity of the Red King's aggression. It might even have seemed that the large sum of money left him by his father[2] was symbolic, for this man knew the power of the purse, and his chief personal characteristic was avarice. He had a dexterity in controlling men by indirect pressure, and though praised by his contemporaries as wise, it was rather in a legalistic cunning that he excelled. He had a personal competence in the details of administration, and a skill in manipulating these to his own advantage, choosing for this work men who were highly competent and pliant agents of his will. It was thus for a rapid growth in the machinery of royal administration that his reign was chiefly notable, and this development, sparsely recorded,[3] forms a link in English constitutional history between the reigns of the Conqueror and Henry II. Thus must it be considered. Yet behind all this institutional advance there may be discerned, dimly but certainly, the short, unlovely figure of this intensely able king, extending his power with ruthless caution at the expense of Church and aristocracy, ever careful to avoid too blatant a breach in the letter of the law, and ready always to cloak with a false *bonhomie* the success of his unscrupulous and effective design.

Self-regarding he thus served England, but it was not only England that he served. With his reign there emerges into prominence that continental problem which was implicit in the circumstances of the Norman Conquest. The fates of Normandy and England had been intertwined ever since the Scandinavian settlements of the tenth century, but with the Conquest England became in a stricter sense a continental power. The Conqueror, Rufus and Henry I spent much of their time in Normandy, and much of their energy on the affairs of the duchy. The union between the duchy and the kingdom was not, it is true, uninterrupted. On his death-bed the Conqueror, following the practice of the Norman aristocracy, bequeathed his lands of inheritance to his eldest, and his lands of conquest to his next surviving son, thus assigning Normandy to Robert and England to Rufus. Robert inevitably sought to add England to his own dominion, and each succession to the English throne was marked, as in 1088 and 1102, by an English rebellion in his favour. His feckless folly handicapped him throughout in his dealings with his brothers, but it was not until 1106 after

[1] No. 1, pp. 163, 164; No. 8. [2] No. 7. [3] Cf. Nos. 43, 62–64

an open battle between him and Henry I outside the walls of Tinchebrai[1] that the issue was settled by his complete defeat. Joined under one rule between 1066 and 1087, formally divided between 1087 and 1106, England and Normandy were henceforth until 1204 to remain part of one realm, and in that realm the interests of England were to be predominant.

England was none the less herself to be affected by this union, and in particular she was brought thereby forcibly into conflict with the two great opponents of Normandy in Europe. The former of these was Anjou. The counts of Anjou during the eleventh century built up a strong principality in western France, and laid the foundation of their future power by securing the city of Tours and holding the county of Touraine against the claims of the counts of Blois. At the same time they hotly resisted the westward expansion of Normandy particularly over the border province of Maine. These rivalries, between Anjou and Normandy over Maine, and between Anjou and Blois over Touraine, were naturally watched with anxiety by the Capetian dynasty in Paris, which was inevitably further disturbed when the power of the English crown was added to the power of the Norman duke. Possessed of compact, though limited, territory, the house of Capet had always striven to prevent a combination against itself of the great fiefs of France, and its object was clearly as far as possible now to balance Anjou against Normandy and to separate the policies of Normandy and England. It was therefore something of a diplomatic triumph when in 1133 the English king obtained the alliance of Fulk V of Anjou in return for his support, and in the same year at Gisors secured from Louis VI a recognition of his own rights as duke of Normandy over Maine and Brittany.

The issue, however, was only postponed and during the ensuing years events precipitated a dynastic crisis of the greatest significance both to England and France. In 1120 Prince William, the son of Henry I, perished in the wreck of the White Ship,[2] and Henry was left with a daughter, Maud, as his sole surviving legitimate child. She had been married early to the emperor, Henry V, but in 1125 she became a widow. Two years later Henry compelled the English barons to recognize her as his heir, and in order further to support her, gave her in marriage to Geoffrey Plantagenet, count of Anjou. Already, however, another claimant was appearing. This was Stephen, grandson of the Conqueror, through his daughter, Adela, who had married a count of Blois. Neither of these two rivals was personally notable. Stephen, courageous, energetic and on occasion prudent, aspired to rule by ecclesiastical sanction and by the support of his magnates. Maud, arrogant and harsh, claimed, as in her charters,[3] to reign as her father's daughter, and it was therefore an hereditary title that in due course she passed on to her son. Neither the one nor the other was capable of translating

[1] No. 9. [2] No. 8, and 6. [3] See No. 46.

into practice the principles of the Anglo-Norman royalty. But the issue between them was none the less of the utmost importance both to the English and the French monarchies. In England the country was faced by the worst of calamities in a feudal State–a disputed succession. In France the ancient antagonism among the fiefs took on a new form. A member of the house of Blois was now claiming not only Touraine but also Normandy and England against the wife of a count of Anjou. And in the Angevin cause the French king saw at last forming before his eyes such a consolidation of French fiefs as might threaten the very existence of Capetian royalty. For these reasons the struggle which began between Stephen and Maud after the death of Henry I not only produced anarchy in England[1] but plunged north-western France into a welter of war. At home the benefits conferred upon England by the strong monarchy established by the Conqueror could be fully appreciated during the disastrous years which marked its decline, and it was fortunate that at least the official system of Henry I was in form retained to be ready for a fresh development when after the treaty which closed the civil war in 1153,[2] the son of Maud succeeded in the next year as sole ruler of England.

Henry II reigned as king for thirty-five years, and was one of the makers of England. His appearance was not prepossessing. Coarsely and sturdily built, he was of middle height, with thick clumsy hands and the arms of a boxer. His hair, worn short, was ruddy and later flecked with white, and his legs were bowed through long standing in the transaction of business. His hard and prominent grey eyes, frequently bloodshot, indicated a shrewd and calculating man of business subject withal to passion.[3] He was a politician rather than a theorist, adapting his aims always to expediency and ever ready to sacrifice good faith to advantage. He was naturally parsimonious and his generosity, which might be lavish, was usually inspired by some ulterior object. He was utterly selfish. He had a wonderful memory which he sought to improve by conversation with the learned, or by assiduous sightseeing when on his travels. He could display kingly manners, and his affability of address was successfully used to win adherence to his plans. His inherent caution was occasionally disturbed, though never mastered, by his ungovernable temper, and if he was, on the whole, a good master, he never trusted his servants. He quarrelled with all his sons, though not necessarily through his own fault, and he was at no time a faithful husband.[4] He was no hero and no genius, nor was he admirable either in temperament or person. But he carried the technique of kingcraft to a very high pitch of competence, and the very selfishness of his politics was adapted to the needs of the age in which he lived. Though he knew private despair and public humiliation, he achieved a large measure of the mundane success he coveted, and he left his mark upon all the countries which he ruled.

[1] No. 1, pp. 199–201. [2] No. 22. [3] Nos. 14–17. [4] Nos. 12, 14–17.

This was a great European prince. Before 1154 he had become count of Anjou, and as such was lord of Touraine. As king of England he became duke of Normandy and count of Brittany. Through his marriage he acquired the duchy of Aquitaine.[1] This mighty empire stretching from the Tweed to the Pyrenees was indeed perhaps the most salient feature in the political structure of Europe during his life, and it inevitably presented a lethal challenge to the kings of France. The Capetian monarchy now found itself confronted with the threat it had hitherto always avoided, and which now took shape in a great confederation of French fiefs rendered the more dangerous through its subjection to a king of England, who was lord over a larger area of France than that possessed by the French kings themselves. It was natural, therefore, that Henry throughout his reign should find himself almost constantly at war with the house of Capet; first with Louis VII and after 1180 with the far more formidable Philip Augustus.[2] His resources, of course, were great, but it was a task to baffle the ability of any ruler to hold together these conglomerate dominions, sundered by an arm of the sea and consisting of peoples who had little in common save in some cases a long tradition of mutual enmity. His experiments in imperial administration were not the least interesting examples of his ability, and particularly noteworthy was his design of ruling his various provinces through his sons–an essay in dynastic federation which was remarkable for the age in which it was attempted.[3] Unfortunately, however, the sons of Henry II, personally in many ways distinguished, were morally and mentally incapable of carrying out in good faith a large and complicated policy, and Philip Augustus was adroit in fomenting disunion among them. His appeal to base motives was successful, and it was probably to the ultimate benefit both of France and England that it should be so. Nevertheless, as the evening of the mighty Angevin empire began to close upon its greatest ruler, an element of true tragedy was to be discerned. The splendour of that far-flung realm faded into betrayal; the web of filial administration was rent by impiety; and at the last the man whose dominion had been founded by fortune and maintained by sagacity found himself bereft of the power for which he had imperilled his soul. He died cursing, ineffectively, the shame that is the lot of a conquered king.[4]

The shadow of that terrible death-bed at Chinon should not, however, be allowed to obscure the importance of Henry's continental position during his life, or the manner in which the prestige thus acquired affected his English realm. This king of England was the most notable secular prince of his day, and his connexions stretched throughout Western Europe. Henry the Lion of Saxony, William of Sicily, and Alfonso, king of Castile, were his sons-in-law; the rulers of Champagne and Flanders were his cousins; Frederick Barbarossa was his ally. His own dominions were renowned not only for their extent but

[1] No. 15, p. 381 [2] Nos. 12, 14, 15. [3] No. 12. [4] No. 15, p. 384.

also as the home of a fresh and flourishing culture. It is unlikely that with his strong sense of reality Henry ever aspired to conquer the whole of France or to win for himself the imperial crown, but neither project was unthinkable, and it is tempting to speculate on what might have been achieved by a crusade led by him and supported by his warrior sons. The prestige of such a man must be reckoned as a factor in his government, and it is on England that the bulk of his vast energy was expended. He seems here to sum up in himself much of the past, and also to concentrate upon his island kingdom many elements derived from his dominions overseas. From Anjou he brought the memory of a compact administration straitly controlled by the count's officials; with Normandy he inherited a financial system capable of being developed and extended; in England he found a tradition of local government not to be matched elsewhere, and the memory of a strong monarchy whose work in providing justice was not less appreciated from the fact that it had been interrupted. Thus were the threads of government placed in his coarse and capable hands, and it was his individual achievement to weave them into a new pattern. Untiringly selfish in his pursuit of power, he gave a new scope to royal administration in England, and in so doing he promoted the interests both of the king and of the kingdom.

The reign of Henry II is best to be considered as marking a stage in English constitutional history, for it was by strengthening the royal administration, and most particularly by making the royal justice directly available to all free men in the land, that this king buttressed the foundations of royalty. What may here be noted is merely the manner in which an identity of interest was thus established between the king and the realm. The expanding royal jurisdiction satisfied the king's lust for power, but it dispensed justice and its efficiency was popular. To the king is to be ascribed an unswerving direction of purpose, to his officials a technical skill in carrying out the royal design, but it was the general acceptance of his measures which alone in the last resort ensured their success. Thus alone was he enabled to withstand all elements of opposition at home; from nobles who found the scope of their private action circumscribed by the encroachments of royal officials; from a strong party in the Church who regarded as immoral and tyrannical the secular interference of the king in ecclesiastical affairs. The quarrel with Becket, the most dramatic and the most disastrous episode of the reign, brought out all that was most violent in the king's character,[1] and the influence of the slain archbishop was to survive the death of his royal antagonist. But neither in 1170[2] nor yet in the rebellion of 1173–1174[3] was Henry's position seriously imperilled. Members of noble houses continued to serve in the royal administration; representative ecclesiastics could support the king against the primate; and Henry II could always rely in England

[1] See especially Nos. 123, 129, 130, 133, 134. [2] No. 12, pp. 337–388. [3] No. 12, pp. 342–356.

on an overwhelming measure of popular acclaim. It was thus that in his reforms he was enabled to create a machinery of government which could form a basis for future constitutional advance. And despite all the reverses he sustained he left the position of the crown in England stronger than he found it.

He has been regarded as an innovator, and so, in some measure, he was; but in truth there was little revolutionary in his policy. He successfully struggled to give to the king an enhanced position in the feudal state, but it was through feudal institutions that he worked,[1] and if he was led into a most spectacular quarrel with the Church, he asserted few ecclesiastical claims that had not been made by his royal predecessors. His financial organization grew out of that used by his grandfather,[2] and his judicial institutions[3] are best to be conceived as the reduction to practice on a vastly extended scale of principles which before had been operative only in a restricted sphere. If his famous reforms[4] were pregnant with future consequence, they none the less derived essentially from the past. He did not inaugurate notions of government: he combined them. He did not originate administrative ideas: he gave them an enlarged application. The first of the Angevins was the greatest heir to the monarchy created by William the Conqueror.

The hearts of kings are proverbially unsearchable, and when these belong to men inhabiting a distant world the task of scrutinizing them becomes well-nigh impossible. The bright light of research seldom irradiates the actual lineaments of those who wielded such power: at best it may reveal a simulacrum of the truth, as it were a dark shadow on a white wall. Nevertheless the investigation is of value, for in the individuality of these rulers is to be found a factor in English history. The men of this age gave great authority to their kings and demanded much from them. The monarch was a public institution,[5] but he was none the less a man whose personal idiosyncrasies were accepted as being an element in politics. The strain on individual character thus produced needs little elaboration. The strange acts and wild passions of these men are indeed to be explained in part as deriving from conditions of life which were highly abnormal. These kings, for instance, were constantly on the move, so much so that the porter of the king's bed had a recognized place at his court.[6] And the king, travelling perpetually from place to place, was never alone: public at his uprising and his worship, in his journeyings and in his judicial acts, at his meals, in his sleep. Fiercely criticized in relation to his responsibilities he was largely uncontrolled by external restraints. His human opportunities were vast, but he must have had much ado to save his soul.

Fortunately, such ultimate judgment is beyond the competence of the historian, but he is none the less called upon to assess the public results of the

[1] Cf. Nos. 58, 266, 268. [2] No. 70, and see Nos. 62–68. [3] No. 58.
[4] Nos. 24, 25, 27, 28. [5] No. 170. [6] No. 30, p. 425.

work of men so placed and so tried. And his final verdict can hardly fail to be impressive. The development of England between 1042 and 1189 would have been very different apart from the personal qualities of the kings who ruled her. They move somewhat portentously across a stage dim-lit: Edward the Confessor, strange compound of pietism, statesmanship and weakness, passes to leave a venerated memory to his successors; William of Normandy, perhaps the most constructive genius ever to occupy the English throne, gives a new direction to the growth of the land he conquers; Henry I, less notable, is none the less a son not unworthy of his father; and Henry II, adding to his inheritance, imparts to it a new value. None of these men was lovable, but none was negligible, and two at least were great. Their private lives were interwoven with English history which cannot be interpreted without reference to their characteristic acts.

(vi) THE POLITICS OF BRITAIN

The Norman Conquest, by establishing in England a new aristocracy and setting up a strong monarchy at its head, profoundly modified also the politics of Britain. In one sense the political development which ensued could be viewed as a simple expansion of power whereby at the end of this period the king of England became overlord also of Scotland, Wales and Ireland. From another point of view this same process might be regarded as the extension of feudal custom and feudal administration over countries where before they had been unknown. But there were other results involved which were at once more important and more durable. Between 1042 and 1189 the political balance of Britain was fundamentally altered, and this change entailed permanent consequences for all that wide area of Britain which in the mid-eleventh century might be called Celtic.

In 1042 the Celtic regions of Britain, knit together in some measure by common traditions, by common sentiments and by a certain community of speech, were of wide extent and strong influence. But they were politically decadent. Thus the strongest unit among them, the kingdom of Alban based upon Perthshire, was in the middle of the eleventh century racked with that civil strife which has been inaccurately immortalized for the delight of posterity in connexion with the names of Duncan, Macbeth and Siward. In Wales the principalities of Gwynned and Powys, of Deheubrath and Morgannwg, each divided into cantrefs, struggled perpetually together. In Ireland the four kingdoms of Leinster, Munster, Connaught and Ulster engaged in endless wars for the doubtful privilege of providing a High King who might exercise a shadowy supremacy over the whole island. Nowhere, over all these wide regions, had tribal organization succeeded in sustaining political unity, or authority preserved political order. Moreover, the position of these Celtic principalities had been further complicated by the Scandinavian settlements. The mighty thrust from the Scandinavian lands which had colonized Iceland, reached Greenland and pushed on to America, had also turned southwards to absorb Shetland and the Orkneys, to ravage Wales, and to devastate much of Ireland. In 1042 Caithness and Sutherland, with most of the Hebrides, were under Scandinavian domination; the place-names of Wales–for example Anglesea and Gresholm, Fishguard and Haverford–bore witness to the earlier incursions; whilst in Ireland the invasions, which had aforetime established a Norse kingdom, had left behind them trading communities of Ostmen settled for instance at Dublin, Waterford, Wexford and Limerick. In the middle of the eleventh century the Celtic lands of Britain were confronted with problems arising out of the earlier Norse settlements, and after 1066 they had also to face a powerful and militant polity newly established in England.

Nowhere was this double tension more clearly displayed than in Scotland. The relations between the kingdom of Alban and the Scandinavian areas to its north had not yet been finally determined, and more doubtful still was the ultimate fate of the two border provinces which separated that kingdom from England and which may thus be very generally designated and described: *Cumbria*, largely Celtic in sentiment, stretching from the Clyde to the Westmorland Fells; and *Lothian*, with strong Anglian traditions, extending from the Forth southward to a boundary as yet undefined. Upon these two provinces the impact of the Norman Conquest was at once to be felt, and the three cardinal questions which were to dominate Anglo-Scottish relations in this period became clearly posed. What should be the political filiations of Cumbria and Lothian? Where should be drawn the frontier between England and Scotland? And, within Scotland, what should be the political position of the kingdom of Alban now extending from the Forth to the Spey? All these vital questions awaited solution while Duncan, Macbeth and Siward played out their famous struggle between 1040 and 1057.[1] But an answer was to be given to all of them in due course by events consequent upon the Norman Conquest of England.

The drama of the Norman Conquest began for Scotland about 1056 when Malcolm Canmore came from Strathclyde to reign in Alban. This young man, son of the murdered Duncan, had lived at Edward's court; he had married a Scandinavian princess;[2] and he had acquired a Celtic kingdom. He was therefore peculiarly attuned to all the chief political questions of the hour. If he could be indifferent to the fate of an earl of Wessex he must none the less have felt himself deeply concerned in the events of 1066, since these directly involved the fate of Alban and his own southern frontiers. Fulford removed some of his chief enemies in England; Stamford Bridge destroyed a Scandinavian king who might well have proved a rival in the north; and Hastings brought him face to

[1] Nos. 1, 2. [2] See Table 16.

face with yet more formidable opponents. He could not ignore the challenge, the more especially when exiles from the dispossessed English aristocracy came flocking to his court.[1] Thus the crisis of the Norman Conquest was reached for Scotland in the late summer of 1066 when the fleet of Harold Hardraada reached Shetland, and it was not passed until some six years later. The Rising of the North of 1069–1070 was undertaken in large measure with Scottish help,[2] and a natural consequence of its suppression was William's invasion of Scotland in 1072.[3] The expedition brought the Norman knights up to the very gates of the Highlands, and without fight the pact of Abernethy was made between the king of Alban and the Conqueror. By it, according to the Anglo-Saxon Chronicle, Malcolm gave hostages to William and became his man. Whether such homage was held to involve the kingdom of Alban itself, or only the lands of Lothian need not here be discussed. The immediate importance of the pact of Abernethy was that by it Malcolm recognized the new Norman order in England. Edgar Atheling left the Scottish court.

The frontier between England and Scotland was not settled at Abernethy. Both Cumbria and Lothian remained, as it were, in equipoise between North and South, and the Conqueror was in fact never able to exercise a continuous or effective rule over many regions which later formed part of England. When in 1086 he made his great survey of the whole of his kingdom he was forced to omit from his description almost all of the modern counties of Cumberland, Westmorland and Northumberland. The amazing detail of the Domesday Survey has often, and justly, been admired, but its limitations ought also to be recognized. The England which is there surveyed is roughly bounded on the north by the Tees and the Westmorland hills. Even in 1086 the problem of Cumbria and Lothian still remained to be solved. Nor was any solution provided for this question until five years later. The campaigns of William Rufus against Scotland in 1091–1092 are somewhat obscure, but they entailed the most permanent achievement of his reign. By agreements, then concluded, the king of Scotland received, on terms, Lothian from the Forth to the Tweed, whilst Rufus annexed to his own dominions Cumbria as far north as the Solway. An English colony was planted in Carlisle and the city fortified as a bastion against the North.[4] The frontier between England and Scotland was at last being defined in a manner which was not indicated by geography, but which was a compromise between conflicting claims; and the boundary thus indicated in the reign of Rufus has, with certain minor modifications, endured to this day.

The removal from Scotland of southern Cumbria, matched as it was by her acquisition of Lothian, altered the political balance of northern Britain. Henceforth the political centre of Scotland gradually ceased to be the ancient kingdom

[1] No. 1, p. 169. [2] No. 1, p. 150. [3] No. 1, p. 154. [4] No. 1, p. 169.

of Alban, between Forth and Spey, and the country tended to fall, more and more, under the sway of kings ruling from Dunfermline and Edinburgh. Indeed, the development of medieval Scotland might in one sense be viewed as the gradual extension over the country of the influence of Lothian and Fife. This process, moreover, took place just at the time when the Anglian characteristics of Lothian were themselves being fortified, and the tendency was consciously developed by the Scottish royal dynasty. The marriage of Malcolm to Margaret, sister of Edgar Atheling, may indeed be regarded as a symbol of the new orientation in the politics of northern Britain. For Margaret, herself the offspring of the Saxon royal house, was to represent in Scotland many of the interests which the English exiles in Lothian were concerned to foster, and as the avowed supporter of the new ecclesiasticism she championed many of the ideas which were implicit in the policy both of William and of Lanfranc.[1] She sought to oppose the Celtic elements in Scottish society, and was the self-styled enemy of all forms of political and ecclesiastical provincialism. Certainly she brought the politics of England and Scotland into closer relation, and it is characteristic of her career that one of her daughters should have married Henry I, thus linking together not only the English and Norman dynasties but also the two reigning royal houses of Britain.[2]

Thus were fostered all the social changes already at work in the north, and southern influence became more apparent in Scotland. Two of Margaret's daughters were educated at the English nunnery of Romsey; and of her sons, four were given the English names of Edgar, Edward, Edmund and Ethelred, whilst two more, Alexander and David, bore names which were not in the Scottish royal tradition.[3] These men, as if inevitably, carried on the work of their mother. They came, not as strangers, into Anglo-Norman England; they held land south of the border as English earls. To Scotland they applied Anglo-Norman feudal custom, and their courts were dominated by Anglo-Norman personalities. Similarly the "Inquisition of David",[4] which in the early twelfth century surveyed some of Scottish Strathclyde has been held, not wholly without reason, to reflect Anglo-Norman principles of administration. It was in short the sons of Margaret who transformed Celtic Scotland into a feudal kingdom in which Celtic customs remained strong but politically subordinate.

The extension to Scotland of Anglo-Norman feudalism raised new problems for the Scottish kings, the more especially when these kings became, in respect of their English lands, tenants-in-chief of the English crown. David I succeeded to the earldom of Huntingdon in 1113, and passed on that dignity to his son Henry in 1136. Henry, deprived of Huntingdon in 1138, acquired the earldom of Northumberland in the next year, and retained it until his death in 1152, when it devolved on his son, Malcolm, who held it until 1157. This Malcolm,

[1] No. 90. [2] No. 1, p. 176. [3] See Table 16. [4] No. 54.

who obtained the Scottish crown in 1153, was recognized as earl of Huntingdon in 1157, and his younger brother, William, also in his turn king of Scotland, succeeded to the Huntingdonshire earldom in 1165, and held it until he was deprived in 1174.[1] Such possessions, which undoubtedly much increased the wealth of the Scottish kings, involved them very closely in English politics. During the civil war of Stephen's reign David invaded England on behalf of himself and of the empress, Maud, and sustained a heavy defeat at the battle of the Standard in 1138.[2] Nevertheless, at the time of his death in 1153 he was in virtual control of most of England north of the Tees. Henry II after his accession was thus faced with a challenge in the North and he was not slow to accept it.

The Scottish dynasty was in truth to be weakened rather than strengthened by its English possessions, for the most powerful and ambitious monarchy in Western Europe was not likely to neglect the opportunity thus presented of extending its claims of overlordship to include the controversial province of Lothian, and even the kingdom of Alban itself. Very early in his reign Henry II deprived Malcolm IV, the young king of Scotland, of the Northumbrian earldom, and in 1173 he was given the occasion to make more extended demands. In that year William the Lion, who had by then succeeded to the Scottish throne, joined the rebellion of Henry II's sons, and was himself taken prisoner.[3] Forced to agree to terms, he was compelled by a treaty ratified at Falaise[4] in 1174 to accept in full the English position. He admitted himself to be an ordinary tenant-in-chief of the English crown, doing homage to Henry II "as the other men of my lord the king are wont". The magnates of Scotland were similarly pledged to do homage to Henry II as against all other men, and as a guarantee of faith the castles of Roxburgh, Berwick, Jedburgh, Edinburgh and Stirling were handed over to English garrisons.

The treaty of Falaise defined in the manner most favourable to England the relations between the Scottish and Anglo-Norman monarchies which had entered on a new phase at the time of the Norman Conquest. Nor did its terms remain inoperative. William the Lion, attended Henry's court on summons, and there he allowed his own tenants-in-chief, on occasion, to seek judgment. It is true that sometimes resistance was offered, but for some fifteen years after the treaty of Falaise the Scottish monarchy was in feudal subjection to England. During the latter part of his reign Henry II exercised rights over Scotland such as were never enjoyed by any English medieval king before or after his time.

The relations thus established between the monarchies of England and Scotland were not to prove permanent, and they were not the most important part of the consequences to Scotland of the Norman Conquest. For Scotland a more notable result was the political subordination of the Celtic elements within her own borders, and partly for that reason the future history of Scotland

[1] See Table 9. [2] No. 11. [3] No. 12, p. 350; No. 13. [4] No. 26.

was to be markedly different from that of Ireland. Nevertheless, the Celtic world to the west of England was also to feel the impact of the Normans, and there too, over Wales and into Ireland, Norman influence was during this period to be extended.

The Norman Conquest was to open a new era in Anglo-Welsh history. During the reign of Edward the Confessor the relations between England and Wales had been dominated by the figure of Griffith ap Llewelyn, prince of North Wales, who, having achieved a predominant position in his own country, had sought to take advantage of the prevailing rivalries among the great English earldoms. His raids upon Herefordshire, for instance, occupy a prominent position in the Anglo-Saxon annals of this time, and the most notable feature of the policy he pursued was his alliance with Ælfgar, earl of Mercia.[1] It was not until after Ælfgar's death that in 1062 Harold felt himself strong enough to take the field against his Welsh adversary, and his overthrow of Griffith[2] undoubtedly facilitated his own seizure of the English crown in 1066. The battle of Hastings therefore not only removed a notable enemy of Wales, but set up a much more formidable adversary in his place. One of the earliest and most remarkable features of the Norman settlement was the establishment of the great Marcher earldoms of Hereford, Chester, and Shrewsbury,[3] and it was from these earldoms that there began at once a persistent penetration into Wales which, within twenty years of the battle of Hastings, had given the Normans all the strategic positions necessary for a further advance. William fitz Osbern, earl of Hereford, for example, had before 1071 planted colonies at Chepstow and Monmouth, and had added Gwent to his possessions. Somewhat later Hugh of Avranches, earl of Chester, extended his power to the river Clywd and provided the means for further encroachments by his cousin, Robert of Rhuddlan, who was for a time to make himself master of Gwynned. Similarly Roger of Montgomery, made earl of Shrewsbury about 1075, acquired the county which has ever since borne his name. It was a most notable advance, and though it met with strong resistance during the earlier years of William Rufus, it was not stayed. With the death of Rhys ap Tudor, prince of South Wales, in 1093 the first stage in the Norman occupation of Wales was concluded.

The general character of that occupation was in fact to be disclosed before the death of Henry I. By 1135 there had already been established in Wales many of those great families which were to dominate much of Welsh history in the feudal epoch. Gilbert fitz Richard of Clare, grandson of Gilbert of Brionne, the count, was in possession of Cardigan;[4] to the east in Radnor was to be found Philip of Briouze, son of a notable Domesday tenant in England; Henry of Beaumont, earl of Warwick,[5] had obtained the lordship of Gower; Bernard of

[1] Nos. 1, 2 [2] Nos. 1, 2. [3] Tables 10, 13, 14. [4] See Table 11. [5] See Table 12.

Neufmarché ruled in Brecknock; and Robert 'fitz Hamon' was established at Cardiff, and later was to pass on his power in Glamorgan to his daughter who married Robert, illegitimate son of Henry I. All these magnates were surrounded by their Norman followers among whom they parcelled out the lands which they had come to control. The feudal organization of the Anglo-Norman State had in fact stretched far beyond Offa's Dyke, and was beginning to enmesh the Celtic land of Wales.

Nowhere were the consequences of this more notable than in Pembrokeshire whose history at this period had a special importance. Before his fall in 1102 Arnulf of Montgomery, son of the first earl of Shrewsbury,[1] had acquired Pembroke, and started the construction of its castle, which he gave into the charge of one of his chief followers, Gerald of Windsor, who himself fortified Carew. At Manorbier, Odo of Barry was established. Moreover, the power of these families and that of their followers was much fortified by their alliances. Gerald of Windsor took to wife Nesta, the daughter of Rhys ap Tudor, and from this marriage may be dated the emergence of a new type among the Norman nobility. For Nesta, who formed other less regular connexions, imparted to her descendants[2] something of the Welsh patriotism of her father, and her sons and grandsons, while sustaining to the full the Norman tradition of conquest, were none the less to exhibit an individual quality in their astonishing adventures in Wales and Ireland. This Norman group in Pembrokeshire, further linked by a marriage between a son of Odo of Barry and a daughter of Gerald of Windsor, was also strengthened in its position by an extensive importation of Flemings into the district during Henry I's reign. These, unlike the Norman nobles, never sought to be a military aristocracy, but they formed a distinct community of industrious farmers and traders, and as such they displaced many of the native inhabitants. Their coming completed the social change which the Normans had begun, and from the beginning of the twelfth century Pembrokeshire began to lose its Celtic character. Welsh gradually ceased to be there the predominant language; and Welsh place-names tended to be replaced by others which, like Hubberston, Lambston and Jordanston, were based upon the names of the new settlers. "Little England beyond Wales" was in process of formation.

The pattern of Norman domination in Wales was always subject to modification, but its main lines were determined by the end of Henry I's reign. The Norman grip on Anglesea, Powys and Cardigan was always precarious, and North Wales was for long to retain much of its independence and many of its native rulers. In the south, however, the story was different. Glamorgan and Gower, Carmarthen and Pembroke yielded up their riches to the invaders, and the region from Manorbier to Cardiff became politically a Norman land. For the remainder of this period the history of Wales is thus to be regarded as in

[1] See Table 13. [2] See Table 15.

one sense forming part of the feudal history of England with the important qualification that feudal disputes when they occurred not only caused (as in England) social disorder, but also gave opportunity for the dispossessed in Wales to rise in revolt. Thus the civil war of Stephen's reign had a double effect on Wales. It caused fluctuations of power among the Norman magnates whereby, for example, Gilbert fitz Gilbert, son of the former lord of Cardigan, became earl of Pembroke.[1] But at the same time the disturbance gave occasion for the rise of Owen of Gwynned and for the Celtic revival which he sponsored in the north. Nor is it remarkable that the reign of Henry II should have proved in Wales as in England to be a time of resettlement. The campaign waged by that king in 1157 against Owen in the north was in the earlier tradition, but with the rise in South Wales of Rhys ap Griffith a new situation developed. For Rhys stabilized his own power by means of an alliance with the Angevin king, and Henry II was, on his side, content to recognize the position of Rhys in return for his vassalage. He treated him as a fellow of the Norman magnates in Wales. A new climate of opinion was in fact beginning to prevail which is exactly represented in Gerald of Wales,[2] the chronicler who, as the son of a lord of Manorbier, combined the sentiments of the Norman aristocracy with an authentic Celtic enthusiasm that he inherited from his Welsh grandmother. Henry II at the end of his reign was overlord of Wales, but he ruled over a country whose essential Celtic character had, by the Norman Conquest, been modified though by no means impaired.

The Norman settlements in South Wales were the base from which took place towards the end of this period a further penetration in the Celtic lands of Britain. For Ireland too at this time invited attack; and in 1166 an opportunity was given when Dermot, king of Leinster, exiled from his realm, sought the aid of Henry II.[3] The Angevin king was at this time too much engaged in the Becket controversy to take any personal initiative in the matter, but he seems to have consented to Dermot's seeking allies among his subjects. As a result Dermot turned to the barons of South Wales, and more particularly to Richard of Clare, son of Gilbert fitz Gilbert, earl of Pembroke, and nicknamed Strongbow.[4] The earl stipulated for the inheritance of Leinster, but took no immediate action. Two of the sons of Nesta, however, Robert 'fitz Stephen' and Maurice 'fitz Gerald', departed to Ireland in 1169, and with Dermot's help took possession of Wexford. In May 1170 Raymond 'the Fat', a trusted vassal of the earl of Pembroke, established himself near Waterford, and in August of the same year Strongbow himself arrived with a considerable force. Before the summer of 1171 he was in possession of the seaport towns of Dublin, Waterford and Wexford; he had overrun Leinster; and had married Eva, the daughter of Dermot.[5] He had in fact ushered in a new era in Irish politics.

[1] See Table 11 [2] See No. 15. [3] No. 12, p. 340. [4] See Table 11. [5] See Table 11.

These conquests were astonishingly rapid, and their success is to be explained partly by Irish disunion, and partly by the superior discipline and military skill of the invaders. Much also was due to the leaders. The sons of Nesta exhibited to the full the Norman capacity for adventure. But Strongbow himself was a man of different mark. A general of ability, he was also a skilled negotiator. He knew how to win battles, but he knew also how to administer a conquered land. He dominated the early Norman enterprise in Ireland, and to him more than to any other single man is due the establishment of the English Pale. He set up a new Norman kingdom at the edge of the western world.

To Henry II this achievement was disquieting. He therefore summoned back the adventurers, and cut off their supplies from England. This action immediately placed Strongbow in difficulties. He had succeeded as king of Leinster, but he could not hold his kingdom against Henry II. He therefore came in person to England to submit, giving up the sea-coast towns which were in fact the key to Ireland, and agreeing to hold Leinster itself as a vassal.[1] From this time forwards the relative importance of Strongbow diminished, but he had prepared the way for further conquests, and in 1172 Henry II determined to take advantage of the situation. With papal approval[2] he invaded Ireland, and immediately took possession of Dublin, Waterford and Wexford, placing in the first town an English colony in which men from Bristol were prominent.[3] He then proceeded to develop his own Irish policy, which was to balance the native against the Norman magnates, and the Norman magnates against each other. Thus Hugh of Lassy was granted the whole of Meath[4] as a counterpoise to the power of Leinster, and at the same time the king received the submission and friendship of many of the Irish chieftains. In 1175 he was to conclude a treaty with the High King himself. Nevertheless, during this period some fresh conquests were made. In Leinster the Norman dominion was pushed as far as Limerick, and John of Courcy was given permission to retain for himself whatever he could conquer in Ulster.[5] In a series of savage battles he managed to reduce most of the province to submission, and subsequently he established in the north a remarkably effective feudal administration. The Norman settlement of Ulster is not the least interesting episode in the Norman government of Ireland.

The partial conquest of Ireland by the Normans which took place during the closing decades of this period will, for many reasons, repay careful study. In one sense a part of the general expansion of the Anglo-Norman State, it none the less from the start exhibited special features which limited its success. It suffered in particular from divided purpose. Two policies might advantageously have been pursued. Either Strongbow and his associates might have been left to work out the settlement of the country; and in this case they might, with the

[1] No. 12. [2] Nos. 160–162. [3] No. 289. [4] No. 267. [5] No. 12, p. 363.

marvellous adaptability of their race, have achieved in Ireland some such political reconstruction as was effected by their predecessors in southern Italy. Alternatively, the king of England might have taken a direct and constant interest in the government of his new realm in an attempt to bring about a Norman settlement of Ireland comparable to the Norman settlement of England. Unfortunately, Ireland was too near to England for the former policy to be tolerated, and too far away for the latter to be made effective. The sons of Nesta were never to play the part of the sons of Tancred, and Henry II was never to perform in Ireland the work of the Conqueror in England. The result was a compromise whereby the various Norman families in Ireland were set against each other, or pitted against the Irish princes. John's short government of Ireland in 1185 was in every way symptomatic of an unhappy future. And Ireland was denied the boons of that ordered administration which elsewhere the Normans at least in some measure conferred upon the lands they ruled.

It would, however, be wrong to allow the bitterness engendered by subsequent history to distort judgment upon the work of the Normans in Ireland. It is true that the warfare involved in the settlement was of quite exceptional brutality, but it was probably no worse than the outrages which had perpetually stained Irish history for more than a century before the Normans came, and it would be a fond fallacy to picture the Norman invasion as a disturbance by ruthless adventurers of a happy and prosperous land. There are perhaps some reasons for thinking that Ireland may have gained more than she lost by the coming of the Normans. At the end of the twelfth century the feudalized districts of Ireland were the least disturbed regions in a distracted country, and the cities undoubtedly benefited from Norman rule. Feudal organization could never in Ireland so modify tribal tradition as to produce an harmonious administration, and the tendency of the new rulers to treat the inhabitants as an inferior race left a legacy of justifiable bitterness. But Ireland did not fail to reap some benefits at least from the *pax Normannica*.

The expansion beyond England of Anglo-Norman feudalism is in fact nowhere to be regarded merely as a progress of crude conquest. Its ecclesiastical implications for instance are not to be ignored. In Scotland, the influence of St. Margaret was as strong on the Scottish Church as it was on the Scottish State, and it was supported by Lanfranc.[1] In Wales, the advent of the Normans entailed in due course the subjection of the Welsh dioceses to Canterbury. In Ireland, the same tendency is to be observed. Whatever views may be held as to the authenticity of the bull *Laudabiliter*,[2] there is no reason to doubt that Henry II's invasion of Ireland was supported by the papacy,[3] and that it was regarded at Rome as directed towards a reformation in the Irish Church, and a closer approximation of that Church to the customs of Western Christendom.

[1] No. 90. [2] No. 159. [3] Nos. 160–162.

The council of Cashel of 1172, summoned during Henry II's short sojourn in Ireland, met under the presidency of a papal legate, and it served the double purpose of reconciling the Irish prelates to the invaders and of inaugurating much needed reforms. Not only administrative order in the State, but also an ecclesiastical discipline conforming to European practice was everywhere a mark of the extension of Anglo-Norman power in Britain during this period.

The consequences of that remarkable expansion were to vary in the several countries which were affected by it. In Scotland, these results were modified by developments within the country which led the Scottish monarchy itself to foster some of the ideas characteristic of the Normans. In Wales, the country by its very proximity to England was brought more directly under the influence of its more powerful neighbour. In both Scotland and Wales, problems were raised during this period which were not to be settled until after the reign of Edward I. In Ireland, the results of the Norman settlements, if perhaps less durable and certainly less happy, were none the less profound. Everywhere, moreover, a general tendency is to be observed in Britain during this period. It is towards the curtailment of Celtic political influence in these islands. This indeed is not the least notable feature which distinguishes the political structure of Britain in 1189 from what it had been in 1042, and there can be little doubt that the chief factor in bringing about this change was the feudal aristocracy established in England after 1066, and the new monarchy it served.

(vii) GOVERNMENT

The main work of this monarchy and this aristocracy was, however, to be done in England. The feudal organization which was set up by the Norman kings and accepted by their greater followers inevitably marked the opening of a new era in English government, but even as the lower ranks of society were less affected than their superiors by the events of 1066–1070, so also did there remain in England almost unimpaired a strong tradition of local administration which had already been crystallized into institutions.[1] It was indeed a characteristic achievement in the Norman aristocracy to utilize existing organs of local government, and it was an essential part of the political genius of the Conqueror, not only to respect local custom, but to develop the institutions of monarchy which he found existing in the land he conquered. In the sphere of constitutional history the Norman Conquest introduced changes which were fundamental and far-reaching, but those changes are only in a very restricted sense to be described as revolutionary.

In posing as the heir to the Confessor, the Conqueror laid claim to a kingship which had enjoyed at least one of the greatest assets which could be possessed

[1] See *English Historical Documents*, vol. I.

by a medieval monarchy. The West-Saxon dynasty had never, despite disasters, lost that prestige which derived from its earlier achievements. There was here at least a tradition of effective government, and the institutions by which this had been maintained were by no means moribund. It was not for nothing that the Conqueror took over the organization of the Old English royal writing-office,[1] that he derived the bulk of his revenue from a tax–the Danegeld[2]–which had for long been regularly levied, or that he utilized in the sheriff an official who had for long served as the chief link between the king and the various local communities which made up the realm.[3] In such spheres of action no break is to be observed at the Conquest, but everywhere there appeared a tendency towards the more efficient employment of institutions already in existence. The commands of the royal Chancery if not more frequently issued were more frequently obeyed; the sheriff advanced towards a position of greater authority in the shire; and the revenue increased. Everywhere a strong monarchical rule is to be seen exercising its power through magnates holding their land under different sanctions from their predecessors. The Norman aristocracy was probably more powerful in England than the nobility it supplanted, but none of its members–even the most mighty–ever succeeded in deflecting royal policy after the manner of the great earls who, under the Confessor, reigned theoretically as the nominees of the king in Northumbria, Mercia, and Wessex. As the most immediate social consequence of the Conquest was the setting up of a new aristocracy, so also the starting-point of constitutional development under the Norman kings is to be found in the changed relationship of that aristocracy with the king.

Edward the Confessor, like his predecessors, governed in consultation with his magnates, and the Anglo-Saxon Chronicle gives many indications of the meeting of his witan or council.[4] The composition of the witan in the earlier half of the eleventh century differed little from what it had been in the tenth. It consisted normally of three classes of persons: great ecclesiastics, great lay nobles, and lesser men who attended either as officials of the royal household or for some special reason at the king's command. It might be consulted by the king on any act of government, on the promulgation of laws, on the levying of taxes, on diplomacy or defence, or in connexion with the solemn ratification of grants of land or privilege. Its function was in the simplest sense to counsel the king, and the king on his part naturally wished to secure the support of those who alone could enable his acts to become operative. In this practical manner only did they exercise control over the monarchy and in the same sense only can they be regarded as playing a part in the choice of the king. Anglo-Saxon kingship was hereditary, but strict rules of primogeniture were not applied to it with any regularity, and the determination as to which member

[1] Cf. p. 800. [2] Nos. 1, p. 120, and 70, p. 525. [3] Nos. 31–40.
[4] No. 1, especially pp. 119, 120, 124, 127, 129, 132.

of the royal house should succeed could always be influenced first by the declared will of the reigning king and secondly in a practical manner by the amount of backing which any claimant could secure from the magnates of the land. Harold and William thus both claimed that they had been nominated by the Confessor[1] and each in turn sought to obtain the support of an assembly of magnates. To assert, however, that these conditions implied that Anglo-Saxon monarchy was 'elective', or that in the witan there was vested a constitutional right to limit the king's authority, is to intrude into the eleventh-century notions derived from later political theory. The king desired the advice and co-operation of his magnates, and if successful he obtained it. It was the strong, and not the weak, king who had a large and powerful witan.

Such was the assembly which William found in England surrounding the king, and at first, it seems, he was content to leave its character unchanged. The council which bore witness to some of his charters in 1068 differed little in character from previous witans.[2] William fitz Osbern and Roger of Montgomery took their place beside Edwin, Morcar and Waltheof; Saxon and Norman prelates attended in company; and among the household officials there were some who had served at the Confessor's court. The transition to a new type of assembly only took place gradually, and it was the result of the general application of feudal principles to the higher ranks of English society. The duty of a feudal vassal included not only military service for his lord, but also the obligation to attend his lord's court, and the court of the Anglo-Norman king must in one sense be regarded simply as the most important feudal court in the land–a court to which the immediate vassals of the king–his tenants-in-chief –were bound in feudal duty, if summoned, to attend.[3] When the *servitia debita* had been imposed not only on the lay magnates, but also on prelates in respect of their temporalities, the feudal character of the council became yet more pronounced, and though the principle was never rigidly or exclusively applied, the *curia regis* came to consist in the first instance of men who were linked to the king through the new conditions under which they held their land.

This assembly met with greater regularity than the witan in the days of Edward the Confessor, but its full sessions were normally confined to the three feasts of Christmas, Easter and Pentecost. These were, moreover, grand occasions. The *curia regis* of the Anglo-Norman kings was not only a council: it was also in the more modern use of the term the court, wherein was displayed the splendour of kingship. A meeting of this court at one of the great festivals of the Christian year was an occasion for magnificence, an opportunity for entertainment, and as such it served an additional purpose. It permitted the magnates of England to maintain personal touch with each other, and it enabled the king to become acquainted with the affairs of all the regions of his realm

[1] See Nos. 1, p. 142, 4.   [2] No. 77.   [3] Cf. Nos. 52, 58.

through intercourse with the men who were responsible for their conduct. Such was the atmosphere, for instance, which surrounded the 'deep speech' held by the Conqueror at his Christmas court at Gloucester, when the Domesday inquisition was planned,[1] and the character of such an assembly can be well judged by the attestation to an instrument given by William at Laycock about 1086 in the presence of an assembly of magnates whose interests covered the whole of England except the extreme north.[2] A contribution towards English political unity may even have been made by these assemblies wherein the new masters of England met together and with their king for mutual entertainment and counsel.

It was, however, not merely on such occasions of special magnificence that the king sought counsel of his magnates, and his *curia* was often of much smaller dimensions. Even in the reign of William the Conqueror it is possible to detect a small group of counsellors who seem to be in more constant attendance on the king. Robert, count of Mortain, Alan, count of Brittany and earl of Richmond, Richard 'fitz Gilbert', William of Warenne, and Henry de Ferrières appear to have been treated by the Conqueror as a sort of inner circle of advisers. Later, Henry I was to develop this principle in a novel manner by raising up a group of 'new men' to do him service.[3] A crowd of fresh names, of which the Clintons and the Bassets were among the most notable, thus appear among the attestations to Henry's charters, and this class through grants of land and privilege speedily advanced to great power. These were more specifically the officials of the king trained to do his business, royal administrators, the nucleus of a new aristocracy of service. They formed a prominent part of the *curia* at its larger sessions, but their real work was done elsewhere. In constant association with the king they were the most effective agents of his will, and able themselves to give their own direction to the details of royal policy.

It would in short be unwise to give too great precision to the composition or functions of the king's council in this age. The essence of government was personal monarchy: the king governed the realm and summoned to his assistance those men who he thought could best help him in his work. It was still a duty rather than a privilege to attend the court, and the council of the king expands and contracts according to his pleasure. In this sense the nucleus of the *curia* was the king's household wherein his most intimate and trusted servants were to be found. Not the least important, or the most appreciated, document relating to the early constitutional history of England is that curious record of the *Establishment of the King's Household*[4] which reflects the conditions of the latter part of the reign of Henry I. The primitive nature of early government is here fully revealed. The chancellor takes his place alongside the king's huntsmen,

[1] No. 1, p. 161. [2] No. 52. [3] No. 8. [4] No. 30.

and prominent officials are stewards, chamberlains, and butlers. The holders of these domestic offices were, moreover, important men. William fitz Osbern himself was *dapifer* to the Conqueror both as duke and king, and Eudo *dapifer* and Haimo *dapifer* were important landowners at the time of Domesday. Hugh and Roger 'd'Ivry', notable tenants-in-chief, were butlers. There is no occasion here to consider what changes in the organization of the royal household occurred in England as the result of the Conquest. Throughout this period the holders of the chief household offices, designated by humble titles, were among the most important men in the land, and among the most influential members of the king's council.

The character of this royal council implied that it was in theory omnicompetent. There was as yet little differentiation of governmental functions, and all categories of secular administration were considered in this body. The trend of constitutional development during this age was, however, towards the formation out of the *curia* of more organized departments of state in which men with special competence were assigned special tasks. Thus before the end of the Conqueror's reign an organized Chancery was in being. The documents it issued were formally derived from the practice which had existed in the Confessor's time, but as Latin gradually replaced English as the language not only of charters but also of writs,[1] so did a new order appear in the *scriptorium* itself. It is improbable, though not impossible, that Edward had a chancellor, but from 1068 onwards there was always an officer with this title appointed by the king to be in charge of the royal clerks, and the office was rapidly to grow in importance. In the primitive *Establishment of the King's Household* he takes the lead among the officials there described.[2] No less a man than Roger, bishop of Salisbury, was chancellor in the reign of Henry I, and Thomas Becket was chancellor to Henry II[3] before, in 1162, he became archbishop of Canterbury.

Finance and justice are always the main concerns of government, and it was therefore naturally in respect of these that the advance towards new constitutional forms was most marked. The establishment of military feudalism in the country involved at the outset one important change in the royal revenue, for the king like every feudal lord might exact money from his tenants by way of the incidents of knight-service,[4] and the charter issued by Henry I in 1100[5] indicates how important these were to the Anglo-Norman king. Indeed, in some quarters the feudal incidents might be regarded as the most legitimate source of the king's supplies, and other levies might be considered as extraordinary, as needing the consent of the taxed. The Saladin tithe[6] levied at the end of the reign of Henry II bore in this sense the character of a new departure in taxational policy, and it was only exacted after special consultation between

[1] Nos. 31-40. [2] No. 30. [3] Nos. 119, 120.
[4] No. 268. [5] No. 19. [6] No. 29.

the king and his council. Feudally speaking, it might be contended that the king like any other feudal lord should 'live of his own'.

The king, however, was always something more than the supreme feudal lord, and his regalian rights enabled him to rely upon sources of revenue peculiar to himself. William was therefore fortunate in succeeding to a monarchy that had been able to create a system of tax collection which had been regularly used to raise the gelds,[1] and more particularly the Danegelds, that were so lamentable a feature of late Old English history. When such a geld was levied, its total amount was decided in the king's council, and this was partitioned in a defined proportion among the various shires, and later (within the shires) among their constituent hundreds. The scheme, though cumbersome, had many advantages, and since it had been operative for a long period, it is not surprising that the Conqueror continued to use it, so that it forms, for instance, the basis of the financial arrangements described in the Domesday Survey. Even in the mechanism of tax collecting there was little change in the period immediately following the Norman Conquest, and the Norman practice of allowing the sheriff to 'farm' his shire,[2] paying the king an agreed sum for the shire and later recouping himself from what he could actually raise from its inhabitants, was almost certainly already in operation in the time of Edward the Confessor. At the centre also the same primitive organization continued. The king had his Treasury at Winchester, and decisions relating to financial policy were decided by the king in consultation with his whole court. There was as yet no separate financial organization.

Not until the reign of Henry I can there be discerned the beginnings of those changes which in time were to produce the English Exchequer.[3] This development was marked in the first instance by a new method of calculation based upon reckoning by counters moved on a squared board, and secondly by a careful system of written accounts recorded upon rolls. To date the change with any precision is impossible. The earliest surviving Pipe Roll[4] is for the year 1130, but there is clear reference to the enrolment of sheriffs' accounts in a writ belonging to an earlier period in the reign of Henry I,[5] and in another text of about the same date allusion is made to the jurisdiction of the 'Barons of the Exchequer'.[6] The growth of this organization can also be watched in certain charters recording royal payments to the abbeys of Tiron and Cluny.[7] By the accession of Henry II the transformation was far advanced and before the death of that king the organization created for the control of royal finance was fully revealed in the *Dialogue of the Exchequer*.[8] Its detailed character can only be ascertained through careful study of that most famous text, but it may at once be generally observed that the organization there described now consisted

[1] Nos. 61, 204–213.
[2] Nos. 70–73.
[3] Nos. 62–68.
[4] No. 71.
[5] No. 62.
[6] No. 64.
[7] Nos. 65–68.
[8] No. 70.

of two related bodies. There was the Lower Exchequer which derived from the earlier Treasury and was concerned with the receipt and payment of money. There was the Upper Exchequer which was a court supervising financial policy and passing judgment on all questions relating to royal finance. The work of the Lower Exchequer was supervised by deputies of the treasurer and the chamberlains. But in the Upper Exchequer the king himself might preside, if his place was not taken by his justiciar, and in this court will be found the great officers of the household, the chancellor, the marshal, the chamberlains, and such other members of the *curia* as the king might summon for this purpose. In one sense therefore the Exchequer even in the reign of Henry II is to be considered as the old omnicompetent *curia regis* acting in a financial capacity. In another sense there is here to be discerned the beginnings of the first of the great separate departments of state.

The royal revenue which the Anglo-Norman kings collected from England by means of the financial organization which they inherited and developed was certainly, if judged by contemporary standards, extremely large. It is, however, impossible to estimate with any accuracy its amount. It has been suggested that at the time of Domesday the annual income from the lands which the Conqueror retained for the profit of himself and his family was in the region of £17,000. In addition the early Norman kings had the moneys which they could exact from their own immediate tenants by way of those feudal incidents whose regulation occupies so much of the 'Coronation Charter' of Henry I. Finally, there was the Danegeld. The right to levy Danegeld must have been regarded by the Conqueror as one of the most valuable legacies he inherited from his Anglo-Saxon predecessors. So valuable was it indeed that its efficient collection was one of the chief motives for the compilation of Domesday Book itself.[1] William I is known to have raised this levy, which was in the nature of a national land tax, at least four times in his reign,[2] and the imposition was extraordinarily heavy. To judge from later practice Danegeld was normally levied at the rate of 2*s*. for every hide of land, but on rare occasions the rate was even higher, and in the notorious geld of 1083 the assessment was at 6*s*. per hide.[3] It must be remembered that many estates, especially those of the Church, obtained exemption from this savage tax,[4] but even so the amount collected must have been very large. The net annual value of Danegeld levied at 2*s*. to the hide in the time of Henry I was probably not less than £2,000.

It would seem therefore that the Conqueror must be credited with an annual revenue of £20,000 or more, and a similar result has been obtained from a study of the Pipe Roll of 31 Henry I. From the sheriffs' farm of the shires–that is to say roughly from the royal lands–Henry I in the last year of

[1] No. 1, p. 161. [2] Cf. Nos. 70–73.
[3] No. 1, p. 160; cf. Nos. 198, 202–204. [4] No. 1, p. 120.

his reign received some £11,000; from Danegeld he obtained about £2,000; and from other revenues, such as the feudal incidents and profits of justice, perhaps another £11,000. If £3,000 be added in respect of those shires which are not included in the surviving text of this Pipe Roll, a total sum of about £27,000 is obtained. After the death of Henry I the royal revenue doubtless sank owing to the ravages of the civil war, but with the improved financial administration of Henry II, and with the increase in the profits of royal justice, it may be supposed that towards the end of his reign the royal revenue was greater than it had been before, although the expenses of government were rapidly increasing. In short, although no precision can be obtained, it may be suggested (albeit with every possible reserve) that the royal revenue was in the time of the Conqueror something over £20,000; that in the time of Henry I it was probably £30,000; and that in the time of Henry II it may have been in the region of £35,000.

To express these sums in terms of modern money would be extremely hazardous. The things which money could then buy were very different and vastly more limited, and even what are now deemed 'necessities' were then otherwise regarded. A predominantly urban community is not, in this respect, to be easily compared with a peasant society subsisting to a large extent upon the products of its own labour. Consequently the attempts which have often been made to estimate the value of medieval money by the simple expedient of multiplying the sums named in the records by a given figure are bound to be misleading. Thus while it has been suggested, in respect of the fourteenth century, that it would be necessary to multiply the medieval figures by forty in order to obtain a rough equivalent of the conditions of 1930, this does not mean that 15*s*. could buy in 1300 what would in 1930 have cost £30, but rather that it would have produced something of the same effect on men's minds: that a buyer would be about equally reluctant to part with this sum, and a seller about equally glad to receive it. Only with the same serious qualification therefore can it be suggested that in order to obtain a rough equivalent of the twelfth-century figures an even higher rate of multiplication would be necessary. The average agricultural wage of that century – 1*d*. a day – can in this sense be compared with the average wage of an agricultural labourer in 1938 – 35*s*. a week – a wage sixty times as great. At the other end of the social scale the chancellor, the highest paid official in the king's household, received shortly after the death of Henry I a salary (in addition to perquisites) of 5*s*. a day,[1] and this, if multiplied by sixty would give an annual income of approximately £5,500. While therefore no exact equivalents can be established and while it is probable that the purchasing power of money was already beginning to fall during the reign of Henry II, some idea of the modern value of the sums

[1] No. 30.

collected by the kings reigning in England between 1066 and 1189 may perhaps be obtained if these be multiplied fifty to sixty times, and though this estimate would still for many purposes be misleading, it may at least help to explain the strong financial position of the Anglo-Norman kings.

The collection of the royal revenue was during this period entrusted to the sheriffs and it was natural therefore that with the growth of monarchical power the authority of the sheriff also increased so that great Norman magnates were ready to hold an office which gave much opportunity for rapid advancement.[1] The sheriffs in Domesday Book were prominent among the despoilers of the Church,[2] and in the time of Stephen an unscrupulous baron, such as Geoffrey 'de Mandeville', found it to his advantage to be sheriff of Essex, London, Middlesex and Hertfordshire.[3] There was also a tendency during the earlier half of the twelfth century for the sheriffdoms to become hereditary[4] and if this had proved a permanent arrangement the royal control over the counties would have been seriously weakened. It is significant therefore that after 1170 Henry II took steps to regain control over his sheriffs, displacing very many of them and substituting others.[5] The success of royal administration was indeed always very dependent upon the reliability of the king's chief agent in the shires, for the sheriff remained responsible to the king, not only for the king's finance, but also for the military organization of the counties. He was the guardian of the king's interests and the king's privileges. As the essential link between the new monarchy and the older institutions of local government, he brought together the two most vital elements in English constitutional growth, and thus he had also his special part to play in the development after the Norman Conquest of the royal justice.

The growth of the judicial power of the king is perhaps the most important of all the English constitutional developments of these years, and it can only be studied in the texts which record its detailed progress.[6] It may, however, be observed that once again the starting-point is in the omnicompetent *curia regis*, acting not only as the highest feudal court in the land, but also as the agent of the king's prerogative powers. No better example of the manner in which the *curia* acted in its judicial capacity could, for instance, be found than in the detailed account of the trial for treason of William of St. Calais, bishop of Durham, in 1088 before the full court of William Rufus.[7] Both the trial, and the document which records it, possess some exceptional features, but the report, whenever it may in fact have been drawn up, illustrates the essentially feudal nature of the *curia* in which both lay and ecclesiastical magnates were present. It was a solemn occasion, but there was none the less a certain informality in the proceedings, and it would be hard to deny even to this

[1] Nos. 37, 45, 46. [2] No. 205. [3] No. 45. [4] Nos. 45, 46
[5] Nos. 47, 48. [6] *e.g.* Nos. 50–60. [7] No. 84.

assembly the character of a deliberative as well as a judicial body. The separation of governmental functions had not as yet been drawn with any precision.

This was not, however, the only type of assembly at which royal justice was dispensed at this time. Among the most notable records of the reign of William the Conqueror are the surviving reports of great pleas held in various parts of England[1] to deal for the most part with disputes arising out of the circumstances of the Conquest itself. These pleas, which were certainly numerous, were normally held in the shire courts, to which Norman magnates were often called from over a wide area, and they were presided over by a justice appointed by the king. These trials are thus of particular interest as showing how the earlier shire administration was preserved and utilized by the Conqueror.[2] But the assemblies which heard these pleas were none the less not ordinary sessions of the shire courts. In another sense they were local sessions of the king's court, summoned by his writ, conducted in his absence by his representative, and having their decisions ratified by royal edict. At these trials, moreover, a procedure was employed that was to be of very great importance in the future. It became the practice for the king's justices to use a jury to help them ascertain the truth respecting facts that were under dispute, and the collective verdict given by selected men upon oath rapidly became a normal feature of such royal pleas.[3] It is very possible that the employment of this device owed something to earlier English practice, particularly in the Danelaw, but its use certainly became much more common in the early Norman period, and it then became specifically associated with the royal administration. The whole country was made familiar with it in the great local pleas of the Conqueror's reign, and it was through such juries that information was in 1086 collected throughout the land for the purpose of compiling Domesday Book.[4]

In justice as in finance the Anglo-Norman king claimed from the start to be possessed of special powers inherent in his royal office. If the *curia regis* as a feudal court was to that extent limited in its operations by the rights of other feudal courts wherein all lords might exercise jurisdiction over their tenants, nevertheless the king always dispensed a justice derived from something higher than feudal suzerainty. He held his pleas on occasion in the shire courts and sent his justices thither to conduct them. He used for his own purpose, and as his own privilege, the sworn jury. His writ, running throughout the land, could initiate legal action and give to any particular plea a special character.[5] The pleas 'reserved' for the king were still not very numerous nor were they well defined, but throughout this period the royal justice was steadily encroaching upon the jurisdictions exercised by the great lords, and in this process there was little difference between the reigns of the Conqueror and Henry I. While the most

[1] Nos. 50–56. [2] Nos. 50, 51, 52. [3] Cf. No. 58. [4] Nos. 215, 216. [5] No. 58.

notable employment of the sworn jury was in 1086, Henry I began to send out justices in eyre to hear his pleas,[1] and while the Conqueror used the shire courts for his own judicial purposes,[2] Henry I sought to regulate the local courts by specific ordinance.[3]

Even the great judicial reforms of Henry II flowed somewhat easily out of these conditions. The Assizes of Clarendon (1166)[4] and Northampton (1176),[5] the Constitutions of Clarendon (1164)[6] and the legal treatise known as Glanville[7] are rightly regarded as fundamental texts providing the indispensable record of a unique constitutional advance. But if the measures which they describe in such detail were to be summarized, particular reference would need to be made to developments which had at least been foreshadowed in the earlier practice of the Anglo-Norman monarchy: to the evolution from the *curia* of a body of professional judges; to the regular mission of such judges throughout the country to hear the royal pleas; to the employment of the jury through the Grand and Possessory Assizes[8] on a far wider scale; and to the issue of royal writs to bring more and ever more cases within the jurisdiction of the royal courts. Here, as in so much else, Henry II was notable for the development rather than for the initiation of ideas, but the progressive application of those ideas was so widespread and so successful as to mark his reign as an epoch in English legal history.

The success of the royal jurisdiction in this age was due in large measure to its popularity. The king, always theoretically the guardian of order, was being enabled to give effect to his power. He could now offer a justice which was more effective than that supplied by any feudal lord, and he could provide remedies that were at once more rapid and more sure. Using the older institutions of local government, he brought these to the service of his own centralized administration, and men became ever more ready to recognize the law that he dispensed as universally applicable. It was a magnificent achievement, and it was made possible only by the fact that the royal authority, established by the Conqueror, had been allowed to grow in strength. Even at the death of Henry II the machinery of royal government, still essentially personal, bore clear traces of its earlier evolution. The *curia regis* was still theoretically omnicompetent, and the *curia regis* could in a sense be seen wherever the king's work was done: in his great councils, in his Exchequer, in his courts of law. It is therefore too early to speak of a separation of legislature, executive and judicature. The king's servants do the king's work; the Exchequer is a court of law as well as a finance bureau; the king's justices are his regular and trusted councillors; and the provision of new remedies for new wrongs is still the essence of law-making. Nevertheless the way has been prepared for a new specialization of administration whereby

[1] No. 1, p. 191.
[2] Nos. 50, 51.
[3] No. 43.
[4] No. 24.
[5] No. 25.
[6] No. 268.
[7] No. 58.
[8] No. 58, pp. 464–476.

to particular men will be allotted the task of giving effect to the specialized activities of a royal government that is becoming ever more multifariously pervasive. That process was, however, more characteristic of a later age, and the main constitutional advance of this period was to establish the monarchy as effectively the paramount authority in England, dispensing a justice increasingly recognized as being binding upon all men, and providing in its thorough administration a force which gave to England a sense of political unity such as she had never before possessed.

(viii) THE CHURCH

By the twelfth century the monarchy had become the bright light in English secular politics, but it would be to denaturalize the history of this age to view those politics in isolation. The history of England in the Middle Ages might almost be conceived as in one sense a part of the history of the Church, and certainly its development in this period was conditioned at every turn by the ecclesiastical coherence then prevailing in Western Europe. It was perhaps the dominant political sentiment of the age that the Church was accepted as all-inclusive: no division of race or kingdom, province or community was held to impair its essential unity; neither pope nor king, baron nor prelate, knight nor peasant could be thought to stand outside it; for all were subject to its rules and all were expected to co-operate in its life.[1] The modern dichotomy of Church and State breaks down in face of such a conception. Athwart the savage ecclesiastical controversies of the period there lay a common acceptance of principles. Pope and king, for instance, might dispute, but they did so not as foreign powers but rather as two members of the same body contending over the authority which they should respectively exercise within it. An archbishop might be slain, and a king do public penance, but neither in the England of the Confessor nor of William I nor of Henry II could there be found any to question the overriding unity of the Church or to deny that it was under papal headship. Whether by force, mansuetude or love, the Church in fact succeeded in compelling an unquestioning allegiance. For the men of this period the conception of Christendom was neither a pious hope nor a threat to national independence. It was a political reality.

It is therefore a cardinal fact in English history that the eleventh century was for the medieval Church the great century of reform, for the endeavour to rid the Church of the abuses, which had grown up within it since the decline of Charlemagne's empire, affected England no less than the rest of Western Europe. Chief among these evils were a decline in clerical morals and 'simony', that is to say the traffic for money in ecclesiastical offices, but the attempt to suppress

[1] Cf. Nos. 170, 171.

these abuses speedily developed into a campaign against clerical marriage and against lay patronage. At first this movement had been under no single direction but had proceeded from several continental centres. Cluny, for instance, concentrated upon a monastic reform, but in Lorraine the secular clergy were also involved, and there it was principally the archbishops and bishops who directed the movement, often with the active support of lay princes. The papacy did not begin to take the lead until after the accession of Leo IX in 1048, and with the papal direction there began to appear a new quality in the movement itself. It was now urged by a papal party that the reforms could only be made effective if a strong central executive was established in the Church. With these men, therefore, support for the political claims of the papacy went alongside an attack on all forms of secular control, and a development of the canon law in the direction of exalting the papal jurisdiction in the Church. At first small in numbers, this section of the reforming movement was later to produce its greatest exponent in Pope Gregory VII, and in due course to dominate the whole Western Church.

Its ultimate triumph was, however, only gradual, and throughout the period 1042–1189 there were always in respect of these questions three opinions in the Church rather than two. Firstly there were those who had a vested interest in the abuses and who resisted the reforms in every shape. Secondly there were the extreme papalists who insisted that the reforming movement was a unity in all its parts: that neither clerical marriage nor simony could be suppressed so long as lay patronage remained, and that no attack on lay control was likely to be successful unless the papacy was given the power to intervene more immediately in every department of secular politics. But there was always also a third party which favoured the reforms in themselves but which contended that these could best be carried out with the help of lay princes and under the direction of local metropolitans and bishops. This was the traditional reforming group, and it could cite in its support many earlier interpretations of canon law. It was to this party that the Conqueror, Henry I and Henry II may be said essentially to have belonged,[1] and the diminishing success of these kings in their ecclesiastical policy is to be explained less by any fundamental change on the part of the kings than by the degree in which the ideas they represented were ceasing to be dominant in the Church at large.

The ecclesiastical policy of the Conqueror was in large measure determined by his inheritance, for the ecclesiastical revival which had taken place in Normandy during the earlier decades of the eleventh century had not only been Cluniac in inspiration, it had also been ducal in direction. William therefore could claim in 1066 to represent in himself the reforming movement in an important province of Christendom and his claim was very generally accepted.

[1] Cf. Nos. 88–106 and particularly 99, 105, 123.

This substantially aided his astute diplomacy in 1066, by which the duke was made to appear as the armed agent of the reforms against an earl of Wessex who, through his association with Archbishop Stigand, had identified himself with the conditions which the reformers denounced.[1] It was not for nothing that William fought at Hastings under a banner blessed by the papacy,[2] but the notion of ecclesiastical government which he brought to England, and which was soon to be developed by Lanfranc, was his own. The Church in its secular organization was to be controlled by the prince and his metropolitan, but, so directed, it was to be made a centre for the spread of the reforms.[3] Perhaps it is not surprising that the Conqueror was in due course not only to be praised, but also denounced, by Hildebrand.[4]

Such was the policy which William and Lanfranc were to make an integral part of the Norman settlement of England. They found in this country a branch of the Church which, like that of Normandy, had developed on highly individual lines. The Church in England on the eve of the Norman Conquest has been very diversely judged. For Stigand himself there can, it would seem, be very little defence, though perhaps, as a pluralist, notoriously avaricious, and spectacularly dependent upon lay support, he presented too easy a target for those who in the eleventh century were anxious to discredit his supporter, the earl of Wessex. There is at least evidence that, despite his success or because of it, he was by no means regarded with general approval even in England: several bishops refused to be consecrated by him,[5] and even Harold in 1066 broke precedent and had himself crowned by the archbishop of York.[6] On the other hand, the evils arising from lay patronage and simony do not appear to have been confined to the archbishop of Canterbury, and a noteworthy passage in two of the Anglo-Saxon Chronicles[7] raises at least the suspicion that these were widespread. Pluralism also was common among the bishops of the reign of the Confessor,[8] although in particular instances there may well have been extenuating circumstances.

The episcopate of the late Old English Church should not, however, be too hastily disparaged. These men, in many cases the immediate successors of the disciples of Dunstan and Ethelwold, usually owed their appointments to the king, but on the whole the Confessor seems here to have used his power wisely, and there is no reason to suppose that the foreign prelates he introduced into England were markedly superior to their native colleagues. An episcopate which included among its members Wulfstan of Worcester can for that reason alone be considered distinguished, and no Church can lightly be regarded as decadent which sponsored a unique and flourishing vernacular culture. It is true that during this period an increasing number of prelates were selected from the

[1] No. 3, 4. [2] No. 4. [3] Nos. 87–106. [4] Nos. 93, 94, 96–98, 102, 105.
[5] Nos. 1, p. 131, 88. [6] Nos. 1, 2. [7] No. 1, p. 112. [8] Nos. 85, 88.

royal household,[1] but such men are not necessarily to be condemned in that after their appointment they often continued to be employed 'on the king's errands',[2] and one of them, Alfred of York, undoubtedly exercised a moderating influence on the secular controversies of the reign. Nor can the Church over which they presided be easily judged as provincial. English bishops were present at several of the great continental councils of the period,[3] and the relation between England and the papacy continued throughout the reign of the Confessor to be close. Peter's Pence, a levy peculiar to England, was regularly paid,[4] and, towards the end of the reign, Nicholas II issued at least two bulls regulating the affairs of two English dioceses.[5] Contact with the reforming papacy had already, it seems, begun in England before the Norman Conquest.

The English Church in the time of Edward the Confessor was not devoid of vitality, but it was distracted by the political misfortunes of the reign, and in 1066 it underwent an upheaval scarcely less drastic than that which destroyed the Old English State. The new aristocracy established by the Conquest entered the Church also, and the reign of William I saw the high places in the Church in England filled by men of foreign birth. In a sense this was a continuation of a policy which had been sponsored by Edward the Confessor, but after the Conquest the process was more rapid even than that which had taken place between 1042 and 1051.[6] Of the twenty-one abbots who took part in the council of London in 1075 only thirteen were English and of these only three remained in office at the death of the Conqueror. The episcopate was even more directly affected, and by 1080 Wulfstan of Worcester was the only bishop of English birth left in England. It was natural that the new king should wish to have trusted compatriots in places of so much influence in his realm, but the new appointments could also be justified on other grounds. The new bishops were for the most part hard-working men, who conscientiously discharged their duties, and many of them left a great reputation behind them. Osmund of Salisbury, Gundulf of Rochester, and Walcher of Durham were for instance remembered for sanctity; Robert of Hereford for scholarship; and Remigius of Lincoln and Walkelin of Worcester left a permanent mark on the sees they ruled. It was this new episcopate which carried through the ecclesiastical changes consequent upon the Conquest, and at its head stood Lanfranc, who, as an ecclesiastical statesman, would have made his mark in any age.

Lanfranc[7] brought a new efficiency into the English Church, not so much by revolutionary change as by adaptive transformation. His model was the Norman Church closely organized under the duke, and in England too he achieved a notable centralization. His dispute with the archbishop of York in 1070[8] was in one sense only the most salient feature of a policy which aimed at

[1] No. 1, pp. 118, 119. [2] Nos. 1, 2, pp. 119, 132, 206. [3] No. 1, pp. 116, 119. [4] No. 82.
[5] Nos. 75, 76. [6] Cf. No. 87. [7] See Nos. 86, 87. [8] No. 87.

destroying the virtual independence enjoyed by so many bishops under the Confessor.[1] But it was also an attempt to remove a potent threat to English unity at a time when the country as a whole was only imperfectly subjected to its new ruler. As duke of Normandy, William had been able to realize the advantage of ruling over a country which was a single ecclesiastical province – that of Rouen with its six dependent bishoprics. In attempting his task of English kingship he found himself aspiring to dominate a land wherein there were two ecclesiastical provinces, each presided over by its own metropolitan. And it is even possible that the Conqueror's support of Lanfranc in 1070 may have been in part dictated by his apprehension that an archbishop of York, acting as head of an independent ecclesiastical province which had as yet not been brought fully under Norman control, might seek to buttress his own position by crowning a rival king – perhaps a Scandinavian, or a member of the Saxon royal house – as legitimate ruler in the north of England.

Certainly, it was only after his own primacy had been effectively acknowledged that Lanfranc could hope to exercise a directing control over the whole Church in England. Nor was it merely in England that his influence was felt. He intervened in the ecclesiastical politics of Ireland,[2] and took some share in the changes in the Scottish Church which followed the marriage of Malcolm with St. Margaret.[3] His letters,[4] models of their kind, spread a web of authority over regions even wider than those the Conqueror swayed. He had in short a high conception of the position of a metropolitan archbishop, and he buttressed this by a wonderful mastery of detail fortified by shrewd political sense. He was not an enthusiast, and he was not a saint, but if some have found his hard and capable precision unattractive, few have been able convincingly to deny his essential greatness.

His policy was perhaps best displayed in the councils he convoked, and the frequency with which these were summoned reflects his energy. In 1072 a 'general council' was held at Winchester; a synod met in London in 1075; in the next year there was another council in Winchester,[5] and during the remainder of the Conqueror's reign at least three other such assemblies were convoked. In these councils was enacted a large mass of legislation relating to the reforms. Thus it was decreed that the marriage of priests was henceforth to be illegal, that no man should henceforth be ordained priest or deacon who was not celibate, but that priests already married need not put away their wives. At the same time important changes were introduced into the organization of the episcopate. Even before the death of the Confessor it had become apparent that many of the English sees were at unsuitable places, and in 1050 the see of Crediton had been moved to Exeter. Now the process was accelerated; the sees of Lichfield, Selsey and Sherborne were in 1075 moved respectively to the urban

[1] Cf. No. 88. [2] No. 87. [3] Nos. 87, 89. [4] Nos. 89, 91, 92, 95, 103, 106. [5] No. 87.

centres of Chester, Chichester and Salisbury, and before 1086 the ancient see of Dorchester was transferred to Lincoln.[1] It was the beginning of a new order, and in it the parishes also were to be affected. At the time of the Norman Conquest many parts of England were still served by communities of priests established at 'old minsters' which supervised large areas.[2] Under Lanfranc a strong stimulation was given to the movement towards the formation of the territorial parish as the ecclesiastical counterpart to the village. The parish served by a single priest and dependent upon a single church advanced towards becoming the normal rural unit of English ecclesiastical life. The secular structure of the medieval English Church was in fact taking shape.

Not less notable were the effects of the Norman Conquest upon English monastic life. In 1066 there were some thirty-five autonomous Benedictine monasteries in England, which, though of varying wealth and importance, together possessed about a sixth of the landed wealth of England. They had shown themselves on the whole hostile to the new régime, so that it is remarkable that after the Conquest no general spoliation took place. A certain amount of pillage occurred about 1070,[3] and some Norman sheriffs were notorious for their encroachments on Church lands,[4] but in general the older English monasteries were probably more prosperous in 1120 than they had been in 1065, and the cathedral monasteries which had been a feature of the Old English Church were actually increased in number from four to nine. The appointment of Norman abbots and in some cases a plantation of Norman monks, must often have caused, as at Glastonbury in 1083,[5] considerable strain, but in general English monasticism did not suffer unduly from the Conquest, and before the death of William I there had taken place in the north a monastic revival sponsored by native as well as foreign monks which established flourishing communities at Durham, Whitby and St. Mary's, York.[6]

Monastic life in England became subjected, however, to fresh foreign influences, and the history of English monasticism between 1066 and 1189 might almost be told in relation to the great European movements associated respectively with Cluny and Cîteaux. At first the process was very gradual. Lanfranc's famous *Constitutiones*, though influential, were essentially a selection of continental practices which he thought suitable for his monks at Canterbury. Similarly, William's own foundation of Battle was an exceptional establishment, and Lanfranc never undertook any systematic increase in the number of English monasteries. Before the death of the Conqueror, however, William of Warenne founded at Lewes the first Cluniac priory in England,[7] and before 1135 more than a dozen such houses had been established in this country. The influence of

[1] No. 87; cf. No. 78.
[2] No. 83.
[3] No. 223; cf. No. 1, pp. 151–153.
[4] Nos. 50, 51.
[5] No. 1, p. 160.
[6] No. 84.
[7] No. 80.

this movement was moreover specifically directed towards destroying the earlier conception of the monastery as an isolated and independent unit. All Cluniac houses were under the direction of the abbot of Cluny and were themselves ruled not by abbots but by priors, whilst the Order itself was removed as far as possible from the control of local bishops and lay magnates. It is probable that Cluniac organization was never as close knit as has sometimes been supposed, but the English Cluniac houses of this period, forming part of a large monastic community that owed allegiance to a single monastic head, none the less introduced a new element into English monasticism.

In the twelfth century, Western Europe was itself swept by a new wave of monastic growth. Its centre was the monastery of Cîteaux, founded in 1098 by a group of Benedictine monks who desired to live a stricter life than their fellows, and the movement attained a unique influence with the advent of St. Bernard and with the subsequent establishment of the daughter-house of Clairvaux. About the same time similar movements were taking place in north-western France, notably at Tiron and Savigny, and in the same spirit a purely English Order was founded by Gilbert of Sempringham, a Lincolnshire knight, which was especially influential in the eastern counties. Such widespread, though related, developments gave to monasticism in the latter part of the twelfth century a different character from what it had possessed before, and no country was more affected by this than England.[1] In 1123, for example, the abbey of Furness was founded on the model of Savigny, and no fewer than twelve monasteries of this family were established in England by 1147, when the Order was merged in the greater community of the Cistercians. The Cistercian growth was itself even more wonderfully rapid.[2] In 1128 Waverley was founded, to be followed by Tintern, while in the north a spectacular development came with the foundation in 1132 of Rievaulx and Fountains.[3] The offshoots of these two Yorkshire abbeys alone produced before 1189 at least twenty-two new houses, and at the death of Henry II English monasticism may be said to have been dominated by Cistercian influence.

The special notes of Cistercian monasticism were simplicity in monastic observance, and a peculiar attitude towards monastic property. The sites of the new monasteries were chosen in places removed from human habitation, and the land around the monastery was cultivated and exploited by the monks themselves and by lay brethren. The typical Cistercian monastery was thus surrounded, not by dependent manors, but by a large unified estate which was gradually brought under cultivation by men who in their abbey were devoted to the simple service of God. There is no doubt that such an ideal made a special appeal to contemporary sentiment,[4] but what gave additional importance to the movement was its organization. Cîteaux produced its legislator in its third

[1] Nos. 115–118. [2] No. 117. [3] Nos. 116, 117. [4] Nos. 117, 118.

abbot, an Englishman named Stephen Harding, and the constitution of the Order was embodied in a remarkable text known as the *Carta Caritatis*.[1] By this each abbey of the Order was directly affiliated to the house from which it had been founded and to no other, but in each case the abbot of the mother-house had the right of inspection over the daughter-monastery. Again, a general chapter of the abbots of the Order was annually held at Cîteaux itself and had considerable powers. In this way a degree of centralization was achieved without loss of that independence which comes from devolution, and in its system of checks and balances the *Carta Caritatis* takes its place in the history of representative institutions.

The history of English monasticism in this age may thus roughly be divided into three periods: the first extending to 1066 when the ancient Benedictine monasteries, such as Glastonbury and Ely, Peterborough, St. Albans and Bury St. Edmunds were predominant; the second was marked by the Norman plantation after the Conquest, and by the establishment of the Cluniac houses; and the third by the advent of the new Orders and by the dominance of Cîteaux.[2] It would of course be easy to describe this growth under the general formula of decay and reform, and there is some truth in this view. In the eleventh century, Cluny was a protest against the threat of secularization to individual Benedictine houses, and Cîteaux in its turn was in some measure a protest against the formalism and splendid ritual of Cluny. But the formula cannot be too strictly applied, in that there were always in the background a number of old-fashioned houses in which a very respectable monastic life was being led outside the reform circle of the hour. And through all these multifarious developments the abiding inspiration remained the seventh-century Rule of St. Benedict which continued to be held as the basis of monastic life alike in the 'unreformed' and in the 'reformed' religious houses of the Cluniacs and Cistercians. Interpretations of the rule might differ, but only within circumscribed limits, and the claims of the 'reformers' to have returned more closely to its primitive institutions were not always justified. Despite the Norman Conquest, and despite the variegated experiments of the mid-twelfth century, there was no essential break in the continuity of Benedictine monasticism in England during this period, and the lavish enthusiasm with which the monasteries were supported by all sorts and conditions of men and women in England during these decades[2] testifies at least to the integral part which they played in the religious life of the age.

The development of the reforming movement, as exemplified in the condition of both the secular and the regular clergy in England, inevitably precipitated in this country as elsewhere a crisis in the relations of Church and State. Under William I the tension was mitigated, not because the Conqueror claimed fewer

[1] No. 115. [2] Nos. 115–118.

regalian rights over the Church than were exercised by his predecessors, but because there had not yet become dominant in the Church itself that party which linked up the cause of reform with a limitation of the rights of princes. The Conqueror was himself a sincere supporter of reform in the Church, and many ecclesiastics in England regarded him as, in this respect, their natural leader.[1] Nor was he unwilling to make at least one innovation in respect of jurisdiction. In, or shortly after, 1072 he issued a writ withdrawing spiritual pleas from the hundred courts and ordering them to be tried before the bishop according to the canons and episcopal laws.[2] Further than this, however, he was reluctant to go, and he resolutely refused to countenance any extension of the political power of the pope within his English realm. He took his stand here, as in so much else, upon tradition, admitting, for instance, his obligation to transmit Peter's Pence as heretofore, but refusing absolutely to do fealty to the papacy for his English kingdom.[3] His desire was clearly to prevent any division of loyalty among his subjects, and his policy was well summed up in the customs which a writer of the next generation attributed to him: in the case of a disputed papal election no pope was to be recognized in England without his consent; no papal letter was to be received in England without his permission; no legislation was to be initiated without his approval by any English ecclesiastical council; and no bishop should excommunicate any of his officials or tenants-in-chief without his leave.

It was a clear-cut position, and its strength derived from the fact that the Conqueror was in fact master in his own realm and used that mastery as a friend to the Church over which he claimed a wide measure of control. Thus only was he enabled to obtain the support of the great bulk of English ecclesiastical opinion, which did not gainsay his fundamental contention that it was the king who should have the deciding voice in the appointment to English prelacies. The circumstances of the Conquest had indeed made this claim imperative, since bishops and abbots had become not only spiritual officials, but also in virtue of their temporalities important tenants-in-chief owing large *servitia debita* of knights in return for their lands.[4] A reforming prince might therefore in his strength demand an overriding temporal allegiance from such men, and even under William Rufus this same position was generally sustained. It was, however, always a situation of some delicacy, and between 1087 and 1100 it changed to the disadvantage of the monarchy. The character of Rufus was not that of his father, and with him it was demonstrated how royal control might operate not to the advantage but to the spoliation of the Church. At the same time there succeeded to the primacy of Canterbury in Anselm a man who enjoyed all the prestige which attaches to sanctity, and who was also unlike Lanfranc a convinced adherent of the extreme papal party in the Church. He

[1] Nos. 6, 7. [2] No. 79. [3] No. 101. [4] Nos. 224–228.

was almost alone in this respect among the prelates in England, and at the council of Rockingham in 1095 he found scarcely a bishop to support him.[1] But he started in his controversial task with an initial moral advantage which he never lost, and it was thus that very gradually he began to gain adherents among the clergy. Henry I, therefore, who on the whole succeeded in maintaining the ecclesiastical policy of the Conqueror, was never in this respect so secure as his father.[2] And on the crucial question of ecclesiastical appointments he was compelled to compromise. A charter of the Conqueror[3] records that William I had given certain lands to Bishop Remigius of Lincoln *cum baculo suo*. Against Anselm such a practice could not be continued. In 1107 a distinction was recognized between the spiritual and temporal functions of prelates, and it was agreed that bishops and abbots should do homage to the king for their lay fiefs, but that no man in future should be invested with the symbols of his spiritual office by the king or any other layman.[4]

The arrangement evaded rather than settled the issue. A strong king could interpret it as implying that homage should precede consecration: a weak king might find that it destroyed his control over ecclesiastical appointments. Thus during the civil war the royal power in ecclesiastical affairs rapidly lapsed, and even in political matters the king had often to submit to the dictates of the Church.[5] Characteristic of this time was Henry of Blois, bishop of Winchester, who might be regarded as a type of ecclesiastic which the reforming movement on its secular side, so to speak, unwittingly called into being. Of princely rank, very able and highly cultured, he thought of the Church as the directing force in Europe, and he conceived it a duty in the episcopate to take an active part in secular politics. This man, an outstanding patron of art and letters, the founder of the hospital of St. Cross, and the great embellisher of Winchester Cathedral, deserves some contemplation as he erects half a dozen fortresses in his diocese and in the course of the war burns his own episcopal city. He was in some sense a portent linking two periods in the history of the Church, and it was in keeping with his influence that no less than four times during the chaotic reign of Stephen, the Church played the decisive part in determining the course of events. Yet more important was the fact that with the decline in monarchical prestige the bishops were coming to regard themselves as papal rather than as royal officials. The barriers which the Conqueror had erected against the political intrusion of the papacy into England had broken down, and thus was the 'freedom of the Church' secured. In 1148 Eugenius III coerced King Stephen by placing England under an interdict,[6] and ecclesiastical pleas began to be taken more regularly to Rome for settlement. A new situation was created with the establishment among the English prelates of a strong party which accorded

[1] No. 107.
[2] Nos. 107, 109–112.
[3] No. 78.
[4] No. 107, p. 673.
[5] Nos. 8, 10, 114.
[6] No. 10.

to the papacy an overriding political loyalty, and although it was ecclesiastical pressure which forced Stephen to recognize Henry of Anjou as his heir,[1] that prince eventually succeeded in England to an ecclesiastical problem much more formidable than any that had vexed his predecessors.

The struggle between Henry II and Thomas Becket has justly fired the imagination of posterity, and its course can best be watched in the documents which record it.[2] Reading these numerous records it becomes plain that it was the exceptional personality of the archbishop which in reality gave a final significance to his astonishing career, every phase of which possesses its own arresting features. The son of a Norman citizen of London winning his way up through the *curia* of Archbishop Theobald to become a chancellor of great magnificence and the friend of his king in itself attracts attention.[3] So also does the man who on becoming archbishop reversed his policy and stood for the rights of the Church against his former master,[4] until after making his magnificent protest at Northampton he fled through a storm of wind and rain in peril of his life.[5] Even the exile between 1164 and 1170[6] is in every way noteworthy as he negotiated with the powers of Europe, pleaded his cause with the pope,[7] or stated his case in full assembly before the kings of England and of France.[8] But it is the final act which has inevitably remained the most familiar: the return in triumph to Canterbury, and the sombre climax in the winter dusk of the cathedral. The account of these events by William fitz Stephen,[9] Herbert of Bosham[10] and Edward Grim[11] defies elaboration, and after the lapse of nearly eight centuries it can still hardly be read without emotion.

Thomas Becket was a great actor on a floodlit stage. Nevertheless, though he had few personal friends and though his methods and lack of moderation[12] have inspired irritation, there is no need to doubt his personal sincerity. In one sense he might, however, be called an innovator, in that without compromise he based his case upon a theory of ecclesiastical law which had only recently won general acceptance in the Church. Thus it was that he counted among his opponents not only the king, but also many members of a most distinguished bench of bishops, some of whom supported consistently a theory of politics[13] which would have been approved by Lanfranc or by the bishops who had formerly gathered at the council of Rockingham. Henry II on his part claimed few, if any, rights which had not been exercised by his predecessors. He wished, in the Church as in the State, to restore the conditions of Henry I, and he claimed for the monarchy its former position as the guardian of the welfare of the Church in England. The Constitutions of Clarendon[14] in which, perhaps unwisely, he reduced his case to writing, reflect with considerable fidelity the

[1] Nos. 10, 114. [2] Nos. 119–158. [3] Nos. 119–121. [4] Nos. 122–128.
[5] No. 129. [6] Nos. 130–147. [7] Nos. 131, 132. [8] No. 144.
[9] Nos. 148, 150. [10] Nos. 149, 151. [11] No. 152. [12] Cf. Nos. 138–143.
[13] Cf. Nos. 126, 127, 129, 140, 142, 150, 151. [14] No. 126.

customary practice of his grandfather. But times had changed, and Henry II could not, like the Conqueror or Henry I, count on the unswerving support of his prelates. His conduct of the struggle,[1] ruthless, brutal and unscrupulous, is thus patent of explanation. For neither he nor the archbishop felt it possible to compromise, and if on both sides high purpose was mingled with petty spite, the final scene in Canterbury Cathedral[2] elevated the drama to the level of tragedy. Becket triumphed in death.[3]

The murder of Becket shocked the conscience of Europe, and not the least tribute to the administration of Henry II is to be found in the manner in which it survived the calamity. For the victory was the archbishop's, and the settlement at Avranches in 1172[4] did but indicate its future consequences. The king's permission of appeals to Rome, however safeguarded, meant that such appeals were in future to become a normal feature of English life, and though the king could easily promise to repeal all new legislation he had made against the Church (since there had been few innovations), in practice the royal authority over the Church, as sustained by his predecessors, was broken. The public penance of the king was symbolic,[5] and though in the latter part of his reign Henry II could delay the process, further concessions by the monarchy had been rendered inevitable. Canon law, as interpreted by the papacy, henceforth became progressively operative in England precisely as in Western Europe generally, and whilst there was always room for uneasy dispute on points of detail, the regalian rights over the Church in England, as claimed and exercised by the Conqueror and Henry I, were abrogated. It was the end of a development whose critical phase occurred between 1070 and 1172, and no student of the documents, which record it, is likely to assign praise or blame indiscriminately to either side. The two great Norman kings could be regarded as friends of the Church; and neither Anselm nor Becket can be judged an enemy to the State. It was a conflict of aspirations reflected above all in rival interpretations of law; and behind all the selfish and unscrupulous ambitions which it provoked, one side might fairly claim to represent a secular justice effectively enforced, whilst the other stood, at least in some measure, as the guardian of those things which should not be rendered to Caesar. Both aspirations, never to be fully realized, were necessary to the development of England, and in the clash between them is probably to be found the most permanent significance of the ecclesiastical politics of this distant age. This ancient controversy, so distorted by individual pride and so distinguished by personal greatness, is perhaps best to be regarded as a chapter in the still unended struggle between the opposed ideals of political order and political liberty.

[1] Cf. Nos. 130, 133, 134. [2] No. 152. [3] No. 157. [4] No. 156. [5] No. 158.

(ix) THE PEOPLE

A medieval observer could remark that society is divided into those who pray, those who fight and those who work, and there was some truth in his trichotomy. The ecclesiastical hierarchy stretching from pope to bishop and abbot, to monk and parish priest was in a real sense a segregated body wielding a power peculiar to itself. Similarly, the aristocratic warrior class, including not only the lords but the knights and serjeants who surrounded them, was a community in itself discharging its own proper function in the state. But the bulk of the population belonged to neither of these groups. It consisted of a peasantry which was largely inarticulate, but which none the less sustained the whole fabric of society upon its shoulders, and which was important above all for its toil. The peasant of this age is indeed hardly to be portrayed as an individual: he is to be regarded more strictly as a member of a community. The English village of the eleventh and twelfth centuries has thus merited the detailed study which has been devoted to it, for it was the basic unit of English social life. Between 1042 and 1189 it was exceptional for any Englishman not to be a villager; and it was equally exceptional for him not to find his life conditioned at every turn by the arrangements of the village in which he lived.

The village of Anglo-Norman England is today presented to the distant gaze of the modern spectator almost as a familiar sight. The thatched cottages cluster round a church which perhaps appears new-white from its recent erection, and around are the hedgeless fields wherein may be descried the peasantry at work upon their scattered strips of land. Here are the meadows for their use, and there the commons where, according to rule, they may graze their beasts. In the distance lies the waste which abuts woodland and forest awaiting reclamation. Nearer the centre stands the larger house of the lord or his bailiff, whence radiates the intricate web of rights and duties which enmeshes the whole community. For this is a village under lordship. It may be termed a manor. It has a lord and tenants, freemen and serfs, a court and custom. As a self-sufficient community it may maintain its inhabitants by co-operative husbandry. As a unit of social administration its arrangements may determine the status of its inhabitants in the land at large. The outlines of such a picture may be hard and the details hidden, but its main features are well known and unmistakable.

Nevertheless, if the scene is familiar it will none the less repay a closer contemplation, and the evidence relating to it, although difficult, is copious. It is, for instance, particularly fortunate that from the late Old English period there has survived in the document known as *Rectitudines*[1] a treatise on estate management which supplies a description of peasant ranks and duties such as

[1] No. 172; cf. 173, 174.

may be compared with the testimony of later surveys compiled, for instance, at Burton Abbey[1] and Peterborough,[2] at Ramsey,[3] Durham[4] and Bury St. Edmunds.[5] And at precisely the most critical point in this period there is Domesday Book which in its entries relating both to 1066 and 1086 discusses village after village and enumerates their peasant population not only as it was twenty years after the Conquest, but also as it was on the day on which King Edward was alive and dead.[6]

Even the most cursory examination of this evidence permits one generalization. It seems clear that the Norman Conquest wrought no such change in the organization and conditions of English peasant life as it promoted in the higher ranks of society. Domesday describes an alien society in alien terms, but it does not suggest that any widespread transformation in the agrarian structure of England took place during the twenty years that followed Hastings, and there is no essential opposition in this respect between the evidence of *Rectitudines* and that of the earlier twelfth-century surveys of manors. On the whole, during the century which opened in 1050 the lot of the English peasantry probably deteriorated owing to the growth of lordship and to the increased efficiency of legal definition, but in some areas, such as the lands of the abbey of Bury St. Edmunds, it seems doubtful whether the conditions of peasant life in the reign of Henry II differed very materially from what they had been in the time of Edward the Confessor. Warfare and local rebellions undoubtedly inflicted hardship upon men whose life was a precarious struggle with the recalcitrant soil, and attempts to define peasant status must often have proved disadvantageous to those whose position depended mainly upon the unwritten compromises of local tradition. But the Normans appear to have been unwilling, or unable, to modify to any appreciable extent the varieties of agrarian structure existing in pre-Conquest England. The events of 1066 caused no fundamental break in the history of the English peasantry.

The use of the term manor in Domesday Book is itself in this respect significant.[7] It should be remembered that the word manor was itself an importation from overseas which for more than a century in this country retained a somewhat esoteric flavour. It came to denote a village organized in a recognized way under lordship, but it possessed no such precise connotation in 1086. The compilers of Domesday described as manors estates and jurisdictions which had little resemblance to each other and less to the facts of English rural life, and even the assumption that the manor was identical in size with the village would be unwarranted. In East Anglia, for example, the majority of villages in 1086[8] were still shared among several lords and farther to the north and west it was no uncommon thing for a 'manor' to comprise several villages.[9] Nothing indeed is

[1] No. 176. [2] No. 177. [3] Nos. 178, 179. [4] No. 180. [5] No. 175.
[6] Nos. 205–213. [7] Cf. Nos. 205, 211. [8] No. 212. [9] No. 180.

more remarkable in the social history of this age than the persistence in this respect also after the Norman Conquest of diverse provincial traditions. The village customs of Kent and Northumbria long remained distinct, and there is abundant evidence to suggest that the exceptional freedom enjoyed by the peasantry in the Danelaw in the twelfth century derived from the intrusion two hundred years earlier of independent Scandinavian warriors whose descendants in the time of Henry II still often bore names unmistakably denoting their Scandinavian ancestry.[1] The villages of England during this period in short never conformed to a uniform scheme of lordship, and while England was divided into 'manors' she never knew a 'manorial system'.

The authentic primary cell of English agrarian life in the eleventh and twelfth centuries was, in fact, not the manor but the village, and the village was in every case the peculiar product of its own environment. Moreover, if the typical village would be hard to discover, so also would a typical village lord. The inhabitants of one of the villages belonging to Ramsey Abbey[2] must, for instance, have entertained very different notions as to what constituted manorial lordship from that possessed by the dwellers in some western hamlet subject to a man whose economic status was hardly to be distinguished from that of a prosperous peasant. Even when the social position of lords of villages was roughly identical, their rights over the peasantry varied according to local custom, and always there remained the basic fact that the village was in one sense a unit of a co-operative husbandry in which lord and peasant shared. This partnership was exemplified for all to see in the open fields of the villages, great hedgeless expanses of arable land in which the villagers held not compact blocks but strips indiscriminately scattered. All were cultivated by common ploughs and, since the modern notion of the rotation of crops was not yet discovered, at least one of these fields was each year left fallow.

Such a system of agriculture, itself obviously of high antiquity, dominated the villages of Anglo-Norman England and affected the lords of manors scarcely less than the peasantry. For the main distinction between the land of the lord and the land of the peasant lay (apart from its extent) simply in the allocation of the labour necessary to maintain it. The lord's land was worked by the peasants of the manor, who thus had to maintain their own holdings and also to contribute both in money and in work to the upkeep of the land of the lord. And the land of every manor could thus be divided into two parts: the demesne land of the lord and the tenant land of the peasantry.[3] But both were intermingled in the strips of the open fields, and both were cultivated by the common ploughs. From one point of view, therefore, the Anglo-Norman village may be regarded as an agricultural association consisting of a lord and serfs; from another point of view it may be considered as a community of

[1] Nos. 180, 212, 217. [2] Nos. 178, 179. [3] Cf. Nos. 172–178.

co-owners in the village. And it is in fact precisely this curious contrast within the manor that constitutes its chief interest. For the peasantry were throughout England graded roughly according to the place they occupied in the manorial economy. Terms varied, and the criteria of freedom were very diverse, but in this respect the *geneat*, the *gebur* and the *cotsetla* of *Rectitudines*[1] have their counterparts in the freemen and sokemen, the villeins and the bordars of Domesday,[2] and again in the free tenants, the villeins and the cottars of the later surveys.[3]

The manor was in short the determinant of feudal peasant status and the threefold distinction thus indicated, though susceptible to endless modifications, will be found in some measure reflected in almost all descriptions of twelfth-century manors in England. There will firstly be a class of free tenants[4]–men who hold their tenements usually in return for a money rent, and who in the Domesday phrase were "free to go with their land where they would".[5] These men were indeed to become more important, when, after the reforms of Henry II, their holdings and their tenures became protected by the king's courts. At the other end of the social scale in the manor were the cottars, men with small holdings usually of about five acres.[6] Their services were correspondingly light and they were sometimes called 'monday-men' because it was often on that day alone that they were compelled to do their forced labour. They sometimes eked out what must have been a precarious existence by providing hired labour, and it is among them that the village craftsmen were usually to be found. Between these two classes were the villeins who, however designated, formed the core of the manorial community.

The typical villein as he appears in the surveys[7] may, with proper reservations, be generally described. He was a man who had a holding in the open fields which was sufficient for the maintenance of himself and his family. He could not be deprived of that holding, and it passed under certain restrictions from him to his son–usually his eldest son but sometimes his youngest. That was the element of freedom in his position. But the villein was also subject to servile work and to servile payments. Certain days in the week he was compelled to work on his lord's land. This was called week-work. At critical times of the year such as harvest he had to perform special agricultural services. These were called boon-works. He might have to provide seed for his lord's sowing, and to send his beasts to graze in the lord's fold. He could be taxed by his lord almost at will, provided that his holding was not taken from him. He paid a fine for giving his daughter in marriage–the *merchet*. He paid another fine, usually his best beast, when he took over his father's land–the *heriot*. He could not leave his land or the service of his lord.

[1] No. 172. [2] Nos. 205, 211, 212. [3] Nos. 176–179. [4] Cf. Nos. 177–180; 217.
[5] No. 212. [6] Nos. 177–179. [7] Nos. 175–179.

In the Anglo-Norman village the average peasant may be said to have lived his life in conditions which can fairly be described as paradoxical. He had to perform servile duties and to make servile payments, but he was not the victim of an arbitrary tyranny and his service was not settled at the caprice of his lord. While this was often heavy, he had the protection of manorial custom against its increase, and in the interpretation of manorial custom he had a share. Essential to the organization of the manor was the manor court wherein manorial custom was appealed to and applied; and to the manor court which was presided over by the lord's steward there came both free tenants and villeins. These were in fact the real judgment-finders in disputed cases, and it is no uncommon thing to find in such a court a villein winning a case against his lord. The villein then was certainly not a free man, but though the lawyers might affect to regard him as a slave, he could not in practice be treated as one. The resolution of this paradox was in fact a matter of adjustment in each particular village. Doubtless, as the weaker party to the arrangement, the peasant, who was hard put to it to find anyone learned or powerful enough to defend his rights, usually suffered in the compromise. But conditions varied from place to place. A vigorous community subject to the distant rule of a lax master might become hardly distinguishable from a group of peasant proprietors. A harsh lord might succeed in treating his peasants merely as the human livestock on his estate.

The evidence which describes the agrarian structure of Anglo-Norman England in this period is copious, but its limitations must be appreciated. The surveys of manors were made by ecclesiastical landlords whose efficient management of their estates might well entail a more rigid enforcement of seigniorial rights than obtained elsewhere. Detailed study of particular localities has already shown how incomplete were many of the generalizations of the past. The co-operative farming, for instance, so characteristic of the medieval manor, often took place alongside of individual enterprise in the open fields; and the man who was compelled to work for so many days a week on his lord's land may have been less heavily burdened than the statistics suggest, in that only part of his day might be required, and even then only one member of his household might be taken from the family holding. In each manor there were infinite gradations of prosperity, and a generalized picture of the medieval village may well fail to take account of the teeming activity which took place therein. Each village was a flux of rising and falling fortunes; and the comparatively easy circumstances of the more prosperous have to be set beside the hard struggle for bare existence which was the lot of the less fortunate.

All alike, however, had to face hardships of which their English descendants know little. The social hygiene of the Roman world was unknown in the Anglo-Norman village where both health and life were preserved with difficulty. Infant mortality was terribly high, and the loss by death in any village was normally so severe that it apparently took two years on an average to add one individual to the community. At the same time the natural desire of lords to prevent the loss of labour consequent upon the marriage of peasants outside their manors was bound to lead to widespread inbreeding. The failure of a crop produced immediate scarcity, and two successive bad harvests might bring on one of those terrible famine pestilences which were so marked a feature of the age. The cottages of the medieval village are dear to the modern sentimentalist. But they would probably have offended both his taste and his nostrils.

There were, however, compensations. Most of these men enjoyed a certain security of tenure, and, apart from an unfortunate minority, they were not dependent upon a precarious wage which they had to defend in a competitive market. The bondage which they endured was tempered in its severity, and though they were strictly forbidden to leave their villages, it is doubtful whether many wished to do so. Flight from the manor was not uncommon, but seigniorial pressure would never have been strong enough to prevent it, had it been general. The majority of the peasants of Anglo-Norman England were probably kept in their villages less by fear of punishment than by a belief that their lot in familiar surroundings was not unduly hard when compared with that of their neighbours. In his own village the peasant had a recognized position, however humble, while to leave the 'villein nest' meant adventuring into a hostile world with no more than a man might carry on his back. Thus they continued in their unending and accustomed routine of labour. Their life, however, was permeated by notions of the supernatural which supplied to their laborious days a background full of terrors, hopes and haunting aspirations that surrounded them almost as closely as the ambient air. No study of the medieval village can in this sense afford to neglect the church which towered so imposingly above the cottage roofs, or the ethical system which it represented. It affected the peasant at every turn. He could not escape it, and doubtless it provided him with consolations. The squalor of his life might exude from the stench of his cottage, his servitude might break him with its incessant demands, but there is no reason to believe that his hardships were not mitigated by a belief in eternity which, though perhaps crude, was none the less vivid and unshaken.

The Anglo-Norman village imparted to the life of its inhabitants something of its own stability. If numbers counted, the peasant was the typical Englishman, and the affairs of his village furnished him with all the major interests of his life. The fields absorbed his energies in a perpetual struggle with the soil; the manor house embodied his temporal allegiance; in the cottages of his neighbours he found his only social contacts; and to the village church he turned for all that transcended his mundane preoccupations. Outside, all was strange. Fifteen or twenty miles from his cottage door there began an unknown world into which he probably never entered, and whose contemptuous judgment he might well ignore. The politics of Church and State affected him only indirectly, and he knew little of the wars of princes. His smaller world was all-demanding, and it was circumscribed. Life in both its natural and supernatural aspects was bounded by familiar landmarks, and its long monotony was punctuated only by the seasons in the surrounding fields, and by their counterparts in the feasts of the Church. Harvest and Michaelmas were but as one celebration, and the miracle of the spring the inevitable prelude to the Easter Mass. And over all was the unending routine of labour which had continued in its accustomed way unchanged from time without memory, and which must have seemed incapable of change.

This immutable rural environment formed the background to the lives of at least nine-tenths of the population of Anglo-Norman England. Town life was in its infancy, and the urban influence on society, though increasing, was throughout this period subordinate to the main stream of English development. In Domesday Book there are some thirty places described as boroughs, and some others, including London and Winchester, were unsurveyed in that record. But the urban population was in its totality relatively small, and it is unlikely that in the time of Edward the Confessor any towns except London, York, Lincoln and Norwich contained more than about five thousand inhabitants. Some of the smaller boroughs were scarcely to be distinguished from large villages, and it would indeed be hard to designate with any precision what then constituted a borough in England. Many of the Domesday boroughs[1] still bore the character of agricultural communities; most of them contained a house area that was apparently usually fortified; and most of them to some degree engaged in trade. And they possessed privileges of very varying extent which marked them off from the surrounding countryside. It has been suggested that only after 1066 did town life develop any of its characteristic later forms in England. Before then, it has been urged, apart from London and perhaps some of the seaports in the south-east, the borough remained essentially an official centre rather than the home of a community predominantly engaged in trade or organized in a special manner adapted to its mercantile pursuits.

This view has, however, been challenged. The arable land surrounding many of the boroughs described in Domesday Book was clearly insufficient by itself to support their population, and in fact trade and commerce had already begun to play a not unimportant part in the England of Edward the Confessor. To London in particular there came traders from Normandy and northern France, from the Low Countries and the Rhineland, and there is evidence to suggest

[1] Nos. 207–209; 211.

that trade with Sweden was conducted from York, Lincoln and Winchester, and perhaps to a lesser degree from Stamford, Thetford, Canterbury, Leicester and Norwich.[1] There is testimony to the activities of Anglo-Saxon merchants as far north as Iceland and as far south as Rome; Chester appears as the centre of a trade in furs which derived from Ireland and Scandinavia;[2] English cheese was exported to Flanders; Droitwich[3] and Norwich were important salt markets; and whilst Gloucester early made a significant render of iron, William of Poitiers speaks specifically of the known skill of English metal workers.[4] Nor is there any reason to suppose that such mercantile activity was not reflected in urban institutions. It is doubtful whether the gild-merchant, as later conceived, existed in England before the Norman Conquest, but the *cnihtengild* in London was at an early date an association of wealthy merchants.[5] Finally it would seem that some at least of the pre-Conquest boroughs possessed the rudiments of a municipal government peculiar to themselves. The court of the *husting* in London, wherein in the twelfth century the aldermen delivered judgment, was certainly an ancient institution; and the *judices* of Chester[6] and York and the *lawmen* of Cambridge, Stamford and Lincoln,[7] all mentioned in Domesday Book, may perhaps have been associated in some measure with borough courts. The controversies relating to the Anglo-Saxon borough relate in the main to an earlier period and need not here be debated. It would, however, seem that while many of the smaller boroughs recorded in Domesday Book have a very rural appearance, in others there had already developed before the Conquest, and apart from foreign influence, some of the features later to be characteristic of the medieval town.

The immediate effects of the Norman Conquest upon English town life were less notable than might have been expected. In some places an actual catastrophe occurred, as at Lincoln where the erection of the new castle involved the demolition of one hundred and sixty houses.[8] The establishment of a more effective monarchy was, however, in time to benefit the English boroughs even as the increased connexion with the Continent was to stimulate their trade. By the time of Henry I two broad classes of boroughs can be seen in England. The majority of these can be described as royal boroughs entirely or predominantly under the control of the king.[9] But after the Conquest there was rapidly growing up a class of seigniorial or *mesne* boroughs which were under the protection or control of one of the new Norman lords. Sometimes the starting-point in this growth was the wresting of privileges by a community from a lord in need of money, but sometimes, as seems for instance to have been the case at Burford in the late eleventh century,[10] the initiative was taken by the lord himself who wished by the establishment of a privileged borough on his lands to

[1] No. 297. [2] No. 209. [3] No. 210. [4] No. 4. [5] Nos. 274–277.
[6] No. 209. [7] No. 211. [8] No. 211. [9] *e.g.* Nos. 288, 289, 291, 295, 300, 302.
[10] No. 286.

increase the revenue which he might obtain from his estates. It is further notable that the materials for English municipal history may be said in one sense to have started with the Norman Conquest, for no genuine borough charter is apparently to be found from the pre-Conquest period. For some time, however, the evidence remains scanty, and it only increases with the advance of the twelfth century. Here too may perhaps be seen reflected another aspect of English municipal history. It was the great expansion of European trade, characteristic of the latter half of the twelfth century which, most of all, contributed to the development of English town life.

During the six-score years which followed the Norman Conquest, the most notable feature in English municipal history was the accumulation by the English boroughs of miscellaneous privileges such as freedom from toll; the right to hold markets; and the acquisition by some of the more important towns of the right to farm for themselves the revenues which the king exacted from them.[1] In respect of such privileges few generalizations can safely be made, since they were a matter for particular bargaining by each individual community. Certain patterns may, however, sometimes be descried. Thus the privileges bestowed in Henry I's charter to Newcastle-upon-Tyne[2] were granted in due course to Alnwick and other places in northern England and southern Scotland; the London charter[3] given by the same king was copied by Oxford[4] and other towns; the customs of Breteuil in Normandy were adopted at Hereford, Shrewsbury, Bideford and other boroughs; and the charter of Henry II to Bristol[5] was later used as a model by Dublin.[6] In general, however, each town in these matters has to be separately considered. The one feature common to all boroughs (though not peculiar to them) was the existence therein of 'burgage tenure', the essential feature of which was the right of the burgess to hold in heredity at a money rent with the freedom to devise, sell or alienate his tenement at will.

Of greater importance was the growth in many boroughs of gilds-merchant. As has been seen, it is an open question to what extent, if at all, these were anticipated in the various gilds of pre-Conquest England, but it is certain that soon after the Conquest there began to appear in many towns privileged associations of merchants closely organized in their own self-interest and aspiring to a monopoly of trade within the boroughs in which they were established. The early charters of Burford[7] suggest that such a body was already in existence in Oxford before the end of the eleventh century, and at York it was certainly established by the time of Henry I.[8] Elsewhere too, the gild-merchant with its monopoly, its oligarchic organization and its fraternalism, was, during the earlier half of the twelfth century, exercising its characteristic influence upon

[1] Nos. 270, 288, 294
[2] No. 298.
[3] No. 270.
[4] No. 300.
[5] No. 284.
[6] No. 289.
[7] Cf. No. 286.
[8] No. 282.

urban growth. Craft gilds, such as that of the weavers in London,[1] also came into existence about this time and probably existed before the death of Henry I at Huntingdon, Lincoln, Oxford and Winchester, but their influence at this period was subordinate. There is, however, a striking analogy to be drawn between the gild-merchant with its alderman, its brethren and its common purse on the one hand, and the mayor, the borough court and the borough treasury on the other. At Leicester,[2] indeed, the personnel of the gild-merchant and the borough court seem to have been identical. Nevertheless, it would be wrong to ascribe too much to the gilds-merchant. The court of the borough–normally more ancient than the gild–was the core of the burghal polity, and some towns, notably London and Norwich, never possessed a gild-merchant at all. It was the older burghal organization, however much it may have been influenced by the gild-merchant, that was subsequently to form the basis of the self-sufficient urban communities of the later Middle Ages.

It was the borough court, for example, which was primarily responsible for operating what was the most important privilege that any twelfth-century English town could receive–the right known as *firma burgi*, whereby the burgesses themselves collected the revenues due from the borough to the king. The earliest evidence for this grant is apparently the charter of Henry I to London,[3] though it seems clear that Lincoln possessed a similar privilege in the same reign.[4] The *firma burgi* might be granted for a term of years and be revocable, or occasionally it might be bestowed in free farm and in perpetuity. Always it was a powerful influence towards the growth of independence and self-government, and it is not impossible that there frequently went with it the right of the burgesses to elect reeves to administer the consequential arrangements within the borough. Municipal independence was in fact, during the reign of Henry II, already progressing, and beginning to encroach even on royal authority. Henry II was chary of seeing its extension, and it was with a somewhat jaundiced eye that he watched his boroughs grow. In 1189 only five boroughs–Lincoln, Cambridge, Shrewsbury, Northampton and Bridgnorth–were certainly being still farmed by their burgesses. The king indeed had some reason for his caution. Already attempts were being made to obtain a still larger measure of autonomy such as was enjoyed by certain continental towns from their possession of a *commune*.[5] The *commune* was a sworn association of burgesses whose object was to offer united resistance to their lords, and ultimately to achieve the position of a collective feudal lordship liable only to the payment of the feudal incidents. It is small wonder that a king of the type of Henry II regarded such designs as constituting a revolutionary conspiracy. Only after his death did London, perhaps alone among English towns, achieve such status in 1191. Even so it was an exceptional attainment. And, quite apart from what

[1] No. 272. [2] Cf. Nos. 292, 293. [3] No. 270. [4] Nos. 294–296 [5] No. 8, p. 302.

may then have been achieved in the capital, it may be said that the greatest period in the history of the self-governing towns of medieval England did not begin before the reign of John.

Among English towns of this period London occupied a special place for, although it did not possess the unique importance it had enjoyed in Roman times, it was still by far the greatest of the English centres of distribution, and its citizens were fully conscious of their privileges and power. Some indication of the importance of London under Edward the Confessor can be seen from the fact that William summoned citizens from the town to meet him at Berkhamsted before his coronation in 1066,[1] and very early in his reign he saw fit to confirm their ancient privileges by charter.[2] A mark of the new régime was the erection of castles within the city such as the Tower of London[3] in the east and Baynard's castle in the south-west. The number of foreign families in London, already considerable, probably increased at this time, and a new official, the justiciar, was established. But speaking generally, the effects of the Norman Conquest upon London were restricted. The English element in the population remained predominant even in the upper ranks of civic society, as is indicated by the names recorded in the remarkable documents relating to the *cnihtengild*.[4] It was perhaps therefore not surprising that, when at the end of the reign of Henry I the Londoners obtained from the king a charter enumerating their privileges, many of its clauses were retrospective.[5] The *firma burgi*, and the right to elect their sheriff, stand out as indicating the manner in which London, strong in its traditional privileges, had succeeded in enhancing its exceptional position under the new government.

The administration of Anglo-Norman London derived in the main from institutions established before the Conquest. The folkmoot of all the citizens still met three times a year, but perhaps it was already regarded as somewhat archaic, and the main business of administration, particularly on its commercial side, was carried on at the *husting*. This court with its Scandinavian name met every Monday at the Guildhall which stood to the west of the present building in the street which since the twelfth century has been named Aldermanbury. It was an aristocratic court in the sense that within it the aldermen formed a class apart with the obligation to know the law and state it, and the aldermen, also, were severally in charge of the city wards, the earliest description of which occurs in a document of the reign of Henry I. These leading citizens were, indeed, largely responsible for the great part the city played in the civil war of Stephen's reign, and it was they who strove to establish the *commune* which was in 1191 actually to be recognized by John. But the real strength of London in this period lay in the self-conscious civic pride which is so admirably reflected in William fitz Stephen's notable description of London in the time of Henry II.[6]

[1] No. 4, p. 230. [2] No. 269. [3] Nos. 279, 281. [4] Nos. 274–277. [5] No. 271. [6] No. 281.

The text is worthy of detailed study for here is portrayed an active and affluent community. Its only plagues we are told were the "immoderate drinking of fools and the frequency of fires". Its matrons were very Sabines; its young men were full of prowess; its merchants were second to none in wealth; and its citizens, like country gentlemen, had hunting rights over four counties. Care must be taken not to allow this enthusiastic description to convey an idealized picture of a city which must have been violent, dirty, and sometimes squalid; but William fitz Stephen's rhetoric was in most cases founded on fact and is often corroborated by legal documents. It reflects the life of a city which would have been a glory to any medieval kingdom.

It seems a far cry from this brilliant metropolis to the bucolic villages of Anglo-Norman England; from them to the royal court; from the Cistercian monastery, newly built perhaps in Yorkshire, to the household of some honorial baron in the western shires. English society in the twelfth century was in truth diversified. Social classes were well defined, and men accepted their place therein. Out of the peasantry, mute and inarticulate, it was rare for a man to move; the warrior conscious of his special duties was conscious also of his privileges; and the clergy were concerned to establish themselves as a separate estate distinct from the laity within the Church. Above moved the king in the criticized glory of regality. Nevertheless this society, so distinctly ordered, was never static. Nor was it wholly segregated in its several parts. The Church offered a career, to a limited extent, open to the talents; St. Anselm was the friend of Hugh of Avranches; and Thomas Becket was the son of a London burgess. It is an epoch of surprises. It is also an epoch of rapid change. A man who in old age was shocked by the news of Becket's murder might have heard from his father in youth an eyewitness account of the battle of Hastings; and the grandson of a thegn who went into exile with Earl Godwine might have been killed in the civil war of Stephen's reign. It is easy to contrast the England of 1160 with the England of 1060, but it is also easy to forget that they were separated by only one hundred years.

This society, so sundered by contrasted activity, yet withal being painfully moulded into a new unity of political and ecclesiastical purpose, challenges attention and escapes description. Life for these men was often violent, usually uncomfortable, always adventurous. Not theirs the happiness of people without history, for they were engaged in hazardous creation and the stakes were high. A society which had seen its aristocracy eliminated was not one to be complacent as to the permanence of wealth. A country, which within a century and a half had experienced incipient anarchy, foreign invasion and a civil war, was not tempted to undervalue the blessings of strong and ordered government. A community, which in the space of three generations had seen a king killed on the Sussex Downs and an archbishop slain in his own cathedral, was not likely to forget that there were causes for which men should be ready to suffer and to die. A sense of urgency thus assailed them, and gave a special quality to their strenuous endeavour. Before their eyes, and through their efforts, they could watch the erection of a new political edifice. But they could not be sure that it would endure. For the floods were still insurgent, and the foundations were but newly laid. And if it fell, who would measure the disaster, and would it ever rise again?

SELECT BIBLIOGRAPHY

of the principal modern works relating generally to English history between 1042 and 1189

(*a*) BIBLIOGRAPHIES

The most useful guide to the literature relating to this period will be found in C. Gross, *The Sources and Literature of English History from the earliest times to about 1485* (2nd ed., London, 1915). For the years 1042–1087 an admirable bibliography is included in F. M. Stenton, *Anglo-Saxon England* (Oxford, 1943), and the whole period is covered in the bibliographies appended to certain chapters of the *Cambridge Medieval History* (vol. III, pp. 625–630; vol. V, pp. 481–591). Bibliographies of the work of particular scholars who made an important contribution to the history of this age are included in *Essays in History presented to R. Lane Poole* (Oxford, 1927), in *Historical Essays in honour of James Tait* (Manchester, 1933), in *Studies in Medieval History presented to F. M. Powicke* (Oxford, 1948), in *Haskins Anniversary Essays* (Boston, 1929), and in P. Lacombe, *Bibliographie des Travaux de M. Léopold Delisle* (Paris, 1902; supplement, 1911). A select list of the works of F. M. Stenton is included in *Sir Christopher Hatton's Book of Seals*, ed. L. C. Loyd and D. M. Stenton (Oxford, 1950). The earlier work on the history of Normandy and on its connexion with England is admirably summarized in E. Frère, *Manuel du Bibliographe Normand* (2 vols., Rouen, 1858, 1860), an excellent book which deserves to be better known in England. Some appraisal of the scholarship which has been devoted to this period will be found in F. M. Stenton, "Early English History, 1895–1920" (*Trans. R. Hist. Soc.*, 4th Series, vol. XXVIII (1946), pp. 7–19), in D. C. Douglas, *English Scholars* (London, 1939, 2nd ed. 1951), and in D. C. Douglas, *The Norman Conquest and British Historians* (Glasgow, 1946).

(*b*) GENERAL WORKS

A survey of the literature which has been devoted to this period, and of the chief interpretations which have been placed upon English history between 1042 and 1189, has been made in the second section of the preceding essay (see above, pp. 9–13).

The best modern treatment of this epoch is contained in F. M. Stenton, *Anglo-Saxon England* (Oxford, 1943), and in A. L. Poole, *From Domesday Book to Magna Carta* (Oxford, 1951). The period also is covered in four chapters of the *Cambridge Medieval History*. These are W. J. Corbett, "England from A.D. 954 to the Death of Edward the Confessor" (vol. III, chap. XV), W. J. Corbett, "The Development of the Duchy of Normandy and the Norman Conquest of England" (vol. V, chap. XV), W. J. Corbett, "England, 1087–1154" (vol. V, chap. XVI), and D. M. Stenton, "England: Henry II" (vol. V, chap. XVII). E. A. Freeman's large *History of the Norman Conquest* (5 vols. and index volume, Oxford, several editions), has been discussed above (pp. 6–7): it covers the period to the death of William the Conqueror in great detail and offers an excellent introduction to the evidence of the chroniclers. It is still indispensable, although the personal conclusions of the author have been subjected to fierce criticism and should be treated with caution. Its sequel, *The Reign of William Rufus and the Accession of Henry I* (2 vols., Oxford, 1882), is in many ways a better balanced book than its more famous predecessor, and, treated with the same caution, will be found of great value. W. Stubbs's wonderful introduction to the chronicle of 'Benedict of Peterborough' (Rolls Series, 1867), which is, in large part, reprinted in Stubbs's *Historical*

Introductions to the Rolls Series (London, 1902), provides what is still perhaps the best general account of the reign of Henry II. Among general histories probably the most useful are J. H. Ramsay, *Foundations of England* (vol. II, London, 1898) and *The Angevin Empire* (London, 1903), but reference may also be made to the later chapters in T. Hodgkin, *The History of England from the earliest times to the Norman Conquest* (London, 1898) and in C. Oman, *England before the Norman Conquest* (8th ed., London, 1937); and to the earlier chapters in G. B. Adams, *The History of England from 1066 to 1216* (London, 1905) and H. W. C. Davis, *England under the Normans and Angevins* (8th ed., London, 1924). D. Jerrold, *Introduction to the History of England* (London, 1949) may also be consulted. Among the older general works the relevant chapters of J. Lingard, *History of England to 1688* (many editions) supply a careful survey of this period; and certain information not easily to be obtained elsewhere is to be found in the edition of F. Palgrave's *Normandy and England* contained in that author's *Collected Works* (vols. I–IV, 1919–1921) where it is supplemented by critical notes and useful genealogies composed by another hand. J. M. Lappenberg's work on early English history still retains some value and can best be studied in the translations made by B. Thorpe, *History of England under the Anglo-Saxon Kings* (2 vols., London, 1881), and *History of England under the Norman Kings* (Oxford, 1857). The modern reader will also gain much from the perusal of Lord Lyttelton's long and documented *History of the Life of King Henry II and of the age in which he lived* (4 vols., London, 1767). The relations between England and the other countries of the British Isles are well set out in J. E. Lloyd, *History of Wales from the earliest times to the Edwardian Conquest* (2nd ed., 2 vols. London, 1912); in G. H. Orpen, *Ireland under the Normans* (4 vols., Oxford, 1911–1923); and in E. Curtis, *History of Medieval Ireland* (2nd ed., London, 1938). The history of Scotland at this time is well surveyed in W. F. Skene, *Celtic Scotland* (3 vols., Edinburgh, 1876-1880), and in R. L. Graeme Ritchie, *The Normans in Scotland* (Edinburgh, 1953). Both these works should be used in connexion with A. O. Anderson, *Scottish Annals from English Chroniclers* (London, 1908), and *Early Sources of Scottish History* (Edinburgh, 1922).

(*c*) GENERAL WORKS ON PARTICULAR ASPECTS OF THE PERIOD

The Scandinavian factor in English history at this time is discussed in F. M. Stenton, *The Danes in England* (Brit. Acad., 1927), and is further considered in a series of works which will be discussed below (pp. 809–811). Vol. I of Steenstrup's pioneer work, *Normannerne* (4 vols., Copenhagen, 1876–1882), was translated into French by E. de Beaurepaire under the title of *Etudes pour servir à l'Histoire des Normands* (Caen, 1880): vols. III and IV deal particularly with England.

No satisfactory history of the Norman duchy and of its early connexions with England exists, but C. H. Haskins, *Norman Institutions* (Harvard U.P., 1918), goes some way to supply this need, and is indispensable for the study of English history at this period. F. M. Powicke, *Loss of Normandy* (Manchester, 1913), also contains much information regarding the twelfth century. J. C. H. R. Steenstrup, *Normandiets Historie under de syv føyrste Hertuger 911–1066* (Copenhagen, 1925, with French summary), sets out the history of the Norman duchy before 1066, but it fails to take account of recent research on this subject, the general trends of which are considered in D. C. Douglas, *The Rise of Normandy* (Brit. Acad., 1946). H. Prentout, *Guillaume le Conquérant* (Caen, 1927), is sometimes suggestive for the Norman reign of Duke William. The most informative discussion of the personal connexions between England and Normandy at this time is contained in the long introductions which T. Stapleton added to his *Magni Rotuli Scaccarii Normanniae* (2 vols., London, 1840, 1844). Other aspects of the relations between Normandy and England at this time are discussed in C. W. David, *Robert Curthose* (Harvard U.P., 1920), and by D. C. Douglas in "The Earliest Norman Counts" (*Eng. Hist. Rev.*, vol. LXI, 1946), in "The

Ancestors of William fitz Osbern" (*ibid.*, vol. LIX, 1944), and in his introduction to *Domesday Monachorum of Christ Church, Canterbury* (London, 1944). Other works of a more detailed nature are Vicomte de Motey, *Robert II de Bellême* (Paris, 1923), Daniel Gurney, *Record of the House of Gournay* (2 vols., London, 1845), and G. H. White, "The sisters and nieces of Gunnor, duchess of Normandy" (*Genealogist*, New Series, vols. XXXVII and XXXVIII, 1920, 1921). L. C. Loyd, "The Origin of the Family of Warenne" (*Yorks. Arch. Journal*, vol. XXXI, 1933) is a definitive study of the early history of a Norman family which played a great part in English affairs. Much information respecting English history is to be obtained from local Norman studies, of which perhaps the most notable is L. Delisle, *Histoire du Château et des Sires de Saint-Sauveur-le-Vicomte* (Valognes, 1867), which contains a large appendix of important documents, whilst the very numerous essays of Charles de Beaurepaire (see *Répertoire bibliographique–de Charles de Beaurepaire*, Paris, 1901, supplement, 1929) are of high quality. Students of English history will also find much of value in more general works such as C. H. Haskins, *The Normans in European History* (Boston, 1915), and most particularly in F. Chalandon, *Histoire de la Domination Normande en Italie et en Sicile 1009–1194* (2 vols., Paris, 1907). The part played by Anjou in English history is discussed in many of the books cited above, and to these must be added Kate Norgate, *England under the Angevin Kings* (2 vols., London, 1887), which should be read in connexion with J. Chartrou, *L'Anjou de 1109 à 1151* (Paris, 1928), and J. Boussard, *Le Comté d'Anjou sous Henri Plantagenet et ses fils* (Paris, 1938). Much work still remains to be done on Norman history, and there is little doubt that its accomplishment would throw a flood of new light upon the Norman Conquest and the Norman settlement of England. In the meantime the best introduction to the material upon which such work must be based is contained in J. H. Round's magnificent *Calendar of Documents preserved in France illustrative of the History of Great Britain and Ireland* (vol. I, 918–1206, London, Public Record Office, 1899). The great French collections, such as "Dom. Bouquet." (*Recueil des Historiens des Gaules et de la France*, 24 vols., folio) and *Gallia Christiana*, of which vol. XI is devoted to Normandy, may also be consulted with great profit by students of English history. Reference may also be made to M. Prou, *Recueil des Actes de Philippe I, roi de France* (Paris, 1908), and to F. Soehnée, *Catalogue des Actes de Henri I, roi de France* (Paris, 1907). An appreciation of the position occupied by Henry II as a continental prince may best be obtained in L. Delisle and E. Berger, *Recueil des Actes de Henri II concernant les provinces françaises et les affaires de France* (4 vols. and atlas of plates, Paris, 1906–1927). The first volume of this magisterial work is an introduction by Léopold Delisle who was probably the greatest French medievalist of his generation.

The military history of the age can be conveniently surveyed in F. Lot, *L'Art militaire et les armées au Moyen Age en Europe et dans le proche Orient* (2 vols., Paris, 1946) which partially supersedes C. W. C. Oman, *History of the Art of War in the Middle Ages* (2nd ed., 2 vols., London 1924). R. Glover, "English Warfare in 1066" (*Eng. Hist. Rev.*, LXVII, 1952) may also be consulted.

The most important general account of English constitutional development at this time is W. Stubbs, *Constitutional History of England*, vol. I (Oxford, many editions). This work, by the hand of a master, retains very much of its value, but it needs to be checked in the light of documentary discoveries made since its original composition. F. Pollock and F. W. Maitland, *History of English Law* (2nd ed., 2 vols., Cambridge, 1898) is likewise a masterly work which illuminates most aspects of constitutional history in this period. These and other works on English government and administration during this period will be further considered below in the Bibliography at p. 395.

The affairs of Church and State in this period were most closely intertwined, but works more specifically devoted to ecclesiastical history will be discussed in the Bibliography at p. 589.

Works on social and economic history are considered in the Bibliography at p. 803.

(*d*) STUDIES OF PARTICULAR POLITICAL PROBLEMS AND PERSONALITIES

Two collective works dealing with persons and families will be found indispensable. *The Dictionary of National Biography* is perhaps less satisfactory for the medieval period than for later centuries, but it contains (apart from the supplements) 186 articles relating to the eleventh century and 377 articles relating to the twelfth. These are of unequal value, but this great co-operative enterprise embodies fine work concerning this period by scholars as distinguished as W. H. Hutton, R. L. Poole, J. H. Round and James Tait. The other general compilation which will be found of great value is *The Complete Peerage of England, Scotland, Ireland, Great Britain and the United Kingdom* (London, 1910 in progress), twelve volumes of which have now been published. The scope of this book is far wider than its title would suggest, and the standard of scholarship displayed therein is (particularly in its later volumes) extremely high. There are few topics relating to the history of Anglo-Norman England which do not find some illustration in it.

Among political studies relating to this period pride of place must be given to those of J. H. Round. His *Calendar of Documents preserved in France* has already been mentioned, but some idea of the productivity of this great scholar may be formed from the fact that he contributed not less than sixty articles to the *English Historical Review*, and that some of his best work is to be found in such periodicals as the *Ancestor* and *The Antiquary*. A very large number of his papers is contained in the *Transactions of the Essex Archaeological Society* and elsewhere, and the best introduction to his work is in the bibliography contained in his posthumous book, *Family Origins* (London, 1930). In addition to those studies, which still remain scattered, Round also collected many of his papers into a number of volumes of which the most relevant to the history of this period are *Geoffrey de Mandeville* (London, 1892), *Feudal England* (London, 1895; reprint, 1909), *The Commune of London and Other Studies* (London, 1899), *Studies in Peerage and Family History* (London, 1901), *Peerage and Pedigree* (2 vols., London, 1910), and *The King's Serjeants and Officers of State* (London, 1911). The more important essays of J. H. Round will be considered in connexion with the topics to which they more particularly refer, but a few of them may here be noted. "Domesday Book" and "The Introduction of Knight Service into England" (*Feudal England*, pp. 3–146, and pp. 225–314) are fundamental studies relating to the reign of William the Conqueror which still remain as indispensable as when they first appeared. In the same volume will also be found valuable papers such as "Normans under Edward the Confessor" (*ibid.*, pp. 317–331), "The Conqueror at Exeter" (*ibid.*, pp. 431–455), and "Walter Tirel and his Wife" (*ibid.*, pp. 465–479). The wide interest of Round's essays is not always indicated by their titles. Thus "The Counts of Boulogne as English Lords" (*Studies in Peerage and Family History*, pp. 147–180) and "The Family of Ballon and the conquest of South Wales" (*ibid.*, pp. 181–215) illuminate much of the political history of Anglo-Norman England, whilst "The Bayeux Inquest of 1133" (*Family Origins*, pp. 201–216) is likewise important, though many of its conclusions must now be checked by reference to H. Navel, "L'Enquête de 1133 sur les fiefs de l'évêché de Bayeux" (*Bull. Soc. Antiq. Norm.*, vol. XIII (1934), pp. 5–50). Round's *Geoffrey de Mandeville* is still the best study of the reign of Stephen.

There is no adequate modern biography of Edward the Confessor, though much of the evidence which could be used to compile one is contained in the notes and commentaries in J. Earle and C. Plummer, *Two of the Saxon Chronicles Parallel* (2 vols., Oxford, 1892, 1898) Episodes in the reign are discussed by B. Wilkinson in "Freeman and the Crisis of 1051" (*Bull. John Rylands Library*, vol. XXII, 1938) and in "Northumbrian separatism in 1065 and 1066" (*ibid.*, vol. XXIII, 1941). P. Grierson's "Relations between England and Flanders before the Norman Conquest" (*Trans. R. Hist. Soc.*, 4th Series, vol. XXIII, 1941) and "A Visit of Earl

Harold to Flanders in 1056" (*Eng. Hist. Rev.*, vol. LI, 1936) are valuable, and there is useful material relating to English history to be found in S. Fest, *The Hungarian Origin of St. Margaret of Scotland* (Debrecen, 1940). R. R. Darlington in "The Last Phase of Anglo-Saxon History" (*History*, vol. XXII, 1937) makes a strong plea for the vitality of the Old English State at the time of its collapse.

The reign of William I is admirably surveyed by Professor Stenton in *William the Conqueror* (New York and London, 1908, 1912, 1915), a notable biography which gives an emphasis to some aspects of the reign different from that given in the same author's *Anglo-Saxon England.* The best account of the battle of Hastings is W. Spatz, *Die Schlacht von Hastings* (Berlin, 1896), and students need today only to be reminded in general terms of the great controversy which took place between J. H. Round and E. A. Freeman on this subject. For the campaign of 1066 and those who took part in it reference may be made to D. C. Douglas, "Companions of the Conqueror" (*History*, vol. XXVIII, 1943), and to G. J. Turner, "William the Conqueror's March on London" (*Eng. Hist. Rev.*, vol. XXVII, 1912). A more general treatment is D. C. Douglas, "The Norman Conquest" (*New English Review*, November 1945). F. M. Stenton, "English Families and the Norman Conquest" (*Trans. R. Hist. Soc.*, 4th Series, vol. XXV, 1943), is a notable essay which deserves careful study. J. H. Le Patourel in "Geoffrey, Bishop of Coutances" (*Eng. Hist. Rev.*, vol. LIX, 1944) sketches the biography of a great figure in Anglo-Norman England, and H. A. Cronne in "The Salisbury Oath" (*History*, vol. XIX, 1934) considers one of the most important episodes in the Conqueror's reign. But most of the special studies relating to the reigns of the Conqueror and of Rufus deal with topics of constitutional and social rather than of political history.

The same concentration of interest is shown in most of the specialized work on the reign of Henry I, but W. Farrer, *An Outline Itinerary of Henry I* (reprinted from *Eng. Hist. Rev.*, vol. XXXIV, 1919), is indispensable for the chronology of the period and for a survey of its political affairs. Much of Round's work concerns the personalities of the period 1100–1135, and two other studies of a similar nature are G. H. White, "The career of Waleran, count of Meulan and Earl of Worcester" (*Trans. R. Hist. Soc.*, 4th Series, vol. XVII, 1934) and H. A. Cronne, "Ranulf des Gernons, Earl of Chester" (*ibid.*, vol. XX, 1937). Reference may also be made to C. W. David, "The Claim of Henry I to be called learned" in *Haskins Anniversary Essays* (Boston, 1929), a subject which, with others, is discussed in V. H. Galbraith's important paper, *The Literacy of the Medieval English Kings* (Brit. Acad., 1935).

On Stephen's reign, Round's work may be supplemented by G. H. White, "King Stephen's Earldoms" (*Trans. R. Hist. Soc.*, 4th Series, vol. XIII, 1930), by H. A. Cronne, "The Honour of Leicester in Stephen's reign" (*Eng. Hist. Rev.*, vol. L, 1935), and by H. W. C. Davis, "The Anarchy of Stephen's reign" (*ibid.*, vol. XVIII, 1903). O. Rössler, *Kaiserin Mathilde* (Berlin, 1897) should also be consulted.

The chronology of the events of the reign of Henry II is well set out in R. W. Eyton, *Court, Household and Itinerary of King Henry II* (London, 1878), a book which is indispensable to the detailed study of this period. The reign as a whole may best be studied in the general works of Lord Lyttelton, W. Stubbs, L. Delisle and D. M. Stenton which have been cited above, or in works devoted more particularly to constitutional and ecclesiastical history.

(*e*) ENGLISH LOCAL HISTORY, 1042–1189

No catalogue of works on English local history can here be given, but full emphasis must be given to the fact that very many local studies have a direct bearing upon the interpretation of the history of this age.

Perhaps the greatest period in the production of English county history was the seventeenth and eighteenth centuries, and a general guide to this work is W. Upcott, *A Bibliographical Account of the Principal Works relating to English Topography* (3 vols., London, 1818). Among the great county histories there described, Dugdale's *Warwickshire* and Nichol's *History of Leicestershire* may be particularly mentioned as especially important. R. W. Eyton, *Antiquities of Shropshire* (12 vols., London, 1854–1860), is of outstanding value for the feudal history of the twelfth century, and the extensive description of Northumberland begun by John Hodgson in 1820 demonstrated the fine results that can be obtained in this field by co-operative endeavour. The more recent *Victoria History of the Counties of England*, which is still in progress, is the most comprehensive work of this nature ever to be organized in any country on a national scale. Of particular value to the student of this period are the general articles which in this work precede the topographical descriptions of each shire. Especially important among them are the translations of Domesday Book, each of which is introduced by an essay that is sometimes of the highest importance.

The principal histories of towns, villages, particular churches and regions can be discovered by reference to W. Upcott (*op. cit.*), to R. Gough, *British Topography* (London, 1768, 1780), and to Gross (*op. cit.*). A selection from among them would be invidious and of little use. Among those works which make a particular contribution to the general history of this period may be cited; J. Bentham, *History and Antiquities of the Cathedral Church of Ely* (2nd ed., Norwich, 1812; supplement, Norwich, 1817), with its notable appendix of charters; W. Tindal, *History and Antiquities of Evesham* (1794), which is important for the history of Domesday Book; J. Tait, *Medieval Manchester and the Origins of Lancashire* (Manchester, 1904); F. M. Stenton, *Types of Manorial Structure in the Northern Danelaw* (Oxford, 1910); C. W. Foster, *The History of Aisthorpe and Thorpe in the Fallows* (Lincoln, 1927); D. C. Douglas, *The Social Structure of Medieval East Anglia* (Oxford, 1927); and J. W. F. Hill, *Medieval Lincoln* (Cambridge, 1948).

Since the earlier half of the nineteenth century, much of the work on English local history has appeared in the publications of local societies. Their productions have taken the form both of articles and of the publication of texts, and many studies of national significance have been published under these auspices. Thus (to take but a few examples) much of the work of James Tait on this period is to be found in the transactions of the Chetham Society; highly important contributions have been made by Sir Frank Stenton to the Lincoln Record Society, and by H. E. Salter to the Oxford Historical Society. Many articles contributed to the transactions of local societies will be recorded individually in the bibliographies in this book, and a useful general introduction to this extensive literature will be found in H. A. Doubleday and W. Page, *A Guide to the Victoria History of the Counties of England* (London, 1903), which may be used in connexion with S. Terry, *Catalogue of publications of Scottish Historical and Kindred Clubs* (Glasgow, 1909).

It may, however, be convenient to list by counties some of the principal societies whose publications merit the special attention of students of this period:

Bedfordshire

Bedfordshire Historical Record Society. Especially important in this connexion for the work of G. H. Fowler on Domesday and on twelfth-century feudalism.

Buckinghamshire

Buckinghamshire Record Society.

Cambridgeshire

Cambridge Antiquarian Society.

Cheshire
  Chetham Society.
Cumberland
  Cumberland and Westmorland Antiquarian and Archaeological Society.
Devonshire
  Devonshire Association for the Advancement of Science, Literature and Art.
  History of Exeter Research Group.
Durham
  Surtees Society.
Essex
  Essex Archaeological Society, especially valuable for the contributions of J. H. Round.
Gloucestershire
  Bristol and Gloucestershire Archaeological Society.
  Bristol Record Society.
Hampshire
  Hampshire Record Society.
Huntingdonshire
  Fenland Notes and Queries.
Kent
  Kent Archaeological Society: its valuable transactions are published under the title of *Archaeologia Cantiana.*
Lancashire
  Chetham Society.
Leicestershire
  Leicestershire Architectural and Archaeological Society.
Lincolnshire
  Lincoln Record Society. Particularly important for the work of C. W. Foster and F. M. Stenton.
London and Middlesex
  Society of Antiquaries of London. The parent of all these societies whose first publications under the title of *Archaeologia,* which are still in progress, appeared in 1770.
  London and Middlesex Archaeological Society.
Norfolk
  Norfolk and Norwich Archaeological Society, whose publications bear the general title of *Norfolk Archaeology.*
  Norfolk Record Society.
Northamptonshire
  Northamptonshire Record Society
Northumberland
  Surtees Society.
Nottinghamshire
  Thoroton Society.
Oxfordshire
  Oxford Historical Society
  Oxfordshire Record Society.
Somerset
  Somerset Record Society.

Staffordshire

William Salt Archaeological Society.

Surrey

Surrey Record Society.

Sussex

Sussex Archaeological Society.

Warwickshire

Dugdale Society.

Wiltshire

Wiltshire Record Society.

Worcestershire

Worcestershire Historical Society.

Yorkshire

Yorkshire Archaeological Society. Publishes an important *Journal*, and also a valuable *Record Series* which includes among other notable works the editions of charters by William Farrar and C. T. Clay.

Thoresby Society. Devoted to the history of Leeds and its neighbourhood.

(*f*) MISCELLANEOUS

The Handbook of British Chronology (R. Hist. Soc., 1939), which includes lists of kings, bishops and nobles, is a book of reference indispensable for the study of this period, and much of the information contained in it is summarized in the *Handbook of Dates for Students of English History* (ed. C. R. Cheney, R. Hist. Soc., 1945). The information respecting the succession of bishops given in W. Stubbs, *Registrum Sacrum Anglicanum* (2nd ed., Oxford, 1897) is also of the highest value.

In respect of archaeology and architecture the most informative general accounts are J. W. Clapham, *English Romanesque Architecture* (vol. I, before the Conquest, Oxford, 1930; vol. II, after the Conquest, Oxford, 1934), and G. Baldwin Brown, *The Arts in Early England* (6 vols., London, 1903–1937). The military architecture of the Norman age is admirably treated in E. S. Armitage, *The Early Norman Castles of the British Isles* (London, 1912). The coinage of the period before the Conquest is dealt with in C. F. Keary, *Catalogue of English Coins in the British Museum* (2 vols., London, 1887, 1893), and that of the post-Conquest period in the same writer's *Catalogue of English Coins in the British Museum: The Norman Kings* (2 vols., London, 1916). On the making of MSS. and their decoration there are many works on particular codices and schools, but a general introduction to the subject can be obtained from E. O. Millar, *English Illuminated MSS. from the tenth to the twelfth century* (London, 1926).

The importance of the testimony of place-names can best be appreciated from the presidential addresses delivered to the Royal Historical Society from 1939 to 1943 by Sir Frank Stenton under the general title of "The Historical bearing of Place Name Studies" (*Trans. R. Hist. Soc.*, 4th Series, vols. XXI–XXV, 1939–1943). These remarkable lectures provide an admirable introduction to such works as E. Ekwall, *Oxford Dictionary of English Place Names* (2nd ed., Oxford, 1940), and to the publications of the English Place Name Society which began in 1924 and still continue.

(*g*) PERIODICAL LITERATURE

The most important periodical is the *English Historical Review* (London, 1886– in progress), which is indispensable for the study of this period; and much fundamental work is contained in the *Transactions of the Royal Historical Society*. Other publications such as *Archaeologia*, the

Antiquaries Journal, the *Ancestor*, the *Economic History Review*, the *Cambridge Historical Journal*, and the *Bulletin of the John Rylands Library*, while mainly concerned with other topics, include articles bearing upon English history in this age; and *History*, the review of the Historical Association, also contains some articles of general interest. Among the numerous American reviews the most useful for students of this period is probably *Speculum*, the review of the Medieval Academy of America, and the *American Historical Review* should not be neglected. The *Revue Historique*, the *Revue Benedictine*, *Le Moyen Age*, the *Revue d'histoire ecclésiastique*, and *Analecta Bollandiana* all include some articles of relevance to English history at this time. But among continental publications of a periodical nature the most important for English history in this period are the transactions of two Norman societies. These are the *Société des Antiquaries de Normandie*, whose long and valuable series of *Mémoires* began in 1825; and the *Société de l'Histoire de Normandie* which is mainly concerned with the critical edition of texts, and which, since its foundation, has produced over a hundred volumes, many of which have a direct bearing upon English history.

NOTE

The original text of all documents printed in this book is, unless otherwise stated, in Latin.

Part I

SELECT CHRONICLES AND NARRATIVES RELATING TO THE HISTORY OF ENGLAND, 1042–1189

SELECT CHRONICLES AND NARRATIVES
RELATING TO THE
HISTORY OF ENGLAND, 1042–1189

Introduction

THE chronicles illustrating this age are so numerous and so extensive that only a fraction of them can be represented in a single volume, but since all this narrative production was closely interrelated, some acquaintance with its general character is essential if the value of any of its parts is to be correctly appraised. Among the chronicles of this age pride of place must be given to the vernacular annals known as the Anglo-Saxon Chronicle which are here printed in full in respect of the three versions which most specifically concern this period and which are discussed in some detail below (pp. 107–110). For the earlier part of this period English narrative history was in fact so dominated by this compilation that other writers such as 'Florence of Worcester' and Henry of Huntingdon are, in so far as they refer to these years, mainly of interest as providing a commentary on the Anglo-Saxon Chronicle upon which they are very largely based. Some additional information may however be obtained from narratives compiled from a local standpoint, such as were made for instance at Abingdon, Ely and Durham, and there are a few important biographies relating to the period of the Conquest. Early in the twelfth century William of Malmesbury, for example, composed what is essentially a translation of a lost vernacular life of Bishop Wulfstan of Worcester written by his chaplain; and Milo Crispin, one of Lanfranc's pupils, wrote (also in the early twelfth century) a biography of the great archbishop. Perhaps the most important, and certainly the most perplexing, of these early biographies is however the strange text known as the *Vita Edwardi Confessoris*. This used to be considered as a product of the years 1066–1075 but it has more recently been referred to the early twelfth century. It is still the subject of controversy, but while most scholars are now disposed to regard it as a nearly contemporary record, it cannot without some reservations be used as a primary source for the Confessor's reign.

The events of the Norman Conquest were also described by a succession of Norman historians among whom the two chief contemporary figures were William of Jumièges and William of Poitiers. The former of these compiled a comprehensive history of the Norman dukes, basing the earliest part of his narrative upon the previous compilation of Dudo of St. Quentin. William of Jumièges, who begins to be a strictly contemporary source with the reign of Duke Robert I (1028–1033), carried his narrative down to 1072. His main interests were always in Normandy, but his work supplies some information respecting England, and it stands in close (though at present undefined) relationship to the biography of William the Conqueror which was made during the lifetime of that king by William of Poitiers. Only part of this has survived, but it is of cardinal importance, both because of the date at which it was composed, and because of the special opportunities possessed by the author of gaining information about his hero. It supplies the best account of the battle of Hastings. In due course the work of both William of Jumièges and William of Poitiers was taken up by a writer of much higher quality. This was Ordericus Vitalis who was born in England about 1075, being the son of one of the Norman counsellors of Robert of Montgomery, first earl of Shrewsbury. Ordericus migrated to Normandy in early boyhood and spent the remainder of his life in the Norman abbey of St. Evroul. He had thus special opportunities for describing the two societies in which he had some share, and he used those opportunities to the full. He was a man of singularly attractive character, and of considerable intellectual distinction. Possessed of a passion for history he wrote with a fluent pen. His book is ill arranged and marred by frequent inaccuracies on points of detail, but it is copious, learned and in the main authoritative, especially after 1072 when the writer ceases to be directly dependent on his predecessors. Though not the most useful of the Latin histories of the time, the *Historia Ecclesiastica* of Ordericus Vitalis is perhaps the most interesting, and probably the most brilliant, of all the historical works relating to the history of England in the twelfth century.

In England a new phase in historiography opened with the reign of Henry I. From 1080 there is but one surviving version of the Anglo-Saxon Chronicle, and as the twelfth century advances this itself begins to be less full. Other writers therefore come into a position of greater relative prominence, since their works are no longer so derivative, but are themselves often of primary value. The earliest in time of this new group of chroniclers was a Canterbury monk named Eadmer who had been in close association with Archbishop Anselm and who shortly after Anselm's death in 1109 put into literary shape the materials respecting his hero which he had previously collected. This resulted in two principal works, a biography of the archbishop, and a larger work styled *Historia Novorum* dealing mainly with the ecclesiastical politics of the time. Meanwhile more general history was beginning to be written elsewhere. Shortly after the Conquest, the general chronicle of Marianus Scotus had been introduced into England by Robert, bishop of Hereford, and 'Florence of Worcester' added to this annals respecting England that after 1082 take on more and more the character of an independent record which in various recensions was later continued down to 1141. Purely annalistic in form, these entries are devoid of any critical distinction, but they are of the highest value as a bare record of fact which is usually reliable, and which sometimes supplies the text of other works which have subsequently been lost. At about the same time important historical work was also being done in the north. The *Historia Dunelmensis Ecclesia* written between 1104 and 1108 by Simeon of Durham is mainly a local history, but the *Historia Regum* ascribed to the same author gives some independent information relating to the period 1119–1129 after which time it was profitably continued by monks of Hexham down to 1153.

The extent and quality of the historical narratives produced in England at this time gives to these Anglo-Norman historians the character of a distinct literary group, and among them one man is eminent. This was William of Malmesbury, a wide reader and a voluminous writer whose miscellaneous production included a *Gesta Pontificum* which supplies some important material respecting the ecclesiastical biographies of the age. His importance however derives in the main from two more general works–the *Gesta Regum* which starting from the fifth century begins to be an independent and a primary authority about the reign of Henry I, and the *Historia*

Novella which deals in greater detail with the period 1100–1142. William of Malmesbury was not an exceptionally gifted writer, and his abilities were not commensurate with his ambition to establish himself as the true successor of Bede. But he is none the less an authentic historian of high quality seeking not merely to narrate but to select, to criticize and to explain. Less brilliant than Ordericus and perhaps less reliable on points of detail than 'Florence of Worcester' he is to be regarded with an especial respect for having consciously approached history from the standpoint of the scholar concerned with problems of cause and effect, and if he was sometimes tempted to exaggerate the magnitude of his own achievement he undoubtedly succeeded in producing a critical commentary on the events of his own time.

It was the corporate achievement of these men to describe the reign of Henry I, and, to a diminishing degree, the reign of Stephen. They cannot precisely be regarded as forming a school, yet there was a certain unity of purpose among them and with their passing occurs a gap in the history of English chronicles. The narrative of William of Malmesbury ends in 1143, and Henry of Huntingdon, who says little about Stephen's reign, stops in 1154. Similarly 'Florence of Worcester' was continued only to 1151, and Simeon of Durham by the Hexham monks only to 1153. For the reign of Henry II it is necessary to refer to a distinct group of chroniclers none of whom wrote much if at all before 1180. This group also however possessed its own coherence, and it was enriched by a fortunate constellation of remarkable men. Some of its numerous members, such as Gervase of Canterbury and Roger of Howden, are of more importance for Richard I than for Henry II, but the chroniclers who commemorated the reign of the first Angevin king were in very truth sufficiently numerous. Among them may be selected for especial mention four outstanding names: Gerald of Wales (Giraldus Cambrensis); Ralph 'de Diceto'; the work conventionally described as 'Benedict of Peterborough'; and William of Newburgh. These men, representative from among many others, give a special distinction to the chronicles of the reign of Henry II.

Their production was manifold. Thus Ralph 'de Diceto' who became dean of St. Paul's about 1180 wrote two works, the *Abbreviationes Chronicarum* and the *Ymagines Historiarum* which in respect of the period after 1183 embody considerable independent information. Gerald of Wales, a far more productive writer, whose published work occupies eight large octavo volumes, is a primary authority for the early history of Wales and Ireland in which he was specially though not exclusively interested, and his account of Henry II's conquest of the latter country is for the English historian probably the most important work he wrote. Still more valuable for English history is the *Gesta Regis Henrici Secundi* traditionally but wrongly assigned to Benedict who became abbot of Peterborough in 1177. This work deals with the period 1170–1192, and is as remarkable for its detail as for its independence. The writer devotes to these twenty-two years a narrative which fills over six hundred pages of print. It has throughout a somewhat official character, is plentifully supplied with dates, and gives the text of many official documents. Its importance can therefore well be imagined, and its merits are fully displayed in the wonderful introduction which Bishop Stubbs added to his edition of it.

It is indeed remarkable that the *Gesta Regis Henrici Secundi* should have any rival as an account of a twelfth-century king. Yet so it is. Less meticulous perhaps, but of a more distinguished mind, was William of Newburgh, a notable writer whose personal career was itself not devoid of distinction. This man was born in 1135 near

Bridlington, and received at least part of his education at the Augustinian priory of Newburgh. When he was between twenty and thirty he married an heiress with much property in Oxfordshire and Berkshire and seemed to be fairly launched on a career of comfortable respectability. The life however apparently left unsoothed within him an itch for less commonplace achievement. At all events in 1182 or 1183 he left his wife, whose comments have escaped the notice of posterity, and entered Newburgh. There he composed his *Historia Rerum Anglicarum* which is largely represented in this volume, and is elsewhere criticized in further detail. Even the most cursory survey of the chroniclers of this age must, however, pay at least a passing tribute to this work. William of Newburgh was a good but not outstanding narrator of events, and his standard of accuracy, though high, is not exceptional. What gives distinction to his book is rather his judgment. He attempts with some success to discriminate among his authorities, and his rejection of the fables of Geoffrey of Monmouth was, for the time, a notable achievement in criticism. His impartiality is to be seen in his treatment of the dispute between Henry II and Becket. His own politics were independent, and his portraits were drawn with fidelity and originality. William of Newburgh may have been over-praised by some of his admirers, but from the latter part of the reign of Henry II he begins to occupy much the same place as had been occupied by William of Malmesbury for the reign of Henry I. A survey of the chronicles of this period may therefore fitly close with an allusion to his work–a remarkable man in a remarkable period of narrative history.

This extensive production illustrates many of the general characteristics of medieval chronicles, and in particular serves to call attention to the close relations between them. There is an intimate connexion not only among the various versions of the Anglo-Saxon Chronicle, but also between them and the narratives of the Anglo-Norman age. 'Florence of Worcester' grafted his English additions on to the existing chronicle of Marianus Scotus, and in due course there were other writers to carry on his own work. Simeon of Durham found his continuators among the monks of Hexham, and the chroniclers of the reign of Henry II based very much of their work upon the writings of their predecessors. Such interdependency deserves some emphasis. It is not solely to be ascribed to the fraternal relations existing within or between monasteries, for whilst most of the chroniclers were monks, some of them such as Henry, archdeacon of Huntingdon, and Ralph 'de Diceto' were secular clerks. Rather it derives from an attitude of mind on the part of these writers towards their subject. Medieval notions of literary propriety, and literary property, were different from those prevailing today. These men lived before the age of footnotes, and in general when they cited a previous writer by name it was not to acknowledge a debt but to give additional weight to a quotation. It is unsound therefore to conclude that because a medieval writer takes material wholesale, and without acknowledgment, from one of his predecessors, he is dishonest or himself wholly derivative. The historians of this age regarded themselves as workers in a common enterprise, as vehicles of a progressive tradition. And in this sense all medieval English chronicles may be considered as forming part of a larger whole, as links in a chain of narrative history to which additions were continually being made by individuals without damage or alteration to what had been forged before.

Some legitimate distinctions may however be made among them in respect of form. The original difference between the chronicle proper and the history, once fundamental though often blurred, still persisted in some measure in twelfth-century

England. In its most primitive form the chronicle can best be regarded as an aid to memory–an attempt to characterize each year by assigning an event to it, and sometimes with this purpose a mechanical structure of years was made, some of the space being left blank to be filled up later by men with greater knowledge than the original compilers. Early tables designed for calculating the date of Easter were frequently thus used, and it was only later that the primitive chronicle so conceived developed into a more comprehensive narrative of events given in order of time. Later still, as this type of writing grew more elaborate, a yet closer approach was made in the chronicle to the causal and topical arrangement proper to a history, until at last, as in the *Gesta Regis Henrici Secundi*, only the annalistic headings remain to remind the reader of the earlier evolution. The original distinction in method may be seen however even in the twelfth century by comparing, for instance, the structure of the Anglo-Saxon Chronicles on the one hand with that of the *Historia Novella* of William of Malmesbury on the other.

The language in which these narratives were composed also commands attention. With the exception of the chronicle of Ethelweard composed in the tenth century, and of some short Northumbrian annals of the same period, almost all the annalistic writings of the late Old English period were in the vernacular, the Latin tongue being kept in the main for biographical composition. After the Norman Conquest this vernacular tradition languished, surviving, in annals, only in the continuations of the Anglo-Saxon Chronicle. From that time forward Latin was in the ascendant, and it is significant that, about 1100, attempts were already being made to translate even the Anglo-Saxon Chronicle into that language. The Anglo-Norman historians seem in fact in this matter to have attempted something like a conscious revival of an earlier tradition, and William of Malmesbury claimed to be the successor of Bede after a long interval not only from the fact that he wrote history as opposed to chronicle, but because he composed his work in the scholar's language which Bede had used. He and his circle were certainly responsible for the resuscitation in England of the Latin chronicle, and in this respect they were followed by their great successors of the reign of Henry II. With the termination in 1155 of the last continuation of the Anglo-Saxon Chronicle, historical prose in the vernacular almost disappeared from England for more than two centuries.

It seems reasonable to suggest that this transition in English historical writing from Saxon to Latin exemplifies one of the cultural consequences of the Norman Conquest. Apart from *L'estorie des Engles*, a poem composed in the mid-twelfth century by Geoffrey Gaimar largely out of material derived from the Anglo-Saxon Chronicle, no attempt in this period seems to have been made to write the history of England in Norman French, and if Saxon was displaced as the language of history it made way not for another vernacular but for the language common to western Christendom. William of Malmesbury, Ordericus Vitalis and their fellows felt themselves part of the Latin and ecclesiastical culture of western Europe and sought to make their own contribution to it. Cosmopolitan in this sense rather than national, these writers therefore did not for that reason find themselves out of sympathy with the people among whom they lived. William of Malmesbury, it is true, painted a savage picture of Anglo-Saxon society. But in general the hostile spirit so evident in William of Poitiers is absent from these men, and even Ordericus, who was closest in touch with Norman traditions, can style himself *Anglicanus* and can mingle with his intense admiration of the Normans a lively sympathy with English affairs. A keen interest in the earlier history of England is in fact a notable characteristic of the Anglo-Norman group of chroniclers and one which they handed on to their successors. It was expressed, for instance, in a conscious antiquarianism which excited their curiosity about the ancient monuments and legends of the English race, and which led them assiduously to study and to use the earlier historical narratives of England. Thus it was natural for William of Malmesbury to take Bede for his model, and for his contemporaries, writing in Latin, to borrow so largely from the Anglo-Saxon Chronicle. Nor should it be forgotten that almost all these Latin authors were born in England and that many of them, such as Eadmer and William of Malmesbury, had at least one English parent. They wrote of a country whose political outlook had very recently been radically changed by events in which they were proud to feel themselves concerned, but it was none the less of their own country that they wrote.

The enduring sense of an English *patria* gives a unity to the historical production of this age which it would not otherwise have possessed. The historical writings of this time fall somewhat easily into the three main divisions separated roughly by the dates 1066 and 1160, Latin replacing Anglo-Saxon as the dominant language of history after the Norman Conquest, and the historians of Henry II only taking up the work of their predecessors after an interval. But without blurring this division it would be well not to give to it too great a precision. Eadmer, the biographer of Anselm and the earliest of the Anglo-Norman group, was born before the Norman Conquest, and the *Historia Pontificalis* of John of Salisbury provides a slender bridge between the Anglo-Norman and the Anglo-Angevin writers. In the Anglo-Saxon Chronicle there is a link between two epochs and two environments. The historical narratives produced in England between 1042 and 1189 reflect, as is proper, the intellectual changes characteristic of an age of transition, but despite their individuality they also represent a consistent and successful endeavour which had for its main objectives not panegyric or propaganda, not the glorification of one race or the disparagement of another, but the honest elucidation of the history of England during these years. In that lies their value, and their especial charm.

SELECT BIBLIOGRAPHY
of Chronicles and Histories

The Descriptive Catalogue of Materials relating to the History of Great Britain and Ireland, ed. T. D. Hardy (3 vols. in 4 parts, Rolls Series, 1862–1871), deals mainly with the manuscripts of the chief narrative sources of English medieval history, and is a mine of information respecting the chronicles of this age. The appendix to vol. I deals also with such publications as had been made at the time of the compilation of this great work. Of more general use to the student will be C. Gross, *The Sources and Literature of English History from the earliest times to about* 1485 (2nd ed., London, 1915). This will be found indispensable for the descriptive list of narrative sources and of the printed editions wherein they can be consulted. The subject is briefly surveyed in two short works: R. L. Poole, *Chronicles and Annals* (Oxford, 1926), and R. R. Darlington, *Anglo-Norman Historians* (London, 1947).

The table which follows indicates the principal chronicles which are of most importance for each reign in this period. It will be recalled how closely many of these works were interconnected, and the manner in which they overlapped. It is in this sense that the names of writers, who are *not* to be regarded as strictly contemporary authorities for the reign in which they are placed, have been printed in italic type.

EDWARD THE CONFESSOR
Anglo-Saxon Chronicle
Malmesbury, William of
'Vita Edwardi'
'Worcester, Florence of'

WILLIAM I
'Amiens, Guy of'
Anglo-Saxon Chronicle
Eadmer
Gaimar
Jumièges, William of
Malmesbury, William of
Ordericus Vitalis
Poitiers, William of
Wace
'Worcester, Florence of'

WILLIAM II
Anglo-Saxon Chronicle
Eadmer
Gaimar
Malmesbury, William of
Ordericus Vitalis
'Worcester, Florence of'

HENRY I
Anglo-Saxon Chronicle
Durham, Simeon of
Eadmer
Hexham, John of
Huntingdon, Henry of
Malmesbury, William of
Ordericus Vitalis
'Worcester, Florence of'

STEPHEN
Anglo-Saxon Chronicle
Canterbury, Gervase of
'Gesta Stephani'
Hexham, John of
Hexham, Richard of
Huntingdon, Henry of
Malmesbury, William of
Newburgh, William of
Ordericus Vitalis
Salisbury, John of (*Historia Pontificalis*)
Torigny, Robert of
'Worcester, Florence of' (continuation)

HENRY II[1]
Canterbury, Gervase of
Diceto, Ralph de
Fantosme, Jordan
Giraldus Cambrensis
Howden, Roger of
Melrose, Chronicle of
Newburgh, William of
'Peterborough, Benedict of'
Rouen, Stephen of
'Song of Dermot'
Torigny, Robert of

[1] The narratives relating particularly to Thomas Becket are discussed below on pp. 698–702

Many of these writers have been several times printed, and some of them are to be found in the great collections made in the seventeenth and eighteenth centuries by scholars such as William Camden, André Duchesne, Henry Savile, Roger Twysden, Thomas Gale and Thomas Hearne. Most of them can however be studied today in good modern editions, and a list follows which is designed to indicate firstly, the best edition of the chief narrative sources of this period and secondly, where a translation, if it exists, can best be found.

'Amiens, Guy of.' *De bello Hastingensi carmen auctore W[idone]*. Printed in F. Michel, *Chroniques Anglo-Normandes*, vol. III, pp. 1–48; and also in J. A. Giles, *Scriptores rerum gestarum Willelmi Conquestoris* (London, 1845), pp. 27–51. The traditional attribution of this poem to 'Guy of Amiens' must now be regarded as doubtful, and its virtue as historical evidence is perhaps less than has sometimes been supposed.

Anglo-Saxon Chronicle. The best edition of the annals relating to this period is in J. Earle and C. Plummer, *Two of the Saxon Chronicles Parallel* (Oxford, vol. I, 1892; vol. II, 1899). Also in *The Anglo-Saxon Chronicle*, ed. B. Thorpe (Rolls Series, vol. I texts, vol. II translation, 1861). This text is discussed in some detail below (pp. 107–109), and a full translation is there given of the three principal versions of this text relating to this period.

Annales Monastici, ed. H. R. Luard, 5 vols. (Rolls Series, 1864–1869).

Canterbury, Gervase of. *The Historical Works of Gervase of Canterbury*, ed. W. Stubbs (2 vols., Rolls Series, 1879–1880).

Diceto, Ralph de. *Opera historica*, ed. W. Stubbs (2 vols., Rolls Series, 1876).

Durham, Simeon of. *Symeonis Monachi opera omnia*, ed. T. Arnold (2 vols., Rolls Series, 1882, 1885). Translated by J. Stevenson, *Church Historians of England*, vol. III, pt. ii (London, 1855).

Eadmer. *Historia novorum in Anglia*, ed. M. Rule (Rolls Series, 1884).

Fantosme, Jordan. *Chronique de la guerre entre les Anglois et les Ecossois en 1173 et 1174*. Printed in appendix to *Chronique des ducs de Normandie par Benoit*, ed. F. Michel (3 vols., Paris, 1836–1844). Another edition, with translation, is in *Chronicles and Memorials of the reigns of Stephen, Henry II and Richard I*, ed. R. Howlett, vol. III, pp. 202–327 (Rolls Series, 1886).

Gaimar, Geoffrey. *L'estorie des Engles solum la translacion Geffrei Gaimar*, edited with a translation by T. D. Hardy and C. T. Martin (2 vols., Rolls Series, 1888, 1889).

'Gesta Stephani.' *Gesta Stephani regis Anglorum*, ed. R. Howlett, in *Chronicles and Memorials of the reigns of Stephen, Henry II and Richard I*, vol. III, pp. 3–136 (Rolls Series, 1886). Translated by J. Stevenson, *Church Historians of England*, vol. V, pt. i (London, 1858).

Giraldus Cambrensis. *Opera*, ed. J. S. Brewer, J. F. Dimock and G. F. Warner (8 vols., Rolls Series, 1861–1891). The more important treatises are translated by R. C. Hoare and T. Wright in Bohn's Antiquarian Library (London, 1863).

Hexham, John of. *Historia Iohannis prioris Hagustaldensis ecclesiae*, ed. T. Arnold, in *Symeonis Monachi opera omnia*, vol. II, pp. 284–332 (Rolls Series, 1885). Translated by J. Stevenson in *Church Historians of England*, vol. IV, pt. i (London, 1856).

Hexham, Richard of. *Historia de gestis regis Stephani et de bello de standardo*, ed. R. Howlett, in *Chronicles and Memorials of the reigns of Stephen, Henry II and Richard I*, vol. III, pp. 139–178 (Rolls Series, 1886). Translated by J. Stevenson, *Church Historians of England*, vol. IV, pt. i, pp. 35–58 (London, 1856).

Howden, Roger of. *Chronica Rogeri de Houedene*, ed. W. Stubbs (4 vols., Rolls Series, 1868–1871).

Huntingdon, Henry of. *Historia Anglorum*, ed. T. Arnold (Rolls Series, 1879). Translated by T. Forester, *The Chronicle of Henry of Huntingdon* (Bohn's Antiquarian Library, London, 1853).

Jumièges, William of. *Gesta Normannorum Ducum*, ed. J. Marx (Soc. de l'Histoire de Normandie, Rouen, 1914). This is the only edition which distinguishes the work of William of Jumièges from that of his later interpolators. It is therefore indispensable. A conflated text will be found in Migne, *Patrologia Latina*, vol. CXLIX, cols. 777–910, and a translation of this conflated text into French is in F. P. G. Guizot, *Collection de Mémoires*, vol. XXIX, pp. 1–316.

Malmesbury, William of. *De gestis regum Anglorum libri quinque; Historiae novellae libri tres*, ed. W. Stubbs (2 vols., Rolls Series, 1887–1889). Translated by J. Stevenson, *Church Historians of England*, vol. III, pt. i (London, 1854); also by J. A. Giles in Bohn's Antiquarian Library (London, 1847).

Melrose, Chronicle of. *Chronica de Mailres*, ed. J. Stevenson (Bannatyne Club, Edinburgh, 1835). Also *Chronicle of Melrose*, Facsimile edition, ed. A. O. and M. O. Anderson (London, 1936). Translated by J. Stevenson, *Church Historians of England*, vol. IV, pt. i (London, 1856), pp. 79–242.

Newburgh, William of. *Historia Rerum Anglicarum*, ed. R. Howlett, in *Chronicles and Memorials of the reigns of Stephen, Henry II and Richard I*, vol. I, pp. 1–408; vol. II, pp. 409–583 (Rolls Series, 1884, 1885). Translated by J. Stevenson, *Church Historians of England*, vol. IV, pt. ii, pp. 297–672 (London, 1856).

Ordericus Vitalis. *Orderici Vitalis angligenae coenobii Uticensis monachi Historiae Ecclesiasticae libri tredecim*, ed. A. Le Prévost (5 vols., Soc. de l'Histoire de France, Paris, 1838–1855). This great edition, to which L. Delisle largely contributed, is indispensable for the study of this period. The text will also be found in Migne, *Patrologia Latina*, vol. CLXXXVIII, cols. 15–984. Translated by T. Forester in Bohn's Antiquarian Library (4 vols., London, 1853–1856).

'Peterborough, Benedict of.' *Gesta Regis Henrici Secundi Benedicti abbatis*, ed. W. Stubbs (2 vols., Rolls Series, London, 1867).

Poitiers, William of. *Gesta Willelmi ducis Normannorum et regis Anglorum*, ed. J. A. Giles, in *Scriptores rerum gestarum Willelmi Conquestoris*, pp. 77–159 (London, 1845). Another edition with notes, and a translation into French, is that by R. Foreville (Classiques de l'Histoire de France, No. 23), Paris, 1952.

Rouen, Stephen of. *Le Dragon normand et autres poèmes d'Etienne de Rouen*, ed. H. Omont (Soc. de l'Histoire de Normandie, Rouen, 1884). Also in R. Howlett, *Chronicles and Memorials of the reigns of Stephen, Henry II and Richard I*, vol. II, pp. 585–781 (Rolls Series, 1885).

Salisbury, John of. *Iohannis Saresberiensis Historiae Pontificalis quae supersunt*, ed. R. L. Poole (Oxford, 1929).

'Song of Dermot.' *The Song of Dermot and the Earl*, edited with a translation by G. H. Orpen (Oxford, 1892).

Torigny, Robert of. *Chronique de Robert de Torigni – suivie de divers opuscules historiques*, ed. Léopold Delisle (2 vols., Soc. de l'Histoire de Normandie, Rouen, 1872, 1873). This is the best edition of a work which is also to be found in R. Howlett, *Chronicles and Memorials of the reigns of Stephen, Henry II and Richard I*, vol. IV, pp. 3–315 (Rolls Series, 1889).

Vita Edwardi Regis. This, the earliest life of Edward the Confessor, was edited by H. R. Luard in *Lives of Edward the Confessor*, pp. 387–435 (Rolls Series, 1858). It is still the subject of controversy, but while the date of its composition is open to some dispute it seems doubtful whether it can be used without caution as a primary authority for the Confessor's reign. For critical comments on this text see M. Bloch, in *Analecta Bollandiana*, vol. XLI, pp. 5–61; R. W. Southern, "The First Life of Edward the Confessor" (*Eng. Hist. Rev.*, vol. LVIII, 1943, p. 385); Henningham, in *Speculum*, vol. XXI, 1946.

Wace. *Roman de Rou*, ed. F. Pluquet (2 vols., Rouen, 1827, 1829); ed. H. Andresen (2 vols., Heilbronn, 1877, 1879). The latter edition is the better, but neither is wholly satisfactory. A partial translation is in E. Taylor, *Master Wace, His Chronicle of the Norman Conquest from the "Roman de Rou"* (London, 1837). Though Freeman relied extensively upon this attractive French poem for his account of the Norman invasion, it is doubtful whether it ought to be included at all among the sources of that period. Composed between 1160 and 1174, it deals with Norman history from the time of Rollo to 1106, the author relying mainly on Dudo of St. Quentin (himself a tainted source), on William of Jumièges and perhaps on William of Malmesbury. J. H. Round showed how untrustworthy the writer is on matters connected with England, and though C. H. Haskins (*Norman Institutions*, Harvard U.P., 1918, pp. 268–272) has given reasons for supposing that on some questions of Norman history Wace may have reproduced a reliable tradition, the history of the Norman Conquest could be written with almost equal fullness, and with much greater safety, without reference to this poem.

'Worcester, Florence of.' *Florentii Wigorniensis Monachi Chronicon ex Chronicis*, ed B. Thorpe (2 vols., London, 1848, 1849). This edition, the best available, is in many ways unsatisfactory. Translated by J. Stevenson in *Church Historians of England*, vol. II, pt. i (London, 1853).

1. The Anglo-Saxon Chronicle (1042-1154)

(i) *The Anglo-Saxon Chronicle*

The most important narrative source of English history for the period 1042–1154 is that which is called "the Anglo-Saxon Chronicle".[1] The title is accurate in view of the fact that the narratives to which it applies were written in the vernacular, but it has none the less led to some confusion, and the manner in which these invaluable narratives are usually presented in translation has rendered it difficult for students to appraise their full value. The most essential prerequisite for comprehending these annals is to recall that the "Anglo-Saxon Chronicle" which was originally compiled progressively, has for this period survived in three principal MS. copies, which, while they are sufficiently alike to be described as 'versions' derived from a common source, nevertheless differ from each other so much, both as to matter and as to interpretation, as to make it necessary to consider them separately, and mutually to compare them. For the years 1042–1065 there exist all three of these recensions; from 1065 to 1079 two of them survive; and it is only after 1079 that the "Anglo-Saxon Chronicle" survives in one copy only. "Nothing", therefore, "is more tantalizing than to find the Chronicle quoted as if it were a single definite authority",[2] and a translated text conflated from all three versions robs this source of much of its value as evidence. For this reason, in the edition which follows, the separate versions, newly translated from the Anglo-Saxon by Miss S. I. Tucker of Bristol University, are placed in parallel columns to enable the reader to form his own judgment alike on their mutual relationship and on the extent of their mutual interdependence.

(ii) *The Three Versions here edited*

The three versions of the Anglo-Saxon Chronicle here edited are derived from three out of six MSS. of the Anglo-Saxon Chronicle which today survive in a more or less complete form. These six MSS. are usually designated by the first six letters of the alphabet, and their earlier history is discussed by Miss Whitelock in volume I of this series. Of these MSS., 'A' (Corpus Christi College, Cambridge MS. 173), the oldest, contains only a few isolated entries relating to the period after the accession of Edward the Confessor; 'B' (Brit. Mus. Cott. Tiber. A. vi) has nothing after 977; whilst 'F' (Brit. Mus. Cott. Domit. A. iii), a bilingual version in Latin and Anglo-Saxon, is of subsidiary importance. In respect of the period dealt with in this volume, there remain therefore versions 'C', 'D' and 'E'. These are very frequently referred to respectively as the "Abingdon Chronicle", the "Worcester Chronicle", and the "Peterborough Chronicle", but in view of the uncertainty which prevails as to where these copies were in fact made, such territorial descriptions are misleading and should be eschewed.

The salient features of these three versions for this period are as follows:

'C' (Brit. Mus. Cott. Tiber. B. i) is a MS. which seems to have been made at Abingdon, and it is written throughout in scripts of mid-eleventh-century date. In describing the political controversies of the reign of Edward the Confessor, it tends to adopt an attitude of hostility to the house of Godwine. This is notable as Godwine seems on the whole to have been friendly to Abingdon. 'C's' attitude on this matter may perhaps be attributed to independent criticism on the part of the writer, or it may in part be due to the fact that in 1056 there was appointed as abbot of Abingdon a certain Rothulf who is described as being a kinsman of the king. Anti-Godwine sentiment is at all events (together with an individual dating method) the most distinguishing feature of version 'C'. 'C' ends in 1066.

'D' (Brit. Mus. Cott. Tiber. B. iv) is, so far as this period is concerned, written in various

[1] A fuller discussion of the earlier development of the Anglo-Saxon Chronicle will be found in vol. I of this series.

[2] See J. Armitage Robinson, *Life and Times of St. Dunstan* (1923), p. 23.

hands, in the twelfth century. Moreover it appears that in the course of transcription a certain amount of interpolation was made. 'D', for instance, includes under 1067 material from a life of St. Margaret of Scotland, and the evident desire of the compiler at this point to trace the descent of Margaret from the Royal House of Wessex suggests that this insertion was originally made after the marriage of Margaret's daughter, Maud, to Henry I in 1100. It has been suggested that this concern with Scottish affairs may indicate that this MS. was designed for presentation to the Scottish court. Where this MS. was written is uncertain. The fact that in the sixteenth century it was discovered at Worcester led its earliest commentators to place its origin at that city, and some modern scholars still consider that Worcester was most probably the place at which it was compiled. Evesham has also been suggested. There is also a distinct probability that much of this chronicle was compiled in the north of England, and perhaps at York. The most prominent personage in this section of 'D' is probably Aldred, who became bishop of Worcester in 1047 and archbishop of York in 1061, and who in 1061 and 1062 held both these sees together.

Whatever may have been the place at which the existing MS. of 'D' was made, it is clear that the text from which it was transcribed contained much northern material relating to this period. There is a tendency in 'D' to give information relating to Scandinavia not to be found in the other versions, and the reference under 1051 to "this northern province" indicates a northern origin at least for this annal. Apart from this, 'D' displays a somewhat impartial attitude to the political disputes of this time, revealing a cool sympathy with the fortunes of Earl Godwine and his family. 'D' ends in 1079.

'*E*' (*Bodleian Library, Laud, Misc.* 636) is a MS. of the twelfth century which was most probably written out at Peterborough. The copyist responsible for this text had however before him a version which was compiled at St. Augustine's monastery in Canterbury at least up to 1061 and probably until 1121. For most of this period 'E' must therefore be regarded as supplying a Canterbury view of events, and unique descriptions of events occurring in the south-east of England are not uncommon in 'E'. It was not until after 1121 that a more definite connexion with Peterborough is to be discerned in this text. Apart from this, the most characteristic feature of 'E' is a very strong bias in favour of Earl Godwine and his family, and the special importance of 'E' to the historian is that it continues after all the other versions have stopped. It is the sole version of the Anglo-Saxon Chronicle surviving in a continuous form from 1080 to the early weeks of 1155 when it ends.

It will have been noted that none of these MSS. contains an 'original' version of the Anglo-Saxon Chronicle. All are copies of texts now lost. Moreover, the lost texts were certainly used by other early writers, and in particular, for this period, in the compilation of the Latin annals which are ascribed to 'Florence of Worcester'. The author of this compilation used however so many sources for his work that it is impossible to reconstruct from his annals the text of the version or versions of the Anglo-Saxon Chronicle which he used, and the lack of any satisfactory edition of his annals makes the task yet more difficult. Certain of the entries in 'Florence of Worcester' relating to the period 1042–1066 deserve however to be compared in this respect with the corresponding annals in the Anglo-Saxon Chronicle.

Although the lost prototypes of the surviving versions of the Anglo-Saxon Chronicle cannot be reconstructed in detail, there is little reason to suppose that the existing MSS. do not supply a faithful reproduction of their contents. Care must be taken to suspect interpolations (especially in 'D'), but these are not numerous. In the three versions of the Anglo-Saxon Chronicle here printed the reader is presented with a contemporary narrative source whose excellence is not excelled by any other narrative produced at that time either in England or in Europe.

(iii) *The Dating of the Anglo-Saxon Chronicle*

The dates given in the Anglo-Saxon Chronicle present the student with problems of some complexity. These problems relate in the main to two topics: (*a*) the dates given to the years, and (*b*) the date at which the year is made to begin. They will be considered in turn.

In general little difficulty is caused to the student of this period when in one or other of the versions a whole annal is assigned to a wrong year. Such errors, when they occur, are in the main due either to simple carelessness on the part of the transcriber, or to the practice of numbering a series of years in advance in the original, with the result that if, for some reason, nothing was recorded in a particular year a whole series of subsequent annals may be wrongly dated. Being mainly mechanical in origin such errors, which sometimes involve a divergence of as much as four years between the versions, may be easily detected and corrected. *In this edition therefore the true year to which the annals refer is placed in each case in large type at their head, whilst the year given in each particular version (whether right or wrong) is given in brackets at the beginning of each version.*

A more serious difficulty arises in respect of the date at which, in the various annals, the year is made to begin. The 'solar year', starting on 1 January, does not appear to be used in the Anglo-Saxon Chronicle, but usually the discrepancy is only slight, since the usual practice in these texts is to make the year to begin at the previous Christmas – that is to say, only seven days before the modern year would start. Broadly speaking, and with certain exceptions hereafter to be noted, this rule applies generally throughout versions 'D' and 'E' in this period. And the tendency of 'E' in later entries to begin the annal with the Christmas court of the preceding year illustrates this practice very clearly.

A different reckoning is however also used sometimes in these annals. By this the year is made to begin on the ensuing Lady Day – that is to say, on 25 March following the 1 January at which the modern year would start. This use became widespread in France during the eleventh century, and it is employed generally in 'C', possibly as a result of the connexion existing between Abingdon and the monastery of Fleury on the Loire. 'C' appears to use this reckoning consistently (and at times demonstrably) between 1042 and 1066, except in the annals for 1055 and 1066, when the year seems to be made to start at Christmas. 'E', which normally begins the year at Christmas, appears to use the Lady Day reckoning in the annals relating to 1073 and 1086, and perhaps in those relating to 1075, 1083 and 1085. *In general therefore, subject to the exceptions noted above, and apart from such cases where the chronology has become widely confused, 'D' and 'E' may be assumed to begin the year on the Christmas Day preceding 1 January, whilst 'C' begins the year on 25 March following 1 January. These practices however only rarely affect the assignment of these annals (as in this edition) to their true year, and any modification of this assignment which may appear necessary will be specially noted at the places where it occurs.*

(iv) *Editions*

There have been many editions made of the various versions of the Anglo-Saxon Chronicle beginning with that produced by Abraham Wheloc at Cambridge in 1643 and reissued in 1644 (*Venerabilis Bedae Historia Ecclesiastica*, pp. 492–562). The best modern edition is by J. Earle and C. Plummer (*Two of the Saxon Chronicles Parallel with supplementary extracts from the others*, 2 vols., Oxford, 1892, 1899). A six-text edition was made by B. Thorpe (*The Anglo-Saxon Chronicle*, 2 vols., Rolls Series, 1861). The translation appended to this latter work is in many ways unsatisfactory; and it is so ill arranged that a student unacquainted with Anglo-Saxon cannot use it to make an adequate comparison between the various versions. It is, in fact, very remarkable that no satisfactory translation of the variant versions of this important historical source for this period, so often quoted, at present exists. The translations made by Ingram (see Everyman's Library, London, 1923), by J. A. Giles (Bohn, 1847), and by J. Stevenson (*Church Historians of England*, vol. II, pt. i, 1853), for instance, give no true idea of the divergences of the versions in the period between 1042 and 1066, and they all to some extent suffer from a confusing conflation between them. The best existing edition of the Anglo-Saxon Chronicle in translation is that made in 1909 by E. C. C. Gomme (1 vol., London, George Bell and Sons), a book that it is now difficult to obtain.

(v) *This Edition*

This edition has been based upon the following plan:

(1) An independent translation is supplied of the three main versions of the Anglo-Saxon Chronicle relating to this period, and these versions are arranged in parallel columns. As explained above, these versions are designated by the letters 'C', 'D' and 'E'. Between 1042 and 1066 all three of these versions exist; between 1067 and 1079 only two remain ('D' and 'E'); after 1079 only one of them ('E') survives.

(2) The annals are assigned to the true years to which they refer, and the true year is indicated in large type at their head. Since however for reasons given above, an annal was sometimes attributed in a particular version to a year other than that to which it properly belonged, the year to which each annal is attributed in each version is also given within brackets at the beginning of each entry.

(3) Dates are given in the modern form. It must however be borne in mind that the Chronicle (as in the case of versions 'D' and 'E') normally begins the year at Christmas before 1 January, whilst sometimes (as is usually the case in version 'C') it starts the year at 25 March following 1 January. In cases where any confusion might arise owing to these practices an explanatory note has been added.

(4) Personal and place-names have, wherever possible, been given in the modern form.

By this plan, an attempt has been made (*a*) to establish the various texts and to facilitate comparison between them; (*b*) to elucidate their chronology; and (*c*) to identify the persons and places to which reference is made. To comment in detail upon the information supplied by the Anglo-Saxon Chronicle would be to rewrite the history of the period to which it refers.[1] The student must be left to form his own judgment on the evidence of what for this period is the most important of his sources.

1042

C and D

(1042) In this year Harthacnut died in this way: he was standing at his drink, and he suddenly fell to the ground with fearful convulsions, and those who were near caught him, and he spoke no word afterwards. He died on 8 June. And all the people then received Edward as king, as was his natural right.[3]

E

(1041)[2] In this year Harthacnut died at Lambeth on 8 June, and he was king over all England two years all but ten days, and he is buried in the Old Minster[4] with King Cnut his father. And before he was buried all the people chose Edward as king in London.[3] May he hold it as long as God will grant it him.[5] And all that year the

[1] A general reference may here perhaps be made to the introduction to this volume.

[2] 'E' is a year wrong at this point.

[3] 'D' reads at this point: "chose Edward and received him as king." The difference of emphasis in the three accounts at this point should be noted.

[4] Winchester.

[5] An indication of contemporary composition.

C

D

E

weather was very distressing in many ways. Storms did much damage to the crops, and more cattle were destroyed during this year than anyone remembered before, both through various diseases and through storms. And in this year Ælfsige, abbot of Peterborough, died, and the monk Arnwig was chosen abbot because he was a very good and a very gentle man.

1043

C

(1043) In this year Edward was consecrated as king at Winchester on Easter Sunday with great ceremony; and Easter was on 3 April.[2] Archbishop Eadsige consecrated him and gave him good instruction before all the people, and admonished him well for his own sake and for the sake of all the people. Stigand the priest was consecrated bishop of the East Angles. And soon after this the king brought all the lands his mother[4] owned forcibly into his own control, and he took from her all that she owned in gold and silver and things beyond description, because

D

(1043) In this year Edward was consecrated king at Winchester on Easter Sunday. And this year, a fortnight before St. Andrew's Day,[3] the king was given advice as a result of which he rode from Gloucester together with Earl Leofric and Earl Godwine and Earl Siward with their retinue to Winchester. And they came unexpectedly upon the lady,[4] and they deprived her of all the treasures which she owned and these were beyond counting, because she had formerly been very hard to the king, her son, in that she did less for him than he wished both

E

(1042)[1]In this year Edward was consecrated king at Winchester on Easter Day with great ceremony. Easter was then on 3 April. Archbishop Eadsige consecrated him and gave him good instruction before all the people, and admonished him well for his own sake and for the sake of all the people. Stigand the priest was consecrated bishop of East Anglia. And soon after this the king brought all the lands his mother[4] owned forcibly into his own control, and he took from her all that she owned in gold and silver and things beyond description, because she

[1] 'E' continues to be a year wrong.
[2] This is correct for 1043.
[3] *i.e.* 16 November, St. Andrew's Day being 30 November.
[4] Emma, successively the wife of Ethelred II and Cnut, and daughter of Richard I, duke of Normandy.

C

she had withheld it too firmly from him. And soon after this Stigand was deprived of his bishopric, and all that he owned was placed in the king's control because he was closest in his mother's counsel, and because, as was suspected, she did as he advised.[1]

D

before he became king and afterwards as well. And they allowed her to stay there afterwards.[1]

E

had withheld it too firmly from him.[1]

1044

C

(1044) In this year Archbishop Eadsige resigned the bishopric because of his infirmity, and consecrated to it Siward, abbot of Abingdon. He did this by the permission and with the advice of the king and of Earl Godwine. Otherwise it was known to few people before it was done, because the archbishop suspected that somebody else would ask for it, or purchase it whom he less trusted and favoured if more people knew about it. In this year there was a very great famine over all England, and corn dearer than anyone ever remembered, so that a sester of wheat went up to 60 pence and even more. And

D

(1045)[2] In this year Bishop Ælfward of London died on 25 July. He had first been abbot of Evesham,[3] and he greatly promoted the good of that monastery while he was there; then he went to Ramsey, and there he passed away. And Manni was chosen abbot and consecrated on 10 August. And in the course of the year Gunnilde, that noble lady, King Cnut's kinswoman,[4] was banished, and she then stayed at Bruges for a long time and then went to Denmark.

E

(1043)[2] In this year Archbishop Eadsige resigned the bishopric because of his infirmity, and consecrated to it Siward, abbot of Abingdon. He did this by the permission and with the advice of the king and of Earl Godwine. Otherwise it was known to few people before it was done, because the archbishop suspected that somebody else would ask for it, or purchase it whom he less trusted and favoured if more people knew about it. In this year there was a very great famine over all England, and corn dearer than any one every remembered, so that a sester of wheat went up to 60 pence and even more. And this

[1] The Annals of St. Mildred, which are here authoritative, add some important information at this point:

So according to the dispensation of God who governs all things, England received the native-born Edward for king. He was the offspring of King Ethelred and Emma. While he was reigning in peace like unto Solomon his own mother was accused of inciting Magnus, king of Norway, to invade England, and it was said that she had given countless treasures to Magnus. Wherefore this traitor to the kingdom, this enemy of the country, this betrayer of her own son, was judged, and everything she possessed was forfeited to the king. (T. D. Hardy, *Catalogue of Materials*, vol. I, p. 381.)

[2] 'D' having omitted the figure '1044' is now a year in advance of the true year; 'E' remains a year behind.

[3] This Evesham history illustrates the connexion of 'D' with the Worcester diocese.

[4] According to 'Florence of Worcester', she was his niece.

C

this same year the king went out to Sandwich with thirty-five ships. And Athelstan the sacristan succeeded to the abbacy of Abingdon. And in the same year King Edward married Edith, daughter of Earl Godwine, ten nights before Candlemas.[1]

D

E

same year the king went out to Sandwich with thirty-five ships. And Athelstan the sacristan succeeded to the abbacy of Abingdon and Stigand obtained his bishopric.

1045

C

(1045) Now in this year died Bishop Bryhtwold on 22 April, and King Edward gave the bishopric to Hereman his priest. And in the same summer King Edward went out with his ships to Sandwich, and there was so large a force collected there that no one had ever seen so large a naval force in this country. And in the same year died Bishop Lifing on 20 March,[5] and the king gave the bishopric to his priest Leofric.

D

(1046)[2] This year died Bryhtwold the bishop in Wiltshire, and Hereman was appointed to his see. In this year King Edward collected a great naval force at Sandwich because of the threat of Magnus of Norway, but the fighting between him and Sweyn of Denmark prevented him from coming.[4]

E

(1043)[2] This year King Edward took as his queen the daughter of Earl Godwine. And in this same year died Bishop Bryhtwold. He held the bishopric thirty-eight years, and Hereman, the king's priest, succeeded to it.[3] And this same year Wulfric was consecrated abbot of St. Augustine's at Christmas-time on St. Stephen's Day by permission of the king and of Abbot Ælfstan because of the abbot's great infirmity.

1046

C

(1046) In this year Earl Sweyn went into Wales, and Griffith the northern king with him, and hostages were given him.

D

(1047)[6] This year Lifing, the eloquent bishop, died on 23 March, and he had three bishoprics, one in Devonshire and one in

E

(1044)[6] This year died Lifing, bishop of Devonshire, and Leofric, the king's priest, succeeded to it. And in this same year

[1] The marriage took place in January 1045, and in 'D' and 'E' it properly appears in the next annal. Its insertion here in 'C' is explained by 'C's' beginning the year at Lady Day (25 March).

[2] 'D' remains one year in advance of the true chronology; 'E' by repeating '1043' at the beginning of this annal becomes two years behind.

[3] This is the bishopric of Ramsbury. Hereman became bishop of Sherborne also, and the two sees were later removed by him to Sarum.

[4] 'D' alone gives these details relating to Scandinavia.

[5] 1046.

[6] 'D' remains one year in advance of the true year; 'E' is still two years behind.

C

When he was on his way home, he ordered the abbess of Leominster to be brought to him and kept her as long as it suited him, and then he let her go home.[2] In this same year Osgod Clapa[3] was outlawed before Christmas. In this same year after Candlemas came the hard winter with frost and snow and every sort of bad weather, so that there was no one alive who remembered so hard a winter, and men and animals died, and birds and fish perished through the great cold and through hunger.

D

Cornwall and one in Worcester. Then Leofric succeeded to Devonshire and Cornwall,[1] and Bishop Aldred to Worcester. And this year Osgod, the staller, was outlawed.[3] And Magnus conquered Denmark.[4]

E

died Ælfstan, abbot of St. Augustine's, on 5 July, and in this same year Osgod Clapa[3] was expelled.

1047

C

(1047) In this year died Bishop Grimketel, the bishop of Sussex, and he lies in Christ Church at Canterbury. And King Edward gave the bishopric to Heca his priest. And in this same year died Bishop Ælfwine on 29 August, and King Edward gave the bishopric to Bishop Stigand. And Abbot Athelstan of Abingdon died in the same year on 29 March—Easter Day was this year on 3 April[9]—and there was a very great

D

(1048)[5] This year was the severe winter, and in the course of this year Ælfwine, bishop of Winchester, died, and Bishop Stigand was raised to his see. Before that in the same year Grimketel, bishop of Sussex, died, and Heca, the priest, succeeded to the bishopric. And Sweyn[7] also sent here asking for help against Magnus, king of Norway, that fifty ships should be sent to his support, but it seemed a

E

(1045)[5] In this year died Grimketel, bishop of Sussex, and Heca, the king's priest succeeded to it. And in this year died Ælfwine bishop of Winchester, on 29 August, and Stigand bishop in the north succeeded to it. And in the same year, Earl Sweyn[6] went out to Baldwin's country,[8] to Bruges, and stayed there all winter, and went away in the summer.

[1] This is the see of Crediton which Leofric was to transfer to Exeter in 1050.
[2] It will be noted that 'C' alone gives this information which is damaging to the family of Godwine.
[3] A Danish notable whose further adventures will be found under 1049 and 1054.
[4] From Sweyn Estrithson.
[5] 'D' remains one year in advance of the true reckoning; and 'E' two years behind it.
[6] Sweyn, son of Godwine.
[7] This is Sweyn Estrithson, son of Earl Ulf by Estritu, sister of Cnut.
[8] *i.e.* Flanders: Baldwin V was count of Flanders at this time.
[9] 1048. This is explained by 'C' using the Lady Day reckoning, or in this instance perhaps closing the year with Easter.

C

pestilence throughout all England in this year

D

foolish plan to everybody and it was hindered because Magnus had a great naval force.[1] And Magnus then drove out Sweyn and seized the country with great slaughter, and the Danes paid him a large amount of money and accepted him as king. And the same year Magnus died.[2]

E

1048

C

(1048) In this year there was a great earthquake far and wide in England, and in the same year Sandwich and the Isle of Wight were ravaged, and the best men who were there were killed. And after that King Edward and the earls went out with their ships. And in the same year Bishop Siward resigned the bishopric[6] because of his infirmity and went to Abingdon, and Archbishop Eadsige[6] succeeded to the bishopric again, and he [Siward] died within eight weeks on 23 October.

D

(1049)[3] This year Sweyn came back to Denmark, and Harold the paternal uncle of Magnus went to Norway after Magnus was dead and the Norwegians accepted him.[5] And he sent to this country to treat about peace. And Sweyn also sent from Denmark and asked King Edward for naval assistance which was to be fifty ships at least, but all the people refused.[8] And this year also there was an earthquake on 1 May in many places – at Worcester and Droitwich and Derby and elsewhere. Also there was a great pestilence among

E

(1046)[3] Battle at Val-ès-Dunes.[4] In this year died Athelstan, abbot of Abingdon, and Sparrowhawk a monk from Bury St. Edmunds succeeded. And in this same year died Bishop Siward, and Archbishop Eadsige succeeded to all the bishopric. And in this same year Lothen and Yrling came to Sandwich with twenty-five ships[7] and captured an indescribable amount of plunder in men and gold and silver so that nobody knew how much it was altogether; and then they went round Thanet and meant to do the same there, but the

[1] This transaction is only recorded in 'D'; 'Florence of Worcester' says the request was supported by Godwine and opposed by Leofric, whose opinion prevailed. (See below, p. 205.)

[2] Magnus died 25 October 1047.

[3] 'D' is still a year in advance of the true reckoning; and 'E' two years behind.

[4] This is an interpolation in Latin; and is wrongly dated. The battle of Val-ès-Dunes between Duke William and his rebellious vassals from Lower Normandy took place in 1047.

[5] Note the details of Scandinavian history given only in 'D'. The reference is to Sweyn Estrithson.

[6] Suffragan of Canterbury.

[7] 'E', being for this period a transcript or a chronicle kept at Canterbury, gives greater details of this raid which particularly affected the south-east.

[8] This may be a repetition of the account given in the previous annal, or there may in fact have been a second request.

C

D

men and beasts; also fire spreading over the country did much harm in Derbyshire and elsewhere.

E

local people firmly resisted them, and prevented them from coming ashore. They kept them from water, and drove them out completely from those parts. So they went off to Essex, which they ravaged, and there they captured people and whatever they could find, and then they went east to Baldwin's country,[1] and sold whatever they had got from their raid, and thence they went east to the country from which they had come.

1049

C

(1049) In this year the emperor[3] collected an immense force against Baldwin of Bruges[5] because he had stormed the palace of Nymegen, and because of many other injuries done by Baldwin. This force which the emperor had collected was beyond counting. Pope Leo[4] was there from Rome and many famous men from many lands. He[3] also sent to King Edward and asked him for naval support—that he would not let Baldwin escape by sea. The king therefore went to Sandwich and stayed there with a large naval force until the emperor obtained

D

(1050)[2] In this year the emperor collected an immense force against Baldwin of Bruges[5] because he had stormed the palace of Nymegen, and because of many other injuries done by Baldwin. This force which the emperor had collected was beyond counting. The pope[4] was in it and the patriarch, and many famous men from many lands. He[3] also sent to King Edward and asked him for naval support—that he would not let Baldwin escape by sea. The king therefore went to Sandwich and stayed there with a large naval force until the emperor

E

(1046)[2] Now in this year was the great synod held at Rheims. Pope Leo[4] was there and the archbishop of Burgundy, and the archbishop of Besançon, and the archbishop of Trèves, and the archbishop of Rheims, and many others both clerks and lay. And King Edward sent there Bishop Dudoc[6] and Wulfric, abbot of St. Augustine's, and Abbot Ælfwine[7] so that they might inform the king of whatever was there decided in the interests of Christendom. And in this same year King Edward went out to Sandwich with a large naval force, and Earl Sweyn[8]

[1] Flanders.
[2] 'D' remains one year in advance of the true reckoning; 'E' by repeating the number '1046' becomes three years in arrears.
[3] Henry III. [4] Leo IX. [5] Baldwin V of Flanders. [6] Of Wells. [7] Of Ramsey.
[8] Sweyn, son of Godwine.

C

from Baldwin all he wanted. Then[1] Earl Sweyn came back again to King Edward and asked him for land to support himself upon. But Harold,[2] his brother, opposed it together with Earl Beorn.[3] They declared they would give up to him nothing that the king had given them. Sweyn came hypocritically and said he would be the king's liegeman, and he asked Earl Beorn for support. But the king refused him in everything. Then Sweyn went to his ships at Bosham, and Earl Godwine came from Sandwich with forty-two ships, and Earl Beorn along with him. And then the king allowed all the Mercians to go home, and they did so. When the king was informed that Osgod[4] lay at Wulpe[5] with twenty-nine ships the king sent for all the ships he could summon from the 'Northmouth'.[6] But Osgod placed his wife in Bruges and turned back again with six ships and the others went to Essex to 'Eadulfsness'[9] and there they did damage, and then turned back to the ships. Then Earl Godwine and Earl Beorn were lying at Pevensey with their ships.

D

obtained from Baldwin all he wanted. Then[1] Earl Sweyn came back who had gone from this country to Denmark, and there committed crimes against the Danes. He came here hypocritically and said he wished to submit to the king, and Earl Beorn promised to help him. Then after the agreement between the emperor and Baldwin many of the ships went home, but the king stayed at Sandwich with a few ships. And Earl Godwine also went with forty-two ships from Sandwich to Pevensey, and Earl Beorn went with him. Then the king was informed that Osgod[4] was at Wulpe[5] with thirty-nine ships, and the king sent for all the ships he could summon from among those which had gone home. And Osgod placed his wife at Bruges, and they went back again with six ships, and the others went to Sussex[8] to 'Eadulfsness',[9] and they did damage there and then returned to the ships, and then a strong wind overtook them so that they were all lost except for four that were killed overseas. While Earl Godwine and Earl Beorn

E

came in with seven ships to Bosham and made peace with the king,[1] and he was promised that he should be restored to every honour that he had previously held. Then Earl Harold[2] his brother and Earl Beorn[3] withstood it, contending that Sweyn was not entitled to any of those things that the king had granted him. He was however given four nights safe-conduct to enable him to get back to his ships. Now it happened during the course of these proceedings that word had come to the king that hostile ships lay to the west and were there ravaging. Then Earl Godwine turned west with two of the king's ships, one of which was captained by Earl Harold and the other by Tosti his brother, and also with forty-two ships belonging to the local people. Then Earl Beorn[7] was appointed to the king's ship that Earl Harold had captained, and they went west to Pevensey and lay there weatherbound. Then within two days Earl Sweyn came there and spoke with his father, and with Earl Beorn and asked him to go with him to the king at

[1] It will be noted that the three accounts of what follows differ as to details, and they cannot wholly be reconciled. Each account provides some information not to be found in the others. The account of 'Florence of Worcester' (below, p. 206) ought also to be consulted.

[2] This is the first mention in the chronicle of Harold, son of Godwine, later to be king of England.

[3] Brother of Sweyn Estrithson: he had been given an English earldom which included Hertfordshire. See Table 3.

[4] Osgod Clapa.

[5] In Flanders.

[6] Of the Kentish Stour.

[7] MS. gives "Harold": an obvious mistake.

[8] A mistake for Essex.

[9] The Naze, Essex.

C

Then Earl Sweyn came treacherously and asked Earl Beorn to accompany him to the king at Sandwich, saying that he would swear oaths to him and be faithful to him. Then Beorn thought that because of their kinship, he would not be betrayed. He took with him three companions and, exactly as if they were going to Sandwich, they rode to Bosham where Sweyn's ships were lying. But he was bound at once and carried on board, and then they went to Dartmouth and there he was put to death, and buried deep. Harold however, his kinsman, fetched him and took him to Winchester and buried him there near Cnut his uncle. And the king and all his host declared Sweyn a scoundrel.[1] He had eight ships before he murdered Beorn, but afterwards all but two deserted him, and he then went to Bruges and stayed there with Baldwin.[2] And in this year Eadnoth[3] the good bishop in Oxfordshire died, and Oswy, abbot of Thorney, and Wulfnoth, abbot of Westminster. And King Edward gave the bishopric to Ulf his priest–which was a bad appointment. And in this same year, King Edward

D

were staying at Pevensey, Earl Sweyn came treacherously and asked Earl Beorn who was his uncle's son to accompany him to the king at Sandwich in order to improve his relations with the king. Beorn went then with three companions because of their kinship, but he was taken to Bosham where Sweyn's ships were lying, and there he was bound and carried on board. Then he was taken to Dartmouth and there Sweyn ordered him to be killed and buried deep. He was found again however and taken to Winchester and buried with Cnut his uncle. A little before this the men of Hastings and its neighbourhood captured two of his ships with their ships, and they killed all the men and brought the ships to the king at Sandwich. Sweyn had eight ships before he betrayed Beorn, but afterwards all but two deserted him.[2] In the same year, thirty-six ships came up the Usk from Ireland and did damage in those parts with the help of Griffith, the Welsh king. The people gathered together against him, and Bishop Aldred was there with them, but they had too little support, and the enemy came on

E

Sandwich in order that he might help him regain the king's friendship. Beorn agreed to do this and they departed as if they were meaning to go to the king. Then as they were riding Sweyn asked him to go with him to his ships for [as he said] his sailors would desert him unless he got there quickly. So they both went to where his ships were lying. When they got there Earl Sweyn asked him to go aboard with him. Beorn refused firmly and so long that the sailors took him and threw him into the boat and bound him and rowed to a ship and put him on board. Then they hoisted sail and ran west to the mouth of the Usk. And they kept Beorn with them until they killed him, and they took the body and buried it in a church. But his friends and his sailors came from London and disinterred him and took him to the Old Minster at Winchester where they buried him with King Cnut his uncle. And Sweyn went east to Baldwin's country and stayed there all winter at Bruges under Baldwin's full protection. And in the same year died Eadnoth, bishop to the north,[4] and Ulf was

[1] *Nithing.*

[2] It will be noted that in describing the foregoing events the versions differ on points of chronology and of fact. Compare also the account given by 'Florence of Worcester' (below, p. 206).

[3] Bishop of Dorchester (Oxfordshire).

[4] Indicates the southern provenance of 'E'; this is the Mercian bishopric of Dorchester (Oxfordshire).

C

paid off nine ships, and they went away, ships and all, and five ships were left behind and the king promised the sailors twelve months' pay. In the same year Bishop Hereman and Bishop Aldred went to Rome, to the pope on the king's business.[1]

D

them by surprise quite early in the morning, and killed many good men there; and the others escaped with the bishop. This was done on 29 July. This year Oswy, abbot of Thorney, died in Oxfordshire and Wulfnoth, abbot of Westminster. And the priest Ulf was appointed as pastor of that bishopric which Eadnoth had held, but he was expelled from it afterwards because he did nothing like a bishop in it, so much that we are ashamed to say anything more about it. And Bishop Siward died who lies at Abingdon. And this year the great minster at Rheims was consecrated; Pope Leo was there and the emperor and they had a great synod there about the service of God. St. Leo, the pope, presided over that synod. It is difficult to know what bishops came to it and in particular what abbots, but two were sent from this country–from St. Augustine's and from Ramsey.

E

appointed bishop

1050

C

(1050) In this year the bishops came home from Rome, and Earl Sweyn was reinstated. And in this same year Archbishop

D

(1051)[2] In this year died Eadsige, archbishop of Canterbury, and the king gave the archbishopric to Robert the Frenchman,[3]

E

(1047)[2] In this year there was a big council at London in the middle of Lent, and nine ships of the sailors were dismissed and five

[1] Possibly to ask the pope to release the king from a vow to go on pilgrimage. This should be referred to 1050. See 'D' and 'E' for that year.

[2] 'D' remains a year in advance of the true chronology; 'E' remains three years behind.

[3] Robert, abbot of Jumièges.

C

Eadsige died on 29 October. Also in this same year died Ælfric, archbishop of York, on 22 January,[1] and his body lies at Peterborough. Then King Edward held a council at London in mid-Lent and appointed Robert[2] as archbishop of Canterbury, and he appointed Sparrowhawk as bishop of London, and gave Rothulf his kinsman the abbacy of Abingdon.[3] In the same year he laid off all the sailors.

D

who had been bishop of London, and Sparrowhawk, abbot of Abingdon, succeeded to the bishopric of London, but it was taken from him before he was consecrated. And Bishop Hereman and Bishop Aldred went to Rome.

E

remained. And in this same year Earl Sweyn came into England. And in this same year was the great synod at Rome, and King Edward sent Bishop Hereman and Bishop Aldred to it, and they got there on Easter eve. And the pope held another synod at Vercelli, and Bishop Ulf went there, and they nearly had to break his staff and would have done so if he had not given more treasure, because he could not perform his duties as he ought. And in this year Archbishop Eadsige died on 29 October.

1051

C

(1051) In this year Archbishop Robert came here from overseas with his *pallium*, and in this same year Earl Godwine and all his sons were driven out of England. He went to Bruges with his wife and with his three sons Sweyn, Tosti and Gyrth. And Harold and Leofwine went to Ireland and stayed there that winter. And in this same year on 14 March,[5] there died the queen-mother, the mother of King Edward and Harthacnut, whose name was Emma, and her body lies

D

(1052)[4] This year died Ælfric, archbishop of York, a man who was very venerable and wise. And in the same year King Edward abolished the tax levied to pay off the Danes which King Ethelred had imposed, that is in the thirty-ninth year after it had been instituted. That tax oppressed all the English people for as long a space of time as we have written. That tax always came before other taxes, which were variously paid, and it oppressed people in many ways. In the same

E

(1048)[4] In this year in Lent King Edward appointed Robert of London to be archbishop of Canterbury, and in the course of the same Lent Robert went to Rome for his *pallium*. And the king gave the bishopric of London to Sparrowhawk, abbot of Abingdon, and he gave the abbacy [of Abingdon] to Rothulf his kinsman. Thus the archbishop came from Rome one day before the eve of the Feast of St. Peter, and occupied his episcopal throne at Christ Church on St. Peter's Day,[6] and

[1] 1051 – evidence of the Lady Day reckoning in 'C'.
[2] Robert, abbot of Jumièges.
[3] He had apparently been bishop of Nidarus. For the significance of this appointment, see above, p. 107.
[4] 'D' remains a year in advance of the true chronology; 'E' three years behind it.
[5] 1052.
[6] 29 June.

C

in the Old Minster near King Cnut.

D

year Eustace[1] who had married King Edward's sister landed at Dover. Then his men went foolishly looking for billets and killed a certain man of the town, and one of the townsmen killed one of their comrades, so that seven of Eustace's men were struck down. And great damage was done on either side with horses and with weapons until the people assembled, and then the men of Eustace fled to the king at Gloucester, who granted them protection. Then Earl Godwine was indignant that such things should happen in his earldom, and he began to gather his people from all over his earldom, and Earl Sweyn his son did the same over all his, and Harold his other son over all his. And they all assembled in Gloucestershire at Langtree,[2] a great and innumerable force all ready to do battle against the king unless Eustace and his men were handed over to them, as well as the Frenchmen who were in the castle. This was done a week before the second Feast of St. Mary.[4] King Edward was then residing at Gloucester. He sent for Earl Leofric,[5] and to the north for Earl Siward[6] and asked for

E

soon after he went to the king. Then came Abbot Sparrowhawk on the way to him with the king's writ and seal to the effect that he was to be consecrated bishop of London by the archbishop. But the archbishop refused and said the pope had forbidden it him. Then the abbot went to the archbishop again about it and asked for the bishopric, and the archbishop refused him resolutely and said that the pope had forbidden it him. Then the abbot went back to London and occupied the bishopric that the king had given him; he did this with the king's full permission all that summer and autumn. Then Eustace came from overseas soon after the bishop, and went to the king and told him what he wished and then went homewards. When he came east to Canterbury, he and his men took refreshment there, and went to Dover. When he was some miles on this side of Dover he put on his corselet and all his companions did likewise.[3] So they went to Dover. When they got there, they wished to lodge where it suited their own convenience. Then one of the men of Eustace came and wished

[1] Eustace 'aux Grenons', count of Boulogne, married Goda, sister of Edward the Confessor, and widow of Drogo, count of the French Vexin. See Table 1.

[2] The hundred in which Beverstone is situated; cf. 'E'.

[3] These details illustrate local knowledge derived from a narrative composed in the neighbourhood.

[4] The Nativity – 8 September.

[5] Earl of Mercia.

[6] Earl of Northumbria.

C

D

their retainers. And they came to him at first with a small force, but after they had understood how things were in the south, they sent north throughout all their earldoms and had a great army called out for the help of their liege lord, and Ralph[1] did the same throughout his earldom; and they all came to Gloucester to the help of the king, though it was late. They were all so much in agreement with the king that they were willing to attack the army of Godwine if the king had wished them to do so. Then some of them thought it would be a great piece of folly if they joined battle because in the two hosts there was most of what was noblest in England, and they considered that they would be opening a way for our enemies to enter the country and to cause great ruin among ourselves. They advised the exchange of hostages, and they issued summonses for London; the folk throughout all this northern province,[2] in Siward's earldom and Leofric's and elsewhere were ordered to go there. And Earl Godwine and his sons were to come there to defend themselves. Then they

E

to stay at the home of a householder against his will, and he wounded the householder, and the householder killed him. Then Eustace got upon his horse and his companions upon theirs, and went to the householder and killed him upon his own hearth, and afterwards they went up towards the town and killed, within and without, more than twenty men. And the townsmen killed nineteen men on the other side and wounded they did not know how many. And Eustace escaped with a few men and went back to the king and gave him a prejudiced account of how they had fared, and the king grew very angry with the townsmen. And the king sent for Earl Godwine and ordered him to carry war into Kent to Dover because Eustace had informed the king that it was more the townsmen's fault than his. But it was not so. And the earl would not consent to this expedition because he was reluctant to injure his own province. Then the king sent for all his council and ordered them to come to Gloucester near the later Feast of St. Mary. The foreigners[3] then had built a castle[4] at Hereford in

[1] Ralph, nicknamed the Timid was the nephew of Edward the Confessor, being the son of Goda by her first husband, Drogo, count of the French Vexin.

[2] 'D' is clearly at this point a transcription of a record compiled at some place in the north.

[3] The Norman colony established in Herefordshire under the leadership of Earl Ralph 'the Timid'.

[4] On this and other castles built about this time in this neighbourhood, see J. H. Round, *Feudal England*, pp. 317–331.

C

D

came to Southwark, and a great number with them from Wessex, but his force dwindled the more the farther they went. And all the thegns of Harold his son were transferred to the king's allegiance, and Earl Sweyn his other son was outlawed. Thus it did not suit him to come to defend himself against the king and against the force that was with the king. Then Godwine went away by night, and next morning the king held a meeting of his council and he and all the army declared him an outlaw, and all his sons with him. And he went south to Thorney and so did his wife, and so did his son Sweyn, and so did Tosti with his wife who was a kinswoman of Baldwin of Bruges, and so did his son Gyrth. And Earl Harold, and Leofwine went to Bristol to the ship which Sweyn had equipped and provisioned for himself. And the king sent Bishop Aldred from London with a force, and they were to intercept him before he got on board, but they could not–or would not. And he went out from the estuary of the Avon, and had such stiff sailing weather that he escaped with difficulty, and he suffered great losses there. He continued his course to Ireland when

E

Earl Sweyn's province, and had inflicted every possible injury and insult upon the king's men in those parts. Then Earl Godwine and Earl Sweyn and Earl Harold came together at Beverstone,[1] and many men with them, intending to go to their royal lord and to all the councillors who were assembled with him so that they should have the advice and support of the king and all the councillors as to how they should avenge the insult to the king and to all the people. Then the foreigners went beforehand to the king and accused the earls so that they were not allowed to come into his sight, because (as they said) they meant to come to betray the king. Earl Siward and Earl Leofric had come there to the king and a large company with them from the north, and Earl Godwine and his sons were informed that the king and the men who were with them meant to take measures against them. And they strengthened themselves firmly in reply, though they were reluctant to have to stand against their royal lord. Then the councillors gave advice that evil doing should cease on both sides, and the king gave the peace of God, and his

[1] In the hundred of Langtree, Gloucestershire.

C

D

sailing weather came. And Godwine and those who were with him went from Thorney to Bruges, to Baldwin's country, in one ship with as much treasure for each person as they could stow away. It would have seemed remarkable to everyone in England if anybody had told them that it could happen, because he had been exalted so high even to the point of ruling the king and all England, and his sons were earls and the king's favourites, and his daughter was married to the king.[1] She was brought to Wherwell and they entrusted her to the abbess. Then forthwith Count William[2] came from overseas with a great force of Frenchmen, and the king received him and as many of his companions as suited him and let him go again. This same year William the priest[3] was given the bishopric of London which had been given to Sparrowhawk.

E

complete friendship to both sides. Then the king and his councillors decided that there should be a meeting of all the councillors a second time at London at the autumnal equinox, and the king ordered the force to be called out both south of the Thames and in the north, all that ever was best. Then Earl Sweyn was declared an outlaw and Earl Godwine and Earl Harold were ordered to come to the meeting as quickly as ever they could make the journey. When they got there they were summoned to the meeting. Then Godwine asked for safe-conduct and hostages so that he could come to the meeting, and leave it without being betrayed. Then the king asked for all those thegns that the earls had had, and they were handed all over to him. Then the king sent to them again and ordered them to come with twelve men into the king's council. Then the earl again asked for a safe-conduct and hostages so that he might be allowed to exculpate himself of all the charges that were brought against him. But he was refused hostages and granted five nights safe-conduct to leave the country. Then Earl

[1] It should be noted that the details given above in 'D' and 'E' in this annal cannot be reconciled. 'D's' version is on the whole much less favourable than 'E's' to the family of Godwine.

[2] Duke William of Normandy, the future King William I. It will be noted that this visit is only asserted by 'D'. It is alleged that on this occasion Edward formally promised him the succession. [3] He was a Norman.

C D E

Godwine and Earl Sweyn went to Bosham and there launched their ships and went overseas and sought Baldwin's protection, and stayed there all the winter. Earl Harold went west to Ireland, and was there all the winter under that king's protection.[1] And as soon as this had happened the king put away the lady who was consecrated his queen,[2] and deprived her of all that she owned, land and gold and silver and everything; and entrusted her to his sister at Wherwell. And Abbot Sparrowhawk was expelled from the bishopric of London, and William the king's priest[3] was consecrated to it, and Odda[4] was appointed earl over Devonshire and Somerset and Dorset and Cornwall; and Ælfgar, son of Earl Leofric, was granted the earldom which Harold had possessed.[5]

1052

C D E

D: (1052)[6] This year on 6 March died the Lady Ælfgyfu, the widow of King Ethelred and of King Cnut. In the same year Griffith the Welsh king[7] was ravaging in Herefordshire so that he came quite close

E: (1052)[6] Now in this year died Ælfgiue Ymma, mother of King Edward and of King Harthacnut. And in the same year the king and his council decided that ships should be sent to Sandwich, and they

[1] See p. 129, n. 1.
[2] Edith, Godwine's daughter.
[3] He was a Norman.
[4] Little is known about him. He was a benefactor to Deerhurst Abbey.
[5] *i.e.* East Anglia.
[6] 'E' has omitted the numbers '1049', '1050', and '1051', whilst 'D' repeats number '1052'. All the versions thus at last become chronologically in harmony and are now arranged to the correct year.
[7] Griffith ap Llewelyn, king of North Wales.

C D E

D

to Leominster and people gathered against him both natives and the Frenchmen from the castle. And very many good Englishmen were killed and Frenchmen too. It was the same day that Edwin and his comrades had been killed thirteen years before. And forthwith

C

(1052)[3] In this year Earl Harold[4] came from Ireland with his ships to the mouth of the Severn near the boundary of Somerset and Devon, and there did much damage, and the local people gathered together against him out of Somerset and Devon, and he put them to flight and killed more than thirty good thegns, apart from other people and immediately after that he went round Land's End.[5] Then King Edward had forty small boats manned which lay at Sandwich[6] in order that they might keep watch for Earl Godwine, who was in Bruges that winter. But despite this, he got into this country without their knowing anything about it. And while he was here in this country he enticed all the men of Kent and all the sailors from the district of Hastings and from the region round about there by the sea-coast,[7] and all Essex and Surrey and much else beside. Then they all said that they would live and die with him. When the fleet that was lying at Sandwich found out about Godwine's expedition, they set out after him and he escaped them[8] and the fleet hurried back to Sandwich, and so homeward to London. When Godwine found out that the fleet that had been lying at Sandwich was on its way home, he went back again to the Isle of Wight, and lay off the coast there long enough for Earl Harold his son to join him. And they would not do any great harm afterwards except that they lived off the countryside. But they enticed all the local people to their side, both along the sea-coast and inland also. And they went towards Sandwich and kept on collecting all the sailors that they met, and so they came to Sandwich with an overwhelming force. When Edward found out about this, he sent inland for more help, but it came very slowly, and Godwine kept on advancing towards London with his

E

appointed Earl Ralph[1] and Earl Odda as their captains. Then Earl Godwine went out from Bruges with his ships to the Isere, and put out to sea a day before the eve of St. John the Baptist's Day[2] so that he came to Dungeness which is south of Romney. Then it came to the knowledge of the earls out at Sandwich, and they then went out in pursuit of the other ships, and a land force was called out against the ships. Then in the course of these events Earl Godwine was warned, and he went to Pevensey, and the storm became so violent that the earls could not find out what had happened to Earl Godwine. And then Earl Godwine put out again so that he got back to Bruges, and the other ships went back again to Sandwich. Then it was decided that the ships should go back again to London, and that other earls and other oarsmen should be appointed to them. But there was so long a delay that the naval force was quite abandoned and all the men went home. Earl Godwine found out about this and hoisted his sail—and so did his fleet—and they went westward direct to the Isle of Wight and there landed, and ravaged

[1] Earl Ralph the Timid.
[2] 24 June.
[3] See p. 125, n. 6.
[4] 'C' and 'D' are identical for most of this annal.
[5] Penwiðsteort.
[6] 'C' adds: "for many weeks".
[7] 'C' adds: "and all the east province".
[8] 'C' adds: "and protected himself wherever he could".

C D

fleet, until at last he came to Southwark where he waited some time until the tide came up. In that interval he treated with the citizens so that they nearly all wanted what he wanted. When Godwine had arranged all his expedition the tide came in and they forthwith weighed anchor and proceeded through the bridge always keeping to the southern bank, and the land force came from above and drew themselves up along the shore, and they formed a wing with their ships[1] as if they meant to encircle the king's ships. The king had also a large land force on his side in addition to the sailors. But it was hateful to almost all of them to fight against men of their own race because there was little else that was worth anything apart from Englishmen on either side; and also they did not wish the country to be laid the more open to foreigners through their destroying each other. Then it was decided that wise men should go between the parties and they made a truce on both sides. And Godwine went ashore and his son Harold and as many of their sailors as suited them, and then there was a meeting of the council, and Godwine was given his earldom unconditionally and as fully and continuously as he had held it at first, and all his sons all that they had held before, and his wife and daughter as fully and continuously as they had held it before. And they confirmed full friendship with them, and promised the full benefits of the laws to all the people. And they outlawed all the Frenchmen who had promoted injustices and passed unjust judgments and given bad counsel in this country, with the exception, as they decided, of as many as the king should wish to have with him, who were loyal to him and to all the people. And Archbishop Robert and Bishop William and Bishop Ulf escaped with difficulty with the Frenchmen who were with them and so got away overseas.[2]

And Earl Godwine and Harold and the queen stayed on their estates. Sweyn had gone to Jerusalem from Bruges and died on the way home at Constantinople, at Michaelmas. It was on the Monday after St. Mary's Day[3] that Godwine came to Southwark with his

E

there so long that the people paid them as much as they imposed upon them, and then they went westward until they came to Portland and there landed, and did whatever damage they could. Then Harold had come from Ireland with nine ships, and he landed at Porlock, and there was a great force gathered there to oppose him, but he did not hesitate to obtain provisions for himself, and he landed and killed a great part of the force that opposed him, and seized for himself what came his way in cattle, men and property, and then he went east to his father, and they both went eastward until they came to the Isle of Wight, and there took what they had left behind them. Then they went on to Pevensey and took with them as many ships as were serviceable and so proceeded to Dungeness. And he took all the ships that were at Romney and Hythe and Folkestone, and then they went east to Dover and landed and seized ships for themselves and as many hostages as they wished. So they came to Sandwich and there they did exactly the same, and everywhere they were given hostages and provisions wherever they asked for them. They went on to the

[1] 'C' adds: "against the north shore".

[2] 'D' ends the annal at this point.

[3] 8 September.

C

ships, and the morning after, on the Tuesday that they came to the agreement which has been stated above. Then Godwine fell ill soon after he landed and recovered again, but he did all too little reparation about the property of God which he had from many holy places. In the same year came the strong wind on the night of the Feast of St. Thomas,[3] and did great damage everywhere. And Rhys the Welsh king's brother was killed.[4]

D

E

'Northmouth',[1] and so towards London, and some of the ships went within Sheppey and did much damage there, and they went to King's Milton and burnt it[2] down to the ground. Thus they proceeded on their way to London in pursuit of the earls. When they came to London the king and earls were lying there with fifty ships ready to meet them. Then the Earls Godwine and Harold sent to the king and asked him legally to return to them all those things of which they had been unjustly deprived. But the king refused for some time for so long that the men who were with the earl were so incensed against the king and against his men that the earl himself had difficulty in calming those men. Then Bishop Stigand with the help of God went there and the wise men both inside the city and without, and they decided that hostages should be arranged for on both sides. And so it was done. Then Archbishop Robert found out about this, and the Frenchmen, so that they took horses and departed, some west to Pentecost's castle, and some north to Robert's castle.[5] And Archbishop

[1] The northern mouth of the Kentish Stour.

[2] 'E' with local knowledge, albeit favourable to Godwine, gives in greatest detail the story of the earl's ravages in the south-east.

[3] 21 December.

[4] Early in 1053.

[5] On these Herefordshire castles, see Round, *Feudal England*, pp. 317–331.

C D E

Robert and Bishop Ulf and their companions went out at the east gate and killed or otherwise injured many young men, and went right on to Eadulfsness,[1] and there got on board a broken-down ship, and he went right on overseas, and left behind him his *pallium* and all the Church in this country. This was God's will, in that he had obtained the dignity when it was not God's will. Then a big council was summoned outside London and all the earls and the chief men who were in the country were at the council. Then Earl Godwine expounded his case, and cleared himself before King Edward his liege lord and before all his countrymen, declaring that he was guiltless of the charges brought against him; and so [he said] were Harold his son, and all his sons. Then the king granted the earl and his sons his full friendship and full status as an earl, and all that he had had. And all the men who were with him were treated likewise. And the king gave the lady[2] all that she had had. And Archbishop Robert was declared utterly an outlaw, and all the Frenchmen too, because they were most responsible for the disagreement between Earl

[1] The Naze, Essex.
[2] Edith, Godwine's daughter, King Edward's wife.

C

D

E

Godwine and the king. And Bishop Stigand succeeded to the archbishopric of Canterbury. And[1] at this time Arnwi, abbot of Peterborough, relinquished his abbacy while well and strong, and gave it to the monk Leofric with the permission of the king and the monks. And this Abbot Arnwi survived eight years and the Abbot Leofric so enriched the monastery that it was called the Golden Borough. Then it grew greatly in land and gold and silver.

1053

C

(1053) In this year the king was at Winchester at Easter, and Earl Godwine with him, and Earl Harold his son and Tosti. Then on Easter Monday as he was sitting with the king at a meal, he suddenly sank towards the foot-stool, bereft of speech and deprived of all his strength. Then he was carried to the king's private room and they thought it was about to pass off. But it was not so. On the contrary, he continued like this without speech or strength right on to the Thursday[2] and then lost his life. And he lies

D

(1053) This year was the big wind on the night of the Feast of St. Thomas,[3] all through Christmas also was there a big wind. And it was decided that Rhys, the Welsh king's brother, should be killed, because he was causing injuries and his head was brought to Gloucester on the eve of the Epiphany.[5] In the same year before All Saints' Day, Wulfsige, bishop of Lichfield, and Godwine, abbot of Winchcombe, and Ægelward, abbot of Glastonbury, all died within one month; and Leofwine succeeded to the

E

(1053) In this year died Earl Godwine on 15 April[2] and he is buried at Winchester in the Old Minster, and Earl Harold his son succeeded to the earldom and to all that his father had had, and Earl Ælfgar succeeded to the earldom that Harold had had.[4]

[1] What follows looks like a Peterborough interpolation.
[2] The Thursday after Easter in 1053 was in fact 15 April.
[3] 21 December 1052.
[4] East Anglia.
[5] 5 January.

C

there in the Old Minster, and his son Harold succeeded to his earldom and resigned the one he had previously held,[1] and to this Ælfgar succeeded. In the course of this year Wulfsige, bishop of Lichfield, died, and Leofwine, abbot of Coventry, succeeded to the bishopric, and Ægelward, abbot of Glastonbury, died, and Godwine, abbot of Winchcombe. Also Welshmen killed a great number of Englishmen of the patrols near Westbury. In this year was no archbishop in the land,[2] but Bishop Stigand held the bishopric in Canterbury at Christ Church and Kynsige at York. And Leofwine and Wulfwi went overseas and had themselves consecrated there. This Wulfwi succeeded to the bishopric that Ulf had had,[3] while Ulf was still alive and expelled.

D

bishopric of Lichfield, and Bishop Aldred succeeded to the abbacy of Winchcombe, and Ægelnoth to the abbacy at Glastonbury. And in the course of the same year died Ælfric, Odda's brother, at Deerhurst, and his body rests at Pershore. And in the course of the same year died Earl Godwine, and he was taken ill while he was sitting with the king at Winchester. And Harold his son succeeded to the earldom his father had had, and Ælfgar succeeded to the earldom that Harold had had.[1]

E

1054

C

(1054) In this year Earl Siward went with a large force into Scotland and inflicted heavy losses on the Scots and routed them, and the king escaped. Also many fell on his side both

D

(1054) In this year Earl Siward proceeded with a large force to Scotland, both with a naval force and with a land force, and fought there with the Scots and routed the king

E

(1053) Battle at Mortemer.[4] In this year died Leo the holy pope of Rome.[5] And in this year was so great a pestilence among cattle that no one remembered anything as bad for many

[1] East Anglia.

[2] An allusion to Stigand's failure to obtain canonical recognition as archbishop of Canterbury. This also explains Leofwine and Wulfric going overseas to be consecrated.

[3] Dorchester.

[4] An addition in Latin. For the battle of Mortemer, see below, no. 7, p. 284.

[5] Leo IX.

C

among Danes and English, his own son also.[2] In the course of this same year the monastery of Evesham was consecrated on 10 October. In the same year Bishop Aldred went south overseas into Saxony, and was received there with great honour.[3] In the same year Osgod Clapa died suddenly as he was lying in bed.

D

Macbeth and killed all the best in the land, and carried off a large amount of plunder such as had never been captured before. But his son Osbern and his sister's son Siward and some of his housecarls, and also some of the king's were killed there[2] on the Day of the Seven Sleepers.[4] In the course of this same year Bishop Aldred went overseas to Cologne on the king's business,[3] and was there received with great honour by the emperor[5] and there he stayed for nearly a year, and the bishop of Cologne and the emperor both gave him entertainment. And he permitted Bishop Leofwine to consecrate the monastic church of Evesham on 10 October. And this year Osgod died suddenly in his bed. And St. Leo, the pope,[6] died, and Victor[1] was elected pope in his stead.

E

years. And Victor[1] was elected pope.

1055

C

(1055) In this year died Earl Siward at York and his body lies in the minster at Galmanho which he himself had built to the glory of God and all his

D

(1055) In this year died Earl Siward at York, and he lies at Galmanho in the minster which he himself had built and consecrated in the name of

E

(1055) In this year Earl Siward died and a meeting of all the councillors was ordered a week before mid-Lent, and Earl Ælfgar was outlawed because he was

[1] Victor II. See No. 2, p. 210.

[2] On the historic Macbeth a general reference may here be made to W. F. Skene, *Celtic Scotland*, vol. I, pp. 395 *et sqq.*, and to Freeman, *Norman Conquest*, vol. II, pp. 363–366.

[3] The purpose of that mission was probably connected with the recall of the Atheling Edward (see under 1057).

[4] 27 July. [5] Henry III. [6] Leo IX.

C

saints.[1] Then after that within a short space there was a council at London, and Earl Ælfgar, son of Earl Leofric, was outlawed without any guilt[3] and he then went to Ireland and there got himself a fleet–it was eighteen ships apart from his own–and then they went to Wales to King Griffith with that force–and he took him into his protection. And then they gathered a large force with the Irishmen and with the Welsh, and Earl Ralph gathered a large force at Hereford town, and there battle was joined. But before any spear had been thrown the English army fled because they were on horseback,[4] and many were killed there–about four or five hundred men–and they killed none in return. And then they went back to the town and burnt it with the famous minster which Athelstan the venerable bishop had had built. They stripped and robbed it of relics and vestments and everything, and killed the people and some they carried off. Then a force was collected from very nearly all over England, and they came to Gloucester, and went a little way out among the Welsh and

D

God and Olaf.[1] And Tosti succeeded to the earldom he had had.[2] And Archbishop Kynsige fetched his *pallium* from Pope Victor. And soon after that Earl Ælfgar, Earl Leofric's son, was outlawed having committed hardly any crime.[3] But he went to Ireland and Wales and got himself a large force and so came to Hereford. But Earl Ralph came against him with a large force but after a little struggle this was put to flight and many people were killed in the flight. The invaders then went to Hereford town and ravaged it, and burnt the famous minster which Bishop Athelstan had built, and killed the priests inside the minster and many others as well, and captured all the treasures and took them away. And when they had done the greatest damage, it was decided to reinstate Earl Ælfgar and give him his earldom, and all that had been taken from him. This devastation happened on 24 October. In the same year died Tremerig the Welsh bishop soon after the devastation. He was Bishop Athelstan's deputy after he became infirm.

E

charged with being a traitor to the king and to all the people of the country.[3] And he admitted this before all the people who were assembled there, though the words escaped him against his will. And the king gave Tosti, son of Earl Godwine, the earldom that Siward had had, and Earl Ælfgar sought the protection of Griffith in Wales, and in this year Griffith and Ælfgar burned down St. Æthelbriht's minster and all the city of Hereford.

[1] Bootham Bar in York was formerly called Galmanhithe. The dedication to St. Olaf illustrates Earl Siward's Scandinavian sentiments. The monastery of Galmanho was subsequently given to St. Mary's, York.
[2] Northumbria.
[3] The several explanations given in 'C', 'D' and 'E' aptly illustrate their attitude to the politics of the king.
[4] Earl Ralph was making them fight after the manner of Norman mounted knights.

C

stayed there, and Earl Harold had a ditch made about the town during that time. Then discussions were held with a view to peace, and Earl Harold and those who were with him came to Billingsley and there confirmed peace and friendship between them. And Ælfgar was reinstated and given all that had been taken from him, and the fleet went to Chester and there waited for their pay which Earl Ælfgar promised them. This slaughter was on 24 October. In the same year died Tremerig, the Welsh bishop, soon after the devastation–he was Bishop Athelstan's deputy after he became infirm.

D

E

1056

C

(1056) Athelstan the venerable bishop died on 10 September, and his body lies in Hereford town, and Leofgar was appointed bishop. He was Earl Harold's priest, and he wore his moustaches during his priesthood until he became a bishop. He gave up his chrism and his cross, his spiritual weapons, and took his spear and his sword after his consecration as bishop, and so went campaigning against Griffith the Welsh king, and they killed him there and

D

(1056) Bishop Ægelric relinquished his bishopric at Durham and went to Peterborough to St. Peter's monastery, and his brother Ægelwine succeeded him. Also Bishop Athelstan died on 10 February, and his body lies at Hereford, and Leofgar who was Harold's priest was appointed bishop, and in his priesthood he had his moustaches until he was a bishop. He gave up his chrism and his cross and his spiritual weapons and took his spear and his sword, and so went

E

(1056) Now died Henry, Emperor of the Romans and his son, Henry, succeeded him.[1]

[1] An addition in Latin. The reference is to the emperor, Henry III.

C

his priests with him, and Ælfnoth the sheriff and many good men with them; and the others fled. This was eight nights before midsummer.[1] It is hard to describe the oppression and all the expeditions and the campaigning and the labours and the loss of men and horses that all the army of England suffered until Earl Leofric came there, and Earl Harold and Bishop Aldred, and made an agreement between them according to which Griffith swore oaths that he would be a loyal and faithful under-king to King Edward. And Bishop Aldred succeeded to the bishopric which Leofgar had held[3] for eleven weeks and four days. In the same year died the emperor Cona.[2] In the course of this year died Earl Odda, and his body lies at Pershore, and he was consecrated monk before his end. He died on 31 August.

D

campaigning against Griffith the Welsh king, and they killed him there and his priests with him, and Ælfnoth the sheriff and many other good men. This was eight nights before midsummer. And Bishop Aldred succeeded to the bishopric that Leofgar had held for eleven weeks and four days. In the course of this year died Earl Odda, and he lies at Pershore, and he was consecrated monk before his end. He was a good man and pure and very noble, and he went hence on 31 August. And the emperor Cona[2] died.

E

1057

C[4]

D

(1057) Prince Edward came to England who was the son of King Edward's brother, King Edmund who was called Ironside because of his valour. This

E

(1057) In this year Prince Edward, son of King Edmund, came to this country and soon after died,[5] and his body is buried in St. Paul's minster in London.

[1] 16 June.

[2] This refers to the emperor, Henry III, who is here confused with his predecessor Conrad II.

[3] Hereford. Aldred, who was already bishop of Worcester, kept the see of Hereford until in 1060 he became archbishop of York.

[4] 'C' has no entry for this year.

[5] The death of the Atheling who was next in the line of succession constitutes one of the unsolved mysteries of the period.

C[1] D E

prince King Cnut had banished to Hungary in order to betray him. But there he became a distinguished man, as God granted it to him and as was his proper destiny, so that he won a kinswoman of the emperor for his wife, and by her begot a noble family. She was called Agatha. We do not know for what reason it was brought about that he was not allowed to visit his kinsman King Edward. Alas, that was a miserable fate and grievous to all this people that he so speedily ended his life after he came to England to the misfortune of this poor realm.[5] In the same year on 30 September died Earl Leofric who was very wise in divine and temporal matters. That was a benefit to all this realm. He lies at Coventry, and his son, Ælfgar, succeeded to his authority. And in the same year died Earl Ralph[6] on 21 December, and he lies at Peterborough. There also died Heca, bishop in Sussex,[7] and Ægelric was elevated to his see. And this year Pope Victor died and Stephen[8] was elected pope.

E: And Pope Victor[2] died, and Stephen[3] was elected pope who was abbot of Monte Cassino. And Earl Leofric died, and Ælfgar, his son, succeeded to the earldom which his father had held.[4]

1058

C[1] D E

(1058) In this year Earl Ælfgar was banished but he got back by violence forthwith through Griffith's help. And a naval force came from Norway.[10] It is tedious to relate fully how things went. In the same year Bishop Aldred consecrated the monastic church at Gloucester that he himself brought to completion to the glory of God and of St. Peter, and so he went to Jerusalem in

E: (1058) In this year died Pope Stephen[8] and Benedict[9] was consecrated pope. This same sent the *pallium* into this country for Archbishop Stigand. And in this year died Heca, bishop in Sussex, and Archbishop Stigand consecrated Ægelric, a monk of Christ Church, as bishop for Sussex, and Abbot Siward[11] as bishop of Rochester.

[1] 'C' has no entry for this year. [2] Victor II. [3] Stephen IX. [4] Mercia.
[5] See p. 135, n. 5. [6] Earl Ralph the Timid.
[7] Selsey, later to be removed to Chichester. [8] Stephen IX. [9] Benedict X.
[10] Nothing further is known of this raid which probably (since the reference is solely in 'D') affected the north of England.
[11] He had been abbot of Chertsey.

C[1] D E

such state as none had done before him, and there he committed himself to God, and also offered a worthy gift for our Lord's tomb; it was a golden chalice worth 5 marks, of very wonderful workmanship. In the same year Pope Stephen[2] died, and Benedict[3] was appointed pope who sent the *pallium* to Bishop Stigand. And Ægelric was consecrated bishop for Sussex, and Abbot Siward[4] was consecrated bishop of Rochester.

1059

C[1] D E

D: (1059) In this year Nicholas[5] was elected pope who had previously been bishop of the city of Florence, and Benedict who was pope there before was expelled. And this year the tower of Peterborough was consecrated on 17 October.

E: (1059) In this year Nicholas[5] was elected pope who had previously been bishop of the city of Florence, and Benedict who was pope there before was expelled.

1060

C[1] D E

D: (1060) In this year there was a great earthquake on the Translation of St. Martin.[8] And King Henry[6] died in France. And Archbishop Kynsige of York died on 22 December, and he lies at Peterborough. And Bishop Aldred succeeded to the office. And Walter succeeded to the bishopric of Herefordshire, and Bishop Duduc also died, who was bishop in Somerset,[9] and the priest Gisa was appointed in his place.[10]

E: (1060) Now Henry, king of the French,[6] died, and Philip[7] his son succeeded him. In this year died Kynsige, archbishop of York, on 22 December, and Bishop Aldred succeeded him. And Walter succeeded to the bishopric of Hereford.

[1] 'C' has no entry for this year. [2] Stephen IX. [3] Benedict X.
[4] He had been abbot of Chertsey. [5] Nicholas II. [6] Henry I. [7] Philip I.
[8] 4 July. [9] Bishop of Wells. [10] Walter, Duduc and Gisa were Lotharingians.

1061

C[1]

D

(1061) In this year Bishop Aldred went to Rome for his *pallium* and received it from Pope Nicholas. And the Earl Tosti and his wife[2] also went to Rome. And the bishop and the earl experienced much hardship when they were coming home. And in this year died Godwine, bishop at St. Martin's; and Wulfric, abbot of St. Augustine's, on 19 March. And Pope Nicholas[3] died and Alexander,[4] who was bishop of Lucca, was elected pope.

E

(1061) In this year died Duduc, bishop in Somerset, and Gisa succeeded him. And in the same year died Godwine, bishop at St. Martin's, on 9 March. And in the same year died Wulfric, abbot at St. Augustine's, in Easter week on 18 April. When word came to the king that Abbot Wulfric was dead, he chose the monk Æthelsige of the Old Monastery for the office; he then followed Archbishop Stigand and was consecrated abbot at Windsor on St. Augustine's Day.[5]

1062

C[1]

D[6]

E[6]

(1062) In this year Maine was subjected to William count of Normandy.

1063

C[1]

D

(1063) In this year after Christmas Earl Harold went from Gloucester to Rhuddlan, which belonged to Griffith, and there he burnt the residence and the ships and all the equipment which belonged to them; and he put him to flight. And then at Rogationtide Harold went with ships from Bristol round Wales,[7] and that people made peace and gave hostages. And Tosti went against them with a land force and they subdued the country. But in the same year in autumn King Griffith was

E

(1063) In this year Earl Harold and his brother Earl Tosti went into Wales with both a land force and a naval force and subdued the country. And that people gave hostages and surrendered, and then went out and killed their king, Griffith, and brought his head to Harold who appointed another king for them.[7]

[1] 'C' has no entry for this year.

[2] Her name was Judith. She was sister to Baldwin V of Flanders and to Maud, wife of William the Conqueror.

[3] Nicholas II.

[4] Alexander II.

[5] Either 26 May (St. Augustine of Canterbury), or 28 August (St. Augustine of Hippo), and probably the former.

[6] 'D' has no entry for this year, and 'E' has only a mention in Latin.

[7] For this Welsh campaign a general reference may be made to Freeman, *Norman Conquest*, vol. II (1870), pp. 465–476.

C[1] D E

killed on 5 August by his own men because of the fight he fought against Earl Harold. He was king over all the Welsh, and his head was brought to Earl Harold, and Harold brought it to the king, and the figurehead of his ship and the ornaments with it. And King Edward entrusted the country to the two brothers of Griffith, Blethgent and Rigwatta, and they swore oaths and gave hostages to the king and the earl, promising that they would be faithful to him in everything, and be everywhere ready on water and on land, and likewise to pay such dues from that country as before had been given to any other king.

1064

C[2] D[2] E[2]

1065

C

(1065) In this year before Lammas, Earl Harold ordered some building to be done in Wales–at Portskewet–when he had subdued it, and there he got together many goods and thought of having King Edward there for hunting. And when it was nearly all got together, Caradoc, son of Griffith, went there with all those he could get, and killed nearly all the people who were building there, and took the goods that were collected there. This slaughter was on St.

D

(1065) In this year before Lammas, Earl Harold ordered some building to be done in Wales–at Portskewet–when he had subdued it, and there he got together many goods and thought of having King Edward there for hunting. And when it was all ready Caradoc, son of Griffith, went there with all the following he could get and killed nearly all the people who were building there, and they took the goods that were got ready there. We do not know

E

[1] 'C' has no entry for this year.

[2] All the chronicles are blank for this year.

C

Bartholomew's Day.[1] And then after Michaelmas all the thegns of Yorkshire went to York and killed all Tosti's housecarls that they could find and took his treasure. And Tosti was then at Britford with the king. And very soon after this there was a big council meeting at Northampton, and likewise one at Oxford on the Feast of St. Simon and St. Jude.[4] And Earl Harold was there and wanted to bring about an agreement between them if he could. But he could not. But all Tosti's earldom unanimously deserted him, and outlawed him, and all those with him who had committed lawless deeds; because first he robbed God, and all those who were less powerful than himself he deprived of life and land. And they adopted Morcar as their earl, and Tosti went overseas and his wife with him, to Baldwin's country, and took up winter quarters at St. Omer. And King Edward came to Westminster at Christmas and consecrated the minster he had himself built to the glory of God and St. Peter and all God's saints.[6] The consecration of the church was on Holy Innocents' Day.[7] And

D

who first suggested this foolish plan. This was done on St. Bartholomew's Day.[1] And soon after this all the thegns in Yorkshire and in Northumberland came together and

E

(1064)[2] In this year all the men of Northumbria came together and

outlawed their Earl Tosti and killed his bodyguard, and all they could get at, both English and Danish, and took all his weapons to York, and gold and silver and all his treasure they could hear about anywhere. And they sent for Morcar, son of Earl Ælfgar,[3] and chose him as their earl, and he went south with all the people of the shire, and of Nottingham, Derby and Lincoln until he came to Northampton. And his brother Edwin came to meet him with the men that were in his earldom, and also many Welsh came with him. Thereupon Earl Harold came to meet them and they entrusted him with a message to King Edward, and also sent messengers with him and asked that they might be allowed to have Morcar as their earl. And the king granted this and sent Harold back to them at Northampton on the eve of St. Simon and St. Jude.[4] And he proclaimed this to them and gave them surety for it, and he renewed there the law of King Cnut. And the northern men did much damage round Northampton while he was gone on their errand, in that they killed people and burned houses and corn and took all the cattle that they could get at–which was many thousands–and captured many hundreds of people and took them north with them so that that shire and many other neighbouring shires were the worse for it for many years. And Earl Tosti and his wife and all those who wanted what he wanted went south overseas to Count Baldwin, and he received them all and there they remained all the winter.[5]

(D) And King Edward came to Westminster at Christmas and had consecrated the minster he had built there to the glory of God and St. Peter and of all God's saints. The consecration of the church was

[1] 24 August.

[2] 'E' having given nothing relating to 1064 places this annal under that figure, thus falling a year behind the true chronology. The bulk of his entry at this place is identical with, although much shorter than, 'D'.

[3] Of Mercia.

[4] 28 October.

[5] 'E' ends his annal at this point.

[6] Westminster Abbey.

[7] 28 December 1065.

C	D	E
he died on the eve of the Epiphany,[1] and was buried on the Feast of the Epiphany[2] in the same minster–as it says below:	on Holy Innocents' Day. And he died on the eve of the Epiphany,[1] and was buried on the Feast of the Epiphany[2] in the same minster–as it says below:	

Now royal Edward, England's ruler
To the Saviour resigns his righteous soul
His sacred spirit to God's safe keeping
In the life of this world he lived awhile
In kingly splendour strong in counsel.
Four and twenty[3] was his tale of winters
That ruler of heroes lavish of riches
In fortunate time he governed the Welshmen
Ethelred's son; ruled Britons and Scots
Angles and Saxons, his eager soldiers.
All that the cold sea waves encompass
Young and loyal yielded allegiance,
With all their heart to King Edward the noble.
Ever gay was the courage of the guiltless king
Though long ago, of his land bereft
He wandered in exile, over earth's far ways
After Cnut overcame Ethelred's kin
And Danes had rule of the noble realm
Of England for eight and twenty years
In succession distributing riches.
At length he came forth in lordly array
Noble in goodness, gracious and upright
Edward the glorious, guarding his homeland
Country and subjects–till on a sudden came
Death in his bitterness, bearing so dear
A lord from the earth. And angels led
His righteous soul to heaven's radiance.
Yet the wise ruler entrusted the realm
To a man of high rank, to Harold himself
A noble earl who all the time
Had loyally followed his lord's commands
With words and deeds and neglected nothing
That met the need of the people's king.

And Earl Harold was now consecrated king[4] and he met little quiet in it as long as he ruled the realm.

[1] 5 January 1066.
[2] 6 January 1066.
[3] Twenty-four years and a half ('C').
[4] Harold was crowned on the day of Edward's funeral.

1066

C

(1066) In this year Harold came from York to Westminster at the Easter following the Christmas that the king died, and Easter was then on 16 April.[3] Then over all England there was seen a sign in the skies such as had never been seen before.[6] Some said it was the star 'comet' which some call the star with hair; and it first appeared on the eve of the Greater Litany,[7] that is 24 April, and so shone all the week. And soon after this came Earl Tosti from overseas into the Isle of Wight with as large a fleet as he could muster, and both money and provisions were given him. And then he went away from there and did damage everywhere along the sea-coast wherever he could reach, until he came to Sandwich. When King Harold who was in London was informed that Tosti his brother was come to Sandwich he assembled a naval force and a land force larger than had ever been assembled before in this country, because he had been told as a fact that Count William from Normandy, King Edward's

D

(1066) In this year King Harold came from York to Westminster at the Easter following the Christmas that the king died, and Easter was then on 16 April.[3] Then over all England there was seen a sign in the skies such as had never been seen before.[6] Some said it was the star 'comet' which some call the star with hair; and it first appeared on the eve of the Greater Litany,[7] that is 24 April, and so shone all the week. And soon after this came Earl Tosti from overseas into the Isle of Wight with as large a fleet as he could muster and both money and provisions were given him. And King Harold his brother assembled a naval force and a land force larger than any king had ever assembled before in this country, because he had been told that William the Bastard[10] meant to come here and conquer this country. This was exactly what afterwards happened. Meanwhile Earl Tosti came into the Humber with sixty ships and Earl Edwin came with a land force and drove him out, and the sailors deserted

E

(1066)[1] In this year the minster of Westminster was consecrated on Holy Innocents' Day,[2] and King Edward died on the eve of the Epiphany[4] and was buried on the Feast of the Epiphany[5] in the newly consecrated church at Westminster. And Earl Harold succeeded to the realm of England, just as the king had granted it to him, and as he had been chosen to the position. And he was consecrated king on the Feast of the Epiphany.[5] And the same year that he became king he went out with a naval force against William[8] and meanwhile Earl Tosti came into the Humber with sixty ships and Earl Edwin[9] came with a land force and drove him out and the sailors deserted him, and he went to Scotland with twelve small vessels and Harold, king of Norway,[11] met him with three hundred ships, and Tosti submitted to him; and they both went up the Humber until they reached York. And Earl Morcar and Earl Edwin fought against them, and the king of Norway had the victory.[12] And King Harold

[1] 'E' having omitted '1065' returns to the true chronology.
[2] 28 December 1065.
[3] Correct.
[4] 5 January 1066.
[5] 6 January 1066.
[6] Halley's comet.
[7] On this feast, see R. Lanciani, *Pagan and Christian Rome* (1893), p. 165.
[8] This is only given in 'E' and perhaps refers to a skirmish off the south-east coast.
[9] He had succeeded his father, Ælfgar, as earl of Mercia.
[10] Note difference of emphasis. 'C' seems to imply that William had some claim to the throne.
[11] Harold Hardraada.
[12] The battle of Fulford took place on Wednesday, 20 September 1066.

C

kinsman meant to come here and subdue this country. This was exactly what happened afterwards. When Tosti found that King Harold was on his way to Sandwich he went from Sandwich and took some of the sailors with him, some willingly and some unwillingly, and then went north to [ ] and ravaged in Lindsey and killed many good men there. When Earl Edwin and Earl Morcar[5] understood about this they came there and drove him out of the country, and then he went to Scotland, and the king of Scots[7] gave him protection, and helped him with provisions, and he stayed there all the summer. Then King Harold came to Sandwich and waited for his fleet there, because it was long before it could be assembled; and when his fleet was assembled he went into the Isle of Wight and lay there all that summer and autumn; and a land force was kept everywhere along by the sea, though in the end it was no use. When it was the Feast of the Nativity of St. Mary[10] the provisions of the people were gone, and nobody could stay

D

him. And he went to Scotland with twelve small vessels and there Harold, king of Norway,[1] met him with three hundred ships, and Tosti submitted to him and became his vassal; and they both went up the Humber until they reached York. And there Earl Edwin and Morcar his brother fought against them: but the Norwegians had the victory.[4] Harold, king of the English, was informed that things had gone thus; and the fight was on the Vigil of St. Matthew. Then Harold our king[6] came upon the Norwegians by surprise and met them beyond York at Stamford Bridge with a large force of the English people; and that day there was a very fierce fight on both sides. There was killed Harold of the Fair Hair[9] and Earl Tosti, and the Norwegians who survived took to flight; and the English attacked them fiercely as they pursued them until some got to the ships. Some were drowned, and some burned, and some destroyed in various ways so that few survived and the English remained in command of the field. The king gave quarter to Olaf,

E

was informed as to what had been done, and what had happened, and he came with a very great force of Englishmen and met him at Stamford Bridge,[2] and killed him and Earl Tosti and valiantly overcame all the invaders. Meanwhile Count William landed at Hastings on Michaelmas Day,[3] and Harold came from the north and fought with him before all the army had come, and there he fell and his two brothers Gyrth and Leofwine; and William conquered this country, and came to Westminster, and Archbishop Aldred consecrated him king, and people paid taxes to him, and gave him hostages and afterwards bought their lands. And[8] Leofric, abbot of Peterborough, was at that campaign and fell ill there and came home and died soon after, on the eve of All Saints. God have mercy on his soul. In his day there was every happiness and every good at Peterborough, and he was beloved by everyone, so that the king gave to St. Peter and him the abbacy of Burton and that of Coventry which Earl Leofric who was his uncle had built,

[1] Harold Hardraada. [2] The battle of Stamford Bridge took place on Monday, 25 September.
[3] 29 September: 'D' gives 28 September.
[4] The battle of Fulford took place on Wednesday, 20 September.
[5] Earls respectively of Mercia and Northumbria.
[6] The note of enthusiasm should be remarked. It is not to be found in 'C'.
[7] Malcolm Canmore. [8] What follows in 'E' has the appearance of being a Peterborough addition.
[9] An error for Harold Hardraada. [10] 8 September.

C

there any longer. Then they were allowed to go home, and the king rode inland, and the ships were brought up to London and many perished before they reached there. When the ships came home, Harold, king of Norway, came by surprise north into the Tyne with a very large naval force–and no little [ ] or more[1]–and Earl Tosti came to him with all those he had mustered just as they had agreed beforehand, and they both went with all the fleet up the Ouse towards York. Then King Harold in the south was informed when he disembarked that Harold, king of Norway, and Earl Tosti were come ashore near York. Then he went northwards day and night as quickly as he could assemble his force. Then before Harold could get there Earl Edwin and Earl Morcar assembled from their earldom as large a force as they could muster, and fought against the invaders and caused them heavy casualties and many of the English host were killed, and drowned and put to flight, and the Norwegians remained masters of the field.[6] And this fight was on the eve of St. Matthew the Apostle, and

D

son of the Norse king, and their bishop and the earl of Orkney and all those who survived on the ships, and they went up to our king and swore oaths that they would always keep peace and friendship with this country; and the king let them go home with twenty-four ships. These two pitched battles were fought within five nights.[2] Then Count William came from Normandy to Pevensey on Michaelmas Eve,[3] and as soon as they were able to move on they built a castle at Hastings. King Harold was informed of this and he assembled a large army and came against him at the hoary apple-tree,[5] and William came against him by surprise before his army was drawn up in battle array. But the king nevertheless fought hard against him, with the men who were willing to support him, and there were heavy casualties on both sides. There King Harold was killed and Earl Leofwine his brother, and Earl Gyrth his brother, and many good men, and the French remained masters of the field, even as God granted it to them because of the sins of the people. Archbishop Aldred and the

E

and that of Crowland and that of Thorney. And he did much for the benefit of the monastery of Peterborough with gold and silver and vestments and land, more indeed than any before or after him. Then the Golden City became a wretched city. Then the monks elected Brand, the provost, as abbot, because he was a very good man and very wise, and sent him to Prince Edgar[4] because the local people expected that he would be king, and the prince gladly gave assent to it. When King William heard about this he grew very angry, and said the abbot had slighted him. Then distinguished men acted as intermediaries and brought them into agreement, because the abbot was one of the distinguished men. Then he gave the king 40 marks of gold as settlement. And he lived a little while after this–only three years. Then all confusions and evils came upon the monastery. May God take pity on it!

[1] The text is corrupt at this point.
[2] 20 September and 25 September.
[3] 28 September. 'E' says 29 September.
[4] Son of the Atheling Edward who died in 1057.
[5] The only narrative contemporary description of the battle. The reference to the apple-tree suggests that the engagement took place at some deserted spot on the Downs.
[6] Battle of Fulford, Wednesday, 20 September.

C

that was a Wednesday. And then after the fight Harold, king of Norway, and Earl Tosti went into York[1] with as large a force as suited them, and they were given hostages from the city with provisions, and so went from there on board ship and had discussions with a view to complete peace, arranging that they should all go with him and subdue this country. Then in the middle of these proceedings Harold, king of the English, came on the Sunday with all his force to Tadcaster,[3] and there marshalled his troops, and then on Monday[4] went right on through York. And Harold, king of Norway, and Earl Tosti and their divisions were gone inland beyond York to Stamford Bridge, because they had been promised for certain that hostages would be brought to them out of all the shire. Then Harold, king of the English, came against them by surprise beyond the bridge, and there they joined battle, and went on fighting strenuously till late in the day. And there Harold, king of Norway, was killed and Earl Tosti, and numberless men with them both Norwegians and English, and the

D

citizens of London wanted to have Prince Edgar as king, as was his proper due; and Edwin and Morcar promised him that they would fight on his side; but always the more it ought to have been forward the more it got behind, and the worse it grew from day to day, exactly as everything came to be at the end. The battle took place on the festival of Calixtus the pope.[2] And Count William went back to Hastings, and waited there to see whether submission would be made to him. But when he understood that no one meant to come to him, he went inland with all his army that was left to him, and that came to him afterwards from overseas, and ravaged all the region that he overran until he reached Berkhamsted. There he was met by Archbishop Aldred and Prince Edgar, and Earl Edwin and Earl Morcar, and all the chief men from London. And they submitted out of necessity after most damage had been done–and it was a great piece of folly that they had not done it earlier, since God would not make things better because of our sins. And they gave hostages and swore

E

[1] On Sunday, 24 September.
[2] Saturday, 14 October.
[3] 24 September.
[4] The battle of Stamford Bridge was fought on Monday, 25 September (cf. below, p. 213).

C

Norwegians fled[1] from the English. There was one of the Norwegians there who withstood the English host so that they could not cross the bridge nor win victory. Then an Englishman shot an arrow but it was no use, and then another came under the bridge and ran him through the corselet. Then Harold, king of the English, came over the bridge and his host with him, and there killed large numbers of both Norwegians and Flemings, and Harold let the king's son Hetmundus go home to Norway with all the ships.[2]

D

oaths to him, and he promised them that he would be a gracious liege lord, and yet in the meantime they ravaged all that they overran. Then on Christmas Day, Archbishop Aldred consecrated him king at Westminster. And he [William] promised Aldred on Christ's book and swore moreover (before Aldred would place the crown on his head) that he would rule all this people as well as the best of the kings before him, if they would be loyal to him. All the same he laid taxes on people very severely, and then went in spring overseas to Normandy, and took with him Archbishop Stigand, and Ægelnoth, abbot of Glastonbury, and Prince Edgar and Earl Edwin and Earl Morcar, and Earl Waltheof, and many other good men from England. And Bishop Odo[3] and Earl William[4] stayed behind and built castles here far and wide throughout this country, and distressed the wretched folk, and always after that it grew much worse. May the end be good when God wills!

E

[1] From here to the end of the annal in 'C' is in a handwriting-and in language-later than the main body of this chronicle.

[2] This is the end of chronicle 'C'.

[3] Odo, half-brother of the Conqueror, being the son of Herluin and Herleva, was bishop of Bayeux from 1049 to 1097. He subsequently became earl of Kent. A sketch of his character appears on pp. 288–289 below.

[4] William fitz Osbern, son of Osbern the steward, was given the Isle of Wight and the earldom of Hereford shortly after 1066

1067[1]

D

(1067) The king came back to England on St. Nicholas's Day.[2] And during the day Christ Church at Canterbury was burnt down. And Bishop Wulfwi died and is buried in his cathedral town of Dorchester. And Edric 'Cild'[3] and the Welsh became hostile, and fought against the garrison of the castle at Hereford, and inflicted many injuries upon them. And the king imposed a heavy tax on the wretched people, and nevertheless caused all that he overran to be ravaged. And then he went to Devonshire and besieged the city of Exeter for eighteen days, and there a large part of his army perished.[5] But he made fair promises to them, and fulfilled them badly; and they gave up the city to him because the thegns had betrayed them. And in the course of the summer, Prince Edgar went abroad with his mother Agatha and his two sisters, Margaret and Christina, and Mærleswegen[4] and many good men with them, and came to Scotland under the protection of King Malcolm, and he received them all. Then[6] the aforesaid King Malcolm began to desire his sister Margaret for his wife, but he and his men all opposed it for a long time; and she also refused, saying that she would have neither him nor any other if the heavenly mercy would graciously grant it to her to please in virginity with human heart the mighty Lord in pure continence through this short life. The king pressed her brother until he said "yes", and indeed he dared not do anything else, because they had come into his control. It then turned out as God had foreseen (otherwise it could not have happened) even as he himself says in his Gospel that not even a sparrow can fall

E

(1067) The king went overseas and took with him hostages and money and came back the next year on St. Nicholas's Day.[2] And that day Christ Church at Canterbury was burnt down. And he gave away every man's land when he came back. And that summer Prince Edgar went abroad, and Mærleswegen,[4] and many people with them, and went into Scotland. And King Malcolm received them all and married the prince's sister, Margaret.

[1] The chronology of the chronicles in respect of the events of 1067–1069 is very confused.
[2] 6 December 1067. [3] A mistake for Edric 'the Wild'. [4] A northern notable.
[5] This campaign took place in the spring of 1068.
[6] Here begins in verse an interpolation from a life of St. Margaret of Scotland. It appears to have been written after 1100, and it is peculiar to 'D'. The marriage between Malcolm and Margaret probably took place in 1070.

D E

into a trap without his providence. The Creator in his foreknowledge knew beforehand what he wished to do through her, because she was destined to increase the glory of God in the land, and set the king right from the path of error, and turn him to the better way, and his people as well, and put down the evil customs that this nation had practised, just as she afterwards did. Then the king received her, though it was against her will, and her behaviour pleased him, and he thanked God who by his power had given him such a consort; and he meditated wisely, like the very sensible man he was, and turned to God and despised every impurity. About this the apostle Paul, the teacher of all nations said, "*Salvabitur vir infidelis per mulierem fidelem sic et mulier fidelis per virum fidelem*", etc. - that is, in our language, "Very often the unbelieving husband is made holy and saved through the righteous wife, and likewise the wife through a believing husband".[1] The aforesaid queen afterwards performed many useful acts in that country to the glory of God, and she also prospered in the State even as was natural to her. She was descended from a believing and a noble family: her father was Prince Edward, son of King Edmund, son of Ethelred, son of Edgar, son of Edred[2] and so on in that royal race.[3] Her mother's family goes back to the emperor Henry who ruled over Rome.[4] And Gytha, Harold's mother, and many distinguished men's wives with her went out to Flatholm and stayed there for some time and so went from there overseas to St. Omer.[5] This Easter the king came to Winchester, and Easter was then on 23 March.[6] And soon after that the Lady

[1] I Corinthians vii. 14.

[2] This Edgar was in fact son of Edmund, Edred's brother.

[3] The insistence on the descent of Margaret from the West-Saxon royal line suggests that the interpolation was made after 1100, in which year Henry I married Margaret's daughter, Maud.

[4] End of the interpolation.

[5] These events probably belong to 1068.

[6] This adds to the chronological confusion of this annal, for it was in 1068 and not in 1067 that Easter fell on 23 March.

D

E

Maud came to this country and Archbishop Aldred consecrated her as queen at Westminster on Whit-Sunday.[1] Then the king was informed that the people in the north were gathered together and meant to make a stand against him if he came. He then went to Nottingham and built a castle there, and so went to York and there built two castles, and in Lincoln and everywhere in that district. And Earl Gospatric and the best men went to Scotland.[2] And in the meanwhile one of Harold's sons came unexpectedly from Ireland with a naval force into the mouth of the Avon, and ravaged all over that district. Then they went to Bristol and meant to take the city by storm but the citizens fought against them fiercely. And when they could not get anything out of the city they went to their ships with what they had won by fighting, and so went to Somerset and landed there. And Ednoth, the staller, fought against them and was killed there, and many good men on both sides. And those who survived went away.[3]

1068[4]

D

(1068) In this year King William gave Earl Robert the aldormanry of Northumberland; but the people of the country surrounded him in the city of Durham and killed him and nine hundred men with him.[5] And soon after that Prince Edgar came to York with all the Northumbrians and the citizens made peace with him. And King William came on them by surprise from the south with an

E

(1068) In this year King William gave Earl Robert the earldom of Northumberland. Then the local people came against him, and killed him and nine hundred men with him.[5] And Prince Edgar came then with all the Northumbrians to York, and the citizens made peace with him. And King William came from the south with all his army and ravaged the city, and killed many

[1] She was crowned on 11 May, which was Whit-Sunday in 1068

[2] These events belong to the summer of 1068.

[3] These events also belong to the summer of 1068.

[4] The chronology of this annal is very confused. Both 'D' and 'E' seem here to be using the Lady Day reckoning, but the arrangement is so haphazard that it is impossible to be certain.

[5] He was murdered 28 January 1069.

D

overwhelming army and routed them and killed those who could not escape, which was many hundreds of men, and ravaged the city, and made St. Peter's minster an object of scorn, and ravaged and humiliated all the others. And the prince went back to Scotland.[1]

E

hundreds of people. And the prince went back to Scotland.[1]

1069[2]

D

After[3] this Harold's sons came from Ireland at midsummer with sixty-four ships into the mouth of the Taw, and landed incautiously. And Count Brian[4] came against them by surprise with no little force and fought against them and killed all the best men who were in that fleet; and the others escaped with a small force to the ships. And Harold's sons went back to Ireland again. Now died Archbishop Aldred of York, and he is buried there in his cathedral city. He died on the day of SS. Protus and Hyacinthus.[6] He occupied the archiepiscopal see with great honour for ten years all but fifteen weeks. Soon after that three sons of King Sweyn came from Denmark with two hundred and forty ships into the Humber, together with Earl Osbeorn and Earl Thurkyl. And there came to meet them Prince Edgar and Earl Waltheof and Mærleswegen and Gospatric with the Northumbrians and all the people riding and marching with an immense army rejoicing exceedingly and so they all went resolutely to York, and stormed and razed the castle and captured an incalculable treasure in it and killed many hundreds of Frenchmen, and took many with them to the ships. And before the naval

E

(1069) In this year Bishop Ægelric of Peterborough had an accusation brought against him, and was sent to Westminster, and his brother Bishop Ægelwine was outlawed. Then between the two feasts of St. Mary[5] they came from the east from Denmark with three hundred ships –that is the sons of King Sweyn and his brother Earl Osbeorn. And then Earl Waltheof went out and he and Prince Edgar and many hundreds of men with them and they met the fleet in the Humber and went to York and landed and won the castles and killed many hundreds of men and took a large amount of treasure on board ship, and kept the chief men in bonds, and lay between the Ouse and the Trent all that winter. And King William went into the shire and ruined it completely. And in the same year died Brand, abbot of Peterborough, on 27 November.

[1] Early spring of 1069. [2] The chronology of this annal is very confused.

[3] 'D' omits to insert any figure for '1069' but seems to begin a new annal starting at Lady Day at this point.

[4] Brian, a count of Brittany. For the family, see C. T. Clay, *Early Yorkshire Charters*, vol. IV (1935), pp. 84 *et sqq.*

[5] *i.e.* between the Assumption and the Nativity–between 15 August and 8 September.

[6] 11 September.

D

men got there the Frenchmen had burned the city, and had also thoroughly ravaged and burnt the holy minster of St. Peter. When the king found out about this he went northwards with all his army that he could collect, and utterly ravaged and laid waste that shire. And the fleet lay all the winter in the Humber where the king could not get at them. And the king was in York on Christmas Day,[1] and so was in the country all the winter. And he came to Winchester that same Easter.[2] And Bishop Ægelric who was at Peterborough had an accusation brought against him, and was taken to Westminster, and his brother Bishop Ægelwine was outlawed.

E

1070

D

(1071) Earl Waltheof[3] made peace with the king. And in the following spring the king had all the monasteries that were in England plundered.[4] And this year there was great famine. And the monastery at Peterborough was plundered: by the men that Bishop Ægelric had excommunicated because there they had taken all that he had. And in the same summer, that fleet came into the Thames and lay there two nights, and then went on to Denmark. And Count Baldwin[6] died, and Arnulf, his son, succeeded him. And the king of the French and Earl William[7] were to be his protectors. But Robert[8] came there and killed Arnulf, his kinsman, and Earl William and routed the king, and killed many thousands of his men.[9]

E

(1070) Earl Waltheof made peace with the king. And in the following spring the king had all the monasteries that were in England plundered.[4] Then in the same year King Sweyn came from Denmark into the Humber and the local people came to meet him and made a truce with him–they expected that he was going to conquer the country. Then there came to Ely, Christian, the Danish bishop,[5] and Earl Osbeorn and the Danish housecarls with them, and the English people from all the Fenlands came to them and expected that they were going to conquer all the country. Then the monks of Peterborough heard it said that their own men meant to plunder the monastery–that was Hereward[10] and his following. That was because they heard it said that the king had given the abbacy to a French abbot called Turold,[11] and he was a very

[1] 1069. [2] 1070. [3] Son of Siward, earl of Northumbria. He held an earldom in the Midlands.
[4] Cf. below, pp. 152–153. [5] Bishop of Aarhus. [6] Baldwin VI, count of Flanders.
[7] William fitz Osbern. [8] Brother of Baldwin VI, and uncle of Arnulf.
[9] Battle of Cassel, 20 February 1071.
[10] Hereward 'the Wake' in respect of whom a general reference may be made to E. A. Freeman, *Norman Conquest*, vol. IV, pp. 455 *et sqq*.
[11] He had previously been a monk of Fécamp, but he came to Peterborough from Malmesbury where he had been abbot.

D

E

stern man, and had then come to Stamford with all his Frenchmen. There was then a sacristan called Yware; he took by night all he could–the Gospels, and chasubles, and copes and robes, and some such small things–whatever he could–and went at once before dawn to the abbot Turold, and told him he was seeking his protection, and informed him how the outlaws were alleged to be coming to the borough. He did all that according to the monks' advice. Then forthwith in the morning all the outlaws came with many ships, and wanted to enter the monastery, and the monks withstood them so that they could not get in. Then they set fire to it and burnt down all the monks' houses and all the town except one house. Then they got in by means of fire at Bolhithe Gate, and the monks came towards them and asked them for a truce, but they paid no attention, and went into the monastery, climbed up to the Holy Rood and took the crown off our Lord's head–all of pure gold–and then took the foot-rest that was underneath his foot, which was all of red gold. They climbed up to the steeple, brought down the crozier (?) that was hidden there–it was all of gold and silver–and took their two golden shrines and nine of silver and they took fifteen great crucifixes, both of gold and silver. They took so much gold and silver, and so many treasures in money and vestments and books that no man can reckon it up to another. They said they did it out of loyalty to the monastery. Then they went on board ship and proceeded to Ely, where they deposited all the treasure: the Danes expected that they were going to overcome the Frenchmen. Then all the monks were scattered and none remained there but one monk who was called 'Tall Leofwine': he was lying ill in the infirmary. Then came Abbot Turold and one hundred and sixty Frenchmen with him, and all

D E

fully armed. When he arrived he found everything burnt inside and out except the church. The outlaws were then all afloat–they knew he would be bound to come there. This was done on 2 June. The two kings, William and Sweyn, came to an agreement. Then the Danes proceeded out of Ely with all the abovementioned treasure, and took it with them. When they were in the middle of the sea there came a great storm, and scattered all the ships carrying the treasure–some went to Norway, some to Ireland, some to Denmark and all that they got there was the crozier and some shrines and some crosses and much of the other treasure, and they brought it to a royal town called ,[1] and then put it all in the church. Then afterwards through their carelessness and drunkenness the church was burnt one night with everything that was in it. Thus was the monastery of Peterborough burnt down and plundered. Almighty God have pity on it through his great mercy! And thus Abbot Turold came to Peterborough, and the monks came back, and performed the service of Christ in the church that had stood a whole week without any kind of service. When Bishop Ægelric heard tell about it, he excommunicated all the men who had done this wicked deed. There was a great famine in the course of the year. And the following summer the fleet came from the north from the Humber into the Thames, and lay there two nights, and then held on this course to Denmark. And Count Baldwin died, and his son, Arnulf, succeeded him, and Earl William was to be his protector, and the king of the French also. And then came Count Robert and killed his kinsman Arnulf and routed the earl and the king, and killed many thousands of his men.

[1] A gap in the MS.

1071

D

(1072)[1] Earl Edwin and Earl Morcar fled away and travelled aimlessly in woods and moors until Edwin was killed by his own men, and Morcar went to Ely by ship. And Bishop Ægelwine and Siward Bearn came there, and many hundred men with them. But when King William found out about this, he called out a naval force and a land force and invested that part of the country from outside and made a bridge and placed a naval force on the seaward side. And they then all surrendered to the king, that is to say Bishop Ægelwine and Earl Morcar and all who were with them except for Hereward and those who could escape with him, and he led them out valiantly. And the king took their ships and weapons and plenty of money and he took all the men prisoner and did as he pleased with them: Bishop Ægelwine he sent to Abingdon and there he died.

E

(1071) Earl Edwin and Earl Morcar fled and travelled aimlessly in woods and moors. Then Earl Morcar went to Ely in a ship, and Earl Edwin was killed treacherously by his own men. And Bishop Ægelwine and Siward Bearn came to Ely and many hundred men with them. And when King William heard about this, he called out a naval force and a land force, and invested that part of the country from outside and made a bridge and went in and placed the naval force on the seaward side. And the outlaws then all surrendered to the king, that is to say Bishop Ægelwine and Earl Morcar and all who were with them except Hereward and those who wished to go with him, and he led them out valiantly. And the king took their ships and weapons and plenty of money, and did as he pleased with the men: Bishop Ægelwine he sent to Abingdon and there he died soon after in the course of the winter.

1072

D

(1073)[2] King William led a naval force and a land force to Scotland, and blockaded that country from the sea with ships. And he went himself with his land force in over the Forth, and there he found nothing that they were any the better for. And King Malcolm came and made peace with King William and was his vassal and gave him hostages, and afterwards went home, with all his force.[3] And Bishop Ægelric died: he was consecrated bishop of York, but it was taken from him unjustly, and he was given the bishopric of Durham and he held it as long as he

E

(1072) King William led a naval force and a land force to Scotland and blockaded that country from the sea with ships. And he led his land force in at the Forth, and there he found nothing that he was any the better for. And the king Malcolm came and made peace with King William and gave hostages and was his vassal, and the king went home with all his force.[3] And Bishop Ægelric died: he was consecrated bishop of York, but it was taken from him unjustly, and he was given the bishopric of Durham, and he held it as long as he wished, and he relinquished it

[1] 'D' omits the figure '1071' and so becomes a year in advance of the true reckoning.

[2] 'D' remains a year in advance of the true reckoning.

[3] This refers to the so-called pact of Abernethy concerning which there has been much dispute. See, for example, W. F. Skene, *Celtic Scotland* (1870), vol. 1, pp. 423 *et sqq*.

D

wished, and he relinquished it later and went to St. Peter's monastery at Peterborough and lived there for twelve years. Then after William conquered England, he had him taken from Peterborough and sent him to Westminster. He died there on 15 October and is buried there in St. Nicholas's Porch.

E

later, and went to St. Peter's monastery at Peterborough and lived there as a monk for twelve years. Then after King William had conquered England, he took him from Peterborough and sent him to Westminster. He died there on 15 October and is buried in that church in St. Nicholas's Porch.

1073

D

(1074)[1] In this year King William led an English and French force overseas, and conquered the country of Maine: and the English damaged it severely: they destroyed vineyards and burned down cities, and damaged the country severely, and made all the country surrender to the king. And afterwards they went home.

E

(1073) In this year King William led an English and French force overseas and conquered the country of Maine: and the English damaged it severely: they destroyed vineyards and burned down cities, and damaged the country severely, and made all the country surrender to the king. And afterwards they went home to England.

1074

D

(1075)[1] In this year King William went overseas to Normandy. And Prince Edgar came from Flanders into Scotland on St. Grimbald's Day.[2] And[3] King Malcolm and Edgar's sister, Margaret, received him with great honour. At the same time the king of France, Philip, sent a missive to him and ordered him to come to him saying he would give him the castle of Montreuil so that he could do daily harm to those who were not his friends. So now King Malcolm and Edgar's sister, Margaret, gave him and all his men great gifts and many treasures consisting of skins covered with purple cloth, and robes of marten's skin, and of grey fur, and

E

(1074) In this year King William went overseas to Normandy. And Prince Edgar came from Scotland to Normandy, and the king reversed his outlawry and that of all his men. And he was in the king's court and received such dues as the king granted him.[4]

[1] 'D' remains a year in advance of the true chronology.
[2] 8 July.
[3] What follows appears to be another interpolation connected with Scotland.
[4] Edgar survived to about 1125.

D

E

ermine, and costly robes and golden vessels and silver and led him and all his naval force out of his jurisdiction with great honour. But on the journey it turned out badly for them when they were out at sea, in that they met rough sailing weather, and the raging sea and the strong wind cast them ashore so that all their ships foundered and they themselves got to land with difficulty and their treasure was nearly all lost. And some of his men were captured by the French, but he and his fittest men went back to Scotland, some walking miserably on foot, and some riding wretchedly. Then King Malcolm advised him to send overseas to King William and ask for his protection, and he did so; and the king granted it to him and sent for him. And again King Malcolm and Edgar's sister gave him and all his men immense treasure, and again very honourably sent him out of their jurisdiction. And the sheriff of York came to meet them at Durham and went all the way with them and had them provided with food and fodder at every castle they came to, until they got overseas to the king. And King William received him with great honour and he stayed there at court and received such dues as were appointed him.

1075

D

(1076)[1] In this year King William gave Earl Ralph[2] the daughter of William fitz Osbern.[3] This same Ralph was Breton on his mother's side, and Ralph his father was English, being born in Norfolk, and the king therefore gave the earldom there

E

(1075) In this year King William gave Earl Ralph[2] the daughter of William fitz Osbern.[3] This same Ralph was Breton on his mother's side, and his father named Ralph was English and was born in Norfolk. Then the king gave his son the

[1] 'D' remains a year in advance of the true chronology.

[2] Ralph 'Guader', earl of Norfolk, lord of Gael in Brittany. For the family, see *Complete Peerage*, vol. IX, pp. 568 *et sqq*.

[3] Emma.

D

and in Suffolk as well to his son. He [Ralph] took the lady to Norwich.[1]

There was that bride-ale
That was many men's bale.

Earl Roger[2] was there and Earl Waltheof[3] and bishops and abbots, and there they plotted to drive their royal lord out of his kingdom. And the king in Normandy was very soon informed about this. Earl Ralph and Earl Roger were the ringleaders in this foolish plot; and they lured the Bretons to their side; and they also sent to Denmark for a naval force. And Roger went west to his earldom[4] and assembled the people for the king's undoing, as he thought, but it turned out to his own great harm. Ralph also wanted to go forward with the men of his earldom, but the castle garrisons which were in England and all the local people came against them and prevented them all from doing anything. On the contrary he was glad to escape to the ships. And his wife remained behind in the castle and held it until she was given safe-conduct, and then she went out of England, and all her men who wished to go with her. And the king afterwards came to England, and captured Earl Roger, his kinsman, and put him in prison. And Earl Waltheof went overseas and accused himself and asked for pardon and offered treasure. But the king made light of it until he came to England and then had him captured. And soon after this two hundred ships came from Denmark, and the commanders aboard were Cnut, son of King Sweyn, and Earl Hakon. And they dared not fight with King William but went to York and destroyed St. Peter's Minster and captured a large amount of property there and so departed. But all who took part in this died–that is to say the son of

E

earldom of Norfolk and Suffolk. Then he took the lady to Norwich.[1]

There was that bride-ale
–Many men's bale.

Earl Roger[2] was there and Earl Waltheof[3] and bishops and abbots, and there they plotted to expel the king from the realm of England. And soon the king in Normandy was informed about this, how it was planned. It was Earl Roger and Earl Ralph who were the ringleaders in this foolish plot; and they lured the Bretons to their side; and also sent east to Denmark for a naval force to help them. And Roger went west to his earldom and assembled his people for the king's undoing, but he was prevented. And Ralph also in his earldom wanted to go forward with his people, but the castle garrisons which were in England and also the local people came against him, and brought it about that he did nothing, but on the contrary went on board ship at Norwich. And his wife was in the castle, and held it until she was given safe-conduct; and then she went out of England and all her men who wished to go with her. And the king afterwards came to England and seized Earl Roger, his kinsman, and put him in prison, and he seized Earl Waltheof as well. And soon after that two hundred ships came from the east from Denmark, and there were two commanders on board, Cnut, son of Sweyn, and Earl Hakon. And they dared not fight with King William but proceeded overseas to Flanders. And the Lady Edith died at Winchester a week before Christmas, and the king had her brought to Westminster with great honour, and laid her near King Edward her husband. And the king was at Westminster that Christmas and all the Bretons who were at the

[1] 'Florence of Worcester' says the marriage feast was held at Exning then in Suffolk, now in Cambridgeshire.

[2] Roger of Breteuil, second son of William fitz Osbern by his first wife and thus brother of the bride. He succeeded his father as earl of Hereford in 1071.

[3] Son of Siward, earl of Northumbria.

[4] Hereford.

D

Earl Hakon and many others. And the Lady Edith who was King Edward's widow died at Winchester a week before Christmas, and the king had her brought to Westminster with great honour and had her laid near King Edward her husband. The king was that Christmas at Westminster; there all the Bretons who were at the marriage feast were sentenced.

Some of them were blinded
And some banished from the land
And some were put to shame
Thus were the traitors to the king
Brought low.

E

wedding feast at Norwich were destroyed.

Some of them were blinded
And some driven from the land
So were the traitors to William
Brought low.

1076

D

(1077)[1] In this year Sweyn, king of Denmark, died, and Harold, his son, succeeded to his realm. King William gave the abbacy at Westminster to Abbot Vitalis who had been a monk at Bernay. And Earl Waltheof was beheaded at Winchester on St. Petronella's Day;[2] and his body was taken to Crowland; and he is buried there. And King William went overseas and led a force to Brittany and besieged the castle at Dol; but the Bretons held it until the king came from France, and then King William went away and lost there both men and horses and incalculable treasure.

E

(1076) In this year Sweyn, king of Denmark, died, and Harold, his son, succeeded to the realm. And the king gave Westminster to Abbot Vitalis who had been abbot of Bernay. And Earl Waltheof was beheaded at Winchester and his body was taken to Crowland. And the king went overseas and led his force to Brittany and besieged the castle at Dol; and the Bretons held it until the king came from France, and William went away and lost there both men and horses and much of his treasure.

1077 and 1078[3]

D

(1078)[3] This year the moon was eclipsed three nights before Candlemas. And Ægelwig, the abbot of Evesham, who was skilled in secular affairs, died on St. Juliana's Day,[4] and Walter was appointed abbot in his place. And Bishop Hereman

E

(1077)[3] In this year the king of the French and William, king of England, came to an agreement, but it held good for only a little while. And in the course of the year London was burned down one night before the Assumption

[1] 'D' remains a year in advance of the true chronology. [2] 31 May.

[3] The chronology is here very confused and it seems possible that two annals have been conflated. The agreement between William and the French king, and the fire at London belong to 1077; the other events recorded to 1078. There was an eclipse of the moon on 30 January 1078. [4] 16 February.

D

died who was bishop in Berkshire and Wiltshire and Dorset. And King Malcolm captured the mother of Mælshæht[2] . . .[3] and all his best men and all his treasure and his cattle; and he himself escaped with difficulty. . . .[5] And this year there was the dry summer; and spreading fire came upon many shires and burned down many villages; and also many towns were burned down.

E

of St. Mary[1] worse than ever it had been since it was founded. And in this year died Ægelwig, abbot of Evesham, on 16 February. And Bishop Hereman also died on 20 February.[4]

1079

D

(1079)[6] Robert, son of King William, deserted from his father to his uncle, Robert, in Flanders[7] because his father would not let him rule his county in Normandy which he himself and King Philip with his consent also had given him; and the chief men in that county had sworn oaths to him and accepted him as liege lord. Robert fought against his father and wounded him in the hand; and his horse was shot under him; and the man who brought him another horse was shot from a cross-bow; his name was Tokig, son of Wiggod;[10] and many were killed there and captured; and Robert came back to Flanders; nor will we write more of the harm he inflicted on his father. . . .[11]

E

(1079)[6] In this same year King Malcolm came from Scotland into England between the two feasts of St. Mary[8] with a great army, and ravaged Northumberland as far as the Tyne, and killed many hundreds of people, and took home much money and treasure and people in captivity. And in the same year King William fought against his son, Robert, outside Normandy near a castle called Gerberoi,[9] and King William was wounded there, and the horse he rode was killed, and William, his son, was wounded there, and many men were killed.

1080

E

In this year Bishop Walcher of Durham was killed at a meeting, and a hundred men with him, French and Flemish. And he himself was born a Lotharingian.[12] The Northumbrians did this in the month of May.[13]

[1] 14 August. [2] Moymaer of Moray. [3] One line missing. [4] 1078. [5] Six lines missing.

[6] 'E' having given many events of 1078 in his annal for 1077 now omits the figure '1078' and comes into harmony with 'D'. Both annalists are now correct.

[7] Maud, wife of William the Conquerer, was sister to Count Robert of Flanders.

[8] Between 15 August and 8 September. [9] MS.: "Gerborneo".

[10] Probably the son of Wigod of Wallingford who is mentioned frequently in Domesday Book.

[11] This is the end of chronicle 'D'. Henceforth 'E' is the sole remaining chronicle.

[12] He came from Liège, and had become bishop of Durham. [13] 13 or 14 May.

1081

E

This year the king led an army into Wales and there liberated many hundreds of men.

1082

E

The king seized Bishop Odo.[1] And there was a great famine.

1083

E

(1083) In this year arose the discord at Glastonbury between the abbot Thurstan[2] and his monks. In the first instance, it came of the abbot's lack of wisdom in misgoverning the monks in many matters, and the monks complained of it to him in a kindly way and asked him to rule them justly and to love them, and they would be loyal and obedient to him. But the abbot would do nothing of the sort,[3] but gave them bad treatment and threatened them with worse. One day the abbot went into the chapter and spoke against them and wanted to ill-treat them, and then sent for some laymen,[4] and they came into the chapter, and fell upon the monks fully armed. And then the monks were very much afraid of them, and did not know what they had better do. But they scattered: some ran into the church and locked the doors on themselves–and they went after them into the monastery and meant to drag them out when they dared not go out. But a grievous thing happened that day–the Frenchmen[4] broke into the choir and threw missiles towards the altar where the monks were, and some of the retainers went up to the upper story and shot arrows down towards the shrine, so that many arrows stuck in the cross that stood above the altar: and the wretched monks were lying round about the altar, and some crept under it, and cried to God zealously, asking for his mercy when they could get no mercy from men. What can we say, except that they shot fiercely, and the others broke down the doors there, and went in and killed some of the monks and wounded many there in the church, so that the blood came from the altar on to the steps, and from the steps on to the floor. Three were killed there and eighteen wounded. And in the same year died Maud, William's queen, the day after All Saints' Day.[5] And in this same year, after Christmas, the king had a great and heavy tax ordered all over England–it was 72*d.* for every hide.[6]

1084

E

(1084) In this year died Wulfwold, abbot of Chertsey, on 19 April.

[1] See below, p. 288.

[2] He had been a monk of Caen.

[3] The dispute concerned chanting and the celebration of Saints' Days.

[4] Household knights.

[5] 2 November.

[6] The *Inquisitio Geldi* (see R. W. Eyton, *Domesday Studies: an analysis and digest of the Somerset Survey*, 2 vols., 1880) was an account of this levy. The inquisition was made in the early months of 1084, and 'E' is perhaps here using the Lady Day reckoning.

1085

E

(1085) In this year[1] people said and declared for a fact, that Cnut, king of Denmark, son of King Sweyn, was setting out in this direction and meant to conquer this country with the help of Robert, count of Flanders, because Cnut was married to Robert's daughter. When William, king of England, who was then in Normandy –for he was in possession of both England and Normandy–found out about this, he went to England with a larger force of mounted men and infantry from France and Brittany than had ever come to this country, so that people wondered how this country could maintain all that army. And the king had all the army dispersed all over the country among his vassals, and they provisioned the army each in proportion to his land. And people had much oppression that year, and the king had the land near the sea laid waste, so that if his enemies landed, they should have nothing to seize on so quickly. But when the king found out for a fact that his enemies had been hindered and could not carry out their expedition–then he let some of the army go to their own country, and some he kept in this country over winter.

Then at Christmas,[2] the king was at Gloucester with his council, and held his court there for five days, and then the archbishop and clerics had a synod for three days. There Maurice was elected bishop of London, and William for Norfolk and Robert for Cheshire–they were all the king's clerics.

After this, the king had much thought and very deep discussion with his council about this country–how it was occupied or with what sort of people. Then he sent his men[3] over all England into every shire and had them find out how many hundred hides there were in the shire, or what land and cattle the king himself had in the country, or what dues he ought to have in twelve months from the shire. Also he had a record made of how much land his archbishops had, and his bishops and his abbots and his earls–and though I relate it at too great length–what or how much everybody had who was occupying land in England, in land or cattle, and how much money it was worth. So very narrowly did he have it investigated, that there was no single hide nor a yard of land, nor indeed (it is a shame to relate but it seemed no shame to him to do) one ox nor one cow nor one pig was there left out, and not put down in his record: and all these records were brought to him afterwards.

1086

E

(1085)[4] The king wore his crown and held his court at Winchester for Easter, and travelled so as to be at Westminster for Whitsuntide and there dubbed his son, Henry, a knight. Then he travelled about so as to come to Salisbury at Lammas:[5] and there his councillors came to him, and all the people occupying land who were of any

[1] A very important annal. On the mutual relationship of the events described in it and in the next annal, see D.C. Douglas, *Domesday Monachorum of Christ Church, Canterbury* (1944), pp. 26–27.

[2] Christmas, 1085.

[3] The inquisition which resulted in Domesday Book. See also Nos. 198–204.

[4] 'E' by repeating the figure '1085' falls a year behind the true chronology. This discrepancy will last until 1089.

[5] 1 August.

E

account over all England, whosoever's vassals they might be; and they all submitted to him and became his vassals, and swore oaths of allegiance to him, that they would be loyal to him against all other men.[1] From there he went into the Isle of Wight, because he meant to go to Normandy. But all the same he first acted according to his custom, that is to say he obtained a very great amount of money from his men where he had any pretext for it either justly or otherwise. He afterwards went into Normandy. And Prince Edgar, Edward's kinsman, left him because he did not have much honour from him, but may Almighty God grant him honour in the future. And Christina, the prince's sister, sought refuge in the convent at Romsey and took the veil.

And in the course of the same year, it was a very severe year, and a very laborious and sorrowful year in England, in cattle plague: and corn and crops were checked, and there was such great misfortune with the weather as cannot easily be conceived – there were such big thunderstorms, and such lightning so that many people were killed and it kept on getting worse and worse among the people, more and more so. May God Almighty make things better when it is his will.

1087

E

(1086)[2] A thousand and eighty-seven years after the birth of our Lord Jesus Christ, in the twenty-first year since William ruled and governed England as God had granted him, it became a very severe and pestilential year in this country. Such a disease came on people that very nearly every other person was in high fever – and that so severely that many people died of the disease. Afterwards because of the great storms that came as we described them above, there came so great a famine over all England that many hundreds of people died a miserable death because of the famine. Alas, how miserable and pitiable a time it was then. Then the wretched people lay driven very nearly to death, and afterwards there came the sharp famine and destroyed them utterly. Who cannot pity such a time? Or who is so hard-hearted that he cannot weep for such misfortune? But such things happen because of the people's sins, in that they will not love God and righteousness. So it was in those days, there was little righteousness in this country in anyone, except in monks alone where they behaved well. The king and the chief men loved gain much and over-much – gold and silver – and did not care how sinfully it was obtained provided it came to them. The king sold his land on very hard terms – as hard as he could. Then came somebody else, and offered more than the other had given, and the king let it go to the man who had offered him more. Then came the third, and offered still more, and the king gave it into the hands of the man who offered him most of all, and did not care how sinfully the reeves had got it from poor men, nor how many unlawful things they did. But the more just laws were talked about, the more unlawful things were done. They imposed unjust tolls and did many other injustices which are hard to reckon up.

[1] The 'Oath of Salisbury' about which there has been much discussion. The reader may be particularly referred to F. M. Stenton, *English Feudalism* (1932), pp. 111–113.

[2] 'E' remains a year behind the true chronology but corrects this in the text.

E

Also, in the same year before autumn, the holy minster of St. Paul, the cathedral church of London, was burnt down, and many other churches, and the largest and noblest part of all the city. Similarly, also, at the same time nearly every chief town in all England was burnt down. Alas, a miserable and lamentable time was this year that brought so many misfortunes into being.

Also, in the same year before the Assumption of St. Mary,[1] King William went from Normandy into France with an army and made war on his own liege lord King Philip, and killed a large part of his men and burnt down the city of Mantes, and all the holy churches that were in the city; and two holy men, who worshipped God living in an anchorite's cell, were burnt to death.

This having been thus done, King William turned back to Normandy. A miserable thing he did, and more miserable was his fate. How more miserable? He fell ill, and he was severely afflicted by it. What account can I give? That fierce death, which leaves alone neither powerful men nor mean, seized him. He died in Normandy on the day after the Nativity of St. Mary,[2] and he was buried at Caen in St. Stephen's monastery: he had built it, and afterwards had endowed it richly.

Alas, how deceitful and untrustworthy is this world's prosperity. He who had been a powerful king and lord of many a land, had then of all the land only a seven-foot measure and he who was once clad in gold and gems, lay then covered with earth. He left behind him three sons. The oldest was called Robert, who was count of Normandy after him, the second was called William, who wore the crown after him in England. The third was called Henry, and his father bequeathed to him incalculable treasure.[3]

If anyone wishes to know what sort of a man he was, or what dignity he had or of how many lands he was lord–then we will write of him even as we, who have looked upon him, and once lived at his court, have perceived him to be.

This King William of whom we speak was a very wise man,[4] and very powerful and more worshipful and stronger than any predecessor of his had been. He was gentle to the good men who loved God, and stern beyond all measure to those people who resisted his will. In the same place where God permitted him to conquer England, he set up a famous monastery and appointed monks for it,[5] and endowed it well. In his days the famous church at Canterbury was built,[6] and also many another over all England. Also, this country was very full of monks and they lived their life under the rule of St. Benedict, and Christianity was such in his day that each man who wished followed out whatever concerned his order. Also, he was very dignified: three times every year he wore his crown, as often as he was in England. At Easter he wore it at Winchester, at Whitsuntide at Westminster, and at Christmas at Gloucester, and then there were with him all the powerful men over all England, archbishops and bishops, abbots and earls, thegns and knights. Also, he was a very stern and violent man, so that no one dared do anything contrary to his will. He had earls in his fetters, who acted against his will. He expelled bishops from their sees, and abbots from their abbacies, and put thegns in prison, and finally he did not spare his

[1] 15 August. [2] 9 September. [3] See below, p. 287.

[4] The remarkable account which follows was clearly written by a man who had attended William's court. It should be compared with the description given below in Nos. 6 and 7.

[5] Battle Abbey. [6] Lanfranc's rebuilding of Christ Church, Canterbury, is meant.

E

own brother, who was called Odo; he was a very powerful bishop in Normandy (his cathedral church was at Bayeux)–and was the foremost man next the king, and had an earldom in England. And when the king was in Normandy, then he was master in this country:[1] and he [the king] put *him* in prison. Amongst other things the good security he made in this country is not to be forgotten–so that any honest man could travel over his kingdom without injury with his bosom full of gold: and no one dared strike[2] another, however much wrong he had done him. And if any man had intercourse with a woman against her will, he was forthwith castrated.

He ruled over England, and by his cunning it was so investigated that there was not one hide of land in England that he did not know who owned it, and what it was worth, and then set it down in his record.[3] Wales was in his power, and he built castles there, and he entirely controlled that race. In the same way, he also subdued Scotland to himself, because of his great strength. The land of Normandy was his by natural inheritance, and he ruled over the county called Maine: and if he could have lived two years more, he would have conquered Ireland by his prudence and without any weapons. Certainly in his time people had much oppression and very many injuries:

He had castles built
And poor men hard oppressed.
The king was so very stark
And deprived his underlings of many a mark
Of gold and more hundreds of pounds of silver,
That he took by weight and with great injustice
From his people with little need for such a deed.
Into avarice did he fall
And loved greediness above all,
He made great protection for the game
And imposed laws for the same.
That who so slew hart or hind
Should be made blind.

He preserved the harts and boars
And loved the stags as much
As if he were their father.
Moreover, for the hare did he decree that they should go free.
Powerful men complained of it and poor men lamented it
But so fierce was he that he cared not for the rancour of them all
But they had to follow out the king's will entirely
If they wished to live or hold their land,
Property or estate, or his favour great,
Alas! woe, that any man so proud should go,
And exalt himself and reckon himself above all men,
May Almighty God show mercy to his soul
And grant unto him forgiveness for his sins.

[1] See above, p. 146. [2] Or "kill". [3] Domesday Book.

E

These things we have written about him, both good and bad, that good men may imitate their good points, and entirely avoid the bad, and travel on the road that leads us to the kingdom of heaven.

We can write many things that happened in the same year. The state of affairs in Denmark was such that the Danes who had been reckoned the most trustworthy of nations became perverted to the greatest untrustworthiness, and the greatest treachery that could ever happen. They chose King Cnut and submitted to him and swore oaths to him, and then basely killed him in a church.[1] Also it happened in Spain that the heathens went and made war upon the Christians and forced much into their power. But the Christian king, who was called Alfonso,[2] sent everywhere into every country and asked for help, and help came to him from every country that was Christian, and they marched and killed and drove off all the heathen people, and conquered their land again through the help of God.

Also in this country in the same year there died many powerful men–Stigand, bishop of Chichester,[3] and the abbot of St. Augustine's,[4] and the abbot of Bath,[5] and that of Pershore:[6] and the liege lord of them all, William, king of England, of whom we spoke before. After his death, his son, called William like his father, succeeded to the realm and was consecrated king by Archbishop Lanfranc at Westminster, three days before Michaelmas day, and all the men in England submitted and swore oaths to him. This having been thus done, the king went to Winchester and scrutinized the Treasury and the treasure that his father had accumulated: it was impossible for anyone to describe how much was accumulated there in gold and silver and vessels and costly robes and jewels, and many other precious things that are hard to recount. The king did as his father told him before he died–gave a part of the treasure for his father's soul to each minster that there was in England–to some minsters 10 marks of gold, to some 6 –and to each country church *60d.* and into every shire were sent 100 pounds of money to be distributed among poor men for his soul: and before he died, he ordered that all the people under his jurisdiction who were in captivity should be set free. And the king was in London at Christmas.

1088

E

(1087)[7] In this year this country was very much disturbed, and filled with great treachery, so that the most powerful Frenchmen who were in this country intended to betray their lord the king and to have as king his brother, Robert, who was count of Normandy. At the head of this plot was Bishop Odo,[8] with Bishop Geoffrey[9] and William,[10] bishop of Durham. The king treated the bishop so well that all England

[1] He was murdered in the summer of 1086.

[2] Alfonso VI of Castile was a great opponent of the Moors in Spain, but the knowledge possessed by the chronicler of his activities seems to be very limited.

[3] He transferred the see of Selsey to Chichester. He should not be confused with the archbishop of the same name.

[4] Scotland. [5] Ælfsige. [6] Thurstan. [7] 'E' remains a year behind the true chronology.

[8] Bishop of Bayeux. [9] Bishop of Coutances: a very large landowner in England.

[10] William of St. Calais. For his trial as a result of these events, see below, No. 84.

E

went by his counsel and did exactly as he wished; and he thought to treat him just as Judas Iscariot did our Lord: and Earl Roger[1] was also in this foolish plot, and a very great number of people with them, all Frenchmen, and this foolish plot was plotted during Lent. As soon as Easter was reached, they marched and ravaged and burned and laid waste the king's demesnes and they ruined the lands of all those men who were in allegiance to the king. And each of them went to his castle and manned it and provisioned it as best he could. Bishop Geoffrey and Robert of Montbrai[2] went to Bristol and carried the plunder to the castle, and then went out of the castle and ravaged Bath, and all the surrounding area, and laid waste all the district of Berkeley. Those who were the chief men of Hereford, and all that shire with them, and the men of Shropshire, with a large force from Wales came and ravaged and burned in Worcestershire until they came to Worcester itself, and intended to burn the town and plunder the monastery, and get the king's castle by force into their hands. Seeing these things, the reverend bishop of Worcester, Wulfstan, was much distressed in mind because the castle had been committed to him to hold; nevertheless, the members of his household marched out, with a few men, from the castle and through God's mercy and the bishop's merits, killed and captured five hundred men and routed all the rest. The bishop of Durham did whatever damage he could everywhere to the north. One of them was called Roger,[3] who threw himself into the castle of Norwich and did always the worst of all throughout all the country. There was also one Hugh[4] who did not mend matters at all, neither in Leicestershire nor Northampton. Bishop Odo, with whom all these affairs originated, went to Kent to his earldom, and injured it severely and utterly laid waste the king's land and the archbishop's and carried all the goods into his castle at Rochester.

When the king understood all these matters, and what treachery they were committing against him, he grew much disturbed in mind. Then he sent for Englishmen and explained his need to them and asked for their help, and promised them the best law that there had ever been in this country, and forbade every unjust tax and granted people their woods and hunting rights–but it did not last any time. But, nevertheless, the Englishmen came to the help of their liege lord the king. They marched towards Rochester, and intended to capture Bishop Odo–they thought that if they had the one who had been the head of the plot they could the better get hold of all the rest. Then they came to the castle at Tonbridge: Odo's soldiers were then in the castle, and many others who meant to support him against the king. But the Englishmen proceeded and stormed the castle, and the men who were in it made truce with the king. The king, with his army, marched towards Rochester, and they thought the bishop was there, but it became known to the king that the bishop was gone to the castle at Pevensey. And the king went in pursuit with his army, and besieged the castle with a very large army for a full six weeks. Meanwhile, the count of Normandy, Robert, the king's brother, collected a very large force and thought to conquer England with the help of the men who were opposed to the king in this

[1] Roger of Montgomery, earl of Shrewsbury. [2] The English form of the name is Mowbray.
[3] Roger Bigot, a large landowner in Norfolk at the time of Domesday Book.
[4] Hugh of Grantmesnil, an independent landowner in Domesday Book, lord of Leicester.

E

country. And he sent some of his men to this country and meant to follow himself. But the English, who guarded the sea, captured some of the men, and killed and drowned more than anyone could count. Afterwards, their food failed in the castle; then they asked for a truce and rendered it up to the king, and the bishop swore he would go out of England and never more come into this country unless the king sent for him, and that he would render up the castle at Rochester. Just as the bishop went and was to render up the castle, and as the king sent his men with him, then the men who were in the castle rose up and seized the bishop and the king's men and put them in prison. In the castle were very good knights–Eustace the Young,[1] and Earl Roger's three sons[2] and all the highest-born men in this country or in Normandy.

When the king understood these matters, he followed with the army that he had there, and sent over all England and ordered that everyone who was not a scoundrel should come to him, French and English, from town and country. Then a great company came to him and went to Rochester and besieged the castle until those inside made a truce and rendered up the castle. Bishop Odo, with the men who were in the castle, went overseas, and the bishop relinquished the dignity that he had in this country.[3]

Then the king sent an army to Durham and had siege laid to the castle: and the bishop made a truce and rendered up the castle, and relinquished his bishopric and went to Normandy. Also, many Frenchmen relinquished their lands and went overseas, and the king gave their lands to the men who were loyal to him.

1089

E

(1089)[4] In this year, the reverend father and consoler of monks, Archbishop Lanfranc, departed this life:[5] but we are confident that he went to the heavenly kingdom. Also, there was a great earthquake over all England on 11 August, and it was a very late year for corn and every kind of crop, so that many people were reaping their corn round about Martinmas[6] and still later.

1090

E

Thirteenth Indiction.[7] (1090) Things having proceeded, even as we have described above concerning the king and his brother and his vassals, the king was considering how he could take vengeance on his brother, Robert, and do most injury to him, and wrest Normandy from him by force. However, by his prudence, or by treasure, he got hold of the castle at St. Valery, and the harbour, and in the same way he got the one at Aumale, and put his retainers into it, and they did injuries to the country in ravaging

[1] Eustace III, count of Boulogne, son of the Eustace who opposed Godwine in 1051.
[2] Robert of Bellême, Hugh and Roger, sons of Roger of Montgomery. See Table 13.
[3] The earldom of Kent.
[4] 'E' by omitting the figure '1088' altogether comes back to the true chronology.
[5] Lanfranc died 24 May. [6] 11 November. [7] Correct.

E

and burning. After this, he got hold of more castles in the country, and placed his knights in them. After the count of Normandy had perceived that his sworn vassals had betrayed him, and rendered up their castles to his detriment, he sent to his liege lord Philip, king of the French, and he came to Normandy with a large army and the king and the count with an immense force besieged the castle in which the king of England's men were. King William of England sent to Philip, king of the French, and he, either for love of him, or for his great treasure, left his vassal Count Robert[1] and his country, and went back to France and so let them be: and in the course of these proceedings, this country was severely injured by unjust taxes and many other misfortunes.

1091

E

(1091)[2] In this year King William held his court at Christmas[3] at Westminster, and afterwards, at Candlemas,[4] he went for his brother's undoing out of England into Normandy. While he was there, an agreement was reached between them, on the condition that the count handed over Fécamp and the county of Eu, and Cherbourg. And in addition to this, the king's men were to be unmolested in the castles which they had taken against the count's will. And the king promised him in return to reduce to obedience Maine which his father had conquered, which had then revolted from the count, and all that his father had beyond it except what he had granted to the king, and that all those in England who had lost their land for the count's sake were to have it by this agreement, and the count was to have all as much in England as was in their agreement. And if the count died without a son born in lawful wedlock, the king was to be heir to all Normandy. By this same agreement, if the king died, the count was to be heir to all England. Twelve of the best men on the king's side and twelve on the count's swore to this agreement though it lasted only a little while after.

During the course of this reconciliation, Prince Edgar[5] was deprived of his lands – of those that the count had handed over to him – and went from Normandy to Scotland to the king his brother-in-law, and to his sister. While King William was out of England, King Malcolm came from Scotland into England and ravaged a great part of it until the good men who guarded this country sent an army against him and turned him back. When King William heard of this in Normandy, he prepared for his journey and came to England, and his brother, Count Robert, with him, and forthwith ordered an army to be called out, both a naval force and a land force; but nearly all the naval force perished miserably before he could reach Scotland, a few days before Michaelmas. And the king and his brother went with the land force, but when King Malcolm heard that an attack by an army was going to be made upon him, he went with his army out of Scotland into the Lothians in England and stayed there. When King William approached with his army, Count Robert and Prince

[1] Robert, duke of Normandy, son of William I.

[2] Here starts the practice of beginning the annal with the Christmas court of the preceding year.

[3] Christmas, 1090. [4] 2 February 1091. [5] Edgar Atheling.

E

Edgar acted as intermediaries and so made an agreement between the kings, so that King Malcolm came to our king and became his vassal to the extent of such allegiance as he had done to his father,[1] and confirmed it with an oath: and King William promised him in land and in everything what he had had under his father.

In this reconciliation, Prince Edgar also was brought into agreement with the king: and the kings separated in great accord, but it lasted only a little while. And Count Robert stayed here with the king till nearly Christmas, and found little to rely on in their agreement: and two days before that festival took ship in the Isle of Wight and went to Normandy and Prince Edgar with him.

1092

E

(1092) In this year King William with a great army went north to Carlisle, and restored the city and erected the castle, and drove out Dolfin[2] who had ruled the country, and garrisoned the castle with his men, and then came here to the south, and sent many peasant people there with their wives and cattle to live there to cultivate the land.[3]

1093

E

(1093) In this year King William was taken so seriously ill in the spring that everywhere he was declared to be dead: and in his affliction he made many vows to God to lead his own life justly, and to protect and secure God's churches, and never more again to sell them for money, and to have all just laws among his people. And the archbishopric of Canterbury which had remained in his own control he committed to Anselm[4] who had been abbot at Le Bec: and to Robert,[5] his chancellor, the bishopric of Lincoln: and he granted land to many monasteries, but he soon took it away when he had recovered, and dispensed with all the good laws he had promised us.

Then, after this, the king of Scotland sent and asked for the fulfilment of the terms that had been promised him, and King William summoned him to Gloucester and sent him hostages to Scotland, and Prince Edgar afterwards; and then he sent back those men who brought him to the king with great honour. But when he came to the king, he could not be granted speech with our king nor given the benefit of the terms that had been promised him: and so they separated with great dissension, and King Malcolm turned back to Scotland. But soon after he came home, he assembled his army and harried England, thus engaging on a foolish and improper project. And Robert, earl of Northumbria,[6] with his men entrapped him by surprise and killed him. He was killed by Moræl of Bamborough, who was the earl's steward and

[1] *i.e.* in 1072. See above, p. 154.
[2] Son of Gospatric, formerly earl of Northumbria.
[3] On these events and their sequel, see above, pp. 41–42.
[4] 4 December 1093. See below, pp. 654–658.
[5] Robert Bloet was apparently consecrated bishop of Lincoln on 12 February 1094.
[6] Robert of Mowbray.

E

godfather of King Malcolm. With him also Edward, his son, was killed, who should have been king after him if he had lived. When the good queen, Margaret, heard of this–that her dearest husband and son were thus betrayed–she was distressed in mind to the point of death, and went to church with her priests and received her rites and in answer to her prayer, God granted that she gave up her spirit. And then the Scots chose Malcolm's brother, Dufenal,[1] as king and drove out all the English who had been with King Malcolm. When Duncan, King Malcolm's son, heard all this had happened in this way (he was at King William's court as his father had given him as a hostage to our king's father and so he had remained here)–he came to the king, and did such homage as the king wished to have from him, and so with his consent went to Scotland with such support as he could get from Englishmen and Frenchmen, and deprived his kinsman, Dufenal,[1] of the kingdom, and was accepted as king. But some of the Scots assembled again and killed nearly all his force and he himself escaped with a few men. Afterwards they came to an agreement, to the effect that he would never again bring Englishmen nor Frenchmen into the country.

1094

E

(1094) King William held his court at Christmas[2] at Gloucester, and messengers came to him from his brother, Robert of Normandy, who informed him that his brother utterly repudiated the truce and terms, unless the king would carry out all that they had arranged by way of agreement, and upon that called him forsworn and faithless, unless he kept to these agreements or went to where the agreement had been made and sworn and cleared himself there.

Then the king went to Hastings at Candlemas,[3] and while he was there waiting for good weather, he had the monastery at Battle consecrated, and deprived Herbert Losinga,[4] the bishop of Thetford, of his pastoral staff: and after that in mid-Lent went overseas to Normandy. After he arrived there he and his brother, Count Robert, agreed to come together peaceably, and they did so–and could not be reconciled. Then again they came together with the same men who had made that settlement, and also had sworn the oaths and they blamed all the breach upon the king, but he would not assent to it, nor further keep to the agreement, and therefore they separated with much dissension.

And the king then conquered the castle at Bures, and captured the count's men inside, and sent some of them to this country. On the other hand, the count conquered the castle at Argentan with the help of the king of France and seized Roger of Poitou[5] in it, and seven hundred of the king's soldiers with him, and then the castle at Le Houlme: and often each of them burned the other party's villages and took people prisoner.

[1] Apparently Donald Bane, whose reign marked a short-lived Celtic reaction against the reforms effected by St. Margaret.

[2] Christmas, 1093. [3] 2 February 1094.

[4] On him, see Freeman, *William Rufus*, vol. I, pp. 354–356. [5] A son of Roger of Montgomery.

E

Then the king sent into this country and ordered twenty thousand Englishmen to be called out to his aid in Normandy: but when they reached the sea, they were ordered to turn back and give for the king's profit the money that they had received: that was half a pound for each man, and they did so.

And the count of Normandy[1] with the king of France and all those that they could assemble went after this towards Eu, in which place King William was; and intended to besiege him inside it, and so proceeded until they came to Longueville. There the king of France was turned from his purpose by intrigue and so afterwards all the expedition dispersed. Meanwhile, King William sent for his brother, Henry, who was in the castle at Domfront; but because he could not go through Normandy in peace he sent ships after him and Hugh, earl of Chester.[2] But when they were to go towards Eu where the king was, they went to England and landed at Southampton, on the eve of All Saints', and stayed here afterwards and were in London at Christmas.

Also in this year the Welshmen gathered together and started a fight with the French who were in Wales or in the neighbourhood and had deprived them of land, and they stormed many fortresses and castles, and killed the men. And after their forces grew they divided themselves into more divisions. Hugh, earl of Shropshire,[3] fought with one of these parties and routed them. But nevertheless all that year the others did not desist from doing all the damage they could.

In the course of this year also, the Scots trapped their king, Duncan, and killed him, and afterwards once more chose his paternal uncle, Dufenal,[4] as king, through whose instruction and instigation he had been betrayed to death.

1095

E

(1095) In this year King William was at Wissant at Christmas[5] for the first four days of the festival, and after the fourth day came into this country and landed at Dover. And Henry, the king's brother, stayed in this country till spring,[6] and then went overseas to Normandy with great treasure, in fealty to the king against their brother, Count Robert: and fought frequently against the count and did him much damage both in land and men.

And then at Easter the king held his court at Winchester, and Earl Robert of Northumbria would not come to court, and therefore the king was very much incensed against him and sent to him and ordered him firmly to come to court at Whitsuntide if he wanted to be entitled to protection.

In this year Easter was on 25 March, and then during Easter on the night of St. Ambrose's Day[7] there were seen nearly all over this country nearly all night very many stars falling from the sky, not by ones or twos but so thickly that nobody could

[1] Robert.

[2] Hugh, son of Richard, *vicomte* of Avranches, became earl of Chester about 1071, and died 27 July 1101.

[3] This is the second son of Roger of Montgomery. He succeeded to the earldom of Shrewsbury on the death of Roger on 27 July of this year. See Table 13.

[4] Donald Bane.

[5] Christmas, 1094

[6] Spring, 1095.

[7] 4 April 1095.

E

count them. After this, at Whitsuntide, the king was at Windsor and all his council with him except the earl of Northumbria:[1] because the king would neither give him hostages nor grant him on pledges to come and go with a safe-conduct. And the king therefore summoned his army and went to Northumbria against the earl: and soon after he got there he overcame many of the earl's household–nearly all the best of them–in a fortress,[2] and placed them in custody and besieged the castle at Tynemouth until he conquered it, and the earl's brother inside it, and all who were with him, and afterwards proceeded to Bamborough and besieged the earl inside it. But when the king saw that he could not take it by force of arms, he ordered a castle to be built in front of Bamborough, and in his language called it "*Malvesin*", *i.e.* in English "Bad Neighbour", and garrisoned it strongly with his men, and then went southwards. Then, soon after the king was gone away south one night the earl went out of Bamborough towards Tynemouth, but those who were in the new castle became aware of this and went after him and fought against him and wounded him and then captured him and killed some who were with him, and took some alive.

Meanwhile it became known to the king that in Wales the Welsh had stormed a certain castle called Montgomery, and killed Earl Hugh's men whose duty it was to hold it, and therefore he ordered another army to be instantly called out, and marched into Wales after Michaelmas and dispersed his army and traversed all the country so that all the army came together at All Saints' at Snowden. But the Welsh always went ahead into mountains and moors so that they could not be reached: and the king then turned homewards because he saw that he could do nothing more there that winter.

When the king came back he ordered Earl Robert of Northumbria to be seized and taken to Bamborough, and both his eyes to be put out, unless those who were within would give up the castle. His wife and Moræl, who was his steward and his kinsman, too, were holding it. Through this scheme the castle was then given up, and Moræl entered the king's court: and through him were discovered many people, both clerics and lay, who had been instigators of rebellion against the king, some of whom the king had ordered to be reduced to captivity before that time. And, afterwards, he ordered it to be announced very peremptorily all over this country that all those who held land of the king must be at court in season if they wished to be entitled to the king's protection. And the king ordered Earl Robert to be brought to Windsor and to be kept in the castle there.

Also in this same year towards Easter, the pope's legate came to this country–that was Bishop Walter, a man very good in the conduct of his life, of the city of Albano, and he gave the *pallium* to Archbishop Anselm at Whitsuntide on behalf of Pope Urban,[3] and he received him at his archiepiscopal see of Canterbury, and Bishop Walter stayed here in this country a long time after during the year, and the Romescot[4] was afterwards sent by him, which had not been done for many years.

This same year also there was much unseasonable weather, so that all over this country the crops ripened very slightly.

[1] Robert of Mowbray.
[2] Newcastle.
[3] Urban II.
[4] Peter's Pence. See No. 82.

1096

E

(1096) In this year King William held his court at Christmas[1] at Windsor, and William, bishop of Durham, died there on New Year's Day.[2] And on the Octave of the Epiphany,[3] the king and all his councillors were at Salisbury. There Geoffrey Bainard[4] accused William of Eu,[5] the king's kinsman, of having been a party to the treason against the king: and fought it out with him, and overcame him in trial by battle, and when he was overcome, the king ordered his eyes to be put out and that afterwards he should be castrated. And his steward, called William, who was son to his mother's sister, the king ordered to be hanged on a gallows. Also, Odo, count of Champagne, the king's uncle,[6] and many others were deprived of their lands there, and some men taken to London and there destroyed.

In this year also there was a very great commotion over all this nation, and many other nations, because of Urban who was called pope though he had no seat at Rome,[7] and an immense host, with women and children, went out because they wanted to fight against heathen nations.[8] By means of this expedition, the king and his brother, Count Robert,[9] came to an agreement, so that the king went overseas and redeemed all Normandy from him for money according as they had come to an agreement; and then the count departed, and with him the count of Flanders[10] and the count of Boulogne, and also many other chief men. And Count Robert and those who went with him stayed the winter in Apulia. But of the people who went by way of Hungary many thousands perished there, and on the way, miserably, and many dragged themselves home towards winter, wretched and hunger-bitten.

This was a very severe year among all the people of England, both because of all sorts of taxes and because of the very severe famine which very much oppressed this country this year.

Also, in this year, the chief men who ruled this country frequently sent armies into Wales, and oppressed many a man very much thereby, but there was no success in it, only destruction of men and waste of money.

1097

E

(1097) In this year King William was in Normandy at Christmas,[11] and went to this country towards Easter, because he thought he would hold his court at Winchester, but he was prevented by bad weather, until Easter Eve,[12] so that he first landed at Arundel, and then held his court at Windsor.

[1] Christmas, 1095. [2] 1 January 1096. [3] 13 January 1096.

[4] Possibly sheriff of York in the time of William the Conqueror. On the family which gave its name to 'Baynard's Castle' in London, see J. Armitage Robinson, *Gilbert Crispin* (1911), p. 38.

[5] Not to be confused with William, count of Eu.

[6] He was the husband of the Conqueror's sister, Adelaide. He was the father of Stephen of Aumale whom the plotters wished to set up as king.

[7] A reference to the earlier struggle between Urban II and the anti-pope Clement III.

[8] The First Crusade.

[9] Robert 'of Jerusalem'. [10] Eustace III. [11] Christmas, 1096. [12] 1097.

E

And after that he went to Wales with a large army and traversed the country widely, by means of some of the Welsh who had come to him and were his guides: and he stayed there from midsummer nearly to August, and had great losses there in men and horses and many other things too. Then the Welshmen revolted from the king, and chose many chiefs from among themselves. One of them who was the most honourable of them was called Caduugaun–he was the son of King Griffith's brother. But when the king saw that he could accomplish nothing of his purpose, he came back into this country and soon after that he had castles built along the Marches.

Then about Michaelmas, on 4 October, there appeared a marvellous star shining in the evening and soon setting. It was seen in the south-west, and the ray that shone from it appeared very long shining south-east, and it appeared nearly all the week in this fashion. Many people said it was a comet.

Soon after this, Anselm, archbishop of Canterbury, got permission from the king –though the king was unwilling so people said–and went overseas,[1] because it seemed to him that in this country little was done according to justice and according to his orders. And the king, after that, at Martinmas,[2] went overseas into Normandy, but while he was waiting for good weather, his court did the greatest damage in the districts where they stayed that ever court or invading army was reported to have done in a land at peace. This was in every respect a very severe year, and over-oppressive with bad weather, when cultivation was due to be done or crops to be got in, and with excessive taxes that never ceased. Also, many shires whose labour was due at London were hard pressed because of the wall that they built about the Tower, and because of the bridge that was nearly all carried away by a flood, and because of the work on the king's hall, that was being built at Westminster, and many a man was oppressed thereby.

Also in this same year, soon after Michaelmas, Prince Edgar went with an army, with the king's support into Scotland, and conquered the country in a severe battle, and drove out King Dufenal:[3] and his kinsman, Edgar, who was son of King Malcolm and Margaret, the queen, he established as king in allegiance to King William, and then came back into England.

1098

E

(1098) In this year at Christmas,[4] King William was in Normandy. And Walkelin, bishop of Winchester, and Baldwin, abbot of St. Edmunds, both died during that time. And in this year also died Turold, abbot of Peterborough.

In the course of this year also in the summer, in Berkshire, at Finchampstead, a pool bubbled up with blood, as many trustworthy men said who were alleged to have seen it.

[1] The breach between the king and Anselm was partly caused by the king's complaint that the military contingent provided by the archbishop was inadequately equipped. See F. M. Stenton, *English Feudalism*, pp. 147–148.

[2] 11 November.

[3] Donald Bane.

[4] Christmas, 1097.

E

And Earl Hugh[1] was killed in Anglesey by sea-rovers[2] and his brother Robert[3] became his heir, even as he obtained it from the king.

Before Michaelmas the sky looked as if it were burning nearly all night. This was a very oppressive year because of all sorts of excessive taxes, and great rains that did not cease throughout the year: nearly all the cultivation perished on marshland.

1099

E

(1099) King William was in Normandy at Christmas[4] and came to this country at Easter,[5] and at Whitsuntide held his court for the first time in his new building at Westminster, and there gave the bishopric of Durham to his chaplain, Rannulf,[6] who had managed his councils over all England, and superintended them. And soon after that he went overseas and drove Count Elias[7] out of Maine, and then established it under his control, and so came back to this country at Michaelmas.

This year also on St. Martin's Day,[8] the tide rose so much and did so much damage that it could not be remembered to have done so much before, and there was on the same day a new moon.

And Osmond, bishop of Salisbury, died in Advent.[9]

1100

E

(1100) In this year King William held his court at Christmas[10] at Gloucester, and at Easter[11] at Winchester, and at Whitsuntide at Westminster.

And at Whitsuntide at a village in Berkshire there was seen blood bubbling out of the earth, as many said who were alleged to have seen it. And after that, in the morning after Lammas,[12] King William when hunting was shot with an arrow by one of his own men, and then brought to Winchester and buried in that diocese–that was in the thirteenth year after his succession to the throne.

He was very strong and fierce to his country and his men and to all his neighbours, and very terrible. And because of the counsels of wicked men, which were always agreeable to him, and because of his avarice, he was always harassing this nation with military service and excessive taxes, so that in his days all justice was in abeyance, and all injustice arose both in ecclesiastical and secular matters. He kept down God's Church, and all the bishoprics and abbacies whose incumbents died in his days he sold for money or kept in his own hands and let out for rent, because he intended to be the

[1] Son of Roger of Montgomery and, like his father, earl of Shrewsbury. See Table 13.

[2] Their leader was Magnus 'Bareleg', king of Norway, son of Harold Hardraada, and he had with him a son of Harold Godwineson–a curious commentary on the battle of Stamford Bridge.

[3] Robert of Bellême, elder brother of Hugh. Up to now he had only held the Norman lands of the family.

[4] Christmas, 1098. [5] Easter, 1099. [6] Rannulf Flambard. He held the bishopric until 1128.

[7] Elias 'de la Flèche'. [8] 11 November. [9] 3 December 1099.

[10] Christmas, 1099. [11] Easter, 1100. [12] 2 August 1100.

E

heir of everyone, cleric and lay, and so on the day he died he had in his own hands the archbishopric of Canterbury, and the bishopric of Winchester and that of Salisbury, and eleven abbacies all let out for rent. And though I prolong it further – all that was hateful to God and just men was all customary in this country in his time: and therefore he was hateful to nearly all his people, and odious to God, just as his end showed, because he departed in the midst of his injustice without repentance and any reparation.

On the Thursday[1] he was killed, and buried next morning: and when he was buried the councillors who were near at hand chose his brother Henry as king, and he forthwith gave the bishopric of Winchester to William Giffard,[2] and then went to London, and on the Sunday after that, before the altar at Westminster he vowed to God and all the people to put down all the injustices that there were in his brother's time,[3] and to maintain the best laws that had stood in any king's day before him. And after that Maurice, the bishop of London, consecrated him king,[4] and all in this country submitted to him and swore oaths and became his men.

And soon after this, the king, by the advice of those who were around him, had Bishop Rannulf of Durham seized and brought into the Tower of London and kept there.[5] Then, before Michaelmas,[6] Archbishop Anselm of Canterbury came into this country as King Henry sent for him on the advice of his council, because he had gone out of this country as a result of the great injustice that King William did him.

And then, soon after this, the king married Maud, daughter of Malcolm, king of Scotland, and of Margaret, the good queen, the kinswoman of Edward, of the true royal family of England, and on St. Martin's Day[7] she was given to him at Westminster with great ceremony, and Archbishop Anselm married her to him and then consecrated her queen.

And Archbishop Thomas of York died soon after this.[8]

In the course of this same year also, in autumn, Count Robert came home to Normandy, and Count Robert of Flanders and Eustace, count of Boulogne, from Jerusalem, and as soon as Count Robert came into Normandy he was joyfully received by all the people, apart from the castles that were garrisoned with King Henry's men, against which he had many struggles and battles.

1101

E

(1101) In this year, at Christmas,[9] King Henry held his court at Westminster, and at Easter at Winchester: and then soon after, the chief men in the country grew hostile to the king, both because of their great untrustworthiness and because of Count Robert of Normandy, who set out to carry war into this country. And the king then sent ships out to sea for the injury and hindrance of his brother, but some of them failed again at this crisis, and deserted from the king and went over to Count Robert. Then,

[1] 2 August 1100 was a Thursday.
[2] He was not consecrated until 1107.
[3] See his charter (No. 19).
[4] 5 August.
[5] He was arrested on 15 August.
[6] 23 September.
[7] 11 November.
[8] 18 November.
[9] Christmas, 1100.

E

at midsummer, the king marched out to Pevensey with all his army against his brother and waited for him there: but meanwhile Count Robert landed at Portsmouth twelve nights before Lammas,[1] and the king with all his army came against him: the chief men, however, went between them and reconciled the brothers on the condition that the king gave up all he was forcibly holding[2] against the count in Normandy and that all in England who had lost their land because of the count should have it again. And Count Eustace[3] also should have his father's land in this country, and every year Count Robert should have 3,000 marks of silver from England, and whichever of the brothers should survive the other, should be heir of all England and of Normandy as well, unless the deceased should have an heir in lawful wedlock. And this twelve of the men of highest rank on both sides confirmed with an oath. And the count afterwards stayed in this country until after Michaelmas: and his men always did much damage wherever they went while the count was staying in this country.

In the course of this year also, Bishop Rannulf escaped by night at Candlemas[4] from the Tower of London, where he was in captivity, and went to Normandy–he was the one through whose contrivance and instigation Count Robert had come to this country this year with warlike intent.

1102

E

(1102) In this year, at the Nativity,[5] King Henry was at Westminster, and at Easter[6] at Winchester. And soon after that there was a disagreement between the king and Earl Robert of Bellême, who had here in this country the earldom of Shrewsbury, that his father, Earl Roger,[7] had had, and authority over a wide area as well, both on this side of the sea and beyond. And the king went and besieged the castle at Arundel:[8] when, however, he could not take it by force so quickly, he had castles made before it and garrisoned them with his men, and then with all his army marched to Bridgnorth and stayed there until he had the castle and deprived Earl Robert of his lands and took from him all he had in England: and the earl went overseas, and the army then turned back home.

Then, after that, at Michaelmas, the king was at Westminster, and all the chief men in this country, cleric and lay: and Archbishop Anselm held a synod of clerics[9] and there they prepared many decrees pertaining to Christianity, and many, both French and English, lost their pastoral staffs and their authority, which they had obtained unjustly or lived in wrongfully.

And in this same year in Whitsun week, there came thieves, some from Auvergne, some from France and some from Flanders, and broke into the monastery of Peterborough and took in it much of value in gold and silver–crosses and chalices and candlesticks.

[1] *i.e.* on 20 July. [2] The so-called 'Treaty of Alton'. [3] Eustace of Boulogne.
[4] 2 February 1101. [5] Christmas, 1101. [6] Easter, 1102. [7] Roger of Montgomery.
[8] Belonging to Robert of Bellême: it had been given by William the Conqueror to Roger of Montgomery. [9] See below, No. 109, p. 674.

1103

E

(1103) In this year, at Christmas,[1] King Henry was at Westminster, and soon after that Bishop William Giffard[2] went out of this country, because he did not wish to receive his consecration uncanonically from Archbishop Gerard of York:[3] and then at Easter the king held his court at Winchester, and after that Archbishop Anselm went from Canterbury to Rome, as he and the king agreed.

In the course of this year also, Count Robert of Normandy came to speak with the king in this country, and before he went away he remitted the 3,000 marks that King Henry had to give him every year by compact.[4]

In this year also, at Finchampstead, in Berkshire, blood was seen coming from the earth. This was a very grievous year in this country through all sorts of taxes, and cattle plague and ruin of crops–both corn and all the produce of trees. Also, on the morning of St. Laurence's Day,[5] the wind did so much damage in this country that no one remembered it ever doing so much before.

In this same year Matthias, abbot of Peterborough, died–he lived no longer than a year after he was abbot. After Michaelmas, on 21 October, he was received as abbot with a procession and on the same day next year he died at Gloucester, and was buried there.

1104

E

(1104) In this year, at Christmas,[6] King Henry held his court at Westminster, and at Easter[7] at Winchester, and at Whitsuntide again at Westminster. This year Whit-Sunday was on 5 June, and on the Tuesday after at midday there appeared four circles all round the sun, of white colour, each intertwined under the other as if they were painted. All who saw them were astonished for they did not remember anything like it before.

After this, an agreement was reached between Count Robert of Normandy and Robert of Bellême whom King Henry had deprived of his lands and expelled from England, and through their agreement the king of England and the count of Normandy became hostile, and the king sent his people overseas into Normandy and the chief men in that country received them and, to the betrayal of their liege lord the count, introduced them into their castles, from which they did many injuries to the count, in ravaging and burning. Also in the course of this year Earl William of Mortain[8] went away from this country into Normandy, but after he had gone he worked against the king, for which reason the king deprived him of everything and confiscated what land he had in this country.

It is not easy to describe the miseries this country was suffering at this time, because of various and different injustices and taxes that never ceased or failed, and

[1] Christmas, 1102. [2] See above, p. 176.

[3] Gerard had a bad character, but the real dispute was that between the king and Anselm on the matter of investiture (see Z. N. Brooke, *English Church and the Papacy*, 1931, p. 163).

[4] See above, p. 173. [5] 10 August. [6] Christmas, 1103. [7] Easter, 1104.

[8] Son of Robert, count of Mortain, uterine half-brother of the Conqueror.

E

always wherever the king went there was complete ravaging of his wretched people caused by his court, and in the course of it often [there were] burnings and killings:

All this was to anger God
And these wretched folk to vex.

1105

E

(1105) In this year, at the Nativity,[1] King Henry held his court at Windsor, and after that in spring[2] he went overseas into Normandy against his brother Count Robert, and in the course of his stay there he won Caen and Bayeux[3] from his brother, and nearly all the castles and the chief men in that country were subjected to him, and then he came back to this country again in the autumn. And what he had won in Normandy remained afterwards in peace, and obedient to him, except those who lived anywhere near William, count of Mortain, who frequently oppressed them as hard as he could because of his loss of lands in this country. And then before Christmas Robert of Bellême came into this country to the king. This was a very grievous year in this country because of the ruin of crops and the various taxes that never ceased, before the king crossed over, and while he was there, and after he came back again.

1106

E

In this year King Henry was at Westminster at the Nativity[4] and there held his court: at that festival Robert of Bellême left the king in hostile fashion and went out of this country into Normandy. Then, after this, before spring, the king was at Northampton: and Count Robert of Normandy, his brother, came there to him, and because the king would not give up to him what he had won from him in Normandy, they separated without coming to an agreement, and the count went back overseas again forthwith.

In the first week of Lent, on the Friday, 16 February in the evening, there appeared an unusual star, and for a long time after that it was seen shining a while every evening. This star appeared in the south-west; it seemed small and dark: the ray that shone from it however was very bright, and seemed to be like an immense beam shining north-east; and one evening it appeared as if this beam was flashing towards the star from an opposite direction. Some said that at this time they saw more strange stars; however, we do not write of it more plainly because we did not see it ourselves. On the eve of *Cena Domini*,[5] that is the Thursday before Easter, two moons were seen in the sky before day, one to the east and one to the west, both full, and the moon on that day was a fortnight old.

[1] Christmas, 1104. [2] 2–8 April 1105.
[3] Bayeux was burnt on 13 April; the surrender of Caen followed.
[4] Christmas, 1105. [5] 21 March.

E

At Easter the king was at Bath, and at Whitsuntide at Salisbury, because he did not wish to hold court on his departure overseas. After that, before August, the king went overseas into Normandy and nearly all who were in that country submitted to his will, apart from Robert of Bellême and the count of Mortain and a few other of the chief men who still held with the count of Normandy: and therefore the king afterwards went with an army and besieged a castle of the count of Mortain called Tinchebrai. While the king was besieging the castle, Count Robert of Normandy came upon the king with his army, on the eve of Michaelmas, and with him Robert of Bellême and William, count of Mortain, and all who agreed with them. But the superiority and the victory were the king's.[1] There the count of Normandy was captured and the count of Mortain, and Robert of Estouteville and they were sent to England and reduced to captivity. Robert of Bellême was put to flight, and William Crispin[2] captured and many together with him. Prince Edgar, who had shortly before gone over from the king to the count, was also captured there: the king afterwards let him go unmolested. Afterwards the king overran everything in Normandy and arranged it according to his pleasure and power.

This year also there were serious and sinful struggles between the emperor of Saxony and his son, and in the course of the struggle the father died and the son succeeded to the throne.[3]

1107

E

(1107) In this year, at Christmas,[4] King Henry was in Normandy and brought it under his control and organized it, and after that in spring[5] came to this country and held his court at Easter at Windsor, and at Whitsuntide at Westminster, and afterwards again at the beginning of August was at Westminster and there he gave and disposed of the bishoprics and abbacies that there were in England or Normandy without ruler or pastor.[6] These were so many that nobody could remember that so many had ever been given together before: and at this same time, among the others who received abbacies, Ernulf, who had been prior at Canterbury,[7] succeeded to the abbacy of Peterborough. This was actually about seven years after King Henry had received the kingship, and that was in the forty-first year after the French had been in control of this country. Many said that they saw various signs in the moon during this year, and its beams waxing and waning contrary to nature.

In the course of this year died Maurice, bishop of London,[8] and Robert, abbot of Bury St. Edmunds,[9] and Richard, abbot of Ely.[10] In the course of this year also, died King Edgar of Scotland on 13 January,[11] and Alexander, his brother,[12] succeeded to the throne with King Henry's consent.

[1] See below, No. 9. [2] William Crispin II, brother of Gilbert Crispin, abbot of Westminster.
[3] Henry IV was deposed on 31 December 1105 and died 7 August 1106.
[4] Christmas, 1106. [5] 1107. [6] Important in relation to the Investiture Contest.
[7] He became bishop of Rochester in 1114 and is reputed to have been the compiler of *Textus Roffensis*.
[8] 26 September. [9] 17 October 1107.
[10] 16 June 1107. After his death, Ely was transformed into a bishopric.
[11] 1107: other authorities give 8 January. [12] Alexander I.

1108

E

(1108) In this year, at the Nativity,[1] King Henry was at Westminster, and at Easter[2] at Winchester, and at Whitsuntide again at Westminster, and after that, before August, he went into Normandy and the king of France, Philip, died on 5 August,[3] and his son, Louis,[4] succeeded to the throne: and there were many struggles between the kings of France and the king of England while he stayed in Normandy.

In this year also died Archbishop Gerard of York[5] before Whitsuntide, and afterwards Thomas[6] was appointed.

1109

E

(1109) In this year King Henry was in Normandy at Christmas[7] and Easter, and before Whitsuntide[8] came here to this country, and held his court at Westminster. There the agreements were completed and the oaths sworn to give his daughter to the emperor[9] in marriage.

In the course of this year there were very many thunderstorms and very terrible they were. And Archbishop Anselm of Canterbury died on 22 March, and Easter Sunday was on the Feast of the Greater Litany.[10]

1110

E

(1110) In this year King Henry held his court at Christmas[11] at Westminster, and at Easter[12] he was at Marlborough, and at Whitsuntide he held his court for the first time at the New Windsor.

In this year before spring, the king sent his daughter overseas with many and various treasures and gave her in marriage to the emperor. On the fifth night in the month of May, the moon appeared in the evening shining bright, and then little by little its light faded until early in the night it was quenched entirely, so much so that neither light nor circle nor anything of it at all was seen: and so it continued until nearly day, and then it appeared full and brightly shining–it was a fortnight old that same day. All that night the sky was very clear, and the stars all over the heaven shining very bright, and fruits were badly damaged by frost that night. After that, in the month of June, a star appeared from the north-east and its beam went out in front of it in the south-west, and it was seen like this for many nights, and later on in the night, after it had risen higher, it was seen going backwards to the north-west.

In the course of this year, Philip of Briouze,[13] William Malet and William Bainard were deprived of their lands.

Also in the course of this year Count Elias died, who held Maine from King

[1] Christmas, 1107.
[2] 1108.
[3] The death of Philip I took place on 29 July.
[4] Louis VI, 'le Gros'.
[5] 21 May.
[6] He was a son of Samson, bishop of Worcester.
[7] Christmas, 1108.
[8] 1109.
[9] Henry V.
[10] 25 April, and see above, p. 142.
[11] Christmas, 1109.
[12] Easter 1110.
[13] Son of William of Briouze, an important tenant-in-chief in Domesday Book.

E

Henry, and did acknowledgment for it, and after his decease the count of Anjou[1] succeeded and held it against the king.

This was a very severe year in this country because of taxes that the king took for the marriage of his daughter, and because of storms by which the products of the soil were badly damaged and the fruits of trees over all this country nearly all perished.

In the course of this year work was begun on the new monastery at Chertsey.

1111

E

(1111) In this year King Henry did not wear his crown at Christmas[2] nor Easter nor Whitsuntide, and in August he went overseas into Normandy because of the disagreement that some people had with him on the boundaries of France, and mostly because of the count of Anjou who held Maine against him, and when he got over there, between them they perpetrated many lawless raids and burnings and ravagings. In this year died Robert, count of Flanders,[3] and his son, Baldwin,[4] succeeded. In the course of this year was a very long winter and troublesome and severe, and as a result all the produce of the soil was very badly damaged, and there was the greatest cattle plague that anyone could remember.

1112

E

(1112) All this year King Henry stayed in Normandy because of the disagreement he had with France, and with the count of Anjou who held Maine against him. And while he was there he deprived the count of Evreux[5] and William Crispin of their land and drove them out of Normandy, and gave their land to Philip of Briouze who had formerly been deprived of his estates. And he caused Robert of Bellême to be captured and put into prison. This was a very good year and very productive in woods and fields, but it was very troublesome and sorrowful because of excessive plague.

1113

E

(1113) In this year King Henry was in Normandy at the Nativity,[7] at Easter[8] and at Whitsuntide; and after that in

H[6]

. . . so that they could speak with difficulty. After that Abbot Peter died at Gloucester on 17 July; and on 5 October

[1] Fulk V. [2] Christmas, 1110. [3] On 4 or 5 October.

[4] Baldwin VII. [5] William, count of Evreux.

[6] This short text to which the title 'H' has been given is a fragment of a lost version of the Anglo-Saxon Chronicle. It is contained in single folio of *Cott. MS. Dom. A. ix* in the British Museum. The original text is printed in *Anglia*, vol. 1, pp. 195–197; and in J. Earle and C. Plummer, *Two of the Saxon Chronicles Parallel*, vol. 1, pp. 243–245.

[7] Christmas, 1112. [8] Easter, 1113.

E

summer he sent Robert of Bellême into this country to the castle at Wareham, and came himself into the country soon after.

H

the king appointed to the office William, who was a monk of the same monastery.

1114

E

(1114) In this year King Henry held his court at Christmas[1] at Windsor, and he did not hold court again in the course of this year. And at midsummer he went with an army into Wales, and the Welsh came and made a truce with the king, and he had castles built among them: and after that, in September, he went overseas into Normandy. In this year late in May there was a strange star with long rays shining for many nights. Also in this same year there was so great an ebb everywhere as nobody could remember before, and so that the Thames, east of the bridge at London, was crossed by people riding and on foot. In the course of this year there were many strong winds in the month of October, but it was extremely strong on the night which was the Octave of St. Martin,[3] and it was reported everywhere in woods and villages. Also in this year the king gave the archbishopric of Canterbury to Ralph, who had been bishop of Rochester. And the archbishop of York, Thomas, died, and Thurstan, who had been the king's chaplain, succeeded him. In this same year the king went towards the sea and meant to cross over but the weather prevented him. Meanwhile he sent his writ to Abbot Ernulf of Peterborough, and ordered him to come to him quickly because he wished to have a secret conversation with him. When he came to him he forced the bishopric of Rochester on him, and so did the archbishops and bishops and the nobility that was in England together with the king: and he resisted a long time

H

(1114) In this year King Henry was at Windsor at Christmas,[1] and wore his crown there; and there he gave the bishopric of Worcester to Theobald, his chaplain. Also he gave the abbacy of Ramsey to Rainold who was a monk of Caen. Also he gave the abbacy of York to Richard who was a monk of the same monastery. Also he gave the abbacy of Thorney to Robert who was a monk of Saint Evroul. Also he gave the earldom of Northamptonshire to David who was the queen's brother.[2] After that Thomas, archbishop of York, died on 17 February. After that the king gave the abbacy of Cerne Abbas to William who was a monk of Caen. Then at Easter he was at Thorpe near Northampton. After that he gave the archbishopric of Canterbury to Ralph who was bishop of Rochester; this man succeeded on 24 February. After that Abbot Nigel of Burton died on 3 May. After that Chichester was burnt down, and the minster there as well. This was on 5 May. Then at Whitsuntide the king was at St. Albans. Afterwards he went with his army into Wales at midsummer and built castles there, and the Welsh kings came to him and became his vassals and swore oaths of allegiance to him. After that he went to Winchester and there gave the archbishopric of York to his chaplain, Thurstan, and the abbacy of Bury St. Edmunds he gave to Albold who was a monk at Bec. This was on 16 August. After that he gave the abbacy of Muchelney to Eadulf, who was a monk in that same monastery, on the Feast of

[1] Christmas, 1113.

[2] David, king of Scotland. See Table 16.

[3] 18 November.

E

but it was of no avail. And the king then ordered the archbishop to conduct him to Canterbury and consecrate him bishop whether he would or no. This took place at the town called 'Burne':[3] it was on 15 September. When the monks of Peterborough heard tell of this, they were more grieved than they had ever been, because he was a very good and gentle man, and did much conducive to good within and without while he was there. God Almighty be with him always!

Then soon after that, the king gave the abbacy[4] to a monk of Séez, called John, at the desire of the archbishop of Canterbury, and soon after, the king and the archbishop of Canterbury sent him to Rome for the archbishop's *pallium*, and a monk, who is[5] called Warner, with him, and the archbishop's nephew, the archdeacon, John; and they got on well there. This took place on 21 September at the town called Rowner:[6] and the same day the king went on board ship at Portsmouth.

H

the Exaltation of the Cross.[1] Also he gave the abbacy of Burton to Geoffrey who was a monk at the Old Minster.[2] At the same time Archbishop Ralph gave the bishopric of Rochester. . . .

1115

E

(1115) King Henry was in Normandy at the Nativity,[7] and while he was there he brought it about that all the chief men in Normandy did homage and swore oaths of allegiance to his son, William, whom he had by his queen, and after that, in the month of July, he came to this country.

In the course of this year there was a winter so severe, what with snow and frost, that nobody then living remembered any more severe, and because of that there was an excessive plague among cattle.

In this year Pope Paschal sent the *pallium* to this country for Ralph, archbishop of Canterbury, and he received it with great honour at his archiepiscopal see in Canterbury. Abbot Anselm,[8] who was a nephew of Archbishop Anselm (and Abbot John of Peterborough),[9] brought it from Rome.

[1] 14 September.
[2] At Winchester.
[3] Probably Westbourne, Sussex.
[4] Of Peterborough.
[5] This has been altered to "was" in the MS., obviously after Warner's death.
[6] In Hampshire, near Gosport.
[7] Christmas, 1114.
[8] Abbot of St. Saba in Rome. He became abbot of Bury St. Edmunds in 1121.
[9] In the margin by a later hand.

1116

E

(1116) In this year King Henry was at St. Albans at Christmas,[1] had the minster there consecrated: and at Easter[2] he was at Odiham. And in the course of this year there was a very bad winter (and severe and long) for cattle and everything. And the king went overseas into Normandy soon after Easter, and there were many raids and robberies and castles taken between France and Normandy. This disagreement was mostly because King Henry was supporting his nephew, Theobald, count of Blois,[3] who was carrying on a war against his liege lord, Louis,[4] king of France.

This was a very toilsome and disastrous year in the matter of the produce of the earth, because of the excessive rains that came shortly before August, and were causing much distress and toil when Candlemas[5] was reached. Also this year was so short of mast[6] that in all this country, and not even in Wales, was any heard tell of. This country and the people also this year were too often severely tormented by the taxes the king took both in cities and outside them.

In this same year, all the church at Peterborough was burnt, and all the buildings except the chapter-house and the dormitory, and in addition most of the town was burnt. All this happened on a Friday–it was 4 August.[7]

1117

E

(1117) All this year King Henry stayed in Normandy because of the quarrel of the king of France and his other neighbours: and then in the summer the king of France and the count of Flanders with him came with an army into Normandy and stayed there one night, and in the morning went back without a fight. And Normandy was very much distressed because of taxes and because of the army King Henry had assembled against them. Also this people was severely oppressed because of this same thing, because of many various taxes.

In the course of this year, on the night of 1 December, there were excessive storms with thunder and lightning and rain and hail. And on the night of 11 December the moon late in the night became as if it were all bloody, and then was eclipsed. Also on the night of 16 December the sky appeared very red as if it were on fire. And on the Octave of St. John the Evangelist[8] there was the great earthquake in Lombardy, because of which monasteries and towers and houses fell down and did much damage amongst people. This was a very disastrous year for corn, because of the rains that hardly ceased nearly all the year.

And Abbot Gilbert of Westminster died 6 December and Faritius, abbot of Abingdon, on 23 February. And in this same year. . . .[9]

[1] Christmas, 1115. [2] 1116.
[3] He was the son of Adela, sister of Henry I, by Stephen, count of Blois. See Table 6.
[4] Louis VI, 'le Gros'. [5] 2 February. [6] Necessary as pasture for swine.
[7] 4 August 1116 was in fact a Friday. [8] 3 January.
[9] More than a line in the MS. is here left blank.

1118

E

(1118) All this year King Henry stayed in Normandy because of the war of the king of France and the count of Anjou and the count of Flanders: and the count of Flanders was wounded in Normandy, and wounded as he was, he went to Flanders. Because of these hostilities the king was very much distressed and lost a great deal both in money and also in land, and the people who troubled him most were his own men, who frequently deserted him and betrayed him and went over to his enemies, and gave their castles up to them for the injury and betrayal of the king. England paid dear for all this, because of the various taxes that never ceased in the course of all this year.

In this year, in the week of the Epiphany, one evening there was very much lightning and excessive thunder after it.

And Queen Maud died at Westminster on 1 May and was buried there. And Count Robert of Meulan[1] also died in the course of the year.

Also in this year, on St. Thomas's Day,[2] there was a wind so very excessively strong that nobody then alive remembered any worse, and its effect was obvious everywhere both in houses and trees.

In the course of this year also died Pope Paschal;[3] and John of Gaeta, whose other name was Gelasius,[4] succeeded to the papacy.

1119

E

(1119) All this year King Henry stayed in Normandy and was very often much troubled because of the war carried on by the king of France and by his own men who had deserted him treacherously and who withdrew until the two kings came together in Normandy with their forces. There the king of France was routed and all his best men captured,[5] and then many of King Henry's men came back to him, and those who had used their castles against him made agreement with him, and some of the castles he took by force.

In the course of this year William, son of King Henry and Queen Maud, went into Normandy to his father and there the count of Anjou's daughter[6] was given him as wife and married to him.

On the eve of Michaelmas there was a great earthquake at some places in this country, though most severe in Gloucestershire and Worcestershire.

In this same year Pope Gelasius[7] died on this side of the Alps and was buried at Cluny, and after him the archbishop of Vienne was elected pope: he was named Calixtus:[8] and afterwards, on the Feast of St. Luke the Evangelist,[9] he came into

[1] Robert of Beaumont, who fought at Hastings, was the son of Roger of Beaumont who appears in Norman history as early as the time of Duke Robert. He was earl of Leicester.

[2] 21 December.

[3] Paschal II. He died 21 January 1118.

[4] Gelasius II. He was elected pope on 24 January 1119 and was consecrated 10 March 1119.

[5] The battle of Brémule, 2 August 1119.

[6] Maud.

[7] Gelasius II.

[8] Calixtus II.

[9] 18 October.

E

France to Rheims, and there held a council, and Archbishop Thurstan of York went to it: and because he had accepted his office from the pope against justice and against the archdiocese of Canterbury and against the king's will, the king refused to let him return to England, and so he lost his archbishopric and went towards Rome with the pope.

Also in this year Count Baldwin[1] of Flanders died of the wounds that he received in Normandy: and after him Charles, son of his father's sister, succeeded to power; he was son of St. Cnut, king of Denmark.

1120

E

(1120) In the course of this year the king of England and the king of France were reconciled, and following their agreement the king's own men in Normandy came into entire accord with him, and so did the counts of Flanders and of Ponthieu.[2] Then, after this, King Henry disposed of his castles and his land in Normandy according to his desire, and so came into this country before Advent.

And on that journey were drowned[3] the king's two sons, William and Richard, and Richard,[4] earl of Chester, and Ottuel, his brother, and many of the king's court –stewards and chamberlains and cupbearers and people of various offices and a very immense number of excellent people with them. Their death was a double grief to their friends–one that they lost this life so suddenly, the other that the bodies of few of them were found anywhere afterwards.

In the course of this year the light came to the Sepulchre of the Lord in Jerusalem twice–once at Easter and the other time at the Assumption of St. Mary[5] as trustworthy people reported who came from there.

And Archbishop Thurstan of York was reconciled with the king through the pope, and came into this country and received his bishopric, though it was very displeasing to the archbishop of Canterbury.

1121

E

(1121) King Henry was at Brampton at Christmas;[6] and after that, before Candlemas,[7] at Windsor. Adela was given to him as wife and then consecrated as queen: she was the daughter of the duke of Louvain.[8]

And the moon was eclipsed on the eve of 5 April, and the moon was a fortnight old.

And the king was at Berkeley at Easter, and after that at Whitsuntide he held

[1] Baldwin VII. [2] William I, count of Ponthieu.
[3] The wreck of the White Ship occurred in the night between 25 and 26 November. See No. 8.
[4] Son of Hugh of Avranches: he became earl of Chester in 1101.
[5] 15 August. [6] Christmas, 1120. [7] 2 February 1121.
[8] Godfrey VII, duke of Lower Lorraine, and count of Louvain.

E

a great court at Westminster, and then in the summer went into Wales with an army: and the Welsh came to meet him, and they made an agreement with him according to the king's desire.

In the course of this year the count of Anjou came from Jerusalem into his country and then sent into this country and had his daughter fetched who had been given as wife to William, the king's son.

And on the night of Christmas Eve there was a great wind all over this country, and that was very obvious in many ways.

1122

E

(1122) In this year King Henry was at Norwich at Christmas[1] and at Easter[2] he was at Northampton.

And in spring, before that, the borough at Gloucester was burnt down while the monks were singing their mass, and the deacon had begun the gospel *Preteriens Jesus*[3] when the fire reached the upper part of the tower, and all the monastery was burnt and all the treasures that were there except a few books and three mass vestments: that was on 8 March.

And after that on the Tuesday after Palm Sunday there was a very big wind, on 22 March.[4] After that came many signs far and wide in England and many illusions were seen and heard. And on the night of 25 July there was a very big earthquake over all Somersetshire and in Gloucestershire. Then on 8 September–that was on St. Mary's Feast Day[5]–there was a very big wind from 9 a.m. till dark night.

This same year died Ralph, the archbishop of Canterbury–that was on 20 October. After that there were many sailors, at sea and on inland waters, who said that they saw in the north-east a great and broad fire near the earth, and it increased in length continuously up to the sky, and the sky opened on four sides and fought against it, as if it was going to quench it, and the fire increased none the more up towards the heavens. They saw this fire at daybreak, and it lasted so long that it was light everywhere–that was 7 December.

1123

E

(1123) In this year King Henry was at Dunstable at Christmas,[6] and messengers of the count of Anjou came there to him,[7] and from there he went to Woodstock, and his bishops and all his court with him.

[1] Christmas, 1121. [2] 1122.

[3] This is the gospel for the Wednesday after the fourth Sunday in Lent, which did in fact fall in 1112 on 8 March.

[4] A day wrong. The Tuesday after Palm Sunday was, in 1122, 21 March

[5] Nativity of the Blessed Virgin Mary.

[6] Christmas, 1122.

[7] To negotiate about the dowry of Henry's widowed daughter, Maud.

E

It happened on a Wednesday (it was 10 January) that the king was riding in his deer-park, and Bishop Roger of Salisbury on one side of him, and Bishop Robert Bloet of Lincoln on the other, and they were riding and talking there. Then the bishop of Lincoln sank down and said to the king, "Lord King, I am dying", and the king dismounted from his horse and caught him in his arms and had him carried home to his lodging: and he soon died. He was taken to Lincoln with great honour and buried before St. Mary's altar, and the bishop of Chester, who was called Robert Pecceth, buried him.

Then, soon after, the king sent his writs over all England, and ordered his bishops and abbots and thegns all to come and meet him for his council meeting on Candlemas Day[1] at Gloucester, and they did so. When they were assembled there, the king ordered them to elect an archbishop of Canterbury for themselves whomever they wished, and he would grant it to them. Then the bishops talked among themselves and said they wished never again to have a monk as archbishop over them, but they all went together to the king and desired that they might elect whomever they wished as archbishop from the secular clerks: and the king granted it to them. That had all been done through the bishop of Salisbury and the bishop of Lincoln before his death, because they never loved the monastic rule but were always against monks and their rule; and the prior and the monks of Canterbury and all the other monks who were there opposed it for a full two days, but it was of no avail, because the bishop of Salisbury was strong and controlled all England, and was against it with all his power and ability. Then they elected a clerk called William of Corbeil–he was canon of a monastery called St. Osyth's[2]–and they brought him before the king, and the king gave him the archbishopric and all the bishops received him: the monks and earls and thegns, nearly all that were there, opposed him.

At the same time the count's[3] messengers left the king without reaching agreement, and cared nothing for his favour.

At the same time there came a legate from Rome called Henry:[4] he was abbot of the monastery of St. Jean d'Angely, and he came for the Romescot.[5] And he told the king it was uncanonical to set a clerk over monks, and especially so when they had previously elected their archbishop in their chapter canonically–but the king would not cancel it because of his love for the bishop of Salisbury. Then the archbishop soon after that went to Canterbury and was received there, though it was against their will, and was there forthwith consecrated bishop by the bishop of London and Bishop Ernulf of Rochester and Bishop William Giffard of Winchester and Bishop Bernard of Wales[6] and Bishop Roger of Salisbury. Then soon, in the spring, the archbishop went to Rome for his *pallium*, and with him went Bishop Bernard of Wales and Sefred,[7] abbot of Glastonbury, and Anselm, abbot of St. Edmunds,[8] and John, archdeacon of Canterbury, and Giffard, who was the king's court chaplain.

At this same time Archbishop Thurstan of York went to Rome at the pope's

[1] 2 February. [2] St. Osyth's, Essex. [3] The count of Anjou.

[4] Henry of Poitou. For his further adventures, see under '1127'. He was the son of William VII, duke of Aquitaine.

[5] Peter's Pence. [6] *i.e.* Bishop of St. David's. [7] He was brother to Archbishop Ralph.

[8] Formerly abbot of St. Saba in Rome. See above, p. 184, n. 8.

E

command and arrived there three days before the archbishop of Canterbury arrived,[1] and was there received with great honour. Then the archbishop of Canterbury came and was there a full week before he could have any conversation with the pope–that was because the pope was given to understand that he had received the archbishopric in opposition to the monks of the monastery and uncanonically. But the thing that overcomes all the world overcame Rome–that is, gold and silver: and the pope relented, and gave him his *pallium*, and the archbishop swore by the heads of SS. Peter and Paul obedience to him in all the things that the pope imposed upon him, and [the pope] sent him home then with his blessing.

While the archbishop was out of the country, the king gave the bishopric of Bath to the queen's chancellor who was called Godfrey. He was born at Louvain. This took place at Woodstock on the day of the Annunciation to St. Mary.[2] Then soon after that the king went to Winchester and was there all Eastertide; and while he was there he gave the bishopric of Lincoln to a clerk called Alexander:[3] he was nephew to the bishop of Salisbury,[4] and the king did all this out of love for the bishop.

Then the king went from there to Portsmouth, and stayed there all over Whitsun week. Then as soon as he had a wind, he went over to Normandy and committed all England to the care and government of Bishop Roger of Salisbury.

Then the king was in Normandy all the year, and then great hostility arose between him and his thegns,[5] so that Count Waleran of Meulan[6] and Amaury[7] and Hugh of Montfort[8] and William of Roumare and many others deserted from him and held their castles against him; and the king resisted them stoutly: and in the course of this same year he won his castle of Pont Aldemer from Waleran and Montfort from Hugh: and afterwards the longer he went on the better he prospered.

In the course of this same year, before the bishop of Lincoln came to his diocese, nearly all the city of Lincoln was burnt down, and an immense number of people, men and women, were burnt to death and so much damage was done there that no one could describe it to another. That was on 19 May.

1124

E

(1124) All this year King Henry was in Normandy: that was because of the great hostilities he had with King Louis of France and with the count of Anjou and with his own men most of all.

Then it happened on the day of the Annunciation to St. Mary[9] that Count

[1] Reference has been made to the dispute between the two archbishops under '1119'. See further Z. N. Brooke, *English Church and the Papacy* (1931), pp. 168–173.

[2] 25 March.

[3] Alexander was consecrated bishop of Lincoln, 22 July 1123. He died 20 February 1148.

[4] Roger, bishop of Salisbury, 1107–1139.

[5] The use of the Old English word in this connexion is curious.

[6] Twin-brother of Robert, earl of Leicester, and son of Robert of Beaumont, count of Meulan and earl of Leicester.

[7] Of Montfort l'Amaury, father-in-law of Waleran.

[8] Of Montfort-sur-Risle, brother-in-law of Waleran.

[9] 25 March.

E

Waleran of Meulan went from his one castle called Beaumont[1] to his other castle of Vatteville: with him went Amaury, steward of the king of France, and Hugh, son of Gervase, and Hugh of Montfort and many other good knights.[2]

Then there came against them the king's knights[2] from all the castles that were thereabouts, and fought against them and routed them, and captured Count Waleran and Hugh, son of Gervase, and Hugh of Montfort and twenty-five other knights, and brought them to the king: and the king had Count Waleran and Hugh, son of Gervase, put in custody in the castle of Rouen, and Hugh of Montfort he sent to England and had him put into grievous bonds in the castle at Gloucester, and he sent as many of the others as he pleased north and south to his castles into custody. Then, afterwards, the king went and gained all Count Waleran's castles that there were in Normandy, and all the others that his opponents were holding against him.

All this hostility was because of the son of Count Robert of Normandy, called William.[3] This same William had married the younger daughter of Fulk, count of Anjou, and therefore the king of France and all the counts held with him, and all the powerful men, and said that the king was wrongfully holding his brother, Robert, in custody, and had unjustly caused his son, William, to flee from Normandy.

In the course of this same year the weather in England was very bad for corn and all products, so that between Christmas and Candlemas it was said that seed wheat for an acre–*i.e.* 2 seedlips–went up to 6 shillings and the barley–*i.e.* 3 seedlips–went up to 6 shillings and the seed oats for an acre–*i.e.* 4 seedlips–went to 4 shillings. That was because the corn was scarce, and the penny so bad that if a man had a pound at a market he could not by any means get the value of 12 pence for it.

In the course of this same year died the blessed Bishop Ernulf of Rochester, who had been abbot of Peterborough previously–that was on 15 March–and after that died King Alexander of Scotland on 23 April, and his brother, David,[4] who was then earl of Northampton, succeeded to the throne and had both together–the kingship in Scotland and the earldom in England. And on 14 December died the pope of Rome, called Calixtus,[5] and Honorius[6] succeeded to the papacy.

In the course of this same year after St. Andrew's Day before Christmas, Ralph Basset,[7] and the king's thegns[8] held a council at Hundcot in Leicestershire, and hanged there more thieves than ever had been hanged before; that was in all forty-four men in that little time: and six men were blinded and castrated. A large number of trustworthy men said that many were destroyed very unjustly there, but our Lord God Almighty that sees and knows all secrets–he sees the wretched people are treated with complete injustice–first they are robbed of their property and then they are killed. It was a very troublous year: the man who had any property was deprived of it by severe taxes and severe courts: the man who had none died of hunger.

[1] Beaumont-le-Roger, on the Risle.
[2] The word 'knight' is here used correctly. Contrast the use of the word 'thegn' in the previous annal.
[3] William nicknamed 'Clito'.
[4] David I, 1124–1153. [5] Calixtus II. [6] Honorius II.
[7] A prominent member of the king's court acting here as itinerant justice.
[8] Note use of the Old English word.

1125

E

(1125) In this year King Henry sent to England from Normandy before Christmas,[1] and ordered that all the moneyers who were in England should be mutilated–*i.e.* that each should lose the right hand and be castrated. That was because the man who had a pound could not get a pennyworth at a market. And Bishop Roger of Salisbury sent over all England and ordered them all to come to Winchester at Christmas.[1] When they got there, they were taken one by one and each deprived of the right hand, and castrated. All this was done before Twelfth Night,[2] and it was done very justly because they had ruined all the country with their great false-dealing: they all paid for it.

In the course of this same year the pope of Rome sent to this country a cardinal called John of Crema.[3] He came first to the king in Normandy, and the king received him with great honour, and commended him to William, archbishop of Canterbury: and he conducted him to Canterbury and he was there received with great honour and with a great procession, and he sang High Mass on Easter Day at Christ's altar, and then he went over all England to all the bishoprics and abbacies that there were in the country and he was received with honour everywhere, and they all gave him great and splendid gifts. And then he held his council at London[4] for a full three days at the Nativity of St. Mary, in September,[5] with archbishops and diocesan bishops and abbots and clerics and laity, and promulgated there the same laws that Archbishop Anselm had previously promulgated, and many more, though it was of little avail. And then he went overseas after Michaelmas, and so to Rome, and with him went Archbishop William of Canterbury and Archbishop Thurstan of York and Bishop Alexander of Lincoln and John, bishop of Lothian,[6] and Geoffrey, abbot of St. Albans, and they were there received by Pope Honorius[7] with great honour, and stayed there all the winter.

In the course of the same year there was so great a flood on St. Laurence's Day[8] that many villages were flooded and many people drowned, and bridges broken down, and corn and meadows utterly ruined, and disease among men and cattle, and there was more unseasonableness in all products than there had been for many years before.

And in the course of the same year died Abbot John of Peterborough on 14 October.

1126

E

(1126) All this year King Henry was in Normandy right up to after harvest time. Then he came to this country between the Nativity of St. Mary[5] and Michaelmas,[9] and with him came the queen and his daughter[10] whom he had previously married to the emperor, Henry of Lorraine,[11] and he brought with him Count Waleran and

[1] *i.e.* Christmas, 1124. [2] 6 January 1125.

[3] An important legatine commission involving jurisdictional controversies. Henry of Huntingdon is pleased to be able to tell a scandalous story respecting the legate's personal conduct while in England.

[4] For its acts, see the comments of Z. N. Brooke in *English Church and the Papacy*, p. 169.

[5] 8 September. [6] Bishop of Glasgow, 1118–1147. [7] Honorius II. [8] 10 August.

[9] Henry arrived in this country on 11 September. [10] Maud. [11] Henry V.

E

Hugh, son of Gervase, and he sent the count to Bridgnorth in custody, and from there he sent him afterwards to Wallingford, and Hugh [he sent] to Windsor and had him put into strict confinement.

And then after Michaelmas, David, king of Scots, came from Scotland into this country and King Henry received him with great honour, and he stayed all the year in this country.

In the course of this same year, the king had his brother, Robert, taken from Bishop Roger of Salisbury and entrusted him to his son, Robert, earl of Gloucester,[1] and had him taken to Bristol and put in the castle there. This was all done on the advice of his daughter, and through the king of Scots, David, her uncle.[2]

1127

E

(1127) This year King Henry held his court at Christmas[3] at Windsor, and David, king of Scots, was there, and all the chief men, both clerics and laymen, that there were in England. And there he [King Henry] caused archbishops and bishops and abbots and earls and all the thegns that were there to swear to give England and Normandy after his death into the hand of his daughter Athelic,[4] who had been wife of the emperor of Saxony;[5] and then [he] sent her to Normandy (and with her went her brother, Robert, earl of Gloucester, and Brian, son of Count Alan Fergant), and had her married to the son of the count of Anjou, called Geoffrey Martel. All the same, it displeased all the French and English: but the king did it to have peace with the count of Anjou and to have help against his nephew, William.[6]

In the course of this same year, in spring, Charles, count of Flanders, was killed by his own men in a church where he lay prostrate and praying to God before the altar, during Mass: and the king of France brought William, son of the count of Normandy, and gave him the county, and the people of that land accepted him. This same William had earlier married the daughter of the count of Anjou,[7] and they were afterwards separated for being within the prohibited degrees of relationship: that was all owing to King Henry of England. Afterwards he married the king of France's sister,[8] and for this reason the king gave him the county of Flanders.

In the course of this same year King Henry gave the abbacy of Peterborough to an abbot called Henry of Poitou,[9] who had possession of his abbacy of St. Jean d'Angely, and all the archbishops and bishops said that it was uncanonical and that he could not have possession of two abbacies. But this same Henry gave the king to

[1] See Table 4.

[2] David I, being the son of Malcolm Canmore and Margaret, was brother-in-law to Henry I, who married his sister Maud. See Table 16.

[3] Christmas, 1126.

[4] Better known by her other name of Maud.

[5] Henry V.

[6] William 'Clito', son of Robert.

[7] Maud, daughter of Fulk V of Anjou; she later became a nun at Fontevrault, where subsequently she was abbess.

[8] The reference is to Joan, daughter of Rainier of Montferrat. She was half-sister to Adelaide of Savoy, wife of Louis VI of France.

[9] See above, under '1123'.

E

understand that he had left his abbacy because of the great disturbance that there was in the country, and that he did it by the advice and permission of Rome and of the abbot of Cluny, and because he was legate in respect of Peter's Pence: but it was none the more like that for all his words–but, on the contrary, he wished to have possession of both: and he had them like that, as long as it was God's will. While a secular clerk, he was bishop of Soissons; then he became a monk at Cluny, then prior in this same monastery, and then he became prior at Savigny; after that, because he was a relative of the king of England and the count of Poitou, the count gave him the abbacy of the monastery of St. Jean d'Angely.

Afterwards, by means of his great stratagems, he then obtained the archbishopric of Besançon and had possession of it for three days, then he justly lost it because he had unjustly obtained it. Then he afterwards obtained the bishopric of Saintes which was five miles from where he was abbot; he had possession of that very nearly a week. Then the abbot of Cluny took him out of that as he had done earlier out of Besançon. Then he bethought himself that if he could get himself rooted in England, he could have everything he wished. He asked the king, and told him that he was an old and broken-down man, and he could not put up with the great injustices and the great disturbances that there were in their country. Then personally and through all his friends he especially desired the abbacy of Peterborough; and the king granted it to him because he was his relative and because he was a principal man in swearing the oath and bearing witness when the son of the count of Normandy and the daughter of the count of Anjou were separated for being within the prohibited degrees of relationship. Thus miserably was the abbacy given, between Christmas and Candlemas, at London, and so he went with the king to Winchester and from there he came to Peterborough, and there he stayed exactly as drones do in a hive. All that the bees carry in, the drones eat and carry out, and so did he: all that he could take inside and outside from clerics and laymen he thus sent overseas and did nothing good there and left nothing good there.

Let it not be thought remarkable, when we tell the truth, because it was fully known over all the country, that as soon as he came there (that was on the Sunday when *Exsurge quare obdormis Domine* is sung),[1] then soon afterwards many people saw and heard many hunters hunting. The hunters were black and big and loathsome, and their hounds were black and wide-eyed and loathsome, and they rode on black horses and black bucks. This was seen in the very deer-park in the town of Peterborough, and in all the woods that there were between this town and Stamford, and the monks heard the horns blow that they were blowing at night. Trustworthy people noticed them at night, and said that it seemed to them there might well be about twenty or thirty hornblowers. This was seen and heard from the time he came there all Lent up to Easter. This was his coming in–of his going out we can say nothing yet. May God provide!

[1] This is the Introit at Mass for Sexagesima Sunday, which in 1127 fell on 6 February.

1128

E

(1128) All this year King Henry was in Normandy because of the hostility that there was between him and his nephew, the count of Flanders. But the count was wounded by a retainer at a fight and, wounded as he was, he went to St. Bertin's monastery and forthwith became a monk there, and lived five days after that, and then died, and was buried there. God have mercy on his soul! That was on 27 July.

In the course of this same year died Bishop Rannulf Passeflambard[1] of Durham, and was buried there on 5 September.

And in the course of this same year the aforesaid Abbot Henry went home, by leave of the king, to his own monastery at Poitou. He gave the king to understand that he would give up the monastery and the land completely, and stay with him in England and in the monastery of Peterborough, but it was not so any the more for that–he did it because he meant to stay there through his great trickery whether it were twelve months or more, and then to come back. God Almighty have mercy on that wretched place!

In the course of the same year Hugh of the Temple[2] came from Jerusalem to the king in Normandy, and the king received him with great honour and gave him great treasures, consisting of gold and silver; and then he sent him to England and there he was received by all good men and they all gave him treasure–and in Scotland also –and sent by him to Jerusalem great property entirely in gold and silver: and he ordered people out to Jerusalem, and then there went with him and after him so large a number of people as never had done since the first expedition in the days of Pope Urban[3]–though it came to little. He said that thoroughgoing war was prepared between the Christians and the heathens. Then when they arrived there it was nothing but lies–thus miserably were all the people afflicted.

1129

E

(1129) In this year the king sent to England for Count Waleran[4] and for Hugh, son of Gervase, and there they gave hostages for themselves, and Hugh went home to his own land, to France, and Waleran remained with the king: and the king gave him all his land except his castle only.

Then the king came to England in autumn and the count came with him, and they became quite as good friends as before they had been enemies.

Then soon by the advice and permission of the king, Archbishop William of Canterbury sent over all England and ordered bishops and abbots and archdeacons and all the priors, monks and canons that there were in all the cells in England, and for all those that had to care for and look after Christianity all to come to London at Michaelmas and there to discuss all God's dues. When they arrived there, the meeting began on Monday and continued right on to the Friday. When it all came out, it

[1] Usually known as Rannulf Flambard.
[2] Hugh 'de Payen', founder of the Templars.
[3] Urban II. The reference is to the First Crusade.
[4] Count of Meulan. See Table 12.

E

turned out to be all about archdeacons' wives and priests' wives, that they were to give them up by St. Andrew's Day, and anyone who would not do so, should forgo his church and his house and his home, and never more have a claim to it: this was ordered by William of Canterbury, the archbishop, and all the diocesan bishops that were in England, and the king gave them all permission to go home, and so they went home, and all the orders availed nothing–they all kept their wives by permission of the king as they had done before.

In the course of this year William Giffard, bishop of Winchester, died, and was buried there on 25 January, and King Henry gave the bishopric after Michaelmas to Henry, abbot of Glastonbury, his nephew,[1] and he was consecrated bishop by Archbishop William of Canterbury on 17 November.

In the course of this year died Pope Honorius.[2] Before he was well dead, two popes were elected there. One was called Peter[3]–he was a monk of Cluny and was descended from the most powerful men of Rome, and the people of Rome, and the duke of Sicily[4] held with him. The other was called Gregory,[5] and he was a secular clerk and was chased out of Rome by the other pope and his relatives. With him held the emperor of Saxony[6] and the king of France[7] and King Henry of England and all those on this side of the Alps.

There now grew up such heresy as there had never been before. May Christ establish counsel for his wretched people!

In the course of this same year on St. Nicholas's eve,[8] a little before day, there was a great earthquake.

1130

D[9]

(1080) Angus[10] was killed by a Scottish army, and there were great casualties on his side. There God's right was avenged on him because he was altogether perjured.

E

(1130) In the course of this year the church of Canterbury was consecrated by Archbishop William on 4 May. These bishops were present: Gilbert 'Universalis' of London; Henry of Winchester; Alexander of Lincoln; Roger of Salisbury; Simon of Worcester, Roger of Coventry, Godfrey of Bath, Everard of Norwich, Seffrid of Chichester, Bernard

[1] This is Henry of Blois, brother of King Stephen, being the son of Stephen, count of Blois, by Adela, sister of Henry I. See Table 6. He administered the revenues of Glastonbury during a vacancy.

[2] Honorius II.

[3] Peter 'de Pier-leoni', who, as anti-pope, took the title of Anacletus.

[4] Roger II.

[5] He later became Innocent II.

[6] Lothair II.

[7] Louis VI.

[8] 5 December.

[9] This entry occurs as an addition to MS. 'D' which ends in 1079. It is there added under 1080, this being due to an obvious scribal error of MLXXX for MCXXX. Perhaps this should be taken into account in considering the original composition of the version of which MS. 'D' is a reproduction, and perhaps also it should be considered in connexion with the theory that 'D' may represent a version of the Anglo-Saxon Chronicle which was prepared for presentation to the Scottish court.

[10] This is Angus, earl of Moray, who in 1130 unsuccessfully rebelled against David I.

D

E

of St. David's, Audoen[1] of Evreux from Normandy, John of Séez.

On the fourth day after that, King Henry was at Rochester and the town was nearly burnt down and Archbishop William consecrated St. Andrew's Cathedral, and the aforesaid bishops with him: and King Henry went overseas into Normandy in autumn.

In the course of this same year, Abbot Henry of Angely[2] came after Easter to Peterborough, and said he had entirely given up the monastery. After him the abbot of Cluny, Peter,[3] came to England by permission of the king and was received everywhere, wherever he came, with great honour. He came to Peterborough, and there Abbot Henry promised him that he would obtain the monastery of Peterborough for him so that it should be subjected to Cluny: but it is said as a proverb "The hedge remains that divides the fields." God Almighty destroy all wicked plans! And soon after that the abbot of Cluny went home to his own country.

1131

E

(1131) This year, after Christmas, on a Sunday night at first sleep, the sky in the north was all as if it was a burning fire, so that all who saw it were afraid as they had never been before–that was on 11 January. In the course of this same year, there was such a great cattle plague all over England as had never been before in anyone's memory–that was among cattle and pigs, so that in a village that had ten or twelve ploughs in action, there was not one left, and the man who had two hundred or three hundred pigs had not one left. After that, the hens died, then the meat and cheese and butter ran short. May God amend it when it is his will!

And King Henry came home to England, before autumn, after the earlier Feast of St. Peter.[4]

In the course of this same year, before Easter, Abbot Henry went overseas to Normandy and there spoke with the king and told him that the abbot of Cluny had ordered him to come to him and hand over to him the abbacy of Angely: and then

[1] He was a brother of Thurstan, archbishop of York. For him, see *Gallia Christiana*, vol. XI, col. 373.
[2] Henry of Poitou, abbot of St. Jean d'Angely.
[3] Peter 'the Venerable'. [4] 29 June.

E

with his permission he would come home–and so he went home to his own monastery, and stayed there right up to Midsummer Day. And the next day after St. John's Day, the monks elected an abbot from among themselves and brought him into the church with a procession, sung *Te Deum Laudamus*, rang the bells, set him on the abbot's throne, and did all such obedience to him as they ought to do to their abbot. And the earl and all the chief men and the monks of the monastery chased the other abbot, Henry, out of the monastery: they had to, of necessity–in five and twenty years they never experienced one good day. Now all his great trickery failed him: now he was forced to creep into his big wallet, into every corner of it, to see whether there were at least one poor trick left so that he could deceive Christ and all Christ's people yet once more. Then he went to Cluny and there was kept, so that he could go neither east nor west–the abbot of Cluny said that they had lost St. John's monastery through him and his great folly. Then he knew of no better remedy for himself than to promise them, and to swear oaths on the relics, that if he might visit England, he would get possession of the monastery of Peterborough for them so that he should appoint a prior from Cluny to it, and the sacristan and treasurer and keeper of the wardrobe, and all the things that were in the monastery, and outside it, he would commit to them. Then he went into France, and stayed there all the year. Christ take counsel for the wretched monks of Peterborough and for the wretched place: now they need Christ's help and that of all Christian people.

1132

E

(1132) This year King Henry came to this country. Then Abbot Henry came and accused the monks of Peterborough to the king, because he wished to put the monastery under the rule of Cluny, with the result that the king was nearly deceived, and sent for the monks. And by the mercy of God and by means of the bishop of Salisbury, the bishop of Lincoln and the other powerful men who were there, the king perceived that he was dealing with treachery. When he could do no more, he wished that his nephew should be abbot in Peterborough, but Christ did not wish it. It was not long after that, that the king sent for him, and made him give up the abbacy of Peterborough, and go out of the country. And the king gave the abbacy to a prior of St. Neot's called Martin. He came into the monastery on St. Peter's Day with great dignity.

1135

E

(1135) In this year King Henry went overseas at Lammas, and the next day, when he was lying asleep on board ship, the day grew dark over all lands, and the sun became as if it were a three-nights'-old moon, with stars about it at midday.

People were very much astonished and terrified, and said that something important

E

would be bound to come after this–so it did, for that same year the king died the day after St. Andrew's Day,[1] in Normandy. Then forthwith these lands grew dark, for everyone who could forthwith robbed another. Then his son and his friends took his body and brought it to England and buried it at Reading. He was a good man, and people were in great awe of him. No one dared injure another in his time. He made peace for man and beast. Whoever carried his burden of gold and silver, nobody dared say anything but good to him.

Meanwhile his nephew, Stephen of Blois, was come to England and went to London. The Londoners received him, and sent for the archbishop, William of Corbeil, who consecrated him king on Christmas Day.

In this king's time there was nothing but disturbance and wickedness and robbery, for forthwith the powerful men who were traitors rose against him. First of all Baldwin of Reviers[2] held Exeter against him and the king besieged it, and then Baldwin came to an agreement. Then the others took and held their castles against him, and David, king of Scotland, began to make war on him. Then, in spite of that, their messengers went between them, and they came together and were brought to agreement, though it was of little use.

1137

E

(1137) This year King Stephen went overseas to Normandy, and was received there because they expected that he would be just as his uncle had been, and because he still had his treasure; but he distributed it and squandered it like a fool. King Henry had gathered a great amount–gold and silver–and no good to his soul was done with it.

When King Stephen came to England he held his council at Oxford, and there he took Roger, bishop of Salisbury, and Alexander, bishop of Lincoln, and the chancellor Roger, his nephews,[3] and put them all in prison till they surrendered their castles. When the traitors understood that he was a mild man, and gentle and good, and did not exact the full penalties of the law, they perpetrated every enormity. They had done him homage, and sworn oaths, but they kept no pledge; all of them were perjured and their pledges nullified, for every powerful man built his castles and held them against him and they filled the country full of castles. They oppressed the wretched people of the country severely with castle-building. When the castles were built, they filled them with devils and wicked men. Then, both by night and day they took those people that they thought had any goods–men and women–and put them in prison and tortured them with indescribable torture to extort gold and silver–for no martyrs were ever so tortured as they were. They were hung by the thumbs or by the head, and corselets were hung on their feet. Knotted ropes were put round their heads and twisted till they penetrated to the brains. They put them in prisons where there were adders and snakes and toads, and killed them like that. Some they put in a "torture-chamber"–that is in a chest that was short, narrow and shallow,

[1] 1 December. [2] Before midsummer 1141 he became earl of Devon.
[3] *i.e.* nephews of Roger, bishop of Salisbury.

E

and they put sharp stones in it and pressed the man in it so that he had all his limbs broken. In many of the castles was a "noose-and-trap"–consisting of chains of such a kind that two or three men had enough to do to carry one. It was so made that it was fastened to a beam, and they used to put a sharp iron around the man's throat and his neck, so that he could not in any direction either sit or lie or sleep, but had to carry all that iron. Many thousands they killed by starvation.

I have neither the ability nor the power to tell all the horrors nor all the torments they inflicted upon wretched people in this country: and that lasted the nineteen years while Stephen was king, and it was always going from bad to worse. They levied taxes on the villages every so often, and called it "protection money".[1] When the wretched people had no more to give, they robbed and burned all the villages, so that you could easily go a whole day's journey and never find anyone occupying a village, nor land tilled. Then corn was dear, and meat and butter and cheese, because there was none in the country. Wretched people died of starvation; some lived by begging for alms, who had once been rich men; some fled the country.

There had never been till then greater misery in the country, nor had heathens ever done worse than then they did. For contrary to custom, they respected neither church nor churchyard, but took all the property that was inside, and then burnt the church and everything together. Neither did they respect bishops' land nor abbots' nor priests', but robbed monks and clerics, and everyone robbed somebody else if he had the greater power. If two or three men came riding to a village, all the villagers fled, because they expected they would be robbers. The bishops and learned men were always excommunicating them, but they thought nothing of it, because they were all utterly accursed and perjured and doomed to perdition.

Wherever cultivation was done, the ground produced no corn, because the land was all ruined by such doings, and they said openly that Christ and his saints were asleep. Such things, too much for us to describe, we suffered nineteen years for our sins.

In[2] all this evil time, Abbot Martin held his abbacy for twenty years and a half, and six days, with great energy, and provided for the monks and the guests everything they needed, and held great commemoration feasts in the house, and nevertheless worked at the church and appointed lands and income for it, and endowed it richly and had it roofed, and brought them into the new monastery on St. Peter's Day[3] with great ceremony–that was A.D. 1140, twenty-three years since the fire. And he went to Rome and was there well received by Pope Eugenius,[4] and obtained there privileges, one in respect of all the lands pertaining to the office of sacristan, another in respect of all the lands of the abbacy, and if he could have lived longer, he meant to do the same in the case of the office of treasurer. And he got back lands that powerful men were holding by force–from William Maudit who held Rockingham Castle, he recovered Cottingham and Easton: from Hugo of Vatteville he recovered Irthlingborough, and Stanwick and 60 shillings each year from Aldwinkle, and he made

[1] *tenserie*.

[2] This paragraph is clearly a later insertion, and the events subsequently recorded in it show it to have been written after the death of King Stephen.

[3] 29 June.

[4] Eugenius III, who succeeded to the papacy in 1145.

E

many monks, and planted a vineyard, and did much building and made the village better than it had ever been before, and was a good monk and a good man, and therefore God and good men loved him.

Now we wish to describe to some extent what happened in King Stephen's time. In his time, the Jews of Norwich bought a Christian child before Easter and tortured him with all the torture that our Lord was tortured with: and on Good Friday hanged him on a cross on account of our Lord, and then buried him. They expected it would be concealed, but our Lord made it plain that he was a holy martyr, and the monks took him and buried him with ceremony in the monastery, and through our Lord he works wonderful and varied miracles, and he is called St. William.[1]

1138

E

(1138) In this year David, king of Scotland, came to this country with an immense army: he meant to conquer this country. And William of Aumale,[2] the earl to whom the king had entrusted York, and the other reliable men with a few men, came to meet him and fought with them and routed the king at the Standard and killed very many of his followers.[3]

[1140][4]

E

(1140) In this year King Stephen meant to capture Robert, earl of Gloucester, King Henry's son, but he could not because he became aware of it.[5]

After that, in spring, the sun grew dark, and the day, about midday when people were eating, so that they lit candles to eat by. That was 20 March,[6] and people were very much astonished. After that, William, archbishop of Canterbury, died,[7] and the king made Theobald archbishop:[8] he was abbot of Le Bec.

After that there arose a great war between the king and Rannulf, earl of Chester, not because he did not give him all that he could ask him (as he did everybody else) but always the more he gave them the worse they were to him. The earl held Lincoln against the king, and deprived him of all that he ought to have had, and the king went there and besieged him and his brother, William of Roumare,[9] in the castle: and the earl got out secretly, and went after Robert, earl of Gloucester, and brought him there with a large army, and they fought fiercely on Candlemas Day[10] against

[1] On this see further A. Jessop and M. R. James, *St. William of Norwich* (1896)

[2] Lord of Holderness.

[3] The battle of the Standard was fought near Northallerton, 22 August 1138. See No. 11.

[4] This annal is made up of notices relating generally to Stephen's reign. The chronology is very confused. On these events, see J. H. Round, *Geoffrey de Mandeville* (1892).

[5] April 1137.

[6] There was an eclipse of the sun on 20 March 1140

[7] 21 November 1136

[8] He was consecrated 8 January 1139.

[9] Earl of Lincoln.

[10] 2 February 1141.

E

their liege lord, and captured him (for his men failed him and fled) and took him to Bristol and put him in prison and fetters there. Then all England was disturbed more than it had been before and there was every evil in the country.

After that came King Henry's daughter[1] who had been empress in Germany and was now countess of Anjou, and came to London: and the Londoners wanted to capture her, and she fled and lost a great deal there.

After that, the bishop of Winchester, Henry, King Stephen's brother, spoke with Earl Robert, and with the empress, and swore oaths to them that he would never again support the king his brother; and he excommunicated all the men who supported him, and told them he would give up Winchester to them and had them come there. When they were in the town, the king's wife came with all her forces, and besieged them[2] so that there was a great famine in the town. When they could endure it no longer, they got out secretly and fled and those outside became aware of it and pursued them and captured Robert, earl of Gloucester, and took him to Rochester and put him in prison there: and the empress fled to a monastery. Then the wise men went between the king's friends and the earl's friends and agreement was reached, the terms being that the king should be let out of prison in exchange for the earl, and the earl for the king, and so they did.

Then, after that,[3] the king and Earl Rannulf came to an agreement at Stamford, and swore oaths and confirmed pledges that neither of them should betray the other: and it came to nothing, because afterwards the king captured him at Southampton through bad counsel, and put him in prison, and soon he let him out through worse counsel, on condition that he swore on the relics and found hostages [to assure] that he would surrender his castles. Some he surrendered and some he did not, and did worse than he ought to have done here.

Then England was very much divided–some supported the king and some the empress, because when the king was in prison the earls and the powerful men expected that he would never get out again, and made an agreement with the empress and brought her into Oxford and gave her the city. When the king was out of prison, he heard this said and took his army and besieged her in the tower, and she was let down at night from the tower with ropes, and she stole out and fled and went on foot to Wallingford.[4]

After that she went overseas, and those of Normandy all deserted from the king to the count of Anjou, some of their own accord and some not of their own accord, because he besieged them till they gave up their castles, and they had no help from the king.

Then Eustace, the king's son, went to France and married the king of France's sister[5]–by which he expected to obtain all Normandy, but he did not prosper much, and by good right for he was a bad man–for wherever he went he did more harm than good. He robbed the lands and levied heavy taxes. He brought his wife to England and put her in the castle in Canterbury. A good woman she was, but she had little

[1] Maud arrived in England in September 1139. Her flight from London took place in June 1141.
[2] August–September 1141. [3] In 1142. [4] December 1142. [5] February 1140.

E

happiness with him, and it was not Christ's will that he should rule long–and he died[1] and his mother as well.

And the count of Anjou died,[2] and his son, Henry, succeeded to the dominions: and the queen of France[3] separated from the king and came to young Count Henry, and he took her as his wife, and all Poitou with her. Then he went with a big army into England,[4] and won castles, and the king went against him with a much bigger army, and all the same they did not fight, but the archbishop and the wise men went between them and made an agreement that the king should be liege lord and king as long as he lived and after his day Henry should be king; they should be as father and son; and there should always be peace and concord between them, and in all England.[5] This, and all the other conditions that they made, the king and the count and the bishop and the earls and powerful men all swore to keep. Then the count was received at Winchester and in London with great honour, and all did him homage, and swore to keep the peace: and it soon became a good peace, such as there never was before. Then the king was stronger than he had been till then, and the count went overseas and everybody loved him because he exacted strict justice and made peace.

1154

E

(1154) In this year King Stephen died,[6] and was buried where his wife and son were buried at Faversham, the monastery they had founded. When the king was dead, the count was overseas, and nobody dared do anything but good to another because they were in such great awe of him. When he came to England, he was received with great honour, and consecrated king on the Sunday before Christmas,[7] and there he held a great court.

That same day that Abbot Martin of Peterborough was to have gone there, he fell ill, and died on 2 January,[8] and the monks within the day chose another from among themselves, whose name is William of Vatteville, a good cleric and a good man, and well loved by the king and by all good men. And they buried the abbot with ceremony in the church; and soon the abbot-elect went (and the monks with him) to Oxford to the king, and he gave him the abbacy; and he went shortly to Lincoln and was there consecrated abbot before he came home, and was then received with great ceremony at Peterborough–with a great procession. And so he was also at Romsey and Thorney and Spalding and Sudbury: and is now abbot, and has made a fine beginning. Christ grant him. . . .[9]

[1] August 1153. [2] 7 September 1151.

[3] Eleanor, wife of Louis VII. Their formal separation took place in March 1152. Her marriage to Henry II took place in May 1152.

[4] January 1153.

[5] The 'Treaty of Winchester' was made on 6 November 1153. See below, No. 22.

[6] He died 25 October 1154. [7] 11 December 1154. [8] 1155.

[9] The MS. is mutilated and ends at this point.

2. Select passages from the annals ascribed to 'Florence of Worcester'

These annals which were compiled at Worcester, and perhaps by a monk of that place named Florence, were originally grafted on to a chronicle of world events written by Marianus Scotus, an Irish monk, who lived at Fulda and later at Mainz. They were probably written towards the end of the first third of the twelfth century, but their author had access to earlier material which he utilized with discretion and care. Thus he used in particular the Anglo-Saxon Chronicles, and it is possible that he had sometimes access to a version of those chronicles which has since been lost. His work in consequence not only assists in the criticism of that invaluable source, with which it should be carefully compared, but also on occasion supplements it. 'Florence of Worcester' was on the whole a very accurate, if somewhat unimaginative, writer, and his work still awaits the detailed criticism it deserves. Good accounts of the work are to be found in R. L. Poole, *Chronicles and Annals* (Oxford, 1926) and in R. R. Darlington, *Anglo-Norman Historians* (London, 1947). No satisfactory edition exists, but the best is that published by the English Historical Society under the editorship of Benjamin Thorpe (2 vols., London, 1848, 1849). A translation from this was made by Joseph Stevenson, in *Church Historians of England*, vol. II, pt. i.

1042.[1] . . . Harthacnut, king of the English, was standing at the wedding-feast given at the place called Lamhithe[2] by Osgod Clapa,[3] a great lord, on the occasion of the joyful marriage of his daughter, Gytha, to Tofig, surnamed Pruda,[4] a Danish magnate. Full of health and mirth, he was drinking with the bride and the guests when suddenly, even in the act of drinking, he fell down, and remained speechless until 8 June when he died. He was carried to Winchester and there buried by the side of King Cnut, his father. His brother, Edward, was proclaimed king in London chiefly by the exertions of Earl Godwine and Lifing, bishop of Worcester. He was the son of Ethelred, whose father was Edgar, whose father was Edmund, whose father was Edward the Elder, whose father was Alfred. . . .

1043.[5] On the first day of Easter, being 3 April, Edward was crowned king in Winchester by Eadsige, archbishop of Canterbury, and Ælfric, archbishop of York, and nearly all the bishops of England. In the same year, fourteen days before the Feast of St. Andrew the Apostle,[6] the king went suddenly and unexpectedly from Gloucester to Winchester accompanied by Earls Leofric, Godwine and Siward, and with their advice took from his mother all the gold, silver, jewels, precious stones and other valuables which she possessed; because she had treated him with parsimony and severity both before he became king and afterwards. Nevertheless he ordered her to live there quietly and had her well supplied with what was necessary. . . .

1044.[7] . . . At a general council which was held about that time in London, Wulmar, also called Manni, a monk of Evesham, was elected abbot of his monastery, and was consecrated on Friday, 10 August. In the same year the noble lady Gunnilde,

[1] The annals, as here given, represent the true chronology. Marianus Scotus, to whose work these notices were added, had a strange chronological theory that the Years of Grace, as commonly reckoned, were twenty-two years wrong. His practice was therefore to place all events twenty-two years before the date on which they occurred. These and other idiosyncrasies of this annalist have here been disregarded. A full solution of all the difficulties which are involved in this text will not be obtained until a new edition of the work has been made.

[2] Lambeth.

[3] See above, pp. 114, 117, 132.

[4] Staller to Harthacnut

[5] Cf. p. 111 above.

[6] 16 November.

[7] Cf. p. 112 above.

daughter of King Wyrtgeorn by the sister of King Cnut, and in turn the widow of Earls Hakon and Harold, was expelled from England with her two sons, Heming and Thurkill. She went over to Flanders, and resided a short time at Bruges, and afterwards reached Denmark. Stigand, the king's chaplain, was made bishop of East Anglia. . . .

1045.[1] . . . In this year Edward, king of the English, collected a very powerful fleet at Sandwich to oppose Magnus, king of the Norwegians, who was planning an invasion of England. His coming was however prevented by Sweyn,[2] king of the Danes, who made war against him. . . .

1046.[3] . . . Osgod Clapa was expelled from England. Magnus, king of the Norwegians, son of the saintly King Olaf, routed Sweyn, king of the Danes, and subdued Denmark to himself. . . .

1047.[4] . . . Sweyn, king of the Danes, sent his ambassadors to Edward, king of the English, requesting him to send his fleet against Magnus, king of the Norwegians. Then Earl Godwine advised the king that he should send at least fifty ships manned with soldiers. This advice however met with the disapproval of Earl Leofric and all the people, and so the king refused to send aid. Afterwards Magnus, king of the Norwegians, having collected a large and strong fleet, fought a battle with Sweyn, and after great slaughter on both sides expelled him from Denmark. Magnus then reigned in Denmark and made the Danes pay heavy tribute to him. Shortly afterwards he died.

1048.[5] Sweyn recovered Denmark, and Harold Hardraada,[6] who was son of Siward, king of the Norwegians, and brother on his mother's side to St. Olaf, and uncle on his father's side to King Magnus, went over again to Norway; and shortly afterwards he sent ambassadors to King Edward making offers of peace and friendship which were accepted. Sweyn, king of the Danes, also sent ambassadors to Edward asking him to dispatch a fleet to his assistance. But although Earl Godwine wished to send at least fifty ships, Earl Leofric and all the people unanimously opposed him. . . .

1049.[7] Leo[8] was pope, being the one hundred and forty-fifth. This was that Leo who made a new hymn about Pope Gregory. The Emperor Henry[9] assembled a great army against Baldwin,[10] count of Flanders, chiefly because he had burnt his beautiful palace at Nymegen. In this expedition went Pope Leo, and very many nobles and magnates from different countries. Moreover Sweyn, king of the Danes, was there at the emperor's bidding, with his fleet, and he swore fealty for that occasion to the emperor. He sent also to Edward, king of the English, and asked him not to let Baldwin escape, if he should take to the sea. The king therefore went with a great fleet to Sandwich, and remained there until the emperor had obtained from Baldwin all that he desired. Meanwhile Earl Sweyn, son of Earl Godwine and Gytha, who had left

[1] Cf. p. 113 above.
[2] Sweyn Estrithson.
[3] Cf. p. 113 above.
[4] Cf. p. 114 above.
[5] Cf. p. 115 above.
[6] Text has erroneously "Harvager".
[7] Cf. p. 116 above.
[8] Leo IX.
[9] Henry III.
[10] Baldwin V.

England and gone to Denmark, because he was not able to marry Edith, abbess of Leominster, whom he had seduced, returned with eight ships, saying falsely that he would not remain a faithful subject to the king. Earl Beorn, son of his uncle, Ulf, the Danish earl who was the son of Sprakling, who was the son of Urse and brother of Sweyn, king of the Danes, promised him to obtain from the king the restoration of his earldom. Count Baldwin having made peace with the emperor, Earls Godwine and Beorn came with the king's permission to Pevensey with forty-two ships. He kept a few ships with him and ordered the rest to return home. When it was told him that Osgod Clapa was lying with twenty-nine ships at Ulpe,[1] he recalled as many as possible of the ships he had dismissed. But Osgod, taking with him his wife whom he had left at Bruges, returned with six ships to Denmark. But some of them went to Essex, and returned having taken much booty from about Eadulfsness.[2] A great storm however overtook them on their return, and sank all but two of them; these were afterwards taken at sea and all on board were slain. While these events were happening Earl Sweyn came to Pevensey, and treacherously asked his cousin, Earl Beorn, to go with him to Sandwich and make his promised peace with the king. Relying on his kinship Beorn took only three companions with him and set out to join his cousin. But Sweyn took him to Bosham where his ships were stationed, and taking him into one had him strongly fettered and borne off to the mouth of the river Dart. There he killed him and threw him into a deep trench which he covered with earth. The six ships were then dismissed. The men of Hastings afterwards captured two of them, and after killing all on board they took them to Sandwich and gave them to the king. Sweyn however fled to Flanders with two ships, and remained there until he was brought back by Aldred, bishop of Worcester, who set him at peace with the king. . . .

1050.[3] Macbeth, king of the Scots, gave alms in Rome. Eadsige, archbishop of Canterbury, died, and Robert, bishop of London, a Norman by birth, succeeded him. Sparrowhawk, abbot of Abingdon, was appointed to the bishopric of London; but before he was consecrated, he was expelled by King Edward. Hereman, bishop of Wilton, and Aldred, bishop of Worcester, went to Rome.

1051. Ælfric,[4] archbishop of York, died at Southwell, and was buried at Medhamstead; Kynsige, the king's chaplain, succeeded him. King Edward released the English from their heavy tax[5] in the thirty-eighth year after his father, Ethelred, had ordered it to be paid to the Danish soldiers. After these things, in September, Eustace the elder, count of Boulogne, who had married Goda, a sister of King Edward, came with a small fleet to Dover. His men, while asking for lodging in a stupid and insolent manner, slew one of the citizens. One of his fellow-citizens who saw the deed avenged it by killing a soldier. The count and his men were very angry about this, and slew men and women and trampled babes and children under the feet of their horses. But when they saw the citizens coming out to oppose them, they began to fly like cowards: seven of them were slain and the rest escaped with difficulty. These betook themselves to King Edward, who was then at Gloucester. Godwine was excessively angry that such things should happen within his jurisdiction. He therefore collected a very large

[1] In Flanders. [2] The Naze, Essex. [3] Cf. p. 119 above. [4] Cf. p. 120 above. [5] Danegeld.

force from his earldom, namely from Kent, Sussex and Wessex. His eldest son, Sweyn, did the same in his earldom, namely from Oxfordshire, Gloucestershire, Herefordshire, Somerset and Berkshire; and his other son, Harold, collected yet another force from his earldom, namely from Essex, East Anglia, Huntingdonshire and Cambridgeshire. King Edward learnt of these things. He therefore sent messengers in haste to Leofric, earl of the Mercians, and to Siward, earl of the Northumbrians, and entreated them to come to him quickly with all the men they could collect, for, as he said, he was in great danger. At first they came with only a few men, but finding out how things stood, they sent swift horsemen throughout their territories and assembled a large army. Likewise, Earl Ralph, son of Goda, daughter of King Edward, assembled as many men as he could from his territory. Meanwhile Godwine and his sons and their respective forces came to Gloucestershire after the Feast of St. Mary's Nativity.[1] They encamped at a place called Langtree, and sent messengers to the king at Gloucester, threatening war unless he gave up Count Eustace and his companions and also the Normans and the men from Boulogne who held the castle at Dovercliff. For a time the king was alarmed and in great distress, not knowing what to do, but when he found that the forces of Earls Leofric, Siward and Ralph were coming in, he stoutly replied that he would in no wise deliver up Eustace and the rest. The messengers thus returned without having obtained their object. When they had departed, the troops with the king entered Gloucester, and so excited were they, and so unanimous in their desire for battle, that if the king had permitted it, they would immediately have attacked Earl Godwine's army. But seeing there were some of the best men in all England in his army and in theirs, Earl Leofric and some others thought it would be great foolishness to fight with their own countrymen. They advised therefore that each side should give hostages, and that on an agreed day the king and Godwine should meet in London to arrange matters. This suggestion was approved, and after negotiations and the exchange of hostages, Earl Godwine went to Wessex, and the king assembled more troops out of all Mercia and Northumbria, and took them on with him to London. Godwine and his sons came up to Southwark with a great host from Wessex, but, seeing that his troops were gradually deserting him, he dared not come to meet the king as arranged, and so he fled in the night. Therefore, when the morning came, the king in his witan, and the whole army, with one accord banished him and his five sons. Immediately he, with his wife, Gytha, and Tosti with his wife, Judith, who was the daughter of Baldwin, count of Flanders, and two of his other sons, namely Sweyn and Gyrth, went to Thorney where his ship lay ready. They speedily loaded her with as much gold, silver and treasure as she could carry, and embarking in haste they went on their way to Count Baldwin in Flanders. But the sons of Godwine, Harold and Leofwine, went to Bristol, and embarking there on a ship which their brother, Sweyn, had prepared for them, they sailed over to Ireland. The king repudiated his queen, Edith, on account of his wrath against her father, Godwine, and sent her without respect with only one female attendant on foot to Wherwell, and delivered her into the custody of the abbess there. After these things Count William the Norman came to England with a host of Normans. King Edward

[1] 8 September.

entertained him and his companions with honours, and sent them back to Normandy laden with gifts. In the same year William, the king's chaplain, succeeded to the bishopric of London which had formerly been given to Sparrowhawk. St. Bardo, archbishop of Mainz, died on 10 June, and was succeeded by Leopold.

1052.[1] Marianus, the chronographer, retired from this life. Algiva-Emma, wife of the kings, Ethelred and Cnut, died at Winchester on 6 March, and was buried there. In the same year Griffith,[2] king of the Welsh, laid waste a great part of Herefordshire. The inhabitants and many Normans from a castle went up against him, but he routed them and slew many of them, and took great booty. This battle was fought on the thirteenth anniversary of the day when the Welsh slew in ambush Edwin, the brother of Earl Leofric. A short time after this Earl Harold and his brother Leofwine, returned from Ireland and entering the mouth of the river Severn they landed on the coasts of Somerset and Dorset,[3] and plundered fields and villages. A great host from Devonshire and Somerset went up against them, but Harold got the victory, killing more than thirty noble thegns and a great number of other men. Then he returned to his ships with the booty and shortly afterwards sailed round Land's End. Then King Edward sent in haste to Sandwich forty ships well found in provisions and manned with picked soldiers, giving them orders to wait and watch for the arrival of Earl Godwine. Despite this, the earl managed to land wholly unobserved in Kent, although he had only a few ships. By means of secret negotiations he won over to his side first the men of Kent and then the men of Sussex, Essex and Surrey, and the shipmen of Hastings and of all that coast. These, and many more besides, all declared they were ready to live or die with him. On the receipt of this news the king's fleet, which lay at Sandwich, pursued him, but he took to flight and concealed himself wherever he could. So the fleet returned to Sandwich, and thence proceeded to London. When Earl Godwine heard this he crossed over to the Isle of Wight, and kept cruising up and down the south coast until his sons, Harold and Leofwine, could join him with their ships. And after their meeting, they left off plundering, confining themselves to getting provisions for their army when they required it. After enticing to their side as many men as they could both on the sea-coast and elsewhere, and taking with them all the shipmen they met, they set sail for Sandwich. Having arrived there, they notified the fact to King Edward who was then staying in London. Thereupon he quickly sent out messengers commanding all those who had not deserted him to come speedily to his assistance. But they were very slow, and did not come in time. Meanwhile, Earl Godwine with his fleet sailed up the Thames against the tide. He reached Southwark on the Feast of the Exaltation of the Holy Cross[4] (which was a Monday) and there waited until the flood tide came up. During this time he had meetings with the citizens of London both in person and by deputy. These he had previously placated by means of many promises, and he brought nearly all of them over to his side. So when everything was arranged and set in order he weighed anchor immediately the tide came up, and sailed up the river along the southern bank, meeting no opposition at the bridge.

[1] Cf. p. 125 above. [2] See above, p. 125.
[3] Doubtless an error for Devonshire: the landing was at Porlock.
[4] 14 September, which in 1052 did in fact fall on a Monday. This is an accurate writer.

The land army also arrived, and putting itself in array along the bank of the river, showed a close and imposing front. Then the fleet made for the northern bank, as though for the purpose of enclosing the numerous fleet and army of the king. But inasmuch as there were very few men of any prowess either with the king or with Godwine who were not Englishmen, nearly all were very reluctant to fight against their kinsmen and fellow-countrymen.[1] This circumstance enabled the wiser sort on both sides to effect a peace between the king and the earl, and both disbanded their troops. The next morning the king held a witan and fully restored Godwine and his wife and all his sons except Sweyn to their former honours; for Sweyn, moved by repentance for the murder of his cousin, Beorn,[2] was gone from Flanders barefoot as far as Jerusalem, and on his return journey homeward he died in Lycia of a disease contracted through extreme cold. The king also took back to honour his queen, Edith, the earl's daughter,[3] and restored her to her former dignity. A firm concord and peace being thus concluded, the king and the earl promised justice to all people, and they banished all those Normans who had introduced unjust laws and given false judgments, and committed many outrages against the English. But they allowed some of them to remain in England: namely Robert the deacon and Richard, son of Scrob,[4] his son-in-law; Alfred, the king's marshal,[5] Ansfrid, nicknamed Cocksfoot, and some others who had been the king's closest intimates, and always faithful to him and to all the people. But Robert, archbishop of Canterbury, William, bishop of London, and Ulf, bishop of Dorchester,[6] with their Normans barely escaped, and crossed overseas. William however, being a man of goodwill, was recalled after a short time and again received his bishopric. Osbern, nicknamed Pentecost,[4] and his companion, Hugh, surrendered their castles, and with the permission of Earl Leofric they passed through Mercia and went into Scotland where they were kindly received by Macbeth, king of Scots. In the same year during the night of the Feast of St. Thomas the Apostle[7] the wind was so violent that it blew down many churches and houses, scattered many trees, and tore up others by the roots.

1053.[8] Rhys, brother of Griffith, king of the South Welsh, was on account of his frequent raids put to death by order of King Edward at a place called "Bulendun", and on the vigil of our Lord's Epiphany[9] his head was brought to the king at Gloucester. In the same year on the Monday after Easter[10] (which was being kept at Winchester) the hand of death came upon Earl Godwine as he was sitting at table with the king as usual. Suddenly seized with a violent disorder, he fell speechless from his seat. When his sons, Earls Harold, Tosti and Gyrth, saw it, they carried him into the king's chamber, hoping that he would soon recover. But he rapidly lost strength and died in great agony five days later. He was buried in the Old Minster.[11] His son, Harold, succeeded to his earldom; and Harold's earldom was given to Ælfgar, the son of Earl Leofric. . . .

[1] *Sed quia ibi et cum rege et cum Godwino erant per pauci, qui fortitudinis aliquid haberent; nisi tantum Angli, pugnare adversus suos propinquos ac compatriotas pene omnes abhorrebant.* [2] See above, pp. 117, 118, 206.
[3] See Table 1. [4] On these men, see Round, *Feudal England*, pp. 317–331. [5] *stratorem.*
[6] Text has "Lincoln"–a sign of later composition: the see of Dorchester was not transferred to Lincoln until 1072. [7] 21 December. [8] See p. 128 above. [9] 5 January.
[10] 12 April. [11] Winchester Cathedral.

1054.[1] . . . Siward, the valiant earl of the Northumbrians, by the king's command marched into Scotland accompanied by many horsemen and a powerful fleet, and fought a battle with Macbeth, king of Scots, and all the Normans we mentioned before. He put him to flight and, as the king had directed, he raised to the throne Malcolm,[2] son of the king of the Cumbrians. However, his own son, and many English and Danes, fell in that battle. . . .

1055.[3] Victor[4] was pope, being the one hundred and forty-sixth. Siward, earl of the Northumbrians, died at York and was buried in the monastery of Galmanho which he had built. His earldom was given to Tosti, brother of Earl Harold. Shortly afterwards the king called his witan to London, and outlawed Earl Ælfgar, son of Earl Leofric, although he had committed no crime. Ælfgar immediately went over to Ireland, and returning with eighteen pirate ships went to Griffith, king of the Welsh, and requested his assistance against King Edward. Griffith immediately collected from every part of his kingdom a numerous army and bade Ælfgar meet him with his own forces at an appointed time. Having met they entered Herefordshire with intent to lay waste the English Marches. Earl Ralph 'the Timid', son of King Edward's sister Goda, assembled an army against them, and falling in with them on 24 October two miles from Worcester ordered the English, contrary to their custom, to fight on horseback. Just before they were about to join battle the earl with his Normans and Frenchmen set the example of flight; the English, seeing this, fled with their commander; and nearly the whole body of the enemy followed them. Four or five hundred were killed and a great number wounded. King Griffith and Earl Ælfgar then entered Hereford in triumph. They slew seven canons who guarded the doors of the cathedral and burned the monastery which Athelstan, that true servant of God and Christ, had built. They also destroyed its ornaments and the relics of St. Ethelbert, king and martyr, and other saints; they killed several citizens and made others prisoners and then, having pillaged and burnt the city, they returned laden with spoil. When the king had been told of this, he ordered an army to be raised from all parts of England. He caused it to congregate at Gloucester and placed it under the command of the valiant Earl Harold. The earl readily obeyed the king's orders and pursued Griffith and Ælfgar, boldly entering the Welsh borders to beyond 'Straddele'. They, knowing him to be a brave and warlike man, dared not risk a battle but retreated into South Wales. Harold therefore left there the greater part of his army with orders to repel the enemy if necessary, and himself returned to Hereford, which he forthwith fortified with gates and bars and with a broad and deep ditch. Meanwhile, negotiations were opened between the parties, and Griffith, Ælfgar and Harold with their attendants met at Billingsley, and peace was agreed between them. They resolved to become good friends, and Earl Ælfgar's fleet sailed to Chester and waited there to receive the pay which he had promised it. But the earl himself went to the king and received his earldom from him. . . .

1056.[5] Athelstan, bishop of Hereford, a man of great sanctity died on 10 February at an episcopal estate called Bosbury.[6] His body was carried to Hereford and buried

[1] See p. 131 above. [2] Malcolm III (Canmore). [3] See p. 132 above.
[4] Victor II. [5] See p. 134 above. [6] Near Ledbury.

in the church which he had built from the foundation. He was succeeded by Leofgar, Earl Harold's priest, who on 16 June in the same year was, with his clerks and Ælfnoth, the sheriff, and many others slain by Griffith, king of the Welsh, at a place called Glasbury after having held the bishopric for eleven weeks and four days. On his death the bishopric of Hereford was committed to Aldred, bishop of Worcester, until a bishop could be appointed. Later this same Aldred in conjunction with Earls Leofric and Harold arranged a peace between King Edward and Griffith, king of the Welsh. . . .

1057.[1] Pope Victor[2] died on 28 July. Prince Edward, son of King Edmund Ironside,[3] returned from Hungary to England at the command of his uncle, King Edward. He had been long in Hungary as an exile. The king had indeed determined to make him heir to the kingdom; but he died at London shortly after his arrival. Earl Leofric, son of Earl Leofwine, died at a good old age on his own estate at Bromley[4] on 31 August. . . . As long as he lived this earl's wisdom stood the kings and people of England in good stead. His earldom was given to his son, Ælfgar. . . . The before-mentioned Earl Ralph died on 21 December, and was buried in the abbey of Peterborough. . . .

1058.[5] . . . Ælfgar, earl of the Mercians, was a second time outlawed by King Edward, but assisted by Griffith, king of the Welsh, and supported by a Norse fleet which came to him unexpectedly, he recovered his earldom by force. . . .

1063.[6] After Christmas Day,[7] Harold, the valiant earl of Wessex, left Gloucester where King Edward was then staying, and by the king's command went with a small troop of horse to Rhuddlan. He was determined to slay Griffith, king of the Welsh, on account of this man's frequent raids into England, and on account of the many insults he had offered to his [Harold's] lord, King Edward. When Griffith heard of his coming he fled with his men and escaped by ship, though only with difficulty. Harold thereupon ordered his palace and his ships and his naval equipment to be burnt and then returned the same day. But about Rogation Week[8] he set out again from Bristol with a naval force and sailed round a good part of Wales. Then his brother, Tosti, met him by the king's orders, and with their united forces they began to lay waste that part of the country. The Welsh were thus compelled to give hostages and to submit. They promised to pay tribute, and they outlawed and renounced their king, Griffith. . . .

1064.[9] . . . Griffith, king of the Welsh, was slain by his subjects on 5 August, and his head together with his ship's prow was sent to Earl Harold who immediately sent them to King Edward. King Edward afterwards gave Wales to Griffith's brothers, Blethgent and Rigwatta, who swore fealty to him and Earl Harold, and promised always to obey their orders by sea and by land, and properly to pay all that their country had previously paid to former kings. . . .

1065.[10] . . . Shortly after the Feast of St. Michael the Archangel, to wit, on Monday, 3 October, the Northumbrian thegns Gamelbearn, Dunstan, son of Athelneth, and

[1] See p. 135 above. [2] Victor II. [3] See Table 1. [4] Staffordshire.
[5] See p. 136 above. [6] See p. 138 above. [7] Christmas, 1062. [8] 26 May.
[9] See p. 139 above. [10] See p. 139 above.

Glonieorn, son of Heardulf, entered York with two hundred men at arms, and in revenge for the execrable slaughter of the noble Northumbrian thegns, Gospatric and Gamel, the son of Orm, and Ulf, the son of Dolfin. Gospatric had been treacherously slain by order of Queen Edith at the king's court on 28 December on account of a quarrel he had with the queen's brother, Earl Tosti; and Ulf had been killed in his own chamber at the instigation of Earl Tosti, although there was peace between them. And another cause of this rising was that Tosti had unjustly laid a heavy tribute on the whole of Northumbria. On the first day the insurgents seized Tosti's Danish *huscarls*,[1] Amund and Ravensuart, as they were escaping and put them to death outside the city walls; on the second day they killed more than two hundred of the earl's tenants on the north side of the Humber, and also broke open his treasury and carried off all his effects. After that nearly all the men in the earldom assembled and went to Northampton to meet Harold, earl of Wessex, and others whom the king at Tosti's request had sent to restore peace among them. There (as also afterwards at Oxford) on the Feast of the Apostles Simon and Jude,[2] when Harold and the others tried to bring about a settlement between them, they unanimously refused, and they outlawed him and all who had taken part with him in his unjust government. After the Feast of All Saints,[3] with the concurrence of Earl Edwin, they banished Tosti from England; whereupon he went at once with his wife to Baldwin, count of Flanders, and passed the winter at St. Omer. After this King Edward's health began gradually to fail, but at Christmas he held his court at London as well as he was able; and on Holy Innocents' Day[4] he caused the church[5] which he had himself built to be dedicated with great splendour to St. Peter, the prince of the Apostles.

1066.[6] On Thursday the vigil of our Lord's Epiphany, in the Fourth Indiction, the pride of the English, the pacific king, Edward, son of King Ethelred, died at London, having reigned over the English twenty-three years six months and seven days. The next day he was buried in kingly style amid the bitter lamentations of all present. After his burial the under-king,[7] Harold, son of Earl Godwine, whom the king had nominated as his successor, was chosen king by the chief magnates of all England; and on the same day Harold was crowned with great ceremony by Aldred, archbishop of York. On taking the helm of the kingdom Harold immediately began to abolish unjust laws and to make good ones; to patronize churches and monasteries; to pay particular reverence to bishops, abbots, monks and clerks; and to show himself pious, humble and affable to all good men. But he treated malefactors with great severity, and gave general orders to his earls, ealdormen, sheriffs and thegns to imprison all thieves, robbers and disturbers of the kingdom. He laboured in his own person by sea and by land for the protection of his realm. On 24 April in this year a comet was seen not only in England but, it is said, all over the world, and it shone for seven days with an exceeding brightness. Shortly afterwards Earl Tosti returned from Flanders and landed in the Isle of Wight. After making the islanders pay tribute he departed and went pillaging along the sea-coast until he came to Sandwich. As soon as King Harold who was then at London heard this, he assembled a large fleet and a contingent

[1] *huscarlas.* [2] 28 October. [3] 1 November. [4] 28 December.
[5] Westminster Abbey. [6] See p. 142 above. [7] *subregulus.*

of horsemen, and prepared himself to go to Sandwich. Tosti, learning of this, took some of the shipmen of that place (whether willing or unwilling) and set his course towards Lindsey, where he burnt many villages and put many men to death. Thereupon, Edwin, earl of the Mercians, and Morcar, earl of the Northumbrians, hastened up with an army and expelled them from that part of the country. Afterwards he went to Malcolm, king of Scots, and remained with him during the whole of the summer. Meanwhile, King Harold arrived at Sandwich and waited there for his fleet. When it was assembled, he crossed over with it to the Isle of Wight, and, inasmuch as William, count of the Normans, was preparing to invade England with an army, he watched all the summer and autumn for his coming. In addition he distributed a land force at suitable points along the sea-coast. But about the Feast of the Nativity of St. Mary[1] provisions fell short so that the naval and land forces returned home. After this Harold Hardraada,[2] king of the Norwegians and brother of St. Olaf, the king, arrived on a sudden at the mouth of the river Tyne with a powerful fleet of more than five hundred large ships. Earl Tosti, according to previous arrangement, joined him with his fleet. Hastening, they entered the Humber and sailing up the Ouse against the stream landed at Riccall. On hearing this, King Harold marched with speed towards Northumbria. But before his arrival the two brother-earls, Edwin and Morcar, at the head of a large army fought a battle with the Norwegians on the northern bank of the river Ouse near York on Wednesday[3] which was the vigil of the Feast of St. Matthew the Apostle. They fought so bravely at the onset that many of the enemy were overthrown; but after a long contest the English were unable to withstand the attacks of the Norwegians and fled with great loss. More were drowned in the river than slain on the field.[4] The Norwegians remained masters of the place of carnage, and having taken one hundred and fifty hostages from York and left there the same number of their own men as hostages they went to their ships. Five days after this, to wit on Monday, 25 September, as Harold, king of the English, was coming to York with many thousand well-armed fighting men, he fell in with the Norwegians at a place called Stamford Bridge. He slew King Harold[5] and Earl Tosti with the greater part of their army and gained a complete victory. Nevertheless the battle was stoutly contested. Harold, king of the English, permitted Olaf, the son of the Norwegian king, and Paul, earl of Orkney, who had been sent off with a portion of the army to guard the ships, to return home unmolested with twenty ships and the survivors, but only after they had sworn oaths of submission and had given hostages. In the midst of these things, and when the king might have thought that all his enemies were subdued, it was told him that William, count of the Normans, had arrived with a countless host of horsemen, slingers, archers and foot-soldiers, and had brought with him also powerful help from all parts of Gaul. It was reported that he had landed at Pevensey. Therefore the king at once, and in great haste, marched with his army to London. Although he well knew that some of the bravest Englishmen had fallen in the two former battles, and that one-half of his army had not yet arrived, he did not hestitate to advance with all speed into Sussex against his enemies.

[1] 8 September. [2] Text has "Harvagra".
[3] 20 September which in fact in 1066 fell on a Wednesday, being the Vigil of St. Matthew.
[4] The battle of Fulford. [5] *i.e.* Harold Hardraada.

On Saturday, 22 October,[1] before a third of his army was in order for fighting, he joined battle with them nine miles from Hastings, where his foes had erected a castle. But inasmuch as the English were drawn up in a narrow place, many retired from the ranks, and very few remained true to him. Nevertheless from the third hour of the day until dusk he bravely withstood the enemy, and fought so valiantly and stubbornly in his own defence that the enemy's forces could make hardly any impression. At last, after great slaughter on both sides, about twilight the king, alas, fell. There were slain also Earl Gyrth, and his brother, Earl Leofwine, and nearly all the magnates of England. Then Count William returned with his men to Hastings. Harold reigned nine months and as many days. On hearing of his death Earls Edwin and Morcar, who had withdrawn themselves from the conflict, went to London and sent their sister, Queen Edith,[2] to Chester. But Aldred, archbishop of York, and the said earls, with the citizens of London and the shipmen planned to elevate to the throne Prince Edgar, nephew of Edmund Ironside, and promised they would renew the contest under his command. But while many were preparing to go to the fight, the earls withdrew their assistance and returned home with their army. Meanwhile Count William was laying waste Sussex, Kent, Hampshire, Surrey, Middlesex and Hertfordshire, burning villages and slaying their inhabitants until he came to Berkhamsted. There Archbishop Aldred, Wulfstan, bishop of Worcester, Walter, bishop of Hereford, Prince Edgar, the Earls Edwin and Morcar, the chief men of London, and many others came to him, and giving hostages they surrendered and swore fealty to him. So he entered into a pact with them, but none the less permitted his men to burn villages and keep on pillaging. But when Christmas Day drew near, he went to London with his whole army in order that he might be made king. And because Stigand, the primate of all England, was accused by the pope of having obtained the *pallium* in an uncanonical manner, William was anointed king by Aldred, archbishop of York. This was done on Christmas Day with great ceremony. Before this (since the archbishop made it a condition), the king had sworn at the altar of St. Peter the Apostle,[3] and in the presence of the clergy and people, that he would defend the holy churches of God and their ministers, that he would rule justly and with kingly care the whole people placed under him, that he would make and keep right law, and that he would utterly prohibit all spoliation and unrighteous judgments. . . .

[1] *Undecimo Cal. Novembris, Sabbato*. This is an error; the battle of Hastings was fought on St. Calixtus's Day, Saturday, 14 October. See above, p. 145.

[2] She had married King Harold. See Table 7.

[3] Westminster Abbey.

3. William of Jumièges: description of the invasion of England by William the Conqueror

This narrative, taken from the seventh book of the *Gesta Normannorum Ducum* of William of Jumièges, is of considerable importance. It was written in, or very shortly after, 1070, so that its author is a contemporary authority. He did not apparently have very much detailed information at his disposal, and his account will not therefore in this respect bear comparison with that of William of Poitiers (see below, No. 4). Nevertheless William of Jumièges is a chronicler of high standing, and what he says, in this place, may be regarded as representing Norman sentiment and Norman opinion about some of the most important events connecting the duchy with England at this crisis. The account of Edward's double bestowal of the English crown on Duke William; the description of Harold's visit to Normandy; the remarks on the battle of Hastings; and the description of William's coronation will be particularly noted. The significance of this account is enhanced by the fact that it is now possible at last to detach this strictly contemporary record from the interpolations which Ordericus Vitalis added to it about half a century later. This was made possible by the research of Léopold Delisle, the results of which were embodied and developed by Jean Marx in his edition of the chronicle of William of Jumièges which appeared in 1914. What follows therefore is a translation of one of the few contemporary narratives of the Norman invasion stripped of all later accretions. Printed: Jean Marx, *Gesta Normannorum Ducum* (Soc. Hist. Norm., 1914), pp. 132–136.

Edward, king of the English, being, according to the dispensation of God, without an heir, sent Robert,[1] archbishop of Canterbury, to the duke, with a message appointing the duke as heir to the kingdom which God had entrusted to him. He also at a later time sent to the duke, Harold[2] the greatest of all the counts in his kingdom alike in riches and honour and power. This he did in order that Harold might guarantee the crown to the duke by his fealty and confirm the same with an oath according to Christian usage. When Harold set out on his mission, he was borne along by the wind until he reached Ponthieu, and there he fell into the hands of Guy, count of Abbeville,[3] who straightway threw him with his retinue into prison. When the duke heard of this he sent messengers, and by force caused him to be released.[4] Harold thereupon tarried with the duke for some time, and performed fealty to him in respect of the kingdom with many oaths.[5] After this the duke sent him back to the king with many gifts.

In due course King Edward completed the term of his happy life, and departed from this world in the year of the Incarnation of our Lord 1065.[6] Then Harold immediately seized the kingdom, thus violating the oath which he had sworn to the duke. Therefore, the duke at once sent messengers to Harold urging him to desist from this mad policy, and to keep the faith which he had pledged with his oath. Harold, however, not only disdained to listen to this message, but seduced all the English people away from obedience to the duke. In these days a star with three long rays appeared. It lit up the greater part of the southern sky for the space of a fortnight, and many thought that this portended a great change in some kingdom.

[1] Robert, abbot of Jumièges, bishop of London, 1044, archbishop of Canterbury, 1051. See above, pp. 120–130.

[2] The Anglo-Saxon Chronicles are silent as to this famous mission and the date. The account here given should be compared with the fuller description in William of Poitiers (see below, No. 4, pp. 217–218) and with the Bayeux Tapestry.

[3] Guy of Ponthieu. An analogy may be found in the description of the dukes of Normandy as counts of Rouen.

[4] *missis legatis, violenter illum extorsit.*

[5] *facta fidelitate de regno plurimis sacramentis.*

[6] Edward died 5 January 1066. See above, p. 142.

Prince William was thus compelled to watch the strength of Harold increasing daily at a time when it was the duke who should have been crowned with a royal diadem. He therefore hastily built a fleet of three thousand ships. At length he brought this fleet to anchor at St. Valery in Ponthieu where he filled it with mighty horses and most valiant men, with hauberks and helmets.[1] Then when a favourable wind began to blow, he set sail, and crossing the sea he landed at Pevensey where he immediately built a castle with a strong rampart. He left this in charge of some troops, and with others he hurried to Hastings where he erected another similar fortress. Harold, rejecting caution, advanced against this, and, after riding all night, he appeared on the field of battle early in the morning.

But the duke had taken precautions against night-attacks by the enemy, and as the darkness approached he had ordered his men to stand by until dawn. At first light, having disposed his troops in three lines of battle, he advanced undaunted against the terrible enemy. The battle began at the third hour of the day, and continued amid a welter of carnage and slaughter until nightfall. Harold himself, fighting amid the front rank of his army, fell covered with deadly wounds. And the English, seeing their king dead, lost confidence in their own safety, and as night was approaching they turned and fled.

The most valiant duke, returning from the pursuit and slaughter of his enemies, came back to the field of battle in the middle of the night. At first dawn, having despoiled the corpses of his enemies and buried the bodies of his dear comrades, he took the road which leads to London. They say that in this battle many thousands of the English perished, and that Christ thus recompensed them for the foul and unjust murder of Alfred, brother of King Edward.[2] At length the most fortunate lord of battle, who was equally eminent in counsel, avoided the city, and taking a by-way to Wallingford, he there brought his troops safely across the river, and bade them at that place lay out a camp. It was from there that he advanced against London. When the advance-guard of his army reached the central square of the city, they found there a large company of rebels who were ready to offer a fierce resistance to them. The Normans, therefore, engaged and inflicted upon the city a great mourning on account of the large number of young men and citizens whom they slew. At length the Londoners saw that they could hold out no longer. Therefore they gave hostages and submitted themselves and all their possessions to their hereditary lord,[3] to their most noble conqueror.[4] His triumph was thus completed after so many dangers, and his wonderful virtues even our praise has not been able adequately to extol. He was chosen king by all the magnates both of the Normans and of the English on Christmas Day; he was anointed with the holy oil by the bishops of the kingdom; and he was vested with the royal crown in the year of the Incarnation of our Lord 1066.[5]

[1] The rhetoric exactly summarizes the significance of the equipment. It was on the specially armed mounted knight that William relied; cf. Bayeux Tapestry (see below, p. 236).

[2] Alfred came to England from Normandy in 1036, and was brutally murdered. It is probable that Godwine was implicated in the crime, and this formed a constant part of the Norman propaganda against Godwine's son, Harold.

[3] The emphasis on the hereditary title is noteworthy. See below, No. 4, pp. 223, 231.

[4] *nobilissimo victori suo*. Is this the earliest application of the name to William? See below, No. 69.

[5] The date is correct: Christmas, 1066.

4. William of Poitiers: "The Deeds of William, duke of the Normans and king of the English"

This work, known as the *Gesta Willelmi ducis Normannorum et regis Anglorum*, was written in, or very shortly after, 1071. Its author was a Norman born near Pont-Audemer. He studied at Poitiers and then returned to Normandy as a soldier. Afterwards, becoming a priest, he was made chaplain to Duke William and archdeacon of Lisieux. His book, about a quarter of which is here reproduced, is written in rhetorical style, is largely coloured by prejudice, and is sometimes repellent in its boastful tone. It was inspired by admiration for the duke, and it tells the story of the invasion of England from the Norman point of view. It is often inaccurate on details relating to the early history of England. Partly for these reasons, it has been somewhat neglected, but in truth it is a source of the highest importance for the history of the Norman Conquest, and it is indispensable in so far as it supplies a unique description of many of its incidents. William of Poitiers did not himself accompany the expedition of 1066, but he was admirably placed to learn about the events which he narrated so soon after they occurred. His remarkable account of the campaign is thus convincing in its details. It provides, together with the Bayeux Tapestry (see below, pp. 232–278), the best contemporary description of the battle of Hastings. The work, which is incomplete in its only known form, has however never been edited with the critical care it deserves, and many problems connected with it, and in particular its relation to the Norman chronicle of William of Jumièges, still await solution. A discussion of some of these will be found in L. Halphen, *Le comté d'Anjou au XI ieme siècle* (Paris, 1906), pp. xii–xiii; and in *Mélanges d'Histoire–offerts à Ferdinand Lot* (1925), pp. 543–548. A critical edition of the work is much to be desired. In the meantime the book of William of Poitiers can be studied most conveniently in J. A. Giles, *Scriptores Rerum Gestarum Willelmi Conquestoris* (London, 1845), pp. 77–159; and it is included also in Migne, *Patrologia Latina*, vol. CXLIX, at col. 1217. Both these texts are derived from the printed version published by A. Duchesne in 1619 in his *Historiae Normannorum Scriptores Antiqui*, pp. 178–213. A translation into French is contained in vol. XXIX of Guizot's *Collection des Mémoires* (1826).

. . . About the same time,[1] Edward, king of the English, who loved William as a brother or a son, established him as his heir with a stronger pledge than ever before. The king, who in his holy life showed his desire for a celestial kingdom, felt the hour of his death approaching, and wished to anticipate its inevitable consequences. He therefore dispatched Harold to William in order that he might confirm his promise by an oath. This Harold was of all the king's subjects the richest and the most exalted in honour and power, and his brother and his cousins had previously been offered as hostages in respect of the same succession. The king, indeed, here acted with great prudence in choosing Harold for this task, in the hope that the riches and the authority of this magnate might check disturbance throughout England if the people with their accustomed perfidy should be disposed to overturn what had been determined. Whilst travelling upon this errand Harold only escaped the perils of the sea by making a forced landing on the coast of Ponthieu where he fell into the hands of Count Guy, who threw him and his companions into prison. He might well have thought this a greater misfortune even than shipwreck, since among many peoples of the Gauls there was an abominable custom utterly contrary to Christian charity, whereby, when the powerful and rich were captured, they were thrown ignominiously into prison, and there maltreated and tortured even to the point of death, and afterwards sold as slaves to some magnate. When Duke William heard what had happened he sent messengers at speed, and by prayers and threats he brought about

[1] The events previously recorded relate to the year 1063. The date of Harold's voyage has not been established with certainty: 1064 seems the most probable year. The only strictly reliable evidence for the journey and the famous oath is contained in the narrative which here follows, and in the Bayeux Tapestry (No. 5).

Harold's honourable release. As a result Guy in person conducted his prisoner to the castle of Eu, although he could at his pleasure have tortured or killed him, or sold him into slavery. Since, moreover, he did this very honourably without the compulsion of force or bribes, William in gratitude bestowed upon him rich gifts of land and money, and then took Harold with proper honour to Rouen. This was the chief city of the Norman duchy, and there William sumptuously refreshed Harold with splendid hospitality after all the hardships of his journey. For the duke rejoiced to have so illustrious a guest in a man who had been sent him by the nearest and dearest of his friends: one, moreover, who was in England second only to the king, and who might prove a faithful mediator between him and the English. When they had come together in conference at Bonneville, Harold in that place swore fealty to the duke employing the sacred ritual recognized among Christian men. And as is testified by the most truthful and most honourable men who were there present, he took an oath of his own free will in the following terms: firstly that he would be the representative[1] of Duke William at the court of his lord, King Edward, as long as the king lived; secondly that he would employ all his influence and wealth to ensure that after the death of King Edward the kingdom of England should be confirmed in the possession of the duke; thirdly that he would place a garrison of the duke's knights in the castle of Dover and maintain these at his own care and cost; fourthly that in other parts of England at the pleasure of the duke he would maintain garrisons in other castles and make complete provision for their sustenance.[2] The duke on his part who before the oath was taken had received ceremonial homage from him, confirmed to him at his request all his lands and dignities. For Edward in his illness could not be expected to live much longer. . . . After this there came the unwelcome report that the land of England had lost its king, and that Harold had been crowned in his stead. This insensate Englishman did not wait for the public choice, but breaking his oath, and with the support of a few ill-disposed partisans, he seized the throne of the best of kings on the very day of his funeral, and when all the people were bewailing their loss. He was ordained king by the unhallowed consecration of Stigand[3] who had justly been deprived of his priesthood by the zeal and anathema of the apostolic see. Duke William therefore having taken counsel with his men resolved to avenge the insult by force of arms, and to regain his inheritance by war. This he determined despite the fact that some of the greatest magnates of Normandy sought to dissuade him from the enterprise, considering it to be too difficult and beyond the resources of Normandy. At this time Normandy possessed in its assemblies (besides bishops and abbots) many illustrious laymen, some of whom might be said to shine as the most brilliant and splendid lights of counsel. Such were Robert, count of Mortain;[4] Robert, count of Eu, the brother of Hugh, bishop of Lisieux,[5] of whom we have spoken before;

[1] *vicarius.*

[2] Note the precise terms of the famous oath as here described. All other elements in the familiar story come from later sources and should be regarded with suspicion. Compare this description with the relevant pictures of the Bayeux Tapestry (see below, pp. 234–235, 251, 252).

[3] The English authorities (who on this matter should probably be followed) say that Harold was crowned by Aldred, archbishop of York (see above, p. 212).

[4] Uterine half-brother of the duke by Herleve, mistress of Robert I and subsequently wife of Herluin, *vicomte* of Conteville. (See Table 2.)

[5] Robert and Hugh were the sons of William, count of Eu, illegitimate son of Duke Richard I. (See D. C. Douglas, *Eng. Hist. Rev.*, vol. LXI, 1946.)

Richard, count of Evreux, the son of Archbishop Robert; Roger of Beaumont;[1] Roger of Montgomery;[2] William fitz Osbern;[3] Hugh the *vicomte*. By the skill and devotion of these men the safety of the duchy might be assured. Indeed the Roman republic, if sustained by such as these, might now be as distinguished as of yore, and might not have to regret the loss of its two hundred senators. None the less let us note that in every deliberation they all deferred to the prudent wisdom of the duke as if the Divine Intelligence had indicated to him what ought to be done and what ought to be avoided. "God gives wisdom to the pious" has said one skilled in divinity, and the duke had acted piously since his childhood, so all obeyed him in whatsoever he ordered unless they were reluctantly forced to admit an overriding necessity. It would be tedious to tell in detail how by his prudent acts ships were made, arms and troops, provisions and other equipment assembled for war, and how the enthusiasm of the whole of Normandy was directed towards this enterprise. Nor did he neglect to take measures for the administration and the security of the duchy during his absence. Further, many warriors came to his support from outside the duchy, some being attracted by his well-known generosity, and all by confidence in the justice of his cause. Such was his moderation and prudence that he utterly forbade pillage, and provided for fifty thousand soldiers at his own cost for a whole month while contrary winds delayed them at the mouth of the Dives. He made generous provision both for his own knights and those from other parts, but he did not allow any of them to take their sustenance by force. The flocks and herds of the peasantry pastured unharmed throughout the province. The crops waited undisturbed for the sickle without being trampled by the pride of the knights or ravaged by the greed of the plunderer. A weak and unarmed man, watching the swarm of soldiers without fear, might follow his horse singing wherever he would.

At that time there sat in the seat of St. Peter at Rome Pope Alexander,[4] who was worthy of the respect and obedience of the whole Church. His decisions were just and good. He had been bishop of Lucca, and had sought no higher place, but through the fervent desire of many of those whose authority counted for most among the Romans, and with the assent of a great council, he was raised to the primacy which entails the headship and mastery of all the bishops of the earth. This he had deserved by reason of his sanctity and learning which caused him to shine from the rising to the setting of the sun. Indeed, the sun does not follow its unchanging course more steadfastly than did Alexander direct his life along the straight path of truth. Wherever he could throughout all the world he corrected evil without compromise. The duke therefore sought the favour of this apostle for the project he had in hand, and gladly received from him the gift of a banner as a pledge of the support of St. Peter whereby he might the more confidently and safely attack his enemy.

With Henry,[5] emperor of the Romans, son of the Emperor Henry[6] and grandson of the Emperor Conrad,[7] the duke entered into a new friendship so that an edict was

[1] Active in the reign of Robert I: still alive in 1086. See Table 12.
[2] Later to be earl of Shrewsbury. See Table 13.
[3] Later to be earl of Hereford: died at the battle of Cassel, February 1071. See Table 10. On this family, see D. C. Douglas, *Eng. Hist. Rev.*, vol. LIX, 1944, p. 66.
[4] Alexander II.
[5] Henry IV.
[6] Henry III.
[7] Conrad II.

issued by which Germany might come to his aid if he asked for it against any enemy. Sweyn, king of the Danes, sent messengers pledging support but, as will be seen later, the king in the event showed himself the friend of the duke's enemies.

Harold on his part, eager for battle by sea or land, guarded the coast with an innumerable army and cunningly sent his spies across the Channel. One of these being captured tried to conceal his errand, but the duke revealed his own high spirit by uttering these words: "It is not necessary", he said, "for Harold to throw away his gold and silver in buying the fidelity and fraud of men like you who come clandestinely among us to ferret out our plans. Quicker than he thinks will he know our designs, and he shall have more certain knowledge of them than he wants, for he shall see me in person. Take him back this message: tell him that if he does not see me within one year in the place which he now strives to make safe against my coming, he may rest quiet for the rest of his days and need fear no harm from me." Some of the magnates of Normandy, appalled by this rash speech, did not conceal their disagreement. In their fear they exaggerated the resources of Harold and minimized their own. They remarked that Harold was blessed with great treasures wherewith he might win the support of dukes and powerful kings; that he had a great fleet and highly skilled sailors who had long experience of the dangers and hazards of sea-warfare; and that in wealth and military strength his country was many times richer than Normandy. Who could hope, they said, that the Norman ships would be ready in time, or that sufficient oarsmen would be found within a year? Would not this new venture irreparably damage the flourishing condition of the province? The resources of the Roman emperor himself [they urged] would be insufficient for such a difficult enterprise.

But the duke restored their courage with these words: "We know Harold's cunning very well. He seeks to alarm us but instead our confidence grows. He spends his money uselessly, squandering his gold and silver without increasing his power. He has not the strength of spirit to promise the least of the things which belong to me, whereas I can better promise both about what is mine and also what he now possesses. Without doubt victory will go to the man who can bestow not only what is his own but also what is held by his enemy. Nor will lack of ships hinder us, for very soon we shall rejoice in the sight of a fleet. That they have experience I do not doubt, but we shall gain it with greater felicity. And wars are won not by numbers but by courage. Besides he will fight to retain what he has wrongfully seized whereas we shall fight to regain what we have received as a gift, and what we have lawfully acquired. Strong in this knowledge we shall overcome all dangers and win a happy victory, great honour and high renown." In such manner did this wise and catholic man, in full assurance that Almighty God would not allow wrong to prevail nor a just cause to fail, seek not so much the increase of his own wealth and glory as the improvement of Christian practice in the country to which he was going.

The whole fleet most carefully equipped had for long waited for a south wind at the mouth of the Dives and in the neighbouring ports, but now by a west wind it was driven thence towards the harbour of St. Valery. But the prince, daunted neither by the delay, nor by the contrary wind, nor by the loss of ships, nor even by the craven flight of many who broke faith with him, commended himself with prayers and gifts and vows to the protection of heaven. In his adversity he prudently concealed his lack of supplies by increasing the daily rations and, as far as he could, he caused those who had perished in the storm to be secretly buried. By varied exhortation he put courage into the fearful, and confidence into those who were cast down. Also he made pious and fervent supplication that the wind which was still adverse might be made favourable to him, and to this end he caused to be brought outside the church the body of Valery himself, that confessor beloved of God. And all those aspiring to set out on the invasion joined with him in this act of Christian humility.

At length the longed-for wind began to blow. All raised their hands and voices in thanks to heaven. Tumultuously encouraging one another they went on board with the utmost haste, and with eager joy began their perilous voyage. So extremely rapid was the launching that even while one was calling for his knight and another for his companion, most of them forgetful alike of followers, companions or provisions were only eager in their haste not to be left behind. The duke vehemently urged on board any that were slow, but cautious lest, if they reached the opposite coast before daybreak, they might have to disembark in confusion at a hostile or unknown port, he gave orders through a herald that when the vessels had reached the open sea they should tarry for a little, and cast their anchors not far from him until they saw a lantern displayed at the masthead of his ship. A trumpet then gave the signal for setting sail. Ancient Greece recalls the story of how Agamemnon, son of Atreus, set out with a thousand vessels to avenge the insult to his brother's bed. We likewise bear witness that William with more ships proceeded to win a royal crown. Everyone knows how Xerxes joined the towns of Sestos and Abydos with a bridge of boats. We tell how William joined the dominion of Normandy and England with a single fleet. Indeed we believe that William is the equal, nay the superior, of Xerxes in power, for Xerxes was vanquished and saw his fleet destroyed by the valour of a few of his enemies, whereas William, who was never overcome at any place, adorned his country with splendid trophies, and enriched it by signal victories.

After a pause in the night the ships weighed anchor. That which carried the duke, more eager than the others for victory, quickly left the rest behind as if held to its course by the will of its master. In the morning an oarsman sent by the duke to the masthead was asked whether he could sight the following fleet but he replied that he could see nothing but sea and sky. Immediately the duke cast anchor. In order to appease among his companions any fear or apprehension he commanded a large repast for himself, and accompanying it with a bumper of spiced wine he dined in good spirit as if he was in a room in his own house. Thus he imparted confidence to his followers, and made them feel sure that they would soon see again their fellows who likewise would be led forward safely under the protection of God. The Mantuan, who is justly held to be the prince of poets for his praise of the Trojan Aeneas, the founder and glory of ancient Rome, would himself have found the splendid and calculated courage of this feast worthy of commemoration. After it the oarsman was sent aloft for the second time and he exclaimed that he now saw four ships; afterwards when he had climbed for the third time he cried out that the numberless masts clustered together looked like trees in a forest. We leave it to the reader to judge how the confident hope of the duke was now turned into joy, and how from the depths of his heart he gave thanks to God for his mercy. Thus, with a favourable wind, they all reached Pevensey, and there without opposition they freely disembarked.

Harold, indeed, had departed into Yorkshire to make war on his brother Tosti, and on Harold, the king of Norway. It is not to be wondered at that Tosti, outraged by injustice and eager to regain the possessions of which he had been deprived, should have brought foreign troops against his brother. Tosti was very different from his brother, Harold, for the latter was stained with vice, a cruel murderer, purse-proud and puffed up with the profits of pillage, an enemy of justice and of all good. Since therefore Tosti could not withstand Harold by the force of his own arms, he had recourse to alliances and diplomacy. Moreover a woman of manly wisdom,[1] loving good and eschewing evil, wished to see the English governed by William whom her husband, King Edward, had adopted as a son and made his heir. For this king was wise and just and good.

Rejoicing greatly at having secured a safe landing, the Normans seized and fortified first Pevensey and then Hastings, intending that these should serve as a stronghold for themselves and as a refuge for their ships. Marius and Pompey the Great, both of whom earned their victories by courage and ability (since the one brought Jugurtha in chains to Rome whilst the other forced Mithridates to take poison), were so cautious when they were in enemy territory that they feared to expose themselves to danger even by separating themselves with a legion from their main army: their custom was (like that of most generals) to direct patrols and not to lead them. But William with twenty-five knights and no more, himself went out to gain information about the neighbourhood and its inhabitants. Because of the roughness of the ground he had to return on foot, a matter doubtless for laughter, but if the episode is not devoid of humour it none the less deserves serious praise. For the duke came back carrying on his shoulder, besides his own hauberk, that of William fitz Osbern, one of his companions. This man was famed for his bodily strength and courage, but it was the duke who relieved him in his necessity of the weight of his armour.

A rich inhabitant of the country who was a Norman by race, being Robert, son of Wimarc, a noble lady, sent a messenger to Hastings to the duke who was his relative and his lord. "King Harold", he said, "has just given battle to his brother and to the king of Norway, who is reputed to be the greatest warrior under Heaven, and he has killed both of them in one fight, and has destroyed their mighty armies. Heartened by this success he now hastens towards you at the head of innumerable troops all well equipped for war, and against them your own warriors will prove of no more account than a pack of curs. You are accounted a wise man, and at home you have hitherto acted prudently both in peace and war. Now therefore take care for your safety lest your boldness lead you into a peril from which you will not escape. My advice to you is to remain within your entrenchments and not at present to offer battle." But the duke replied to the messenger thus: "Although it would have been better for your master not to have mingled insults with his message, nevertheless I thank him for his advice. But say this also to him: I have no desire to

[1] The reference is apparently to Edith, daughter of Earl Godwine and wife of Edward the Confessor.

protect myself behind any rampart, but I intend to give battle to Harold as soon as possible. With the aid of God I would not hesitate to oppose him with my own brave men even if I had only ten thousand of these instead of the sixty thousand I now command."[1]

One day when the duke was visiting the guards of his fleet, and was walking about near the ships, he was told that a monk had arrived sent to him by Harold. He at once accosted him and discreetly said: "I am the steward of William, duke of Normandy, and very intimate with him. It is only through me you will have an opportunity of delivering your message. Say therefore what you have to say to me, and I will deliver a faithful report of your message, for no one is dearer to him than I am. Afterwards through my good offices you may in person say to him whatever you wish." The monk then delivered his message without further delay, and the duke at once caused him to be well housed and kindly entertained. At the same time he carefully considered with his followers what reply he ought to make to the message.

The next day, seated in the midst of his magnates, he summoned the monk to his presence and said: "I am William, by the grace of God prince of the Normans. Repeat now therefore in the presence of these men what you said to me yesterday." The envoy then spoke: "This is what Harold bids you know. You have come into his land with he knows not what temerity. He recalls that King Edward at first appointed you as his heir to the kingdom of England, and he remembers that he was himself sent by the king to Normandy to give you an assurance of the succession. But he knows also that the same king, his lord, acting within his rights, bestowed on him the kingdom of England when dying. Moreover, ever since the time when blessed Augustine came to these shores it has been the unbroken custom of the English to treat death-bed bequests as inviolable. It is therefore with justice that he bids you return with your followers to your own country. Otherwise he will break the friendship and the pacts he made with you in Normandy. And he leaves the choice entirely to you."

When the duke had heard this message he asked the monk whether he would conduct his messenger safely into Harold's presence, and the monk promised that he would take as much care for his safety as for his own. Then the duke ordered a certain monk of Fécamp to carry this message forthwith to Harold: "It is not with temerity nor unjustly but after deliberation and in defence of right that I have crossed the sea into this country. My lord and kinsman, King Edward, made me the heir of this kingdom even as Harold himself has testified; and he did so because of the great honours and rich benefits conferred upon him and his brother and followers by me and my magnates. He acted thus because among all his acquaintance he held me to be the best capable of supporting him during his life and of giving just rule to the kingdom after his death. Moreover his choice was not made without the consent of his magnates since Archbishop Stigand, Earl Godwine, Earl Leofric, and Earl Siward confirmed it, swearing in his hands that after King Edward's death they would serve me as lord, and that during his lifetime they would not seek to have the country in

[1] The numbers of troops given here and elsewhere in this narrative should be read with caution.

any way occupied so as to hinder my coming. He gave me the son and the nephew of Godwine as hostages. And finally he sent me Harold himself to Normandy that in my presence he might personally take the oath which his father and the others had sworn in my absence. While he was on his way to me Harold fell into a perilous captivity from which he was rescued by my firmness and prudence. He made himself my man by a solemn act of homage, and with his hands in mine he pledged to me the security of the English kingdom.[1] I am ready to submit my case against his for judgment either by the law of Normandy or better still by the law of England, whichever he may choose; and if according to truth and equity either the Normans or the English decide that the kingdom is his by right, let him possess it in peace. But if it be decided that in justice the kingdom should be mine, let him yield it up. Moreover, if he refuses these conditions, I do not think it right that either my men or his should perish in conflict over a quarrel that is none of their making. I am therefore ready to risk my life against his in single combat to decide whether the kingdom of England should by right be his or mine."

We have been careful to record all this speech in the duke's own words rather than our own, for we wish posterity to regard him with favour. Anyone may easily judge that he showed himself wise and just, pious and brave. On reflexion it will be considered that the strength of his argument was such that it could not have been shaken by Tully himself, the glory of Roman eloquence; and it brought to nought the claims of Harold. The duke (it will be seen) was ready to accept the judgment prescribed by the law of nations, since he did not desire that his enemies, the English, should perish because of his quarrel but rather he wanted to decide the issue by means of a single combat and at the peril of his own life. When Harold advanced to meet the duke's envoy and heard this message he grew pale and for a long while remained as if dumb. And when the monk had asked more than once for a reply he first said: "We march at once," and then added, "We march to battle." The envoy besought him to reconsider this reply, urging that what the duke desired was a single combat and not the double slaughter of two armies. (For that good and brave man was willing to renounce something that was just and agreeable to him in order to prevent the death of many: he wished for Harold's head, knowing that it was defended by less fortitude than was his own, and that it was not protected by justice.) Then Harold, lifting up his face to heaven, exclaimed: "May the Lord decide this day between William and me, and may he pronounce which of us has the right." Thus, blinded by his lust for dominion, and in his fear unmindful of the wrongs he had committed, Harold made his conscience his judge and that to his own ruin.

In the meantime trusty knights who had been sent out by the duke on patrol came back in haste to report the approach of the enemy. The king was the more furious because he had heard that the Normans had laid waste the neighbourhood of their camp, and he planned to take them unawares by a surprise or night attack. Further, in order to prevent their escape, he sent out a fleet of seven hundred armed vessels to block their passage home. Immediately the duke summoned to arms all those within the camp, for the greater part of his host had gone out foraging. He

[1] *Sic mihi per manus suas dedit, sua manu securitatem mihi regno Anglico firmavit.*

himself attended Mass with the greatest devotion, and fortified both his body and soul by partaking of the Body and Blood of our Lord. With great humility he hung round his neck the relics on which Harold had sworn the oath he had now broken, and whose protection he had therefore lost. The duke had with him two bishops from Normandy, Odo, bishop of Bayeux, and Geoffrey, bishop of Coutances; and there were also with him many secular clergy and not a few monks. This company made ready to fight for him with their prayers. Anyone but the duke would have been alarmed at seeing his hauberk turn to the left when he put it on, but he merely laughed and did not allow the unlucky omen to disturb him.

Although no one has reported to us in detail the short harangue with which on this occasion he increased the courage of his troops, we doubt not it was excellent. He reminded the Normans that with him for their leader they had always proved victorious in many perilous battles. He reminded them also of their fatherland, of its noble history, and of its great renown. "Now is the time", he said, "for you to show your strength, and the courage that is yours." "You fight", he added, "not merely for victory but also for survival. If you bear yourselves valiantly you will obtain victory, honour and riches. If not, you will be ruthlessly butchered, or else led ignominiously captive into the hands of pitiless enemies. Further, you will incur abiding disgrace. There is no road for retreat. In front, your advance is blocked by an army and a hostile countryside; behind you, there is the sea where an enemy fleet bars your flight. Men, worthy of the name, do not allow themselves to be dismayed by the number of their foes. The English have again and again fallen to the sword of an enemy; often, being vanquished, they have submitted to a foreign yoke; nor have they ever been famed as soldiers. The vigorous courage of a few men armed in a just cause and specially protected by heaven must prevail against a host of men unskilled in combat. Only be bold so that nothing shall make you yield, and victory will gladden your hearts."

He then advanced in good order with the papal banner which had been granted to him borne aloft at the head of his troops. In the van he placed foot-soldiers equipped with arrows and crossbows; in the second rank came the more heavily armed infantry clad in hauberks; and finally came the squadrons of knights in the midst of whom he rode himself, showing invincible courage and in such a position that he could give his orders by hand or by voice. If any ancient writer had described the host of Harold he would have said that at its passage the rivers became dry and the forests were turned into plains. From all the provinces of the English a vast host had gathered together. Some were moved by their zeal for Harold, but all were inspired by the love of their country which they desired, however unjustly, to defend against foreigners. The land of the Danes who were allied to them had also sent copious reinforcements. But fearing William more than the king of Norway and not daring to fight with him on equal terms, they took up their position on higher ground, on a hill abutting the forest through which they had just come. There, at once dismounting from their horses, they drew themselves up on foot and in very close order. The duke and his men in no way dismayed by the difficulty of the ground came slowly up the hill, and the terrible sound of trumpets on both sides signalled the beginning of the battle. The eager boldness of the Normans gave them the advantage of attack, even as in a trial for theft it is the prosecuting counsel who speaks first. In such wise the Norman foot drawing nearer provoked the English by raining death and wounds upon them with their missiles. But the English resisted valiantly, each man according to his strength, and they hurled back spears and javelins and weapons of all kinds together with axes and stones fastened to pieces of wood. You would have thought to see our men overwhelmed by this death-dealing weight of projectiles. The knights came after the chief, being in the rearmost rank, and all disdaining to fight at long range were eager to use their swords. The shouts both of the Normans and of the barbarians were drowned in the clash of arms and by the cries of the dying, and for a long time the battle raged with the utmost fury. The English, however, had the advantage of the ground and profited by remaining within their position in close order. They gained further superiority from their numbers, from the impregnable front which they preserved, and most of all from the manner in which their weapons found easy passage through the shields and armour of their enemies. Thus they bravely withstood and successfully repulsed those who were engaging them at close quarters, and inflicted loss upon the men who were shooting missiles at them from a distance. Then the foot-soldiers and the Breton knights, panic-stricken by the violence of the assault, broke in flight before the English and also the auxiliary troops on the left wing, and the whole army of the duke was in danger of retreat. This may be said without disparagement to the unconquerable Norman race. The army of the Roman emperor, containing the soldiers of kings accustomed to victory on sea and land, sometimes fled on the report, true or false, that their leader was dead. And in this case the Normans believed that their duke and lord was killed. Their flight was thus not so much shameful as sad, for their leader was their greatest solace.

Seeing a large part of the hostile host pursuing his own troops, the prince thrust himself in front of those in flight, shouting at them and threatening them with his spear. Staying their retreat, he took off his helmet, and standing before them bareheaded he cried: "Look at me well. I am still alive and by the grace of God I shall yet prove victor. What is this madness which makes you fly, and what way is open for your retreat? You are allowing yourselves to be pursued and killed by men whom you could slaughter like cattle. You are throwing away victory and lasting glory, rushing into ruin and incurring abiding disgrace. And all for naught since by flight none of you can escape destruction." With these words he restored their courage, and, leaping to the front and wielding his death-dealing sword, he defied the enemy who merited death for their disloyalty to him their prince. Inflamed by his ardour, the Normans then surrounded several thousands of their pursuers and rapidly cut them down so that not one escaped. Heartened by this success, they then furiously carried their attack on to the main body of the English host, which even after their losses scarcely seemed diminished in number. The English fought confidently with all their strength, striving in particular to prevent the attackers from penetrating within their ranks, which indeed were so closely massed together that even the dead had not space in which to fall. The swords of the bravest warriors hewed a gap in some places, and there they were followed by the men of Maine, by the French, by the Bretons and the men of Aquitaine, and by the Normans who showed the greatest valour.

A certain Norman, Robert, son of Roger of Beaumont, being nephew and heir to Henry, count of Meulan, through Henry's sister, Adeline,[1] found himself that day in battle for the first time: he was as yet but a young man and he performed feats of valour worthy of perpetual remembrance. At the head of the troop which he commanded on the right wing, he attacked with the utmost bravery and success. It is not, however, our purpose, or within our capacity, to describe as they deserve the exploits of individuals. Even a master of narrative who had actually been present that day would find it very difficult to narrate them all in detail. For our part we shall hasten to the point at which, having ended our praise of William the count, we shall begin to describe the glory of William the king.

Realizing that they could not without severe loss overcome an army massed so strongly in close formation, the Normans and their allies feigned flight and simulated a retreat, for they recalled that only a short while ago their flight had given them an advantage. The barbarians thinking victory within their grasp shouted with triumph, and heaping insults upon our men, threatened utterly to destroy them. Several thousand of them, as before, gave rapid pursuit to those whom they thought to be in flight; but the Normans suddenly wheeling their horses surrounded them and cut down their pursuers so that not one was left alive. Twice was this ruse employed with the utmost success, and then they attacked those that remained with redoubled fury. This army was still formidable and very difficult to overwhelm. Indeed this was a battle of a new type: one side vigorously attacking; the other resisting as if rooted to the ground. At last the English began to weary, and as if confessing their crime in their defeat they submitted to their punishment. The Normans threw and struck and pierced. The movements of those who were cut down to death appeared greater than that of the living; and those who were lightly wounded could not escape because of the density of their formation but were crushed in the throng. Thus fortune crowned the triumph of William.

There were present in this battle:[2] Eustace, count of Boulogne;[3] William, son of Richard, count of Evreux;[4] Geoffrey, son of Rotrou, count of Mortagne;[5] William fitz Osbern;[4] Haimo, *vicomte* of Thouars;[6] Walter Giffard;[7] Hugh of Montfort-sur-Risle;[8] Rodulf of Tosny;[9] Hugh of Grantmesnil;[10] William of Warenne;[11] and many other most renowned warriors whose names are worthy to be commemorated in

[1] See Table 12.

[2] The list which follows is, with the Bayeux Tapestry, the most important piece of testimony providing express evidence as to those individuals who were indubitably "companions of the Conqueror". Concerning it, and the men mentioned therein, see D. C. Douglas in *History*, vol. XXVIII, p. 129. Such express evidence, vouching the presence of particular persons at Hastings, can be found in the case of less than thirty-five persons.

[3] The man who was partly responsible for the troubles in England in 1051. See above, pp. 121, 206, 207.

[4] See Table 2.

[5] Not to be confused with *Mortain*.

[6] Thouars in Poitou. On this remarkable man, see H. Imbert, *Histoire de Thouars* (Niort, 1871), pp. 45 *et sqq*.

[7] The younger Walter Giffard. He took part in the mutilation of Harold's body. The family came from Longueville-sur-Scie, and was to receive large estates in England, particularly in Berkshire.

[8] Later constable of Dover Castle. On the family, see D. C. Douglas, *Domesday Monachorum of Christ Church, Canterbury*, p. 70.

[9] A powerful family in middle Normandy.

[10] A family destined to be powerful in England. They came from Le Grand-Mesnil (Calvados, arr. Lisieux; cant. St.-Pierre-sur-Dives).

[11] Later earl of Surrey. On the family, see L. C. Loyd, in *Yorks. Archæol. Journal*, vol. XXXI, pp. 97–113, and C. T. Clay, *Early Yorkshire Charters*, vol. VIII (1950). This man founded at Lewes the first Cluniac monastery in England. (See below, No. 80.)

histories among the bravest soldiers of all time. But Duke William excelled them all both in bravery and soldier-craft, so that one might esteem him as at least the equal of the most praised generals of ancient Greece and Rome. He dominated this battle, checking his own men in flight, strengthening their spirit, and sharing their dangers. He bade them come with him, more often than he ordered them to go in front of him. Thus it may be understood how he led them by his valour and gave them courage. At the mere sight of this wonderful and redoubtable knight, many of his enemies lost heart even before they received a scratch. Thrice his horse fell under him; thrice he leapt upon the ground; and thrice he quickly avenged the death of his steed. It was here that one could see his prowess, and mark at once the strength of his arm and the height of his spirit. His sharp sword pierced shields, helmets and armour, and not a few felt the weight of his shield. His knights seeing him thus fight on foot were filled with wonder, and although many were wounded they took new heart. Some weakened by loss of blood went on resisting, supported by their shields, and others unable themselves to carry on the struggle, urged on their comrades by voice and gesture to follow the duke. "Surely", they cried, "you will not let victory slip from your hands." William himself came to the rescue of many. . . .

Evening was now falling, and the English saw that they could not hold out much longer against the Normans. They knew they had lost a great part of their army, and they knew also that their king with two of his brothers and many of their greatest men had fallen. Those who remained were almost exhausted, and they realized that they could expect no more help. They saw the Normans, whose numbers had not been much diminished, attack them with even greater fury than at the beginning of the battle, as if the day's fighting had actually increased their vigour. Dismayed at the implacable bearing of the duke who spared none who came against him and whose prowess could not rest until victory was won, they began to fly as swiftly as they could, some on horseback, some on foot, some along the roads, but most over the trackless country. Many lay on the ground bathed in blood, others who struggled to their feet found themselves too weak to escape, while a few although disabled were given strength to move by fear. Many left their corpses in the depths of the forest, and others were found by their pursuers lying by the roadside. Although ignorant of the countryside the Normans eagerly carried on the pursuit, and striking the rebels in the back brought a happy end to this famous victory. Many fallen to the ground were trampled to death under the hooves of runaway horses.

But some of those who retreated took courage to renew the struggle on more favourable ground. This was a steep valley intersected with ditches. These people, descended from the ancient Saxons (the fiercest of men), are always by nature eager for battle, and they could only be brought down by the greatest valour. Had they not recently defeated with ease the king of Norway at the head of a fine army?

The duke who was following the victorious standards did not turn from his course when he saw these enemy troops rallying. Although he thought that reinforcements had joined his foes he stood firm. Armed only with a broken lance he was more formidable than others who brandished long javelins. With a harsh voice he called to Eustace of Boulogne, who with fifty knights was turning in flight, and was about to give the signal for retreat. This man came up to the duke and said in his ear that he ought to retire since he would court death if he went forward. But at the very moment when he uttered the words Eustace was struck between the shoulders with such force that blood gushed out from his mouth and nose, and half dead he only made his escape with the aid of his followers. The duke, however, who was superior to all fear and dishonour, attacked and beat back his enemies. In this dangerous phase of the battle many Norman nobles were killed since the nature of the ground did not permit them to display their prowess to full advantage.

Having thus regained his superiority, the duke returned to the main battlefield, and he could not gaze without pity on the carnage, although the slain were evil men, and although it is good and glorious in a just war to kill a tyrant. The bloodstained battle-ground was covered with the flower of the youth and nobility of England. The two brothers of the king were found near him, and Harold himself stripped of all badges of honour could not be identified by his face, but only by certain marks on his body. His corpse was brought into the duke's camp, and William gave it for burial to William, surnamed Malet, and not to Harold's mother, who offered for the body of her beloved son its weight in gold. For the duke thought it unseemly to receive money for such merchandise, and equally he considered it wrong that Harold should be buried as his mother wished, since so many men lay unburied because of his avarice. They said in jest that he who had guarded the coast with such insensate zeal should be buried by the seashore. . . .

It would have been just if wolves and vultures had devoured the flesh of these English who had rightly incurred their doom, and if the fields had received their unburied bones. But such a fate seemed cruel to the duke, and he allowed all who wished to do so to collect the bodies for burial. Then, having arranged for the honourable interment of his own men, he left Hastings in charge of a brave commander, and proceeded to Romney, where he punished at his pleasure those who had previously killed some of his men after a struggle.

Then he marched to Dover, which had been reported impregnable and held by a large force. The English, stricken with fear at his approach, had confidence neither in their ramparts nor in the natural strength of the site, nor in the number of their troops. This castle is situated on a rock adjoining the sea, and it is raised up by nature and so strongly fortified that it stands like a straight wall as high as an arrow's flight. Its side is washed by the sea. While the inhabitants were preparing to surrender unconditionally, our men, greedy for booty, set fire to the castle, and the greater part of it was soon enveloped in flames. The duke, unwilling that those who had offered to surrender should suffer loss, gave them a recompense in money for the damage of the castle and their property; and he would have severely punished those who had started the fire if their numbers and base condition had not prevented their detection. Having taken possession of the castle the duke spent eight days adding new fortifications to it.

Owing to foul water and bad food his knights were there stricken with severe dysentery, and many were brought by weakness almost to the point of death. But this adversity did not daunt the duke. Posting a guard in Dover he left there his sick, and himself went forward to tame the enemies he had conquered. Not far from Dover the men of Canterbury came out to meet him in order that they might give him hostages and swear allegiance. The mighty capital itself now began to tremble, and realizing that resistance would be followed by utter ruin, it hastened to submit in order to avoid destruction. The next day the duke went on to the Broken Tower,[1] and there he was stricken with the sickness that had previously afflicted his troops. Occupied with the general good, and fearful lest his army should lack anything necessary to it, he would not brook delay for the sake of his health, although it was the chief desire and the common need of all that this best of leaders should be restored.

Meanwhile Stigand, archbishop of Canterbury, who had the greatest influence with the English owing to his wealth and position, took counsel with the sons of Ælfgar[2] and other magnates how they might resist the duke. They had set up Edgar the Atheling as king, a boy in years who was sprung from the noble race of King Edward. Their chief desire was to have as king not a stranger but a fellow-countryman. But he who was destined to become their master advanced without fear, and established himself not far from London in a place where he knew they often met. This city is watered by the Thames, which supplies harbourage to many ships which bring thither the riches of foreign lands. Its citizens could themselves supply a numerous and formidable force, and they had now been joined by so many troops that they could hardly be housed even in this large town. Some of them indeed made a sortie, but an advance guard of five hundred Norman knights bravely drove them back within the walls, and then burnt all the buildings on this side of the river in order to inflict a double blow on the pride of their stubborn foes. The duke, who was following, went on without opposition, and having crossed the Thames by ford and bridge arrived at Wallingford.

There the metropolitan bishop, Stigand, came to him and surrendered. He swore fidelity and renounced the Atheling whom he had rashly nominated as king. The duke then proceeded on his way and when he was in sight of London the principal citizens came out to meet him.[3] They surrendered themselves and their city into his hand, like the citizens of Canterbury before them, and gave him such hostages as he asked. Further, the bishops and the lay magnates begged him to assume the crown. "We are accustomed to obey a king," they said, "and we desire to have a king as lord."

The duke therefore took counsel with those Normans who were of proven wisdom and fidelity, and explained to them why he was reluctant to accede to the demand of the English. Whilst the country was still unsettled and so much resistance remained to be crushed, he would prefer the peace of the kingdom to its crown. Besides, if God were to accord him this honour, he would wish to be crowned with his wife. It therefore seemed foolish to him to show undue haste in reaching for the peak of achievement. In short, he had no lust for dominion, and cherishing the sanctity of his marriage vows he desired to keep them holy.

His familiar counsellors, however, although they respected his motives and his wisdom, none the less urged him to take the crown, for they knew that this was the fervent desire of his whole army. In this debate, moreover, there was present Haimo

[1] Apparently near Canterbury.
[2] Edwin and Morcar.
[3] These negotiations took place at Berkhamsted.

from Aquitaine, the *vicomte*[1] of Thouars. He was as famous for his speech as for his strong right arm. This man, after expressing his admiration for the modesty of the duke in asking his knights whether he should become a king, went on to say: "Never, or very rarely, can knights have been asked for their opinion on such a matter. Nor is it necessary to prolong a discussion about something we all desire to be accomplished as soon as possible. Wise and prudent men, moreover, however much they might desire to increase their own wealth and dignity through the advancement of their leader, would never seek to raise him to the peak of monarchy if they were not assured that he was in every way suited nobly to discharge his duties as king." The duke, therefore, after further consideration, yielded to their fervent wishes in the hope that after he had begun to reign, men would hesitate to rebel against him, or if they did so, would be more easily crushed.

Having taken this decision, he sent forward to London picked men to build a fortress in that city and to make suitable preparations for the coming of the royal splendour. Meanwhile he waited on the outskirts of the city, and so free was he from any opposition that he might, if he had wished, have occupied his leisure in hunting and hawking.

On the day appointed for the coronation the archbishop of York,[2] a wise, good and eloquent man, famed for justice and for his mature prudence, demanded of the English in a fitting oration whether it was their will that William should be crowned as their lord. All without the least hesitation shouted their joyous assent, as if heaven had given them one will and one voice. Then the bishop of Coutances in like manner addressed the Normans, and they showed the same eagerness as the English. Nevertheless, those who for safety were keeping guard outside the abbey, being armed and mounted, thought that the shouting boded some ill, and so without reason they started to set fire to the city.

William, the duke, was hallowed king by the said archbishop of York, a man equally esteemed for his holy life and his spotless reputation. He it was who set the royal crown upon the duke's head, and led him to the throne in the presence of a great company of bishops and abbots assembled in the church of St. Peter the Apostle which is graced with the tomb of King Edward. This was done on Christmas Day in the year of our Lord 1066. The duke had refused to be crowned by Stigand, archbishop of Canterbury, because he knew that the just zeal of the apostolic see had stricken Stigand with anathema. The insignia of royalty became him as well as the quality of his rule, and his sons and grandsons by a just succession will reign over the English land. This land he has gained as the legal heir with the confirmation of the oaths of the English. He took possession of his inheritance by battle, and he was crowned at last with the consent of the English or at least at the desire of their magnates. And if it be asked what was his hereditary title, let it be answered that a close kinship existed between King Edward and the son of Duke Robert whose paternal aunt, Emma, was the sister of Duke Richard II, the daughter of Duke Richard I and the mother of King Edward himself. . . .[3]

[1] *praeses*. On the man, see above, p. 227, n. 6. [2] Aldred. [3] See Table on p. 2.

5. The Bayeux Tapestry

The Bayeux Tapestry is a roll of stitchwork executed in many colours. It is some 19½ inches wide, and in its present state it is some 23 feet long. From at least as early as 1476 it has been among the possessions of the cathedral of Bayeux.

The main theme of the Tapestry concerns the personal relations between the Conqueror and Earl Harold. In one sense it may be regarded less as an account of the Norman Conquest than as the drama of Harold's broken oath and its consequences. It begins with Harold's voyage to France, probably in 1064, and in its present condition (for something has been lost) it ends with the battle of Hastings. There is also a decorative margin at the top and bottom of the roll.

The Bayeux Tapestry has been the source of a voluminous literature which is summed up in Marquet de Vasselot, *Bibliographie de la Tapisserie* (1935). The two most useful books on the Tapestry for the student of English history are F. R. Fowke, *The Bayeux Tapestry* (London, 1875), and the much shorter but wholly admirable treatment of the subject by Sir Eric Maclagan, *The Bayeux Tapestry* (King Penguin Books, London, 1943). Both these books contain reproductions of the Tapestry based upon photographs made in 1871 for the British government, and now preserved in the Victoria and Albert Museum. It is from these photographs that the plates which here follow are ultimately derived. Both the works mentioned above contain a translation of the headings in the Tapestry, together with much critical material, and Sir Eric Maclagan has added to his introduction a useful bibliographical note. A. Levé, *La Tapisserie de la Reine Mathilde dite La Tapisserie de Bayeux* (Paris, 1919), may also be consulted with profit if it be studied in connexion with the review of this work by R. N. Sauvage in *Bibliothèque de l'Ecole de Chartes*, vol. LXXXII, 1921.

The criticism of the Bayeux Tapestry as a work of art falls outside the scope of this note. Its value as historical evidence must, however, be emphasized. There has been considerable dispute about the date of its composition. A. Marignan (*La Tapisserie de Bayeux: les méthodes du passé*, 1902) suggested that the style of arms, armour, etc., indicate that it was composed in the latter half of the twelfth century, and this theory was popularized in England by H. Belloc, *The Bayeux Tapestry* (1914). This view is not now generally accepted. Most scholars have adhered to the opinion expressed by Freeman (*History of the Norman Conquest*, vol. III, App. 'A') and by J. H. Round (*Eng. Hist. Rev.*, vol XXX (1915), pp. 109–111) that the work was executed within living memory of the Conquest.

It will be noted that in the Tapestry prominence is given to Odo, bishop of Bayeux, and apparently also to certain of his knights (see in particular Plates XXXVI, XLVII, XLVIII, XLIX, LI, LVII–LIX, LXXII), and it is thought that Odo was the man responsible for having the Tapestry made. He (or some other) employed a designer, who was a great artist, and who, although his name will probably never be known, must be regarded as the most important person connected with the Tapestry. Concerning the actual executants, it has been argued with great plausibility that these were English women who in the eleventh century were famous for their needlework. It will be noted that in the headings there are a certain number of English letters, and that some of the Latin place-names seem to derive from English forms.

It may be accepted, therefore, without much misgiving that the main body of the Bayeux Tapestry constitutes a primary source for the history of England in this age, and one which, in this respect, deserves to be studied alongside the accounts given in the Anglo-Saxon Chronicles and in William of Poitiers (see above, pp. 142–146 and pp. 217–231). The borders of the roll (on which see H. Chefneux in *Romania*, vol. LX (1934) offer a fine commentary on contemporary manners and customs, and folk-lore.

The scope of the Tapestry may be judged by the fact that it is said to contain representations of

623 persons,
202 horses and mules,
55 dogs,

505 other animals,
37 buildings,
41 ships and boats,
49 trees.

It is small wonder therefore that the Tapestry can be, and has been, extensively used by students of arms and armour, of architecture, costume, and folk-lore. In this place, however, it is primarily as a first-hand description of the Norman Conquest that this notable work of co-operative art will be considered. Its importance in this respect can only be appraised by detailed examination. The whole of the surviving Tapestry is represented in the plates that follow. These have been given their conventional numbers for the sake of reference, and a translation of the legends, together with a brief commentary is here added.

Plate I (p. 239). KING EDWARD. WHERE HAROLD

Important for the architecture and more particularly for the portrait of the king. One of the subordinate figures is probably Earl Harold.

Plate II (p. 239). DUKE OF THE ENGLISH AND HIS KNIGHTS RIDE TO

The dogs wear collars fitted with leash-rings. The mane of Harold's horse is ornamented.

Plate III (p. 240). BOSHAM CHURCH.

Note the architecture of the church, and (in this and the next plate) the meal in the house. There seems here no suggestion that Harold's voyage was unpremeditated or taken without the knowledge of the king. This fact (if it were sufficiently established) would have an important bearing on the history of the succession question in England (see above, pp. 215, 217, 218).

Plates IV, V, VI (pp. 240, 241). HERE HAROLD CROSSES THE SEA AND WITH HIS SAILS FULL IN THE WIND ARRIVES IN THE LAND OF COUNT GUY.

These designs are very realistic: Harold and his friends partially undress in order to get on board. The design of the ships should be studied. Note that there is no indication of shipwreck. "Count Guy" is Guy I, count of Ponthieu (1053–1100).

Plate VII (p. 242). HERE GUY ARRESTS HAROLD

Harold is fully dressed, and the spear in his hand suggests that he may resist arrest.

Plates VIII, IX (pp. 242, 243). AND LEADS HIM TO BEAURAIN AND THERE HOLDS HIM.

The realistic portrayal of Harold's followers is masterly.

Plate X (p. 243). WHERE HAROLD AND GUY CONFER.

The conference is possibly about the amount of Harold's ransom. Guy sits upon a throne which, as it seems, has the characteristic dog's head ornamentation. The figure on the right may be a prophetic representation of the messenger of Duke William who is about to appear, but more probably it represents an Englishman eavesdropping before escaping to summon help.

Plates XI, XII (p. 244). WHERE THE MESSENGERS OF DUKE WILLIAM CAME TO GUY. THE MESSENGERS OF WILLIAM.

Guy stands in some defiance. Over the head of a small dwarf-like figure who holds the horses appears the name TUROLD, which, however, perhaps refers to the rearmost of the two armed messengers to whom it is also attached. This has been thought to be that Turold who held from Bishop Odo in England in 1086, and the suggestion is interesting from the fact that if indeed Odo ordered the Tapestry some of his vassals might be expected to appear prominently in it. (See also Plates XLVIII, XLIX, LVII, LVIII, LIX.) It has even been guessed that the little figure placed with the horses might represent the designer of the Tapestry. The building on Plate XII must represent Guy's dwelling at Beaurain.

Plate XIII (p. 245). HERE CAME THE MESSENGER TO DUKE WILLIAM.

William is seated on a throne very similar to that used by Guy of Ponthieu. The messenger appears to be an Englishman, and is perhaps the same man who is portrayed on the right of Plate X. The chronological sequence of the events depicted on the last five plates is probably confused.

Plates XIV, XV (pp. 245, 246). HERE GUY LEADS HAROLD TO WILLIAM, DUKE OF THE NORMANS.

The building on the left of Plate XIV possibly refers to the previous scene, and may represent Duke William's palace at Rouen. The attitude of the chief figures is noteworthy, and Duke William may here be depicted in a characteristic attitude. The drawing supports the statement of William of Poitiers that Guy surrendered Harold in person.

Plates XVI, XVII, XVIII (pp. 246, 247). HERE DUKE WILLIAM CAME WITH HAROLD TO HIS PALACE.

One of the most dramatic scenes in the whole Tapestry. The tower-like structure in the middle of Plate XVII perhaps represents the gate of the palace with a watchman looking out. The palace which extends to Plate XVIII is spacious, being surmounted by seventeen semi-circular arches. William is seated. Harold is speaking with vehemence. The attitude of the spectators indicates an occasion of importance. The subject under consideration must be conjectural, but taking this plate in connexion with Plate I it has been suggested that it was most probably a message from King Edward relating to William's eventual succession to the English throne.

Plate XVIII (p. 247). WHERE A CLERK AND ÆLFGYVA.

The most mysterious picture in the Tapestry. Much has been written about it (see Freeman, *Norman Conquest*, vol. III, App. 'A'), and no wholly satisfactory explanation has been supplied. Ælfgifu is a purely English name and what the lady was doing in Normandy must remain a matter of conjecture. The similarity of attitude between the clerk and the semi-obscene figure in the lower margin will not escape notice, nor will the absence of a verb in the legend. Perhaps the dovecot and the doves in the upper border have an erotic significance, and the whole episode may possibly refer to some scandal, then notorious, but now advantageously forgotten.

Plates XIX, XX (p. 248). HERE DUKE WILLIAM AND HIS ARMY CAME TO LE MONT-SAINT-MICHEL

A new chapter in the story. Harold, after the arrangements shown on Plates XVI, XVII, joins the Norman duke in the Breton wars. The structure at the top of Plate XX is possibly a representation of the abbey of le Mont-Saint-Michel to which reference is made in the legend. An ingenious, though perhaps hazardous, suggestion has been put forward that the host stopped at Bayeux on the way, and that the building here depicted is the priory of Saint-Vigor at Bayeux which was rebuilt by Bishop Odo, and filled with monks from le Mont-Saint-Michel.

Plates XX, XXI (pp. 248, 249). AND HERE THEY CROSSED THE RIVER COUESNON AND CAME TO DOL. AND HERE DUKE HAROLD DRAGGED THEM OUT OF THE QUICKSAND.

A most romantic section. The Couesnon, which runs into the sea by the still dangerous quicksands of le Mont-Saint-Michel, divides Normandy from Brittany. Harold is represented as of great stature, as he is described by the chroniclers. Note the care taken to prevent the precious armour getting wet.

Plate XXII (p. 249). AND CONAN TURNS IN FLIGHT.

This is Conan II, duke of Brittany, who died in 1066. The town from which a man is seen escaping is Dol, and the two birds underneath it are doubtless meant to symbolize a peaceful submission.

Plates XXIII, XXIV (p. 250). HERE THE KNIGHTS OF DUKE WILLIAM FIGHT AGAINST THE MEN OF DINAN.

The castle of Rennes is represented on the left of Plate XXIII and that of Dinan in the centre of Plate XXIV. The methods here employed for storming a castle deserve careful study.

Plates XXIV, XXV (pp. 250, 251). AND CONAN REACHED OUT THE KEYS. HERE WILLIAM GAVE ARMS TO HAROLD.

The keys of the citadel are handed out at the end of one lance and received at the end of another. The knighting of Harold by William is important as having a considerable bearing on the Norman Conquest. Harold receives arms from his overlord, and carries the banner which he is now entitled to bear. Harold undoubtedly was considered, after receiving knighthood in this fashion, as being bound to support the interests of his overlord. Both men are fully armed and wear hauberks.

Plates XXVI, XXVII (pp. 251, 252). HERE WILLIAM CAME TO BAYEUX. AND HAROLD MADE AN OATH TO WILLIAM.

One of the most important scenes in the whole Tapestry. It should be studied in connexion with the account of the famous oath given in William of Poitiers (see above, p. 218). It will be noted that there is no suggestion of treachery: the relics are not concealed but fully exposed, and the bones may be seen at the bottom of the reliquary. On the altar the Host is also fully exposed.

Plates XXVIII, XXIX (pp. 252, 253). HERE DUKE HAROLD RETURNED TO ENGLISH LAND.

The first climax in the story has been reached and passed. The scene now shifts to England. The ship is interesting. Harold, it seems, is leaning against the mast looking towards the shore. The erection to the right of Plate XXVIII may be Harold's house at Bosham and the figure looking out to sea may be a woman.

Plates XXIX, XXX (p. 253). AND HE CAME TO KING EDWARD.

An extremely interesting picture in that Harold's attitude indicates dejection and shame. The attendant with the axe may even suggest that the earl is in custody, and the king is evidently giving a reprimand. This scene (whatever conclusions may be drawn from it) should be taken into careful consideration in all attempts to interpret the relations between the Confessor and Earl Harold towards the close of the former's reign.

Plates XXX, XXXI (pp. 253, 254). HERE THE BODY OF KING EDWARD IS CARRIED TO THE CHURCH OF ST. PETER.

Westminster Abbey is here displayed, and its recent completion is indicated by the man on the roof who is engaged in fixing a weather-cock to the east end. The style of the early abbey will be noted. The funeral procession is of great simplicity. Stigand appears to be absent, for the leading priest wears a simple cope. The body of the king is borne on a bier by eight nobles: it is still uncoffined. It is about to be carried to the place in the abbey where it still remains. Above, a hand is stretched out of heaven in benediction.

Plate XXXII (p. 254). HERE KING EDWARD IN BED SPEAKS TO HIS LIEGEMEN. AND HERE HE DIES.

A highly important picture. Its position in this series after the funeral may be due to a simple misplacement. On the other hand, it may be deliberate to indicate the indecent haste of the obsequies, as who might say: "King Edward was buried almost before he died." However this may be, the death-bed scene here depicted deserves the most careful study: nor should it be dissociated with those in Plates I–III and XXIX, XXX. It has been suggested that Edward's hand outstretched towards that of a man who is apparently Harold indicates that Edward was delivering the kingdom to the earl of Wessex. In the lower picture the prelate is possibly Stigand. The bed seems to consist simply of sacks laid upon a board.

Plates XXXII, XXXIII (pp. 254, 255). HERE THEY GAVE THE KING'S CROWN TO HAROLD. HERE SITS KING HAROLD, KING OF THE ENGLISH.

Once again the extreme haste of the proceedings is indicated. Harold's formal coronation is depicted. They are offering him the sword, and he carries the sceptre and the orb. The officiating prelate is interesting since he is specially named as Stigand, and this, though probably inaccurate, is of great significance to the criticism of the Tapestry as a whole. According to the English evidence (which should probably here be accepted) Harold was crowned not by Stigand but by Aldred, archbishop of York. The Norman tradition (see above, p. 218) is that Harold was crowned by Stigand with whom he had been closely associated, a fact which, if true, would have weakened the position of the new king. For this reason this picture has been taken to indicate that the designer of the Tapestry was not an Englishman. However this may be, the close connexion of Harold with Stigand, the schismatic archbishop, and its influence on the contemporary opinion respecting the disputed succession is indisputable.

Plates XXXIII, XXXIV (p. 255). THESE MEN WONDER AT THE STAR.

At the very time that some are watching the coronation, another crowd is shown as looking at the portent in the sky (see Anglo-Saxon Chronicle, above, p. 142). Note how the two crowds are deliberately brought together in juxtaposition and are represented in contrasted attitudes. The picture of Harold to the right of Plate XXXIV is somewhat mysterious; perhaps he is having the portent explained to him by a soothsayer. Perhaps he has heard of Tosti's landing. At all events, as will be noted, he has already exchanged his sceptre for a javelin.

Plate XXXV (p. 256). HERE AN ENGLISH SHIP CAME TO THE LAND OF DUKE WILLIAM.

The artistic significance of this picture is that it transfers the action once again to Normandy. The ship carries the news of Edward's death and of Harold's coronation. The realistic treatment of the man wading ashore half-clad is interesting.

Plates XXXVI, XXXVII, XXXVIII, XXXIX (pp. 256–258). HERE DUKE WILLIAM ORDERED SHIPS TO BE BUILT. HERE THEY DRAG THE SHIPS TO THE WATER.

The Norman preparations for invasion now occupy the Tapestry. William takes counsel with his magnates, and the figure beside him is probably Odo. The messenger with the tidings from England shows signs of fear. The duke has determined on invasion, and the ensuing sequences show the rapid construction of ships for that purpose. The importance of these pictures to the student of the history of shipbuilding needs no emphasis. The cutting of the trees, the shaping of the wood, and the assembly of the ships themselves are all depicted. The small size of the vessels is clearly indicated both here and in the ease with which they are dragged to their launching.

Plates XL, XLI (pp. 258, 259). THESE MEN CARRY ARMS TO THE SHIPS AND HERE THEY DRAW A CART WITH WINE AND ARMS.

The arms displayed include swords, lances, axes, helmets, and hauberks. The weight of the hauberk, the characteristic equipment of the fully armed knight, is well seen by the fact that it is carried on a pole thrust through its sleeves and supported on the shoulders of two men. Note the wine cask in the carts with the helmets and spears above–a touch of realism.

Plates XLI, XLII, XLIII (pp. 259, 260). HERE DUKE WILLIAM CROSSED OVER THE SEA IN A GREAT SHIP.

Compare this with the graphic account given by William of Poitiers (see above, p. 221). Note particularly that no less than ten horses are depicted as being carried in the vessel.

Plates XLIV, XLV, XLVI (pp. 260, 261). HE CAME TO PEVENSEY. HERE THE HORSES GO OUT OF THE SHIPS.

The vessel to the right of Plate XLIV is the duke's ship with its lantern. In all this sequence the presence of the horses in the ships is emphasized.

Plates XLVI, XLVII, XLVIII (pp. 261, 262). HERE THE KNIGHTS HASTEN TO HASTINGS TO FIND FOOD.

Note the full armour, the shape of the shields. The horses have no armour.

Plates XLVIII, XLIX (pp. 262, 263). THIS IS WADARD.

It is suggested that this figure which is given such unnecessary prominence is that Wadard who was subsequently a tenant of Odo in Oxfordshire (see also Plates XI, LVII, LVIII).

Plates XLIX, L (p. 263). HERE THE MEAT IS COOKED AND HERE THE SERVANTS SERVE. HERE THEY HAVE DINNER.

The joint of meat is being boiled; the lesser articles of food are being roasted. Roasted birds impaled on arrows in place of skewers are offered to the diners who take hold of them with their hands.

Plate LI (p. 264). HERE THE BISHOP BLESSES THE FOOD AND DRINK. BISHOP ODO. WILLIAM. ROBERT.

A realistic picture which supplies another instance of the prominence given to Odo in the Tapestry. The portraits of the king and his two uterine half-brothers (see Table 2) are interesting. The seated figure on the right is Robert, count of Mortain.

Plate LII (p. 264). [WILLIAM] ORDERS A CASTLE TO BE DUG AT HASTINGS. THE CAMP.

The word castle here signifies a mound or rampart. The English word "*at*" is used instead of the Latin "*ad* ", and the camp is "*ceastra*". These facts have been cited in favour of the theory that the Tapestry was made in England.

Plates LIII, LIV (p. 265). HERE NEWS ABOUT HAROLD IS BROUGHT TO WILLIAM. HERE A HOUSE IS BURNT.

Perhaps the "news" concerned the result of the battle of Stamford Bridge which William could hardly have known when he left Normandy. Note the woman and child escaping from the burning house.

Plates LIV, LV, LVI, LVII (pp. 265–267). HERE THE KNIGHTS GO OUT FROM HASTINGS AND ADVANCE TO GIVE BATTLE TO KING HAROLD.

The knights for the most part carry lances. The duke carries a mace.

Plates LVII, LVIII, LIX (pp. 267, 268). HERE DUKE WILLIAM ASKS VITAL IF HE HAD SEEN HAROLD'S ARMY.

This may well be Vitalis, a tenant of Bishop Odo in Kent (see Plates XI, XLVII, XLIX). Vital points eagerly to his scouts who have taken up their position behind a spinney on the crest of a hill. Mr. Belloc suggests that this is Telham Hill.

Plate LX (p. 268). HERE ONE INFORMS KING HAROLD ABOUT THE ARMY OF WILLIAM.

The armour of the mounted messenger deserves study.

Plates LX, LXI, LXII, LXIII, LXIV (pp. 268–270). HERE DUKE WILLIAM EXHORTS HIS FOLLOWERS TO PREPARE THEMSELVES MANFULLY AND WISELY AGAINST THE ARMY OF THE ENGLISH.

See the account given by William of Poitiers (above, p. 225). Note the archers preceding the knights.

Plates LXV, LXVI (p. 271).

The battle is joined. Note the English fighting on foot. Some are with battle-axes; some have darts which they throw. Harold rides to the battle but dismounts to fight. On all these details the Tapestry is confirmed by the account given by William of Poitiers (see above, pp. 225–226).

Plates LXVII, LXVIII, LXIX (pp. 272, 273). HERE FELL LEOFWINE AND GYRTH, THE BROTHERS OF KING HAROLD.

For Leofwine and Gyrth, see Table 7. Note the border of wounded and slain men.

Plates LXIX, LXX, LXXI (pp. 273, 274). HERE FELL TOGETHER ENGLISH AND FRENCH IN THE BATTLE.

The climax of the battle scenes and a most striking piece of composition. The Saxon battle array on the top of the hill is beginning to disintegrate in Plate LXXI.

Plate LXXII (p. 274). Here Bishop Odo, holding a club, encourages the young soldiers.

Once again the bishop is brought into prominence. Does he carry a club rather than a sword because it was forbidden to churchmen to shed blood?

Plates LXXII, LXXIII (pp. 274, 275). Here is Duke William.

Compare this scene with the account of William of Poitiers (see above, p. 226). Perhaps this is the moment when the duke rallies his troops who are discomfited by a false report that he is slain. In the lower margin emphasis is given to the part played by the archers at this stage of the battle.

Plate LXXIII (p. 275). E[us]tace.

On the part played by Eustace, count of Boulogne, in the battle see William of Poitiers (above, pp. 228–229). The two accounts corroborate each other very neatly at this point.

Plates LXXIII, LXXIV, LXXV (pp. 275, 276). Here the French fight and those who were with Harold fell.

The co-operation between the archers and the fully armed mounted knights is here well brought out.

Plates LXXVI, LXXVII (pp. 276, 277). Here King Harold was slain.

Harold probably appears twice in these two plates. In Plate LXXVI he seems to be plucking some object, perhaps an arrow, from his eye. In Plate LXXVII he is being cut down by a Norman knight. He fights on foot wielding a battle-axe to the last.

Plates LXXVIII, LXXIX (pp. 277, 278). And the English fled.

A vivid representation of the rout (cf. William of Poitiers, above, p. 228). In the lower border it will be seen that the corpses are being stripped of their armour.

I
EDWARD REX: VBI: hAROL

II
DVX: ANGLORVM: ETSVI MILITES: EQVI TANT: ADE

III
BOSHAM: ECCLESIA:

IV
HIC HAROLD: MARE NAVIGAVI

T: ETVE LIS: VENTO: PLENIS VE-
NIT: INTE RRA:
VVIDONIS
COMITIS

HIC: APPREHENDIT: VVIDO: HAROLDV

AD BEL REM:

IX
BI EVM:TEN VIT:

X
VBI:HARO LD: ⁊VVIDO:PA RABO LANT:

XI
VBI:NVNTII:VVILLELMI: DVCIS: VENE
TVROLD

XII
ERVNT:ADVVIDO
NE
NVN TII

XIII
VVILLELMI
+HIC VENIT: NVNTIVS: AD WIL
GELMVM DVCEM

XIV
HIC: WIDO: AD DVXIT HAR OLDVC

XV
ADVVILGELM VM: NORMANNO RV M: DVCEM

XVI
HIC: DVX: VVILGELM:

XVII
:CVM HAROLDO:VENIT:ADPA
LATIV SVV

XVIII
VBI:VNVS:CLERICVS:ET:
ÆLFGY VA
HIC:VVILL

XIX
.EM:DUX:ET EXERCITUS:EIUS:VENERUNT:ADMON

XX
E MICHAELIS
ET HIC:TRANSIERUNT:FLU
HIC:HAROLD:
DEARE

XXI
VMEN: COSNONIS: ET VENERVNT
AD DOL: ET: C
DVX: TRAHEBAT: EOS:
ENA

ONAN:
FVGA VER
TIT
RE

XXIII
HIC MILITES
VVILLELMI:DVCIS:PVG
NAN
ED
NES

XXIV
NT:CONTRA
DINANTES:ET:CV

XXV
NAN: CLAVES: POR REXIT: HIC: WILLELM:
DEDIT: HAROLDO:
ARMA
HIC

XXVI
VVILLELM VENIT: BAGIAS
UBI

XXVII
AROLD:SACRAMENTUM:FECIT:
VVILLELMO DUCI:
HIC HAROLD:DUX:

XXVIII
REVERSUS: EST

XXIX
ANGLICAM:TERRAM:ET
VENIT:AD:EDVVAR

XXX
RDV:
REGEM:
HIC PORTATVR:C

XXXI
ORPVS:EADWARDI:REGIS:AD:ECCLESIAM:SCI
PETRI APLI

XXXII
HIC EADWARDVS:REX
IN LECTO:ALLOQVIT:FIDELES:
HIC DEDERVNT:HAR
CORO NA
ET HIC: DEFVNCTVS
EST

XXXIII
ROLDO:
REGIS
HIC RE SIDET: HAROLD
REX: AN GLORVM:
STIGANT
ARCHI EPS

ISTI MIRANT STELLA
HAROLD

XXXV
HIC:NAVIS:ANGLI
CA:VENIT.I
WILLELM

XXXVI
HIC:WILLELM
DUX:IU
NAVES:EDI
FICA
INTER
MI:DU
RAM
CIS

XXXVII
IUSSIT
ARE :

XXXVIII
HIC

TRAHVNT:NAVES:ADMA RE:

ISTI PORTANT:ARMAS:AD
TR
CV

XLI
NAVES: ET HIC
AHVNT: CARRVM
M VINO: ET ARM IS:
+ HIC: VVILLELM: DVX
IN M

XLII
MAGNO: NAVIGIO:
MA

XLIII
ARE
TRAN

XLIV
SIVIT
ETVENIT
ADPEVENESÆ :-

XLV
HIC EX

EXEVNT: CABALLI DENAVIBVS ETHIC: MILIT

XLVII
TES: FESTINA VERV NT: HESTINGA: VT CIB

XLVIII
CIBVM. RAPERENTVR:
HIC: EST: V

XLIX
:VVAD AR D:
hIC:COQVI
TVR:CARO
ET hIC: MINISTI

NISTRAVERVN
MINISTRI
hIC FECERVN: PRANDIVM:
ET
POT

LI
HIC·EPISCOPVS:CIBV:ET
TV: BE NE DIC IT·
ODO:EPS:
ROTBERT:·ISTE·IV
WIL LELM:

LII
VSSIT: VT FO DERETVR:CASTELLVM:AT·HESTENGA CEAST

LIII
STRA
HIC:NVNTIATVM EST:
WILLELMO DE HAROLD:
HIC

LIV
OMVS:IN
ENDITVR:
HIC:MILITES: EXIERVNT:D

LV
DE HESTENGA:
ET VENERVNT

LVI
AD PRELIVM: CON TRA:

LVII
HAROL DVM:REGE: HIC: V VILLELM:DVX INT

LVIII
NTERROGAT:VITAL: SIVI DISSET EXE
HAROLDI

LIX
ER CI
TV
ISTE

LX
NVNTIAT:HA ROLDVM
REGE
DE·EXER
CITV
VVILLELMI
DVCIS
HIC WILLELM:

LXI
ELM:DUX ALLOQUI TUR:SU IS:MILITI BUS:UT PR

LXII
PREPARA RENT SE:VI RILI TER

LXIII
ETSAPIENTEAR: ADPRELIVM:

LXIV
CON RA:AN GLORVM EXER

LXV

LXVI

LXVII
HIC CECI
DERVN

LXVIII
RVNT LEVVINE
ET: GYRD: FRATRES: H

LXIX
S HARO L DI REGIS: HIC CECI

LXX
CI DERVNT SIMVL: ANGLI ET FRA NCI

LXXI
CI: INPRELIO:

LXXII
ODO EPS: BACVLV TENENS: CONFORT:
HIC EST
TAT
PVE
ROS

LXXIII
IUS
DUX
HIC FRAN
CI
PUGNAN

LXXIV
ETCECI
DE

LXXV
RVNT QVIERANT: CVM hAROLDO:

LXXVI
AROLDO:
hIC
hARO L D: R

LXXVII
REX: INTERFEC
TVS: EST

LXXVIII
ET FVGA: VERTERVNT

LXXIX
ANGLI

6. An account of the death and character of William the Conqueror, written by a monk of Caen

This description is contained in an addition to some manuscripts of the Norman chronicle of William of Jumièges. It was apparently written within a few years of the Conqueror's death, and was perhaps the work of a monk of St. Stephen's, Caen. Its simplicity inspires confidence, and it supplies information not to be obtained elsewhere. It has been printed as a long footnote in T. D. Hardy, *Catalogue of Materials* (Rolls Series, 1865), pp. 14–16; and in William of Jumièges, *Gesta Normannorum Ducum*, ed. J. Marx (Soc. Hist. Norm., 1914), pp. 145–149.

CONCERNING THE DEATH OF WILLIAM, DUKE OF THE NORMANS AND KING OF THE ENGLISH, WHO CAUSED HOLY CHURCH TO LIVE IN PEACE

In the year of our Lord 1087, King William of most pious memory, when returning from the sack and burning of Mantes, began to be afflicted with weakness. His stomach rejected food and drink, his breathing became difficult, and he was shaken with sobs. Thus his strength began to ebb away. He therefore ordered a little dwelling to be prepared at the church of St. Gervase, which is in the suburbs of Rouen, and there in his weakness he betook himself to bed. Who shall reveal the anxiety then felt for the state of the Church, and for its impending afflictions, and who shall describe the tears then poured out to hasten the divine pity? The king did not grieve so much by reason of his approaching death, as because he knew the future. He declared that after his death disasters would visit his Norman homeland, and subsequently events were to show that he spoke truth.[1] Then there came to console the king venerable prelates and many other servants of God. Among these were William,[2] archbishop of the aforesaid city, and Gilbert, bishop of Lisieux,[3] and John, the doctor, and Gerard, the chancellor,[4] and also Robert, count of Mortain, the king's brother, in whom the king reposed great confidence because he was his close kinsman. Wherefore the king ordered the same Robert, who was then advanced in years, to summon to his side the officials of his household,[5] and he commanded them to enumerate one by one all the things which were in his household, to wit crowns and arms, vessels and books, and ecclesiastical vestments. And, as it seemed good to him, he declared what ought to be given to churches, to the poor, and finally to his sons. He allowed William, his son, to have his crown, his sword, and his gold sceptre studded with gems. Wherefore Archbishop William and others who were present were afraid lest the king should be too harsh to his first-born son, Robert, since they knew that a wound frequently cut and cauterized may cause a greater pain to him who bears it. For this reason trusting in the invincible patience which the king had always shown they gently urged him through Archbishop William that he would not disdain their counsel. At first the king showed some bitterness at this intervention, but, after a little, somewhat rallying his strength, he seemed to consider the great injuries he had received from Robert, and then he spoke: "Since he has disdained to come here himself, it is with your witness and with the witness of God that I shall act. With such testimony I declare that I

[1] An obvious allusion to the disturbances in Normandy in the time of Duke Robert II.
[2] William 'Bonne-Ame', archbishop of Rouen, 1079–1110.
[3] Gilbert Maminot, bishop of Lisieux, 1077–1101.
[4] Made bishop of Hereford, 1096.
[5] *ministros camerae suae.*

forgive him all the sins he has committed against me and I grant him the whole duchy of Normandy. This, before God and in the presence of the magnates of my court, I previously promised him. It will be your duty however to admonish him. I have pardoned him so often that he has learnt to take advantage of my leniency, and now he has brought down his father's grey hairs in sorrow to the grave. By so doing he has broken the commands of God and incurred the wrath of him who is our common Father." Having spoken thus, the king asked that the Visitation and the Unction of the Sick should be celebrated, and Holy Communion was administered to him in due form by the hand of the archbishop. Thus he departed this life, and, as we believe, went happily to his rest. He died on 10 September[1] in the fifty-ninth year of his age, having reigned over England for twenty-two years.

This king excelled in wisdom all the princes of his generation, and among them all he was outstanding in the largeness of his soul. He never allowed himself to be deterred from prosecuting any enterprise because of the labour it entailed, and he was ever undaunted by danger. So skilled was he in his appraisal of the true significance of any event, that he was able to cope with adversity, and to take full advantage in prosperous times of the false promises of fortune. He was great in body and strong, tall in stature but not ungainly. He was also temperate in eating and drinking. Especially was he moderate in drinking, for he abhorred drunkenness in all men and disdained it more particularly in himself and at his court. He was so sparing in his use of wine and other drink, that after his meal he rarely drank more than thrice. In speech he was fluent and persuasive, being skilled at all times in making clear his will. If his voice was harsh, what he said was always suited to the occasion. He followed the Christian discipline in which he had been brought up from childhood, and whenever his health permitted he regularly, and with great piety, attended Christian worship each morning and evening and at the celebration of Mass. And so, at last, it seemed to everyone that he could be given no more honourable grave than in the church which out of love he had built at Caen to the honour of God and of St. Stephen, the first martyr. This, indeed, he had previously arranged. Therefore in that church he was buried, and a monument of gilded silver was erected over his tomb by his son, William, who succeeded him as king of England.

[1] The Anglo-Saxon Chronicle (above, p. 163) gives, by a different reckoning, 9 September, as also does Ordericus Vitalis (below, p. 289). This date seems correct. The anniversary was celebrated on 9 September in the abbey of Jumièges (*Rec. Hist. Franc.*, vol. XXIII, p. 421).

7. Ordericus Vitalis: "The Ecclesiastical History"

The following essay on the life and death of William the Conqueror comes from the elaborate history written between 1123 and 1141 by Ordericus Vitalis, a man who was born in England in 1075, and who at an early age became a monk in the Norman abbey of St. Evroul. It was the custom of Ordericus, after the manner of Thucydides, to place speeches into the mouths of the chief personalities in his story in order thereby to illustrate their character and policy. The speech which here follows must be read in this sense. The whole description, though not contemporary, is of great interest as representing the considered opinion respecting the Conqueror formed by an acute observer who lived much of his life under his rule. Further information respecting Ordericus Vitalis (see above, p. 98) will be found in the magnificent introduction by L. Delisle included in *Orderici Vitalis Historia Ecclesiastica* (ed. A. Le Prévost, Soc. Hist. Franc., 5 vols., Paris, 1838–1855), and the passage printed below is in vol. III, pp. 227–249, of that work. A translation into English, which with some modifications is here followed, is given in T. Forester, *The Ecclesiastical History of Ordericus Vitalis*, vol. II (1854), pp. 401–418.

The king, who during his whole life had followed the advice of wise counsellors, had feared God as became his faithful servant, and had been the unwearied protector of holy mother Church, maintained his exalted reputation to the end. His death was worthy of his life. To the very last, through all his illness, his intellect was clear and his conversation lively; repenting of his sins he confessed them to the priests of God, and humbly strove to appease his wrath according to the rites of the Christian Church. The bishops, abbots, and men of religion never left him, and were indefatigable in opening to the dying prince the salutary doctrines of eternal life. When the noise of Rouen, which is a populous place, became insupportable to the sufferer, the king gave orders that he should be conveyed out of the city to the church of St. Gervase, standing on a hill to the west, which his grandfather, Duke Richard, had given to the monastery of Fécamp. There Gilbert, bishop of Lisieux,[1] and Guntard, abbot of Jumièges, with some others, well skilled in medicine, carefully watched over him, devoting themselves zealously to their master's welfare both spiritual and temporal.

At length, his disorder continually increasing, and perceiving that inevitable death was becoming imminent, he became anxious about the future which was veiled from his sight. Therefore reflecting on this with deep concern, he was frequently moved to sighs and groans. He summoned to his side his sons, William Rufus and Henry, who were in attendance on him with some of his friends, and gave them many wise and prudent directions for the government of his realms. Robert, his eldest son, had long before entered on a course of repeated quarrels with his father,[2] and had recently taken umbrage in consequence of some new follies, and retired to the court of the king of France.

The wise king hastened to make provision for the future welfare of himself and others, ordering all his treasures to be distributed among the churches, the poor, and the ministers of God. He exactly specified the amount to be given to each, and gave directions to the notaries to reduce it to writing in his own presence. He also contritely sent large donations to the clergy of Mantes, to be applied to the restoration of the churches he had burnt. He gave admonitions to all who were present relative to the maintenance of justice and good faith; about keeping the law of God and peace; about the privileges of the churches; and about observing the rules of the fathers. His

[1] Gilbert Maminot, bishop of Lisieux, 1077–1101.

[2] Cf. Anglo-Saxon Chronicle, above, p. 159.

eloquent discourse, worthy to be held in everlasting remembrance, and at times interrupted by tears, was to the following effect.

"I tremble," he said, "my friends, when I reflect on the grievous sins which burden my conscience, and now about to be summoned before the awful tribunal of God, I know not what I ought to do. I was bred to arms from my childhood, and am stained with the rivers of blood I have shed. It is out of my power to enumerate all the injuries which I have caused during the sixty-four[1] years of my troublous life, for which I am now called to render account without delay to the most righteous Judge. At the time my father went into voluntary exile, entrusting to me the duchy of Normandy, I was a mere youth of eight years, and from that time to this I have always borne the weight of arms. I have now ruled this duchy fifty-six years,[2] amidst the difficulties of incessant wars. My own subjects have often conspired against me, and shamefully exposed me to serious losses and great injuries. They have perfidiously put to death Turchetil my guardian, Osbern,[3] son of Herfast, steward of Normandy; Count Gilbert,[4] the father of his country, and many others, who were the pillars of the State. In these trials I had proof of the fidelity of my people: often by night I was secretly taken from the chamber of my palace by my uncle, Walter,[5] through fear of my own relations, and conducted to the dwellings and retreats of the poor, that I might escape from discovery by the traitors who sought my death.

"The Normans, when under the rule of a kind but firm master, are a most valiant people, excelling all others in the invincible courage with which they meet difficulties, and strive to conquer every enemy. But under other circumstances they bring ruin on themselves by rending each other. They are eager for rebellion, ripe for tumults, and ready for every sort of crime. They must therefore be restrained by the strong hand of justice, and compelled to walk in the right way by the reins of discipline. But if they are allowed to take their own course without any yoke like an untamed colt, they and their princes will be overwhelmed with poverty, shame, and confusion. I have learnt this by much experience. My nearest friends, my own kindred, who ought to have defended me at all hazards against the whole world, formed conspiracies against me, and nearly stripped me of the inheritance of my fathers.

"Guy, son of Rainald, duke[6] of Burgundy, by my aunt Adeliza, returned me evil for good. I had kindly received him on his arrival from a foreign country, and treated him with the regard due to an only brother, giving him Vernon, Brionne, and an important part of my Norman territories. Notwithstanding this, he did all in his power to injure me, both by word and deed, calling me bastard, degenerate and unworthy to reign, and defaming me as if I had been his enemy. Need I add more? Breaking his fealty, he rebelled against me, seduced from my service Rannulf of Bayeux,[7] Haimo 'dentatus',[8] Nigel of the Cotentin,[9] and many others, forcing them by his nefarious counsels to be partakers of his perjury. Regardless therefore of the

[1] Inaccurate: William was born in 1027 or perhaps 1028.
[2] Inaccurate: William became duke of Normandy in 1035.
[3] Father of William fitz Osbern who became earl of Hereford shortly after the Conquest. (See Table 10.) On him, see D. C. Douglas, *Eng. Hist. Rev.*, vol. LIX, p. 66.
[4] Father of Richard fitz Gilbert of Tonbridge and of Clare. (See Table 11.)
[5] Brother of Herleva. (See Table 2.)
[6] Count, not duke, of Burgundy.
[7] Rannulf, *vicomte* of the Bessin.
[8] Father of Haimo, sheriff of Kent. (See below, p. 428.)
[9] Nigel, *vicomte* of the Cotentin.

homage and fealty which he had sworn to me, he strove to strip me of the whole of Normandy. Thus, while I was yet a beardless youth, I found myself compelled to take up arms against him, and to fight on the plain of Val-ès-Dunes[1] against my cousin and liegeman. Then, by the help of God, the righteous Judge, I conquered my foes between Caen and Argences, and having by his permission utterly defeated them, I obtained entire possession of my paternal rights. I then laid siege to the fortress of Brionne, in which Guy, who fled wounded from the field of battle, had shut himself up, and I did not depart until I had driven the public enemy out of Normandy, and obtained possession of all his strongholds.

"Shortly afterwards, a still more grievous calamity befell me. My uncles,[2] Mauger, archbishop of Rouen, and his brother, William, to whom I had gratuitously given Arques and the county of Talou, treated me with contempt as a bastard, and induced King Henry and Ingelram, count of Ponthieu,[3] to take up arms against me. I received this intelligence in the Cotentin, and lost no time in beginning my march contrary to the advice of most of my counsellors. Sending forward to Arques some light troops who were eager for the fray, I followed myself with the main body, which was far from considerable, to lay siege to the castle. But before I reached the country between the two rivers, the Sie and the Garenne, the advanced guard fell in with Count Ingelram pushing forward to occupy the fortress. Although he fought bravely as a valiant knight, they killed him and routed his squadrons.[4] Pressing the siege closely, I compelled the perjured count to go into banishment, and did not permit him to return to the domains he lost during all the days of his life. I also, by virtue of a papal decree, deposed the insolent archbishop, who neither observed his fealty to me, nor his duty to God, and raised to the see the venerable monk, Maurilius,[5] who was providentially sent from Florence, an Italian city.

"Henry,[6] in all his royal power, and in the fervour of his chivalric spirit, was often incited by my enemies to trample me under his feet as a defenceless man. He endeavoured to crush me, and to assert unjust rights against me. He made frequent invasions of my territory at the head of large armies, but he was never able to glory either in the spoils of war or in the captives he took from among my subjects. He often crossed my frontiers with great military pomp, and terrible threats, but he never returned to his own kingdom without sorrow and shame. He brought in his train numbers of brave men who – alas! – never saw their own country again, since they fell by my sword, or were killed by my followers.

"On one occasion[7] King Henry was so enraged against me that he invaded my land with a vast army in two divisions so that he might overwhelm it by a double attack. He led one body of troops himself into the diocese of Evreux, and ravaged the

[1] The battle of Val-ès-Dunes took place in 1047, and Duke William was victorious with the aid of the French king. An interesting description of the battle is given in the *Roman de Rou* of Wace (ed. H. Andresen, vol. II (1879), pp. 172 *et sqq.*).

[2] Mauger, archbishop of Rouen (1037–1055), and William, count of Arques, were sons of Duke Richard II of Normandy.

[3] Ingelram of Ponthieu, brother-in-law of William, count of Arques, was himself elder brother of Guy, count of Ponthieu, who figures in the Bayeux Tapestry. For the family, see C. Brunel, *Recueil des Actes des Comtes de Ponthieu* (Paris, 1930).

[4] This revolt took place in 1053.

[5] Maurilius, archbishop of Rouen, 1055–1077.

[6] Henry I, king of France, 1031–1060.

[7] February 1054.

whole country on this side of the Seine, while he gave the command of the other division to his brother, Odo, with Rainald of Clermont, and the two counts, Ralph of Montdidier, and Guy of Ponthieu,[1] who had orders to enter Normandy by the fords of the Epte, and, after raiding Brai, Talon and the whole province of Rouen, to continue their devastations to the sea-coast. Receiving intelligence of these movements, I lost no time in preparing to meet them. Stationing myself with part of my troops along the bank of the Seine against the king's tents, I kept him in check, and was ready to fall upon the enemy at whatever point he attempted to ravage my territories. Meanwhile, I detached against Odo and his division, Robert, count of Eu,[2] with Roger of Mortemer, and other distinguished warriors, who encountered the French near the castle of Mortemer. Battle was then joined, and a desperate engagement ensued, in which the carnage was enormous, for the combatants on both sides were full of ardour and resolved to yield only with their lives. On one side, the French made furious assaults, inspired by the hope of gaining the spoils of victory; on the other, the Normans struck home, animated by their determination to repel the enemy and defend their lives and possessions. This battle was fought beyond the Seine in the winter season, before Lent, eight years after that of Val-ès-Dunes.[3] Guy,[4] count of Ponthieu, was taken prisoner and Odo, Rainald, and others were put to flight, owing their escape to the speed with which they ran away. Count Ralph would also have been taken, if Roger, my commander, had not favoured his escape on account of the fealty he had formerly sworn to him. In acting thus, in the hour of the count's utmost need, he paid him a noble and legitimate service, receiving him in his castle where he entertained him three days, and afterwards conducting him in safety to his own territories. Nevertheless, for this breach of his duty to me, I banished Roger from Normandy, but, being soon afterwards reconciled with him, I then restored him all his domains, except the castle of Mortemer, in which he had sheltered my enemy. This I think he justly forfeited. So I granted it to his cousin, William de Warenne,[5] one of my loyal young vassals. Guy, count of Bayeux,[6] was detained a captive during my pleasure; but two years afterwards I received his fealty on the terms of his being always my liegeman and doing military service every year, wherever I should appoint, with a hundred knights.[7] I then heaped favours upon him and dismissed him in peace thus honoured.

"As soon as I received certain intelligence of the issue of the battle of Mortemer, I dispatched Ralph of Tosny to the king of France with an account of what had occurred on the left bank of the Seine. On hearing the news, which reached him in the dead of the night, King Henry lost not a moment in putting his troops in motion, and, having made a precipitate retreat, from that hour he has never reposed for a single night on my territories.

[1] Guy, count of Ponthieu, 1053–1101.

[2] Robert, count of Eu, being a grandson of Richard I, duke of Normandy, survived until after 1086. For the family, see D. C. Douglas in *Eng. Hist. Rev.*, vol. LXI, pp. 135 *et sqq.* Robert held extensive possessions in England, particularly in Sussex.

[3] The correct date of the battle is February 1054.

[4] Successor of Ingelram.

[5] Later received large estates in England, particularly in Sussex. First earl of Surrey, and founder of Lewes Priory. (See below, No. 80, p. 605.)

[6] A mistake for Ponthieu.

[7] If this statement could be taken at its face value, it would provide evidence of an early imposition of the feudal *servitium debitum* by Duke William.

"Thus, from my very infancy, I have been continually involved in numberless troubles, but, by God's mercy, I have freed myself from them all with the highest honour. I became in consequence an object of jealousy to all my neighbours, but by his aid in whom I always put my trust, none of them were able to prevail against me. The Bretons and Angevins have found this; the French and Flemings are witnesses of it; the men of Maine have severely felt it.

"Geoffrey Martel, count of Anjou,[1] Conan, duke of Brittany,[2] and Robert the Frisian, count of Flanders,[3] engaged in perfidious enterprises against me; but as God was my protector, though they made great efforts and laid many snares for me, they were never able to accomplish their designs. I have placed on my brow a royal diadem, which none of my predecessors wore, having acquired it by the grace of God, not by hereditary right.[4] It would be difficult for me to recount my labours beyond sea, and the perilous conflicts in which I have been engaged with the people of Exeter,[5] Chester, and Northumbria,[6] with the Scots[7] and Welsh,[8] Norwegians, Danes[9] and other adversaries who attempted to deprive me of the crown of England: in all which I obtained the victory. But much as human ambition is disposed to triumph in such successes, I am a prey to cruel fears and anxieties when I reflect with what barbarities they were attended. I therefore humbly entreat you, the priests and ministers of Christ, to commend me in your prayers to Almighty God for the forgiveness of the sins with which my conscience is burdened, and that through his inexhaustible mercy he will vouchsafe to grant me salvation among his elect. I direct my treasure to be given to the churches and the poor, that what was amassed in crime may be dispersed among the saints and applied to holy uses. For you ought to remember how dearly I have loved you, and how stoutly I have defended you against all your enemies.

"I have never injured the Church of God, which is our mother, but have always paid her, as circumstances demanded, due honour. I never sold ecclesiastical dignities. I prohibited simony, which I always detested. In the election of prelates my choice was directed by meritorious conduct and wise doctrine, and, as far as it has been in my power, the government of the Church has been committed to the most worthy. This may be truly proved by my selection of Lanfranc, archbishop of Canterbury; of Anselm, abbot of Bec; Gerbert, abbot of Fontenelles; Durand, abbot of Troarn; and many other doctors of my realm, whose praise, I think, is spread to the ends of the earth. Such were the associates with whom I conversed, and in whose society I learnt the maxims of wisdom and truth; so that I always delighted to receive their counsels.

"Nine abbeys of monks[10] and one of nuns,[11] founded in Normandy by my predecessors, have, under God's blessing, been augmented by my care, nobly enriched with the splendid endowments of various kinds I have conferred upon them. Moreover, during the time I have governed the duchy, seventeen convents of monks and

[1] Count of Anjou, 1040–1060. [2] Died 1066. [3] Count of Flanders, 1071–1111.
[4] Contrast William of Poitiers (above, p. 231). [5] See above, p. 147. [6] See above, p. 150.
[7] See above, p. 154. [8] See above, p. 147. [9] See above, p. 157.
[10] The reference is probably to the abbeys of St. Ouen; St. Wandrille; Jumièges; Fécamp; le Mont-Saint-Michel; Bernay; Holy Trinity, Rouen; Cerisy; and Le Bec Hellouin.
[11] Montivilliers.

six of nuns have been erected, in which the work of God is regularly performed, and large alms are daily distributed for the love of the supreme King. With such fortresses Normandy is well protected, and in them men are taught to combat devils and the sins of the flesh. By God's inspiration all these abbeys have been either of my creation or foundation, and I became their zealous benefactor and kind promoter. Moreover, all the endowments, whether in lands or other revenues, which my barons have given to God and his saints, for the good of their souls, both in Normandy and England, I have graciously confirmed. And I have gratuitously ratified by my princely authority the charters granting them, against all claims and pretensions.

"Such have been my cares from my earliest years, and these duties I leave to my successors to be observed in all time to come. In these, my sons, be sure to follow my example, that you may be honoured for ever before God and men. I especially exhort you, who are my own flesh, to cultivate unceasingly the society of good and wise men, and to submit to their rule in all things, if you desire to possess lasting glory. From the teaching of pious philosophers you will learn to distinguish good from evil; to adhere to justice on all occasions; and to avoid iniquity; to spare the humble, the poor, and the pious, and to war-down the proud and malicious:[1] to refrain from injuring simple folk; to frequent with devotion the services of holy Church; to love the worship of God above all riches; and to observe unweariedly the divine law by day and night, in prosperity and adversity.

"Before I fought against Harold on the heath of Senlac,[2] I granted the dukedom of Normandy to my son Robert, because he was the eldest. He has already received the homage of nearly all the barons of this land. The grant thus made and ratified I cannot annul. But I know for certain that the country which is subject to his dominion will be truly wretched. He is proud, silly and prodigal, and will have long to suffer severe misfortune.

"I appoint no one my heir to the crown of England, but leave it to the disposal of the eternal Creator, whose I am, and who ordereth all things. For I did not attain that high honour by hereditary right, but wrested it from the perjured King Harold in a desperate battle, with much effusion of human blood; and it was by the slaughter and banishment of his adherents that I subjugated England to my rule. I have persecuted its native inhabitants beyond all reason. Whether gentle or simple, I have cruelly oppressed them; many I unjustly disinherited; innumerable multitudes, especially in the county of York, perished through me by famine or the sword. Thus it happened: the men of Deira and other people beyond the Humber called in the troops of Sweyn, king of Denmark, as their allies against me, and put to the sword Robert Comyn and a thousand soldiers within the walls of Durham, as well as others, my barons and most esteemed knights, in various places. These events inflamed me to the highest pitch of resentment, and I fell on the English of the northern shires like a ravening lion. I commanded their houses and corn, with all their implements and chattels, to be burnt without distinction, and large herds of cattle and beasts of burden to be butchered wherever they were found. It was thus that I took revenge on multitudes of both sexes by subjecting them to the calamity of a cruel famine; and by so doing –alas!–became the barbarous murderer of many thousands, both young and old, of

[1] Cf. Virgil, *Æneid*, VI, 853: *parcere subjectis et debellare superbos.*
[2] Ordericus appears to be the first to give this description to the battle of Hastings.

that fine race of people.[1] Having, therefore, made my way to the throne of that kingdom by so many crimes, I dare not leave it to anyone but God alone, lest after my death worse should happen by my means. I trust that my son, William, who from his earliest years has always attached himself to me, and has been dutiful under all trials to the best of his power, may live long and prosperously in the influence of the Spirit of God. Should it be the divine will that he succeed to the throne, may his reign be illustrious!"

While King William discoursed thus, with much more to the same effect, the bystanders who cautiously scanned the dim prospects of the future, were lost in amazement. Henry, his youngest son, hearing that no provision was made for him out of the royal wealth, said sorrowfully to the king: "And what, my father, do you give me?" To which the king replied: "I bequeath to you five thousand pounds of money from my Treasury."[2] Upon which Henry said: "What shall I do with this money, having no corner of earth which I can call my own?" To which the king answered: "My son, be contented with your lot, and trust in the Lord. Suffer patiently your elder brothers to precede you. Robert will have Normandy, and William England. But you, also, in your turn, will succeed to all the dominions which belong to me, and you will surpass your brothers in wealth and power."[3] After he had said this, the king, fearing lest in such extended territories some sudden tumults might burst forth, addressed a letter to Lanfranc, the archbishop, on the appointment of a successor to the throne, and affixing his seal, gave it to his son, William Rufus, commanding him to embark for England without delay. He then kissed him, and, giving him his blessing, directed him to hasten his departure and cross the sea to secure the crown. The prince lost no time in riding to the port of Wissant, and there he received intelligence of his father's death. Henry was equally prompt in securing the money allotted to him. He had it carefully weighed that there might be no deficiency, and, summoning his intimate friends in whom he could confide, sought a place of safety in which to deposit his treasure.

Meanwhile the physicians and royal attendants in charge of the dying prince, together with the nobles who had come to visit him, took an opportunity of speaking in favour of the captives who were detained in prison, humbly entreating him to have pity on them and grant their release. The king replied to them: "I have long kept in captivity Morcar, the noble English earl; in this I have been unjust, but my fear has been that if he were liberated he would raise disturbances in the kingdom of England. I threw into prison Roger of Breteuil who opposed me with bitter animosity, and stirred up against me his brother-in-law, Ralph 'de Guader', and many others,[4] and I swore that he should not be set free as long as I lived. In like manner I imprisoned many persons to punish them for their own offences, and others to prevent their causing rebellions. Justice requires this; and the divine law, through Moses, commands the rulers of the world to restrain the guilty that the innocent may not perish. I am now, however, at the point of death, and as I hope to be saved, and,

[1] See above, pp. 151, 161, 162.
[2] Perhaps the equivalent of £250,000 to £300,000 today.
[3] A clear indication that this was written after 1106 when Normandy and England were again united.
[4] See Anglo-Saxon Chronicle (above, pp. 156, 157).

by God's mercy, absolved from my sins, I order that the prison doors shall be forthwith thrown open, and all the prisoners, except my brother, the bishop of Bayeux, be released. Let them go free, for the love of God, so that he also may have mercy on me. They are, however, to be liberated only on condition that they first take an oath to my ministers, that for the security of the realm they will use every means to preserve the peace both in Normandy and in England, and will steadfastly resist the enemies of tranquillity to the utmost of their power."

When Robert, count of Mortain, heard that by the king's decision his brother was condemned to perpetual imprisonment he was much distressed. Herluin of Conteville[1] had married Herleva, the concubine of Duke Robert, by whom he had two sons, Odo and Robert.[2] William, who was first duke and afterwards king, had heaped honours and possessions on his father-in-law both in Normandy and England, and had enriched with large domains his sons, Ralph, born of another wife,[3] and Robert and Odo, his own uterine brothers. For, having expelled from Normandy on slight pretences William, surnamed Warlenc, count of Mortain, son of Count Mauger,[4] he had conferred the county of Mortain on Robert, son of Herluin, and his own brother. Moreover, on the death of Hugh, bishop of Bayeux, son of Count Rodulf,[5] he gave that bishopric to his brother, Odo, whom he afterwards made earl of Kent in England. At length King William arrested him in the Isle of Wight, on account of his overweening pride, as I have before fully related, and, having detained him four years in prison, was unwilling, such was the insolence of Odo, to release him even when he was himself at the point of death. In consequence, the count of Mortain, of whom I have lately spoken, was sorely afflicted, and, by his own supplications and those of his friends on behalf of his brother, wearied the suffering prince.

The king was exhausted by the numerous solicitations from so many quarters for the release of the bishop of Bayeux; but at length he said: "I wonder that your penetration has not discovered the character of the man for whom you supplicate me. Are you not making petitions for a prelate who has long held religion in contempt, and who is the subtle promoter of fatal divisions? Have I not already incarcerated for four years this bishop, who, when he ought to have proved himself exemplary in the just government of England, became a most cruel oppressor of the people and destroyer of the convents of monks? In desiring the liberation of this seditious man you are ill-advised, and are bringing on yourselves a serious calamity. It is clear that my brother, Odo, is an untrustworthy man, ambitious, given to fleshly desires, and of enormous cruelty; and that he will never be converted from his whoredoms and ruinous follies. I satisfied myself of this on several occasions, and therefore I imprisoned, not the bishop, but the tyrannical earl.[6] There is no doubt that if he is

[1] He was *vicomte* of Conteville, and took as his first wife, Herleva, the former mistress of Robert, duke of Normandy, the mother of the Conqueror.

[2] See Table 2. For a fuller discussion of these relationships, see D. C. Douglas, *Domesday Monachorum of Christ Church, Canterbury* (1944), pp. 33–36.

[3] Fredesendis, second wife of Herluin.

[4] This relationship is improbable. The "Count Mauger" to whom Orderic seems here to refer is Mauger, a son of Duke Richard I, but it is unlikely that this man was the father of William 'Warlinc'. For the county of Mortain at this period, see Douglas, in *Eng. Hist. Rev.*, vol. LXI, pp. 141–145.

[5] Rodulf of Ivry, stepson of Duke William Longsword.

[6] Compare this with the distinction made in the report of the trial of William, bishop of Durham (below, No. 84, p. 618).

released, he will disturb the whole country and be the ruin of thousands.[1] I say this not from hatred, as if I were his enemy, but as the father of my country, watching over the welfare of a Christian people. It would indeed give me inexpressible and heart-felt joy to think that he would conduct himself with chastity and moderation, as becomes a priest and minister of God."[2]

When all the friends of the bishop pledged themselves for his reformation, the king further said: "Whether I will or not, your petition shall be granted, but after my death there will immediately be a violent change in affairs. It is against my own judgment that I permit my brother to be liberated from confinement, for be assured that he will cause the death or the grievous injury of many persons. Further, as I have declared the forfeiture of all the lands of Baudri, son of Nicholas, as a punishment for his folly in quitting my service and going to Spain without my licence, I now restore him his domains for the love of God. I do not think that a braver knight exists, but he is prodigal and inconstant, and loves to wander in foreign countries."

Thus King William, though tormented with excruciating pains in his intestines, preserved throughout the full possession of his clearness of intellect and power of expressing himself with his usual vivacity; and gave with readiness useful counsels to all who addressed themselves to him on the affairs of the kingdom.

At length, on Tuesday, 9 September, the king woke just when the sun was beginning to shed his rays on the earth, and heard the sound of the great bell of the cathedral of Rouen. On his inquiring what it meant, his attendants replied: "My lord, the bell is ringing for Prime in the church of St. Mary." Then the king raised his eyes to heaven with deep devotion and lifting up his hands said: "I commend myself to Mary, the holy mother of God, my heavenly Lady, that by her blessed intercession I may be reconciled to her well-beloved Son, our Lord Jesus Christ." Having said this he instantly expired. The physicians and others who were present, who had watched the king all night while he slept (his repose being broken neither by cries nor groans), seeing him now expire so suddenly and unexpectedly, were much astonished, and became as men who had lost their wits. Nevertheless, the wealthiest of them mounted their horses and departed in haste to secure their property. But the inferior attendants, observing that their masters had disappeared, laid hands on the arms, the plate, the robes, the linen, and all the royal furniture, and leaving the corpse almost naked on the floor of the house, they hastened away.

[1] An allusion to the war of 1088. (See above, pp. 165, 166.)

[2] This estimate of Odo is of considerable interest and has been generally endorsed. It may, however, also be noted that Odo was a great benefactor to Bayeux, and to some extent a patron of the arts and of scholarship.

8. William of Malmesbury: "The Deeds of the Kings of the English" and "The Modern History"

The passages which follow are taken from two works by this very voluminous writer: the *Gesta Regum Anglorum* and the *Historia Novella*. Some notice of this author has been given above (pp. 98, 99), and further information concerning him will be found in Stubbs's edition of these two works, and also in R. R. Darlington, *Anglo-Norman Historians* (London, 1947). The *Gesta Regum Anglorum* was finished in 1125 but two new recensions appeared between 1135 and 1140. The *Historia Novella* was written in 1140–1142. For the reign of Henry I and subsequently, William of Malmesbury may be considered therefore as a contemporary source. In the passages here printed will be found his opinion of the Norman Conquest, his estimate of Henry I, his account of the wreck of the White Ship and his description of two important councils held during the reign of Stephen. He was personally present at one, at least, of these councils. The text is printed in *Willelmi Malmesbiriensis–Gesta Regum Anglorum*, ed. W. Stubbs (Rolls Series, 2 vols., 1887–1889), and the section references here supplied are to that edition. Translations of these works are to be found in J. A. Giles, *William of Malmesbury's Chronicle* (1847) and in J. Stevenson, *Church Historians of England*, vol. III, pt. i (1854). These have been used in preparing the version which follows.

(a) *On the English and the Normans*[1]

This[2] was a fatal day for England, a melancholy havoc of our dear country brought about by its passing under the domination of new lords. For England had long ago adopted the manners of the 'Angles' which had been very various at different times. In the first years after their arrival they were barbarians in their look and manners, warlike in their usages, heathens in their rites; but after embracing the faith of Christ, in process of time and by degrees, owing to the peace which they enjoyed, they came to regard arms as only of secondary importance, and gave their whole attention to religion. I say nothing of the poor, whom meanness of fortune often restrains from overstepping the bounds of justice; I omit men of ecclesiastical rank whom respect for their sacred profession, or fear of shame, sometimes restrains from straying from the true path; I speak of princes who from the greatness of their power might have full liberty to indulge in pleasure. Some of these in their own country, and some at Rome, changing their habit, obtained a heavenly kingdom and a saintly communion; and many during their whole lives, to outward seeming so managed their wordly affairs that they might disperse their treasures on the poor, or divide them among monasteries. What shall I say of the multitudes of bishops, hermits, and abbots? Does not the whole island blaze with so many relics that you can scarcely pass a village of any consequence but what you hear the name of some new saint? And of how many have all records perished? Nevertheless, with the lapse of time, the love of learning and of religion decayed, and some years before the coming of the Normans it had declined. The clergy, contented with a very slight measure of learning, could scarcely stammer out the words of the sacraments, and a person who understood grammar was an object of wonder and astonishment. The monks mocked the rule of their order with fine vestments and with the use of every kind of food. The nobility, given up to luxury and wantonness, did not go to church in the early morning after the manner of Christians, but merely in a casual manner heard matins and Mass

[1] *Gesta Regum Anglorum*, SS. 245, 246.
[2] The day of the battle of Hastings.

from a hurrying priest in their chambers amid the blandishments of their wives. The common people, left unprotected, became a prey to the more powerful who amassed riches either by seizing the property of the poor or by selling their persons to foreigners. Nevertheless it is the manner of this people to be more inclined to dissipation than to the accumulation of wealth. There was one custom repugnant to nature which they adopted: namely to sell their female servants when pregnant by them, after they had satisfied their lust, either to public prostitution or to foreign slavery. Drinking in parties was a universal custom, in which occupation they passed entire days and nights. They consumed their whole fortune in mean and despicable houses, unlike the Normans and the French who in noble and splendid mansions live with frugality. The vices attendant upon drunkenness followed in due course and these, as is well known, enervate the human mind. Hence it came about that they engaged William more with rashness and fury than with military skill, and so they doomed themselves and their country to slavery by giving him an easy victory in a single battle. For nothing is less effective than rashness; and what begins with violence is quickly checked. The English at that time wore short garments, reaching to the mid-knee; they had their hair cropped, their beards shaven, their arms laden with gold bracelets, their skin adorned with punctured designs[1]; they were wont to eat until they became surfeited and to drink until they were sick. These latter qualities they imparted to their conquerors; as to the rest they adopted their manners. I would not, however, have these bad propensities ascribed to the English universally. I know that many of the clergy at that time trod the path of sanctity, and I know that many of the laity of all ranks and conditions were well-pleasing to God. Far be it from me to be unjust: my accusation is not indiscriminate. But as in peace the mercy of God often cherishes both the bad and the good together, so also does his severity sometimes include them both in tribulation.

The Normans–that I may speak of them also–were at that time, as they are now, exceedingly particular in their dress, and delicate in their food, but not to excess. They are a race inured to war, and can hardly live without it, fierce in attacking their enemies, and when force fails, ready to use guile or to corrupt by bribery. As I have said, they live with economy in large houses; they envy their equals; they wish to vie with their superiors; and they plunder their subjects though they protect them from others. They are faithful to their lords though slight offence gives them an excuse for treachery. They weigh treason by its chance of success, and change their opinions for money. They are the most polite of peoples; they consider strangers to merit the courtesy they extend to each other; and they intermarry with their subjects. After their coming to England they revived the rule of religion which had there grown lifeless. You might see churches rise in every village, and, in the towns and cities, monasteries built after a style unknown before; you could watch the country flourishing with renewed religious observance; each wealthy man counted the day lost in which he had neglected to perform some outstanding benefaction.[2]

[1] This should be compared with the pictorial evidence of the Bayeux Tapestry (see above, p. 235).
[2] This should be compared with the description of the Normans given by Ordericus Vitalis (above, No. 7, p. 282).

(*b*) *On the death of William Rufus*

In[1] the thirteenth year, which was the last of his life, there were many adverse events, but the most dreadful incident was that the devil visibly appeared to men in woods and secret places, and spoke to them as they passed by. Moreover, at Finchampstead in Berkshire, a well flowed so freely with blood for fifteen whole days that it discoloured a neighbouring pool. The king heard of it and laughed. Nor did he heed his own dreams, or take note of what others saw concerning him.

Many visions are recorded as having been seen, presaging his death, and three of these being vouched for by the testimony of creditable witnesses I shall myself record. Eadmer, the historian of our times,[2] a man noted for his veracity, says that Anselm, the noble exile, with whom religion was also banished,[3] came to Marcigny that he might communicate his sufferings to Hugh, abbot of Cluny.[4] There, when the conversation turned upon King William, the abbot said: "Last night that king was brought before God; and was finally judged to have incurred the dire sentence of damnation." How he came to know this he neither explained at the time, nor did any of those who heard him ask; nevertheless these words coming from a man who was so respected convinced many of those present that they were true. Hugh led such a life and had such a character that all took heed of what he said, and valued his counsel, even as though an oracle from heaven had spoken. And soon after the king was slain (as we shall relate) and there came a messenger to beg the archbishop to resume his see.

The day before the king died, he dreamed he was let blood by a surgeon, and that the stream reaching to heaven clouded the light and obscured the day. Calling upon St. Mary for protection, he suddenly awoke, and told his attendants they were not to leave him. Thus they watched with him for several hours even unto daybreak. Shortly afterwards, just as the day began to dawn, a certain foreign monk came to Robert, son of Haimo, one of the chief magnates at the court, and told him that he had that night dreamed a strange and fearful dream about the king. "The king", he said, "came into a certain church with threats and boasting as is his custom. He looked contemptuously on those present, and then seizing the crucifix he gnawed the arms and almost tore away the legs. The image endured this for a while, but at last struck the king with its foot so that he fell backwards, and from his mouth as he lay on the ground came out such a flame that the smoke touched the very stars." Robert, thinking this dream ought not to be neglected, ventured to tell it to the king with whom he was very intimate. William burst into long laughter, and said: "He is a monk and dreams for money. Give him a hundred shillings." None the less he was not unmoved, and hesitated a long time whether he should go out hunting as he had planned, and his friends urged him not to take the risk of testing the truth of these omens. He therefore did not hunt before dinner, but attended to serious business instead, hoping by occupation to dispel his uneasiness. And they say that he soothed his cares with more food and wine than usual. After dinner he went into the forest with a very small number of attendants. Among these the most intimate with the

[1] *Gesta Regum Anglorum*, SS. 331, 332, 333.
[2] See below, No. 107.
[3] See below, Nos. 108–112.
[4] Hugh I, 1044–1109.

king was Walter, surnamed Tirel, who had come from France attracted by the liberality of the king. This man alone remained with him, while the others were widely scattered in the chase. The sun was now setting, and the king drawing his bow let fly an arrow which slightly wounded a stag which passed before him. He ran in pursuit, keeping his gaze rigidly fixed on the quarry, and holding up his hand to shield his eyes from the sun's rays. At this instant Walter, forming in his mind a project which seemed fine to him, tried to transfix another stag which by chance came near him while the king's attention was otherwise occupied. And thus it was that unknowingly, and without power to prevent it (oh, gracious God!), he pierced the king's breast with a fatal arrow. When the king received the wound, he said not a word, but breaking off the shaft of the arrow where it stuck out of his body, he fell upon the ground and thus made more speedy his own death. Walter immediately ran up, but finding the king senseless and speechless, he leapt quickly on his horse, and escaped at full gallop. Indeed, there was none to pursue him. Some connived at his flight. Others pitied him. And all were intent on other matters. Some began to fortify their dwellings; others to plunder; and the rest went to look for a new king. A few countrymen recovered the body and took it on a cart to the cathedral at Winchester, the blood dripping from it all the way. Here it was committed to the ground within the tower, attended by many of the magnates, but mourned by few. Next year the tower fell,[1] but I forbear to mention the different opinions about this lest I should seem to assent too readily to unsupported trifles, the more especially as the building might have fallen through imperfect construction even if he had not been buried there.[2] He died in the year of the Incarnation of our Lord 1100 on 2 August, aged above forty years. He formed mighty plans which he would have brought to effect, could he have spun out the tissue of fate, or broken through the violence of fortune. Such was the energy of his mind that he was bold enough to promise himself any kingdom whatsoever. Indeed the day before his death when asked where he would keep Christmas, he said "in Poitou". For the count of Poitou[3] who wished to go to Jerusalem was said to be anxious to pawn his territory to the king of England. Thus not content with what he had inherited, he was lured on by the hope of greater glory, and grasped at honours which were not his by right. He was a man much to be pitied by the clergy for throwing away a soul which they could not save. He earned the love of hired soldiers for he was lavish in his gifts to them. But by the common people he is not to be mourned because he allowed them to be plundered. I remember no council being held in his time wherein the health of the Church might be strengthened by the correction of abuses. He delayed long in appointing to ecclesiastical offices, either for the sake of the money he gained thereby, or because he wished to consider the merits of those who might be advanced. Thus on the day he died he held in his own hands three vacant bishoprics, and twelve vacant abbeys.

[1] The tower fell in 1107.

[2] The whole tone of the foregoing description is interesting, and perhaps all the mysteries connected with the death of William Rufus have not yet been fully explained.

[3] William VII, count of Poitou.

(c) *On the character of Henry I*

Henry,[1] the youngest son of William the Great, was born in England in the third year after his father's coming to this country. He was a child who enjoyed the ardent good wishes of all, for to him the kingdom seemed to pertain as of right since he was the only one of William's sons who was born when his father was a king. He was early instructed in the liberal arts, and so throughout imbibed the sweets of learning that no warlike disturbance and no pressure of business could ever erase them from his noble mind. Although he never read much in public, nor displayed his attainments except sparingly, yet his learning (as I can affirm), though obtained by snatches, assisted him much in the science of government, according to the saying of Plato: "Happy would be the commonwealth if philosophers were kings or kings philosophers." Thus considerably imbued with philosophy, he learnt by degrees how to restrain the people with lenity, and only to employ his troops when there was a pressing emergency. In this manner was he trained by learning in his early years to the hope of the kingdom, and often in his father's hearing made use of the proverb: "An unlettered king is a crowned ass." They say also that his father, observing his disposition, never omitted any means of encouraging his lively prudence; and that once when he had been ill used by one of his brothers and was in tears, he consoled him by saying: "Don't cry, my boy, you too will be a king."[2] . . . On the violent death of King William after the solemnization of the royal funeral he was chosen king, though some small dissensions had arisen among the magnates which were allayed mainly by the exertions of Henry, earl of Warwick,[3] a man of unblemished integrity with whom he had long been in the closest intimacy. He immediately issued an edict[4] throughout England annulling the illegal practices of his brother and of Rannulf.[5] He remitted taxes, released prisoners, drove the unnaturally vicious from the court, and restored the nightly use of lights within the palace which in his brother's time had been discontinued. He renewed the operation of the ancient laws, confirming them with his own oath, and that of the magnates so that they should not be evaded. A joyful day then seemed to dawn upon the people when the light of fair promise shone forth after such repeated clouds of distress. And, that nothing might be wanting in the universal joy, Rannulf,[5] that sink of iniquity, was cast into prison and speedy messengers were sent to recall Anselm. Wherefore amid universal rejoicings Henry was crowned king at London on 5 August, that is to say, four days after his brother's death. These acts were the more carefully carried out lest the magnates should be induced to repent their choice, as a rumour prevailed that Robert, count of Normandy,[6] was about to reach home on his return from Apulia. Soon afterwards the friends of the king and particularly the bishops persuaded him to give up his pleasure in mistresses, and to take a lawful wife. Therefore on St. Martin's Day[7] he married Maud, daughter of Malcolm, king of Scotland, to whom he had been greatly attached. He little regarded the

[1] *Gesta Regum Anglorum*, SS. 390, 393, 411.

[2] On the exaggerated claims made for Henry I's alleged learning, further reference may be made to C. W. David in *Haskins Anniversary Essays* (1929), p. 45, and to V. H. Galbraith, *Literacy of Medieval English Kings* (1935).

[3] Henry of Beaumont, son of Roger of Beaumont, became earl of Warwick in 1088. (See Table 12.)

[4] See below, No. 19.

[5] Rannulf Flambard, bishop of Durham, chief minister of William Rufus.

[6] Robert, eldest son of William the Conqueror.

[7] 11 November.

marriage portion if he could possess her whom he so ardently desired. For though she was of noble descent, being grand-niece of King Edward by his brother Edmund,[1] yet she possessed but little fortune, being an orphan deprived of both parents. . . . [Henry] was active in providing what conduced to the strength of his dominion, and firm in defending it. He refrained from war so long as he could do so with honour, but when he resorted to arms he was a most severe requiter of injuries, dispelling danger by his energy and courage. He was constant alike in his enmities, and in his general benevolence, giving too much rein to his anger in the one case and displaying his royal magnanimity in the other. For he reduced his enemies even to ruin, and he exalted his friends and dependants so that all men envied them. Does not philosophy propound this to be the first and greatest concern of a good king, "to spare the suppliant and war-down the proud"?[2] Inflexible in the administration of justice he ruled the people with moderation, and with a seemly dignity restrained the great. He ruthlessly sought after robbers and counterfeiters, and signally punished them when caught. Nor was he negligent in matters of less importance. When he heard that traders refused broken money, though of good silver, he commanded that the whole of it should be broken or cut in pieces.[3] The measure of his own arm was used to correct the false ell of traders, and he made that arm the standard for all England. He made it a rule for the followers of his court that no matter on which of his estates he might be, they should observe his orders as to what they should take without payment from the country folk, and how much and at what price they should purchase; and he punished those who transgressed this rule by heavy fines or even loss of life. At the beginning of his reign, that he might awe transgressors, he usually decreed punishment by mutilation, but later he resorted more to fines. Thus in consequence of the rectitude of his conduct, as is natural to man, he came to be feared by the magnates and beloved by the common people. If at any time the better sort, regardless of their plighted oath, wandered from the path of fidelity, he immediately recalled them to the straight road by the wisdom of his unceasing exertions; the refractory he brought back to reason by the wounds which he inflicted upon their bodies. I cannot easily describe how close a watch he kept on such persons and he allowed nothing to go unpunished which had been to the detriment of his dignity. Normandy was the chief source of his wars, and there in the main he resided, yet he also took special care of England so that none dared rebel by reason of his prudence and courage. Rebellions among his nobles never caused him to be treacherously attacked by his attendants, save only once when a certain chamberlain of plebeian birth, but distinguished as the keeper of the king's treasure, was detected in such an attempt, and, after confession, suffered a bitter penalty.[4] With this exception the king remained

[1] See Table I. [2] Virgil, *Æneid*, VI, 853.

[3] Apparently to avoid any cause for broken money not to be accepted, and also to enable anyone to test the quality of the coins issued.

[4] Suger (*Vita Ludovici Grossi*, ed. A. Molinier, p. 88), describing the set-backs of Henry I in 1118–1119, remarks: "To increase his distress he suffered domestic misfortunes and he feared so much the secret plots of his chamberlains and of the keepers of his chamber that frequently he changed the position of his bed. Often tormented by nightly fears, he multiplied his guards and ordered that his sword and shield should hang near him as he slept. Among these conspirators was one Henry, the most intimate of his household, whom the liberality of this prince had made rich and famous. More famous still was he made by his treachery and although being convicted of such a horrible treason he deserved hanging, yet such was the excess of generosity on the part of the king that he was only condemned to blinding and castration."

secure throughout his life: fear restrained the minds of all and admiration controlled their conversation.

He was of middle stature, neither unduly short nor tall; his hair was black and set back on his forehead; his eyes were mildly bright; his chest brawny; his body well fleshed. He was facetious in proper season, and even when preoccupied with business he was pleasant in company. He was not personally pugnacious, for he seemed to recall the saying of Scipio Africanus: "My mother bore me to be a commander not a soldier."[1] Therefore he preferred to gain his ends by diplomacy rather than by the sword, and in this he was inferior in wisdom to no king of modern times, and indeed might without exaggeration be said to have in this matter surpassed all his predecessors. If he could, he made his conquests without violence, and if that was unavoidable, with as little bloodshed as possible. Throughout his life he was wholly free from carnal desires, for as we have learnt from those who were well informed, his intercourse with women was undertaken not for the satisfaction of his lusts but from his desire for children.[2] Thus he did not condescend to carnal intercourse unless it might produce that effect. Wherefore he was the master of his passions rather than their slave. He was plain in his diet, seeking rather to satisfy his hunger than to sate himself with a multitude of delicacies. He drank simply to allay his thirst, and he deplored the least lapse into drunkenness both in himself and others. His sleep was heavy and marked by much snoring. His eloquence was rather natural than premeditated, and deliberate rather than fluent.

(*d*) *On the wreck of the White Ship*, 25 *November* 1120

By[3] Maud, Henry had a son named William, who with the fondest hope and surpassing care was educated and destined for the succession. When he was barely twelve years old, all the free men of England and of Normandy, of every rank and condition, to whatever lords they were subject, were obliged to submit themselves to him by oath and homage.[4] While still a boy he was betrothed to the daughter of Fulk, count of Anjou,[5] and received her in wedlock although she was herself scarcely of marriageable age. His father-in-law not only bestowed on him the county of Maine as her dowry, but also, on going to Jerusalem,[6] committed his county to the king on the understanding that if he returned it should be restored to him, but otherwise it should pass to his son-in-law. Many provinces thus looked forward to the rule of this boy; and it was confidently expected that in him the hopes of England, like the tree cut down, might again through this youth blossom and bring forth fruit. But God saw otherwise, for this illusion vanished into air, since he was already hastening to his doom. This was the more tragic since already by the exertions of his father-in-law, and of Theobald, son of Stephen, and of his aunt, Adela,[7] Louis, king of France, had,

[1] Derivation uncertain.

[2] He had two or possibly three legitimate children, at least eight bastard sons, and at least eleven illegitimate daughters. (See Table 4.)

[3] *Gesta Regum Anglorum*, S. 419.

[4] Cf. the oath at Salisbury (above, p. 162).

[5] Maud, daughter of Fulk V of Anjou, betrothed to Prince William, became later abbess of Fontevrault. (See Table 4.)

[6] He was to become titular king of Jerusalem.

[7] See Table 4.

in return for his homage, conceded to the lad the legal possession of Normandy. The prudence of his truly careful father so contrived that the homage, which from the extent of his dominion he himself disdained to perform, should not be refused by his son, who was a youth of delicate habit and not very likely to live. In negotiating these matters the king spent four years, continuing the whole of that time in Normandy.[1] Nevertheless the calm of this brilliant and carefully arranged peace, this anxious and universal hope, was destroyed in an instant by human fate. On 25 November the king gave orders for his return to England, and set sail from Barfleur just before twilight on the evening of that day. But the young man who was just over seventeen and himself a king in all but name, commanded that another vessel should be prepared for himself, and almost all the young nobility, being his boon companions, gathered round him. The sailors, too, who had drunk overmuch, cried out with true seamen's hilarity that they must overtake the ship that had already set out since their own ship was of the best construction and newly equipped. Wherefore these rash youths, who were flown with wine, launched their vessel from the shore although it was now dark. She flew swifter than an arrow, sweeping the rippling surface of the deep, but the carelessness of her drunken crew drove her on to a rock which rose above the waves not far from the shore. All in consternation rushed on deck, and with loud cries got ready their boat-hooks in an endeavour to force the vessel off, but fate was against them and brought to naught their efforts. The oars too, lashing ineffectively, crashed against the rock,[2] and the battered prow remained fixed. Then the waves washed some of the crew overboard and the water entering the vessel through chinks in its side drowned others. A boat was, however, at last launched and the young prince was taken into it. He might easily have reached the shore in safety had not his bastard sister, the countess of Perche,[3] now struggling with death in the larger vessel implored his assistance. She cried out that her brother should not abandon her so heartlessly. Whereupon, touched with pity, he ordered his boat to return to the ship that he might rescue his sister, and it was thus that the unhappy youth met his death; for the boat overcharged by the multitude that leapt into her capsized and sank and buried all indiscriminately in the deep. One rustic alone, floating all night upon a mast, survived until the morning to describe the dismal catastrophe. No ship ever brought so much misery to England; none was ever so notorious in the history of the world. There perished with William: Richard,[4] another of the king's sons whom a woman of no rank had borne him before his accession, a brave youth who was dear to his father from his obedience; Richard, earl of Chester,[5] and his brother, Otuel,[6] tutor to the king's son; the countess of Perche, the king's daughter; the countess of Chester, the king's niece and sister to Theobald; and indeed almost every person of consequence about court, whether knight or chaplain or young nobleman training to

[1] April 1116–1120.

[2] Cf. Virgil, *Æneid*, V, 206.

[3] Maud, whose mother was a certain Edith of whom nothing is known, married Rotrou 'the Great', count of Perche, who shortly after 1114 received the Bellême fiefs.

[4] His mother was Ansfride, the widow of a knight of Abingdon Abbey.

[5] Richard, son of Earl Hugh, became earl of Chester in 1101. (See Table 14.)

[6] Sometime called Othuer or Other. He witnessed several royal charters earlier in the reign. After his death some of his lands went to Westminster Abbey (J. Armitage Robinson, *Gilbert Crispin*, p. 156).

arms.[1] For, as I have said, they had all rushed together expecting no small addition to their prestige if they could either amuse or show their devotion to the young prince. The calamity was increased by the difficulty of finding the bodies which could not be discovered by the various persons who sought them along the shore. Delicately nurtured as they were they became food for the monsters of the deep. The death of this youth, being known, produced a remarkable change in politics. His father renounced the celibacy he had maintained since Maud's death, since he was now anxious for heirs by a new consort. The lad's father-in-law returning home from Jerusalem[2] faithlessly espoused the party of William,[3] son of Robert, count of Normandy, giving him his daughter[4] in marriage, and the county of Maine. For his indignation had been aroused by the fact that his other daughter's dowry had been detained in England after the death of the prince.

(e) *Concerning a council held at Winchester*, 29 *August* 1139

On[5] the appointed day almost all the bishops of England with Theobald, archbishop of Canterbury, who had succeeded William, came to Winchester. Thurstan, archbishop of York, excused himself on account of the malady with which he was afflicted; for he was so enfeebled as to be hardly able to guide his steps. The others apologized for their absence by letter by reason of the war. The bull of Pope Innocent[6] was first read in the council whereby even from 1 March, if I remember rightly, he had enjoined the administration of his anxious charge to the lord bishop of Winchester[7] as legate in England. This was received with much goodwill as the bishop had shown his forbearance and had not proclaimed himself as legate with precipitate vanity. Next followed, in the council, his address in the Latin tongue directed to the learned, on the disgraceful detention of the bishops: among whom the bishop of Salisbury[8] had been seized in the chamber of his palace, and the bishop of Lincoln[9] in his dwelling; furthermore the bishop of Ely,[10] fearing similar treatment, had escaped the calamity by a hasty flight to Devizes. The legate observed that it was a dreadful crime for the king to have been so led astray by sinister persons as to have laid violent hands on his subjects, and especially on bishops in the security of his court. Further, to the king's disgrace must be added the crime of despoiling churches of their possessions under pretext that the bishops were criminals. He added that the king's outrage against the law of God was a matter of such pain to him that he would rather have himself suffered grievous injury both in person and property than have the episcopal dignity so basely humiliated. The king, however (he concluded), after repeated admonitions had agreed to amend his fault and consented to the council being summoned. Wherefore the archbishop and the rest should deliberate about what ought to be done, and for his own part he would not be deterred from putting into

[1] Among others who perished there were according to Ordericus Vitalis (ed. Le Prévost, vol. IV, pp. 411–419): Dietrich, nephew of the emperor, Henry V; Geoffrey, son of Gilbert of Laigle; the two sons of Ivo of Grantmesnil and their cousin, William of Rhuddlan; William Bigot the steward; Geoffrey Ridel; Hugh 'de Molines'; Gilbert of Exmes; Ralph of Pont-Echaufré; Robert Mauduit; and Gisulf the king's scribe. Robert of Torigny (ed. L. Delisle, vol. II, p. 159) adds that there were also drowned "many magnates, stewards and chamberlains". On this matter see also W. Farrer, *Outline Itinerary of Henry I* (London, 1920), pp. 89, 90.

[2] In January 1122.
[3] William Clito.
[4] Sibyl.
[5] *Historia Novella*, SS. 471–477.
[6] Innocent II.
[7] Henry of Blois. (See Table 6.)
[8] Roger.
[9] Alexander.
[10] Nigel.

execution whatever might be the sentence of the council either from friendship with the king who was his brother, or from fear of loss of property or even of life.

When he had expatiated on these matters the king, confident in his own cause, sent certain earls[1] into the council to demand why he should be summoned. The legate briefly replied: that when he recollected that he was in subjection to the faith of Christ he ought not to be displeased if when guilty of a crime, such as the present age had never before witnessed, he was required by the ministers of Christ to make amends; that it was the act of a heathen age to imprison bishops and divest them of their possessions; that if he would listen to his advice as legate he would give him such counsel by God's authority as neither the Church of Rome nor the French king's court nor even Count Theobald,[2] their common brother, could reasonably oppose. Indeed they ought to welcome the counsel he was prepared to give. At present therefore (he continued) the king would act prudently if he would either account for his conduct or submit to canonical judgment; it was indeed what he owed to the Church by whose fostering care, and not by military force, he had been promoted to the kingdom. The earls retiring after this speech, returned shortly afterwards with their answer, and they were accompanied by Aubrey of Ver,[3] a man deeply versed in legal affairs. He reported the king's answer and stressed the case against Bishop Roger, for Bishop Alexander whom he supported had departed. But this he did with moderation and without using violent language, though some of the earls who were standing by repeatedly interrupted his speech by casting reproaches on the bishop.

The sum of what Aubrey had to say was as follows: that Bishop Roger had greatly injured King Stephen; that he seldom came to court and that his people presuming on his power had often raised up tumults; that they had frequently, and very recently at Oxford,[4] attacked the attendants and even the nephew of Earl Alan[5] as well as the servants of Hervey 'de Liuns',[6] a man of such high nobility and so extremely haughty that he had never deigned to visit England though King Henry had invited him; that the injury done to this man therefore doubly recoiled upon King Stephen through whom he had come to England; that the bishop of Lincoln had been the author of a riot excited by his followers out of enmity to Alan; that the king had proved beyond all reasonable doubt that the bishop of Salisbury secretly favoured his enemies, though for the nonce he had cunningly concealed his hostility; that in particular this bishop had refused permission to Roger of Mortemer and the king's soldiers who were with him to remain even a single night in Malmesbury, although they were under the greatest apprehension from the garrison of Bristol; that it was in every one's mouth that, as soon as the empress should arrive, the bishop would join her party with his nephews and let her use his castles; that Roger in short had been imprisoned, not as a bishop but as the king's servant, who had administered his affairs and received his wages; that the king had not taken their castles by violence, but that both bishops had surrendered their castles voluntarily to escape the punishment due to the disturbance

[1] On the earls of King Stephen, see G. H. White in *Trans. R. Hist. Soc.*, 4th Series, vol. XIII (1930), pp. 51–82.

[2] Count of Blois. (See Table 6.)

[3] He derived from Ver in the Cotentin and perished in a riot in London in May 1141. He was the father of Aubrey 'de Vere', created first earl of Oxford in 1142.

[4] Or Lincoln.

[5] Alan III, a count of Brittany and earl of Richmond. He died 15 September 1148.

[6] Possibly Lyons la Forêt (Eure).

they had created in the court; that the king had found some trifling sums of money in the castles which must lawfully belong to the king since Bishop Roger had collected it from the revenues of the Exchequer in the time of King Henry, the king's uncle and predecessor; that the bishop had readily relinquished this money as well as the castles, being conscious of those crimes of which the king had plenty of evidence; and that therefore it was his will that the conditions entered into between himself and the bishops should remain in force.

In opposition to this speech of Aubrey, Bishop Roger rejoined that he had never been the minister of King Stephen or received his wages. This spirited man, who blushed at being cast down by adversity, further threatened that if he could not have justice from the council in respect of the property which had been taken from him, he would carry the case to a higher court.[1] The legate, mildly as usual, observed that every allegation against the bishops ought to be made, and the truth investigated in an ecclesiastical court before passing sentence contrary to the canons on innocent persons; that the king therefore ought to do what was necessary in the civil court, that is reinvest the bishops with their property; otherwise being dispossessed they were by the law of nations[2] not compelled to plead.

Many arguments of this kind were used on both sides, and then the case, at the king's request, was adjourned until the next day; and afterwards on the morrow it was adjourned for another day to await the arrival of the archbishop of Rouen.[3] When he came all were anxious to hear what he had to say. "I would be willing", he said, "for the bishops to have their castles if they could prove by the canons that they ought to possess them. But as they cannot do this, it is the height of impudence to contend against the canons. Even admitting that it is just for them to possess castles, yet as the times are critical, they ought as magnates to deliver up the keys of their fortifications in an emergency to the king whose duty it is to wage war for the security of all." Thus the whole plea of the bishops was shaken, for either according to the canons it was unjust for them to have castles, or if that was allowed them by the king's indulgence, then they ought to yield to the emergency of the time and give up the keys.

To this Aubrey added that the king knew that the bishops had privily determined that some of their number should proceed to Rome against him. "The king", he concluded, "advises you strongly not to presume to do this, for if any person shall go from England to any place in opposition to his will and dignity, perhaps it will not be so easy for him to return. He is himself the injured party and, knowing the justice of his case, of his own accord he summons you to Rome."

When the king, partly advising and partly threatening, had sent this message it became clear what was his plan. In consequence the council broke up since he would not submit to canonical censure. The bishops moreover deemed it inadvisable to enforce it against him for two reasons: first because it was a rash act to excommunicate the king without the knowledge of the pope; and secondly because they believed (and some of them with reason) that swords were unsheathed against them. It was no

[1] Compare the pleadings in the trial of William of St. Calais (below, No. 84, p. 609).
[2] *jure gentium.*
[3] Hugh III, archbishop of Rouen, on whom see *Gallia Christiana*, vol. XI, cols. 43–48.

longer a joking matter but a struggle of life and death. The legate and the archbishop were still, however, anxiously observant of their duty. They humbly prostrated themselves before the king in his chamber, entreating him to take pity on the Church, and to consider his soul and his reputation. They begged him not to allow a schism to be opened between his royalty and the priesthood. But the king, although in some measure he removed the odium of his former conduct by condescendingly rising to meet them, yet through ill advice, he carried none of his fair promises into effect.

(*f*) *On a council held at Winchester*, 7 *April* 1141

On[1] the second day after the Octave of Easter,[2] a council began with great parade at Winchester, consisting of Theobald, archbishop of Canterbury, all the bishops of England, and many abbots; the legate[3] presiding. Such as were absent accounted for it by messengers and letters. As I was present at the holding of this council, I will not deny posterity a true account of its proceedings: I perfectly remember that on the same day, after the letters were read by which some excused their absence, the legate called the bishops apart, and discoursed with them in secret of his design; then the abbots, and, lastly, the archdeacons were summoned. Of his intention nothing transpired publicly, though what was to be done engrossed the minds and conversation of all.

On the third day of the week,[4] the speech of the legate ran nearly to this effect: That, by the condescension of the pope, he acted as his vicegerent in England: wherefore by his authority the clergy of England were assembled at this council, to deliberate on the peace of the country, which was exposed to great danger; that, in the time of King Henry, his uncle, England had been the peculiar abode of peace so that, by the activity, spirit, and zeal of that most excellent man, the natives, of whatever power or dignity, dared make no disturbance; also by his example each neighbouring king and prince also yielded to peace, and either persuaded or compelled his subjects to do the like; moreover, that this king some years before his death had caused the whole realm of England as well as the duchy of Normandy to be constrained by the oaths of all the bishops and barons to the allegiance of his daughter, once empress, who was his only surviving issue by his former consort. This he did in case he should fail of male offspring by the wife he had espoused from Lorraine. "Adverse fortune", continued the legate, "was envious of my most excellent uncle and suffered him to die in Normandy without male issue. Therefore, as it seemed long to wait for a sovereign in Normandy who delayed in her coming to England, we provided for the peace of the country, and my brother was allowed to reign. And although I gave myself as surety between him and God, that he would honour and advance holy Church, and uphold good laws, yet it now gives me shame to say how he conducted himself in the kingdom. Justice was no longer enforced against the presumptuous; peace was brought to naught almost within a year; bishops were made captive and robbed; abbeys were sold; churches were stripped of their treasures;

[1] *Historia Novella*, SS. 492–497.
[2] 7 April.
[3] Henry of Blois, bishop of Winchester.
[4] 8 April.

and the counsels of the wicked prevailed, while those of the good were despised. You know how often I addressed him both by myself and through the bishops, and most especially in the council held last year, but it brought me nothing but odium. Of course I must love my mortal brother, but I have still greater regard for the cause of my immortal Father. Wherefore since God has pronounced judgment on my brother by permitting him without my design to fall into the hands of the mighty, I have invited you all to assemble here, lest the kingdom should fall to decay through want of a ruler. The matter was privately discussed yesterday before the greater part of the clergy of England to whom, of right, it principally pertains to choose and crown the sovereign. Wherefore as is fitting, invoking God's help, we elect as ruler of England and Normandy the daughter[1] of that peaceful, glorious, rich, good and incomparable king,[2] and we promise her fidelity and support."

When all present had either applauded his sentiments, or by their silence assented to them, he added: "We have dispatched messengers for the Londoners asking them to meet us in this business, because from the importance of their city in England they are as it were nobles. We have sent them a safe-conduct, and I hope they will not delay their arrival beyond tomorrow. Wherefore let us grant them indulgence until that time."

On the fourth day of the week[3] the Londoners came. When they had been introduced to the council they argued that they were sent from what they call their *commune*,[4] and not to dispute but rather to beg that their lord the king might be liberated from captivity. They said that all the barons who had been received into their *commune*[5] most earnestly solicited this from the lord legate, from the archbishop, and from all the clergy who were present. The legate answered them copiously and eloquently, repeating the arguments which he had used on the previous day. He added also that if the Londoners were to be considered as nobles, and as among the magnates of England, it ill became them to side with those persons who had deserted their lord in battle. It was by the advice of these men, he concluded, that the king had dishonoured holy Church, and now they only pretended to favour the Londoners in order that they might defraud them.

A certain person whose name, if I rightly remember, was Christian now stood up and gave a document to the legate. He was, as I heard, one of the queen's clerks. The legate perused this document in silence for a time and then declared in a loud voice that it would be both unlawful and improper for it to be read in so great an assembly. For (as he said) it was both surprising and offensive, and it was witnessed by a man who in the preceding year and at a similar council had insulted the venerable bishops. The clerk, however, was not daunted by the legate but with sublime confidence he read the letter out loud. This was its purport: "The queen earnestly entreats the whole clergy present, and especially the bishop of Winchester, the brother of her lord, to restore to his kingdom the said lord whom wicked men and even his vassals had cast into chains." The legate answered this message as he had previously answered the Londoners, and the latter after conferring together declared that they would

[1] Maud. [2] Henry I. [3] 9 April.

[4] *a communione quam vocant Londoniarum.*

[5] *omnes barones qui in eorum communionem jamdudum recepti fuerant.*

communicate the decree of the council to their fellow-townsmen, and give it such support as they were able. On the fifth day of the week[1] the council broke up, many of the royal party having first been excommunicated, and more especially William Martel, who had formerly been butler to King Henry and was at that time butler to Stephen. For this man had sorely exasperated the legate by pilfering much of his property.

[1] 10 April.

9. Description of the battle of Tinchebrai given by a priest of Fécamp

This remarkable description is given in a letter written by a priest of Fécamp to a priest of Séez. The author, who was perhaps chaplain to Robert of Estouteville, was clearly in a position to know at first hand exactly what happened, and equally certainly his letter was written very shortly after the event. This description must therefore take precedence over all other surviving accounts of the battle. These are in truth less than satisfactory. That of Ordericus Vitalis (ed. Le Prévost, vol. IV, p. 224) is the fullest, but it is vague and for the most part uninformative. Henry of Huntingdon (ed. Rolls Series, 1879, p. 235), who was followed by Robert of Torigny (ed. L. Delisle, vol. I, p. 127), writes thus:

> "Upon the king laying siege to the castle of Tinchebrai,[1] the duke of Normandy, with Robert of Bellême and the count of Mortain and all their retinue, advanced against him. The king on his side had with him almost all the chief men of Normandy and the best soldiers of England, Anjou and Brittany. He was therefore not unprepared. After sounding shrill trumpets, the duke with his small force boldly charged the king's more numerous army and since the duke and his troops had been well trained in the wars of Jerusalem,[2] their onslaught upset the royal array. William, count of Mortain, moreover, harassed it at several points and threw it into confusion. The king and the duke, with great part of their troops, fought on foot that they might make a more sustained attack; but the Breton knights bore down upon the flank of the duke's force which, unable to resist the charge, was presently routed."

The tactics of the battle of Tinchebrai have been much discussed by modern writers, and this literature is admirably criticized by C. W. David in *Robert Curthose* (Harvard U.P., 1920), Appendix F. Professor David points out that while it is generally agreed that the determining episode in the struggle was a surprise charge of Breton knights, nevertheless infantry played a much larger part in the engagement than is often recognized. The letter which follows further strengthens this conclusion. The letter itself was printed by L. Delisle in his great edition of Robert of Torigny (vol. I, p. 129), but a line from it was there unfortunately omitted, destroying the sense. This identical omission was repeated when H. W. C. Davis re-edited this letter as a new source in *Eng. Hist. Rev.*, vol. XXIV, p. 728 (cf. *ibid.*, vol. XXV, p. 296). Professor David (*op. cit.*, p. 247) supplied from the MS. the text of the missing line which is here embodied in the version which follows in its proper context.

To his lord, the priest of Séez, the priest of Fécamp, sends greeting and prayers. I bring you good news, my lord, inasmuch as I realize you are eager for tidings in this matter. Our lord king fought with his brother at Tinchebrai on 28 September at the third hour. Thus was the battle disposed. In the first line were the men of the Bessin, the Avranchin and the Cotentin, and these were all on foot. In the second line was the king with his very numerous barons and these likewise were on foot.[3] Seven hundred mounted knights were placed with each line; and besides these the count of Maine, and Alan Fergaunt, count of Brittany, flanked the army with about a thousand mounted knights. All the camp followers and servants were removed far to the rear of the battle. The whole army of the king may be reckoned as having consisted of about forty thousand men. When the battle had lasted only an hour, Robert of Bellême turned and fled, and all his men were dispersed. The count himself was captured, and the count of Mortain with his barons, and my friend, Robert of Estouteville. The rest all disappeared in flight. Wherefore the land became subject to the king. Nor must I fail to tell you about this marvel: that the king in the battle lost only two men; and only one was wounded, namely Robert of Bonnebosc. When I came to the king, he received me very graciously at Caen, and he willingly granted all those things which he had exacted from our land. And now, thank God, peace is restored in the land. Let us pray that it may continue, and that God may grant us good health in mind and body. Farewell.

[1] Dep. Orne, arr. Domfront.

[2] Robert had been on crusade.

[3] It will be noted that in 1141 King Stephen with his barons fought on foot at the battle of Lincoln (see below, No. 10, p. 307).

10. Henry of Huntingdon: Some events of the reign of Stephen described in "The History of the English"

The *Historia Anglorum* of Henry, archdeacon of Huntingdon, does something to bridge the gap between the great chroniclers of the Anglo-Norman age and the group of writers who cover the reign of Henry II. Accordingly passages from the eighth and final book of his *Historia* are here given as illustrating the reign of Stephen. The author was probably born shortly after 1080. The son of a priest, he was brought up in the household of Robert Bloet, bishop of Lincoln, and promoted to the archdeaconry of Huntingdon at the age of thirty. He travelled widely during his life, and probably lived on into the reign of Henry II. The first draft of the *Historia Anglorum* came down only to 1129, but the work was extended in successive editions to 1154. As a whole it is a well-planned work, but the author had a commonplace mind. There is throughout a surprising weakness in his treatment of ecclesiastical affairs, and in this he may be supplemented for the reign of Stephen from William of Malmesbury (see above, pp. 298–303). A good account of Henry of Huntingdon is given in the *Dictionary of National Biography*, and there are valuable notes concerning him in R. L. Poole, *Chronicles and Annals* (1926), and in R. R. Darlington, *Anglo-Norman Historians* (1947). The Latin text is given in the Rolls Series (ed. T. Arnold, 1879), and an English translation was made by T. Forester (London, 1853).

(a) *The Accession of Stephen*

. . . So[1] on the death of the great King Henry[2] the verdict of the people was freely expressed concerning him, as is usually the case after the death of a notable personage. Some said that he was eminently distinguished for three splendid qualities: great wisdom, for he was most deep in counsel, keen foresight and outstanding eloquence; success in war, for besides other fine achievements he had overcome the king of France;[3] and riches, for he was more wealthy than any of his predecessors. Others, however, taking a different view, attributed to him three vices: gross avarice through which, though himself wealthy like all his ancestors, he devoured the poor by tolls and exactions, entangling them in the toils of his informers; cruelty in that he put out the eyes of his kinsman, the count of Mortain,[4] during his captivity, about which nothing could be known until death revealed the king's secrets, and other examples of greed were also cited which I forbear to mention; and also incontinence, for like Solomon he was perpetually enslaved by the rule of women. Such diverse opinions were freely expressed by the common people. But in the terrible times which followed later through the insensate treachery of the Normans, whatsoever King Henry had done, whether in the manner of a tyrant or of a true king,[5] appeared most excellent in comparison with their evil deeds. For without delay came Stephen, younger brother of Theobald, count of Blois, a man of great resolution and audacity, who, although he had sworn an oath of fealty for the realm of England to the daughter of King Henry,[6] trusting in his strength, shamelessly tempted God and seized the crown of the kingdom. William, archbishop of Canterbury,[7] who had been the first to swear allegiance to the king's daughter, alas! crowned Stephen king, wherefore God visited him with the same judgment which he had inflicted on him who had stricken Jeremiah, the great priest;[8] namely, that he should not live out the year. Roger, the

[1] Ed. Arnold, p. 255. [2] Henry I. [3] Louis VI, 1108–1137.

[4] The reference is probably to Henry I's half-brother, William, count of Mortain and earl of Cornwall, who fought against Henry at Tinchebrai in 1106 and was thereafter imprisoned for many years.

[5] *vel tyrannice vel regie.* [6] Maud, daughter of Henry I.

[7] William of Corbeil, archbishop of Canterbury, 1123–1135.

[8] A confused and inaccurate reference to Jeremiah xx. 2, and xxviii. 16.

great bishop of Salisbury, who had been the second to take the aforesaid oath and had ordered all the others to do likewise, contributed everything in his power to secure for him the crown. He, too, by the just judgment of God was afterwards taken captive by him whom he had made king and in dire torments came to a wretched end. But why tarry? All those who had sworn fealty, whether prelates, earls or magnates, offered to accept Stephen and paid homage to him. This indeed was an evil sign, that the whole of England should so suddenly and without delay or struggle, and, as it were, in the twinkling of an eye, submit to Stephen. So, after his coronation at Christmastide, he held his court at London.

Meanwhile the body of King Henry lay still unburied in Normandy, for he died on 1 December. . . . At last the royal remains were transported to England and buried within twelve days of Christmas in the abbey of Reading which King Henry had founded and endowed with great possessions. Thither came King Stephen, after holding his court in London that same Christmastide, to meet the body of his uncle, and William, archbishop of Canterbury, with many prelates and lay magnates. There they buried King Henry with the honour due to so great a man. From thence King Stephen proceeded to Oxford where were recorded and confirmed the covenants which he had granted to God and the people and to holy Church on the day of his coronation. . . .[1]

(*b*) *The battle of Lincoln and its consequences*

. . . In[2] the sixth year[3] of his reign during the Christmas season,[4] King Stephen laid siege to Lincoln, the fortifications of which Rannulf, earl of Chester,[5] had seized by guile. The king maintained the siege up to the Purification of St. Mary,[6] whereupon the said Rannulf brought with him Robert,[7] the son of King Henry and his own father-in-law, and other powerful nobles to raise the siege. But after the intrepid earl had successfully crossed a marsh which was almost impassable, the very same day he attacked the king with his troops drawn up in battle array. He himself had set the first line in order, which consisted of his own retainers; the second was led by the man whom King Stephen had disinherited,[8] while Robert, the great earl, commanded the third. On the flanks of the army were placed bands of Welshmen, greater in courage than in knowledge of arms. At that point the earl of Chester, a man of prowess in war and clad in shining armour, thus addressed Earl Robert and the other barons. . . .[9]

[Earl Robert] had scarcely made an end of speaking when the whole army, raising their hands to heaven with a tumultuous cry, swore not to seek refuge in flight, and, closing their ranks, advanced in arms against the foe in splendid order. In the meantime King Stephen, overwhelmed with a flood of cares, was hearing Mass with great devotion. But when, in making the accustomed offering to God and worthy of a king,

[1] See below, No. 20.
[2] Ed. Arnold, p. 268.
[3] 1141.
[4] Christmas, 1140.
[5] A strong supporter of Maud in the north.
[6] 2 February 1141.
[7] Robert, earl of Gloucester. (See above, pp. 201–202.)
[8] William of Roumare, who had been recently invested by Stephen with the earldom of Lincoln, but had been refused his rights as custodian of the castle. The earl of Chester had aided him in the seizure of the castle.
[9] Here follow two of Henry of Huntingdon's fictitious speeches, a brief one put into the mouth of the earl of Chester and a much longer reply ascribed to the earl of Gloucester, in which among other things he rehearses the grievances of the rebel barons against the king, and slanders the character of the latter's chief adherents.

he was handing the wax taper[1] to Bishop Alexander, it broke; a sign of the rupture of the king's reign. The pyx, also, which contained the Body of the Lord,[2] snapped its chain and fell upon the altar while the bishop was present: this was a token of the king's downfall. Nevertheless, he set forth with great energy and made his dispositions for battle with the greatest circumspection. He himself took up the centre position in the midst of a host of mailed knights, who were dismounted and drawn up in close formation. The earls with their knights he stationed on horseback in two lines, but this force of cavalry appeared below strength. For these spurious and factious earls[3] had brought with them few soldiers, while the king's own army was very large and one particular body was entrusted with the royal standard. Then, as King Stephen lacked a strong voice, Baldwin fitz Gilbert, a man of the highest rank and a brave warrior, was charged with addressing a speech of encouragement to the assembled host. . . . Already before the close of this address were heard the shouts of the advancing enemy, the blast of the trumpets and the thud of the horses as they trampled the ground beneath their hooves.

The battle had begun. The troops of the disinherited barons who were in the van broke through the lines of the royal army, in which were stationed Earl Alan,[4] the count of Meulan,[5] Hugh, earl of East Anglia[6] [*sic*], Earl Simon,[7] and the earl of Warenne,[8] with such force that it was scattered, as it were, in the twinkling of an eye and divided into three. For some of them were slain, others taken prisoner and yet others took to flight. The force commanded by the earl of Aumale and William of Ypres charged the Welsh as they were advancing on the flank and put them to flight. But the forces of the earl of Chester drove back this troop of horsemen and it was scattered in a moment like the first line. Thus all the king's horse fled and with them fled William of Ypres, who had been born in Flanders, ranked as an earl and was a man of valour. As an experienced soldier, perceiving that it was impossible to bring succour to the king, he deferred his aid to better times. And so King Stephen was left alone with his infantry in the midst of the enemy. The latter encircled the royal army and attacked it from all sides, as if they were assaulting a castle. Thenceforth the battle was seen to rage horribly around the royal defences, helmets and swords gleamed as they clashed, and the dreadful noise re-echoed from the hills and the walls of the city. The cavalry, furiously charging the royal column, slew some and trampled down others, while yet others were dragged away captive. No respite, no breathing-space was given, except in the quarter where the most valiant king had taken his stand and the foe recoiled from the incomparable ferocity of his counter-strokes. Perceiving this and envious of the king's glory, the earl of Chester threw himself upon him with the whole weight of his men-at-arms. Even then the lightning strokes of the king were made manifest, and, wielding his great two-handed battle-axe, he slew some and cut down others. Then a fresh shout arose and every man rushed at the king while he in

[1] The battle of Lincoln was fought on 2 February, and the ceremony here referred to formed part of the traditional rites of the Feast of Candlemas.

[2] The Reserved Sacrament.

[3] *ficti et factiosi consules*: a reference to Stephen's creation of titular earls without jurisdiction over counties or earldoms.

[4] Alan, a count of Brittany.

[5] Waleran, count of Meulan. (See Table 12.)

[6] Hugh Bigot, earl of Norfolk.

[7] Simon 'de St. Liz', earl of Northampton. (See Table 9.)

[8] William.

turn thrust back at them all. At length his battle-axe was shattered by repeated blows, whereupon he drew his trusty sword, well worthy of a king, and with this he wrought wonders, until it too was broken. At sight of this William 'de Chesney', a very valiant knight, rushed upon him and, seizing him by the helmet, shouted with a loud voice, "Hither, all of you, hither, I hold the king." Everyone flew to his aid and the king was taken prisoner. Baldwin, who had made a speech of exhortation, was also captured, pierced with many wounds, and by his determined resistance gained immortal honour. Richard fitz Urse was likewise taken prisoner, who had also acquitted himself valiantly and gained great glory both in giving and receiving blows. Until the king was captured his troops continued the struggle, for they were so hemmed in on all sides that flight was impossible. Thus the whole army was either slain or captured.[1] The city[2] in consequence was given over to pillage in accordance with the laws of war, and the king was brought back to it in his wretched plight.

The judgment of God having been thus executed against the king, he was brought to the empress and imprisoned in the castle of Bristol. The empress was recognized as ruler by the whole people of England except in Kent, where the queen and William of Ypres continued to fight against the empress with all their might. The latter was first acknowledged by the Roman legate, the bishop of Winchester,[3] and next by the men of London. But she was swollen with insufferable pride by her success in war, and alienated the affections of nearly everyone. Therefore either by crafty men or by God's will – though all human activity is subject to God's design – she was driven out of London. With a woman's anger she forthwith ordered the king, the Lord's Anointed, to be bound with fetters; and after some days with her uncle, the king of Scots, and her brother, Robert, and with all their forces, she besieged the castle of the bishop of Winchester. But the bishop called for help to the queen and William of Ypres, and to almost all the magnates of England. Great armies were thus marshalled and there were daily encounters, not indeed the strife of armies, but the desultory skirmishes of patrols. In such combats deeds of heroism were not lost, as so often in the blind confusion of a battle, but each man's valour was manifest and won due renown. Thus this pause seemed in a sense agreeable to both sides as a means of displaying glorious deeds. At length the arrival of the army from London, and the vast increase in the opponents of the empress, compelled her to retreat. Many were taken prisoner in this flight, among them Robert, the brother of the empress. It was in his castle that the king lay imprisoned.[4] With his capture, therefore, the king was able to regain his freedom, by mutual exchange. Thus the king who by God's judgment had been made a wretched captive was by His mercy wonderfully liberated and received by the magnates of England with great rejoicing. . . .

(c) *The coming of Henry of Anjou and the end of the reign of Stephen*

. . . When[5] the illustrious duke, Henry, driven onwards by a gale, had reached the shores of England[6] the earth quivered with sudden rumours like reeds shaken by a breeze. The

[1] The actual casualties in the battle were not large: not more than a hundred knights being slain.
[2] Lincoln. The citizens had taken part in the battle on the king's side.
[3] Henry of Blois, bishop of Winchester, the king's brother.
[4] Bristol. [5] Ed. Arnold, p. 285. [6] 1153.

report spreading far and wide, gave joy and exultation to some, dread and dejection to others. But the pleasure of those who rejoiced was somewhat tempered by the fact that he had brought few men with him,[1] while the distress of his enemies was not a little relieved at his meagre following. Moreover, both sides marvelled at the fact that he had ventured to cross a tempestuous sea in mid-winter; what his own party considered heroism, the opposition judged to be temerity. But the energetic young prince, detesting delay most of all things, gathered together his forces, both those he found in England and those he had brought with him, and laid siege to the castle of Malmesbury. And because the virtues of such a man are many and great, they must be but briefly related, lest the full toll of his deeds should entail excessive prolixity. In short, then, having besieged the castle (for he never brooked delay in his operations) he presently assaulted and took it by storm. After the town had been captured, the exceedingly strong keep of the castle, which was still held for the king by Jordan, remained to be starved out. From thence the said Jordan sallied forth in great haste to inform the king of what had befallen. Distressed by messengers of evil tidings, the king's countenance fell and was contorted with grief. Nevertheless, he was not slow in collecting all his forces and pitched his camp not far from Malmesbury. On the morrow of his arrival he positioned his troops for battle, the army including a body of knights specially chosen for valour and their experience in war. It was indeed a huge army, packed with a host of barons, exceedingly formidable and of splendid appearance, its banners glittering with gold; but God, in whom alone is perfect safety, had withdrawn his presence from them. For the floodgates of heaven were opened and heavy rain drove in their faces, and in addition to this downpour, God visited them with such bitter cold and violent gusts of wind, that it seemed as if the Almighty himself were fighting for the duke. Nevertheless, they kept their formation, though harassed and tormented by the elements as if they were contending against the very power of God. The army of the young duke was stationed in line over against them, trusting more in its valour than in its numbers, but especially fortified by the grace of God, which the justice of the cause, for which it stood in arms, had in mercy procured for it.

The army was drawn up on the banks of a tributary of a river, not far from the walls of the town [of Malmesbury], which was so flooded by the torrents of rain and snow that those who attempted to ford it were so numbed by the icy cold that they could not regain the bank. The young and noble duke stood at the head of his troops, clad in armour worthy of so great a prince, which, in a figure, showed forth the excellence of his mind by the nobility of his bodily form, so that we may say, not so much that his arms became him, but that the elegance of his person shed lustre upon his arms. He and his men had the storm at their backs, while the wind and rain drove in the faces of the king and his troops, so that they could hardly support their armour or handle their spears, soaked with the rain.

And because God had contrived that his son should gain possession of the land without bloodshed, when neither side could cross the river and the king could no longer endure the floods, he marched back to London, having failed in his operations

[1] 140 knights and 3,000 foot-soldiers.

and his discomfiture complete. The keep of the castle, which the duke had been besieging, was thereupon surrendered to him, and in high spirits he hastened to accomplish the purpose for which he had come, namely, the relief of the garrison at Wallingford, now like to perish from famine. Accordingly, having collected a body of troops to transport provisions into the beleaguered camp, God so favoured his undertaking that he was enabled to execute his plan and effect a peaceful entry. For although there were several castles in the vicinity held by the royal troops, by God's will they were unable to prevent him either coming or going. This occupied but a short space of time and then the valiant duke, having gathered together all the knights who had espoused his cause, laid siege to the castle of Crowmarsh. Making an excellent start to this arduous and difficult enterprise, he erected a strong earthwork encircling both the king's castle and his own army, so that the only way of retreat open to his own troops lay through the castle of Wallingford and the besieged had none whatever. Upon hearing this the king, concentrating all the forces at his command, moved up to threaten the duke's position. But the latter, unmoved by fear, although his forces were inferior in number to those of the king, ordered the earthwork he had erected for the protection of his army, to be forthwith levelled with the ground. Then, raising the siege, he arranged his forces in good order and marched against the king. Accordingly, when the royal troops saw the serried ranks of the enemy unexpectedly confronting them they were smitten with sudden panic. The king, however, unsubdued by fear, commanded his troops to march forth from their camp in battle order. Whereupon the nobles, nay rather the traitors of England, arose and discussed terms of peace among themselves. They loved indeed nothing better than discord, but were unwilling to commit themselves to battle; for they desired to raise up neither one nor the other of the claimants to the throne, lest by vanquishing the one they might become entirely subject to the other. They preferred that, each being kept in fear of the other, the royal authority should not be effectively exercised against them. The king and the duke, therefore, becoming aware of the treachery of their followers, were reluctantly compelled to make a truce between themselves. But God in his accustomed manner protected the honour of the young prince. For the royal castle,[1] which the duke had been besieging, was razed to the ground in accordance with the terms of the truce. Afterwards the king and the duke conferred together alone on an island in the river concerning the conclusion of a permanent peace between them, where both complained bitterly of the betrayal of their barons. Here only the preliminaries of peace negotiations were dealt with, their completion being deferred to a later stage.

The dispute between them was not yet settled, when each returned to his quarters, but soon light dawned serenely on the fortunes of the great duke. For it chanced that his two most powerful enemies, namely, Eustace, the king's son, and Simon, earl of Northampton, were by the providence of God removed from this world when they least expected it, and this both at the same time. In consequence of this unforeseen event the courage and hope of all those in arms against the duke began to wane. Both the young men succumbed to the same disease in the same week. Earl Simon

[1] *i.e.* Crowmarsh.

was buried at Northampton. He was a standing example of all that was unlawful and dishonourable. The king's son was buried in the abbey at Faversham, which his mother had founded. He was a tried warrior but obdurate in the things pertaining to God. He dealt very harshly with the higher clergy, persecuting them in a ruthless manner. In this fashion God removed these formidable adversaries from the path of Henry, his elect, and then of his bounty prepared the way for his accession to the throne in tranquillity.

The third siege undertaken by the duke was that of the castle of Stamford. The town was captured immediately, but the garrison of the castle resisted and sent messengers to the king begging for aid. But the king was engaged in besieging the castle of Ipswich, which Hugh Bigot was holding against him. As he was unwilling to raise the siege or to send help to the garrison of Stamford, the latter castle surrendered to Prince Henry, while Ipswich in its turn surrendered to the king. Leaving Stamford, the duke of Normandy marched to Nottingham, which he took forthwith; but the enemy, who held the castle, set fire to the town. Stricken with grief and pity at the burning of the town, the duke moved his army on to another place.

In the meantime Archbishop Theobald was holding important consultations with the king on the subject of the treaty to be concluded with the duke. He had frequent conversations in person with the king and negotiated with the duke through intermediaries. The archbishop found an ally in Henry, bishop of Winchester, who had taken the lead in promoting the disastrous dissensions in the kingdom by bestowing the crown upon his brother, Stephen. But now, repenting of his action when he saw everything in ruins through rapine, fire and slaughter, the bishop of Winchester sought to put an end to these great evils by establishing concord between the two leaders. It was, however, chiefly by the providence of God, who maketh peace and giveth all good things, that the scourge with which England had been deservedly afflicted was finally withdrawn. So God granted a happy issue to the enterprise of the bishops, and by His favour a treaty was solemnly concluded[1] and peace shone forth in all serenity through their endeavours. What boundless joy! What a happy day! when in the city of Winchester, in the midst of a splendid procession of prelates and nobles and with the acclamations of a countless host of spectators the illustrious young prince was conducted by the king himself and received with all honour. For the king duly acknowledged him as his adopted son and made him heir to the kingdom. From thence the king escorted the duke to London, where he was received with no less joy by the assembled throng of people and with brilliant processions, as befitted so great a prince. Thus, by God's mercy, he contrived to bring to a close the gloomy night, that had darkened the ruined realm of England, and to herald the dawn of peace.

These things accomplished, the king and his new son parted in love and joy, though destined soon to meet again; for the peace was ratified before Christmas. On the Octave of Epiphany[2] they met at Oxford, when the duke had already spent nearly a year in the conquest, nay rather in the recovery, of England. There, by the king's command, the magnates of the realm paid homage and at the same time promised the fealty due to their liege lord to the duke of Normandy, saving only the honour and

[1] See below, No. 22. [2] 13 January 1154.

allegiance owing to the king during his lifetime. At this splendid gathering there were fresh rejoicings, after which the magnates departed with joy and gladness to their own homes. After a brief interval the king and the duke met once more at Dunstable where a small cloud obscured the brightness of the day. For the duke was displeased because the castles, constructed everywhere after the death of King Henry and put to evil uses, had not been demolished in accordance with the provisions of the treaty so firmly made between them and solemnly ratified. Many of them indeed had been already razed to the ground, but others held by his own followers had been spared by the indulgence or duplicity of the king, and this appeared to weaken the mutual execution of the treaty. But when the duke complained of this to the king, he suffered a rebuff. Nevertheless, desirous of maintaining a good understanding with his adopted father, he reluctantly let the matter drop, lest the light of peace should be extinguished. So both parties separated amicably. Not long afterwards with the king's permission the victorious duke returned to Normandy.

Such were the deeds of Henry, that most energetic of young men, during his second visit to England.[1] Let no one be wroth with me for having committed to writing but a few of his many glorious acts. For it would have needed many volumes to have covered in detail the history of so many and great kings and the series of events that have occurred throughout so many ages. I have therefore chosen rather to compress into one volume an abridgment of history, so that the events of the past may not altogether be concealed from those who come after. Now let us return to our subject.

Returning to France in triumph, the duke was received by his mother,[2] his brother and all the peoples of Normandy, Anjou, Maine and Poitou with the joy and honour due to him. Moreover, King Stephen, now for the first time reigning in peace, was, thanks to his adopted son, strong enough to maintain the authority due to his royal state. But alas! for the dire fury of mortals and their abominable perversity. Certain sons of men, "whose teeth are spears and arrows, and their tongue a sharp sword"[3] were at great pains to sow the seeds of discord between the king in England and the duke abroad. The king could scarcely resist their persuasions and in course of time, as some supposed, he was on the point of yielding to them, listening to their evil counsels not unwillingly, but more than was right, though he pretended to reject them. But the judgment of the sons of men was one thing, and that of the Almighty another; and He, as was fitting, perfected what He had begun, and brought to naught the counsels of wicked men and their perverse machinations. When therefore the king had besieged and taken the castle of Drax near York, and also demolished many other castles, he marched to Dover for the purpose of conferring with the count of Flanders.[4] While in conference with him the king was seized with mortal sickness and died eight days before the Feast of All Saints.[5] He was interred in the abbey of Faversham next to his wife and son after a troubled and unhappy reign of nearly nineteen years.

[1] According to the *Gesta Stephani*, ed. R. Howlett, *Chronicles and Memorials of the reigns of Stephen, Henry II and Richard I*, vol. iii (Rolls Series, 1886), p. 129, Henry had first visited England in 1147. If this statement could be accepted, the campaign of 1153 took place during his third visit, but this chronology is rejected by J. H. Round in *Eng. Hist. Rev.*, vol. v, p. 747.

[2] Maud, the empress. [3] Psalms lvii. 5. [4] Thierry. (See Table 18.) [5] 25 October 1154.

Thereupon Archbishop Theobald and a great many of the magnates of England hurriedly sent messengers to the duke of Normandy as their new lord, entreating him to come without delay and take possession of the kingdom. Impeded, however, by the winds and waves and by many other causes, it was not until a few days before Christmas that he landed in the New Forest,[1] accompanied by his wife,[2] his brothers,[3] many great magnates and a strong force of troops. Thus England was left without a king for about six weeks, and yet by God's grace perfect peace prevailed, either through love or fear of the king whose coming was expected. When he had disembarked, he proceeded to London,[4] where, as befitted so great and blessed a prince, he was crowned king[5] and installed on the throne of England in pomp and majesty amidst universal rejoicing, while many wept for very joy. . . .[6]

[1] Possibly at Lymington, but more probably at Southampton, see R. W. Eyton, *Court, Household and Itinerary of King Henry II*, p. 2, n. 4.

[2] Eleanor, duchess of Aquitaine.

[3] Geoffrey and William.

[4] He broke his journey at Winchester, see Eyton, *loc. cit.*

[5] 19 December 1154.

[6] The chronicle ends with a poem in heroic hexameters glorifying the new king.

11. Richard of Hexham: Account of the battle of the Standard

This is a valuable narrative, and since it was written before 1154, it is nearly contemporary with the events it describes. It supplies an account not only of the Scottish invasion but also of the conditions in the north of England at the time of the anarchy. For the author, whose sentiments are strongly anti-Scottish, see above, pp. 98-100. The narrative is printed in R. Howlett, *Chronicles and Memorials of the reigns of Stephen, Henry II and Richard I* (Rolls Series, 1886), vol. III, pp. 151 *et sqq.*; and it is translated in J. Stevenson, *Church Historians of England*, vol. IV, pt. i, pp. 35-58.

On 10 January, King David's nephew, William, the son of Duncan,[1] with a portion of King David's army, made a nocturnal attack upon a fortress called Carham, in the king of England's[2] territory, and having plundered the neighbourhood around, proceeded to storm the castle. Afterwards the king himself and his son, Henry, arrived with a further reinforcement, and applying the whole strength of their resources attempted to carry the town by various assaults with battering machines and other implements, and after that laid siege to it for three weeks. Yet he gained no advantage but, on the contrary, every attempt proved injurious to himself: for the knights and others who were in the fortress, most ably defending themselves and the town, killed his standard-bearer and many others of his men, under his own eyes, and wounded many more. The king, perceiving the uselessness of his efforts, and the many and daily increasing losses to himself and his troops, at length raised the siege, and rushed with his whole force to devastate Northumberland. And then that execrable army, more atrocious than the whole race of pagans, neither fearing God nor regarding man, spread desolation over the whole province, and murdered everywhere persons of both sexes, of every age and rank, and devastated towns, churches, and houses. For the sick on their couches, women pregnant and in childbed, infants in the womb, innocents at the breast, or on the mother's knee, with the mothers themselves, decrepit old men and worn-out old women, and persons debilitated from whatever cause, wherever they met with them, they put to the edge of the sword or transfixed them with their spears; and by how much more horrible a death they could dispatch them, so much the more did they rejoice. The mournful lamentation of the Psalmist then plainly received its fulfilment, "O God, the heathen are come into thine inheritance. Thy holy temple have they defiled, and made Jerusalem an heap of stones",[3] and, indeed, the whole remaining portion of that psalm. It is said that in one place they slew a multitude of children together, and having collected their blood into a brook which they had previously dammed back, they drank the mixture, of which the greater part was pure blood. It is said, also, that in the church they shattered the crucifixes with every mark of dishonour, in contempt of Christ and to their own infamy; they dug up the altars, and near them, yea, upon them, they slaughtered the clergy and innocent children. Wherefore we may again not unfitly exclaim in lamentation with the Psalmist, "O God, Thou hast cast us out, and scattered us abroad; Thou hast also been displeased, and hast not turned unto us again",[4] and so on as there follows. That infamous army received accessions from the Normans,

[1] See Table 16. [2] Stephen. [3] Psalms lxxix. 1. [4] Psalms lx. 1.

Germans, and English, from the Northumbrians and Cumbrians, from Teviotdale and Lothian, from the Picts, commonly called Galwegians, and the Scots, and no one knew their number; for multitudes of their own accord allied themselves with those above mentioned, either from love of plunder, or opportunity of revenge, or from the mere desire of mischief with which that region was rife. Overrunning the province, and sparing none, they ravaged with sword and fire almost all Northumberland as far as the river Tyne, excepting the towns and the sea-coast which lies on the eastern side, but this they designed to devastate on their return. A portion of that army also crossed the Tyne, and massacred numberless persons in the wilds, laying waste in the same way the greater part of the territory of St. Cuthbert[1] on the west side.

While these things were being perpetrated by his followers, the king of Scots with a considerable force occupied Corbridge. At this period a monastery of the Cistercian rule, founded the same year on the property of Ralph of Merlay, was destroyed, and very many others were overwhelmed with the heaviest afflictions. Wherefore the monastery at the mouth of the river Tyne, called in English Tynemouth, in order to secure itself and its inmates in this urgent need, paid to the king of Scotland and his men 27 marks of silver. In this raging and tempestuous period, that noble monastery of Hexham (although in the midst of the conflict, and placed as it were on the very route of these ruffians, so as to be surrounded by them on every side) yet on account of the renowned merits of its tutelary saints, Andrew the apostle, and Wilfrid, bishop and martyr, and of its other patrons, Saints Acca, Alcmund, and Eata, bishops and confessors, and the other saints who reposed within that church, offered the most tranquil security to its people and those who took refuge in it, and afforded them all a perfectly safe asylum from hostile assaults. Nevertheless, at first the Picts rushed with impetuous haste to the river Tyne, on which the town stands, and would have destroyed it, as they had others; but just as they were about to cross this river, two of their number were killed by their own countrymen, and on this the others retired in fear. Moreover, two of the same tribe of Picts came by chance upon an oratory of St. Michael the archangel, situated on the northern bank of the river Tyne, and attached to the aforesaid church of Hexham; thereupon they broke open the door, and carried off what they found. But the vengeance of God overtook them; for, given up to the evil one, they were bereft of reason, and, as the madness drove them, tore night and day, in the sight of all, through forest and country, and both perished by a horrible death; the one first battering his own face with stones, and then having his legs cut off by someone, the other drowning himself in the Tyne. These events struck terror into some of the army, and they did not venture to make any further attempt upon the possessions of the church of Hexham. Thereupon David, king of Scotland, and Earl Henry, his son, guaranteed to that monastery, its brethren, and all belonging to it, security from themselves and all their followers; and this they confirmed by their charters, which are preserved in that church, the sole condition being that the monastery should keep the peace towards him and his. Thus that noble church, founded by St. Wilfrid, preserved its ancient and wonted lustre in this

[1] Bishopric of Durham.

and other storms of battle and became a secure place of refuge to numberless poor as well as rich, to whom it afforded the necessaries of life, and the preservation of their property.

Meanwhile, about the Feast of the Purification of St. Mary,[1] Stephen, king of England, arrived with a great number of earls and barons, and a large force of horse and foot. On hearing this the king of Scots left Northumberland, and rapidly retreated with his army to his own territory. He marched to Wark, and afterwards lay in wait with his troops in some wilds near Roxburgh, with a design to ensnare the king of England, who, he hoped, would take up his quarters at Roxburgh. He directed the citizens to receive him favourably and to make a show of good faith; but he also directed that when he with his army should steal up by night, and a number of soldiers whom he had placed in the town should make a sudden sally and join him with the townsmen, they should all unite in encompassing the king of England unawares on every side, and should cut him off with all his men. But the Lord, who knoweth the thoughts of man that they are but vain, brought to naught all these devices. For the king of England crossed the river Tweed and did not proceed to Roxburgh, but devastated and burnt a great portion of the territory of the king of Scots; and then, because many of his knights declined to take arms and carry on the war (for it was now the beginning of Lent) and also because the king of Scots and his men dared not give battle, he retired with his troops to the south of England, since his own army was short of supplies. . . . But on the Friday of the week following the celebration of Easter,[2] the king of Scots, with his execrable army, once more returned to Northumberland, and with no less ferocity and cruelty than he had previously exhibited, he devastated first the sea-coast of the county, which on the former occasion had been left undisturbed, and all those other portions besides which anywhere had escaped uninjured, and after that the greater part of the territory of St. Cuthbert, on the eastern side, between Durham and the sea. And both on this and the former occasion he in like manner destroyed, together with the husbandmen, many farms of the monks who served God and St. Cuthbert day and night. But St. Cuthbert at length took pity on his servants; for, in the midst of these enormities, the king with his retinue took up his abode near Durham, and there, a serious mutiny having arisen on account of a certain woman, the life of the king and his suite was placed in jeopardy by the Picts. While he was alarmed about this, he suddenly heard a false report that a large army was approaching from the south of Britain. Wherefore, leaving his provisions behind, he fled with all his forces towards his own country. On his march he reached Norham which is the territory of St. Cuthbert, and he laid siege to it, seeking to reduce it by various plans and devices. And while he remained there occupied with the siege, he sent his nephew, William, son of Duncan, on an expedition into Yorkshire with the Picts and a portion of his army. These gained the mastery owing to the sins of the people of that region, and destroyed by fire and sword the greater part of the possessions of the splendid church of Southerness in the district of Craven. Then taking no account of rank, age, sex or condition, they barbarously massacred children and kindred in the sight of their relatives, masters in the sight of

[1] 2 February. [2] 15 April.

their servants, servants before the eyes of their masters, and husbands in the sight of their wives. Afterwards (horrible to relate) they carried off as booty noble matrons and chaste virgins together with other women. These they drove before them naked, fettered and herded together, lashing them with whips, and goading them with their spears. Such atrocities occur in all wars but very seldom to such an extent. These women were distributed with the other plunder, but afterwards a few were, out of pity, restored to liberty at the church of St. Mary at Carlisle. The Picts, however, carried off those that fell to their share into their own country. And finally these brutal men, making no account of adultery, incest and such crimes, when tired of abusing these poor wretches, made them their slaves or sold them like cattle to other barbarians.

The king of Scots and his men received these tidings with great exultation, and applied themselves with still greater energy to the capture of the fortress before them. The townsmen at first defended themselves with great vigour, but they were few in number and had only nine knights among them. Moreover they were inexperienced in such struggles and soon began to despair of receiving help from their lord, Geoffrey, bishop of Durham. Therefore in dismay they surrendered to the king while the wall was still in good condition, though the tower remained very strong, and though their provisions were still abundant. As a result, the soldiers, and those who were in the town, incurred great odium, because they had made a feeble resistance and had too readily given up the castle; and not only were they censured, but their lord also, because he had not garrisoned his fortress according to his means, and as the necessities of the period required. The knights retired with their men to Durham. So the king, having captured the town, and taken the provisions which were there stored up in much abundance, intimated to the bishop that if he would desert Stephen, king of England, and swear fealty to his party, he would restore the castle to him, and make good the damage which it had sustained. This the bishop refused, and the king, therefore, caused the town to be dismantled.

While these events occurred there, about Rogation time,[1] the soldiers sallying from the town of Wark seized under their walls King David's supplies, which had to pass close by them, together with the wagons and the attendants. The king, much enraged at this, hastened with his whole force to besiege them, and he proceeded to assail it by batteries and with all the means in his power. But by God's blessing all his endeavours were in vain. Many of his men were wounded and disabled, and some slain; likewise, in the conflicts which before this siege had been fought with the king's son, Henry, some were killed, others wounded or taken prisoner, and ransom received for them. Blessed be God over all, who protecteth the righteous, but overthroweth the wicked! The king then, perceiving that his attempts upon the town were useless, caused the crops to be consumed on the ground, and then levying from his own country, and whencesoever else he could, a larger force than ever before, he united his troops into one body. Moreover Eustace, son of John, one of the barons of the king of England, who held a very strong fortress in Northumberland, called Alnwick, and who had long secretly favoured the king of Scots, now openly showed

[1] 9 May.

his treachery, and threw off his allegiance to his lawful sovereign, the king of England. With his whole strength he gave his aid to the Scots against the realm of England. Leading with him no inconsiderable number of fighting men, he marched with the king of Scots to ravage Yorkshire. He also made arrangements to give up to the king of Scots and his party another strong castle of his at Malton, situated in that province on the river Derwent, not far from York, of which we shall have to say more hereafter. King David then, consigning the siege of Wark to two of the thegns (that is to say, his barons), with their retainers, marched with most of his army to Bamborough, where, having taken an outwork of the castle, he killed nearly a hundred men. And then having destroyed the crops around that place, and around William Bertram's town of Mitford, and in many other parts of Northumberland, he crossed the river Tyne. Entering the territory of St. Cuthbert, he there waited for a portion of his army which had not yet joined him, and at his summons the Picts, and Cumbrians, and the men of Carlisle and the adjoining district, came to him without delay. The whole army being thus assembled, he regarded it with unbounded exultation; for it appeared to him immense and invincible, and in truth it was very large, consisting of more than twenty-six thousand men. His heart and the hearts of his men were lifted up, and putting their trust in themselves and their numbers, and having no fear of God, they spoke boastfully and proudly. They threatened to destroy not only Yorkshire, but the greater part of England; for, with such a host, they did not imagine that anyone would venture, or be able to resist them. These events occurred within the Octave of the Nativity of St. Mary;[1] and the king then passing by Durham, destroyed the crops as far as the river Tees, and, according to his usual practice, caused the towns and churches which had previously escaped uninjured to be dismantled, plundered, and burnt. Crossing the Tees, he began a similar career of violence. But God's mercy, being moved by the tears of innumerable widows, orphans, and victims, no longer permitted such wickedness to remain unchastised. For whilst he and his men were engaged in this course of outrage, information of his crimes and his designs was conveyed to the men of Yorkshire, both by common report and by sure intelligence. Whereupon the barons of that province, to wit, Archbishop Thurstan (who, as will presently appear, greatly exerted himself in this emergency), William of Aumale, Walter of Ghent, Robert 'de Bruce', Roger of Mowbray, Walter Espec, Ilbert of Lassy, William 'de Percy,' Richard of Courcy, William Fossard, Robert of Estouteville, and other powerful and wise men, assembled at York, and anxiously deliberated as to what course should be pursued at this crisis. Much irresolution was caused by distrust of each other, arising from suspicions of treachery, by the absence of a chief and a leader of the war (for their sovereign, King Stephen, encompassed by equal difficulties in the south of England, was just then unable to join them), and by their dread of encountering with an inadequate force so great a host. It appeared indeed as if they would actually have abandoned the defence of themselves and their country, had not their archbishop, Thurstan, a man of great firmness and worth, animated them by his counsel and exhortations. For, being the shepherd of their souls, he would not, like a hireling on the approach of the wolf, seek

[1] 8–15 September.

safety in flight, but rather, deeply pitiful at the dispersion and ruin of his flock, he applied all his energy and labours to counteract these great evils. Wherefore, by the authority of his divine commission, and the royal warrant with which on that occasion he was provided, he boldly urged them, by their loyalty and their honour, not to allow themselves through cowardice to be prostrated at one blow by utter savages, but rather, with their dependants, to seek God's favour by true repentance, and to turn with all their heart to him whose wrath these many and heavy evils proved that they deserved. Thus they should act with the confidence and courage demanded in so pressing an emergency. If they acted thus devotedly, trusting in God's mercy, he assured them of victory; for that infamous people were directing their hostile endeavours against God and holy Church rather than against them, and therefore supporting a cause unrighteous and accursed. But their own battle was a just and most holy one, inasmuch as they were encountering peril in defence of holy Church and of their country; and if so be it should please God that this contest should not terminate without the loss of some of them, yet, by those who were fighting with such an object, death was not to be feared, but rather desired. He promised them also that the priests of his diocese, bearing crosses, should march with them to battle together with their flocks, and that he also, God willing, would be present with his men in the engagement.

At this period of perplexity, one of the nobles of that province, Bernard 'de Baliol', sent to them by the king of England, arrived with a number of knights; and, on the king's part and his own, he greatly aroused their energy to the same effect. Thus incited by the charge of the king and their archbishop, coming unanimously to one decision, they returned to their own estates; and shortly after they met at York, each fully equipped and armed for battle. Having there made private confession, the archbishop enjoined on them and the whole populace a three days' fast with alms-giving; after which he solemnly absolved them, and gave them God's blessing and his own. And although he was himself so greatly reduced by age and infirmity, that he had to be carried on a litter where need was, yet, in order to animate their courage, he would readily have accompanied them to the field of battle. But they compelled him to stay behind, begging that he would employ himself in interceding for them by prayers and alms, by vigils and fasts, and other sacred observances; while they (as God would deign to aid them, and as their position demanded) would cheerfully go forth against the enemy, in defence of God's Church, and of him who was his minister. So he consigned to them his retainers together with his cross and the standard of St. Peter; and they proceeded to Thirsk, from whence they dispatched Robert 'de Bruce' and Bernard 'de Baliol' to the king of Scots, who was then, as has been said, devastating the territory of St. Cuthbert. They very humbly and courteously besought him that he would at least desist from his acts of ferocity; and faithfully promised him that if he would accede to their request, they would obtain for him from the king of England the earldom of Northumberland, which he claimed for his son Henry. But he, together with his followers, with a hardened heart, spurned their request, and disdainfully taunted them. They therefore returned to their associates, Robert abjured the homage he had rendered to the Scottish king, and Bernard the fealty he had sworn to him on one occasion when he had been taken prisoner. All the nobles, therefore, of that province, and William of Ferrières from Derbyshire, and other eminent and prudent men, made a compact amongst themselves, which they confirmed by oaths, that not one of them in this difficulty would desert another while he had the power to aid him; and thus all would either perish or conquer together. At the same time, the archbishop sent to them Ralph, surnamed 'Novellus', bishop of Orkney, with one of his archdeacons, and other clergy, who as his delegates should impose penance and give absolution to the people who daily flocked to them from every quarter. He also sent to them, as he had promised, the priests with their flocks. While thus awaiting the approach of the Scots, the scouts whom they had sent forward to reconnoitre, returned, bringing the information that the king with his army had already passed the river Tees and was ravaging their province in his wonted manner. They hastened to resist them; and, passing the village of Northallerton, they arrived early in the morning at a plain distant from it by about two miles. Some of them soon erected, in the centre of a frame which they brought, the mast of a ship, to which they gave the name of the Standard; whence those lines of Hugh 'Sotevagina', archdeacon of York:

> Soldiers, today shall fight or fall
> Strong in the Standard's right
> Its holy Sign, confessed by all,
> Shall fortify our might.

On the top of this pole they hung a silver pyx containing the Host, and the banner of St. Peter the apostle, and John of Beverley and Wilfrid of Ripon, confessors and bishops. In doing this, their hope was that our Lord Jesus Christ, by the efficacy of his Body, might be their leader in the contest. They also provided for their men a certain and conspicuous rallying-point, by which they might rejoin their comrades in the event of their being cut off.

Scarcely had they put themselves in battle array when tidings were brought that the king of Scots was close at hand with his whole force, ready and eager for the contest. The greater part of the knights, then dismounting, became foot-soldiers, a chosen body of whom, interspersed with archers, were arranged in the front rank. The others, with the exception of those who were to dispose and rally the forces, mustered with the barons in the centre, near and around the Standard, and they were guarded by the rest of the host, who closed in on all sides. The troop of cavalry and the horses of the knights were stationed at a little distance, lest they should take fright at the shouting and uproar of the Scots. In like manner, on the enemy's side, the king and almost all his followers were on foot, their horses being kept at a distance. In front of the battle were the Picts; in the centre, the king with his knights and English; and the rest of the barbarian host poured roaring around them.

As they advanced in this order to battle, the Standard with its banners became visible at no great distance; and at once the hearts of the king and his followers were overpowered by extreme terror and consternation; yet persisting in their wickedness, they pressed on to accomplish their evil ends. On the Octave of the Assumption of St. Mary, being Monday, 22 August,[1] between the first and third hours, the struggle

[1] Correct.

of this battle was begun and finished. For numberless Picts being slain immediately on the first attack, the rest, throwing down their arms, disgracefully fled. The plain was strewed with corpses; very many were taken prisoner; the king and all the others took to flight; and at length, of that immense army all were either slain, captured, or scattered as sheep without a shepherd. They fled like persons bereft of reason, away from their own country instead of towards it, thus entering the land of their enemies. But wherever they were discovered, they were put to death like sheep for the slaughter; and so, by the righteous judgment of God, those who had cruelly massacred multitudes, and left them unburied, giving them neither their country's nor a foreign rite of burial (leaving them a prey to dogs, birds, and wild beasts), were themselves either dismembered and torn to pieces or left to decay and rot in the open air. The king also, who, in the haughtiness of his mind and the power of his army, seemed but a little before to raise his head even to the stars of heaven, and who had threatened ruin to the whole of England, fled dishonoured and meanly attended, and barely escaped with his life. The power of divine vengeance was most plainly exhibited in this, that the army of the vanquished was incalculably greater than that of the number of the slain; for, as many affirm, of that army which came out of Scotland alone, more than ten thousand were missing; and in various localities of the Deirans, Bernicians, Northumbrians, and Cumbrians, many more perished after the fight than fell in the battle.

The army of the English thus, by God's help, with a small loss, easily obtained the victory, and took possession of the spoil, which was found in great abundance. Afterwards it was rapidly disbanded; and all returning to their homes, restored with joy and thanksgiving to the churches of the saints the banners which they had received. They had gone forth to this battle in their gayest array, and with costly splendour, as to a royal marriage. Some of the barons, with a portion of the army, marched to Eustace's town, called Malton, mentioned above; and, having destroyed the suburb, they lay siege to it, because, during the fight, the soldiers had sallied from it by orders of their lord, and set fire to many villages. A truce of eight days was arranged, after which the siege continued. Only the ground on which the above battle was fought was the possession of St. Cuthbert, the whole surrounding district being owned by others; and this occurred not by design of the combatants, but by the dispensation of Providence; for it may clearly be observed that divine justice would not long allow to go unpunished the iniquity that had been perpetrated in the territory of his holy and beloved confessor and bishop, but would speedily visit it with wonted vengeance.

12. William of Newburgh: "The History of England"

The *Historia Rerum Anglicarum* of William of Newburgh, of which the major part of Books II and III is here given, is one of the most important authorities for the reign of Henry II. For the period 1154–1170 it is indeed the most valuable general account that we possess, for other chroniclers who write of that period such as Ralph 'de Diceto', Gervase of Canterbury, and Roger of Howden are not strictly contemporary in their narratives at this point. From 1170 to 1189 William's *History* is less satisfactory as a general narrative, for it has numerous gaps and omissions. For this period the work of William of Newburgh, though still independent, must take second place to the *Gesta Regis Henrici Secundi*, which was formerly, though wrongly, ascribed to Benedict, abbot of Peterborough.

William of Newburgh, of whom some account is given above (pp. 99, 100), was born at Bridlington, Yorkshire, in December 1135 or 1136, and his life appears to have been spent entirely within the borders of Yorkshire and Durham. In his prefatory epistle he describes himself as "William, canon of Newburgh", an Augustinian priory founded by Roger 'de Mowbray' in 1145. According to Leland, who followed Bale and older scholars, his name was William Pettit or 'Parvus', but the latter appears to have been a nickname. There is some ground for thinking that his surname was Rufford or Rufforth, derived from a village of that name situated some five miles west of York. In all probability his whole life was spent as an inmate of the Augustinian house at Newburgh. He is reported to have died at the age of seventy-two in 1208, but there is no proof of this. It is, moreover, unlikely that he survived beyond the year 1198, since his *History* concludes with the early part of the reign of Richard I, on which it is very detailed. The work was undertaken at the request of Ernald, abbot of the neighbouring Cistercian monastery of Rievaulx, and is dedicated to him. It begins with the Norman Conquest and ends in 1197. From internal evidence much of it would appear to have been written soon after the events recorded; in any case the work, as it has come down to us, was begun before 1196 and completed soon after that date. It was apparently never revised.

Like most medieval chronicles, the *History* is in a sense a composite work, being based by the author on other chronicles, though the material incorporated from these sources has been recast. The first three chapters of Book I, for example, are based upon Simeon of Durham; for the whole of Stephen's reign William follows closely the *Historia Anglorum* of Henry of Huntingdon; the account of the feudal revolt of 1173–1174 is taken chiefly from Jordan Fantosme's metrical chronicle, while the history of the Third Crusade and of the events leading up to it is summarized from the *Itinerarium Regis* of Richard of London.

The merits of Newburgh as a historian have often been extolled; he has even been compared with Roger of Wendover and Matthew Paris of the succeeding century. A juster appreciation would be content with pointing to his general conscientiousness and his freedom from prejudice. So far as the material available to him permitted, he does on the whole present a balanced and accurate narrative of events. Moderation and impartiality are perhaps the most strongly marked characteristics of his work. His style is generally clear and readable, and his criticism often surprisingly objective. For instance, his attitude to Archbishop Thomas Becket is judicious, though his account of the causes of the fatal strife between king and prelate is not very well informed and leaves much unexplained. Moreover, in this as in other matters his work is interesting as a presentation of the point of view of a northern writer.

Nevertheless the work contains serious errors both of fact and judgment, due no doubt partly to the lack of a final revision. The proportions of the *History* are very unequal; in some sections, for example, the years between 1174 and 1183, and the last days and death of Henry II, the narrative is rather thin; in others, such as those dealing with the feudal revolt of 1173–1174, the Scottish campaign culminating in the battle of Alnwick and the capture of the king of Scots, the 'conquest' of Ireland (though here the author is dependent to a large extent on the writings of Gerald of Wales), and the continental campaigns of 1188, the narrative is expanded to considerable dimensions. A notable sketch of the character and policy of Henry II is given in Book III, chap. XXVI.

There is an excellent account of William of Newburgh by Professor Bruce Dickins in the *Transactions of the Yorkshire Dialect Society* (vol. v, pt. 35), and the article on him by Kate Norgate in the *Dictionary of National Biography* should also be consulted. The Latin text of his *History* is contained in *Chronicles and Memorials of the reigns of Stephen, Henry II and Richard I*, vols. I and II (ed. R. Howlett, Rolls Series, 1884). A translation into English by J. Stevenson is included in *Church Historians of England*, vol. IV, pt. ii.

Book II

CHAPTER I. OF THE BEGINNING OF THE REIGN OF HENRY II

In[1] the year of our Lord 1154, after the death of King Stephen, Henry, grandson of the elder Henry[2] by his daughter, the late empress,[3] came over from Normandy and took possession of his hereditary kingdom, being acclaimed by all and crowned and

[1] This is the beginning of 'Book II' of the *History* (ed. Howlett, *op. cit.*, vol. I, p. 101).
[2] Henry I. [3] Maud, widow of the emperor Henry V. (See Table 6.)

anointed king, while throughout England the people shouted "Long live the king". Indeed, so many evils had sprung up in the previous reign that after their unhappy experiences the people hoped for better things from the new monarch, especially when they saw he possessed remarkable prudence, constancy and zeal for justice, and at the very outset already manifested the likeness of a great prince. First he issued an edict against the mercenaries who under King Stephen had streamed into England from foreign parts, as much for the sake of booty as for the profession of arms, especially the Flemings, of whom a great host then infested the land. These he ordered to return to their own country and appointed a day after which to prolong their stay in England would be attended with certain danger. Terror-stricken by this edict, they slipped away in so short a time that they seemed to have vanished in a moment like phantoms, while many marvelled at the haste of their departure. Next he ordered the newly erected castles, which had not been standing in the days of his grandfather, to be razed to the ground, with the exception of a few sited in advantageous places, which he desired either to retain for himself or to be maintained in the hands of peaceful men for the defence of the realm.

In these early days, also, he paid due regard to public order and was at great pains to revive the vigour of the laws in England, which seemed under King Stephen to be dead and buried. Throughout the realm he appointed judges and legal officials to curb the audacity of wicked men and dispense justice to litigants according to the merits of their case; he himself, whether engaged in pleasure or in affairs of State, jealously watched over the royal interests. For as often as any of his judges acted either too leniently or too harshly and he was alarmed at the complaints of the men of the shire, he applied the remedy of a royal ordinance to amend effectively their negligence or excess.

Such were the first acts of the new monarch, which earned the praise and thanksgiving of peace-loving men but induced the murmuring and perturbation of the wicked. The ravening wolves were put to flight or turned into sheep, or, even if they were not really changed, they were made through fear of the law to dwell harmlessly with the sheep. Swords were beaten into ploughshares and spears into pruning-hooks,[1] and none now girded himself to battle, but all with God's favour tasted the joys of peace which they had previously longed for, whether they pursued their pleasures or were intent upon their business.

CHAPTER II. HOW KING HENRY II BROUGHT THE CROWN LANDS BACK TO THEIR FORMER STATE

As the king considered the royal revenue, which in the time of his grandfather had been abundant, was now deficient, because the crown lands had for the most part been alienated to numerous other lords through the weakness of King Stephen, he commanded that these lands should be surrendered wholly unimpaired by those who held them and restored to their former right and status. Those indeed who had hitherto been prominent in possession of royal towns and villages, produced for their security charters which they had either extorted from King Stephen or obtained in return for services rendered. But because the charters of an usurper ought by no means to prejudice the rights of the lawful king, they could in no wise secure themselves by

[1] Isaiah ii. 4.

these instruments. At first they were highly indignant, then, stricken with terror and grief, all unwillingly they made full restitution of the lands they had usurped and long held in possession as if by a firm title. And since throughout the shires of the kingdom all men yielded to the king's will, with one exception, of whom brief mention will be made later, the king journeyed to the regions beyond the Humber and summoned William, earl of Aumale,[1] who had been the real king there under Stephen, on a similar charge and with the same weight of authority as the others. After long hesitation and seething with indignation the earl with a troubled mind at last submitted to superior forces and delivered up in great vexation whatsoever crown lands he had retained in possession for several years, more particularly that famous and noble castle called Scarborough whose site we know to be as follows. . . .[2]

CHAPTER IV. OF THE SIEGE AND SURRENDER OF BRIDGNORTH AND HOW THE KING OF SCOTS RESTORED THE NORTHERN PARTS OF ENGLAND TO KING HENRY

So having achieved his purpose in Yorkshire the king returned to the mountainous parts of England,[3] where he met with resistance only from Hugh Mortimer, a man powerful and of noble birth, who had already for many years been in possession of the royal castle of Bridgnorth. When this man was ordered to rest content with his own lands and to surrender those which he occupied belonging to the crown, he obstinately refused to do so and prepared to resist with all his might. But subsequent events showed that his arrogance and indignation were greater than his courage. For the king rapidly gathered together an army and besieged Bridgnorth, and after attacking it in strength for some days he obtained its surrender and granted pardon to the earl, whose heart a little before had been like the heart of a lion, but who now became a humble suppliant. Moreover the king took occasion to summon the king of Scots,[4] who was treating as his own property the northern counties of England, namely Northumberland, Cumberland, and Westmorland, formerly acquired by David, king of Scots, in the name of the empress, Maud, and her heir, bidding him not to defraud the king of England of so large a part of his realm, for the king of England would not patiently suffer these lands to be dismembered, since justice demanded that what had been acquired in his name should be restored to him. Prudently calling to mind how the king of England had manifested the justice of his cause in this matter with great strength, the king of Scots restored the lands in question in their entirety, although he might have raised as an objection the oath sworn to his grandfather, David, when he received from him the insignia of knighthood. In return for this surrender he received from King Henry the earldom of Huntingdon which belonged to him of ancient right.[5] Matters having been thus settled, England enjoyed for a time peace and security throughout her borders. Moreover in all parts of his realm the king won the renown of a monarch who ruled over a wider empire than all who had hitherto reigned in England, for it extended from the far border of Scotland to the Pyrenees.

[1] One of Stephen's partisans who fought on his side in the battle of the Standard (1138) and was created earl of York. His earlier career is narrated in Book I, chap. XII, of William of Newburgh's *History*.

[2] Chap. III, omitted here, contains a detailed description of the castle.

[3] 1155.

[4] Malcolm IV, 1153–1165.

[5] The earldom came into the hands of the Scottish royal house through the marriage of David I with Matilda, daughter of Waltheof, the last Saxon earl, executed by William the Conqueror in 1076.

CHAPTER V. OF THE WAR AGAINST THE WELSH AND HOW THEY RETURNED TO THE KING'S OBEDIENCE

Not many days had passed when a dispute arose between the king and the Welsh, a restless and barbarous people, either because the king in his power made unaccustomed demands upon them, or because through unwonted arrogance they denied to so great a prince his wonted rights, trusting more than was justified in the protection of their well-wooded mountains and valleys; or even perhaps on account of their turbulence and their secret forays across the neighbouring English border. Gathering a huge force from all England, the king resolved to invade Wales in the region which seemed easiest of access.[1] The Welsh in their turn assembled their forces and stood guard on their frontiers; their light armed levies warily refrained from advancing into the plain to engage the mailed knights in pitched battle and they lay hidden in the woods keeping watch on the narrow passes. . . .

So, with the king entering enemy territory and contending hard against the difficult nature of the country, the campaign had an inauspicious opening. For part of the army, marching incautiously through forest and marshland, was caught in an ambush which the enemy had laid for it *en route* and placed in dire peril. There fell Eustace, son of John, a great man and very aged, and distinguished among the highest magnates of the realm for wealth and wisdom, together with Robert of Courcy, a man of equal rank and many another. But those, who escaped the danger, supposed that the king also had fallen with the rest, when in fact by God's grace he had already escaped and reached a place of safety. To the troops following up behind and hastening to reach the pass they reported the king's death, and induced no small part of the army to flee ingloriously, thunderstruck at the horror of the rumour; insomuch that Henry of Essex, a man of the highest distinction and the king's standard-bearer by hereditary right, lowered the royal standard, which should have served to rally the army's courage, and took to flight, proclaiming the king's death to all whom he met. For this offence he was afterwards publicly accused by a certain noble of dishonourable treason and by the severity of royal justice adjudged to trial by combat and vanquished by the said noble.[2] The king, however, of his mercy commuted the sentence of death and ordered him to become a monk at Reading, confiscating his very large patrimony to the Exchequer. But more of this anon.

The king therefore swiftly hastened towards his routed army and so gladdened it with the sight of his countenance that the confused ranks, recovering their senses and their strength, again drew together in order and learned to be more wary in future of hostile ambushes. When the king made preparations to invade the enemy from the sea also and had ordered a considerable fleet of ships to be made ready, the enemy sent envoys with overtures for peace and shortly afterwards their chieftains came to the king as suppliants. With the intent to curry favour with so great a prince, they delivered over to him certain border fortresses and offered him their oaths of homage; soon gentle peace smiled again through the clouds of war, the army returned home rejoicing and the king addressed himself to other affairs or to his pleasures.

[1] 1157.

[2] These events occurred in 1163.

CHAPTER VI. HOW NICHOLAS, AN ENGLISHMAN, WAS MADE POPE OF ROME[1]

In the first year of the reign of King Henry II died Pope Anastasius, the successor of Eugenius, after having been pope for one year only. He was succeeded by Nicholas, bishop of Albano, who, changing his name with his fortune, was called Adrian.[2] Of him it should be told how he was raised, as it were, from the dust to sit in the midst of princes and to occupy the throne of apostolic glory. By birth an Englishman, his father was a certain clerk of limited resources who, having abandoned the world together with his son of tender age, became a monk at St. Albans. But when the son grew to adolescence, being unable to attend school on account of his poverty, he hung about the monastery for the sake of the charity daily dispensed there. At which his father was ashamed and, rebuking his indolence with bitter taunts, drove him forth destitute of comfort in high indignation. Left to himself and impelled by dire necessity to try some venture, he went to France, being honourably ashamed to dig or beg in England. Faring but indifferently in France,[3] he travelled farther afield, wandering beyond the Rhone into the region called Provence. In that country there is a noble monastery of regular canons called after St. Rufus.[4] Being come to this place and finding occasion to tarry there, he was at pains to commend himself to the brethren by rendering them what services he could. And because he was attractive in person, pleasant of countenance, prudent in speech and diligent in obedience he gained the favour of all. Being entreated to take the habit of a canon-regular, he settled there for many years, vying with the foremost in the discipline of the rule. Being also of keen intelligence and fluent in speech, he made considerable progress in knowledge and eloquence by constant and diligent study. Hence it came to pass that on the death of the abbot the brethren unanimously and canonically chose him for their father. After he had presided over them for some time, the monks, repentant and indignant at having raised up a foreigner to rule over them, later became faithless and hostile towards him. Gradually their hatred became so violent that they now regarded with anger the man who had a little earlier found favour in their sight. At length they concerted and put foward charges against him and summoned him before the apostolic see. But when Eugenius of pious memory, who then occupied the papal chair, had heard the complaints of these rebellious sons against their father and taken note of the prudence and modesty with which the abbot defended himself, he set himself earnestly to the task of restoring peace between the two parties, reproaching them severely and urging them again and again to cease their fratricidal strife and to keep the unity of the spirit in the bond of peace.[5] Then he sent them back reconciled to their abbey. Malice,

[1] This chapter in William of Newburgh's *History* is the chief contemporary source for the early life of this remarkable Englishman, the other being the official life by the papal chamberlain, the English cardinal, Boso, who was also Adrian's secretary. The Latin text of this is printed in J. M. Watterich, *Pontificum Romanorum Vitae*, vol. II (Leipzig, 1862), pp. 323 *et seq.* Another source of later date is the *Gesta Abbatum Monasterii Sancti Albani* ascribed to Matthew Paris (ed. H. T. Riley, Rolls Series, pp. 112–113). Modern lives are those by A. H. Tarleton, *Nicholas Breakspear, Englishman and Pope* (London, 1896), and H. K. Mann, reprinted 1914, from the same author's *Lives of the Popes in the Middle Ages*, vol. IX, pp. 236–340. See also R. L. Poole, "The Early Lives of Robert Pullen and Nicholas Breakspeare", in *Essays in Mediaeval History presented to T. F. Tout* (1925), and G. W. Greenaway, *Arnold of Brescia* (Cambridge, 1931), pp. 147 *et seq.*

[2] 3 December 1154. The popes here mentioned are Anastasius IV, Eugenius III, and Adrian IV.

[3] Matthew Paris, *op. cit.*, p. 112, records that he first went to Paris to study; R. L. Poole, *op. cit.*, pp. 65–66, doubts the truth of this statement.

[4] At Avignon.

[5] Ephesians iv. 3.

however, that knows no quiet, could not long remain silent, and the storm broke out again with redoubled fury. Again an appeal was made to the same venerable pontiff, whose ears were still ringing with the complaints and murmurs of the brethren. Surveying each party with kindly and prudent eyes, he spake unto them: "I know, brethren, where the seat of Satan lies; I know what arouses this storm among you. Depart, choose for yourselves a father with whom you may, or rather will remain at peace; for this man shall be a burden to you no longer." So sending the monks away but retaining the abbot in the service of St. Peter, the pope consecrated him bishop of Albano, and not long after, having made proof of his industry, appointed him as a legate enjoying plenary powers among the wild and savage peoples of Denmark and Norway. Having executed his office among these barbarians with wisdom and efficiency, he returned to Rome in joy and gladness and was received with honour and in triumph by the pope and cardinals. Not many days later on the death of Anastasius, successor of Eugenius, being elected by an unanimous vote, he assumed the papacy, changing his name from Nicholas to Adrian. Not unmindful of his early training and chiefly in memory of his father, he honoured the church of the blessed martyr, Alban, with gifts and endowed it with lasting privileges.

CHAPTER VII. FOR WHAT REASON THE KING'S BROTHER, GEOFFREY, REBELLED AGAINST HIM AND HOW HE WAS RECONCILED

So then, the Welsh being pacified and subdued, all England dwelt in peace and security; nevertheless it was reported to the king that his brother, Geoffrey, had raised a revolt in his dominions overseas.[1] The cause of the dissension between the brothers was as follows. The illustrious count of Anjou[2] had begotten three sons, Henry, Geoffrey, and William, by the late empress, Maud. Since therefore both the paternal and the maternal inheritances would fall exclusively to Henry as the eldest son, the said count was unwilling that provision for the others should be wholly dependent upon their brother's favour, for he knew not what disposition Henry might show towards them. Accordingly, towards the end of his life he made a will bequeathing the county of Anjou to his second son [Geoffrey]. But, because the issue of events in England was at that time doubtful,[3] he argued: "When Henry obtains his mother's inheritance in full right, namely Normandy together with England, he may cede his entire paternal inheritance to his brother, Geoffrey. In the meantime then let Geoffrey be content with the three considerable castles of Chinon, Loudun, and Mirabeau."[4] And because Henry was by chance absent at that time but would soon return, the count adjured the bishops and magnates present not to give his body burial until his son had taken an oath that he would in no wise violate his father's will. At length, when the count was dead, the son arrived for the funeral ceremony and learnt of his father's solemn charge. For long he hesitated; at last, overborne by a general outcry against allowing his father's unburied corpse to suffer corruption to his own eternal and inexpiable disgrace, he gave way and took the oath demanded of him, though not without weeping. After the funeral the will was declared. For a time indeed

[1] 1156. [2] Geoffrey V. [3] Through the civil war raging between Stephen and Maud.
[4] All three castles are in Touraine.

Henry concealed his anger. But when he had come to his kingdom he took care, it is said, to inform the pope how he had been forced to swear he knew not what. And because oaths or vows extorted under pressure are not binding unless perchance they are ratified by a subsequent agreement, he easily obtained, so it is said, absolution from his oath. For the necessity of making an oath or a vow under pressure does not imply an equal need to fulfil what is sworn or vowed, but free will alone determines the necessity. Secure in this opinion he would not make satisfaction to his brother out of respect either to his father's will or for his own oath. At this his brother grew angry and having, as he supposed, fortified against all contingencies the three castles above named bequeathed him by his father, he created disorder in the adjacent provinces. The king, however, hastily gathering an army, besieged the castle of Chinon, so named because its strength was such that in its fortifications and defences nature and the labours of man seemed to vie with each other; in a short time he obtained its surrender. To his brother, now humbled and penitent, the king granted pardon and, having stripped him of his castles, in order to remove any occasion for arrogance, bestowed upon him a simple estate, from which he might derive the advantages of his labours. While he lay stricken with grief, first accusing his brother's harshness and then bewailing the cruelty of fortune, all unexpectedly a happier event occurred to cheer him. For the citizens of the famous city of Nantes, owning no definite lord nor any in whom they could find a congenial master, and being attracted by his diligence and vigour, chose him for their liege and undoubted lord and delivered to him the city with the adjacent province. But not long after he had performed this happy function an untimely death overtook him; thereupon the earl of Richmond,[1] who at that time virtually governed the greater part of Brittany, entered and took possession of the city as if it were his by right.[2] When the king heard this, he issued an edict commanding the revenues of the earldom of Richmond to be paid into the Exchequer and forthwith crossed from England into Normandy, claiming the city of Nantes by right of succession to his brother. So completely did he strike terror into the earl by the magnitude of his preparations that the earl, whose resistance had been broken, scarcely attempted even a lukewarm defence but yielded to the king's insistence by relinquishing the city. . . .

CHAPTER XII. HOW THE KINGS OF FRANCE AND ENGLAND WHO WERE AT LOGGERHEADS MADE PEACE

So, after his return from the expedition to Toulouse,[3] Henry II, king of England, enjoyed but a brief respite. For in the following year[4] which was the eighth of his reign, the hostility engendered between him and the king of France at the time of this expedition grew more serious for various reasons and at last flared up anew, disturbing the peace of the subject provinces with turbulent insurrections. At length vast armies were mobilized by both parties on the adjacent frontiers, camps were set up over against each other and both monarchs halted their troops, since it appeared dangerous to advance and dishonourable to retreat. Each monarch and his army were more ready to avoid battle than to engage in it, because of the doubtful issues of the arbitrament of

[1] Conan, a count of Brittany and earl of Richmond.
[2] 1158.
[3] Related in chap. X, omitted here.
[4] 1161.

war. So the men of peaceful disposition, taking advantage of this pause in operations to sow the seeds of peace, set to work conscientiously and cautiously, lest the pride and ambition of the two monarchs should involve the slaughter of innocent peoples. And because, as is so often said, negotiations for peace for the most part proceed better under cover of the shield of war, the kings were easily persuaded to adopt a course which at first they would not even deign to hear. Thus the two monarchs made peace and their subjects returned home. In the very same year Theobald, archbishop of Canterbury, died, and Thomas, the king's chancellor, succeeded him in the following year.[1]

CHAPTER XIII. OF THE COMING OF HERETICS INTO ENGLAND AND HOW THEY WERE EXTERMINATED

In those days there came to England certain exponents of error believed to be of the sect popularly known as Publicani.[2] Taking their origin without doubt in times past from an unknown founder in Gascony, they instilled the poison of their false teaching into many lands. Indeed so many are said to have been infected with this pest throughout the length and breadth of France, Spain, Italy, and Germany that, as the Psalmist saith,[3] they seemed to be multiplied beyond number. When the bishops of the churches and the lay rulers of the provinces act too leniently towards them, these wicked foxes come forth from their holes and, leading astray the simple folk by a show of piety, lay waste the vineyard of the Lord of hosts the more grievously for being unimpeded. But when the zeal of the faithful is kindled against them at the fire of the Lord, they slink back into their fox-holes and become less of a nuisance; still, however, they cease not to work injury by sprinkling their poison in secret. Rustics and ignorant boors and men dull of understanding, who have once drunk deep of this draught, are so imbued with it that they become intractable to all discipline; so it rarely happens that any of them are converted to the right way when they are discovered and dragged out of their lairs. Of a truth England has always been free from this and other pestilential heresies, although so many heresies have run riot in other parts of the world. This island, indeed, in the days when it was called Britain on account of the Britons, its original inhabitants, sent forth Pelagius, the future heresiarch in the East, and in course of time allowed his errors to come back into the country: to exterminate them the church of Gaul with pious foresight twice sent the blessed Germanus[4] hither. But when the English nation occupied this island after the Britons had been driven out, and it was no longer called Britain but England, the bane of heretical pravity never again burst forth, nor up to the reign of King Henry II was it introduced from elsewhere, for the purpose of propagation and expansion. Then indeed by God's favour the pest, which had already crept into the land, met with such opposition that it must fear to approach this island again.

There were, however, rather more than thirty persons, both men and women, who, dissimulating their errors, came hither as if in peace for the purpose of propagating

[1] Consecrated archbishop 3 June 1162. (See below, No. 121.)

[2] Albigenses or Cathari.

[3] Psalms iii. 1.

[4] St. Germanus of Auxerre (*c.* 378–448) visited Britain in 429 and 447 for the purpose of combating the Pelagian heresy. An account of his life and work by W. Bright is given in Murray's *Dictionary of Christian Biography and Literature* (London, 1911).

their noxious teaching, their leader being a certain Gerard, whom they all looked up to as teacher and master; for he alone among them had a smattering of learning, but the others were ignorant folk, unlettered and wholly uncultivated, peasants of German race and tongue. Sojourning for some time in England they only deceived one wretched woman with their lying whispers and, so it is said, having bewitched her with certain spells they joined her to their coterie. For they could not long lie hidden but were detected by certain men curious to explore to what strange sect they belonged, then seized and held in public custody. The king, however, being unwilling either to discharge them or to punish them without examination, ordered an episcopal synod to meet at Oxford. Here they were solemnly charged concerning their religion; the one among them who seemed literate, undertaking their common defence and speaking for them all, replied that they were Christians and reverenced the apostolic teaching. Interrogated successively concerning the articles of the Holy Faith, they answered rightly concerning the nature of Christ, the heavenly Physician; but concerning the saving remedies whereby he condescends to heal our human infirmity, that is, the Divine Sacraments, they answered perversely. Holy Baptism, the Eucharist, and Holy Matrimony they abhorred, and the Catholic unity sustained by these divine aids they wickedly dared to disparage. When they were pressed by texts taken from Holy Scripture, they answered they believed what they had been taught but were unwilling to dispute about their faith. Admonished that they should do penance and be united to the body of the Church, they spurned all sound advice. They laughed at the threats, with which in all piety they were confronted to induce them to recover their senses through fear; making wrongful use of the Lord's words: "Blessed are they which are persecuted for righteousness' sake, for their's is the kingdom of heaven."[1] Wherefore, lest the poison of heresy should be more widely dispersed, the bishops took the precaution of having the accused publicly proclaimed heretics and handed them over to the king to be subjected to corporal punishment. He commanded that the mark of heretical infamy should be branded upon their foreheads and in the sight of the people they should be beaten with rods and expelled from the city, sternly forbidding anyone to presume to offer them hospitality or supply any comfort. Sentence having been passed, they were led away rejoicing to suffer just punishment, their master marching in front with rapid strides and chanting, "Blessed are ye when men shall revile you".[2] To such an extent did this deceiver mislead the minds of those seduced by him. The woman, however, whom they had perverted in England, deserted them through fear of punishment and on confession of her error obtained pardon and reconciliation. Next this hateful band were branded upon their foreheads and suffered stern justice. To mark his primacy of office their chief endured the shame of being twice branded, first on his forehead and then on his chin. Then with their clothes cut off to the waist they were publicly flogged and with resounding blows driven forth from the city into the intolerable cold, for it was winter-time. None shewed the slightest pity on them and they perished miserably. This pious severity not only purged the realm of England of this pest which had lately crept into it, but also prevented further inroads through the terror stricken into the heretics. . . .

[1] Matthew v. 10. [2] Matthew v. 11.

CHAPTER XVI. OF THE KING'S WRATH AGAINST THE VENERABLE THOMAS, ARCHBISHOP OF CANTERBURY

Before the year of this council[1] closed the king's wrath was kindled against the venerable Thomas, archbishop of Canterbury, and this was the disgraceful origin of the many and great evils which surely followed.

This same Thomas was a Londoner by birth, a man of keen intelligence and ready eloquence, of comely countenance and fine manners. Second to none in his efficient discharge of business, he had been foremost in the service of Theobald, archbishop of Canterbury. From the latter he had received the archdeaconry of Canterbury at the time Roger[2] was promoted to the archbishopric of York. When Henry II inherited the kingdom on the death of Stephen, as related earlier, he did not suffer the king's business to be deprived of the services of so well qualified a man, but made him high chancellor of the realm. Distinguishing himself in this office he performed such signal service to the State, and won the king's affection and regard to such a degree, that he seemed to share the throne with him. Some years had elapsed in his secular service, when lo! he was enlisted in the service of the Church, and at the king's will he was elected archbishop of Canterbury.[3] Soon, reflecting piously and prudently how great was the responsibility of such an office, he was suddenly so changed both in dress and manners that some said, "This is the finger of God",[4] while others said, "This is a change wrought by the right hand of the Most High."[5] In the second year after his promotion he was present at the council of Tours, where it is related that, being unable to endure the pricks of conscience, he secretly resigned into the pope's hands the archbishopric, which he had received not honestly and canonically, as it were, but by the agency and at the hands of the king. The pope, approving his action, reimposed the burden of pastoral office upon him at the Church's hand and healed the over-scrupulous prelate of the wound of a troubled conscience.

After the bishops had returned from the council to their own sees, the royal power and the priesthood became at variance in England, and no small commotion arose concerning the prerogatives of the clerical order.[6] The judges informed the king, busy enough with the care of the realm and with ordering evildoers to be banished without fear or favour, that many offences against public order, namely theft, rapine, and homicide were very often committed by clerks, whom the vigorous arm of the secular jurisdiction could not reach. Finally it was declared in the king's hearing that more than a hundred murders had been committed by clerks within the borders of England during his reign. Deeply moved on this account the king in a violent passion enacted laws against evildoers among the clergy, wherein he certainly showed zeal for public justice, though his intemperate ardour exceeded proper bounds. Yet the blame for this lack of moderation on the king's part lies at the door of the bishops of our time, inasmuch as they were the cause of it. For the sacred canons enjoin that not only criminous clerks, that is, those charged with heinous crimes, but also those accused of petty offences should be degraded, and the English Church contains many thousands of such, like the unnumbered chaff among a few grains of corn, yet how many for

[1] The council of Tours (1163), treated by William of Newburgh in Book II, chaps. XIV and XV, omitted here.
[2] Roger of Pont l'Evêque. (See below, pp. 357–359.)
[3] 24 May 1162.
[4] Exodus viii. 19.
[5] Psalms lxxxvii. 10.
[6] See below, Nos. 123–129.

several years past have been deprived of office in England? The bishops indeed, while they pay more attention to defending the liberties and privileges of the clergy than to correcting and rooting out their vices, judge that they do God and the Church service if they protect against public discipline those criminous clerks, whom they either refuse or neglect to curb with the vigour of canonical censure, in accordance with the obligations of their office. Hence the clergy, who are called to inherit the Lord's portion and ought in deed and word to shine as lights in the world, like fixed stars in the firmament of heaven, have liberty and licence to do what they will with impunity, and neither reverence God, whose judgment seems to tarry, nor the men who have authority over them, especially since episcopal oversight is so slack, while the prerogative of holy orders exempts them from secular jurisdiction.

When therefore the king had enacted certain new laws against the chaff among our sacred order, that is to say, for the examination or punishment of criminous clerks in which, as has been said, he exceeded proper bounds; he believed that these laws would become effective if they were confirmed by the assent of the bishops. So, summoning them with the intention of obtaining their assent at all costs, he either persuaded them by flattery or terrified them by threats that with one exception they deemed it expedient to yield obedience to the royal will, and affixed their seals to the document embodying the new constitutions.[1] All but one, I say, for the archbishop of Canterbury was alone unbending and withstood every assault. Then the king's anger waxed more vehement against him in proportion as he seemed indebted to the royal patronage for what had been given and received. Wherefore the king became hostile to him and, seeking every possible occasion to attack him, demanded an account of all his former acts as chancellor of the realm.[2] The archbishop replied with undaunted freedom that, having fully discharged his secular office, he had been transferred to the service of the Church unconditionally by the very monarch he had served, and that old charges ought not to be brought up against him to suit the occasion rather than for the purpose of ascertaining the truth. As the causes of the king's fury were daily aggravated, on the day the archbishop was due to answer more fully to the allegations brought against him, he ordered the solemn office for St. Stephen's Day, namely "Princes did sit and speak against me and the ungodly have persecuted me",[3] to be duly chanted in his presence at the celebration of the Mass. Next he came to court carrying with his own hands the silver cross that was customarily borne before him, and when certain of the bishops present wished to undertake the office of carrying the cross in front of their metropolitan, he refused; neither would he allow any other to carry the cross in that public assembly, however often entreated. These events acted like tinder to the already blazing fury of the king. On the following night the archbishop secretly fled and crossed overseas, and being honourably received by the king of France and his magnates and bishops he abode with them for a time. But the king of England, raging beyond all reason and indulging his unbridled fury more than was becoming to a monarch, took an undignified and paltry revenge on all the archbishop's kinsfolk by banishing them from the soil of England.

Though indeed many persons, being readier in affection than sparing in prudence,

[1] Constitutions of Clarendon, 25 January 1164. (See below, No. 126.)
[2] At the council of Northampton (7 October 1164). (See below, No. 129, p. 726.)
[3] Psalms cxix. 23—the opening words of the Introit.

are wont to approve everything done by those they love and commend, yet I by no means consider that the actions of this venerable prelate are worthy of commendation, although they may have proceeded from laudable zeal, because no profit accrued therefrom, but on the contrary they only the more inflamed the king's anger, and from this so many evils afterwards arose: for the same reason that I cannot commend the blessed prince of the apostles in that, when he had already reached the summit of apostolic perfection, he compelled the Gentiles to become Jews after his own example; in which affair the teacher of the Gentiles declares him worthy of reprimand, although it is agreed that he acted thus from commendable piety. . . .

CHAPTER XVIII. OF THE SECOND EXPEDITION TO WALES AND THE CONQUEST OF BRITTANY

In the year in which Pope Alexander, as related earlier, returned from France to Apulia,[1] a fresh dispute arose between the king of England and the Welsh, which was a matter of great concern to both parties. For when this lawless and savage race, wantonly breaking their treaty and thus exposing to danger the hostages they had given in pledge of their covenant, created a disturbance on the English border, the king gathered together a huge army, both from his kingdom here and from his dominions overseas, and crossed the enemy's frontier in great strength. Although he was unable to penetrate farther on account of the insuperable difficulties of the country, yet he succeeded in checking their forays and so strictly confined their activities that they were forced to sue for peace.

Having thus withdrawn his army from Wales, the king was called away to other business, and crossed overseas to provide for the future advancement and endowment of his sons, a task to which he was favourably inclined. For, having begotten four sons of Eleanor, formerly queen of France, he meditated leaving to Henry, his first-born and successor, the kingdom of England, the duchy of Normandy, and the county of Anjou, while Richard was to be established in Aquitaine and Geoffrey in Brittany; his fourth and youngest son, John, he surnamed 'Lackland'. Having also three daughters by the same queen, he betrothed one to the king of Spain,[2] another to the duke of Saxony,[2] while the third, being not yet of an age to marry, he purposed in due time to bestow upon the king of Sicily.[2] As he meditated the establishment of his son in Brittany, he was already preparing the design by force and cunning, for he had not yet subdued the land to his authority. He had, however, two means of entry into that province already prepared for him, namely the city of Nantes and the castle of Dol. It happened also that Conan, earl of Richmond, who governed the greater part of Brittany, died leaving as his heir an only daughter by the sister of the king of Scots. Uniting this girl, still unripe for marriage, to his youthful son, he reduced the maiden's whole inheritance to his power. There were, however, in Brittany certain nobles of such great wealth and power that they would never condescend to submit to the governance of any man. As for many years past they had contended together in a hostile spirit through lust of power and impatience of subjection, this once flourishing region had become so devastated and impoverished that a barren wilderness now appeared where fruitful fields had stood. And when the weaker were oppressed by

[1] Pope Alexander III returned in 1165.

[2] See below, p. 381.

the stronger, they entreated help from the king of England and submitted to his authority of their own free will. To this party the king brought prompt and generous succour and succeeded in subduing the men of power and substance, who were hitherto deemed unconquerable by reason of the greatness of their resources and the almost inaccessible nature of their strongholds. Thus in a short time he acquired the whole of Brittany, the warmongers were either expelled or tamed, and the king so regulated and pacified the land throughout its borders that its people dwelt in peace and the wasted lands little by little returned to fertility.

CHAPTER XIX. ON THE DEATH OF MALCOLM, THE MOST PIOUS KING OF SCOTS

About this time[1] Malcolm, the most Christian king of Scots, whom we have pertinently mentioned in the preceding book,[2] departed this life at the summons of Christ. Far from losing his kingdom he rather changed it for one in which he would consort with the angels. For heavenly angels carried away from earth this man of angelic purity, for he was like an earthly angel of whom the world was not worthy. Even in his tender years he was a youth of singular gravity, and afterwards, amid the pride and luxury of empire, a man of transcendent and unexampled piety; so he was translated from his virgin body to the presence of the Lamb, the Virgin's Son, there to follow him whithersoever he should go. Indeed he was snatched away by a premature death[3] lest the evil of the times should sully his singular innocence and purity, when so many opportunities and incentives might urge a youthful monarch to a contrary disposition. Nevertheless, amid his sublime virtues his noble soul did not lack some trifling blemishes incurred through regal luxury, but these he suffered patiently rather than took pleasure in. Wherefore the visitation of heaven dealt with him persuasively rather than forcibly, chastising him in fatherly fashion and refining his impurities. For some years before his death he fell into a state of weakness and, in addition to his other troubles, suffered from such excruciating pains in his extremities, that is, in his head and feet, that it seemed that any penitent sinner would assuredly be purified by such correction. Hence it is manifest that this child of God experienced the severity of paternal chastisement, not merely for the purpose of purification but also for testing and increasing his virtues. So he slept with his fathers and was buried at a place called Dunfermline in Scotland, renowned for the burial of its kings.

His brother, William,[4] succeeded him. He was a man better equipped, so it seemed, to deal with worldly affairs, but not destined to be more fortunate than his brother in the government of his kingdom. It was his aim not merely to use but to enjoy the things of this world, which his brother would use simply as a means to piety, and so in a praiseworthy manner. Though he endeavoured to surpass his brother's standards in temporal dignity, yet he was never able to match his fame even in worldly happiness. For a long time he shunned the benefits of marriage, whether to raise up issue or as a remedy for incontinence, whereas his brother preferred the higher state of pious and holy virginity. At length, however, moved by saner counsels he took to wife the daughter of a certain foreign noble[5] and afterwards not only amended his way of life but also reigned more successfully. . . .

[1] 1165. [2] Book I, chap. XXV. [3] He died on 9 December 1165.
[4] William, surnamed 'the Lion', 1165–1214. (See Table 16.)
[5] Ermengarde, daughter of the count of Beaumont.

CHAPTER XXII. OF THE LONG-STANDING VACANCY IN THE CHURCH OF LINCOLN

In the fourteenth year of the reign of Henry II, being the year of our Lord, 1167, Robert, bishop of Lincoln,[1] the successor of Alexander, died. The revenues of the see were paid into the Exchequer, and the church was bereft of pastoral care for nearly seventeen years, that is, from the fourteenth year of this king's reign until his thirtieth; insomuch that it was mildly credited that no one would be appointed bishop there in future. More especially was this the case by reason of the prophecy of a certain lay brother at Thame, who consistently proclaimed that on the death of the bishop previously named there would be no future bishop of Lincoln. For this man, so it is said, was endowed with the spirit of prophecy both on account of the merit of his saintly life and because of the fulfilment of many similar predictions. In consequence of this many people believed that he would not be deceived in this matter either. But after a short time faith in this prophecy appeared to waver, when Geoffrey, the king's natural son, was elected bishop of the aforesaid church out of compliment to the king. But when, content with the ample revenue of the see and being ignorant how to feed the Lord's flock though skilled in shearing them, he deferred the hour of canonical consecration in order to indulge his pleasures the more freely and so occupied the church of Lincoln a long time under the title of bishop-elect, credence in the words of the aforesaid brother again revived in many minds. After a short space this was brought home more forcibly to many people, when the king, moved to repentance at having thus through family affection promoted a young man of fastidious tastes and scarcely suitable for so exalted an office, again sequestrated the revenues of the see to the Exchequer after his son had at last been prudently persuaded to surrender the right and title of bishop-elect. Nevertheless the falsity of this prophet's predictions and conjectures was subsequently manifested, as will be related in its proper place. . . .

CHAPTER XXIV. OF THE QUARREL AND RECONCILIATION BETWEEN THE KINGS OF FRANCE AND ENGLAND

In the sixteenth year of the reign of Henry II this monarch and the king of France, who had for some time been at enmity together, once again made peace through the mediation of men of peaceable disposition.[2] This was the cause of their discord.

While King Stephen was formerly occupied with tumults in England, the count of Anjou invaded Normandy and took possession of it, with the exception of Gisors and two other castles as it were dependent on it, which yielded to the power of the king of France. In process of time Henry II, king of England, son of the said count, not being prepared to suffer this curtailment of his rights to his Norman inheritance, realized the necessity of employing diplomacy rather than force in this affair. At length through the agency of that diligent man, Thomas, his chancellor, he so arranged matters with the king of France that the latter's daughter by the daughter of the king

[1] Robert 'de Chesney' died 26 January 1167. The see remained vacant until 1173, when Geoffrey, son of Henry II, was elected. He resigned the see in January 1182, never having been consecrated. Subsequently (July 1189) he was appointed archbishop of York, but not consecrated till August 1191.

[2] 6 January 1169.

of Spain, whom he had married subsequently to his divorce from Eleanor,[1] should be betrothed to Henry, the eldest son of the king of England, and the fortresses mentioned above should be ceded as her dowry. These, however, were to be guarded by the Templars, as it were in sequestration, until the two children, who could not yet contract a marriage, being still under age, should in due time be able to live together. In the meantime the king of England was to have the guardianship of both. But after some years had passed, King Henry, impatient of further delay, celebrated the marriage between the two children prematurely[2] and received the castles from the Templars. Whereupon the French waxing highly indignant and accusing the king of duplicity and the Templars of treachery, the affair led to disputes and war. But having learnt by frequent experiments that violence could effect nothing against the power of the king of England, and their anger gradually cooling, they at last agreed that on certain conditions peace should be made. Accordingly a treaty was concluded, not however a lasting peace but a truce, as afterwards appeared. To be sure the two kings mentioned above were never long at peace together, their respective peoples having grown accustomed to suffering for the follies committed through the arrogance of their monarchs.

CHAPTER XXV. OF THE CORONATION OF 'HENRY III' AND THE MARTYRDOM OF ST. THOMAS

In the year of our Lord 1170, being the seventeenth of the reign of Henry II, the king caused his son, Henry, while yet of tender age, to be solemnly anointed and crowned king at London at the hands of Roger, archbishop of York.[3] For the venerable Thomas, archbishop of Canterbury, was still an exile in France, the king being not yet appeased, although the pope and the king of France had been at pains to effect a reconciliation between them. When he had received news of this, the archbishop, being jealous for the rights of his church, speedily informed the pope, by whose favour and countenance he was supported, alleging that the coronation had been performed to the prejudice of himself and his see. So he obtained letters of stern reprimand for the purpose of constraining both the archbishop of York, who had performed this office in another's province, and the bishops, who had consented to it by their presence. King Henry indeed remained in England but a short time after his son's coronation and then crossed overseas. There, urged by the frequent admonitions of the pope and the importunate entreaties of the illustrious king of France that he would at least condescend to be reconciled to the exiled prelate after seven long years of banishment, he at length yielded. So a solemn reconciliation was effected between them,[4] which was the more desirable and acceptable since it was late in coming. While therefore the king remained abroad, the archbishop returned to his diocese with the permission and favour of the king.[5] But unknown to the king he carried with him letters obtained from the pope and directed against the archbishop of York and the other bishops who had participated in that most unfortunate coronation. These letters were destined to be destructive of the concord recently established and provocative of yet greater discord.

[1] Louis VII of France married as his second wife Constance, daughter of Alfonso VII, king of Castile, by whom he had Margaret, the princess mentioned in the text.

[2] 2 November 1160.

[3] 14 June 1170.

[4] 22 July 1170. (See below, No. 146.)

[5] 1 December 1170. (See below, Nos. 148, 149.)

These letters decreeing the suspension of the bishops having been previously dispatched to England, the archbishop himself followed, burning with zeal for justice, but whether fully informed of the situation, God knows. For it is not permitted to one of my lowly station to judge hastily the actions of so great a man. I think nevertheless that the blessed Pope Gregory,[1] in view of the partial and still recent reconciliation with the king and in consideration of the time and the terms of the agreement, would have acted with greater leniency and have deemed it proper to have ignored those matters which might be tolerated without danger to the Christian Faith, in accordance with the words of the prophet: "He that is prudent shall keep silence at such time, for it is an evil time."[2] Therefore I neither judge the actions of the venerable prelate at this juncture to be worthy of commendation nor do I presume to censure them; but this I say, that if through some slight lack of moderation in his zeal this holy man went to excess in this affair, this was purged away in the fire of his sacred passion, which is known to have followed. Hence, although men of piety are to be loved and praised by us who recognize our marked inferiority to them, yet we should by no means cherish and commend them for the things in which they have shown their human frailty but rather for those in which we should imitate them without scruple. For who can say that they should be imitated in all their actions, when the Apostle James, saith, "In many things we all stumble"?[3] Wherefore they should be commended not for all their actions, but with prudence and caution that God's prerogative may be kept inviolate, in whose praises indeed none can be too active, however much he strive.

So then, on account of the irregularity mentioned above—would that it had been ignored at the time!—the bishops were suspended at the instance of the venerable Thomas from the exercise of all episcopal functions by the authority of the apostolic see, and the king, exasperated by the complaints of certain among them, waxed furious and indignant beyond measure, and keeping too little restraint upon his fiery and ungovernable temper poured forth wild words from the abundance of a distracted mind. Upon which four of his magnates standing by, men of noble birth and renowned in arms, were incensed to commit a villainous crime out of zeal for the rights of their temporal lord. Quitting the royal presence forthwith and crossing the seas with as much speed as if they were hastening to a solemn banquet, goaded on with the fury they had engendered, they arrived at Canterbury on the fifth day after Christmas, where they found the venerable archbishop occupied in the celebration of that holy festival with religious joy. Having forced their way into his presence just as he had dined and was seated with certain honourable clerics, and omitting any salutation but holding out the terror of the king's name, they commanded rather than entreated or admonished him to relax forthwith the suspension of the bishops who had complied with the will of the king, to whose contempt and shame this act redounded. When the archbishop replied that the sentence of a higher power could not be annulled by a lower one, and that it was not his business to pardon persons suspended not by him but by the pope, they raised their voices high and uttered threatening speeches. Undismayed by such threats uttered by men in a loud and frenzied fury, the archbishop

[1] Pope Gregory the Great, 590–604.
[2] Amos v. 13.
[3] James iii. 2.

answered with singular freedom and assurance. Wherefore being yet more incensed against him, they hastily retired and flew to arms – for at their first entry they were unarmed – preparing themselves with loud clamour and indignation for the perpetration of a most atrocious crime. By his friends the venerable archbishop was persuaded to avoid the madness of these inhuman monsters by retiring into the church. But as he would not readily agree, being prepared to brave every danger, at the moment when his enemies broke in and pressed upon him he was dragged by the friendly violence of his companions to the protective bulwark of the church.[1] The monks were solemnly chanting vespers to the praise of Almighty God as he entered the sacred temple of Christ, himself shortly destined to become an evening sacrifice. For thither the satellites of Satan pursued him, neither showing reverence as Christians to his sacred order nor respect for the sanctity of the place or the season, but assaulting the high priest as he stood in prayer before the holy altar, these most wicked Christians slew him with the sword with the utmost cruelty during the very festival of the Nativity of Christ.[2] When the deed was done, they withdrew as if in triumph and departed with unholy joy. But recollecting that their action might possibly prove displeasing to the king on whose behalf they had shown such zeal, they retreated to the northern parts of England and there remained for a time, until they could more fully ascertain the disposition manifested by their monarch towards them.

Moreover, the frequent miracles which ensued manifested how precious in the sight of the Lord was the death of the blessed prelate, and how great the atrocity of the crime committed against him by reason of the time, the place and the person. Indeed the tidings of so great an outrage were rapidly spread abroad through almost all the regions of the Latin world, sullying the reputation of the illustrious king of England and so tarnishing his fair fame among the monarchs of Christendom that he was assailed with almost universal execration and deemed a suitable object for public odium, since it could scarcely be credited that the deed had been perpetrated against his will and without his command. Having learned what had been done by his followers and realizing the blot cast upon his fame and the almost indelible stain on his character, his grief was such that, so it is related, for several days he tasted nothing. Moreover he reflected that, whether he pardoned the murderers or not, men would be only too ready to think evil of him. For if he should spare these villainous wretches, he would appear boldly to countenance so great a crime by the weight of his authority; while if he should punish them for what they were alleged to have done at his express command, he would on every side be termed a scoundrel. For this reason he deemed it better to pardon them and so, looking equally to his own good name and their safety, he ordered them to present themselves before the apostolic see for the purpose of undergoing solemn penance. Accordingly this was done. Pricked in conscience they set out for Rome and were directed by the lord pope to do penance at Jerusalem where, it is related, they all ended their lives after passing several years diligently making reparation according to the measure appointed them; but of this hereafter.

While almost everyone laid the death of the blessed martyr at the king's door, and the French nobles more especially, who had always been jealous of his good fortune,

[1] See below, No. 152. [2] 29 December 1170.

were inciting the holy see against him as the true and undoubted author of this cruel outrage, the king sent envoys to Rome[1] in order to soften by submissive entreaty the displeasure raging against him. Arriving at Rome, where all men joined in execration of the king of England, they were admitted only with difficulty.[2] Consistently maintaining, however, that this dreadful outrage had been committed neither at the command nor with the consent of their master, they at length obtained this request that legates *a latere* vested with plenary powers should be sent by the pope to France.

After careful investigation and inquiry into the matter they were either to allow the king to clear his name or to punish him with ecclesiastical censure if he were found guilty; and so it was done. For two cardinals, namely the venerable Albert, who afterwards presided over the Roman Church[3] and Theodinus were dispatched from the holy see and came to France. A solemn synod[4] of ecclesiastics and lay nobles was held within the territory of the king of England at which was undertaken the formal absolution of the said monarch, who appeared there in all humility, firmly protesting that the deed, which had sullied his fame, had taken place against his wishes and orders, and that never before had he grieved so much over anything. Indeed he did not deny that the murderers had possibly taken occasion to dare such a frenzied act from some words he had incautiously let fall at a time when, having received tidings of the suspension of the bishops, he was filled with anger beyond measure and spoke all too imprudently. "And on this account," said he, "I do not shrink from the Church's discipline; decide what you will, I will accept it in all piety and fulfil your decree." This said, casting off his clothes he submitted himself naked to ecclesiastical discipline after the manner of public penitents. Deeply affected at this spectacle of humility in so great a prince the cardinals shed tears for very joy, many of the bystanders weeping with them and praising God, and so the council was dissolved, the king's conscience being quietened and his character partially vindicated. Richard, prior of Dover, thereupon succeeded the blessed Thomas in the cathedral church of Canterbury.

CHAPTER XXVI. OF THE SUBJUGATION OF THE IRISH BY THE ENGLISH[5]

In those days under pretext of military service the English secretly crept into the island of Ireland, intending afterwards as their forces increased in strength to invade it and to occupy no small part thereof once it had been subdued by their arms.

Ireland, so we have heard, ranks second in importance to Britain among the islands, but, as the venerable Bede observes,[6] far excels it in the serenity and salubrity of its climate. It abounds wonderfully in pasturage and fisheries, and the soil would be fertile enough if it did not lack the industry of a skilful cultivator; but its people are

[1] According to the *Gesta Regis Henrici Secundi*, vol. I, p. 19, the embassy consisted of the archbishop of Rouen, the bishop of Evreux, the bishop of Worcester and Richard Barre.

[2] See text of their letter to Henry II, dated 28 March 1171, given in *Gesta Regis Henrici Secundi*, vol. I, pp. 20–22.

[3] As Pope Gregory VIII. He reigned only two months, October to December 1187.

[4] Synod of Avranches, held 28 September 1172. (See below, No. 156.)

[5] The chief contemporary narratives of the conquest of Ireland in the reign of Henry II are the two works of Gerald of Wales, *Topographia Hibernica* and *Expugnatio Hibernica* in *Giraldi Cambrensis Opera*, ed. J. F. Dimock, Rolls Series, vol. v, pp. 205–461.

[6] Bede, *Historia Ecclesiastica*, Book I, chap. I. The lines which immediately follow in this paragraph are a paraphrase of Bede's remarks.

uncivilized and barbarous in their habits, almost wholly ignorant of law and order, slothful in agriculture and in consequence live more on milk than on bread. Moreover nature has conferred upon this island above all other lands this singular favour and gift, namely that it produces no venomous animal or noxious reptile; for, should any such be carried thither from elsewhere, a sure and speedy death awaits it with the first breath drawn from Irish air. Again, whatever is brought thence is proven to avail as an antidote against poison.

It is indeed a singular fact with regard to this island that while Britain, equally an island in the ocean and severed from it by only a short distance, has experienced so many disasters in war, has so often fallen a prey to foreign nations and been subjected to alien domination, having been subjugated and occupied first by the Romans, next by the Germans, then by the Danes and finally by the Normans, yet Ireland, being difficult of access to the Romans–though they had dominion even over the Orkney Isles–has been rarely and only half-heartedly attacked by any nation in war, has never been conquered and subdued, never made subject to a foreign power[1] until the year of our Lord 1171, which was the eighteenth of the reign of Henry II, king of England. For the assertion of the Britons that the island was made subject in obedience to Arthur is a fable like the other stories which they have wantonly invented concerning him out of pure lust of lying. But it is easy to explain how the Irish by falling under the dominion of the king of England have put an end to their long, uninterrupted and, as it were, inborn freedom, since the occurrence is within recent memory. In fine, the reason for the changed condition of this nation and land is as follows.

Ireland, being divided into several kingdoms after the ancient usage of Britain and accustomed to own numerous kings, was perpetually torn asunder by their feuds and, in proportion as she was free from foreign war, from time to time suffered miserably at the hands of her sons who tore her vitals in pieces as they rushed to mutual slaughter. It chanced that a certain king[2] of that land was grievously beset by the attacks of the neighbouring princes and through lack of strength was on the point of experiencing the dire cruelty of his enemies. Whereupon, having taken counsel, he hastily sent his son into England[3] for the purpose of securing armed assistance from a band of vigorous young men attracted thither by the hope of a substantial reward. Sustained by their efforts, at first he began to breathe again, then he gained strength and finally succeeded in triumphing over his enemies. Nor did he suffer his allies to depart but bestowed upon them such liberal rewards that, forgetful of their own people and their fathers' house, they chose to make their dwelling there. But when the fiercest peoples of all Ireland began to rage and storm against the said king for having admitted the English into the island, the latter, fearful because of the smallness of their numbers, summoned from England such as were oppressed by poverty or greedy of gain and by this means gradually increased their strength. And because they had as yet no leader and were as sheep without a shepherd, they invited over from England a powerful noble called Earl Richard[4] to become their commander. Being a man of

[1] It is not perhaps altogether surprising that the chronicler omits to mention the bull *Laudabiliter*, alleged to have been granted by Pope Adrian IV in 1155, empowering Henry II to exercise authority in Ireland. (See below, No. 159.) [2] Dermot, king of Leinster. [3] This is an error; Dermot himself came.
[4] Richard of Clare, earl of Pembroke, 'Strongbow'.

spirit and extravagant beyond his family means, and having already squandered his ample revenues and almost exhausted his patrimony, being also harassed by his creditors and in consequence more ready for greater enterprises, he readily accepted the invitation. Accordingly, having drawn to himself in his own domains a numerous and hardy band of young warriors,[1] he made ready a fleet to transport him to Ireland. But when he was on the point of setting sail, there came messengers from the king who on their master's orders forbade his crossing.[2] Nevertheless he would not stay behind out of regard for any property he possessed in England, but incontinently crossed over to Ireland and delighted his expectant allies by his long-awaited arrival. Forthwith uniting forces he deemed it expedient to venture some offensive action in order to strike terror into the barbarians for the future. With daring impetuosity he threw his forces against Dublin,[3] a maritime city and the capital of all Ireland, and by reason of its celebrated harbour the rival of our own London in commerce and sea-borne trade. Having bravely and speedily assaulted and captured the city, he compelled many who dwelt farther afield to enter into a treaty with him through fear of his power. By building fortresses on suitable sites and extending his dominion by degrees, he persistently harassed the neighbouring provinces which strove to preserve their ancient liberty. Next, affecting to show some small regard for this barbarous people by entering into kinship with them, he took to wife the daughter of the king, his ally, and received a considerable portion of the kingdom as her dowry.[4]

When these auspicious successes had become known to the king of England, he was moved to anger against the earl for having attempted so great an enterprise, not only without consulting him but even in defiance of him, and also because the earl had taken to himself the glory of so noble a conquest, which ought rather to have been ascribed to the king as his superior. Accordingly he confiscated to the Treasury all the earl's family estates in England and, lest any reinforcements should be sent to Ireland from England, he forbade all communication by sea. Threatening even sterner measures against him, he forced the earl, now almost a king, to return speedily to his good graces. In consequence he extorted from him that most famous city of Dublin and the greater part of the lands he had acquired but, leaving him with the residue and restoring to him unimpaired his estates in England, he bade him rest content. These things accomplished, this same earl, who shortly before had prodigally squandered his patrimony and possessed hardly anything save his title to nobility, now became renowned for his wealth both in England and Ireland, and passed his days in great prosperity, until some years later he was carried off by a premature death.[5] By this event was plainly manifest the vanity of human fortune, which in this man's case so quickly vanished, and the fallacy with which he deceived himself when his possessions suddenly eluded his grasp. From his Irish booty, which he had greatly coveted and for which he had so strenuously toiled, even at the peril of his safety,

[1] 200 knights and upwards of 1,000 foot-soldiers.

[2] Dermot had paid homage to Henry II for his kingdom of Leinster in 1169; hence Henry was bound by feudal contract to safeguard the territories of his vassal. For political reasons he was not desirous of increasing the power of a great magnate like the earl of Pembroke.

[3] August 1170.

[4] Large estates in Leinster with the reversion of the whole kingdom on Dermot's death.

[5] He died in April 1176.

he carried nothing away with him at his departure but, bequeathing his hard-earned and perilous acquisitions to his ungrateful heirs, he left by his fall a salutary lesson to many.

Shortly afterwards[1] the king of England crossed over to Ireland with a large army and, through the terror his coming inspired, subdued without bloodshed the kings of the island who had hitherto been in rebellion against him. Having settled affairs in accordance with his will he returned to England the same year[2] in joy and safety.

CHAPTER XXVII. HOW "HENRY III" REBELLED AGAINST HIS FATHER AND STIRRED UP THE KING OF FRANCE AND OTHERS AGAINST HIM

In the year of our Lord 1173, being the twentieth of the reign of King Henry II, when the king had returned from Ireland to England[3] and shortly afterwards crossed over from England to Normandy, a foul and detestable strife arose between him and his son, 'Henry III', whom two years earlier, as related above,[4] he had caused to be solemnly crowned and anointed king. When this prince grew to manhood he desired to obtain the reality of kingship as well as the oath of allegiance and title of the same, and at the least to reign jointly with his father. Certain persons indeed whispered in his ear that he ought now by rights to reign alone, for at his coronation his father's reign had, as it were, ceased. Moreover he was highly indignant because his father had but sparingly supplied him with money to meet the expenses of his royal state. So his anger was kindled against his father and he secretly fled to his father-in-law, the king of France, an act calculated to arouse his father's ill-will.[5] Being graciously received by the French king, not so much because he was his son-in-law as because he had deserted his father, he put his whole trust in his counsel. Thus encouraged and incited against his father by the virulent exhortations of the French, he was not in the least deterred from violating the law of nature by the example of the accursed Absalom.

Having discovered his son's treachery and knowing whither he had fled, his father sent to the king of France certain eminent men who in pacific terms demanded the return of his son by paternal right, and promised that if anything should appear to require amendment in respect of his son, it should speedily be rectified with the advice of the French king. At these words the king of France asked, "Who is it that sends such a message to me?" They replied, "The king of England." "It is false," he answered, "behold! the king of England is here present, and he sends no message to me through you. But even if you still call king his father who was formerly king of England, know ye that he, as king, is dead. And though he may still act as king, this shall be speedily remedied, for he resigned his kingdom to his son, as all the world bears witness." Thus foiled in their design the envoys returned to their lord. Soon after, the younger Henry, devising evil against his father from every side by the advice of the French king, went secretly into Aquitaine where his two youthful brothers, Richard and

[1] October 1171.

[2] Actually Henry returned in April 1172. See *Gesta Regis Henrici Secundi*, vol. I, p. 30.

[3] April 1172, not 1173, as here implied: the king sailed for Normandy in May 1172. See R. W. Eyton, *Court, Household and Itinerary of King Henry II*, p. 167.

[4] Chap. XXV. (See above, p. 336.)

[5] 8 March 1173.

Geoffrey, were living with their mother, and with her connivance, so it is said, he incited them to join him and brought them back with him to France. For their father had granted in possession for his lifetime Aquitaine to the one and Brittany to the other. For this reason the younger Henry was taught by the French to believe that the men of Aquitaine might be more easily won over to his side through Richard, and the Bretons similarly through Geoffrey. He also allied himself with the count of Flanders,[1] his father's cousin, a man of great power, glorying beyond measure in the confidence reposed in him by the numerous and warlike people whom he governed. This man was also enticed by large promises with the help of the French king. At the same time many powerful and noble magnates, both in England and beyond the seas, either impelled by sheer hatred, which up to then they had concealed, or seduced by vain and empty promises, proceeded to desert the father for the son and to make every preparation for war.[2] Among them were the earl of Leicester,[3] the earl of Chester, Hugh Bigot,[4] Ralph of Fougères[5] and several others formidable from the greatness of their wealth and the strength of their fortresses. Many others, less confident of their resources and power, showed a hostile attitude by retiring into France in order to remain neutral. To these was added a more ferocious enemy, the king of Scots,[6] who was on the point of dispatching across the English border his savage and cruel people, prepared to spare neither sex nor age. Thus, while so many and great magnates deserted the elder king and drove all men against him as with one heart and mind, there were yet a few who loyally and firmly adhered to him, but the rest wavered around him in uncertainty, fearing in all conscience to be swallowed up in the victory of the younger monarch. Then at long last the elder king realized, for so it was commonly reported, how unadvisedly, nay rather, how foolishly he had acted by prematurely appointing his successor; but he had little expected that those who hankered after a new régime would so eagerly follow his son. Uneasy therefore at the troubled state of affairs, while enemies from within and without were pressing upon him, he placed little trust in those who appeared to take his side but yet remained inactive in order to curry favour with his son. Accordingly he summoned to his aid mercenary troops from Brabant called Rutians, in view of the fact that he had an abundant hoard of money in the royal Treasury which in such a crisis ought not to be used sparingly.

CHAPTER XXVIII. WHAT BEFELL AT AUMALE, AT CHÂTEAUNEUF AND VERNEUIL

In the month of June,[7] when kings are wont to go to war, the neighbouring princes, having assembled their forces from every quarter, advanced in a hostile manner against the king of England under the pretext that they were only jealous for the rights of the son against his father. Indeed nothing could be more absurd than this jealousy, for in reality they engaged in this affair either to satisfy a private grudge like the king of France, or to secure advantage for themselves like the count of Flanders. Actually the king of England was ill-prepared to withstand the assault of so many enemies on

[1] Philip, count of Flanders, prepared to sustain the rebels by raising a large fleet to invade England.
[2] See the long list of the younger Henry's partisans given in *Gesta Regis Henrici Secundi*, vol. I, pp. 45 *et seq.*
[3] Robert of Beaumont, the third earl.
[4] Earl of Norfolk.
[5] Castellan of a fortress on the Norman frontier of Brittany.
[6] William the Lion. (See below, pp. 348–350, 374–376.)
[7] June 1173.

account of the disturbances among his subjects in England, by which he was extremely hard pressed. When therefore by reason of his military inferiority he could not oppose his assailants in the field, he prudently took care to fortify and garrison the border fortresses. So the king of France, having encircled with his army the town of Verneuil, which lacked nothing needful to withstand a lengthy siege, resolved not to proceed farther until the town was taken or surrendered. But the count of Flanders, attacking with his forces from the side of Flanders, laid siege to Aumale, which had been strongly garrisoned, albeit in vain, since the count of Aumale, the lord of that town, like many others, wavered in his allegiance to the elder king. It was certainly believed that he had a secret understanding with the count of Flanders because the town had hardly been assaulted before it was quickly taken, and when he was made prisoner by the count of Flanders, together with all the troops sent hither by the king to serve as a garrison, he surrendered his other castles as well. Heartened by this auspicious opening to the campaign the Flemish army advanced to greater objectives and attacked in strength the royal fortress called Châteauneuf, assaulting it with engines of war for several days. When at last it surrendered, the count of Flanders nevertheless took no pleasure therein. For his brother, Matthew, count of Boulogne, whom he was pleased to regard as his future successor, since he never had or hoped to have issue by his own wife, was wounded in the knee by an arrow during the siege of that town. His wound growing worse, he took to his bed and died after a very few days under medical treatment.[1] His death grieved his brother so much that he soon afterwards abandoned the expedition and returned in sorrow to his own land, reproaching himself for this untoward event and imputing it to the fact that he had ventured for the sake of a worthless son to engage in hostilities against his royal cousin, who had never done him any injury but on the contrary had frequently showered benefits upon him. On this being brought to the knowledge of King Henry, he reckoned that he was now for the time being delivered from one-half of his military anxieties and soon gained greater confidence against the remaining half. So, having concentrated his mercenary forces, together with as many others as felt bound not to desert him in his hour of extreme need, he sent a message to the king of France, who had already wasted the greater part of the summer in besieging Verneuil, to this effect: that he should either raise the siege or shrink not from fighting a decisive battle on a certain day. At first the French, who are by nature both fierce and arrogant, especially since they appeared to be superior in numbers and equipment, scoffed at his message, calculating that he would by no means dare to act upon it. But when they realized that he was approaching them undaunted with his army in battle order, then for the first time they began to suspect he would attempt to force a decision. Hastily summoning his magnates their king proceeded to hold a council of war on the spot. A bishop and an abbot were sent to meet the king of England and to ascertain from his own mouth whether he came intending to fight; in the meantime as a temporary measure the king of France drew up his army in battle array. And lo! the envoys as they journeyed met the king of England fully armed and with a small bodyguard proceeding some furlongs ahead of his army; he showed complete confidence in himself and was issuing orders, concerning I know not

[1] July 1173.

what. When they informed him that the king of France wished to receive an assurance concerning the battle, with a fierce countenance and in a terrible voice he replied, "Go, tell your king that I am here in person." And when they had returned in haste and reported the ferocity and stubborn resolution of the monarch who was even then rapidly drawing nigh, the king of France and his magnates took counsel together and determined for the present to retire and avoid a battle, though they would fight in defence of the inheritance of their fathers. So striking camp[1] they retreated into France, with their formidable forces still fully armed and drawn up in ranks, lest they should appear to be in flight. In this manner the men, who shortly before seemed like lions in the ferocity of their disposition and the roar of their boastful voices, were suddenly discovered running away and flying like hares. The king of England, however, remained content with the inglorious flight of his proud and arrogant enemies and was unwilling to press them harder or to pursue their retreat; but turning his army aside to pillage the enemy's camp, he entered the town in joyful solemnity to congratulate his men there on the valour they had displayed. An abundance of corn, wine and victuals was discovered in the camp together with a variety of equipment which their adversaries in their hasty flight were unable to carry away with them.

CHAPTER XXIX. OF THOSE WHO WERE MADE PRISONER AT DOL

Although the king's extremely powerful enemies abroad, namely the king of France and the count of Flanders, had been thus by God's will repulsed, his enemies at home by no means remained quiet. Many of these latter met together by arrangement, and uniting forces obtained possession of the town of Dol which indeed belongs by right to Brittany, though it is included within the boundaries of Normandy. At this news the Brabançons in the king's service speedily arrived before the town and joined battle with the rebels, upon which a multitude of them took refuge in the town. Soon afterwards the town itself was taken[2] and they were forced to retire within the narrow limits of a single fort. While they were thus besieged, the news was carried with the utmost speed to the king then stationed at Rouen. Oblivious of food and sleep, by relays of post-horses he covered a large tract of country and arrived so quickly that he seemed to have flown. While he was conducting an assault upon the fort the besieged host, unable to endure their straitened circumstances, begged for mercy. Accordingly the king agreed to spare them in life and limb, but when the fort had surrendered he consigned to prison the nobles captured therein. There the earl of Chester and Ralph of Fougères, with about a hundred other magnates, fell by God's judgment into the hands of the king whom they had pursued with the most cruel hatred. Nevertheless they were treated by him much more mercifully than they deserved, although for a time they remained in chains. But the two mentioned above, who seemed the more distinguished among the prisoners, obtained their release by satisfying the king that they would from henceforth maintain their loyalty. The magnanimity of this great monarch in this affair towards these most disloyal traitors and his most bitter enemies is beyond doubt justly worthy of admiration and applause.

[1] 9 August 1173. [2] 20 August 1173.

CHAPTER XXX. OF THE SIEGE OF LEICESTER, THE WAR AGAINST THE KING OF SCOTS AND THE CAPTURE OF THE EARL OF LEICESTER

While these things were being enacted by the king in person or by those about him in his dominions overseas, similar events were taking place in England. For when the earl of Leicester, who had been the first to desert the king, had seduced many others by his bad example, upon receipt of the king's mandate Richard of Lucé, who then governed England,[1] hastily gathered an army and besieged Leicester.[2] The town was taken and burnt, but he forbore to attack the castle because he was called away on more urgent business and forced to retire. Moreover the king of Scots, having perceived how hard pressed the king of England was in Normandy, crossed the English border with an enormous force of his barbarous and bloodthirsty people and laid siege to the city of Carlisle, devastating the adjacent county with rapine and slaughter. But having discovered that a large army from the north of England was advancing against him, he raised the siege and after frightful devastation in the county of Northumberland retreated to his own land before the approach of our barons. The latter, however, advanced with their forces across the river Tweed, which marks the boundary between the realms of England and Scotland; meeting no resistance they retaliated against the enemy's country. Soon they were recalled to southern England by hasty messengers, though not before the ferocity of the hostile king had prudently been tamed by the conclusion of a temporary truce; for by cunning dissimulation our commanders had up till then kept hidden from him the news they had received.

The earl of Leicester with a hostile fleet from Flanders had landed on the east coast of England and, being welcomed by his fellow-conspirator, Hugh Bigot,[3] a powerful and crafty man, he remained there some time with the army he had brought. Presently, with the guidance and co-operation of this same Hugh, the army advanced upon the city of Norwich[4] and broke into it with very little trouble, since it was without a garrison and stricken with sudden panic. After pillaging its wealth the army returned to its camp laden with spoils. At Hugh's instigation the earl of Leicester in like manner turned against Dunwich, a celebrated town on the sea-coast noted for various kinds of merchandise, intending to take it by assault; but being dismayed at the courage of the inhabitants, who were prepared as one man to withstand the enemy's attack, he judged that he dared venture nothing against them and retreated barren of success. But Hugh, having made as much use of this army as he desired, then intimated to the earl that he ought to conduct the foreign troops he had brought over to England into lands and castles pertaining to his own jurisdiction. Nevertheless the earl hesitated long, because he could not traverse hostile territory to reach Leicester without great peril from the enemy who was said to be watching his march. At last, trusting in the number and

[1] Justiciar of England, 1154–1179.

[2] July 1173.

[3] Earl of Norfolk. (See above, p. 343.)

[4] William of Newburgh seems to have confused the invasion of East Anglia in 1173 with that which took place in 1174; see *Gesta Regis Henrici Secundi*, vol. I, p. 68, Ralph 'de Diceto', *op. cit.*, vol. I, p. 381. The siege of Norwich took place during the latter campaign, and was therefore not in the sequence of events leading up to the battle of Fornham. (See below, p. 347, n. I.)

valour of his allies – for he had about eighty picked horsemen and four or five thousand valiant infantry – and reckoning also that no one would oppose him on the way, because he had many friends among those who appeared to favour the king's side, he set out boldly with all his forces, taking with him his wife and a certain French noble called Hugh 'de Châteauneuf'. But the barons of the royal party were at Bury St. Edmunds watching his movements with a considerable force, and when they had come up with him, they led forward their army drawn up in battle order against his troops. The latter, unable to wheel either to the right or to the left, made a virtue of necessity and boldly pushed on with all speed using their cavalry as a screen. And so began a desperate battle,[1] the king's troops fighting for glory and the rebels for safety; but victory fell to the royal army. The earl was taken captive with his wife, a woman of masculine disposition, and the aforesaid Hugh 'de Châteauneuf', together with almost all the cavalry, but nearly the whole host of infantry was annihilated. The more illustrious prisoners were sent to the king in Normandy while the rest were dealt with in accordance with his wishes.

CHAPTER XXXI. OF THE DEFECTION OF DAVID OF SCOTLAND AND CERTAIN OTHERS FROM THE KING[2]

This unfilial madness of the son against his father raged for nearly two years; the more notable events of the first year have already been described in the preceding narrative. For a short time indeed during the winter there was a cessation of hostilities on the Continent, but in England this was not the case. For the troops occupying the fortresses of the earl of Leicester, after they had remained quiet for some time on account of the mishap which had overtaken their lord, again became restive as if they burned to avenge him. Having been joined by a multitude of miscreants they proceeded to harass the neighbouring counties by their forays; and so that they might act with greater confidence under a prince of high renown, they chose as their leader and captain, David, earl of Huntingdon,[3] brother of the king of Scots, who was, as it were, rampaging about successfully and advancing to higher fortune. In addition 'Earl Ferrars' and a noble called Roger of Mowbray now openly declared their long concealed intention and joined the other rebels. Scarcely restraining, even during the sacred season of Lent, the impulse of their pent-up fury, after the solemnities of Eastertide they broke out in wicked and daring adventures. Nor did the younger king at that time cease to entice those English magnates, who outwardly appeared to cling to his father, by promises and secret letters or even to move them by threats in order to win them over by any means whatsoever to his own party. For this cause there are said to have been only a few nobles then left in England who were not wavering in their allegiance to the king and would not be ready to desert him for a time, unless some check should speedily be placed on their intentions.

[1] Battle of Fornham, fought on 17 October 1173. The site lies on the road between Thetford and Bury St. Edmunds.

[2] 1174.

[3] Grandson of David I and third son of Henry, earl of Northumberland and Huntingdon. (See above, p. 324.)

CHAPTER XXXII. OF THE KING'S COMING INTO ENGLAND AND WHAT THE SCOTS DID THERE

In the second year therefore from the beginning of this strife the war against the elder king of England was again renewed with all their might by his most powerful enemies, namely the king of France, the count of Flanders, and the king of Scots. The count of Flanders, already forgetful of his brother's death and, so it is said, ambitious to secure possession of the English county called Kent, for which he had indeed recently done homage to the younger king, was preparing a fleet to transport his forces to England together with the young Henry. But the king of France was also engaged in preparing an army drawn from all quarters for the invasion of Normandy. When these preparations became known, the elder king of England chose rather to imperil his dominions overseas than the safety of his English realm which, however, he prudently thought should be fortified. For he foresaw that, while he was absent abroad and, as it were, non-existent, no one would offer any opposition to the man who was expected to be his successor. So, forestalling the movements of his enemies, he was speedily conveyed to England together with a considerable force of cavalry and one troop of Brabançons.

In the meantime[1] the king of Scots with an immense number of his own barbarous people and no small force of mercenary cavalry and infantry hired from Flanders, crossed the English border[2] and obtained possession of two royal fortresses in Westmorland named Burgh and Appleby which he found ungarrisoned. Departing thence he determined once again to attack the city of Carlisle, but the frightened citizens having given an undertaking that they would surrender the city to him on a certain day[3] unless in the meantime sufficient reinforcements were sent them by the king of England, he diverted his army to attack a certain fortress on the river Tyne called Prudhoe. There the aforementioned Roger of Mowbray came to him begging for help. For after two of his fortresses had been valiantly stormed and captured by Geoffrey, the natural son of the king of England and at that time bishop-elect of Lincoln, he had difficulty in maintaining possession of a third called Thirsk. This Roger indeed had a long time ago given his eldest son as a hostage to the king of Scots who was then meditating an incursion into Yorkshire, and had engaged to assist him in everything. In return he had received from the king a pledge that he should never be deprived of help in any necessity whatsoever that might arise. Indeed, after the king of Scots had laboured in vain for some days at Prudhoe with considerable loss to his own men, hearing that the men of Yorkshire were raised in arms against him, he crossed the Tyne and invaded Northumberland. Everything was consumed by the Scots, to whom no food was too filthy to eat, even that fit only for dogs, and while they sought out their prey it was the delight of that inhuman nation, more savage than wild beasts, to cut the throats of old men, to slaughter little children, to disembowel women and to commit other atrocities of a kind too horrible to mention. So, while this army of monstrous bandits was let loose upon this wretched province and the

[1] April 1174.

[2] See the very detailed account of the Scottish campaign of 1174 in Jordan Fantosme, *Chronique de la guerre entre les Anglois et les Ecossois en 1173 et 1174* in *Chronicles and Memorials of the reigns of Stephen, Henry II and Richard I*, vol. III, pp. 300–362.

[3] At Michaelmas.

barbarians were revelling in their inhumanity, the king of Scots himself, attended and guarded by a more honourable and civilized body of soldiery, wasted his time in keeping watch over a very strong castle called Alnwick, lest perchance a band of soldiers should break out from it and so disturb the robbers who were pillaging all round them.

CHAPTER XXXIII. OF THE CAPTURE OF THE KING OF SCOTS

While these events were taking place on the northern frontier of England, the magnates on the king's side in the county of York, highly indignant that the Scots should have attacked the English border, came together at Newcastle-on-Tyne with a strong body of cavalry.[1] Indeed the occasion was so urgent that they had no time to collect their infantry. They arrived there on a Friday, worn out with their long and arduous journey. While they were there consulting together as to what should be done, the more prudent among them argued that much had already been accomplished, since the king of Scots upon learning of their arrival had beat a hasty retreat; that this ought to suffice for the time being, considering the numerical inferiority of their forces, and that it was neither safe for themselves nor profitable to the king of England to advance any farther, lest perchance they should seem to be exposing their scanty numbers to be devoured like bread by the immense host of barbarians. They further pointed out that they had no more than four hundred horse while the enemy's army was estimated at more than eight thousand armed men. To this the more impetuous replied that these malignant foes ought to be attacked by every possible means and that they ought not to despair of victory, which beyond a doubt would fall to the side of justice. Ultimately the opinion of the latter prevailed, because God so willed that the issue should be ascribed more to divine providence than to human power or prudence. The valiant warriors, among whom the leaders were Robert of Estouteville, Rannulf 'de Glanville', Bernard 'de Balliol' and William 'de Vesci',[2] somewhat refreshed by a night's sleep, set out early in the morning hastening onwards at such a speed that they appeared to be propelled by some force of nature. For they covered twenty-four miles in five hours, a thing which seemed scarcely possible for men burdened with the weight of arms. While on the march they are said to have been enveloped in so dense a fog that they hardly knew where they were going. Then the more cautious among them, using as a pretext the peril of the journey, argued that certain danger awaited them unless they immediately turned back. In reply to this said Bernard 'de Balliol', a man of nobility and courage, "Let him who wills retreat, but I will go forward even though none should follow me, for I will not brand myself with perpetual infamy." While they were thus marching onwards, suddenly the mist cleared and they saw in front of them the castle of Alnwick, which they rejoiced to think would afford them a safe retreat if they were hard pressed by the enemy. And lo! the king of Scots with a squadron of sixty horsemen or more was on guard in the open fields not far off, as if in complete security and fearing nothing less than an incursion of our men, while the hosts of the barbarians together with part of the cavalry, were widely dispersed for purposes of plunder. At

[1] July 1174. [2] Sheriff of Northumberland.

sight of our men he at first thought that they were some of his own returning from pillage. But soon, having carefully observed our banners, he at last understood that our men had dared what he could not have suspected they would have attempted. Nevertheless he was by no means affrighted; indeed, being encompassed by an army so vast, though less concentrated, he did not even condescend to doubt that our scanty force would easily be encircled and engulfed by the host which lay scattered around him. Fiercely clashing his arms on the spot and encouraging his men by word and example, he cried, "Now will be made manifest which of us knows the art of war." Hurling himself foremost on the enemy while the others followed after, he was soon intercepted by our men and being thrown from his horse, which was killed under him, he was taken prisoner[1] together with nearly all his troops of horsemen. For those who could have escaped by flight, disdained to do so when they saw that their king was taken, but gave themselves up of their own free will into the hands of their enemies in order to be made prisoners with him. Certain Scottish nobles also, who chanced at that time to be away, though not far off, on hearing what had befallen, returned presently at full gallop and threw themselves rather than fell into the hands of their enemies, deeming it honourable to share their lord's peril. But Roger of Mowbray, who was present when the king was taken, escaped and took refuge in Scotland. In the evening our magnates brought back their royal prisoner with joy to Newcastle, whence they had set out that very morning, and caused him to be kept in the strictest custody at Richmond with the intention of sending him at a convenient opportunity to their illustrious lord, the king of England. This battle was happily won by God's favour on Saturday, 13 July, in the year of our Lord 1174, and the tidings were soon carried far and wide and received with gladness throughout all the shires of England, the church bells ringing in joyful celebration.

CHAPTER XXXIV. WHAT BEFELL THE ARMY AND LAND OF SCOTLAND AFTER THE CAPTURE OF ITS KING

The king of Scots having been thus delivered into the hands of his enemies, the manifest vengeance of God did not allow his bloodstained army to depart unpunished. When the capture of their king was known for certain, the barbarians were at first thunderstruck and desisted from plunder, but soon after, as if goaded by the Furies, they turned against each other the sword–now drunk with innocent blood–which they had drawn against their foes. For they had with them in their army a great number of Englishmen, since the towns and boroughs of Scotland are known to be inhabited by men of our nation. So, seizing this opportunity, the Scots disclosed their inborn hatred against them, which they had previously concealed through fear of the king, and slew as many as they lighted upon, while those able to escape took refuge in the royal fortresses.

There were also present in that army two brothers named Gilbert and Uctred,[2] lords of the province of Galloway, with a numerous troop of their own people. They

[1] According to Jordan Fantosme he surrendered to Rannulf 'de Glanville'.

[2] Uctred was a kinsman of Henry II, being the son of an illegitimate daughter of Henry I. This may explain the jealousy between the two brothers and the subsequent history of events; see *Gesta Regis Henrici Secundi*, vol. I, p. 80.

were sons of Fergus, formerly chieftain of that province, and succeeded their father at his death, the king of Scots, who is the liege lord of that land, dividing the inheritance between them. But Gilbert, the elder son, aggrieved at being deprived of the whole of his paternal rights, had always hated his brother in his heart, although for a time fear of the king restrained the impulse of the anger he had conceived. But when the king was taken prisoner, being delivered from this fear Gilbert[1] presently laid hands upon his unsuspecting brother and murdered him, not by a straightforward death but with excruciating tortures in order to gratify his insatiable hatred. Forthwith he invaded his brother's territory and wrought considerable carnage there, barbarian raging horribly against barbarian. The brother, however, who had been so impiously slain, left a son, Roland by name, a brave and energetic youth who with the help of his father's friends resisted his uncle's furious attacks with all his might. Thus the whole realm of Scotland was thrown into dire confusion by God's just dispensation, who meted out to the wicked the measure which they themselves had dealt to others; that is to say, those who a little before had disturbed the quiet of an innocent people and thirsted for the blood of Englishmen, by a most admirable decree suffered retribution at each other's hands.

CHAPTER XXXV. OF THE MEMORABLE HUMILIATION OF THE KING OF ENGLAND AND OF ITS CONSEQUENCES

King Henry II had by this time returned from Normandy,[2] prepared to hurl himself in person against his son who was expected to arrive there with the Flemish forces. But calling to mind how greatly he had sinned against the church of Canterbury, he hastened thither as soon as he had landed, and prayed before the tomb of the blessed Archbishop Thomas, shedding copious tears. Having entered the chapter of the monks he prostrated himself on the ground and most humbly entreated their pardon; at his own urgent petition this man who stood so high in rank was beaten with rods by all the brethren in turn.[3] On the following night it was said in a dream to a certain venerable old monk of this same church, "Hast thou not seen today this great miracle of a king's humility? Know that the issue of these events will shortly declare how greatly his royal humility has pleased the King of kings." I learnt this indeed from a most reverend and upright man, Roger, abbot of Byland, who in the relation of it declared that he had positively heard the story from a trustworthy person, who by chance was living in Kent at that very time. Verily he who touches the mountains and they smoke,[4] soon showed how much he valued the devotion of that smoking mountain. For on that same day, and so it is said at that very hour, in which the mountain gave forth smoke at Canterbury, God of his goodness overthrew the king's most mighty enemy, the king of Scots, on the extreme border of England;[5] as though the reward of his pious action might not seem to have followed the action itself but rather to have accompanied it, and no one should be suffered to remain in doubt concerning this point.

Departing from Canterbury, the king hastened to London and having sent the

[1] According to the *Gesta Regis Henrica Secundi* (*loc. cit.*, *ante*) Malcolm, the son of Gilbert, shared responsibility for the crime, giving the actual order for the execution.

[2] 8 July 1174. [3] 12 July 1174. (See below, No. 158.) [4] Psalms cxliv. 5. [5] See above, pp. 349, 350.

army on before him against Hugh Bigot, he himself made a short stay there for blood-letting. And lo! about the middle of the night a very swift courier sent by Rannulf 'de Glanville' came knocking at the outer door of the king's lodging.[1] Rebuked by the porter and the guards and bidden to keep quiet, he knocked yet more loudly, announcing that he brought good tidings, which it was meet the king should hear that very night. His importunate insistence at last prevailed, especially as they hoped he was the bearer of a good report. Once admitted within the precincts he similarly overcame the opposition of the royal chamberlains and was introduced into the royal bed-chamber, where he went boldly up to the king's couch and roused him from sleep. The king awakening cried, "Who art thou?" Whereupon he answered, "I am the manservant of Rannulf 'de Glanville', your faithful liegeman, by whom I have been sent to your highness, and I come as the bearer of good tidings." "Our Rannulf, is he well?" asked the king. "He is well, my lord," replied the youth, "and behold, he holds your enemy, the king of Scots, captive in chains at Richmond." The king, verily astonished at the news, said, "Speak on." But he merely repeated the message. "Hast thou no letter for me?" asked the king. Forthwith he produced a sealed letter containing a narrative of the order of events. The king, instantly inspecting it and leaping from his bed deeply moved, gave thanks, with tears of devotion, to him who alone doeth wondrous things. Then, hastily summoning the attendants of his household, he made them partakers of his joy. Moreover in the morning came other couriers confirming the good news, but only the one who had first arrived received a reward. These good tidings were immediately published abroad and joyfully acclaimed by the people, while the bells rang throughout all London.

CHAPTER XXXVI. OF THE SIEGE OF ROUEN AND THE CRAFTY ASSAULT OF THE BESIEGING ARMY

In the meantime the king of France with a formidable army invaded Normandy from the east, that is to say, where it seemed to lie open to attack, through the castles having been taken by the count of Flanders. The said king advanced upon Rouen, the capital of that province, and laid siege to it. Rouen is one of the most famous cities of Europe, situated on the great river Seine, by which the trade of many regions is carried to that city. By that same river and the spur of the mountains lying opposite, it is so well protected that hardly a third part of it can be effectively blockaded by a single army. Moreover the younger King Henry and the count of Flanders, supported by vast forces, were watching for an opportunity of crossing the Channel with the fleet they had made ready in the port of Boulogne, from which there is the shortest crossing to England. Upon learning that the elder King Henry was already stationed in England, doubtless prepared to withstand their attack with fierce resistance, they deemed it would by no means be safe for them to cross the Channel thither. So they changed their plan, thus rendering ineffectual the whole equipment of the fleet they had already prepared. Reflecting how great an undertaking the siege of Rouen would be and what spoils might be gained from the storming of the city, they transported their mighty and terrible forces to that area, and vastly increased the strength of the

[1] The narrative here follows closely the account of Jordan Fantosme. (See below, No. 13.)

besieging army. In truth so great an army had not been seen in Europe for very many years past, yet on account of the difficult approaches to the city it could scarcely blockade a third of it.

By a bridge across the river there was both free access to the city from the country and likewise egress from the city to the country, and all manner of necessities were transported thereby into the city in abundance, while the hostile army close at hand looked on with envy. And perhaps (to quote from the poet) "Sicilian tyrants have found no greater torment than envy."[1] When brave and high-spirited men beheld this going on quite close to them almost every day, without their having the power to prevent it, they bore it with considerable vexation. The engines being ready and in position a full-scale attack was launched upon the city. For this purpose the army was divided into three, and the natural day was also split up into eight-hour periods, so that men might relieve each other in turns, that is, those who had been refreshed taking the place of those who were weary. Thus the assault was continuously maintained in order that the defenders of the walls should not be given the slightest breathing-space either by day or night. But this provision was made in vain; for the citizens, counteracting this design by a similar art and precaution, also divided their numbers into three, and by a careful disposition of their forces repelled a continuous succession of hostile attacks. Thus they provided an effective remedy against the intolerable labour and weariness by which, it was believed, they would be overpowered. After the struggle had continued unabated for many days and neither side had in any degree relaxed their efforts, came the feast-day of St. Laurence.[2] Out of reverence to that distinguished martyr, whom he was wont to venerate with singular devotion, the king of France ordered that a respite for the city on that day should be solemnly proclaimed. This favour the citizens gratefully accepted and enjoyed the all too brief interval of peace in the most joyful manner. Young men and maidens, old men and children, as much in joyful celebration of the feast-day as to annoy the enemy, chanted with melodious voices within the city, while outside on the banks of the river a troop of soldiers engaged in a tournament in full view of the enemy. Then, so it is related, the count of Flanders came to the king and said, "Behold! the city, on which we have already expended so much labour, lies open for us to take, while those within are singing and dancing and those without disport themselves in unconcerned security. Let the army therefore silently take up arms, and let the scaling ladders be quickly placed against the wall, and we shall be in possession of the city before the men disporting themselves outside the town for our annoyance are able to regain it." "Far be it from me", replied the king, "to sully my royal honour with so foul a stain: for thou knowest I have granted a respite to the city for this day out of reverence to the most blessed Laurence." Whereupon all the magnates present rebuked his mildness with bold familiarity, quoting, "Who asks whether it be deceit or valour in an enemy?"[3] and at last he acquiesced. So, not by the sound of the trumpet nor by the voice of a herald, but by the whispers of the commanders, alone in their tents, was the army summoned to the storming of the city.

It chanced, however, by the will of God that certain clerks were at that same hour

[1] Horace, *Epist.* I, 2. [2] 10 August. [3] Virgil, *Æneid*, II, 390.

passing the time in some way or other in the lofty tower of a certain church within the city, from which it was the custom to give a signal to the citizens to man the wall against hostile attacks by ringing a very ancient but wonderfully sonorous bell. One of these clerks, happening to look out of the window and casting his eyes over the besieging army encamped in tents, was at first struck by the unusual silence pervading the camp, as though some mystery were afoot. Presently, peering cautiously from his lofty vantage-point, he observed the enemy's secret preparations. And when he had pointed out the fact to his companions, they immediately gave the well-known signal to the city by ringing Ruvell, for so that bell was called. At the sound of the bell both sides made haste to gather their forces. The besieging army, already prepared for battle, rushed forward from the camp and advanced against the city wall with scaling ladders, while the citizens, stirred to action by the unexpected peril, seized their arms and with ardent spirit and excited movements endeavoured to repel the assailants. Those also, who were exercising themselves outside the city, came running up with surprising speed. Already the enemy had succeeded in scaling the wall by the ladders placed against it, already their shouts of triumph were heard on the summit; when lo! they were strongly counter-attacked and hurled back by the citizens. A most bitter hand-to-hand struggle took place on the wall, weapons and bodies came into violent contact and much blood was shed on either side. At length those who had proudly ascended the wall were thrust headlong down again. Nightfall put an end to the battle, and the army which had violated the truce retired in confusion to its camp after suffering far greater losses than it had inflicted. The king of France threw the blame upon the count of Flanders, but the stain of such foul treachery is to be attached more to the person of the king himself. In conclusion, rest assured that from that day forward the besieged acted with greater confidence and the besiegers with less hope and more negligence.

CHAPTER XXXVII. HOW THE KING RESTORED PEACE TO ENGLAND AND RELIEVED ROUEN

In the meantime,[1] King Henry the elder, remaining in England, summoned the governors of the castles belonging to the earl of Leicester, whom he had brought with him bound from Normandy, and admonished them for their lord's safety to deliver up these castles from which they made war upon the adjacent shires. When they begged permission to confer with their lord, it was denied them; whereupon they stated they would only obey the king's will if their lord were definitely released. The king replied, "I will not bargain with you in this matter, but it will be well for you to do what I wish." And, so it is related, laying his hands on the sacred relics he swore an oath, saying, "So may God and these sacred relics be my helper, but the earl of Leicester shall taste nothing until you comply with my wishes in respect of his castles: but go, depart with all speed." Then, perceiving that their lord was threatened with sure and swift destruction if they maintained further resistance, they forthwith agreed to deliver up the fortresses.[2] Earl David, however, who had been their leader, left the castle of Huntingdon, which soon afterwards surrendered to the king, and fled in fear

[1] July 1174. [2] 31 July 1174.

to Scotland. Hugh Bigot and 'Earl Ferrars', terrified at the king's successes, made a treaty of their own accord, offering security for keeping the peace and maintaining their loyalty.

Affairs having been thus settled in England by God's favour in accordance with the king's will, he speedily crossed the seas with a mighty army,[1] taking with him the king of Scots, who had shortly before been handed over to him, the earl of Leicester and the other distinguished prisoners. While throughout Normandy the people rejoiced exceedingly at his speedy and happy return, he entered Rouen in great pomp and in full view of the enemy. Grievously alarmed at the news of the capture of the king of Scots received by messenger a few days earlier, the enemy were stunned at the king's unexpected and triumphant return from England. Nevertheless, confident in the strength of their countless host, they persisted in the siege. Then the king secretly and by night sent out a troop of Welshmen brought over from England, in order that under cover of a dark wood they might observe from convenient vantage-points by what road supplies were conveyed to this great army. For the men of this race are nimble and skilled in woodcraft. Seizing their opportunity the Welsh burst forth out of the woods, attacked the convoy and, after putting to flight the horsemen by whom it was drawn and destroying all the equipment and provisions with huge slaughter of men and beasts, retired again into the woods. Whereupon it was noised abroad that the woods were full of Welshmen, and the hostile army suffered hunger for two whole days in consequence of the interception of the convoy. In these circumstances the siege was abandoned, and the princes departed with their vast army, carrying away no other reward but dishonour for such great labour. They kept their ranks intact, however, in order to repel danger if perchance the enemy should press upon their rear. In this manner whatever was devised or attempted against the king of England by the malice of his enemies was turned to his glory by the favour of God towards him.

CHAPTER XXXVIII. OF THE RECONCILIATION OF THE KINGS AND THE TRANQUILLITY OF THEIR REALMS

While God thus smiled favourably on this monarch in all things accomplished by him or about him, his enemies were so terrified and humbled by his many brilliant successes that they began to sue for peace. The very same men now made themselves mediators in restoring peace who had formerly been the chief in fomenting discord. Accordingly a grand parley[2] took place between the parties in which the deadly enmity of the princes and the disquietude of the provinces were alike appeased. The count of Flanders restored to the king of England his lawful possessions of which the chances of war had deprived him, while over and above this he claimed from the count in future the pledge of loyal friendship and homage. Moreover that most ungrateful son was restored to his father's good graces, promising his future obedience and filial devotion by the surety of many offered for his loyalty. Not only so, but the king, adopting a new precaution against these ungrateful and suspected sons, bound

[1] 8 August 1174.

[2] This took place on Michaelmas Day, 1174, between Tours and Amboise. See *Gesta Regis Henrici Secundi*, vol. I, p. 77; *Chronica Rogeri de Hoveden* (Rolls Series), vol. II, p. 67.

them to himself by an oath of homage prudently exacted and solemnly performed. For it was the father's desire that he, who had through lack of respect broken the strongest tie of nature like a spider's web, should at least be bound by what is held honourable and profitable according to the civil law and the law of nations. And since it is written, "A threefold cord is not quickly broken",[1] the violator of nature in the natural law, which ought to be observed towards a father, should at least keep faith out of consideration for honour and the double bond of oath and fealty, and beware in future lest the same sentence should justly be pronounced against him by his father–henceforth not his father only but also his liege lord–as was declared of old by the Lord of lords to his disobedient people through the prophet, "If I be a father, where is mine honour? and if I be a master, where is my fear?"[2]

His youthful brothers also, whom he had seduced from their allegiance to their father at the instigation of the French, he brought back to him: in any case there was little question about them, since they were excused on the ground of their tender age. Moreover, at the instance of the king of France and the other princes present, the illustrious king of England unconditionally released the earl of Leicester and the other prisoners, with the exception of the king of Scots, and on their release restored to them their goods and honours. He intended also in his own good time to act towards the said king of Scots with both prudence and clemency. But in due course, when it seemed as though he had forgotten the injuries wrought against himself by those ungrateful and faithless men, he suddenly ordered the walls of Leicester to be thrown down, and the fortresses of all who had deserted him to be razed to the ground: thus providing for the future by breaking the horns of the proud, lest they should attempt anything of a similar kind on any subsequent occasion. Last of all he also released the king of Scots on condition that hostages should be given for the execution of the agreements made between them. Being come to England, he appointed the city of York for the ratification of these same covenants. On his arrival there, attended by a great concourse of his magnates, the king of Scots came to meet him with all the peers of his realm, as had been arranged. In the church of the most blessed prince of the apostles all the Scots lords did homage and allegiance to the king of England as their overlord, that is to say, at their own king's command they bound themselves by a solemn pledge to stand with him and for him against all men.[3] The king of Scots himself also, in the presence of the whole multitude of nobles of both realms and in the customary manner, solemnly acknowledged the king of England as his lord and himself as his vassal and liegeman. He also handed over to him as pledges in lieu of hostages the three principal fortresses of his kingdom, namely Roxburgh, Berwick, and Edinburgh.[4] These things accomplished, the people enjoyed the long-desired peace, and the king of England by reason of his success in so many enterprises became renowned to the ends of the world. Thus ended this more than civil war between father and son, and fraught with so much peril to so many people. With this narration we also bring the second book of our history to a conclusion.

[1] Ecclesiastes iv. 12. [2] Malachi i. 6. [3] See below, No. 26.

[4] This statement is misleading; two other castles were surrendered, Jedburgh and Stirling, and many hostages also given. (See below, No. 26.)

Book III

CHAPTER I. OF THE COUNCIL OF LONDON AND THE STRIFE BETWEEN THE ARCHBISHOPS

In the year 1175 from the fullness of time in which Truth was born on the earth, which was the twenty-second of the reign of King Henry II, a provincial council was held at London[1] by Richard, archbishop of Canterbury and legate of the apostolic see, in full session with his suffragans and other ecclesiastical persons.

In the following year,[2] however, Cardinal Hugh,[3] legate of the apostolic see, came to England, though I know not for what purpose. Intending to hold a general council for the whole of England, supported by the goodwill of the king, he summoned the ecclesiastics of both provinces, that is to say, of Canterbury and York, to meet at London. On the day fixed for the meeting of the council, when the legate was about to go in procession with the insignia of his office, a violent quarrel arose between the two archbishops concerning priority of session in the council. Verily the apostolic precept "in honour preferring one another" has been so violated by the bishops of our time, that laying aside their pastoral care, they contend with one another for pre-eminence with equal obstinacy and vanity; and nearly every controversy between the bishops is concerned with precedence in honours.

In short, the archbishop of York,[4] being the first to arrive, took possession of the chief seat, basing his claim to it on the ancient decree of St. Gregory, by whom it was laid down that he who was first consecrated should be regarded as the chief metropolitan of England.[5] But the archbishop of Canterbury, like a man who has suffered an injustice, refused to take the lower seat and solemnly lodged a complaint in respect of the seat which had been already occupied. Thereupon, his clergy showing themselves fiercely jealous for his dignity, a mere strife of words developed into a brawl. The archbishop of York, however, because the party of his adversaries was the stronger, was ejected with ignominy from the seat he had prematurely occupied. Displaying his torn hood to the legate as proof of the violence used against him, he then summoned the archbishop of Canterbury together with certain of his clergy to answer before the holy see. Thus, while the two metropolitans were at variance, everything was thrown into confusion, and the council did not complete its business but was dissolved, and those who had been summoned to it and had attended there returned home. . . .

CHAPTER II. OF THE DEATH OF THE KING OF FRANCE

In the year of our Lord 1180, being the twenty-seventh of the reign of Henry II, king of England, and the forty-fourth of Louis, king of France, the said king of France died.[6] He was a man of fervent devotion towards God and singular mildness

[1] 18 May 1175.

[2] An error in dating; the correct year is 1175; see *Gesta Regis Henrici Secundi*, vol. 1, p. 104. But Newburgh is correct in his date for the council.

[3] Hugo Pierleone, cardinal deacon of St. Angelo.

[4] Roger of Pont l'Évêque, archbishop of York, 1154–1181, formerly archdeacon of Canterbury. (See below, pp. 358–359.)

[5] An arrangement in conformity with Pope Gregory the Great's original plan for the ecclesiastical organization of England, which was never at any time in operation.

[6] 18 September 1180.

towards his subjects, and also one who highly reverenced men in holy orders. He was, however, rather more simple than became a monarch; and in some of his actions he most clearly expressed the truth of the apostle's words, "Evil communications corrupt good manners."[1] Indeed, by putting undue trust in the counsels of certain nobles who cared too little for what is honourable and just, he frequently sullied his otherwise admirable character with no small stain; as, for instance, when he maintained the cause of a worthless son against a noble father and supported this unnatural enmity with all the resources of his kingdom. He was succeeded by his son, Philip,[2] borne to him by the daughter of the most illustrious Count Theobald,[3] whom he had married as his third wife. For, following upon the divorce between himself and Eleanor, who, having left him with two daughters, as has been fully related in its place,[4] then contracted a marriage with the king of England, the king of France took a consort of the royal blood of Spain.[5] She in like manner died, leaving him with two daughters, the elder of whom, as is well known, became the wife, albeit childless, of Henry, the younger king of England. . . .[6]

CHAPTER V. OF THE ALTERATION OF THE COINAGE OF THE REALM AND THE DEATH OF THE ARCHBISHOP OF YORK

In the twenty-seventh year of the reign of King Henry II the coinage of the realm in England was changed on account of its having been corrupted by forgers.[7] This measure proved necessary at the time for reasons of public welfare, but was too great a burden on the poor and the husbandmen.

In the following year, being the year of our Lord 1181 and the twenty-third of the pontificate of Pope Alexander, this venerable pontiff died and was succeeded by Lucius.[8]

In the same year also died Roger, archbishop of York,[9] a learned and eloquent man, and in worldly affairs prudent almost to singularity. In his episcopal office indeed, that is, in the cure of souls, he was less conscientious; but he was zealous to good purpose in the preservation and advancement of those things which God had not joined to his office but which the world had added to it for God's sake. Certainly, in temporal goods he so raised the archbishopric of York that he left to his successors hardly any anxieties in respect either of the increase of their revenues or the grandeur of their buildings. Further, he used his opportunities for the aggrandisement of his finances to such an extent, and so excelled in his management of them that he rarely overlooked or neglected a chance to improve them. Instead of ecclesiastics of eminence, with whom the church of York was formerly studded as with jewels, he preferred to benefices beardless youths or even boys, still under the master's rod and more suited by their age

> "to build toy houses, to yoke mice to a little cart,
> to play at odd and even, and to ride a hobby-horse"[10]

[1] I Corinthians xv. 33.
[2] Philip Augustus, 1180–1223.
[3] Alice, daughter of Theobald, count of Champagne.
[4] Book I, chap. XXXI.
[5] See above, p. 336, n. 1.
[6] See above, pp. 335, 336.
[7] November 1180.
[8] Lucius III, 1181–1185; 30 August 1181.
[9] 26 November 1181.
[10] Horace, *Sat.*, II, 3, 247.

than to sustain the character of Church dignitaries. And this he did with the intent that until they became of age he might undertake the care of their persons and appropriate the entire revenues of their benefices. Christian philosophers, that is to say, men of the religious Orders, he abhorred to such a degree that he is reported to have said that Thurstan[1] of happy memory, the former archbishop of York, had never committed a more grievous sin than when he built the abbey of Fountains, that shining mirror of Christian philosophy. Perceiving that some of those present were shocked at this remark, he added, "You are laymen and cannot comprehend the meaning of the term." He was wont also to say that an ecclesiastical benefice ought rather to be conferred on a dissolute priest than on a monk. This rule he openly and scrupulously kept all his days, and in nearly everything he made the lot of the monks worse than that of the secular clergy. Moreover, in this astonishing blindness–for he was in other respects extemely acute–he thought he rendered obedience to God, which is proved by the following incident.

There came to him as he lay on his bed in his last illness and nigh to death the prior of a certain religious house, who was well known to me for a good and upright man, humbly entreating that he would deign to confirm by the attestation of his own seal the pious bequests of honest men which his saintly predecessors, moved by love for God, had confirmed to the said house by their original charters. To this request he replied, "Behold! I lay dying and, as I fear God, I dare not do what you ask"; so firmly did he stick to his opinion that a grant of this nature could be made to any rather than to men of religion. But he made clear at his end that it had been his intention during his lifetime to shear rather than to feed the Lord's sheep. For as he lay at the point of death this prelate of advanced years had in his treasury more than a few thousand marks of silver, while so many of Christ's poor were suffering from starvation. When he could no longer brood over his riches, he tardily bequeathed them as a legacy, one part to the poor, a second part to the churches and yet a third among the servants of his household and his relatives. But after his death the king through his officers seized what was found and extorted what was not forthcoming from those to whom it had been granted, saying that treasure hoarded up till death was the sole property of the crown. Verily this was done by God's judgment in order that others might be frightened by this example and might learn to lay up for themselves treasures in heaven, where indeed neither thieves creep in nor robbers break in to steal.[2]

The judgment of God was also made manifest immediately afterwards in the case of John, the archdeacon, a crafty and avaricious man who had been the archbishop's counsellor and confidant in all things. He died the day after his master, bequeathing his wealth to the king. So these two men, inseparable in life, were in death divided only by the shortest possible interval. The archbishop died in the twenty-eighth year of his episcopate; forthwith the revenues of the archbishopric were paid into the Exchequer and the see of York remained vacant for ten years.

[1] Archbishop of York, 1131–1139, the hero of the battle of the Standard in 1138. He resigned the see of York in 1139 and died the following year. (See above, No. 11.)

[2] Matthew vi. 20.

CHAPTER VII. OF THE DEATH OF KING 'HENRY III' AND OF HIS BROTHER, GEOFFREY

In the year of our Lord's Incarnation 1183, which was the thirtieth of the reign of Henry II, king of England, 'Henry III', the younger king of England, met an untimely death,[1] untimely, that is to say, in respect of his age, but too late by consideration of his acts. For he had sullied his early years by an indelible stain, after the manner of the accursed Absalom, as has been related earlier.[2] On his coming to manhood he would not change his youthful conduct and, as at first he violated nature, so now he also violated his solemn compacts and rebelled against his father a second time.

The cause of this rebellion was as follows. His father had committed the government of the duchy of Aquitaine to his son, Richard, and had also delivered to his other son, Geoffrey, now approaching manhood, the whole of his wife's domain, that is to say, Brittany, while Henry, his first-born, was either keeping watch over or advancing the interests of his father's empire. But on the occasion of some feud which had broken out among his brothers, Henry waxed indignant because his father had appointed his brother, Richard, governor of Aquitaine. Having made an alliance with his brother, Geoffrey, count of Brittany, and some magnates from Aquitaine, he provoked his father by his warlike movements. Their father, after having vainly endeavoured to coax his rebellious sons with conciliatory messages, made preparations to combat their wicked designs and crossed the borders of Aquitaine with an army.[3] Shortly after, by God's judgment, the younger Henry was stricken with fever in vengeance for his double treachery, and the spirits of all who had conspired with him in like manner began to droop. His malady growing more serious and his physicians despairing of his life, he was smitten with remorse and sent to his father, humbly confessing his fault and begging as a last favour from his affectionate father that he would condescend to visit his dying son. On receipt of this message his father's bowels yearned over him but, being persuaded by his friends that it would not be safe for the king to trust himself to those wicked conspirators who were about his son's person, although it would be a fatherly act to visit him in his sickness, these timid counsels prevailed and the king did not go.[4] Instead he dispatched to his son a familiar ring as a token of mercy and forgiveness and a pledge of his paternal affection. On receiving the ring the son kissed it and immediately expired while the archbishop of Bordeaux stood by. His body was borne in a long funeral cortège to his father, who thereupon affectionately came to meet it and ordered it to be carried to Normandy for interment at Rouen.[5] Such was the end of this turbulent youth, born indeed for the ruin of many, yet so beloved and amiable to his followers - as it is written, "the number of

[1] 11 June 1183.

[2] See above, p. 342.

[3] A more detailed and accurate account of the quarrel between Henry II and his sons is given in *Gesta Regis Henrici Secundi*, vol. 1, pp. 291–298.

[4] Probably the king doubted the truth of the message and suspected that a trap had been laid for him; see *Gesta Regis Henrici Secundi*, vol. 1, p. 300.

[5] This is the second interment, which took place on 22 July 1183. The young king died at Martel, a village between Limoges and Cahors, on 11 June, and the body was first buried at Le Mans, *Gesta Regis Henrici Secundi*, vol. 1, pp. 301, 303–304.

the unwise is infinite"[1]–that many remarkable things were uttered concerning him. Finally, after his death certain persons, moved by love of falsehood and the most shameless vanity, spread abroad the rumour that cures of sickness were worked at his tomb,[2] doubtless in order that it might be believed either that he had a just cause against his father or that his final repentance was well pleasing to God.

The father, however, tempering the grief he felt for the loss of his son by the consideration that an enemy had been destroyed, steadfastly pressed on against the other conspirators, who were stunned by the death of their leader; in a short time he subdued them all and admitted his son, Geoffrey, back into favour. Nevertheless the latter remained ungrateful for all the proofs he received of his father's affection and by no means laid aside his hostile intentions, as later appeared. For a short while afterwards he continued to waver and vacillate with regard to his father, courting by every possible means the friendship of the French,[3] whom he knew to be jealous of his father's fame. When he could not obtain from his father the county of Anjou –despite the vain solicitude of the French king in the matter–because Richard, his elder brother, would on no account yield it to him, he allied himself with the French, as though by their power he might extort from his father what he had not obtained by soft entreaties. Thus, while engaged in active service under the king of France, he made great efforts to annoy his father, but in the midst of them he was overwhelmed by the weight of God's judgment and ended his activities together with his life at Paris.[4] There he was buried with but few regrets from his father, to whom he had been an undutiful son, but with sore grief to the French to whom he had been highly acceptable. A posthumous son was born to him by the only daughter of the count of Brittany;[5] and when the king, the child's grandfather, had ordered his own name to be given him, the Bretons objected and by solemn acclamation he was named Arthur in Holy Baptism. In this manner the Bretons, who are said to have long expected the advent of the fabled Arthur, now in high hope rear a true one, in accordance with the beliefs of certain prophets[6] enshrined in their great and famous legends of Arthur.

CHAPTER VIII. OF THE DEATH OF THE ARCHBISHOP OF CANTERBURY AND OF THE INSTITUTION OF THE BISHOP OF LINCOLN

Within a year of the death of Henry, the young King, Richard, archbishop of Canterbury, the successor of the venerable Thomas, also departed this life.[7] He was a man of only modest learning but worthy of praise for the innocence of his life, prudently keeping within the measure of his own capacity and not straying into the field of great affairs. He was succeeded by Baldwin,[8] a monk and a learned man, and formerly abbot of Ford, whence he had been made bishop of Worcester. Moreover

[1] Ecclesiastes i. 15.

[2] For these alleged miracles see the account given by Thomas Agnellus, in his panegyric of the young king, "*De morte et sepultura Henrici regis junioris*", printed in Radulph 'de Coggeshall', *Chronicon Anglicanum* (ed. J. Stevenson, Rolls Series, 1875), pp. 263–273.

[3] These events are misplaced; they took place in 1185 and should therefore be taken in conjunction with the narrative given in chap. XIII, cf. *Gesta Regis Henrici Secundi*, vol. 1, pp. 307–350.

[4] 19 August 1186.

[5] 29 March 1187. (See above, p. 333.)

[6] An allusion to the prophecies of Merlin regarding Arthur's return.

[7] 27 February 1184.

[8] Archbishop of Canterbury, 1185–1190.

in the same year[1] Walter of Coutances was made bishop of Lincoln after the see had been vacant for nearly seventeen years. Thus was brought to naught the prophecy, or rather the conjecture, of the lay brother of Thame who had prophesied of his own will rather than by the spirit of God that the church of Lincoln would never again possess a bishop.[2] This prediction, on account of the long-standing vacancy of the see, had such an effect upon many people that the aforesaid Walter, having been duly consecrated, arrived in his see with considerable trepidation. However, he did not for long enjoy possession of it for, having been elected archbishop of Rouen shortly afterwards,[3] he bade farewell to his newly espoused church being allured by the blandishments of a fairer form. Herein may be contemplated how strong is the influence of ambition for honours and how greatly it surpasses the love of money, even in the most avaricious of men.[4] Indeed it is sufficiently well known that to the same extent in which the church of Rouen excels that of Lincoln in rank and honour it yields to it in temporal advantages. Nevertheless the man who so highly coveted the see of Lincoln for the sake of its ample revenues preferred to leave it and to ascend to a higher office with more modest wealth rather than by retaining it to take a lower seat endowed with greater riches. It is reported indeed that he hesitated for a long time, carefully deliberating whether he would choose to be more eminent or more wealthy, but at last the ambition of a higher throne triumphed over the love of a more abundant revenue. On his translation the see of Lincoln again remained vacant for some years.[5]

CHAPTER IX. OF THE EXPEDITION AGAINST ROLAND AND OF CERTAIN EVENTS IN IRELAND

After the death of Henry, the young king, Henry II, the illustrious king of England, crossed over to England[6] and led his army into the most distant confines of his kingdom against Roland, prince of Galloway. For on the death of his uncle, Gilbert, who, as it has been related above,[7] had basely murdered his brother, Uctred, at the time the king of Scots had been captured by our forces, this same Roland, prevailing against his uncle's sons by the fortune of war, had claimed for himself the whole province of Galloway. Having received an appeal from Gilbert's sons, the king of England commanded Roland to restore their paternal inheritance to his cousins. Upon his contemptuous rejection of this command the king, moved to anger, marched against his lands with a mighty army both of horse and foot.[8] But receiving some very gratifying reports from Ireland at this juncture, he was elated with the news and became more accommodating. Wherefore, obtaining satisfaction from Roland, he soon withdrew his army. In order, however, that the nature of this intelligence from Ireland may be better explained, a few facts relative to the state of affairs in that country should be given, now occasion offers.

[1] *i.e.* 1183, the year of the death of the young King Henry. Walter of Coutances was consecrated bishop of Lincoln on 3 July 1183.
[2] See above, p. 335.
[3] 24 February 1185.
[4] This is a partial and misleading account of the character of Walter of Coutances, the statesman-prelate.
[5] Actually for two years only.
[6] This is misleading; Henry had already been in England from 10 June 1184 to 16 April 1185. The crossing referred to here was on 27 April 1186.
[7] See above, p. 351.
[8] August 1186.

It has been recorded above[1] how Earl Richard was compelled to relinquish his Irish acquisitions to the king, which the latter by an opportune crossing to Ireland settled according to his pleasure. But on his return to England[2] the military commanders whom he had left there in charge of the government of this conquered province, covetous either of booty or of fame, by degrees extended the boundaries allotted to them. Among them one named John of Courcy, joined by a strong force of foot and horse, thought to make a hostile incursion into the Irish province called Ulster, which is separated from the kingdom of Scotland only by a narrow strait. It chanced that there had arrived from Scotland a most eloquent man named Vivian, a legate of the apostolic see. Having been honourably received by the king and the bishops of that province, he was for the time being sojourning in a city on the sea-coast called Down. The approach of the enemy, however, being known beforehand, the Irish consulted the legate as to what ought to be done in such a crisis. He replied that they should certainly fight in defence of their country and gave his solemn blessing to those about to engage in battle. Thus inspired they rushed boldly into the fray, but being easily overwhelmed by the mail-clad knights and archers, they turned tail and fled.[3] In consequence the city of Down was taken. Then the Roman legate took refuge with his followers in a church renowned for the relics of its saints. But this prudent man had provided for his safety and had ready to hand letters from the king of England addressed to his commanders in Ireland, in order that being protected by their good offices he might fulfil the object of his legation among the barbarians. Obtaining peace and security by this authority he journeyed to Dublin and, acting with assurance in the joint names of the lord pope and the king of England, he summoned hither the bishops and abbots of Ireland and held a general council. When however he wished to act with the customary Roman licence among these churches of uncivilized habits, the royal commanders declared that he must either depart or act in concert with them; whereupon he returned to Scotland, his coffers but lightly laden with the Irish gold he had so much coveted.

In their turn John of Courcy and his men, who had taken Down and the adjacent territory, were afterwards attacked in vain by the kings of Ireland. Then having stormed Armagh, reputed to be the chief see of Ireland in honour of St. Patrick and other native saints whose sacred relics repose there, he reduced the whole province to obedience. The men of this province are reported to have been up to then superstitious beyond all the other peoples of Ireland in their manner of keeping Easter. For, as I have learnt from a certain venerable bishop of that nation, they imagined that they did God service by lavishing on the most sumptuous banquets in the festal season of Easter, as it were in honour of the risen Lord, what they had amassed by theft and rapine during the course of the year. Intense rivalry ensued among them lest perchance any one of them should be outdone by another in the preparation and serving of their courses. The conquest of the country, however, duly put an end to this most superstitious practice no less than to their status as freemen.

[1] Book II, chap. XXVI. (See above, pp. 340–342.) For a fuller account of the events narrated here, see Gerald of Wales, *Expugnatio Hibernica*, *op. cit.*, Lib. II, cap. 17 and 18.
[2] April 1172.
[3] January 1177.

Among the magnates of the English king then serving in Ireland, Hugh of Lassy was esteemed the chief and the most powerful. After the death of the most energetic Earl Richard,[1] the king had conferred upon Hugh very extensive possessions there and had committed to him the administration of the royal domains. But in a short time he so extended his boundaries, and prospered and increased so much in the magnitude of his wealth and power that he soon became formidable, not only to his enemies but also to his fellows, that is to say, the other magnates of the crown. For he even treated them as enemies if by chance they were lacking in obedience. He now appeared to regard himself as a rival to the king of England in his realm of Ireland; insomuch that he was said to have provided for himself a royal crown. When these things were reported to the king, he recalled him to England, whereupon he scorned to obey the royal command[2] and by this act of disobedience gave credence to the popular suspicion. Shortly afterwards, however, as though fortune favoured the king, the said Hugh was slain by the treachery of a certain youthful servant of his household belonging to the party among the Irish in league with him.[3] Having quitted his fortress for the country for the sake of exercise and being separated from his escort by about a stone's throw, he by chance bent down to examine something on the ground; whereupon this perfidious wretch, rejoicing in that he had acquired the long-sought opportunity, struck him violently on the head with an axe and cleft it in two. The escort ran up in a vain effort to avenge their lord, but the assassin escaped with the aid of an adjacent wood and his own fleetness of foot. The news of this event gave immense joy to the king of England, who as has been mentioned,[4] was then stationed on the farthest borders of his kingdom; and in due course the affairs of Ireland were settled by him with greater caution. . . .

CHAPTER XIII. HOW THE PATRIARCH[5] RETURNED HOME WITH HIS MISSION UNFULFILLED

At his coming into England,[6] therefore, the venerable patriarch was fully occupied with the business which had brought him hither. Having been received by the king with the honour due to his rank, he made known the cause of his arduous journey; and in order that the king might gird himself for this so holy warfare as one ordained by God and earnestly entreated by all the people to abase the pride of the most vile Saladin, he exhorted him to that end with the whole weight of his high authority. The king willingly acknowledged the soundness of his advice and promised an answer after a fitting interval for deliberation, and in consequence the patriarch remained for some little time in England. But when the king put forward as an excuse the undoubted and very great dangers to his own kingdom which would arise from his

[1] Richard of Clare, earl of Pembroke. (See above, pp. 340–342, 363.)

[2] Hugh obeyed two such summonses of recall in 1181 and 1184.

[3] 25 July 1186.

[4] See above, p. 362.

[5] Heraclius, patriarch of Jerusalem, was sent in September 1184 by Baldwin the Leper, the Byzantine emperor, to the pope and the monarchs of Western Europe to raise help against the threat to the Holy Land from Saladin, the Moslem prince. Details of his journey and of the political and military situation in Palestine are given by William of Newburgh in Book III, chaps. X–XII, omitted here.

[6] 1185.

expedition to the East, and promised to raise a handsome sum of money in aid of the Eastern Church instead of going in person, the patriarch at length returned to France far less sanguine than at his coming. The king also crossed overseas to deal with his affairs on the Continent.[1] And because the seeds of a fatal discord between himself and the king of France were germinating at the instigation of the devil, who strove by every means to induce the Christian princes, by wasting their strength in mutual conflict, to bring the least possible aid to the land and city, whence issued the salvation of all men and which was now exposed to manifold dangers, the patriarch returned home with his mission unfulfilled.[2]

CHAPTER XIV. OF THE DISCORD BETWEEN THE KINGS AND THE SUBSEQUENT ARMISTICE

The evil consequences of the discord which arose between the kings[3] involved many peoples; for, as each nation strove enthusiastically for its own monarch, so their hostility was aroused and directed against each other as if each man sought his own profit and glory or was intent on avenging his own injuries. Accordingly whole hosts of armed men, animated with the most ferocious temper, gathered together from the various provinces in opposite directions at a castle called Châteauroux[4] with the incredibly mad intention of pouring out their own blood in a libation to the glory, or rather to the pride, of their respective monarchs. For what is more insane than to be jealous, not for one's own vainglory but for that of another, and what more unjust or more deplorable than that so many thousands of Christians should put themselves in danger for the advantage, or even the mere pride of a single individual? When the two great armies had gazed upon each other from their opposite camps with a glowering countenance for several days, and while the men of peaceful disposition among them busied themselves in vain in the endeavour to arrange either a peace or an armistice, and could do no more than beat the air, at last there dawned the dread and fateful day in which battle must be joined. The troops were drawn up in battle order and the shock of the first encounter was not far off, when lo! more, it is said, from the whispered consultations of the commanders than through open parley, a truce for several days was proclaimed to each army by the voice of a herald.[5] Manifestly this voice sounded sweeter in the ears of every man than the sound of the trumpet calling to battle. As a result the nations, who a short while ago were barking at each other in enmity, and the peoples, who before were imagining vain or rather insane things, by the favourable dispensation of God returned home with bloodless joy. But the king of England having disbanded his army remained overseas more for the purpose of consolidating peace than of arousing warlike passions. For on account of his age[6] he was now sick to death of war, but eventually he was drawn on to warlike designs not from desire but by necessity alone. . . .

[1] 16 April 1185.
[2] August 1185.
[3] 1187.
[4] Philip Augustus, the French king, was besieging Richard and John in the castle, while Henry II was marching to relieve it.
[5] 23 June 1187.
[6] Henry II was now fifty-four.

CHAPTER XXIII. HOW THE KINGS TOOK THE CROSS TOGETHER WITH MANY OF THEIR NOBLES

This melancholy report of the ill management of affairs in the East[1] in a short time became known throughout the world and bred astonishment and horror in the hearts of all Christians. Nevertheless it aroused the spirit of many to seize the glorious opportunity it seemed to offer of exercising their valour. Among such, Richard, count of Poitou, the son and future heir of the king of England, chancing to receive the bearer of these ill tidings towards the close of day, at once and without any further deliberation conceived this laudable intention with his whole heart. Whereupon, early the following morning, so it is said, he solemnly received the sign of the cross as an earnest of his forthcoming pilgrimage and expedition. When the king, his father, heard this, he maintained silence until his son's arrival. And when he came a few days later, the king said: "You should by no means have undertaken so arduous an enterprise without consulting me; nevertheless I will in no wise oppose your design, but I will take steps to ensure that you carry it out well and truly." It was then, however, winter-time and as yet not one of the greater princes had taken the Lord's sign, but all were wavering in uncertainty in this matter. Nevertheless they continuously experienced the stimulus of the fear of God to this end. At length,[2] the archbishop of Tyre, arriving from the East with yet graver news to report, publicly bewailed both the present and the imminent misfortunes of the Eastern Church in such a manner that the mighty kings of France and England met in solemn conclave on the borders of their territories, with the bishops and a large concourse of their peers, for the purpose of consulting what they should do to deliver the land of Jerusalem out of the hand of its enemies. And although, as has been related above,[3] the kings had been at enmity a little while before and had not yet brought their hostility to a conclusion, but had merely suspended it for the time being by an armistice, yet in that colloquy, so long as with true religious devotion they sought not their own interests but the things of Christ, none but the faintest recollection remained of their former animosity; on the contrary, all rivalry and dissension were so stilled for the sake of Christ that one might have supposed them dead and buried, whilst with equal ardour and zeal they forwarded the work of Christ. Thus rising to a lofty fervour of devotion they received from the hand of the aforesaid archbishop the sign of the King of kings, intending soon to gird themselves for his warlike service; so they consecrated to this same noble warfare not only their substance but their persons also. Their example was followed with joyful devotion by the duke of Burgundy, the count of Flanders, and the count of Champagne, together with many other noble peers of both the realms of France and England and a vast number of knights. These also deemed it glorious to wear the Lord's sign on their shoulders and for his sake to expose themselves to labours and perils. Next, having appointed a time for the start of their journey, they decreed the following measures as necessary for the provision and preparation of so great an expedition and undertaking, and after these had been put into writing by the bishops, they were directed to all the provinces of both kingdoms.

[1] The capture of Jerusalem and the conquest of almost the whole of the Holy Land by Saladin in 1187, narrated by William of Newburgh in Book III, chaps. XVII and XVIII, is omitted here.

[2] 1 January 1188.

[3] Book III, chap. XIV. (See above, p. 365.)

Statutes of the kings on taking the cross

The lamentable report of the destruction of the land of Jerusalem and the capture of the Holy Cross has come to the ears of the Roman Church and the whole of Christendom. Wherefore the lord pope and the Roman Church, desirous of relieving this misery, have ordained with the customary compassion of the apostolic see the best remedy for all who shall take the cross, that is to say, that from the day on which anyone shall take the cross he shall be wholly released from the penalties laid upon him in consequence of his sins, provided he has repented and made confession of them, and in like manner for the sins he has forgotten.

Therefore, as God's providence ordains, the kings of France and England, together with an immense host of archbishops, bishops and barons of both lands, have taken the cross of the Lord, and by their common counsel it has been enacted that every man, whether clerk or layman, shall give for one year a tenth part of all the revenues and movables, which he now possesses, excepting this year's harvest, for the relief of the land of Jerusalem: and from next year's harvest he shall in like manner give a tenth. The books and wearing apparel and the vestments and all the portable equipment of the chapels of the clergy and their mounts and the ornaments of their churches are to be excepted, and in like manner the apparel and horses and arms of the knights and the precious stones of both orders.[1] But whosoever shall take the cross, whether clerk or layman, shall give nothing, and he shall receive from his tenants a tenth of their land, with the exception of burgesses and villeins, unless they shall take the cross with the consent of their lords. We, therefore, trusting in God's mercy, do remit to all those who lawfully pay this tithe a half of the penance laid upon them; we also remit the tithes which they have not so far paid, as the law demands, and the sins they have forgotten. But if there be any doubt whether any man has not paid his lawful tithe, let the truth of the matter be investigated by seven lawful men of his neighbourhood,[2] and let it be ordered that this shall be legally carried out under pain of anathema.

It has also been enacted by the lord kings and granted by the archbishops, bishops and all the barons that every clerk or layman who shall take the cross, if he has previously mortgaged his rents, shall have this year's profits entire; and at the end of the year let his creditor again have the rents in such a manner that the proceeds he shall receive therefrom may be reckoned towards the payment of the debt, for interest shall not be raised upon debts contracted before the cross was taken, so long as the debtor shall be on pilgrimage. Moreover all men, both clerks and laymen, who set out on this pilgrimage, may lawfully mortgage their rents, whether derived from ecclesiastical or other sources, up to a term of three years, so that their creditors may be secure thereof no matter what may happen to the debtors. With regard, however, to the money of all those who may die on this pilgrimage, which they have taken with them for the maintenance of their servants, or as an aid to the land of Jerusalem, or for the sustenance of the poor, let it be apportioned in accordance with the advice of discreet men who shall be appointed for this purpose.

It has also been enacted that no man shall swear outrageously, or play at dice or

[1] Cf. Ordinance of the "Saladin Tithe", cap. I. (See below, No. 29.)

[2] The sworn inquest procedure. (See below, Nos. 24, 25, 58.)

games of chance, and that none shall wear minever or vaire[1] or sable or scarlet, that all men, both clerks and laymen, shall be content with two dishes of the food that is brought, and that none shall take any woman with him on pilgrimage except a laundress, who shall go on foot and of whom no suspicion can be entertained, and that no man shall wear clothes slashed or trimmed with lace.

CHAPTER XXIV. OF THE EXACTION OF TITHES AND HOW THE EMPEROR AND HIS FOLLOWERS TOOK THE CROSS

On the dissolution of the assembly in which the kings had taken the sign of the Lord[2] and decreed these ordinances with the assent of all the bishops and nobles present, the illustrious king of England made a speedy crossing to his own kingdom and there held a solemn council at a convenient place.[3] With the unhesitating approbation of the prelates and lay magnates of England he confirmed what had been resolved on the Continent.[4] Then the archbishop of Canterbury,[5] the bishops of Durham and Norwich and many lay nobles of the realm, fired by the king's example, solemnly accepted the sacred sign of the cross. Many indeed acted thus from pure devotion but others with less sincerity, that is to say, either by orders from the king, or so that they might commend themselves more readily to the monarch by anticipating his command. Moreover a vast multitude of clergy and knights, burgesses and villeins, in all parts of the country took care to follow the example of the king and the nobles, just as had occurred in the provinces of France. Tithes were also exacted according to the form prescribed, and preparations were made with the most vigilant care for the necessary expenses of so large an expedition.

Nor did Frederick, the Roman emperor,[6] long endure to be found in this respect less devout or less active than the kings mentioned above. Having summoned the chief men of his empire, he revealed to them the design conceived in his great mind, and, solemnly decorating the crown of his imperial majesty with the symbol of the Lord's humiliation, he presented this most saving emblem to the rulers and peoples under him. So great an ardour of faith and devotion then burned among the great chieftains and the most warlike peoples of Germany for the undertaking of that most perilous expedition for the sake of Christ, that it might rightly be said, "This is the finger of God."[7] And so almost all nations bearing the name of Christian were seething with fervour in the immense preparations for hastening the start of their proposed journey.

CHAPTER XXV. OF THE RUPTURE OF THE TREATY BY THE KING OF FRANCE, AND OF THE DEATH OF THE KING OF ENGLAND WHICH FOLLOWED[8]

While the devotion of the faithful princes and peoples thus burned within them, the malice of the ancient enemy did not rest from seeking to spoil what had been so well begun. For when the illustrious king of England was quietly residing in his own realm

[1] Another kind of fur. [2] 1188. [3] Council of Geddington, held 11 February 1188.
[4] A reference to the Ordinance of the "Saladin Tithe". (See below, No. 29.)
[5] Baldwin, archbishop of Canterbury, 1185–1190; see above, p. 361, for his election.
[6] Frederick I (Barbarossa), emperor, 1152–1190. [7] Exodus viii. 19.
[8] Cf. with this chapter the accounts of the last days and death of Henry II given by Gerald of Wales and in the *Gesta Regis Henrici Secundi*. (See below, Nos. 14 and 15.)

and, as befitted so great a monarch, was making all kinds of preparation for the forthcoming expedition, the king of France, incited by I know not whom, broke faith in the treaty solemnly concluded between them and intended to last until the return of both monarchs from the East. Showing no reverence for the sign of the Lord, which they had both received as allies, he was suddenly inflamed with passion and, so it is said, through the treachery of certain vile traitors, occupied like an unexpected usurper the noble castle of Châteauroux, which belonged to the king of England.[1] Elated at this success and altering, or rather extinguishing, the plan for an expedition to Jerusalem, he aspired to undertake yet greater exploits. But these events speedily became known to the king of England, who strove to act with moderation for the sake of the sacred enterprise they had jointly undertaken. Being on the point of crossing the Channel he sent on before him certain men of high rank[2] with a conciliatory message to this violator of treaties. The latter, however, not only remained rigid and unyielding to all flattery, but with an arrogance even more unbridled applied himself to his evil designs. As soon as the king of England had crossed overseas, through the good offices of certain well-disposed men the two monarchs duly met together,[3] the king of England intending to lay a complaint against the breach of the treaty and the injury done to himself, while the king of France was disposed to reply as if in justification of his actions. Yet, as it were, under cover of confidence in his own uprightness he was secretly working iniquity, as he gave us to understand from what followed. For Richard, son of the king of England and at that time count of Poitou, who, as mentioned above,[4] had been the first to take the cross, being enticed and estranged, it is believed, by the cunning of the French, deserted his father in the solemn colloquy of the kings and went over to the enemy's camp.[5] While the situation grew ever more serious, the father, shocked by this betrayal, and having all in vain uttered words of peace to those who hated peace, left the conference,[6] scarcely knowing whom he could trust now that he had experienced the ingratitude of his son.

War was immediately begun by both sides,[7] but with unequal forces and resolution. For Richard, whom his father had set over the duchy of Aquitaine, led his father's army over to the side of the king of France. Many also of the magnates of Normandy, Anjou and Brittany, their loyalty extinguished, openly deserted the father for the son and for his sake swelled the army of the French. Whence it came to pass that, with the exception of the mercenaries, only a small number came to the assistance of the king of England, and even those about him were wavering in their loyalty. And so the king of France, with the count of Poitou and immense forces, invaded the territory of the king of England without opposition and marched towards

[1] 16 June 1188.

[2] The embassy consisted of Baldwin, archbishop of Canterbury, and St. Hugh, bishop of Lincoln. See *Gesta Regis Henrici Secundi*, vol. II, p. 40.

[3] Two conferences seem to have been held between the kings at this time, the first at Chatillon on 7 October and the second between Bonsmoulins and Soligny on 18 November; both were inconclusive. See *Gesta Regis Henrici Secundi*, vol. II, pp. 49 *et seq.*

[4] In Book III, chap. XXIII. (See above, p. 366.)

[5] This took place in the second conference held in November. Richard did homage to Philip Augustus for his continental possessions. See *Gesta Regis Henrici Secundi*, vol. II, p. 50.

[6] William of Newburgh makes no mention of the further conference between the kings held at La Ferté Bernard, 1–4 June 1189. (See below, No. 14, p. 377.)

[7] 3 January, 1185.

the city of Le Mans where the said king was then stationed with his army. Upon ascertaining this and reviewing his troops, he recognized that he was too greatly outnumbered to run the risk of fighting a battle and, fearing to be besieged by the enemy, he set fire to the city,[1] sacrificing much of his equipment, and retreated to a place of greater safety. After this the army which seemed to be following him melted away. Then John, his youngest son, whom he loved most tenderly, abandoned his father lest he should become estranged from his brethren and less than a brother to them. Having gained possession of the city of Le Mans and its castle,[2] the enemy by a rapid advance also took the city of Tours and its castle by storm,[3] and proceeded in turn to lay siege to the city of Angers. Rendered desperate by so many misfortunes, and especially troubled in spirit by the defection of his youngest son, whose untimely promotion,[4] which he had planned through his peculiar affection for him,[5] appeared to have alienated his eldest son [Richard], the king's troubles gave him understanding and showed him that the hand of the Lord was stretched out against him, and that he was the true author of the sudden and marked change in his fortunes which had occurred as a punishment for his evil deeds. At length, as a result of his heavy sorrow, he caught a fever which, gaining in strength, after some days put an end to his life at Chinon.[6]

Such was the end of this famous King Henry, the most renowned among the kings of the earth and second to none of them either in the extent of his riches or, until recently, in the good fortune of his enterprises. His enemies indeed, when they heard of his indisposition, began to conduct themselves with greater moderation and, having hastily agreed to a truce,[7] suspended operations; when lo! it was announced that the star was set that had formerly shone so brightly. Distressed at the news the count of Poitou bewailed his loss, and as an expiation for the undutiful conduct he had displayed towards his father during his lifetime proved himself though tardily to be a son in the respect he paid at his father's funeral. Even the king's enemies, who had always been envious of his valour and high renown, are said to have praised and lamented him in death, and it was manifest to the minds of all men how vain and deceitful are earthly honours, when so pitiable a fate suddenly overtook one who a little while ago had shone resplendent throughout the world. His body, as he himself on his death-bed with pious devotion had directed, was borne to that famous and noble nunnery called Fontevrault, and there, in the presence of his sons and a host of nobles, it was buried with regal splendour. For during his lifetime he had especially favoured this nunnery, distinguished by the title of a famous religious Order,[8] and had endowed it with such great privileges that, in accordance with the favours he had bestowed upon it and also

[1] See the graphic account of the storming and burning of the city in Gerald of Wales given below, No. 15, pp. 382–383.

[2] 12 June 1189.

[3] 3 July 1189.

[4] On 4 June in the conference at La Ferté Bernard Henry had threatened to make John his successor and to wed him to Alice, the French king's sister, whom Henry held in wardship and who had been betrothed to Richard; see Howden, *op. cit.*, vol. II, p. 363.

[5] See the king's utterance on learning of John's treachery recorded by Gerald of Wales below, No. 15, p. 384.

[6] 6 July 1189.

[7] Obtained by Henry at the price of almost complete surrender, 4 July, two days before his death; see *Gesta Regis Henrici Secundi* for the terms of the agreement, below, No. 14, pp. 378–379.

[8] The mother-house of the Order of Fontevrault, founded in 1101 by Robert of Arbrissel, a Breton by birth and a wandering preacher in Anjou, Touraine and Poitou. The nuns kept the Rule of St. Benedict.

with his own wishes, it was most fitting he should there obtain a resting-place for his body in expectation of the final resurrection.

I ought not, I think, to pass over in silence what I remember to have heard from a certain venerable man who asserted that he had received the story[1] from a devout brother of the same house. A certain worthy brother of our congregation, who entertained an abundant affection for the king of England as the chief patron of our abbey, was wont to make earnest supplication to Almighty God for his welfare, and when he was desirous to learn what would happen to the said king either through the mercy or through the judgment of the supreme Governor, prior to the time the kings had taken the sign of the cross, he received in a dream the following response from the Lord concerning the king he loved. "He shall lift up my sign above him, but amidst torment he shall endure torment; for the offspring of his wife's womb shall rise up against him, and at the last he shall be veiled among those who wear the veil." The truth of this revelation was made doubly clear in the devotion wherewith this monarch assumed the sign of the cross and in the events which followed, even unto his interment among the veiled nuns, as the foregoing narrative has made manifest.

CHAPTER XXVI. OF THE CHARACTER OF KING HENRY

Of a truth this king was well known both for the many virtues which adorned his royal person and no less for certain vices most unbecoming in a Christian prince. Prone to lasciviousness he exceeded the bonds of marriage; in this indeed he followed the pattern of his ancestors, though in excesses of this kind he yielded the palm to his grandfather. With his queen he had relations for a time sufficient to raise up issue, but when she ceased to bear children, he begat illegitimate offspring by following his own lusts. Like his grandfather he loved the delights of the chase more than was meet, but in the punishment of those who transgressed the laws safeguarding wild animals[2] he was milder than his grandfather. For the latter, as has been said in its due place,[3] made little or no distinction in his public sentences between those who slew men and those who slew beasts. His grandson, however, punished transgressors of this sort with imprisonment or temporary exile.

To that perfidious nation and enemy of Christians, the Jews, he gave undue encouragement on account of the liberal and advantageous terms he received from their usurious transactions, and this to such an extent that they showed themselves violent and insolent towards Christians and inflicted great injuries upon them. In financial exactions he was somewhat immoderate, but the unrestricted growth of this evil in later times justified him in this respect and was a token that he maintained due bounds; with the exception that he allowed vacant bishoprics to remain for a long time unfilled in order to enjoy the emoluments accruing therefrom, and confiscated to the Treasury the revenue that should properly have been devoted to ecclesiastical uses. Yet he strove, it is said, to defend this far from kingly action by this excuse: "Is it not better that this money should be expended on the necessities of affairs of State, rather than be consumed in the pleasures of the bishops? For the prelates of our

[1] This story is also narrated in the *Gesta Regis Henrici Secundi*, vol. II, p. 55, and by Howden who ascribes it to a Cistercian, *op. cit.*, vol. II, p. 356.

[2] The Forest Laws. (See below, No. 28.)

[3] Book I, chap. III.

time portray very little of the character of those of old, but are negligent and slack in the duties of their office and embrace the world with both arms." In which speech without doubt he branded our bishops with disgraceful calumny, while he shielded his own actions with a vain and foolish reason. Certainly he grievously failed in his duty to the church of Lincoln,[1] which is known to have been kept long vacant for the sake of its large revenues. Nevertheless some years before his death, in order to expiate this crime of his, he took care to provide a conscientious shepherd[2] for the church of this diocese.

By Queen Eleanor he had illustrious sons but, as the preceding narrative has revealed, in them the father was most unfortunate. This, we may believe, duly occurred by God's judgment by virtue of a double cause. For the said queen had formerly been the consort of the king of France[3] but, growing weary of her union with him and aspiring to marriage with the king of England, she sought grounds for a divorce. Freed by law from her first husband after the fashion of the Church, by a certain unlawful dispensation,[4] if I may so call it, Henry thereupon made her his wife. So it came to pass by God's careful deliberation that he raised up from her distinguished offspring to his own ruin. It was also just that he, who through his inordinate love for his sons is acknowledged to have injured many others while he exerted himself unduly for their advancement, should have been punished by their wicked rebellion and premature deaths. All this however manifestly occurred by the admirable dispensation of the heavenly Judge. Moreover because, as I believe, he had not yet sufficiently repented the severity and unfortunate obstinacy which he had shown towards the venerable Archbishop Thomas, the end of this great prince was in my opinion so wretched. So that while the Lord in his stern righteousness did not spare him in this life, in the next, as may be piously believed, he prepared for him forgiveness.

In his exalted position in the State he was most diligent in defending and promoting the peace of the realm; in wielding the sword for the punishment of evildoers and the maintenance of peace and quiet for honest men, he was a true servant of God. He was the champion and defender of ecclesiastical interests and liberties, as became evident after his death. In his ordinances he took great care of the poor, the widows and orphans, and in several places gave liberal alms with a bountiful hand. He showed particular respect to monks and ordered that their property should be protected by law, equally with that of his demesne lands. At the very beginning of his reign with exemplary piety he reformed the ancient and inhuman custom with regard to shipwrecks, and ordered that humane treatment should be accorded to mariners rescued from the perils of the deep. On those who in any way assaulted them or dared to appropriate their possessions, he imposed heavy penalties. He never laid any grievous burden on his realm of England or on his lands overseas, until the recent tithe for the purpose of an expedition to Jerusalem,[5] which was in fact also levied in other countries. He never laid tribute on churches or monasteries on pretext of some necessity like other monarchs, but even preserved their immunity from tolls and public charges with religious fervour. He abhorred bloodshed and the sacrifice of men's lives, and strove diligently to keep the peace, wherever possible by gifts of money, but with

[1] See Book II, chap. XXII, above, p. 335.
[2] St. Hugh, consecrated bishop 1186.
[3] Louis VII.
[4] *illicita licentia.*
[5] The "Saladin Tithe", 1188. (See below, No. 29.)

armed force if he could not secure it otherwise. With these and other good qualities adorning his royal person, he was nevertheless not acceptable to many who had eyes only for his bad qualities. Ungrateful men and those bent on evil courses cavilled unceasingly against the wickedness of their own monarch and would not endure to hear good spoken of him. To such men especially the hardships of the days that followed alone brought understanding. Indeed the experience of present evils has revived the memory of his good deeds, and the man, who in his own time was hated by almost all men, is now declared to have been an excellent and profitable prince. Solomon also, that peace-loving king, who raised the people of Israel to the pinnacle of honour and amassed proverbial riches, was not wholly acceptable to his own people, as may well be inferred from the following words addressed to his son [Rehoboam]: "Thy father made our yoke grievous, now do thou make our yoke lighter, and we will serve thee."[1] Moreover this same son replied to his people when they complained, threatening them with youthful levity: "My little finger is thicker than my father's loins; my father made your yoke heavy; I will add to your yoke. My father chastised you with whips, but I will chastise you with scorpions."[2] This remark, I repeat, was uttered by him in levity, but not lightly may it be applied to our own times; rather it fits them most appropriately. Yet this foolish people makes less complaint now when it is chastised with scorpions than it did some years ago when it was chastised with whips. Henry II, illustrious king of England, duke of Normandy and Aquitaine and count of Anjou, died in the thirty-fifth year of his reign, in the second year from that in which he took the cross and at the close of the second year of the Christians' warfare in the East.

[1] 1 Kings xii. 4. [2] 2 Chronicles x. 11.

13. Jordan Fantosme: Description of the capture of William the Lion, king of Scots

The metrical chronicle of Jordan Fantosme, written in French, was composed before 1183. The following passage gives an indication of its character, and introduces several important personages. It should be compared with the account of William of Newburgh (above, pp. 351, 352), which may perhaps be derived from it. It is printed in *Chronique des ducs de Normandie par Benoit*, ed. F. Michel, vol. III, Appendix IV, pp. 608–610, and also (with a translation which is here followed) in *Chronicles and Memorials of the reigns of Stephen, Henry II and Richard I* (Rolls Series), vol. III, pp. 365–373.

Thus they accompanied the king as far as Westminster.
The Londoners make rejoicings at the coming of their lord.
They give him presents, they pay him great respect.
But he was pensive and somewhat distracted
On account of the king of Scotland who had acted madly,
And Roger of Mowbray, a noble warrior,
Who were laying waste his land by night and by day.
But before the right hour came for going to bed,
There came a piece of news from which he gained great honour.
The king had entered his own chamber
When the messenger came; he had gone through much fatigue:
He had neither drunk nor eaten for three days of the week,
Nor slept a wink on account of the certain news,
But by day and night fatigues himself with journeying.
He has acted very wisely, he will have a good gift.
The king was leaning on his elbow and slept a little,
A servant at his feet was gently rubbing them;
There was neither noise nor cry, nor any who were speaking there,
Neither harp nor viols nor anything was sounding at that hour,
When the messenger came to the door and gently called.
And says the chamberlain: "Who are you there?"
"I am a messenger, friend; now come more this way.
"Lord Rannulf 'de Glanville' sent me here
"In order to speak with the king, for great need he has of it."
And says the chamberlain: "Let the business be till the morning."
"By my faith!" said the messenger, "but I will speak to him forthwith.
"My lord has in his heart sorrow and vexation:
"So let me enter, good chamberlain."
And says the chamberlain: "I should not dare to do it.
"The king is asleep: you must withdraw."
Whilst they are speaking the king has awaked,
And he hears a crying at that door: "Open! open!"
"Who is that," said the king, "can you tell me?"
"Sire," said the chamberlain, "you shall know directly.

"It is a messenger from the north, very well you know him.
"A man of Rannulf 'de Glanville's': his name is Brien."
"By my faith!" said the king, "now am I very uneasy:
"He is in need of aid, let him come in here."
The messenger, who was very well bred, entered,
And saluted the king, as you may shortly hear:
"Sire king, may God who dwells in Trinity save you,
"Your person first and then all your intimate friends!"
"Brien," said the king, "what news do you bring?
"Has the king of Scotland entered Richmond?
"Has Newcastle-upon-Tyne been seized, and the fortifications?
"Odinel 'de Umfravile' been taken or driven away,
"And all my barons ousted from their estates?
"Messenger, by thy faith! tell me the truth.
"Badly have they served me, so now may they be punished for it."
"Sire," so said the messenger, "hear me a little.
"Your barons of the north are right good people.
"On behalf of my lord kindly listen to me,
"He sends to you by me salutation and friendship,
"And my lady much more, with whom you are well acquainted,
"He sends you word by me, that you would do wrong to torment yourself.
"The king of Scotland is taken and all his barons."
And says King Henry: "Do you speak the truth?"
"Yes, sire, truly, in the morning you will know it:
"The archbishop of York, a wise, learned man,
"Will send you two private messengers;
"But I started first, who know the truth.
"I have hardly slept during the last four days,
"Neither eaten nor drunk, so I am very hungry:
"But, in your kindness, give me a reward for it."
And the king replied: "You would be wrong to doubt it.
"If you have told me the truth, you are rich enough.
"Is the king of Scotland taken? tell me the truth."
"Yes, sire, by my faith! On a cross may I be crucified,
"Or hanged by a rope, or burnt on a great pile,
"If tomorrow, before noon, all be not confirmed."
"Then," says King Henry, "God be thanked for it,
"And Saint Thomas the Martyr and all the saints of God!"
Thereupon the messenger went to his hostel,
He has abundance to eat and to drink,
And the king is so merry and joyful that night
That he went up to the knights and awoke them all:
"Barons, wake up. It has been a good night for you.
"Such a thing I have heard as will make you glad:
"The king of Scotland is taken, so it has been told me for truth.

"Just now the news came to me, when I ought to have been in bed."
And the knights say: "Now thank the Lord God;
"Now is the war ended, and your kingdom in peace."
This night seemed very fine to King Henry.
Next day, before noon, the news again reached him
From the archbishop of York, whom they call Roger,
Who salutes his lord and who cares for the loyal.
When the king saw the messengers, never was he more delighted,
And perceives that they say the same thing, so he answered them:
"Last night I heard the news when I was very irritable;
"To him who brought it to me a reward shall be given."
He took a little stick, to Brien he gave it.
Ten librates of his land for the trouble which he has had.

14. "The Deeds of King Henry II": The last days and death of Henry II

This account of the last days and the death of Henry II is taken from the work known as the *Gesta Regis Henrici Secundi*. This work, perhaps the most valuable chronicle for the latter part of the reign of Henry II, was for long erroneously ascribed to Benedict, abbot of Peterborough, who was not, however, the author. Some notice of it has been given above (p. 99), and the reader is referred for further information to the long preface which William Stubbs added to his edition of it (2 vols., Rolls Series, 1867). That wonderful essay, it may be added, not only discusses the chronicle but contains what is probably the best modern account of Henry II's reign. The passage here translated occurs in that edition in vol. II at pp. 67–71.

Thus the conference ended[1] and Philip, king of France, departed and took La Ferté Bernard and then in turn Montfort,[2] Maletable, Beaumont and Ballon, where he stayed for three days after its capture. Then coming to Le Mans on the Sunday he feigned to move against Tours. On the Monday following, when the king of England and his men appeared to be at a safe distance from the farthest point of the French king's advance, the latter arranged his army in line of battle in preparation for an attack upon the city [Le Mans]. Seeing which, Stephen of Tours, the seneschal of Anjou, set fire to the suburb. But the fire immediately grew to immense proportions and leaping across the city walls set the city itself aflame. At which sight the French advanced to a certain stone bridge, where Geoffrey 'de Bruillon' and many of the English king's men with him ran to meet them in an effort to destroy the bridge. Here a great struggle took place, and many were slain on both sides in the fight.

In it also the aforesaid Geoffrey was captured and wounded in the leg, and many others of the English king's army were taken. The rest incontinently took to flight, desiring to retreat into the city. But the French forced an entry together with them; seeing which the king of England, despairing of his lot and breaking his promise, fled from the city with seventy knights. For he had promised the citizens that he would not leave them in the lurch, in the first place because his father's body rested there, in the second because he himself was born there and loved the city above all others. The French king, however, pursued him for three miles, and had the river[3] by which the French crossed not been running enormously high, they would have pursued the other fugitives with such swiftness that, as is commonly asserted, they would all have been taken prisoner. In this flight, moreover, many Welshmen were slain.

The English king, however, came with a small retinue to Chinon and withdrew into the fortress there. But the remnant which remained of the king's household retired into the citadel of the castle at Le Mans. At once the king of France besieged the citadel and assaulted it both by his engineers and by missiles of war; at length within three days the citadel surrendered with thirty knights and sixty men-at-arms.

Departing thence, Philip took Montdoubleau by the surrender both of the fortress and of the demesne. For the *vicomte* of Châteaudun, the occasion of this ruin, nay rather the chief cause of it, being armed lay wait in ambush for the unarmed Geoffrey, count of Vendôme, and so grievously wounded him that at first his life was despaired

[1] At La Ferté Bernard, 4 June 1189.

[2] Montfort-le-Rotrou; all four were castles in the province of Sarthe.

[3] River Sarthe.

of; but by the grace of God he was fully restored to health. The king of France, however, took this outrage deeply to heart because the aforesaid *vicomte* was bound in honour to him not to injure or oppress any of the king's men, either in coming or going during the siege of Le Mans.

Departing thence, there was surrendered to the French king the fortress of Trou together with Roches L'Evêque, Montoire, Chartre, Château du Loir, and the fortresses of Chaumont, Amboise and Rochecorbon. At length, in the week following the Feast of the Nativity of St. John the Baptist, on the sixth day of the week, namely the morrow of the Feast of the Apostles Peter and Paul,[1] he came to Tours.

On the Sunday next following, Philip, count of Flanders, William, archbishop of Rheims, and Hugh, duke of Burgundy,[2] came to the king of England, who was then at Saumur, rather of their own initiative than at the king's will, to make a settlement between them. But the king of France had warned them before they set out on their journey that he would notwithstanding prepare an attack upon the city from the fortress of St. Martin, to which he had retired across the river Loire.

On the following Monday[3] about the third hour the city[4] was taken by storm by an assault from the bank of the Loire in consequence of the low level of the river, the volume of water being reduced beyond measure, and ladders being placed against the walls; within the city eighty knights and a hundred men-at-arms were taken prisoner. For shame! On the one hand the men of Poitou laid a plot for their lord, the king of England, on the other the Bretons surrendered to the king of France, having obtained letters-patent from him that he would on no account come to terms with the king of England, unless the Bretons were allowed to go in peace. But the king of England, placed in a difficult position, made peace[5] with Philip, king of France, on this wise.

"Henry, king of England, has put himself in all things at the advice and will of Philip, king of France, to the effect that, whatsoever the king of France has provided and decreed, the king of England will wholly perform without opposition. First, the king of England again paid homage to the king of France because, as related above, he had surrendered his dominions to the king of France, who had requited him at the beginning of this truce. Secondly, the king of France has appointed that his sister Alice, whom the king of England holds in wardship, shall be surrendered and handed over to the custody of one of five [barons] whom Earl Richard[6] shall choose. Moreover, the king of France has provided that his sister shall be granted safe-conduct on the oath of the men of the land for her marriage to Earl Richard on his return from Jerusalem, and that Earl Richard shall have the fealty of the men of his father's lands both on this side of the Channel and beyond. Also, none of the barons or knights, who have withdrawn their allegiance from the king of England in the recent war and have come over to Earl Richard, shall in future return to the king of England, except within the last month before the king sets out for Jerusalem. The time-limit for this journey shall be mid-Lent. So the said kings and Richard, count of Poitou, shall meet on that date at Vézelay. Also, all the townsfolk of the demesne vills of the king of

[1] 30 June 1189.

[2] This does not agree with the account given in Gerald of Wales (see below, No. 15), where Hugh of Burgundy is replaced by Theobald, count of Blois.

[3] 3 July.

[4] Tours.

[5] At Colombières, 4 July.

[6] Richard, count of Poitou, the future Richard I.

England in all lands of the French king shall be quit by their lawful customs and shall not be impleaded in any matter unless they have trespassed by a felony. Also, the king of England shall pay 20,000 marks in silver to the king of France; and all the barons of the king of England shall swear to stand by the king of France and Earl Richard and to assist them to the utmost of their power against the king of England, if he does not fulfil these agreements. Also, the king of France and Earl Richard shall take possession of the city of Le Mans and the castles of Château du Loir and Trou; or if the king of England shall prefer, the king of France and Earl Richard shall hold the castles of Gisors, Pacy and Nonancourt, until everything is carried out as the king of France has appointed above."

Henry, king of England, died in the year of our Lord 1189, in the month of July, on the sixth day of the month, within the Octave of the Apostles Peter and Paul, in the nineteenth lunation, on the fifth day of the week, at Chinon. He was buried at Fontevrault in the abbey of the nuns who served God there.

The day after his death, when he was borne to burial, he lay in state robed in royal splendour, wearing a gold crown on his head, gauntlets on his hands and a gold ring on his finger, holding the sceptre in his hand, with gold-braided shoes and spurs on his feet, girded with his sword, and his face uncovered.[1] When this had been reported to Earl Richard, his son, he came post-haste to meet the cortège. At his coming blood began to flow forthwith from the dead king's nostrils as if his spirit was moved with indignation. Whereupon the said earl weeping and lamenting followed his father's corpse in procession as far as Fontevrault where it was given burial.

[1] Gerald of Wales gives a very different picture of the scene. (See below, No. 15.)

15. Gerald of Wales (Giraldus Cambrensis): "Concerning the Instruction of a Prince"

The following passages on the antecedents, reign and character of Henry II, are taken from the work *De Principis Instructione* by Gerald of Wales. Gerald 'de Barri' or Gerald of Wales was a voluminous writer of mixed Norman and Welsh ancestry. Born about 1147, he became a secular clerk and archdeacon. Trained in the schools of Paris, he was a courtier and man of affairs with pronounced Celtic sympathies and prejudices. He was first brought into contact with Henry II in or before 1176. After 1184 when he became a royal chaplain permanently attached to the court he grew to know the king well. He was an eyewitness of many of the great events of the last five years of the reign. Disappointed by the king's refusal to confirm his election to the see of St. David's, he conceived a strong personal antipathy for Henry II, but there is no evidence that this was reciprocated. In his book on "the Instruction of a Prince" he took a belated literary revenge for his real or imagined wrongs, and the work "from different points of view may be regarded as a political pamphlet or a historical tragedy": the theme is the follies and vices of the princes of his own time and more particularly of Henry II and his sons. The work centres round the personality and policy of Henry II. The rise and fall of Henry II he strives to represent as God's retribution for the crimes and wickedness of princes. The tone is therefore didactic and homiletic, but despite bias and inaccuracy it is not only graphic and colourful, but informative and circumstantial.

Concerning Gerald of Wales, there is a large literature. Reference may here only be made to J. E. Lloyd, *History of Wales* (2nd ed., London, 1912), vol. II, chap. XV. Much of Gerald's work, but not the *De Principis Instructione*, has been translated in *The Historical Works of Giraldus Cambrensis* (ed. T. Wright, London, 1905). The Latin text of all these works will be found in the standard edition thereof, *Giraldi Cambrensis Opera* (8 vols., Rolls Series, 1861–1891). The passages here reproduced will be found in vol. VIII of that edition at pp. 158–175, 282–297, and 304–306, and the treatise as a whole is discussed at pp. xli–xlviii.

To judge from the fortunate issues of chance, Henry II, king of the English, seemed to have obtained divine favour in almost everything, not only from the beginning of his reign, but even from his first year and his very birth, and this more by grace than as a reward for his merits. In the first place, William, the only son and heir of King Henry I, was drowned,[1] and to our Henry, as the king's grandson by his eldest daughter,[2] both the duchy of Normandy and the kingdom of England descended by hereditary right. But when King Henry I departed from this world and the young Henry was left the heir as a lad of fifteen years, Stephen of Blois, the king's nephew on his sister's[3] side, took the crown of the kingdom unlawfully. After a reign of nineteen years, and a little after the death of that noble knight, Eustace, his son,[4] King Stephen died. All obstacles having thus been removed from Henry's path, everything that had been unjustly withheld from him, now that he was a grown man, was wholly restored to him.

Accordingly Henry II was forthwith raised to the throne, and among the very first events, by a sign of happy omen, all those who had before this been oppressors of the kingdom and disturbers of the peace of the realm, including not only the foreigners but even his own brothers[5] and later their sons, were suddenly and, as it were, by a miracle destroyed by death. From the peace-loving king all obstacles to tranquillity and quiet were thus removed by the admirable favour of fortune. Thus

[1] In the wreck of the White Ship, 1120. (See above, No. 8.)

[2] Maud. (See above, pp. 305 *et sqq.*)

[3] Adela, daughter of William the Conqueror, married Stephen, count of Blois.

[4] In 1153. (See above, pp. 203, 310.) [5] Geoffrey, count of Nantes, died 1158, and William, died 1164.

happily reigning, he not only brought strong peace with the aid of God's grace to his hereditary dominions, but also triumphed victoriously in remote and foreign lands, a thing of which none of his predecessors since the coming of the Normans, not even the English kings, had proved capable. . . .[1]

Furthermore, he vigorously extended his dominions overseas in Gaul and Aquitaine; to Anjou, Maine and Touraine, which he had inherited from his father, and Poitou and the whole of Gascony as far as the Pyrenees, which had fallen to his lot by marriage,[2] he added Auvergne, Berri and Gisors, together with the Vexin, which had formerly been taken from Normandy.

Moreover, he aspired to extend his rule, not only to France, making full use of the good nature of the simple and saintly King Louis,[3] but even also to the Roman empire, through the occasion of the long war and inexorable discord between the Emperor Frederick[4] and his subjects. Having often been invited by the whole of Italy and the city of Rome, an opening for this was afforded him by way of the Alps and the valley of Maurienne,[5] but he could not obtain effective control there. Indeed, he was sometimes wont, since "his mouth spoke from a full heart", to let fall spirited and ambitious words among his intimates to the effect that the whole world was too small a prize for a single courageous and powerful ruler. Thus, throughout the world the fame of his honoured name was so spread abroad that it abounded in glory above the kings, princes and liegemen of the whole earth and to the terror of the nations. Moreover the princes of all lands, both Christian and heathen, such as the German king, Frederick,[4] the Greek emperor, Manuel,[6] Noureddin in his time and afterwards Saladin, and the princes of Asia and Europe, even of Spain, both Christian and infidel,[7] were accustomed to visit him and honour him with presents and to send frequent embassies. . . .

. . . His three daughters, whom he had by the noble Queen Eleanor, he gave in marriage in three widely separated regions of Europe. The eldest[8] he bestowed in Saxony to Henry, duke of Saxony; the second,[9] in Spain to Alfonso, king of Toledo and Castile; the third and youngest,[10] in Sicily to be the wife of William, king of the Two Sicilies. .

By the same Eleanor he had in addition six illustrious sons, of whom two died prematurely and at a tender age. The other four[11] who grew to manhood, rejoiced their father's heart more in time of flowering than in time of fruiting, more in the stalk than in the ear of harvest, more in childhood than in maturity. . . . Doubtless it came to pass by the just and admirable vengeance of God that he deserved to be punished for his grave excesses and irregularities through his own offspring, whom he had begotten less lawfully than was fitting,[12] and that his lands and even his last breath

[1] Here follows an account of Henry's wars against the Irish and the Scots.

[2] To Eleanor of Aquitaine.

[3] Louis VII.

[4] Frederick I (Barbarossa), 1152–1190.

[5] A reference to the treaty made between Henry and Humbert, count of Maurienne in 1173.

[6] Manuel Comnenus, 1143–1180.

[7] The Moorish emirs and chieftains of the caliphate of Cordoba.

[8] Maud, married Henry the Lion.

[9] Eleanor, married Alfonso IX of Castile.

[10] Joan, married William II of Sicily, 1166–1189.

[11] Henry, Richard, Geoffrey and John.

[12] A reference to Eleanor's first marriage to Louis VII of France and its subsequent annulment. (See above, p. 372.)

should be disturbed with anxiety, as saith the prophet Naaman [*sic*], "The sword shall not depart from the house of the impious man", and again, "God shall raise up thy seed against thee."[1]

In the first place, as is sufficiently well known, he basely stole Queen Eleanor from his liege lord, Louis, king of the French, and then married her. In course of time and by an evil fortune he had by her the offspring above mentioned. By them also, as we have said, on account of this and other grave offences, some of which we shall recount hereafter, and because adversity engenders understanding, God willed he should be humbled and called to repentance, or if he proved obdurate, the father should be punished by his own brood and the torturer tormented by his own victims.[2] From the beginning even unto the end he was an oppressor of the nobility, weighing justice and injustice, right and wrong by his own convenience, a vendor and procrastinator of justice, shifty and cunning in speech, a ready breaker not merely of his word but also of his plighted troth, an open adulterer, ungrateful and impious towards God, the hammer of the Church and a son of perdition. . . .[3]

. . . From the time of this odious crime, this wicked infamy and sacrilege, the revolving wheel of fortune began to run swiftly down to its lowest point and was only slowly raised again to its normal height. The royal state began to weaken a little and the strength of the ruler to decline from day to day. For although after grave and desperate afflictions, by divine permission and also by way of proof, he seemed at times to rise again and mount up courageously to greater heights of glory, yet his sons, now grown men, frequently rose in revolt against him and day by day enticed the hearts of his nobles away from him until he could find no abiding state of happiness or enjoyment of security. . . .

By 1 June[4] [1189] all negotiations for peace between the English king and the count of Poitou[5] had led not to an agreement but to unrelenting hostility, and thus the divine vengeance was excited. After many castles in Maine had been destroyed, at length Le Mans itself was reached by the king of France and the count of Poitou with their armies. Therefore, when the townsfolk had been evacuated, the hostile armies prepared for battle. But while the opposing forces were not yet fully engaged but made as it were by sallies the preliminaries of battle, the English king as usual evaded military combat as long as he could. Recalling his men within the walls, he ordered the whole suburb adjoining the city, which though not comparable to it in dignity yet matched it in grandeur and in the abundance and variety of its merchandise, to be laid waste by fire, lest it should hinder the defence of the city or give advantage to the enemy. But the wind, which before this had been blowing away from the city, now suddenly changed and blew in the contrary but prevailing direction, and, increasing in strength, carried the hungry flames from the suburb into the

[1] II Samuel xii. 10, 11; words of the prophet Nathan.
[2] *carne carnificem cruciari.*
[3] In this career of wickedness and violence, Gerald continues, the culminating point was the king's persecution and murder of Thomas Becket, of which event a brief account is given in the passage omitted here.
[4] Actually 4 June, being Trinity Sunday.
[5] Richard, the king's son.

heart of the city. At once the fire raged with the utmost fury and spread to many parts of the city, so that the king was compelled to abandon it as fast as he could with his men, many being lost together with the city through the precipitancy of his retreat.

Thus having been put to flight by the French king and his son, the king reached a certain hill about two miles distant, from the summit of which he could look back on the burning city; and turning his face away he uttered this blasphemy, and that no less shamelessly than on another occasion, "Since thou, O God, to crown me with confusion and increase my dishonour, hast basely taken from me this day the city I have loved best in all the world, wherein I was born and bred and my father lies buried, and the body of St. Julian lies entombed, I also will assuredly recompense thee, as far as I am able, by withholding from thee that which thou lovest best in me." And more also which it is more fitting for a prudent man to pass over in contempt than to put into writing. . . .

At length, however, the pace of the pursuit slackened through the count of Poitou being thrown from his horse when it was pierced with a knight's lance. The same night the king reached Fresnay and the next day crossed from thence into Anjou. But when the opposing army had subdued Maine, it at once advanced on Touraine, and, as it were, tempting fortune in the ferocity of its attack and exploiting its success, took the noble city of Tours by storm.

When this had been accomplished, a parley was arranged between the kings for the Friday[1] not far from a little town in Touraine called Azai. But on the very day the meeting should have taken place at Azai the English king took to his bed, fatally smitten with an acute fever. The French king and the count of Poitou, however, would give no credence to this sickness, supposing that according to the king's habit it was counterfeit or designed to frustrate them; and on the morrow they blockaded the town with strong forces. At this, on the invitation of the English king, who still wished to secure the benefits of peace, his kinsfolk William, archbishop of Rheims, Philip, count of Flanders, and Theobald, count of Blois,[2] with certain others, were summoned to meet him in his camp. But when the king of France perceived that by a propitious turn of events God had already delivered his enemy into his hands, he would listen to no proposal for peace until the English king had in all things placed himself at Philip's mercy. This Henry promised to do, saving his honour and the crown and dignity of his kingdom. Whereupon the king of France answered that the surrender must be made unconditionally, nor would he allow any reservation to be made unless he himself of his mercy granted it. At length after many disputes and much coming and going of the negotiators, since necessity knows no law, an agreement was reached between them,[3] but not without much heart-searching and indignation on Henry's part which served to increase his malady. . . . The negotiations having been thus completed and set in writing, a treaty of peace was drawn up in agreement with the French king redounding in every way to the profit of the count of Poitou

[1] 30 June 1189.

[2] See above, No. 14, for the discrepancy between Gerald and the account given in the *Gesta Regis Henrici Secundi*.

[3] See above, No. 14.

but to the shame and loss of the king of England. The terms were then presented for the latter's hearing and consideration. The first clause concerned the surrender which he had made, the second provided that all who had taken the count's side against his father should owe allegiance for all their lands to the son alone and not to his father, unless by chance they wished to return to the king of their own free will. But when the king had read the names of those in the list, and first of all came the name of his son, John, as though beside himself in consternation, he sat up on the bed on which he was lying and gazing round fiercely said: "Is it true that John, my very heart, whom I have loved before all my sons, and for whose advancement I have endured all these ills, has deserted me?" When he discovered that this was indeed the case, he sank back upon his bed and, turning his face to the wall and groaning aloud, cried, "Now let all things go as they will, I care no longer for myself or for anything else in the world." And, as those who were present have borne witness positively, nothing provoked more the gravity and violence of his disease, nothing hastened his death more than this sudden and unexpected grief. . . .

It was included, moreover, in the treaty that he should receive from his son the kiss of peace and put away all anger and indignation from his heart. When this had been done, or rather counterfeited, and the kiss of peace had been given, as the count took leave of his father he overheard him say in a low voice, "God grant I die not before I have worthily avenged myself on thee!" So, withdrawing from the camp, the count carried back these words as a measure of the concord established between himself and his father, and aroused thereby the great mirth and astonishment of the French king and the whole court.

When matters had thus been settled, the king caused himself to be carried to the castle of Chinon, where on the fifth day of the week his strength further declined, and on the seventh day after he had taken to his bed, the very day the doctors call the crisis, he lay stricken to death. His groans ever increasing, he spake these words as from a full heart and wrung from the remnant of his thoughts by the violence of his malady and the gravity of his grief and indignation, "Shame, shame on a conquered king!" and so he laboured in his death-agony. At length, uttering words of dire calamity, the herald of his own confusion, he passed away and went to his last resting-place, overwhelmed and oppressed with grief rather than succumbing to a natural death. . . .

We will first unfold the things concerning the death of this great prince which occur to us as being worthy of note and attention and as a fearful example to all great men; then we will deal with the signs foretelling his death and diverse visions and revelations. In the first place it is noteworthy that, although in nearly every year he had two or three archbishops and five or six bishops in attendance upon him at court, yet at his end there was no bishop to give him counsel, no one of authority to give him consolation. To be sure, all who reverence God's Church and his ministers, the chosen representatives of Christ, are sustained in their last moments by priestly consolation. Those, however, who do not, but make themselves sons of perdition rather than of the Church, as we often see, are deprived of such consolation at the end.

When the corpse was laid out on the ground, all and sundry indulged their greed, as at such times they are wont to do, so that for some while the body was exposed naked and without any clothing, until a certain lad ran up and covered it as best he could with a short cloak, woven of fine thread, though it only reached to the knees, of the kind young men used to wear in summer. Thus was fulfilled, as often seems to be the case, the nickname bestowed upon him in his youth before he was king and while he was yet duke. Indeed he first introduced the short cloak from Anjou to England, where, from the time of his grandfather, Henry I, it had been the custom to wear long cloaks reaching down to the ground. For this reason he was commonly called Henry Curtmantel.

At this time also, when the body was to be taken from Chinon to Fontevrault for burial, it was difficult to find anyone to wind it in a shroud, to fix the horses in the hearse or to follow the funeral procession with fitting obsequies. When the body had already been carried into the great church of the nuns, the report of his death flying swiftly across the border brought the count of Poitou post-haste to attend his father's funeral. As he entered the church and approached the bier, his father's face lay unveiled, the cloth that had covered it having been laid aside. To all of them it appeared still to retain its colour and wonted look of fierceness. The count gazed on it with real and strong emotion and then knelt down before the altar in prayer, remaining there, however, scarcely longer than the space of a Paternoster. But at the very moment he had entered the church, as those present saw and bear witness, blood began to flow from the dead king's nostrils and ceased not so long as his son remained there; insomuch that the bystanders and those attending the bier were scarcely able to wipe it away and cleanse the mouth and face with the cloth. As to the meaning of this sign or portent, for it invites comment, let the diligent reader direct his attention thereto and seek out for himself by careful inquiry from the physicians the scientific reason for such an occurrence.

On the morrow, when the body was carried to the high altar for burial, there was scarcely to be had, as was fitting, a ring for his finger, a sceptre for his hand or crown for his head; in a word scarcely any insignia of royalty but what had been begged for the purpose. Even these were hardly suitable since for an orphrey only an old one could be found. And since the saddest state of the unfortunate man is that he once knew happiness, this also completed the tale of his adversity, that amidst his many treasures, both in England and across the sea, greater by far than was wont, he died a pauper; and that he who had heaped up riches as high as a tower and deep in the bowels of the earth, and had acquired the widest realms, yet knew not for whom he gathered them, should have left them crammed with gold and silver to the man he hated most in all the world. And thus by the discriminating vengeance of God while his son, the instrument and author of his death, succeeded him in all his dominions, like another Tantalus, surrounded by his own riches, he did not escape the misfortunes of poverty.

16. Gerald of Wales: Character of Henry II, king of England

The Latin original of this passage is to be found in the *Expugnatio Hibernica* of Gerald of Wales (*Giraldi Cambrensis Opera*, Rolls Series, 1867, vol. v, pp. 302–306), a work dedicated to Henry II's son, Richard, count of Poitou. The first part was later transcribed by Gerald himself in the *Liber de Principis Instructione*, *op. cit.*, pp. 214–215.

Henry II, king of England, was a man of reddish, freckled complexion with a large round head, grey eyes which glowed fiercely and grew bloodshot in anger, a fiery countenance and a harsh, cracked voice. His neck was somewhat thrust forward from his shoulders, his chest was broad and square, his arms strong and powerful. His frame was stocky with a pronounced tendency to corpulence, due rather to nature than to indulgence, which he tempered by exercise. For in eating and drinking he was moderate and sparing, and in all things frugal in the degree permissible to a prince. To restrain and moderate by exercise the injustice done him by nature and to mitigate his physical defects by virtue of the mind, he taxed his body with excessive hardship, thus, as it were, fomenting civil war in his own person.

In times of war, which frequently threatened, he gave himself scarcely a modicum of quiet to deal with those matters of business which were left over, and in times of peace he allowed himself neither tranquillity nor repose. He was addicted to the chase beyond measure; at crack of dawn he was off on horseback, traversing waste lands, penetrating forests and climbing the mountain-tops, and so he passed restless days. At evening on his return home he was rarely seen to sit down either before or after supper. After such great and wearisome exertions he would wear out the whole court by continual standing. But since "above everything moderation is beneficial in life"[1] and no remedy is good by itself alone, the swelling of his feet and legs, aggravated by injuries sustained in spurring on his refractory horses, brought on other bodily ailments, and without doubt old age, the mother and handmaid of many evils.

In stature he was of middle height, and in this he was matched by none of his sons, for the two eldest were a little above the average, while the two youngest stopped short of it. Except when troubled in mind or moved to anger, he was a prince of great eloquence and, what is remarkable in these days, polished in letters.[2]

He was a man easy of access and condescending, pliant and witty, second to none in politeness, whatever thoughts he might conceal within himself; a prince so remarkable for charity that as often he overcame by force of arms, he was himself vanquished through showing too great compassion. Strenuous in warfare, he was very prudent in civil life. But always he dreaded the doubtful arbitrament of war, and with supreme wisdom, in accordance with the ancient comic poet, he essayed every method before resorting to arms.[3] For those lost in battle he grieved more than any prince, and was more humane to the dead warrior than to him who survived; the dead indeed he mourned with a grief far greater than the love he bore the living. When difficulties

[1] Terence, *And.* I, 34.
[2] Here the transcription in the *Liber de Principis Instructione* ends.
[3] Terence, *Eun.* IV, 7, 19.

pressed hard upon him, none was more amicable, but none sterner once safety was regained. He was fierce towards those who remained untamed, but merciful to the vanquished, harsh to his servants, expansive towards strangers, prodigal in public, thrifty in private. Whom he had once hated he scarcely ever loved, but whom he had once loved he scarcely ever called to mind with hatred. He delighted beyond measure in birds of prey, especially when in flight, and in hounds pursuing wild beasts by their keen scent, both for their resonant and harmonious voices and for their swift running. Would he had given himself as much to his devotions as he did to the chase![1]

After the grievous injuries inflicted upon him by his sons, at the instigation it is said of their mother,[2] he became an open violator of the marriage bond. By a certain inconstancy of nature he was habitually prompt to break his word. For as often as his affairs became difficult he would repent in word rather than in deed, and so the more easily accounted his oath null and void than his deed. In all his affairs he showed cautious anticipation and restraint, so much so that the remedy to some extent exceeded the need, and he appeared dilatory in maintaining law and justice. Only by the grievous importunity of his counsellors would he give proper attention to all matters of business. Finally, while the justice which God bestows freely and without price was sold for money, he pre-eminently turned everything to his own profit and left many heirs to Gehazi[3] both in Church and State.

He was most diligent in guarding and maintaining peace, liberal beyond comparison in almsgiving and the peculiar defender of the Holy Land;[4] a lover of humility, an oppressor of the nobility and a contemner of the proud, "filling the hungry with good things and sending the rich empty away, exalting the humble and putting down the mighty from their seat".[5] By his detestable usurpations in the things pertaining to God he was highly presumptuous; out of zeal for justice, but not informed by knowledge, he joined together, or rather confounded the laws of Church and State, making them both one.[6] As a son of the Church, from whom he acquired the sceptre of royalty, he was either forgetful of his sacramental unction or ignored the fact that he had received it, devoting scarcely an hour to the divine mysteries of the sacred Host, and that very time, perchance through pressure of affairs of State, he passed more in taking counsel and in discussion than in his devotions. The revenues of vacant benefices he paid into the public treasury and as the whole lump may be spoilt by a little leaven, whilst he confiscated the revenues which Christ claims for himself, new difficulties continually arose and he was forced to pour forth his whole treasure, bestowing on the impious soldiery the moneys which should have been given to the priesthood. Through his consummate prudence he devised many changes and ordered them with foresight, but the issue of events was not always favourable and often seemed to work to a contrary end. Never did a great misfortune arise which was not brought about by familiar causes.

On his legitimate children he lavished in their childhood more than a father's

[1] Nevertheless, he heard Mass every day. [2] Eleanor of Aquitaine.

[3] The servant of the prophet Elisha who attempted to extort money from Naaman, after he had been healed of his leprosy, II Kings v. 20–27.

[4] Henry duly took the cross for the Third Crusade, but died before the expedition sailed. (See above, pp. 366–368.)

[5] *Magnificat*, 7, 8.

[6] A reference to Henry's projects in the Constitutions of Clarendon. (See below, No. 126.)

affection, but in their more advanced years he looked askance at them after the manner of a stepfather; and although his sons were so renowned and illustrious he pursued his successors with a hatred which perhaps they deserved, but which none the less impaired his own happiness. And because man's prosperity is neither enduring nor perfect, through the outrageous malice of fortune he incurred a sword when he ought to have obtained joy. He found strife instead of safety, ruin instead of repose, ingratitude instead of constancy, and the utmost confusion instead of peace and tranquillity.[1] Whether by some breach of the marriage tie or as a punishment for some crime of the parent, it befell that there was never true affection felt by the father towards his sons, nor by the sons towards their father, nor harmony among the brothers themselves.

Once he had subdued those who had oppressed the realm and disturbed its peace, among whom were his brothers and sons as well as others, including both his own servants and strangers, he for long afterwards governed in all things according to his will. Would that from beginning to end he had recognized this to be a mark of divine favour to himself by deeds appropriate to its worth, or at least had done so at the very end! Although he was daily set amidst a host of faces, he never again forgot anyone whom he had once closely scrutinized. Anything he had once heard worthy of remembrance he could never obliterate from his mind. So he had at his fingers' end both a ready knowledge of nearly the whole of history and also practical experience of almost everything in daily affairs. To compress much in a few words, if he had to the very end remained a chosen vessel to the Lord and had turned himself to his obedience, he would have been beyond comparison among the princes of this world for his many natural gifts.

[1] *unde habere debuerat gaudium, inde gladium; unde securitatem, inde securim; unde pacem, inde pestem; unde fortitudinem, inde ingratitudinem, unde quietem et tranquillitatem summa cum inquietudine suscipiens turbationem.*

17. Walter Map: Character of Henry II, king of England

The following passages, descriptive of the character and personality of Henry II from the pen of Walter Map, may be regarded as complementary to the longer account from that of his friend and 'fellow-countryman', Gerald of Wales, given above. It is indeed probable that Map's description, contained in his satirical commentary, *De Nugis Curialium* (*Of Courtiers' Trifles*), was written in imitation of Gerald's *Liber de Principis Instructione*, which was known to him.

Sprung from the Anglo-Norman aristocracy of the 'Welsh Marches' on the Herefordshire border, Walter Map was born about 1140 and was thus some seven years older than Gerald. As a young man he was introduced as a clerk into Henry II's household and travelled with the court both in England and in the continental lands of the Angevin empire. He may be regarded as one of the king's intimate counsellors and his record is therefore that of an eyewitness. In 1179 he was sent to Rome as the royal ambassador to the Third Lateran Council. As an ecclesiastic he received substantial preferment in the Church, culminating in his appointment as archdeacon of Oxford in 1197. His efforts to obtain the see of Hereford two years later were frustrated. He outlived Henry II by many years, and his death is conjecturally placed in the first decade of the twelfth century.

The *De Nugis Curialium* is a racy work, rich in local colour, legends, traditions and anecdotes, in which the author unconsciously reveals much of his personality, for example, his wit and humour, his literary knowledge (especially of the classics), and his prejudice against the Monastic Orders, particularly the Cistercians, including the illustrious apostle of the Order, St. Bernard. Here again a judicious comparison may be drawn with Gerald of Wales. The work was composed over a long period between 1181 and 1193. The section here presented comes near the end and was written after the death of Henry II; in all probability it was the last to be completed. The work has survived in a single MS. in the Bodleian Library, and the most recent edition of the Latin text is that of Dr. M. R. James, in the series *Anecdota Oxoniensia*, vol. XIV (1914). The relevant passages will be found on pp. 237–242. English versions have been published by Dr. James for the Cymroddorion Society (London, 1923) and by F. Tupper and M. B. Ogle (London, 1924). The introductions to these editions contain additional information on the man and his work.

When Henry began to reign he was about twenty years old, and he reigned for thirty-six years unconquered and unshaken, except by the sorrows his sons inflicted on him, which, it is said, he bore with a bad grace, so that he died through their hostility. Also this king caused great uneasiness to the most virtuous Louis in addition to the aforesaid wrong,[1] which the Lord remembered and avenged upon both the king and his sons, so it is believed.

I witnessed the beginnings of his reign and the following years in which his life was praiseworthy in many things. He was a little over medium height, a man blessed with sound limbs and a handsome countenance, one upon whom men gazed closely a thousand times, yet took occasion to return. In physical capacity he was second to none, incapable of no activity which another could perform, lacking no courtesy, well read to a degree both seemly and profitable, having a knowledge of all tongues spoken from the coasts of France to the river Jordan, but making use only of Latin and French. In making laws and in ordering the affairs of government he showed discrimination, and was clever in devising new and undiscovered legal procedure; he was easy of approach, modest and humble; the discomforts of dust and mire he suffered patiently; though vexed by the importunity of suitors and litigants and provoked by injustice, he bore all in silence. Nevertheless he was ever on his travels, moving by intolerable stages like a courier, and in this respect he showed little mercy to his household which accompanied him. He had great experience of dogs and birds and was a very keen follower of hounds; in night-watches and labours he was unremitting. As often as the

[1] A reference to Henry's marriage with Eleanor of Aquitaine, formerly wife of Louis VII.

vain images of pleasure disturbed his slumbers, he used to revile his body, because neither labour nor abstinence availed to break or weaken it. I, however, used to ascribe his distresses not to his infidelities but to his fear of growing too plump.

I have heard that his mother[1] taught him to protract all men's business, to hold fast for a long period whatever possessions fell into his hands and so enjoy the fruits of them, and to keep in suspense those who coveted them, endorsing this opinion by the following parable: "The untamed hawk, when raw meat is frequently offered to it and then snatched away or hidden from it, becomes more greedy and prone to obey and to cling closer." She taught him also that to be frequently in bed was to be rarely prepared for public audience, and that he should bestow nothing on any man on another's evidence unless he had seen and known him, and much worse advice of this kind. But I confidently impute to her teaching all his unattractive qualities. . . .

. . . Moreover the said King Henry II was distinguished for many virtues and infamous for some vices. One fault he derived from his mother's teaching, as I have said before, is this. He was dilatory in settling the affairs of his subjects, whence it befell that many died before they could bring their suits to a conclusion, or withdrew from court sorrowful and empty-handed, impelled by hunger. Another fault was that when he was taking his ease, which was seldom, he did not permit himself to be seen as good men desired, but, shutting himself up within doors, he was accessible only to those who seemed unworthy of such approach. A third fault was that, impatient of repose, he did not scruple to disturb almost half Christendom. In these three respects he erred; yet in others he was exceedingly good and lovable. No man surpassed him in gentleness and friendliness. As often as he went abroad he was seized by the crowd, carried about by force from place to place whither he would not, and what is remarkable, he gave ear patiently to each man singly, and though assailed at one time by the shouts of the mob, and at another violently dragged and pushed about, yet for this he brought no charge against any man nor used it as an excuse for anger. When he was too hard pressed he fled in silence to havens of peace. He did naught insolently or pompously, but was temperate, moderate and virtuous, faithful and wise, liberal and victorious, bringing honour on good men.

I lately crossed the Channel with him in a fleet of twenty-five vessels, reserved for his crossing without charge. But a storm scattered them all and drove them upon rocks and shores inhospitable to ships, with the exception of his own ship which, by God's grace, was brought safely into port. In the morning therefore the king sent and recompensed each sailor according to the estimate of his loss, although he was not bound to do this, and the total sum was large. Perchance another king would not have paid this just debt.

[1] Maud, the empress.

Part II

GOVERNMENT AND ADMINISTRATION

GOVERNMENT AND ADMINISTRATION

Introduction

THE texts which are here printed have been selected as having a special reference to the history of the English constitution between 1042 and 1189. They have been arranged as follows. In the first place, there appears a series of important public documents which set forth the position of the king in the feudal State, and indicate the principles of his government (Nos. 18–29). Secondly, there follows (No. 30) the earliest description of the king's household as the centre of administration. Thirdly (Nos. 31–49), there is included evidence relating to local government and to the office of the sheriff. Fourthly, there is presented (Nos. 50–60) evidence for the growth of royal jurisdiction in this period, as illustrated more particularly in the reports of trials and in legal treatises. And fifthly (Nos. 61–73), there are included texts concerning the development of the royal financial administration during this age.

A short survey of the constitutional development thus evidenced has been attempted above (pp. 49–60), and here it will suffice to note that whilst the chronicles of the period reflect the intellectual preoccupations of the age, its records are the natural product of the developing system of royal administration. The great records of the time, such as Domesday Book and the early Geld Rolls, are themselves the outcome of a government which exercised an omnicompetent control over all the departments of administration–a *curia* whose miscellaneous character can nowhere be more clearly seen than in the *Establishment of the King's Household* (No. 30). The financial records of the twelfth century such as the *Pipe Rolls* (Nos. 71–73) are at once a product and an illustration of the practice of the Exchequer whose operations are described with such fidelity in the *Dialogue of the Exchequer* (No. 70). And the Assizes of Henry II are at the same time the result of, and the evidence for, the growth of royal justice under the first Angevin king. Although, therefore, the history of the English constitution in this period is illustrated in all types of material appearing in this book, it must be based in the first instance upon documentary sources and especially upon the records of the royal administration.

SELECT BIBLIOGRAPHY

of Records and Modern Works relating to English Government and Administration (1042–1189)

(a) RECORDS AND CONTEMPORARY TREATISES

The earliest 'Public Records' of which the text has been preserved are the *Northamptonshire Geld Roll* (see below, No. 61) and the Geld Inquest relating to the south-western shires of 1084. The latter text is printed at the beginning (pp. 1–75) of vol. IV (1806) of the Record Commission's edition of Domesday Book. Domesday Book itself (see below, pp. 847–878, and separate Bibliography, pp. 810, 811) is "the earliest record of which the official copy has always remained in public custody". The continuous history of the Public Records, however, began with the practice of enrolment, and at once the earliest, and the most important, rolls of this period are the *Pipe Rolls* (see below, Nos. 71, 72 and 73). The earliest surviving Pipe Roll is that for 31 Henry I which was edited by Joseph Hunter in 1833 (reprinted by H.M. Stationery Office, 1929). A gap then occurs in the surviving series which, however, recommences in 1155. The Pipe Rolls of 2, 3, and 4 Henry II were edited by Joseph Hunter in 1844 (reprinted H.M. Stationery Office, 1931) and the work has been carried on by the Pipe Roll Society which has edited the Pipe Rolls for the whole of the remainder of the reign of Henry II. These volumes, whose publication extended from 1884 to 1925, provide perhaps the most important single source for the reign of Henry II, and the introductions to them, no less than twelve of which are by J. H. Round, supply a mass of information not to be obtained elsewhere. Other Public Records of this period are subordinate to those cited above, but mention may be made of the *Rotuli de Dominabus et Pueris et Puellis* (ed. J. H. Round, Pipe Roll Soc., vol. XXXV, 1913) which were compiled to ascertain the rights of the king over widows, minors and wards on whom he had claims. Two Exchequer Memoranda-books drawn up in the earlier part of the thirteenth century contain official documents relating to the twelfth century. These are *Liber Niger Scaccarii* (ed. T. Hearne, 2 vols., Oxford, 1728; 2nd ed. London, 1771), and *Liber Rubeus de Scaccario* (ed. H. Hall, under the title of *The Red Book of the Exchequer*, 3 vols., Rolls Series, 1886). This latter edition was much criticized on its appearance, and a prolonged controversy ensued to which the most important contributions were J. H. Round, *Studies in the Red Book of the Exchequer* (London, 1888), and H. Hall, *Red Book of the Exchequer: a reply to Mr. J. H. Round* (London, 1898). Both the *Liber Niger* and the *Liber Rubeus* contain the *Cartae* of knight-service, for which see below (Nos. 224–234).

The laws of the Anglo-Saxon kings were edited by F. Liebermann in *Die Gesetze der Angelsachsen* (3 vols., Halle, 1903–1916), a magisterial work in which the learned editor's notes contain much information relating to this period. A J. Robertson, *The Laws of the Kings of England from Edmund to Henry I* (Cambridge, 1925), gives text and translation of the principal laws issued by royal authority at this time. The chief constitutional edicts of the Anglo-Norman period and of the reign of Henry II are printed below (Nos. 18–29) and in each case the source from which they are derived is indicated. Texts of most of these can be conveniently studied in W. Stubbs, *Select Charters and other illustrations of English Constitutional History to the reign of Edward I* (Oxford, 1870; 9th ed., 1913). These, and other royal and private charters, are further considered below in a separate Bibliography (below, pp. 804–809).

During the twelfth century four important treatises respecting English government and administration were issued. These were:

(i) *Leges Henrici Primi*, a somewhat confused compilation relating to royal and private jurisdiction, which was edited in Liebermann, *op. cit.*, vol. I, pp. 544–611) and further discussed by him in *Über das englische Rechtsbuch Leges Henrici* (Halle, 1901). See also below, No. 57.

(ii) *Constitutio Domus Regis*. The text of this is contained in both the *Liber Niger* and the *Liber Rubeus* of the Exchequer, and it is translated and discussed below (No. 30).

(iii) *Dialogus de Scaccario* which is translated in full below (No. 70) and there discussed. The best edition of the original text is that made by A. Hughes, C. G. Crump and C. Johnson (Oxford, 1902). Another excellent edition, with text, translation and notes is that of C. Johnson. (Nelson's Medieval Classics, London, 1950.)

(iv) *Tractatus de Legibus et Consuetudinibus Regni Angliae* ascribed to Rannulf 'de Glanville'. Much of this appears in translation below (Nos. 58 and 268). The best edition of the original is G. E. Woodbine (Yale U.P., 1931).

(*b*) MODERN WORKS

The most important general work on the constitutional history of England in the Middle Ages is W. Stubbs, *The Constitutional History of England in its Origin and Development* (3 vols., Oxford, 1874–1878; many subsequent editions). This great book is, in respect of this period, of particular value for the years 1066–1189, and it has been a starting-point of research in this field ever since its first publication. Naturally, it has on many topics been superseded, particularly through the discovery and fresh appreciation of documents relating to Anglo-Norman feudalism, and some of the points on which it needs the revision to which it was never subjected by its author are indicated in C. Petit-Dutaillis, *Studies and Notes supplementary to Stubbs's Constitutional History* (translation, 3 vols., Manchester, 1908). Despite the change of emphasis which has taken place in the interpretation of English constitutional history in the Middle Ages, Stubbs's *Constitutional History* remains a standard secondary authority for this period. No other book can be adequately used as a substitute for it.

In 1895 there appeared F. Pollock and F. W. Maitland, *History of the English Law before the time of Edward I* (2nd ed., 2 vols., Cambridge, 1898). This masterly work is modern in its approach, and it exhibits to the full the genius of Maitland who was responsible for most of it. There are few problems relating to the constitutional history of England between 1042 and 1189 which are not in some measure illuminated in the course of its six opening chapters, and the work is particularly valuable for its discussion of the judicial reforms of the reign of Henry II. It has been supplemented, but not superseded, by W. S. Holdsworth, *History of English Law*, 12 vols. (1922–1938).

Maitland's lectures on constitutional history were posthumously printed (F. W. Maitland, *The Constitutional History of England*, Cambridge, 1908, and later editions). The earlier part of this book deals with the Norman and Angevin periods but, since it was never revised by the author, it lacks the authority of his other work. The latest general treatment of this subject to be based upon original authorities is J. E. A. Jolliffe, *The Constitutional History of Medieval England* (London, 1937).

G. B. Adams, *The Origin of the English Constitution* (enlarged edition, Yale U.P., 1920), is a brilliant study of the place of the king in the feudal State, and directs attention to the fact that the constitutional development of this age cannot be appraised apart from the establishment of Anglo-Norman feudalism. The changes which were thus involved are further treated in all general works, and to these may be added in this connexion F. Liebermann, *The National Assembly in the Anglo-Saxon Period* (Halle, 1913), and C. H. Haskins, "Quelques problèmes de l'histoire des institutions anglo-normandes" (*Congrès du Millénaire de la Normandie*, vol. I, pp. 562–570, Rouen, 1912). Works relating more specifically to Anglo-Norman feudalism are considered below in a separate Bibliography (see p. 811).

The royal household, its composition and its constitutional significance are discussed in a number of works. L. M. Larson, *The King's Household in England before the Norman Conquest* (Madison, 1904), is useful for the reign of Edward the Confessor. Studies of the royal household in the Anglo-Norman period are mostly based upon "The Establishment of the King's Household" (below, No. 30). Among these G. H. White, "The Household of the Norman Kings" (*Trans. R. Hist. Soc.*, 4th Series, vol. XXX (1948), pp. 127–156), is particularly valuable, and much information relative to this period is to be found in J. H. Round, *The King's Serjeants and Officers of State* (London, 1911). Reference should also be made to L. O. Pike, *Constitutional History of the House of Lords* (London, 1894) and to L. W. Vernon Harcourt, *His Grace the Steward and Trial of Peers* (London, 1907). Concerning the chancellor and the Chancery there is a large literature, the most useful summary of which is probably to be found in the introduction to H. W. C. Davis, *Regesta Regum Anglo-Normannorum*, vol. I (Oxford, 1913). Further studies of importance are R. Drogereit, "Gab es eine angelsachsische Königskanzlei?" *Archiv für Urkundenforschung*, vol. VI, pp. 335–436 (Leipzig, 1913), J. H. Round, "Regenbald, priest and chancellor" (*Feudal England*, pp. 421–430), W. H. Stevenson, "An Old-English Charter of William the Conqueror" (*Eng. Hist. Rev.*, vol. XI, 1896), V. H. Galbraith, "Girard the chancellor" (*ibid.*, vol. XLVI, 1931), F. E. Harmer, *Anglo-Saxon Writs* (Manchester U.P., 1952). The household of Henry I can be studied in W. Farrer's *Itinerary* of that king, and that of Henry II in R. W. Eyton, *Court, Household and Itinerary of King Henry II* (London, 1878). R. S. Hoyt, *The Royal Demesne in English Constitutional History* (Cornell U.P., 1950) is an excellent study of one aspect of royal administration and finance.

The king's household, forming the nucleus of the *curia regis*, was the centre of royal administration. From it other more specialized organs of government were evolved. Chief of these was the Exchequer. The starting-point of all detailed work on this subject remains the great treatise which Thomas Madox produced in the early years of the eighteenth century (*The History and Antiquities of the Exchequer of England*, London, 1711; 2nd ed., 2 vols., London, 1769). Of modern works the most illuminating are R. L. Poole, *The Exchequer in the Twelfth Century* (Oxford, 1912), and the introduction to the 'Oxford' edition of the *Dialogus de Scaccario* (Oxford, 1902). Valuable information is also to be obtained in the introduction by Charles Johnson to the Pipe Roll of 2 Richard I (*Pipe Roll Society*, New Series, vol. I, 1925), and the Norman Exchequer of the English kings is discussed in a long and valuable treatise by L. Delisle entitled "Des revenues publics en Normandie au douzième siècle" (*Bibliothèque de l'Ecole de Chartes*, vols. X, XI, XIII (1848–1852)). The financial system of the Anglo-Saxon monarchy is described briefly in F. M. Stenton, *Anglo-Saxon England*, and has engaged the attention of many writers on Domesday Book (see Bibliography, pp. 810, 811). There are many particular studies of the institutional innovations of the twelfth century, among which may be mentioned: J. H. Round, "The Origin of the Exchequer" (*Commune of London and Other Studies*, 1899, pp. 62–97); the same writer's "The Weigher of the Exchequer" (*Eng. Hist. Rev.*, vol. XXVI, 1911); and C. H. Haskins, "The Abacus and the King's Curia" (*ibid.*, vol. XXVII, 1912). G. H. White's "Financial Administration under Henry I" (*Trans. R. Hist. Soc.*, 4th Series, vol. VIII, pp. 56–78) is valuable and should be read in connexion with R. W. Southern, "Rannulf Flambard and early Anglo-Norman Administration" (*ibid.*, 4th Series, vol. XVI, 1933). The financial administration under Henry II must be studied in direct relation to the *Dialogues de Scaccario* and to the Pipe Rolls (see below, Nos. 70–73). Further reference may usefully be made to the tables contained in J. H. Ramsay, *Revenues of the Kings of England* (Oxford, 1925).

The growth of the royal jurisdiction in this age has been the subject of a considerable literature. The best introduction to this theme is to be found in the opening chapters of F. Pollock and F. W. Maitland, *History of English Law*; and T. F. T. Plucknett, *Concise History of the Common Law* (3rd ed., London, 1940) is also of high value. About royal justice before the Norman Conquest much information is to be gained from the elaborate notes appended to F. Liebermann's monumental *Die Gesetze der Angelsachsen* (3 vols., Halle, 1903–1916), and the same subject is treated more generally in the course of F. W. Maitland, *Domesday Book and Beyond* (Cambridge, 1897), and in P. Vinogradoff, *English Society in the Eleventh Century* (Oxford, 1908). The judicial functions of the *curia regis* are well brought out in G. B. Adams, *Council and Courts in Anglo-Norman England* (Yale U.P., 1926). The great pleas of the age are mostly dealt with in M. M. Bigelow, *Placita Anglo-Normannica* (Boston, 1879), and much information derived from these and other sources is contained in M. M. Bigelow, *History of Procedure in England* (London, 1880). The literature specially concerned with some of the more important of these trials is particularly noted in connexion with the reports of them printed in this book (see below, Nos. 50–56). The origin of the jury, and its early use, are discussed in the works of Stubbs, Vinogradoff, Maitland and Stenton cited above, and its employment at the time of Henry II can best be studied in the treatise of 'Glanville' (see below, No. 58), and in G. E. Woodbine's notes to his edition of that text. Reference may also be made to N. D. Hurnard, "The Anglo-Norman Franchises" (*Eng. Hist. Rev.*, vol. LXIV, 1949). The interconnexion between royal and ecclesiastical jurisdiction in this age is considered in all the works devoted to the latter and is set out with particular clarity in Z. N. Brooke, *The English Church and the Papacy* (Cambridge, 1931). The jurisdictional aspects of the dispute between Henry II and Becket are discussed in many of the works on the ecclesiastical history of the age (see Bibliography, pp. 594, 595).

In the sphere of local administration the characteristic achievement of the Norman monarchy was to utilize the existing institutions of the shire and hundred. The evolution and functions of these have been considered in vol. I of this Series, and they have been exhaustively treated in the works of Stubbs and Maitland, and again in H. M. Chadwick, *Anglo-Saxon Institutions* (Cambridge, 1905). W. A. Morris, *The Frankpledge System* (Harvard U.P., 1910) is also interesting in this respect. The essential link between the monarchy and local government, and also between the financial and jurisdictional administration of the crown, was the sheriff whose functions are therefore very fully discussed in all the general constitutional histories of England at this time. W. A. Morris, *The Medieval English Sheriff to 1300* (Manchester, 1927), is indispensable on this question.

A. SELECT DOCUMENTS OF A GENERAL NATURE RELATING TO THE ROYAL ADMINISTRATION

THE texts which here follow may be regarded as the cardinal documents relating to English constitutional history in this period. Being general in their nature, they cannot be classified under particular headings of administration. They have all been frequently printed, and are here introduced separately.

18. The "Laws of William the Conqueror"

This document appears in its earliest form in the *Textus Roffensis*, ed. T. Hearne (1720), a manuscript of the earlier half of the twelfth century. It is probably a compilation of legal enactments made at various times by the Conqueror, apart from his confirmations of earlier laws and customs. The document is thus very miscellaneous in content. Note may be made of the introduction of trial by battle, in cases where Normans were concerned, as an alternative to the Anglo-Saxon system of wager-at-law and ordeal. The Latin text is printed in F. Liebermann, *Die Gesetze der Angelsachsen*, vol. I, p. 486, and in W. Stubbs, *Select Charters* (ed. 1913), pp. 98–99. An English translation appears in E. F. Henderson, *Select Historical Documents of the Middle Ages* (1896), pp. 7–8.

Here is set down what William, king of the English, established in consultation with his magnates after the conquest of England:

1.[1] First that above all things he wishes one God to be revered throughout his whole realm, one faith in Christ to be kept ever inviolate, and peace and security to be preserved between English and Normans.

2. We decree also that every freeman shall affirm by oath and compact that he will be loyal to King William both within and without England, that he will preserve with him his lands and honour with all fidelity and defend him against all his enemies.

3. I will, moreover, that all the men whom I have brought with me, or who have come after me, shall be protected by my peace and shall dwell in quiet. And if any one of them shall be slain, let the lord of his murderer seize him within five days, if he can; but if he cannot, let him begin to pay me 46 marks of silver so long as his substance avails. And when his substance is exhausted, let the whole hundred in which the murder took place pay what remains in common.

4. And let every Frenchman who, in the time of King Edward, my kinsman, was a sharer in the customs of the English, pay what they call "scot and lot", according to the laws of the English. This decree was ordained in the city of Gloucester.

5. We forbid also that any live cattle shall be bought or sold for money except within cities, and this shall be done before three faithful witnesses; nor even anything old without surety and warrant. But if anyone shall do otherwise, let him pay once, and afterwards a second time for a fine.

6. It was also decreed there that if a Frenchman shall charge an Englishman with perjury or murder or theft or homicide or 'ran', as the English call open rapine which cannot be denied, the Englishman may defend himself, as he shall prefer, either by the ordeal of hot iron[2] or by wager of battle. But if the Englishman be infirm, let him find another who will take his place. If one of them shall be vanquished, he shall pay

[1] The conventional numeration of the paragraphs is retained for purposes of reference. This has no place in the original.

[2] For various ordeals, see below, No. 58, pp. 476–478.

a fine of 40 shillings to the king. If an Englishman shall charge a Frenchman and be unwilling to prove his accusation either by ordeal or by wager of battle, I will, nevertheless, that the Frenchman shall acquit himself by a valid oath.

7. This also I command and will, that all shall have and hold the law of King Edward in respect of their lands and all their possessions, with the addition of those decrees I have ordained for the welfare of the English people.

8. Every man who wishes to be considered a freeman shall be in pledge[1] so that his surety shall hold him and hand him over to justice if he shall offend in any way. And if any such shall escape, let his sureties see to it that they pay forthwith what is charged against him, and let them clear themselves of any complicity in his escape. Let recourse be had to the hundred and shire courts as our predecessors decreed. And those who ought of right to come and are unwilling to appear, shall be summoned once; and if for the second time they refuse to come, one ox shall be taken from them, and they shall be summoned a third time. And if they do not come the third time, a second ox shall be taken from them. But if they do not come at the fourth summons, the man who was unwilling to come shall forfeit from his goods the amount of the charge against him–'ceapgeld' as it is called–and in addition to this a fine to the king.

9. I prohibit the sale of any man by another outside the country on pain of a fine to be paid in full to me.

10. I also forbid that anyone shall be slain or hanged for any fault, but let his eyes be put out and let him be castrated. And this command shall not be violated under pain of a fine in full to me.

19. The "Coronation Charter" of Henry I (5 August 1100)

This famous charter was issued by Henry I at the beginning of his reign, and since in the surviving copies the address and witnesses vary, it is probable that it was circulated to every shire. It can best be regarded as a bid for support by the new king, who here makes promises which he hopes will be acceptable to various sections of the community and in particular to the lay magnates. Its contemporary significance may thus easily be over-emphasized, but it was later to be cited as an important precedent. It is particularly informative as evidence of feudal custom and especially of the relations between the Anglo-Norman kings and their tenants-in-chief. Its testimony respecting the 'feudal incidents' is also noteworthy, as is also its illustration of the manner in which feudal rights might be abused. It has been many times printed. The best edition is probably that contained in F. Liebermann, *Die Gesetze der Angelsachsen*, vol. I, p. 521. It is also printed in C. Bémont, *Chartes des Libertés anglaises* (1892), pp. 3–6, and in W. Stubbs, *Select Charters* (ed. 1913), pp. 117–119.

Henry, king of the English, to Samson the bishop, and Urse of Abbetot, and to all his barons and faithful vassals, both French and English, in Worcestershire, greeting.

1.[2] Know that by the mercy of God and by the common counsel of the barons of the whole kingdom of England I have been crowned king of this realm. And because the kingdom has been oppressed by unjust exactions, I now, being moved by reverence towards God and by the love I bear you all, make free the Church of God; so that I will neither sell nor lease its property; nor on the death of an archbishop or a bishop or an abbot will I take anything from the demesne of the Church or from its vassals during the period which elapses before a successor is installed. I abolish all the

[1] A reference to the system of frankpledge, see below, p. 460.

[2] The conventional numeration of paragraphs is retained for purposes of reference. This has no place in the original.

evil customs by which the kingdom of England has been unjustly oppressed. Some of those evil customs are here set forth.

2. If any of my barons or of my earls or of any other of my tenants shall die, his heir shall not redeem his land as he was wont to do in the time of my brother, but he shall henceforth redeem it by means of a just and lawful 'relief'. Similarly the men of my barons shall redeem their lands from their lords by means of a just and lawful 'relief'.[1]

3. If any of my barons or of my tenants shall wish to give in marriage his daughter or his sister or his niece or his cousin, he shall consult me about the matter; but I will neither seek payment for my consent, nor will I refuse my permission, unless he wishes to give her in marriage to one of my enemies. And if, on the death of one of my barons or of one of my tenants, a daughter should be his heir, I will dispose of her in marriage and of her lands according to the counsel given me by my barons. And if the wife of one of my tenants shall survive her husband and be without children, she shall have her dower and her marriage portion, and I will not give her in marriage unless she herself consents.[2]

4. If a widow survives with children under age, she shall have her dower and her marriage portion, so long as she keeps her body chaste; and I will not give her in marriage except with her consent. And the guardian of the land, and of the children, shall be either the widow or another of their relations, as may seem more proper. And I order that my barons shall act likewise towards the sons and daughters and widows of their men.

5. I utterly forbid that the common mintage,[3] which has been taken from the towns and shires, shall henceforth be levied, since it was not so levied in the time of King Edward. If any moneyer or other person be taken with false money in his possession, let true justice be visited upon him.

6. I forgive all pleas and all debts which were owing to my brother, except my own proper dues, and except those things which were agreed to belong to the inheritance of others, or to concern the property which justly belonged to others. And if anyone had promised anything for his heritage, I remit it, and I also remit all 'reliefs' which were promised for direct inheritance.

7. If any of my barons or of my men, being ill, shall give away or bequeath his movable property, I will allow that it shall be bestowed according to his desires. But if, prevented either by violence or through sickness, he shall die intestate as far as concerns his movable property, his widow or his children or his relatives or one of his true men shall make such division for the sake of his soul, as may seem best to them.

8. If any of my barons or of my men shall incur a forfeit, he shall not be compelled to pledge his movable property to an unlimited amount, as was done in the time of my father and my brother; but he shall only make payment according to the extent of his legal forfeiture, as was done before the time of my father and in the time of my earlier predecessors. Nevertheless, if he be convicted of breach of faith or of crime, he shall suffer such penalty as is just.

[1] See below, p. 412, n. 3.
[2] See below, No. 268, p. 941.
[3] *monetagium*: mintage is here apparently used in the sense of a forced levy to prevent loss to the king from depreciation of the coinage.

9. I remit all murder-fines which were incurred before the day on which I was crowned king; and such murder-fines as shall now be incurred shall be paid justly according to the law of King Edward.

10. By the common counsel of my barons I have retained the forests in my own hands as my father did before me.[1]

11. The knights, who in return for their estates perform military service equipped with a hauberk of mail, shall hold their demesne lands quit of all gelds and all work; I make this concession as my own free gift in order that, being thus relieved of so great a burden, they may furnish themselves so well with horses and arms that they may be properly equipped and prepared to discharge my service and to defend my kingdom.

12. I establish a firm peace in all my kingdom, and I order that this peace shall henceforth be kept.

13. I restore to you the law of King Edward together with such emendations to it as my father made with the counsel of his barons.

14. If since the death of my brother, King William, anyone shall have seized any of my property, or the property of any other man, let him speedily return the whole of it. If he does this no penalty will be exacted, but if he retains any part of it he shall, when discovered, pay a heavy penalty to me.

Witness: Maurice, bishop of London; William, bishop-elect of Winchester;[2] Gerard, bishop of Hereford; Henry the earl;[3] Simon the earl;[4] Walter Giffard; Robert of Montfort-sur-Risle; Roger Bigot; Eudo the steward; Robert, son of Haimo; and Robert Malet.

At London when I was crowned. Farewell.

20. Charter of Stephen addressed generally (probably 1135)

This charter is of uncertain date but was probably issued in 1135 at the time of Stephen's coronation. It is vague and formal in its terms, but the reference to Edward the Confessor is of interest. It has been many times printed, notably in W. Stubbs, *Select Charters* (ed. 1913), p. 142.

Stephen (by the grace of God), king of the English, to the justices, sheriffs, barons, and to all his servants and liegemen, both French and English, greeting. Know that I have granted, and by this present charter confirmed, to all my barons and vassals of England all the liberties and good laws which Henry, king of the English, my uncle,[5] granted and conceded to them. I also grant them all the good laws and good customs which they enjoyed in the time of King Edward.[6] Wherefore I will and firmly command that both they and their heirs shall have and hold all these good laws and liberties from me and from my heirs freely, fully and in peace. And I forbid anyone to molest or hinder them, or to cause them loss or damage in respect of these things under pain of forfeiture to me.

Witness: William Martel.

At London.

[1] cf. below, No. 28.
[2] William Giffard. He was not consecrated until 11 August 1107.
[3] Henry of Beaumont, earl of Warwick. See Table 12.
[4] Simon 'de St.-Liz', earl of Huntingdon. See Table 9.
[5] Henry I.
[6] Edward the Confessor.

21. Charter of Stephen addressed generally (1136)

Many copies of this charter have survived, and a description of the original, which is now in the possession of the dean and chapter of Salisbury, is given by R. L. Poole in *Hist. MSS. Comm., Report on MSS. in Various Collections*, vol. 1 (1901), p. 384. The circumstances in which it was granted are discussed in J. H. Round, *Geoffrey de Mandeville* (1892), pp. 19–23. The bid on the part of the king for ecclesiastical support will be specially noted, and in this sense the charter may be compared with Nos. 19 and 20 above. The large number of important witnesses called in support of the charter is also noteworthy. This represents a very full session of the king's court, and in the Hereford copy of the charter it is described as having been given *in communi concilio*. The charter has been printed many times. It will be found in W. Stubbs, *Select Charters* (ed. 1913), pp. 143, 144.

I, Stephen, by the grace of God, and, with the assent of the clergy and people, elected king of the English,[1] and consecrated thereto by William,[2] archbishop of Canterbury and legate of the holy Roman Church, and confirmed by Innocent,[3] pope of the holy Roman See, out of respect and love towards God, do grant freedom to holy Church and confirm the reverence due to her.

I promise that I will neither do nor permit anything to be done simoniacally in the Church, or in ecclesiastical affairs. I allow and concede that jurisdiction and authority over ecclesiastical persons and over all clerks and their property, together with the disposal of ecclesiastical estates, shall lie in the hands of the bishops. I grant and decree that the immunities of churches confirmed by their charters, and their customs which have been observed from antiquity, shall remain inviolate. I grant also that all ecclesiastical possessions and tenures, which were held on the day King William, my grandfather, was alive and dead, shall be free and quit of all dues and from the claims of all litigants. But if the Church shall hereafter seek to claim possessions which it held before the death of the said king, but of which it is now deprived, I reserve to my own pleasure and decision whether the matter is to be discussed, or the property restored. But whatsoever has been bestowed upon the churches since the death of the said king by the generosity of kings or the munificence of princes, whether in alms or by purchase, or by any other alienation on the part of the faithful, I duly confirm. I promise that I will keep peace and do justice to all men, and preserve them as far as I am able.

I reserve for my own use the forests which William, my grandfather, and William, my uncle, established and maintained. All others, which King Henry added to them, I restore and surrender to the churches and the kingdom free from molestation.

If any bishop or abbot or other ecclesiastical person shall have made reasonable disposal of his property, or intended so to dispose of it before his death, I allow that this shall be firmly maintained. But if he be prevented by sudden death, let such disposal of his property be made for the salvation of his soul at the discretion of the Church. But when sees are vacant and without shepherds, I will commit them and all their possessions into the hand and keeping of the clerks and pious men of the said church, until a new pastor may be canonically appointed.

I wholly annul all exactions, injustices and 'miskennings',[4] whether wrongfully imposed by the sheriffs or by any other person.

[1] The whole charter may be regarded as an exotic diplomatic form.
[2] William 'de Corbeil'. [3] Innocent II.
[4] A penalty imposed for a mistake in reciting a formula in a process of litigation.

I will observe good laws and the ancient and lawful customs in respect of pecuniary exactions for murder and pleas and other causes, and I command them to be observed and established.

All these things I grant and confirm saving my royal and lawful dignity.

Witness: William, archbishop of Canterbury; Hugh, archbishop of Rouen;[1] Henry, bishop of Winchester; Roger, bishop of Salisbury; Alexander, bishop of Lincoln; Nigel, bishop of Ely; Everard, bishop of Norwich; Simon, bishop of Worcester; Bernard, bishop of St. David's; Audin, bishop of Evreux;[2] Richard, bishop of Avranches;[3] Robert, bishop of Hereford; John, bishop of Rochester; Æthelwulf, bishop of Carlisle; Roger the chancellor; Henry, the king's nephew; Robert, earl of Gloucester; William, earl 'de Warenne'; Rannulf, earl of Chester;[4] Robert, earl of Warwick;[5] Robert 'de Vere'; Miles of Gloucester; Brian, son of the count, and Robert 'd'Oilly', constables; William Martel and Hugh Bigot and Humphrey 'de Bohun' and Simon 'de Beauchamp', stewards; William of Aubigny and Odo Martel, butlers; Robert of Ferrières; William Peveril of Nottingham; Simon of St.-Liz; William of Aumale; Payn, son of John; Haimo of St. Clare and Ilbert 'of Lassy'.

At Oxford, in the year of the Incarnation of our Lord, 1136, and in the first year of my reign.

22. Charter of Stephen describing the conditions of the "Treaty of Winchester", made between the king and Henry, son of the Empress Maud (later Henry II), at the conclusion of the civil war (November 1153)

This charter is important as marking the end of the civil war,[6] and as determining the succession to the throne of England. It deserves study also with reference to the feudal conditions prevailing in England at the time, and in this sense it may be compared in particular with No. 257. The long list of important witnesses is also significant. It has been suggested that this charter only relates some of the terms of this arrangement. This charter is discussed in J. H. Round, *Studies in Peerage and Family History* (1901), pp. 147–180, by C. T. Clay in *Early Yorkshire Charters*, vol. VIII, pp. 15, 16, and by A. L. Poole, *Domesday Book to Magna Carta*, p. 165. Printed: L. Delisle and E. Berger, *Recueil des Actes de Henri II*, vol. I, p. 61; *Hist. MSS., Comm. 12th Rep.*, App. IX, p. 119.

Stephen, king of England, to the archbishops, bishops, abbots, earls, justiciars, sheriffs, barons, and to all his liegemen of England, greeting.

Know that I, King Stephen, have established Henry, duke of Normandy, as my successor in the kingdom of England, and have recognized him as my heir by hereditary right; and thus I have given and confirmed to him and his heirs the kingdom of England.

The duke in return for this honour and gift and confirmation which I have made to him, has done homage to me, and given me surety by oath. He has sworn that he will be my liegeman, and that he will guard my life and honour by every means in his power according to the agreements made between us which are described in this charter.

I also have given an oath of surety to the duke, that I will guard his life and honour

[1] Hugh of Amiens, archbishop of Rouen, 1130–1164.
[2] 'Andoenus', bishop of Evreux, 1113–1139.
[3] Richard I, bishop of Avranches, 1134–1142.
[4] See Table 14.
[5] See Table 12.
[6] See above, p. 311.

by every means in my power, and that I will maintain him as my son and heir in all things, and that I will do all I can to guard him against all men.

William, my son, has done liege homage and given surety to the duke of Normandy, and the duke has granted him to hold from him all the lands which I held before I acquired the kingdom of England, whether in England or in Normandy or in other places. He is also to hold whatever came with the daughter of the earl of Warenne,[1] whether in England or in Normandy, and whatever pertains to those honours. And the duke will put William, my son,[2] and the men of that honour into possession of all the lands, villages and boroughs and revenues which the duke has now in his demesne, and especially those which pertain to the honour of the earl of Warenne, particularly the castle of Bellencombre, and the castle of Mortemer: the agreement being that Reginald of Warenne[3] shall, if he wish, keep the castle of Bellencombre and the castle of Mortemer, giving the duke hostages in respect of it; but if Reginald does not wish to do this, then other liegemen of the earl of Warenne agreeable to the duke shall keep the said castles likewise giving the duke good hostages.

The duke shall return to him the other castles, which belong to the count of Mortain,[4] at my pleasure, when he can, for safeguard and with safe hostages, it being understood that all hostages shall be returned without dispute to my son when the duke comes into possession of the kingdom of England.

The duke has agreed to the increment which I have given to my son, to wit, the castle and the town of Norwich with 700 librates of land, it being understood that the revenue of Norwich itself is included within those 700 librates; and the whole county of Norfolk, except what pertains to churches and prelates and abbots and earls, and excluding particularly the third penny which pertains to Hugh Bigot as earl, and excepting in all things the rights of the royal justice which are reserved.

Also, in order to increase my thanks and to strengthen my love towards him, the duke has given to my son, William, all those things which Richer of Laigle had from the honour of Pevensey. And besides this castle and town of Pevensey, and the service of Faramus, apart from the castle and town of Dover, and which pertains to the honour of Dover, the duke has confirmed the church of Faversham with its appurtenances and will confirm all the other things given or returned by me to other churches by the advice of holy Church, or through my own intention.

The earls and barons of the duke, who were never my men, in consideration for the honour which I have done to their lord, have sworn homage to me, saving only the agreements made between me and the duke; and the others who in previous times had done homage to me, and performed fealty to me as to their lord.

If the duke goes back from his promises, these shall altogether break their service to him until he corrects his errors; and my son also, following the counsel of holy Church, shall act likewise in similar circumstances.

My earls and my barons have done liege homage to the duke saving their fealty

[1] Isabel, daughter of William third earl of Warenne, married William of Blois, son of King Stephen. After his death she married in 1164 Hamelin, an illegitimate son of Geoffrey of Anjou by an unknown mother.

[2] A younger son of the king. He died in 1159.

[3] Younger brother of William, the third earl. He was ancestor of the Warennes of Wormegay.

[4] William, son of the king, was also count of Mortain.

to me so long as I live and have the kingdom with a similar understanding that if I go back from my promises they shall altogether break their service to me until I correct my errors.

The citizens of towns and the men of castles, which I have in my demesne, have likewise by my order done homage and given surety to the duke saving the fealty which they owe to me so long as I live and have the kingdom. Those who keep the castle of Wallingford have done me homage, and have given me hostages that they may keep their fealty to me.

And I have given surety to the duke concerning castles and fortifications, according to the counsel of holy Church, so that the duke on my death may not here suffer loss or hindrance in his acquisition of the kingdom.

The Tower of London and Windsor Castle have with the counsel of holy Church been given into the keeping of Richard of Lucé. But the said Richard has sworn in the hand of the archbishop, and has given his own son as pledge, that on my death he will hand over these castles to the duke.

Likewise, with the counsel of holy Church, Roger of Lucé is keeping the castle of Oxford, and Jordan 'de Buselo' is keeping the castle of Lincoln; and they are the liegemen of the duke, and have sworn and have given hostages in the hand of the archbishop that when I die they will hand over these castles to the duke without any dispute.

The bishop of Winchester[1] has pledged himself in the hand of the archbishop, and in the presence of the bishops, that when I die he will hand over the castle of Winchester and the fortification of Southampton to the duke.

But if any one of those to whom castles have been entrusted shall make delay, or shall go away from the castle to which he has been appointed, then, with the counsel of holy Church, another custodian shall be appointed in his place until he returns.

And if anyone who keeps my castles shall show himself contumacious or a rebel, to wit, concerning the castles which pertain to the crown, then the duke and I making common cause shall wage war upon him until he has been compelled to give satisfaction to both of us.

The archbishops, bishops and abbots of the kingdom of England, by my order, have sworn fealty to the duke. And those who shall henceforth be made bishops or abbots in the kingdom of England shall do the same.

And the archbishops and bishops severally have undertaken that if either of us departs from these agreements, they will visit him with the justice of the Church until he has corrected his errors and returned to the proper observation of this pact.

The mother of the duke,[2] and his wife, and his brothers, and all his men to whom this applies have likewise given sureties about this.

In all the business of the kingdom I will act with the advice of the duke.

But in the whole kingdom of England, both in that part which pertains to the duke and in that part which pertains directly to me, I shall exercise royal justice.

All these were witnesses: Theobald, archbishop of Canterbury; Henry, bishop of Winchester; Robert, bishop of Exeter; Robert, bishop of Bath; Jocelyn, bishop of

[1] Henry of Blois, bishop of Winchester, brother of the king.

[2] Maud, the Empress.

Salisbury; Robert, bishop of Lincoln; Hilary, bishop of Chichester; William, bishop of Norwich; Richard, bishop of London; Nigel, bishop of Ely; Gilbert, bishop of Hereford; Walter, bishop of Chester; Walter, bishop of Rochester; Geoffrey, bishop of St. Asaph's; Robert, prior of Bermondsey; Otun, knight of the Temple; William, earl of Gloucester; Reginald, earl of Cornwall; Baldwin, earl of Devon; Roger, earl of Hertford; Patrick [earl of] of Salisbury; William of Aumale, the earl; Aubrey the earl; Roger, earl of Clare; Richard, earl of Pembroke;[1] Richard of Lucé; William Martel; Richard of Le Hommet; Reginald of Warenne; Manasser Biset; John of Norwich; Richard of Canville; Henry of Essex.

At Westminster.

23. Charter of Henry II addressed generally (19 December 1154)

This charter issued by Henry II immediately after his coronation may be modelled on that issued by Stephen in 1135 (above, No. 20). Henry merely confirms in vague terms the customs more specifically allowed in Henry I's charter issued at the beginning of his reign (No. 19). This text has been frequently printed, notably in W. Stubbs, *Select Charters* (ed. 1913), p. 158.

Henry (by the grace of God), king of the English, duke of the men of Normandy and Aquitaine, and count of the Angevins to all his earls, barons and liegemen, both French and English, greeting. Know that for the honour of God and holy Church, and for the common restoration of my whole realm, I have granted and restored, and by this present charter confirmed, to God and to holy Church, and to all my earls, barons and vassals all concessions, gifts, liberties and free customs, which King Henry, my grandfather, granted and conceded to them. Likewise all evil customs, which he abolished and relaxed, I also grant to be relaxed and abolished in my name and in that of my heirs. Wherefore I will, and firmly command, that holy Church and all my earls, barons and vassals shall have and hold all these customs, gifts, liberties and freedom from pecuniary exactions, freely and unmolested, fully, rightly and in peace from me and my heirs for themselves and their heirs, as freely and peaceably and fully in everything as King Henry, my grandfather, granted and conceded to them and confirmed by his charter.

Witness: Richard of Lucé.

At Westminster.

24. The Assize of Clarendon (1166)

This important document is the first of the great legislative enactments of the reign of Henry II. It was issued at the council held at Clarendon in the early part of the year 1166 and probably in February. The assize is the earliest official document providing evidence for the great administrative changes introduced by Henry II, and particularly for those effected in the sphere of local jurisdiction. The visitations of the itinerant justices are here seen to have become regular, and increased powers of police jurisdiction have been given to them. The sworn inquest is here applied extensively for the settlement of criminal cases. Indeed the assize may be regarded as a landmark in the history of the jury, since it supplies evidence of the existence of the use of juries of presentment and recognition as a normal part of the administration of local justice. The assize is also of interest for the light it throws upon the changes introduced about this time in the formal procedure in criminal cases whereby the ancient processes of compurgation and trial by ordeal were now to be supplemented by recourse to the previous record and reputation of the accused. The Latin text of the assize is to be found in the appendix to Roger of Howden's *Chronica* (ed. W. Stubbs, Rolls Series, 1871), vol. II, p. cii. A slightly different version of the text is printed in the main body of the chronicle (*op. cit.*, vol. II, p. 248). It is the former of these two versions which is reproduced in W. Stubbs, *Select Charters*

[1] This is 'Strongbow' (see above, No. 12, pp. 340–342).

(ed. 1913), p. 170. An English translation is given in Adams and Stephens, *Select Documents of English Constitutional History*, p. 14. The text has been frequently discussed, and particular reference may be made to F. Pollock and F. W. Maitland, *History of English Law*, vol. I, pp. 137 *et sqq.*; M. M. Bigelow, *History of Procedure in England* (1880), pp. 99 *et sqq.*; G. B. Adams, *Origin of the English Constitution* (1912), pp. 112 *et sqq.*

Here begins the Assize of Clarendon made by King Henry II with the assent of the archbishops, bishops, abbots, earls and barons of all England.

1.[1] In the first place the aforesaid King Henry, on the advice of all his barons, for the preservation of peace, and for the maintenance of justice, has decreed that inquiry shall be made throughout the several counties and throughout the several hundreds[2] through twelve of the more lawful men of the hundred and through four of the more lawful men of each vill upon oath that they will speak the truth,[3] whether there be in their hundred or vill any man accused or notoriously suspect[4] of being a robber or murderer or thief, or any who is a receiver of robbers or murderers or thieves, since the lord king has been king. And let the justices inquire into this among themselves and the sheriffs among themselves.[5]

2. And let anyone, who shall be found, on the oath of the aforesaid, accused or notoriously suspect[4] of having been a robber or murderer or thief, or a receiver of them, since the lord king has been king, be taken and put to the ordeal of water,[6] and let him swear that he has not been a robber or murderer or thief, or receiver of them, since the lord king has been king, to the value of 5 shillings, so far as he knows.

3. And if the lord of the man, who has been arrested, or his steward or his vassals shall claim him by pledge within the third day following his capture, let him be released on bail with his chattels until he himself shall stand his trial.

4. And when a robber or murderer or thief or receiver of them has been arrested through the aforesaid oath, if the justices are not about to come speedily enough into the county where they have been taken, let the sheriffs send word to the nearest justice by some well-informed person that they have arrested such men, and the justices shall send back word to the sheriffs informing them where they desire the men to be brought before them; and let the sheriffs bring them before the justices. And together with them let the sheriffs bring from the hundred and the vill, where they have been arrested, two lawful men to bear the record of the county and of the hundred as to why they have been taken, and there before the justice let them stand trial.

5. And in the case of those who have been arrested through the aforesaid oath of this assize, let no man have court or justice or chattels save the lord king in his court in the presence of his justices; and the lord king shall have all their chattels.[7] But in the case of those who have been arrested otherwise than by this oath, let it be as is customary and due.

[1] The conventional numeration of the paragraphs is retained for purposes of reference. This has no place in the original.

[2] *i.e.* through the visitation of the itinerant justices; for a discussion of the restoration and subsequent experiments in the development and reorganization of the eyre system, see pp. 59, 60.

[3] The sworn inquest is here applied to criminal jurisdiction in the form of the 'accusing jury' or jury of presentment, operating within the hundred unit in conjunction with the frankpledge system.

[4] *rettatus vel publicatus*. Note the importance here attached to the previous record of the accused.

[5] *i.e.* the sheriff is here left with certain powers of criminal jurisdiction.

[6] *juisam aquae*; for the various ordeals in operation, see account given in Glanville's treatise, below, No. 58, pp. 476–478.

[7] The king claims the sole right to the profits of jurisdiction in this new procedure.

6. And let the sheriffs, who have arrested them, bring them before the justice without any other summons than that they have from him. And when robbers or murderers or thieves, or receivers of them, who have been arrested through the oath or otherwise, are handed over to the sheriffs, let them receive them immediately and without delay.[1]

7. And in the several counties where there are no gaols, let such be made in a borough or some castle of the king at the king's expense and from his wood, if one shall be near, or from some neighbouring wood at the oversight of the king's servants, to the end that in them the sheriffs may be able to guard those who shall be arrested by the officials accustomed to do this, or by their servants.

8. Moreover, the lord king wills that all shall come to the county courts to take this oath, so that none shall remain behind on account of any franchise which he has, or any court or soke,[2] which he may have, but that they shall come to take this oath.

9. And let there be no one within his castle or without, nor even in the honour of Wallingford, who shall forbid the sheriffs to enter into his court or his land to take the view of frankpledge[3] and to see that all are under pledges; and let them be sent before the sheriffs under free pledge.

10. And in cities or boroughs let no one hold men or receive them into his house or on his land or in his soke, whom he will not take in hand to produce before the justice, should they be required; or else let them be in frankpledge.

11. And let there be none in a city or a borough or a castle or without it, nor even in the honour of Wallingford, who shall forbid the sheriffs to enter into their land or their soke to arrest those who have been accused or are notoriously suspect of being robbers or murderers or thieves or receivers of them, or outlaws, or persons charged concerning the forest;[4] but the king commands that they shall aid the sheriffs to capture them.

12. And if anyone shall be taken in possession of the spoils of robbery or theft, if he be of evil repute and bears an evil testimony from the public and has no warrant, let him have no law.[5] And if he has not been notoriously suspect on account of the goods in his possession, let him go to the ordeal of water.

13. And if anyone shall confess to robbery or murder or theft, or to harbouring those who have committed them, in the presence of the lawful men or in the hundred court, and afterwards he wish to deny it, let him not have his law.[6]

14. Moreover, the lord king wills that those who shall be tried by the law and absolved by the law, if they have been of ill repute and openly and disgracefully spoken of by the testimony of many and that of the lawful men, shall abjure the king's

[1] *i.e.* speed and promptitude of action on the part of the sheriff are essential for the success of the new procedure.

[2] Rights of private jurisdiction often granted by privilege or charter; this clause is directly aimed at the limitation of the franchises of feudal courts and the scope of their jurisdiction.

[3] Customarily taken twice a year by the sheriff as a measure of local police jurisdiction.

[4] Offences against the Forest Law. For Henry II's *Assize of the Forest*, see No. 28.

[5] *i.e.* criminals taken red-handed and without surety are to be punished without trial.

[6] The case is not to be tried after the accused has once pleaded guilty to the offence. In all these clauses the particular importance attached both to the past record of the accused and to local opinion concerning him should be noted.

lands,[1] so that within eight days they shall cross the sea, unless the wind detains them; and with the first wind they shall have afterwards they shall cross the sea, and they shall not return to England again except by the mercy of the lord king; and both now, and if they return, let them be outlawed; and on their return let them be seized as outlaws.

15. And the lord king forbids that any vagabond, that is, a wanderer or unknown person, shall be given shelter anywhere except in a borough, and even there he shall not be given shelter longer than one night, unless he become sick there, or his horse, so that he can show an evident excuse.

16. And if he shall remain there longer than one night, let him be arrested and held until his lord shall come to give surety for him, or until he himself shall procure safe pledges; and let him likewise be arrested who gave him shelter.

17. And if any sheriff shall send word to another sheriff that men have fled from his county into another county, on account of robbery or murder or theft or the harbouring of them, or on account of outlawry or of a charge concerning the king's forest, let him (the second sheriff) arrest them; and even if he knows of himself or through others that such men have fled into his county, let him arrest them and guard them until he has taken safe pledges for them.

18. And let all the sheriffs cause a record to be made of all fugitives who have fled from their counties; and let them do this before the county courts and carry the names of those written therein before the justices, when next they come to them, so that these men may be sought throughout England, and their chattels may be seized for the needs of the king.

19. And the lord king wills that from the time the sheriffs shall receive the summons of the itinerant justices to present themselves before them, together with the men of the county, they shall assemble them and make inquiry for all who have newly come into their counties since this assize; and they shall send them away under pledge to attend before the justices, or they shall keep them in custody until the justices come to them, and then they shall present them before the justices.

20. Moreover, the lord king forbids monks or canons or any religious house to receive any men of the lower orders as a monk or a canon or a brother, until it be known of what reputation he is, unless he shall be sick unto death.[2]

21. Moreover, the lord king forbids anyone in all England to receive in his land or in his soke or in a house under him any one of that sect of renegades who were branded and excommunicated at Oxford.[3] And if anyone shall so receive them, he himself shall be at the mercy of the lord king, and the house in which they have dwelt shall be carried outside the village and burnt. And each sheriff shall swear an oath that he will observe this, and shall cause all his officers to swear this, and also the stewards of the barons and all knights and freeholders of the counties.

22. And the lord king wills that this assize shall be kept in his realm so long as it shall please him.

[1] A new feature in criminal law administration; even those who have been acquitted on a particular indictment are not regarded as free and lawful men if their past record is shady.

[2] This provision is virtually a corollary to clause 16 of the Constitutions of Clarendon, 1164 (see No. 126).

[3] The sect mentioned were Cathari. cf. above, No. 12, pp. 329, 330

25. The Assize of Northampton (1176)

This document should be compared with the Assize of Clarendon, since in the form in which it has come down to us, it is in the main a recapitulation and enlargement of the decisions taken at Clarendon in 1166. It should be noted, however, that the penalties for various offences are here more severe, and that the powers assigned to the justices are substantially enlarged at the expense of the sheriffs. This may be held to reflect the changes consequent upon the Inquest of Sheriffs in 1170 (see No. 48). Nor is there much doubt that this assize should be considered in connexion with the organization of the system of itinerant justices, since the assize is drawn up in the form of instructions to six groups of justices appointed to operate in newly delimited circuits. The latter clauses of the assize contain new legislation of importance. The king claims the right to have certain cases respecting the feudal incidents brought to king's courts, and it makes provision for the employment of the sworn inquest for their resolution. Here also is the first mention in an official document of the recently instituted 'possessory' assizes of *Mort d'Ancestor* and *Novel Disseisin*, although the latter was certainly in operation as early as 1166. The Assize of Northampton was passed early in 1176, probably at the council of Northampton held in January of that year. The Latin text is to be found in *Gesta Regis Henrici Secundi* (ed. W. Stubbs, Rolls Series, 1867), vol. II, p. 89, and it is printed also in Stubbs, *Select Charters* (ed. 1913), p. 179. A translation is in G. B. Adams and H. M. Stephens, *Select Documents of English Constitutional History* (1901), p. 20.

These are the assizes made at Clarendon and afterwards revised at Northampton.

1.[1] If anyone has been accused before the justices of the lord king of murder or theft or robbery or of harbouring men who do such things, or of forgery or arson by the oath of twelve knights of the hundred or, if knights be not present, by the oath of twelve free and lawful men and by the oath of four men from each vill of the hundred,[2] let him go to the ordeal of water,[3] and if he fail, let him lose one foot. And at Northampton it was added for the sake of stern justice that he shall likewise lose his right hand with his foot, and shall abjure the realm and within forty days be banished from the kingdom. And if he shall be cleared of guilt at the water, let him provide sureties and remain in the kingdom, unless he has been accused of murder or some other base felony by the common report of the county and of the lawful knights of the country; moreover, if he has been accused in the aforesaid manner, although he may have come safely through the ordeal of water, nevertheless let him depart from the realm within forty days, and let him take his chattels with him, saving the rights of his lords, and let him abjure the realm at the mercy of the lord king.[4] Moreover, this assize shall remain in force from the time the assize was made at Clarendon continuously up to the present time and from now on, so long as it shall please the lord king, in cases of murder and treason and arson and in all the aforesaid articles, except in cases of petty thefts and robberies, which have been committed in time of war,[5] as of horses and oxen and lesser things.

2. Item, let no one either in a borough or in a vill entertain in his house for more than one night any stranger for whom he is unwilling to be responsible, unless there be a reasonable excuse for this hospitality, which the host of the house shall show to his neighbours.[6] And when the guest shall depart, let him leave in the presence of the neighbours and by day.

3. If anyone shall have in his possession the spoils of murder or theft or robbery or forgery, and shall confess the fact or any other felony, which he has committed,

[1] The conventional numeration of paragraphs is retained. This has no place in the original.
[2] No. 24, clause 1.
[3] No. 24, clause 2.
[4] No. 24, clause 14.
[5] A reference to the recent fighting in England between the king and the feudal magnates in the rebellion of 1173–1174.
[6] No. 24, clause 15.

before the reeve of the hundred or borough and in the presence of lawful men, he cannot afterwards deny it before the justices.[1] And if he shall also confess anything of this kind in their presence without having the spoils thereof in his possession, he cannot deny this either before the justices.

4. Item, if any freeholder has died, let his heirs remain possessed of such 'seisin'[2] as their father had of his fief on the day of his death; and let them have his chattels from which they may execute the dead man's will. And afterwards let them seek out his lord and pay him a 'relief'[3] and the other things which they ought to pay him from the fief. And if the heir be under age, let the lord of the fief receive his homage and keep him in ward[4] so long as he ought. Let the other lords, if there are several, likewise receive his homage, and let him render them what is due. And let the widow of the deceased have her dowry and that portion of his chattels which belongs to her.[5] And should the lord of the fief deny the heirs of the deceased 'seisin'[2] of the said deceased which they claim, let the justices of the lord king thereupon cause an inquisition to be made by twelve lawful men as to what 'seisin' the deceased held there on the day of his death.[6] And according to the result of the inquest let restitution be made to his heirs. And if anyone shall do anything contrary to this and shall be convicted of it, let him remain at the king's mercy.

5. Item, let the justices of the lord king cause an inquisition to be made concerning dispossessions[7] carried out contrary to the assize, since the lord king's coming into England immediately following upon the peace made between him and the king, his son.

6. Item, let the justices receive oaths of fealty to the lord king between the Octave of Easter and the final term, the Octave of Pentecost, from all who wish to remain in the kingdom, namely from the earls, barons, knights and freeholders, and even villeins. And whoever shall refuse to take an oath of fealty may be arrested as an enemy of the lord king. The justices shall also order that all who have not yet paid homage or allegiance to the lord king shall come at a time appointed for them and pay homage and allegiance to the king as their liege lord.[8]

7. Item, let the justices determine all suits and rights pertaining to the lord king and to his crown through the writ of the lord king, or of those who shall be acting for him, of half a knight's fee or under, unless the dispute is so great that it cannot be determined without the lord king, or is such as his justices shall refer to him, or to those who are acting for him, by reason of their uncertainty in the case. Let them, nevertheless, apply themselves to the utmost to act in the interest of the lord king. Let them also hold the assize for wicked robbers and evildoers throughout the counties

[1] No. 24, clause 13.

[2] The technical term describing legal possession or tenure of a fief (see below, p. 472).

[3] Payment made by the heir to the lord before entering into possession of a fief (see below, pp. 548, 549, 940).

[4] Wardship, another of the incidents of feudal tenure (see below, pp. 547, 940).

[5] See No. 19.

[6] A reference to the newly instituted assize of *Mort d'Ancestor*, one of the three possessory assizes (see below, pp. 472, 473, 942). This clause, while safeguarding the legitimate rights of feudal lords, enacts that disputes concerning testamentary disposition of property should be brought before the king's court and decided by the sworn inquest procedure.

[7] Assize of *Novel Disseisin* (see below, pp. 475, 476).

[8] This clause is primarily of political significance; the king desired the renewal of the oath of homage from those who had lately been in arms against him. None the less the wide terms of reference are remarkable.

they are about to traverse, for this assize is enacted in accordance with the advice of the king, his son, and his vassals.

8. Item, let the justices see to it that the castles which have been destroyed are utterly demolished, and those which are due for destruction are razed to the ground. And if they do not do this, the lord king will have the judgment of his *curia* upon them, as on men who have held his commands in contempt.

9. Item, let the justices make inquiry concerning 'escheats',[1] churches, lands and women, who are in the gift of the lord king.[2]

10. Item, let the bailiffs of the lord king answer to the Exchequer both for the revenue from the assize and also for all the profits they make in their bailiwicks, with the exception of those pertaining to the sheriffdom.

11. Item, let the justices make inquiry concerning the custody of castles, as to who owes service for them, and how much, and where,[3] and afterwards let them send word to the lord king.

12. Item, let a thief be handed over to the sheriff of the place where he is arrested for safe-keeping. And should the sheriff be absent, let the accused be brought to the custodian of the nearest castle, and let him keep him in ward until he may deliver him to the sheriff.[4]

13. Item, let the justices cause search to be made according to the custom of the land for those who have fled from the kingdom; and unless the fugitives be willing to return within the appointed time and stand trial in the king's court, let them henceforth be outlawed; and let the justices report the names of the outlaws at Easter and at Michaelmas to the Exchequer, and from thence let their names be sent to the lord king.[5]

26. The Treaty of Falaise (December 1174)

In the autumn of 1174 William the Lion, king of Scotland, having supported the rebellion of the sons of Henry II, was captured near Alnwick. He was brought as a prisoner to Normandy, and at Falaise he was forced in December 1174 to agree to the terms which are set out below. The text which records them is of interest as an intensely feudal document; and the savage treaty which it embodies marks the climax of the power over Scotland by kings of England in the Middle Ages. It was to be renounced by Richard I in 1190. This record is given in Rymer's *Foedera*, vol. I (1704), pp. 39 *et sqq.*, where it is printed from a documentary source, and it was also included in the *Gesta Regis Henrici Secundi* (ed. Rolls Series, vol. I, pp. 96–98). A similar document was apparently drawn up shortly afterwards at Valognes on 8 December, and this is contained in the *Liber Niger Scaccarii* (ed. Hearne (1728), vol. I, pp. 36–40): this is almost identical with the Falaise text except that there are some additional witnesses.

This is the agreement and treaty which William, king of Scots, made with his lord king, Henry, the son of Maud, the empress. William, king of Scots, has become the liegeman of the lord king (Henry) against every man in respect of Scotland and in respect of all his other lands; and he has done fealty to him as to his liege lord, as all the other men of the lord king (Henry) are wont to do. Likewise, he has done homage to Henry the king,[6] son of King Henry, saving only the fealty which he owes to the lord king, his father.

[1] The reversion of a fief to the lord, generally through failure of an heir. cf. pp. 937, 938.
[2] A reference to the feudal incident of wardship (see p. 940).
[3] A reference to castle-guard (see No. 243).
[4] cf. No. 24, clause 17.
[5] cf. No. 24, clauses 14 and 18.
[6] The young king, crowned as his father's heir in 1170, died without issue in 1183.

And all the bishops and abbots and clergy of the king of Scots and their successors shall do fealty to the lord king (Henry) as to their liege lord, in the same way as the lord king's other bishops are wont to do; and they shall likewise do fealty to Henry the king, his son, and to his heirs.

And the king of Scots, and David, his brother, and his barons and other men, have granted to the lord king (Henry) that the Scottish Church shall make such submission to the English Church as it ought to do, and as it was wont to do in the time of the lord king's predecessors, kings of England. Likewise, Richard, bishop of St. Andrews, and Richard, bishop of Dunkeld, and Geoffrey, abbot of Dunfermline, and Herbert, prior of Coldingham, have granted that the English Church should have such rights in Scotland as it ought to have, and that they will themselves not oppose any of the rights of the English Church. And they have pledged themselves in respect of this admission by performing liege fealty to the lord king and Henry, his son.

Likewise the other Scottish bishops and clergy shall do so by a pact made between the lord king (Henry) and the king of Scots, and David, his brother, and his barons.

The earls also and barons and such other men holding land from the king of Scots as the lord king (Henry) may select, shall also do homage to the lord king as against all men, and shall swear fealty to him as their liege lord, in the same way as his other men are wont to do. And they shall do the same to Henry the king, his son, and to his heirs, saving only the fealty which they owe to the lord king, his father. Likewise, the heirs of the king of Scots, and of his barons, and of his men shall do liege homage to the heirs of the lord king (Henry) against all other men.

Further, the king of Scots and his men shall not receive, either in Scotland or in any of his other lands, any exile from the lands of the lord king who has been expelled therefrom by reason of felony, unless he wishes to justify himself in the court of the lord king (Henry), and to submit to the judgment of his court. Otherwise, the king of Scots and his men shall take such a one as quickly as they can and bring him to the lord king (Henry) or to his justiciars or to his bailiffs in England.

Again, if there comes to England any fugitive expelled as a felon from the lands of the king of Scots he shall not be received in the lands of the lord king (Henry) unless he wishes to justify himself in the court of the king of Scots, and to submit to the judgment of his court. Otherwise such a one shall be delivered to the men of the king of Scots by the bailiffs of the lord king (Henry) wherever he is found.

Further, the men of the lord king (Henry) shall continue to hold the lands which they held, and which they ought to hold, from the lord king (Henry) and from the king of Scots and from their men. And the men of the king of Scots shall continue to hold the lands which they held, and which they ought to hold, from the lord king (Henry) and from his men.

In order that this treaty and pact with the lord king (Henry) and Henry the king, his son, and their heirs, may be faithfully kept by the king of Scots and his heirs, the king of Scots has delivered to the lord king (Henry) the castle of Roxburgh, and the castle of Berwick, and the castle of Jedburgh, and the castle of Edinburgh, and the castle of Stirling to be held by the lord king (Henry) at his pleasure. And the king of Scots shall pay for the garrison of these castles out of his own revenue at the pleasure of the lord king (Henry).

Further, in pledge of the aforesaid treaty and pact, the king of Scots has delivered to the lord king (Henry) his brother, David, as a hostage, and also the following:

Earl Duncan	Richard Comyn	Robert Frembert
Earl Waldewin	Walter Corbet	Robert 'de Burneville'
Earl Gilbert	Walter Olyfard	Hugh Giffard
The earl of Angus	John 'de Vals'	Hugh Rydal
Richard of Morville, the constable	William of Lindsay	Walter Berkele
	Philip 'de Coleville'	William 'de la Haye'
Niz, son of William	Philip of Valognes	William 'de Mortemer'

When the castles have been handed over, then shall William, king of Scots, and David, his brother, be released. And (again after the castles have been handed over) the earls and barons aforesaid shall be released, but only after each one has delivered his own hostage, to wit, his legitimate son if he has one, or otherwise his nephew or nearest heir.

Further, the king of Scots and his barons aforesaid have guaranteed that with good faith and without evil intent and without excuse, they will see to it that the bishops and barons and other men of their land, who were not present when the king of Scots made his pact with the lord king (Henry) and with Henry the king, his son, shall do the same liege homage and fealty as they themselves have done. And the barons and men, who were not present at this agreement, shall give such hostages as the lord king (Henry) shall determine.

Further, the bishops, earls and barons aforesaid have covenanted with the lord king (Henry) and with Henry the king, his son, that if the king of Scots shall by any mischance default in his fealty to the lord king (Henry) and his son, and shall thus break the aforesaid agreement, then they, the aforesaid bishops, earls and barons will hold to the lord king (Henry), as to their liege lord, against the king of Scots and against all men hostile to the lord king (Henry). And the bishops shall place the land of the king of Scots under interdict until the king of Scots returns to the lord king (Henry) in his fealty.

The king of Scots and David, his son, and all the aforesaid barons, as liegemen of the lord king (Henry) and of Henry the king, his son (saving only their fealty to the lord king, his father), have given full sworn assurance that the aforesaid treaty shall be strictly observed by them in good faith and without any evil intent.

And these are the witnesses: Richard, bishop of Avranches;[1] John, dean of Salisbury; Robert, abbot of Malmesbury; Ralph, abbot of Montebourg; Herbert, archdeacon of Northampton; Walter of Coutances; Roger, the king's chaplain; Osbert, clerk of the chamber; Richard, son of the lord king, and count of Poitou;[2] Geoffrey, son of the lord king, and count of Brittany; William, earl of Essex;[3] Hugh, earl of Chester;[4] Richard of Le Hommet, the constable; the count of Meulan;[5]

[1] Richard III, bishop of Avranches, 1171–1182.
[2] Subsequently Richard I, king of England.
[3] William 'de Mandeville'.
[4] Styled 'of Kevelioc'. See Table 14.
[5] Robert, count of Meulan, being the son of Waleran, count of Meulan, who was twin brother to Robert of Beaumont, earl of Leicester. See Table 12.

Jordan Tesson; Humphrey 'de Bohun'; William of Courcy, the seneschal; William, son of Aldhelm, the seneschal; Alfred of Saint-Martin, the seneschal; Gilbert Malet, the seneschal.[1]

At Falaise.

27. The Assize of Arms (1181)

This document illustrates the military reforms effected by Henry II. Its intention was to re-create the ancient 'fyrd' as an efficient force supplementary to the feudal levies. The measure was also applied to the continental lands ruled by Henry II. It will be noted that the jury system is to be employed in the application of the assize. The text of the document is to be found in the *Gesta Regis Henrici Secundi*, vol. I, p. 261, and in Howden's chronicle. It has many times been separately printed, notably in W. Stubbs, *Select Charters* (ed. 1913), pp. 183, 184. It is translated in Adams and Stephens, *Select Documents of English Constitutional History*, pp. 23–25.

1.[2] Let every holder of a knight's fee have a hauberk,[3] a helmet, a shield and a lance. And let every knight have as many hauberks, helmets, shields and lances, as he has knight's fees in his demesne.

2. Also, let every free layman, who holds chattels or rent to the value of 16 marks, have a hauberk, a helmet, a shield and a lance. Also, let every free layman who holds chattels or rent worth 10 marks have an 'aubergel'[4] and a headpiece of iron, and a lance.

3. Also, let all burgesses and the whole body of freemen have quilted doublets and a headpiece of iron, and a lance.

4. Moreover, let each and every one of them swear that before the Feast of St. Hilary[5] he will possess these arms and will bear allegiance to the lord king, Henry, namely the son of the Empress Maud, and that he will bear these arms in his service according to his order and in allegiance to the lord king and his realm. And let none of those who hold these arms sell them or pledge them or offer them, or in any other way alienate them; neither let a lord in any way deprive his men of them either by forfeiture or gift, or as surety or in any other manner.

5. If anyone bearing these arms shall have died, let his arms remain for his heir. But if the heir should not be of age to use the arms, should the need arise, let him who has him in ward likewise have the custody of his arms, and let him find a man who can use them in the service of the lord king, until the heir be of age to bear arms, and then let him have them.

6. Let every burgess who has more arms than he ought to have according to this assize, sell them or give them away or otherwise bestow them on such a man as will retain them for the service of the lord king of England. And let none of them keep more arms than he ought to have according to this assize.

[1] The document dated at Valognes, and given in the *Liber Niger Scaccarii*, adds the following witnesses: Reginald 'de Curtenai'; Fulk Paynel; Geoffrey 'de Pertico'; William of Le Hommet; Jordan of Le Hommet; Ingelram of Le Hommet; Ralph Tesson; Roger, his brother; Robert Bertram; Richard of Vernon; William Vavasur; Robert of Mortemer; Robert, son of Bernard; Rannulf Puhere; Bertram of Verdun; Roger Bacun. It is interesting to observe that for the ratification at Valognes, Richard of Le Hommet, the famous constable of Henry II, brought in his relatives as witnesses, for Le Hommet, the ancestral home of the family, is very close to Valognes.

[2] The conventional numeration of paragraphs is retained for purposes of reference. This has no place in the original.

[3] *loricam*. For the hauberk, see Bayeux Tapestry, Plate XL (p. 244).

[4] A less elaborate and less costly counterpart to the *lorica*.

[5] 13 January.

7. Item, let no Jew keep in his possession a hauberk or an 'aubergel', but let him sell them or give them away or otherwise dispose of them that they may remain in the king's service.

8. Item, let no one carry arms out of England except by order of the lord king; neither let anyone sell arms to anyone who will carry them out of England.

9. Item, let the justices cause oaths to be sworn by lawful knights and other free and lawful men of the hundreds or boroughs,[1] as many as they deem fit, who shall have chattels of such value as makes it necessary for him to have a hauberk, an 'aubergel', a lance and a shield, according as has been said, namely that, one by one, they will give the names of all in their hundreds and neighbourhoods and boroughs who have 16 marks either in chattels or rent, and likewise of those who have 10 marks. And afterwards let the justices cause to be enrolled all those who have sworn on oath and others, who have this amount of chattels or rents, and also what arms they ought to possess according to the value of their chattels or rents, and afterwards, in their presence and in the hearing of them as a body, let the justices cause this assize concerning the bearing of arms to be read, and let them swear on oath that they will have these arms according to the aforesaid value of chattels and rents and that they will hold them in the service of the lord king in accordance with the said assize at the command and allegiance of the lord king, Henry, and of his realm. If indeed it should happen that any of those who ought to possess these arms are not present in the county at the time the justices shall be in that county, let the justices appoint him a time in another county to come before them. And if he shall not have come to them in any county through which they shall pass, and shall not have been in this land, let a time be appointed him at Westminster in the Octave of Michaelmas there to take his oath, as he values his life and all his possessions. And let order be given him to have arms according as he ought to have before the Feast of St. Hilary.[2]

10. Item, let the justices cause it to be announced throughout all the counties through which they shall pass, that those who have not these arms, according as has been said, the lord king will seize their persons, but will on no account take from them their land or their chattels.

11. Item, let no one swear concerning lawful and free men who has not 16 marks or 10 marks in chattels.

12. Item, let the justices command throughout all the counties that no one, as he values his life and his possessions, may buy or sell any ship with intent to take it out of England, or may export timber or cause it to be exported out of England. And the king commands that none shall be accepted for the oath of arms except a free man.

28. The Assize of the Forest (1184)

This document is the first official act of legislation relating wholly to the forest. It is sometimes cited as the Assize of Woodstock, since Henry II is known to have made legislation dealing with the forest at a council held there in 1184. Nevertheless the assize in its present form is composite in character, the text of the several clauses being derived from a variety of sources: some are restatements or modifications of earlier decrees, and some, for instance, article 12, are additions formulated at Woodstock in 1184. The whole document should be compared with the account of the forest given in the *Dialogue of the Exchequer* (No. 70). Though it is not possible to give any accurate

[1] An employment of the jury of recognition for administrative purposes.
[2] 13 January.

estimate of the size of the territory comprised within the jurisdiction of the forest at this time, it was very considerable, and it formed an integral part of the social and economic structure of the country. To supervise its administration there existed a hierarchy of officials: the forest justices, the wardens and master foresters, the verderers and woodwards. The arbitrary and severe character of their administration tended to be felt as a grievance among all classes of the community. The account of the forest in Anglo-Norman times given by Stubbs, in his *Constitutional History*, vol. I, has now been largely superseded, and the reader is referred for further information to C. Petit-Dutaillis, *Studies . . . supplementary to Stubbs's Constitutional History*, vol. II, and more particularly to *Select Pleas of the Forest*, ed. G. J. Turner (Selden Soc., 1899). The Latin text of the Assize of the Forest can most conveniently be studied in W. Stubbs, *Select Charters* (ed. 1913), pp. 186–188.

This is the assize of the lord king, Henry, son of Maud, concerning the forest, and concerning his deer in England; it was made at Woodstock with the advice and assent of the archbishops, bishops, barons, earls, and magnates of England.

1.[1] First he forbids that anyone shall transgress against him in regard to his hunting-rights or his forests in any respect; and he wills that no trust shall be put in the fact that hitherto he has had mercy for the sake of their chattels upon those who have offended against him in regard to his hunting-rights and his forests. For if anyone shall offend against him hereafter and be convicted thereof, he wills that full justice be exacted from the offender as was done in the time of King Henry, his grandfather.

2. Item, he forbids that anyone shall have bows or arrows or hounds or harriers[2] in his forests unless he shall have as his guarantor the king or some other person who can legally act as his guarantor.

3. Item, he forbids anyone to give or sell anything to the wasting or destruction of his own woods which lie within the forest of King Henry: he graciously allows them to take from their woods what they need,[3] but this is to be done without wasting and at the oversight of the king's forester.

4. Item, he has commanded that all who have woods within the bounds of the royal forest shall install suitable foresters in their woods; for these let those to whom the woods belong act as sureties, or let them find such suitable sureties as can give redress if the foresters shall transgress in anything which pertains to the lord king. And those who have woods without the bounds of the forest visitation[4] but in which the venison of the lord king is covered by the king's peace, shall have no forester, unless they have sworn to the assize of the lord king, and to keep the peace of his hunt and to provide someone as keeper of his wood.

5. Item, the lord king has commanded that his foresters shall have a care to the forest of the knights and others who have woods within the bounds of the royal forest, in order that the woods be not destroyed; for, if in spite of this, the woods shall be destroyed, let those whose woods have been destroyed know full well that reparation will be exacted from their persons or their lands, and not from another.

6. Item, the lord king has commanded that all his foresters shall swear to maintain his assize of the forest, as he made it, according to their ability, and that they will not

[1] The conventional numeration of paragraphs is retained for purposes of reference. This has no place in the original.

[2] *leporarios*.

[3] *i.e.* for firewood; the right of felling trees on one's own property was strictly limited according to the Forest Law, and anyone who exceeded the customary rights committed the crime of 'wasting'; cf. the sections on the forest in the *Dialogue of the Exchequer*, given below, No. 70, pp. 526–528.

[4] The visitation or 'regard' was a regular part of the administration of the forest and took place once every three years. The 'regarders' were twelve knights appointed by the sheriff in obedience to the royal mandate and constituted a commission of inquiry into all forest matters.

molest knights or other worthy men on account of anything which the lord king has granted them in respect of their woods.

7. Item, the king has commanded that in any county in which he has venison, twelve knights shall be appointed to guard his venison and his 'vert'[1] together with the forest; and that four knights shall be appointed to pasture cattle in his woods[2] and to receive and protect his right of pannage.[3] Also the king forbids anyone to graze cattle in his own woods, if they lie within the bounds of the forest, before the king's woods have been pastured; and the pasturing of cattle in the woods of the lord king begins fifteen days before Michaelmas and lasts until fifteen days after Michaelmas.[4]

8. And the king has commanded that if his forester shall have demesne[5] woods of the lord king in his custody, and those woods shall be destroyed, and he cannot show any just cause why the woods were destroyed, the person of the forester himself and not something else shall be seized.

9. Item, the king forbids that any clerk shall transgress either in regard to his venison or to his forests; he has given strict orders to his foresters that if they find any such trespassing there, they shall not hesitate to lay hands upon them and to arrest them and to secure their persons, and the king himself will give them his full warrant.[6]

10. Item, the king has commanded that his 'assarts',[7] both new and old, shall be inspected, and likewise both 'purprestures'[8] and the wastes of the forest; and that each shall be set down in writing by itself.

11. Item, the king has commanded that the archbishops, bishops, earls, barons, knights, freeholders and all men shall heed the summons of his master-forester to come and hear the pleas of the lord king concerning his forests and to transact his other business in the county court, if they would avoid falling into the mercy of the lord king.[9]

12. At Woodstock[10] the king commanded that safe pledges shall be taken from any who shall be guilty of one transgression in respect of the forest, and likewise if he shall trespass a second time; but if he shall transgress a third time, for this third offence no other pledges shall be taken from him nor anything else, except the very person of the transgressor.

13. Item, the king has commanded that every male attaining the age of twelve years and dwelling within the jurisdiction of the hunt, shall swear to keep the king's peace, and likewise the clerks who hold lands in lay fee there.

[1] The privilege of using wood in the forest.
[2] *ad agistandum boscos suos*; the knights were called *agistatores*.
[3] *panagium*, the right of feeding swine in the woods.
[4] *i.e.* from 15 September to 14 October inclusive.
[5] Not all royal forests lay within the royal demesne.
[6] An important clause which indicates Henry II's desire for a clarification and adjustment of the position of clerical offenders against the Forest Law. Clerks detected in the act of poaching are now to be charged in the king's court, and 'benefit of clergy' is not to be regarded as a valid plea against arrest by the forest officials. In this reform Henry was unsuccessful, and the provision was generally unpopular among churchmen; see C. Petit-Dutaillis, *op. cit.*, pp. 181–182, and G. J. Turner, *op. cit.*, pp. lxxxvii *et seq.*
[7] Forest clearings.
[8] Encroachments on royal land.
[9] This clause was annulled by the barons in *Magna Carta*, clause 44.
[10] This would appear to suggest that the earlier articles are recapitulations of existing legislation.

14. Item, the king has commanded that the mutilation of dogs[1] shall be carried out wherever his wild animals have their lairs and were wont to do so.

15. Item, the king has commanded that no tanner or bleacher of hides[2] shall dwell in his forests outside of a borough.

16. Item, the king has commanded that none shall hereafter in any wise hunt wild animals by night with a view to their capture, either within the forest or without, wheresoever the animals frequent or have their lairs or were wont to do so, under pain of imprisonment for one year and the payment of a fine or ransom at his pleasure.[3] And no one, under the same penalty, shall place any obstruction whether alive or dead[4] in the path of his beasts in his forests and woods or in other places disafforested by himself or his predecessors.

29. Ordinance of the "Saladin Tithe" (1188)

This document is a notable example of an early attempt to raise money by extraordinary taxation based upon the unit of personal property. The money was needed to finance the expedition to be raised from the lands of the Angevin empire to wage the Third Crusade, and the measure here enacted was the result of an agreement between Henry II and Philip Augustus of France earlier in the year. The content of the document should therefore be compared with the account given by William of Newburgh of the agreement between the two kings in his *Historia* (see above, No. 12, pp. 367, 368). Apart from this the chief point of interest is the employment of the sworn inquest procedure in each locality to determine the extent of individual liability, as had already been done in the Assize of Arms (see above, No. 27).

The text of the ordinance is to be found in Stubbs, *Select Charters* (ed. 1913), p. 189. An English translation is given in Adams and Stephens, *Select Documents of English Constitutional History*, pp. 27–28.

1.[5] This year each man shall give in alms a tenth of his revenues and movables with the exception of the arms, horses and garments of the knights, and likewise with the exception of the horses, books, garments and vestments, and all appurtenances of whatever sort used by clerks in divine service, and the precious stones belonging to both clerks and laymen.

2. Moreover, let this money be collected in each parish in the presence of the parish priest, the rural dean, one Knight Templar, one Knight Hospitaller, a servant of the lord king and the king's clerk, a servant of the baron and his clerk, and the clerk of the bishop; excommunication having been previously pronounced by the archbishops, bishops, and rural deans, each in every parish, upon anyone who shall not lawfully have paid the aforesaid tithe in the presence and with the knowledge of those who ought to be present, as has been said. And if anyone to their knowledge shall have given less than he ought, four or six lawful men shall be chosen from the parish, who shall declare upon oath what amount he ought to have declared; and this sum shall then be added to the smaller amount he has given.

3. Moreover, clerks and knights who have taken the cross shall not pay this tithe, except for their own property and demesnes; and whatsoever their vassals

[1] *Expeditatio mastivorum*, the clipping of their claws to prevent the dogs being used for hunting.

[2] *dealbator coriorum*.

[3] A glaring inconsistency appears between the comparatively mild penalties decreed for forest offences in this clause, and those implied in clause 1 (see also Petit-Dutaillis, *op. cit.*, pp. 175, 181).

[4] Presumably is meant a live beast used as a decoy or a dead one used as a bait in a snare.

[5] The conventional numeration of paragraphs is here retained for purposes of reference. This has no place in the original.

owe, shall be collected for their need by the aforesaid, and the whole shall be paid over to them.

4. Moreover, the bishops by their letters in each parish of their dioceses shall cause a proclamation to be made on Christmas Day and on the Feasts of St. Stephen and St. John that each man shall gather together at home the aforesaid tithe before the Feast of the Purification of the Blessed Virgin,[1] and on the following day and thereafter, in the presence of the aforesaid, let each man make payment at the place to which he has been summoned.

[1] 2 February 1189.

B. THE KING'S COURT AND HOUSEHOLD

THE *curia regis* was the central organ of royal government in the Anglo-Norman age. Its relation to the institutions of Anglo-Saxon England has been discussed above (pp. 49–53), and much of the constitutional history of England in this period is to be seen in the manner in which this body, originally omnicompetent in theory, threw off specialized bodies to discharge specialized judicial and financial functions. This process is evident in the texts which are included in separate sections below (Nos. 50–60 and Nos. 61–70). The starting-point of this process was a body which was primitive in its composition, and which could be regarded as a court in all senses of the term. Its nucleus was the royal household. The composition of the royal household and its organization are described in the important *Establishment of the King's Household* here printed, which reflects conditions towards the end of the reign of Henry I.

30. The "Establishment of the King's Household" (*Constitutio Domus Regis*)

This text, usually cited as the *Constitutio Domus Regis*, describes the establishment of the king's household shortly after the death of Henry I. It is of unique importance as revealing a very early stage in the growth of royal administration which is still here organized in connexion with the king's household. Here can be seen the origins of many of the great offices of State, many of which existed in Normandy before the Conquest. But the arrangements here described are primitive in their simplicity, and many holders of what will subsequently be these offices of State are seen in company with the king's personal servants and with his humble retainers. The document has recently been discussed at length in a remarkable essay by Mr. G. H. White, "The Household of the Norman Kings" (*Trans. R. Hist. Soc.*, 4th Series, vol. XXX (1948), pp. 127–155). He points out that the officials here described can be roughly divided into five groups of diminishing importance. The first group would include the chancellor, the stewards, the master-butler, the master-chamberlains, the treasurer, and the constable. The second group would include the three master-dispensers, the master of the writing office, the clerk of the spence, and the deputy of the master-chamberlain. The third group would include the deputy constables (Henry 'de la Pomerai' and Roger 'd'Oilly') and the master-marshal. The fourth group would include the deputy dispensers. And the fifth group would include minor officials such as the porter of the king's bed, and the ministers to the king's sport.

All these can be graded according to their pay and allowances. The highest paid official is the chancellor, who receives 5 shillings a day together with "1 lord's simnel loaf and 2 salted simnel loaves and 1 sextary of clear wine, and 1 sextary of ordinary wine, and 1 fat wax candle and 40 pieces of candle". The lowest paid officials receive 1 penny a day. To assess these wages in terms of modern money would be rash (see above, p. 56), but it would probably not be too hazardous to consider the penny as here representing not less than forty, and not more than sixty, times as much as it does today.

This document has been much discussed. Besides the paper of G. H. White mentioned above, it is considered in R. L. Poole, *The Exchequer in the Twelfth Century* (Oxford, 1912), wherein on pp. 96, 97 and 98, extracts from it are translated. A more detailed consideration will be found in J. H. Round, *The King's Serjeants and Officers of State* (London, 1911); and in 1950 Mr. Charles Johnson produced an admirable text with an excellent translation (appendix to *Dialogus de Scaccario*, ed. C. Johnson, London, 1950). The text is also printed in T. Hearne, *Liber Niger Scaccarii* (1728), vol. I, pp. 341–359; and in H. Hall, *Red Book of the Exchequer* (1896), pp. 808–813. Mr. White has shown that these two versions were copied, not from the original manuscript, but from an earlier copy. In general the *Red Book* version has here been followed except where indicated in the footnotes.

THIS IS THE ESTABLISHMENT OF THE KING'S HOUSEHOLD

The chancellor shall receive 5 shillings a day, and 1 lord's simnel loaf, and 2 salted simnel loaves, and 1 sextary of clear wine, and 1 sextary of ordinary wine, and 1 fat wax candle and 40 pieces of candle.

The master of the writing office used at first to receive 10 pence a day and 1 salted simnel loaf, and half a sextary of ordinary wine, and 1 fat wax candle and 12 pieces of candle; but King Henry increased the allowance of Robert 'of the Seal'[1] to the extent that on the day when that king died, Robert was receiving 2 shillings and 1 sextary of ordinary wine and 1 salted simnel loaf, and 1 small wax candle and 24 pieces of candle.

The chaplain in charge of the chapel and of the relics shall have the provision of two men; and the four servants of the chapel shall each receive double food, and for each of the two packhorses assigned to the chapel they shall have an allowance of a penny a day, and also a penny a month for shoeing. For their service of the chapel they shall have 2 wax candles on Wednesday, and 2 on Saturday; and 30 pieces of candle; and 1 gallon of clear wine for Mass; and 1 sextary of ordinary wine on Maundy Thursday for the washing of the altar; and on Easter Day 1 sextary of clear wine for Communion, and 1 of ordinary wine.

CONCERNING THE STEWARDS

The[2] steward shall receive the same as the chancellor if they live outside the king's household; but if they live within the king's household, they shall receive each day 3 shillings and 6 pence, and 2 salted simnel loaves, and 1 sextary of ordinary wine and a candle.

The clerk of the issue of bread and wine shall receive 2 shillings a day and 1 salted simnel loaf and 1 sextary of ordinary wine and 1 small wax candle and 24 pieces of candle.

CONCERNING THE DISPENSERS

The master-dispenser of bread who is permanently in office shall receive 2 shillings and 10 pence each day, if he lives outside the king's household, and 1 salted simnel loaf, and 1 sextary of ordinary wine and 1 small wax candle and 24 pieces of candle; but if he lives within the king's household he shall receive 2 shillings and half a sextary of ordinary wine and 1 candle.

CONCERNING THE DISPENSERS WHO SERVE BY TURN[3]

If they live outside the king's household they shall receive 19 pence daily and 1 salted simnel loaf, and 1 sextary of ordinary wine and 1 fat wax candle and 20 pieces of candle. If they live within the king's household they shall receive 10 pence and half a sextary of ordinary wine and a candle.

CONCERNING THE NAPERERS

The naperer shall receive the customary allowance of food. He shall have 3 halfpence a day for his man and 1 penny a day for his packhorse, and 1 penny a month for its shoeing.

The usher of issues shall have the same except for the payments in respect of the packhorse.

The counter of bread shall have the customary food.

[1] *de Sigillo*, an important official of the court of Henry I and a witness to many of his charters.

[2] In both MS. transcripts this paragraph is placed later in the text. G. H. White has shown that this was a blunder, and he has restored it to its proper position as above (cf. *Trans. R. Hist. Soc.*, 4th Series, vol. XXX, p. 133, n. 2 and 4) – a brilliant emendation.

[3] *i.e.* acting as deputies to the master-dispensers.

CONCERNING THE FOUR BAKERS WHO SERVE IN PAIRS BY TURN

The two who serve in the king's house shall live in the king's household; and the two that are travelling ahead shall have 40 pence to procure a bushel of Rouen[1] out of which they must render 40 lord's simnel loaves and 140 salted simnel loaves and 260 ordinary loaves from the bakery. They shall receive a lord's simnel loaf for four men; a salted simnel loaf for two; a baker's loaf for one.

CONCERNING THE WAFERER[2]

The waferer[3] shall have the customary allowance of food and 3 halfpence a day for his man.

The keeper of the tables[4] shall receive the same together with a packhorse and its allowances.

The bearer of the alms-dish shall live in the king's household.

CONCERNING THE DISPENSERS OF THE LARDER

The master-dispenser of the larder shall receive the same allowance as the master-dispenser of bread and wine. Similarly, the dispensers of the larder who serve by turn shall receive the same allowance as the dispensers of bread and wine who serve by turn. The larderers who serve by turn shall receive the customary food, and they shall have 3 halfpence a day for their man. The usher of the larder likewise. The slaughter-men shall similarly have the customary food.

CONCERNING THE COOKS[5]

The cook of the king's kitchen shall live in the king's household, and he shall receive 3 halfpence a day for his man. The usher of the same kitchen shall have the customary food and 3 halfpence a day for his man. The keeper of the vessels[6] shall live in the king's household and shall receive 3 halfpence a day for his man, and also a packhorse with its allowances. The scullion[7] of the same kitchen shall have the customary food. The cook for the king's private household and the dispenser likewise. Ralph 'de Marchia', who before his death was cook to the king [Henry I], lived in the king's household[8] and received 3 halfpence for his man.

CONCERNING THE GREAT KITCHEN

Oinus[9] Pochard shall have the customary food and 3 halfpence a day for his man. Two cooks shall likewise have the customary food and 3 halfpence a day for their man. The servants of the same kitchen shall have the customary food. The usher of the turnspit shall have the customary food and 3 halfpence a day for his man. The turnspit likewise. The keeper of the dishes receives the same and also a packhorse with its allowances. The carter of the great kitchen shall have double food and a just allowance for his horse. The carter of the larder likewise. The servant who takes in the beasts killed in the chase shall live in the king's household and shall receive 3 halfpence a day for his man.

[1] Of corn. [2] Heading omitted in the *Liber Niger*. [3] *nebularius*. [4] *bordarius*.
[5] Heading omitted in the *Liber Niger*. [6] *vasarius*. [7] *sumelarius*.
[8] The reading is corrupt in both texts at this point, but the meaning is clear.
[9] This from the *Liber Niger* The *Red Book* has *dominus*, which is obviously wrong.

CONCERNING THE BUTLERY[1]

The master-butler shall be as the steward, and they shall both have the same allowance.[2] The master-dispenser of the butlery shall be as the master-dispenser of bread and wine. The dispensers of the butlery who serve by turn shall be as the dispensers of issue except that they shall have one candle more, for they have 1 small wax candle and 24 pieces of candle. The usher of the butlery shall have the customary food and 3 halfpence a day for his man. The keepers of the wine barrels[3] shall live in the king's household, and each one of them shall receive 3 halfpence a day for his man. The keeper of the wine-butts[4] shall have the customary food and 3 pence for his man, and half a sextary of ordinary wine and 12 pieces of candle. The cellarman shall have the customary food, but Sereius shall have besides this 3 halfpence a day for his man, and 2 packhorses with their allowances.

CONCERNING THE KEEPERS OF THE CUPS[5]

Four serve together in turn, of whom two shall live in the household, and each one shall have for his man 3 halfpence a day. The other two shall have the customary food and likewise 3 halfpence a day for their men.

CONCERNING THE FRUITERERS

The fruiterer shall live in the king's household and shall receive 3 pence a day for his men. The carter shall have the customary food and an allowance for his horses.

The master-chamberlain[6] is the equal of the steward in his allowance. The treasurer shall be as the master-chamberlain if he is at the court and is serving in the Treasury.[7] William Mauduit[8] shall have 14 pence a day and shall live always in the king's household, and he shall have 1 fat wax candle and 12 pieces of candle, and 3 packhorses with their allowance. The porter of the king's bed shall live in the king's household and shall receive 3 halfpence a day for his man, and 1 packhorse with its allowances. The chamberlain who is on duty shall receive 2 shillings a day and 1 salted simnel loaf and 1 sextary of ordinary wine and 1 small wax candle and 24 pieces of candle. The chamberlain of the candle shall receive 8 pence a day and half a sextary of ordinary wine. The king's cutter[9] shall live in the king's household, and shall receive 3 halfpence a day for his man. The chamberlains who do not receive an allowance shall live in the

[1] The heading comes from the *Liber Niger*.

[2] Both texts are somewhat corrupt at this point, but the meaning is plain.

[3] *hosarii*. Hosa is probably a wine vessel in the shape of a boot. See J. H. Round, *King's Serjeants*, p. 177.

[4] *buttarius*.

[5] *de escantionibus*. For these obscure officials who early disappeared in England, see J. H. Round, *King's Serjeants*, p. 61.

[6] For the office of the master chamberlain, see No. 252.

[7] On this entry, see R. L. Poole, *Exchequer in the Twelfth Century*, pp. 25, 26.

[8] He was the son of William Mauduit, a tenant-in-chief in Hampshire in 1086, and he held a chamberlainship of the Exchequer which passed to his son. On him, see G. H. White, *op. cit.*, pp. 145, 146; R. L. Poole, *Exchequer*, p. 97; Round, *Commune of London*, p. 82.

[9] *tallator*. But is he a cutter of clothes – a tailor – or a cutter of tallies? The authorities seem to disagree with themselves and with each other. Hearne, *Liber Niger* (1728), took the latter view. Hall said first he was a tailor (*Court Life under the Plantagenets*, p. 244) and later (*Red Book*, p. ccxcix) a tally cutter. Round said first (*Studies in Red Book*, p. 33) a tally cutter and later a tailor (*King's Serjeants*, p. 257). G. H. White (*op. cit.*, p. 146) neatly sums up the matter. R. L. Poole, *Exchequer*, p. 97, has 'tailor', ignoring the alternative, and this is perhaps decisive.

king's household if they wish. The ewerer[1] shall have double the customary food, and when the king goes on a journey he shall receive a penny a day for drying the king's clothes, and when the king takes a bath[2] he shall have 4 pence except on the three feasts of the year.[3] About the wages of the washerwoman there is some doubt.

The constables have their allowances as do the stewards. William, son of Odo, shall have 1 lord's simnel loaf and 1 sextary of clear wine and 1 wax candle and 24 pieces of candle. Henry 'de la Pomerai', if he lives outside the king's household, shall have 2 shillings a day and 1 salted simnel loaf and 1 sextary of ordinary wine, and 1 small wax candle and 24 pieces of candle. If he lives within the household, he shall have 14 pence, and half a sextary of ordinary wine and a candle at discretion. Roger 'd'Oilly' likewise.

CONCERNING THE MARSHALSHIP[4]

The master-marshal, to wit, John, has similar payment; and he shall also have tallies for the gifts and allowances which are made from the Treasury of the king and from his chamber; and he shall have tallies against all the king's officials as a witness to all these things. The four marshals who serve the men of the king's household–clerks and knights and serjeants–when they go billeting, or when they stay outside the king's household on the king's business, shall have 8 pence each day, and a gallon of ordinary wine, and 12 pieces of candle. When they live within the household they shall have 3 pence a day for their man and a candle. But if any of the marshals be sent on the king's business he shall only have 8 pence a day. The serjeants of the marshals, when they are sent on the king's business, shall each have 3 pence a day, but not when they are living in the king's household. The ushers, if they are knights, shall live in the king's household, and they shall have 3 halfpence a day for each of their men, and 8 pieces of candle. Gilbert Goodman and Rannulf shall live in the king's household, and shall have 3 halfpence a day for their men. The other ushers, who are not knights, shall live in the king's household without further allowances.[5] The watchmen shall have double food and 3 halfpence for their men, and 4 candles; and besides this each one of them shall receive in the morning 2 loaves and a tray of meat, and a measure of beer. The stoker of the fire shall live always within the king's household, and from Michaelmas until Easter he shall have 4 pence a day for the fire. The usher of the chamber shall receive, on each day that the king travels, 4 pence for the king's bed. The keeper of the tents shall live in the king's household, and when the tents have to be carried, he shall receive an allowance for a man and a packhorse.

Each[6] one of the horn-blowers shall have 3 pence a day. And there are twenty servants each of whom receives 1 penny a day. Each keeper of the greyhounds[7] shall

[1] *aquarius.*

[2] King John's bathman had only a halfpenny a day, but he received a bonus of 5 pence when the king took his bath, an event which normally occurred once a fortnight (see A. L. Poole, *Obligations of Society*, 1946, p. 78).

[3] Christmas, Easter, Pentecost.

[4] This heading does not occur in the *Liber Niger*. For the section which follows, see *Complete Peerage*, vol. x, Appendix G, and J. H. Round, *Commune of London*, pp. 302–320.

[5] This sentence is from the *Liber Niger*. The *Red Book* version is confused at this point.

[6] On what follows relating to the king's sport, see J. H. Round, *King's Serjeants*, chap. V.

[7] *veltrarii.*

have 3 pence a day, and 2 pence for his men, and a halfpenny a day for each greyhound. The keeper of the kennels[1] shall have 8 pence a day. The knights-huntsmen shall each receive 8 pence a day. The hunt-servants[2] shall each receive 5 pence. The leader of the bloodhound[3] shall receive 1 penny a day and 1 halfpenny for the bloodhound. The keeper of the running hounds[4] shall receive 3 pence a day. The huntsmen of the stag-hunt[5] shall each receive 3 pence a day; and there shall be 1 penny for each four of the greater staghounds, and 1 penny for each six of the lesser staghounds. Two men each receiving 1 penny a day shall attend to the greater staghounds, and two men each receiving 1 penny a day shall attend to the lesser staghounds. Each one of the keepers of the small hounds[6] shall receive 3 pence a day. The huntsmen of the wolf-hunt[7] shall have 20 pence a day for horses and men and dogs, and they are required to maintain 24 running hounds and 8 greyhounds; and they shall have 6 pounds a year wherewith to buy horses; but they themselves say it ought to be 8 pounds. The bowman who carries the king's bow shall have 5 pence a day, and the other bowmen likewise. Bernard, Ralph 'le Robeur', and their fellows shall each have 3 pence a day.

[1] *mueta regis.* [2] *catatores.* [3] *ductor liemarii.* [4] *bernarii*
[5] *venatores del garrede.* [6] *braconarii.* [7] *luparii.*

C. THE SHERIFF AND LOCAL GOVERNMENT

AS the *curia regis* was the central organ of royal administration, so, throughout this period, was the sheriff the chief agent of the king in local government. No feature of the constitutional history of this age can be studied apart from the sheriff, and for a study of his activities the reader may be referred generally to W. A. Morris, *The Medieval English Sheriff to 1300* (Manchester, 1927).

Evidence for the functions and activities of the sheriff, and of the local courts, in which much of his work was done, can therefore best be sought in the texts relating generally to the royal government (Nos. 18–29), and more particularly in the texts concerning judicial (Nos. 50–60) and financial (Nos. 61–70) administration. The documents which follow in this place illustrate more simply the continuity of this office and those courts throughout this period.

Nos. 31–34 below provide evidence of the sheriff in the time of Edward the Confessor and indicate the type of business he was at that time directed by writ to perform. They also illustrate the manner in which the Conqueror in the early years of his reign took over the institution of the Old English shrievalty and used it for his own purposes.

The duties of the sheriff were exercised largely in the ancient courts of shire and hundred, and these too were maintained and efficiently conducted by the Norman kings. The mandate of Henry I (No. 43) is a classic example of this policy. Many of the hundred courts at this time passed into private hands (see Nos. 41–44). The manner of procedure in these courts is outlined, albeit with some confusion, in the *Leges Henrici Primi* (below, No. 57), which also gives information respecting certain feudal relations at this period, and in particular indicates the duties of the sheriff in relation to the older institution of the tithing and newer organization of frankpledge.

The sheriff under Edward the Confessor was usually a landowner of second-rate importance, and subordinate in position of course to the earl. After 1070 his personal importance increased. The shrievalty of the period 1070–1100 included some of the most powerful men in the land, and here is an indication both of the co-operation of king and magnates at this period and also of the design of the new governors of England to utilize pre-Conquest institutions. Characteristic of the new shrievalty are Haimo, sheriff of Kent (Nos. 39, 222), who was son of Haimo 'Dentatus', a Norman prominent as early as 1047; Urse of Abbetot, sheriff of Worcester; Edward of Salisbury, sheriff of Wiltshire; Baldwin of Meules, sheriff of Devon, who was the son of Count Gilbert of Brionne and brother to Richard 'fitz Gilbert'; Robert Malet, sheriff of Suffolk, who was lord of Graville-Sainte-Honorine; Roger Bigot, sheriff of Norfolk; and Hugh of Port-en-Bessin, sheriff of Hampshire. All these were tenants-in-chief of the king, and landowners of the first rank. It will be noted also that some of them were *curiales*, holding offices in the royal household. Roger Bigot, for instance, was steward to William Rufus, and Haimo, sheriff of Kent, was steward both to that king and his father. Robert Malet was a royal chamberlain, and so possibly was Edward of Salisbury.

The power of the sheriff, when possessed by persons of this standing, was very great, and it was often abused. In Domesday Book sheriffs appear among the chief despoilers of the Church, and about 1077 the Conqueror set up a commission to investigate such depredations. The institution of this commission and some of its acts are given below (Nos. 38–40). Later it became the policy of Henry I to appoint as sheriffs 'new men' who owed everything to his favour, such as Gilbert (see No. 42) who was made sheriff of Surrey, and later also of Cambridgeshire and Huntingdonshire. A closer connexion between the shrievalty and the household is also characteristic of this reign. In 1130 the majority of the English sheriffs were not only new men but were also officials of the household.

This policy of centralization could not, however, be consistently sustained. Not all the great feudal families who had acquired sheriffdoms in the time of the Conqueror could be ejected from their office, and in many cases the office itself became hereditary. During the civil war both Stephen and Maud were ready to purchase the support of magnates by fresh grants of sheriffdoms to be held by hereditary tenure. Of such grants the instruments printed below as Nos. 45 and 46 may serve as examples.

The development of the royal centralized administration under Henry II which was specially notable in the spheres of finance and justice (Nos. 50–70), depended largely upon resumption by the king of an effective control over the official who was so directly responsible for its conduct. That is the chief constitutional importance of the Inquest of Sheriffs of 1170. The instrument instituting this inquest appears below as No. 48, and it is followed (No. 49) by one of the two surviving copies of an original return made in respect of the inquiry.

31. Writ (in Anglo-Saxon) of Edward the Confessor addressed to Bishop Grimketel, Earl Ælfgar, and Toli, sheriff of Suffolk (1042–1047)

Interesting for its address. Toli was still apparently acting as sheriff as late as 1065. Printed: F. E. Harmer, *Anglo-Saxon Writs* (1952), p. 155.

Edward the king to Grimketel the bishop and Ælfgar the earl and Toli and all my thegns in Suffolk, greeting. I make known to you that I will that the soke of the eight and a half hundreds that pertains to Thingow shall be held . . . by St. Edmund[1] with sake and soke as fully as my mother held it. And I forbid that any man shall take away anything that I have already given her.

32. Writ (in Anglo-Saxon) of Edward the Confessor addressed to Tofi, sheriff of Somerset, respecting a sale of land (1061–1066)

Interesting as illustrating the activities of the sheriff in the time of the Confessor. Tofi as sheriff survived the Norman Conquest (see No. 33). Printed: J. M. Kemble, *Codex Diplomaticus*, No. 839.

Edward the king greets Harold the earl and Tofi his sheriff and all his thegns in Somerset in friendly fashion. And I make known that Alfred has sold to Giso the bishop the land of Lutton peacefully and quietly: he did this in my presence at Parret, and in the present of Edith, my wife, Harold the earl and many others who were there present with us. We also wish that the same bishop shall hold that land with all its appurtenances which the bishop possesses with sac and soc as freely as any of his predecessors as bishops ever held anything. And if anything be taken away from it unjustly we ask that it may be restored. Nor shall it be done otherwise.

[1] The abbey of Bury St. Edmunds.

33. Writ (in Anglo-Saxon) of "William the King and William the earl" addressed to Giso the bishop, Eadnoth the staller, and Tofi the sheriff (March–December 1067)

An important writ of the Conqueror issued during his absence from England in 1067, and showing the maintenance of pre-Conquest officials in the local government at the beginning of the reign. Tofi had been sheriff of Somerset under Edward the Confessor (see No. 32). Printed: W. Hunt, *Two Chartularies of the Priory of St. Peter at Bath* (1893), p. 36.

William the king and William the earl to Giso the bishop and Eadnoth the staller and Tofi the sheriff and all my thegns in Somerset, greeting. I make known that I have granted to Abbot Wulfwold and the church of St. Peter at Bath the land at Charlcombe as fully and freely as it ever was. And I forbid anyone to take away anything of what I have given him. God keep you.

34. Writ (in Anglo-Saxon) of Edward the Confessor respecting the lands of Regenbald, his priest

This document and the two instruments which immediately follow it (Nos. 35 and 36) are of exceptional importance for the history of the effects of the Norman Conquest on central and local administration. Regenbald was employed in the writing office of Edward the Confessor, and it is clear that he continued to serve in the chancery of William the Conqueror. He is therefore to be regarded as one of the men who were responsible for the continuity of diplomatic practice through this period of crisis. It will be further noted that the writ is addressed to the earls and the sheriffs as responsible for local administration. Printed: *Archaeologia*, vol. XXVI (1836), p. 256; F. E. Harmer, *Anglo-Saxon Writs* (1952), p. 213.

Edward the king greets in friendly fashion his bishops, his earls, his sheriffs and all his thegns in the shires where Regenbald, his priest, has land and men. And I make known to you that I will that he should have sake and soke, and toll and team and infangenthef both within the burh and without, as fully and completely as any of his ancestors before him originally in the time of King Cnut. I will that his wite shall be the same as a bishop in all respects, and I will favour no man who takes from him any of the things that I have granted him.

35. Writ (in Anglo-Saxon) of William I respecting the possessions of Regenbald (1067)

This instrument should be compared with No. 34 to which (as will be noted) it is similar in form. It is, moreover, addressed not to Norman but to English authorities, the obvious inference being that Norman administration had not yet been set up in the district. Here the Conqueror is to be seen in the earliest period of his English reign addressing his new subjects not only in their own language but according to the forms with which they were familiar. Eadrich and Bristrich represent the power of the sheriff. The new Norman sheriff has not yet been appointed. This instrument is discussed in J. H. Round, *Feudal England*, pp. 422, 423. It is printed in *Archaeologia*, vol. XXVI (1836), p. 256.

William the king greets Hereman the bishop, Wulfstan the bishop, Eustace the earl and Eadrich and Bristrich and all his thegns in Wiltshire and Gloucester in friendly fashion. And I make known to you that I have granted Regenbald, my priest, the land at 'Esi' and the land at Latton,[1] and all the things that belong to them both within the town and without, with sake and soke as fully as they were in the hands

[1] The relevant entry from Domesday Book (vol. I, fol. 68b) runs: "Regenbald the priest holds Latton and 'Aisi'. Two thegns held it for 2 manors. *T.R.E.* Earl Harold joined it into one. It used to pay geld for 9 hides."

of King Harold. Let him be free to dispose of them today or hereafter as may be most acceptable. And I will favour no one who takes from him any of the things I have granted him out of my friendship.

36. Writ (in Anglo-Saxon) of William I respecting the possessions of Regenbald (1067)

See above, Nos. 34 and 35. Printed: *Archaeologia*, vol. XXVI (1836), p. 256.

William the king greets all his liegemen well. And I make known to you all that I have granted Regenbald, my priest, all his land as fully and as completely with sake and soke as he had it under Edward, my kinsman.[1] And I will not permit that any man should deprive him of it on the penalty of losing my friendship.

37. Writ of William I to Baldwin, sheriff of Devon (probably 1070–1071)

Illustrates the early establishment and duties of Baldwin, sheriff of Devon. This Baldwin was typical of the new shrievalty established after the Norman Conquest. He was an important Norman noble, being the son of Gilbert of Brionne, the count, and brother to Richard 'fitz Gilbert', lord of Tonbridge and Clare. Printed: Dugdale, *Monasticon Anglicanum*, vol. III, p. 377.

William, king of the English, to Baldwin, sheriff of Devonshire, and to all his barons and ministers in that province, greeting. Know that I have granted to the monks of Battle the church of St. Olaf at Exeter with the lands of Sherford and 'Cheneberie', and with all other lands and things which pertain to that church. Wherefore I will and order that they hold it freely and in peace, and that it may be free from the burdens of all earthly service, and from all pleas and claims, and from all obligations to shires and hundreds, and from aids and gifts and gelds and danegelds and expeditions. Let them hold it with sake and soke and toll and team and infangenthef, and let it be free of works on castles and bridges as if it were my own demesne alms.

Witness: Thomas, archbishop of York, and William fitz Osbern.[2]

At Winchester.

38. Writ of William I setting up a commission to inquire into the conduct of his sheriffs and to restore such lands as they had taken from the Church (1077)

This important writ throws much light on the position of the sheriff in the time of the Conqueror and of his relation to the king. Printed: M. M. Bigelow, *Placita Anglo-Normannica*, p. 4, but there placed in a wrong context. For the true date and significance of this instrument, see the two texts which immediately follow (Nos. 39 and 40).

William (by the grace of God), king of the English, to Lanfranc, archbishop of Canterbury, and Geoffrey, bishop of Coutances, and Robert, count of Eu, and Richard, son of Count Gilbert, and Hugh of Montfort-sur-Risle and to all his other magnates of England, greeting. Summon my sheriffs by my order and tell them from me that they must return to my bishoprics and abbacies all the demesne, and all the

[1] The emphasis in an official document of this date on the Conqueror's kinship to the Confessor is significant.

[2] MS. "Osbert". The surviving text is from a late *inspeximus*. If Osbern is the correct reading, the date of the writ must be before February 1071, and this date is accepted by Davis (*Regesta Regum Anglo-Normannorum*, No. 58) and by W. A. Morris, *Medieval English Sheriff*, p. 47.

demesne-land which my bishops and abbots, either through carelessness or fear or greed, have given them out of the demesne of my bishoprics and abbacies; which they have consented to hold; or which they have seized by violence. And unless they return those things belonging to the demesne of my churches which they have up to now wrongfully held, you are to compel them willy-nilly to make restitution. And if anyone else, or if any one of you,[1] to whom I have addressed this instrument of justice, is liable to the same accusation, let him likewise make restitution of whatever he holds of the demesne of my bishoprics and abbacies, lest any one of you holding anything by a similar wrong might be the less able to coerce any sheriff or other person who in like manner possesses the demesne of my churches.

39. Writ of William I in favour of the abbey of St. Augustine at Canterbury (1077)

This writ is interesting as illustrating the action taken in a particular case in connexion with the commission respecting the conduct of the sheriffs, set up by the previous instrument. It is printed in Dugdale, *Monasticon Anglicanum*, vol. I, p. 142.

William (by the grace of God), king of the English, to Lanfranc, archbishop of Canterbury, and Geoffrey, bishop of Coutances, and Robert, count of Eu, and Hugh of Montfort-sur-Risle, and to his other magnates of England, greeting. I command and order you that you cause St. Augustine and Abbot Scotland to be repossessed of the borough of Fordwich, which Haimo the sheriff[2] now holds, and also of all the other lands which Æthelsige,[3] whom I sent into exile,[4] either by carelessness or fear or greed gave away or allowed to be alienated. And if anyone has taken away anything of them by violence, you are to compel him willy-nilly to restore it. Farewell.

Witness: Odo, bishop of Bayeux, at the dedication of Bayeux.[5]

40. Writ of William I in favour of the abbey of Bury St. Edmunds (1077)

Interesting as a particular example of action taken in respect of the commission on the conduct of sheriffs set up by William in 1077 (see No. 38). For the date, see the previous instrument. Printed: D. C. Douglas, *Feudal Documents from the Abbey of Bury St. Edmunds* (1932), pp. 56, 57.

William (by the grace of God), king of the English, to Robert, count of Eu, and Hugh of Montfort-sur-Risle, and Richard, son of Count Gilbert, greeting. Act so that by my order the lands and men of St. Edmund may remain quit and in peace as they were on the day on which I crossed the sea. And cause by my precept the men of St. Edmund, whom Peter of Valognes[6] holds for whatever reason in captivity, to be released and to go free. Afterwards dispense firm justice between the abbot and the aforesaid Peter and all others who did wrong to St. Edmund after I crossed the sea.

[1] Richard fitz Gilbert, and Hugh of Montfort-sur-Risle, had both despoiled the church of Canterbury (see below, No. 50).
[2] Sheriff of Kent.
[3] Alsinus.
[4] *fugitivus meus.*
[5] The rededication of Bayeux Cathedral took place in 1077.
[6] Sometime sheriff.

41. Writ of William II granting a hundred court to be held in fee-farm by the abbey of Thorney (1087–1100)

Illustrates the manner in which private jurisdiction might be exercised in the hundred court, from which the sheriff would in such case be excluded. Printed: Stubbs, *Select Charters* (ed. 1913), p. 122; Davis, *Regesta Regum Anglo-Normannorum* (1913), p. 139.

William, king of the English, to all the sheriffs and barons of Huntingdonshire, greeting. Know that I have granted the hundred of Normancross to the abbot and monks of Thorney to be held in fee-farm for an annual rent of 100 shillings which I order them to pay to my sheriff at Huntingdon. And I forbid any of my officers to do them injury or insult in respect of this.

42. Writ of Henry I addressed to Gilbert, sheriff of Surrey (1100–1107)

Interesting as illustrating the early appointment by Henry I of a sheriff of the new type. Gilbert, who owed everything to the king's favour, was subsequently sheriff also of Cambridgeshire and Huntingdonshire. Printed: J. Armitage Robinson, *Gilbert Crispin* (1911), p. 141.

Henry, king of the English, to Gilbert, sheriff of Surrey, greeting. I order and command you to give quittance to the land of St. Peter of Westminster and of Abbot Gilbert which is in my demesne within the park and the forest of Windsor, and particularly 8 hides of the manor of Pyrford which my father granted to the same church to be for ever quit from all geld and scot and all other things. And in particular I call them quit of the new geld on account of hidage and of all other gelds, as my father and my brother granted it by their writs.

Witness: R. Bigot at Bushley.

43. Charter of Henry I concerning the holding of the courts of shire and hundred (26 July 1108–August 1111)

This document is interesting for many reasons. It illustrates in particular the policy of the Anglo-Norman monarchy towards the pre-Conquest institutions of local government. It illustrates also the authority of the sheriff in the courts of shire and hundred, and the concern of a strong king to control and regulate his power. The arrangements for the settlement of disputes among members of the Norman aristocracy are also noteworthy. This document has been extensively discussed. Particular reference may perhaps be made to G. B. Adams, *Political History of England* (1905), vol. II, pp. 151–153 and to the same writer's *Origin of the English Constitution* (1922), pp. 380–384. The text is printed in F. Liebermann, *Die Gesetze der Angelsachsen*, vol. I, p. 524, and in Stubbs, *Select Charters* (ed. 1913), p. 122.

Henry, king of the English, to Samson the bishop[1] and Urse of Abbetot[2] and to all the barons of Worcestershire, both French and English, greeting.[3] Know that I grant and order that henceforth my shire courts and hundred courts shall meet in the same places and at the same terms as they were wont to do in the time of King Edward,[4] and not otherwise. And I do not wish that my sheriff should make them assemble in different fashion because of his own needs or interests. For I myself, if ever I shall wish it, will cause them to be summoned at my own pleasure, if it be necessary for my royal interests. And if in the future there should arise a dispute

[1] Samson, bishop of Worcester, 1096–1112.
[2] Sheriff of Worcester before 1086 and a notorious despoiler of church lands.
[3] The mandate was probably sent to many addressees.
[4] Edward the Confessor.

concerning the allotment of land, or concerning its seizure, let this be tried in my own court if it be between my tenants-in-chief. But if the dispute be between the vassals of two different lords let the plea be held in the shire court; and if it be not there settled, let the matter be decided by the duel. And I will and order that the men of the shire so attend the meetings of the shire courts and hundred courts as they were wont to do in the time of King Edward: nor may anyone claim excuse or quittance from me from following my pleas and my judgments as they then did.

Witness: R[ichard], bishop of London;[1] and Roger the bishop;[2] and Rannulf the chancellor; and R[obert], count of Meulan.[3]

At Reading.

44. Confirmation by Henry I of the rights of the bishop of Lincoln in the wapentake of Well in Lincolnshire (1123–1133)

This example of private jurisdiction exercised in the court of a wapentake is interesting for the manner in which it shows such jurisdiction was on occasion enforced by royal command. The king was interested in the maintenance of these arrangements inasmuch as the bishop paid him a yearly sum for exercising his jurisdiction in the wapentake court. Printed: *Registrum Antiquissimum of Lincoln Cathedral*, vol. 1 (Lincoln Rec. Soc., 1931), p. 41.

Henry, king of the English, to all the barons and vavassors and to all the lords who hold land within Well wapentake, greeting. I order you all to come to the pleas and to the wapentake of the bishop of Lincoln, who holds it from me, when you are summoned thereto by his officers. And I command you to render to him all the rights and customs which you owe to him in respect of your lands in that wapentake, as well and as fully as ever you did to Bishop Robert or to his predecessor, and as you now justly owe them. If you do not do this, he will himself continue to fine you by judgment until you perform your duty, lest I should lose the money which the bishop owes me in respect of this.

Witness: [Roger] bishop of Salisbury; G[eoffrey] the chancellor.

At Fareham.[4]

45. Charter of Stephen in favour of Geoffrey 'de Mandeville', earl of Essex and hereditary sheriff (Christmas, 1141)

After obtaining late in 1140 his charter of creation from Stephen (No. 255), Geoffrey 'de Mandeville' changed sides in the civil war and about midsummer, 1141, extracted a charter of increased grants from the empress. A few months later, by similar tactics, he once more obtained from Stephen new concessions in the charter here printed. This charter thus aptly illustrates the conditions of the anarchy, but its main importance lies in its description of the knight-service on a great honour in 1141. The list of knights, with their fees here given, forms so to speak a link between the description of the Canterbury barony in 1093–1096 (No. 222) and the returns made by the barons in 1166 (see below, Nos. 224–234). It will be further noted that Geoffrey is here made hereditary sheriff of London, Middlesex, Essex and Hertfordshire. The tendency of the shrievalties to become hereditary created a grave danger to the royal authority in the shires, and it was checked by Henry II. The reference to the Tower of London is also of interest. This charter is printed and discussed in J. H. Round, *Geoffrey de Mandeville*, p. 140.

Stephen, king of the English, to his archbishops, bishops, abbots, earls, justices, sheriffs, barons, and all his servants and liegemen, both French and English, of the whole of England, greeting. Know that I have rendered and firmly granted to Geoffrey,

[1] Richard of Beaumais was consecrated bishop of London, 26 July 1108.
[2] Of Salisbury.
[3] Robert of Beaumont (see Table 12). He fought at Hastings.
[4] Near Portsmouth.

earl of Essex, all the holdings which he held from whomever he held them on the day on which I was withstood at Lincoln and captured.[1] And besides this I have given and granted to him 300 librates of land, to wit Maldon and Newport and Depden and Bonhunt and 'Inga' and 'Phingria'; and Chatley with all its appurtenances for 100 pounds; and Writtle for 120 pounds; and Hatfield for 80 pounds; with all the appurtenances of the aforesaid manors. And besides this I have given and granted to him and his heirs in fee and heredity to be held from me and my heirs 100 librates of escheated lands,[2] to wit all the land which Robert of Bampton held in Essex, that is to say Rainham, and Great Holland and Amberden and Woodham and Easton which Picard of Domfront held; and Ickleton with all its appurtenances for 100 pounds. And besides I have given and firmly granted to him in fee and in heredity 100 pounds of land to be held by Arnulf 'de Mandeville' from the same Earl Geoffrey, that is to say Anstey and Braughing and Ham with all their appurtenances, and 100 solidates of land in Hatfield to complete these 100 librates. And besides this I have given and granted to him the ward of the Tower of London, with the castle which is attached to it, to have and to hold by him and his heirs from me and my heirs with all things and liberties and customs pertaining to the aforesaid Tower. And I have given him the offices of justice and sheriff in London and Middlesex in fee and heredity to be held of the same 'farm' by which his grandfather, Geoffrey 'de Mandeville,' held them, to wit for 300 pounds; and the offices of justice and sheriff in Essex and Hertfordshire to be held by the same 'farm' at which his grandfather held them, except that the demesne-lands which were given to the same Earl Geoffrey or to another shall be deducted from the aforesaid 'farm' and shall be accredited to him and to his heirs at the Exchequer. And besides this I have firmly granted to him that he may set up and maintain any castle wherever he wishes on his land. And besides this I have given to the same Earl Geoffrey and firmly granted in fee and heredity to him and his heirs, to be held of me and my heirs, 60 enfeoffed knights, among whom Arnulf 'de Mandeville' shall hold 10 in fee and heredity from his father. These are: the service of Graaland 'de Tany' for 7½ knights; and the service of William, son of Robert, for 7 knights; and the service of Brian, son of Ralph, for 5 knights; and the service of Robert fitz Gerold for 11 knights; and the service of Ralph fitz Gerold for 1 knight; and the service of William of Troisgots for 6 knights; and the service of Maurice 'de Chiche' for 5 knights; and the service of Ralph Maudit for 2 knights; and the service of Gilbert 'de Inga' for 1 knight; and the service of William, son of Hervey, for 3 knights; and the service of William of Eu for 1½ knights; and the service of William of Beuzeville for 2 knights; and the service of Matthew Peverel for 4 knights; and the service of Adam 'de Sumeri' from the fee of Elmdon for 3 knights; and the service of Rannulf Brito for 1 knight.[3] And whatever the charter of the queen[4] confirmed to him, that also have I given and granted. All the aforesaid holdings, whether held in demesnes or by enfeoffed knights, and the wardship of the Tower of

[1] 2 February 1141.

[2] *i.e.* lands forfeited by those who broke their feudal contracts by rebelling against their lord, or for other reasons.

[3] The total is correct, 60 knights.

[4] Charter given at midsummer 1141, and printed in Round, *op. cit.*, p. 88. The present instrument is an attempt to outbid the empress of the services of Geoffrey.

London with the castle which is attached to it, and the offices of justice and sheriff I have given and firmly granted with all the aforesaid things and customs and liberties to Earl Geoffrey and his heirs to be held in fee and in heredity from me and my heirs in return for his service. Wherefore I will and firmly order that he and his heirs after him shall have and hold all such holdings and grants as freely and quietly and honourably as does any earl in the whole of England hold his possessions in the fullness of freedom and honour and quiet.

Witness: Maud the queen; and Henry, bishop of Winchester; and William, earl of Warenne; and Gilbert, earl of Pembroke; and Gilbert, earl of Hertford; and William, earl of Aumale; and William, earl of Sussex; and Earl Alan; and Earl Robert of Ferrières;[1] and William of Ypres; and William Martel; and Baldwin, the son of Gilbert; and Robert 'de Vere'; and Pharamus; and Richard of Lucé; and Turgis of Avranches; and Adam 'de Belum'.

At Canterbury.

46. Charter of the Empress Maud to William 'de Beauchamp', hereditary sheriff of Worcestershire (1141)

This intensely feudal document illustrates the conditions of Stephen's reign and should be compared in this respect with Nos. 45 and 255. The reference to the hereditary shrievalty of Worcestershire is particularly notable, as are also the feudal changes involved in the civil war. The Latin text is printed with a commentary in J. H. Round, *Geoffrey de Mandeville* (1892), p. 313.

Maud the empress, daughter of King Henry, and Lady of the English, to the archbishops, bishops, abbots, earls, barons, justiciars, sheriffs, servants, and all her liegemen, both French and English, of the whole of England, greeting. Know that I have given and restored to William 'de Beauchamp' in hereditary right the castle of Worcester with its moat, to be held by him and his heirs from me and my heirs in chief. I have given and restored to him the shrievalty of Worcestershire, and the forests with all their appurtenances, to be held by him in fee and heredity by the same 'farm' which his father, Walter 'de Beauchamp,' paid for them. And for this the same William has become my liegeman[2] against all mortals and particularly against Waleran, count of Meulan.[3] Nor can the same Count Waleran conclude an agreement with me respecting the aforesaid possessions unless the same William may hold from me in chief, or unless William of his own free will and pleasure shall wish to hold from the count. And besides this I have given and restored to him the castle and the honour of Tamworth to hold as well, peacefully, quietly, fully, honourably and freely as ever Robert the dispenser, the brother of Urse of Abbetot, shall have held the same castle and honour. And I also give and restore to him Weston and Luffenham in Rutland with all their appurtenances as his right without plea. I give and grant to him by way of addition 60 librates of land out of the acquisition of England for his service. And again I give and restore to him the constableship, which Urse of Abbetot held, and the dispensership as Walter, his father, held it by heredity from my father, King Henry. And I further give and grant to him the lands and inheritance of his

[1] Further information repecting the earldoms here mentioned will be found in G. H. White, "King Stephen's Earldoms" (*Trans. R. Hist. Soc.*, 4th Series, vol. XIII, p. 51).

[2] *meus ligius homo.*

[3] Twin brother of Robert who became earl of Leicester in 1118.

nearest kin who fought against me in my war, and they shall not be able to make agreement with me in this matter, unless there are some of their nearer kindred who in the same war have fought on my behalf. Wherefore I will and firmly order that William and his heir after him may hold this of me or of anyone else well and honourably and in heredity, peace, freedom and quiet, in wood and plain, in meadow and pastures, in forests and chases, in warrens and droves, in waters and mills and fish-ponds and pools and marches and saltpans and ways and paths, in fairs and markets within borough and without, within city and without, and everywhere with sake and soke, and toll and team and infangenthef and with all customs, liberties, and quittances.

These are the witnesses: Bernard, bishop of St. David's; and Nigel, bishop of Ely; and Robert, earl of Gloucester; and Milo, earl of Hereford; and Brian, son of the count; and Humphrey 'de Bohun'; and John, son of Gilbert; and Walkelin Maminot; and Milo 'de Beauchamp'; and Geoffrey of Vatierville; and Stephen 'de Beauchamp'; and Robert of Colleville; and Isnard 'Park'; and Geoffrey of Abbetot; and Gilbert the archdeacon; and Nicholas, son of Isnard.

At Oxford.

47. Account given in the "Deeds of King Henry II" of the proceedings involved in the Inquest of Sheriffs (1170)

For the author of this account, see above, pp. 99, 377. The narrative serves as an introduction to the documents which immediately follow. The account is printed in the edition of the *Gesta Regis Henrici Secundi* by W. Stubbs (vol. II, p. 4). The changes in the personnel of the shrievalty which ensued may thus be set out, the table being based upon that given by Stubbs, *op. cit.*, vol. II, pp. lxvii–lxviii:

County	*Went out*	*Stayed in*	*Came in*
Berks.	Adam of Gatmere	—	Hugh of Buckland
Oxon.			Alard Banastre
Beds.	Hugh 'de Loya'	—	David the archdeacon
Bucks.	William, son of Richard	—	William, son of Richard
Cambs.	Philip of Daventry	—	Elvard 'de Beach'
Hunts.			Warin of Bassingbourne
Cumb.	—	Robert Troit	—
Derbys.	Robert, son of Ralph	—	William, son of Ralph
Notts.			
Devon	—	Robert, son of Bernard	—
Corn.			
Dorset	Robert Puckerall	—	Alfred of Lincoln
Som.			
Essex	Nicholas the clerk	—	Robert Mantell
Herts.	Stephen 'de Beauchamp'	—	—
Hants	Richard, son of Thurstan	—	Hugh of Gonneville
Leics.	William Bassett	—	Bertram of Verdun
War.			
Lincs.	Philip 'de Kyme'	—	Walter of Grimsby
London	R., son of Berengar	—	John Bienvenutte
Middx.	William, son of Isabel	—	Baldwin the clerk

County	*Went out*	*Stayed in*	*Came in*
Northumb.	William 'de Vesci'	—	Roger of Estouteville
Norfolk Suffolk	Ogier the steward	—	Wimar the chaplain William Bardulf
Northants.	Simon, son of Peter	—	Robert, son of Sawin
Rutland	—	Richard of Le Hommet	—
Salop	Geoffrey of Ver	—	William the clerk
Stafford	—	Hervey Stratton	—
Surrey	—	Gervase of Cornhill	—
Sussex	Roger Hai	—	Reginald 'de Warenne'
Wilts.	—	Richard of Wilton	—
Worcs.	William 'de Beauchamp'	—	Hugh Puhier
Lancs.	William 'de Vesci'	—	Robert 'de Herleberga'
Gloucs.	—	Gilbert Pipard	—
Hereford	William 'de Beauchamp'	—	Walter the clerk
Yorks.	Rannulf 'de Glanville'	—	Robert of Estouteville

So when the Easter ceremonies were ended, the king proceeded to London. There he held a great council for the coronation of his eldest son, Henry, and for amending the laws of his kingdom. Moreover at this time he removed from office almost all the sheriffs of England and their bailiffs because they had evil entreated the men of his realm. And all the sheriffs and their bailiffs gave pledges to do right to their lord the king and to the men of his realm and to make proper recompense for their exactions. Afterwards the king caused all the men of the realm, including earls, barons, knights, freeholders and even villeins in every shire to swear on the Gospels to give true testimony concerning the things of which the sheriffs and their men had deprived them, and also to what amount, and how much by process of law and how much without, and for what trespass.

But the people of England suffered considerable loss in this matter, since after the inquisition had taken place the king restored some of the sheriffs to office, and they afterwards imposed even heavier exactions than before.

48. The Inquest of Sheriffs (Easter, 1170)

The following document is the text of the commission given by Henry II in 1170 to the body of itinerant barons set up to inquire into the administration of the sheriffs throughout the shires of England as a result of complaints made against their conduct. The royal commissioners are authorized to make a thorough investigation of the whole system of local justice and administration. The Latin text may be studied most conveniently in Stubbs, *Select Charters* (ed. 1913), pp. 175–178. An English translation is given in Adams and Stephens, *Select Documents of English Constitutional History*, pp. 18–20.

In the first place the barons itinerant shall exact bond and surety from all sheriffs who have been sheriffs since the lord king last crossed over to Normandy,[1] and from all who since that time have been their bailiffs or officials, whatsoever bailiwick

[1] *i.e.* since March 1166.

they have held from them; and from all who since that time have held the hundreds of the barons, which they themselves hold in the county, whether at 'farm' or in custody; that on a day the barons shall have appointed for them, they will appear before the lord king to do justice and to make amends to him and his men what they ought to amend. And if the sheriffs cannot appear before them on account of sickness, let them send in their place those who may answer for them, and let these give bond and surety sufficient for the sheriffs and for themselves, that they will perform in the presence of the lord king that which the sheriffs ought to perform at the appointed day.

Afterwards they shall exact an oath from all barons and knights and freemen of the county, that they will speak the truth concerning that which shall be asked of them on behalf of the lord king, and that they will not conceal the truth out of love for any man, or from hatred, or for bribe or reward, or from fear or from any promise or for any cause.

This is the manner of the inquest:

1.[1] In the first place let inquiry be made concerning the sheriffs and their bailiffs as to what and how much they have received from each hundred and from each vill and from each man, since the lord king crossed over to Normandy, by reason of which the land and the people have been oppressed; and what they have received by a judgment of the county or hundred, and what without a judgment. And let that which they ascertain has been taken by a judgment be written down separately; and let inquiry be made concerning all exactions, both as to the cause and the evidence.

2. Likewise let inquiry be made as to what and how much land the sheriffs or their bailiffs have bought or mortgaged.

3. Likewise let inquiry be made concerning the archbishops, bishops, abbots, earls, barons, sub-tenants, knights, citizens and burgesses, and their stewards and officers as to what and how much they have received from their lands since the above date, from their several hundreds and their several vills, and from each of their men, both with judgment and without, and let them write down separately all these exactions and their causes and occasions.

4. And likewise let them inquire concerning those men who since that date have held in custody from the lord king other bailiwicks, whether of an archbishopric, or of a bishopric, or of an abbey, or of a barony, or of any honour or escheat, as to what and how much they have acquired in that bailiwick.

5. And likewise let inquiry be made concerning the king's bailiffs, who have traversed his land to do the king's business, as to what has been granted them; and what they have ascertained from this inquiry, let them put into writing.

6. Also concerning the chattels of those who have fled on account of the Assize of Clarendon[2] and the chattels of those who have been undone through that assize, let inquiry be made as to what has been done and what has issued from it in the several hundreds and the several vills, and let it be accurately and carefully written down.

[1] The conventional numeration of paragraphs has been retained for purposes of reference. It has no place in the original.

[2] No. 24.

And likewise let inquiry be made whether anyone has been unjustly accused in that assize for reward or promise or from hatred or other unjust cause, and whether any accused person has been released or any accusation withdrawn for reward or promise or love, and who received the reward for it, and likewise let this also be written down.

7. And let inquiry be made concerning the aid for marrying the king's daughter, as to the amount issued from the several hundreds and the several vills and from each man, whether in payments or in pardons, and to whom it was handed over and delivered.

8. And let inquiry be made as to what and how much the foresters and their bailiffs and officers have received, since the aforesaid date, in their bailiwicks, in whatsoever way they have taken it or on whatsoever occasion, and whether they have remitted any of the king's rights for reward or promise or out of friendship for any man. And concerning transgressions of the forest, and concerning those who have trespassed in his forests and injured his stags and hinds and other wild beasts; and what they ascertain from this, let them write down carefully. And if the foresters or their bailiffs have arrested anyone or have taken anyone by bond and surety, or have accused anyone, and afterwards have released him without trial on their own responsibility, let inquiry be made as to who have done these things, and let their names be recorded.

9. And let all who have been accused concerning any right be placed under bond and surety to attend before the lord king on the day which shall be appointed them, and to do right and to make amends to the king and his men for what they should amend, and let those who lack sureties be kept in custody.

10. And let inquiry be made whether the sheriffs or any of their bailiffs, or the lords of the vills or their bailiffs, have restored any of the things which they have taken, or have made any peace with their men, since they have heard of the coming of the lord king, in order to prevent any complaint thereof reaching the lord king or his justices.

11. And let inquiry be made concerning fines and amercements, whether anyone has been released for reward or love from what he had been first amerced, and by whom this has been done.

12. And likewise let inquiry be made throughout all bishoprics as to what and how much and for what cause the archdeacons or deans have taken unjustly and without trial, and let all this be written down.

13. Let inquiry be made as to those who owe homage to the lord king and have not paid it, either to him or to his son, and let their names be recorded.

14. Let inquiry be made concerning the demesnes of the lord king, whether the houses are enclosed with ditches and hedges, and whether there are granaries there and cowsheds and sheepfolds and other outhouses and stock, as the lord king commanded before he crossed the sea.

15. And after they have been examined, let my sheriffs and officers be employed about the rest of my affairs and let them swear on oath to apply themselves lawfully to the inquisition to be made throughout the lands of the barons.

49. Return made in compliance with the Inquest of Sheriffs (1170)

This text is the best surviving copy of an original return made to the royal commissioners in compliance with the instructions set out in the text of the commission (No. 48). The returns are for the counties of Norfolk and Suffolk and are written on a number of scraps of parchment found in the Public Record Office in 1889 and pronounced by J. H. Round to be fragments of the original returns to the Inquest from these counties; see Round, "The Inquest of Sheriffs (1170)" in *The Commune of London* (London, 1899), pp. 125–136. The identification was not accepted by Hubert Hall, who printed the fragments as an appendix to his edition of *The Red Book of the Exchequer* (Rolls Series, vol. II, 1896); see Preface, pp. cc–ccxi. Round's arguments, however, are now generally accepted as conclusive. Many of the returns throw an interesting light on the feudal relations between individual tenants-in-chief of the crown and their sub-tenants. It is therefore plain that the scope of the Inquest included the fiscal relations between private landholders in addition to those between the crown and its tenants-in-chief (Round, *op. cit.*, pp. 127–129).

THE EARL OF ARUNDEL'S MANOR

This is the inquest for the manor of the earl of Arundel in Snettisham, namely what his men have paid since our lord, the king of England, last crossed over to Normandy. When the earl marched forth to defend the Welsh Marches on several occasions, the men of his demesne paid 100 shillings, and Richard, son of Atrac, and his fellows paid for one socage 3 marks voluntarily. Richard the chamberlain, of Buckenham, received these moneys. Later, however, the men of the earl's demesne paid 40 marks for the discharge of the earl's debts, and Richard, son of Atrac, and his fellows paid 4 marks, and this of their own free will; and Richard the chamberlain, of Buckenham, received these moneys.

When the earl returned from France, the men of the earl's demesne again paid 10 marks, namely 5 marks to Richard the chamberlain, and 5 marks to the Jew of Rising. Once again Richard, son of Atrac, and his fellows gave 3½ marks, namely 2 marks to Richard the chamberlain, and 20 shillings to Deulebeny the Jew.

Again, the men of the earl's demesne paid 8½ marks, and Richard and his fellows gave 3 marks for one socage to redeem the earl's lands from the Jews; and this they did of their own free will. Deulebeny, the Jew of Rising, received these moneys.

These are the sums of money which the burgesses of [Castle] Rising have paid to their lord, the earl, since the king crossed overseas.

William Mercer	22*s.* 5*d.*	Gomannus	11*d.*
Sweyn Mercer	22*s.* 5*d.*	Hacetus	3*s.* 6*d.*
Manduerus	17*s.* 10*d.*	Eudo and his fellows	3½ marks
Hardekinus	5 marks, 6*s.* 6*d.*	Wulnoth	16*d.*
Richard Mercer	9*s.*	Richard Fisher	8*s.* 1*d.*
William Skinner	18*d.*	William, son of Leif	5*s.*
Hervey	2*s.*	Richard Lorimer	40*d.*
Airicus (Ælfric)	28*d.*	William Hardegrey	12*d.*
Geoffrey Mercer	2*s.*	Roger Miller	13*d.*
John Large	3*s.*	Hangot	10*d.*
Richard, son of Ivetta	9*s.* 3*d.*	Osbert Gendry	4*d.*
William Swan	9*s.* 4*d.*	Acerus	8*d.*
Hubert Testor	2*s.* 11*d.*	Robert Bucel	26*d.*
Anchetinus Cook	18*s.* 8*d.*	Edwin	7*d.*

Alan Bishop	17*d.*	Siolf	5*d.*
Asselac	8*d.*	Roger Florast	4*s.* 6*d.*
Osbert	8*d.*	Ralph	28*d.*
Ivetta	19*d.*	John	5*d.*
Adam, son of Elviva	4*s.* 8*d.*	Seman	16*d.*
Wulfet	6*d.*		

They paid all these sums to the earl of Arundel of their own free will to redeem his land from the Jews. They paid them to Nicholas the steward.

The village of Roydon, which belongs to the soke of Rising, paid as much within four years after the king's passage overseas. For the four armies going against Wales they paid 10 marks. On the other hand, they gave the earl of their own free will 11½ marks to redeem his land from the Jews.

The men of Kenninghall, on the demesne of the earl of Arundel, on two occasions of their own free will gave the earl 10 marks for the defence of the Welsh Marches, and they voluntarily gave 5 marks to discharge the earl's debt to the Jews. Also in the last expedition to France they voluntarily gave the earl 5 marks.

The men of Wymondham, on the earl's demesne, on two occasions freely gave the earl 15 marks for the defence of the Welsh Marches. And later they voluntarily gave 10 marks to discharge the earl's debts. For the last expedition to France they paid the earl 10 marks.

The men of Buckenham and of the soke of the earl's demesne on two occasions voluntarily gave 20 marks for the defence of the Welsh Marches. To redeem the earl's debts they voluntarily gave 10 marks. When the king sent the earl to Saxony with his daughter they gave the earl 10 marks voluntarily, and when the earl returned from the last French campaign they gave him 10 marks voluntarily.

After the lord king crossed the seas, the men of John 'L'Estrange' in Hunstanton and Ringstead paid 40 shillings to the earl of Arundel for a fee of three knights.

Fifteen days before the Purification of St. Mary next following,[1] it will be four years ago that the servants of the earl of Arundel seized 405 sheep of Matthew of Candos and transported them as far as Snettisham and kept them fourteen weeks. In course of transit 2 died; they had in their charge 18 ewes and 80 lambs; and a sum of 2 shillings was paid over to these servants. In fact nothing was due to the earl. The earl's bailiffs reply that they seized the aforesaid chattels on account of default of service on the part of Anelald of Bidon, the earl himself admits this and complains of Anelald.

Amaury 'de Beaufou' has paid the earl of Arundel, after the king's last crossing to Normandy, 9 shillings for a fee of three knights by order of the king's writ from overseas. Again Amaury has paid the earl 40 shillings for a judgment.

Robert of Bavent has paid the earl of Arundel 6 marks in money and horses, when he was keeper of the Welsh March.

After the king's crossing overseas Cecilia of Holme paid the earl of Arundel 2 marks for the Welsh campaigns; and on his return from the last French campaign

[1] 19 January.

10 shillings by order of the king's writ from overseas; and for discharging the earl's debt to the Jews 10 shillings.

Hugh, son of Ralph of Harling, has paid the earl of Arundel [10] marks for a fee of two knights for the campaign in England and for the campaign [in Normandy?] . . . .[1] And for a certain privilege of his which the earl restored to him, he gave him of his own free will 5 marks.

Adam, son of Alfred, voluntarily gave the earl 40 shillings by order of the king's writ from overseas.

After the king's crossing Godfrey, son of Aubert, paid the earl 4 marks for the campaign; and afterwards by order of the king's writ from overseas he paid the earl 20 shillings on his return from Saxony. Robert 'de Seingis' gave the earl 20 shillings for an aid.

Hervey 'de Ingelose' has paid the earl of Arundel . . .[1] for scutage [and] by order of the king's writ from overseas 4 pounds for four knights for the last French campaign.

The land of William of le Quesnay at Stoke has paid the earl of Arundel 20 shillings by order of the king's writ, and 20 shillings to Ralph for purchase.

From the land of William of Courcy at Dersingham his men have paid the earl of Arundel for several campaigns $4\frac{1}{2}$ marks.

After the king's last crossing overseas and after the assize[2] the men of Robert of Mileham at Wootton and Newton paid the earl of Arundel 60 shillings for the first Welsh campaign, 6 pounds for the second Welsh campaign and 60 shillings for the third. And on the earl's return from Saxony they gave him 60 shillings as an aid. Richard and Toco the chaplain, received these moneys at the order of William the steward.

Robert 'de Bavent' has paid 1 mark for pannage to Richard, the earl's clerk, to be given for the king's daughter's [marriage]. . . .[1] After the earl's return from Saxony Robert 'de Bavent' paid him 20 shillings by order of the king's writ from overseas as his fellows have done.

From the fief which Rannulf 'de Glanville' has in his keeping in Helhoughton and in Wramplingham in fee of the earl of Arundel, he has paid the earl's bailiffs by command of the king 30 shillings for a knight's fee and a half, and 30 shillings for a knight's fee and a half to Ralph 'de Monchensey' for dubbing him knight.

Matthew of Candos has paid 5 shillings for a quarter of a knight's fee as an aid to the earl of Arundel, and 6 shillings to Ralph 'de Monchensey' for dubbing him knight, and from the demesne of Holkam 10 shillings as an aid to the earl.

Elias of Heckingham has paid the earl of Arundel 30 shillings for a knight's fee and a half for the last Welsh campaign, and this by order of the king's writ; and 30 shillings for knighting Ralph 'de Monchensey', and to Anelald of Bidon 20 shillings.

William Malherbe has paid the earl of Arundel since the king's crossing overseas 7 pounds for a fee of three knights and a half for the king's host.

[1] Mutilated in MS.
[2] The Assize of Clarendon, 1166.

William Malherbe has paid the earl of Arundel on his return from Saxony 50 shillings as an aid; and to Ralph 'de Monchensey' 50 shillings for knighting him after the king's crossing overseas.

Robert, son of Ansgar of Wymondham, has paid the earl 20 shillings by order of the king's writ from overseas since his return from the French campaign. For the marriage of the king's daughter he gave 1 mark; and nothing more since the king crossed over to Normandy.

William 'le Velter' of Burnham . . .[1] has paid the earl's bailiff 60 shillings for three knights' fees on the earl's return from overseas on the last French campaign, by order of the king's writ which he brought; and nothing more to the earl since the king's crossing.

BARONY OF HENRY OF RYES

The men of Aldeby have paid to Avellina, wife of Henry of Ryes, 30 shillings for the Welsh campaign; for knighting Hubert of Ryes 2 marks; and for the marriage of his sister 40 shillings. And after Lord Reginald of Warenne received Hubert's land, they paid him 1 mark.

The lady Avellina, wife of Henry of Ryes, took from Newton, after the king went overseas, 28 marks, with a good conscience.

After Lord Reginald of Warenne received the land of Hubert of Ryes in wardship, he received from the said vill for the marriage of Henry of Ryes's daughter 5 marks, and for the stock of the manor 5 marks.

From the land of William of le Quesnay at Wroxham for knighting Hubert of Ryes 1 mark, and for the marriage of Henry's daughter at the king's command 2 marks, and for the Welsh campaign 2 marks.

From the land of William, son of Baldry of Tunstall, for the marriage of Henry of Ryes's daughter 2 shillings, $3\frac{1}{2}$ pence, and for the two campaigns in Wales 4 shillings, 7 pence.

After the lord king crossed overseas, Ralph 'de Bevill' paid the lady Avellina 1 mark as an aid at the lord king's command from overseas. And for the marriage of the daughter of Henry of Ryes, at the lord king's command, 1 mark, and for the maintenance of knights in the Welsh Marches 1 mark.

From the fief of Henry of Ryes now in the custody of Reginald of Warenne, the soke Hockering, Reginald had . . .[2] for payment of Hubert of Ryes's debt to Abraham the Jew and for redeeming his certificate; also 10 marks for the marriage of Hubert's sister and for the stock of the manor . . .[2] voluntarily.

Rannulf 'de Schalines' after the king's crossing overseas paid 6 marks, three for the marriage of his lord's daughter and three for the knighting of his son, Hubert of Ryes, at the order of his liege lady by the king's writ from overseas; and for holding the Welsh Marches he paid 3 marks.

Osbert of Wattisham has paid 2 marks to Hubert of Ryes for his sister's marriage at the king's command, 2 marks for an aid, and 4 marks for the king's needs in the Welsh campaign.

The lady Avellina, wife of Henry of Ryes, took from Somerton 10 marks for

[1] Nearly two lines erased in MS. [2] Illegible in MS.

knighting her son. After Lord Reginald of Warenne received Hubert's land in wardship, the men of the said vill gave to their lord, Reginald, for the marriage of Henry's daughter 10 marks of their own goodwill.

Richard, son of Radbod, paid Henry of Ryes 1 silver mark for his daughter's marriage by order of the king's writ from overseas and 10 shillings for the defence of the Welsh March.

After our lord king's crossing overseas the lord Alexander of Drayton paid at his lord's command through the king's writ from overseas 6 marks, three for the marriage of his lord's daughter and three for knighting his son, Hubert of Ryes. Also he paid 3 marks for the upkeep of the Welsh March.

. . . [two lines of MS. illegible] . . . ½ mark as an aid for the needs of Hubert of Ryes and 10 shillings for the defence of the Welsh March . . . [two lines of MS. illegible] . . . ½ mark as an aid for the needs of Hubert of Ryes, and 1 mark for the defence of the Welsh March.

BARONY OF ROBERT, SON OF HUGH

Fetcham is part of the demesne of Robert, son of Hugh, in Depwade hundred. And the men there say that, after the lord king's most recent crossing over to Normandy, they paid the said Robert, their lord, 13 shillings for the campaign of the lord king in Wales; and 20 shillings for an aid to discharge his debt to the Jews of their own free will.

After the king's crossing overseas Robert, son of Mordant of Denton, paid his lord, Robert, son of Hugh, 8 shillings, 9 pence for the two campaigns in Wales for a third of a knight's fee.

After the king's crossing Roger of Docking paid for the Welsh campaign to Robert, son of Hugh, 2 silver marks for one knight's fee.

After the king's crossing Roger 'de Tofts' paid his lord, Robert, son of Hugh, two parts of 1 mark for one expedition to Wales, and two parts of another mark for another expedition to Wales for two parts of a knight's fee.

Babingley is part of the demesne of Robert, son of Hugh, in Freebridge hundred. The men there say that, after the lord king's crossing to Normandy, they paid the said Robert, their lord, 10 shillings for an aid, and voluntarily to redeem him from his debt to the Jews; and to the said Robert they paid 1 silver mark for the lord king's expedition to Wales.

Topcroft is part of the demesne of Robert, son of Hugh, in . . .[1] When the king last crossed over to Normandy, Robert paid . . .[1] 20 shillings and 33 shillings as an aid, and. . . .[1]

Item, Denton is part of the demesne of Robert, son of Hugh, in the half hundred of Earsham. The men there say that, after the lord king's crossing to Normandy, they paid the said Robert, son of Hugh, their lord, 10 shillings for the lord king's Welsh campaign; and they gave him voluntarily as an aid to discharge his debts to the Jews 16 shillings, 8 pence. Item, for scutage 5 shillings.

[1] MS. mutilated.

BARONY OF ROBERT OF VALOGNES

Since the king last crossed over to Normandy and made his assize, Walter of Sapiston was reeve of Robert of Valognes at Fakenham, and through his ill custody his lord's hay crop perished, and so by the verdict of a jury he paid 40 shillings recompense to his lord. Afterwards he was 2 silver marks short in his reckoning, and these he restored to his lord by judgment. Likewise Godfrey the clerk was his servant, and he was 3 marks short in his reckoning and restored them to his lord by judgment; also for encroachment on his lord's land legally proven against him he paid his lord 16 shillings, 8 pence by judgment. Robert Shepherd had custody of his lord's sheepfold and was 46 shillings short in his rent, and this sum he paid his lord by judgment. Ralph, son of Loveday, was his lord's servant, and he was 30 shillings short in his reckoning, and this sum he repaid his lord by judgment. Brian had charge of his lord's grove and warren, and the deterioration of the warren was assessed at 30 shillings, and this sum he repaid his lord by judgment. The whole soke of the demesne at Fakenham entered a legal plea concerning a certain pastureland against their lord, but could not secure judgment in proof; so they paid the lord 52 shillings by judgment. Gilbert Nep had charge of his lord's apiary, and through his mismanagement his lord's loss was assessed against him at 9 shillings, 8 pence, and this sum he repaid his lord by judgment. Hugh Painter was his lord's swineherd, and the deterioration of the piggery in his charge was assessed at 5 shillings; and this he paid his lord by judgment. Walter Cobbe had the keys of the lord's grange in his charge and was deficient in his reckoning, whence the loss was assessed at 18 shillings, 4 pence, and this sum he repaid his lord by judgment. Likewise Leofwine had the keys of the lord's grange, and he showed a deficiency in the profits of the grange which was assessed at 28 shillings; this sum he repaid his lord by judgment.

For the marriage of the lord king's daughter the men of the soke of Fakenham paid their lord 3 marks. The men of Robert of Valognes at Rushworth [?] paid 10 shillings to the said Robert and 1 mark for the king's army.

THE "EARL OF CLARE"

Since the last assize which the lord king made when he crossed the Channel to go into Normandy, the earl of Clare had from the land of Robert of Briceurt, namely for three knights' fees 8 pounds from each assize held in the last two years at the four terms in each year.

Again for a certain scutage the earl had 30 shillings, and again a second time another 30 shillings, and for the said moneys the earl's servants seized a certain horse. But though they have received the moneys, they still retain the horse.

Again at the third term the earl had 60 shillings for a certain aid. And for the marriage of the king's daughter the said earl had 3 marks, which his servants received.

The men of the earl of Gloucester at Wells [-on-Sea] and Warham paid the earl 3 marks for the expedition to Normandy and 2 marks for the campaign in Wales.

William of le Quesnay paid 60 shillings for a fee of three knights to Earl Richard for an aid, and afterwards 40 shillings.

THE BISHOPRIC OF ELY

In the hundred of Milford and the half hundred of Dereham and in the soke pertaining to the fief of the bishop of Ely, the bishop had 18 marks; and again 6 marks which Achard his reeve received, and this was a grievance. And to the said Achard 30 shillings again as a grievance; and again for discharge of the bishop's debts 40 shillings by Achard, and this as a grievance. And after the bishop's death they paid 4 marks, and William of Dereham received the money and handed it over to William of Walsham on the order of Walter, son of Hugh, the archdeacon's steward. Achard the reeve and Payn the priest during the illness of the bishop increased the 'farm' to 8 pounds by reason of which the men were so heavily burdened that, unless it be amended, they will all be paupers.

UNCERTAIN BARONIES

Ralph 'l'Estrange' paid Hugh of Cressy for a fee of two knights which he holds of him, for his wife's dowry, 10 marks for a scutage; and for a relief William of Walton paid 100 shillings to his liege lady, and she to the earl of Warenne.

Since the lord king crossed over into Normandy, Henry 'de Novilla' paid 4 marks and 2 shillings for the five Welsh campaigns, and for the one campaign across the seas 2 marks for one journey, because he stayed behind on account of illness. For one other journey he found a certain knight who went in his place, and he gave him his freedom, because it was not yet in his power to go with him.

The men of William of Courcy at Little Saxham paid nothing to the sheriff and the king's reeves except 16 pence, which they paid for strengthening the castle at Orford, namely to Walter the reeve and his servants. For the marriage of the king's daughter half a silver mark. For the king's army at the four terms 1 silver mark after the king's passage.

BARONY OF WILLIAM, SON OF ALAN

The verdict of the men of Mileham. When the village fell into the custody of John 'l'Estrange' and Ralph, his brother, there were in the aforesaid village only sixteen ploughs, and now according to their testimony there are twenty-eight in the village. Moreover, the men of the village assert that, in respect of men newly enfeoffed and of woodland and other things in the custody of John 'l'Estrange' and Ralph, his brother, the village has been improved to an extent worth more than 40 marks of silver. This, indeed, all the men of the vill testify on oath.

Moreover, the men of this same vill assert that they have paid their lord, John 'l'Estrange', 9 pounds for an aid voluntarily in one year and in another year 45 shillings voluntarily.

The verdict of the knights of John 'l'Estrange' concerning the payments made to their lord, John, since the lord king last crossed over to Normandy; Herbert, 300 shillings; Brian 'Canis', 3½ marks; William of Palgrave paid Geoffrey of Ver 1 mark for the levy coming from Sporle.

FROM THE FIEF OF ROGER 'DE BERKELEY'

Reginald of Dunham paid his lord, William of le Quesnay, 1 mark for the Welsh campaign.

This is the description of the land of Waleran 'de Iveri' in the soke of Docking. The men of the soke of Docking have paid Waleran 'de Iveri' 20 marks unjustly, since the king last crossed the Channel; and unjustly indeed, because in the time of King Henry [I] they paid nothing except a just rent.

These are the services of watch and ward in the castle of Rockingham:

At the castle keep, 11 shillings, 3 pence.
From Alexander of Somersham for castle-guard, 15 pence.
At the Abbot of Coleby, 5 shillings.
At Isham, 5 shillings.
At Harewood, 5 shillings.
At Heverdon, 15 shillings.
At Melchbourne, 5 shillings.
At Standon, 5 shillings.
At Syston, 1 mark.
At the Abbot of Wroxton, ½ mark.
At Aldewinkle, 2 shillings, 6 pence.

These are the places where the services are due.

And if one of them shall have died, his heir owes to the collector 100 shillings; indeed it is unjust to collect from us, unless our lord or we ourselves owe anything.

D. JUDICIAL ORGANIZATION

THE growth of royal justice is among the most important developments in the constitutional history of this period. It is here evidenced firstly in reports of trials, and secondly in legal treatises. Among the many topics to be studied in these texts may be mentioned the position claimed by the king as the ultimate source of justice; the relation between royal and private jurisdiction; the progressive employment of the jury as a means of legal proof; the evolution out of the *curia regis* of a body of professional justices; and the missions of these justices through the country to hear the king's pleas. The 'grand' and 'possessory' assizes of Henry II as described by 'Glanville' are noteworthy as marking the end of a long process whose detailed significance can only be appreciated through the study of the individual texts themselves.

(*a*) REPORTS OF TRIALS

50. Report of a trial held on Pinnenden Heath (near Maidstone) at an uncertain date[1] but probably either in 1072 or between August 1075 and July 1076

This is the 'best documented', and not the least important, trial of the reign of William the Conqueror. It was held before the shire court of Kent which was afforced for the purpose by notable personages from elsewhere, and it was presided over by Geoffrey, bishop of Coutances. The dispute concerned the alleged robbery of lands belonging to the archbishopric of Canterbury and other Kentish churches by Odo, bishop of Bayeux and earl of Kent, and other magnates. The proceedings occupied three days, and deserve careful study. Not their least noteworthy feature was the appeal made to Old English precedent. There is a considerable modern literature respecting the trial which is discussed in most of the general histories of England at this time. Much consideration has also been given to the date at which the trial was held and to the various accounts which record its proceedings. In this respect special reference may be made to W. Levison, "A Report of the Pennenden Trial" (*Eng. Hist. Rev.*, vol. XXVII (1912), pp. 717–720); D. C. Douglas, "Odo, Lanfranc and the Domesday Survey" (*Essays . . . in honour of James Tait* (1933), pp. 47–57); J. H. Le Patourel, "The Date of the Trial at Penenden Heath" (*Eng. Hist. Rev.*, vol. LXI, pp. 378–388); and the same writer's "The Reports of the Trial on Penenden Heath" (*Studies . . . presented to F. M. Powicke* (1948), pp. 15–26). Of the four principal accounts of the trial, one (which is here followed) is printed in the last-named work; another in H. Wharton, *Anglia Sacra* (1691), p. 334; a third in M. M. Bigelow, *Placita Anglo-Normannica* (1879), p. 5, and a fourth in Levison, *op. cit.*

In the time of the great King William, who conquered England by his arms and subjected it to his sway, it happened that Odo, bishop of Bayeux, who was the brother of that king, came to England some time before Lanfranc, archbishop of Canterbury. He established himself in the county of Kent very strongly and exercised great power therein. Moreover, because in those days there was no one in that shire who could resist so powerful a magnate, he attached to himself many men of the archbishopric of Canterbury, and seized many of the customary rights which pertained to it. These he annexed wrongfully to his own lordship. Not long afterwards, the aforesaid Lanfranc, who was then abbot of Caen, himself came to England by the command of the king, and by the grace of God was made archbishop of Canterbury and primate of the realm of England. When the archbishop had resided here for some

[1] An appreciation of the difficulties in dating this trial may be obtained by referring to the annals printed below (No. 87). There this date is given as the third year of Lanfranc's archiepiscopate, *i.e.* 29 August 1071 to 28 August 1073, and another early account gives the date as 1072. On the other hand, Ernost, bishop of Rochester, was apparently present at the trial, and Ernost was consecrated bishop after 29 August 1075, and he died 15 July 1076 (see below, No. 87). These are among the many points considered by J. H. Le Patourel in *Eng. Hist. Rev.*, vol. LXI, pp. 378–388.

time he discovered that his church lacked many of its ancient possessions and that these had been dissipated or alienated through the negligence of his predecessors. He therefore diligently collected accurate information, and then, hastening to the king, he energetically stated his case. The king thereupon gave orders that the whole shire court should meet without delay, and that there should be brought together not only all the Frenchmen in the county, but also and more especially those English who were well acquainted with the traditional laws and customs of the land. This assembly met in due course at Pinnenden. At this trial very many questions were raised between the archbishop and the bishop of Bayeux relating both to the ownership of particular estates and also to the legal customs of the country; and at the same time many points were mooted concerning the customary rights to which the king and the archbishop were respectively entitled. So numerous indeed were the matters in dispute that all the business could not be transacted in one day, and for that reason the court of the shire was held in continuous session for three whole days at this place. During these three days Lanfranc, the archbishop, proved his title to many lands which were then held by men of the bishop, to wit: Herbert, son of Ivo, Thorold of Rochester, Ralph of Courbépine,[1] and others of his vassals. He vindicated his rights in these lands and in the customs which went with them against the bishop of Bayeux himself, and against the aforesaid men of the bishops and against others also. These were the lands in question: Detling; Stoke; Preston; Denton; and many other smaller estates. And against Hugh of Montfort-sur-Risle,[2] he vindicated his rights in Ruckinge and Brook; and against Ralph of Courbépine, 60 solidates in the island of 'Grean'. Over all these lands and others the archbishop vindicated his rights so completely that on the day on which the trial ended there was not a man in the whole kingdom of England who could claim any jot or tittle of them.

In this plea the archbishop not only proved his right to these and other lands; he also vindicated afresh the liberties of his church and the customary jurisdiction which he was entitled to exercise, to wit: sake and soke, toll and team, flymenafyrrmth, grithbryce, forsteal, hamfare and infangenthef,[3] with all other customs like to these and less than these, on land and water, in woods and ways and meadows, within city and without, within borough and without, and everywhere in the land. And verdict was passed in his favour by all the worthy and wise men who were present, and by the whole court of the shire, who all gave judgment that just as the king himself held his lands in every way freely and quit from tribute, so also did the archbishop of Canterbury.

At this plea there were present: Geoffrey, bishop of Coutances,[4] who was there representing the king, and who presided over this trial; Lanfranc, the archbishop, who pleaded and justified his plea; the earl of Kent, that is to say, the aforesaid Odo, bishop

[1] For these men, see D. C. Douglas, *Domesday Monachorum of Christ Church, Canterbury* (1944) *passim*.

[2] On this man, who was constable of Dover Castle and on his family, see Douglas, *op. cit.*, pp. 65–70.

[3] These are traditional formulae of jurisdiction. Too precise a meaning should not be given to them. Sake and soke may be taken to signify here jurisdiction in general; toll and team were probably primarily connected with rights to fines and warranties; girthbryce concerns house-breaking; forsteal possibly the launching of the pursuit of a criminal; hamfare is again probably house-breaking; and infangenthef normally signifies jurisdiction over thieves caught on one's own estates.

[4] Bishop of Coutances, 1048–1093. He was an important administrator in England and chief of the Domesday commissioners.

of Bayeux; Ernost, bishop of Rochester;[1] Ægelric, bishop of Chichester,[2] a man of great age and very wise in the law of the land, who, by the command of the king, was brought to the trial in a wagon in order that he might declare and expound the ancient practice of the laws; Richard of Tonbridge;[3] Hugh of Montfort-sur-Risle; William of Arques;[4] Haimo the sheriff;[5] and many other barons both of the king and the archbishop; and many men of the aforesaid bishops; and other men of other shires; and many men both French and English of great authority from the county of Kent.

In the presence of all these men, it was further fully proved that the king of the English could claim in all the lands of the church of Canterbury no customary dues save only three. If any men of the archbishop are arrested in the act either of digging up the royal roads which lead from city to city, or of felling trees so close to those roads that an obstruction is caused, then shall they fall under the jurisdiction of the king's officer, whether they had previously given surety or not, and they shall be fined by him according to justice. The third custom concerns any man who commits homicide or any felonious act on the king's highway: if caught in the act and arrested forthwith, he shall be punished by the king; if however he is not caught in the act but, being suspected, absconds without giving any surety, the king shall have no jurisdiction over him. In the same trial it was shown that the archbishop justly exercises many customary rights over certain lands both of the king and the earl. From the beginning of Lent[6] to the Octave of Easter, anyone who sheds blood shall be punished by the archbishop;[7] and at all times, both during Lent and otherwise, anyone who commits adultery shall pay either the whole or half the penalty to the archbishop, to wit, during Lent the whole, and outside Lent either the whole or half. The archbishop shall also have in the same lands whatever pertains to the cure of souls.

When the king heard the judgment given in this plea, and had been made aware of those who ratified it, and when he had learnt the many reasons which could be adduced in support of it, he gave thanks, and joyfully confirmed the judgment with the assent of all his magnates, and ordered that it should be steadfastly and completely upheld. Wherefore this has been written down so that it may in the future be kept in perpetual remembrance, and so that those who shall hereafter succeed to the Church of Christ in Canterbury may know of it; and may be aware of the rights they hold from God in the same church; and may have knowledge of what things the kings and magnates of the realm may exact from them.

[1] Bishop of Rochester, appointed after 29 August 1075, died 15 July 1076.

[2] See above, No. 1, p. 136.

[3] Richard fitz Gilbert, son of Gilbert of Brionne, the count, and brother of Baldwin of Meules, sheriff of Exeter.

[4] To be distinguished from William, count of Arques. See Douglas, *Domesday Monachorum of Christ Church, Canterbury*, pp. 43, 44.

[5] Sheriff of Kent, son of Haimo 'Dentatus'. See above, p. 428.

[6] *Ab illo die quo clauditur alleluia.*

[7] These jurisdictional rights of king and archbishop were described in 1086 as follows: "Over the city of Canterbury the king has sake and soke except over the land of Holy Trinity and of the monastery of St. Augustine. The archbishop claims jurisdiction over the roads outside the city on both sides wherever his estates lie. In cases of adultery throughout the whole county of Kent, the king has jurisdiction over the man and the archbishop over the woman, but on the lands of Holy Trinity, the king has jurisdiction over neither." (See Douglas, *Domesday Monachorum of Christ Church, Canterbury*, p. 98, and cf. Domesday Book, vol. 1, fol. 2.)

51. Plea respecting the liberties of the abbey of Ely held at Kentford, Suffolk (2 April 1080)

This famous trial illustrates many of the problems of the Norman settlement and the methods adopted to solve them. It is of particular interest for its description of the court, and the depredations of the sheriffs are noteworthy. It is discussed by E. Miller in "The Ely Land Pleas in the reign of William" (*Eng. Hist. Rev.* (1947), vol. LXII. The text is printed in M. M. Bigelow, *Placita Anglo-Normannica* (1879), p. 22.

In the year of the Incarnation of our Lord 1080 in the eleventh Indiction, the Epact being 26, on 2 April, an inquiry was held concerning the liberty of the abbey of Ely. There was a danger that this liberty might be entirely extinguished since it had been neglected for fourteen years owing to the restrictions imposed by King William, and since it had been almost destroyed by the unjust exactions of his officials. But at the time when Godfrey the monk was in charge of the possessions of the saint,[1] the king was moved by godly piety to give his attention to these matters. He therefore gave orders to his attendant magnates through the bishop of Bayeux[2] that they should investigate these matters at an assembly held at Kentford which should consist of the shire courts of the three adjacent shires. Many took part in the pleadings which then ensued, and we have written down the names of some of those who brought this dispute to an end in the belief that the settlement they made was final:

Four abbots with their followers, both French and English, to wit, Baldwin, abbot of Bury St. Edmunds; Wulfwold, abbot of Chertsey; Ulfketil, abbot of Crowland; Alfwold, abbot of St. Benet of Holme.

The emissaries of the king, to wit, Richard, son of Count Gilbert;[3] Haimo the steward;[4] Tihel of Helléan.[5]

The sheriffs likewise with their followers, to wit, Picot;[6] Eustace;[7] Ralph;[8] and Walter who appeared on behalf of the sheriffs Roger[9] and Robert.[10]

Hardwin; Guy; Wimer; Wihumer; Odo; Godric; Norman; Colsweyn; Godwine; and many other respected French knights, and Englishmen also from the four shires of Essex, Hertford, Huntingdon and Bedford.

This is the settlement of the liberty of Ely: that it ought to be respected even as the holy queen[11] possessed it at the beginning; and as it was protected by the privileges granted by the kings, Edgar, Ethelred and Edward; and as it was restored by holy saints and particularly by Ethelwold; and as it was copiously redeemed by money from the later encroachments of laymen. Solemn anathema was jointly pronounced and recorded in writing against all those who out of malice should deny it. And lest anyone by false pleading should be able to disturb the definite results of this most thorough investigation, the king with careful forethought associated himself with the verdict, strengthened it with his orders, and confirmed it by his edicts. He added grants of his own, and ratified these privileges by his charters, one of which relating to these matters he caused to be drawn up as follows:

[1] Etheldreda, queen and saint, to whom the abbey of Ely is dedicated. [2] Odo.
[3] Richard 'fitz Gilbert' of Tonbridge and Clare. [4] Also sheriff of Kent, see Nos. 39, 50.
[5] Dep. Morbihan, arr. Pontivy, cant. Josselin. The name survives in Helion's Bumpstead (Essex).
[6] Sheriff of Cambridgeshire. [7] Sheriff of Huntingdonshire. [8] Ralph Bainard, sheriff of Essex.
[9] Roger Bigot, sheriff of Norfolk. [10] Sheriff of Suffolk. [11] Etheldreda, see above.

William, king of the English, to all his faithful vassals, and to his sheriffs in all the shires in which the abbey of Ely holds lands, greeting. I order that the abbey shall possess in all its lands all its customary rights over all its men. That is to say sake and soke, toll and team, and infangenthef, hamsocne, grithbryce, fihtwite and fyrdwite,[1] within borough and without, and all those forfeitures for which compensation can be paid. Let the abbey hold these, I say, as it held them on the day on which King Edward was alive and dead, and as they have been proved by my order at Kentford by several shire courts held before my barons, to wit, Geoffrey, bishop of Coutances; and Baldwin the abbot; and Alsi the abbot; and Wulfwold the abbot; and Ivo Taillebosc; and Peter of Valognes; and Picot the sheriff; and Tihel of Helléan; and Hugh 'de Hosdeng'; and Jocelyn of Norwich; and many others.

Witness: Roger Bigot.

52. Record of the judgment given by William I in his court in a plea between the abbey of Fécamp and William of Briouze (*circa* 1086)

This record illustrates with particular effect a trial in the reign of William the Conqueror, and the manner in which an attempt was made to provide a legal solution of the many problems arising out of the Norman settlement. The lands in question were in Sussex, where both the abbey and William were large landowners. The text is also interesting as revealing the composition of a session of the *curia regis* towards the close of the Conqueror's reign, and in this respect it may be compared with No. 77. This text is printed in H. W. C. Davis, *Regesta Regum Anglo-Normannorum* (1913), p. 127, and is summarized in J. H. Round, *Calendar of Documents preserved in France* (1899), p. 37.

King William held a court at Laycock, a manor of William of Eu, and there decided a plea concerning the claims which William of Briouze had made respecting the possessions of the abbey of Holy Trinity [Fécamp]. The trial lasted one Sunday from morning until evening, and there were present with the king his sons and all his barons. There it was decided and agreed, as to the wood of Hamode, that it should be divided through the middle, both the wood and the land in which the villeins had lived and which belongs to the wood; and by the king's command a hedge was made through the middle of the wood, and our part remained to us[2] and William's to him. As to St. Cuthman's rights of burial, it was decreed that they should remain inviolate; and by the king's command the bodies which had been buried in William's church were exhumed by William's own men and taken to St. Cuthman's church for lawful burial. And Hubert the dean restored the money which he had received for burials and wakes and for tolling the bells, and for all dues for the dead; and he swore first through the mouth of a relative that he had not taken more. As to the land at 'Udica' which William had claimed from Holy Trinity for his park, it was adjudged that the park should be destroyed; and it was destroyed. As to the warren which he had made on the land of Holy Trinity, it was adjudged that it should be destroyed; and it was destroyed. As to the toll which he took at his bridge from the men of Holy Trinity, it was adjudged that it ought not to be paid, because it was never paid in the time of King Edward;[3] and by the king's command what had there been

[1] See above, p. 450. [2] *i.e.* the abbey of Fécamp: this is a Fécamp record.
[3] The appeal to pre-Conquest custom is characteristic and interesting.

taken in toll was returned, the toll collector swearing that he had not taken more. As to the ships which go up [the river] to St. Cuthman's harbour, it was adjudged that they should be quit for 2 pence for each ascent and descent [of the river], unless they should make another market at William's castle. As to the road which William had made on the land of Holy Trinity, it was adjudged that it should be destroyed; and it was destroyed. As to the ditch which William had made to bring water to his castle, it was adjudged that it should be filled up; and it was filled up; and the land remained the abbot's. As to the marsh, it was decreed that it should be the abbot's as far as the hill and the salt pits; and it was so. As to the eighteen gardens it was adjudged that these should belong to Holy Trinity. As to the weekly toll, it was adjudged that the whole should belong to the saint but that William should have half on Saturday. All these things remained free and quit to the church at Fécamp; and in respect of them William placed his pledge in the king's hand, he being in the king's mercy.

These barons saw the conclusion of this business:

The sons of the king: William and Henry.

The archbishops: Lanfranc and Thomas.

The bishops: William of Durham; Walkelin of Winchester; Remigius of Lincoln; Geoffrey of Coutances; Robert of Chester; Robert of Hereford; Osmund of Salisbury; Maurice of London.

The earls: Robert [count] of Mortain; Alan the Red;[1] Roger of Montgomery.[2]

The barons: Richard, the son of Count Gilbert;[3] Baldwin, his brother;[4] Roger Bigot; Henry of Ferrières; Bernard of Neufmarché; William of Eu; Hugh of Port-en-Bessin; Richard 'Goiz'; Eudo the steward; Robert the dispenser; Robert, son of Tetbald; William of Perci; Robert of Rhuddlan; Nigel of Thorpe; Roger of Courcelles; Alfred of Lincoln; William of Falaise; Henry of Beaumont.[5]

The abbots: Serlo of Gloucester; Thurstan of Glastonbury.[6]

The monks of Holy Trinity: William and Rahere and Bernard, son of Ospac.

The laymen: William 'Malcunduit'; Godfrey, his brother; Sotriz; Leviet; Richard 'de Bodes'; Geroldin.

53. Charter of Henry I respecting a suit to be held in the court of the abbot of Thorney (1107–1111)

A lord was entitled to hold a court for his feudal tenants, but as early as the time of Henry I the king was taking notice how seigneurial justice was administered. This charter should be compared with the remarks of Glanville (see also No. 58, p. 471) on the practice of Henry II. It shows that Henry II's reforming procedure in this matter as in so many others was guided by custom which had prevailed at a much earlier date. Printed: F. M. Stenton, *Facsimiles of Early Charters in Northamptonshire Collections* (Northants. Rec. Soc., 1930), p. 12.

Henry, king of the English, to Hugh the sheriff and Geoffrey Ridel and Aubrey the chamberlain, greeting. If the abbot of Thorney can show that he has not failed to do right to Robert, his man, and to his father, then I order that the plea

[1] A count of Brittany, and earl of Richmond (Yorks.).
[2] Earl of Shrewsbury. See Table 13.
[3] Richard fitz Gilbert of Tonbridge and Clare. See Table 11.
[4] Sheriff of Exeter. See Table 11.
[5] See Table 12.
[6] Cf. No. 1, p. 160.

should be held in the court of the aforesaid abbot, that is to say, the plea about the land and corn of Charwelton. And in regard to the disgrace which was done to Osbert the monk, despite my peace and despite my writ, do full right to the abbot when he shall wish to bring a plea in this matter, in order that I may hear no further complaint of default of right.

54. The "Inquisition of David" respecting the lands of the see of Glasgow (*circa* 1124)

This curious text is included in a history of the see of Glasgow, which in turn is contained in a MS. of thirteenth-century date. It is there prefaced by a long preamble. The record which follows may probably be assigned to the approximate date of 1124, at which time David, later to be David I, king of Scots, was lord of Cumbria, and earl of Huntingdon. The importance of this text has probably sometimes been exaggerated by some of the numerous writers who have discussed it. But it is none the less of considerable interest, particularly perhaps as testimony of the use of the sworn inquest by a Scottish prince who was deeply influenced by Norman customs. The procedure here revealed may thus be profitably compared with that employed in many of the Norman trials in England.[1] The most convenient place where the text can be studied in print is in A. C. Lawrie, *Early Scottish Charters prior to A.D. 1153* (1905), pp. 46, 47. It is fully annotated at pp. 299–204 of that work.

This is the inquisition made by David, prince of Cumbria, concerning the lands pertaining to the church of Glasgow.[2] Wherefore David, lord of the region of Cumbria, moved chiefly by love of God, but also by the love and admonition of a monk, caused an inquiry to be made concerning the lands pertaining to the church of Glasgow in each of the provinces of Cumbria[3] which were subjected to his rule and his power. (For he did not rule over the whole of Cumbria.) He did this because he was jealous that there should be restored to that church those possessions which in ancient times it had held, and because he desired to leave a sure record of these things to his successors and to posterity.

He therefore caused an inquiry to be made according to his power by means of the help and participation of the elders and of the wisest men of the whole of Cumbria,[4] and their findings on these matters will be written below:

(Here are the lands):[5] Cardowan; 'Camcar'; 'Lengartheyn'; Barlanark; Kinclaith; 'Chefcanenuat'; Carntyne; Carmyle; 'Quendal'; 'Abercarf'; Machan; 'Planmichel'; Stobo; Eddleston; Ancrum; 'Treuercunum'; Lillesleaf; Ashkirk; Hoddam; 'Edyngaham'; 'Abermelc'; Dryfesdale; 'Colehtoun'; 'Trevertrold'; Esbie; 'Brumescheyed'; 'Treuergylt'; in Peebles 1 carucate of land and a church; in Traquair 1 carucate and a church; in Morebattle 1 carucate and a church.

These lands were declared on oath to belong to the church of Glasgow by a sworn verdict given at the command of the aforesaid prince by Echtred,[6] son of Waltheof; Gille, son of Brod; Leysing and Oggo, judges of Cumbria;[7] Halden, son of Eadulf.

(Those[8] who are witnesses of this business, having heard and seen what was done

[1] Cf. especially Nos. 51, 52.
[2] Written in the margin.
[3] *Cumbrensis regionis*. The translation is difficult but none of the places mentioned below appears to have been in 'Cumberland'.
[4] Cf. prologue to the *Inquisitio Eliensis* (No. 215).
[5] The identifications which follow are taken from A. C. Lawrie's book.
[6] These are the named jurors. Cf. *Inquisitio Eliensis* (below, No. 215, pp. 882, 883).
[7] *Cumbrenses judices*. Perhaps 'lawmen' would be a proper translation. See the description of Lincoln in Domesday Book (below, No. 211).
[8] Sir Archibald Lawrie regarded this as a "spurious addition": the names are none the less interesting as indicating the extent to which the Scottish court was permeated by Anglo-Norman influence.

are: Maud the countess,[1] who granted this on her own behalf; William, the nephew of the aforesaid prince; Gospatric, the brother of Dolfin; Waltheof, his brother; Gospatric, the son of Ictred; Gospatric, the son of Alden; Oswulf, the son of Eadive; Maccus, the son of Undweyn; Uhctred, the son of Scot; Ulchel, the son of Alstan; Hugh of Morville; Payn of Briouze; Obert 'de Ardena'; Gervase Ridel; Guy of Cahagnes; Berengar Engaine; Robert Corbet; Walter 'de Lindeseya'; Robert 'de Burnevilla'; Rainad 'de Muscans'; Walter, son of Winemar; William the huntsman; Alan of Percy; Walter of Brouay.)

55. Suit of Richard 'de Anesti' against Mabel 'de Francheville' (1158–1163)

This text contains the plaintiff's record of the costs and charges incurred in his suit to recover certain lands bequeathed to him by his uncle, William of Secqueville. The defendant in possession of the estate was William's daughter by a second marriage contracted by him in violation of a previous betrothal to Alfreda of Troisgots. The pope had already declared this previous betrothal binding and had pronounced the second marriage null and void. This sentence had been promulgated at an ecclesiastical synod held in London. The plaintiff claimed the lands on the ground of this decision. The record illustrates the delay and expense which might be incurred in obtaining a verdict. In view of the complications involved, litigation was protracted for five years, and the circumstances of the case may be regarded as exceptional. On this case and the persons involved, see *Victoria County History*, vol. XX, *Essex*, vol. I, p. 379; W. F. Farrer, *Honors and Knights Fees*, vol. III, p. 271; D. M. Stenton in *Camb. Med. Hist.*, vol. VI, p. 588; F. Pollock and F. W. Maitland, *History of English Law*, vol. I, p. 158. The text which follows is printed in M. M. Bigelow, *Placita Anglo-Normannica*, pp. 311 *et sqq*.

These are the expenses which I, Richard 'de Anesti', incurred in gaining possession of the land of my uncle. First of all I sent one of my men to Normandy to obtain the king's writ to put my adversaries on trial. This man spent half a mark on the journey. When my messenger had brought me the writ I took it to Salisbury that it might be sent back sealed with the queen's seal; in this journey I spent 2 silver marks.

On my return thence, hearing that Ralph Brito was obliged to cross the Channel, I followed him as far as Southampton to speak with him and to ask him to convey the king's writ to the archbishop for me, because I knew that the suit ought to be transferred to the archbishop's court. In that journey I spent 22 shillings, 7 pence, and lost a palfrey, which I had bought for 15 shillings. Returning thence with the queen's writ, I went to Ongar and handed the writ to Richard of Lucé.[2] And when he had given me audience, he appointed a day, the eve of St. Andrew,[3] for my suit to be heard at Northampton. Before that day arrived, I sent Nicholas, my clerk, for Geoffrey of Troisgots and Alfreda, his sister, because she was my uncle's widow. Them he found at Burnham in Norfolk. This journey cost me 15 shillings and the loss of a packhorse, which I had bought for 9 shillings.

On my return I went with my friends and helpers to Northampton to plead my case, and on that journey I spent 54 shillings. There another day was appointed me at Southampton a fortnight later; on that journey I spent 57 shillings and lost a packhorse worth 12 shillings. After this came Ralph Brito from Normandy bringing me the king's writ transferring the suit to the archbishop's court. This writ I took to Archbishop Theobald, whom I found at Winchester, and on that journey I spent 25 shillings, 4 pence. Then the archbishop appointed me the Feast of St. Vincent,[4] and

[1] Countess of Huntingdon and wife of Earl David. She was the daughter of Simon 'de St.-Liz', earl of Huntingdon. See Table 9. [2] The king's justiciar. [3] 29 November. [4] 22 January.

the case was heard at Lambeth. There the case was adjourned until St. Valentine's Day.[1] On this journey I spent 8 shillings, 6 pence, and the case was heard at Maidstone.

Here the Feast of SS. Perpetua and Felicitas[2] was appointed me. But before that day arrived I went to the bishop of Winchester to ask him to bear witness to the decree of nullity which had been previously decreed in a synod at London.[3] This journey cost me a silver mark. The bishop having agreed to testify, I went on the appointed day all prepared to plead my case at Lambeth. There I spent 37 shillings, 6 pence, and the case was adjourned till the Monday following *Laetare Jerusalem*.[4] Before this I went for Master Ambrose, who was then with the abbot of St. Albans in Norfolk; on that journey I spent 9 shillings, 4 pence. I sent also Samson, my chaplain, for Master Peter 'de Mileto' at Buckingham. On this journey he lost his palfrey for which I recompensed him with a silver mark; he had spent there 7 shillings.

Having obtained the services of these clerks, I came with my counsel at the appointed day to London, spending on the journey 5 silver marks. Here the day *Quasi modo geniti*[5] was set for me, before which I sent my brother, John, overseas to the king's court, since it was told me that my adversaries had secured a writ from the king giving them leave not to plead until the king should return to England. For this cause I sent my brother for another writ, lest my suit should be held over on account of my adversaries' writ. In this journey my brother spent 3 silver marks. Meanwhile I myself went to Chichester to speak with Bishop Hilary and to get him to witness to the decree of nullity made in his presence by the bishop of Winchester in the synod at London. This I received in letters sent by him to the archbishop testifying to the decree. On that journey I spent 14 shillings, 4 pence. So I came to London on the appointed day with my clerks, my witnesses and my counsel. There I remained four days, pleading my suit each day. This journey cost me 103 shillings.

Then the case was adjourned till Rogationtide. And when I appeared at Canterbury on the appointed day, my adversaries declared they would not plead because of the summons to the king's army for the war of Toulouse. On that journey I spent 8 shillings and I returned thence without a day being fixed for further hearing. . . .

[Finally after many further delays and fruitless journeys and two appeals to Rome, the plaintiff obtained a writ summoning the case before the king's court.]

We came then to the king at Woodstock, where we remained eight days; and *at length* by grace of the lord king and by the judgment of his court my uncle's land was adjudged to me. There I spent 7 pounds, 10 shillings and 6 pence.

These are the presents which I gave to my counsel and to the clerks, who assisted me in the archbishop's court, namely 11 silver marks. In the court of the bishop of Winchester 14 silver marks, to Master Peter 'de Mileto' 10 marks and a gold ring worth half a silver mark. To Master Robert 'de Chimay' 1 mark. In the king's court I have spent in gifts, in gold and silver and in horses, 17½ marks. To Master Peter of Littlebury I gave 40 shillings. To the other counsel from among my friends, who had come regularly to the hearings of my suit, I gave in silver and in horses 12½ marks.

[1] 14 February. [2] 7 March.
[3] The declaration of nullity of his uncle's marriage with Adeliza.
[4] Fourth Sunday in Lent. [5] First Sunday after Easter.

56. Suit of Baldwin, archbishop of Canterbury, against the abbot of Bury St. Edmunds (1185–1189)

From this text it appears that the Grand Assize was in full operation, though here the claimant refused to prosecute, and accordingly judgment could not be pronounced. The conflicting evidence of the charters produced in the case is also noteworthy. Printed: M. M. Bigelow, *Placita Anglo-Normannica* (1879), pp. 238–240, from the chronicle of Jocelyn of Brakelonda, ed. J. G. Rokewode (Camden Soc., 1840), p. 37.

A murder had been committed on the manor of the monks of Canterbury called Monk's Eleigh[1] which lay in the hundred of the abbot of St. Edmunds.[2] The archbishop's men were unwilling that this murder should be tried in the abbot's court. The abbot, however, laid a complaint before the king, alleging that Archbishop Baldwin[3] had laid claim to the liberties of our church by obtaining a new royal charter for the church of Canterbury after the death of St. Thomas.[4] The king replied that he had never issued any charter to the prejudice of our church nor would he take from St. Edmunds anything which belonged to it. On hearing this the abbot said to his intimate counsellors: "It is better that the archbishop should bring a suit against me than I one against the archbishop.[5] I will put myself in seisin of this liberty and defend my cause with the help of St. Edmund whose rights are attested by our charters."

So early next morning, with the assistance of Robert of Cockfield, the abbot sent a body of about eighty armed men to the village of Brent Eleigh and caught the three murderers unawares and brought them bound to St. Edmunds, where they were cast into the lowest prison. When the archbishop complained of this, the justiciar, Rannulf 'de Glanville', ordered the accused to find sureties and to stand trial in the proper court, and summoned the abbot to attend the king's court there in order to answer the charges of violence and injury which the archbishop had made against him. On several occasions the abbot presented himself without offering any excuses. At length the case was heard before the king in the chapter-house at Canterbury, and the charters of both churches were openly read. Whereupon the king remarked: "These charters are of great antiquity and derive from King Edward.[6] I know not what to say except that the charters are at variance with each other." To this the abbot answered: "Whatever may be said about the charters, we are in possession now, and have been up to this day. Wherefore I desire in this matter to put myself upon the sworn verdict of the two shire courts, namely Norfolk and Suffolk, since the charters grant this right." But Archbishop Baldwin, having first taken counsel with his men, replied: "The men of Norfolk and Suffolk bear great love towards St. Edmund, and the greater part of the two shires are under the jurisdiction of the abbot. Therefore I will not accept their verdict." At this the king rose up in anger, and as he left the court he said, "Let him take who can." Thus the case was postponed and to this day it is still under judgment.

[1] Illega.

[2] Monk's Eleigh was within the "eight and a half hundreds of the abbey of Bury St. Edmunds". In it, however, the archbishop of Canterbury had land. An interesting and a typical case of disputed jurisdiction.

[3] Baldwin became archbishop of Canterbury in 1185.

[4] Thomas Becket was canonized within three years of his death in 1170.

[5] Because under the Grand Assize (see below, p. 466) the burden of proof lay with the claimant, and the defendant retained possession until the claimant had established his case.

[6] Edward the Confessor.

(*b*) LEGAL TREATISES AND STATEMENTS OF PROCEDURE

57. The "Laws of King Henry I" (*Leges Henrici Primi*)

This treatise was written early in the twelfth century as a supplement to a digest of Old English Laws known as the *Quadripartitus*. It reflects a transitional period in the history of English jurisprudence. It is incompetent in draughtsmanship and frequently very vague in its terms. Nor can it be regarded as being beyond question authoritative. It must therefore be used with caution. With these qualifications it may, however, be consulted with profit in respect of the procedure adopted in local and feudal courts during the first quarter of the twelfth century. But its usefulness is further limited by the fact that the confusion of its language and arrangement makes it impossible to supply more than a very rough rendering of the author's probable meaning in translation; and the passages which here follow should be read with this in mind. The text as a whole is discussed by F. Liebermann in *Über das englische Rechtsbuch Leges Henrici* (Halle, 1901), and many comments on its feudal implications are made in the course of F. M. Stenton's *English Feudalism* (1932). The text is printed in full in F. Liebermann, *Die Gesetze der Angelsachsen* (Halle, 1898), vol. I, pp. 544–611. Extracts therefrom (including some of those which appear below) are printed in W. Stubbs, *Select Charters* (ed. 1913), pp. 123–126.

VII, 1. According to ancient custom, and as lately established by the beneficent rule of the king,[1] the general pleas of the shire court shall be held at the recognized terms and times throughout the different provinces of England. Nor shall anyone be burdened further unless the needs of the king and the convenience of the realm demand that meetings shall be more frequent.[2]

VII, 2. There shall take part in these meetings bishops, earls, sheriffs,[3] representatives,[4] hundred men, aldermen, stewards, reeves, barons, vavassors, town reeves and other lords of land. And these shall diligently labour so that the humble may not suffer their wonted injuries through lack of punishment being meted out to evildoers, or through the crimes of oppressors, or through the subversion of judgments.

VII, 3. The true laws of Christianity ought to be dealt with first; then the pleas of the king; and lastly the needs of individuals which are held to be worthy of consideration. And all disputes which are brought to the notice of the shire court shall be settled thereat, either by amicable arrangement or by the rigour of judgment.

VII, 4. The shire moot and the borough moot ought to meet twice a year; and the hundred moot and the wapentake moot twelve times a year. And seven days notice must be given of the meetings unless the public weal, or those things necessary to the efficiency of the king's government demand greater speed.[5]

VII, 5. And if, owing to lack of judges or by any other chance, a matter which should be dealt with by the hundred court is delayed beyond two or three or more meetings of that court, let it be brought to a just settlement.

VII, 6. And if anyone, by lack of right, or by violence, shall so disturb his plea in the hundred court or in any other properly appointed place that it is brought for hearing into the shire court, let him lose it, or otherwise make such amends as may be just.

VII, 7. Any one of the barons of the king, or any one of the barons of any other man taking part in the shire court according to law shall there be entitled to speak in respect of all the land (and the men upon it) which in that shire he holds in demesne. And it shall be likewise done if his steward shall there properly represent him. If either

[1] Henry I. [2] See the writ printed above, No. 43.
[3] The term used is, however, *vice-domini* not *vice-comites*.
[4] *vicarii*. [5] Cf. No. 43.

the baron or his steward be absent from necessity, then the reeve and the priest and four of the better men of the village shall represent all those who shall not have been summoned by name to the plea.[1]

VII, 8. Likewise we have decreed what should be done concerning the time and place and manner of judgment in the hundred court, and concerning the just hearing of the causes of individuals, and concerning the presence either of the lord and his steward, or of the priest and reeve and four good men.

VIII, 1. If, however, there be need of a specially full session of the hundred court, let there be summoned twice a year to the hundred court all the freemen who are 'hearth-fast' and householders so that they may decide, among other things, whether the tithings are complete, and who for any reason has left them, or whether any of them are over-full.[2]

VIII, 1*a*. Let there be in each tithing one man as leader over the other nine; and likewise in each hundred let there be one of the better men who may be called alderman, and let him be zealous to promote with all vigilance the observance of the laws of God and man.

VIII, 2. It is provided for the common welfare that each man, who wishes to be held fully worthy of his were and his wite and his law, shall be in a hundred from the twelfth year of his age, and also in a tithing or frankpledge.[3] Hired men, mercenaries and wage-earners shall however be in the surety of their lords.

VIII, 3. And let every lord have with him those who are subject to his jurisdiction, so that he may hold them to justice for their crimes, or if necessary plead on their behalf.

VIII, 4. It has been said of those who do not hold land that if they serve in another shire and visit their kindred, then shall their kindred be responsible for them to public justice, and if they incur fines their kindred shall make payment for them.

XIX, 2. Over all the lands which the king has in his demesne he has also the jurisdiction. But out of certain lands the king has given manors and the jurisdiction over them as well. And out of other lands the king has given manors but retained the jurisdiction in his own hand. Nor are the royal rights of jurisdiction inevitably alienated when manors are given: rather it is a matter for individual arrangement.[4]

XXIX. The judges for the king are the barons of the shire who hold free lands

[1] *i.e.* a lord shall be responsible for his men, and if the lord or his steward be absent, then the priest, the reeve and four of the more prominent men of the village to which the man belongs shall be made responsible for him.

[2] Early evidence of the sheriff's *tourn*, which was regularized in the time of Henry II. It seems clear that at least from the time of Henry I the sheriff presided over two sessions of the hundred court each year, which all freemen of the hundred were required to attend in order that inquiry should be made respecting the condition of the tithings in the hundred.

[3] The tithing was recognized as an institution of the realm as early as the Laws of Cnut. On this was based the Anglo-Norman institution of frankpledge, and the present passage illustrates the process. Frankpledge has been defined as "a system of compulsory collective bail fixed for individuals, not after their arrest for crime, but as a safeguard in anticipation of it". This bail was collected at the sheriff's *tourn* when "View of frankpledge" is held. (See W. A. Morris, *The Frankpledge System*, 1910.)

[4] The distinction is here apparently between *franchised* jurisdiction, *i.e.* jurisdiction granted by the king to favoured individuals, and *feudal* jurisdiction, *i.e.* that jurisdiction which was inherent in feudal lordship.

therein. Through them are to be judged the causes of individuals by means of alternate pleadings. But villeins and cottars and farthingmen[1] and those who are base-born and without property are not to be numbered among the judges of the laws.

XXXI, 3. In the business of the shire court there shall take part bishops, earls and other powers,[2] who shall declare with just consideration the laws of God and man.

XXXI, 4. No man may dispute the judgment of the king's court, but it shall be permitted to men who have knowledge of the plea to appeal against the judgment of other courts.

XXXI, 5. No man may be convicted in a capital plea by evidence alone.[3]

XXXI, 7. Each man is to be judged by his equals[4] and by men of the same province.

XXXII, 2. No man shall sit in judgment on his lord, and in the case of the lord to whom he owes liege homage, he shall not do this even if the king is interested in the plea.[5]

XXXIII, 1. If anyone has a plea to bring forward in his court, or in any place properly appointed for such purpose, let him call together his equals[6] and his neighbours, in order that by the judgment they may thus be compelled to give, he may be able fully to prove the justice of his cause in a manner which cannot be disputed.

XLIII, 6. Whoever holds his lands from several lords shall be chiefly responsible to the lord from whom he holds his chief residence and who is his liege lord.

XLIII, 6*a*. If a man has given homage to several lords, and is seized and impleaded by one of them, then his liege lord, from whom he holds his residence, may be his pledge by right against all the others, nor can the liege lord be denied the 'manbot'[7] of his man. . . .

XLIII, 8. If the lord takes away from his man the land or the fief by reason of which he is that lord's man, or if the lord deserts his man in the man's mortal need, then may the man make the lord suffer forfeiture of his rights over him.

XLIII, 9. None the less, the man must suffer insult and injury from his lord for thirty days in time of war, and for a year and a day in time of peace; but during the interval he may demand justice from his lord by legal process through his equals,[8] his neighbours, his household officials or through strangers.

LV, 1. Every lord is allowed to summon his men, so that he may do justice upon them in his court. If the man be resident in a manor far from the honour from which he holds, he shall none the less go to the plea if the lord summon him. But if his lord holds several fiefs, he cannot legally compel a man of one honour to go to the court of

[1] Probably holders of quarter virgates. [2] *potestates.*
[3] *i.e.* formal proof, such as compurgation or the ordeal, will be required.
[4] Or 'peers', the Latin word is *pares.*
[5] On this and the subsequent statements of feudal rights and duties, the comments in F. M. Stenton, *op. cit.*, should be consulted.
[6] *pares.* [7] The fine paid if the man be killed. [8] *Compares.*

another, unless the plea to which the lord summons him concerns a man of that honour.

LV, 2. If the man holds of several lords and honours, he owes more to him from whom he holds his dwelling, and he shall be judged by that lord to whom he shall owe liege homage.

LV, 3. Every man owes duty to his lord for the lord's life and limbs and earthly honour, and for the keeping of the lord's counsel honestly and with profit saving only his fealty to God and to the prince of his country. Theft and treachery and murder and what is against God and the Catholic faith are not to be condoned or demanded. But faith shall be kept to all lords, except in respect of these things, and chiefly to him who is a man's liege lord. And the permission of the liege lord must be obtained before his man makes any other his lord.

58. The legal treatise known as 'Glanville': "Concerning the Laws and Customs of the kingdom of England": Methods of Trial in operation during the reign of Henry II

Here follow passages from this treatise relating to methods of trial in operation during the reign of Henry II. The author's discussion of feudal tenures will be found below, No. 268. The treatise itself was written about 1190, and though it has been traditionally assigned to Rannulf 'de Glanville', justiciar of England from 1180 to 1189, it is by no means certain that he was the author of the work According to F. W. Maitland[1] it was written by Rannulf's nephew, Hubert Walter, but this too has been disputed.[2] Whoever may have been its author the treatise is of the first importance as supplying a contemporary account of the legal practice of the king's court in the reign of Henry II, and sheds a great deal of light upon the judicial reforms made by that king. The work enables us to see how the heterogeneous mass of laws and customs derived from a variety of sources was slowly being welded into a living, growing body of law.

The work deals with the initiation and procedure of litigation and trial both in civil and criminal law, though the space devoted to the former is so much greater that it may be regarded as disproportionate. Here we possess detailed information as to the operation of the royal *curia* and the shire courts, the relevance or validity for the twelfth century of older forms of proof or witness, such as compurgation or wager-at-law and the various ordeals, the operation of trial by battle or the duel, introduced by the Normans, and the new judicial instruments devised or developed by Henry II, such as the application of the sworn inquest procedure to the ascertainment of legal fact in questions of land disputes, and also its increasing use in criminal cases as provided for in the great legislative enactments of the reign, the Assize of Clarendon and the Assize of Northampton, and from which the jury system is derived. Further, the working of the Grand Assize and the various possessory assizes is explained in detail, and the vast extension of the writ system is illustrated by copious citation of the writs appropriate to the various circumstances.

Accounts of this treatise will be found in all standard works on the history of English law, and reference may be specially made to Pollock and Maitland, *History of English Law*, vol. I, chap. VI; W. S. Holdsworth, *History of English Law*, vol. II, pp. 188–192, and M. M. Bigelow, *History of Procedure in England* (1880). The best edition of the treatise is that by G. E. Woodbine (Yale U.P., 1931), and the passages which follow are taken from pp. 42–44, 58–70, and 149–179 of that edition. A translation of the whole treatise was made by J. Beames in 1812.

(a) *Concerning the pleas which pertain to the king's court*

BOOK I. *Chap. I.* Pleas are either criminal or civil. The former are divided into such as appertain to the crown of the lord king, and those which belong to the sheriffs of shires. The following pleas belong to the crown of the lord king:

[1] Pollock and Maitland, *History of English Law*, vol. I, pp. 162–165.

[2] This ascription of authorship has been questioned by D. M. Stenton (*Camb. Med. Hist.*, vol. V, pp. 578–579). She argues in favour of a return to the older view that the author was Rannulf 'de Glanville' himself. The case depends on the interpretation of a passage in the chronicle of Roger of Howden (ed. Rolls Series, vol. II, p. 215).

Chap II. The crime which in legal parlance is called lese-majesty as tending to the death of the king, or the moving of a sedition against his person or his realm or in his army; or again the fraudulent concealment of treasure trove; or again the pleas concerning a breach of the king's peace: homicide, arson, robbery, rape, falsifying, and other pleas of a similar nature. These crimes are either punished capitally or with loss of members. We must, however, exclude the crime of theft which belongs to the sheriffs, and is discussed and determined in the shire courts. It also pertains to the sheriff, in case of default by the lords [of feudal courts] to take cognizance of brawling, assault and battery, unless the accuser makes specific complaint that the offence was committed against the king's peace.

Chap. III. Civil pleas are divided into such as are discussed and determined only in the king's court, and such as fall within the jurisdiction of sheriffs of shires. In the former court are discussed and determined all such pleas as concern baronies, advowsons of churches, questions of status and dower, when the woman has been entirely debarred from receiving it; for breach of fine made in the king's court; concerning the performance of homage and the receiving of reliefs, and concerning purprestures[1] and debts owing by lay persons. These pleas relate to ownership only: concerning those which refer to possession, and which are debated and decided by recognitions we shall speak in the proper place.[2]

Chap. IV. The following pleas pertain to the sheriffs: the plea concerning the right of freehold, when the courts of the lords are proved to have failed in doing justice, the procedure of which we shall discuss in another place,[3] and the plea concerning villeins born: such pleas being in each instance sanctioned by the king's writ.[4]

Chap. V. When anyone complains to the king or his justices concerning his fee or his freehold, if the complaint be such as ought to be determined in the king's court, or if the king is pleased that it should there be decided, then the party making the complaint shall have the following writ of summons:[5]

Chap. VI.

The king to the sheriff greeting. Command [*Praecipe*] *N.* that without delay he render to *R.* one hide of land in such-and-such a village, of which the said *R.* complains that the aforesaid *N.* has dispossessed him: and unless he do so, summon him by good summoners to attend before me or my justices on the day after the

[1] Encroachments on crown lands which, when resumed into the hands of the sheriff, were accounted for separately from the 'farm' of the county, see *Dialogue of the Exchequer* (below, p. 546). The intense activity of Henry II's government in this field, made more necessary by the alienation of crown lands under Stephen, led to a number of suits in respect of such usurpations.

[2] See below, p. 472.

[3] See below, p. 471.

[4] On writs generally, see Pollock and Maitland, *op. cit.*, vol. I, pp. 150–151; G. B. Adams, *The Origin of the English Constitution*, pp. 76 *et sqq.*; M. M. Bigelow, *History of Procedure* (1880), chap. IV.

[5] The famous writ 'Præcipe quod reddat'. In principle the same as the writ of right ('De recto tenendo') see below, p. 471; the writ 'Præcipe' was simpler in character and more direct in procedure. It constituted "a more direct interference with the private jurisdiction of the feudal baron" (Adams, *op. cit.*, p. 80). It transferred the suit immediately from the baronial to the royal court. It does not require the lord to do justice to the claimant in his own court, but entirely ignores the lord's right of jurisdiction. For detailed discussions of its basis and working ,see Pollock and Maitland, *op. cit.*, vol. II, pp. 62–65; Adams, *op. cit.*, pp. 80–82, 103 *et seq.*; Bigelow, *History of Procedure*, pp. 77–83.

Octave of Easter at such-and-such a place to show why he has failed to do this. And let him have there the summoners and this writ. Witness: Rannulf 'de Glanville'. At Clarendon.

Chap. VII. The party summoned either appears on the appointed day or makes default, or sends a deputy or makes an essoin, or does neither of these things. If he neither appears nor sends a deputy, let his adversary, the claimant, appear before the justices on the day appointed, and present his case against him, and he shall wait thus in court for three days. Should, however, the defendant not have come by the fourth day and the summoners are present and have affirmed that they have properly summoned him, and offer to prove the same according to the decision of the court, then the defendant shall again be summoned by another writ at an interval of at least fifteen days. This will be the writ which calls him to answer both to the capital charge and to his default at the summons. In this manner therefore three summons shall be issued. Should he not appear at the third summons or send a deputy, the tenement shall be taken into the king's hands, and it shall remain there for fifteen days. And if the defendant come not within the said fifteen days, possession will be adjudged to the claimant, so that from henceforth the defendant shall not be heard again, except in a suit on the question of ownership authorized by the king's writ of right. But if during the fifteen days he shall wish to redeem his tenement by surety, he shall be ordered to attend on the fourth day, and he shall have there what by law he is entitled to; and so he may recover possession if he come. But if he appear at the third summons and shall admit he received those previously sent to him, he instantly forfeits possession, unless he can save the day by the king's warrant and by a writ which he can instantly produce.

Chap. VIII.

The king to his justices greeting. I warrant that *N.* was at such-and-such a place on such-and-such a day at my command in my service, and therefore he could not be present that same day at our assizes; I therefore charge you not to place him in default on account of his absence. Nor should he suffer loss in anything. Witness, etc.

Chap. IX. If he shall deny all the summonses, he shall for each one of them obtain the oath of twelve men in corroboration; if one of these compurgators should fail on the appointed day, or a just objection should be made to the person of any of them, without the vacancy being filled, the defendant shall forfeit possession from that moment on account of his default. But if the oaths shall be proved to be sufficient, he shall that very day answer to the suit. . . .

(*b*) *Concerning ownership: trial by battle, and the Grand Assize*

Book II, *Chap. III.* [When the ownership of land is disputed] it shall be for the tenant to choose by what method he shall defend himself against the man who claims his land; he may either do so by means of the duel,[1] or he may put himself upon the king's Grand Assize,[2] to ascertain which of the disputants has the greater right to the land. If he choose the former method of procedure, he must deny the right of the claimant

[1] On the duel as a method of proof, see G. Neilson, *Trial of Combat* (1890). [2] See below, p. 466.

word for word, as the claimant has set it forth, and this he must either do himself or through some other proper person. And here we must observe that after the tenant has once offered the duel, he must abide by his choice and cannot afterwards put himself upon the assize.

In this stage of the suit the tenant may again avail himself of three reasonable 'essoins' with respect to his own person and the same number with regard to the person of his champion. When all permissible 'essoins' have expired, it is necessary before the duel can take place that the claimant should appear in court accompanied by his champion armed for the contest. Nor will it suffice if he then produce any champion, other than one of those upon whom he originally put the proof of his claim. Nor can any other contend for him after the duel has been offered.

If he who offered the duel should in the interval pending the suit happen to die, a distinction is to be made. If he died a natural death, and this is vouched for by the neighbourhood, as it ought always to be if there is any doubt, then the claimant may in the first place turn to one of those upon whom he originally placed his proof, or to another suitable person, even if he have not as yet named any other, provided that such other be an unobjectionable witness. Thus the plea may begin again. If, however, his death was occasioned by his own fault, his principal shall lose his case. It may be asked whether the champion of the claimant can substitute another in court to make that proof which he took upon himself. According to the law and ancient custom of the realm he cannot appoint any other unless it be his legitimate son, and it must also be observed that the champion of the claimant must be such a person as is a proper witness to the fact. Nor is it lawful for the claimant to prosecute his appeal in his own person, because such claim is not allowed, except by the intervention of a proper witness who had both seen and heard the fact.

The tenant may defend himself either in his own person, or if he choose by any other unobjectionable witness. But if he has produced a champion, and such champion should die in the interval, it may be asked what the law is, and whether the tenant may defend himself by another champion, or whether he ought to lose his suit or only his possession. We must here have recourse to our former distinction. It should further be remarked that the champion of the tenant cannot substitute another in court for the purpose of undertaking the defence, unless it be his son.

It frequently happens that a hired champion is produced in court who has undertaken the proof for the sake of a reward. If the adverse party should object to such, alleging him to be an improper witness, because he has accepted a reward to undertake the proof, and should add that he is prepared to prove this accusation against the champion either by himself or by another who saw the champion take the reward, then the party shall be heard on this charge, and the principal duel shall be postponed. If the champion of the claimant should be convicted on this charge and conquered in the duel, then his principal shall lose his case and the champion himself, being conquered, shall lose his law, that is to say, he shall never again be admitted in court as a witness for the purpose of making proof by duel for any other person. But with respect to himself he may be admitted, either in defending his own body, or in prosecuting any atrocious injury, as being a violation of the king's peace. He may also defend by duel his right to his own fee and inheritance.

The duel being finished, a fine of 60 shillings shall be imposed upon the party conquered in the name of recreance, and besides this he shall lose his law. And if the champion of the tenant shall be conquered, his principal shall lose the land in question, with all the fruits and produce found on it at the time the fee was taken into possession, and never again shall the plea concerning this land be heard in court. For those matters which have once been determined by duel in the king's court remain for ever unalterable. . . .

Chap. VI. But if the tenant should prefer putting himself upon the king's Grand Assize, the claimant must either adopt the same course or decline it. If the claimant has once conceded in court that he would put himself upon the assize, and has so expressed himself before the justices sitting on the bench,[1] he cannot afterwards retract, but must stand or fall by the assize.

But if he is unwilling to put himself upon the Grand Assize, he ought in such case to show some cause why the assize should not proceed between them, such as that they were of the same blood and sprung from the same kindred stock whence the inheritance itself descended; and if the claimant make this objection, the tenant will either admit its validity or deny it. If he admit it in court, the assize shall thereby cease, so that the matter shall be verbally pleaded and determined in court; because it shall then be lawfully examined which of the parties is the nearer to the original stock and as such the heir most justly entitled to the inheritance. In this manner the nearer heir shall prove his title, unless his adversary can allege in court any reason why such an heir has lost his right either for a time or in perpetuity, or that any ancestor of his had done so; as, for example, that he has given or sold or exchanged the land in question, or has alienated it by any other means which the law allows; or if the heir or any of his ancestors has committed felony, and so wholly forfeited his rights; a circumstance that will be treated more fully hereafter. Should the suit on any of these grounds be delayed (the manner of pleading having such a tendency), the matter may be properly brought to the decision of the duel. But if he who has put himself on the assize deny all relationship between himself and the claimant, or at least insist that they were not sprung from the same stock from which the inheritance descended, then recourse must be had to the common kindred of both parties, who for this purpose are to be called into court, in order that the relationship of the parties to the suit may be investigated in the light of their testimony. If the kindred unanimously affirm that the parties have descended from the same stock from which the inheritance descended, their assertion on this point is conclusive. But if one of the parties strongly persist in asserting the contrary, then recourse shall be had to the neighbourhood, and if its testimony coincides with that of the kindred, it must be accepted without reserve. The same course must be adopted if the kindred are found to differ in their testimony, for then the verdict of the neighbourhood shall be accepted as conclusive. This inquest having been made, if it is proved that the parties are unquestionably of the same stock from which the inheritance descended, the assize shall cease and the suit must proceed in the manner already described. But if the contrary should appear to the court and to the king's justices, then the claimant who made the objection that both parties sprang

[1] *coram justiciis in banco sedentibus.*

from the same stock, in order maliciously to forestall the assize, shall lose his case. Should nothing intervene to impede the progress of the assize, then the question shall be as finally settled by the assize as it would have been by the duel.

Chap. VII. The [grand] assize is a certain royal benefit bestowed on the people and emanating from the clemency of the prince with the counsel of his magnates. So effectually does this procedure preserve the lives and the civil condition of men that every man may now legally retain possession of his freehold, and at the same time avoid the doubtful event of the duel.[1] Moreover, by this means men may escape the severe punishment of an unexpected and premature death, or at least the opprobrium and lasting infamy of that dreadful and ignominious word that so disgracefully sounds from the mouth of the vanquished champion.[2]

This legal institution emanates from perfect equity. For justice, which after many and long delays is scarcely ever demonstrated by the duel, is advantageously and speedily attained through this institution. The assize does not allow so many essoins as the duel, and by this procedure both the labour of man and the expenses of the poor are saved. Besides, since the testimony of many credible witnesses is of more value in judicial proceedings than that of one only, so this institution relies to a greater degree on equity than does the duel. For whilst the duel proceeds on the evidence of one juror, this assize requires the oaths of at least twelve lawful men. These are the proceedings leading up to the assize. The party who puts himself on the assize should in the first instance, in order to prevent his adversary from subsequently impleading him, sue for a writ for keeping the peace[3] during the interval when the suit is pending between the parties concerning the tenement for which the tenant has put himself upon the assize. . . .

Chap. X. By means of such writs the tenant may protect himself and may put himself upon the assize until his adversary, appearing in court, obtains another writ to the effect that four lawful knights of the shire and of the neighbourhood may choose twelve lawful knights from the same neighbourhood who shall declare upon their oaths which of the litigating parties has the greater right to the land in question. The writ for summoning the four knights is as follows:

Chap. XI.

> The king to the sheriff greeting. Summon by good summoners four lawful knights of the neighbourhood of Stoke, that they attend before me or my justices at Westminster on the Octave of Easter to elect on their oaths twelve lawful knights of that neighbourhood who know the truth better than they themselves. The latter shall declare on their oaths whether *M.* or *R.* has the greater right to

[1] *est autem assisa illa regale* quodam beneficium clementia principis de consilio procerum populis indultum, *quo vitae hominum et status integritati tam salubriter consulitur, ut in iure quod quis in libero soli tenemento possidet retinendo, duelli casum declinare possint homines ambiguum.* The words printed in roman would seem to imply that this assize was established by a definite act of legislation. J. H. Round (*Eng. Hist. Rev.*, vol. XXXI, p. 268) has proved that this was so, and that the Grand Assize dates from the council of Windsor in 1179. See also Pollock and Maitland, *op. cit.*, vol. I, p. 47; Adams, *op. cit.*, p. 127; and D. M. Stenton, *Camb. Med. Hist.*, vol. V, p. 587.

[2] The conquered champion had to confess his defeat by publicly proclaiming himself *recreant*, a craven or coward.

[3] Writ 'De pace habenda'.

one hide of land in Stoke, which *M.* claims against *R.* by my writ, and for which *R.* the tenant, has put himself upon my assize, and who prays that a recognition[1] be made as to which of them has the greater right to that land. And you shall cause their names to be enrolled. And summon by good summoners *R.* who holds the land, that he be there at that time to hear the election, and you shall have there the summoners, etc. Witness, etc.

Chap. XII. On the appointed day the tenant may 'essoin' himself and again have recourse to three reasonable 'essoins'. And this appears but right since, as we have explained in a former part of this treatise, as often as anyone appears in court, and there performs what the law requires of him, he may again recur to his 'essoins'. But then it may happen that as many, if not a greater, number of 'essoins' may intervene in the remedy of the Grand Assize as in the duel, which is by no means compatible with what we have earlier laid down. Let us suppose then that the tenant has lodged three successive 'essoins' against the election of the twelve by the four knights. After these three 'essoins' and upon the tenant appearing in court, one or more of these four knights may on the same day lodge an 'essoin'; and if this be conceded the tenant might again, after the 'essoins' of the four knights had expired, 'essoin' himself afresh, and thus the assize could scarcely or never be brought to a conclusion. We should therefore observe that a certain just regulation has been made whereby the court is authorized to expedite the suit upon the four knights appearing in court on the day appointed for them, and being prepared to proceed to the election of the other twelve knights. Upon such an occasion, whether the tenant appear or not, the four knights shall nevertheless proceed upon their oaths to elect the twelve. But if the tenant himself were present in court, he might possibly have a just cause for objecting to one or more of the twelve, and concerning this he might be heard in court. Therefore it is usual in his absence not to confine the number of those elected to twelve, but to add as many more as may incontrovertibly satisfy the absent party when he returns to court. For jurors may be objected to for the same reasons as witnesses in the courts christian[2] are justly rejected. It should also be observed that if the party who has put himself upon the Grand Assize appear, although not all the four knights are present, the twelve may be elected by one of the four associating with himself two or three other knights from the same shire, if these should happen to be in court, even if these have not been summoned for the purpose, provided always that this is agreed to both by the court and by the litigating parties. But for greater caution and to prevent all possible quibbling, it is usual to summon six or more knights to the court for the purpose of making the election. Indeed, if the object be to expedite the proceedings, it will be better to follow the direction of the court than to observe the accustomed course of the law. It is therefore at the discretion and judgment of the king or his justices so to modify the proceeding as to render it more beneficial and equitable.

Chap. XIII. Any person may put himself upon the assize concerning a service or land and also concerning demands of service and concerning the right of advowson

[1] A recognition is a formal declaration on oath to determine a point at issue.

[2] The ecclesiastical court, whether of the bishop or of the archdeacon, where procedure in respect of recognitions was perhaps already more firmly fixed.

to any church. Nor is the party confined to this remedy as against a stranger, but he may utilize it also against his lord for the purpose of ascertaining whether the lord has the greater right to retain the object in question as part of his demesne, or whether the tenant may more justly hold it of him. It is easy to frame a writ adapted to these varied circumstances.[1]

Chap. XIV. The election of the twelve knights having been made, they should be summoned to appear in court prepared upon their oaths to declare which of the parties, namely the tenant or the claimant, possesses the greater right to the property in question. And let the summons be made by the following writ:

Chap. XV.

> The king to the sheriff greeting. Summon by good summoners those twelve knights (naming each) that they attend on such a day before me or my justices at such a place, prepared on their oaths to declare whether *R.* or *N.* has the greater right to one hide of land (or in the subject matter of dispute) which the aforesaid *R.* claims against the aforesaid *N.*, and of which the aforesaid *N.*, the tenant, has put himself upon our assize, and has prayed a recognition which of them has the greater right to the thing in question; and in the meantime let them view the land or tenement itself, of which service is demanded. And summon by good summoners *N.* the tenant, that he be there at that time to hear that recognition.

Chap. XVI. On the day fixed for the recognition, whether the tenant appear or absent himself, the recognition shall proceed without delay; nor shall any 'essoin' avail the tenant, because his presence not being requisite the recognition may proceed without him, since if he were present he would be precluded from alleging any reason why the Grand Assize upon which he had put himself should be deferred. It is otherwise with respect to the absence of the claimant. If he should 'essoin' himself the assize shall for that day be deferred, and another day shall be given in court; because although a party may lose by his default, no one can gain anything in his absence.

Chap. XVII. When the assize proceeds to make recognition, if none of the jurors know the truth of the matter, and shall have declared as much on oath in court, then recourse must be had to others until such can be found who do know the truth of it. If, however, some of them know the truth of the matter and some not, the latter are to be rejected and others to be summoned to court, until twelve at least can be found who are unanimous. But if some of the jurors should decide for one party and some of them for the other, then others must be added until twelve at least can be obtained who agree in favour of one side. Each of the knights summoned for this purpose ought to swear that he will neither utter falsehood nor knowingly conceal the truth. With respect to the knowledge requisite on the part of those put on oath, they should be acquainted with the merits of the case, either from what they have personally seen and heard, or from the declarations of their fathers, or from other sources equally entitled to credence as if falling within their own immediate knowledge.

Chap. XVIII. When the twelve knights, who have appeared for the purpose of making recognition, entertain no doubt about the truth of the matter, then the assize

[1] For enlargement of the writ system, see Adams, *op. cit.*, pp. 111–112; Pollock and Maitland, *op. cit.*, vol. II, pp. 558–567; Bigelow, *Placita Anglo-Normannica*, pp. 315–320.

should proceed to ascertain whether the claimant or the tenant has the greater right to the land in dispute.

If they decide in favour of the tenant, or make any other declaration by which it should sufficiently appear to the king or his justices that the tenant has the greater right to the land in dispute, then by the judgment of the court he shall be for ever released from the claim of the claimant, and the claimant shall never again be heard in court concerning the matter. For those disputes which have been once lawfully determined by the king's Grand Assize shall upon no subsequent occasion be revived.

But if by this assize the decision of the court go in favour of the claimant, then his adversary shall lose the land in question, which shall be restored to the claimant, together with all the fruits and produce found upon the land at the time of its possession.

Chap. XIX. A punishment is ordained for those who rashly swear in this assize, and it is with much propriety inserted in that royal institution. For if the jurors shall by the due course of law be attainted or by legal confession be proved to have perjured themselves in court, they shall be despoiled of all their chattels and movables which shall be forfeited to the king, although by the great clemency of the prince their freehold tenements are spared. They shall also be thrown into prison and there be detained at least for one year. In short, deprived for ever of their law they shall justly incur the mark of perpetual infamy. This penalty is justly ordained in order that a similarity of punishment[1] may deter men in such a case from the unlawful use of an oath.

It should also be observed that the duel shall never be offered in a case where the Grand Assize is not applicable, and the converse of this proposition equally holds.

If the land in question be adjudged to the claimant, he shall be sent to the sheriff of the shire where the land is situated in order to recover his possession, and for this purpose he shall have the following writ:

Chap. XX.

> The king to the sheriff greeting. I command you that without delay you deliver possession to *M.* of one hide of land in such-and-such a village which he claims against *R.*, for which the said *R.* put himself upon my assize, because the said *M.* has proved his right to that land in my court by recognition. Witness, etc.

Chap. XXI. If there are no knights to be found in the neighbourhood or in the shire itself, or fewer than twelve, who are acquainted with the truth of the matter in dispute, what steps shall then be taken?[2] In view of this situation, shall the tenant for this reason alone prevail against the claimant? If this be answered in the affirmative, shall the claimant lose his right, supposing that he has any? A doubt may be entertained on this subject. Let us suppose that two or three lawful men, or even more, provided the number be fewer than twelve, who are witnesses to the fact, offer themselves in court to prove it. Let us even suppose that they are of such an age as to be qualified to make proof by duel, and that they make use in court of such words on

[1] *i.e.* similar to that of the defeated party in the duel.

[2] The Grand Assize was a new institution when Glanville wrote this account of it, and the situation posed in this chapter had not yet arisen; accordingly it is treated hypothetically. See G. E. Woodbine's edition, p. 205.

account of which a duel is usually awarded. After all this it may still be doubtful whether any of them shall be heard upon the subject. . . .

BOOK XII. *Chap. I.* Pleas of right are directly, and in the first instance, begun in the king's court[1] where, as we have said, they are discussed and determined. But some pleas of right, although not in the first instance begun in the king's court, are sometimes transferred thither when the courts of different lords are proved to have failed in doing justice. In this case such pleas may through the shire court be transferred from thence to the chief court of the king. . . .

Chap. II. When therefore a person claims any freehold tenement or a service as held of another by free service he cannot draw the person holding it into a suit without the king's writ or that of his justices. He shall therefore have a writ of right directed to the lord from whom he claims to hold. If the plea concerns land, the writ shall be as follows:

Chap. III.

The king to the earl of *W.* greeting.[2] I command you without delay to grant full right to *N.* concerning ten ploughlands in Middleton which he claims to hold from you by the free service of one knight's fee for every service; or by the free service of 100 shillings a year for every service; or by the free service of which twelve ploughlands make a knight's fee for every service; or which he claims to belong to his free tenement that he holds from you in the same village or in Morton, by the free service, etc., or by the service, etc.; or which he claims to hold of you as the free marriage portion of *M.* his mother; or in free burgage; or in frankalmoign; or by the free service in the king's host with two horses at his own cost for every service; or by the free service of finding you one cross-bowman in the king's host for forty days for every service; of which *R.* the son of *W.* had dispossessed him; and unless you do so, the sheriff of Nottingham will do so, lest I should hear any further complaint about this through default of justice. Witness, etc.

But writs of right of this kind are infinitely diversified for different causes. . . .

Chap. VI. These suits are wont to be conducted in the courts of lords, or of those who fill their places according to the reasonable customs prevailing in the courts, which are so numerous and various that it is scarcely possible to reduce them to writing.

Chap. VII. These courts are proved to have failed in doing justice in the following manner.[3] Upon the claimant's complaining to the sheriff in the shire court and producing the king's writ, the sheriff shall send one of his officers to the lord's court on the day appointed the parties to the suit by the lord of such court, in order that the officer in the presence of four or more lawful knights of the shire, who by the sheriff's

[1] Because they are initiated by the writ 'Præcipe' already discussed in Book I, chap. VI. See pp. 463, 464.

[2] The writ of right ('De recto tenendo'). For full accounts of method of procedure, see Pollock and Maitland, *op. cit.*, vol. II, pp. 62–63; Adams, *op. cit.*, pp. 78–80, 100 *et seq.* and 129; Bigelow, *History of Procedure*, pp. 157–168.

[3] This should be compared with No. 43, which shows that this procedure was already adopted early in the reign of Henry I. The essence of Henry II's reforms in this respect probably consisted in its more frequent and regular application.

command shall attend there, may hear and see the proof of the claimant, namely that such court has failed to do him justice in his suit. The claimant must prove this by his own oath and that of two others who have heard and known the fact, and shall swear with him.

After such formality pleas are generally transferred from these courts to the shire court and there finally terminated after a fresh discussion, without any contradiction or recovery being allowed to such courts or to the lords of them or their heirs, in respect of the plea in question. . . .

Chap. XXIII. I omit here any discussion of the manner or the right of conducting or terminating these or other pleas in the various shire courts, both because of the different customs which prevail in different shires–for each observes its own peculiar customs–and also because the brevity of my treatise does not permit me to deal with any save those customarily discussed and determined in the king's chief court. . . .

Chap. XXV. Moreover it should be observed that according to the custom of the realm no one is compelled to answer in his lord's court for any free tenement he may possess, except at the command of the king or his chief justice,[1] that is, if it be claimed as held by lay fee. . . .

(*c*) *Questions of possession: the possessory assizes of Henry II*

Book XIII, *Chap. I.* Having explained the general course of proceedings which usually occur in court when questions of right[2] are concerned, it now remains to speak of the steps which should be taken when possession[3] alone is in question. Since these questions of possession are under the beneficial provisions of the law of the realm, which is termed an assize, usually decided by a recognition,[4] our subject leads us to treat of the different kinds of recognition.

Chap. II. There is one species of recognition which is called *Mort d'Ancestor*,[5] another *Darrein Presentment*,[6] another whether a tenement be an ecclesiastical fee or lay fee,[7] another whether anyone was possessed of a freehold on the day of his death, as of fee or of pledge, another whether anyone be under age or of full age, another whether anyone has died possessed of a certain freehold, as of fee or of ward, another whether anyone presented the last parson to a church by virtue of the fee that he held in his demesne or by virtue of wardship. And others of a similar kind, which frequently arise in court when the parties are present, are with their consent and that of the court examined in order to settle the point at issue. There is also another recognition which is called *Novel Disseisin*.[8]

[1] This passage has occasioned much comment. It might appear that here Glanville denies the competence of baronial courts in cases between the lord and his vassals; and certainly the statement goes further than the writ 'Præcipe' (see above, p. 463). See Adams, *op. cit.*, pp. 96–105; Woodbine, *op. cit.*, p. 273.

[2] *i.e.* 'best right', ownership. The distinction is of course between ownership which is a matter of right, and possession which is a matter of fact.

[3] The technical term is 'seisin'.

[4] See above, p. 468, n.

[5] See below, p. 473.

[6] *de ultima presentatione*. See below, p. 474.

[7] The assize *Utrum*. See below, p. 474.

[8] See below, p. 475.

When[1] therefore anyone dies possessed of a freehold in his demesne as of fee, the heir may justly claim the possession of his ancestor, and if he be of full age he shall have the following writ:

Chap. III.

The king to the sheriff greeting. If *G.* the son of *O.* shall make you security for prosecuting his claim, then summon by good summoners twelve free and lawful men of the neighbourhood of such-and-such a village to attend before me or my justices on such-and-such a day, prepared to declare on oath if *O.* the father of the aforesaid *G.* was possessed of his demesne as of fee of one virgate in that village on the day of his death, if he died after my first coronation[2] and if *G.* be the nearer heir. And in the meantime let them view the land, and you shall cause their names to be enrolled. And sumonm by good summoners *R.* who holds the land, that he be there to hear such recognition, and you shall have there the summoners and this writ. Witness, etc. . . .

Chap. VII. The writ of *Mort d'Ancestor* having been received by the sheriff, and security having been given by the claimant in the shire court to prosecute his claim, the proceeding comes to an assize in this manner. In the first place, twelve free and lawful men of the neighbourhood are to be elected according to the form expressed in the writ, both parties being present, as well the claimant as the tenant, or even in the latter's absence, provided he has been summoned at least once. He must be summoned once in order that he may be present and hear who are elected to make such recognition. Some of them he may, if he wishes, reasonably object to, and they shall in that case be excluded from the recognition. But if he should not appear in court at the first summons, he shall not be awaited any longer, but even in his absence the twelve jurors shall be elected and then sent by the sheriff to take a view of the land or other tenement in question. Yet the tenant shall have one summons of this account. The sheriff shall also cause the names of the twelve jurors elected to be enrolled, and having done this, he shall cause the tenant to be summoned to appear on the day appointed by the king's writ or that of his justices, to stand before the king or his justices, and to hear the recognition. But if the claimant be of full age, the tenant may 'essoin' himself on the first and second day, but on the third day he cannot do so. . . . On the third day, therefore, whether the tenant appear or not, the assize must be taken, and if the jurors should decide for the claimant, possession shall be adjudged to him, and the sheriff shall be directed to put him into possession by the following writ:

Chap. VIII.

The king to the sheriff greeting. Know that *N.* has in my court proved his claim to the possession of so much land in such-and-such a village by a recognition of *Mort d'Ancestor* against *R.*, and therefore I command you to cause him to enter into possession without delay. Witness, etc. . . .

[1] Glanville proceeds now to describe the assize of *Mort d'Ancestor*. This was instituted by the Assize of Northampton (No. 25, clause 4). For detailed discussion, see Pollock and Maitland, *op. cit.*, vol. II, pp. 56–62; Adams, *op. cit.*, pp. 126 *et seq.*

[2] Legal limit thus fixed at 1154. See Pollock and Maitland, *op. cit.*, vol. II, p. 51, for subsequent changes.

Chap. XVIII. It remains to speak of the recognition of *Darrein Presentment.*[1] If upon the vacancy of a church there be a controversy concerning the presentation, it may be decided by a recognition of *Darrein Presentment* upon either of the litigating parties requiring it in court. On such an occasion he shall obtain the following writ:

Chap. XIX.

The king to the sheriff greeting. Summon by good summoners twelve free and lawful men of the neighbourhood of such-and-such a village to attend before me or my justices on such-and-such a day, prepared to declare on oath what patron presented the last parson who has died to the church of such-and-such a village, which is said to be vacant, and of which *N.* claims the advowson. And you shall cause their names to be enrolled. And summon by good summoners *R.*, who has prevented that presentation, to attend there to hear the recognition. And have there, etc. Witness, etc.

Chap. XX. As to the 'essoins' allowed in this species of recognition, they may be understood from what has previously been said. Upon the recognition proceeding, whether both the parties be present or even if one of them be absent, the person to whom on his own or on his ancestor's behalf the last presentation shall be adjudged, is understood thereby to have proved his right to the possession of the advowson itself, so that upon his presentation the bishop of the place shall institute the first parson, if a proper person, into the vacant church, which he shall retain during his whole life upon his patron's presentation, whatever may afterwards happen to the right of advowson. . . .

Chap. XXIII. It remains to treat of the recognition to ascertain *whether* a tenement be a lay or an ecclesiastical fee.[2] Upon either of the parties desiring to have such recognition, it shall be effected by the following writ:

Chap. XXIV.

The king to the sheriff greeting. Summon by good summoners twelve free and lawful men of the neighbourhood of such-and-such a village to attend before me or my justices on such-and-such a day prepared to declare upon oath *whether* one hide of land, which *N.* the parson of the church of that village claims as held in free alms by his church against *R.* in that village, be the lay fee of the said *R.* or an ecclesiastical fee; and in the meantime let them view the land, and you shall cause their names to be enrolled. And summon by good summoners the aforesaid *R.* who holds that land, that he be there at that time to hear the recognition, and have there, etc. Witness, etc.

[1] This is bound up with the question of advowson and rights of presentation to churches. The advowson was treated as a piece of real property. By the Constitutions of Clarendon (No. 126) Henry II had decreed that a proprietary action for advowson must be brought before the king's court. See F. W. Maitland, *Roman Canon Law in the Church of England*, pp. 62–64; Makower, *Constitutional History of the Church of England*, pp. 435–436 and footnotes. Then, in or about 1179, this new possessory assize called *Darrein Presentment* was instituted to determine the actual fact concerning possession, its function being limited to this end; see Pollock and Maitland, *op. cit.*, vol. I, p. 148; vol. II, p. 137; Holdsworth, *op. cit.*, pp. 179, 190.

[2] Instituted by the Constitutions of Clarendon, 1164, No. 126, clause 9. Its object was to determine in which court, *whether* civil or ecclesiastical, cases of dispute concerning land should be heard; see Pollock and Maitland, *op. cit.*, vol. I, pp. 144–145, 246–248.

Chap. XXV. Neither in this recognition nor in any other, except the recognition of the Grand Assize, are more than two 'essoins' permitted. For a third 'essoin' is never allowed except where it can be judicially ascertained whether an illness be genuine or not.[1] As this is not usually done in recognitions they necessarily preclude a party from lodging a third essoin. The recognition we are now discussing proceeds in the manner prescribed for other recognitions. Yet it should be further observed that, if by the said recognition a tenement be proved to be an ecclesiastical fee, it cannot afterwards be treated as a lay fee, although it may be claimed by the adverse party to be held of the church by a stipulated service. . . .[2]

Chap. XXXII. Finally it remains to discuss that species of recognition which is called *Novel Disseisin.*[3] When anyone therefore unjustly and without a judgment has dispossessed another of his freehold; and the case falls within the king's assize, or in other words, within the time appointed for this purpose by the king with the advice of his magnates[3] (which is sometimes a greater period and sometimes a less), this ordinance comes to the aid of the person dispossessed, and he shall have the following writ:

Chap. XXXIII.

The king to the sheriff greeting. *N.* has complained to me that *R.* has unjustly and without a judgment dispossessed him of his free tenement in such-and-such a village since my last voyage into Normandy; therefore I command you that, if the aforesaid *N.* should make you security for prosecuting his claim, then you shall cause possession of that tenement to be restored to him, together with the chattels taken on it, and you shall cause the tenement with the chattels to be in peace until the Sunday after Easter, and in the meantime you shall cause twelve free and lawful men of the neighbourhood to view the land, and have their names enrolled. And summon them by good summoners to appear before me or my justices prepared to make the recognition. And put *R.* (or his bailiff, if he cannot be found) under safe pledge to be there at that time to hear such recognition, and have there, etc. Witness, etc.

Chap. XXXIV. But writs of *Novel Disseisin* are varied in different modes according to the diversity of tenements in which dispossessions are committed. . . .

Chap. XXXVIII. In this species of recognition no 'essoin' is permitted.[4] For the first day, and that whether the party committing the dispossession is present or not, the recognition shall proceed, because it spares no person, neither one of full age,

[1] *Nisi ubi potest judicari de infirmitate utrum sit languor vel non.*

[2] The assize *Utrum* cannot determine the question of ownership or give a title to the land. It is merely a preliminary process distinguishing between the respective competencies of civil and ecclesiastical courts. See Pollock and Maitland, *loc. cit., ante.*

[3] Appears in the extant version of the Assize of Northampton, 1176, clause 5, but was instituted at least ten years earlier, probably at the council of 1166, which issued the Assize of Clarendon, Nos. 24, 25. The date may be approximately determined by the Pipe Rolls for the reign of Henry II, where the phrase "*pro dissaisina super assissam Regis*" constantly recurs, *e.g.* Pipe Roll 12 Henry II, pp. 63, 65, and 13 Henry II, p. 134; 14 Henry II, *passim.* See Pollock and Maitland, *op. cit.*, vol. 1, pp. 145–146, 148 *et seq.* For earlier writs resembling the writ of *Novel Disseisin*, see M. M. Bigelow, *Placita Anglo-Normannica* (1879), pp. 128, 130, 169 and 170. This assize was intended to be a speedy process for remedying violent evictions; cf. also Bigelow, *History of Procedure*, pp. 169–183.

[4] Because of the necessity for a speedy judgment.

nor a minor, nor will it even await a warrantor.[1] But if a party should acknowledge such dispossession in court, naming at the same time a warrantor, the recognition shall thereby cease, and the person who has thus confessed shall be amerced to the king. The warrantor shall afterwards be summoned, and the plea proceed between him and the person who has on this occasion nominated him as warrantor.

It should also be noted that the unsuccessful party, whether appellant or appealed,[2] shall in every instance be amerced to the king on account of the violent dispossession. In addition, if the appellant should not keep his day, then also his sureties are to be amerced to the king. The same rule prevails with respect to the person of the other party, should he absent himself at the appointed day. The penalty inflicted by this ordinance is merely an amercement to the king.

In this recognition the party who has proved that he has been recently dispossessed, may obtain that the sheriff should be directed, with the authority of the king's writ and that of his justices, to restore to him the chattels and the produce of which he has in the meantime been deprived. In no other recognition does the judgment of the court usually make any mention of chattels or produce; and unless the sheriff has taken steps to compensate him for the loss of chattels and produce, then the party who complains of it shall obtain the following writ:

Chap. XXXIX.

The king to the sheriff greeting. I command you that you compel *N.* justly and without delay to render to *R.* his chattels, since *R.* complains that *N.* took them unjustly and without a judgment, etc.

(*d*) *Concerning criminal pleas which belong to the crown*[3]

BOOK XIV, *Chap. I.* Having thus far explained those civil pleas which are dealt with in court, it remains to treat of criminal pleas. When therefore anyone is charged with the king's death or with having promoted sedition in the realm or in the king's army, either a particular accuser will appear or not. If no particular accuser should appear, but public fame alone accuses him, then from the first the accused shall be safely attached either by suitable pledges or by imprisonment. The truth of the fact shall then be investigated by means of many and various inquiries and interrogations made in the presence of the justices. The probable circumstances of the case shall be taken into consideration, and each conjecture, whether it tends in favour of the accused or against him, shall be weighed. He must purge himself by the ordeal[4] or entirely absolve himself from the crime imputed to him. But if on the trial by the ordeal, a

[1] In this respect it differed from the assize *Mort d'Ancestor*.

[2] The terms are unusual in a civil action. Perhaps the allusion to *violence* explains their employment in this connexion.

[3] It should be noted that Glanville's exposition of criminal law is not only much shorter but more elementary and fragmentary than his treatment of civil suits. This final book of the treatise is indeed almost academic in character, *e.g.* little attempt is made to indicate the profound changes introduced into criminal procedure by the Assize of Clarendon. See Woodbine, *op. cit.*, p. 294.

[4] No. 24, clause 2. Here the ordeal by water (hot or cold) is made consequent upon the verdict of a jury and applied to those proved guilty of the charge. Stubbs, *Select Charters* (ed. 1913), p. 169; Pollock and Maitland, *op. cit.*, vol. II, pp. 598–599.

person is convicted of a capital crime, then the judgment is of life and members which are at the king's mercy, as in other pleas concerning felony.[1]

If, however, a particular accuser should appear in the first instance, he shall be attached by sureties (if he can produce them) that he will prosecute his suit. But if he is unable to bring forward sureties, it is usual to trust to his solemn promise,[2] as in all pleas concerning felony, for it is customary in such cases to trust in his good faith, lest by enacting too hard a security others might be deterred from making similar accusations. When security has been taken from the accuser that he will prosecute his plea, then the party accused is, as we have observed, usually attached by safe and secure pledges; or if he cannot produce any pledges, he shall be confined in prison. But in all pleas of felony the accused is customarily permitted pledges, except in a plea of homicide where for the purpose of striking terror it is otherwise ordained. The next step usually taken is to appoint a day for the parties, pending which the usual 'essoins' may be lodged.

At length the accuser should put forward his charges, namely that he had seen, or by some other method of proof in court, that he knew for absolute certainty that the accused had conspired or done something against the king's life, or moved a sedition in the realm or in the army; or had consented or given counsel or delegated an authority for such a purpose. And the accuser must allege that he is prepared to prove his charge according to the direction of the court.

If the accused in due manner in court shall deny everything the accuser has asserted, it is usual to decide the plea by the duel. And it must be observed that from the moment the duel is offered in pleas of this kind, neither of the parties can add or take away from the words employed in offering the duel; nor can either retract his statement without being regarded as vanquished and liable to the penal consequences. Nor can the parties be in any way reconciled to each other in future except by the king's permission or that of his justices. But if the appellant be vanquished he shall be amerced to the king. What other penalties and disgrace he shall incur if vanquished have been sufficiently described.[3] On the other hand, if the accused be vanquished the judgment that awaits him has been mentioned a little earlier, to which may be added the confiscation of all his chattels and the perpetual disinheritance of his heirs.

Every free man of full age is admissible as an accuser in a prosecution of this kind. Should, however, a minor move such an appeal, he shall be attached in the manner we have before stated. A rustic[4] is also admissible; but a woman shall not be permitted to make an accusation in any plea of felony unless in some exceptional instances of which we shall presently speak. Moreover, the accused may in pleas of this kind decline the duel either on account of age, or by reason of his being adjudged to have received a 'mayhem'.[5] The age of the party in such a case ought to be sixty years or upwards.

[1] No. 24, clauses 5 and 14; No. 25, clause 1. The latter provision marks an advance on the earlier. Here it is enacted, as a result of growing scepticism as to the efficacy of the ordeal, that even those who have emerged successfully from the ordeal shall, if of ill repute, be required to fly the realm as outlaws in cases of homicide and felony. Greater weight is now attached to the previous record of the accused than to particular proof.

[2] *fidei suae religioni solet committi.*

[3] See above, p. 466.

[4] *rusticus, i.e.* a serf or unfree villein.

[5] Bracton defines 'mayhem' as "when anyone has been so affected in any part of his body as to be unable to fight".

'Mayhem' signifies the fracture of any bone, or an injury to the head, either by wounding or abrasion. In such a case the accused is obliged to purge himself by the ordeal, that is by the hot iron if he be a freeman, and by water if he be a rustic.

Chap. II. A plea concerning the fraudulent concealment of treasure trove is customarily treated in the manner and order stated above, where a particular accuser appears. But if a man is accused of this crime by public fame only, it is not customary by the law of the land for him to purge himself by the ordeal (although by the assize a different course may be adopted) unless he has been first convicted or has confessed in court that he has found and taken some kind of metal in the place in question. But if upon this he be convicted, the presumption being against him, he shall be obliged to purge himself by the ordeal of the charge that he had found or taken anything from the place in question. In other respects the proceedings are as described above.

Chap. III. When anyone is accused of homicide the judgment is regulated by, and proceeds on, the distinction laid down above.[1] It should, however, be observed that it is not customary to set free upon pledges a person accused of this crime except by the royal prerogative. There are two species of homicide. The first is called murder, which is secretly perpetrated out of sight and out of hearing of all save the murderer and his accomplices, and in such a manner that the hue and cry[2] cannot at once be made after the offenders as ordained by the assize.[3] To make an accusation of this kind no one is admissible unless he be of the blood of the deceased,[4] and the nearer heir may exclude the more remote from the appeal.

There is also another species of homicide which is called simple homicide. In this suit no one is admissible to prove the accusation unless he be a blood relation of the deceased or connected with him by the tie of homage or lordship, so that he can speak of the death upon the testimony of his own eyes. It should also be observed that a woman is to be heard in this suit accusing anyone of her husband's death, if she speak as an eyewitness to the fact, because husband and wife are one flesh. And it is generally admitted, as will presently be shown, that a woman may be heard in accusing anyone of having committed an injury against her person. It is at the choice of the accused either to abide by the woman's proof, or to purge himself by the ordeal[5] from the crime imputed to him. A person accused of homicide is also sometimes compelled to undergo the legal purgation, if he was taken in flight by the crowd pursuing him, and this be legally testified in court by the sworn testimony of the shire.

Chap. IV. The crime of arson is proceeded upon, discussed and terminated under the form and order previously described.

Chap. V. The crime of robbery may also be passed over as this suit has no special peculiarities.

Chap. VI. The crime of rape is that in which a woman charges a man that he has violated her by force while in the king's peace. A woman having suffered such violence is bound to go at once to the nearest village and there declare to reputable men the injury she has received, showing them any effusion of blood that has taken place and

[1] *i.e.* the distinction between an accusation by a particular person and by public fame.
[2] *non assequatur clamor popularis.*
[3] No. 25, clause 7.
[4] A relic of the ancient blood feud. See Pollock and Maitland, *op. cit.*, vol. II, pp. 485–486, esp. p. 486, n. 3.
[5] *Iudicium Dei.*

any tearing of her garments. Next she must do the same before the reeve of the hundred. And lastly she should make public complaint of her injury in the shire court. The accusation being made, judgment is as has previously been laid down. A woman accusing anyone of such a crime is heard in the same manner as is customary in respect of any other personal injury which has been done her. But it should be understood that it is at the choice of the accused in such a case either to submit to the burden of making purgation, or to rebut the woman's proof against him. It should likewise be remarked that if anyone be convicted in such a suit, he will be judged in a similar manner to that in the foregoing suits.

Nor will it suffice if after judgment the malefactor wishes to take to wife the woman he has defiled. For in that case it might frequently happen that men of servile condition would use the occasion of having once defiled a woman to bring perpetual disgrace upon a woman of noble birth. Similarly, men of high rank would be disgraced by women of base blood, and thus unworthily blacken the fair fame of their lineage. Previous to the judgment, however, it is not uncommon for the woman and the accused to be reconciled by means of a marriage, but this can only be done by the licence of the prince or his justices and with the consent of the relatives.

Chap. VII. The crime of falsifying includes many particular offences, as for example, false charters, false measures, false money, and others of a similar nature which embraces all such falsifying for which a person ought to be accused and, if convicted, condemned. The manner and order of prosecuting these different species of crime may be sufficiently ascertained from what has gone before. One thing, however, ought to be observed, namely that if a person be convicted of falsifying a charter, it becomes necessary to distinguish whether it be a royal or a private charter, because in the former case the party, when convicted of this offence, shall be condemned as guilty of lese-majesty.[1] But if the charter be a private one, then the person convicted is to be dealt with more leniently as in other minor crimes of falsifying, where the guilty are punished by loss of members only, according to the will and disposition of the king.

Chap. VIII. As to thefts and other pleas which fall within the jurisdiction of the sheriff, they are conducted and determined according to the various customs of different shires[2] and may not properly be dealt with in the scope of the present treatise, which is solely concerned with the subject of the king's court.

59. Accounts given by Ralph 'de Diceto' and in the "Deeds of King Henry II" of the changes made by Henry II in judicial organization between 1176 and 1179

The itinerant visitations of the king's justices, in fitful and occasional operation under Henry I, were restored in the early years of Henry II, but it would appear that they did not become regularized in their procedure until Henry II had reorganized the power of his sheriffs in 1170 (see Nos. 47 and 48). The council of Northampton of 1176 marks the beginning of a vigorous attempt to put the eyre system on a permanent basis, and in 1179 a further reorganization took place. The accounts of these changes here given come from Ralph 'de Diceto', *Ymagines Historiarum*, and the *Gesta Regis Henrici Secundi*, both edited by W. Stubbs for the Rolls Series.

---

[1] Cf. T. F. Tout "Mediaeval Forgers and Forgeries", in *Bulletin of John Rylands Library*, vol. v (1920), pp. 208 *et seq.*

[2] *i.e.* in the county court; local variations still persisted in the twelfth century.

(i)

The[1] king on the advice of the king, his son,[2] and in the presence of the bishops, earls, barons, knights and his other vassals, and with their consent, appointed justices for the six regions of his kingdom, three for each region, who swore on oath to preserve the king's justice in each. This was done at Northampton on 26 January.[3]

(ii)

At[4] the beginning of the year 1176 the lord king, son of the Empress Maud, and the king, his son,[2] held court at Windsor. . . . And before the Purification of St. Mary[5] about the Feast of the Conversion of St. Paul[6] the lord king came to Northampton, and there he held a great council concerning the statutes of the realm in the presence of the bishops, earls and barons of the land. On the advice of his son, King Henry, and of the earls, barons and knights who were his vassals, he caused this assize[7] to be written down and ordered it to be kept. He divided his kingdom into six parts and appointed three justices for each part; these are their names and the shires he divided between them. . . .[8] Afterwards he caused all the aforesaid justices to swear on the Gospels that they would keep the assizes here subscribed, and would cause them to be kept inviolate by the men of the realm.

(iii)

The[9] bishops, earls and magnates of the realm being assembled at Windsor, the king by their common counsel and in the presence of the king, his son,[2] divided England into four parts. For each part he appointed wise men[10] from his kingdom and later sent them through the regions of the kingdom assigned to them to execute justice among the people. These are the names of those whom the king set over his people and the names of the shires assigned to them:

Richard, bishop of Winchester[11] Richard, the king's treasurer[12] Nicholas, son of Thorold Thomas Basset Robert of Witfield	Southamptonshire, Wiltshire, Gloucestershire, Dorset, Somerset, Devon, Cornwall, Berkshire, Oxfordshire.
Geoffrey, bishop of Ely Nicholas, the king's chaplain Gilbert Pipard Reginald of Wisbech, the king's clerk Geoffrey Hose	Cambridgeshire, Huntingdonshire, Lincolnshire, Leicestershire, Warwickshire, Worcestershire, Herefordshire, Staffordshire, Shropshire.

[1] Ralph 'de Diceto', *op. cit.*, vol. I, p. 404. [2] Henry, the young king. [3] 1176.
[4] *Gesta Regis Henrici Secundi*, *op. cit.*, vol. I, p. 106.
[5] 2 February. [6] 25 January. [7] The Assize of Northampton (see above, No. 25).
[8] Here follow the names: they are all, significantly, officers of the Exchequer.
[9] *Gesta Regis Henrici Secundi*, *op. cit.*, vol. I, p. 238. This refers to the year 1179.
[10] *i.e.* judges. [11] Richard of Ilchester; see below, pp. 500, 506, 507.
[12] Richard fitz Nigel, author of the "Dialogue of the Exchequer" (No. 70).

John, bishop of Norwich Hugh Murdac, the king's clerk Michael Belet Richard Peck Ralph Brito	Norfolk, Suffolk, Essex, Hertfordshire, Middlesex, Kent, Buckinghamshire, Bedfordshire.
Godfrey of Lucé[1] John Comyn[2] Hugh of Gloucester Rannulf 'de Glanville'[3] William 'de Bendings' Alan 'de Furnelles'	These are the six justices appointed in the king's court to hear the pleas of the people. To them also were assigned the following shires: Nottinghamshire, Derbyshire, Yorkshire, Northumberland, Westmorland, Cumberland and between the Ribble and the Mersey.[4]

(iv)

The[5] king of England, seeking to benefit those least able to help themselves, found that the sheriffs, while involved in public duties and fiscal business, were mindful of their own interests. Wherefore, becoming more and more anxious for the common weal, at certain times he entrusted the administration of justice in his realm to other loyal subjects. This he did in order that the coming of public officials of authority throughout the shires might strike terror into the hearts of wrongdoers, and that those who cheated him of the taxes and thus affronted the king's majesty might incur the royal displeasure. . . . Moreover, as time passed, the king was most assiduous in meting out justice to every man and, in order to provide more particularly for his subjects, he wished to test the loyalty of many of his servants. Diligently he sought out those who were lovers of justice in their various callings, and inquired among a countless host of men for one who was not corrupted by office. Thus, steadfast in his purpose, he again and again made changes in personnel while maintaining an unchanged opinion. . . . For at one time the king made use of the abbots, at another of the earls, at another of the tenants-in-chief, at other times of the servants of his household and his most intimate counsellors to hear and judge cases. At length, after the king had appointed to office so many of his vassals of such diverse callings, who proved harmful to the public weal, and yet he had not quashed the sentence of any official; when he could find no other aid beneficial to the interests of his private affairs, and while he was yet reflecting on the things of this world, he raised his eyes to heaven and borrowed help from the spiritual order. Thus he took care to provide for men's needs by setting apart from the generality of mankind those who, albeit they live among men and watch over them, yet possess qualities of insight and boldness superior to those of an ordinary man. Accordingly, passing over all who could easily become subject to worldly vicissitudes and resorting to the sanctuary of God, the king appointed the bishops of Winchester, Ely and Norwich chief justiciars of the realm. Perhaps he did this with

[1] Bishop of Winchester, 1189.
[2] Archbishop of Dublin, 1183.
[3] Justiciar of England, 1180, and probably author of *Tractatus de Legibus et Consuetudinibus regni Angliae*. See No. 58.
[4] *i.e.* Lancaster.
[5] Ralph 'de Diceto', *op. cit.*, vol. I, p. 434.

the calculation that even if the others, whom he had long before set up as judges, had shown scant respect for him as reigning monarch, these ecclesiastics would at all events show reverence more attentively and assiduously towards God, the King of kings, the Creator of mankind, the Judge of all hearts and the Recompenser of men's works. So, they should turn neither to the left hand nor to the right, they should neither oppress the poor in their judgments nor presume to favour the cause of the rich by taking bribes. If then these prelates should occupy themselves in secular business, contrary to the ordinances of Canon Law, and should be called to account for this, let them instantly oppose to the rigour of the canons the importunity of the king, his good intentions, and his actions pleasing to God and meet for the praise of men. . . . So, by the aforesaid bishops and their fellow justices pleas were determined by the mediation of justice. Certain cases were, however, reserved for hearing by the king, and the procedure of royal administration was restored on 27 August at Westminster.

60. Account in the "Deeds of King Henry II" of the provision of justices to hear pleas (*clamores hominum*) (1178)

The following account printed in the *Gesta Regis Henrici Secundi* (vol. I, pp. 207–208) records a further change in judicial organization in 1178. This was the provision of a group of justices, five in number, to hear pleas designated *clamores hominum*, which may be interpreted in a non-technical sense as 'common pleas'. This innovation did not, however, constitute the establishment of a new court of central jurisdiction, as was formerly supposed,[1] since the procedure is known to have been operated through the justices of the Exchequer, which was still regarded as the chief central court.[2] The justices assigned to this new task continued to follow the king and the *curia regis* about the country, and the new provision was plainly regarded as a step towards the closer association of the *curia regis* and the local courts presided over by the itinerant justices. It is also apparent that the experiment of dividing the realm into six regions to be visited by eighteen justices operating in fixed circuits had not succeeded in providing speedy and impartial justice.

So the lord king, while sojourning in England, examined the judges, whom he had appointed,[3] as to whether they had dealt discreetly and well with the men of the realm. And when he had learnt that the land and its people had been overmuch burdened by the great multitude of judges, for they were eighteen in number; on the advice of the wise men of his realm he chose five only, namely two clerks and three laymen, all members of his private household. These five he commanded to hear all the complaints of the realm[4] and to do right judgment, and that they should not depart from the king's court, but should remain there for the purpose of hearing the complaints of the people,[5] so that if any case should come before them which they could not bring to a decision, it should be presented to the king, and determined as might seem good to him and the wise men of the realm.

[1] Stubbs, *Constitutional History*, vol. I, p. 644; Pollock and Maitland, *History of England Law*, vol. I, pp. 153–154; Adams, *Origin of the English Constitution*, pp. 168–170.

[2] D. M. Stenton, *Camb. Med. Hist.*, vol. v, pp. 585–586.

[3] See above, p. 480.

[4] *omnes clamores regni.*

[5] *clamores hominum.*

E. ROYAL FINANCE

THE development of royal financial administration in this period which is discussed above (pp. 53–57) is here illustrated under three main heads. In the first place the Old English financial system, whose operation can best be watched in Domesday Book (below, Nos. 205–213), is displayed in the earliest of the surviving geld rolls. In the second place is exhibited some of the evidence relating to the origin of the Exchequer in England. Thirdly, the Exchequer is displayed at work in the time of Henry II. By far the most important document in this section is the *Dialogue of the Exchequer*, which is here printed in full in a new translation (No. 70). Finally, some representative extracts are added from the Pipe Rolls (Nos. 71–73) as being the most notable of the Exchequer records of this period.

(*a*) EVIDENCE RELATING TO THE ANGLO-SAXON FISCAL SYSTEM

61. The Northamptonshire Geld Roll (1068–1083, and probably 1072–1078)

This document is of interest first in displaying the system of finance operating in the time of Edward the Confessor, and secondly as showing how this was utilized with little modification by William the Conqueror. Edward the Confessor, like his predecessors, was wont to meet any financial needs which could not be satisfied from the revenues of his private estates by levying a general land tax or 'geld'–and of all gelds the Danegeld was the most important. Liability to such gelds was assessed by the expedient of assigning to each shire a certain round number of geldable units, which in Wessex, Essex and the southern Midlands were termed 'hides'. By the time of Edward the Confessor these units had ceased to have any but the most general relationship to the agricultural actualities in the shire. This general assessment of the shire was subsequently subdivided in round numbers among the hundreds in the shire, and it is this subdivision that is illustrated in the present text. It is interesting to observe that whereas the "County Hidage", a document drawn up in the early years of the eleventh century, assigns to Northamptonshire 3200 hides; in this text the shire is divided into 22 hundreds, 4 hundreds and a half and 2 double hundreds–making 32 "hundreds" in all. This correspondence may be held to indicate the continuation of an older system. It must, however, be noted that the actual hidage in the time of Edward the Confessor, as here described, is held to be only 2663½ hides. Perhaps the tax-paying capacity of Northamptonshire had fallen during the earlier half of the eleventh century. A further deterioration is also to be observed in what is perhaps the most striking feature of this document–the reiterated entries of "waste". The clue to this is probably to be found in the entry of the Anglo-Saxon Chronicles (see above, p. 140), which describes the savage harrying of Northamptonshire by Earl Morcar's northern levies in 1065. More than a decade afterwards, it seems, the results of this terrible visitation were sufficiently serious to affect the tax-paying capacity of the shire. This document is printed, translated and annotated in A. J. Robertson, *Anglo-Saxon Charters* (1939), pp. 231–237, 481–484. It is also printed in H. Ellis, *General Introduction to Domesday Book* (1833), vol. I, pp. 182–187. The record is discussed in J. H. Round, *Feudal England*, pp. 147–156, and in the *Victoria County History: Northamptonshire*, vol. I, p. 259. It is further considered in F. M. Stenton, *Anglo-Saxon England*, p. 636.

To Sutton hundred belong 100 hides as was the case in King Edward's time, and of these 21⅔ hides have paid geld, and 40 hides are in demesne,[1] and 10 hides are the king's own food rent and 28⅓ hides are waste.

To Warden hundred belong 100 hides as was the case in King Edward's time, and of these 18 hides less 1 yardland have paid geld and 40 hides are in demesne and 41 hides and 1 yardland are waste.

To Cleyley hundred belong 100 hides, as was the case in King Edward's time, and

[1] 'Inland', *i.e.* land exempt from the geld. The round numbers at which the 'inland' is assessed points to a systematic reduction of geld liability–perhaps due to the large amount of 'waste'.

of these 18 hides have paid geld and 40 hides are in demesne and 42 hides are waste.

To 'Gravesende' hundred[1] belong 100 hides as was the case in King Edward's time, and of these 18½ hides have paid geld and 35 hides are in demesne and 5 hides are the king's own food rent land and 41½ hides are waste.

To 'Eadboldesstowe' hundred[2] belong 100 hides, as was the case in King Edward's time, and of these 23½ hides have paid geld and 45 hides are in demesne and 5 hides are the king's and 26½ hides are waste.

To 'Egelweardesle' hundred belong 100 hides as was the case in King Edward's time, and of these 16½ hides have paid geld and 40 hides are in demesne, and from 6½ hides at Norton not a penny has been received – Osmund[3] the kings' secretary owns that estate – and 37 hides are waste.

To Foxley hundred belong 100 hides, as was the case in King Edward's time, and of these 16 hides have paid geld and 30 hides are in demesne and 21 hides are the king's own land and 33 hides are waste.

To Towcester hundred belong 100 hides as was the case in King Edward's time, and of these 19 hides have paid geld and 40 hides are in demesne and 30 hides are the king's own land and 21 hides are waste.

To Huxloe hundred belong 62 hides as was the case in King Edward's time, and of these 8 hides have paid geld and 15 hides are in demesne and 39 hides are waste.

To Willybrook hundred belong 62 hides as was the case in King Edward's time, and of these 7 hides have paid geld and 11 hides are in demesne and 13 hides are waste. All this belongs to half the hundred, and the king owns the half hundred which has paid no geld.

To the double hundred of Upton Green[4] belong 108½ hides as was the case in King Edward's time, and of these 50 hides have paid geld, and 27 hides are in demesne and 29½ hides are waste, and of the 100 hides 2½ hides have not paid geld, and that estate is owned by Richard Engayne.[5]

To the double hundred of Navereslund[6] belong 100 hides as was the case in King Edward's time, and the amount of land belonging to this double hundred which has paid geld is 29 hides and 1 hide, and 59 hides are in demesne and 11½ hides are waste, and of these 160 hides, 8 hides have not paid geld, and that estate is owned by the lady, the king's wife.[7]

To Navisford hundred belong 62 hides as was the case in King Edward's time, and the land which has paid geld amounts to 15 hides, and 14 hides are in demesne and 33 hides are waste.

To Polebrook hundred belong 62 hides as was the case in King Edward's time, and of these 10 hides have paid geld and 20 hides are in demesne and 32 hides are waste.

To the hundred and a half of Nobottlegrove belong 150 hides, of which 45 hides less half a yardland are occupied and have paid geld and 72 hides are in demesne and 33 hides and half a yardland are waste, and it was the same in King Edward's time.

[1] Now part of Fawsley hundred.
[2] Now part of King's Sutton hundred.
[3] Probably Osmund who became bishop of Salisbury in 1078.
[4] Now Nassaborough hundred. [5] Holding in 1086. [6] Now part of Huxloe hundred.
[7] Edith, widow of Edward the Confessor, has been suggested, but the reference is almost certainly to Maud, wife of William the Conqueror, who died in 1083.

There is a hundred and a half attached to Guilsborough, and it consists of 150 hides, and of these 16 are occupied and have paid geld, and there are 68 hides in demesne and 66 hides are waste. And it was the same in King Edward's time.

To Spelhoe hundred belong 90 hides, and of these 20½ hides are occupied and have paid geld and 25 hides are borough-land[1] and from 10 hides belonging to Abington -Richard's[2] land-not a penny has been received, and from 6 hides belonging to Moulton-William's[3] land-not a penny has been received, and 28½ hides are waste.

To Witchley west hundred belong 80 hides, and it was the same in King Edward's time, and of these 10 hides have paid geld and 40 hides are in demesne and 30 hides are waste.

To Witchley east hundred belong 80 hides as was the case in King Edward's time, and of these 15 hides have paid geld and there are 34 hides in demesne and 31 hides waste.

To 'Stotfalde'[4] hundred belong 100 hides, as was the case in King Edward's time, and of these 9 hides and half a yardland have paid geld and there are 40 hides in demesne and 50 hides and 3½ yardlands are waste.

To Stoke hundred belong 40 hides as they did in King Edward's time, and of these 17½ hides have paid geld and 10½ hides are in demesne and 12 hides are waste.

To the hundred and a half attached to Higham belong 150 hides as was the case in King Edward's time, and of these 50 hides less half a hide have paid geld and 44 hides are in demesne and 56 hides are waste and 10 hides in addition belong to Hamfordshoe.

To Mawsley[5] hundred belong 80 hides, and of these 12 hides have paid geld, and there are 30 hides in demesne and 30 hides waste, and 8 hides which have not paid geld are owned by the king.

To Corby hundred belong 47 hides as was the case in King Edward's time, and of these 7½ hides have paid geld and 11½ hides are in demesne and there are 12 hides and 1 yardland of the king's food-rent land which are waste and have not paid geld and 5 hides have not paid geld-of these the Scottish king[6] owns 3 hides and the lady[7] 1½ hides and Urs[8] half a hide-and 11 hides less a yardland are waste.

To Rothwell hundred belong 60 hides as was the case in King Edward's time, and of these 10 hides have paid geld and 20 hides are in demesne and 15 hides have not paid geld-the king owns 7½ hides and the king's wife[8] and Earl Robert's wife[9] and William Engayne own 7½ hides.

To Hamfordshoe hundred belong 90 hides as was the case in King Edward's time, and of these 25 hides have paid geld (and 26 hides are) in demesne and 39 hides are waste.

To Orlingbury hundred belong 80 hides as was the case in King Edward's time,

[1] *i.e.* lands belonging to the borough of Northampton, which lies within this hundred.

[2] Richard Engayne. [3] William Engayne. [4] Now part of Rothwell hundred.

[5] Now part of Orlingbury hundred.

[6] A surprising entry. The kings of Scotland were to hold large estates in Northamptonshire at a later date, so an interpolation might be suspected. But it is not impossible that some land was here held by the Scottish king even at this date. [7] Queen Maud. [8] Unidentified.

[9] Maud, wife of Robert, count of Mortain, half-brother of the Conqueror.

and of these 29½ hides have paid geld and 24½ hides are in demesne and 5 hides owned by William Engayne and Witeget the priest have not paid geld, and 21 hides are waste.

To the hundred and a half belonging to Wymersley belong 150 hides as was the case in King Edward's time, and of these 41 hides have paid geld and 60 hides are in demesne and 49 hides are waste.

(*b*) EVIDENCE RELATING TO THE ORIGIN OF THE EXCHEQUER

62. Writ of Henry I in favour of the abbot of Westminster (*circa* 1100–Easter, 1116)

Important for the early history of royal finance. R. L. Poole (*Exchequer in the Twelfth Century* (1912), p. 37) observes: "Here we have several features of interest. First the king orders the sheriff to make a payment of alms such as those for which, when the Pipe Rolls are preserved, we find him regularly asking for allowance as a deduction from his 'farm'. Secondly, the order was recorded on the roll . . . Thirdly, the order is changed into a permanent charge by the addition of the words '*et hoc quoque anno*'." Printed by J. Armitage Robinson, *Gilbert Crispin*, p. 149. Translated by R. L. Poole, *op. cit., loc. cit.*

Henry, king of the English, to Richard 'de Monte'[1] greeting. Cause the abbot of Westminster to have 10 shillings of my alms, as it is in my rolls. Witness: the bishop of Salisbury at Cannock. And this every year.[2]

Witness the same.

63. Writ of Henry I in favour of Holy Trinity, London (1100–May 1118)

One of the earliest references to the royal 'Exchequer' and to the barons of its upper court. Printed: Madox, *History of the Exchequer* (ed. 1711), p. 188. Discussed by R. L. Poole, *Exchequer in the Twelfth Century*, p. 39.

Henry, king of the English, to Roger, bishop of Salisbury, and to the barons of the Exchequer[3] greeting. Know that I have ratified the gift which Queen Maud, my wife, gave and granted to the canons of Holy Trinity, London, to wit, 25 pounds 'blanch' which she gave them from the 'farm' of the city of Exeter. And I order you so to constrain the sheriff that he gives it to them, as you would do this out of my own 'farm'.

Witness: Geoffrey 'de Clinton'.

At Winchester.

64. Writ of Henry I in favour of the abbot of Westminster (July 1108–1127)

An early reference to the royal Exchequer, and to the barons of the Exchequer who are here entrusted with judicial powers. Printed: J. Armitage Robinson, *Gilbert Crispin*, p. 149. Translated and discussed in R. L. Poole, *Exchequer in the Twelfth Century*, p. 39.

Henry, king of the English, to Richard, bishop of London, greeting. I bid you do full right to the abbot of Westminster concerning the men who forcibly, by night, broke into his church of Wenington. And unless you do it, my barons of the Exchequer[4] will cause it to be done in order that I may hear no further complaint about it for lack of right.

[1] The sheriff.
[2] *et hoc quoque anno.*
[3] *baronibus scaccarii*
[4] *barones mei de scaccario.*

65. Charter of Henry I in favour of the monks of Tiron (1114–1120)

This, and the three following charters, form an interesting series relating to the early royal Exchequer. Here Henry I between 1114 and 1120 gives 15 marks annually from his Treasury at Winchester. Then in July 1141 the Empress Maud confirms this and adds 5 marks. In 1152–1154 Henry, count of Anjou, confirms this again. And finally in 1156–1157 Henry II confirms the original 15 marks which he orders to be paid annually from the Treasury at the Exchequer. Printed: L. Merlet, *Chartularium de Tirone* (1883), vol. I, p. 43, and discussed by R. L. Poole, *Exchequer in the Twelfth Century*, p. 40.

Henry (by the grace of God), king of the English and duke of the Normans, to the archbishops, bishops and all his barons and liegemen of the whole of England and Normandy, greeting. Know that I have given to God and to the monks of Tiron, for the safety of my soul and of the souls of my children, of my father, of my mother, of my ancestors and my successors, 15 marks of silver for the shoes of the monks, the same to be received annually for ever at Michaelmas from my Treasury at Winchester.

Witness: Rannulf the chancellor; Geoffrey, archbishop of Rouen; John, bishop of Lisieux; Robert 'de Haia'; Nigel of Aubigny.

At Caen.

66. Charter of the Empress Maud in favour of the monks of Tiron (July 1141)

For the significance of this text, see No. 65. Printed: L. Merlet, *Chartularium de Tirone* (1883), vol. I, p. 109.

Maud the empress, daughter of King Henry and lady of the English, to the archbishops, bishops, abbots, earls, barons, justices, sheriffs, and all her servants, both French and English, greeting. Know that I have granted and given to the monks of Tiron in perpetual alms 15 marks of silver which my father, King Henry, gave them to be received each year from the Treasury at Winchester. And I have added to these 5 marks of silver in perpetual alms each year for the souls of my father and mother and of my ancestors and for my own soul. And I grant these 20 marks of silver to them from the 'farm' of Winchester, at Michaelmas 10 marks and at Easter 10 marks. Wherefore I will and firmly order that whoever shall hold my 'farm' of Winchester shall pay these marks to them annually at the aforesaid terms.

Witness: Robert, bishop of London and chancellor; David, king of Scotland; William 'de Sablaillo'; Payn 'de Clara-Valle'.

At Oxford.

67. Confirmation to the abbey of Tiron by Henry, count of Anjou (later King Henry II), of a payment from the Treasury of Winchester (1154)

For the significance of this text, see No. 65. It is printed in Delisle and Berger, *Recueil des Actes de Henri II* (1916), vol. I, p. 79.

Henry, duke of the Normans and of the men of Aquitaine, and count of the Angevins, to all archbishops, bishops, earls, barons, justices, sheriffs, and to all his liegemen and friends, both French and English, greeting. Know that I have granted and confirmed to the monks of Tiron in perpetual alms 20 marks of silver to be annually paid from my Treasury at Winchester, to wit, 15 marks which King Henry gave them and my mother confirmed to them, and another 5 marks which Maud the empress, my mother, gave to them in addition, as her charter testifies. Wherefore I will and firmly order that they shall have every year from the 'farm' of Winchester, at Michaelmas 10 marks and at Easter 10 marks. And whoever shall hold the 'farm' of Winchester must pay this sum to them at the aforesaid terms without any default.

Witness: Philip, bishop of Bayeux; Arnulf, bishop of Lisieux; William, bishop of Le Mans; Richard of Le Hommet, the constable; Geoffrey 'de Claers'.

At Le Mans.

68. Confirmation of an annual grant of 15 marks by Henry II to the monks of Tiron for their shoes (1156–1159)

For the significance of this text, see No. 65. It is printed in Delisle and Berger, *Recueil des Actes de Henri II*, vol. I, p. 214.

Henry, king of the English, and duke of the Normans and of the men of Aquitaine, and count of the Angevins, to the archbishops, bishops, abbots, earls, barons, justices, sheriffs, ministers, and to all his liegemen in all England and Normandy, greeting. Know that I have granted and confirmed to God and to the monks of Tiron in perpetual alms, for the safety of my soul, and the souls of my ancestors and successors, 15 marks of silver for their shoes. Let them receive this from my Treasury at my Exchequer yearly at Michaelmas for ever, as King Henry, my grandfather, gave it to them, and confirmed it to them by his charter. Wherefore I will and firmly order that they shall have this every year well and in peace at the aforesaid term without any default.

Witness: Philip, bishop of Bayeux; Arnulf, bishop of Lisieux; Thomas the chancellor;[1] Robert of Neufbourg; Jollan the steward; Hugh 'de Claers'.

At Le Mans.

69. Charter of Robert, earl of Leicester, for the abbey of St. Léger at Préaux making reference to his exchequer (29 January 1121–December 1135)

This important charter is particularly interesting as supplying a very early reference to the private exchequer of a great baron, and also for its early ascription to William I of the title of Conqueror. It is printed in A. du Monstier, *Neustria Pia* (1663), p. 524, and there can be little doubt that the printed version, even if not completely accurate, gives an adequate representation of the lost original whose authenticity can hardly be called in question.

I also Robert, earl of Leicester, grant to the aforesaid church of St. Léger the village of 'Sturia' freely as Roger of Beaumont, my grandfather, and my father, Robert, count of Meulan, granted it to the same church; and this I do with the consent and confirmation of King William, the conqueror of the English,[2] and of the second King William, his son. Furthermore I give and grant to the same church 8 librates in 'Stracfort', and in 'Herdeberga' 40 solidates annually; and 8 pounds and 6 shillings which used annually to be paid to my exchequer,[3] as my father gave and granted it. And I do this for the souls of King William the Conqueror, and of his wife, Maud the queen, and of their son, the second King William; and as a memorial in the future

[1] Thomas Becket.
[2] *Willelmi regis expugnatoris Anglorum.*
[3] *et ad scaccorium meum octo libras et sex solidos per annum.*

for the souls of Henry the king and of his wife, Adela, the third queen; and for the soul of Maud, the second queen of the English and of her son, William; and for the souls of my grandfather, Roger of Beaumont, and of his wife, Adeline;[1] and for the soul of my father, Robert, count of Meulan.

I, Henry, king of the English, grant the aforesaid gift to the same church of St. Léger and with my own hand confirm it with this sign.
The sign of Adela, queen of the English.
The sign of Waleran,[2] count of Meulan.
The sign of Robert,[3] earl of Leicester.
The sign of Robert. . . .

[1] See Table 12.

[2] Waleran of Beaumont, son of Robert of Beaumont, and twin brother of Robert 'le bossu', earl of Leicester. See Table 12.

[3] Robert 'le bossu', earl of Leicester.

(c) EVIDENCE RELATING TO THE WORK OF THE EXCHEQUER IN THE TIME OF HENRY II AND BEFORE

70. The "Dialogue of the Exchequer" (*Dialogus de Scaccario*)

This monumental work, which is here presented in full, is written in the form of a dialogue between *Master* and *Disciple*, both of whom are presumed to be officials of the Exchequer. Its primary object is to explain the system whereby the accounts of the sheriffs were audited and enrolled; it thus serves as a valuable commentary on the Pipe Rolls.[1] It explains the origin of the Exchequer and describes the constitution and organization both of the Higher and Lower Exchequers, enumerating the various offices and duties and privileges attached to them, detailing the complicated calculations which regularly took place with the aid of tallies and counters moved on the chess-board, the testing of the coins paid into the Treasury by the processes of weighing and combustion, the method of recording or enrolling accounts, the various writs of summons issued to compel or excuse attendance–in short, all the multifarious business normally transacted in the Exchequer at its two half-yearly sessions at Easter and Michaelmas. In the second book, the treatise branches out into a description of the major sources of the royal revenue and of the different methods of collecting them, including also the manner of recovering debts owing to the king. It thus throws considerable light on the fiscal rights of the crown. The importance of the treatise for the whole subject of Anglo-Norman and Angevin administration can scarcely be overestimated.

The treatise is extant in several MSS. which were used or cited by the great antiquaries of the seventeenth century, Camden, Coke, Spelman and Selden. The work was first printed by Thomas Madox as an appendix to his *History and Antiquities of the Exchequer* in 1711. This text was reprinted by Stubbs in the early editions of his *Select Charters*. In 1875 F. Liebermann published an exhaustive critical study of the work in his *Einleitung in den Dialogus de Scaccario* (Göttingen, 1875). This has become the foundation of all subsequent study of the subject. The definitive text of the *Dialogue*, based on the collation of all the extant MSS., is to be found in the Oxford edition by A. Hughes, C. G. Crump and C. Johnson, published in 1902. This text has been followed in the preparation of the present version.[2]

At one time the treatise was ascribed to Gervase of Tilbury, but the true authorship was established in 1711 by Thomas Madox, who showed that it was the work of Richard fitz Nigel, bishop of London and treasurer of the Exchequer from about 1160 to 1198. This identification is now universally accepted. The work was probably undertaken in 1177, but from internal evidence it appears not to have been completed until 1179. Richard was also the author of the historical work to which he refers in the text of the *Dialogue* as the *Tricolumnis*. This is no longer extant.

Born before 1130, Richard fitz Nigel came in the third generation of a family long employed in the service of the Anglo-Norman kings and no less distinguished in the hierarchy of the English Church. He was the great-nephew of the famous Roger, bishop of Salisbury,[3] the organizer of the Exchequer under Henry I. His father was Nigel, bishop of Ely, prominent both in the *curia regis* and in the Exchequer, who in 1158 purchased for his son the office of treasurer. It is not clear, however, that Richard was in sole possession of it before 1162. In 1160 he had been promoted archdeacon of Ely, and thereafter he became successively a canon of St. Paul's and dean of Lincoln. In 1189 he was elected and consecrated bishop of London. He retained both the see and the treasurership until his death in 1198. He served as an itinerant justice in the south-western counties in 1179 and again in Norfolk, Suffolk and Essex in 1194,

[1] See below, Nos. 71–73.

[2] For the convenience of readers the traditional chapter headings have been preserved, though there is no authority for them in the early MSS. and they have been omitted by the editors of the Oxford text.

[3] See the references made to him by the author in the text of the *Dialogue* below, pp. 516, 517.

but appears to have played little part in politics. He may be described as a practical man of affairs, liberally educated, but in no sense a profound scholar. He knew the Latin classics fairly well and had read the *Institutes* of Justinian. His acquaintance with the *Corpus Iuris Civilis* appears to have been severely limited. The Latin of the *Dialogus* is in the main the straightforward Latin of the twelfth century and shows few traces of facility in classical construction.

The *Dialogue of the Exchequer* is thus the work of an experienced fiscal administrator, a high officer of the crown, whose statements may be regarded as fully trustworthy within the limits of his knowledge. In his retrospective surveys and in his digressions into points of law he is often in error, but full confidence and admiration may be accorded to his detailed exposition of the practice of the Exchequer in the twelfth century. In the words of F. W. Maitland (Pollock and Maitland, *History of English Law*, vol. 1, p. 162): "That such a book should be written, is one of the most wonderful things of Henry's wonderful reign."

The Latin text may be studied in the definitive edition by Hughes, Crump and Johnson, referred to above. It is also included in the first eight editions of Stubbs, *Select Charters*. The admirable text produced by Charles Johnson in 1950 (*Dialogus de Scaccario*, London, 1950) is accompanied by an illuminating introduction and by an excellent translation.

THE DIALOGUE OF THE EXCHEQUER

Preface

It is necessary to be subject in all fear to the powers ordained by God, and at the same time to obey them. For all power is of God the Lord. It is not therefore unreasonable or improper for ecclesiastics to take service under kings, as supreme, and under other powers, and to preserve their rights, especially in matters not inconsistent with truth and honour. But they should be served for the preservation, not only of those honours through which the glory of regal majesty shines forth, but also of the worldly wealth which pertains to them by virtue of their office. The former confer renown upon them, the latter gives power. Moreover the abundance of resources, or the lack of them, exalts or humbles the power of princes. For those who are lacking in them become a prey to their enemies, whilst those who are well supplied with them despoil their foes. Although it may chance that such wealth accrues to kings, not by some established legal right, but sometimes from the laws of their country, and at other times from the hidden designs of their own hearts, or even on occasions from their own arbitrary acts, nevertheless their actions ought not to be discussed or condemned by their subjects. For they whose hearts and the motions thereof are in the hand of God, and to whom the sole care of their subjects has been by God himself committed, stand or fall by God's judgment and not by a human one. Let no one, therefore, however rich, delude himself that he will go unpunished if he act otherwise, for of such it is written: "Mighty men shall be mightily tormented."[1] Therefore, no matter what may be, or appear to be, the origin or manner of acquisition of wealth, those who by their office are appointed to keep the revenues should not be remiss in caring for them. But careful diligence in collecting, conserving and distributing them befits those who are about to render account, so to speak, of the state of the realm whose security depends upon its wealth. We know indeed that chiefly by prudence, fortitude, temperance, justice and other virtues are kingdoms ruled and laws maintained; wherefore the rulers of the world must stand firm in these with all their strength. But it happens now and then that what is conceived with sound counsel and excellent intent

[1] Wisdom vi. 6.

may be the more expeditiously undertaken if funds are available, and what seemed difficult is easily carried out by adopting a particular routine method of business. Money is necessary, not only in time of war, but also in time of peace. For in the former case, revenue is expended on the fortification of towns, the payment of wages to the soldiers, and in many other ways, according to the status of the persons concerned, for the maintenance of the realm; in the latter case, although weapons of war are laid aside, churches are built by devout princes, Christ is fed and clothed in the persons of the poor, and the Mammon of this world is distributed in other acts of charity. The glory of princes consists in mighty deeds both in peace and war, but it excels in those where, in return for an earthly outlay, there follows an eternal and blessed reward.

Wherefore, illustrious king,[1] greatest of earthly princes, inasmuch as I have often witnessed thy glory, both in peace and war, not sparing thy treasure, but diligently providing for legitimate expenses according to the place, the time and the person, I have dedicated to your highness this little work, which is not concerned with matters of high policy, nor written in a pretentious manner, but is written in rustic style and deals with the procedure to be observed in your Exchequer. Moreover, I have from time to time noted thy solicitude for these things, so much so that, through the agency of certain wise and intimate counsellors, thou didst summon the late bishop of Ely[2] to give his views on the question. Nor was it out of place that a man of thy great intelligence, a prince of such singular power should, among his other cares of State, pay heed to this also. To be sure, the Exchequer has evolved its rules, not by hazard, but by the deliberations and decisions of great men; and if those rules be observed in every particular, the rights of individuals will be maintained, and the revenue due to the Treasury will come to thee in full, and this thy hand, which ministers to thy most noble mind, may suitably expend.

Book I. *Prologue*

In the twenty-third year[3] of the reign of King Henry II, while I was sitting at the window of a turret overlooking the river Thames,[4] a certain man, speaking with deliberation, said unto me, "Master, hast thou not read that there is no advantage in keeping knowledge or treasure hidden?" And when I made answer to him, "I have so read", straightway he continued, "Why therefore dost thou not teach others the knowledge of the Exchequer thou art said to possess so fully, and commit it to writing lest it perish with thee?" Whereupon I replied, "Lo! brother, thou hast now for a long time sat at the Exchequer and nothing is hidden from thee, for thou are over-conscientious; and the same is probably true of the others who have seats there." Then answered he, "Just as those who walk in darkness and grope with their hands frequently stumble, so many sit here who see but do not perceive, and hear

[1] Henry II.

[2] *ut missis a! atere tuo viris discretis de eodem dominum tunc Eliensem conueneris*. The reference is to Nigel, bishop of Ely, the author's father, who was treasurer of the Exchequer from 1154 to 1158.

[3] *i.e.* 1177, the year ending, according to the Exchequer rule, at Michaelmas. See above, p. 490, for discussion of probable limits of composition, also R. L. Poole, *Exchequer in the Twelfth Century* (1912), p. 8.

[4] The text gives no indication as to the exact venue of the *Dialogue*; claims might be made for Westminster or the Tower of London; it is not at all certain that the Exchequer normally resided in London at this time; on these questions, see Hughes, Crump and Johnson, *op cit.*, pp. 43–45.

but do not understand." Then said I, "Thou speakest irreverently, for neither is the knowledge required so great nor does it concern such great matters; but perchance those who strive after great things have minds like the claws of an eagle which cannot hold small prey, but do not allow great ones to escape." And he answered, "So be it, but though eagles fly high, they rest and refresh themselves in lowly places; and for this reason we beg you to explain to us those things of humble import which may profit even the eagles themselves." To which I replied, "I have been afraid to compose a work on these things, because they are subject to the bodily senses and are debased by daily usage, nor is there, nor can there be in them a discussion of abstract principles or a pleasing appearance of novelty." He answered, "Those who delight in novelties and pursue abstractions have Aristotle and the works of Plato; let them hear them. But write not thou of theoretical but of practical things." To which I objected, "It is impossible to relate what thou dost ask except in homely speech and ordinary words." "But", said he, as one roused to wrath–for a mind consumed with longing brooks no delay–"writers on the arts[1] have appropriated many ideas and have concealed them under strange words, lest they should seem to know too little about many things and in order that the art of composition might be made more difficult of apprehension. But thou art not undertaking a work on philosophy, but a treatise on certain laws and customs of the Exchequer; and since these are matters of common interest, common words must of necessity be employed, so that the style may bear relation to the things of which we are speaking. Moreover, although it is often permissible to invent new names, nevertheless I beg that thou wilt not scorn to use the conventional terms for the objects described, so that no new difficulty may arise to disturb us through the use of unaccustomed words." Then said I, "I see that thou art angry, but compose thyself; I will do what thou dost urge. Arise then and sit down opposite me, and ask me questions concerning the things which puzzle thee. But if thou dost propound anything unheard of, I shall not blush to confess my ignorance; but let us both agree together like prudent men." "Thou hast met my wishes," he cried, "for although an old man learning his alphabet is a disgraceful and ridiculous sight, I will nevertheless begin with the very groundwork of the subject."

I. What the Exchequer is, and what is the reason for this name

Disciple. What is the Exchequer?

Master. The Exchequer is a quadrangular board about ten feet in length and five in breadth placed before those who sit around it in the manner of a table. Running round it there is a raised edge about the height of four fingers, lest anything placed upon it should fall off. Above the board is placed a cloth purchased at the Easter term–not an ordinary cloth, but a black one marked with stripes which are the space of a foot or a hand's breadth distant from each other. Within the spaces counters are placed according to their value, and of this we shall speak elsewhere. But although such a board is called an 'exchequer',[2] nevertheless this name is applied also to the

[1] The seven liberal arts of the schools.

[2] The cloth appears to have been ruled into squares which at a later date were coloured black and white like a chess-board.

court which sits with the Exchequer so that if anyone obtains anything through its judgment, or anything is determined by common counsel, this is said to have been done "at the Exchequer" of such-and-such a year.[1] Thus as men say today "at the Exchequer", so they formerly said "at the tallies".

D. What is the reason for this name?

M. No truer one at present occurs to me than that it has a shape similar to that of a chess-board.

D. Would the ancients in their wisdom have so named it for its shape alone? For it might for a similar reason have been called a draught-board.[2]

M. I was right to call thee conscientious. There is another but less obvious reason. For just as in a game of chess there are certain classes of pieces and they move or stand still by definite rules or within certain limits, some being first in dignity and others in place,[3] so in this, some preside while others sit in virtue of their office and none is free to depart from the established rules, as will be manifest from what follows. Again, as in chess the battle is joined by the kings, so in this it is chiefly between two men that the conflict takes place and the battle is waged, namely, the treasurer and the sheriff who sits there to render his account,[4] while the others sit by like umpires to watch and judge the proceedings.

D. It is then the treasurer who receives the account, although there are many others present who are of higher rank?

M. That the treasurer should receive the account from the sheriff is manifest from the fact that the said account is required from him whenever it shall please the king: for what he had not received could hardly be demanded of him. Nevertheless, there are some who say that the treasurer and the chamberlains are only answerable for what is entered in the rolls as being "In the Treasury", and for this alone an account may be demanded of them. But the more correct view is that they should answer for all that is written in the roll,[5] as will be readily understood from what follows.

II. That there is an Upper Exchequer and a Lower Exchequer: but both have the same origin

D. Is the Exchequer, in which such a conflict takes place, the only one?

M. No. There is a Lower Exchequer which is also called the 'Receipt'[6] where the money received is counted over, put down in writing and notched on tallies, so that afterwards at the Upper Exchequer an account of it may be rendered. Both have the same origin,[7] however, for whatever is declared payable at the greater Exchequer is paid here, and what has been paid here is accounted for there.

[1] *factum ad scaccarium illius vel illius anni.*

[2] *tabularium.*

[3] *presidentibus aliis et aliis precedentibus*; because on the chess-board the pawns are arranged in front of the other pieces.

[4] *qui assidet ad compotum.*

[5] *Sunt tamen qui dicant thesaurarium et camerarios obnoxios tantum hiis que scribuntur in rotulis 'In thesauro' ut de hiis compotus ab eis exigatur. Set verius creditur ut de tota scriptura rotuli respondeant:* that is, they are answerable not only for actual receipts, but also for the correctness of the roll, and must make good any loss caused by erroneous entry.

[6] *Recepta.*

[7] *Una tamen est utriusque origo.* On the interpretation of this phrase, see Poole, *op. cit.*, p. 60, n. 3, where he argues that *origo* means here no more than 'basis' or 'principle'.

III. As to the nature or arrangement of the Lower Exchequer according to the several offices

D. What is the nature or arrangement of the Lower Exchequer?

M. I see that thou canst not bear to remain ignorant of any of these things. Thou shouldst know then that the Lower Exchequer has its own personnel, distinguished from each other by the nature of their offices, but devoted to the king's interests with a single mind, due regard, nevertheless, being paid to equity. All these discharge their duties, not in their own names but in those of their superiors,[1] with the exception of two, namely the knight who conducts the 'assays' and the melter.[2] Their offices depend solely on the authority of the king; hence they seem to belong more to the Upper than to the Lower Exchequer, as will be explained below.

There sits the clerk of the treasurer with his seal and also two knights of the chamberlains. There is also a certain knight who may be called the 'silverer',[3] because his office is to preside at the testing of the silver. Then there is the melter[2] who does the testing. There are also four tellers[4] to count the money, and the usher of the Treasury and the watchman. These are their duties. When the money has been counted and placed in boxes,[5] each containing a hundred pounds, the clerk of the treasurer affixes a seal and records in writing[6] the amount received, and from whom and for what reason. He also writes on the tallies made by the chamberlains for a receipt of the money. Further, not only does he place his seal on the sacks of money, but also, if he wishes, on the chests[7] and the several boxes in which are placed the rolls and tallies; he carefully supervises all the offices subordinate to him, and nothing is hidden from him. These are the duties of the knights, who are also called chamberlains, because they serve in the place of the chamberlains. They carry the keys of the chests–for each chest has two locks of a different pattern, neither of which the key of the other will fit–and they bear the keys of them. Each chest is girded with a fixed strap, on the top of which, when the locks are closed, the seal of the treasurer is placed, so that neither of the chamberlains can have access except by their joint consent. Also it is their duty to weigh the money after it has been counted and placed, a hundred shillings at a time, in wooden bowls, lest there be any error in the counting, and then finally to put them in boxes by the hundred pounds, as has been said. But if any bowl is found to be deficient in anything, it is not made good by guesswork but is straightway thrown back upon the pile of coins waiting to be counted. . . .[8] The chamberlains also make the tallies for the receipts, and have, in common with the clerk of the treasurer, the duty of disbursing the money received, either by order of the king's writ or at the command of the barons,[9] but only after consultation with their superiors. These three,[10] all together or by turns, are sent with

[1] The officials of the Lower Exchequer are deputies, holding their appointments, not directly from the king, but each from his superior whom he represents.

[2] *fusor.* [3] *argentarius.* [4] *computatores.*

[5] *forulos*; in its classical meaning boxes or shelves to contain books, see Hughes, Crump and Johnson, *op. cit.*, p. 167.

[6] The Receipt Roll of the Exchequer.

[7] *archis.*

[8] The passage here omitted bears no relation to the argument of the section and, in the opinion of the editors of the Oxford edition, may almost certainly be regarded as a later interpolation. See Hughes, Crump and Johnson, *op. cit.*, p. 168.

[9] The barons (or justices) of the Exchequer.

[10] *i.e.* the two chamberlains and the treasurer's clerk.

the treasure when it is required. These three have the principal charge of all business transacted in the Lower Exchequer.

D. I perceive then that these men are allowed to disburse the treasure received in accordance with the king's writ or with an order from those who preside, but only after consultation with their superiors.

M. They are permitted, I say, to the extent that they are entrusted with the payment of those who serve in the Lower Exchequer, and with the purchase of the small necessities of the Exchequer, such as the wooden bowls and other things which will be mentioned below; but not otherwise. When anyone brings a writ from the king or a charter for the payment of money, by the order of their superiors the sum explicitly named in the writ may be paid to him, with the understanding that before he leaves he shall count the money he has received. But if anything be wanting, the recipient shall return to the counter where the money was paid, and take an oath on this wise, namely that he has brought back as much as he received, without adding "to the best of my knowledge and belief", as is done in other cases. This done, the remainder shall be handed over to him after it has been counted by the regular tellers in the presence of all. But if, being duly acquainted with the rule, he has already passed through the doorway of the Treasury, no answer shall be made to him, no matter who he is or how great the loss.

The duties of the knight-silverer and the melter are bound up together, and pertain rather to the Upper Exchequer, and for this reason will be explained there with the other offices. The duties of the four tellers are as follows. When money is sent to the Exchequer to be counted, one of them carefully mixes the whole lot together in order that the better coins may not lie in one pile and the inferior coins in another, but may be mixed so that they achieve the correct weight.[1] This done, the chamberlain weighs in the scales as much as is needed to balance a pound of the Exchequer. But if the number shall exceed twenty shillings (in weight) by more than sixpence in the pound, it is considered unfit to be received; if, however, the excess is limited to sixpence or less, the money is accepted and carefully counted by the tellers, a hundred shillings at a time as described above. If the coins are on account of the 'farm'[2] and are to be tested, forty-four shillings are gathered up from the pile and then put into a purse[3] by themselves. On this the sheriff puts his mark, so that the test commonly called the 'assay' may afterwards be made of them, as will become clear from what follows. It will also be the duty of those who preside over the receipt on the authority of their superiors, that is, of the clerk of the treasurer and of the chamberlains, to put aside from the money received the lumps of tested silver and the pence paid in as the 'farm' in separate piles. Certain marks are then affixed on the bags containing them, so that if the king desires silver vessels to be made for the service of the house of God or for use in his own palace, or perchance money for use overseas, they may be taken from this source.

D. There is one point in what thou hast said that strikes me.

[1] *ut non seorsum meliores et seorsum deteriores sint set mixti ut ponderi respondeant*; the meaning is that the same number of heavy pennies would weigh more than a pound, the same number of light ones less.

[2] *firma*, the fixed sum or rent paid by the sheriff by way of composition for the profits of jurisdiction in the shire.

[3] *loculum*, purse or coffer, or some receptacle.

M. Tell me what it is.

D. Thou saidst, if I remember rightly, that money is sometimes brought to be paid into the Exchequer which is judged unfit for acceptance, namely if, on being weighed against the pound weight of the Exchequer, the deficiency is found to be more than sixpence. Inasmuch, then, as every coin of this realm ought to have the image of the king stamped upon it, and all moneyers are bound to work according to the same weight, how can it happen that every piece they make is not of the same weight?

M. Thou hast raised an important point, and one which needs further investigation. It can indeed happen through forgers and clippers or cutters of coins. Thou knowest, moreover, that English money can be detected as false in three respects, namely false in weight, false in quality and false in the stamping. These different kinds of falsification are not, however, visited by an equal punishment. But more of this anon.

D. Pray continue to relate the offices as thou hast begun.

M. It is the duty of the usher to admit or exclude as is necessary, and to be diligent in guarding everything which is confined within the doors; wherefore, for keeping the door he receives two pence for each writ of issue. He provides the boxes to put the money in, the rolls, tallies and other things which become necessary each year, and for each box he is paid two pence. He furnishes the whole receipt office with wood suitable for the tallies of receipt and account, and once a year, that is at the Michaelmas term, he receives five shillings for the wood of the tallies. He provides at the expense of the Treasury the wooden bowls, knives, purses, straps and other small necessaries. At the same term two shillings are due for providing the ink used in both Exchequers during the whole year, and these by ancient right the sacristan of the cathedral church of Winchester[1] claims for himself. The duty of the watchman is the same there as elsewhere, namely to guard most carefully at night the treasure and everything housed in the Treasury building. This concludes the several duties of those who serve the Lower Exchequer. They have regular payments while the Exchequer is in session, that is from the day on which they are called together until the day the court rises. The clerk of the treasurer in the Lower Exchequer has five pence a day. The scribe of the said treasurer in the Upper Exchequer has likewise five pence a day. The scribe of the chancellor, five pence. The two knights who bear the keys have each eight pence a day by reason of their knighthood.[2] For they claim they must needs be equipped with the necessary horses and arms, so that when they are sent with the treasure they may the more readily execute their duties. The knight-silverer has twelve pence a day; the melter, five pence. The usher of the Greater Exchequer, five pence. The four tellers, each three pence, if they are in London; if at Winchester each has two pence, since they are usually taken from there. The watchman has one penny; and for the light of each night spent guarding the treasure, a halfpenny.

D. Why does the usher of the Treasury alone receive no pay?

M. I do not rightly know; perhaps, however, he is paid nothing because he is

[1] For the MS. variants here and their interpretation, see Hughes, Crump and Johnson, *op. cit.*, p. 170. R. L. Poole (*op. cit.*, p. 79) regards the reading "Westminster" as of higher authority.

[2] The customary payment for a knight.

known to receive a fee for keeping the door and providing the boxes and tallies, or possibly because he is known to serve, not the king, but the treasurer and the chamberlains in guarding the door of their building. In this way then has the arrangement of the Lesser Exchequer or receipt office been carried out.

D. I have been so well satisfied in this respect that nothing seems lacking. Now, therefore, pray proceed concerning the Greater Exchequer.

IV. What is the authority of the Upper Exchequer, and whence it took its origin

M. Although the offices of those who sit in the Greater Exchequer may seem to differ in certain functions, yet the purpose of all the offices is the same, namely to watch over the king's interests, due regard being paid, however, to equity, according to the established rules of the Exchequer. The arrangement or ordering of the latter stands confirmed both by antiquity and by the authority of the magnates who have seats there. It is said to have been introduced by King William at the time of the Conquest of England, though its constitution was taken from the Exchequer overseas.[1] But the two differ in many and almost the most important respects. There are also some who believe it existed under the Anglo-Saxon kings, adducing as evidence for this view the fact that husbandmen and men already grown old on the crown estates–men whose memory in these matters is hoary–have learned from their fathers and know very well how much they are bound to pay for every pound for the 'blanching' of their 'farm' rent.[2] This reasoning, however, is conclusive only for the payment of the 'farm' and not for the session of the Exchequer. [But those who assert that the 'blanching' of the 'farm' began in Anglo-Saxon times are confronted by the fact that in Domesday Book, which contains a careful survey of the whole kingdom and states the value of each manor, both in the time of King Edward and in the time of King William, under whom it was compiled, there is absolutely no mention of the 'blanching' of the 'farm'. Whence it seems probable that after that survey was made in the time of the aforesaid king, the custom of 'blanching' the 'farm' was instituted by those zealous for his interests for the reasons noted below.][3] But at whatever time the Exchequer came into being, it is certain that it is confirmed by the authority of the magnates, so that no one is permitted to break its laws or to oppose them by any foolhardiness. For it has this privilege in common with the court of the lord king,[4] in which he in his own person gives judgment, that no one is allowed to contradict a record or dispute a judgment passed therein. Moreover, the

[1] *i.e.* in Normandy. Here the author is asserting the tradition held in official circles in his own day. For a full discussion of the question of the origin of the Exchequer, see Hughes, Crump and Johnson, *op. cit.*, pp. 13–43; R. L. Poole, *op. cit.*, pp. 57 *et seq.*

[2] *quantum de albo firme pro singulis libris soluere teneantur*; 'blanching' was the process of combustion of a sample or of the whole of a given sum of money to test the correct weight and standard of the coins; see below, pp. 514 *et sqq.* Money paid in and so tested was said to be 'blanched' or 'in blank'.

[3] The passage here placed in square brackets is rejected by the editors of the Oxford edition as of questionable authenticity. It does, however, contain the notable statement that no reference is made in Domesday Book to the 'blanching' of the 'farm'. This is such a gross error that, if the passage is really genuine, as Poole was inclined to think, the author of the *Dialogue* must have known that the statement was wrong from his own experience as an official in the Exchequer; see Hughes, Crump and Johnson, *op. cit.*, p.171; Poole, *op. cit.*, pp. 60–62; J. H. Round, *Commune of London* (1899), pp. 65 *et seq.*

[4] The distinction between the king's *curia* and the Exchequer was gradually becoming clearer during the reign of Henry II; on this point, see Hughes, Crump and Johnson, *op. cit.*, p. 171.

authority of this court is so great, both on account of the excellence of the king's image, which is by law inseparable from his seal kept in the Treasury,[1] and also by virtue of those who have seats there, as mentioned above, and by whose ability the whole state of the realm is preserved in safety. For there sits the chief justice of the lord king, next in rank to the king by virtue of his judicial status, together with the greater magnates of the realm, who share the king's inmost secrets; so that whatever shall be established or determined in the presence of these great men abides by an inviolable right. In the first place there sits, or rather presides in virtue of his office, the first man in the kingdom, namely the justiciar. With him there sit, solely by command of the king and with temporary and limited authority, certain of the greatest and most prudent men in the kingdom, whether they be clerks or laymen from the king's court. They sit there, I repeat, to interpret the law and to decide disputed points which frequently arise from incidental questions. For the superior science of the Exchequer consists not in its methods of reckoning but in the multiplicity of its judgments. It is easy enough, when the amount in demand has been set down and the sum handed in has been placed underneath it for the purpose of comparison, to discover by subtraction whether the debt has been paid or if anything remains. But when one begins to make a detailed investigation of the moneys which come into the Treasury in various ways, and are due for different accounts and are not collected by the sheriffs in the same manner, to be able to discover if the latter have acted in any wise other than they should, this is in many ways a serious business, and for this reason the science of the Exchequer is said to be superior. But the judgments on doubtful or partially doubtful points, which frequently come up, cannot be comprehended under one heading of a treatise, because all kinds of doubtful points have not yet come to light. Nevertheless, certain matters, which we know have been brought up and settled, we shall notice below in their proper place.

V. What the duties of the president are, and those of all who sit there officially; and what the arrangement of the seats

D. What are the duties of this most distinguished member of the court?

M. Nothing can more truly be said of him than that he supervises everything, both in the Lower and the Upper Exchequers, and that all the subordinate offices are arranged according to his will, in such wise, however, that they duly turn out to the advantage of the lord king. Moreover, his pre-eminence is to be seen in this among other things, that he can cause a writ of the lord king to be drawn up with his own attestation, authorizing the delivery of any amount from the Treasury, or the accounting to anyone of what he knows by the king's mandate ought to be so accounted. Or, if he prefer, he may draw up a writ of his own and get others to witness concerning these matters.[2]

D. Great is this man to whose fidelity the care of the whole realm, nay, rather the

[1] *Propter regie ymaginis excellentiam que in sigillo eius in thesauro indiuidua lege seruatur*; the passage means only that the seal has a portrait of the king on it.

[2] That is, he may either issue a writ in the king's name, *e.g. Henricus rex*, etc., and ending with his own name as witness, *e.g. Teste A. B.*, or he may choose the other style and begin his writ with his own name and end it with the names of other witnesses.

very heart of the king is entrusted. For it is written: "Where your treasure is, there will your heart be also."[1] But now, please, proceed concerning the others.

M. Dost thou wish me to proceed with them according to their rank and dignity, or according to the arrangement of the seats?

D. According to the order by which each one by right of office has attained his seat. For it will be easy, I imagine, to deduce the rank from the duties of the office.

M. That thou mayst understand in what order they are arranged, know that on the four sides of the Exchequer board four seats or benches[2] are placed. At the head of the board, that is on the broad side, and in the middle, not of the bench,[3] but of the Exchequer table, is the place of the chief officer of whom we spoke above. In the first place on his left by virtue of his office sits the chancellor, if he should happen to be present; next to him the knight whom we call the constable; next to him two chamberlains, the nearest being the one who, judging from his seniority in years, is considered the more venerable; after them the knight who is commonly called the marshal. When these are absent, however, others are sometimes put in their places, or perchance even when they are present, if indeed the dignity of those sent by the king is so great that the others ought to give place to them. Such is the arrangement of the first bench. In the second bench, which is on the long side of the Exchequer table, there sits at the head the clerk or other servant of the chamberlains with the 'recauta',[4] that is the counter-tallies from the receipt office. After him – though in between are some who do not sit there by right of office but are sent by the king – there is a place, almost in the middle of the long side of the Exchequer, for the man who sets down the amounts by placing the counters. Next to him come some who are not there *ex officio* but whose presence is nevertheless necessary; finally, at the end of the row sits the clerk who presides over the writing office, and he is there by right of office. That completes the arrangement of the second bench.

Immediately on the right of the presiding justice sits the present bishop of Winchester,[5] formerly archdeacon of Poitiers, by right of office under the new constitution.[6] He sits there in order to be next to the treasurer and to give careful attention to the writing of the roll. After him, at the head of the third bench on the right, sits the treasurer, who has to attend most carefully to everything done there, being bound, as it were, to give an account of all these transactions, should the need arise. Next to him sits his clerk, the scribe of the roll of the Treasury; after him a second scribe, of the roll of Chancery; after him the clerk of the chancellor, who with his own eyes always sees to it that his roll corresponds to the other in all particulars, so that not one *iota* is lacking, and that the order of the entries does not differ. After him, almost at the end of the bench, sits the clerk of the constable, a great man withal and much in evidence at the court of the lord king, holding here an office which he performs in person or, if it appear to the king that his presence is more

[1] Matthew, vi. 21.

[2] *scanna*.

[3] Because the bench ran down the room.

[4] The name given to the stock from which the tally was split, and which served as evidence if the tally was lost.

[5] Richard of Ilchester, one of Henry II's most trusted officials with a wide experience in the field of administration.

[6] The reorganization of the Exchequer since the accession of Henry II, see p. 521.

necessary elsewhere, through a discreet clerk. This is the description of the third bench.

On the fourth bench opposite the justiciar, there sits at the head Master Thomas, surnamed Brown,[1] with a third roll, which has been added under the new constitution[2] by our lord the king. Wherefore it is written: "A threefold cord is not quickly broken."[3] After him come the sheriff and his clerks, who sit there to render account with tallies and other necessaries. This then is the arrangement of the fourth bench.

D. Has the scribe of Master Thomas a seat with the other scribes?

M. He has his seat, not indeed with the others, but above them.

D. Why so?

M. Because from the beginning the seats were so arranged that the scribe of the treasurer should sit beside him, lest anything should be written which should escape his eye, and in like manner the scribe of the chancellor beside the scribe of the treasurer, so that he might faithfully copy what the latter wrote. Again, the clerk of the chancellor was of necessity put next to his scribe, lest he should make a mistake. So there was no place left in that row of seats which the scribe of Master Thomas might occupy; instead he was given a seat perched higher up so that he might overlook and watch the scribe of the treasurer, who is the first to write, and might copy from him whatever is necessary.

D. He would need to have the eyes of a lynx so as not to make a mistake; for an error in these matters is said to be most serious.

M. Although he might sometimes make a mistake in copying, through being so far away, yet when the rolls are corrected and a comparison is made between all three versions, it will be easy to correct the errors.

D. Enough has thus far been said about the order of seating; now, please, proceed to relate their respective duties, beginning from the left of the president.

The duties of the chancellor

M. In that order the chancellor is first; he is as great a man at the Exchequer as he is at court, so that nothing important is done, or ought to be done, without his consent and advice. But this is his office when he sits at the Exchequer; to him pertains the custody of the royal seal, which is kept in the Treasury and is not removed therefrom, except when by order of the justiciar it is taken by the treasurer or the chamberlain from the Lower to the Upper Exchequer and then only for the purpose of discharging Exchequer business. This accomplished, it is put in its case, which is then sealed by the chancellor and handed over to the treasurer for safe keeping. When it is needed again, it is presented to the chancellor before the eyes of all in a sealed condition; it should never be removed either by the chancellor or anyone else on any other occasion. Likewise to him, through his deputy,[4] belongs the custody of the roll of Chancery, and, as seemed good to these great men of the State, the chancellor is held equally responsible with the treasurer for all that is written on the roll, save only

[1] A fuller account of the career and character of this official is given in the text on p. 512 below.
[2] See p. 521.
[3] Ecclesiastes iv. 12.
[4] *per suppositam personam*; the reference is to the chancellor's clerk, who acts as his deputy.

what is recorded as having been received "in the Treasury".[1] For although he may not dictate what the treasurer writes, nevertheless he writes together with him,[2] and if the latter makes a mistake, it is permissible for the chancellor or his clerk to rebuke him in moderation and to suggest what he ought to write. But if the treasurer shall persist in his error and refuse to alter it, the chancellor may, if he is fully confident in his opinion, argue the point before the barons, so that the latter may give judgment as to what ought to be done.

D. It seems probable that the keeper of the third roll[3] is also bound by the same rule in respect of his entries.

M. It is not only probable but actually the case, for the authority of the third roll is equal to that of the other two in respect of their entries, because it so pleased the author of the system.

The duties of the constable

It is the duty of the constable at the Exchequer to bear witness, together with the president, in the case of royal writs concerning the issue of treasure, or to any reckonings by those who render account. For in all writs of this kind it is proper according to ancient custom that the names of two witnesses should be subscribed. Likewise, when the king's soldiers come to the Exchequer for their pay, whether they form the garrison of the king's castles or not, it is the function of the constable, accompanied by the clerk of the constabulary, whose duty it is to know their terms of service, and the marshal of the Exchequer, to reckon up their wages and to take their oath concerning arrears of pay[4] and to cause the residue to be paid to them. For the wages of all persons whatsoever, whether they be keepers of hawks or falcons or hunting dogs, pertains to his office, if he be present, unless perchance the lord king has previously assigned someone else to this duty; but the king cannot easily be deprived of the constable's services on account of greater and more urgent business. . . .[5] He likewise shares with the other magnates the privilege that no important step should be taken without his being consulted.

The duties of the chamberlains

The duties of the chamberlains are bound up with those of the treasurer, for they are recognized as serving under one and the same dispensation of reward or loss, and they will and refuse the same thing in respect of the king's honour, so that the act of any one of them may not be declared invalid by either of the others. The treasurer receives the accounts on his own behalf and theirs, and according to the nature of the sums in demand he dictates the words to be written in the roll; in all these matters they are bound in an equal bond of fellowship. It is the same with regard to the other acts performed either by him or them, whether in respect of written entries or receipts or tallies or expenditure, saving their loyalty to the lord king.

[1] See above, p. 494. [2] *licet enim non prescribat ut thesaurar ius, conscribit tamen.*
[3] *i.e.* Master Thomas Brown, see above, p. 501. [4] *retractis*; *i.e.* payments held back.
[5] The following sentence is bracketed in the Oxford edition as being out of place in this section; it should have been placed in the section dealing with the marshal: "It is to be noted that the marshal of the Exchequer appropriates from the wages of the garrison knights what pertains to him by right of office, but not from those who serve in the field (*commeantibus*)." There seems to be no evidence in support of the distinction made here; see Hughes, Crump and Johnson, *op. cit.*, p. 174.

The duties of the marshal

It is the duty of the marshal more particularly to put away in his box the tallies of the debtors, which the sheriff hands in, and which are also noted in the roll. Also he puts therein the royal writs dealing with the computation, remission or payment of the moneys demanded of the sheriff through the summons. On the box is written the name of the county to which the contents relate, and separate boxes should properly be provided for the several counties by the sheriff who renders his account to the marshal.

D. There is a point here which troubles me.

M. I quite foresaw it. But wait a little; everything will be plain from what follows. Likewise if any debtor, failing to pay the amount for which he has been summoned, shall become liable to arrest, he is handed over to the marshal for safe keeping; and when the Exchequer is adjourned for that day, the latter shall, if he so desire, send the prisoner to the public gaol.[1] He shall not, however, be put in chains or cast into a dungeon, but be lodged by himself or over the lower gaol. For although he be insolvent, nevertheless he has not on this account deserved to be numbered with the transgressors[2] [that is, provided he is not a knight. For concerning knights held for debt there is in existence a royal ordinance which will be noticed below in treating of the sheriff].[3] It is likewise the duty of the marshal, when the account of the sheriff, or custodian or whatsoever person sits to render account has been completed, to receive an oath from him in public that to the best of his knowledge he has rendered a true account. But if the sheriff, or other person accounting, is liable for any debt, he shall add that he will not depart from the Exchequer, that is, from the suburbs[4] of the town in which it is sitting, without permission from the barons,[5] unless he intends to return on the same day. Likewise the marshal shall receive from the keeper of the king's seal the writs of summons made out against the term fixed for the next Exchequer, duly numbered and sealed with the royal seal, and shall deliver them with his own hand to the usher of the Upper Exchequer to be dispatched throughout England. So thou hast had pointed out to thee the offices of those who sit on the first bench.

The duties of the maker of tallies

Now at the head of the second bench the serjeant of the chamberlains comes first, be he clerk or layman; his duties can briefly be disposed of in word though not in deed. He produces the tallies from the Treasury against the sheriff or other accountant, and when necessary he changes or reduces or adds to the tally, according as the process of accounting demands, and joins it to the counter-tally of the sheriff. After this has been done at the Easter term, he returns the longer tally to the sheriff to be brought back again at the Michaelmas term. But at the Michaelmas term, when the full total

[1] The Fleet prison, when the Exchequer sat in London.
[2] *cum sceleratis deputari*; cf. Isaiah liii. 12.
[3] The passage in square brackets reads like a marginal gloss on the original text; the reference is to Book II of the *Dialogue*; see below, p. 562.
[4] *leugata*; cf. Fr. *banlieue*.
[5] Of the Exchequer; see above, p. 495, n. 9.

has been entered upon the roll, the sheriff hands this same longer tally to the marshal to be replaced in his box.[1]

D. I marvel at thy saying that a tally, once offered and accepted for an account, need be offered again at another account.

M. Marvel not, because whatever has been exacted from, or paid by the sheriff at the Easter term, he must needs be summoned again; not indeed that what has been already paid should be paid again, but that the sheriffs may present themselves to render account, and that the tally offered for the payment previously made may be recorded in the roll, and thus the sheriff may be absolved from the debt. For so long as he has the tally in his possession, he will not be acquitted, but will always be liable to summons.

D. All this seems necessary. But proceed, please, concerning the duties.

M. Nay rather, since we have mentioned tallies, consider briefly the process of cutting tallies. There is then one kind of tally called a tally simply, another called a memoranda tally. The length of a genuine tally is the distance between the tip of the forefinger and the thumb when fully extended; and at one end there is a fairly small hole bored in it. But the memoranda tally, which is always made for payments that are 'blanched',[2] is somewhat shorter because, after the 'assay', by which the 'farm' is 'blanched' the original memoranda tally is broken in pieces, and then for the first time a tally of full length is issued when the tally of combustion has been tied to it.[3] The manner of cutting is as follows. At the top of the tally a cut is made, the thickness of the palm of the hand, to represent a thousand pounds; then a hundred pounds by a cut the breadth of the thumb; twenty pounds, the breadth of the little finger; a single pound, the width of a swollen barleycorn; a shilling rather narrower, yet so that converging cuts remove some of the wood and leave there a little furrow; a penny is marked by a single cut without removing any wood. On the edge where the thousand is cut, no other number should be put, except perhaps the half-way mark, and this by removing the middle part of that incision and putting it lower down. Similarly one would cut a hundred pounds, if there are no thousands; and in the same way for twenty pounds, and for twenty shillings which we call a pound. But if several thousands or hundreds or scores of pounds are to be notched, the same rule should be observed, so that on the more exposed edge of the same tally, that is, on the edge which is placed uppermost when the tally has been inscribed, the larger number must be cut, and on the other edge the smaller. But on the obverse side the higher number is at the top, and on the converse side always the smaller number, that is, the pence. There is no special notch to signify a mark of silver at the Exchequer, but it is set down in shillings. But a mark of gold is cut in the middle of the tally like a pound. A gold piece is not cut exactly like a silver piece, but by cutting with the knife perpendicularly into the middle of the tally, not obliquely as is done in the case

[1] The shorter tally was called a "memoranda"; the sheriff accounted at Easter for only half of his 'farm' and a like proportion of the other debts. Since the full total of these could not then be known, the memoranda tally might require alteration; see Hughes, Crump and Johnson, *op. cit.*, pp. 175-176; also below, p. 514.

[2] See above, p. 498, n. 2.

[3] An obscure and difficult passage, which has been variously interpreted; see Hughes, Crump and Johnson, *op. cit.*, p. 176. The Latin text reads: *Memoranda vero, que de firma blanca semper fieri solet, paulo breuior est quia, facto essaio per quod firma dealbatur, prima illa confringitur et, apposita sibi talea combustionis, talee longitudinem tunc primo meretur.*

of the silver piece. So therefore the arrangement of the positions and the variations in the incisions determine what is gold and what is silver. For the rest thou mayst learn all these things more easily by looking at tallies than by word of mouth.

D. What remains of this will be made clear by ocular demonstration. Now, please, proceed concerning the offices.

M. After the tally-cutter and a few discreet men sent by the king, who come in between, as we have said above, sits the man who by the king's command makes the reckoning by placing coins used as counters.

The duties of the calculator[1]

This office is indeed perplexing and laborious enough; yet without it seldom or never could the business of the Exchequer be carried on. It belongs, however, to none of those who sit there officially, but to him whom the king or the justiciar shall order to execute it. I call it laborious, for other offices are fulfilled by the tongue or hand or both, but in this "the tongue, the hand, the eyes and the mind are unwearied in labour".

But the system of this is according to the usual course of the Exchequer, not by the rules of arithmetic.[2] Thou wilt remember, I presume, my saying[3] that on the Exchequer table there was placed a cloth marked by stripes in the spaces between which coins are put in piles. Now the calculator sits in the middle of his side of the table so as to be visible to all, and so that his working hand may have free play. He has already set at his right hand in the lower space a pile of pennies, from eleven down; in the second space a pile of shillings from nineteen down, and in the third, of pounds. This last pile ought indeed to be placed opposite and directly facing him, because in the usual accounts of the sheriff it is the middle column. In the fourth space is the pile of the scores, in the fifth, of the hundreds; in the sixth, of the thousands; in the seventh, which is but rarely needed, the tens of thousands. I say *rarely*, because this is when the account for the receipts of the whole realm is received from the treasurer and the chamberlains by the king, or at his command by the magnates of the whole kingdom. Moreover, the calculator is allowed to put down a silver halfpenny[4] in place of ten shillings, or a gold halfpenny[4] in place of ten pounds, in order that the reckoning may be more rapidly made. He must take care, however, lest his too ready hand anticipate his tongue, or the converse; but as he counts, he must place the counters and indicate the number so that no mistake be made. The total required from the sheriff having been thus arranged in piles, the amount already paid in either "to the Treasury"[5] or otherwise is similarly arranged in piles below. But if it be a 'farm by tale'[6] which is demanded of him, or any other debt which can be discharged 'by tale' only, a simple subtraction of the lower from the higher total shall be made, and he shall be held responsible for the residue. The method will be different, however, if he has come to 'blanch his farm', as will be shown more fully in treating of the sheriff's business.[7]

[1] These duties fell at a later date to the marshal.

[2] A reference to the contrast between the old methods of the *abacus* and those of the new arithmetic introduced by the Arabs.

[3] See above, p. 493.

[4] The *obolus aureus* and *obolus argenteus* were in reality counters used to represent ten pounds and ten shillings respectively; see Poole, *op. cit.*, p. 84, n. 2.

[5] See above, p. 494.

[6] *firma numero.*

[7] See below, p. 542.

D. Spare a moment thy running pen that I may be allowed to say a few words.

M. "It is thy turn to throw the dice, nor may speech be denied thee."

D. It seems I am given to understand that the same penny used as a counter may represent now a penny, now a shilling, now a pound, now a hundred pounds, now a thousand pounds.

M. So it may, but only under certain conditions. If the coins with which it was placed have been taken away, it can at the will of the calculator be brought about that what represents a thousand may by gradual descent represent a unit.[1]

D. So it is when a man of the people, since he is human and cannot be otherwise, ascends from the depths to the summit,[2] and worldly goods are bestowed upon him at the will of the ruler, and then later by Fortune's caprice he is cast down again into the depths, he yet remains what he had once been, although he seem to himself, by right of rank and status, to be utterly changed in nature.

M. Thou shouldst know that thy parable does not fit every case; but in truth, whatever others may think, I am well pleased that thou dost draw further conclusions from them. For it is praiseworthy to seek the flowers of mystic meaning amidst the thistles of worldly affairs. Not only in the points thou hast raised, but also in the full description of the Exchequer, there are certain places where are concealed sacred mysteries. The diversity of offices, the authority of the judicial power, the stamp of the royal image, the issue of summonses, the composition of the rolls, the accounting of stewardships, the exaction of debts, the condemnation or acquittal of the accused, are all symbols of the strict account to be revealed when the books of all shall be opened and the doors closed. But enough of this. Now let us proceed concerning the offices. Next to the calculator sits first, by right of office, the clerk who presides over the king's writing office.

The duties of the clerk who presides over the writing office

To him it falls to find suitable scribes for the roll of Chancery and for the king's writs which are drawn up in the Exchequer, and also for writing the summonses, and to see that they are properly executed. These duties indeed, although they may be explained in a few words, can hardly be fulfilled without infinite pains, as they know who have learnt by their own experience of such matters. That concludes the duties of those placed on the second bench.

The office of the archdeacon of Poitiers, now bishop of Winchester[3]

D. If I remember rightly, first at the right hand of the president sits the bishop of Winchester. I should like to have his office explained to me, for he is a great man and ought not to be occupied save with great matters.

M. He is without doubt a great man and intent on great matters. Thus is he pulled

[1] This appears to be the meaning of the passage, which remains somewhat obscure; the Latin text is as follows: *Sic est quibusdam tamen appositis. Itemque fieri potest eisdem demptis, si calculatori placeat, ut qui mille significat gradatim descendens unum significet.*

[2] The reference is to the wheel of Fortune.

[3] Richard of Ilchester. He is repeatedly mentioned in the Pipe Rolls as *scriptor curie*. As clerk presiding over the *scriptorium*, he was apparently head of the chancellor's staff in the Exchequer. The office does not seem to have become permanent.

in many directions, as is more fully shown in *Tricolumnis*.[1] Before the time of his promotion, when he was serving in a subordinate capacity in the king's court, he seemed from his loyalty and industry to be indispensable to the king's business, being prompt and efficient in the reckoning of accounts, in the writing of the rolls and the drawing up of writs. Wherefore a place was found for him at the treasurer's side, so that together with the latter he might attend to the writing of the rolls and all such matters. The treasurer indeed is distracted by so many and such great cares and anxieties through all this business that he may be pardoned if at times sleep steals in upon such arduous labours. Nay, in human activities hardly anything is absolutely perfect.

D. What is it thou art saying? I do not even know what *Tricolumnis* is.

M. It is a little book which I composed in my youthful years, a tripartite work dealing with the history of the kingdom of England under the illustrious king of the English, Henry II. I called it *Tricolumnis* because I wrote it throughout in three columns. In the first I treated of several matters concerning the Church of England and some rescripts of the apostolic see. In the second column I discoursed of the famous deeds of the aforesaid king, which are past man's belief. In the third many matters, both public and private, are dealt with, including the judgments of the king's court. If by chance this book should fall into thy hands, see that thou lose it not, for it may be useful to posterity and entertaining to those interested in the state of the realm under the said king. For although this king "is sprung from kings of ancient lineage",[2] and has expanded his empire in triumphant conquest far and wide, nevertheless, it is a yet greater feat that by his mighty deeds he has surpassed the title of fame so prodigally bestowed on him. But enough of this; now let us pursue the matter in hand.

D. So be it, if it please thee. Saving then the reverence due to the treasurer, it seems derogatory to his dignity that his word alone is not trusted in all things.

M. God forbid! nay rather in this way he is spared labour and assured of indemnity. For it is not because among so many and such great men who sit at the Exchequer, either he or any other is not trusted, but that for such great matters and affairs of State under so distinguished a monarch, it is fitting that many and great men should be appointed, not merely for the king's profit but also to promote his glory and honour.

D. Proceed, please, concerning the offices.

The duties of the treasurer

M. The duties of the treasurer, and his cares and anxieties, can hardly be expressed in words, though mine were "the pen of a ready writer".[3] For in everything which is done, either in the Lower or the Upper Exchequer, he must show careful diligence. From what has been said before, however, it will be fairly clear where his chief care lies, namely in receiving the accounts of the sheriffs and in the writing of the roll, so much so that he cannot be released from these duties while the Exchequer is still sitting. According to the nature of the business he dictates[4] the words for the writing of his roll, from which afterwards the same words are copied on to the other rolls, as

[1] A tripartite history, now no longer extant. See below, p. 537.
[2] Horace, *Odes*, I, 1.
[3] Psalms xlv. 2.
[4] To his scribe.

mentioned above. He must take care that there be no mistake in the amount, the occasion or the person, lest anyone be discharged who is not quit of payment, or one who ought to have been acquitted be summoned again. For so great is the authority of his roll that no one is allowed to dispute or alter it, unless perchance the mistake is so glaring that it is manifest to all. Nor even then may it be changed except by the common counsel of the barons and in their very presence, so long as the Exchequer of that roll shall last. But the writing of the roll of the previous year, or even of the current year, once the Exchequer has risen, may not lawfully be changed by anyone save the king,[1] whose will is law in these matters. Likewise it is the treasurer's right to associate himself with his superiors in all great affairs, and to let nothing be hidden from him.

The duties of the scribe of the treasurer

It is the duty of the scribe who is nearest the treasurer to prepare the rolls for writing;[2] they are made from sheepskin, and not without reason. Their length amounts to two membranes, not chosen at random, but from large ones carefully provided for this purpose, the breadth a little more than a span and a half. The rolls are then ruled from the top almost to the bottom and on both sides, the lines being drawn at a suitable distance from each other, and at the top of the roll are marked the counties and bailiwicks whose accounts are listed below. A medium-sized space about the width of three or four fingers having been left, in the middle of the line is inscribed the name of the county which is to be dealt with first. Then, at the head of the following line is set down the name of the sheriff, followed by this form of words, "such-and-such a sheriff renders account of the 'farm' of such-and-such a county". Then, a little farther on in the same line is written "in the Treasury", and nothing else is added until the account has been completed, for an urgent reason which is made plain in the part treating of the sheriff.[3] Next, at the head of the following line, is set down how much of the 'farm' of the county has been expended in alms and fixed tithes and also how much in salaries. After these, at the head of the lower line, are noted under the demesne-lands[4] those which the munificence of kings has bestowed on churches or on those who performed military service for them, and, among the estates of the crown, which are 'blanched' and which are accounted 'by tale'.[5]

D. It surprises me that thou sayest certain estates are given 'blanched' and others 'by tale'.

M. Let us proceed for the present with the duties of the scribe, and when we come to deal with the sheriff, please ask me about this.[6] After the demesne-lands a space of one line is left in order that the data may appear distinct by their very nature, and then are noted down the sums ordered to be expended from the 'farm' through the king's writs, because these are not fixed by rule but are occasional. Certain payments also, which are allowed without writs, are accounted for by the custom of the

[1] That is, mistakes in the roll may be corrected during the session in which the roll is drawn up, but not later, except by royal authority.

[2] This passage is important for the evidence it affords as to the construction and composition of the Pipe Roll of the Exchequer; see Hughes, Crump and Johnson, *op. cit.*, pp. 48–52, 179–180.

[3] See below, pp. 546 *et sqq.*

[4] *in terris datis*, see below, Nos. 71–73.

[5] See above, p. 505.

[6] See below, p. 542.

Exchequer, which will be explained below.[1] Thus the account of the principal 'farm' of the county[2] is completed. After this another space is left of about six or seven lines for the reckoning of 'purprestures' and 'escheats'[3] under this form of words, "the same sheriff renders account of the 'farm' of 'purprestures' and 'escheats'", also in the same place an account of all the 'farms' of manors and of the rents of woods which are owed and paid annually. After this the accounts are set down in their order, except for those of certain cities, towns and bailiwicks whose accounts are longer because they have their own fixed alms, salaries or grants of demesne-land,[4] and to the custodians of these special writs of summons are directed concerning their debts to the king. Moreover, their accounts are made up after the account for the counties in which they are situated has been altogether completed. Such are Lincoln, Winchester, Meon, Berkhamsted, Colchester and several others.

D. I marvel thou hast said that certain fixed revenues are called 'farms' but others, rents.

M. 'Farms' are of manors, but rents only of woods.[5] For the produce of manors is justly called firm and immutable, because through agriculture it is renewed and recurs each year, and besides this it constitutes an assured revenue by the perpetual law of custom. But that which by a law made every year is due from woods, which are daily cut down and perish, is not so firm or fixed a demand but is subject to rise and fall frequently, though not yearly; this is called rent, and thus by elision these rents are said to be assessed.[6] There are some, however, who believe that what is paid by individuals is called rent, while a 'farm' is the aggregate of these rents: hence 'farm' is a collective noun like 'crowd'. For this reason, they believe, rent is assessed as an annual payment to indicate it is not 'farm'. After these fixed payments another blank space is left, and then comes the account of the debts for which the sheriff has been summoned; first, however, are recorded the names of the judges responsible for determining them. Finally, a record is made of the chattels of fugitives from justice and of those who have been mutilated for their offences. When all this has been filled in, the account of that county is complete. The scribe must take care not to write anything in the roll of his own accord, but only what he has heard from the treasurer's dictation. But if perchance through negligence or some other mishap he should happen to make a mistake in the writing of the roll, either in the name or in the amount or in the occasion, in which the chief significance of the entries consists, he may not presume to erase the entry but may cancel it by drawing underneath a thin line and writing the requisite words on the same line immediately after. For the writing of the roll has this in common with charters and other public documents, that it ought not to be erased; and for this reason care has been taken to make the rolls of sheepskins, for they do not easily yield to erasure without the fault becoming apparent.

[1] See below, p. 543.

[2] *compotus de corpore comitatus.*

[3] See below, pp. 546, 547.

[4] *terras datas*. See below, Nos. 71–73.

[5] The distinction here made is somewhat arbitrary and by no means fits all the circumstances of the Exchequer system in Henry II's reign.

[6] The Latin text here reads: *set est in eis* ascensus *et* descensus, *licet non annuus, frequens tamen,* census *dicuntur, et sic per afferesim redditus hos* censeri *dicunt.* The words given in roman indicate the nature of the elision.

D. Does this scribe provide the rolls at his own expense or at that of the Treasury?

M. At the Michaelmas term he receives five shillings from the Treasury and the scribe of the Chancery likewise other five. From these sums they provide the parchments for both rolls, for the writs of summons and for the receipt rolls of the Lower Exchequer.

The duties of the scribe of the Chancery

The care, labour and zeal of the remaining scribe, seated at the side of the scribe of the treasurer, consist chiefly in this, namely that he copy the other roll word for word, observing the order prescribed. Also it is his duty to draw up the writs of the king concerning the outlay of the Exchequer,[1] but only for those payments which, in the opinion of the barons during the session of the Exchequer, ought to be made by the treasurer and chamberlains. Notwithstanding, he writes the writs of the king concerning the reckoning or remission of those sums which the barons have decreed should be allowed or remitted at the Exchequer.[2] It is his duty also, when the accounts of the sheriffs have been completed, and the taxes due to the king, for which writs of summons are issued, are determined, to write out the same with diligent and painstaking discrimination to the intent that they may be dispatched throughout the realm; for it is through them and by their sanction that the Exchequer of the ensuing term is convoked.

VI. The wording of the writs of the king drawn up at the Exchequer, whether concerning issues of treasure or computation or remission

D. Under what form of words are writs of the king concerning issues of treasure drawn up?

M. The treasurer and chamberlains do not expend the money received, except on the express order of the king or of the presiding justice. For when the general account is demanded of them, they must have the authority of the king's writ for the issue of the money. This is the wording of it: "H[enry] king, etc., to *N.* the treasurer and such-and-such, chamberlains, greeting. Pay from my treasure to such-and-such a man such-and-such a sum. Witness the following at *N.* at the Exchequer."[3] Moreover, "at the Exchequer" is added in order to distinguish them from the writs which are drawn up in the *curia regis*. It is also necessary that, when a writ for the issue of treasure is made, as we have indicated, the same scribe shall make a copy[4] thereof, commonly called a counter-writ, and this the clerk of the chancellor shall retain in his own possession as a testimony of the payment made through the original writ of the king kept by the treasurer and chamberlains.[5] Also, writs for crediting or remitting what the barons have decreed shall be credited or remitted, the will of the king having been previously ascertained, are drawn up under this form of words: "H[enry], by the grace of God, king, etc., to the barons of the Exchequer, greeting. Credit such-and-such a man or men with such-and-such a sum which he expended on such-and-such a business of mine. Witness the following here at the Exchequer." Likewise:

[1] Writ of issue or *liberate*.

[2] Writs of *computate* and *perdono*.

[3] Specimen writ of *liberate*.

[4] *rescriptum*.

[5] All writs issued at the Exchequer were in duplicate; only in the case of writs of *liberate* did the original remain in the hands of the treasurer and chamberlains.

"The king to the barons of the Exchequer, greeting. I remit to this man" or "I quit-claim so-and-so for such-and-such. Witness the following here at the Exchequer." Copies of all these writs shall remain with the aforesaid clerk as a proof that the writs have been issued. For the original writs of computation and remission are shut up in the marshal's boxes once the accounts of the sheriffs have been made up: for the rest, they are not to be displayed openly, unless a dispute arise concerning them. Moreover, what we say of the writs of the king is likewise to be understood of the writs of the presiding justice, but only when the king is absent, and the laws of the realm are established by the impress of the seal of the justiciar and the cases cited, in order that those summoned before the court may be condemned or acquitted. For the rest, so long as the king remains in England, the writs of the Exchequer shall be drawn up in the name of the king with the witness of this same justiciar and of some other magnate. But the form of words in writs of summons will be more fully indicated below under the heading of summonses.[1]

The duties of the clerk of the chancellor

Although the clerk of the chancellor, who sits next to him, serves, not in his own name, but in that of another, he is nevertheless occupied in great matters and distracted in many ways, so that from the very beginning of the reckoning even unto the end he cannot be torn away, unless perchance he be inclined to take things easy the while, in which case a discreet deputy is in the meantime substituted for him. After the treasurer he has the first charge of all Exchequer business, and is more particularly concerned with the writing of the rolls and the writs, for in these he is chiefly versed. He watches too lest the pen of his scribe should make a slip while he follows the other scribe[2] at an equal pace. Likewise he carefully inspects the roll of the previous year which is set before him, until the sheriff has discharged the debts which are set down there and for which he is summoned. Again, while the sheriff is sitting to render his account, and after the fixed payments from the county have been credited and recorded, the clerk receives from the sheriff the writ of summons to which the king's seal is affixed, and presses the sheriff for the debts there listed, proclaiming in public and saying: "Render from this person so much, and from that so much." But the debts discharged and paid in full the said clerk cancels by drawing a line through the middle (of the writ), so that a distinction may be made between what has been paid and what remains to be paid. The clerk also keeps the counter-writs of those issued at the Exchequer. He also corrects and seals the writs of summons drawn up in the manner mentioned above. In short, his labours are infinite and the greatest of all next after those of the treasurer.

D. "Here Argus would be more useful than Polyphemus." [3]

The duties of the clerk of the constabulary

M. The clerk of the constabulary is a great and busy man in the *curia regis*; at the Exchequer also he is associated with the magnates in all matters of importance, and with his assent the king's business is conducted. Moreover he is sent by the king to

[1] See below, pp. 532 *et sqq.*
[2] The scribe of the treasurer; see above, p. 502.
[3] Cf. Gervase of Tilbury, *Otia Imperialia*. See *R. de Coggesall Chronicon*, Rolls Series (1875), p. 423.

the Exchequer at the terminal sessions with the counter-writs, but only of those issued at the *curia*. He also, together with the constable, attends to the payment of the knights and certain others, as above mentioned,[1] and at times his duties are fairly onerous, although they may be expressed in a few words. Nevertheless, he frequently performs his office through a deputy, as does the chancellor, since on account of more important business they cannot easily go far from the king's presence. That completes the description of the offices of those placed on the third bench at the right hand of the president.

As to Master Brown

Next, at the head of the fourth bench, which is placed opposite the justices, sits Master Thomas, surnamed Brown. His authority at the Exchequer is not to be despised. For it is a great and strong proof of his loyalty and discretion that he was chosen by a prince of such excellent talents to keep, contrary to ancient custom, a third roll in which to record the laws of the realm and the secrets of the king, and which he may retain in his own possession and carry whithersoever he will. He even has his own clerk in the Lower Exchequer, who sits next to the clerk of the treasurer, and has full authority to record receipts and expenditure in the Treasury.

D. Are then his good faith and discretion so well known to the king that none other is considered his equal in this work?

M. He was a great man at the court of the king of Sicily,[2] provident in counsel and almost the chief participant in the royal secrets. In the meantime a new king[3] arose who did not know him, one who took to himself evil associates and persecuted his own father in the person of the latter's servants. This man, therefore, with the change in his fortunes, was compelled to provide for his own safety. Many countries lay open to him, together with the highest honours; nevertheless, having been frequently invited by Henry, the illustrious king of the English–since bare rumour is less than the very truth–he chose rather to return to his native country and his hereditary and liege lord. Accordingly, having been received by the king in a manner becoming to both of them, because in Sicily he had been employed in great affairs, here also he was appointed to important business in the Exchequer. In this way, then, he acquired at one and the same time a seat there and an office of dignity,[4] being associated with the magnates in all important business. This completes the account of the different functions of all who by right of office sit in the Greater Exchequer. It follows next, if I mistake not, that we should proceed to narrate the privileges appropriate to their seats there.

D. Nay, if it please thee, there are still to be explained the duties of the knight called the 'silverer' and also the duties of the melter: for they have been deferred until now because they seem to be bound up together and to belong to the Greater Exchequer.

M. I see that the recollection of promises made does not escape thee, whence

[1] See above, p. 497.

[2] Roger II (the Great), 1127–1154. [3] William I (the Bad), 1154–1166.

[4] This office also, like that held by Richard of Ilchester, seems to have been a temporary one and filled only during Master Brown's lifetime; no record remains of the appointment of a successor; see Hughes, Crump and Johnson, *op. cit.*, pp. 26–27.

I conceive the confident hope that thou wilt not forget what I have already said to thee. I thought indeed that I had fully satisfied thee concerning the offices, seeing I have omitted none of those who have seats at the Exchequer. But those, of whom thou dost remind me, have no permanent seats allotted to them; rather they perform their duties at the command of the president or the treasurer.

The duties of the knight-silverer

The knight-silverer, then, carries from the Lower to the Upper Exchequer the purse of silver which is to be tested, as we remarked above. When he has delivered it, sealed with the seal of the sheriff, he shakes out on the Exchequer table in the sight of all, the forty-four shillings which he had previously marked when they were taken from the pile.[1] Having mixed them together so that they correspond to the proper weight, he puts in one scale of the balance a pound weight and in the other as many coins as are needed. This done, he counts them so that it may be evident from the number whether they are of the correct weight. But whatever the weight may prove to be, he puts into a cup by itself one pound, that is, the twenty shillings, of which a test is to be made, but the remaining twenty-four shillings he puts back into the purse. Likewise, in addition to the pound to be tested, two pence are given to the melter, not from the Treasury but from the sheriff's own money, as a reward for his labour. Next, two other sheriffs are chosen by the president or, if he be absent, by the treasurer, in order that they, together with the knight-silverer and the sheriff whose money is to be tested, may proceed to the fire for the 'assay'. There the melter, duly forewarned and having made the necessary preparations, awaits their coming. There again, in the presence of the melter and the representatives of the barons, the coins are carefully counted and handed over to the melter.

The duties of the melter

Taking the coins in his own hand, the melter counts them and arranges them in a bowl of burnt cinders which is in the furnace. Then, following the rules of the melter's art, he reduces them to a lump, melting and purifying the silver. But he must be careful not to stop before the process is complete nor to injure and reduce the silver by unnecessary melting, since in the former case the king, in the latter the sheriff, would suffer loss. He should, however, take every precaution and exercise all diligence that the silver be not damaged but only thoroughly refined; moreover, those who have been sent there by the barons should pay heed to this very thing. When the test-piece has been made, the silverer takes it to the barons, accompanied by the others, and then weighs it in the sight of all against the pound weight mentioned above. Moreover, he then makes good what the fire has consumed by adding coins out of the purse until the test-piece balances the pound weight. Next, the test-piece is marked with chalk in these words, "Yorkshire. The pound lost in the fire so many or so many pence", and then it is called an 'assay'; for it is not marked unless it has been previously agreed that it should be so marked. But if the sheriff whose 'assay' it is shall challenge it on the ground that too much has been consumed, perhaps by over-

[1] See above, p. 496.

heating, or by the melting of the silver into lead; or if the melter himself shall admit that for some reason or other the test has failed, another twenty shillings shall be counted out from the remainder left in the purse in the presence of the barons, as described above, and the test shall be repeated in the same manner. Hence it must be clear to thee for what reason, out of the huge pile of coins placed there, forty-four shillings were originally put aside in the purse on which the sheriff's seal has been fixed. It must be noted indeed that the melter receives two pence for the 'assay', as mentioned above. But if by any chance the test shall be made twice, or even a third time, he shall receive nothing more, but shall remain content with the two pence already received.

D. I marvel that such care should be shown by so many great men in the testing of a single pound, since neither great gain nor grievous loss can result therefrom.

M. This is done, not only for the sake of this particular pound, but also of all those which are paid in together with it by the same sheriff under the same account, that of the 'farm'. For, according to the amount which this pound has lost through the refining fire, the sheriff will know how much is to be subtracted from his total for every other pound; so that if he should pay a hundred pounds 'by tale' and the test-pound shall be twelve pence short, only ninety-five pounds shall be credited to him.

D. Now I begin to see that no small profit may accrue from these transactions, but to whom it ought to go, I know not.

M. It was once said, and it should be always understood, that in all these matters the interest of the king alone is to be served. But although the amount lost in the test of burning is subtracted from the sheriff's tally, it is nevertheless recorded separately on another shorter tally, in order that the treasurer and the chamberlains may answer for the total thereof. It must also be realized that it is by means of this tally "of combustion" that the 'farm' of the sheriff is 'blanched'; wherefore, in evidence of this, it always remains attached to the greater tally.

D. A question strikes me here, not unlike the one I remember asking when we were dealing with the Lower Exchequer, namely why one pound should fall shorter than another, since the standard of all those engaged in minting money ought to be the same.

M. To this, as to the former question, it is a sufficient answer that this can be done through false moneyers and clippers of coin. Moreover, there were some who believed – and I do not disagree with them – that the coins of the realm are not lawful if the pound, when tested, falls short by more than sixpence from its proper weight even if 'in tale' it be of full number; and also that money of this kind, when brought to the Exchequer, ought to be confiscated to the Treasury, unless perhaps the coins are new and not in current use, and the superscription betrays their author.[1] In that case the moneyer shall be strictly called to account for his work, and according to the established laws he shall be condemned or acquitted without loss to the sheriff. But if, after the coins have been proved and re-proved by testing, the moneyer has been condemned and punished, the money shall be reduced to a molten lump by the

[1] The name of the moneyer formed part of the inscription of the coin.

melter of the Exchequer in the presence of others skilled in this art, and its weight shall be credited to the sheriff. . . .[1] On the other hand, if any sheriff had brought coins, a pound of which when burnt kept within four or five pence or less, and they seemed newly minted and not of current usage, they were similarly judged illegal, as exceeding the common standard;[2] wherefore they, like the others, could be impounded.

There are likewise at the Exchequer fixed payments made at the set terms without a writ from the king. Such is the salary of the *nauclerus*, to wit, the master of the king's ship called *esnecca*,[3] who receives twelve pence a day. For this and similar payments tallies are made by the chamberlains, since they have no writs for them. Moreover the knight-silverer keeps the 'recauta' of these, that is to say, the counter-tallies. Likewise he and the melter may, when it becomes necessary and the amount of money delivered at the Exchequer is too much for the tellers to handle, be brought in to aid them in the counting at the request of the chamberlains. This, however, is voluntary on their part, not compulsory. This completes the description of the duties of the knight-silverer and the melter.

D. What are the tokens of a test completed or of one not completed?

M. I do not really know, nor have I troubled myself about these things. So long indeed as a dark film can be seen hovering about on the surface of the now molten silver, the test is considered incomplete. But when certain minute grains, as it were, rise up from the bottom to the top and there dissolve, it is a sign that the test is complete.

VII. By whom, and for what purpose, the testing of silver was instituted

D. By whom, and for what reason was this process of testing or combustion instituted?

M. In order that this may be made clear to thee, we must begin a little further back. In the primitive state of the kingdom after the Conquest,[4] so we have learned from our fathers, payments were made to the kings from their estates not by weights of gold or silver, but through provisions in kind alone. From these were supplied the daily necessities of the royal household, and those who had been appointed for this task knew how much came in from the individual estates. Besides this, for the wages and gratuities of the knights and other needs, there grew up the custom of exacting cash payments from the pleas of the realm, from covenants made with the king and from cities and castles where agriculture was not practised. This system persisted during the whole reign of King William I and down to the time of King Henry, his son: what is more, I have myself met certain persons who remember seeing provisions being carried to court at stated times from royal manors. The officials of the king's

[1] The following passage, omitted in the text, is taken by the editors of the Oxford edition to be a marginal gloss subsequently interpolated: "But all this is almost abolished now and much relaxed, since in money matters all men sin together. When however money shall achieve the required standard as fixed by law, it will be necessary to observe the law as originally constituted."

[2] *i.e.* having more than the usual alloy.

[3] A word of Scandinavian origin meaning a 'snake' ship or fast man-of-war.

[4] For the credibility of this account of the development of the 'farm' of the county and the method of payment, see Hughes, Crump and Johnson, *op. cit.*, pp. 31 *et seq.* and 187; R. L. Poole, *op. cit.*, pp. 27 *et seq*; Round, *op. cit.*, pp. 66 *et. seq.*

household knew precisely from which counties wheat was due, from which divers kinds of meat, or fodder for horses, or any other necessaries. After these had been paid according to the accepted measure for each commodity, the royal officials credited them to the sheriff and compounded them for a sum of money; namely for a measure of wheat sufficient to bake bread for a hundred men they allowed one shilling; for the carcass of a grazing ox, one shilling; for a ram or a sheep, four pence; for the fodder of twenty horses, likewise four pence. But as time passed and the said king[1] was occupied in suppressing rebellion overseas and in distant parts of his dominions, it came to pass that the sums needed to meet these expenses were paid in coin. Meanwhile a host of farmers flocked to court, lodging complaints or, what was even more of a nuisance to the king, they frequently accosted him on his travels, holding up their ploughs in token of the decay of agriculture. For they were oppressed by innumerable burdens because they had to transport provisions great distances from their own homes. The king favourably received their complaints and, with the approval of his magnates, dispatched throughout the realm men whom he knew to be wise and prudent. The latter, traversing their circuits[2] and examining the individual manors thoroughly with their own eyes, made an estimate of the provisions which were due from them and expressed them in terms of money. They resolved, also, that the sheriff of a particular county should be responsible to the Exchequer for the sum-total to be raised from all the crown manors in that county, adding that he should pay according to a scale, that is, at the rate of an additional sixpence for each pound due. For they judged that in course of time it might easily come to pass that money of full weight might deteriorate in standard. Nor were they deceived in their opinion. In fact they were compelled to decree that the 'farm' of the manors should be paid, not merely by rate, but by weight, which could not be done without adding a great deal. This rule of payment was observed in the Exchequer for several years; wherefore in the ancient annual rolls of that king[1] there will often be found written, "in the Treasury a hundred pounds according to scale", or "a hundred pounds according to weight".[3] In the meantime there arose a man of prudence, far-sighted in counsel, eloquent in discourse and, by the grace of God, remarkably qualified to deal with great affairs. It may be said that in him was fulfilled what is written, "the grace of the Holy Spirit knows no belated efforts".[4] Being summoned to court by this same king, unknown yet not ignoble, he taught by his example "how extreme poverty can be most fruitful of heroes".[5] This man, therefore, increasing in favour with the king, the clergy and people, was made bishop of Salisbury; he enjoyed the highest offices and honours in the kingdom, and acquired a most profound knowledge of the Exchequer; so much so that, as without doubt the rolls themselves make manifest, it flourished mightily under him. From his legacy,[6] indeed, I have received by direct inheritence[7] the little knowledge which I possess. Upon this point I refrain from saying much at

[1] Henry I. [2] Presumably a reference to an itinerant commission.
[3] This statement is not confirmed by the surviving Pipe Roll of 31 Henry I.
[4] A quotation from St. Ambrose, *Commentary on St. Luke's Gospel*, I, 39.
[5] Lucian, *Pharsalia*, I, 165; note the play upon the name of Roger 'le Poer'.
[6] *stillicidiis*, droppings of moisture, in this case used in the sense of 'leavings'.
[7] *per traducem*, lit. a shoot of the vine, the meaning here being that the author of the *Dialogus* is a branch of the 'old vine', *i.e.* his great-uncle, Roger, bishop of Salisbury, through his father, Nigel, bishop of Ely. See Hughes, Crump and Johnson, *op. cit.*, pp. 9, 10.

present, since, as became the nature of his rank, he left to posterity a memory which gives proof of a most noble mind. Subsequently on the king's orders he came to the Exchequer; and after having sat there for several years, he discovered that, by the method of payment described above, the claims of the Treasury were not fully met. For although it seemed to receive its due in weight and number, yet it by no means did so in substance. Thus it did not follow that for one pound paid in twenty shillings cash, even if they corresponded to a pound in weight, a pound of silver was actually paid; for the debtor could have paid in one mixed with copper or some other ore, since no test was made. In order therefore that the interests of the king and the public weal might at one and the same time be protected, the king himself took counsel on the matter, and it was ordained that the 'assay' or testing of the 'farm' by fire should take place in the manner described above.

D. In what way does it protect the *public* interest?

M. Because the sheriff, finding himself personally at a loss by the burning of the debased coins, takes good care, when he is about to account for the 'farm', that the moneyers placed under him do not exceed the limits of the appointed standard. And when he has detected them in this offence, they are duly punished, that others may be frightened by the example made of them.

D. Ought then a 'blanched farm' to be paid from all the counties, or should an 'assay' be performed?

M. No; only those which by ancient right are named as pertaining to the crown pay in this manner. Those, however, which come into the possession of the crown through some incidental cause, discharge their dues 'by tale' alone. Such are Shropshire, Sussex, Northumberland and Cumberland. It is open to the sheriff to pay, instead of a 'blanched farm', the weight of tested silver, and so escape any loss by combustion, provided, however, that the king's melter shall judge it to be worthy of acceptance. Thou hast an answer now to thy question, by whom and for what purpose the 'assay' was instituted.

D. I perceive that by this is fulfilled the text: "The fire shall try every man's work of what sort it is."[1] But now, pray proceed in thy discourse.

M. So be it. It follows, I believe, in accordance with the order of the plan laid down, that we proceed to treat of the privileges of those who sit at the Exchequer, whether by right of office or by order of the king.

D. I marvel greatly why, when thou wert dealing with the offices, thou didst either refrain of set purpose from speaking of the usher of the Greater Exchequer and his duties, or else forgetfulness overtook thee and thou didst pass him over.

M. I congratulate thee on recollecting what has gone before; verily, the glory of the teacher is in the progress of the pupil. Thou knewest that the aforesaid usher received his pay with the other officials, and therefore thou art right to ask what his duties are. They are as follows.

The duties of the usher of the Upper Exchequer

The usher alone, and without a colleague, guards the door of the hall in which the Exchequer sits, except when he takes with him servants from his own house to aid

[1] I Corinthians iii. 13.

him in discharging the burden of his office. He also guards the door of the secret chamber[1] adjoining the Exchequer hall. Thither the barons retire when a doubtful point is laid before them in the Exchequer, which they would rather debate in private than in public. But the chief reason why they withdraw is, lest the process of accounting at the Exchequer should be hindered; so, while they are deliberating in private, the usual course of reckoning accounts proceeds. Indeed, should any question arise, it would be referred to them. The usher is permitted with impunity to refuse entry at his pleasure to any persons, even those of great authority, if their presence is not necessary to the work in hand. Only those, who sit at the Exchequer by right of office or by mandate of the king, are allowed freedom of access to either chamber.[2] If, however, they are persons of authority, who may not fittingly enter by themselves, they may bring with them one or two attendants into the outer hall of the Exchequer; but only the principal officers of the Exchequer enter the privy chamber. All others are excluded, except when they are summoned by their superiors to discharge the king's business. Likewise the usher receives the writs of summons drawn up and sealed by the marshal at the adjournment of the Exchequer of that term, and carries them, in person or by a trusty messenger, throughout England, as we have said.[3] He also, at the president's order, summons before the latter the sheriffs who are standing about in groups outside the hall, when their presence is required. Likewise it is his duty to attend to certain small necessaries in the Exchequer hall, such as covering and preparing the benches around the Exchequer table and the like. From all this, I think, the duties of all who sit at the Exchequer should be clear to thee. I will now show what are their rights and privileges by virtue of their sitting there.

VIII. What are the rights and privileges of those who sit at the Exchequer

I have still greater need now to be spared the backbiting tongue and the envious tooth, lest they leap upon me and tear me in pieces. For scarcely anything would be brought home to thy understanding if I thought it right to insist on the use, not of the usual terminology, but of a choice arrangement of words or of newly coined phrases.[4]

D. The use of novel terms is the one thing I warned thee to avoid from the beginning, and thou didst give me the assurance that thou wouldst employ common and customary words to explain ordinary things, lest strange novelties should confuse elementary instruction. Pray, then, complete thy task as thou hast begun. But if in the course of thy progress the jealous mind or carping tongue of the critic should catch thee out, thou mayst hold him to this, "Let him who is without sin", in his own writings, "first cast a stone" at thee.[5]

M. I gladly obey, so long as that rule is observed. The privileges of those sitting at the Exchequer consist in many things. For those who sit there by the king's order, whether they be clerks or lay courtiers, are not summoned for any other cases before any judges whatsoever from the day the Exchequer assembles up to the day the court

[1] *ostium thalami secretorum.*

[2] *i.e.* both the Exchequer proper and the inner chamber.

[3] See above, p. 503.

[4] *non usitatis vocabulis, set exquisito verborum scemati, vel confictis nominibus duxerimus insistendum*: the author is here apologizing for the barbarous and uncouth terms he is forced to use in describing the rank and privileges of those who sit at the Exchequer.

[5] John viii. 7.

rises, and if by chance they have received a summons, they are excused attendance by virtue of their official position. But if those present in the Exchequer have suits elsewhere in which they are plaintiffs and not defendants, they have the option of having their cases conducted by proxy, or of postponing the day of trial without prejudice to their case. But if the judge before whom they bring their suit, whether ecclesiastical or civil, in ignorance of this law, shall cite any one of them after the summons to the Exchequer has been issued, and shall perchance by his judgment deprive the absent suitor of his possessions or rights, by the authority of the king and by virtue of the session his suit shall revert to the stage it was in before the summons. But the judge has not for this cause deserved punishment, for he has merely discharged his duty, although in this instance his judgment is ineffectual on the ground of the public interest. But if he has been summoned in such wise that the day of decision, appointed for him and determined by law, shall precede the day of his summons to the Exchequer, he cannot 'essoin' himself for that reason, or evade the sentence of the judge, or treat it as invalid, even though the two days be so close together that he is compelled to set out on his journey at once. In that case he may provide for himself a proctor or attorney,[1] and he himself shall hasten to court and attend to the king's business without misgiving. Moreover, the barons of the Exchequer shall pay nothing by way of tolls and customs for the victuals of their households bought in cities, towns and ports. But if a revenue officer should exact payment for them, even if only one of the baron's servants is present and willing to pledge his faith that the victuals have been bought for his master's use, then the money exacted shall be restored to the baron in its entirety, and the unjust collector shall pay a fine appropriate to the rank of the injured person. Likewise, if any man, even if he be of high rank in the kingdom, shall take leave of his senses and injure anyone sitting at the Exchequer with taunts and insults, this outrage being committed in the presence of the president, it shall be visited on the spot with the penalty of a fine. But if the president be absent, and the man stoutly denies the alleged offence, but his fellows who sit with him affirm unanimously that he did use the words with which he is charged, he shall nevertheless be forthwith judged guilty to the extent of a fine payable to the king whom he serves, unless he hasten to forestall sentence by begging for mercy. If, however, those who sit at the Exchequer shall vex each other with mutual insults or recrimination, let them make peace again through the mediation of others of their rank serving with them, in such wise that satisfaction be made by the one who in their judgment has injured an innocent person. But if he will not agree to this, but still persists in his folly, let the case be referred to the president, and afterwards let both parties accept his decision as just. For the rest, if through the devil, the instigator of all evil, who cannot endure to gaze unmoved on the joyful spectacle of fraternal concord, it should come to pass that an occasion for discord should arise among the principal officers themselves, and thence–which God forbid–the quarrel should develop into an insulting brawl, spurred on by Satan, and peace cannot be restored by their colleagues in office, then cognizance of all these matters shall be taken by the king himself. The latter shall punish the outrage according as God, in whose hand it is, shall inspire his heart; lest

[1] *Procuratorem vel responsabilem*; the former is an agent in an ecclesiastical court, the latter in a civil court. The terms are also used by Glanville in the same sense.

those who are set over others should appear to be able to do with impunity what they decree should be punished in others.

D. From this is manifest the saying of Solomon, "Death and life are in the power of the tongue",[1] and likewise that of James, "The tongue is a little member and boasteth great things."[2]

M. So it is, but let us proceed with the privileges.

Common assessments[3] are made from time to time throughout the counties by itinerant justices (whom we call perambulatory or wandering justices). The assessments are said to be *common* because, when the total sum required from the county is known, it is distributed in common among those who have estates in the county, and calculated by hides of land, in order that when the time comes for payment at the Exchequer nothing may be lacking thereof. From these charges all those sitting at the Exchequer by the king's mandate are entirely exempt, so that not only is nothing exacted from lands they hold in demesne, but also nothing from any of the fiefs held of them. If, however, one of them sitting there holds an estate, whether at fee-farm, or in wardship, or in pledge for a money payment,[4] he will not be exempt but on the contrary be subject to the common law for them. Besides these privileges, and over and above them, he will be exempt at the Exchequer from murder-fines,[5] scutages and Danegeld. Further, what pertains to him shall be deducted from the fixed total and credited to the sheriff in these words: "Pardoned by the king's writ to such-and-such a person, such-and-such a sum", although in fact he has no writ corresponding to this. Moreover, a man whom the king pardons anything must take care not to demand it afterwards from his sub-tenants; he had better be mindful of the words, "Forgive and ye shall be forgiven",[6] because, should he be detected in this, the king, emulating the teaching of the Gospel,[7] will neither let him go nor forgive him his debt, but will perchance punish him a hundredfold. For he is known to have abused the favour bestowed upon him, when he impudently exacts from others what has been freely remitted to himself.

D. It has been said, if I remember aright, that whoever sits at the Exchequer by royal mandate is exempt by reason of that fact from certain legal decisions. It was also added, if I recollect truly, that the Exchequer sits at the Easter term; not, however, that the proceedings there are finally terminated, but that their consummation is deferred to the Michaelmas term. Since therefore it is possible, nay, frequently happens, that someone is summoned to it by royal mandate at the Easter term, and by the Michaelmas term he has either died or been transferred by order of the king to other affairs of State, or, as some judge to be more weighty, he has been considered unworthy to perform such exalted duties through having in the meantime incurred the king's displeasure; in such a case, I ask, does he who is quit at the Easter term – when but little is finally settled but the whole procedure is renewed through the issue of a second summons – deserve to be acquitted at the Michaelmas term, even when he has forfeited his seat in the Exchequer and the favour of his monarch?

[1] Proverbs xviii. 21. [2] James iii. 5.

[3] The term used for any assessment made on the county as a whole, whether for purposes of taxation or by way of amercement.

[4] If the tenant-in-chief were free from a particular exaction he had no right to demand a levy from his sub-tenants on this ground. [5] See below, p. 523. [6] Luke vi. 37. [7] Matthew xviii. 23 *et seq.*

M. Numerous reasons may possibly be discovered for taking either side of this question, but thou must know it is the privilege of regal generosity, once the favour of acquittance has been granted, always to incline to the more lenient view, even when it entails pecuniary loss. Indeed, the principle of royal gifts and pardons is one and the same, namely that just as the king's gifts ought not to be revoked or reclaimed, so also his remissions, which are commonly called pardons, cannot be declared invalid. One who has in any way earned his quittance at the preceding term is therefore free and quit at the term in which the accounting is completed.

D. Certain statements of thine trouble me. First, because thou dost assert that anything is remitted to anyone under this form of words, "in remission of debts through the king's writ to such-and-such a person for such-and-such", when nevertheless he has not obtained a writ of remission from the king. For I do not see how it can happen that the entry in the roll is not then discovered to be false.

M. Not without cause does it trouble thee, for it has long troubled me; and so, I believe, the reason why this entry is made is not yet clear to everyone. Wherefore, although what thou dost ask is no great matter, yet it is unusual and does seem absurd that what is always remitted without a writ is said to have been remitted through the king's writ. For this reason I once solicited the opinion of the bishop of Ely[1] on this very point, as being a man highly skilled in his office, and whose memory should be blessed to all eternity. This man, the illustrious treasurer of Henry I, king of the English, and nephew of the bishop of Salisbury, mentioned above,[2] had a knowledge of the Exchequer unrivalled in his own day. He was also pre-eminent in matters pertaining to the privileges of his rank, and enjoyed so high a reputation that almost alone in the realm he so lived and died that no envious tongue dares to blacken his fair fame. Further, at the insistent petition of the illustrious king, Henry II, he reformed the system of the Exchequer which had been wellnigh destroyed through the continuance of the time of warfare for many years.[3] Like another Esdras,[4] the zealous restorer of the Bible, he renewed the whole structure of its constitution. Indeed, this prudent man thought it better to make known to posterity the laws established in antiquity rather than by maintaining silence to cause the passage of new ones. For the modern age in its quest for money has scarcely decreed laws more lenient than preceding ones. From him then I received an answer of this nature concerning the matter.

"Brother, he who has ears eager to hear, may easily find the tongue of a critic; and even he who has not, will not easily escape the same. It was thus that there came to King Henry I a certain man with the tongue of a serpent, saying to him, 'Your barons who sit at the Exchequer, why do they not pay the dues which arise from their lands? For some have fixed payments at the Exchequer for sitting there; some also on account of their office have estates and the fruits thereof, whence therefore a heavy loss to the Treasury results.' When, therefore, urging the profit that would accrue to the monarch, he incessantly pressed his point, his words at last possessed the king's mind to such an extent that he ordered all the fixed dues to be paid by everyone and

[1] The author's father. [2] Roger, bishop of Salisbury. See above, pp. 516, 517.
[3] *i.e.* the civil war of Stephen's reign.
[4] An error for Nehemiah; the reference is to II Maccabees ii. 13.

to be remitted to none, unless any of them obtained an express mandate from him to this effect. And so it was done. But with the passage of time, when the king remembered the counsel of Achitophel,[1] he repented of having acquiesced. He therefore decreed that all the aforesaid allowances should be credited to those who served there, considering the loss of a small sum of money as nothing in comparison with the great honour gained. So he dispatched his writ to the Exchequer to the effect that those sitting there should by a perpetual law be freed from these dues. By this writ, therefore, from that time onwards they were said to be 'pardoned by the king's writ'. And so it came to pass that the favour granted to our forefathers is still preserved to their posterity."

I myself recollect seeing in my own day a payment similar to this, which in course of time was credited to those deserving quittance under a similar form of words. For our lord, King Henry II, in the Michaelmas term of the twenty-fourth year of his reign,[2] commanded that the Knights Templars, the Knights Hospitallers and the monks of the Cistercian Order, to whom by the privilege of a royal charter he had long since granted the favour of quittance in all money payments, saving jurisdiction over life and limb, should thenceforth be quit of all pecuniary dues throughout the several counties, in such wise that thereafter they should not be compelled to produce their charters in the Exchequer. And the authority of royal piety decreed that thus once for all they should be set free from all these burdens at the discretion of the barons, that those, who have passed to the cultivation of the virtues of a higher life and are bound rather to devote their leisure to prayer, should not be forced on that account to make a tedious and unprofitable delay with their charters at the Exchequer. So, by the advice and deliberation of the barons there present, a writ of the lord king was drawn up in these terms: "I quit-claim the Knights of the Temple of five marks exacted from their tenants for default, and I forbid that from henceforth anything shall be exacted or taken in money payments from them, or from their tenants or their lands. Witness here the following." And in like manner for the Knights Hospitallers and the aforesaid monks. By the authority of this mandate therefore they will henceforth be quit throughout the several counties of all pecuniary dues, so that it may be written in the roll, "pardoned by the king's writ", namely the writ we have mentioned above.

D. I have understood well enough what has been said. Now, please, delay not to explain what are meant by scutage, *murdrum* and Danegeld. They seem indeed to be barbarous terms, but they concern me the more because thou sayest that the officials of the Exchequer are exempt from them.

IX. What scutage is, and why it is so called

M. It happens sometimes, when the realm is threatened or attacked by enemies, that the king ordains that a certain sum, usually one mark or one pound, shall be paid from each knight's fee, and from this source are derived the soldiers' wages and gratuities. For the king prefers to expose foreign mercenaries rather than his native knights to the fortunes of war. And so this sum, which is paid in the name

[1] The true identity of this counsellor remains hidden.
[2] 1178.

of shields is called 'scutage'.[1] Those who sit at the Exchequer are quit of this charge.

X. *What 'murdrum' is, and why it is so called*

Next, *murdrum*,[2] properly speaking, is the concealed death of a man where the slayer is unknown. For *murdrum* means the same as 'concealed' or 'hidden'. Now in the primitive state of the kingdom, after the Conquest, the remnant of the conquered English secretly laid ambushes for the Normans whom they distrusted and hated, and far and wide, in woods and remote places, when opportunity presented itself, they slew them in secret. When, to avenge their deaths, the monarchs and their ministers had for some years taken violent measures against the English with various refinements of torture, and yet the latter had not altogether ceased their attacks, at length the following plan was devised, namely that the hundred in which a Norman was found slain in this way–no evidence being found as to the identity of the slayer–should be condemned to pay into the Treasury a large sum of tested silver; some indeed to the extent of thirty-six pounds, others, forty-four pounds, according to the different localities and the frequency of homicide. It is said that this was done so that the imposition of a general penalty might make it safe for wayfarers, and each man might hasten to punish so great a crime and to hand over to justice the man by whose fault such an enormous indemnity was imposed on the whole neighbourhood. You must know that those who sit round the Exchequer table are exempt from these charges, as we have said above.

D. Ought not the concealed death of an Englishman, like that of a Norman, to be reckoned for *murdrum*?

M. By the original institution it ought not to be so reckoned, as thou hast heard. But, with the English and Normans dwelling together and alternately marrying and giving in marriage, the races have become so fused that it can scarcely be discerned at the present day–I speak of freemen alone–who is English and who is Norman by race. I except, however, the bondmen, who are called villeins, and are not permitted, if their lords object, to change their status. For this reason invariably, when anyone is found slain in this manner nowadays, it is punished as murder,[3] except in the case of those who can be proved to be of servile status, as we have said.

D. I marvel that a monarch of singular excellence and high courage[4] should have shown such mercy towards the English race subjugated and distrusted by him that, not only did he preserve in safety the peasants who practised agriculture, but even left to the great ones of the kingdom their manors and extensive possessions.

M. Although this may not pertain to the business under discussion, and to which I have committed myself, I will nevertheless freely expound what I have learned concerning them from native Englishmen.[5] After the conquest of the kingdom and

[1] On scutage, see p. 558.

[2] For the history of *murdrum* or the murder-fine, see Hughes, Crump and Johnson, *op. cit.*, pp. 193–194; Pollock and Maitland, *op. cit.*, vol. II, pp. 485–487.

[3] If the coroner's jury could prove that the deceased was an Englishman, the hundred was released from the murder-fine.

[4] William the Conqueror.

[5] This passage is a somewhat lengthy digression purporting to give an explanation of the land settlement made after the Norman Conquest and to formulate a legal theory to comprehend the sweeping changes it involved. See detailed commentary in Hughes, Crump and Johnson, *op. cit.*, pp. 195–196.

the just overthrow of the rebels, when the king and his magnates made a tour through the new territories, careful investigation was made as to the identity of those who had contended against the king in war and had saved themselves by flight. To all such, and even to the heirs of those who had fallen in battle,[1] all hope of recovering the lands, estates and revenues, which they had previously possessed, was precluded; for they considered it a great boon even to enjoy the privilege of life under their enemies. Those indeed who had been summoned to war, but had not yet joined the host, or had taken no part in the battle through preoccupation with their domestic affairs or some other indispensable business, contrived in course of time to obtain lands for themselves, according as by their devoted service they gained the favour of their lords, and this without hope of hereditary possession, but solely at their lords' pleasure. But with the lapse of time, becoming hateful to their lords, they were everywhere driven from their possessions and could find no one to restore to them the lands of which they had been deprived. In consequence there came before the king a general complaint from the native English to the effect that, since they had become hateful in the sight of all men and been despoiled of their property, they would be compelled to cross over to foreign parts. At length counsel was taken on these matters, and it was decreed that whatsoever, by virtue of their merits and the interposition of a legal covenant, they had been able to obtain from their lords, the same should be conceded to them by inviolable right.[2] Nevertheless, they might claim nothing for themselves by right of hereditary succession from the time of the conquest of their nation. Indeed, with what prudent consideration this provision was made is manifest, especially since they would thus be bound, in order to consult their own advantage, to strive thereafter by every means to purchase the goodwill of their lords by devoted services. So then, anyone belonging to the conquered race, who possesses estates or anything of the kind, has acquired them, not because they seemed to be due to him by hereditary right, but only by virtue of his merits or through the conclusion of some convenant.

D. I am not quite clear what is a 'centuriate' or hundred.

M. Wait but a little, and thou shalt know hereafter in the proper place. . . .[3] Now let us proceed to treat of Danegeld, and pay attention for a little space, that the reason for this name may be made clear to thee.

XI. What Danegeld is, and why it is so called

"Our island content with its own, has no need of the goods of strangers;
Therefore, with very good right, our ancestors have called it
Truly the lap of riches, the home, too, of every delight."[4]

[1] *i.e.* those who fought against William at Hastings.

[2] By this decree two types of tenure were recognized, tenure by favour of the lord (*meritis exigentibus*) and tenure under contract (*interveniente pactione*), and a title was thus afforded to these precarious tenants. Confirmation of this is found in Bracton; see Pollock and Maitland, *op. cit.*, vol. I, pp. 372–383.

[3] The phrase here omitted runs, "this is in the chapter on Domesday Book (*libro iudiciario*)", and is palpably a marginal gloss. In any case the reference is wrong, since the hundred is treated in Book I, chap. XVII of the *Dialogues*, not in chap. XVI, the one dealing with Domesday Book, see below, p. 530.

[4] These lines are possibly the author's own composition, though they are reminiscent of passages in John of Salisbury's *Policraticus* (Book VIII, chap. VII, ed. C. C. J. Webb, vol. ii, p. 268) and Ralph 'de Diceto', *Opera* (ed. W. Stubbs, Rolls Series, vol. I, p. 10).

For this cause she has suffered countless injuries from foreign foes, for it is written: "Marked jewels attract the thief."[1] For pirates from the adjacent islands made incursions and depopulated our shores, carrying off gold and silver and all manner of precious things. But when the king and the native English came up in battle array in defence of their people, the pirates took to flight overseas. Chief among these robbers, and always the most ready to inflict injury, was that warlike and numerous race of Danes, who in addition to the greed common to all robbers, pressed on the more eagerly because they had some claim by ancient right to the lordship of this realm,[2] as is more fully related in the *History of the Britons*.[3] So, in order to keep them at bay, it was decreed by the English kings that by a perpetual law two shillings in silver should be levied on each hide of land in the kingdom for the use of the brave warriors who mustered to patrol and guard the shores, in order to repel the attacks of the enemy.[4] Since, therefore, this revenue was instituted chiefly on account of the Danes, it is called 'Danegeld'. Under the native kings, then, as has been said, this tax was paid annually, up to the time of King William I, of the race and people of the Normans.[5] For in his reign both the Danes and other pirates by land and sea restrained their hostile incursions, recognizing as true what is written: "When a strong man armed keepeth his palace, his goods are in peace."[6] They also recognized that men of surpassing valour do not suffer injuries to go unpunished. When, therefore, the land had long been quiet under the rule of this same king, he was unwilling that a tax levied under the pressing needs of a time of war should continue to be paid annually, nor yet on account of unforeseen mischances did he desire it to be wholly remitted. Thus it was rarely paid in his day or in that of his successors,[7] that is, when wars or rumours of wars arose through relations with foreign peoples. But whensoever it is paid, those who sit at the Exchequer are exempt from it, as has been said. The sheriffs, also, although they are not reckoned among the barons of the Exchequer, are quit of it in respect of their demesne-lands on account of the labour of collecting the tax. Moreover, you must know that the demesne-lands of any man are those cultivated at his own expense or by his own labour, and likewise those held by his villeins in his name. For villeins, according to the custom of the realm, may not only be transferred by their lords from their present holdings to other places, but even their persons may lawfully be sold or otherwise disposed of, since they themselves and the lands they till for the benefit of their lords, are rightly reckoned part of the demesne. Likewise, it is asserted by those who were well acquainted with the ancient privileges of the Exchequer through personal experience, that the barons are exempt from

[1] Seneca, *Ep.* 68, 4.

[2] An allusion to the mythical king, Danus, in whose right the Danes claimed the island of Britain.

[3] Possibly a reference to the lost work from which Geoffrey of Monmouth drew material for his *Historia Britonum*.

[4] This interpretation follows the *Laws of Edward the Confessor*, cap. 11, rather than the statement in the Anglo-Saxon Chronicle, traditionally accepted, that the original object of Danegeld was to buy off the Danes; see *English Historical Documents*, vol. I.

[5] The author seems ignorant of the fact that the tax was abolished by Edward the Confessor and was not paid annually in pre-Norman times.

[6] Luke xi. 21. It is not of course strictly true that there were no Danish invasions during William's reign, but the typical piratical raids had for some years ceased.

[7] This statement is contradicted by the Pipe Roll of 31 Henry I (see No. 71), where Danegeld is recorded as an annual payment. Under Henry II it was collected only in the second and eighth years of the reign.

payment for 'assarts' of the forest in respect of their demesne-lands. With them we also agree, with the reservation that they may be said to be quit of those 'assarts' which were in being before the day the illustrious King Henry I departed this life. For if they were quit of all 'assarts', no matter when they were made or might be made, the barons would seem to be free to cut down their woods in the area of the royal forest at their own will and pleasure; which in fact they can by no means do with impunity, unless the consent of the king or of the chief forester has first been obtained. Further, those who have their homes in the forest may not even take from their own woods what they need for use in their own homes, except under the supervision of those appointed to guard the forest.[1] There are, however, many who prove by their arguments that no one is exempt from these 'assarts' by right of sitting at the Exchequer. If any one of them should by some misfortune commit an offence against the king for which he deserved to be punished by a fine, he would not be freed from that penalty, except by a special mandate from the king. Since then the making of an 'assart' is an offence against the king's forest, he who is thus guilty of it and is punished for it, ought not, so they say, to be acquitted except by the express mandate of the king. Now although this reasoning is subtle and may seem to some almost convincing, yet the objection may be made that the penalty for 'assarts' is fixed and general for those who err in this particular, namely that for the clearance of one acre sown with wheat one shilling is paid, but for an acre sown with oats, six pence, by immemorial custom. Moreover, from these particulars a sum-total arises, for which the sheriff is held to account at the Exchequer, just as a sum-total arises from the two shillings or one shilling fixed for the different hides of the county, which is called a common assize.[2] Because, then, in these respects the 'assart' bears a distinct resemblance to the common assize, as has been said, it would seem that the barons of the Exchequer may not unjustly be considered similarly quit from 'assarts', as they are from the other common assizes. Moreover, the authority of custom and ancient usage, which is not to be despised, is opposed to those who raise this objection. For those with hoary memories recollect that this was the practice in past times. I myself, who speak with thee, have known in these latter days Robert, earl of Leicester,[3] a prudent man, learned in letters and well versed in matters of law. This man, possessing a natural talent, became also a serious rival to his father in wisdom. His diligence was proven in many matters by our present king, Henry II. He gained such favour and power with the king, who is deceived neither by specious sagacity nor by concealed ineptitude, that by the king's command he not only obtained the office of president of the Exchequer but was made justiciar of the realm. Once when the visitation of the forests, commonly called the 'regard',[4] was impending–it takes place every third year–he obtained from the king a writ granting him exemption from all charges laid upon his land in respect of 'assarts', with an express statement of the amount due from them. When this writ was produced and read in public in the Exchequer, everyone was aghast with astonishment, saying, "Does not this earl weaken our privileges?" While those who sat there looked at each other expectantly,

[1] See above, No. 28.
[2] See above, p. 520.
[3] Robert of Beaumont, justiciar of the realm, 1154–1167. See Table 12.
[4] See above, No. 28.

Nigel, then bishop of Ely,[1] of blessed memory arose and said in modest fashion, "My lord earl, by this writ it appears that thou hast impaired the dignity of the Exchequer, seeing thou hast obtained thereby a mandate from the king in respect of dues from which thou art already exempt by right of sitting at the Exchequer. From this it may now be inferred by an argument *a fortiore* that anyone who does not obtain a writ from the king in respect of his 'assarts' will soon become answerable for payment. But, with all due respect, this method of securing acquittance is pernicious, because it may be taken as a precedent. When therefore, as happens in doubtful cases, some were of one opinion and others of the contrary, there was put forward as a stronger argument in this matter the yearly roll[2] of the time of the aforementioned great king under whom the dignity and science of the Exchequer are said to have flourished exceedingly; and something was discovered there which seemed to support the bishop's assertion concerning the dignity of those sitting in the Exchequer. On hearing this and after deliberating for a little space within himself, the earl answered thus: "I admit that I obtained a writ from the king concerning these matters, but not with the intention of impairing your rights. Rather I did so that I might thus without trouble avoid the importunate and excessive demands, made without the knowledge of the king, by the minions of Alan 'de Neville'."[3] So, renouncing his writ, he chose rather to be acquitted through the privilege of his seat in the Exchequer. In after days, when the aforesaid bishop was unable to be present through infirmity[4] and I myself took his place, as well as I could, at the Exchequer, it happened that 'assarts' were paid there. When therefore the amount levied on his demesne had been paid, I made a public protest, asserting the privilege of exemption. Accordingly, by the common counsel and consent of all, the sum already paid was returned to me. Keeping back, therefore, the amount which had been raised from his demesne, I restored to his villeins in full what had been levied on each of them, in order that the memory of this transaction might survive and bear witness to it.

D. With all due respect one should not employ examples but reasons in the discussion of these matters.

M. That is so. But it sometimes happens that the causes of events and the reasons for opinions are hidden, and then it suffices to adduce examples relating to them, especially those taken from the experience of prudent men, whose deeds are circumspect and not performed without reason. Nevertheless, whatever we have said about these matters, arguing for this privilege or against that, thou mayst rest assured that in this case we have taken nothing as definite, except what the authority of the king has ordained to be observed. To be sure, the organization of the forests and also the punishment or acquittal of transgressors against them, whether it be a pecuniary or a corporal penalty, is kept separate from the other judgments of the realm and is subject solely to the will of the king, or that of some official specially appointed for this purpose. It abides indeed by its own laws, which, it is alleged, are not based upon

[1] The author's father. The incident recorded seems to have taken place in 1166–1167; see Hughes, Crump and Johnson, *op. cit.*, p. 198.
[2] *i.e.* the Pipe Roll of the Exchequer.
[3] *Alaniorum exactionem.* The phrase is obscure in meaning. *Alaniorum* may conceivably be derived from 'Alanus' and be a reference to Alan 'de Neville', the chief justiciar of the forest under Henry II, whose name is frequently mentioned in the Pipe Rolls of the reign.
[4] The bishop of Ely retired from public life in 1164 and died in 1169.

the common law of the realm but upon the will and disposition of the monarch; in such wise that whatsoever has been done in accordance with its laws, may be termed not *absolutely* just, but *just according to the law of the forest.* The forests also are the sanctuaries of kings and their chief delight. Thither they repair to hunt, their cares laid aside the while, in order to refresh themselves by a short respite. There, renouncing the arduous, but natural turmoil of the court, they breathe the pure air of freedom for a little space; whence it is that they who transgress the laws of the forest are subject solely to the royal jurisdiction.

D. From earliest childhood I have learned that it is wrong to remain in shameful ignorance rather than to seek reasons for statements made. In order then to elucidate them more fully, tell me without delay what is a forest and what an 'assart'.

XII. What is the king's forest, and what the reason for this name

M. The king's forest is a safe refuge for wild beasts; not every kind of beast, but those that live in woods; not in any kind of place, but in selected spots, suitable for the purpose. Wherefore such a place is called *foresta,* as it were *feresta,* that is, an abode for wild beasts,[1] the *e* in *feresta* being changed into an *o.*[1]

D. Is there a royal forest in each county?

M. No. Only in well-wooded ones, where there are hiding-places and rich pasture for wild beasts. Nor does it matter to whom the woods belong, whether to the king or to the magnates of the realm; the wild animals can none the less roam about free and unharmed.

XIII. What an 'assart' is, and why it is so called

'Assart' is the common name for what are called clearings in the works of Isidore;[2] that is, when groves or thickets in the forest suitable for pasture or lairs for animals are cut down, and after the trees have been felled and torn up by the roots, the land is dug up and cultivated. But if the groves are cut down in such a way that anyone, standing and leaning against the stump of an oak or other tree that has been felled, can, as he looks around, see five others that have been cut down, it is termed a 'waste', that is, a place laid waste, and is so called by contraction. Such an outrage, moreover, even if committed in one's own woods, is considered so grave an offence that a man may never be acquitted thereof, even by right of a seat at the Exchequer, but he must on the contrary be amerced according to the competence of his rank. Thus far I have expounded in bare outline, as far as brevity and conciseness allow, what has come into my mind at short notice concerning the privileges of those sitting at the Exchequer. But for the rest, I have fixed no limit in these matters for the liberality of kings which they may not overstep; for all men are disposed, on account of the favour entrusted to them, to promote the glory of their own rank, especially those among them who are truly wise. But that greatest of temporal princes, the illustrious king of the English, Henry II, ever strives to increase the privileges of his servants, knowing full well that benefits bestowed on them win glory for his name by titles of undying fame. Now then, let us turn our ready pen to other subjects.

[1] The etymology of this derivation is, of course, absurd.

[2] Isidore of Seville.

D. It follows logically, if I mistake not, and as I have gathered from what has been said before, that thou shouldst now proceed to deal with the king's seal and Domesday Book, the former of which, if I remember rightly, is kept in the Treasury and never leaves it.

M. Nay, rather, both of them are kept there, along with many other things.

XIV. That 'thesaurus' sometimes means the money itself, and sometimes the place where it is kept

Thou shouldst know, moreover, that *thesaurus* sometimes means money in coin, as well as gold or silver plate of various kinds and changes of raiment. In accordance with this meaning it is said: "Where your treasure is, there will your heart be also."[1] But the place in which it reposes is also called *thesaurus,* because it is equated to *auri thesis,* to wit, the place of gold. Wherefore, if a man asks where something is, the answer he receives appears incongruous, "It is in the *Treasury*", that is, in the place where the treasure is kept. Money in coin and other things mentioned above, once they have been deposited in a safe place, are not taken out again except by the king's order, when they are to be sent to him to be distributed for necessary purposes. But there are several things deposited in the chests of the Treasury which are carried around, locked up and guarded by the treasurer and the chamberlains, as has been more fully shown above.[2] Such are the king's seal, which thou hast inquired about, Domesday Book and the so-called exactory roll, which some call the writ of the 'farm'. Likewise the great annual rolls of accounts,[3] a multitude of charters, the counter-tallies and the rolls of receipts, the royal writs for issue of treasure and several other things which are necessary for the daily use of the Exchequer when it is in session.

XV. What use is made of the royal seal which is in the Treasury

What should be the use of the royal seal is manifest from the foregoing. With it are sealed the summonses which are issued and the other mandates of the king pertaining by rights to the Exchequer. Nor is it taken elsewhere, but is kept by the chancellor through a deputy, as has been explained above.[4] Moreover, it has stamped upon it the same image and inscription as the seal of the *curia* which follows the king around,[5] so that each may be recognized as having equal authority of command, and he who has acted contrary to either may be similarly judged guilty. Further, the book about which thou dost inquire is the inseparable companion of the royal seal in the Treasury. From Henry, formerly bishop of Winchester,[6] I received the following account of the reason for its compilation.

XVI. What Domesday Book is, and for what purpose it was composed[7]

When that renowned conqueror of England, King William–a near kinsman to this same prelate–had subjugated the farthest limits of the island and thoroughly tamed

[1] Matthew vi. 21.
[2] See above, pp. 495, 503.
[3] *i.e.* the Pipe Rolls of the Exchequer.
[4] See above, p. 501.
[5] The Great Seal of the *curia* followed the king, while the seal of the Exchequer remained with the Exchequer, wherever it moved.
[6] Henry of Blois, brother to King Stephen, bishop of Winchester.
[7] This chapter must be regarded as largely conjectural rather than as serious history.

the minds of the rebels by the terror of his vengeance, lest a further opportunity of wrongdoing should again be accorded them, he ordained that the people subject to him should submit to written laws and customs. Accordingly, the laws of the English having been set before him in their triple form, that is, Mercian law, Danish law and the law of the West Saxons, some he rejected while others he approved, adding to them also those laws of Neustria overseas, which seemed most efficacious for preserving the peace of the realm. At length, lest aught should be lacking to the full sum of his foresight, after taking counsel he dispatched the most prudent men in his court on circuit throughout the kingdom. In this manner, and by these agents, a careful survey was made of the whole country, of its woods, pastures and meadows, as well as of its arable land. All this was set down in common language and compiled in a book, in order that each man, being content with his own rights, should not with impunity usurp the rights of another.[1] The survey was made by counties, hundreds and hides, the king's name being written at the head of the list, followed in turn by the names of other magnates set down according to the dignity of their rank, that is, the names of the tenants-in-chief of the king. Further, after the individual names have been arranged in order, numbers are placed against them, by means of which, in the course of the book below, the matters which concern them may more easily be found. This book is called by the English "Doomsday", that is, by metaphor, the day of judgment. For just as the sentence of that strict and terrible Last Judgment cannot be evaded by any art or subterfuge, so, when a dispute arises in this realm concerning facts which are there written down, and an appeal is made to the book itself, the evidence it gives cannot be set at naught or evaded with impunity. For this cause we have called this same book "Doomsday", not because it passes judgment on any doubtful points raised, but because it is not permissible to contradict its decisions, any more than it will be those of the Last Judgment.

D. Please explain what a county is, what a hundred and what a hide. Otherwise what thou hast said will not be at all clear to me.

XVII. What a hide is, what a hundred and what a county, according to the common opinion of them

M. Countrymen know this better. Indeed, as we have learned from them, a hide in its primitive form consisted of a hundred acres. But the hundred consists of several hundred hides, though the number is not definitely fixed. For one hundred may contain a great many hides, another fewer. Hence thou wilt often find in the ancient charters of the Anglo-Saxon kings that a hundred is called a 'centuriate'. The county is made up of hundreds in the same way, that is to say, some of more, others of less, according as the land was divided by the wise men of old. The county, then, is called after the count,[2] or, alternatively, the count after the county. It is the count, moreover, who receives the third part[3] of the profits of jurisdiction in each county. For the full amount demanded from the sheriff in the name of his 'farm' does not come wholly

[1] For a discussion of the Domesday Inquest, see below, pp. 847–851.
[2] To be more properly translated 'earl'; the literal translation has been kept in this passage in order to show the author's etymological derivation.
[3] The third penny.

from the rents of lands, but in great part from pleas, and of these the count receives the third part.[1] He is said to be thus named because he is associated with the Treasury and is a companion [*comes*] in receipt thereof. Again, the sheriff [*vice-comes*] is so called because he takes the place of the count in those pleas in which the latter participates by virtue of his dignity.

D. Are there in every county counts who receive these dues?[2]

M. By no means: only those men receive them whom the liberality of kings creates earls in return for services rendered or for distinguished probity, and to whom by reason of that dignity it decrees that these profits are to be granted, to some by hereditary right and to others for life only.

XVIII. What the exactory roll is

The exactory roll[3] is that in which are noted down distinctly and carefully the 'farms' of the king arising from the several counties, the sum-total of which may not indeed be diminished, but is frequently augmented through the diligent labours of the justices. The reason for the remaining rolls, such as the annual rolls and the others mentioned above,[4] which are kept in the Treasury and never leave it, is clear enough from the previous discourse. It remains then for us to turn to the greater and more indispensable institutions of the Exchequer, in which, as has been already said,[5] is contained the higher, more profitable and more advanced science of the Exchequer.

Book II

M. Hear me, brother, and with attentive ear give heed to what I say unto thee. Thou wilt not regret thy willingness to expend a short space of time snatched from leisure upon matters of business. For there are some who are not ashamed to say in their hearts, "He that increaseth knowledge increaseth sorrow."[6] To such learning is a burden and it is a pleasure to play the fool. For this cause the truth is far removed from them, because they shrink from the pleasant labour of acquiring knowledge and so stumble into error. Thus they become blind in heart and, all unconscious of the perils of the road, they fall headlong down a precipice. Nevertheless, brother, let no day find thee idle, lest perchance the lot of human weakness, which is more prone to evil, catch thee off thy guard and subject thee to a worse fate. But if at any time thou hast nothing to do, devise for thyself some honest occupation, that thy mind, being always employed, may be more ready for instruction. Give ear, then, a little to those matters in which thou hast involved us; not in order to reap from them the fruits of labour, but only that thou mayst not remain idle.

D. I fear that the shades of approaching night may put a sudden stop to the business under discussion, and that, many cardinal points having been omitted, thou wilt hasten to rid thyself of an importunate questioner.

M. Nay, I rather feared that after long silence thou wert convulsed with long suppressed laughter on account of the rusticity of my style, or perchance that thou

[1] The third penny.
[2] For difficulties in the interpretation of this passage, see Hughes, Crump and Johnson, *op. cit.*, pp. 203–205.
[3] Not now extant; from 9 Richard I onwards the sheriff's 'farm' appears on the Pipe Roll.
[4] See above, pp. 501, 502. [5] See above, p. 499. [6] Ecclesiastes i. 18.

wert silently cogitating how, without offence to me, thou couldst withdraw from the discussion which thou hast forced upon us. For this cause I confess I had almost brought my discourse to an untimely end. Nevertheless, as thou art still willing to learn and thy diligent attention has not yet begun to flag, I will proceed in the way we have started. For the purpose, then, of keeping to the order of our prearranged plan, we must speak in the first place concerning summonses, namely from what materials and how and with what object they are issued; and, in order that these matters may be made plainer to thee, let the last of these three points be demonstrated before the first, that is, with what object they are issued.

I. Summonses are issued in order that the Exchequer may be held

After a writ of summons, sealed with the image of royal authority, has been dispatched, those whose attendance is necessary are convoked to the place named.[1] For they are not obliged to come unless the summons has first been sent. Some, moreover, attend to sit as judges, others to pay and be judged. The barons, whom we mentioned above, sit and act as judges either by virtue of their office or by mandate of the king. But the sheriffs and many others in the kingdom discharge their accounts and are judged accordingly. Of these, some are liable for voluntary payments, others for compulsory ones. Concerning the latter we shall speak more fully below in treating of the sheriff.[2] Now, as there are a great number of such persons in all the counties, it should be specifically stated in each case in the summons how much is due to be paid at the forthcoming term, and the cause thereof added, as if it were said: "Thou shalt have from so-and-so such-and-such a sum for such-and-such a reason." But if anything should be demanded from the sheriff, when he is sitting to render account, in respect of any debtor in his county, of whom, however, no mention was made in the summons, he will not be held liable for it, but will rather be excused, because the summons has not preceded the demand. Summonses are issued, therefore, in order that the king's 'farm' and the dues demanded for a variety of reasons may flow into the Treasury. There are indeed some revenues which must necessarily be transmitted through the hand of the sheriff, even though no summons be issued concerning them, but these are casual[3] rather than fixed or definite payments, as will appear from what follows.

How summonses are drawn up

First, it must be told how, and by what rules they are drawn up, and secondly, from what materials. Thou shouldst know, then, that after the adjournment of the Exchequer of the term in which the summonses are made out, the debts owing to the king throughout the several counties are copied from the great roll[4] of that particular year by the clerks of the treasurer and recorded in shorter rolls together with the causes. This done, those whom we have called the principal officers[5] withdraw to one side and, as each county is brought forward, they decide for how much

[1] The place where the Exchequer should sit was not determined until the summons was issued.

[2] See below, pp. 542 *et sqq*.

[3] Examples of these, given by Madox, are treasure trove, chattels of felons and fugitives, and chattels of usurers dying intestate.

[4] The Pipe Roll.

[5] *i.e.* the barons of the Exchequer.

each debtor in the county should be summoned, the status of the debtor, the nature of the business and the reason why he is liable to the king, all being taken into consideration. The official annual roll,[1] also, from which the debts have been extracted, is held open before the treasurer or his clerk, lest perchance there be any kind of error made in the process of copying. There is also another clerk[2] who carefully records the assessment agreed upon in respect of the debt for which a summons is made out in these words: "H[enry], king of the English, to such-and-such a sheriff, greeting. See to it, as thou lovest thyself and all that is thine, that thou attend at the Exchequer in such-and-such a place on the day after Michaelmas, or on the day following the Octave of Easter, and that thou hast there with thee whatsoever thou owest for the old 'farm' or for the new, and specifically the debts mentioned below, namely ten marks from so-and-so for such-and-such a cause" and so on. Moreover, after all the debts, together with the occasions thereof, contained in the greater annual roll, have thus been set down in due order, the lesser rolls of the itinerant justices[3] are likewise produced. From these are extracted the dues owing to the lord king in the several counties by dint of their labour and industry.[4] These, having been assessed by the greater barons, are recorded in the summonses. After these points have been duly set down in order, the summons ends with these words: "and all these thou shalt have with thee in money, tallies, writs and quittances, or they will be deducted from thy 'farm'. Witness, such-and-such a person here at the Exchequer". . . .[5] Moreover, because a new disease should be treated by new remedies, the following addition was made to the summonses by a new decree issued subsequent to the reign of King Henry I, namely "If perchance thou [the sheriff] art summoned for the debt of anyone who has no land or chattels in thy bailiwick, and thou knowest in whose shire or bailiwick he holds them, thou shalt thyself signify the fact by thine own writ to that sheriff or bailiff, and it shall be carried by thy messenger, who shall deliver it to the sheriff concerned, in the county court, if possible, or in the presence of many witnesses." This addition was rendered necessary by the somewhat ridiculous and wasteful subterfuge of certain persons. For when the appointed seasons for the issue of the summonses became known, before the summons concerning his debt had arrived in the county, a man would empty his barns and alienate his money or transfer it to a safe place, and thus, sitting empty-handed in his house, would await in confidence the arrival of the sheriff and the other officers. By this device the authority of a royal summons was for many years evaded, and that not without loss. For the sheriff, to whose jurisdiction the debtor had removed, together with his property, through fear of this summons, dared not lay hands on the debtor's possessions, since he had no orders to this effect. For this reason, therefore, the abovementioned clause was for some years inserted in the summonses. Afterwards no one had any ground for the subterfuge that every debtor should not render satisfaction in every way, except him whom the direst poverty excuses. When, moreover, it had

[1] The Pipe Roll. [2] The scribe of the chancellor; see above, p. 500.

[3] The Assize Rolls kept in the Treasury of the Exchequer.

[4] This statement is presumably intended to cover new debts incurred through the judicial proceedings of the eyres. These, like the old ones copied from the Pipe Roll, are assessed by the barons.

[5] The eight lines of the Latin text here omitted are regarded as suspicious by the editors of the Oxford edition and dismissed as a later gloss or interpolation; see Hughes, Crump and Johnson, *op. cit.*, p. 207.

become clear to all sheriffs and debtors that by this means a stop could be put to their sophisticated insolence, it was judged no longer necessary to insert this clause, nor is it inserted now. Nevertheless, the method of coercing debtors, wherever they may have betaken themselves, described above, persists among the sheriffs and is still observed, as though established by a perpetual law.

D. I have already heard from many others, that the Exchequer is summoned twice a year, namely at the Easter term and at the Michaelmas term. Thou hast also said, if I recollect aright, that the Exchequer is not held unless the summonses have been previously sent out. Since, then, the summonses are made out at each term, I beg thee, please, to disclose whether the same rule is observed in both summonses or, if there be a difference in the form of words, what it is and why it is so.

II. How the summonses differ according to the term

M. It is a great proof of thy progress that thou hast already learnt what questions to ask in these matters. Beyond all doubt it is certain that the Exchequer is convened and held twice in the year, being preceded, however, as has been said above, by summonses. Thou dost recollect very well the terms of each session. Note, however, that in the Easter term it is not the settlement but the review of accounts that is discharged by the sheriffs. Wherefore hardly any of the business transacted there on that occasion is committed to writing, but the whole of it is reserved for the other term, when the separate items are set down in order in the great annual roll.[1] Notes on some matters of importance, however, which frequently arise, are at that term written down separately by the clerk of the treasurer,[2] so that before the Exchequer of that term rises, a decision may be taken concerning them by the greater barons. Indeed, on account of their large number these matters could not easily be brought to mind, unless they were committed to writing. Furthermore, the proportion of the 'farm' which the sheriff has paid into the Treasury is entered there, and then, if he has paid in full, on the same line is added, "And he is quit." If he has not, the debt is clearly entered on the line below, so that he may know how much of the total for that term is lacking, and forthwith render satisfaction in money or security in accordance with the decision of the presiding barons. For every sheriff is bound to pay at that term one-half of the 'farm' accruing from his county that year. Thou shouldst know, moreover, that the form of words in these summonses is not changed, except in so far as the term and place are concerned; when, for instance, the barons have ordered the Easter session of the Exchequer to be held in one place and the Michaelmas session in another. But although the same form of words is observed in both summonses, the form of entry of the debts extracted[3] is different. For in the summons made out against the Easter term it shall simply be stated: "From such a one thou shalt exact ten pounds", because the year is said to begin then. And from this summons the sheriff shall not be acquitted, unless he either pay on the spot or give security for the ten pounds. But when the summons is to be drawn up for the Michaelmas term, in which the year is closed and terminated and also the annual roll is made up, there shall be added to the said ten pounds another ten or more, according

[1] The Pipe Roll. [2] In this record we probably have the origin of the treasurer's memoranda roll.
[3] From the Pipe Roll of the previous year.

as the presiding officers shall think fit; and in the roll it shall be recorded, "From so-and-so thou shalt exact twenty pounds." But he who had paid ten pounds of this very sum at the Easter term, and now pays ten pounds in coin and produces a tally for the ten pounds already paid, is considered worthy of acquittal from the summons, for it is stated in the summons, "thou shalt have all these in money and writs and tallies". Thou shouldst know, besides, that, after a summons has been made out, if when it is checked some error is discovered therein, it must not be cancelled by drawing a line under it nor erased, because the writ is open; rather, the summons in which the error was made ought to be entirely blacked out, so that the writing may be indecipherable. The reason for this will readily occur to thee, if thou hast reflected upon these matters.

D. Since, as thou sayest, the writ is open, and is thus dispatched to the sheriff and may remain for a long time with him and his officials, the safe custody of the summons is entrusted solely to his good faith. He could with impunity efface, alter or diminish it at his pleasure, since no copy of it remains with the barons.

M. Perhaps he could if he wished, but it would be a proof of lunacy if of his own accord he were to court such great dangers, especially since he could not thus annul the debts he owed to the king, and scarcely even defer them. For all the debts for which summonses are drawn up, are noted down and carefully preserved elsewhere,[1] so that no one by this device could be delivered from his debts, even with the connivance of the sheriff. Indeed we have seen how, for a greater safeguard in this affair, copies of all the summonses were made by the archdeacon of Poitiers, now bishop of Winchester. Nor are the originals ever at any time sent out, unless copies of them have been made and carefully corrected. Moreover, during the reading of the summons by the clerk of the chancellor, while the sheriff was sitting to render account, the clerk of the archdeacon,[2] inspecting his copy of the summons, was watching him, lest he deviated from the truth. In course of time, however, when the number of debts enormously increased, so much so that one membrane of parchment was barely long enough for a single summons,[3] this manifold and onerous labour was given up, and they were content, as of old, with the original summons alone. So now thou hast had, I think, as briefly as possible an explanation as to how, and for what purpose, summonses are issued. We are now free to consider from what sources they are compiled, although this also is for the most part already clear from what has gone before.

For what debts summonses are issued

The illustrious king of the English, Henry, is the second of the kings bearing that name, but in the management of affairs he is believed to be second to none in modern times by virtue of his intelligence. For from the very beginning of his reign he applied his whole mind to this, that by manifold victories he might destroy rebels and malcontents, and altogether seal the hearts of men with the blessings of peace and

[1] The old debts could be traced from the Pipe Roll of the previous year, while any new debts incurred would be shown on the eyre rolls of the itinerant justices or by the counter-writs (*contrabrevia*) from the *curia*.

[2] This is the sole mention of this official in the treatise.

[3] The growing length of the writs of summons may be accounted for by the practice of including year after year the debts remaining over from the previous year; cf. the vast increase in the length of the Pipe Rolls during the reign of Henry II.

confidence. Although the fame of his great deeds has now spread far and wide among all nations, so that it may seem superfluous to insist on them, yet there is one thing I cannot pass over in silence, by which alone his singular probity and unexampled goodness are established.

> "This was no work of man, but rather of pitying Godhead,
> That with a few, himself–nay, the whole world–he resisted."

D. How it can be called a great work to resist himself, I do not see, unless thou make it plain.

M. Although this does not pertain to the task we have undertaken or purposed, nevertheless, remembering that noble monarch, I dare not pass over these things and preserve my peace of mind. Thou mayst perceive, then, how marvellously this man withstood himself in these affairs, even against the sons of his own body, nay rather against the sole hope and peculiar glory of his soul, next after God. When his children were young, and by reason of their tender age flexible beyond measure like wax, and prone to every impulse of the mind, they were seduced by the evil counsels of the pertinacious little foxes,[1] who finally turned them against their father as against an enemy. Indeed, "A man's enemies have become they of his own household"[2] and those who guarded his person have taken counsel against him, saying unto his sons and his enemies, "Persecute him, and take him for there is none to deliver him."[3] Thou mightest say that in them was fulfilled the word of the prophet, "I have nourished and brought up children and they have rebelled against me."[4] When, therefore, the wife was raging against her husband, the sons against their father, the servants without cause against their master, wouldst thou not say with ample justification that a man was at war with himself? To be sure, against so great a host of enemies[5] the magnitude of divine grace alone sustained him; and as though the Lord were fighting on his side, he vanquished almost all the rebels in so short a time that he was far more strongly established than before, and that through the very circumstance which should have weakened him. For the mightiest of those, who had conspired against him in all his virtue, came by this to know that the club can be wrested from the hand of Hercules only with difficulty. Moreover, after his enemies had been taken, an unexampled compassion spared the instigators of so outrageous a crime; with the result that few of them sustained forfeiture of their possessions and none of their rank or their lives. If thou wert to read the vengeance which David visited upon the murderers of his son, Absalom,[6] thou wouldst say that Henry had dealt far more leniently than he; and yet of David it is written: "I have found in him a man after mine own heart."[7] Although the noble king could find an abundance of precedents, and might have taken most condign vengeance against them, he preferred nevertheless to spare rather than to punish the vanquished in order that even against their will they might live to see his kingdom grow in greatness. Long live the king then, and may he go happy and glorious, and in return for the grace bestowed upon him may he merit

[1] An allusion to Henry II's queen, Eleanor, and Louis VII, king of France.
[2] Cf. Matthew x. 36.
[3] Psalms lxxi. 9.
[4] Isaiah i. 2.
[5] A reference to the feudal revolt of 1173–1174.
[6] Cf. I Kings ii. 5.
[7] Acts xiii. 22.

grace from on high. Long live also his noble offspring[1] in obedience to their father and not unlike to him; and since they are born to rule over the nations may they learn both by their own example and their father's how glorious it is to spare the vanquished and overthrow rebels. However, let us proceed with the task we have undertaken. But shouldst thou desire to be more fully instructed concerning these and his other mighty acts, take a look, please, at the little book[2] of which we spoke.

When, therefore, peace had been restored, after the shipwrecked state of the kingdom, the king strove to renew the times of his grandfather, and choosing discreet men he divided the realm into six parts[3] in order that the justices selected, whom we call itinerant, might pass through it on circuit, and re-establish the laws which had been abandoned. So, giving the king abundant opportunity of seeking advice in the several counties, and exhibiting full justice to those who considered themselves wronged, they spared the poor both labour and expense. In such cases, furthermore, it came to pass that different offences were for the most part punished in different ways, according to the nature of the charges, so that some suffered corporal punishment, others a money penalty. The fines exacted from offenders, then, are carefully recorded in the eyre rolls[4] which, when the Exchequer is in session, are handed over to the treasurer in the presence of all. Moreover, the justices must see to it that they deliver the rolls to the treasurer correct and in good order, for, once they have been handed over, it is unlawful even for the justices themselves to change one *iota*, even in a matter in which the justices are of one mind.

D. It is remarkable, seeing they are the authors of their own writings and nothing may be done without their diligence and labour, that they have not the power to change their own writing, even when they are agreed upon any matter.

M. Inasmuch as time for correction has been allowed them, and they are acquainted with the established rule, it is their own fault. For the full payment will be exacted either from the individual debtors, if they have been found liable in this respect, or from the justices themselves. Thus, if they have entered anyone in their roll as liable to pay twenty pounds, and after the bond has been delivered to the treasurer it shall be discovered that he is only liable for ten, then the justices themselves shall make good the remainder, because their entries, made and corrected with deliberation, may not be revoked after the roll has been handed over. The treasurer, however, causes the debts marked in the rolls he has received to be carefully and plainly recorded for each county in the great annual roll,[5] together with the cases to which they relate. The names of the justices are first set down, as already mentioned, so that in this way a distinction may be made between the various exactions. From these lists the summonses are made out as follows: "For the pleas of such-and-such, *N.*[6] From so-and-so, so much", according to the previous assessment of the barons.

Thou hast now learnt, I think, as far as is necessary, the sources, the manner and

[1] The absence of any reference to the death of the young king, Henry, at this place is perhaps an indication that the work was written before 1183.

[2] *Tricolumnis*. See above, p. 507.

[3] A reference to the reorganization of local justice at the council of Northampton (26 January 1176); see above, No. 59, p. 480.

[4] See above, p. 533.

[5] The Pipe Roll, Nos. 71–73.

[6] Here the name is given.

the purpose of the summonses. Now let me pass to the duties of the sheriff. But thou must pay careful attention to what must now be told, because, as I said in the beginning, in these particulars the higher science of the Exchequer consists.

III. Concerning the manifold duties of the sheriff

All sheriffs and bailiffs, therefore, to whom summonses are directed, are bound by the same legal sanction, that is to say, by the authority of a royal mandate, to the effect that on the day named and at the place appointed they shall gather together and discharge their debts. In order that this may be clearer to thee, consider more carefully the wording of the summons itself. For it reads: "See to it, as thou lovest thyself and all that is thine, that thou attend at the Exchequer at such-and-such a time and place, and that thou hast with thee whatsoever thou owest for the old 'farm' and for the new, as well as the debts written below." Give heed, then, for two things are said which fit in respectively with the two which follow; for this, "See to it, as thou lovest thyself", relates to "That thou attend there at such-and-such a time and place", but the other, "As thou lovest all that is thine", seems to refer to this, "And that thou have there with thee all these debts written below"; as if it were openly said, "Whosoever thou art that receivest a summons, thy absence, unless it can be excused by unavoidable and legitimate causes, will redound to the peril of thine own head. For thou wilt appear thus to have spurned the royal mandate and to have acted disrespectfully and in contempt of the king's majesty if, when thou hast been summoned concerning the business for which thou art bound to him, thou hast neither come nor sent anyone to make an 'essoin' for thee. But if it is thy fault that the undermentioned debts have not been paid, then the other debts for which thou hast been summoned shall be taken from the 'farm' due from thee, and the latter shall be made good from thy chattels and the revenues of thy estates. Thou thyself, in the meantime, if the barons have so decreed, shall be lodged in a safe place under liberal surveillance."[1] When, therefore, the aforesaid summons has been received by the sheriff, on the day named let him come and present himself to the president, if the latter chance to be there, or if he be absent, to the treasurer. Then, having paid his respects to the greater barons, let him have that day free on the understanding that he will return to the Exchequer on the following day and every day thereafter. But if perchance he neither comes nor sends in advance a valid excuse, on the first day he shall be condemned to pay to the king a hundred shillings of silver for each county, on the next, ten pounds of silver, on the third, as we have learnt from our predecessors, whatsoever movables he possesses shall be at the mercy of the king. But on the fourth day, because he is now by this convicted of contempt towards the king's majesty, he shall lie at the sole mercy of the king, not only in respect of his property, but also of his person. There are some, however, who believe that for the whole total a pecuniary penalty alone will suffice, namely, that on the first day absentees should be amerced to the extent of a hundred shillings, on the second, likewise a hundred shillings, and so thereafter for each day another hundred shillings. With them I do not disagree; that is, however, provided that the king, who is wronged thereby, has given his consent thereto.

[1] *sub libera custodia*; that is, restricted to a given area as opposed to strict confinement.

Moreover, it is likely enough that the king will be willing to allow a sentence of this kind, since his singular indulgence "is slow to punish and swift to reward".[1]

D. It is the lot of an imprudent and an impudent listener to interrupt the flowing pen before the appointed end of the narrative, and so I have thus far forborne, revolving in my mind the while a question which somewhat troubles me. For thou didst say that if it was the sheriff's fault that the debts recorded were not paid, then they ought to be deducted from the 'farm' which he is about to pay. If then the sheriff has disbursed the whole sum due from him through the king's writ, either in public works[2] or otherwise, what is to be done?

M. When by the king's order he has expended the 'farm' of the county on the king's private household,[3] or on public works or on any other undertaking, if he is then found remiss in paying his debts, he shall be detained on oath, wherever the barons shall decide, until he shall make good his debts, as he would have done for his 'farm'.

D. Since a grievous loss, both to his movable and immovable property, and also to his own person, befalls a sheriff who has been summoned, but has neither come nor sent an 'essoin', unless he explains his absence as involuntary and unavoidable; I beg thee to disclose without delay what reasons he can put forward as sufficient excuse for his absence once he has been summoned.

IV. For what causes the absence of the sheriff is considered worthy of condonation

M. There are many kinds of 'essoins'[4] whereby the absence of the sheriff is considered permissible, provided, however, that the reason and nature of the excuse have been previously signified, and that the money due to the king, being already in hand, is sent forward on the appointed day through lawful men. The latter, presenting to the president the letter of 'essoin' and affirming the causes of their master's absence to be unavoidable, shall also, if it be the president's pleasure, confirm the same with an oath taken in their own person. But if the sheriff or any other official of his, who has been summoned, cannot attend through infirmity, he may add in the letter of 'essoin' directed to the Exchequer, "And since I cannot come, I send you these my servants *N.* and *N.* that they may take my place and discharge my office, I myself being prepared to ratify their actions."

Moreover, he who sends an 'essoin' must see to it that one or both of those sent be a knight or other layman joined to him by ties of blood or in some other way, that is, one to whose loyalty and discretion he does not hesitate to commit himself and his interests. For it is not proper that clerks alone should undertake this task, because if they act wrongly, it is not seemly that they should be arrested for debt or mistakes in rendering accounts. If, however, a sheriff who has been summoned shall

[1] Cf. Ovid, *Epist. ex Ponto*, I, ii, 123.

[2] For the nature of these, see below, pp. 544, 545.

[3] *camera curie*; the department of the Chamber constituted part of the king's household. Wholly independent of the Exchequer, it became in the thirteenth century a formidable rival to it. Payments made thereto escaped audit, nor did the officials in charge of it render any accounts to the Exchequer.

[4] This account of the nature and operation of 'essoins' should be compared with that given by Glanville, see above, No. 58, pp. 465–468, 473–475.

chance to be absent, being hindered, not by infirmity but by some other cause, he can perhaps even then escape the customary penalty. Nevertheless, none can be admitted to take his place in the completion of his account, neither his eldest son nor his steward, even though he may direct his writ to the effect that he would ratify what so-and-so should perform on his behalf. But solely by the authority of the king's mandate or that of the president, if the king be absent, can another be admitted to complete his account. If, however, he be engaged on some other business assigned to him by the lord king, he himself in person may nominate someone present at the Exchequer who can and should manage the affairs of the absent sheriff, in accordance with what has been said above.[1] Furthermore, the writ in question, whether of the king or of the president, or of the sheriff lodging an 'essoin', shall be kept in the marshal's box previously mentioned,[2] as a testimony of this matter. But if the sheriff, being indispensable to the king in other matters, shall be summoned by him to go outside the realm or, having received permission to deal with his private affairs, shall have arranged to go abroad, let him first go to the president and by word of mouth delegate his duties at the Exchequer to any lawful man he pleases. This done, he is neither compelled to send a writ nor to make an 'essoin' during his absence. When the sheriff excuses himself on the ground of infirmity, and his account comes to be entered in the annual roll, it shall read as follows: "William, sheriff of London, for whom Robert, his son, renders account of the 'farm' of London." But if through the king's mandate another is substituted for him, or he himself, as previously stated, has indicated to the president by word of mouth someone to act for him, then in all respects it is to be recorded as if he himself, in his own person, were sitting to render account.

D. Is infirmity alone sufficient excuse for one who has been summoned to be absent with impunity?

M. Far from it; for there are many 'essoins' allowed at the Exchequer, but this is the more usual both in litigation and in other business, whether ecclesiastical or civil. Then again, thou shouldst remember what has been said, in order to understand that no 'essoin' permits the retention of the royal revenue collected from the county in the sheriff's keeping with impunity or the withholding of it from the Exchequer on the appointed day. The money having been first dispatched, the sheriff may be excused through illness as aforesaid. Likewise, he will be excused if his first-born son, whom he has declared to be his heir, should be thought nigh unto death; likewise, if his wife should be in peril through the onset of her travail in child-birth, or if for some other cause she should be nigh unto death, he may be excused; for she is part of his own flesh. Likewise, if he who is commonly called his liege lord, that is, the person to whom alone by right of lordship he is so bound that he owes service to none other against him,[3] saving only to the king, if such a one shall summon him to his aid when legal proceedings have been taken against the lord in respect of his fief or of the greater part of it, or for any other reason which seems to redound to the detriment of the lord's status or of his body, he may be excused, provided, however, the said lord is unable to postpone the case any longer or otherwise avert litigation. But if

[1] See above, p. 539. [2] See above, p. 503. [3] On liege homage, see Nos. 57, 268.

that same lord shall bring a suit of this kind against another, and it is within his power to postpone the day of hearing without irreparable damage, if in such a case he shall summon the sheriff of the lord king, as being also his vassal, then the latter shall not be bound to comply, because he cannot for this reason be excused from the Exchequer. Again, if that same lord weighed down by his infirmity shall desire to make a will in the presence of his men and shall call in the sheriff for this purpose together with his other vassals, the sheriff shall be excused. Again, if his lord or his wife or son shall die and he shall have to make the necessary arrangements for the funeral, he shall deserve to be excused. There are also many other 'essoins' permissible for the absence of a sheriff, or even necessary and established by law, which I do not deny nor exclude; nay, when they are judged by the greater barons to be sufficient, I willingly admit them. For the sake of example, however, I have included those which at the moment came to mind as being the more common.

D. I seem to understand from this that a knight who is a sub-tenant, or some other discreet man, may be made a sheriff or other bailiff by the king, even though he hold nothing from the king but only from others.

M. This privilege belongs to the authority of public office, that no matter whose vassal any man in the realm may be, nor for whom he may perform military or other service, if he be judged indispensable to the king, he may lawfully be taken and seconded to the royal service.

D. From this indeed I perceive that that is true which is written, "Dost thou not know that the hands of kings stretch to the uttermost?"[1] But now, please, delay not to deal with the activities of the sheriff; for, being warned by thee, I have concentrated the whole of my attention on these matters, knowing that in them, as has been said before,[2] the higher knowledge of the Exchequer should be sought.

M. I congratulate thee on remembering what has gone before; by this, I confess, thou hast added an incentive to my laggard pen. Know, then, that unless an 'assay' has first been made and the debts for which the sheriff was summoned have been paid, he is not allowed to take his seat to render account.[3] But once he has arrived and already taken his seat, the other sheriffs are excluded and he sits there alone with his officials, ready to make answer to the questions put to him. Furthermore, he shall see to it that, either on that very day or on the previous one, it has been made known to the debtors in his county on what day he is due to sit at the accounting table. Also he shall proclaim to them by the voice of a crier around the Exchequer building and the town and its neighbourhood that he will be sitting there at such-and-such a time. Then, all being seated and paying attention, the treasurer, who, as previously stated,[4] by right of office sits opposite to the sheriff, asks him whether he is ready to render his account. On his answering, "I am ready", the treasurer proceeds, "Tell me, then, in the first place, if the alms, tithes, fixed payments and the lands farmed out are the same this year as in the past?" If he reply that they are the same, then let the scribe of the treasurer carefully follow the roll of the previous year in transcribing these fixed payments, while at the same time the treasurer is watching "lest perchance the

[1] Ovid, *Heroides*, 17, 166. [2] See above, p. 499.
[3] The sheriff first pays money into the Treasury and accounts for it afterwards.
[4] See above, p. 494.

hand of the scribe should commit an error". And since I recollect having said enough concerning the order of writing in the section on the duties of the scribe of the treasurer, I omit the details now.

D. Pray proceed then concerning the matters thou hast deferred until treating of the sheriff's duties, namely, how it is that some lands are granted by the king 'blanched' and some 'by tale'; for this has troubled me from the beginning.

M. It is clear enough to thee, I trust, from what has been said, how it is that certain 'farms' are paid 'blanched' and others 'by tale'. To be sure, a 'farm' is paid 'blanched' when it has been 'blanched' by the 'assay'.

V. How it is that some estates are given 'blanched', some 'by tale'

Moreover, the author of this system, and the reason for its institution, are sufficiently well known. We have stated previously that a 'farm' is paid 'by tale' when it is proved correct by counting alone without recourse to the 'assay'. Accordingly, when the king has conferred an estate upon anyone, together with the hundred court and the pleas arising therein, the estate in question is said to have been granted 'blanched'; but when the king has merely granted the estate, retaining for himself the hundred court in which the 'farm' is declared 'blanched', and not settling the hundred court and the 'blanching' upon it, it is said to have been granted 'by tale'. Moreover, it is fitting that he, to whom such an estate has been granted, shall deliver to the Exchequer at the Michaelmas term the writ or charter issued in respect of the grant, in order that it may be accounted to the sheriff: otherwise it will not be entered in the great annual roll nor credited to the sheriff. Moreover, it shall be recorded in this manner; after the alms, tithes and fixed payments of both kinds, at the head of the line: "To lands farmed out to so-and-so, *N.* twenty pounds 'blanched' in such-and-such a place, and to so-and-so *N.* twenty pounds 'by tale' in such-and-such a place." Note also that if perchance among the lands so farmed out, thou shouldst find written, "To so-and-so and so-and-so ten pounds 'blanched'", or "'by tale' by an allowance from the king", and he who has profited by such an allowance shall die, no opportunity is given to his wife or his children or any kinsman of his to claim any rebate on account of this loan, except by favour of the king. The same holds good if the entry runs, "To so-and-so ten pounds during the king's pleasure."

VI. The things which should be credited to the sheriff, namely alms, tithes, payments of both kinds and lands farmed out

D. What are they which thou hast termed "payments of both kinds"?

M. Some of the payments are charitable ones made to the poor, as when, out of pure charity, a penny a day, or two or more, are accorded to someone by the king for food and clothing. But some are payments for service, so that they are received as wages. Recipients of such are the guardians of the royal chapels, the minstrels,[1] the slayers of wolves and the like. These then are miscellaneous payments made for diverse causes, but are nevertheless reckoned among the fixed charges. . . .[2] When all these

[1] *tibicines.*

[2] Five lines are here omitted, which are taken by the editors of the Oxford text to be a later interpolation.

have been set down in order, the treasurer inquires of the sheriff whether, in addition to the fixed payments, he has expended anything from the 'farm' of the county through the king's writs. Then, one by one, the sheriff hands over to the chancellor's clerk the writs of the king dispatched to him. Having read them aloud the clerk delivers them to the treasurer for him to record them appropriately in his roll, in accordance with the form in which the writs have been drawn up. For, as has been said,[1] it is the scribe of the treasurer who writes first, and the others, who write with him, copy his entries. This done, the sheriff shows, not through the writs, but through the established rule of the Exchequer, whether he has expended anything which ought to be credited to him; such are the payments to the king's approvers and likewise those expended in carrying out sentences and holding trials.

VII. The things which should be credited to the sheriff solely by custom of the Exchequer, that is, without a writ

Notice also that the enforcement of the penalties of the law pronounced against anyone is here usually termed the sentence, but judgments are the ordeals of the hot iron and of water. The payments to the approvers are therefore made for this reason. On account of the vast wealth of this realm, and likewise on account of the inclination to drunkenness inborn in the native population, which is always accompanied by lust, it happens that theft, whether open or secret, and also homicide and crimes of various kinds are frequently committed at the instigation of harlots, so that there is nothing that those who submit to their counsels will not dare or attempt. When, therefore, anyone notoriously accused[2] of these crimes is arrested by the royal officials who keep watch over the peace of the realm–by reason of the numerous host of criminals and in order that the land may thus be purged of malefactors–the justices sometimes agree upon this; that if anyone of this sort shall confess his crime and be willing to challenge his accomplices in the same, and by engaging in wager of battle shall succeed in proving the charge brought against the other or the others concerned in it, then he may escape the death he has deserved and his person may go free, provided he withdraw from the realm and wholly forfeit and abjure the right to return.[3] Some, moreover, by an agreement previously entered into with the justices, do not get off scot free, even though they may prove their charges, but while escaping hanging or some other disgraceful kind of death, which they confess they have deserved, they are nevertheless punished with mutilation of members and become a wretched spectacle among the people; thus they serve as a deterrent to the rash escapades of like-minded offenders through the terror caused by their examples. Since, then, the criminal charge brought against him has been proved, and he can yet save his life; and since likewise whatsoever is calculated to promote the peace of the realm doubtless redounds to the advantage of the king, he is called a king's approver. From the day, however, on which he is accepted for the purpose of proof up to the fulfilment of his promise, or until his failure to do so, he receives from the Treasury one penny per day for victuals, and this is credited to the sheriff solely by custom of the Exchequer. But if order shall be given for the said approver to be transferred to

[1] See above, p. 501. [2] Cf. above, No. 24. [3] Cf. above, No. 25.

another place, to the intent that, before the justices there assembled, he may the more conveniently carry out his promise, or perchance failing to do so, may receive condign punishment for his crimes; in that case, only the sum expended in transporting vehicles thither and providing him with victuals at the rate of a penny a day shall be credited to the sheriff by custom; but anything beyond, only by the king's writ. There are, besides, in certain counties many who, as a privilege of their estates, may take vengeance upon condemned persons, in such wise that some are punished by hanging, others by mutilation of members or otherwise according to the measure of the crime committed. On the other hand, there are some counties wherein those who are to be condemned in this manner are only punished when the money has already been paid out in cash from the Treasury. Whatsoever then is paid by the sheriff to men of hateful greed, who receive it in return for the shedding of blood, for the purpose of carrying out these sentences or judgments, is credited to him by custom of the Exchequer, that is to say, not by writ of the king. There is also another charge which ought to be credited to the sheriff by custom alone. When in the opinion of the greater barons the king's treasure should be removed from one place to another, and has need of vehicles and lesser things of this kind, the sheriff, on the orders of the treasurer or the chamberlains or their servants sent for this purpose, provides what is needed from his 'farm', and this is duly credited to the sheriff without a writ. The treasurer himself, however, or any one of the aforesaid who ordered this to be done, bears witness to it in the presence of the greater barons. In such a case there shall be written in the roll,[1] "For such-and-such needs of the Treasury such-and-such through so-and-so or so-and-so." Likewise, if a "royal fish",[2] a turbot[3] or a whale,[4] or another of the kind is caught, the amount expended by the sheriff on salting it and providing other things necessary is credited without a writ. Likewise the amount spent in cultivating and vintaging the vines on the demesne-lands of the king, and in providing vessels and other necessities, is credited without a writ on the oath of the sheriff; concerning which oath, how it is taken, whether on one occasion or more often, we will speak below.[5] These then are the things which at present occur to us as due to be credited to the sheriff by custom alone. Now let us proceed to treat of the other matters pertaining to the account of the principal 'farm' of the county.

VIII. In what order the sums expended in public works by a writ from the king of indeterminate amount are to be credited to the sheriff

It happens sometimes that the king gives orders to the sheriff through his writ to provide from his 'farm' what is necessary for the fortification of castles or for the construction of houses and the like, and this is to be done under the supervision of two or three men whose names are mentioned in the writ. At the end may be added a clause, brief but necessary to those drawing up the account, "and it shall be credited to thee at the Exchequer". When therefore the time has come for the sheriff to render his account, those chosen to be clerks of the works also attend. Whereupon, after they have taken an oath in public that to the best of their knowledge the sum named has

[1] Entries regarding the removal of the royal treasure are often met with in the Pipe Rolls.
[2] Originally any fish of unusual size, in practice limited to sturgeon and those of the whale genus.
[3] *rumbus.* [4] *cetus.* [5] See below, p. 566.

been expended on that work to the king's advantage, a royal writ shall be issued at the Exchequer under witness of the president and of another whom he shall name. In the writ shall be specified the amount to which they have borne witness and likewise the names of the clerks. Then, finally, it shall be credited to the sheriff. But if by means of this expenditure the king's business has been completed, both the first writ concerning the provision of the amount necessary, which was addressed to the sheriff, and this last writ issued at the Exchequer are put away in the marshal's box in respect of the accounts settled. But if any work still remains to be done, the sheriff shall retain the writ addressed to him until the work has been completed, in order that he may have authority to supply the amount required for its completion, but the other writ shall be shut up in the marshal's box as stated. Accordingly, when there is recorded in the annual roll, "To such a work one hundred pounds", there should subsequently be added, "by the king's writ and under the supervision of the following". For if there were no writ from the king containing the express amount and the names of the overseers, the entry on the roll reading "by the king's writ" might appear to be false.

D. I am so fully satisfied by this explanation that I willingly pass over points about which I had just now opened my mouth to inquire. For when the king's writ concerning the sum necessary for such-and-such a work has been delivered to the sheriff, and there is added, "And it will be credited to thee at the Exchequer", or this, "Provide from thy 'farm'"–which is of almost equal authority–it seems superfluous that he should be put to the trouble of getting another writ. But I did not then understand that the amount must be expressly stated in the writ itself, in order that it might thus correspond in form of words to the authoritative annual roll.

IX. That no one is acquitted from debt through a royal writun, less it states the amount, even though it may give the cause

M. Understand likewise that the business of the Exchequer is different from other business. For in many cases it may be said that "explicitness does harm, but generalities are harmless"; but here on the contrary "explicitness helps and generalities are a source of trouble". For example, if a man be in debt to the king for a hundred pounds, and delivers to the Exchequer a writ to the effect that he is quit of his debt, even though the words "the whole debt" are added and the writ explicitly mentions the occasion, if the amount is not stated he will not be acquitted, but for this reason his case will rightly be postponed until another summons has been issued. For it should properly have been written in the roll, "Pardoned by the king's writ to so-and-so one hundred pounds"; but because what has not been previously specified in the writ has not been actually cancelled, the debtor is put to much trouble to seek the means whereby he may secure quittance. Thus in these matters "generalities are a source of trouble".

D. With all respect to the president and his associates, it does not seem that the king's mandate has been altogether executed in this case. For a man whom the king has ordered to be acquitted, adding also the reason for which he was indebted to the king, is nevertheless not acquitted thereby.

M. Nay, rather, may regard be paid to the subtlety of thy over-conscientious mind in these matters. Thou shouldst indeed have known that to be ignorant of the law is no help to those who have most need of the law. He, therefore, who is in debt to the king, should diligently inquire by what means he may be freed therefrom, that is, in accordance with the established rule concerning such things. But if he has neglected to do so, let him lay it to the charge not of the president but of himself. For even the president is not permitted to change one *iota* of the writ delivered to him. Since then the debtor is not thereby acquitted, let him hasten to obtain what is necessary.

D. I perceive that these precautions are chiefly observed for this reason, that they be not contradictory to the writing in the roll. But now, proceed forthwith concerning other matters.

M. When therefore all the allowances have been set down which are either fixed by rule or are to be credited through the writs of the king or by custom of the Exchequer, then the account is left, as it were, uncompleted, and attention is turned to other debts. For the words, "And he is quit", or the alternative, "And he still owes", by which indeed the accounting is considered closed, may not be entered in the roll, until satisfaction has been given for everything contained in the summons. The reason for this procedure will be clear enough from what follows. After the account for "the body of the county", that is, for the principal 'farm'–which, as has been said, is left unfinished until the end–and after a small space has been left blank, there is set down the account of the old 'farm' of the county, that is to say, whatever had by any chance been left over from the previous year; but this shall only be done if the sheriff who was then in office has been removed. But if the same man continue in office for the present year, let him render satisfaction for the old 'farm' before beginning to account for the new.[1] In the beginning of the roll the words, "For the old ['farm']" will be carefully and distinctly inscribed, and afterwards, "For the new". For thou must know that the outgoing sheriff is to be summoned for the old 'farm' like any other debtor, not for his own particular share, but for the whole, because it is the 'farm', the payment of which ought not to be deferred. But for a debt of the old 'farm', for which a sheriff in office is held responsible, it is sufficient to issue a summons under this form of words, "Whatsoever thou owest for the old 'farm' and the new"; concerning which enough has been said above.

X. Concerning extinctions and usurpations,[2] or, as we more usually term them, 'escheats' and 'purprestures'

Moreover, after these entries, a space of about six lines being left blank, there follows the account in respect of extinctions and usurpations,[2] which are more commonly termed 'escheats' and 'purprestures'. In the middle of the line a heading in capital letters is made, "Concerning 'purprestures' and 'escheats'", but at the beginning of the line below is written, "The same sheriff renders account of the 'farm' of 'purprestures' and 'escheats', namely ten pounds from this man and twenty pounds from

[1] To prevent the sheriff from obtaining quittance for his new 'farm' before arrears on the old one have been paid.

[2] *De excidentibus et occupatis. Excidentia* is a classicism for *escaete*; *occupata*, used in this sense, is a term borrowed from Roman Law.

that"; and then successive entries, according as they have been previously set down in the roll of the itinerant justices, "Total, one hundred pounds". Then, at the end of the line where the total is put, there is written, "In the Treasury twenty pounds in so many tallies; and he owes four score pounds", or "He has paid them into the Treasury and is quit". But thou wilt learn the order of these entries better by ocular demonstration than by a verbal description, however ingenious.

D. What these 'escheats' and 'purprestures' are, and for what reason they flow into the Treasury, I cannot understand, unless thou explain it more fully.

M. It happens sometimes through the negligence of the sheriff or of his officials, and also through the prolongation of a time of war, that those dwelling near estates known as crown lands encroach on some portion of the latter and treat it as their own property. When therefore the itinerant justices, acting on the oath of lawful men,[1] have seized such lands, they are valued separately from the 'farm' of the county, and handed over to the sheriffs that they may answer for them separately; these we call 'purprestures' or encroachments. When such lands are seized, they are taken, as has been said, from those in possession, and thereupon fall to the Treasury. But if the man from whom the 'purpresture' is taken be the doer of the deed, then at the same time he shall be punished by a heavy fine, unless the king pardon him. If, however, he be not the doer of the deed but his heir, then the forfeiture of the estate alone is sufficient penalty. To be sure, this, like many other things, is a proof of the king's mercy, inasmuch as so heinous an offence on the part of the father is not visited upon the son, who, until the inquest was made, was enriched at the expense of the power of the State.

Next, 'escheats' is the term commonly used to describe property which reverts to the Treasury on the death of the king's tenant-in-chief for want of an heir.[2] Moreover, the accounts for these are drawn up at the same time as the 'purprestures' under one head; in such wise, however, that the names of the individual tenants are set down in order. But when the head of the family, whether knight or serjeant, holding of the king in chief, dies leaving children, of whom the first-born is a minor, then his revenue returns to the Treasury. In this case it is not called simply an 'escheat' but an 'escheat with heir'.[3] Hence, neither is the heir removed from the inheritance nor the inheritance from the heir, but, having been placed under royal wardship together with his inheritance, during his minority both he and the other children receive what is needful from their inheritance through the officials of the king. The residue, however, which issues therefrom, falls to the king's interest. The accounts for the latter, moreover, are rendered separately, because they are due to the Treasury not by perpetual right but by a temporary one. For when the heir, now a minor, shall have attained his majority[4] and shall know how to dispose of his property for himself and his family, he shall obtain from the king's bounty what is due to him by hereditary

[1] By the sworn inquest procedure, see Nos. 24, 26.

[2] For 'escheats', see below, No. 268. It is to be noted that the classification given in the following pages differs from that put forward by Glanville; the latter, however, seems to accord better with contemporary custom.

[3] The use of this term seems peculiar to the *Dialogue*, the usual one being *custodia* (wardship).

[4] In the case of a military tenant, on completing his twenty-first year, in that of a tenant by socage, on the completion of his fifteenth.

right; some freely, as it were by sole favour of the monarch, others on promise of a definite sum concerning which, when the account is rendered, it shall be stated in the annual roll: "So-and-so renders account for one hundred pounds as a 'relief'[1] for his father's lands. In the Treasury so much, and he owes so much." Moreover, no further account shall be entered in the annual roll, since thereafter it does not revert to the Treasury. Nevertheless, so long as it remains in the hand of the king it shall thus be entered in the annual roll: "Such-and-such a sheriff renders account for the 'farm' of such-and-such an 'honour'" (that is, if it be a barony).[2] "In the Treasury so much, and for the maintenance of the children of so-and-so, so much by writ of the king"; and this shall be drawn up there at the Exchequer according to custom, adding also "He owes so much", or "And he is quit". But if it be a minor holding, consisting of one, or two, or three manors it shall be stated as follows, "Such-and-such a sheriff" or "Such-a-one, *N.*"–the man to whom the king has entrusted the custody of that property–"renders account for the 'farm' of that land *N.* which belonged to so-and-so *N.*, and which the king now has in his possession", or "which is in the hand of the king, together with the heir. In the Treasury so much, and he owes so much", or "And he is quit". Notice, besides, that so long as that 'honour' or manor, together with the heir, shall remain in the hand of the king, all the alms and charitable bequests to the poor, which were instituted by former lords solely out of charity, shall be paid in full to those to whom they are due, and shall be credited to the custodian[3] at the Exchequer. But the liveries of servants, who were regarded as necessary to the lords for the discharge of certain offices and were appointed for that purpose, shall be paid at the king's discretion while he is in possession. Furthermore, when the inheritance has come into the heir's possession, he ought to follow in his father's footsteps, in such wise that, during the lifetime of those for whom these payments were instituted by his father, he may make due provision for them. Afterwards he may make use of their services or dispense with them at his pleasure.

D. Thou didst say, if I recollect aright, that if anyone holding in chief from the king should die and leave a minor as his heir, the latter on attaining his majority at length obtains from the king what is due to him, either freely, or else on the promise of a money-payment; also, thou dost term such payment a 'relief'. Say, then, whether a 'relief' ought to be exacted for the same amount from every estate held of the king in chief, or, if for a different sum, wherefore it is so.

M. It seems that I have armed thee to my own ruin: for by drawing conclusions from what has been already said, thou dost vex me with barbed questions. Know then that a different amount arises from the 'reliefs' due to the king according to the different status of the tenants. For some of them hold in chief from the king fiefs of the crown, namely greater and lesser baronies.[4] If then a father in possession of a fief of this kind die, leaving an heir already of full age, the latter shall give satisfaction for his lands, not according to a fixed amount, but according to the terms he can obtain from the king. But if the heir be a minor placed under wardship, he shall await his

[1] *relevium*, see Nos. 21, 268.

[2] The writer appears to equate the holder of a barony with the holder of an 'honour': for the true nature of an honour, see F. M. Stenton, *English Feudalism*, pp. 50–53, 97–99.

[3] The guardian of an estate held in wardship.

[4] *baronias scilicet maiores seu minores.*

majority, at which time he will obtain his paternal inheritance like an heir of full age, either freely, as has been stated,[1] or at the good pleasure of the king. But if anyone holding a knight's fee of the king should die–such fief not being a fief from the king but rather one held of some barony which has accidentally lapsed to the crown, such as a bishopric when the see is vacant–the heir of the deceased tenant, being of age, shall pay for a knight's fee a hundred shillings, for two, ten pounds and so forth, according to the number of knights the inheritance owed to the lord before it lapsed to the Treasury. If, however, there is left an heir who is a minor, the amount issuing from his inheritance shall flow into the Treasury by right of wardship during his minority, as stated above. If he be already of age at his father's death, he shall pay a hundred shillings for each knight's fee or proportionally less, that is to say, fifty shillings for half a knight's fee, and so forth. Nor should it be hidden from thee that one who is in wardship for several years, together with the fruits of his possession, will not be liable to pay a 'relief' when he comes of age.

D. In this respect the law judges in favour of the wards, and decrees what is agreeable to a good conscience.

M. That is so; but let us proceed with our undertaking.

There is also a third kind of 'escheat' which flows to the Treasury by perpetual right. When any tenant-in-chief of the king, conscious of having committed a crime, whether charged therewith or not, forsakes everything and seeks to save his life by flight; or having confessed or been convicted of the said charge, he is judged worthy to forfeit both his land and his life; then everything which belongs to him by right is immediately confiscated, and all his revenues are paid into the Exchequer by the sheriff by an annual, or rather perpetual right; also, the profits obtained from the sale of his movables go to the king. Likewise, if a man of any status whatsoever, be he villein or freeman of any lord whatsoever, moved by fear of the stricter law[2] which the king has ordained for felons, has fled from his dwelling,[3] and has neither presented himself for trial nor excused himself within the limits fixed and defined by law; or again if, as a result of the neighbourhood raising "the hue and cry" against him, he has been suspect and afterwards taken and convicted as guilty of the crime by the established law of the assize;[4] in such cases all his movables fall to the Treasury, but his immovables revert to his lords. The value of his movable goods, however, shall be handed over by the sheriff at the Exchequer and set down in the roll as follows, "Such-and-such a sheriff renders account for the chattels of fugitives and of those mutilated through the assize held in such-and-such a place, *N.* namely five (pounds) from this one, and ten (pounds) from that one", and so forth, for each man separately, the names and the amounts arising from the chattels of each being explicitly stated. Furthermore, at the end the sum-total shall be set down, and near the end of the line where the total is put shall be written, "In the Treasury forty pounds in so many tallies, and he owes ten pounds", or "And he is quit". These, brother, are the receipts mentioned above[5] which must be brought to the Exchequer and accounted for there,

[1] See above, p. 548.
[2] Assize of Northampton, an amended and stricter version of the Assize of Clarendon; see above, Nos. 24, 25.
[3] A case falling within the provisions of the Assize of Northampton, clause 13, see above, No. 25.
[4] *i.e.* by the sworn inquest procedure.
[5] See above, p. 532.

even though no summons has been previously issued. The same applies to treasure dug up from the earth or otherwise discovered. Similarly, when anyone in possession of an estate held in lay fee or any citizen has publicly practised usury and died intestate, or even if, while failing to make restitution to those whom he has defrauded, he is known to have made a will in respect of his ill-gotten gains, but has not yet distributed them, but has rather kept them in his own hands – because he is so intent on amassing money that the lust for possessions has not left him – in such a case his wealth and all his movables are immediately confiscated and handed over by the officials to the Exchequer without a summons. But the heir of the deceased may rejoice in the fact that he still retains his father's estate and his movables, which were wellnigh lost to him.

D. Arising from the previous remarks about usurers, a grave question strikes my mind which I should like, please, to see more fully dealt with. For thou hast said, "When anyone in possession of an estate held in lay fee or any citizen has publicly practised usury, etc." From these words it would appear that a certain distinction of persons can be made between offenders of this kind, and that there is one provision for clerks and another for laymen, though they are guilty of the same offence. Likewise, from the phrase "has publicly practised usury" it can be inferred that there are certain transactions of the kind which are 'not public', and I am altogether ignorant whether anyone addicted to such practices would be subject to the law concerning public usury.

M. In vain did I think to satisfy thee with brief and commonplace answers, when from such thou dost elicit a question the solution of which has hitherto eluded some of the most expert. I do not, however, agree with thy remark, "From thy words it would appear that the status of clerks and laymen is unequal, though they are equally guilty." For, as they differ in rank, so also in guilt, according to the proverb: "The higher the step, the greater the fall." To some also it would seem that they are unequal in good works and merit. For the laity not being constrained by the obligation of vows, seem to merit ampler indulgence, even as in wrongdoing those who are bound by a vow of religion the more grievously offend. But enough of these matters. On the contrary, from what has gone before, thou hast a complete answer to the first part of thy question. For inasmuch as a clerk practising usury forfeits the privilege of his order, he becomes liable to the same penalty as a layman who offends in this way, namely that at his death all his movables are due to the Treasury. Indeed, we have learnt from the legal experts that the royal power has no right against a clerk or Christian layman, who thus offends, while he is yet alive, for there remains time for repentance; but such a one is rather referred to an ecclesiastical court, there to be condemned according to the nature of his rank. Moreover, upon his death all his goods shall fall to the king, the Church having no claim upon them; unless, as has been stated, he has truly repented while yet alive and, having made a will, has entirely disposed of what he intended to bequeath as a legacy.

It remains now for us to explain what we call 'public usury' and what is 'not public', and then, whether those who offend in either are bound by the same law. We call it then 'public' or 'common usury' when, after the manner of the Jews, anyone is due by covenant to receive in the same kind more than he has lent, as, for example, a pound in return for a mark, or for a pound of silver two pence each week as interest[1] besides the principal. But that form of usury is 'not public', but equally to be condemned,[2] when anyone receives a manor or a church in return for a loan and, the principal remaining intact, appropriates to himself the profits thereof until the principal has been repaid. This kind of usury seems to be more venial on account of the labour and expense usually bestowed upon agriculture, but beyond a doubt it is sordid and rightly to be accounted as usury. But if the creditor, being avaricious and intent upon the ruin of his soul, has seen fit to have the matter so expressed in writing that it reads, "Be it known to all men that I, *N.*, owe *N.* one hundred marks of silver, and for these hundred marks I have pledged to him such-and-such a piece of land for ten pounds, until such time as I or my heir shall pay to him or his heir the aforesaid hundred marks"; and then, after the death of the creditor, the tenor of this infamous charter shall come to the notice of the king or his justiciar; first, the detestable practice of usury will be condemned, and the creditor, detected as a usurer by his charter shall be judged unworthy of his movables. If, however, the holder of the estate shall by some means obtain from the king the restitution of the property thus alienated from him, he shall be under obligation to the king for the whole of the principal, even if the creditor has been in possession thereof for two years or more. Nevertheless, the liberality of the king usually makes some allowance for the amount of the principal, chiefly on account of the gift of especial grace which he is considered bound to show to his liegemen by virtue of his superior status, and secondly, because by right of his regal authority he is about to take into his possession all the goods of that creditor or usurer who had grown rich to the grievous loss of a faithful vassal. There are also many other things which pertain individually to the Treasury but cannot be easily brought together under one head, because they are not fixed but occasional. The accounts of 'escheats' of this third kind, however, are set down not above, after the 'farm', but below, after all the pleas, and before the chattels of fugitives; so that by their actual position[3] they seem to pertain to the Treasury on account of the enormity of the offences.

D. I marvel at what thou hast said, for it does not seem possible to reconcile it with what has gone before. For since the lords of villeins are permitted, not only to transfer them, but also to dispose of them in any way whatsoever, as stated above,[4] and since they are justly deemed lords, not only of their chattels, but also of their bodies, it is a matter for surprise why the lord of the chattels and of the man, who has committed no offence against the law, should be deprived of his possession. For it would seem but just that the royal ordinance should punish an outrage in the person of the offender, but that the movables, together with the estates themselves, should be granted to the lords for their use.

M. What troubles thee troubles me also; but I think it superfluous to waste more time over these matters, since they are foreign to our undertaking. But in order to satisfy thee, know that this is so, solely on account of the king's assize.[5] Nor indeed

[1] The recognized rate of interest charged by the Jews.
[2] Already condemned by the council of Tours in 1163.
[3] An indication that the author's classification of 'escheats' is loose and purely arbitrary.
[4] See above, p. 525.
[5] Assize of Clarendon, clause 3; see above, No. 24.

is there anyone who would presume to act counter to a royal ordinance made in the interest of the public peace. But if the chattels of villeins condemned through the assize were to go to their lords–perchance because the burning thirst of human covetousness is to be found among them–some of the lords would, for the sake of a modicum of gain, contrive the death of their tenants, however innocent. For this reason the king himself, to whom also the general care of his subjects has been entrusted by God, has thus ordained, in order that by this means the guilty, rendering satisfaction to the law, should be punished in their own persons and that, their movables having been retained by him, they should not be exposed to their natural enemies, that is to say, their lords. Indeed, as we have already observed, the king's ordinance alone, issued under the compulsion of necessity and for the peace of the realm, is the chief answer to this question.

D. I perceive that this is not done without cause. Now please proceed. There remains indeed something which I could wish to be more fully dealt with. For thou hast said that the movables of fugitives and of those mutilated through the assize are delivered to the Exchequer without a summons and are entered in the annual roll in their place. Thou didst not say, however, what ought to be done with the chattels of robbers or thieves, namely whether they pertain to the king, or to whom they ought by right to go.

M. The situation of robbers, who are also thieves, is different from that of those who steal in secret. Again, there are two kinds, both of the latter and of the former, from each of which the chattels fall to different persons in a different way. Some robbers, indeed, like some thieves, are without the benefit of the law, outlaws, as we usually call them, some not. They become outlaws when, having been lawfully summoned, they do not appear, and are awaited and even sought for throughout the lawful and appointed terms, and yet they do not present themselves for trial. For this cause the chattels, and also the lives of such felons, are recognized as being in the hands of those who arrest them, nor can they by any right whatsoever pertain to the king. In the case, however, of robbers who have not yet sunk to this depth of wretchedness, their goods, when they are arrested, flow to the Treasury; but, in the case of thieves, they go to the sheriff in whose jurisdiction they have been caught and punished. But if the sheriff considers the case of a thief worthy of being referred to the king's court for judgment, none of the thief's possessions are due to him but everything to the king. If, however, anyone pursues the thief who has robbed him, and having caught him, brings him before the itinerant justice in the king's court,[1] or even before the county court,[2] and shall prove him guilty of theft in accordance with the decision of the law; then the stolen goods shall first be made good to the injured party out of the chattels of the thief, if they be sufficient for this purpose, following upon the swearing of an 'affidavit' or oath by the claimant at the pleasure of the justice of the lord king.[3] Afterwards, in addition, by the far-sighted institution of those zealous for peace, the claimant shall receive from the thief's goods as a recompense for his labour and expense a sum equal to what he had originally lost through the guile of

[1] The king's court held by the itinerant justice was a court of first instance.
[2] Because theft came within the sheriff's jurisdiction.
[3] The procedure known as "appeal of theft", see Pollock and Maitland, *op. cit.*, vol. II, pp. 158 *et seq.*

the thief. The prudent provision of this twofold restitution was not unjustly called by men of old *solta et persolta* or *prosolta*.[1] For first of all, restitution is made to him of what had been stolen, which for this cause is called *solta*. Next, what is added to defray labour and expense is termed *pro-* or *persolta*. When these payments have been made, the residue of the property shall go to the Treasury.

D. Certainly, these things seem necessary. But now, according to thy promise, please proceed to deal with the rents of woods.

M. I congratulate thee, since I perceive that thou hast borne in mind both the value of what has been said and the sequence of what is to come. It remains then for me to meet thy wishes according to my powers.

XI. Concerning the rents of woods and how they ought to be computed

After the account of 'purprestures' and 'escheats' there follows the account for the rents of woods, brief and succinct enough, under this form of words, "The same sheriff" or "Some other person *N*. renders account for twenty pounds for the rent of such-and-such a wood or forest in Northamptonshire. He has paid it into the Treasury and is quit." There are, however, some forests from which the tenth part of the fixed rents is paid to the mother-churches, as, for example, from Wiltshire and Hampshire to the church of Salisbury, and from Northamptonshire to the church of Lincoln. The reason for this payment, so I have heard, is as follows. Almost the whole or the greater part of what is paid for the forests comes from pleas and exactions. So then by the granting of tithes illicit profits seem to be to some extent redeemable. In such cases, however, the accounts are rendered in this manner: "So-and-so renders account for twenty pounds for the rent of such-and-such a forest. In the Treasury eighteen pounds"–and at the beginning of the next line is entered–"And in fixed tithes to such-and-such a church forty shillings." Then, at the end of the same line, a little apart from the other entry, is written, "And he is quit." Recollect also that it was once told thee that all debts, and likewise the payments made to the Treasury, are to be entered separately from the rest of the writing, so that the eye in conjunction with the mind, may more easily take them in, inasmuch as summonses are made out for what is due, and quittances for what has been already paid.

After careful computation of the principal 'farm', whether of the old or the new,[2] and likewise after the computation of 'purprestures', 'escheats' and wood-rents, all of which are paid regularly each year, as has been stated, there follows the account of profits from pleas and covenants, for which, after leaving a small space, a heading is made in the middle of the line to denote to which justices they belong.

XII. Concerning pleas and covenants; in what order the accounts for them are drawn up, when the amounts on demand are paid

By pleas we mean amercements incurred by offenders, but by covenants, voluntary payments. When therefore the demand for these is at hand, the summons is first delivered to the chancellor's clerk who presses the sheriff for each item in turn,

[1] *i.e.* paid and doubly paid.

[2] See above, p. 546.

saying: "Render from so-and-so ten pounds for such-and-such a cause." But if the amount demanded has been paid into the Treasury, it will be entered thus in the annual roll, "*N.* renders account for ten pounds for such-and-such a cause", and the whole sum will be set down in order, "He has paid into the Treasury, and he is quit." But if he is quit through the king's writ, provided, as we have said,[1] the amount is stated in the writ, the entry will read, "*N.* renders account for ten pounds", and the cause will be added. Then a little farther on in the same line, "In remission by the king's writ to the said *N.* ten pounds; and he is quit." But if he be summoned for a hundred [shillings], when nevertheless the amount of the debt entered in the annual roll is ten pounds, and he has paid the hundred [shillings] in cash, or has obtained a writ from the king for them, it will read, "*N.* renders account for ten pounds; in the Treasury a hundred shillings, and he owes a hundred shillings", or "Pardoned through the king's writ to the said *N.* a hundred shillings, and he owes a hundred shillings." Note also that in all accounts respecting pleas and covenants each debtor shall answer for himself, so that each may undertake the burden of debt in his own name, if he has not given satisfaction for it or, alternatively, obtained quittance if he has paid the whole of it, except in cases of the common assizes, Danegeld and murder-fines. For the sheriff renders account of these, and is himself set down in the roll, in respect of them, either as quit or as still in debt. But if the sheriff has been changed, his successor will nevertheless be summoned to answer for the same, and if he fails to meet them, he will be distrained through the 'farm' he is due to pay. For whoever succeeds to the burden of that office when the sheriff is changed, receives from his predecessor copies of the list of debts owing to the king in that county, in order that, when he has received the summons delivered to him, he may by this means know from whom the debts are to be collected. To the sheriff, therefore, is directed the general account, and to him alone pertains the distraint of individuals; and the sheriff, who was in office when the account was made, will be written down in this manner as either quit or still in debt.

D. I bear in mind what ought to be done when anyone summoned for debt brings a king's writ explicitly stating the required amount. But if he brings to the Exchequer a charter of the king in respect of quittance for things of the same kind, which may read thus, "I will therefore that he hold all these freely and quit of pleas and murder-fines and of such-and-such, and the like"; will he not be pardoned?

M. To be sure, he will be; but the entry will not read, "Pardoned by charter of the king", or "by privilege of this charter or that", but rather "by the king's writ". If, however, the charter is not specific, but contains this, "Let him possess the aforesaid freely and quit of all exactions and secular service",[2] he will nevertheless not be quit of his debts thereby, or entered as pardoned; for those who sit at the Exchequer are unwilling to annul a particular debt by a general acquittance.

D. This subtlety is pernicious enough; for he who is free from the sum of the parts deserves also to be acquitted from the parts of the whole.

M. What thou sayest is true, nor do I disagree. Nevertheless, I am telling what is

[1] See above, p. 533.

[2] *seculari servitio*; perhaps an indication that the author had chiefly in mind gifts in 'frankalmoign' to ecclesiastics.

actually done, not what perhaps ought to be done. When therefore satisfaction has been given for everything contained in the summons, either in cash or through writs of the king, the form of entry mentioned above should always be employed. When, however, anyone who has not paid the whole of the amount demanded of him, but only part of it, or even nothing, the reason why he has defaulted is at once to be inquired of the sheriff. If the latter shall answer that he has made diligent search for the chattels of the person in question and has been unable to find them, the treasurer will intervene, saying, "Take care, for thou shalt confirm the truth of this matter by taking a corporal oath to the effect that thou hast sought and could not find wherewith these demands might be satisfied." If to this the sheriff answer, "I am prepared to do so", the taking of the oath will be deferred until the account is completed, so that, having been once given, it may suffice for many similar cases. Much has already been said concerning this oath near the beginning,[1] and something yet remains to be said in its proper place.[2]

XIII. Concerning the different kinds of persons who are insolvent, in respect of whom the oath is offered by the sheriff, and under what form of words it may be given

Here again a distinction must first be made with regard to debts and debtors, in order that it may be clear to thee in which cases the swearing of an oath is permitted and in which cases not. For if a knight or other free man or a villein or any person of whatsoever status or sex is held bound to the king for any debt, which, however, must be the penalty for an offence and not a voluntary payment, the treasurer will be content with the proffered oath of the sheriff to be taken at the close of proceedings. Moreover, the man or woman, against whom the action has failed through poverty, will again be entered in the annual roll as a debtor for the same amount as in the previous one. The case is different if the debtor in question be a citizen or burgess, that is, if he be a citizen by birth, or has become subject of his own free will to the laws of his fellow-citizens through necessity. In such cases it is not enough for the sheriff, if any debtor has not made satisfaction for the required amount, to pay in for the movables alone or to proffer an oath that he has sought them and found none, in order thus to be quit at the Exchequer. He must also confiscate their houses and estates and any rents due from the city, and let them out to others, so that by this means the money due to the king may be raised. But if no one be found to undertake these obligations, inasmuch as men of the same condition mutually refrain from acting against each other, let the sheriff block up their houses and fasten them with bolts and cause their estates to be diligently cultivated. But if in the meantime they shall pay what is demanded, the property shall be restored to them unimpaired, as being the rightful owners, by the hand of the sheriff.

D. I cannot be too much surprised that, when the guilt is equal, "our law should more severely oppress this class of men".

M. The bulk of the possessions of those who have estates and live by agriculture, consists of flocks, cattle and crops, and of similar things which cannot easily escape the notice of their neighbours. But with those who engage in commerce, who are

[1] See above, p. 503. [2] See below p. 568.

sparing in their expenses and strive with all their strength and by every means to multiply their possessions, the acquisition of ready money is the prime consideration. For by this means commerce is the more easily carried on, and their gains can easily be deposited in safe and secret places. Whence it often happens that a rich man may be reputed poor because his hidden wealth is not suspected. For this reason then this law bears more hardly against them, for a superabundant source of wealth does not appear to be easily exhausted.

D. What a common assessment is, and who may answer for it and at what point, is to a great extent clear from the foregoing.[1] Now, please, explain fully about the aids or gifts of cities or boroughs; how the accounts for them are rendered and who are chiefly to be summoned or distrained in respect of them; for the manner of distraint is already plain from what has been said already.

M. I rejoice that thou art mindful of this, and thereby I confess thou dost encourage me the more. Know then that it is of great importance whether the gift or aid of a city is fixed by the justices at so much a head, according to the number of the citizens dwelling therein, or whether the citizens offer the justices an amount worthy of the monarch and it is accepted by them. For in these two cases the method of distraint is different. For if the gift has been fixed by the judges according to the number of individuals, and any one of them be insolvent, the aforesaid law concerning insolvent citizens is put into operation, namely that he be deprived of houses and rents until payment is made. But if the citizens have declared, "We will give a thousand [pounds] to the king", and this sum is considered worthy of acceptance, they themselves must see to it that the said amount is forthcoming at the appointed times. If, however, they begin to make excuses, alleging the poverty of some of those who were liable for part of this sum, then a careful inquiry is to be made, that is, through the sheriff's oath, as to whether, at the time the gift or aid was determined by the said citizens, the persons in question were obviously incapable of paying. If such is found to be the case, let them provide others from whom the previous sum may be raised, or else let what remains of the debt be apportioned among them. But if indeed, at the time the aid was determined, they were wealthy but, by the law of fortune, fickle by nature, they have now become in need, a delay is to be accorded them until, by the grace of God, they grow rich again.

D. I perceive that, while preserving moderation in all things, thou dost hold fast always to the king's interests.

M. Thou dost recollect what should be done in the case of citizens or burgesses who are insolvent. But if perchance a knight or other freeman, lapsing from the dignity of his rank–which God forbid–has proceeded to amass money through public merchandise or the basest form of profit-making, that is to say, through usury, and has not paid the amount required of him of his own free will, the sheriff will not be acquitted solely by an oath that he has found nothing. Indeed, when he has imparted this information to the president, the latter shall impose upon him strict orders that, for the amount demanded of him the defaulter shall find sureties for payment at the appointed term. But if he refuses to do so, all his revenues will be confiscated, since

[1] For the 'common assessment', see above, p. 520.

in this respect he may rightly be considered "like to those who increase their state as best they can".[1]

D. It is certainly fitting that a degenerate knight or other freeman, who renounces his rank for a base profit, should be punished beyond the measure of the common law for freemen. But now please explain what should be reckoned among the chattels of one in debt to the king, and whether the sum-total of everything should be taken away by the sheriff, until the amount required is raised; when, that is, the original debtor has not paid the sum of his own free will.

XIV. What chattels of debtors are to be sold, when they do not pay up themselves, and what order is to be observed in the sale

M. Thou dost plunge me into a sea of questions; God knows, I do not, where I shall emerge. Know then that here again a distinction of persons must necessarily be made, as will be clear from what follows. I would, nevertheless, that thou wouldst spare me in this matter and not compel me to put forward views displeasing to many.

D. So long as thou dost not stray from the path of the established law, thou wilt not incur the just reproach of the prudent. But if the law's decrees seem grievous to any man, let him be wroth with him who made the law, not with thee.

M. From the beginning I became indebted to thee through my undertaking. "Whence it is that I am held bound to obey thee in any petition, though unwilling." The chattels, then, belonging to debtors who do not pay demands made of them of their own free will, and which may lawfully be sold, are those goods which are movable and move themselves. Such are gold and silver, and vessels made therefrom, also precious stones, changes of raiment, and the like. Also both kinds of horses, namely those which have been broken in and those which are untamed, herds of oxen and flocks of sheep, and others of the same kind. The nature of produce also, and of some victuals is movable, so that they too may be freely sold, deducting only the necessary expenses of the debtor for victuals, in such wise that provision may be made for his bare needs, not for a surfeit, and nature be satisfied, not extravagance. Nor are these needs provided for the debtor alone, but also for his wife, his children and the household he maintained whilst living at his own expense.

D. Why sayest thou of *some* victuals?

M. Victuals prepared by them for daily use and suitable for consumption as they are, such as bread and drink, may on no account be sold. Only those victuals then, which, contrary to common usage, have been kept back for sale by the lords themselves, may lawfully be sold; such as salted meat, cheese, honey, wine and the like. Note also that if the insolvent debtor has once obtained the belt of knighthood, when the rest of his chattels have been sold, he shall none the less retain a horse, and that, not just any horse, but one of those in common use; lest having once attained the rank of knight, he should be compelled to go on foot. But if he be a knight of the kind who "delights in the glory of arms and takes pleasure in using them", and has earned the right to be reckoned a man of war, then all his bodily armour, together with the horses necessary for his profession, shall be wholly exempt from sale, so that, when

[1] Horace, *Epist.* I, i, 45.

need arises, he can be summoned to the service of the king and the realm, equipped with arms and horses.

"If, however, this man whom the law has partially favoured", having heard of the needs of the king or of the realm, shall lurk in hiding and absent himself, or shall not appear when summoned–provided, however, that he serve not at his own expense but at the king's–and if also he give no plausible excuse for his absence; then those in charge of the sale shall not spare these appurtenances but, resting content only with a single horse on account of his knightly rank, he shall live in subjection to the common law. Furthermore, the sheriff shall take care to warn his distraining officers to observe this order in respect of the things to be sold. First, the debtor's movables are sold; let them spare, however, as much as possible, the plough oxen by means of which agriculture is practised, lest being deprived thereof the debtor be still further reduced to want in the future. But if the sum required cannot be raised otherwise, the plough oxen are not to be spared. When therefore all the saleable things belonging to him personally have been put up for sale, and the debt is not yet made good, they may enter the lands of his villeins, and lawfully sell their chattels, observing always the aforesaid order and rule. For these are known to belong to the lord, as stated above.[1] This done, whether the required sum has been raised or not, our law orders the distraining officers to have respite, unless perchance 'scutage' be required from the lord. For if a tenant-in-chief, who is under obligation to the king for 'scutage', has not discharged it, not only his own chattels but also those of his knights and their villeins everywhere are sold, because the matter of 'scutages' in great part concerns his knights,[2] since they are due to the king only for the knights and by right of military service. Yet I myself, whose memory is not yet hoary, have seen how, for the individual debts of those who were defaulters, not only their own chattels but also those of their knights and villeins were lawfully sold. But the decree of the illustrious king has ordered this to be observed only in respect of 'scutage', due regard being paid to the sequence that first the debtor's goods, and next those of others are to be sold. But if the knights have paid their lord the 'scutage' due from their fiefs, and are willing to prove this by proffering a bond of security, the law forbids their chattels to be put up for sale in order to make good the dues demanded from their lords.

XV. That the sheriff must first take from the debtors of a defaulting debtor the sum due to the king

Likewise the sheriff is to be admonished to make diligent and careful search to the best of his ability whether there be anyone in his county in debt to the said debtor on account of money lent to him or deposited with him. If this is found to be the case, the sum demanded from his creditor, that is, the man bounden to the king for debt, shall be exacted from that debtor, and he shall be prevented by authority of the crown from being made answerable for it to his creditor.

[1] See above, p. 551.
[2] If a tenant-in-chief were unable to recover it from his sub-tenant, he might plead this as a valid excuse for non-payment of 'scutage'.

XVI. That the sheriff may seize what is demanded from the estates of a defaulter, even though he has in any way alienated them since the time he was held bound to the king for them

Likewise if a debtor has leased his estate or the rents thereof to another, since the time he became bound to the king, or has given it as a pledge for money, or even–which perhaps to thee will seem absurd–has transferred his rights of ownership[1] by sale; if means cannot otherwise be found to make restitution to the king, then, no matter who the person is or by what title he obtained possession, none the less what pertains to the king shall be taken from him, saving the proprietary rights of the lord who has recently entered into possession thereof with a just title. Unless perchance the said debtor has at the beginning of his own free will paid to the king the amount received for the estate, in which case the purchaser's right of possession will be secure. Moreover, the reason for this, although it may seem to thee somewhat perverse and operating too much in the king's favour, thou wilt manifestly approve as wholly just according to the law of the land. For whosoever is detected as having committed an offence against the king's majesty is condemned by the king in one of three ways, according to the nature of his offence. For petty offences he is sentenced to forfeit his entire movable goods; for more serious offences his immovable property, such as his estates and revenues, are confiscated, with the result that he is deprived of his inheritance. But if it is a question of major offences or of the greatest or most heinous crimes, he is sentenced to forfeit his life or members. Accordingly, when anyone is condemned at the king's pleasure in respect of his movables, sentence is passed upon him by the judges in these words: "This man is at the mercy of the king in respect of his money." This is tantamount to their having said "the whole of his wealth". For the indefinite propositions of laymen are to be regarded as equivalent, not to the particular purposes to which they may be more safely applied, but always to a universal signification. Because then the chattels of that estate, which the debtor afterwards alienated, had been adjudged at the mercy of the king, and the debtor had not made good the sum demanded, it would seem unjust that he should be allowed to alienate what was not his own to the loss of the Treasury.

XVII. That it is unlawful for the sheriff to accept money owing to himself from those who are insolvent, and what should be done if perchance he has accepted it

Likewise the sheriff is to be admonished in connexion with the oath demanded of him concerning insolvent debtors, or rather which he himself is deemed to have offered of his own free will in order to be delivered from the summons issued to him; namely that he do not accept in the meantime from any debtor who has not paid the king, anything that was justly owing to himself. For it is hardly likely that the sheriff could not find the means to pay the sum due to the king from among the chattels of a man who, willingly or unwillingly, has discharged his debt to the sheriff himself. If, however, before taking the oath, the sheriff has either himself recollected, or been reminded by another that he has received something from such persons, or even after taking the oath, provided the Exchequer is still in session for that day, that is to say, while his account is still fresh, and if he comes forward publicly and states

[1] *dominium*.

in apologetic tones that he had previously forgotten having received any such sum, and confirms it on oath, he shall be acquitted on payment of the amount received in the name of the debtor. But if, which God forbid, the fact shall have become known through someone else, after the sheriff has taken his oath and after the Exchequer has risen, then he shall not be acquitted simply on payment of what he has received, but, having been judged to lie at the mercy of the king on account of his offence, he shall suffer amercement.

Finally, let the sheriff be warned that, after receiving the summons, he shall make diligent inquiry throughout the neighbourhood whether the insolvent debtor has not grown rich, in the case of a man, by taking a wife, or in the case of a woman, by marrying someone richer, or either of them in some other way, to the extent that he or she may make good the demands made upon them. If this is found to be so, on account of the sheriff's oath the defaulter shall be compelled to pay. If, on the contrary, none of these things has been discovered, the sheriff can then with a clear conscience take an oath concerning these matters, and thus avert the threatened loss of his possessions.

XVIII. How a husband is to be called to account for a wife, or a wife for a husband, if he or she be insolvent

D. Should a husband be called to account for a wife, who was under obligation to the king and has already died, or ought a woman who survives her husband to be called to account for him?

M. Thou hast heard often enough that "He who is joined to a woman is made one body", but in such manner that he is her head.[1] He may therefore rightly be called to account for her, for "The wife hath not power of her own body, but the husband."[2] But if the husband has had children by her, to whom by the wife's right the inheritance is due, and, the wife being already dead, the money due to the king has not yet been paid; then the husband is to be called to account and distrained in the heir's name; but not otherwise. On the other hand, a woman, surviving her husband and having children and remaining in widowhood with them, is to be summoned and distrained by right of the children to whom the inheritance is due, in such wise, however, that her dowry is spared, because it is the price of her virginity.[3] If, however, she forsakes her children, and marries a second husband, the lawful heir is to be summoned for his father's debt. Nevertheless, if a woman has committed an offence and is held bound to the king for it, and, her former husband being dead without children, she transfers herself and her inheritance to another, her debt is to be required from her second husband. This then is the answer to thy question, and in this manner a husband is to be summoned on account of his wife, and a wife on account of her husband. Moreover, thou mayest be assured that the lawful heir, who succeeds to a debtor, is always to be called to account for him, to the intent that he may accept the liabilities as well as the assets. The villein and the man who dies without inheritance, after their chattels have been sold, are alone freed from debt by "death's last

[1] Cf. I Corinthians vi. 16; Ephesians v. 23. [2] I Corinthians vii. 4.

[3] *premium pudoris est*: the woman is to be summoned as representing the infant child of the debtor, even though she may not occupy the legal position of guardian of the minor or of his inheritance.

throw". Such debts, however, are not cancelled in the annual roll, wherein debts are normally entered, except through the king's writ, that is, when this course has been recommended to the king by the treasurer on the ground that it is useless to enter them in the roll, since no agreement could possibly secure payment of the money due for them.

XIX. That there is not the same method of distraint for the barons of the king as for others in respect of amercements

In this connexion thou shouldst know that, in reclaiming debts due to the king and in distraint of debtors, the conditions do not apply equally to the barons of the king and to others who are indiscriminately punished for their offences by fines to the king. Concerning those, then, who hold nothing of the king in chief the above-mentioned rule is observed. But if one holding a barony of the king, after receiving a summons, shall in his own person, or by the hand of his steward, who is commonly called the 'seneschal', give a pledge to the sheriff under this form of words, namely that on the day his account is due, he will give security to the barons of the Exchequer for this sum and for this summons; then the sheriff may rest content.

XX. What is to be done when the steward, who has pledged himself to render satisfaction, does not appear

If, however, after being summoned on the day of the account by the voice of the crier, the lord neither comes nor renders satisfaction in person or through another, the sheriff will be adjudged to have done his duty. Nevertheless, after the case has been carefully noted down by itself in the Exchequer rolls at the instance of the treasurer as a matter of importance, it will be reserved for the end of the session, to the intent that, after consideration has been given to it, the offender may then be more severely punished. But if, after the sheriff's account has been completed, the offender shall come and render satisfaction, he may be acquitted by the favour of those in session and the indulgence of the law. It is indeed necessary that the sheriff should receive his oath in the county court in full view of all men; because, if perchance the taker of the oath should afterwards try to hedge and deny that he has taken it, the record of the county will suffice for the whole burden of proof against him. If, however, the sheriff shall admit that the oath was made to him on some other occasion, he will be deemed to have taken no action. The sum demanded will thereupon be straightway taken from his 'farm', in order that he may comply with the summons which runs in this respect, "or they shall be taken from thy 'farm'".

XXI. What is to be done in the case of a knight who comes but does not give satisfaction; and what in the case of one who is not a knight

If, however, one who does not deny that he gave an oath comes on the appointed day but does not render satisfaction, he will, if he is a lord, be detained at the Exchequer so long as it is in session; having taken an oath to the marshal, as narrated above,[1] to the effect that he will not quit the suburbs[2] of the town without permission from the

[1] See above, p. 503. [2] *a leugata ville.*

barons. But after the dissolution of the Exchequer of that term, if he has not yet given satisfaction, he will be lodged in a safe place under liberal surveillance,[1] until such time as the king himself, if he be present, or the president, together with the others in session, may decide what is to be done with a man, who has admitted that he promised on oath to render satisfaction, but has in no wise done so. But if his knight or his steward shall come, but shall not make satisfaction, he will be arrested for breaking his oath and handed over to the custody of the marshal, as one who deserves to be bound and cast into prison after the dissolution of the Exchequer, whether he be a knight or no. A knight, however, who fails to make satisfaction for his own debt, after he has pledged his word to do so, will be kept, after the Exchequer has risen, under liberal surveillance,[1] not in a prison cell, but within the precincts of the prison buildings, upon giving in person an oath that he will not depart from thence without permission from the king or the president. For the illustrious king, whose renown is worthy of remembrance, has ordained that any man who enjoys the dignity of knighthood may not be sent to prison for his own debt, when he is accounted a pauper both by the sheriff and his neighbours, but he will be kept apart under liberal surveillance[1] within the precincts of the prison building. But, on the contrary, whosoever by order of his lord[2] has pledged himself to the sheriff in the manner aforesaid, and has come but has not discharged his debt; the law has decreed that such a one, be he knight or no, shall be seized and cast into prison when the Exchequer rises. And since any baron[3] is free to pledge the word of his official for a debt required from himself, so that he may in the meantime be delivered from the attentions of the sheriff and arrange his affairs more conveniently; lest the authority of the royal mandate should thus in great measure be evaded, it has been decreed that on the arrest of one who, by failing to make good the debt, has brought judgment upon himself as being guilty of breaking his pledged word, the sheriff shall straightway direct his officers to survey the estates of the principal lord,[3] and to sell his chattels as best they can, and to produce the sum required at the Exchequer of that term. Finally, the person arrested for breaking faith shall pay a fine according to his means, and shall not be permitted, even though the lord order it, to take any further oath concerning that debt.

XXII. How a lord is to be punished, who has wilfully exposed a knight in order that he himself may in the meantime remain free

Furthermore, lest the principal lord may presume upon this with impunity, if he should by chance again be summoned for that debt, he shall not obtain the benefit of a respite through the oath of a substitute, but solely through his own. There are, however, some who believe that he may by no means obtain from the sheriff a respite in respect of his debt until the Exchequer meets, even through his own oath. This respite indeed is considered a great benefit by those in debt to the Treasury, for they can in the meantime dispose more favourably of their possessions and make the necessary preparations for a payment deferred for some while. But these objectors

[1] *sub libera custodia*; see above, p. 538, n.

[2] The distinction drawn here is between a knight summoned as a tenant-in-chief for his own debt, and a steward summoned for the debt of his lord.

[3] *i.e.* the tenant-in-chief.

assert rather that, upon receipt of the summons, it is lawful for the sheriff to lay hands immediately upon their chattels, in accordance with the common law for ordinary debtors. I confess that I do not altogether disagree with them, provided, however, it appears probable from the evidence of many witnesses that the lord contrived to expose his knight to such hazards, in order that by this means he himself might in the meantime go free. Moreover, the most convincing proof to be brought against a lord in such a case is, when he is judged both by the sheriff and his neighbours to be wealthy and abounding in possessions, and well able to pay.

D. It is in truth only fitting that one who has abused the favour accorded to him to the detriment of him who granted it, should forfeit the same.

M. In our previous discourse,[1] to some extent a distinction was drawn further between the chattels which are to be sold and those which are not, and likewise between the persons to whom discretion is to be granted and those to whom it may not; that is, in the case where debtors who are subject to the king for amercement are insolvent. It remains for me to show what ought to be done concerning voluntary payments, when they also remain unpaid.

XXIII. What is to be done with those who make voluntary offerings when they also do not pay

Thou shouldst know then concerning voluntary payments to the king, that some are offered for an immediate benefit, some in expectation of future benefits. We term it payment for an immediate benefit, when it is accepted by the king, and he who offers it receives something from the king in return for it, as, for example, when anyone in return for some privilege, for a manor or a farm, or for the wardship of a minor, to be enjoyed until he comes of age, or for anything else which may appear to redound to his advantage or honour; when such a one offers the king of his own accord a hundred pounds or a hundred marks, and with the king's consent after the offering, obtains forthwith the desired concession. Concerning those, therefore, who bind themselves of their own free will, and who, once the bargain with the monarch has been made, enter into possession, our law decrees that, so long as they discharge their obligations,[2] they may use and enjoy the benefits bestowed upon them. But if, after being summoned concerning the debt due to the king, they shall cease from making payment, let them forthwith be deprived of their gains; provided, however, that if, while the Exchequer remains in session, they shall give satisfaction for the same, what has been taken from them may be restored wholly unimpaired. Note also that any person, of whatsoever rank or sex, will always be subject to this rule in respect of voluntary payments, namely tha the shall make good the summons or forfeit the benefit conferred upon him; unless the king himself, out of regard for a service rendered or for the debtor's poverty, shall grant him an indulgence beyond the terms of the common law. So it is when, in respect of a large sum offered at any Exchequer, the king agrees to pay some part of the debt himself and notifies the barons of this through his writ.[3]

[1] See above, pp. 557, 558.

[2] Payment was customarily made in instalments, though occasionally by an annual fixed sum.

[3] The procedure known as 'attermination'.

On the other hand, offerings are said to be made 'in expectation', when anyone, for the sake of obtaining justice in respect of some farm or revenue, offers a certain sum to the king, not, however, for the primary purpose of getting justice done–lest thou wax hot with passion and declare that justice in this case is venal–but that it be done without delay. Nevertheless, thou shouldst know that not everything thus offered to the monarch is accepted by him, even though it may seem to you to exceed due measure. For to some he shows the fullness of justice freely, out of regard for a service rendered or solely out of charity; but to others, by the law of human circumstance, he will not yield either for love or money, while in the meantime the rights of those who are known to be in possession are standing in the way. Or perchance the personal merits of those who make such requests by no means warrant this, because they are accused of having committed some offence, either against the realm or against the king in person. Moreover, concerning such persons the illustrious king has thus ordained that before their rights are granted, that is to say, before they have obtained it by a verdict or, after the case has been decided wholly against them and they have abandoned all hope, they shall pay nothing in the nature of offerings, but it shall suffice for the sheriff to reply concerning such persons: "They have not yet had justice done." Nevertheless, let the sheriff take steps lest it befall that, through the debtor's own fault, his case is not brought up for judgment, that is, if he neglects to put himself on trial, in order that by this artifice the king may be defrauded of the money promised him. For where this has been discovered, the subterfuge will not avail him, but he shall be distrained in all things, just as if he had obtained a favourable verdict. Furthermore, it is a sign of wilful procrastination on his part when he holds back the king's writ and does not make use of it. Nevertheless, through the compassion of the monarch, it is customary to deal more leniently[1] with those who default after promising a money payment, lest, having been frustrated in their hopes and deprived also of their possessions without having gained any advantage, they be consumed by a double misfortune.

XXIV. As to 'reliefs' not paid voluntarily

There are likewise sums of a third kind received, which seem not altogether rightly to be reckoned among voluntary payments,[2] but at the Exchequer are rather termed 'Fines'. On the death of one holding a barony[3] in chief of the king and leaving an heir, the said heir engages with the king for what amount he can, in order to obtain entry into his paternal rights; this fine we commonly call a 'relief'.[4] If it be a barony, the amount of the 'relief' is determined by the king at will. But if it be a question of an 'escheat',[5] which has fallen into the hands of the king through lack of an heir or otherwise, the heir shall pay to the king in the name of a 'relief' only the amount he would have paid to his lord, that is, a hundred shillings. There are, however, some who believe that those under obligation to the king for 'reliefs', who do not pay when summoned, are subject to the rules respecting free-will offerings, that is to say, unless they pay, they will be deprived of the benefits acquired. But it accords more

[1] The practice known as 'abatement'.
[2] Because, as one of the incidents of feudal tenure, the 'relief' is bound by the customary feudal law.
[3] See above, pp. 548, 549. [4] See above, p. 548. [5] See above, pp. 514, 515.

with the truth to say that the procedure in cases of 'relief' is the same as that for amercements. For the fact that the inheritance is due to the sons by right of succession seems to exclude them from the rule concerning voluntary payments.

XXV. What is to be done concerning the offering of birds, and at what time a summons should be issued for them

Again it sometimes happens that for some reason or other there are promised to the king 'royal birds', namely, hawks and falcons. If he who makes such a promise specifically states "a hawk of the present year" or "a moulted one", and shall also expressly mention the place of origin, saying, "I will give an Irish hawk, a Spanish or a Norwegian", he must make good his promise. But if neither he who promises, nor he to whom it is promised, shall specify, it shall be at the discretion of the donor, whether he shall pay a moulted bird or not. If, however, the bird be judged sound and whole by the royal falconers, it will be accepted, no matter where it was hatched. Further, if, having been summoned to the Exchequer, the donor shall bring thither one worthy of acceptance, and there be no one there at the time to receive it, he is not bound to deliver any other bird than the one he has chosen, namely, whether moulted or one with this year's plumage, even though the summons be deferred for a year or two or more. But if after summons he have in some way contrived that payment be deferred, he shall pay one that has moulted, according to the number of years for which the delay has been granted him. Furthermore, concerning these birds, no summons is issued against the Easter term, because they are rarely used in summer. For at that time they are carefully guarded, being shut up in mews, in order that, after their old feathers have moulted, the splendour of their plumage may return and their youth be renewed like the eagle's. To be sure, those due to the king are summoned against the Michaelmas term, to the intent that with the approach of winter they may be made fit for the king's service. Finally, in the distraint of those who of their own accord make such a promise, but do not redeem it, the aforesaid rule concerning voluntary offerings shall be observed.

XXVI. Concerning the queen's gold

Besides this, those who bind themselves to the king of their own free will to pay ready money, should know that they are in like manner bound to the queen, even though it has not been expressly stated. For although it be not explicit, nevertheless it is implied in the promise; so that one who has promised one hundred or two hundred marks to the king, is in like manner under obligation to the queen to the extent of one mark of gold for a hundred marks of silver promised to the king, two marks for two hundred, and so forth. Moreover, in collecting them the sheriff will in all things employ the same rule which he used in the case of debts owing to the king, not, however, before, but after the latter have been collected. Accordingly, when summonses are issued concerning debts due to the king, a clerk of the queen is present, appointed for this purpose, and he inserts in the summons: "From so-and-so thou shalt take a hundred marks for such-and-such a cause, and one mark of gold for the needs of the queen." Furthermore, the amounts called for are received separately at the Exchequer by her officials appointed for this purpose. Know also that even though the king should renounce the half or the whole of the sum promised to him, or even delay sending a summons for it, nevertheless, in those matters which pertain to the queen, it shall be done in all things according to her pleasure. Thus, if she be unwilling, what is due to her may neither be remitted nor postponed, but the amount in the summons shall be paid, and those who do not pay may be compelled to do so in the manner aforesaid.

D. Is anything due to the queen from sums of under one hundred marks promised to the king?

M. To some it seems right that it should hold good for an amount not less than ten marks, so much so that he who has promised ten to the king should be under obligation to the queen for one ounce of gold. Others say "No", but only on a hundred or more promised in the beginning. Concerning these matters, then, for the present forbear with moderation, because, the question being not decided, the answer is in suspense. To be sure, on the queen's part litigation concerning this is being carried on against debtors, and the case is still *sub judice*.[1] Further, from the amercements of Jews and the redemption fees paid by moneyers,[2] the queen should have her portion in accordance with the above-mentioned procedure, just as has been stated in the case of free-will offerings.

D. In the case of pecuniary fines and voluntary offerings, are both clerks and laymen coerced by the same law without distinction?

M. In voluntary offerings the same law is applicable to all, namely that whether the defaulter be clerk or layman, he shall forgo his advantage until he has made good his debt. The same rule is applied also in the case of all other debts due to the king from clerks by any covenant, namely when they have omitted to claim the privilege of their order and of free possession.[3] In the case of those who, on the contrary, do make this claim, please ascertain what ought to be done from learned and God-fearing laymen; for at present I pass over these things on purpose, lest I be said to have dictated my own rules and more lenient laws to men of my profession.

D. Thou hast said, if I recollect aright, that baronies and manors frequently fall into the king's hands. I wish, therefore, thou wouldst please explain in what manner the revenue from 'escheats' flows into the Treasury; whether in one way or in different ways.

XXVII. That 'farms' are to be accounted for in one way and wardships in another, and that the oath is to be given under a different form of words

M. When a barony or other great fief falls into the hands of the king, by his command or that of the president, discreet men of both orders[4] are dispatched thither. These men, traversing the different areas, bring the revenues of the same to a total,

[1] "*Adhuc sub judice lis est*", Horace, *Ars Poetica*, 78.

[2] *de redemptione monetariorum*; the payment made by a moneyer or minter of coins on obtaining office by the death of a previous holder, or consequent upon a change of coinage involving the manufacture of new dies.

[3] *sue dignitatis et libere possessionis privilegium*; lands held in 'free alms' by clerics were customarily regarded as free from amercements.

[4] *utriusque ordinis viri*; *i.e.* both clerks and laymen.

and arrange that the sheriff or some other person shall be held responsible for it at the Exchequer. When therefore the individual appointed for this purpose accounts satisfactorily for this amount in coin or writs or tallies, and later testifies that it is a true account, he deserves to be acquitted. Moreover, it shall be written thus in the annual roll concerning it: "So-and-so renders account for the 'farm' of such-and-such an 'honour'. In the Treasury so much; and he is quit"; or "And he owes". But when the king has entrusted the custody of his 'escheat' to someone in good faith, namely that the latter shall pay into the Exchequer the revenues thereof; then, after the reckoning has been made, the oath shall not be given under the aforesaid form of words, but rather to the effect that he has paid into the Exchequer to the best of his knowledge as much as he received from it in coin or any other things whatsoever; except only such victuals as have been bestowed upon him, without his having procured them under the name of presents.

D. Does such a custodian then obtain the necessities of life from these revenues?

M. Although it is written: "Thou shalt not muzzle the mouth of the ox when he treadeth out the corn",[1] nevertheless, except by express command of the king, he will receive nothing from them. For whoever he be, he shall serve the king in these matters at his own expense. Furthermore, concerning such a one it shall thus be entered in the annual roll: "So-and-so renders account for the income of such-and-such an honour on his affirmation."

When therefore[2] all the aforesaid dues, whether fixed or occasional, have been duly accounted for, and the separate items have in due sequence been set down in writing in the official roll, all those who have seats there are called together for the completion of the account of the principal 'farm', which is entered at the head of the roll and completed in the following order. The 'farm' paid for the current term by the sheriff, for which an 'assay'[3] has been made, is first distributed by the calculator into numbered piles and placed in the spaces marked by the stripes. Next, after allowance has been made for the process of combustion, as related above,[4] the coins are 'blanched', and the little tally of combustion added to them, although it is not being reckoned to the sheriff. The sum remaining over is then inscribed on a tally. Likewise, the amount paid at the Easter term and 'blanched' is inscribed on the same tally. Similarly, the amount of combustion for that term is joined together with the combustion of the final term, in order that there may be one tally for both payments and in like manner one tally of combustion. This done, the treasurer brings forth the exactory roll, which we mentioned above,[5] and causes the total due from that county to be arranged above in piles and in order. From this then is first deducted the amount paid into the Treasury and 'blanched', and next the sum the king has bestowed 'blanched' upon anyone out of the 'farm' of the county. After this again, the amount of the other payments made through the king's writ or otherwise is arranged in piles, and these are 'blanched' by the deduction of twelve pence from each pound, just as that paid into the Treasury is 'blanched' by combustion. Then the expenses set out

[1] Deuteronomy xxv. 4.

[2] At this point the author resumes his exposition of the procedure of computation at the Exchequer interrupted by the long series of digressions on the sums accruing from amercements, escheats, wardships, etc.

[3] See above, pp. 513–515. [4] See above, p. 514.

[5] See above, p. 531.

below are deducted from the total above, and if the sheriff has fully earned his quittance, at the end of this same account there is written in clear letters, "And he is quit", or else below at the beginning of the lower line, "And he owes". Then finally, the account having been completed, the total of the payments made to the Treasury is set down in the place where we said long since[1] "In the Treasury" was written, and which had been up till then left blank for this purpose, lest perchance the scribe might be obliged to erase an entry. This, especially with regard to numbers and names and accounts, is, as we said long ago,[2] to be avoided.

XXVIII. That an oath as to the truth of an account, once given by the sheriff, suffices once and for all

The account for the principal 'farm' of the county[3] having been completed in the manner narrated above, the oath of the sheriff is received by the marshal once for all under the form described above,[4] and after being thus acquitted he is dismissed. There have been some, however, who believed that a separate oath should be given by the sheriff for each separate item needing confirmation, that is, he should pledge his faith as often as he made an assertion which could only be confirmed by his oath. But this seemed to men learned and skilled in the divine law[5] a pernicious subtlety indeed, because once he had given his oath, he had upon his conscience rendered a lawful account for everything. For this reason, after a while this opinion, together with its author, came deservedly under condemnation, and they rest content with one oath, that is a pledge once given, because they are one in the confession of one Faith.

D. I perceive by thy already lagging pen that the end of our discussion speedily draws nigh. But though the shades of approaching night and the extended labour of a protracted undertaking summon us elsewhere and compel us to take breath awhile, nevertheless I would desire thee, if it can be done, to strengthen the mind of thy pupil, which up till now has been in suspense and wavering at thy words, by showing how it is–as I recollect thou didst say at the beginning[6]–that the whole description of the Exchequer is a sort of inner sanctuary of sacred mysteries which are to be revealed when the books of all are opened and the gates shut.

M. What thou dost ask is a great matter and one needing further investigation, nor by my undertaking did I become thy debtor to the extent of expounding these things. For the present, then, I pass over them, reserving them for the discussion of another day. I fear indeed that if I were to impose a new burden upon one already charged with so many, thou wouldst succumb under the weight. Likewise, if I were to add the study of a new subject to what has already been said and should be committed to memory, I might drive thee to hate both. Be content therefore with what has already been said and which thou hast elicited from me. For herein thou hast, as much as my feeble memory allows, an exposition, as it were from first principles, of whatsoever seemed most weighty to thee in respect of the science of the Exchequer. But as to

[1] See above, p. 508.
[2] See above, p. 509.
[3] *de corpore comitatus*; see above, p. 509.
[4] See above, p. 555.
[5] Decision of points connected with the taking of oaths came within the province of the Canon Law.
[6] See above, p. 506.

explaining the various details which in course of time must necessarily come to light, for that, neither one man's strength nor perhaps even his lifetime would suffice. For from diverse and unusual cases either no system at all can be devised, or one hitherto unknown; whence it might happen that I should probably be exposed to the tongues of slanderous critics, while perchance with the passage of time many doubtful points may arise and questions hitherto unheard of be propounded. And when the critics shall find nothing here concerning these or similar points, they may begin to mock at me, saying: "This man began to build and was not able, or knew not how to finish."[1] Nor do I wholly disagree with them. I have followed myself, indeed, the worst of masters. Nevertheless, at thy behest I have done what I could without a guide and without a pattern. For I have laid my axe to a wild and virgin forest and hewn from it timber for a king's edifice worthy to be shaped by the tools of a more experienced craftsman. When, therefore, from these materials there shall arise the structure of a regal palace, may he who laid the foundations merit the first, if not the chief thanks. Farewell, illustrious king.

* * *

(*d*) SELECT PASSAGES FROM THE PIPE ROLLS

The Pipe Rolls record the accounts made up each year in the Upper Exchequer between the king and his sheriffs. Certain other accounts and accountants are mentioned in them, but they are subordinate, and the chief matters described in respect of each shire in the Pipe Rolls concern on the one hand the king, and on the other hand the sheriffs of the shire.

The Pipe Roll was always made up at Michaelmas when the sheriffs were obliged to attend at the Upper Exchequer for the purpose. Each Pipe Roll thus bears the date of the regnal year in which a particular Michaelmas fell, and the accounts it contains are those of the twelve months immediately preceding that Michaelmas.

It is not certain when the Pipe Rolls began to be compiled regularly: they were, however, an essential part of the practice of the royal Exchequer. The earliest surviving Pipe Roll is that for 31 Henry I. After that there is a gap in the surviving texts, but the series recommences with 2 Henry II, and thereafter continues without interruption to the end of the reign and beyond.

Physically a Pipe Roll consists of a number of membranes each of which is made up of two pieces of sheepskin sewn together and inscribed on both sides. Each membrane thus composed was termed a 'pipe', and each 'pipe' was joined to its fellows by a fastening at its head. A Pipe Roll therefore is not a roll in the sense that it consists of a number of membranes sewn continuously end to end: it is a roll in the sense that it consists of a number of membranes fastened together at their tops and then rolled up.

A Pipe Roll, being primarily concerned with the accounts of the sheriffs, opens properly, in respect of each shire, with an account of the sheriff's 'farm' of that shire. The sheriff 'farmed' the shire in the sense that, being responsible for the royal revenue

[1] Luke, xiv. 30.

therefrom, he did not account separately for all its items, but paid in respect of all normal contributions a lump sum or composition. The account of the 'farm' occupies the first section of the Pipe Roll for any shire, but the manner in which this account is set out needs to be carefully noted if the information there given is to be read aright. The amount of the 'farm' is *not* stated. Instead there will be found, first a statement as to the amount which the sheriff has actually paid into the Treasury or Lower Exchequer, and secondly a statement of the disbursements and allowances he has made on the authority of the king. If the total of all these items adds up to the sum for which he 'farms' the shire, then he will be recorded as being "quit" (see below, pp. 572, 576, 578). If he still has some money in hand, this sum will be recorded at the close of this section of the roll after the words "and he owes" (see below, p. 572). If he has overpaid on the year's working, the words "he has a surplus" will be entered.

The sheriff made his payments in cash, not in the Upper Exchequer where the account was balanced, but in the Lower Exchequer or Treasury to which he was called for this purpose, not only at Michaelmas, but also at Easter. A Pipe Roll will thus record payments made both at Michaelmas and at the previous Easter. If the sheriff paid cash at the Treasury, this might be done in three ways: in 'blanched' money (see below, p. 572); in money reckoned by weight; or in money reckoned, as at present, *numero* or 'by tale'. 'Blanched' money was money of standard weight and fineness, and the methods of testing it are described fully in the *Dialogue of the Exchequer* (see above, pp. 513-515).

For money payments made by the sheriff at Easter he obtained specific receipts in the form of 'tallies'. A tally was a stick of wood notched to represent the amount paid and then split longitudinally. One part was given to the sheriff, the other was kept in the Exchequer. When the account was taken at Michaelmas, the sheriff was required to produce his tallies, and these were compared with their counterparts in the Exchequer.

It will be noted that the disbursements of the sheriff, recorded in connexion with his 'farm', mainly concerned such items as alms, tithes, liveries and "lands granted out"–that is to say, lands which had once belonged to the royal demesne but which had since passed into private possession. Moreover, most of these allowances are described (see pp. 572, 575, 578) as 'fixed', that is to say, they were in the nature of standing orders, carried on from year to year. A comparison between the openings of the Pipe Rolls for Staffordshire in 1186 and 1187 (see pp. 575, 578) will illustrate this point, and the difference in the initial cash payment noted in the two cases is to be explained by the variation in the amount of the disbursements recorded as having been authorized from the unrecorded total of the 'farm'.

The sheriff's account at Michaelmas (which is the subject of the Pipe Roll) could thus be met in four ways: (i) by producing cash; (ii) by producing tallies in respect of the payments made to the Treasury at the previous Easter; (iii) by securing an admission (based on the record of a previous roll) that a deduction from the 'farm' was a 'settled' arrangement; or (iv) by producing the king's writ authorizing a special payment to be made on the king's behalf. All these methods are recorded in the extracts from the rolls printed below.

The account of the sheriff's 'farm' was the most important item in the Pipe Roll, and it therefore naturally comes first. But it occupies only a small section of the roll. It is followed in each shire by a record of particular items of account, which are recorded separately as not being included in the 'farm'. Such are the 'purprestures' and 'escheats'. 'Purprestures' were rents charged for encroachments on the royal demesne. 'Escheats' (on which see above, pp. 547, 548) include lands and goods of tenants-in-chief who leave no heir, and the possessions of those who for one reason or another, criminal or otherwise, have forfeited their property. In this second section of the roll will also be found accounts of the debts owing to the king, including fines which have been imposed in his court. Sometimes it will be seen that the sheriff has been able to collect these debts in full; sometimes only a part has been collected; on occasion the debtor has fled to another county and the duty of collection is therefore passed on to another sheriff (see p. 577).

This long section of the roll stretches from the end of the account of the sheriff's 'farm' to the heading "New pleas and new agreements". It is carried on from year to year until the payments are finally discharged, so that a debt here recorded may have been originally incurred many years before. A comparison between the two Staffordshire records printed below will reveal many debts in respect of which the sheriff had only partially succeeded in obtaining payment.

Under the heading "New pleas and new agreements" the account is given of special transactions relating to the year just completed. These, like the preceding items, are of a miscellaneous character. Among them will be noted, for instance, the quasi-voluntary payments made in order to obtain the benefits of royal justice, or to appease the king's anger or to obtain his favour. Here also will be found the murder-fines imposed upon hundreds in which a murderer has escaped detection.

Finally in the Pipe Roll will be recorded special levies of a larger and more important character, which it has been the business of the sheriff to collect. A levy of Danegeld (see below, p. 574) may be taken as an example of this, or a general tallage (see below, p. 581) or the 'scutage' taken in connexion with the Galloway expedition (see below, p. 582).

The Pipe Rolls, taken in conjunction with the *Dialogue of the Exchequer*, are the chief sources for the conduct of royal finance in the twelfth century. But the incidental information, which they supply on other matters, is very extensive. Thus they are of particular value as evidence for the history of great families, since frequently the replacement of one person by another supplies a date for the death of important individuals. Perhaps for the general historian the most valuable entries are those relating to special payments by royal writ, for these often supply information respecting the king's movements and his acts.

It should not, however, be supposed that the complexities of the Pipe Rolls, or the evidence they supply, can be appraised by means of a short note or by means of the selected passages which are all that can be included in this volume. Students desiring to explore further the intricacies of medieval accountancy and royal finance in the twelfth century may be directed in the first instance to Charles Johnson's admirable introduction to the Pipe Roll for 2 Richard I (Pipe Roll Soc., New Series, vol. I, 1925), and to R. L. Poole, *The Exchequer in the Twelfth Century* (Oxford, 1912). For all students of this subject the *Dialogue of the Exchequer* (above, No. 90) is an indispensable text.

The surviving Pipe Rolls relating to the period with which this volume is concerned have all been printed and they fill thirty-one substantial volumes. The Pipe Roll for 31 Henry I, and those for 2, 3, and 4 Henry II, have been reprinted from the editions made thereof by Joseph Hunter for the Record Commission in 1833 and 1844 respectively. The Pipe Rolls from 5 Henry II onwards are being printed by the Pipe Roll Society.

71. The Pipe Roll of 31 Henry I: The account of Gloucestershire

This is the account of Gloucestershire taken at Michaelmas 1130 in respect of the preceding twelve months. It is printed at pp. 76–80 of H.M. Stationery Office reprint (1929) of Joseph Hunter's edition of 1833.

GLOUCESTERSHIRE

Miles of Gloucester accounts for 80 pounds and 14 pence 'blanch' for the old 'farm' of the shire. He has paid this in the Treasury. And he is quit.

The same sheriff accounts for the new 'farm' of the shire. He has paid 222 pounds and 13 shillings by weight in the Treasury. And he has disbursed:

In fixed tithes 6 pounds 'by tale'.

In fixed alms 11 pounds, 2 shillings and 11 pence 'by tale'.

In fixed liveries 4 pounds, 11 shillings and 3 pence 'by tale'.

In liveries for a knight and serjeants and a door-keeper and a watchman in the castle of St. Briavels 14 pounds, 5 shillings and 7½ pence 'by tale'.

In the livery of Walter of Pavilly, the clerk, 9 pounds, 2 shillings and 6 pence 'by tale'.

In the livery for Wibert Savage 76 shillings 'by tale'.

To the earl of Gloucester 20 pounds 'by tale' for his share of the county.

In land for cultivation which has been taken within the park of Alveston, 72 shillings 'by tale'; and for the tithe of the same land 8 shillings 'by tale'.

For the transport of wine by the king's writ to Worcester and Bridgnorth 12 shillings and 10 pence 'by tale' to Gilbert of Argentan.

And he owes 16 pounds and 9 shillings and 10 pence 'blanch'.[1]

The same sheriff accounts for the 'farm' of the manor of 'Edefield'. He has paid 15 pounds in the Treasury. And he is quit.

The same sheriff accounts for the profits of the forest of Cirencester. He has paid 40 shillings in the Treasury and is quit.

Hugh, the son of William, son of Norman, accounts for 13 pounds for the forest of Dean and for the hedges of Hereford. He has paid this in the Treasury. And he is quit.

The same sheriff accounts for 420 pounds of the old debt of his father in respect of his land and his office. He has paid 50 pounds in the Treasury. And he owes 370 pounds.

The same sheriff owes 100 pounds for the debt of his father in respect of the plea concerning the deer of Carmarthen (?).

Robert of Saltmarsh owes 13 pounds of the old 'farm' of Painswick. And for this he ought to make payment to the king of 45 marks of silver. But he has altogether defaulted.

Henry, son of Humphrey, owes 6 shillings and 8 pence of the old 'farm' of Painswick for the third year.

And the same Henry owes 10 pounds of the old 'farm' of Painswick for last year.

And the same Henry owes 10 pounds of the same 'farm' for this year.

William of Fécamp owes 100 marks of silver in respect of the land of his father which Robert, son of Nigel, holds.

[1] This is the end of the account of the 'farm'. For its method, see above, p. 569.

The burgesses of Gloucester owe 30 marks of silver if they can recover through the justice of the king the money which was taken from them in Ireland.

Geoffrey, son of Engenulf, the cook, owes 100 marks of silver in respect of the plea concerning 'Bada'; and 100 marks of silver in respect of the plea of 'Dami' of Hallingbury.

Thierry the miller of 'Popelicercrha' owes 15 marks of silver in respect of the plea of 'Cerui'.

Gilbert of Mesnières accounts for 5 marks of silver in respect of the plea of Miles of Gloucester and of Payn, son of John. He has paid 4 marks of silver in the Treasury. And he owes 1 mark of silver.

Roger, son of Osbert the priest, accounts for half a mark of gold in respect of the grant of the land and of the churches of his father. He has paid 60 shillings in the Treasury in respect of this half mark of gold. And he is quit.

Sabricht the canon accounts for 10 pounds, 4 shillings and 6 pence in respect of the plea concerning the money of Roger of Berkeley. He has paid 10 marks of silver in the Treasury. And he owes 71 shillings and 2 pence. And the bishop of Worcester is pledge.

And the same Sabricht owes 20 marks of silver in respect of the treasure of Roger of Berkeley.

The same sheriff accounts for 6 pounds, 6 shillings and 8 pence in respect of 1 murder-fine in the hundred of 'Botelawia'; and for 110 shillings in respect of the plea of Payn, son of John.

For the works in the Tower of Gloucester (he has disbursed) 7 pounds, 6 shillings and 2 pence.

He has pardoned by writ of the king to Herbert, son of Dudeman, the sum of 42 shillings, and in the demesne of the king 48 shillings and 6 pence.

Geoffrey 'de Maisi' accounts for 20 marks of silver in respect of the land which his father held from the earl of Gloucester. He has paid 10 marks of silver in the Treasury and he owes 10 marks of silver.

Aelfric, son of Godric, accounts for 15 marks of silver in respect of his father's land and office. He has paid in the Treasury 40 shillings and he owes 12 marks of silver.

Elias Giffard accounts for 100 marks of silver in respect of the 'relief'[1] of the land of his father. He has paid 36 pounds, 13 shillings and 5 pence in the Treasury. And he owes 30 pounds.

The same Elias accounts for 10 pounds from the bishop of Durham which the daughter of Geoffrey, the bishop's brother, paid him. He has paid 100 shillings. And he owes 100 shillings.

The same sheriff accounts for 42 pounds and 10 shillings in respect of the last Danegeld. He has paid 75 shillings in the Treasury.

By the writ of the king he has pardoned the following payments:

To the bishop of Winchester, 36 shillings.

To the earl of Gloucester, 30 pounds and 13 shillings.

In the demesne of the church of Cirencester, 42 shillings and 6 pence.

[1] The customary due paid by the incoming heir for admission to his inheritance, see No. 19.

To Brian, son of the earl, 41 shillings and 6 pence.

In the demesne of the abbey of Caen, while it was in the king's hand. 42 shillings.

The sum is 38 pounds and 15 shillings.

And he is quit.

The same sheriff accounts for 34 shillings in respect of the last aid from the city. He has pardoned the earl of Gloucester 34 shillings by writ of the king. And he is quit.

The same sheriff accounts for 26 shillings and 8 pence for the last aid from borough of Winchcomb. By writ of the king he has pardoned the earl of Gloucester 26 shillings and 8 pence. And he is quit.

Geoffrey 'de Maisi' accounts for the 'farm' of Bisley. He has paid 6 pounds and 10 shillings in the Treasury. And by writ of the king he has disbursed 10 shillings to Hugh 'villanus'.

New pleas and new agreements

The monks of Gloucester account for 100 pounds in respect of the land of 'Sotora' which the king granted to them. They have paid 20 pounds in the Treasury. And they owe 80 pounds.

John of Sudeley accounts for 10 marks of silver, in respect of the plea of his wife. He has paid 40 shillings in the Treasury. And he owes 7 marks of silver.

Simon the dispenser owes 40 marks of silver in respect of the plea which the king brought against Odard of Carlisle, his sister's husband.

The same sheriff accounts in respect of Danegeld. He has paid 95 pounds, 19 shillings and 4 pence in the Treasury.

By writ of the king he has pardoned the following payments:

To the bishop of Winchester, 36 shillings.
To Humphrey 'de Parco', 4 shillings.
To William, son of Robert, 8 shillings.
To Eustace of Breteuil, 10 shillings.
To Henry, son of Humphrey, 8 shillings.
To Walter of Beauchamp, 2 shillings.
To Osbert, son of Pointz, 2 shillings.
To Geoffrey, son of Engenulf, 3 shillings and 6 pence.
To Gilbert of Mesnières, 30 shillings.
To Brian, son of the earl, 37 shillings.
To William Arcar, 10 shillings and 6 pence.
To Grimbald the physician, 10 shillings.
To the archbishop of York, 40 shillings.
To the abbot of Eynsham, 28 shillings.
To the abbess of Caen, 42 shillings.
To the earl of Warwick, 20 shillings.
To Henry of Ferrières, 18 shillings.
To Henry 'de Lamara', 3 shillings.
To the countess of Warwick, 14 shillings.
To Walter, son of Richard, 4 pounds and 18 shillings.

To Peveril of Beauchamp, 68 shillings.
To Ralph the butler, 8 shillings.
To William (?) Patric, 20 shillings.
To Patric 'de Cadurc', 42 shillings.
To the prior of Llanthony, 5 shillings.
To Miles of Gloucester, 10 pounds and 11 shillings.
To Rabel of Tancarville, 46 shillings.
To Elias Giffard, 36 shillings.
To Payn, son of John, 28 shillings.
In the demesne land of Odo 'de Vilers', 44 shillings.
In the king's demesne of Painswick, 6 shillings.
In the king's demesne of Newnham, 2 shillings.
In the king's demesne of the land of Roger of Berkeley, 36 shillings and 4 pence.
To the earl of Gloucester, 30 pounds and 13 shillings.
To the abbot of Cirencester, 42 shillings and 6 pence.
To the bishop of Salisbury, 25 shillings.
To Robert 'de Sigillo', 5 shillings and 6 pence.
To Richard the clerk, 10 shillings.
The sum is 80 pounds, 72 shillings and 4 pence.

And he is quit.

The same sheriff accounts in respect of the aid from the shire. He has paid 13 pounds, 3 shillings and 8 pence in the Treasury. By the writ of the king he has pardoned the earl of Gloucester 33 shillings and 4 pence and the bishop of Salisbury 3 shillings. And he is quit.

The same sheriff accounts for the aid from the borough of Winchcomb. He has paid 46 shillings and 8 pence in the Treasury. By the writ of the king he has pardoned the earl of Gloucester 13 shillings and 4 pence. And he is quit.

The same sheriff accounts for the 'old pennies'[1] which were Sabricht the priest's. He has paid 59 shillings in the Treasury. And he is quit.

72. The Pipe Roll of 32 Henry II: The account of Staffordshire

This, the account of Staffordshire, taken at Michaelmas 1186, in respect of the preceding twelve months, is printed in vol. XXXVI of the Pipe Roll Society's publications (1914) at pp. 145–147.

STAFFORDSHIRE

Thomas Noel[2] accounts for the 'farm' of Staffordshire. He has paid in the Treasury 80 pounds and 109 shillings and 1 penny 'blanch'

He has disbursed:

In fixed alms 1 mark to the knights of the Temple.

In fixed liveries half a mark to the canons of Llanthony for the keeping of the king's houses at Cannock.

In lands granted to the monks of Bordesley, 10 pounds 'blanch' in Tardebigg. And in Trentham 30 pounds 'blanch' concerning which Geoffrey Savage accounts below. And in Meretown 8 pounds 'blanch' concerning which Roger Muisson

[1] The debased and unreformed coins of the reign of Henry I before 1125. [2] The sheriff.

accounts below. And to William 'de Herovilla' 60 shillings 'blanch' in Wednesbury.

For enclosing the court around the king's houses in Kinver 42 shillings by writ of the king. And for repairing the gaol at Stafford 5 shillings by the writ of Rannulf 'de Glanville'. And for transferring the treasure from Burton to Chester 6 shillings and 11 pence.

And he is quit.[1]

Concerning purprestures and escheats

The same sheriff accounts for 33 shillings and 4 pence for the 'farm' of Broome. And for 1 mark for the 'farm' of Rowley Regis. And for 3 shillings for a building in Stafford. He has made payment in the Treasury by means of 3 tallies. And he is quit.

Geoffrey Savage renders account for 30 pounds 'blanch' in respect of the 'farm' of Trentham. He has paid into the Treasury 14 pounds and 2 shillings 'blanch'.

He has disbursed:

In lands given to the knights of the Temple in Keele, 43 shillings and 7 pence.

To John the chaplain, 100 shillings.

In fixed liveries to ten serjeants, 9 pounds, 3 shillings and 6 pence.

In pastures which the king granted to John Lestrange, 8 shillings and 8 pence.

The same renders account for 60 shillings 'by tale' in respect of the new market at Trentham. He has paid into the Treasury. And he is quit.

Roger Muisson accounts for 8 pounds 'blanch' for the 'farm' of Meretown. He has paid into the Treasury. And he is quit.

Robert 'de Broc' owes 3 marks in respect of rent of the forest of Cannock for last year.

The same accounts for 6 pounds, 13 shillings and 4 pence in respect of the rent of the same forest of Cannock for this year. He has paid this in the Treasury. And he is quit.

The same accounts for 50 shillings and 4 pence in respect of the pannage[2] of the same forest. He has paid this in the Treasury. And he is quit.

The same sheriff accounts for 6 pounds in respect of the increase of Walsall. And for 3 shillings and 6 pence in respect of the house of Walter the reeve in the cemetery of Stafford. He has paid in the Treasury by means of 2 tallies. And he is quit.

The same sheriff accounts for 3 shillings in respect of the profits of the mill at Cradley. And for 13 shillings and 4 pence in respect of the prebend of Penkridge. He has paid in the Treasury by means of 2 tallies. And he is quit.

The same sheriff accounts for 10 pounds in respect of the assize of the borough of Newcastle.[3] He paid 8 pounds in the Treasury.

He disbursed in gifts 40 shillings to the wife of Ralph of London by writ of the king.

And he is quit.

William, son of Guy, owes 2 war-horses in respect of the amercement of the king in connexion with the forest.

[1] This is the end of the account of the 'farm' of the county by the sheriff. It should be compared with the account of the same 'farm' in the following year. See below, p. 578.

[2] The privilege of feeding swine in the woods.

[3] Newcastle-under-Lyme.

Gervase Paynel accounts for 22 pounds that he may be quit of the pledge made by the earl of Leicester to Aaron the Jew, and that he may not be distrained for that pledge. He has paid in the Treasury 7 pounds, 6 shillings and 8 pence. And he owes 14 pounds, 13 shillings and 4 pence.[1]

The same sheriff owes 21 shillings in respect of the wastes and the assarts and the purprestures and the pleas of the forests of Staffordshire through Thomas, son of Bernard. But this money must be collected from the sheriff of Worcestershire.

Eugenia, the wife of Thomas, son of Bernard, accounts for 60 shillings in respect of the old 'farm' of Kinver on behalf of her husband. Also for 45 shillings for the 'farm' of the same Kinver for a quarter of a year. She has paid into the Treasury. And she is quit.

The same sheriff accounts for half a mark in respect of the amercement of Roger, son of Nicholas of Lichfield. He has made payment in the Treasury by means of 2 tallies. And he is quit.

Ernald the priest owes 1 mark for false pleading. Richard Miles the forester owes half a mark for default.

Robert of Beaumais owes 1 mark in respect of the sale of wood from the forest. But the debt should be collected in Shropshire.

Robert, son of Payn, accounted for half a mark because he did not prosecute his claim. He has paid this in the Treasury. And he is quit.

Concerning pleas of court

Alice, who was the wife of Robert of Bec, owes 10 pounds for the recognition[2] of 1 knight's fee against Robert of Stafford by the pledge of Geoffrey Savage.

Alina of Darlaston owes 2 marks in respect of the right given her in the king's court against Walter of Caverswall concerning the land of Olnea.

Adam of Alveley accounts for 10 shillings for the recognition[2] of 1 hide of land in Appleton against the son of Odo. He has paid this in the Treasury. And he is quit.

William of Englefield accounts for 50 shillings in order to have the land which Fulk Paynel held at 'farm'. He has paid this in the Treasury. And he is quit.

Geoffrey Savage owes 100 pounds for goods distrained[3] by the sheriff.

New pleas and new agreements made through Ralph, son of Stephen, and Miles Musgrove and their fellows

Hugh Travers accounts for 1 mark for dispossession. He has paid this in the Treasury. And he is quit.

Robert 'de Pierrefite'[4] owes half a mark for making a false charge.

Concerning the offerings of the court[5]

William, son of Turkill, owes 20 shillings for right concerning 10 marks which he claims against the prior of Staines.

[1] See also below, p. 579.
[2] By the sworn inquest.
[3] *pro nammis excussis.*
[4] See also below, p. 579.
[5] Gifts or offerings made to the king were entered on the Fine Roll, and if not paid were reckoned as a due to be collected by the sheriff; see also below, p. 579.

William of Sandford owes 1 mark for right concerning 5 marks against Robert of Tamhorn by the pledge of John of Sandford. But he has not yet had right.

The same sheriff accounts for 43 shillings and 5 pence concerning the profit of the land of Simon 'le Sage' which belongs to the fee of the bishop of Chester. He has paid this in the Treasury. And he is quit.

73. The Pipe Roll of 33 Henry II: The account of Staffordshire

This, the account of Staffordshire taken at Michaelmas 1187, in respect of the preceding twelve months, is printed in vol. XXVII of the Pipe Roll Society's publications (1915) at pp. 148–153.

STAFFORDSHIRE

Thomas Noel[1] accounts for the 'farm' of Staffordshire. He has paid in the Treasury 88 pounds and 6 pence 'blanch'.

He has disbursed:

In fixed alms 1 mark to the knights of the Temple.

In fixed liveries half a mark to the canons of Llanthony for the keeping of the king's houses at Cannock.

In lands granted to the monks of Bordesley 10 pounds 'blanch' in Tardebigg. And in Trentham 30 pounds 'blanch' concerning which Geoffrey Savage accounts below. And in Meertown 8 pounds 'blanch' concerning which Roger Muisson accounts below. And to William 'de Herovilla' 60 shillings 'blanch' in Wednesbury.

And he is quit.[2]

Concerning purprestures and escheats

The same sheriff accounts for 33 shillings and 4 pence for the 'farm' of Broom; and for 1 mark for the 'farm' of Rowley Regis. He has made payment in the Treasury by means of 2 tallies. And he is quit.

Geoffrey Savage accounts for 30 pounds 'blanch' in respect of the 'farm' of Trentham. He has paid into the Treasury 14 pounds and 23 pence 'blanch'.

He has disbursed:

In lands given to the knights of the Temple in Keele, 43 shillings and 7 pence.

To John the chaplain, 100 shillings.

In fixed liveries to ten serjeants, 9 pounds, 2 shillings and 6 pence.

In pasture which the king granted to John Lestrange, 8 shillings and 8 pence.

And he is quit.

The same Geoffrey renders account for 60 shillings 'by tale' in respect of the new market at Trentham. He has made payment into the Treasury. And he is quit.

Roger Muisson renders account for 8 pounds 'blanch' for the 'farm' of Meretown. He has paid into the Treasury. And he is quit.

Robert 'de Broc' accounts for 3 marks in respect of rent for the forest of Cannock for the third year. He has paid this in the Treasury. And he is quit.

The same Robert accounts for 6 pounds, 13 shillings and 4 pence for rent for

[1] The sheriff.

[2] The end of the account of the county 'farm'. This should be compared with the account of this 'farm' in the previous year. See above, pp. 575, 576.

the same forest of Cannock for this year. He has paid in the Treasury. And he is quit.

The same Robert accounts for 116 shillings and 3 pence in respect of the pannage of the forest of Cannock. He has paid in the Treasury. And he is quit.

[The same sheriff] accounts for 6 pounds in respect of the increase of Walsall. And for 3 shillings and 6 pence in respect of the house of Walter the reeve in the cemetery of Stafford. He has paid in the Treasury by means of 2 tallies. And he is quit.

The same sheriff accounts for 3 shillings in respect of the profits of the mill at Cradley. And for 13 shillings and 4 pence for the prebend of Penkridge. He has made payment in the Treasury by means of 2 tallies. And he is quit.

[William], son of Guy, owes 2 war-horses in respect of the amercement of the king in connexion with the forest.

[Gervase] Paynel accounts for 14 pounds, 13 shillings and 4 pence that he may be quit of the pledge made by the earl of Leicester to Aaron the Jew, and that he may not be distrained for that pledge. He has paid 5 marks in the Treasury. And he owes 11 pounds, 6 shillings and 8 pence.[1]

The same sheriff owes 21 shillings in respect of the wastes, the assarts, the purprestures and the pleas of the forest of Staffordshire through Thomas, son of Bernard.

Ernald the priest owes 1 mark for false pleading. Richard Miles the forester owes half a mark for default.

Robert of Beaumais accounts for 1 mark for the sale of wood in the forest. He has paid half a mark into the Treasury. And he owes half a mark.

Concerning pleas of the court

Alice who was the wife of Robert of Bec accounts for 10 pounds for the recognition of 1 knight's fee against Robert of Stafford by the pledge of Geoffrey Savage. She has paid 6 pounds in the Treasury. And she owes 4 pounds.

Alina of Darlaston owes 2 marks in respect of the right given her in the king's court against Walter of Caverswall concerning the land of Olnea. But she has not yet had right.

[Geoffrey] Savage accounts for 100 pounds for goods distrained[2] by the sheriff. By writ of the king the said Geoffrey has been pardoned 100 pounds. And he is quit.

[Robert] 'Pulerefice'[3] owes half a mark for making a false charge.

Concerning the offerings of the court[4]

[William, son of] Turkill, owes 20 shillings for right in respect of 10 marks which he claims against the prior of Staines.

William of Sandford owes 1 mark for right concerning 5 marks against Robert of Tamhorn by the pledge of John of Sandford. But he has not yet had right.

[1] See above, p. 577.
[2] *pro nammis excussis.*
[3] Appears in the previous roll in the guise of Robert 'de Pierrefite'; see above, p. 577.
[4] See above, p. 577, n. 5.

New pleas and new agreements through Robert Marmion, Ralph of Arden, Hugh Pantulf, William, son of Stephen, and Thomas Noel

The same sheriff[1] accounts for 1 mark from Totmonslow for murder.[2]

And for 1 mark from Eitroph Hasting because he first denied what he afterwards admitted.

And for 40 shillings from William of Birmingham because he did not have what he had pledged.

He has made payment in the Treasury by means of 3 tallies. And he is quit.

The same sheriff accounts for 2 marks from Gerard of Stafford in respect of the pledge of Robert the Frenchman. And for 1 mark from William the Frenchman for the same. And for 1 mark from Margaret 'de la Barre' for false accusation.

And for 1 mark from Hereward of 'Huneswurth' for false witness.

The king has granted by his writ 5 marks from the amercements of the above to the brethren of the Hospital of Jerusalem.

And he is quit.

The same sheriff accounts for 20 shillings from 'Pirhulle' hundred for murder. He has paid 18 shillings in the Treasury. And he owes 2 shillings.

The same sheriff accounts for 1 mark from Cuttleston hundred for murder. He has paid 12 shillings and 8 pence in the Treasury. And he owes 8 pence.

Hugh of Comberford accounts for 10 marks for 'novel disseisin'.[3] He has paid 44 shillings and 4 pence in the Treasury. And he owes 4 pounds and 9 shillings.

Simon, son of Ailwin, accounts for 2 marks for the same. He has paid half a mark into the Treasury. And he owes 20 shillings.

Concerning those who have paid in full

The same sheriff accounts for 10 pounds and 3 shillings and 4 pence in respect of petty amercements from those men whose names and debts and delinquencies are noted in the roll of the aforesaid, and which they have paid in the Treasury. He has made payment in the Treasury by means of 30 tallies. And he is quit.

Gamel of 'Deruereslawa' owes half a mark because he did not have 'Suanhilda' whom he had pledged.

Godwin, son of Chilla, owes half a mark for 'novel disseisin'.

Richard Wagtail accounts for half a mark because he withdrew from his appeal. He has paid 12 pence in the Treasury. And he owes 5 shillings and 8 pence.

Concerning the pleas of the forest through Robert 'de Broc', William of Stanton and Robert of 'Haselea'

John of Perton accounts for 20 shillings for keeping dogs in the forest without a warrant. He has paid this in the Treasury. And he is quit.

Concerning those who have paid in full in respect of pleas of the forest

The same sheriff accounts for 66 shillings in respect of petty amercements for the forest. He has paid in the Treasury, and he is quit.

[1] Thomas Noel; see above, p. 578.
[2] The *murdrum* or murder-fine; see above, p. 523.
[3] See above, No. 58.

Robert of Walton owes 2 shillings for new purpresture.

The same sheriff accounts for 63 shillings and 4 pence in respect of petty amercements for the forest. He has paid in the Treasury by means of 9 tallies. And he is quit.

The same sheriff accounts for 4 pounds, 2 shillings and 3 pence in respect of the assarts of Staffordshire. He has paid in the Treasury 40 shillings and 9 pence. And he owes 41 shillings and 6 pence.

Concerning the pleas of the court

Guy of Swinfen renders account for 1 mark for making his complaint against Henry of Perry in the king's court instead of in the shire court. He has paid in the Treasury. And he is quit.

Concerning the tallage of the demesne lands of the king and of those lands which were then in the king's hands; through Robert Marmion and his associates as aforesaid[1]

The same sheriff accounts as follows:

For 15 pounds, 4 shillings and 8 pence for the gift of Newcastle.[2] He has paid 8 pounds and 10 shillings in the Treasury. And he owes 6 pounds, 13 shillings and 8 pence.

For 13 pounds for the gift of the borough of Stafford. He has paid 6 pounds and 10 shillings in the Treasury. And he owes 6 pounds and 10 shillings.

For 55 shillings in respect of the gift of Meretown. He has paid 53 shillings. And he owes 2 shillings.

For 103 shillings and 8 pence for the gift of Penkridge. He has paid 52 shillings in the Treasury. And he owes 51 shillings and 8 pence.

For 46 shillings and 8 pence for the gift of Cannock. He has paid 23 shillings and 4 pence in the Treasury. And he owes 23 shillings and 4 pence.

For 4 pounds and 17 shillings for the gift of Kinver. He has paid this in the Treasury. And he is quit.

For 71 shillings for the gift of Rugeley. He has paid 35 shillings and 6 pence into the Treasury. And he owes 35 shillings and 6 pence.

For 58 shillings and 4 pence for the gift of Clent. He has paid 29 shillings and 2 pence in the Treasury. And he owes 29 shillings and 2 pence.

For 34 shillings for the gift of Wolverhampton. He has paid 17 shillings in the Treasury. And he owes 17 shillings.

For 36 shillings for the gift of Bilston. He has paid 18 shillings in the Treasury. And he owes 18 shillings.

For 17 shillings for the gift of Willenhall. He has paid this into the Treasury. And he is quit.

For 63 shillings and 8 pence for the gift of Tettenhall. He has paid 31 shillings and 10 pence in the Treasury. And he owes 31 shillings and 10 pence.

For 40 shillings for the gift of Bromley. He has paid 20 shillings in the Treasury. And he owes 20 shillings.

[1] See above, p. 580

[2] Newcastle-under-Lyme.

For 42 shillings for the gift of Walsall. He has paid 21 shillings in the Treasury. And he owes 21 shillings.

For 74 shillings for the gift of Swinford. He has paid 37 shillings in the Treasury. And he owes 37 shillings.

For 24 shillings and 8 pence for the gift of Penkhull. He has paid in the Treasury. And he is quit.

For 43 shillings and 4 pence for the gift of Tamworth. He has paid 28 shillings and 4 pence in the Treasury. And he owes 15 shillings.

For 100 shillings for the gift of Wigginton. He has paid 60 shillings in the Treasury. And he owes 40 shillings.

For 4 pounds, 7 shillings and 4 pence for the gift of Aldridge. He has paid 44 shillings in the Treasury. And he owes 43 shillings and 4 pence.

For 20 shillings for the gift of 'Lench'. He has paid 10 shillings in the Treasury. And he owes 10 shillings.

The same sheriff owes 40 shillings for the gift of Arley.

Concerning the chattels of outlaws

The same sheriff accounts as follows:

For 15 shillings for the chattels of Lefwin of 'Hopwas' for harbouring outlaws.
For 6 shillings and 9 pence for the chattels of Richard of Great Barr for the same.
For 8 shillings and 2 pence for the chattels of Ordric of Great Barr for the same.
For 11 pence for the chattels of William Prutel for the same.
For 19 shillings and 3 pence for the chattels of William of Featherstone.
For 5 shillings for the chattels of Anschill of Madeley.
For 17 shillings and 8 pence for the chattels of Ralph of Himley.
For 14 pence for the chattels of William the clerk of Swinford.
For 12 shillings for the chattels of Aldred of Ketley.

For half a mark for the chattels of Adam and Robert of Pipe. The sum is 4 pounds, 12 shillings and 7 pence. He has paid this in the Treasury by means of 10 tallies. And he is quit.

The same sheriff renders account for 43 shillings and 5 pence for the profit of the land of Simon 'le Sage', which is of the fee of the bishop of Chester. He has paid this into the Treasury. And he is quit.

The same sheriff renders account for 28 shillings and 9 pence for the profit of Coton, which was in the possession of William, son of Alan, for a whole year and for a quarter of a year. He has paid this into the Treasury. And he is quit.

The same sheriff renders account for 8 shillings and 1 penny for the profit of the land of Ralph of Himley for three-quarters of a year. He has paid this into the Treasury. And he is quit.

Concerning the scutage of the knights of Staffordshire who did not go with the king on the expedition to Galloway

The bishop of Chester renders account for 15 pounds of the scutage of his knights. He has paid 14 pounds in the Treasury. And he owes 20 shillings.

Bertram of Verdun renders account for 20 shillings of the scutage of 1 knight. He has paid this into the Treasury, and he is quit.

Robert 'de Broc' and William of Stanton and Robert of 'Haselea' render account for 6 pounds and 4 shillings and 2 pence in respect of the pannage of Herefordshire in Wales. And for 110 shillings and 9 pence of the pannage of Gloucestershire. And for 6 shillings for the pannage of Bushley in Worcestershire. And for 48 shillings and 2 pence for the pannage of Shropshire. The sum is 14 pounds and 9 shillings and 1 penny. They have made payment for this in the Treasury by means of 4 tallies. And they are quit.

Part III

THE CHURCH

THE CHURCH

Introduction

THE material for the history of the Church in England presented in the following pages is divided into three sections arranged in chronological order. The first section covers the period 1042–1089, the reigns of Edward the Confessor and William the Conqueror, and ends with the death of Archbishop Lanfranc; the second section runs from 1089 to 1154 and covers the reigns of William II, Henry I and Stephen, including the conflicts between Church and State during the primacies of Archbishops Anselm and Theobald; the third section comprises the whole reign of Henry II (1154–1189) and includes the struggle between that king and Archbishop Thomas Becket.

(i) 1042–1089 (Nos. 74–106). In this section evidence is provided for the condition of the Church in England on the eve of the Norman Conquest and for the far-reaching changes in its structure and organization made by William I and Lanfranc in the years following the latter's consecration as archbishop of Canterbury in 1072. In the first place a number of papal bulls and royal charters are given to illustrate the relations between the crown, the papacy and the English episcopate, both before and after the Conquest. Notable texts included are the writ of William the Conqueror effecting a separation between the jurisdiction of spiritual and secular courts and an early report of the trial of William of St. Calais, bishop of Durham, for high treason in the court of William Rufus. This is followed by a selection of material relating to the life and work of Lanfranc. It includes the earliest and most accurate account of his life and training as a monk at Le Bec and of the circumstances of his elevation to the see of Canterbury, together with a record of his archiepiscopal administration in the "Acts of Lanfranc". A selection of his correspondence is also included, together with the more important letters passed between Pope Gregory VII and King William I, which throw light on the pope's demand for William's fealty for the crown of England made in 1080. The text of William's letter rejecting the claim is also given.

(ii) 1089–1154 (Nos. 107–118). The relations between Crown and Church under William II and Henry I, more particularly the dispute between William Rufus and Archbishop Anselm and the controversy between Anselm and Henry I over Lay Investiture, are illustrated at some length by passages drawn from Eadmer's *Historia Novorum in Anglia* and by some of the letters of king and archbishop incorporated in that work. These in turn are followed by certain select passages from the surviving fragment of John of Salisbury's *Historia Pontificalis* (a work invaluable for the history of Anglo-papal relations in the troubled reign of Stephen) centering round the personality and policy of Archbishop Theobald. The great monastic revival, already in progress at this time on the continent of Europe, and destined to become one of the chief features of English religious life in the twelfth century, is here evidenced by the "Charter of Love", the foundation statute of the Cistercian Order, and by other texts illustrative of the growth and expansion of the Order in England in its early days.

(iii) 1154–1189 (Nos. 119–171). The history of the English Church during the reign of Henry II is dominated by the contest between the king and Thomas Becket over the question of "criminous clerks". The course of the struggle is documented in the following pages with passages drawn from the various contemporary biographers of the archbishop, and from the correspondence between Becket and his opponents, and between both parties and Pope Alexander III (Nos. 119–158.) For this struggle the key documents are the Constitutions of Clarendon (No. 126), William fitz Stephen's account of the council of Northampton in 1164 (No. 129) and Edward Grim's narrative of the murder of the archbishop (No. 152): all these will be found below translated in full. The Becket material is followed by a number of documents indicating the attitude of the papacy towards Henry II's invasion and conquest of Ireland. Notable among these is the text of the Bull *Laudabiliter* (No. 159), in the name of the English pope, Adrian IV, which has occasioned much controversy among scholars. Part III concludes with a selection from the works of John of Salisbury designed to provide illustrations of the working of the ecclesiastical system as seen through the eyes of one of the most gifted writers, experienced administrators and impartial critics of the age.

SELECT BIBLIOGRAPHY

of works relating to the History of the Church in England between 1042 and 1189

I. ORIGINAL SOURCES

(*a*) PRINTED COLLECTIONS OF A GENERAL CHARACTER

The majority of the great collections relating to the general history of the Church are cited, in so far as they relate to England, in C. Gross, *Sources and Literature of English History* (see above, p. 85). Special mention may here be made of Carl Mirbt, *Quellen zur Geschichte des Papsttums und des Römischen Katholizismus* (4th ed., Tübingen, 1924)–a discriminating selection from among papal bulls and official letters, canons of Church councils, the various compilations of canon law and the statutes of monastic Orders. The principal guide to papal chronology at this time is Philipp Jaffé, *Regesta Pontificum Romanorum* (2nd ed. by W. Wattenbach and S. Loewenfeld, 2 vols., Leipzig, 1885–1888). Contemporary *Lives* of the popes of this time will be found in L. Muratori, *Rerum Italicarum Scriptores* (vol. III, Milan, 1723) and also in J. M. Watterich, *Pontificum Romanorum Vitae* (2 vols., Leipzig, 1862). But of all the collections of papal acts, two are of transcendent importance for the elucidation of English history in this age. The one is W. Holtzmann, *Papsturkunden in England* (2 vols., Berlin, 1930, 1936), an indispensable work containing a number of hitherto unpublished papal bulls and rescripts of the eleventh and twelfth centuries. The other is *Registrum Papae Gregorii VII*–the sole surviving papal register before the time of Innocent III. It has twice been edited: firstly by P. Jaffé under the title *Monumenta Gregoriana* (Bibliotheca Rerum Germanicarum, vol. II, Berlin, 1865), and secondly by E. Caspar in *Monumenta Germaniae Historica* (2 vols., Berlin, 1893). Whilst the latter edition is generally to be preferred, the former is by no means superseded since it alone contains many of Gregory's letters which were never embodied in his *Register*. The official correspondence of later popes of this period has largely to be studied in various volumes of Migne's vast *Patrologia Latina*: the letters of Urban II are, for example, to be found in vol. CLI of that work; those of Innocent II in vol. CLXXIX; and those of Alexander III in vol. CC. The fact that the editing of this huge undertaking often leaves much to be desired does not make the work less indispensable, or diminish the debt of gratitude owed by all students to its organizer. It should be noted, also, that all these collections of papal acts may be supplemented from the publications of English local record societies (see above, pp. 90–92) which often include records emanating from the papal *curia*.

The Church councils of the period, and their acts, can most conveniently be studied in the French edition of C. J. Hefele's *Conciliengeschichte* which was prepared by H. Leclercq, *Histoire des Conciles* (Paris, 1907 *et sqq.*): vol. V of this work (2 parts, 1912, 1913) relates to the councils of the eleventh and twelfth centuries. Much of the English evidence is more elaborately displayed in David Wilkins, *Concilia Magnae Britanniae et Hiberniae* (4 vols., London, 1737). The character of this great book, and also the extent to which it now stands in need of revision, are discussed in F. M. Powicke, *Sir Henry Spelman and the Concilia* (Oxford, 1930), in E. F. Jacob, "Wilkins' Concilia and the Fifteenth Century" (*Trans. R. Hist. Soc.*, 4th Series, vol. XV, 1932), and in D. C. Douglas, *English Scholars* (1939), chap. X. The conciliar legislation of the Norman province can be surveyed in G. Bessin, *Concilia Rotomagensis Provinciae* (Rouen, 1727), which may be regarded as a revised edition, much augmented, of an earlier work by F. Pommeraye, *Sanctae Rotomagensis Ecclesiae Concilia* (Rouen, 1677).

An indispensable work of a more general character is the great collection made by Henry Wharton under the title *Anglia Sacra* (2 vols., London, 1691, together with a small supplementary volume issued in 1695). In the opinion of William Stubbs, Wharton "did for the elucidation of English church history more than any one before or since". *Anglia Sacra* contains, amidst a wealth of other material, the *Lives* of bishops and other ecclesiastical dignitaries, many of which are not printed elsewhere.

For the history of monasticism in England during the period the most important collection is the *Monasticon Anglicanum* attributed to William Dugdale (new ed., 6 vols. in 8, London, 1817–1830, reprinted 1846). G. Schreiber, *Kurie und Kloster im 12ten Jahrhundert* (2 vols., Stuttgart, 1910) contains material useful for the illustration of English monastic history, and L. Holsten, *Codex Regularum Monasticarum* (2nd ed., 6 vols., Vienna, 1759), is still the most complete single collection of monastic rules available. The Constitutions of Odo, abbot of Cluny, are printed in Migne, *Patrologia Latina*, vol. CXLIX, and new light is thrown on English monastic history at this period by the new edition of Lanfranc's *Monastic Constitutions* edited by M. D. Knowles (London, 1951). Much material also exists for the study of the Cistercian Order in England. The older works have for the most part been superseded by the magnificent collection of J.-M. Canivez, *Statuta Capitulorum Generalium Ordinis Cisterciensis* (Louvain, 1933): vol. I of this work contains the definitive text of the primitive Cistercian statutes. Among other books relating to the original sources of Cistercian history may be mentioned P. L. Januschek, *Origines Cistercienses* (vol. I, Vienna, 1877), and P. Guignard, *Monuments primitifs de la règle cistercienne* (Dijon, 1878), whilst the collection of Cistercian statutes made by J. T. Fowler and printed in *Yorks. Archaeol. Journal* (vol. IX, 1886); vol. X (1889); and vol. XI (1891) is of particular relevance to English abbeys of the Order. Mention may also be made of F. M. Powicke's edition of Walter Daniel's *Life of Ailred of Rievaulx* (London, 1950). For the original sources relating to the Carthusian Order the principal work is C. Le Coulteux, *Annales Ordinis Cartusiensis ab anno 1084 ad annum 1429* (8 vols., 1887–1891). An indication of the vast body of original literature concerning particular monasteries may be obtained by reference to L. H. Cottineau, *Répertoire topo-bibliographique des abbayes et prieurés* (2 vols., Mâcon, 1935), whilst there is an admirable bibliography relating to all aspects of English monastic history at this period appended to M. D. Knowles, *Monastic Order in England* (Cambridge, 1940). The great series of general chronicles relating to English history between 1042 and 1189 (see above, pp. 103–105) are of course in themselves of cardinal importance as evidence for the history of the Church in England.

(*b*) MATERIAL RELATING MORE ESPECIALLY TO PARTICULAR TOPICS

The career and policy of Lanfranc are fairly fully illustrated in a considerable mass of original material. The oldest account of his early life is to be found in Gilbert Crispin's *Life of Herluin*, splendidly edited by J. Armitage Robinson in *Gilbert Crispin, Abbot of Westminster* (Cambridge, 1911). This early life was used by Gilbert's younger relative, Milo Crispin, for his *Vita Lanfranci*, which is included in *Lanfranci Opera* (ed. J. A. Giles, 2 vols., Oxford, 1844), and this collection also contains the greater part of Lanfranc's illuminating correspondence. For the chief events of his career as archbishop the essential guide is the short Latin narrative added to the annal for 1070 in version 'A' of the Anglo-Saxon Chronicle: it is printed as an appendix to vol. I of J. Earle and C. Plummer, *Two of the Saxon Chronicles Parallel* (Oxford, 1892). The relations between Lanfranc, the Conqueror and the Papacy are evidenced, not only in the archbishop's correspondence, but also in the *Registrum Papae Gregorii VII* cited above.

The life and character of Anselm, archbishop of Canterbury, can best be appreciated from a perusal of his own writings–his theological works and his voluminous correspondence. These are to be found in Migne, *Patrologia Latina*, vols. CLVIII and CLIX, and a new edition—still incomplete—is that of F. S. Schmitt (*S. Anselmi Opera Omnia*, London, 1949, etc.) wherein the text is excellent but the annotation often faulty or inadequate. Eadmer's *De Vita et Conversatione Anselmi* (ed. M. Rule, Rolls Series, 1884) partakes of the character of hagiography, but none the less presents a convincing portrait of the archbishop, whilst the same writer's *Historia*

Novorum (see above, pp. 98, 104) is a large-scale history designed to place the archbishop in the setting of the ecclesiastical politics of his time. In this work the Investiture Controversy in England is fully described, and the same controversy is further evidenced in the letters of Ivo of Chartres which have been translated into French and annotated by L. Merlet (*Lettres de Saint Ives, évêque de Chartres*, Chartres, 1885). But the most interesting English contribution to the literature of the Investiture Controversy is probably to be found in a series of tractates which have been described as *Tractatus Eboracenses*. Six of these tractates were published in *Mon. Germ. Hist., Libelli de Lite*, vol. III (1897), and eighteen of the remainder in an appendix to H. Böhmer, *Kirche und Staat in England und in der Normandie im XI und XII Jahrhundert* (Leipzig, 1899). Their author (if, indeed, they are all by one hand) has been styled the "Anonymous of York", but he should more probably be associated with Rouen, and the tractates themselves are of special interest for their exaltation of the spiritual functions and privileges of the king at the expense of the papacy and the episcopate. They are fully discussed in G. H. Williams, *The Norman Anonymous of 1100 A.D.* (Harvard Theological Studies, No. XVIII, 1951).

The original material relating to the history of Thomas Becket is considered elsewhere in the book (see below, pp. 698–702). Here reference need only be made to the great collection of that material made by J. C. Robertson and J. B. Sheppard (7 vols., Rolls Series, 1875–1885). Vols. I–IV of this collection contain the contemporary Latin biographies of the archbishop; vols. V–VII are entirely concerned with his correspondence. Even this elaborate compilation does not exhaust the material relating to the archbishop, and in addition there needs to be mentioned the biography in old French verse written by Guernes de Pont-Sainte-Maxence (*La Vie de Saint Thomas le martyr*, ed. E. Walberg, Lund, 1922) and the Icelandic saga of Becket published in the original and with an English translation by E. Magnússon (*Thómas Saga Erkibyskups*, Rolls Series, 2 vols., 1875, 1883). The state of the Church in England at the time of Becket and Henry II could be copiously illustrated also from the correspondence of other men. The letters of Gilbert Foliot, bishop of London, are of particular importance in this respect. They are to be found in J. A. Giles, *Gilberti episcopi . . . epistolae* (2 vols., Oxford, 1845) and in Migne, *Patrologia Latina*, vol. CXC. Neither of these editions is, however, wholly satisfactory, and the forthcoming edition of Foliot's letters promised by Mr. C. N. L. Brooke is awaited with great interest: it will probably necessitate the re-dating of many of the letters of Thomas Becket himself. The correspondence of Arnulf, bishop of Lisieux, is likewise of importance for the ecclesiastical history of this period and should be studied in the edition by F. Barlow (Camden Soc., 3rd Series, vol. LXI (1939)). Finally the letters of John of Salisbury will repay careful study. They will be found in Migne, *Patrologia Latina*, vol. CXCIX, and also, as edited by J. A. Giles, in *Iohannis Saresberiensis Opera*, vols. I and II (Oxford, 1848).

It has seemed convenient to arrange much of this material in relation to three great archbishops of Canterbury, but there remains, of course, a mass of evidence which is not susceptible to such classification. Thus much information respecting the northern province and its religious houses will be found both in the works of Simeon of Durham (ed. T. Arnold, Rolls Series, 2 vols., 1882–1885) and also in the collection made by James Raine of the *Historians of the Church of York*, vols. II and III (Rolls Series, 1879–1894), whilst much information is to be derived from H. H. E. Craster, "A contemporary record of the pontificate of Rannulf Flambard" (*Arch. Aeliana*, 4th Series, vol. VII, 1930). The importance of the *Historia Pontificalis* of John of Salisbury for the ecclesiastical politics of the reign of Stephen has already been indicated (see above, p. 102), and much of the correspondence of Henry, bishop of Winchester, is published in an appendix to L. Voss, *Heinrich von Blois, bischof von Winchester* (Berlin, 1932). Many of the letters of St. Bernard of Clairvaux (Migne, *Patrologia Latina*, vol. CLXXXII) are addressed to English correspondents, and throw light on the condition of the English Church in his time. Finally, there remains to be noted the considerable biographical material relating to the leading English ecclesiastics of this age. Thus, William of Malmesbury in his *De Gestis Pontificum* (ed. N. E. S. A. Hamilton, Rolls Series, 1870) supplies informative biographies of many prelates, both of the Anglo-Saxon and Anglo-Norman periods; and in his *Vita Wulfstani* (ed. R. R. Darlington, Camden Soc., vol. XL, 1928) the same author presents an admirable account of the greatest bishop of the late Old English Church, the work being of especial value in that it is essentially a Latin version of an earlier *Life* in Anglo-Saxon written by Coleman, who was Wulfstan's own chaplain. Many other shorter biographies of this nature are to be found in Henry Wharton's *Anglia Sacra* cited above, and, as a further example of this literature, there may be mentioned the *Magna Vita Sancti Hugonis Episcopi Lincolniensis* (ed. J. F. Dimock, Rolls Series, 1864), which is the chief authority for the Carthusian bishop, Hugh of Lincoln, perhaps the greatest figure in the English Church after the death of Thomas Becket.

No adequate documentation can of course be attempted in this place of the contribution made by English ecclesiastical writers to the revival of theological and philosophical scholarship characteristic of this age. Much material relating to this can, however, be obtained in the collected works of Lanfranc and Anselm cited above, and the letters of Osbert of Clare (ed. E. W. Williamson, Oxford, 1929) are here of particular value. Walter Map's entertaining satirical commentaries are best to be studied in the edition by M. R. James of that writer's *De Nugis Curialium* (*Anecdota Oxoniensia*, vol. XIV, Oxford, 1914), whilst English translations of the work were published by Dr. James for the Cymroddorion Society (London, 1923) and by F. Tupper and M. B. Ogle under the title *Master Walter Map's Book "De Nugis Curialium"* (London, 1924). But among English writers of the twelfth century John of Salisbury is probably the outstanding figure. His two great treatises, the *Policraticus* and the *Metalogicon* (for which see below, Nos. 170, 171), are now available in the definitive editions of C. C. J. Webb, *Iohannis Saresberiensis Episcopi Carnotensis Policraticus* (2 vols., Oxford, 1909) and *Iohannis Saresberiensis Episcopi Carnotensis Metalogicon* (Oxford, 1929).

II. MODERN WORKS

(*a*) DICTIONARIES AND WORKS OF PRIMARY REFERENCE

The *Dictionary of National Biography* (see above, p. 88) contains many good notices of personages prominent in the English Church at this time (*e.g.* Lanfranc, Anselm, Henry of Winchester, Gilbert of Sempringham), while the *Dictionary of English Church History* (ed. S. L. Ollard and G. Crosse, London, 1912) is even more valuable. To these may be added the *Catholic Encyclopaedia* (15 vols. plus an index, New York, 1908–1914; supplement, 1922), and J. J. Herzog's *Realencyklopädie fur protestantische Theologie und Kirche* (3rd ed., ed. A. Hauck, 24 vols., Leipzig, 1896–1913) contains some excellent articles on English Church history. The *Dictionary of Christian Antiquities* (ed. W. Smith and S. Cheetham, 2 vols., 1876, 1880) is now being gradually superseded by the *Dictionnaire d'Archéologie Chrétienne et de Liturgie* (ed. F. Cabrol and H. Leclercq, 14 vols., Paris, 1907 *et sqq.*). A complete list of English bishops and their sees may be obtained from W. Stubbs, *Registrum Sacrum Anglicanum* (2nd ed., 1897) or from the *Handbook of British Chronology* (ed. F. M. Powicke, Charles Johnson and W. J. Harte, R. Hist. Soc., London, 1939). Much of the statistical information there given is also printed in smaller compass in *Handbook of Dates for Students of English History* (ed. C. R. Cheney, London, 1945), including a select bibliography on works of chronology, a complete list of the popes, ecclesiastical and legal calendars and tables for Easter.

(*b*) WORKS RELATING GENERALLY TO THE ECCLESIASTICAL HISTORY OF ENGLAND IN THE PERIOD 1042–1189

Some of the large general histories of the Church are of value to the student of English affairs. Among these may be mentioned vols. VIII and IX of the *Histoire de l'Église*, edited by A. Fliche and V. Martin (Paris, 1946 *et sqq.*) and vol. II of P. Hughes, *History of the Christian Church* (London, 1948). H. H. Milman, *History of Latin Christianity* (4th ed., 9 vols., London, 1883) still repays study, particularly in regard to the struggle between Henry II and Becket.

J. Lingard's *History and Antiquities of the Anglo-Saxon Church* (2 vols., London, 1845) retains much of its original value. W. Hunt, *The English Church from its Foundation to the Norman Conquest* (London, 1901), and W. R. W. Stephens, *The English Church from the Norman Conquest to the accession of Edward I* (London, 1901), supply competent narratives. The scope of F. Makower's *Constitutional History and Constitution of the Church of England* (London, 1895) is indicated by its title.

Such works will, however, be found of less service to the student of the main trends of English ecclesiastical history in this period than are certain individual studies. Thus the best introduction to the English Church in the time of Edward the Confessor will be found in an excellent, if perhaps somewhat tendentious, article by R. R. Darlington, "Ecclesiastical Reform in the late Old English Period" (*Eng. Hist. Rev.*, vol. LI, 1936), and this may be supplemented by the same writer's "Aethelwig, abbot of Evesham" (*ibid.*, vol. XLVIII, 1933). The crucial and controversial question of the effects of the Norman Conquest on English ecclesiastical life may most profitably be approached by means of comparing these articles with chapter XVIII of Sir Frank Stenton's *Anglo-Saxon England* (see above, p. 85) and with chapters III–XIV of M. D. Knowles's *Monastic Order in England* (see below, p. 595). Again, the best introduction to the history of the Church in England between 1066 and 1189 is contained in Z. N. Brooke, *The English Church and the Papacy* (see below, p. 594), whilst the European setting of English ecclesiastical events during this age can be most readily appraised through the medium of A. Fliche, *La Réforme Grégorienne* (3 vols., Louvain, 1924–1937). All the particular works cited in this paragraph are of the highest standard of scholarship: taken together they supply a better general account of the main course of English ecclesiastical development between 1042 and 1189 than is to be obtained through any or all of the general Church histories relating to this period.

(*c*) THE CHURCH IN SCOTLAND, IRELAND AND WALES (1042–1189)

For Celtic Christianity in general the reader may be confidently referred to the classic study of L. Gougaud, *Les Chrétientés celtiques* (Paris, 1911). An English version of this remarkable work was published under the title of *Christianity in Celtic Lands* (London, 1922).

The ecclesiastical history of Scotland in this age is elaborately surveyed in the second volume of W. F. Skene, *Celtic Scotland* (Edinburgh, 1887), a pioneer work which still remains of great value. A more modern treatment is J. T. Dowden, *The Medieval Church in Scotland: its Constitution, Organization and Law* (Glasgow, 1910). Much information may be obtained from G. G. Coulton, *Scottish Abbeys and Social Life* (Cambridge, 1933). M. B. MacGregor, *Sources and Literature of Scottish Church History* (Glasgow, 1934) is an elaborate, if somewhat uncritical, bibliography. M. Morgan, "The organization of the Scottish Church in the Twelfth Century" (*Trans. R. Hist. Soc.*, vol. XXIX, 1947) throws light on the parochial system as applied to Scotland.

For the ecclesiastical history of Anglo-Norman Ireland vols. I and II of G. H. Orpen, *Ireland under the Normans* (Oxford, 1911) are indispensable. W. A. Phillips, *History of the Church of Ireland from the earliest times to the present day* (vol. II, Oxford, 1934), supplements the information given in the best of the older works on this subject: G. T. Stokes, *Ireland and the Anglo-Norman Church* (2nd ed., London, 1892). Some of the literature surrounding the crucial question of the alleged bull *Laudabiliter* and Henry II's ecclesiastical activities in Ireland is indicated below on p. 776.

The best account of the Church in Wales in this period is contained in J. E. Lloyd, *History of Wales* (see above, p. 86). J. W. Willis-Bund, *The Celtic Church of Wales* (London, 1897) is generally useful, while the same author's article on "The Religious Houses in South Wales after 1066" (*Archaeologia Cambrensis*, 5th Series, vol. VII (1890)) is a more specialized study of Celtic monasticism in a period long past its prime. J. Conway Davies, *Episcopal Acts and Cognate Documents relating to Welsh Dioceses* (Cardiff, 1946) brings together a large amount of scattered material and is prefaced by a valuable introduction.

(*d*) SPECIAL STUDIES AND MONOGRAPHS RELATING TO THE CHURCH IN ENGLAND

(i)

The best works on the Anglo-Norman Church in its secular aspect are H. Böhmer, *Kirche und Staat in England und in der Normandie im XI und XII Jahrhundert* (Leipzig, 1899), and Z. N. Brooke, *The English Church and the Papacy* (Cambridge, 1931). Both these books are replete with erudition lucidly displayed, and the former is criticized in, though not superseded by, the latter. Brooke's study is particularly valuable for its exposition of ecclesiastical law and jurisdiction and for its survey of the whole field of the relations of Church and State in the eleventh and twelfth centuries. It may be supplemented by reference to the later chapters in R. L. Poole's brilliant *Lectures on the History of the Papal Chancery down to the time of Innocent III* (Cambridge, 1915).

(ii)

Reference to specific questions of Anglo-papal relations during the reign of William the Conqueror is made in J. P. Whitney, *Hildebrandine Essays* (Cambridge, 1932), and in *Studi Gregoriani raccolti da G. B. Birino* (3 vols., Rome, 1947). The nature and circumstances of Gregory VII's claims over the English crown are explained in Z. N. Brooke, "Pope Gregory VII's demand for fealty from William the Conqueror" (*Eng. Hist. Rev.*, vol. XXVI, 1911). All studies of these questions tend to emphasize the importance of the co-operation at this time between the king and Lanfranc. The best available biography of the great archbishop is that of A. J. Macdonald, *Lanfranc: a Study of His Life, Work and Writing* (Oxford, 1926). This is a full-scale treatment which, incidentally, seeks to vindicate the archbishop from the charges of forgery brought against him by H. Böhmer in *Studien zur Geschichte der Theologie und der Kirche*, vol. VIII, pt. i (Leipzig, 1902). Lanfranc's attitude to the papal schism is discussed by F. Liebermann in *Eng. Hist. Rev.*, vol. XVI (1901), and his Monastic Constitutions are considered by J. Armitage Robinson in *Journal of Theological Studies*, vol. X (1909). Some of Lanfranc's controversial writings are critically reviewed by R. W. Southern in *Studies presented to F. M. Powicke* (Oxford, 1948).

(iii)

The short biography of *Anselm* by R. W. Church (London, 1888, and later editions) has a perennial charm, while other lives worthy of note are M. Rule, *Life and Times of St. Anselm* (2 vols., London, 1883), and J. M. Rigg, *Saint Anselm of Canterbury* (London, 1896).

(iv)

The modern literature dealing with English ecclesiastical history in the reign of Henry II is very extensive, especially on the crucial question of the relations between Church and State. M. D. Knowles, *Archbishop Thomas Becket: a Character Study* (Brit. Acad., 1949) is a brilliant and penetrating essay which offers an admirable introduction to the archbishop and his stormy career, while the same author's *The Episcopal Colleagues of Archbishop Thomas Becket* (Cambridge, 1951) is of high importance. T. F. Tout, "The Place of St. Thomas of Canterbury in English History" (*Bulletin of the John Rylands Library*, vol. VI, no. 3, 1921) attempts to assess the significance and the results of the archbishop's policy. A biography of Becket worthy of its subject still remains to be written. W. H. Hutton, *Thomas Becket* (2nd ed., Cambridge, 1926) will, however, be found of interest, J. Morris, *Life and Martyrdom of St. Thomas Becket* (2nd ed., London, 1885), is the work of a fervent admirer, whilst J. C. Robertson, *Becket* (London, 1859), is prejudiced in the opposite direction. An elaborate study by a French Catholic writer is A. L'Huillier, *Saint Thomas de Cantorbéry* (2 vols., Paris, 1891, 1892). E. A. Freeman, "St. Thomas of Canterbury and his biographers" (*Historical Essays*, 1st Series, 3rd ed., London, 1875) is valuable for its criticism both of the contemporary *Lives* of the saint and of the work of some modern historians: in regard to the former of these topics it may be read in conjunction with L. Halphen, "Les

Biographes de Thomas Becket" (*Revue historique*, vol. CII, 1909), and E. Walberg, *La tradition hagiographique de Saint Thomas Becket avant la fin du XII siècle* (Paris, 1929). Some of the more controversial episodes in Becket's career are discussed in numerous scattered works. Among these pride of place must be given to F. W. Maitland's "Henry II and the Criminous Clerks" which originally appeared in the *English Historical Review* for April 1892, and was subsequently included in the same author's *Roman Canon Law in the Church of England* (Cambridge, 1898). L. B. Radford, *Thomas of London before his Consecration* (Cambridge, 1894) throws light on Becket's work as chancellor. Reference may also be made to J. H. Round, "The Alleged Debate on Danegeld in 1163" (*Eng. Hist. Rev.*, vol. v, 1890), to L. Halphen, "Les entrevues de Louis VII et Henri II durant l'exil de Thomas Becket en France" in *Mélanges offerts à M. Charles Bémont* (Paris, 1913), to Z. N. Brooke, "The Effect of Becket's Murder on Papal Authority in England" (*Camb. Hist. Journal*, vol. II, no. 3, 1928), and to M. Cheney, "The Conference of Avranches, and the Spread of Canon Law in England" (*Eng. Hist. Rev.*, vol. LVI, 1941). The results of some of these studies are summarized, but not noticeably modified, in Mlle R. Foreville's long work, *L'Eglise et la Royauté en Angleterre sous Henri II, Plantagenet, 1154–1189* (Paris, 1946). E. A. Abbott, *St. Thomas of Canterbury, his Death and Miracles* (2 vols., London, 1899), is the best account of the posthumous fame, and the legends, of the martyred archbishop.

(v)

Works on the history of the secular clergy and on parochial life in this period are not very numerous. The development of the parochial system in England is discussed by F. M. Stenton in *St. Frideswide and her Times* (*Oxoniensia*, vol. I (1936)) and in the introduction to his *Documents illustrative of the Social and Economic History of the Danelaw* (Brit. Acad., 1920), by M. Deanesly in the introduction to the *Descriptive Catalogue of the Charters and Muniments of the Marquis of Angelsea* (William Salt Soc., 1937), and by D. C. Douglas in the introduction to *Domesday Monachorum of Christ Church, Canterbury* (London, 1944). A. Hamilton Thompson, *The Historical Growth of the English Parish Church* (Cambridge, 1911), is an account by an expert in the subject, and R. A. R. Hartridge, *A History of Vicarages in the Middle Ages* (Cambridge, 1935), is an exhaustive survey. Additional information on the lives of parish priests and their flocks may be gleaned from G. G. Coulton, *Social Life in Britain from the Conquest to the Reformation* (Cambridge, 1915), and from H. S. Bennett, *Life on the English Manor* (Cambridge, 1937). Episcopal administration may be studied in I. J. Churchill, *Canterbury Administration* (2 vols., London, 1933), and there is much material relating to this period to be found in K. Edwards, *The English Secular Cathedrals in the Middle Ages* (Manchester, 1949). One important aspect of the manifold activities of a medieval bishop at this time is dealt with by Professor Stenton in "Acta Episcoporum" (*Camb. Hist. Journal*, vol. III, no. 1, 1929), and in C. R. Cheney, *English Bishops' Chanceries* (Manchester, 1950).

(*e*) MONASTICISM

It is fortunate that the history of monasticism in England during this period has recently been written at length and with great erudition in a single authoritative book. M. D. Knowles, *The Monastic Order in England* (Cambridge, 1940) may be regarded as a work which sustains the highest traditions of English historical scholarship. It can serve as a guide to all aspects of the subject with which it deals, and its extensive references and bibliographies give full indication of the directions in which more particular investigations may proceed. The same writer's *Religious Houses of Medieval England* (London, 1939) also carries authority but is more limited in scope, whilst in "The Cultural Influence of English Medieval Monasticism" (*Camb. Hist. Journal*, vol. VII, 1943) Professor Knowles has attempted a revaluation of the contribution made by the monks to the arts and letters of medieval England. An admirable short account of English monasticism is that of A. Hamilton Thompson in *Camb. Med. Hist.*, vol. v, chap. XX; and in the first two volumes of G. G. Coulton's erudite and controversial work, *Five Centuries of Religion* (Cambridge, 1923) there will be found much of interest relating to English monastic history in this period. Cuthbert Butler, *Benedictine Monachism* (London, 1927), may usefully be consulted on general questions, and most aspects of English monasticism receive illustration in Rose Graham's remarkable *English Ecclesiastical Studies* (London, 1929). M. Heimbucher, *Die Orden und Kongregationen der Katholischen Kirche* (2nd ed., 3 vols., Paderborn, 1907–1908) is an exhaustive work of general reference.

The standard work on the general history of the Cluniac Order is E. Sackur, *Die Cluniacenser* (2 vols., Halle, 1892, 1894). Joan Evans, *Monastic Life at Cluny, 910–1157* (Oxford, 1931) is perhaps the best account available in English, but much valuable material is also to be found in the work of Miss Rose Graham cited above.

The early history of Cîteaux is sketched in W. A. P. Mason, "The Beginnings of the Cistercian Order" (*Trans. R. Hist. Soc.*, New Series, vol. XIX (1905)), and this should be compared with U. Berlière, "Les origines de Cîteaux et l'Ordre Bénédictin du XII siècle" (*Revue d'Histoire Ecclésiastique*, vols. I and II). A. M. Cooke contributed a paper on "The Settlement of the Cistercians in England" to the *Eng. Hist. Rev.* (vol. VII (1893)), and J. S. Fletcher, *The Cistercians in Yorkshire* (London, 1919) is useful for the northern houses of the Order. Two papers by Sir Maurice Powicke, "Ailred of Rievaulx" (*Bulletin of John Rylands Library*, vol. I, nos. 3 and 4) and "Maurice of Rievaulx" (*Eng. Hist. Rev.*, vol. XXXVI (1921)) have in this respect a wide general interest.

The best work on the English Carthusians is M. Thompson, *The Carthusian Order in England* (London, 1930). For the Gilbertine monks Rose Graham, *St. Gilbert of Sempringham and the Gilbertines* (London, 1901), should be consulted, together with Mary Bateson, "Origin and Early History of Double Monasteries" (*Trans. R. Hist. Soc.*, New Series, vol. XIII (1899)). Lina Eckenstein, *Women under Monasticism* (Cambridge, 1896), and Eileen Power, *Medieval English Nunneries* (Cambridge, 1922) illuminate the part played by women in the 'religious' life of the Middle Ages. On the history of the "White Canons", J. C. Dickinson, *The Origin of the Austin Canons* (London, 1950) and H. K. Colvin *The White Canons in England* (Oxford, 1951) should be consulted.

An appreciation of English monastic history in this age can best be obtained by supplementing such general accounts as that of Professor Knowles by reference to some of the many studies which have been devoted to the history of particular monasteries. These are too numerous to permit citation in this place. A guide to this large literature is the *Répertoire topo-bibliographique* of L. H. Cottineau cited above.

(*f*) LEARNING AND LITERATURE

No attempt can here be made to supply a bibliography of the modern literature concerned with the contribution made by the Medieval Church to the culture and political theory of the age. The best introduction to this vast subject would perhaps be the brilliant article of A. Hamilton Thompson, "Medieval Doctrines to the Lateran Council of 1215", which is chapter XIX in *Camb. Med. Hist.*, vol. VI. The significance of Sir Maurice Powicke's delightful *The Christian Life in the Middle Ages and other essays* (Oxford, 1935) is indicated by its title. More specialized studies are O. von Gierke, *Political Theories of the Middle Age* (ed. F. W. Maitland, Cambridge, 1927); W. H. V. Reade, "Philosophy in the Middle Ages" (*Camb. Med. Hist.*, vol. V, chap. XXIII); and W. Ullmann, *Medieval Papalism* (London, 1949). For the twelfth-century Renaissance and the part played therein by English ecclesiastics reference may be made in the first instance to H. Rashdall, *The Universities of Europe in the Middle Ages* (ed. F. M. Powicke and A. B. Emden, 3 vols., Oxford, 1936), to C. H. Haskins, *Renaissance of the Twelfth Century* (Harvard U.P., 1927), to Bishop Stubbs's essay on "Learning and Literature at the Court of Henry II" (*Seventeen Lectures on Medieval and Modern History* (3rd ed., Oxford, 1900), and to V. H. Galbraith, *The Literacy of the Medieval English Kings* (Brit. Acad., 1935). A more particular study of considerable value is that of Adrian Morey, *Bartholomew of Exeter* (Cambridge, 1937), while mention may be made of the recent contribution of H. Liebeschütz, *Medieval Humanism in the Life and Works of John of Salisbury* (London, Warburg Institute, 1950).

Sir John Sandys, *History of Classical Scholarship*, vol. I (3rd ed., Cambridge, 1903) still remains of great use for students of this period, while other aspects of the literary activity of this age are described with sensitive erudition by F. J. E. Raby in *Christian Latin Poetry* (Oxford, 1927) and *Secular Latin Poetry in the Middle Ages* (2 vols., Oxford, 1934). Nor can it be doubted that many, in the future as in the past, will make their happy entrance into the literary world of twelfth-century England by means of R. L. Poole's fascinating *Illustrations of the History of Medieval Thought and Learning* (revised edition, London, 1920). Especially valuable in respect of John of Salisbury and his circle, this book may be supplemented by articles in the same writer's *Studies in Chronology and History* (Oxford, 1934). The work of this great scholar remains as fresh and as stimulating as when it first appeared.

A. THE CHURCH IN ENGLAND, 1042–1089

THE material here set out relates to the Church in England between the accession of Edward the Confessor and the death of Lanfranc. It is arranged in two sections: the former containing miscellaneous material, and the latter including texts relating particularly to the life and policy of Lanfranc.

(a) MISCELLANEOUS DOCUMENTS RELATING TO THE CHURCH IN ENGLAND (1042–1089)

74. Bull of Pope Victor II in favour of Chertsey Abbey (1055–1057)

This document is of interest as being the first of the medieval series of papal privileges to English churches. The beginning of this series in the reign of Edward the Confessor is of some significance. It is printed in W. Holtzmann, *Papsturkunden in England*, vol. I (1930), p. 221.

Victor, the bishop, servant of the servants of God, to his dearest son, Edward, king of the English, and to all his magnates greeting and apostolic benediction. We make known to you our privilege which, by the apostolic authority and by the authority of the Roman Church, we have granted to the monastery of St. Peter which is called Chertsey, and which we have committed to writing so that it may remain firm and unchanged for ever. By apostolic authority we command and order that all things which are there situate or appurtenant, whether in monastic buildings, or lands, or arable, or pastures, or cattle, or free men, or serfs, or bondwomen, or laws, or customs, or debts, or payments, or tithes, or fisheries, or woods, or warrens – indeed everything which by writing or bequest, or by the testimony of the memory of good men, has been given by the faithful or by kings to St. Peter in that monastery – shall be so confirmed that no one may dare to diminish or lessen or disperse them on any excuse, judgment or authority. But if anyone moved by the promptings of the devil shall wish to break this our privilege of St. Peter, and shall presume to diminish the goods of this church by encroachment, let him be condemned by God and St. Peter, and in so far as it is permitted to us, let him be excommunicate and cut off from the community of the faithful. Shall it be done? Let it be done. Does it please? It pleases. Do you commend it? We commend it. Let it be established. Thrice we say "Let it be done."[1]

75. Bull of Pope Nicholas II addressed to Wulfwig, bishop of Dorchester (3 May 1061)

This bull, "one of the earliest genuine documents issued by a pope during the reformation of the Church in the eleventh century", is of particular interest as indicating the manner in which the reforming papacy intervened in England before the Norman Conquest. The reference to Edward's mission to the pope confirms the statement in the Anglo-Saxon Chronicle. The Latin text is printed in *Registrum Antiquissimum of the Cathedral Church of Lincoln* (Lincoln Rec. Soc.), ed. C.W. Foster and K. Major, vol. I, pp. 186–187.

Nicholas, the bishop, servant of the servants of God, to Wulfwig, bishop of Dorchester, and to his successors subsequently in perpetuity to be canonically appointed there in his place. The charge has been laid upon us to watch with the utmost care over all the churches of God and over all holy places, lest they suffer any loss in what is needful to them. But their revenues should be for their own use. It thus

[1] *Fiat? fiat. Placet? placet. Laudatis? laudamus. Hoc sit stabile. Fiat. fiat. fiat.* The whole document is verbose and rhetorical.

behoves us to provide with singleness of purpose for such holy places that they may continue to possess those things which have been assigned to them. Since therefore you, dearest son, have asked us to confirm by the writing of our official document of privilege, with the messengers of King Edward and with our own friendly letters, those things which justly and lawfully belong to the aforesaid church (of Dorchester); we on our part, gladly consenting, do now grant this charter of our own will and as a grant freely made by the apostolic see. And we confirm that there should pertain to you and to your successors to be subsequently canonically appointed in your place, all those things which the aforesaid church of Dorchester has possessed and now possesses: and especially the diocese of Lindsey and the churches of Stow with Newark and its appurtenances which, as we have heard from our legates and have learnt from the written testimony of our predecessors, Ailric, archbishop of York, wrongfully seized. And we confirm to the aforesaid church (of Dorchester) whatever it may in the future by divine and human law be able to acquire; and all its property and possessions both movable and immovable; and all its buildings, villages and lands; and its churches with their revenues and tithes; and all holy things which the pious devotion of the faithful has conferred or will confer in gifts for the salvation of the living and the dead. By the authority of this, our apostolic see, over which by the favour of God we preside, and by our own inviolable edict, we order that neither king nor archbishop, nor duke, nor marquis, nor count, nor viscount, nor any other person great or small, of whatever station or degree, shall presume to disturb or defraud the aforesaid church (of Dorchester) or you, dearest brother, or your successors; or to set up anything contrary to the holy canons. Both you and your successors are to hold and possess, by the authority of this charter and by the apostolic sanction, all those things which, as we have said, the aforesaid church (of Dorchester) well and firmly held from its foundation. If, therefore, despite our hope, anyone should attempt to infringe this our privilege, or to break the precept ratified by apostolic authority, let him know himself bound with the chain of anathema; and if he does not repent and make satisfaction, let him have his part with Judas, the traitor, and with Dathan and Abyrom. But as for him who shows himself watchful in all things, and a guardian of what has been ordained in this our privilege for the worship of God, let him be blessed by our most merciful Lord God, and let him deserve to become a partner in eternal life. Given 3 May by the hand of Bernard, bishop of the holy church of Palestrina, in the year of the Incarnation of our Lord 1061, and in the third year of the pontificate of Nicholas the pope, it being the fourteenth Indiction.

76. Bull of Pope Nicholas II addressed to Giso, bishop of Wells (25 April 1061)

This bull is of particular interest as indicating the manner in which the reforming papacy intervened in England during the reign of Edward the Confessor. It is "the oldest papal document which still remains in the English Church to which it was directed". Together with the document which follows, it affords evidence of the relations between the Anglo-Saxon Church and the papacy in the decade immediately preceding the Norman Conquest. It is displayed in facsimile in *Nouveau Traité de Diplomatique*, vol. V (1762), p. 283; and in G. Hickes, *Linguarum Veterum . . . Thesaurus*, vol. I (1705), p. 177. It is printed in W. Holtzmann, *Papsturkunden in England*, vol. II (1936), p. 131.

Nicholas, the bishop, servant of the servants of God, to Giso, his beloved brother, and his fellow-bishop, and through him to the church of Wells, and to his successors there in perpetuity to be appointed in his place. It belongs to our pontificate to provide for the needs and just desires of all churches and to lend a ready ear to their petitions. You, dearest brother, when you received consecration as bishop by the ministration of our humility in the very basilica of the patriarch, asked that we should confirm by the writing of our privilege to your church, and to you, and to your successors in perpetuity, all those things which justly and legally pertain to the aforesaid church. Gladly acceding to your request, by the decree of this our statute, and by the edict of the apostolic church freely given, we grant and confirm to you as aforesaid, and to your successors there to be for ever canonically appointed in your place, whatever pertains to the bishopric of the aforesaid church, both what it now possesses, and also whatever it may in the future be able to acquire with the sanction of divine and human laws: to wit, the episcopate itself with all its possessions and appurtenances, movable and immovable; fortifications; houses; villages; lands; churches with their revenues and tithes; and all things which it has acquired by the holy offerings which the faithful have made for the salvation of the living and the dead. By the authority of this our apostolic see over which by the favour of God we preside, and by our own inviolable edict, we order that neither king, nor duke, nor marquis, nor count, nor viscount, nor any other person, great or small, of whatever station or degree, shall presume, against our privilege, to disturb or to defraud the aforesaid bishopric in its possessions or you, dearest brother, or your successors; or to set up anything contrary to the holy canons; or in any wise to harm or diminish or alter the confirmation of your episcopate. If, against our hope, anyone shall attempt to go against this our privilege and against those things which have been ordered and stablished by the apostolic authority, and after canonical warning from you shall not desist, let him know that he is to be bound for ever by the chain of anathema, unless he repents and makes proper restitution. But as for him who shows himself watchful in all things, and a guardian of what has been ordained in this our privilege for the worship of God, let him be blessed by our most merciful Lord God, and by our blessed St. Peter, prince of the apostles, and deserve to become a partner in eternal life.

(*Rota*)[1] (*Benevalete*)

Given at Rome, 25 April, in the year of the Incarnation of our Lord Jesus 1061, by the hand of Humphrey, bishop of the holy church of Silva Candida, and *bibliothecarius* of the apostolic see, in the third year of the pontificate of Pope Nicholas, it being the fourteenth Indiction.

77. Solemn diploma given by William I to Giso, bishop of Wells (? May 1068)[2]

An initial suspicion rests on all the solemn diplomata of William the Conqueror, but this document is generally accepted as being genuine in substance, although, since it is preserved in no copy earlier than the fifteenth century, it contains copyist's errors and is on occasion, in consequence, somewhat confused. It is of particular interest, not only for its archaic form, but more especially as displaying the first phase of William's government of England. Its witnesses reveal the Whitsuntide *curia* of

[1] A confirming formula set down in the design of a wheel.

[2] In the dating clause below, the year of grace is 1067, but the Indiction gives 1068: the latter must be correct, as Whitsuntide 1068 is almost the only time when the witnesses could have met together. Accepting this date, the list of witnesses becomes a powerful argument in favour of the authenticity of the charter, for at the worst this list must have been copied from some genuine document. In any case, therefore, it supplies the record of this important session of the *curia regis*.

1068, and among them will be found both Saxon and Norman magnates. This charter is printed in *Proc. Somerset Archaeol. Soc.*, vol. XXXIII (1877), p. 56, together with comments upon it by E. A. Freeman and others. It is also printed in J. Earle, *Land Charters and other Saxonic Documents* (1888), p. 431.

✠ Our Lord Jesus Christ reigning for ever! I, William, by the grace of God king of all Britain, following the footsteps of my ancestors who fostered the integrity of the catholic and apostolic faith, do now propose to make Jesus Christ a sharer in those things which by his gift I seem to possess in this vale of tears, and at the same time I propose to change them by him from earthly and temporal things into heavenly and eternal possessions. I have been moved also by the pious prayers of Giso, the bishop, respecting 30 hides in the place which by the inhabitants is called Banwell: these Duduc, the bishop, his predecessor gave to God for the sake of his soul, but King[1] Harold, inflamed with avarice, took them away. Now I restore them to St. Andrew the apostle to make proper increase of the dignity of the church, not only in respect of the demesne of the bishop, but also in respect of the sustenance of the brothers of the church of Wells. I restore them in full liberty and with all their appurtenances, that is to say, in woods, fields, meadows and fisheries, for my own sake and for the souls of my father, and of my predecessor, King Edward, and of all who stand by me faithfully. I acquit this gift of my bestowal from all fiscal burdens and tributes except three, to wit, military service, and bridge building and castle building. If any should desire to maintain and increase this my gift, may God increase to him the goods of this world and also the joys of heaven. But if, against my hopes, anyone, moved by the devil, dares to break or diminish this, may his memory disappear from the land, and may his name be blotted out of the book of the living. The boundaries of the aforesaid land are as follows:

[Here follows a long and detailed description in Anglo-Saxon, which is of purely local interest.]

In order that what we do may be held firm and unbroken by succeeding posterity, we have confirmed it by the charter of this privilege in the year of our Lord 1067[2] in the seventh Indiction. And we add below the names of many witnesses by whose counsel these matters have been settled, lest by becoming old and hidden these acts might be brought to no effect if they had not given their consent. If anyone shall despoil God and St. Andrew of this gift of my humility, let him be struck by an unbreakable curse, and let him be subjected to eternal damnation.

✠ I William, king of the English, confirm my gift with the sign of the cross.
✠ I Maud[3] the queen with the same sign add my confirmation.
✠ I Stigand the archbishop[4] agree and subscribe.
✠ I Aldred the archbishop[5] confirm it.
✠ I Odo the bishop,[6] the king's brother, corroborate it.
✠ I Hugh the bishop[7] adhere to it.
✠ I Geoffrey the bishop[8] also sign.
✠ I Herman the bishop[9] consent to it.

[1] A copyist's error. If not it is suspicious, for William's chancery was normally careful not to give to Harold the title of king.
[2] *rectius*, 1068, see above.
[3] She arrived in England after Easter 1068.
[4] Of Canterbury.
[5] Of York.
[6] Of Bayeux.
[7] Of Lisieux.
[8] Of Coutances.
[9] Of Sherborne.

✠ I Leofric the bishop[1] do not deny it.
✠ I Ægelmaer the bishop[2] agree to it.
✠ I William the bishop[3] praise it.
✠ I Ægelric the bishop[4] confirm it.
✠ I Walter the bishop[5] favour it.
✠ I Wulfsige[6] the bishop have confirmed it.
✠ I Remigius the bishop[7] have also signed it.
✠ I Athelnoth, abbot.[8]
✠ I Leofweard, abbot.[9]
✠ I Wulfwold, abbot.[10]
✠ I Wulfgeat, abbot.
✠ I William, 'dux'.[11]
✠ I Waltheof, 'dux'.[12]
✠ I Eadwin, 'dux'.[13]
✠ I Robert, brother of the king.[14]
✠ I Roger, 'princeps'.[15]
✠ I Walter Giffard.
✠ I Hugh of Montfort-sur-Risle.
✠ I William 'de Curcello'.
✠ I Serlo 'de Burgh'.
✠ I Roger 'Derundel.'
✠ I Richard, the king's son.[16]
✠ I Walter Fleminc.
✠ I Rambriht Fleminc.
✠ I Thurstan.
✠ I Baldwin 'de Wartenbiege'.
✠ I Othelheard.
✠ I Aymery.
✠ I Tovi the 'minister'.[17]
✠ I Dinni.
✠ I Ælfgeard Thorne.
✠ I William 'de Walville'.
✠ I Bondig the staller.[18]
✠ I Robert the staller.[19]
✠ I Robert 'd'Oilli'.
✠ I Roger the butler.
✠ I Wulfweard.
✠ I Herding.
✠ I Atsor.
✠ I Brixi.
✠ I Brihtric.[20]

78. Charter of William I in favour of Remigius, bishop of Lincoln (1070–1087)

This charter, which by the best authorities is accepted as genuine, is interesting for many reasons, among which may be specially noted its reference to the transference of the see of Dorchester to Lincoln, and also its allusion to the fact that Remigius was invested by King William with the symbols of his episcopal office. This was one of the practices to which Anselm and the reforming party in the early twelfth century were most opposed. Before becoming bishop of Dorchester in 1067 or 1068 Remigius had been almoner of Fécamp. Printed, with facsimile, in *Registrum Antiquissimum of Lincoln Cathedral*, ed. C. W. Foster and K. Major, vol. 1, p. 3.

William, king of the English, to T. the sheriff and to all the sheriffs in the bishopric of Remigius, the bishop, greeting. Know that I have transferred the seat of the bishopric of Dorchester to the city of Lincoln by the authority and counsel of Alexander, the pope, and his legates, and by the authority and counsel of Lanfranc, the archbishop, and other bishops of my kingdom. Know also that I have given him there land free and quit of all customs sufficient to construct a mother-church for the whole bishopric and its buildings. Moreover, wishing to give something to this church for the salvation of my soul, I grant in the first place two manors, namely Welton and

[1] Of Exeter. [2] Of Elmham. [3] Of London. [4] Of Selsey.
[5] Of Hereford. [6] A scribal error: possibly for Wulfstan, bishop of Worcester.
[7] Of Dorchester, later of Lincoln. [8] Of Glastonbury. [9] Of Michelney.
[10] Of Chertsey. [11] William Rufus. [12] Son of Earl Siward.
[13] Earl of Mercia. [14] Robert, count of Mortain. [15] Roger of Montgomery.
[16] This son of the Conqueror very soon after this died in the New Forest.
[17] Sheriff of Somerset.
[18] Also staller to Edward the Confessor.
[19] Robert 'fitz Wimarc', also staller to Edward the Confessor.
[20] The composition of this *curia* should becompared with the description of the king's household given above, No. 30.

Sleaford with their appurtenances, and then the churches of three of my manors with their lands and tithes, namely Kirton, Caistor and Wellingore. I also add all the tithe of the whole render of the same manors, and two churches in Lincoln, namely St. Lawrence and St. Martin. At the prayer and demand of Bishop Remigius I grant besides to the same church a certain manor which is called Leighton [Bromswold] which Earl Waltheof formerly gave to the aforesaid bishop through my hands; and yet another manor called Wooburn which I formerly gave him with his episcopal staff.[1] With the grant and consent of the aforesaid church, I grant in perpetuity with all their appurtenances, and by royal authority I confirm to him four churches, namely Bedford and Leighton [Buzzard] and Buckingham and Aylesbury, which his predecessors held and which I had given him to possess for ever. Witness, Lanfranc the archbishop and E. the sheriff.

79. Writ of William I concerning spiritual and temporal courts (1072–1076, and probably April 1072)

This famous writ is preserved in two copies, the one is the *Registrum Antiquissimum of Lincoln Cathedral* (Lincoln Rec. Soc., ed. C. W. Foster and K. Major, vol. XXVII, p. 1), and the other in a cartulary of St. Paul's Cathedral, London (see M. Gibbs, *Early Charters of St. Paul's* (1939), p. 10). It has been many times reprinted, and the St. Paul's version (which is here followed) is printed in W. Stubbs, *Select Charters* (ed. 1913), pp. 99–100.

William, by the grace of God king of the English, to Ralph Bainard, Geoffrey of Manneville, and Peter of Valognes, and to all his other liegemen in Essex, Hertfordshire and Middlesex greeting.[2] Be it known to you and to all my liegemen who are in England that by the common council and counsel of the archbishops, bishops, abbots, and of all the magnates of my kingdom, I have ordained that the episcopal laws shall be amended, because before my time these were not properly administered in England according to the precepts of the holy canons. Wherefore I order, and by my royal authority I command, that no bishop or archdeacon shall henceforth hold pleas relating to the episcopal laws in the hundred court; nor shall they bring to the judgment of secular men any matter which concerns the rule of souls; but anyone cited under the episcopal laws in respect of any plea of crime shall come to the place which the bishop shall choose and name, and there he shall plead his case, or answer for his crime. He shall not be tried according to the law of the hundred court, but he shall submit to the justice of God and his bishop in accordance with the canons and the episcopal laws. Moreover, if anyone, puffed up with pride, shall refuse to come to the bishop's court, he shall be summoned three times, and if, after this, he shall still fail to appear, he shall be excommunicated; and if the strength and justice of the king and his sheriff shall be needed to carry this into effect, this support will be forthcoming. Anyone failing to appear at the bishop's court after one summons shall pay the appropriate penalty according to episcopal law. By virtue of my authority I also forbid any sheriff or reeve or official of the king or any layman

[1] *quod sibi olim cum episcopali baculo concesseram.*

[2] The Lincoln version is addressed: "William, by the grace of God, king of the English, to the earls, sheriffs, and all Frenchmen and Englishmen, who hold lands in the bishopric of Bishop Remigius." Sir Frank Stenton here observes: "these variant addresses suggest that copies of the writ were sent in the first place to the principal local agents of Anglo-Norman administration, the sheriffs, and that an example was kept in each cathedral church".

to interfere with the laws which pertain to the bishop; nor in these cases shall any layman bring another man to justice until the judgment of the bishop has been given. Judgment shall not be given except at the seat of the bishop or in some place that the bishop shall appoint for this purpose.

80. Charter of William 'de Warenne',[1] founding the priory of Lewes in Sussex (1078–1082)

This is the true foundation charter of the first Cluniac monastery to be founded in England. Concerning other charters alleged to have been granted to Lewes Priory by William of Warenne, many of which have been proved to be forgeries, see L. C. Loyd, "The Origin of the Family of Warenne" (*Yorks. Archaeol. Journal*, vol. XXXI, pp. 97–113) and C. T. Clay, *Early Yorkshire Charters*, vol. VIII (1949), pp. 59–62. The present document is preserved in the original and is, for many reasons, of peculiar interest. It is here included as a very notable foundation charter: the mention of Cluny will be noted, and also the part played by King William in the transaction. Printed: C. T. Clay, *op. cit.*, pp. 54, 55, with facsimile.

Be it known to all the faithful that I, William 'de Warenne,'[1] and Gundrada, my wife,[2] for the redemption of our souls, and with the advice and assent of our lord, William, king of the English, give to God and to the holy apostles Peter and Paul at the place called Cluny where the lord abbot Hugh[3] presides, the church of St. Pancras in the same land of the English with all the things which pertain to it; and 2 carucates of land belonging to us in Swanborough[4] with the villeins attaching to them; and 1 carucate of land which is named; and the village of Falmer,[4] where there are 3 carucates belonging to us, with all the things pertaining to it, even as my wife aforesaid held it.

In the name of our Lord Jesus Christ, I, William,[5] by the grace of God king of the English, moved by divine inspiration, and for the sake of the safety of my kingdom and the salvation of my soul, and at the fervent request and petition of William of Warenne and Gundrada, his wife, confirm with our seal the gift here recorded which they make to the holy apostles of God at the place called Cluny. With my royal authority I ratify it in order that it may remain firm and unimpaired. I grant this gift in such a manner that I may have the same rights in it as I have in the other alms which my magnates give with my assent, to wit, that I may have in respect of these alms what I have in others.

✠ the sign of William, king of the English.
✠ the sign of Maud, queen of the English.
✠ the sign of William the count, the son of the king.[6]
✠ the sign of William 'de Warenne'.
✠ the sign of Gundrada, the wife of William 'de Warenne'.
✠ the sign of Robert of Beaumont.[7]

[1] Later first earl of Surrey. The absence of the title shows that he had not yet received this dignity.

[2] She was, it seems, sister to Gerbod, earl of Chester. There has been much controversy respecting this lady, who has been falsely alleged to have been a daughter of William the Conqueror. On her the curious should consult R. E. Chester Waters, *Gundrada de Warenne* (Exeter, 1884); and C. T. Clay, *op. cit.*, pp. 4–7.

[3] (St.) Hugh I, abbot of Cluny, 1049–1109.

[4] In Sussex.

[5] William the Conqueror.

[6] Later William II (Rufus), king of England.

[7] See Table 12. Robert of Beaumont, who fought at Hastings, became count of Meulan not later than December 1081. The fact that he has not that title here suggests that this charter was issued before that date.

✠ the sign of Henry of Beaumont.[1]
✠ the sign of Robert Giffard.
✠ the sign of Roger of Mortemer.
✠ the sign of Geoffrey 'de Calvomonte'.
✠ the sign of Ralph the steward.
✠ [2] the sign of Maurice the chancellor.

81. Penances imposed for various sins on Normans who took part in the invasion and conquest of England (1070)

This little penitentiary was issued by Ermenfrid, bishop of Sitten, during his visit to England in 1070. Its topical interest will be apparent, and it is important in many ways. Its homely particularity and its realism are both notable. It is printed in G. Bessin, *Concilia Rotomagensis Provinciae* (Rouen, 1717), pp. 50, 51, and in D. Wilkins, *Concilia Magnae Britanniae et Hiberniae*, vol. I (1737), p. 366.

This is an institution of penance according to the decrees of the bishops of the Normans, confirmed by the authority of the pope through his legate Ermenfrid, bishop of Sitten. It is to apply to those men whom William, duke of the Normans [? commanded],[3] and who gave him military service as their duty.

Anyone who knows that he killed a man in the great battle[4] must do penance for one year for each man that he killed.

Anyone who wounded a man, and does not know whether he killed him or not, must do penance for forty days for each man he thus struck (if he can remember the number), either continuously or at intervals.

Anyone who does not know the number of those he wounded or killed must, at the discretion of his bishop, do penance for one day in each week for the remainder of his life; or, if he can, let him redeem his sin by a perpetual alms, either by building or by endowing a church.

The clerks who fought, or who were armed for fighting, must do penance as if they had committed these sins in their own country, for they are forbidden by the canons to do battle.[5] The penances of the monks are to be determined by their rule, and by the judgment of their abbots. Those who fought merely for gain[6] are to know that they owe penance as for homicide. But those who fought as in a public war[7] have been allotted a penance of three years by their bishops out of mercy.

The archers who killed some and wounded others, but are necessarily ignorant as to how many, must do penance as for three Lents.

Apart from the actual battle, anyone who before the consecration of the king killed those who resisted as he was going through the countryside for the sake of food, must do penance for one year for each man he so killed. But if it was not for food, but merely for plunder that he was foraging, he must do penance for three years for each man he then killed.

[1] See Table 12.
[2] The cross before the 'sign' of Maurice may have been made by Maurice himself.
[3] The text is deficient at this point: the word *iussu*, however, appears.
[4] Hastings.
[5] This evidence of clerks and monks fighting at Hastings is important. The comments of Odo, bishop of Bayeux (see above, Bayeux Tapestry, Plate LXXII) would have been interesting.
[6] *tantum praemio.*
[7] *in publico bello.*

Those who have killed men after the consecration of the king must do penance as for homicides wilfully committed, always with this exception, that if the men thus killed or wounded were in arms against the king, then the penalties will be as before stated.

Those who committed adulteries or rapes or fornications must do penance as if these sins had been committed in their own country.

Concerning the violation of the church likewise. Let those who stole from churches restore what they stole to the church they robbed if they can. If they cannot, let them restore it to some other church. And if they will not restore it, then the bishops have decreed that they may not sell it, nor may anyone buy it.

82. Allocation of the liability to pay Peter's Pence in East Kent in the eleventh century

This document, which was drawn up shortly after the Norman Conquest at the instigation of Lanfranc, most probably represents an assessment which had already been in force before the Conquest. The regular payment of this exceptional levy from England in the reign of Edward the Confessor is well established. This text provides evidence as to the manner in which it was allocated among various estates, boroughs and churches in a section of the diocese of Canterbury. Printed in D. C. Douglas, *Domesday Monachorum of Christ Church, Canterbury* (1944), p. 80. Translated in *Victoria County History: Kent*, vol. III, p. 257.

ROME-SCOT FROM EAST KENT

From St. Augustine's [abbey], 50 shillings.
From Dover, 10 shillings.
From Hugh of Montfort-sur-Risle, 22 shillings and 6 pence.
From Maidstone, 10 shillings.
From Limminge, 7 shillings.
From Milton Regis, 20 shillings.
From Bishopsbourne, 6 shillings.
From Chartham, 4 shillings.
From Aldington, 20 shillings.
From Chilham, 3 shillings and 8 pence.
From Barham, 2 shillings and 9 pence.
From Monkton, 7 shillings and 3 pence.
From 'Godwinesburne', 16 pence.
From Teynham, 22 pence.
From Westwell, 3 shillings.
From Wickham, 12 pence.
From Elham, 2 shillings.
From Thanet, 6 shillings and 5 pence.
From Seasalter, 3 shillings.
From Brabourne, 3 shillings and 3 pence.
From Little Chart and Pluckley, 2 shillings and 7 pence.
From Northwood (of the archbishop), 12 shillings.
From Wingham, 14 shillings and 4 pence.
From Stalisfield, 12 pence.
From Wye, 7 shillings.

From East Chart, 4 shillings and 7 pence.
From Ickham, 5 shillings.
From Stowting, 2 shillings.
From Godmersham, 3 shillings and 6 pence.
From Westgate (Canterbury), 3 shillings.
From Coldred, 2 shillings.
From Faversham, 7 shillings.
From Charing, 7 shillings.
From Petham, 4 shillings.
From Adisham, 12 shillings and 8 pence.
From Throwley, 18 pence.
From Mersham, 2 shillings and 8 pence.
From Eastry, 11 shillings and 2 pence.
From 'Bilice', 4 shillings.
From Folkestone, 5 shillings.
From Preston, 16 pence.
From Appledore, 5 shillings and 9 pence.
From the city,[1] 20 shillings.
From Boughton-under-Blean, 16 pence.
From Boughton Aluph, 8 pence.

83. Parochial organization in Kent at the time of the Norman Conquest

This text illustrates a transitional stage in the evolution of the medieval English parish. The churches which head the sections are the ancient baptismal churches which served wide areas. Out of the districts so served were the later parishes carved. The transition was apparently not complete in the reign of William I. It will be noted how some of the 'parish churches' are designated by the saints to whom they are dedicated; some by the layman who has apparently built them, or to whom they belong; whilst others are named by reference to the villages they serve. The development has begun whereby the region served by a community attached to a minster church makes way for the parish served by a single priest, supported by the revenues of a single church, and normally coincident with the village of which it was the ecclesiastical counterpart. Printed and discussed in D. C. Douglas, *Domesday Monachorum of Christ Church, Canterbury* (1944), pp. 8–13, 78–79; translated in *Victoria County History: Kent*, vol. III, p. 256.

To St. Martin of Dover there belong these churches: St. Peter's; St. Mary's; five minsters within the city; Charlton; Denton; 'Niwantun'; two churches in Ewell; 'Itun'; another church in Ewell; Walton; West Cliffe; Northbourne; St. Margaret at Cliffe; Guston.

To Folkestone there belong: Ethelwulf's church; 'Bilicean'; 'Circetun'; Swingfield; Alkham; Fleet; Higham; Asholt; Lydden; Woolverton.

To Lympne there belong: St. Lawrence's church; St. Martin's church; Ivychurch; St. Benet's church; Lydd; Siwold's church; Newchurch; two churches in Hythe; Ælsi's church;[2] Blaceman's church[3]; 'Mertumnescirce'; Dymchurch; Ordgar's church; Bilsington; Bonnington; Aldington; Street; Sellinge; Kingston; Wootton; Swarling church.

[1] Canterbury.
[2] Ælsi held Eastbridge within four miles of Lympne from Earl Godwine (*Domesday Book*, vol. I, fol. 13b).
[3] 'Blaceman' was established as a landowner within five miles of Lympne in the time of the Confessor (*ibid.*, fol. 13).

To Lyminge belong: Wittersham; St. Peter's church; St. Martin's church; 'Stanford'; Horton; Stowting; Bircholt; Stelling; Acrise; Paddlesworth.

To Newington belong: Hartlip; Rainham; Upchurch; Stockbury; Halstow; Sexburga's minster; 'Niwecyrce'.

To Teynham belong: Doddington; Stone; Selling; Iwade.

To Wingham belong: Ash; Nonnington; Ratling; Womenswold; Walmestone; 'Eadredestun'.

To Maidstone belong: Boxley; Detling; Thornham; Aldington; Hollingbourne; 'Welcumeweg'; Lenham; Boughton Malherbe; Ulcombe; Leeds; Langley; Sutton; Chart; Headcorn; Frinsted; Goudhurst; Marden.

To Wye belong: Ashford; Crundale; Brook; Trimworth; Hinxhill; 'Brixiestun'; Eastwell; Hawkhurst.

To Charing belongs: Egerton.

To [1] belong: Wilmington; Challock; Bridge; Barham; the other Barham; the minster at Herne; Garrington; Nackington; Hernehill.

84. Trial of William of St. Calais, bishop of Durham, in the court of King William II

The authorship of this tractate is unknown, but it was clearly written by someone connected with the church of Durham, and it would seem to have been compiled by an eyewitness of the events it describes. It has, indeed, been generally accepted as an authentic contemporary description of this important trial, and it is considered in that light, and further discussed, in this sense, by C. W. David, in *Eng. Hist. Rev.*, vol. XXXII, 1917; by E. A. Freeman, *William Rufus* (1882), vol. I, pp. 89–117; and by G. B. Adams, in *Council and Courts in Anglo-Norman England* (1926), pp. 43–70. A recent, and remarkable, article by H. S. Offler (*Eng. Hist. Rev.*, vol. LVI, 1951) has, however, challenged the view that this is a record contemporary with the events it describes, and suggests that it was concocted for polemical purposes at a later date, and should be referred to "the second quarter of the twelfth century". If this conclusion were accepted, the evidence of this text on matters of detail would clearly have to be scrutinised with caution, but in any case the record remains of value as an early description of the activities of the Anglo-Norman *curia regis*. The text has been printed in *Monasticon Anglicanum* (1817), vol. I, p. 244, and in the Rolls Series edition of the works of Simeon of Durham (vol. I, pp. 170–195). A translation is given in J. Stevenson, *Church Historians of England*, vol. III, pt. ii.

CONCERNING THE UNJUST PERSECUTION OF WILLIAM,[2] BISHOP OF DURHAM, BY WILLIAM THE KING, SON OF WILLIAM THE GREAT KING

In the year of our Lord 1080, Walcher, bishop of Durham, was killed by the men of his diocese, and after six months and ten days he was succeeded by William, who was elected bishop of Durham on 9 November, and ordained on 5 January at Gloucester by Thomas, archbishop of York, in the presence of William the king[3] and of all the bishops of England. This William who was made bishop of Durham had been one of the clergy of Bayeux; he became a monk in the monastery of St. Calais; he was then successively prior of the cloister, major prior, and abbot of the monastery of St. Vincent; and finally he was translated to the bishopric of Durham by King William, who had found him assiduous in the conduct of difficult business. He was a man of acute mind, being supple in counsel and of great eloquence and wisdom. Moreover, he had read in the *Ecclesiastical History of the English People*[4] and in the

[1] Name omitted: the minster church here involved was probably at Eastry.
[2] *Deiniusta vexatione Willelmi episcopi.*
[3] William I.
[4] By Bede.

Life of St. Cuthbert[1] that, before the time of St. Cuthbert and for many years afterwards, a convent of monks had served God in the church of Durham, but that subsequently, together with nearly all other churches and monasteries it had been destroyed by the pagans. He therefore determined to restore the ancient monastic practice in the capital church of his diocese. Wherefore he went to Rome at the bidding of King William, and faithfully reported to Pope Gregory[2] the ancient and present state of the church at Durham. Coming back with the apostolic command and authority, he restored the monastic life around the body of St. Cuthbert at Pentecost on 28 May in the third year of his episcopate and in the seventeenth year of King William's reign. On the death of this king, his son, William, was consecrated king on 26 September [1087], and from him as from his father the bishop had great honour. But a dispute broke out between the king and the magnates of England so that there was great disturbance in the land, and as a consequence the bishop, being surrounded by enemies, incurred the anger of the king to such an extent that he was exiled. This affair is narrated in due order in the little book[3] which here begins.

King William the younger formally dispossessed the bishop of Durham of his possessions and of the lands of his church on 12 March,[4] and, as far as he could, caused his men and his property to be seized. He also ordered that the bishop himself should be taken prisoner and prepared ambushes for him. With the help of God, the bishop escaped from these traps and reaching Durham he immediately sent a messenger to the king with the following letter:

> To William the king, his lord, William, bishop of Durham, sends greeting and faithful service. Know, my lord, that your men of York and Lincoln hold my men in captivity; that they have seized my lands; that if they had been able they would have seized me also; and that they say they have done these things by your order. I claim then from you, as my lord, that you cause my men and my lands and my cattle to be restored to me, as to your man and vassal whom you have never formally accused of any breach of duty, and who has never failed to render you just service. If, afterwards, you formally accuse me of any breach of duty, I shall be ready under a safe-conduct to come to your court at an agreed time and there to do you justice. But I beseech you not to treat me basely or with dishonour by reason of the advice of my enemies, and I beg you not to keep me unjustly out of my possessions. It is not for everyone to judge bishops, and I offer you such full justice as is consistent with my order. If, however, in the meantime you wish to have my service and the service of my men, I offer this to you at your pleasure.

When the king had seen the bishop's messenger and heard the letter read, he distributed the lands of the bishop among his barons. Further, he sent word to the bishop saying that he might come to the king's court on the understanding that, if he did not wish to remain there, he would be allowed to return unmolested to Durham. On receipt of this message, the bishop prepared to go to the king, and sent a messenger to York asking the sheriff for a peaceful passage to the court. But Ralph Paynel, who was then sheriff, refused to grant such passage either to the bishop or to his messengers

[1] By Bede [2] Gregory VII. [3] *libellus.* [4] 1088.

or to his men; and he seized the bishop's messenger who was returning from the king, and having killed his horse afterwards allowed him to depart on foot. Besides this, the sheriff ordered the king's liegemen that on behalf of the king they should inflict damage on the bishop whenever and wherever they could. The bishop was thus unable to attend the king either in person or by deputy, and for more than seven weeks he saw his lands being destroyed and laid waste without having a remedy. At length the king sent to the bishop the abbot of St. Augustine's with an order that, in accordance with his previous command, the bishop should now come to the king's court with the abbot. But the bishop, fearing the anger of the king and the plots of his enemies, replied that he could not come without a safe-conduct, and he sent his messenger to the king with the following letter:

> To his lord William, king of the English, William, bishop of Durham, sends greeting and faithful service. Know, my lord, that after I left your court I immediately sent a messenger with a letter to you in which I presented to you my service, which was offered to you as to my king and lord; and I sent you also a rebuttal of the charges which had been made against me. I further asked of your mercy that you should cause to be restored to me my men and lands and cattle which your sheriffs had taken from me, as far as they could, at Howden and Wellton and at other places in Yorkshire and which had been apportioned between Count Odo[1] and Count Alan,[2] and this without any reason being given on your part, and at a time when I was always ready to justify myself before you. I asked, also, that this restitution should be made to me as your man and vassal who had never failed in his duty but had tried to serve you faithfully, and who still wished to do so. It did not then please you to restore my property to me, as I had asked and as seemed just to me. Nevertheless you offered me your peace so that I could come to you, abide with you and return from you in safety. This you offered me by writ; and in the same writ you commanded your liegemen throughout England that all my possessions should remain unmolested until you knew whether I should remain with you. But when I sent this writ to Ralph Paynel, not only did he deny me peace, but on your behalf he formally renounced my service, and on the morrow he ravaged the lands of our church; he distributed my possessions; and he sold some of my men and held others to ransom. Further, the men of this same Paynel arrested the monk who was carrying your writ and killed his horse. In addition to all this, I learnt that you had given away part of my estates, and when I sought to acquaint you with these things Paynel refused my men passage through your lands. Now you have sent me a letter through the abbot of St. Augustine's bidding me come to you. But I beseech you, and, as my king and my lord I request you, that you will return to me my possessions which were taken from me without good cause, and without any legal judgment being pronounced against me. Then gladly will I come to your court, and consistently with my order I will submit to whatever may be judged as just. If I am able to persuade you on this matter I shall give thanks to God and to you. But if it does not please you to restore my property, I shall none the less be ready to come under a safe-conduct to your court,

[1] Odo, count of Champagne.
[2] Alan I, 'the Red' of Richmond, Yorks., a count of Brittany.

and there to make my defence in the presence of all your barons. I shall show that I have neither made nor received any pledge which could do harm to your body or your lands or your honour; nor have I ever consciously revealed your secrets; nor have I ever concealed any threat of damage to you, but rather have I always by word or messenger or letter informed you of it as quickly as I could. Thus I have acted consistently since the day when I last left your court. Therefore in all sincerity I ask you that I may come with this abbot freely and without fear of the designs of my enemies or of the uninstructed rabble, and without doubts about the efficacy of your writ or the faith of your barons. Wherefore I pray you that you will send me a pledge that will conduct me with your honour and my safety to your court, and will likewise ensure my safe return. For although I firmly trust your word that no harm will be inflicted upon me by your orders, yet if against your will harm should befall me, it would profit me little if I should subsequently be avenged. If, moreover, I come to you without having had my possessions restored, I shall in the meantime make no plea save that which shall establish my innocence.

When the king had read this letter he sent a safe-conduct to the bishop and pledged his faith that the bishop should be molested by none of his men until he was safely returned to Durham after his visit to the king. Then the bishop went to the king and pleaded that the king should do justice to him as a bishop. But the king replied that if the bishop would waive the pledge of temporary peace and would plead in lay fashion as a feudal tenant, the king would consent in this manner to try him; but if the bishop refused to plead in this manner he should be conducted back to Durham. The bishop therefore asked the archbishop of York and the bishops who were present to give him counsel, but they replied that the king had forbidden it. Then the bishop formally demanded from his archbishop, by virtue of the duty which he owed him, whether he was unable to give him counsel, but the archbishop having consulted the king, declined to do so. The bishop therefore begged the king that he would allow his archbishop and his primate, and the bishops, his peers, to give him advice, but the king absolutely forbade it. The bishop finally offered to purge himself before the king from the charges of crime and breach of faith, and when the king refused to accept this defence he returned to Durham. Meanwhile the king seized more than seven hundred of the bishop's men and much plunder. Wherefore the bishop again sent his messenger to the king with the following letter:

To William, king of the English, William, bishop of Durham, sends greeting, and if the king wishes it, service also. Be it known to you, dearest lord, that often by messages and letters, I have asked your mercy, offering to purge myself in your court from the charges of infidelity and breach of faith by the process of law proper to my order. When I could not prevail upon you to consent to this, I came to you, but the counsel of my enemies was too strong for me, and it availed me little. Now since I earnestly desire to regain your love which I have unjustly lost, I demand from you, my lord and king, that within the security of your peace you will do justice to me as to your man and your bishop according to the process of law proper to my order. And if you still hold to your decision that I must plead in lay fashion, I am prepared to submit in the first instance to a fair trial of this kind. But I make this condition, that before anyone is permitted to inflict punishment upon me as a result of this trial, I shall be allowed, under the security of your pledged peace, to appeal against this judgment according to the rights of my order and in a place where canon law is administered. I further promise to abide by whatever judgment is there canonically pronounced, whether it be imprisonment or loss of office, or (as God may justly grant) the restoration of your favour and affection. In token of this I am ready to give you a suitable pledge. If, however, you deny me this, and are resolutely determined not to try me, allow me at least to clear myself in your court from the charges of perjury and breach of faith. Your father, who gave me the land I hold, was such a lord as allowed me to possess my lands with honour, and he promised yet further to enrich me, but now I have no wish to hold any land from you against your will.

When the king had read this letter, he caused the monk who had brought it to be thrown into prison, and he sent troops against the bishop. But after these troops had visited the bishop's lands with fire and pillage, some barons entered into negotiations with the bishop, and the following sworn pact was made between them.

Count Alan and Roger of Poitou,[1] and Count Odo have pledged their faith to the bishop of Durham on the Nativity of Holy Mary[2] that they will conduct him in safety to the court of the king on the condition that if the king is unwilling to try him according to bishop's law by such judges as ought to try bishops, then the aforesaid counts will conduct the bishop back to Durham as soon as the bishop wishes it. If such judgment be pronounced against the bishop as seems to him unjust, and he appeals against it, and if the king and his judges wish to have their judgment confirmed in the place where the trial of prelates should be concluded, then the bishop shall be conducted safely back to his castle. If, however, the king proves that no appeal can justly be made and the bishop agrees; or if no appeal in fact arises; or if an appeal is made by the king and his judges to have their judgment confirmed in a proper place, and the bishop is unable or unwilling to accept this; then without delay the king shall find a harbour and as many ships as may be necessary for the bishop and his men; and the bishop himself shall choose the harbour somewhere between Exeter and Sandwich; and the bishop and his men shall have the safe-conduct of the king until they reach dry land beyond the sea. And they shall be allowed to take with them gold and silver, horses, clothes, arms, dogs and hawks and all such things as are seemly for them to take away from the country. And the bishop and his men shall not be compelled either by force or fraud to make any other agreement save that which they have here made with Roger of Poitou.

The bishop on his side has pledged his faith to Roger of Poitou that if he be conducted back to his castle and during his absence the castle has been strengthened either in its garrison or in its fortification, then the bishop will cause such additional armament to be totally removed lest the bishop should have unfair profit or the king unfair loss. And until Michaelmas when the bishop starts on his journey to the king, he

[1] Son of Roger of Montgomery, first earl of Shrewsbury.

[2] 8 September.

shall not do damage to the king nor wittingly treat of things which might be to the king's hurt.

Besides this, seven men of the bishop at his command swore to Roger of Poitou, who in this matter acted for the king, that if the bishop refused proper legal satisfaction as aforesaid, and chose to go into exile, they would give up the castle of Durham to the king. The bishop on his part pledged his faith to Roger of Poitou that he would be the faithful servant of the king so long as the pact with the counts was in force, and that he would use no guile save that which he might legitimately employ in his legal action against the king. The counts pledged their faith to the bishop that the king would observe his pact, and that the trial should not be postponed after the next Michaelmas except with the bishop's agreement or for such period as might be arranged between the legal advisers of the king and the bishop. Moreover, if it should happen that any man or horse of the bishop should fall sick, they should enjoy the king's peace so long as they were detained by illness, and afterwards they should be allowed either to rejoin the bishop or, with the bishop's consent, to remain peacefully with the other men of the king and do fealty to him. But if the king should break the agreement in any way either through the agency of the counts or through that of any of his men, they should take no profit from this breach of contract until the bishop had freely and without compulsion absolved them.

After these agreements had been accepted by both parties it was at length arranged that the trial should begin on 2 November [1088], and on that day the bishop came to Salisbury. Thereupon Urse of Abbetot, one of the servants of the king, bade him come into the king's presence, but instead the bishop sent his representatives to the king and asked that he might first be allowed to speak with certain of his brother bishops who were there, for none of them, they say, had dared to offer him a kiss of greeting or such advice as the bishop had already received from his metropolitan. But the king forbade this, and since no one of them bestowed on him this symbol of brotherhood, as is prescribed by church law, the bishop inquired of the archbishops whether he should come into the king's presence robed in his ecclesiastical vestments; and he said: "Nothing shall here be transacted except canonically and consistently with my order, so it seems to me that the custom of the church demands that I should make my plea vested and in the presence of vested prelates so that in due canonical form I may reply to the charges brought against me."

To which Lanfranc replied: "Clothes do not cloak truth, and clad as we are we shall be able to judge the rights of the king and yours."

The bishop then rose and prayed the king that he would give him back his bishopric which had been unjustly taken away. The king made no reply, but Lanfranc said: "The king has taken nothing away from your bishopric. Nor have any of his men. Nor have you seen any writ of his which ordered you to be deprived of anything pertaining to your bishopric."

"I have seen Ralph Paynel," retorted the bishop, "and I see him here now, and he it was who at the king's command robbed me of all my bishopric in the county of York. Moreover, when by messenger and letters I prayed the king that my possessions should be returned, and when I asked the king to give me fair trial as his bishop in respect of the accusations which were made against me, the king gave me back nothing, but distributed the lands of my church among his barons. Afterwards I offered to justify myself in person at the king's court, but the king not only kept what he had taken from me, but further ordered that what remained should be seized, and he sent letters to his barons in the neighbourhood ordering them to do me what harm they could. And as if this was not enough, the king sent counts and barons with troops who laid waste all my bishopric. He also took from me the lands and men and cattle of St. Cuthbert, and compelled me for a time to leave my see. Even the tenants of the church who were my liegemen and who held whatever they possessed by tenure from the church, made private war against me by command of the king, but despite this they still continue to hold their lands peacefully from the king, and now I see them here with the king gathered against me."

Then Lanfranc spoke: "The king has summoned you to justify yourself before him, and it is for that purpose that his barons have conducted you to this place. Do you therefore first give him satisfaction, and afterwards you may make what demands you please."

The bishop replied: "My lord archbishop, are you saying this as judgment or as advice?"

"Certainly I am not pronouncing judgment," responded Lanfranc, "but if the king will listen to my advice he will quickly cause judgment to be made."

Then the laymen, stirred up by the words of Lanfranc, primate of all England, cried out together against the bishop, exclaiming that it was wrong that the king should reply to the bishop before the bishop had answered the charges of the king; and for a long time they continued vociferously to expostulate with the bishop. When silence had been restored, the bishop said: "My lord barons and laymen, I beg you will allow me to address my remarks to the king, and to the archbishops and bishops, for I have nothing to say to you. Nor have I come here to be judged by you. Indeed I entirely refuse to accept your judgment. But if it please the king and the archbishops and the bishops to associate you with them in this matter, it would not become me to criticize them."

Then the king said: "I had hoped that the bishop would first answer the charges I have brought against him, and I am very surprised that he has spoken of anything else."

And Count Alan and Earl Roger interposed: "We brought the bishop here solely that he should answer the king's charges."

"I am very ready to do so," said the bishop, "even though I have been robbed of my possessions, but only if I am to be judged canonically, for in this trial I shall in no way transgress the law of my order."

Then Roger Bigot addressed the king: "You ought", he said, "to tell the bishop of what you accuse him, and then, if he is ready to defend himself, we shall be able to pass judgment upon him in the light of his reply. But if he refuses to answer your charges, you should take such action as your barons advise."

The bishop answered: "I have said, and I shall continue to say, that I utterly repudiate the judgment of laymen, and whatever is contrary to canon law. Nor will I answer any accusation until either my bishopric is restored to me, or it has been canonically shown that I ought to be charged, defended and judged before such restitution is made."

Then Hugh of Beaumont[1] rose up at the command of the king and charged the bishop in these words: "The king now makes this accusation against you. When he heard that his enemies were come upon him and when his men, to wit, the bishop of Bayeux and Earl Roger and many others sought to rob him of his kingdom and his crown, he took arms against them by your counsel, and as I myself heard, he commanded you to join his expedition. You replied that you would willingly assist him with the seven knights who were with you, and that you would send without delay for more from your castle. But afterwards you fled from his court without his leave, and took away some of your household, and thus you failed him in his necessity. Now therefore it is his will that you should make such amends to him as his court shall judge right, and later, if it be necessary, the king will have other complaints to make against you."

"You can say what you like, Hugh," answered the bishop, "but I will not reply to you further today; nor will I answer any other accusation; nor will I enter any plea until it has been formally decided that I ought to plead without my possessions being returned to me or before I have been canonically restored to my bishopric. After that I will of my own free will reply to the accusations of the king, and will show that whatever I have done, I have done lawfully and justly, so that on no count can I be found guilty."

At this there was a great uproar among the laymen, who repeatedly shouted insults and protests against the bishop, but he himself said nothing. Whereupon Geoffrey of Coutances spoke: "My lord archbishops, it would be better if we did not pursue this matter any further at present. Let us rather retire and call together a committee of bishops and abbots with certain barons and counts in order that it may be decided whether the bishop should be reinstated before he is judged on the charges made against him by the king."

But Lanfranc opposed this suggestion: "There is no necessity for us to retire," he said. "Let the bishop and his men retire, and we who remain, both clergy and laymen together, may thus on an equal footing consider what course should be adopted."

"I willingly retire," said the bishop, "but I solemnly tell you, archbishops and bishops, that whatsoever you do in my trial you must do canonically and in due order. Nor should you associate with you in your judgment those whom the decretals and canons forbid to undertake the trial of bishops."

"Go!" said Lanfranc. "Whatever we do will be justly done."

And Hugh of Beaumont called out to the bishop: "If today I cannot judge you and your order, you and your order will never again judge me."

"See to it", replied the bishop, "that those who remain behind in this place appoint ecclesiastical judges to try me according to canon law, for otherwise I shall refuse to accept judgment."

And thus with his men he left the court, and the king with his bishops and magnates and sheriffs, together with his officials, huntsmen and other servants, remained behind in judgment.

After a long delay the bishop was recalled and Thomas, archbishop of York, thus

[1] No Hugh of Beaumont is known in this connexion, and it has been suggested that this is a mistake for Henry of Beaumont. In this case, however, Henry of Beaumont would be styled earl of Warwick, if, as is generally supposed, he received that dignity before November 1088.

addressed him: "My lord bishop, our lord archbishop and the court of the king has decided that you should answer the king's charges before he reinvests you with your fief."

The bishop replied: "It is with my bishopric that I have asked to be reinvested, for it is of my bishopric that I have been robbed, and that without any summons or judgment. I left this court that I might be judged about my bishopric and on that I now demand your verdict. Not one word has today been spoken by me or anyone else about my fief."

The archbishop of York replied: "The court decides that the king need restore nothing to you before you justify yourself before him."

"Will someone versed in canon law", asked the bishop, "tell me whether this is a canonical judgment? For I never heard that a judgment of this kind had the sanction either of ecclesiastical custom or of the law of the Church, and if I accepted an uncanonical judgment I should sin alike against holy Church and against the sacred order of the priesthood. Although perhaps I should do myself little immediate harm, yet in the future many might be led astray by my example. Therefore I ask for authoritative ruling that this is right."

"The judgment is a just one," declared Lanfranc, "and you must either accept and obey it, or else argue against it in this court."

"With the king's permission," replied the bishop, "I should like to consult some of these bishops whether I ought to accept or reject this judgment."

Lanfranc retorted: "The bishops are your judges and it is not for them to tender you advice."

"I beg the king to grant me this favour," repeated the bishop, "and I ask the bishops here present for their brotherly counsel."

"Consult your own followers," said the king, "for you will have no further advice from any member of my court."

"From these seven men", said the bishop, "I shall have little counsel that can weigh against the strength and wisdom of the whole kingdom which I now see arrayed against me."

And so he left the court with his men.

When he returned he said to the archbishop: "I reject the judgment which has been pronounced against me, because I hold it to be against the canons and against the law of our Church. For I have not been summoned canonically, but have been coerced by the king's troops, and I have been deprived of my bishopric and now I am being constrained to plead my cause in a lay court outside my own province and in the absence of my fellow-bishops in that province. Moreover, my enemies, who have refused to speak with me or to give me counsel or the kiss of peace, now judge me in respect of words that I have never uttered. They are in fact at the same time my accusers and my judges. I find that the law of our Church forbids me to accept a judgment of this nature, and even if in my weakness I were disposed to accept it, my archbishop and my primate, out of their respect for the order of priesthood, would in their charity prevent me. Therefore, because I know that the king's hostility has made you all my enemies, I appeal to the apostolic see, to the holy Roman Church, to the blessed Peter, and to his vicar. May I always be ready to abide the just verdict which he will give in my case! For the most ancient decrees of bishops, and of the successors of the apostles, have reserved to him the authority to decide on all the greater ecclesiastical questions."

Lanfranc answered: "We are not judging you about your bishopric, but about your fief, and in like manner we passed judgment in the court of this king's father on Odo, bishop of Bayeux. For that king did not then summon to trial the bishop of Bayeux, but his earl and his brother."

The bishop replied: "My lord archbishop, you have not today heard me mention my fief nor the fact that I possess one. It is about my bishopric that I have made my complaint."

"I may not have heard you speak of your fief," retorted the archbishop, "but I know you have a great fief and it is in respect of it that we now judge you."

"My lord archbishop," said the bishop, "I now understand that you have ignored all that I have said, and have judged me according to your own preconceived ideas. God has made you wise and famous, and perhaps in this matter your wisdom is so exalted that I in my littleness cannot comprehend it. But I have made my appeal to the apostolic see and there, with the king's leave and yours, I will go."

"Leave the court," said the archbishop, "and the king after consultation with his liegemen will tell you his pleasure."

After an interval the bishop was called back and Hugh of Beaumont rose and said to him: "My lord bishop, you have refused to reply to the charges which through me the king brought against you, and now you summon the king to Rome as if he were himself a litigant. Therefore the court of the king and his barons have decided that you have forfeited your fief."

The bishop answered: "I am ready in any place, where justice prevails and not violence, to purge myself of the charges of crime and perjury; and this sentence which you have pronounced against me, I shall show to be false and unjust in the court of the Church of Rome."

"I and my peers", retorted Hugh of Beaumont, "are ready to give effect to our judgment in this court."

The bishop replied: "I shall enter no plea in this court, because I can here say nothing so well that the flatterers of the king will not distort it; and these same men show no respect for apostolic authority when, after my appeal, they still try to impose upon me a judgment which is not legal. But I will go to Rome to seek the help of God and of St. Peter."

The king said: "Although you will not accept the judgment of my court, yet in very truth you will give me your castle."

The bishop answered: "In the agreement which I made with you it was agreed that I should not give up my castle unless I refused to obey a canonical judgment, or unless, in the case of an appeal, I refused to answer that appeal in the place where it should properly be heard. But now an appeal has been made and I am ready to continue my case in the Roman Church to which ever since apostolic times has belonged the final authority in ecclesiastical trials."

"By the Face of Lucca!" cried the king, "you will never go out of my hands until I have your castle."

"My lord king," said the bishop, "I suffered three of your servants to rob me of the lands and cattle of the church, and with a hundred of my knights present and under arms I offered no resistance to them. Now nothing remains out of my bishopric except the capital city of my diocese, and this also you wish to take away from me. I put my trust in God but again I do not oppose you. But in the name of God and of St. Peter and of his vicar, our lord the pope, I say to you that you should not take this from me. Moreover I am ready to give you hostages and proper pledges to make certain that my men who remain there while I go to Rome will keep the place faithfully for you, and, if you wish it, will do you faithful service."

"You can be very certain", retorted the king, "that you will not return to Durham, nor will you remain in Durham, nor will you leave my custody, before you have yielded up your castle freely into my hands."

"I place my trust", replied the bishop, "in the honour of your counts who pledged me that I should be conducted safely back to my castle. They are now present in this court, and know well what was agreed between us."

Then Lanfranc said to the king: "If the bishop continues to refuse you his castle, you may justly take him into custody, because the safe-conduct would no longer protect him. He seeks to show that your barons are breaking faith with him, but in fact it is he who has broken faith."

Then Ralph Peverel and all the laymen present started to shout together: "Seize him! Seize him! Well has he spoken, this trusty old liegeman."[1]

At this, Count Alan rose up and said: "I brought the bishop from his castle and led him to the king's court on the understanding that I would conduct him safely back to his castle, if the king refused to do him such justice as his bishop, as could not legitimately be disputed; and if the king offered him such justice and the bishop was either unwilling or unable to abide by it, then the king at the bishop's choosing was to offer him and his men a harbour between Exeter and Sandwich and ships, and the bishop and his men were to be given a safe-conduct until they reached dry land beyond the seas. Now I earnestly pray my lord the king that he will not compel me to break my faith for, if I did so, no one would henceforward place any trust in my honour."

When Counts Roger and Odo were making this request Archbishop Lanfranc intervened and said: "The king has himself given you quittance of your pledge, for he has offered the bishop full justice, and in your hearing the bishop has refused it. The bishop has furthermore unjustly summoned the king to Rome. By such action the bishop admits that we have delivered a judgment according to law, and he has refused to accept it. The king will certainly in due course furnish him with ships and a safe-conduct."

"I must solemnly remind you, counts," said the bishop, "that you are pledged to bring me back to Durham, for the king has refused me justice, as I am prepared to show in the Roman Church."

"No further delay can be tolerated," said Lanfranc. "When judgment is pronounced in this court, it is necessary that in this court it should be either accepted or answered. You must therefore either accept the court's verdict, or, in this place, show good reason for refusing to do so."

[1] *vetulus ligaminarius*; the meaning is uncertain.

The bishop replied: "Without doubt I appeal against this judgment, and I propose to sustain my appeal at Rome, both because it is my duty to do so, and because in that court justice and not violence prevails. And since from fear of the king not one of you dares to testify on my behalf, I call as my witness the written law of the Church, which assures me that I ought to go to Rome, and that the final verdict in this case ought to proceed from the Roman pontiff."

"You can talk as much as you please," said the king, "but you will not go out of my hands until you have yielded me your castle."

To which the bishop replied: "Since you have robbed me of my bishopric and all my possessions, nothing that I can do is likely to prevent you from robbing me also of my bishop's seat."

A day was therefore fixed for the bishop to leave his city and for the king to install his own men there. Then the bishop said: "My lord king, I wish to know whether you propose to leave me anything out of my bishopric to enable me to live."

But Lanfranc answered him: "Are you going to Rome to bring damage to the king and dishonour to all of us? Remain on your lands, and the king will return you all your bishopric except your city, provided always that you will accept the judgment of his barons which they have pronounced in his court."

"I have appealed to the apostolic see", replied the bishop, "because in this court I can obtain no justice. And my decision to go to Rome stands."

"If you go to Rome without the king's permission", said the archbishop, "we will tell him what ought to be done with your bishopric."

The bishop answered: "Up to the present you have told him nothing good about me, and you have been free to tell him what you wished. But before I leave this place I am ready before all these barons to clear myself of all charges of crime and perjury. I have never to my knowledge acted so as to do harm to the king's person or to his lands. Nor have I ever associated myself with any scheme that might prove to his detriment. Immediately I have heard anything to his loss I have warned him of it as soon as possible, and I faithfully helped him against his enemies. All this I shall legally prove. For I will show that in my fealty I held Dover and Hastings which he had almost lost; that on his behalf I pacified London which was on the point of rebellion; and that I brought twelve of the more important citizens of London to him in order that he might persuade them to influence the others. These things I will prove by the testimony of his own barons, if he will allow them to give it. Therefore I earnestly beg him to listen to my defence; that afterwards he will allow me to show my service to him; and that he will graciously allow some of the bishops here present to testify on my behalf."

So the bishop continued to argue, but the king was firm in his refusal. Then Lanfranc said to the bishop: "You would do better to throw yourself on the king's mercy, and if you do so, I will gladly myself go to his feet in your interest."

"I ask his mercy", said the bishop, "solely that for the love of God and of holy Church he will cause to be revised those judgments which have here been promulgated to the loss of the Church, to the confusion of the priesthood, and to the disgrace of Christian law. In that case I will freely serve him and, if it please him, I will make him payment out of my property."

"Throw yourself without reservation on his mercy", repeated Lanfranc, "and do not further question the judgment of this court."

"God forbid", declared the bishop, "that I should accept any uncanonical judgment or one that violates the law of the Church."

Then the king said: "The bishop must give me his promise that he will not seek to do me damage this side of the sea, and that my brother will not, to my loss, and against the will of the sailors, keep the ships which I have provided."

"My lord," answered the bishop, "the counts pledged their faith to me that neither I nor any of my men should be compelled to enter into any further undertakings in addition to those we made at Durham; and I will not give the promise you now ask of me except under compulsion."

And Reginald Paynel added: "Yes, your counts did make this promise, as the bishop says, and it should be kept."

"Be silent," said the king, "I will not lose my ships because of anyone's pledge. But if the bishop will make this promise to me, I will not require any further undertaking from him."

"We have already made many promises to your barons," said the bishop, "and I ought not to make more. Nor ought you to ask me to do so."

Then the king exclaimed in wrath: "By the Face of Lucca, you will not cross the sea this year before you make this promise about my ships."

"I will promise this and much more", replied the bishop, "rather than be kept here in captivity, but let all present take note that I do this under compulsion and against my will."

The bishop then made the required promise and asked for ships and a safe-conduct. But the king said: "You shall not have a safe-conduct until I know that I have received your castle. Until then you will stay at Wilton, and afterwards, but not before, you shall have your ships and your safe-conduct."

The bishop replied: "Since I have no longer any power to do what I wish or what I ought to do, I will act as you command under compulsion, although I know your orders to be unjust."

Then William 'de Merlao' rose and said to the king: "My lord, before the bishop came to this court, his men robbed my lord, the bishop of Coutances, of two hundred head of cattle which were in your keeping; and my lord, the bishop of Coutances, asked that they might be restored to him, but this was refused. Afterwards Walter 'de Haiencorn', acting on your instructions, ordered that the restoration should be made, and still it was refused. Now therefore we pray you that you will cause the cattle of my lord to be restored."

"You may now judge for yourselves, barons," said the king, "whether I justly accused this bishop or not."

But Lanfranc interposed: "It would be unjust if you now accused him further, because now he no longer holds any land from you. And you are pledged to give him his safe-conduct."

On the morrow the bishop, who had retired to consider his choice of a harbour, returned and requested Count Alan that he would find him harbourage and ships at

Southampton. When the king heard this, he said to the bishop: "You must clearly understand that you will not go overseas before I have your castle. For lack of such a precaution I have been much harassed by the bishop of Bayeux, so see you to it that my men are put in possession of the castle of Durham on 14 November. If my men have the castle in their possession on that day then you will get your safe-conduct and your ships without any further questions or delay."

The king therefore, in the hearing of Count Alan and of his other barons, ordered Gilbert the sheriff to deliver to the bishop on 21 November at Southampton as many ships as might be necessary to transport the bishop and his men. But the bishop said to Count Alan: "My lord count, you and your men who have pledged your faith for my safety must see that I am not molested after that date. And as long as I remain in England a trusty man should be attached to my person to ensure that I am not harassed. By these means your honour may be saved and additional persecution avoided."

"The king will do this for you", said Count Alan, "through one of his own servants."

The bishop thus remained at Wilton with Robert of Conteville, who was instructed to provide for his necessities and in due course to conduct him to Southampton, where he might receive his ships and wait for a favourable wind.

On 14 November Ivo Taillebosc and Ernesius 'de Burone' took the castle of Durham into the king's hand, and dispossessed the bishop of his church and his castle and all his land. And they sent Helpo, the king's crossbowman, to the bishop's men with a sealed writ of the king in the following words:

> William, king of the English, to all his liegemen in all England greeting. Know that the bishop of Durham and all his men have my peace throughout the whole kingdom of England, and that they have my permission to cross the sea. Wherefore I forbid all men under my authority to do them harm.

The men of the bishop hoped that the promise of the counts, together with the sealed writ of the king which had been brought by Helpo, would protect them, but Ivo Taillebosc none the less seized two of the bishop's knights and forced them to answer for the cattle of the bishop of Coutances, although it had been decided in the king's court that no action lay against them. Also Ivo Taillebosc, despite the safe-conduct, caused a horse belonging to one of the bishop's knights to be seized. Nevertheless the bishop demanded that Gilbert and Robert should deliver the ships to him on 21 November and that he should be allowed to cross with Roger of Mowbray who was making a passage at that time. But they replied that they would hand over no ship, asserting that the king had ordered them to keep the bishop in captivity, and that he was not to leave the kingdom before fulfilling the king's demands. Thus did they detain the bishop until 26 November, and that day Robert brought him to Southampton. When he arrived the bishop asked to go immediately on board since there was a favourable wind blowing. But the aforesaid servants of the king denied him both the ships and the crossing until the next day when they saw that the wind had failed. Only then did they deliver the ships to him and give him permission to sail. The bishop therefore who had paid his passage money had to tarry once more waiting for a favourable wind.

Later there came to him Osmund, bishop of Salisbury, and Robert 'de Insula' and Richard 'de Cultura', and they summoned him on behalf of the king to come to the king's court in London at Christmas and there to answer for his monk Geoffrey. For this monk (they alleged) had disposed of five hundred and thirty-nine of the bishop's beasts and had reduced the fortifications of the castle during the time that the bishop was standing his trial. The bishop was further summoned to answer for the conduct of certain of his men who (it was said) had killed one of the king's men. The bishop replied, however, to the king's emissaries in these words: "None of these things were done by my orders; and I and my retinue have a safe-conduct. I cannot, moreover, go to the king's court because he has robbed me of everything, so that I have even had to sell my horses to buy food. But if the king will allow me and my men to depart, and thus honour the pledges of his counts, I will by the mercy of God go to the Roman Church where out of my necessity I have made my appeal. But if the king will not permit this, then, rather than be arrested, I will defend myself before you concerning the actions which you impute to my men, and I will show you by my oath that none of these things were done by my orders, although I could justly have given such orders, since before the king dispossessed me I was at liberty to do what I wished with my own."

The king's emissaries therefore refused to hand over the ships to the bishop, who continued to protest. "The king", he said, "has taken away all my lands and possessions, and now, if he desires to take away my retinue also, I will not gainsay him, but with his leave will cross the sea alone."

And he sent one of his knights to the king asking him, for the love of God and St. Peter, for permission to depart for Rome. Then the king sent the bishop of Winchester and Hugh of Port-en-Bessin and Geoffrey 'de Traileio' with orders that the bishop should send the monk Geoffrey to Durham about the aforesaid forfeitures, and that he should himself come to London to justify himself there at Christmas before the king. To these emissaries in turn the bishop made reply: "In accordance with the pact I made with the king's counts I have remained continually in the king's custody. And the counts have pledged their faith to me that if Durham Castle was handed over to the king, I and such of my men as cared to follow me should have safe-conduct and a passage overseas without further delay. Durham is now in the king's hands, and we have come to this port where by the king's orders we have received ships and paid for our passage; and we seek to go to Rome to the apostolic see. Anyone therefore who detains us will commit a grievous sin. None the less I am ready, if it be made a condition of my departure, to defend myself before you upon my oath and to show that none of the things of which you speak were done either by my orders or with my knowledge. Nor have I derived from these actions so much as the price of a loaf of bread. If after this the king keeps back my followers, they must suffer whatever the king inflicts upon them, because for myself I am inflexibly determined to go to Rome as soon as I am released from my bondage."

Then the king's servants caused the bishop to be guarded night and day, and the bishop in his distress sent to Counts Alan and Roger and Odo asking them for his baggage; and he adjured them by the faith in which they were baptized, and by the faith which they had pledged him, that they should deliver him from his captivity, and procure for him ships and a passage without further delay. He asked further that he should be recompensed for the loss and damage which he had unjustly sustained.

At last, therefore, by the intercession of the counts, the king allowed the bishop to depart overseas.

In the eighth year of his bishopric [William of St. Calais] was expelled from England, but he was honourably received by Robert the king's brother, count of the Normans, and he undertook the ecclesiastical charge of all Normandy. After three years he was reconciled to the king and received back his bishopric. This restitution was made on the anniversary of his exile in the presence of the king, the king's brother and a host of the English who were then proceeding to Scotland against King Malcolm. On 11 September, in the second year after his return, he demolished to its foundation the old church which Ealdhun the bishop had built, and in the next year, that is to say in 1093, he began to build a new and better cathedral. This was done in the thirteenth year of his episcopate and in the eleventh year after he had brought back monks to Durham. In that year he and Prior Turgot, who was second to him in the church, laid the first stones on 11 August, and Malcolm, king of Scots, was also present joining in this foundation. In the third year after the church had been begun, the bishop was taken gravely ill at Windsor at Christmastide. He was visited often by Anselm, archbishop of Canterbury of blessed memory, and having confessed his sins he received the archbishop's absolution and repeated benedictions. He was anointed by Thomas, archbishop of York, Walkelin, bishop of Winchester, and John, bishop of Bath. He died on the night of 2 January, that is to say in 1096, and in the thirteenth year after the monks had been brought back to Durham. His body was brought from Windsor to Durham on 16 January, and it was buried in the chapter of the monks.

85. Official declaration by Wulfstan, bishop of Worcester, of the acts of a synod held at Worcester in 1092

This important document is notable as representing a characteristic act of the greatest prelate in the late Old English Church. It took place within three years of his death and it illustrates the policy of a surviving member of the Anglo-Saxon episcopate during the period of the Norman ecclesiastical settlement. The intense conservatism of the document will be noted. The text may also be regarded as an early and outstanding example of that class of documents known as "*Acta Episcoporum*" (see below, Nos. 163–169). It was printed by H. Wharton in *Anglia Sacra*, vol. I (1691), pp. 542, 543, and by T. Hearne in *Hemingi Chartularium Ecclesiae Wigorniensis*, vol. II (1723), p. 527. Wharton's text is here translated.

I, Wulfstan, by the grace of God, bishop of Worcester, ordered a synod to meet at the monastery of St. Mary in those crypts which I myself built from their foundations, and which later by the mercy of God I dedicated. This synod was held in the year of the Incarnation of our Lord 1092 in the fifteenth Indiction. To this synod there came by summons all the wisest persons of the three shires of our diocese, namely Worcestershire, Gloucestershire and Warwickshire. This was done because I, being of great age, was conscious of the weakness of my body, and knew that the end of my life was near. I therefore desired that all the affairs of the church committed to my care should be canonically settled, and that anything which needed amendment should be corrected and amended according to the wise counsel of these men.

While in our humility we were presiding over this synod, there arose a dispute between two priests, namely Alfnoth, priest of St. Helena's and Ala, priest of St. Albans, concerning the parishes and customary rights of their churches; and the controversy between these priests for long occupied the attention of the holy synod.

I, therefore, being anxious for the matter to be decided according to the canons, ordered certain elders who knew the ancient constitution of the churches and parishes of Worcestershire to declare the truth about the most ancient constitution, not only of the aforementioned two churches, but also of all the churches in the city of Worcester.[1]

When the argument between the aforementioned priests took place, a protest was made in the holy synod by the sons of the Church, to wit the monks, who complained that they had suffered loss of revenues owing to the long-standing controversy between the two priests.

I therefore ordered that a verdict should be given concerning the constitution of the other churches, in so far as this affected that of the mother-church. And I further ordered that the following should examine this matter: Thomas the prior; Alfære the writer; Godricpirl the chamberlain; Uhtred the chanter; Ægelric the archdeacon; Edwin, his brother; Ægelmar the priest; and several others whom I chose for this purpose. All of these took common counsel together and reported to the holy synod as follows.

They declared that in the whole city of Worcester there was no parish which did not pertain to the mother-church. They stated further that the mother-church had possessed the vicariate of St. Helena's from the time of King Ethelred and Archbishop Theodore who had then founded it, and there established Bosel as first bishop in the year of the Incarnation of our Lord 680 in the seventh Indiction. This settlement, dating from the days of the aforesaid Bosel, was preserved unbroken by the clerics serving in that place through all the reigns of the bishops of this holy church down to the time of Archbishop Oswald, who with the mandate of King Edgar and by the authority of the pious father, Dunstan, archbishop of Canterbury, changed the congregation of the mother-church and transferred it from the irregular discipline of clerks into the regular discipline and rule of monks. This was done in the year of the Incarnation of our Lord 969 in the twelfth Indiction.

In the time of the pious father Oswald, Wynsius the priest was the vicar of this holy mother-church at St. Helena's. This man, on the injunctions of St. Oswald, renounced the world, and with many others who as clerks served this church, he assumed the garb of monastic discipline. He then gave up the keys of St. Helena's of which hitherto he had had charge as vicar, and made over to the monks for their common use the lands, tithes and other revenues pertaining to that church. Wherefore, after Wynsius had become a monk (together with many others who followed his example of their own free will), the lands, burial-rights and other ecclesiastical perquisites passed into the hands of the monks who now occupied the mother-church: they had previously been held in severalty by the clerks, but they now passed into the

[1] This procedure should be compared with that followed in secular pleas; cf. No. 50.

ownership of the monks and were assigned for their common use. This was done with the assent of King Edgar and of the saints Dunstan and Oswald, archbishops.

In the third year after Wynsius the priest had become a monk, the blessed Oswald made him prior over the monks of the church with the assent of the same king. At the same time Oswald granted to him and all his successors as priors of the same mother-church that they should be deans over all its churches and priests. Thus no one was to set himself up as dean or archdeacon over the churches and priests subjected to the monks except the prior of the church of the monks; and the prior, as supreme dean of the bishop, was to pay to the bishop all the ecclesiastical revenues due from these churches.

The jurors concluded: "We are witnesses to these things which we have learnt from our predecessors and which we have seen in our own time, both under your predecessor Aldred and also in the period of your own rule as bishop."

I, therefore, Wulfstan, having hearkened to this true testimony have ended the dispute between the priests. And I have confirmed this just settlement by my record and seal, and with the witness of the holy synod, taking care that no dissension or scandal may arise between the monks and any other ecclesiastical person concerning these things relating to this holy mother-church. May eternal life in heaven be given to all those who uphold this settlement! And may those who strive to break or worsen it be condemned to everlasting torment with the devil and his angels! Amen.

(*b*) MATERIAL RELATING TO THE LIFE AND POLICY OF ARCHBISHOP LANFRANC

86. Gilbert Crispin: Life of Herluin, abbot of Le Bec

The subject of this biography was the founder and first abbot of the famous monastery of Le Bec-Hellouin. Its author was himself a monk at Le Bec with Lanfranc, and he subsequently joined Lanfranc in England after the latter had become archbishop. Gilbert Crispin became abbot of Westminster in 1085 or 1086, and he continued to hold this office until his death in, or soon after, 1117. Although in this work he is chiefly concerned with Herluin, his narrative is also the earliest and most authoritative source for the Norman career of Lanfranc, and Milo Crispin drew from it most of his material for his *Life of Lanfranc*. Gilbert alone would appear to have given the true story of Lanfranc's coming to Le Bec and his profession as a monk there, and he also tells us something of Lanfranc's relations with William, duke of Normandy, and of the negotiations leading up to his appointment as archbishop of Canterbury in 1070. Not less valuable are the sidelights thrown on the genius and character of the great archbishop. The Latin text was edited with an admirable introduction by J. Armitage Robinson in his *Gilbert Crispin, Abbot of Westminster* (Cambridge, 1911), pp. 95-102.

There was a certain man of Italian birth named Lanfranc, who was universally acclaimed with the love and respect due to him as supreme master of the Latin tongue, the knowledge of which he had restored to its former state. Even Greece too, the mistress of the nations in the liberal arts, gratefully acknowledged his pupils and marvelled at their prowess. This man left his native land and came to Normandy, where he attracted a band of scholars of high renown.[1] Deeming it, however, a vain thing to secure the favour of mortal men, and recognizing that all things come to naught save God who is eternal and those who wait upon him, the learned man

[1] Lanfranc was born at Pavia in Lombardy soon after 1000. He left Italy about 1036, when he had already established a reputation there as a lawyer. He studied theology under his future opponent, Berengar of Tours, and then set up as a teacher in the cathedral school of Avranches. The dates throughout are very uncertain. See R. W. Southern, "Lanfranc of Bec and Berengar of Tours" in *Studies in . . . History presented to F. M. Powicke* (1948).

steadfastly applied his mind to win his love. So he followed the plan of doing God's will, which he had found to be the more perfect in his studies; forsaking everything and renouncing even his liberty in order to follow him who said: "If any man will come after me, let him deny himself, and take up his cross and follow me."[1] And because he now desired to become as lowly as once he had been great, he thought to find a place where there were no men of letters to hold him in honour and esteem. Accordingly he came to Le Bec, which was considered to be the poorest and most despised of all monasteries. It chanced that at the moment he arrived, the abbot[2] was occupied in building an oven, working at it with his own hands. His lowly demeanour and dignity of speech gained Lanfranc's respect, and there he was made a monk.

Then might have been witnessed a godly rivalry between the two men. The abbot, who had grown old as a layman before being made a clerk, regarded with awe the eminence of such a teacher now placed under his governance. Lanfranc, however, displayed no arrogance over his learning, but was humbly obedient in everything, observing, admiring and commending the grace which God had granted the abbot in understanding the Scriptures. The abbot, on his part, showed him fitting reverence, while Lanfranc endeavoured to give him his entire obedience. Both had to live together as members of a family, the one engaged in active pursuits, the other in the life of contemplation. The abbot was skilful in settling disputes of a worldly character and far-sighted in matters pertaining to the abbey's external affairs: no one could have been more prudent or efficient in constructing buildings and procuring the necessities of life, saving his obligations towards holy religion. . . .

But the other, the great teacher, gave all his time to silence and solitude in the cloister, cultivating the fallow fields of his heart with the seed of God's word by constant reading and often watering them with the fragrant tears of repentance. So for three years he dwelt in solitude, unvisited by men, rejoicing in his anonymity, unknown to all save to the very few with whom he occasionally conversed. But once his identity was discovered, the rumour spread far and wide, and the fame of the distinguished scholar soon published the name of Le Bec and Abbot Herluin abroad throughout the world. Clerks, the scions of noble houses and the foremost masters of the Latin schools flocked thither,[3] while lay magnates and many men of high lineage bestowed numerous lands upon the church of Le Bec out of love for Lanfranc. Forthwith the abbey was enriched with furniture, possessions and the persons of noble and honourable men. Within the abbey religion and learning increased apace; without, the supply of all necessities began to flow in abundance. Thus was fulfilled the vision seen in the monastery a few days before this great man entered the religious life. In the valley wherein the abbey stood there was seen to rise a fountain whose waters gushed forth even to the summit of the hills and, flowing in every direction, flooded the whole plain. The fountain was the abbot, sprung up, as it were, in the enclosed valley of humility; the waters, overflowing on every side, were the monks who

[1] Matthew xvi. 24.
[2] Herluin, founder of Le Bec and first abbot.
[3] Among the scholars of Le Bec at this time were included the future Pope Alexander II; Anselm and Theobald, later archbishops of Canterbury; Ivo, bishop of Chartres, the great canonist; Gilbert Crispin, abbot of Westminster, the author of this account, and many others destined to high preferment in the English and Norman churches.

received from him the increase of religion, that is to say, the discipline of divine learning, whereby many of them afterwards received promotion from that very house in lands far and wide.

Lanfranc was also chosen by William, duke of Normandy, to be his chief counsellor and to administer the affairs of the whole duchy.[1] Thanks to the duke, God instantly turned a great calamity, which one day suddenly overtook him, into a cause for unexpected rejoicing, and that in a manner worth relating. Through accusations brought by certain informers the duke was violently incensed against Lanfranc[2] and gave orders that he should be driven out of the monastery and banished from the duchy. Nor could he sate his passion by this sentence, but ordered a vill of the said monastery called Parque to be burned, and this savage order was duly carried out. At the departure of him who was all the joy and solace of the brethren, deep sorrow remained. Because no better mount was to be had, Lanfranc was offered a horse lame in one leg and a single servant for escort. So the brethren were instant in prayer according to the word of the prophet Jeremiah, "Waiting in silence for the salvation of the Lord."[3] As he took his departure Lanfranc straightway met the duke coming the opposite way and greeted him as his lord, while his lame nag bobbed his head towards the ground at every step. Conscious of his innocence, he was not unhopeful of his cause, if an opportunity of speech with the duke could be secured. At first the duke turned his face away but, moved by divine clemency, he immediately looked back at Lanfranc with compassion, and with a kindly gesture permitted him to come forward and speak. Thereupon Lanfranc addressed him with a timely jest, "At your command I am turning my steps from your duchy, hindered by this useless quadruped. Give me a better horse that I may the better obey your command." Smiling the duke replied, "What man ever demanded from an offended judge a reward before the crime he was charged with has been expiated?" Then at last the skilled advocate craved audience and received it. Commending the settlement of his cause to him who hath made eloquent the tongues of babes,[4] and with the active assistance of the monks who were praying to God for him, he so successfully pleaded his cause that in a short while he brought it to the desired conclusion. He was instantly restored to full favour and was accorded a promise that thereafter he should not suffer the injustice of being forced to clear himself from any accusation. Then followed kisses and embraces of gratitude, with which arguments he altogether undermined the whole case of his adversaries. Even the property, which the duke had just previously ordered to be ravaged, he now gave a promise to restore with substantial increase. A messenger was sent on post-haste to inform the monks of Lanfranc's return. Their sorrow was turned into joy: not once only, as is the Church's custom, but continuously and throughout the day, and by all men everywhere the *Te Deum Laudamus* was chanted, not only with the lips but from the very heart. The abbot[5] could hardly credit the unexpected

[1] A palpable exaggeration; Lanfranc at this time was merely one of the host of Norman ecclesiastics whose help and advice William occasionally accepted in his efforts to promote reforms in the life and administration of the local churches.

[2] Lanfranc strongly disapproved of William's marriage to Maud, which had been already condemned by Rome as being within the prohibited degrees. Herfast, the duke's chaplain, appears to have stirred up trouble for Lanfranc at William's court; see A. J. Macdonald, *Lanfranc* (1926), pp. 34–36.

[3] Lamentations iii. 26.

[4] Cf. Psalms viii. 2.

[5] Herluin.

issue of events until the return of him whose absence for a single day had seemed to the monks in their anxiety to have lasted for several years. Their joy was the more increased because complete restitution was made for the property which had been destroyed, and confirmation was also obtained from their lord of the many lands bestowed upon the said church. . . .

Not long afterwards, on account of the increase in the number of its inmates, there was fulfilled in the abbey the word of the Lord through the prophet Isaiah, saying, "The place is too strait for me; give place to me that I may dwell."[1] Because the size of the buildings was indeed too restricted to accommodate the crowd of monks who were now gathered there, and the site of the abbey was detrimental to their health, the venerable Lanfranc began to urge Abbot Herluin to erect a larger monastery and more spacious premises on a different site. But the abbot was greatly alarmed at the mere suggestion of undertaking so ambitious an enterprise, being mistrustful of his strength in his declining years. Lanfranc lost no opportunity of exhorting, encouraging and often urging him to do this, but the abbot utterly refused to agree, until the choir of the abbey church fell in as a sign from heaven. In his great distress and confusion at this untoward event the abbot was again approached by Lanfranc with words of consolation, beseeching him to agree now to begin the construction of larger buildings. Finally the abbot gave way; putting his whole trust in God and relying chiefly upon the aid of his counsellor, whose labours were always productive of benefits to him, he commenced the erection of a monastery and outbuildings on a new and healthier site, on a grander and worthier scale, and of a dignity to which many richer abbeys did not attain. To this enterprise the abbot devoted not only his own resources, which were very small, but most of all his faith in God. By contributions from every quarter his resources were so augmented that, from the day the foundations were laid, up to the placing of the last stone, neither material nor money was lacking. Those whose responsibility it was to control expenditure have borne witness that very often the funds available each week were less than the sum due to the workmen, yet whenever the time for payment came, God provided sufficient for the purpose.

When three years had passed and only the church remained to be completed, the venerable Lanfranc, the author of the enterprise, was promoted abbot of the church of Caen,[2] having been constrained to accept by the entreaties both of the duke and of the prelates of Normandy. The progress of the building was for a time retarded, but his advice and liberal aid were always available whenever they were needed.[3] The church of Le Bec had now at last so many and great resources and flourished so mightily under the skilful guidance of its abbot, that no lack of funds caused the work to flag. Indeed by the time it was finished the prosperity which followed through this speeding up of the work compensated for the previous delay.

In the meantime William, duke of the Normans, taking possession of his

[1] Isaiah xlix. 20.

[2] The actual date of Lanfranc's appointment as abbot of Duke William's new foundation of Caen is still uncertain, owing to the contradictions implicit in the various accounts extant. He was probably appointed in 1063, three years after the commencement of the building operations at Bec referred to in the text above, but he does not appear to have been formally invested as abbot until the eve of the expedition for the Norman Conquest of England, *i.e.* July 1066.

[3] As the abbey church at Caen was also in process of building, Lanfranc could probably spare little financial aid for Bec.

hereditary kingdom of England, subjugated the rebel forces to his authority by force of arms. After this he turned his attention to the improvement of the condition of the churches there. Having sought the advice of Pope Alexander,[1] a man of upright life and great experience, and having also obtained the willing assent of all the magnates of the realm, both English and Norman, King William adopted the plan, which he alone had first conceived, and appointed Lanfranc to this task.[2] Overcome by a variety of arguments the latter was translated to England and undertook the office of archbishop of Canterbury which carried with it the primacy of the islands across the seas. Endowed with a wide extent of property and enriched with gold and silver, he fulfilled the command laid down in the book of Exodus, "Honour thy father and thy mother, that thy days may be long in the land"[3] and in every way showed himself well disposed towards his ghostly father[4] and mother-church.

His translation to England was foreshadowed to Abbot Herluin in a vision after this manner a few days before the invitation to him arrived. It seemed to the abbot as if he had in his orchard an apple-tree whose spreading branches were laden with abundance of fruit. The form and flavour of the apples were of surpassing loveliness. King William demanded the tree, desiring to transplant it to one of his own orchards. When the abbot was reluctant and entreated that this tree at least might be spared, the king, because he was master, overcame his opposition and carried off the tree. But its roots could not all be torn up, and from those which remained there immediately sprouted forth suckers which grew up into tall trees. A little later on in the dream the king came back to rejoice with the abbot over the abundance of fruit his tree had borne, and the abbot, sharing his delight, replied that he too had had splendid offshoots from it. The king then invited him to come and see for himself the increase of the tree which had been transplanted, but other cares–I know not what–prevented him from making the journey. Moreover, all these things came to pass in the issue of events, just as the vision indicated, save that the abbot did not actually go to see what he had been told.

The abbot's orchard was the church of Le Bec and the great tree Lanfranc, the excellent teacher, who sustained by his doctrine and example not only Le Bec but also all the other churches throughout the land. When invited by King William through his abbot (to whom he owed obedience under God) to cross the seas to deliver instruction to the English, he obeyed all unwillingly the orders reluctantly given him by his abbot. The abundance of fruit he afterwards brought forth there is widely attested by the renewal everywhere of ecclesiastical ordinances.[5] The monastic Order, which had wholly lapsed into worldly corruption, was reformed in accordance with the discipline of the most approved houses; clerks were compelled to live under canonical rule; the idle vanities of barbarian customs were forbidden to the laity, and they were instructed in the true faith and the right way of life.

This fruit, so dear to God for its sweetness and fragrance, whose odour filled the

[1] Alexander II, 1061–1073.
[2] He was formally elected on 15 August 1070 and solemnly consecrated a fortnight later on 29 August.
[3] Exodus xx. 12. [4] *i.e.* the pope.
[5] Probably a veiled reference to Lanfranc's "Monastic Constitutions".

Church of God throughout the world, and which the abbot had so gladly perceived even though absent, he afterwards yet more joyfully felt when he was present with Lanfranc during his subsequent visit to England. . . .[1] After a prosperous voyage the ship anchored in the port of Dover . . . and five days later the abbot reached Lanfranc[2] in safety.

How each man vied with the other in proffering him his humble submission! The archbishop, who exercised apostolic authority over the churches across the Channel humbled himself before his former abbot like any other monk, seating himself in the second place after the abbot everywhere, except at the solemn celebration of the Mass, and kissing his hand when he received anything from him, save when the other hurriedly snatched it away. To the abbot was accorded the more honourable seat and the right of command in everything. He pardoned the archbishop's servants when they were at fault, and ordered other matters in the household according to his pleasure. The archbishop had the title of lord, but the abbot exercised the authority. The more crowded his court and the more numerous the persons of high degree, both in Church and State, who waited upon him, so much the more humble service did the archbishop render the abbot in the sight of all men. The whole court marvelled greatly, and the English more especially, that an archbishop of Canterbury should so humble himself before any mortal man. Let those then, who appear contumacious towards their superiors, take this as a pattern of obedience, when a man occupying so exalted an office among the nations of his own accord stooped to bear the yoke of humility and obedience. . . .[3]

87. "The Acts of Lanfranc"

This record, written in Latin, is appended to the annal for 1070 in version 'A' of the Anglo-Saxon Chronicle. It is of high importance particularly in respect of questions of chronology. It is printed by J. Earle and C. Plummer in *Two of the Saxon Chronicles Parallel*, vol. I, p. 287.

In this year[4] Lanfranc, abbot of Caen, at the instigation of King William, and by the command of Pope Alexander, came to England, and undertook the primacy of the kingdom of England in the church of Canterbury, being chosen by the senior members of that church together with the bishops and magnates, the clergy and the people of England in the court of the king.[5] When he came to Canterbury, the chapter of Christ Church came in procession honourably to meet him, and they were accompanied by the chapter of St. Augustine's Abbey led by Scotland who was abbot-elect of that house. According to ancient custom, all the bishops of the kingdom of England came to his consecration, or if they could not come they sent by messengers written excuses humbly explaining their absence. Not many days afterwards Thomas came to Canterbury in order to be consecrated archbishop of York. When Lanfranc, with the suffragan bishops whom he had summoned to the

[1] Herluin's visit to England took place some time between 1072 and 1075. The passage here omitted contains a lengthy description of the Channel crossing, Robinson, *op. cit.*, pp. 100–101.

[2] *i.e.* at Canterbury.

[3] Lanfranc duly returned the abbot's visit; in 1077, the year before Herluin's death, he came to Le Bec to consecrate the new church of the abbey. Gilbert gives a long description of the pomp and splendour which accompanied the ceremony, see Robinson, *op. cit.*, pp. 104 *et seq.*

[4] 1070.

[5] The careful mention of all the parties who might claim to have rights in the appointment is notable.

ceremony, sat robed before the altar of Christ, with the whole chapter as is customary on such occasions standing in the choir honourably vested in their albs, Thomas was led forward to be examined. But when Lanfranc bade him proffer his oath of obedience, Thomas replied that he would by no means do so because he was not aware that his predecessors had ever done so to the predecessors of Lanfranc; and although Lanfranc showed him that this profession of obedience had since ancient times always been exacted, Thomas persisted in his refusal. Lanfranc therefore rose up, and Thomas went away without being consecrated. He went to the king and made his protest, but Lanfranc followed him almost immediately, and showed that he and the Church had good reason for making their demand.[1] Nor did he cease from his expostulations until Thomas, albeit with much reluctance, returned to Canterbury and there humbly performed what Lanfranc asked of him. Not long afterwards Lanfranc demanded a profession of obedience from all the bishops of the kingdom of England, and received it.

In the second year of his ordination[2] Lanfranc went to Rome, and Pope Alexander so far honoured him that, contrary to custom, he rose to meet him and gave him two *pallia*[3] as a sign of his especial affection. One of these *pallia* Lanfranc took according to the Roman custom from the altar [of St. Peter], but the other, in which the pope had been wont to say Mass, he received from the hands of the pope himself. Thomas raised afresh the question of the primacy of Canterbury and of the subjection of certain bishops thereto, and in the presence of the pope initiated a plea which afterwards was terminated in England, as Lanfranc wrote briefly and finally to Pope Alexander. In this year also Lanfranc held a general council at Winchester in which he deposed Wulfric, abbot of New Minster, and made many ordinances concerning the proper observance of Christian monastic life.[4] After a few days he consecrated at London, Osbern, bishop of Exeter, and Scotland, abbot of St. Augustine's in Canterbury.

In the third year[5] at Gloucester Lanfranc consecrated Peter as bishop of Lichfield or Chester. In this year also a great plea was held in the place which is called Pinnenden,[6] and there Lanfranc proved by argument that he and his church held all their lands and customs, on land and sea, as freely as the king held his. Only three exceptions to this were admitted: if the king's road was dug up, or if a tree was felled so as to fall across it, or homicide was committed or blood was shed upon it, then anyone who was arrested for these crimes, and had given a pledge in respect of them, should pay his penalty to the king. Otherwise the archbishop was to be free from interference by royal officials.

In the fourth year[7] at London Lanfranc consecrated Patrick to be bishop of Dublin, a city in Ireland. He received his profession of obedience and gave him memorable letters which were to be passed on to the kings of Ireland.

[1] It was in connexion with this controversy that there were produced the forged documents purporting to justify the supremacy of the see of Canterbury over that of York.

[2] Lanfranc was consecrated 29 August 1070. His second year thus ran from August 1071 to August 1072.

[3] The *pallium* was a small vestment of wool worn over the shoulders and bestowed by the pope on metropolitans.

[4] *multa que de Christianae religionis cultu seruanda instituit.*

[5] August 1072–August 1073.

[6] See above, No. 50.

[7] August 1073–August 1074.

In the fifth year[1] Lanfranc held a general council in London and by general request confirmed its decisions in his letters.

In the sixth year[2] he gave to Ernost the church of Rochester to rule and consecrated him in London. Ernost had been a member of the chapter of Christ Church. Lanfranc held a council at Winchester. Ernost in this same year departed this life.

In the seventh year[3] Lanfranc gave the church of Rochester to Gundulf the monk and consecrated him at Canterbury. In this year also Thomas, archbishop of York, sent letters to him asking that two bishops might be sent to consecrate a certain clerk who had brought to Thomas letters from the Orkney Islands requesting that this clerk might be hallowed as bishop of these islands. Lanfranc assented to this petition, and ordered Wulfstan, bishop of Worcester, and Peter, bishop of Chester, to go to York in order that, with Thomas, they might do their utmost to carry through this important business.

In the eighth year[4] he held a council at London, and there he deposed Ailnoth, abbot of Glastonbury.

In the eleventh year[5] he held a council at Gloucester, and there Thomas, archbishop of York, by the order of the king and with the consent of Lanfranc, consecrated William as bishop of Durham. He did this because he could not find a suitable coadjutor from among the Scottish bishops who were his subordinates. In this consecration there took part: Lanfranc, who presided, and also the bishops Wulfstan, Osbern, Giso and Robert. At this time Lanfranc sent to Bishop Donald in Ireland letters which were stuffed with the marrow of holy doctrine.

In the sixteenth year[6] at Canterbury Lanfranc consecrated Donatus his monk to rule over the church of Dublin. He did this on the petition of the king, the clergy and the people of Ireland to whom he sent letters of exhortation. In this year also he held a council at Gloucester, in which he deposed Ulfketel, abbot of Crowland. On one and the same day at Canterbury he consecrated Robert to be bishop of Chester and William to be bishop of Elmham. At Winchester he consecrated Maurice to be bishop of London, and a few days later Maurice presented himself with worthy gifts at his mother-church at Canterbury.

In the eighteenth year[7] when King William died overseas, Lanfranc chose his son William as king, even as his father had desired, and hallowed him and crowned him in the church of the blessed Peter[8] which is in the western part of London. In the same year in the metropolitan see of Canterbury he examined and consecrated Godfrey to be bishop of Chichester and Guy to be abbot of St. Augustine's and John to be bishop of Wells. The day after this, in the company of Odo, bishop of Bayeux, the brother of the king, who had come to Canterbury, Lanfranc brought Guy to St. Augustine's Abbey and demanded of the monks whether they would accept Guy as their true abbot and pastor. Unanimously and with fervour the monks replied that they would neither obey nor receive him. Lanfranc thereupon entered, leading the abbot with him, and when he saw that the monks were determined to resist and

[1] August 1074–August 1075.
[2] August 1075–August 1076.
[3] August 1076–August 1077.
[4] August 1077–August 1078.
[5] August 1080–August 1081.
[6] August 1085–August 1086.
[7] August 1087–August 1088.
[8] Westminster Abbey.

would refuse obedience, he ordered that all who were not willing to obey the abbot should leave his presence. Almost all of them departed, and then Lanfranc, together with his own followers, set the new abbot honourably on his throne and gave the abbey to his charge. He transferred Ælfwin, prior of St. Augustine's, and other selected monks to Christ Church in Canterbury that they might henceforth serve God in that place. But those who were more vehement and had been the ringleaders, he ordered to be sent to the castle and there to be imprisoned. After these acts Lanfranc returned home, but very soon he learnt that the monks of St. Augustine's who had departed from his presence had assembled at the encampment which is next to the church of St. Mildred. The archbishop gave them until the ninth hour to return to their monastery, and promised that if they did so they should not be punished. If, however, they delayed longer he assured them that they should return not as free men but as renegades. At these tidings they were in two minds whether to return or to stay. When, however, dinner-time came and they were hungry, most of them, regretting their obstinacy, sent to Lanfranc and promised him full obedience. These Lanfranc spared, ordering them to return to their monastery and there to swear obedience to their new abbot. So they went back, and on the body of St. Augustine swore that henceforth they would be faithful and obedient to Abbot Guy. Those, however, who remained obdurate, Lanfranc scattered among the monasteries of England, and continued to chastise them until he compelled them to make profession of obedience. About the same time, Lanfranc arrested one of these monks named Alfred, who, having made his escape, was wandering about: he was thrown into prison at Canterbury with several of his accomplices who had plotted against the new abbot. There, heavily fettered, they were compelled for many days to learn the strict discipline of their Order. After all these monks had been sufficiently punished, as was thought, and had promised to make amends, Lanfranc took pity on them, and ordered them to be brought back from the places to which they had been sent and to be reconciled to their abbot.

In the same year[1] there was further dissension against the abbot. Lanfranc thereupon caused one of the malcontents named Columbanus to be brought before him. "Would you kill your abbot?" asked Lanfranc. "Certainly I would if I could," replied the monk. Lanfranc thereupon caused him to be tied naked in front of the great door of St. Augustine's, and there to be flogged in view of all the people. Afterwards his hair was shaved, and he was driven from the city. Thus did Lanfranc enforce obedience, and so long as he lived he broke down the opposition of the rest by dread of his name.

In the nineteenth year[2] died Lanfranc, the venerable archbishop, and he was buried in the metropolitan cathedral of Canterbury. He occupied his archbishopric for eighteen years, nine months and two days. His acts, his buildings, his alms and his labours are in part commemorated in the lection which is read each year on the anniversary of his death. For they were very many. After his death the monks of St. Augustine's openly resisted their abbot, Guy, and the citizens of Canterbury rose up against him and tried to kill him by armed force in his house. The members of his

[1] *i.e.* August 1087–August 1088.
[2] The nineteenth year of Lanfranc's archbishopric began in August 1088. He died 24 May 1089.

household defended him, and a scuffle ensued which did not end until many had been wounded and a few killed on both sides. The abbot barely managed to escape unharmed, and flying to the mother-church in Canterbury he sought help. Walkelin, bishop of Winchester, and Gundulf, bishop of Rochester, both suffragans of Canterbury, therefore came to the city with certain nobles whom the king had sent for the purpose of imposing proper punishment for so great an offence. When they had examined the causes of the rising, they decided that the monks could not be freed from blame, and so they ordered that those monks who had openly rebelled, should undergo chastisement openly in the presence of the people. But the prior and monks of Christ Church, moved by pity towards their Order, opposed this judgment, for they feared that if these guilty monks were chastised in public, it might bring contempt upon the monastic life itself and on those who followed it. It was therefore agreed that only a select company should be present when the punishment was carried out, and that it should take place in church. Two monks of Christ Church, Guy and Norman, were summoned and these inflicted the punishment ordered by the bishops. Then these rebel monks were scattered through the monasteries of England, and in their place twenty-four monks of Christ Church were transferred to the monastery of St. Augustine under a prior named Anthony who had formerly been sub-prior at Christ Church. The citizens who had violently forced an entrance into the abbot's house were then arrested, and those who could not prove themselves innocent of having taken part in that assault were blinded.

After the death of Lanfranc Christ Church was without a pastor for four years, nine months and nine days, and during that period it suffered many misfortunes. In the year of our Lord 1093, on 6 March, the archbishopric of Canterbury was given to Anselm, abbot of Le Bec. He was an upright man, being both good and full of learning. He was indeed the most notable man of his time. For many reasons he was for some time unwilling to undertake the charge that had been laid upon him, but at length he came to Canterbury on 23 September and on 4 December he was hallowed.

88. Profession of obedience made by Wulfstan, bishop of Worcester, to Lanfranc, archbishop of Canterbury (? 1070 or shortly after)

This text is of cardinal importance for the study of effects of the Norman Conquest on the Church in England. The fact that Wulfstan, the most respected prelate of the Anglo-Saxon Church, made his profession of obedience to Lanfranc is itself of some political significance, and the references to Stigand have a direct bearing upon the interpretation of the reign of Edward the Confessor and upon the ecclesiastical circumstances of the invasion and establishment of the Conqueror. Printed by R. R. Darlington, in *Vita Wulfstani* (Camden Soc., 1928), Appendix, p. 190.

This custom of holy religious observance prevails: when a bishop is consecrated he should reverently go to the metropolis [of his province] and there make profession of obedience to the metropolitan; he should also leave a written profession of the same obedience to the metropolitan and his successors. But at the time when I, Wulfstan, was ordained bishop of the Hwiccas in the city of Worcester, Stigand had seized the holy church of Canterbury to which all my predecessors had been subjected; by force and guile he had expelled the metropolitan from his see; and in contempt of the apostolic see he had rashly presumed to wear the *pallium* which he had seized. For this reason he was summoned, excommunicated and condemned by the Roman pontiffs, Leo,[1] Victor,[2] Stephen,[3] Nicholas[4] and Alexander.[5] Nevertheless, in the hardness of his heart he persisted in his obduracy. During this time therefore orders were given throughout England by the popes forbidding anyone to reverence him as bishop; further, no one was to go to him for ordination. For this reason some bishops of the English at that time went for consecration to Rome, and others to France, whilst others again had recourse to their fellow-bishops at home. But I went to Aldred, bishop of the church of York, and I have put off making my profession of canonical obedience down to this day. Now, therefore, I, a bishop, and according to the canons, offer to you, Lanfranc, metropolitan of the holy church of Canterbury, my profession of obedience to your orders and to those of your successors. And as God is my witness I promise to keep my pledge.

89. Letter from Lanfranc, archbishop of Canterbury, to Pope Alexander II (? 1070)

This letter was written by Lanfranc shortly after his consecration as archbishop of Canterbury, which took place on 29 August 1070. It is presented here as of interest for the light it throws upon the circumstances of his election and for the self-portrait it unconsciously reveals. It is printed in the original Latin in J. A. Giles, *Lanfranci Opera* (1844), Ep. 3, pp. 19–21, who has also given an English translation thereof at the end of his introductory memoir of the life of Lanfranc, *op. cit.*, pp. xiv–xvi. It is also given in English in A. J. Macdonald, *Lanfranc* (1926), pp. 67–69. The present version is based on both of these.

To Pope Alexander, the chief shepherd of holy Church, Lanfranc, an unworthy prelate, canonical obedience. I know no one, holy father, to whom I can with greater propriety unfold my troubles than to you, who are the very cause of these calamities. For when William, duke of Normandy, drew me forth from the monastery of Le Bec, where I had assumed the religious habit, and appointed me to preside over that of Caen,[6] I found myself unequal to the task of governing a few monks. Therefore I cannot comprehend by what dispensation of the Almighty I have been promoted at your behest to undertake the supervision of an innumerable multitude. The aforesaid prince, after he had become king of England, tried every means to bring this about, but laboured in vain, until your legates, Ermenfrid, bishop of Sitten, and Hubert,[7] cardinal of the holy Roman Church, came to Normandy, caused the bishops, abbots and magnates of that land to be assembled, and in their presence and by virtue of the authority of the apostolic see commanded me to undertake the government of the church of Canterbury. Against this I pleaded in vain my incapacity and unworthiness, my ignorance of the language and of the barbarous people. My plea did not avail. What need of further words! I gave my consent, I came, I took the burden upon me, and such are the cares and troubles, the discomfort of mind I daily endure, so great are the annoyance, the suffering, the losses caused me by different persons pulling me in opposite directions, the harshness, avarice and baseness

[1] Leo IX. [2] Victor II. [3] Stephen IX.
[4] Nicholas II. [5] Alexander II. [6] See above, p. 629, n. 2.
[7] Subdeacon of the Roman Church and on numerous occasions sent as legate to Normandy and England; see below, pp. 641 *et sqq*.

that I see around me; so dire is the peril to which in my view holy Church is exposed, that I grow weary of my life, and lament that it has been prolonged to witness such times. But bad as is the present state of things when I look around me, I feel the future will be still worse. That I may not detain your highness, whose time must be fully occupied by other weighty matters, longer than is necessary–since it was beyond dispute by your authority that I became charged with these duties–I entreat you in God's name and for the sake of your own soul, by the same authority to release me from them and grant me leave to return once more to the monastic life which I love above all other. Do not, I pray, spurn this my petition, for I only ask what is right and necessary to my well-being. You should remember, and indeed never forget, how ready I have always been to entertain in my monastery your kinsfolk and others who came bearing letters of introduction from Rome. I instructed them in both sacred and secular learning as well as I was able to teach or they to learn; and many other things I might mention in which I have been of service to you or your predecessors when time or circumstances allowed. My conscience bears witness that I do not say this boastfully or by way of reproach, or to obtain favours from you beyond what is due to my obedience. My sole object in writing this letter is to put forward a just and valid reason why for Christ's sake I should obtain the favour I am seeking at your hands. If, however, you should be guided by the interests of others and decide to refuse my request, it is greatly to be feared you may run the risk–which God forbid–of committing a sin by the very act you consider well-pleasing to God. For I have met with no spiritual success in these parts either directly or indirectly, or, if any, it is so slight that it cannot possibly be weighed against my misfortunes. But enough of this for the present. When I was at Rome and by God's grace had the pleasure of seeing you and conversing with you, you invited me to visit you again the following year at Christmas and to spend three or four months in your palace as your guest. But God is my witness, and the angels, that I could not do so without great personal inconvenience and to the detriment of my affairs. For this there are many different reasons, too long to be related in a short letter; but, should the heavenly powers preserve my life and circumstances permit, I long to visit you and the shrine of the holy apostles and the holy Roman Church. To this end I entreat you to pray the divine mercy that long life may be granted to my lord the king of England and peace from all his enemies. May his heart ever be moved by love for God and holy Church with all devotion of spirit. For while he lives we enjoy peace of a kind, but after his death we may scarcely hope to experience either peace or any manner of good.

90. Letter from Archbishop Lanfranc to Margaret, queen of Scots (? 1072–1075)

This letter appears to have been written in answer to an appeal from the queen for help in educating and organizing the religious life of Scotland in conformity with the traditions and usages of the Western Church. The mere fact that such correspondence took place indicates the commanding position and prestige which Lanfranc had acquired in the wider ecclesiastical world of the West by his consecration to Canterbury. The letter itself is interesting in the indication it gives that Lanfranc had a softer side to his nature, where the exigences of Anglo-Norman politics were not directly concerned; his sincere and tender passion for souls is nowhere more strongly manifest. Queen Margaret, the recipient of the letter, was the daughter of Edward the Atheling and granddaughter of Edmund Ironsides, and a sister of the unfortunate Edgar Atheling, the last male representative of the house of Egbert (see Table 1). Her marriage to Malcolm III (Canmore), king of Scots, probably took place in 1069 after she and her brother had taken refuge at the Scottish court. Lanfranc's letter is printed in J. A. Giles, *Lanfranci Opera*, vol. II, p. 59. The translation here followed is by W. F. Hook, *Lives of the Archbishops of Canterbury*, vol. II, p. 152. The same version is given in A. J. Macdonald, *Lanfranc* (1926), p. 196.

Lanfranc, the unworthy primate of the holy Church of Canterbury, to Margaret, the illustrious queen of Scots, greeting and benediction. The small compass of a letter is insufficient for declaring with what joy you have filled my heart, O Queen, well pleasing to God, by your excellent epistles which you have sent me. With what pleasantness do your words flow forth, proceeding from the inspiration of the Holy Spirit. I believe, indeed, that what you have written is said not by you but for you. Truly by your mouth has he spoken who said to his disciples, "Learn of me, for I am meek and lowly of heart." From this teaching of Christ it has proceeded that, born of royal ancestors, royally educated and nobly wed to a noble king,[1] you choose me, a man of foreign extraction, vile, ignoble, involved in sins, as your father, and pray me to consider you as my spiritual daughter. I am not what you think me to be, but may I become so! Lest you remain deceived, pray for me that I may be worthy as a father to pray to God and be heard for you. May there be between us an interchange of prayers and benefits! I bestow little indeed, but I hope to receive much more myself. Hence, therefore, may I be your father and you my daughter. I send to your illustrious husband and yourself, our dearest brother, Master Goldwin, and two other brethren, according to your request, because he himself would not be able to accomplish alone what is requisite for God's service and your own. And I beg and entreat that you may endeavour quickly and perfectly to complete what you have undertaken for God and your own souls. If you are able or desirous to finish your work by means of others, we greatly desire these our brethren to return to us, because they are very necessary to us in the offices of our church. Your will, however, be done, since in all things and for all things, we desire to obey you. May Almighty God bless you and mercifully absolve you from all your sins!

91. Letter from Archbishop Lanfranc to Herfast, bishop of Elmham (? 1073)

This letter illustrates Lanfranc's conception of his duty and right as primate to superintend the personal and public conduct of his suffragans. It is written to Herfast, bishop of Elmham, who had long been his opponent, ever since, in fact, they had clashed at Duke William's court in Normandy. The dispute, which provided an opportunity for Lanfranc to express his displeasure with the bishop so vigorously, was a complicated one between Herfast and the abbot of Bury St. Edmund's and involved the intervention of Pope Gregory VII. Lanfranc was commanded to rebuke the bishop and to take steps to prevent any encroachment on the liberties of the abbey. This Lanfranc complied with in a letter no longer extant, soon following it up with the letter given below. The Latin text was printed by J. A. Giles, *Lanfranci Opera* (1844), Ep. 26, p. 47, who, however, wrongly gave the name of the recipient as *Herebert*. But Herbert of Losinga, the only bishop of this name, was not consecrated till 1091. The mention in the letter of the dispute with Abbot Baldwin would appear to sanction the emendation to Herfast. The translation is that of W. F. Hook, *Lives of the Archbishops of Canterbury*, vol. II, pp. 154–155.

Lanfranc, by divine mercy, the unworthy archbishop of the church of Canterbury, to Bishop H[erfast], knowledge with humility, and understanding with sobriety. Berard, a clerk, and one of the household of Abbot Baldwin, delivered to you our letter relating to his affairs, which, as he afterwards informed me, you impudently ridiculed and, in the hearing of many, spoke very vilely and said much that was

[1] Malcolm III, king of Scots, 1057–1093.

discreditable to me, declaring most positively that for me you would do nothing in that matter.[1] For this, at another time and place, account shall be rendered. I now charge you, however, not to grasp at anything belonging to St. Edmund, unless you can show by authentic documents that it has been sought by your predecessors. Dismiss the said Berard in peace and unharmed, until the matter shall come to our hearing and receive a decision agreeable to canonical authority and our judgment. Give over dice playing, not to speak of graver misconduct and worldly sports, in which you are said to waste the whole day. Study theology and the decrees of the Roman pontiffs, and give special attention to the sacred canons. There, indeed, you will find that whereof you are ignorant. In reading through them you will discover how vain is your expectation of escaping ecclesiastical discipline. In the decrees it runs thus: "In every province let him attend to the regulations of his metropolitan in all things." At the council of Nicæa: "The confirmation of everything done in each province is to be left to the metropolitan by the bishop." At that of Antioch: "In every province it is fitting that the bishops acknowledge the metropolitan bishop as having charge of the whole province, for since all who have any business resort from all parts to the metropolis, it is right that he should have the precedence." At the council of Toledo: "It is proper that each should receive rules of discipline from the place where he received the honour of consecration, in order that, in accordance with the decrees of the fathers, the see which is the mother of each one's priestly dignity should be the mistress of his ecclesiastical rule." And a little after: "If anyone violates these decrees, let him for six months be debarred from the communion, and undergo penitential correction as the metropolitan may direct." There are many other passages on the precedence and powers of primates and archbishops, both in the aforesaid writings and in other authentic books of the orthodox fathers which, if you had read more attentively and, having read, had remembered, you would not think disrespectfully of your mother-church, nor have said what you are reported to have said. Nor would anyone in his senses have considered this to have been a rash presumption in the diocese of another, when through God's mercy this one island, which they call Britain, is manifestly the diocese of our single church.

Remove from your company and from your household Herman, the monk, of whose life so many scandalous reports are circulated, for I desire him to live under rule in a monastery or, if he refuse, to depart from this realm of England.

92. Letter from Archbishop Lanfranc to Stigand, bishop of Chichester (1070–1089)

This letter is of interest as illustrating Lanfranc's struggle to re-establish a uniform ecclesiastical administration throughout the dioceses of the province of Canterbury. Certain clerks of the diocese of Chichester had been fined by the bishop's archdeacons. These clerks held livings in the gift of Canterbury, and the archbishop claimed the right to deal with their alleged misdeeds himself in the course of his visitation of his estates. In future such clerks are forbidden to attend the synods of the diocese of Chichester or those of any other diocese. The reference to archdeacons is an indication that this feature of diocesan organization, which had almost lapsed prior to the Norman Conquest, was now in process of revival as a normal part of ecclesiastical administration; see on this point, H. Böhmer, *Kirche und Staat in England und in der Normandie im XI und XII Jahrhundert* (1899), p. 44. The Latin text of this letter is printed in J. A. Giles, *Lanfranci Opera* (1844), Ep. 30, p. 50; the translation is that of W. F. Hook, *Lives of the Archbishops of Canterbury*, vol. II, pp. 156–157, with minor alterations.

[1] The dispute between the bishop and the abbot of Bury St. Edmunds.

The clergy on my estates in your diocese have complained to me that on certain occasions they have been mulcted by your archdeacons, and that some of my tenants have paid the fines which have been imposed on them. Your fraternity ought to remember that, contrary to the customs of my predecessors and yours, I made to you certain concessions, and gave direction that they might attend your synods to receive religious instruction and advice, though not to discuss or debate. Should any, however, be guilty of any crime, we especially provided that punishment should be postponed until we had ourselves examined the case, in order that we might determine whether to pardon the offender or to punish him.

We command you therefore to make immediate restitution, and to warn your officials not to presume thus far in future and to take care to preserve good relations. We expressly enjoin those of our priests dwelling beyond the borders of Kent never more to attend any synod, whether held by you or any other bishop, and not to hold themselves responsible to you or your officials for any crime they may commit. For we ourselves, when we visit our estates, are bound in the exercise of our pastoral authority to make inquiry with respect to their character, both moral and intellectual. The chrism alone may they receive from you, and they shall pay the fees customary for the same. For while we are determined to preserve unimpaired those rights which have been handed down to us from our predecessors, God forbid that we should desire to withhold from others their due.

93. Letter from Pope Gregory VII to William I, king of England (4 April 1074)

The first of Gregory VII's letters to William I. Printed: P. Jaffé, *Monumenta Gregoriana* (1865), p. 89; E. Caspar, *Registrum Papae Gregorii VII*, vol. I (1893), p. 101.

Gregory the bishop, servant of the servants of God, to William, king of the English, greeting and apostolic benediction. We have learnt from your letters, dearest son, of your grief at the death of our predecessor Alexander[1] of blessed memory, and likewise of your joy at the report of our accession. We believe that without doubt you cleave with all your heart to your mother, the holy Roman Church, and love her with all your strength as you ought. For seeing you were grievously distressed at the tidings of her bereavement and now rejoice in her consolation at our accession; and since you humbly and firmly beg in your letters to be informed of our present state, you display the affection of a good son, a son who loves his mother from his heart. Accomplish therefore in deeds what you profess with your mouth. Fulfil in very earnest what you promise, that you may conform to the word of him who is Truth itself, saying: "If a man love me, he will keep my word",[2] and again, "The proof of love is in deeds." Your mother's words are these, and others like unto them; cease not to strive after righteousness,[3] nay rather, after God in all things, whenever opportunity allows, and have regard for the churches entrusted to your keeping, that you may effect the salvation of your own soul, wipe out the stain of your sins and so instil the perfume of virtue that you may say with the apostle, "We are a sweet savour of Christ."[4] We beg, advise and admonish you to place the honour of God and everything which pertains to him before your own honour and

[1] Alexander II, who died 21 April 1073.
[2] John xiv. 23.
[3] The Hildebrandine *iusticia*.
[4] II Corinthians ii. 15.

all worldly affairs; for this is assuredly a matter through neglect of which princes of your rank very often perish and are cast down to hell. And so, beloved, we have impressed these things upon you, because we deem that you alone among kings cherish above all others what we have earlier written. . . .[1] We admonish you to watch over the revenues of St. Peter which are collected in England[2] as if they were your own; and thus we entrust them to your generosity as if they were yours; so may you find in Peter a pious and gracious creditor, and beseech him to whom, as will be evident, you have already paid a great deal, to aid you in discharging your debt. Given at Rome, 4 April, in the twelfth Indiction.[3]

94. Letter from Pope Gregory VII to William I (21 March 1077)

The occasion of this epistle was the intercession of William on behalf of the deposed bishop of Dol. Though unwilling to comply with the king's request in this matter, the pope shows his desire to meet the king's wishes in every possible contingency. He also announces his decision to send a legate to discuss the general relationship between crown and papacy. The letter is printed in P. Jaffé, *Monumenta Gregoriana* (1865), p. 265, and in E. Caspar, *Registrum Papae Gregorii VII*, vol. I (1893), p. 323.

There is no doubt on our part that your highness will agree wholeheartedly with our decision. For although many excellent virtues have been implanted in you by the grace of God, nevertheless this is the brightest and most renowned, and the one that chiefly commends your fame to God and men, namely that among your other activities you love and approve justice, and are prompt to execute it. In the meantime you should know that your excellence and well-known devotion are most pleasing to us, and that we embrace both you and whatsoever redounds to the glory of your highness under God, and hold you ever in our heart with great fervour and deep affection. Moreover, we are ready to agree and to meet your wishes in everything you have asked of us, so far as we are able and dare in accordance with God's will. But because we have determined to send our aforesaid son, Hubert,[4] to you, we deem it unnecessary to write further unto you. Wherefore, we neither doubt nor desire your excellency to doubt that, in everything he relates to you on our behalf, he will faithfully adhere to the text of our letter and our explicit words. May Almighty God, through the merits and at the intercession of the apostles Peter and Paul and all the saints, grant you and the most gracious Queen Maud, your wife, and your illustrious sons, pardon and remission from all your sins and, when he shall order your release from the cares of this world, cause you to pass to his eternal kingdom and true glory. Given at Bianello, 21 March, in the fifteenth Indiction.[5]

95. Letter from Archbishop Lanfranc to Wulfstan, bishop of Worcester, and Peter, bishop of Chester (1072–1085)

This letter is evidence of Lanfranc's claims to the effectual primacy of all churches of the British Isles. Paul, earl of the Orkneys, had applied to Thomas, archbishop of York, the nearest metropolitan, for the consecration of a suffragan bishop for the islands. Archbishop Thomas, following upon the settlement of the vexed question of the metropolitical jurisdiction in Britain, was compelled to refer the request to Lanfranc, with the suggestion that the bishops of Worcester and

[1] Cf. Gregory's eulogy of William in a letter to Archbishop Lanfranc, dated 20 November 1073, *Registrum*, I, 31, p. 49 (Jaffé): "most beloved king and singular son of the holy Roman Church".
[2] Peter's pence. [3] 1074.
[4] Subdeacon of the Roman Church, see below, pp. 642–647. [5] 1077.

Chester might be ordered to assist him in the consecration of Earl Paul's nominee. In this letter Lanfranc accordingly gives orders and instructions to the two bishops to attend at York for this purpose. But they are to keep copies of Thomas's letter in view of a possible revival of his claim to metropolitical authority over Scotland and the islands. The letter is printed in J. A. Giles, *Lanfranci Opera* (1844), Ep. 15, p. 35, and is to be dated after 1075 and before 1086, probably in 1077, as stated in the *Acta Lanfranci*.[1] The translation here given is by W. F. Hook, *Lives of the Archbishops of Canterbury*, vol. II, p. 153.

Lanfranc, by the grace of God, archbishop of the holy church of Canterbury, to his venerable brothers, Wulfstan, bishop of Worcester, and Peter, bishop of Chester, greeting. Our venerable brother, Thomas, archbishop of York, has intimated to us that a certain clerk from the Orkneys has come to him, whom he states to have been chosen to the episcopate of that country at the nomination of Earl Paul; and since of ancient custom the right of consecrating the bishops of those islands is his, he has begged me to send him two of my suffragans that they may be able, together with him, to celebrate so great a sacrament. We entreat and command you, therefore, to proceed thither without any delay and in pursuance of our order, as is proper, to complete so solemn a mystery. For it is not fitting that one coming hither for consecration, and with all humility requesting it, should through want of coadjutors depart from such a realm as this unconsecrated. The term of this consecration the bearers of these presents will point out. And that you be not solicitous in thinking that either he or his successors should from this precedent, at some time or other, endeavour to seize metropolitical jurisdiction over your churches,[2] having regard to the future, I have taken care to transmit to you the letter which he sent me; and I charge that this, as well as the present one I am sending you, be preserved among the archives of your churches for future reference.

96. Letter from Pope Gregory VII to William I (4 April 1078)

Occasioned by the reported indisposition of John, archbishop of Rouen, and his alleged inability to fulfil his episcopal functions. The case is to be examined by the papal legate, Hubert, whom the pope is sending to Normandy. The letter is printed in P. Jaffé, *Monumenta Gregoriana* (1865), p. 315; E. Caspar, *Registrum Papae Gregorii VII* (1893), vol. II, p. 380.

Gregory, the bishop, servant of the servants of God, to William, king of the English, greeting and apostolic benediction. The care of our office demands that we should hasten to provide pastors for widowed churches. But, because among the kings we embrace you with peculiar affection, both for the moral probity after which you strive and for the liberal foresight with which you are endowed, it is fitting we should take especial care for the churches committed to you in your realm by divine dispensation. Wherefore, we have determined to succour in this way the church of Rouen, which, so we have learned, has long been deprived of a shepherd through infirmity. We send to you our dearest son, Hubert, subdeacon of the holy Roman Church, whom we have known by experience to be loyal both to us and to you. Let him come to the aforesaid archbishop, together with the ecclesiastics, the bishops, abbots and monks of the said church, and examine with diligent and pious deliberation whether the archbishop is well enough to exercise his pastoral office as he should. . . .

[1] See above, No. 87, p. 633.
[2] Worcester and Chester were two of the sees over which Thomas of York had claimed jurisdiction.

97. Letter from Pope Gregory VII to Archbishop Lanfranc (25 March 1079)

The first of a series of letters written between 1079 and 1082 on which see A. J. Macdonald, *Lanfranc*, pp 224, 225. Printed: P. Jaffé, *Monumenta Gregoriana* (1865), p. 377; E. Caspar, *Registrum Papae Gregorii VII*, vol. II (1893), p. 443.

Gregory, the bishop, servant of the servants of God, to Lanfranc, archbishop of Canterbury, greeting and apostolic benediction. We are the more astonished, beloved, because we little expected that you would not have taken the trouble to visit us since the time when, albeit unworthy, we took upon our shoulders the priestly yoke of the apostolic see. We should indeed have resolved long since to take a grave view of this matter, had not our apostolic clemency and the ancient pledge of our love hitherto restrained us. Verily, as we have ascertained from a reliable source, your presence has been denied to us either through fear of the king – whom indeed we have always peculiarly cherished above others of that rank – or mainly through your own fault. Moreover, if the memory of our former love for you had survived or the affection you owe to your mother, the Roman Church, had been kept in mind, nothing, neither fear of the secular power nor inordinate regard for any other person would have withheld you from our presence. But if the king, newly swollen with pride or provoked by wilfulness or insolence, has taken this measure against the holy see, we shall treat it the more seriously because it has caused him to act in a manner unworthy of our love. Nevertheless, your reverence can avert these consequences for him by this means, namely if by careful explanation and firm warning you counsel him not to presume unjustly against the Roman Church, the mother of all, nor wantonly to dare anything contrary to the power of religion, nor to restrict further you or any other devoutly desiring to visit the apostolic see. So, then, it behoves your reverence prudently to correct your excess of negligence and to hasten as often as possible to present yourself before us in accordance with our wishes and oft-repeated commands: to the intent that these and other matters may be discussed personally between us, and as a result of our conversation and by the divine favour the interests of the Church may be promoted. Given at Rome, 25 March, in the second Indiction.[1]

98. Letter from Pope Gregory VII to Hubert, subdeacon of the Roman Church (23 September 1079)

The matter at issue is the same as in the preceding letter, namely William's alleged refusal to allow his bishops freedom of access to Rome. It appears from the text, however, that the legate, Teuzo, had infringed the diplomatic proprieties by adopting a more intransigent attitude to the king over this question than the pope deemed advisable in view of the general political situation. Accordingly Hubert is charged with the task of effecting an accommodation with the king. The letter is printed in P. Jaffé, *Monumenta Gregoriana* (1865), pp. 379–380, and in E. Caspar, *Registrum Papae Gregorii VII*, vol. II (1893), pp. 458–459.

Gregory, the bishop, servant of the servants of God, to his dear son in Christ, Hubert, subdeacon of the holy Roman Church, greeting and apostolic benediction. We marvel greatly – and you may regard it as wholly displeasing to us – that you have hitherto made so great delay and neglected to return to the apostolic see. No excuse, indeed, may be regarded as sufficient, unless you have been prevented from

[1] 1079.

returning either by sickness or lack of facilities. . . . Wherefore, in the knowledge that we desire your presence for many reasons, hasten your return as best you can. You have informed us that Teuzo, as legate on our behalf, has spoken against the king of England. This, you should know, is not by our command. Nevertheless, the Roman Church has many things whereof to complain against him. For none of all the kings, not excepting those that are heathen, has dared to act against the apostolic see in the way he has unblushingly done; none has been so irreverent or shameless as to forbid the bishops and archbishops to frequent the threshold of the apostles. Wherefore, we would have you diligently admonish him on our behalf not to strive so ardently to diminish the honour of the holy Roman Church, honour the like of which he would not release his own subjects from the obligation of according to himself; so, by paying the honour due to blessed Peter, he may gain his favour. For, mindful of our former love for him and in imitation of the apostolic clemency, we have hitherto spared his fault, so far as we may on God's authority. If, however, in this and similar cases, which are well known to you, he will not restrain himself, let him know of a certainty that he will grievously provoke against him the wrath of blessed Peter. . . .

99. Letter from Pope Gregory VII to William I (24 April 1080)

This letter marks the opening of a new phase in the relations between the pope and the king of England. Gregory VII was now on the point of opening negotiations for the recognition of the supremacy of the papacy over the secular kingdoms of the West, and the letter is the prelude to the formal demand for William's fealty which was to be made during the year. Consequently the pope is concerned to create a favourable atmosphere for the negotiations, and he makes an appeal to William's sense of gratitude for past favours. The letter is printed in P. Jaffé, *Monumenta Gregoriana* (1865), pp. 414–416. This letter, and the other letters which follow in this correspondence, are discussed in relation to the negotiations between William I and the papacy in A. J. Macdonald, *Lanfranc* (1926), pp. 220–231; Z. N. Brooke, *The English Church and the Papacy* (1931); H. Böhmer, *Kirche und Staat in England und in der Normandie im XI und XII Jahrhundert* (1899), pp. 126–140; and F. M. Stenton, *Anglo-Saxon England* (1943), chap. XVIII.

Gregory, the bishop, servant of the servants of God, to William, king of the English, greeting and apostolic benediction. I believe it is known to you, most excellent son, how great was the love I ever bore you, even before I ascended the papal throne, and how active I have shown myself in your affairs; above all, how diligently I laboured for your advancement to royal rank. In consequence I suffered dire calumny through certain brethren insinuating that by such partisanship I gave sanction for the perpetration of great slaughter. But God was witness to my conscience that I did so with a right mind, trusting in God's grace and, not in vain, in the virtues you possessed. For the higher you climb (in rank and power) the better disposed you should show yourself towards God and holy Church, even as now there is matter for thanksgiving to him. Now, therefore, I give you, as to a very dear son and one faithful to St. Peter and ourself, and in a few words, my advice as to how you should conduct yourself in future, just as I would in private converse. For when it pleased him who exalteth the humble, that our holy Mother-Church should raise me, though all unwilling and reluctant, as God is my witness, to the government of the apostolic see, impelled by the obligations of my office "to cry aloud and spare not",[1] and bound by ties of love and fear, I could not henceforth conceal from myself the

[1] Isaiah lviii. 1.

shameful iniquities the Church endures through her most reprobate sons. By *love*, I say, because St. Peter had kindly nurtured me from boyhood in his household,[1] and our Lord God in his love, finding as it were something of value in me, had chosen me as his vicar to govern our holy Mother-Church; by *fear*, because the law of God thunders forth terribly, saying, "Cursed be the man that keepeth back his sword from blood",[2] that is to say, he that removes from his teaching the destruction of this mortal life.

Now, therefore, son most beloved and ever worthy to be embraced in Christ, when you behold your mother in great tribulation and are constrained by the inevitable necessity of bringing succour to us, I desire you to act as such, and I advise you strongly in true and not counterfeit charity, and for your own honour and safety, to give full obedience. . . .[3] As with God's help you have well merited the title of "jewel of princes",[4] so by the justice of your rule and the character of your obedience you may deserve well of all the princes of the earth. And as, to the end of time, princes will win salvation by the example of your obedience, so without doubt you are destined to be the chief of princes in future glory. But even if some of them are unwilling to be saved, nevertheless your reward shall by no means be diminished, neither in the glory of the eternal kingdom nor in this present world, where victory, honour, power and a more than heavenly exaltation shall be bestowed upon you and your heirs. Put your own case as an example to yourself. For just as you would wish to be duly honoured by one whom you had raised up from the state of a poor and wretched servant to be a powerful monarch, so you yourself, whom God of his grace has transformed from poverty and servitude to sin–in which state indeed we are all born–to be a powerful king, should hasten with the utmost diligence to honour Jesus as your protector and all-powerful helper. Nor let the swarm of evil princes hinder you from this; for wickedness is the portion of many and virtue of the few. It is more glorious for the tried warrior to stand in the battle when many take to flight; more precious is the jewel which is rarely found. Yea rather, the more the potentates of this world, blinded by their pride and impious deeds, rush headlong into the deep, so much the more should you, who are dearer to God than they, be uplifted in devotion by humility and obedience, that it may come to pass as it is written, "He that is unjust, let him be unjust still; and he which is filthy, let him be filthy still; and he that is righteous, let him be righteous still."[5] I could write yet more to you by way of exhortation; but seeing you have sent me ambassadors, together with our son, Hubert, who have wholly delighted me with evidence of your prudence, honesty and justice, I have deemed that enough has been said to a wise man. I trust that Almighty God, as written above, will condescend to work in you and through you to his honour. Those matters, however, which have been insufficiently dealt with in this letter,[6] we commit to your ambassadors to relate to you by word of mouth. May Almighty God, our Father, deign of his mercy so to inspire and implant in your heart,

[1] A reference to Gregory's eaaly education at Rome.
[2] Jeremiah xlviii. 10.
[3] Lacuna in MS.
[4] *gemma principum.*
[5] Revelations xxii. 11.
[6] Presumably the claim for the recognition of papal overlordship in England and for the payment of Peter's Pence.

beloved son, that whatever increase your realm and power in this world may receive as a reward for your virtues, he may hereafter effectually bring you with all saintly kings to the heavenly realms whose joy surpasseth knowledge. Amen. . . . Given at Rome, 24 April, in the third Indiction.[1]

100. Letter from Pope Gregory VII to William I (8 May 1080)

This letter, which was brought to England by the subdeacon, Hubert, together with Gregory's formal demand for fealty, followed hard upon the preceding letter. In it Gregory expounds the Hildebrandine tenets on the relations between Church and State, accompanied by the use of the familiar metaphors of the sun and moon, as the basis of his claim on William's obedience. It is printed in P. Jaffé, *Monumenta Gregoriana* (1865), pp. 410–421, and E. Caspar, *Registrum Papae Gregorii VII*, vol. II, pp. 505–507.

Gregory, the bishop, servant of the servants of God, to William, king of the English, greeting and apostolic benediction. We believe it is not hidden from your wisdom that the apostolic and royal dignities excel all others in this world, and that Almighty God has apportioned his governance between them. For as he has appointed the sun and moon as lights greater than all others to show forth the beauty of the world to human eyes at diverse seasons, so, lest the creature whom his beneficence created for this world in his own image should be drawn into error and mortal peril, he has provided that he should be governed by the apostolic and royal powers through their diverse offices. Yet, according to the difference between the greater and the less, the Christian religion has so disposed that after God the royal power shall be governed by the care and authority of the apostolic see. Although, dearest son, you are not ignorant of this, yet, in order that it may be ineradicably implanted in your mind for your salvation, Holy Scripture bears witness that the apostolic and pontifical authority must represent all kings, Christian and others, before the judgment seat of God and render an account to him for their sins. If then I am to represent you in the great judgment day before the righteous Judge, the Creator of all creation, in whom is no deceit, do you prudently and carefully consider whether I should not or cannot take diligent pains for your salvation, and whether you should not or cannot without delay render obedience to me, in order to possess the land of the living. Take care therefore to stand fast, to love God and place his honour before your own; serve God with a pure mind and love him with all your strength and in fullness of heart. Believe me, if you love God with a pure mind, as you now hear and as Holy Scripture commands; if you place God's honour before your own in everything, he who knows no love that is counterfeit, who is powerful also to set you up, will both here and hereafter embrace you and extend to you his kingdom with his own Almighty arm. Given at Rome, 8 May, in the third Indiction.[1]

101. Letter from William I to Pope Gregory VII (? 1080)

This letter contains William's famous refusal of fealty to the pope. Gregory VII's demand for William's fealty is not specifically mentioned in the pope's surviving letters to the king. It was probably conveyed verbally by the papal legate, Hubert, who was in England in 1080. William's answer here given is in every way notable. "No statesman has ever settled a major issue in fewer words or more conclusively."[2] A text is in *Lanfranci Opera* (ed. J. A. Giles) (1844), p. 32.

---

[1] 1080. [2] F. M. Stenton, *Anglo-Saxon England* (1943), p. 667.

To Gregory, most excellent shepherd of holy Church, William, king of the English and duke of the Normans, greeting and friendship. Your legate, Hubert, most holy father, coming to me on your behalf, has admonished me to profess allegiance to you and your successors, and to think better regarding the money which my predecessors were wont to send to the Church of Rome. I have consented to the one but not to the other. I have not consented to pay fealty, nor will I now, because I never promised it, nor do I find that my predecessors ever paid it to your predecessors. The money has been negligently collected during the past three years when I was in France; but now that I have returned by God's mercy to my kingdom, I send you by the hands of the aforesaid legate what has already been collected, and the remainder shall be forwarded by the envoys of our trusty Archbishop Lanfranc when the opportunity for so doing shall occur. Pray for us and for the state of our realms, for we always loved your predecessors and it is our earnest desire above all things to love you most sincerely, and to hear you most obediently.

102. Letter from Pope Gregory VII to Hugh, bishop of Die, and Amatus, bishop of Oléron (1081)

This extract shows Gregory VII still maintaining his high opinion of William I, despite the latter's refusal of fealty. Printed: P. Jaffé, *Monumenta Gregoriana* (1865), pp. 478; E. Caspar, *Registrum Papae Gregorii VII*, vol. II, p. 579.

The king of the English, although in certain matters he does not comport himself as devoutly as we might hope, nevertheless in that he has neither destroyed nor sold the churches of God; that he has taken pains to govern his subjects in peace and justice; that he has refused his assent to anything detrimental to the apostolic see, even when solicited by certain enemies of the cross of Christ; and that he has compelled the priests on oath to put away their wives and the laity to forward the tithes they were withholding from us–in all these respects he has shown himself more worthy of approbation and honour than other kings. . . .

103. Letter from Archbishop Lanfranc to Pope Gregory VII (? 1081)

The chronology of the correspondence between pope and archbishop during the years 1079 to 1082 is difficult to determine owing to the fact that at least one, and possibly two, of Gregory's letters are no longer extant. It would seem, however, that this letter is a reply to one of Gregory's lost letters written during the second half of the year 1080 rather than to that of 25 March 1079, printed above, No. 97. In his reply Lanfranc defends himself against the charge of negligence in coming to Rome and promises obedience in everything according to the canons, a qualification of considerable importance. In the final paragraph the archbishop refers to the pope's recent claim on William and in diplomatic terms indicates his substantial agreement with William's views. The original Latin is printed in *Lanfranci Opera* (ed. J. A. Giles), Ep. 11, vol. I (1844), pp. 32–33, and the translation here given is based upon Z. N. Brooke, *The English Church and the Papacy* (1931), p. 131.

To the venerable Gregory, supreme shepherd of the holy and universal Church, Lanfranc, a sinner and unworthy prelate, pays service and due obedience. I have received with due humility the letter which your excellency caused to be conveyed to me by Hubert, subdeacon of your palace. The purport of the letter was, with paternal kindness, to find fault with my conduct, for that having been advanced to the honour of the episcopate, I have no longer that respect for the holy Roman Church and for yourself in particular, which I professed before my elevation to the post of honour, for which, as is well known, and as I do not deny, I was indebted to the apostolic see. I ought not to misrepresent your words, venerable father, nor do I wish to do so, but I must say that I cannot in conscience understand what absence or distance of place, or exalted station, be it ever so great, can have to do with this matter. I am ready to yield obedience to your commands in everything according to the canons, and if by God's blessing I shall have at any time the pleasure of conversing with you personally, I will endeavour to make it evident, by deeds rather than words, that my affection for you, instead of being diminished, has on the contrary increased, although yours –excuse me for saying so–is evidently not towards me what once it was. The verbal message brought by your legate[1] I recommended as best I could to my lord the king. I advised him,[2] but I could not persuade him. The reason why he could not assent to your wishes in all points he will himself make known to you, by word of mouth to your legate, and by letter to yourself.[3]

104. Letter from Pope Gregory VII to Archbishop Lanfranc (? 1082)

Printed: P. Jaffé, *Monumenta Gregoriana* (1865), p. 494; E. Caspar, *Registrum Papae Gregorii VII* vol. II (1893), p. 600.

Gregory, the bishop, servant of the servants of God, to Lanfranc, archbishop of Canterbury, greeting and apostolic benediction. Often have we invited you by apostolic legations to come to Rome as proof of your loyalty and Christian devotion. Hitherto you have forborne to do so, abusing our patience, so it appears, either through pride or negligence, since you have put forward no canonical reason. For the labour or danger of the journey is insufficient excuse for your absence, when it is well known that many from a great distance, though weak and infirm of body and scarcely able to rise from their beds, have nevertheless out of their ardent love for St. Peter made haste to approach his threshold in vehicles. Wherefore we command you on apostolic authority that, putting aside every engagement or empty foreboding –four months' grace after the receipt of this our mandate being granted–you be sure to attend at Rome on the Feast of All Saints[4] in the present year, and delay no longer to make amends for the charge of disobedience so long preferred against you. If, however, the apostolic mandate moves you not, and you ignore it and choose to remain in contempt thereof, and are not ashamed to run the risk of disobedience, which according to the testimony of the blessed Samuel is as the sin of witchcraft,[5] then rest assured that you will be deprived of the favour of blessed Peter and stand wholly rebuked by his authority. So then, if you do not visit us within the appointed term, you will be suspended from all episcopal functions.

[1] Hubert. The reference is to the legation of 1080 conveying Gregory's demand for William's fealty; see above, p. 646.

[2] This remark might be regarded as indicating Lanfranc's private opinion on the question of fealty; more probably it should be interpreted in the sense that the archbishop had by virtue of his office felt constrained to advise the king to comply with the pope's demands, whatever his personal views on the matter; see A. J. Macdonald, *Lanfranc* (1926), p. 225.

[3] See above, No. 101.

[4] 1 November.

[5] I Kings xv. 23.

105. Letter from Pope Gregory VII to William I (? 1083)

Another letter notable for the eulogistic terms used by the pope towards the king of England, despite his rebuff at William's hands in the matter of his claim to fealty. Printed: P. Jaffé, *Monumenta Gregoriana* (1865), p. 518; E. Caspar, *Registrum Papae Gregorii VII*, vol. II, p. 630.

Gregory, the bishop, servant of the servants of God, to William, king of the English, greeting and apostolic benediction. The common love and sincere devotion we bear towards the blessed apostle Peter has long since united us in friendship, and this has grown in mutual strength from the fact that while I have observed that your devotion to the apostolic see surpasses that of others of your rank, your illustrious highness has on your part credited me with having striven more than any of my predecessors to promote the honour of the said see. In brief, as in evil natures, desire for, or denial of, the same thing often engenders deadly discord, so in good things it will be found that the same zeal and fervour of spirit may join in one bond of love those who are widely separated in different lands. Although, indeed, certain persons of regal authority complain unduly and oft-times murmur against us that their grievances are to some extent ignored, and that they are not cherished by the apostolic see nor honoured by us in word or deed; this is a matter of small regret to us and with God's help will be so in future. Verily we trust that your highness will ever diligently maintain the same devotion towards holy Church and the same zeal for righteousness, and even with God's help extend them in future. Wherefore it is meet and right that we should persevere in the same course of love, or rather increase more and more with the passage of time as our merits grow.

106. Letter from Archbishop Lanfranc to Hugh the cardinal (1084)

This letter, written to a partisan of the anti-pope Clement III, is of interest in illustrating Lanfranc's attitude towards the papal claims. Printed: *Lanfranci Opera* (ed. J. A. Giles), p. 79; translated: A. J. Macdonald, *Lanfranc* (1926), p. 228.

I have received and read your letter which you sent me by the bearer of mine, and some things in it have displeased me. I do not approve of your vituperation against Pope Gregory, or of your calling him Hildebrand and his legates bad names, or of your advocacy of Clement. For it is written that a man should neither be praised nor condemned in his lifetime nor his neighbours disparaged. What men are now is as yet unknown to mankind, and also what they will be in the sight of God. Yet I do not believe that the emperor[1] would have ventured to take so grave a step without good reason, nor do I think that without the help of God he would have been able to achieve so great a victory.[2] I do not recommend your coming to England unless you first obtain permission from the king of the English. For our island has not yet rejected the former nor pronounced judgment as to whether it should obey the latter.[3] When the arguments on both sides have been heard, if it so happen, it will be possible to see more clearly what ought to be done.

[1] Henry IV, 1056–1106.
[2] A reference to Gregory's final expulsion from Rome by the Imperial army in the autumn of 1084.
[3] *i.e.* decided between Gregory VII and Clement III.

B. THE CHURCH IN ENGLAND
1089–1154

THE dominant personality in the English Church at this time was Anselm, archbishop of Canterbury, whose life and policy were described at length by Eadmer in two works, the "Modern History" (*Historia Novorum in Anglia*) and the "Life of Anselm" (*De Vita et Conversatione Anselmi*). Eadmer was a very voluminous writer, and only a small portion of his work can, for reasons of space, be included in this volume. His writings are here represented by a part of the *Historia Novorum*: the *Vita Anselmi* is more hagiographical in tone, and whilst it contains much matter of great interest it covers much of the ground traversed in the *Historia Novorum*. Anselm died 21 April 1109; and a description of the Church in England in the reign of Stephen is given by John of Salisbury. Perhaps, however, the most important feature in the internal history of the Church at this time was the establishment and rapid development in England of the Cistercian Order, which is here separately evidenced in four independent texts.

(*a*) MATERIAL RELATING TO THE LIFE AND POLICY OF ARCHBISHOP ANSELM

107. Eadmer: "The History of Modern Times in England" (*Historia Novorum in Anglia*)

The *Historia Novorum in Anglia* by Eadmer, a monk of Christ Church, Canterbury, has long been recognized as one of the chief authorities for English history in the reigns of William II and Henry I. It is a contemporary narrative and treats of certain aspects of the political and ecclesiastical history of the period in great detail. It is, moreover, the chief narrative source for the history of the Investiture Controversy in England.

Eadmer was born about 1064. One, at least, of his parents was English. He was reared from early childhood in the monastery of Christ Church at Canterbury, where he first made the acquaintance of Anselm during the latter's visit to England in 1071. Thus began a long and ripening friendship. After Anselm's appointment as archbishop of Canterbury in 1093, Eadmer became his intimate companion, both in England and during Anselm's successive periods of exile on the Continent.

Eadmer was thus peculiarly fitted to record the chequered fortunes of his master throughout Anselm's career, and the circumstances in which much of his literary work was performed can best be judged from a note which he included in his *Vita Anselmi*:

> I had just taken this work[1] in hand, and transferred a considerable portion of it from the rough draft in wax when Father Anselm privately requested me to inform him what it was that I was writing on my tablets. I was disposed rather to veil the thing in silence than to unveil it to him, when he desired me either to desist from my undertaking and turn to something else, or forthwith to show him my manuscript. I readily obeyed, for I had already enjoyed his help and profited by his corrections in some few writings of mine, and I hoped that with his real kindness he would correct what needed correction, and, if any stories had not been arranged in proper order, he would put each in its right place. Nor was I disappointed. He corrected some passages in my little book and cancelled others; he changed the place of some and left others where they were. Great was my delight and great my pride–but after some few days the archbishop called me to him, and desired me utterly to destroy the quires on which I had written my work, for he deemed it altogether unbecoming that his praise should redound to posterity through my writings. This view I reluctantly accepted; for I dared not disobey his command utterly, but neither did I wish to lose all the fruit of my labours. I therefore complied with his wishes literally by destroying the quires which he had mentioned, but I did not do so until I had transferred their contents to others. This action of mine was perhaps not wholly free from the sin of disobedience.

The first recension of the *Historia Novorum* was probably produced soon after 1109. It comprised four books, and carried the story down to the death of Anselm. A fifth book was added some

[1] *De Vita et Conversatione Anselmi Archiepiscopi Cantuariensis*, ed. M. Rule (Rolls Series, 1884), pp. 422, 423: translated *ibid.*, p. lxvi.

time between 1121 and 1124, and the sixth and final book appeared not long before Eadmer's death which is conjectured to have taken place in 1144. Except in the first two books Eadmer undertook very little revision or improvement of his text. Among the major events which are discussed in the passages which follow are the circumstances in which Anselm became archbishop; his quarrel with William Rufus and the council of Rockingham; his relations with Henry I; and the settlement of the Investitures question in England ratified at the Concordat of Bec in 1107.

The *Historia Novorum* thus preserves an historical form and sequence, but it is by no means a full-scale history of the period like that of William of Malmesbury. It is rather a history of the English Church during Anselm's primacy, with the saintly archbishop always in the forefront of the stage. Consequently the proportions of the narrative are not entirely satisfactory. For example, in Eadmer's account of the council of Rockingham,[1] admirable in many other respects, the causes of the change in the attitude of the lay magnates towards the king and the archbishop do not emerge with sufficient clarity. Moreover, the story of the tyrannical conduct of Rufus in his dealings with the English Church is told almost exclusively from the standpoint of the monks of Canterbury, who admittedly suffered most from the depredations of the royal officials. On the other hand, Eadmer frequently displays a masterly power of dramatic narrative whenever, as was usually the case, he was an eyewitness of the events he records. Excellent examples of his prowess as a dramatic writer are to be found in his graphic account of the election of Anselm[2] and in his detailed exposition of the arguments used on either side in the debates in the council of Rockingham. In this respect the narrative in Book II is vastly superior to that in Books III and IV, where Eadmer's treatment of the successive phases of the Investiture Controversy–much the more interesting and important topic to the modern student because of its constitutional significance–is characterized by a deficiency in dramatic sense and insight. It is probable that he did not fully comprehend the motives actuating king and archbishop in their diverse policies and, being a contemporary, he certainly failed to measure or appreciate the greatness of the issues involved. Nevertheless, the prime interest of his subject-matter, the simplicity and unity of the work, his general trustworthiness on points of detail and, not least, his habit of incorporating in the text of his narrative letters and official documents–though these are not always quoted accurately or arranged in the right order–these qualities render Eadmer's *Historia* of the highest value.

The Latin text is printed in the Rolls Series (ed. Martin Rule, 1884). For elucidation of specific points reference may be made to R. W. Church, *St. Anselm* (1870, and later editions), to W. F. Hook, *Lives of the Archbishops of Canterbury*, vol. II, pp. 169–276, to P. Hughes, *History of the Christian Church*, vol. II (London, 1947, 1948); and above all to Z. N. Brooke, *The English Church and the Papacy* (Cambridge, 1931).

Book I

On[3] the death of King William, his son, William, succeeded him in the realm of England. Endeavouring to forestall his brother, Robert,[4] in gaining possession of the crown, he found that Lanfranc, without whose consent he could by no means ascend the throne, was not altogether willing to satisfy his desire in the matter. Fearing, therefore, lest any delay in his coronation might entail the loss of the coveted title, he made the following promises on oath to Lanfranc, both for himself and on behalf of all whom he could muster; namely first, to maintain justice, mercy and equity in all his dealings throughout the realm, if he should become king; secondly, to defend the peace, freedom and security of the Church against all men; and, thirdly, to obey the orders and accept the advice of the archbishop in everything. But once he had become established in the kingdom, he forsook his promises and lapsed into evil ways. Whereupon, being humbly reproved by Lanfranc and charged with breach of faith towards him, the king flared up into a passion and said, "Who among men can fulfil all his promises?" From this time forth he was unable to look the archbishop straight in the eyes, although in some matters to which his self-will inclined him, he preserved moderation out of respect for the archbishop during his lifetime. For this same Lanfranc was a man highly skilled in laws both human and divine, and the government of the whole kingdom waited upon his word. But how grievous a calamity befell

[1] See below, pp. 660–668. [2] See below, pp. 653–657. [3] Rolls Series edition, p. 25.

[4] Eldest son of the Conqueror, succeeded to the duchy of Normandy on his father's death.

the churches as a consequence of his death, I may show in a few words, omitting a great deal.

Forthwith the king showed openly the disposition which during the archbishop's life he had kept hidden in his breast. For soon–if I may omit his other vile deeds–he attacked the church of Canterbury, the mother-church of all England, Scotland and Ireland, and also of the neighbouring islands. He caused an inventory to be made by his officials of all that belonged to it, both within and without, and after fixing an allowance for the monks who served God there, he offered the remainder of the property to be assessed and reckoned as part of his demesne. So he put up the church of Christ for sale, granting the power of lordship over it to the highest bidder, no matter how great the damage incurred thereby. Every year in lamentable succession a new assessment of values was made; for the king would permit no agreement to remain settled, but whoever promised more ousted him who was paying less, unless perchance the former tenant, in voidance of the original contract, raised his price to that of the second bidder. Moreover, every day one might see the most abandoned of men engaged in exacting money for the king, tramping about the cloisters of the monastery with cruel and intimidating looks in contempt of the religion of God's servants, issuing orders on all sides, uttering threats, lording it over everyone and manifesting their power to the uttermost. What scandals, discords and irregularities arose from this it pains me to record. Certain monks of the church were dispersed abroad at the outbreak of the trouble and sent to other houses, while those who remained behind suffered many tribulations and indignities. What shall I say of the tenantry of the abbey, who were ground down with such misery and devastation that, but for the evils which followed, I might hazard a guess whether they could have been more cruelly oppressed if left with a bare subsistence?

Nor were such deeds confined to Canterbury. The same barbarity raged in every daughter-church in England which at that time fell into widowhood through the death of her spouse, whether bishop or abbot. This king was indeed the first to bring this baleful oppression against the Church of God, having inherited no such tradition from his father; he alone, when churches fell vacant, kept them in his own hands. For he would name no successor so long as he could exact from them through his officials whatever price he deemed feasible. Thus, wherever one looked, misery abounded and this wretched state of affairs lasted for nearly five years[1] in the church of Canterbury, every increasing, ever deteriorating and becoming more deplorable. . . .

In[2] the meantime, all the chief men of the realm being assembled, as was the custom, at the king's court to keep Christmas,[3] it chanced that some of the greatest of them found themselves of one mind in lamenting the fate of the church [of Canterbury], the common mother of the realm, in that, having lost her shepherd, she was being subjected to continuous oppression, and that of a kind without precedent. So they took counsel together in this matter and their decision, which perchance may seem remarkable to posterity, was as follows: humbly to beseech their lord the king to

[1] About this time Anselm, abbot of Le Bec, was invited over to England by Hugh of Avranches, earl of Chester. Already there was talk of his being designated primate in succession to Lanfranc. After five months' sojourn in the country, during which he had his first meeting with the king, the latter refused him permission to return to Normandy to attend to the affairs of his abbey.

[2] Rolls Series edition, p. 29.

[3] 1092.

allow prayers to be offered to God in all the churches of England that he would move the king to raise up the church of Canterbury from dire desolation by the appointment of a worthy pastor. When in concert together they laid this suggestion before the king, he showed some indignation; nevertheless he assented thereto, adding that, whatever the Church might ask, he himself would undoubtedly do what he chose in the matter. On receipt of this reply, the bishops, being the party most concerned, sought advice from Anselm, but only with difficulty were they able to persuade him to arrange the form and substance of the prayers. For he, as an abbot, was reluctant in such a case to perform the function of the bishops. But pressure was brought to bear on him on the ground that he knew the matter was of crucial importance to the Church of God; so he drew up the form of prayer in their hearing, and with praise for the good sense and perspicacity of his mind all the magnates of the realm departed home at the adjournment of the court. Accordingly prayers were offered throughout all the churches of England.

Just then it happened one day that one of the chief magnates, being engaged in private audience with the king and treating of this matter among others, spoke his mind as follows: "I know no man of such proven sanctity as Anselm, abbot of Le Bec. Indeed he loves nothing more than God and, as is patent in all his ways, he seeks nothing of a temporal character." To this the king replied mocking, "Not even the archbishopric of Canterbury?" The other answered, "That least of all in my opinion and that of many other men." Whereupon the king protested solemnly, "If he had the slightest hope of obtaining it, he would dance and clap his hands as he rushed to embrace it. But", he added, "by the Holy Face of Lucca"–his customary oath–"neither he nor anyone else at this juncture shall be archbishop except myself." At the moment he thus spake a grievous sickness laid hold of him, and he took to his bed. His malady daily increasing, he drew nigh unto death. What need of further words! All the magnates of the realm flocked to court, bishops, abbots and lay barons, in expectation of his death. The sick man was bidden to meditate upon the salvation of his soul, to open the prisons, to set free the captives and to loosen their chains, to pardon debtors, to restore freedom to the churches so long subjected to royal servitude through the sees being kept vacant, especially the church of Canterbury, the oppression of which, so they alleged, was universally acknowledged to be the most monstrous indignity against Christianity in England.

At this time Anselm, wholly ignorant of these events, was dwelling in a certain town not far from Gloucester where the king lay sick. He was thereupon ordered to come to the king with all speed to support and fortify the dying man with his presence.[1] On receipt of these tidings he came in haste and entered the royal chamber. He was asked what counsel he deemed most wholesome for the soul of the dying man. He first begged to be told what advice had been given to the sick monarch by those in attendance before his arrival. He listened, approved, and added: "It is written, 'Begin by making confession to the Lord.' Wherefore it seems to me that first he should make full confession of all sins he has knowingly committed against God and should promise that, if he recovers, he will amend them all without dissimulation, and

[1] 6 March 1093.

then without delay he should give orders for everything to be done as you have advised." The substance of this advice was approved and Anselm was charged with the duty of hearing the king's confession. The king was informed of what Anselm had recommended to be most expedient for his soul's salvation. Without delay he agreed and with a contrite heart promised to perform all that in Anselm's opinion was required, and also for the remainder of his life to deal justly and compassionately. He pledged his faith to this and took his bishops to witness between himself and God, sending some of them to promise this, his vow to God, upon the altar in his stead. An edict was drawn up and sealed with the royal seal, to the effect that all prisoners without exception should be set free in all his dominions, all debts should be irrevocably cancelled, all offences heretofore committed should be pardoned and consigned to perpetual oblivion. Furthermore, good and holy laws, the inviolable maintenance of rights and such a searching inquiry into wrongdoing as might deter others, were promised to all men. Amidst universal rejoicing and praise to God, unceasing prayer was offered for the health of the king.

In the meantime certain good men advised the king to release the mother-church of the kingdom from her recent widowhood by the appointment of a new shepherd. He willingly acquiesced and admitted that he had made up his mind to do so. Accordingly they began to seek for a man worthy of the honour. Everything, however, waited on the king's nod and he himself proclaimed Anselm to be the man most worthy of the office; with one voice all welcomed his decision. Aghast at this nomination, Anselm grew pale; and while he was being hurried along to the royal presence to receive investiture of the archbishopric by ring and staff at the king's hands, he resisted with all his might, alleging that many obstacles prevented his acceptance. Then the bishops came forward to meet him and, leading him apart from the multitude, addressed him as follows: "What art thou about? What meanest thou by this? Why dost thou strive against God? Thou seest that religion has wellnigh perished in England, that everything has fallen into confusion and all manner of wickedness is rampant, and we, the bishops, the appointed rulers of God's Church, stand in peril of eternal death through this man's tyranny; and yet, when thou couldst bring succour, thou scornest to do so. What art thou dreaming of, thou paragon of men? Whither have thy wits strayed? The church of Canterbury, in whose oppression we all are oppressed and destroyed, summons thee to deliver her from bondage and us from anxiety; yet thou wouldst prefer thine own ease and quiet to undertaking her liberation and the relief of our distress, thou wouldst refuse to share in the labours of thy brethren."

To these remonstrances he answered, "Bear with me, I pray you, bear with me, and give me your attention. I admit that what you have said is true; many are your tribulations and great is your need. But consider, I beg you. I am already an old man and unable to sustain earthly cares. I can scarcely perform my own duties; how can I undertake the administration of the whole Church in England? For that matter, ever since I became a monk, as my conscience bears witness, I have shunned all worldly business, nor could I ever direct my mind thereto by reason of my profession as a monk, for there is naught therein in which I could ever take pleasure or love. Wherefore, give me leave to remain in peace and do not entangle me in public business, which I have never loved and for which I am not fitted." They reply, "Only do thou accept the primacy of the Church without hesitation and go before us in the path of God, informing and commanding us how to act, and we will give our firm support to thee, for we shall not be found wanting in obeying and executing thy commands. Do thou pray to God for us and we will take charge of thy secular business for thee." "What you ask", he replied, "is impossible. I am abbot of a monastery in another land, with an archbishop to whom I owe obedience, a temporal prince to whom I am subject, and monks for whom I must provide counsel and help. Thus I am strictly bound by all these ties; I cannot desert my monks without their consent, nor remove myself from my prince's dominion without his permission; nor can I withdraw obedience from my archbishop without peril to my soul unless absolved by him." "All these matters", they complain, "are of small account and may be easily arranged." To this he answered, "It is no use, what you purpose shall not be accomplished."

At this they seized him by force and brought him to the bedside of the sick king, to whom they openly declared his obstinacy. Almost weeping with sorrow the king spake unto him, "O Anselm, what art thou about? Why dost thou deliver me to everlasting torment? Recollect, I pray thee, the firm friendship my father and my mother had for thee, and which thou didst always reciprocate, and by that token, I beseech thee, suffer me not, their son, to perish both in soul and body. For I am certain that I shall so perish if I end my life holding the archbishopric in my possession. Succour me, therefore, father, and receive the archbishopric through the retention of which I am so greatly confounded, and dread lest I be yet further confounded in eternity." At these words some of the bystanders were moved with compassion and began to upbraid Anselm for making excuses and showing reluctance to shoulder so heavy a burden at this juncture, importuning him angrily and in some confusion, saying, "What madness has possessed thy mind? Thou art frightening the king to death, in that thou art not afraid to embitter his dying hours by thine obstinacy. Rest assured then that all the disorders, all the acts of oppression, all the crimes which will follow, one after the other in England, will be laid to thy account, unless thou avert them by accepting the pastoral charge this day." In this dire extremity Anselm turned to two of his monks, Baldwin[1] and Eustace, there present with him, and said unto them, "Ah, my brethren, why do you not help me?" This he spake, for before God I lie not, he was afterwards wont to say that he was so straitened with anxiety, that if the choice had been given him, saving his reverence for God's will, he would gladly have died rather than have been raised to the archbishopric. Baldwin then answered, "If this be according to the will of God, who are we to speak against it?" and immediately burst into tears, while the blood gushed forth from his nostrils, openly testifying to all those present with what sorrow of heart the words had been forced from him amid tears. At this reply Anselm said, "Alas! your staff is soon broken." Then the king, feeling that all their labour was being expended in vain, bade them all fall at Anselm's feet, whether perchance they might thereby constrain him to give consent. But lo! as they prostrated themselves, he in turn fell on his knees before them and

[1] Baldwin of Tournai-sur-Dives, later placed in charge of the archbishop's household at Canterbury and, together with Eadmer, a companion of his exile; see below, p. 667.

would not budge from his first refusal. At length, incensed against him and vexed at themselves for their irresolution in allowing his objections to defeat their purpose for so long, they raised the cry, "Bring hither the pastoral staff! the pastoral staff!" And, seizing his right arm, some of them dragged him forward while others pushed him from behind, and so they forced him struggling to the king's bedside. But when the king held out the staff to him, he closed his fist against it, and would not receive it. The bishops then tried to wrench open his fingers, which he kept firmly fixed in the palm of his hand, in order to place the staff therein. But after some moments spent in this vain endeavour, while Anselm cried out with the pain he was suffering, the index finger which they had succeeded in raising being once more immediately closed by him, finally the staff was placed against his clenched fist and held there by the hands of the bishops. While the crowd shouted "Long live the bishop!" and the other bishops, together with the clergy, began to chant in a loud voice the *Te Deum Laudamus*, the elected prelate was carried rather than led into the church near by, still resisting with all his might and crying out, "It is naught that you are doing; it is naught that you are doing." The formalities of the Church customary on such an occasion having been complied with, Anselm returned to the king, and thus addressed him, "I tell thee, my lord king, that thou wilt not die of this sickness, and therefore I wish thee to know how easily thou mayst alter what has been done with me; for I have neither acknowledged nor do I acknowledge its validity." Having thus said, he withdrew from the royal chamber and retraced his steps, the bishops together with the lay magnates escorting him. Turning upon them he upbraided them in these words, "Do you realize what you have done? You have yoked together in the plough the untamed bull and the old and feeble sheep, and what good will come of it? The untameable ferocity of the bull, unless he break the yoke, will so tear in pieces the sheep, which produces wool, milk and lambs, by dragging her hither and thither through briars and thickets, that she will never be of use either to herself or to anyone else, while she can furnish none of these things. Why so? Because you have thoughtlessly yoked the sheep to the bull. Reflect that the plough is the Church, according to the word of the apostle saying, 'Ye are God's husbandry, ye are God's building.'[1] In England this plough is managed and drawn by two oxen which excel all others, namely the king and the archbishop of Canterbury, the former by jurisdiction and rule over the things of this world, the latter by teaching and governance in the things of God. One of these twain, Archbishop Lanfranc, is dead, and the other, possessed of the ferocity of an untameable bull, already as a young man was predestined to the plough; and now in place of the dead ox you would join me, an old and feeble sheep, to the untamed bull. You understand well enough what I mean; you might have paused in this affair to consider whether I would wish to be paired with him, and having reflected upon it at the very beginning, you should have forborne. But as you have not, behold! I predict that after I have been worn out by diverse injuries inflicted at the king's hands, the royal tyranny will grind me down to a greater degree than you now deem possible, me, from whom some will look to be provided with the fleece and milk of the word of God and lambs for his service; and the joy,

[1] I Corinthians iii. 9.

which you now feel at the hope of my being able to afford you some relief, will be turned again in many to grievous mourning, when they find they cannot obtain through me the customary counsel and hoped-for succour. All that you will have gained from this, is that the Church, which you have been at such great pains to raise up from widowhood, will sink back therein, even when her shepherd is still alive; which is a worse state of affairs, whichever way one looks at it. And to whom shall these evils be charged if not to you, who have so thoughtlessly joined the ferocity of the king to my weakness? So, once I have been crushed, none of you will dare to cross his path in anything, and beyond a doubt he will not hesitate to trample you underfoot at his will." At these words his tears began to flow and, unable to conceal his sorrow of heart, he dismissed the assembly and returned to his lodging. All this took place on the First Sunday in Lent, 6 March, in the year of our Lord 1093. The king thereupon commanded that without delay or loss he should be invested with everything pertaining to the archbishopric, both within and without, and with the city of Canterbury, which Lanfranc had held in fee from the king, together with the abbey of St. Albans, which not only Lanfranc, but his predecessors also, were known to have held in free alms of the church of Christ at Canterbury, by perpetual right for the redemption of the king's soul. . . .[1]

Meanwhile,[2] as Anselm had foretold, the king recovered from his sickness, and soon he broke all the good resolutions he had then made and ordered them to be regarded as null and void. Indeed he ordered the prisoners who had not yet been released to be guarded more strictly than usual, while those who had been set free were to be imprisoned again if they were recaptured. Old debts, which had already been cancelled, were exacted again in full; pleas of the crown and criminal suits were revived in the ancient form and heard and examined by men who cared more for the subversion of justice than for its maintenance and defence, more for the oppression of the poor and the exaction of money than for the suppression of crime. Then arose such misery and devastation throughout the realm that whoever remembers it cannot, I ween, recall having seen anything like it in England before. Indeed all the evil the king had done before he was sick seemed good in comparison with the evil he did when restored to health. But should any man desire to know the origin of these things, he may reflect upon the king's reply to the aforesaid bishop of Rochester,[3] when the latter, in private discourse with the king during his convalescence, warned him to act more circumspectly towards God in everything: "Be assured, bishop, that by the Holy Face of Lucca, God shall never have good from me in return for the evil he has brought upon me."

Accordingly, after Anselm had received the letters dispatched from Normandy mentioned above, and the king had returned from a conference at Dover with Robert, count of Flanders, to Rochester, where Anselm then was, the latter carried off the king in private and had speech with him as follows, "My lord king, my mind is still in doubt whether I should agree to accept the archbishopric or not. Nevertheless,

[1] At the king's petition Anselm duly obtained permission to take up his archiepiscopal office from the duke of Normandy and the archbishop of Rouen, while his monks at Bec also released him from his abbacy.

[2] Rolls Series edition, p. 38.

[3] Gundulf.

if reason should incline me to undertake it, I wish you to know summarily beforehand what I desire you to do for me. First, I desire you to restore all the lands held by the church of Canterbury–over which I have been chosen to bear rule–in the time of Archbishop Lanfranc of blessed memory without any suit or controversy, and that you will consent to do right and justice in respect of the other lands held by the said church before his time, but subsequently lost and not yet recovered. In addition, I desire that in things pertaining to God and religion you will listen to my advice in preference to that of others; and inasmuch as I take you for my earthly lord and protector, so you on your part should take me for your spiritual father and ghostly counsellor. Moreover, in the matter of the Roman pope, Urban, whom you have not hitherto recognized as lawfully elected, but whom I have accepted and still accept, I desire you to offer him due obedience and submission.[1] I warn you to take care in this matter, lest scandal should arise in the future. On all these points I beg you to make your opinion known, so that, having ascertained it, I may be sure of my future course." Thereupon the king summoned to him William, bishop of Durham,[2] and Robert, count of Meulan,[3] and bade Anselm repeat his statement in their presence. He duly complied and, in accordance with the advice of his counsellors, the king made answer as follows: "I give back to you in their former state all the lands the church possessed under Lanfranc, but at present I will make no agreement with you concerning the possessions which were not held under the late archbishop; nevertheless, on these and other points I will trust you only so far as I ought." Thereupon the king closed the interview and they parted from each other.

A few days later the king received letters from the Normans consenting to his request respecting Anselm,[4] as we have mentioned above. And coming to his town of Windsor he summoned Anselm thither with the intent that he should no longer refuse to accept his election as primate of the whole realm and, as a personal favour to the king, should agree to the alienation of the church lands which the king had granted to his vassals at Lanfranc's death to be held by hereditary right in return for stipulated service to the crown. But Anselm, being unwilling to consent to the spoliation of a church with which he had not yet been invested, would by no means make the bargain about the lands which the king sought. Wherefore, by reason of this discord between himself and the king, the first point, concerning his election, remained undecided. At this Anselm rejoiced, hoping that by this chance he might by God's grace be relieved of the burden of the archbishopric. For he had already resigned his charge as abbot of Le Bec, which he had received with the pastoral staff, on account of his absolution therefrom described above; and now he rejoiced to see an opportunity of escaping the burden of episcopal office. Nevertheless, after a long interval, when the king could no longer endure the clamour of the universal lamentation about the ruin of the churches, he caused Anselm to attend him at Winchester, where a council of magnates had been convened, and there, by dint of many fair

[1] A reference to the schism between Urban II and Clement III, the anti-pope. England had not yet officially recognized either claimant, though Anselm, as abbot of Bec, had given his allegiance to Urban; see below, pp. 659 *et sqq*.

[2] William of St. Calais; see above, No. 84.

[3] Robert of Beaumont; see Table 12.

[4] *i.e.* agreeing to his release.

promises to the Church of God for the future, he succeeded in persuading Anselm to undertake the alluring office of primate of the Church in England. So then, invested after the manner and example of his predecessor, he became the king's liegeman in accordance with the custom of the land, and, like Lanfranc in his time, he was granted possession of the whole archbishopric.

After this he came to Canterbury on 25 September[1] and amidst the enthusiasm of the monks, the clergy and the whole people he was enthroned as primate of the Church of God with great solemnity. But on that very day there came to Canterbury an envoy from the king named Rannulf,[2] the principal agent of the royal will. Disdaining every consideration of piety and modesty, he incontinently brought a suit against the archbishop, and in his harshness and insolence was not afraid to disturb the Church's joy. All were deeply offended at this untoward event, complaining indignantly at the insult offered to so great a man, in that he was not allowed to spend even the first day of his dignity in peace. Their indignation was augmented by no small grief because the case in question pertained to the jurisdiction of the Church, and in no wise came within the province of royal justice. . . .

During the king's stay in a certain town called Gillingham,[3] three miles from Shaftesbury, Anselm visited him and made known his desire to go to the Roman pope to obtain his *pallium*. "From which pope", inquired the king, "do you seek it?" For it was reported in England that there were then two claimants to the Roman see in dispute with each other, who were dragging the Church of God along with them in schism, namely Urban, formerly Odo, bishop of Ostia, and Clement,[4] who as archbishop of Ravenna had been called Guibert. This matter (to say nothing of other parts of the world) had for several years so preoccupied the Church in England that since the death of Gregory of venerated memory, formerly called Hildebrand, up to this present day, she had been unwilling to become subject or obedient to the pope in anything. But Urban had long since been recognized as vicar of the blessed Peter in Italy and France, and Anselm also, when abbot in Normandy, had acknowledged him as pope. Moreover, Anselm being a most distinguished personage though not of the highest rank, had received letters from Urban and sent replies to him as the supreme shepherd of holy Church. Accordingly, to the king's question as to which pope he desired to ask for the use of the *pallium*, he answered, "Pope Urban." At this the king asserted that Urban had not yet been acknowledged as rightful pope, and that it was not in accordance with his custom or that of his father that any man should be recognized as pope in the realm of England without his leave or approval. If anyone tried to infringe his prerogative in this, it would be tantamount to depriving him of his crown. Astonished at this, Anselm then reminded him of the incident related earlier,[5] namely what he had told the king at Rochester, before he would consent to become archbishop, that, as abbot of Bec, he had acknowledged Urban as pope and would on no account withdraw his obedience and submission. Upon

[1] 1093.
[2] The notorious Flambard, chancellor of England in 1094, bishop of Durham, 1099–1128; see above, No. 1, p. 175.
[3] February 1094.
[4] Clement III, anti-pope, had been elected in 1080 with the support of the emperor, Henry IV, during the lifetime of Gregory VII. See above, No. 106.
[5] See above, p. 658.

hearing this the king was moved to great anger, protesting that the archbishop could by no means at one and the same time maintain his allegiance to the crown and his obedience to the apostolic see against the king's will. Anselm then begged that the case should be postponed for further examination, saving the right which he had put forward respecting his submission and obedience to the Roman Church; a council should be summoned consisting of the bishops, abbots and all the magnates of the realm, and it should be determined by their common consent whether or no he could maintain his allegiance to his earthly sovereign, while reserving the reverence and obedience he owed to the apostolic see. "If it be proved", he said, "that this cannot be done, I confess I would rather go into exile, until such time as you acknowledge the pope, than refuse obedience to blessed Peter and his vicar for a single moment." So a postponement was granted, and by royal decree almost all the magnates of the realm gathered together at Rockingham on 11 March[1] for the purpose of discussing this matter.

Accordingly a great council was held in the church of the castle there on the Lord's Day beginning at the first hour of the day.[2] The king and his associates sat apart, diligently weaving their designs against Anselm. But the latter summoned the bishops, abbots and lay magnates from the king's inner council and in the presence of a numerous concourse of monks, clergy and laity addressed them on this wise: "My brethren, children of God's Church, I speak to all of you gathered here in the Lord's name; I beg you to listen and give me the benefit of your advice in the matter which you have been assembled here to discuss. What that matter is, will those who are not yet fully conversant with it, please briefly note? A certain question has arisen between our lord the king and myself which seems to be creating some dissension. For when recently I begged leave of him to visit Urban, the pontiff of the apostolic see, in order to obtain my *pallium* in keeping with the custom of my predecessors, he replied that he had not yet acknowledged the said Urban as pope and so he was unwilling for me to go to him for that purpose. 'Furthermore,' said he, 'if you recognize the said Urban or any other as pope, or persist in doing so, in my kingdom without my approval or authority, you will be acting contrary to the allegiance you owe me, and in this respect you could not offend me more if you tried to deprive me of my crown. Wherefore, be assured that you shall have no part in my realm unless I have proof by an open declaration that, as I wish in the matter, you will refuse all submission and obedience to Urban.' Upon hearing this I was astounded for, as you know, I was an abbot in another land and by God's grace I have dwelt in concord with all men. Indeed it was with no expectation of, or desire for the archbishopric, but impelled by certain reasonable arguments, which I may by no means pass over here, that I came to this land. For at the time of the king's illness all you who were present with him urged him to provide for the good estate of the church of Canterbury, his mother and yours, by appointing an archbishop before his death. What more need I say? Having accepted this advice, it pleased both him and you to choose me for this office. I made several objections in my eagerness to decline the archbishopric, but you

[1] This date is given in error; the council opened on 25 February 1095; see Preface to Rolls Series edition, p. lxii.

[2] 25 February 1095.

would not agree. I protested among other things that I had acknowledged this Urban, concerning whom this dispute has now arisen, as pope, and that I would not withdraw my obedience from him for a moment during his lifetime; and no one on this occasion ventured to contradict me. But what followed? You seized hold of me and compelled me to undertake every man's burden, when, worn out with bodily weakness, I was scarcely able to resist. By this action you perhaps supposed that you had forced me to serve your purpose. But how little I desired it, how unattractive I have found it, what small pleasure I have taken therein, I deem it superfluous at present to declare, since no good can come of it. Nevertheless, lest any should be shocked at me, not knowing my conscience in this affair, I confess, I speak the truth, that had the choice been given me that day, saving my reverence for God's will, I would rather have been cast upon a funeral pyre to be burned than have been exalted to the rank of archbishop. Nevertheless, seeing you were so importunate in your wishes, I trusted myself to you and took up the burden you imposed on me, relying on the hope of your promised assistance.[1] Lo! now an occasion is here to which the case applies, when you should support my burden by the hand of your counsel. It was to this end that on the day the aforesaid challenge was issued to me, I begged for a postponement till today, to the intent you should meet together and examine by common counsel whether or no I can maintain my obedience to the apostolic see in keeping with my allegiance to the king. I repeat, I begged for a postponement and I received it, and lo! you are here by the grace of God. I therefore beseech and warn you all, but more especially you, my brethren and fellow-bishops, that, after due and careful study of the matter, you tender me reliable advice, so that I neither do anything contrary to my obedience to the pope nor offend against the loyalty I owe to the lord king. For to me it is indeed a serious thing to despise and deny the vicar of blessed Peter, and likewise a serious thing to violate the fealty which, under God, I promised to the king; but it is a no less serious assertion that it is impossible for me to keep the one without violating the other."

To this the bishops answered, "The advice you seek from us you already have in your possession, for we know you are prudent in heavenly things and a lover of the good; for this reason you do not need our counsel in so deep a matter. If indeed, waiving every objection, you will frankly refer the sum of your deliberations to the pleasure of our lord the king, we will be instant in watching over your interests as we should our own. Nevertheless, if you bid us do so, we will relate your words to our lord the king, and when we have learned his opinion about them, we will inform you thereof." The archbishop agreed, and they did as they had promised. Thereupon, because it was a Sunday, the king commanded that the whole question should be deferred until the morrow, and that Anselm should return to his lodging and be prepared to attend the council again early on the following morning. So it was done, and we returned early next day as arranged.

Seated in the midst of the magnates and the thronging multitude, Anselm thus opened the proceedings, "My lords and brethren, if you are now prepared to offer me the advice on the case before us which I asked of you yesterday, I will receive it."

[1] *i.e.* the offer made by the bishops at the time of Anselm's consecration to relieve him of the burden of his secular duties; see above, p. 655.

But the bishops replied, "Our answer today is the same as yesterday, namely that if you will unconditionally submit the sum of your deliberations to the pleasure of the lord king, you will receive from us prompt and sound advice, such as we have learnt to be advantageous to ourselves. If, however, you expect from us advice which, under God, by no means meets with the king's approval, you look for it in vain, because you will find we shall never support you in such a case." Having thus said, they were silent and hung their heads, as if to receive what was coming to them. Then Anselm lifted up his eyes and with animated countenance and inspiring voice spoke thus. "Since you, the shepherds of the Christian flock, and you, who are called the princes of the people, refuse to give counsel to me, your father, except at the bidding of one man, I turn to the supreme shepherd and prince of all, I will hasten to 'the Angel of great counsel'[1] and receive from him the counsel I will follow in this my cause, yea rather, his cause and that of his Church. To Peter, the most blessed prince of the apostles, he saith, 'Thou art Peter, and upon this rock I will build my Church, and the gates of hell shall not prevail against it. And I will give unto thee the keys of the kingdom of heaven; and whatsoever thou shalt bind on earth shall be bound in heaven; and whatsoever thou shalt loose on earth shall be loosed in heaven.' . . .[2] These are God's words, these are God's counsels. These I approve and accept, and from them I will by no means depart. Know ye, therefore, all of you, that in the things that are God's I will render obedience to the vicar of the blessed Peter, and in those which pertain of right to the earthly dignity of my lord the king, I will render him both faithful counsel and service to the best of my understanding and capacity." With these words the archbishop concluded his speech.

All those seated round him were dismayed beyond measure and rose up in haste and with great clamour, giving vent to their anger in confused voices, so that one might have supposed they were declaring him guilty of death. Turning upon him in altercation the bishops cried out, "Be assured, we will by no means transmit such words of thine to the king", upon which they retired to the king's chamber. Since therefore no one remained whom he could safely trust to report his words to the king, Anselm went in person and delivered his message by word of mouth. The king, raging with anger, peremptorily inquired of the bishops and magnates what could be said in contradiction of the archbishop's words, but he received no guidance. Aghast at the turn of events and divided among themselves, they stood apart in groups of two or three or four, earnestly taking counsel and discussing how they might compose an answer refuting the archbishop's argument, which would allay the king's anger without directly impugning the declared word of God. Meanwhile Anselm sat by himself, putting his whole trust in the innocency of his heart and the mercy of God. The deliberations of his adversaries being unduly protracted, leaning against the wall he fell into a gentle sleep. After long delay the bishops returned from the king, together with some of the lay barons, and thus addressed him; "Our lord the king, ignoring other matters, desires from you an immediate decision on the question discussed between you at Gillingham and postponed at your request to the present time. The matter is perfectly plain and needs no argument. Nevertheless, you should

[1] Cf. Isaiah ix. 6 (Septuagint version). [2] Matthew xvi. 18.

know that the whole realm cries out against you for endeavouring to detract from the honour of the sovereign power of our common lord. For whoever impairs the customs of the royal prerogative, at the same time deprives him of his crown and kingdom: we judge that the one cannot properly be held without the other. We beseech you to think over the matter again, cast off your obedience to this Urban, who is of no profit to you, now that the lord king is offended with you, and who could not hinder you, once peace had been made between you; shake off the yoke of servitude and as a free man, as becomes an archbishop of Canterbury, anticipate in all your actions the pleasure and commands of the lord king. Acknowledge your fault in what you have done amiss and, that you may obtain the king's forgiveness, comply with his wishes in everything he asks of you, like a wise man; so may your enemies, who now deride you in your misfortunes, be put to shame when they see your rank exalted. This is our request, this is our advice, this we declare and affirm to be necessary to you and your interests." The archbishop answered, "I have listened to your counsel but, if I pass over the rest in silence, I will in no wise deny my obedience to the pope. Already the day declines towards evening; if it please you, let this matter be deferred until tomorrow, so that I may turn it over in my mind and make answer as God shall see fit to inspire me." Suspecting therefore that either he knew not what to reply, or else through fear he was beginning to waver from the intransigent position he had hitherto maintained, the bishops returned to the king and urged him on no account to grant a postponement but, in the light of the recent examination of the case, to order that, if the archbishop would not consent to his designs, final sentence should forthwith be passed upon him.

The king's spokesman and protagonist in this business was the aforesaid William, bishop of Durham,[1] a witty and fluent speaker rather than one endowed with true wisdom. He was the chief author and instigator of the discord between the king and Anselm, and had promised William he would contrive that Anselm should either wholly renounce his obedience to the Roman pope or resign his archbishopric by the surrender of the ring and staff. Relying on this promise, the king congratulated himself, calculating that, if Anselm abjured the pope, he would be discredited in the kingdom, or, if he maintained his allegiance, he might be justly banished from the realm. For what the king desired most of all was to deprive Anselm of all authority for exercising religion. For he had a misgiving that he was not in complete possession of the royal dignity so long as anyone in all the land was said, even in spiritual matters, to hold any power, or to be in a position to do so, except through him. Appreciating the king's hearty desire, the bishop of Durham employed every artifice to drive the archbishop, wearied as he was by false accusations, from the kingdom; having calculated, it was alleged, that on Anselm's departure he would himself be made archbishop. Accordingly, after he had persuaded the king not to grant the postponement Anselm had requested, he approached the archbishop with several members of his entourage who have borne witness to his words, saying, "Give ear to the king's complaint against you. He alleges that in your own interest you have infringed his prerogative, in that you have recognized Odo, bishop of Ostia, as pope in England without his

[1] William of St. Calais; see above, No. 84.

authority and, having thus injured him, you now seek a delay whereby you may demonstrate by fresh arguments that this infringement is lawful. First, if you please, reclothe him with the due dignity of his sovereignty and only after that talk of a postponement. Otherwise, you may know that he will call down upon himself the hatred of Almighty God, and we, his vassals, will connive at the imprecation, if he do but grant for an hour the adjournment till tomorrow for which you ask. Therefore make answer to our lord king here and now, or without doubt you shall forthwith receive the sentence which shall avenge your presumption. Nor should you deem it a matter of jest, nay, to us it is rather a matter of great pain; and no wonder! For that which your lord and ours regards as the chief prerogative of his rule, and in which he assuredly excels all other monarchs, you unjustly rob him of, so far as you are able, breaking the oath of fealty you took to him and involving all his friends in this great distress." Anselm listened to him patiently and then replied as follows to this monstrous accusation: "Whoever would prove that, because I will not renounce the obedience of the venerable and supreme pontiff of the holy Roman Church, I am violating my faith and oath to my earthly sovereign, let him present himself, and he shall find me prepared in the name of the Lord to answer him as I ought, and where I ought." At these words the bishops stared at each other and, finding no apt rejoinder, they again repaired to the king. For they at last understood what they had not at first perceived, nor suspected that Anselm had perceived, namely that the archbishop of Canterbury can neither be judged nor condemned by any man save the pope alone; nor can he be compelled by any man, except the pope, to answer any accusation against his will. Meanwhile there arose a murmur among the whole multitude[1] at the injury done to so great a man, many of the bystanders complaining among themselves in whispers. But no one dared to speak openly in his favour through fear of the king. At last a single knight stepped forward from the throng and knelt before the archbishop, saying, "Lord and father, through me thy suppliant sons entreat thee not to let thy heart be troubled by what thou hast heard; but be thou mindful of the blessed Job, how he vanquished Satan on a dunghill[2] and avenged Adam whom the devil had overcome in Paradise." Anselm received these words with a friendly smile, for he perceived that the people were of the same opinion as himself. So we were glad thereof and became easier in our minds, being confident that, as it is written, "The voice of the people is the voice of God". Were I to attempt to describe one by one the threats, the reproaches, the insults, the false accusations hurled at the archbishop, I fear I should be thought to exaggerate. But all these things he bore with equanimity out of loyalty to the apostolic see, and by God's help overcame them with invincible arguments, proving that he stood firmly established in the truth and had God for his authority in everything which the business entailed. When the king perceived all this, he was exasperated "even to the dividing of his spirit",[3] and said to the bishops, "What is this? Did you not promise me that you would deal with him wholly according to my will, that you would judge him and condemn him?" To this the bishop of Durham made answer, "He spoke each word so quietly and without passion that he might have been thought ignorant and deficient in common sense." Then he added,

[1] *i.e.* of the laity, as opposed to the bishops and clergy.
[2] *in sterquilinio*, Job ii. 8 (Vulgate).
[3] Hebrews iv. 12.

"It is now night; give order to repair to our lodging, and now that we have learnt his reasons, we will cogitate the matter on your behalf until morning." Thereupon at the king's command we again repaired to our lodging.

Returning early next morning, we took our seats in our accustomed place, awaiting the king's command. But when Anselm and his companions inquired of the king what sentence was to be passed against him, they received no reply. Being asked what conclusion he had come to during the night, William of Durham confessed that he could find no argument to shake that of Anselm, "especially", he added, "in view of the fact that his whole case rests on the word of God and the authority of St. Peter. Indeed, it seems to me that we must have recourse to violence in order to crush him. If he will not acquiesce in the king's wishes, the ring and the staff should be taken from him, and he should be expelled from the kingdom." This speech was wholly unacceptable to the lay magnates. "Then what does please you", said the king, "if these words do not? While I live, I will not endure an equal in my realm. And if you knew that he had such strong support for his case, why did you allow me to bring this suit against him? Go, take counsel together, for by God's countenance, if you do not condemn him as I desire, I will condemn you." To this replied Robert,[1] one of the king's most intimate associates, "I admit that I know not what to say concerning our deliberations. For after we have spent all day conferring among ourselves with pain and toil and have arranged how matters should hold together, he for his part just goes to sleep, suspecting no evil; and the moment the case is put before him, with one breath of his lips he breaks it as if it were a cobweb." "And what do my bishops say?" inquired the king. They answered, "My lord, we regret we cannot do your bidding in this matter. He is primate not of this realm only, but also of Scotland and Ireland and of the adjacent islands, and we are his suffragans. Wherefore it is clear to us that we cannot lawfully judge him or condemn him, even if any crime could be brought against him, which cannot now be proved." Said the king, "What then remains to be done? If you have no power to judge him, could you not at least withdraw from him your oath of obedience and refuse him your fraternal friendship?" "This we can certainly do, since you order it," came their reply. "Make haste then, and do as you say with all speed. And when he sees that he is scorned and forsaken by all men, he may be ashamed and lament that he has followed Pope Urban to the contempt of me, his liege lord. And to the intent that you may do so with greater safety, lo! I myself do first wholly withhold my confidence from him and all protection throughout my realm, and will henceforth never put further trust in him nor in his cause; nor will I longer hold him as archbishop or ghostly father."

From now on many and diverse stratagems were employed against the archbishop in order to deflect him from the course he had set for his conduct, but they were of no avail. At length the bishops, accompanied by the abbots, reported the king's decision to him and, in keeping with the royal will, conveyed to him the formal withdrawal of their obedience indicated above. He answered them, "I hear what you say. When, however, you refuse me all the obedience, faith and friendship which you owe me both as primate and as your spiritual father, because I maintain my submission and

[1] Robert of Beaumont, count of Meulan (see above, p. 658, and Table 12). In later years he was one of Anselm's bitterest opponents.

allegiance to the blessed Peter, prince of the apostles, you act unjustly. But far be it from me to recompense you in kind. I will assuredly endeavour to show you paternal and fraternal charity, provided you do not refuse it; I will strive to turn you from this gross error into which you have fallen and, by the authority committed to me by God, to recall you, as sons and brothers of the holy mother-church of Canterbury, to the path of rectitude. As for the king, who has deprived me of all protection within his realm and declares he will no longer have me as archbishop or ghostly father; to him I solemnly promise, as far as in me lies, every safety with my faithful service, and I will have a diligent care for his soul like a father, if he will condescend to permit me. I will still retain for the service of God the authority, title and office of archbishop of Canterbury no matter what oppression may chance to vex me in everyday affairs." To this the king rejoined, "What the archbishop says runs wholly counter to my mind; no man shall be mine who chooses to be his. Wherefore you, the barons of my realm, do you also forthwith refuse him all faith and friendship as the bishops have done, to the end it may be made manifest what profit he hath gained by maintaining his allegiance to the apostolic see in contempt of my wishes." The barons protested, "We were never his men and we cannot abjure the fealty we have never sworn to him. He is our archbishop: he has to govern religion in this land, and in this respect we, who are Christians, cannot deny the authority of his office while we live here, especially as no stain of offence is attached to him to compel us to act otherwise in regard to him." Smothering his anger, the king bore with this answer, taking care to refrain from contradicting their argument openly, lest they should take too great offence. The bishops, as witnesses of this scene, covered their faces in confusion, for they perceived that the eyes of all men were turned upon them and that their apostasy was, not without justice, universally detested. If you had been present there, you might have heard this or that bishop dubbed now by one man, then by another, with some nickname, accompanied with exclamations of indignation, such as "traitor Judas", "Pilate" or "Herod", and the like. A little later the king asked them one by one whether they had in fact renounced all submission and obedience to Anselm unconditionally, or only in so far as he claimed it by the authority of the Roman pope. Some gave one answer, others the contrary. Those who professed that they had renounced their duty to their archbishop fully and unconditionally, the king commanded to be seated honourably as his faithful friends and liegemen. But those who dared to affirm that they had refused submission and obedience to Anselm solely in respect of instructions issuing from the pope, he branded as traitors and enemies of his will and, in a paroxysm of rage, ordered them to await sentence of condemnation in a corner of the castle. Thus terror-stricken and doubly covered with confusion, they fled and skulked in a corner of the building. Soon, however, they found the wholesome and familiar counsel on which they were wont to rely; that is to say, they gave a large sum of money and were restored to the king's favour.

Now Anselm, realizing that the king had deprived him of all protection in England, demanded that a safe-conduct should be accorded him and his companions to enable them to reach a seaport and quit the land. At this request the king was sore troubled. For although he ardently desired Anselm's departure, nevertheless he did not wish him to leave while still in possession of the archbishopric, lest from this a new scandal should arise worse than the first. Yet it seemed impossible to dispossess him of it. Thus perturbed in mind, he forbore to seek advice from the bishops, who, he complained, had brought him to this sorry pass, but entered into consultation with the lay magnates as to what ought to be done. They advised that the archbishop should be told to retire to his lodging in peace and quiet and that he would receive the king's answer to his petition on the morrow. It was done as they suggested, and we repaired to our lodging, to the misgiving even of many of the king's servants. For they assumed that Anselm was about to quit England and they were full of sorrow. He, on the contrary, was cheerful and eager, for he hoped by crossing overseas to escape the disorders and cares of the world, as he had always longed to do. While therefore his mind was wavering between the prospect of leaving England and fear of remaining in the kingdom, lo! early next morning the magnates came to him direct from the king, saying, "Our lord the king desires you to wait upon him." We mounted up, we went and took our seats in our accustomed places, eager to learn the final issue of the business. There was no delay; the peers of the realm, attended by some of the bishops, came up to our father and delivered their message as follows: "Moved by ancient ties of friendship, we lament that this dispute has arisen between our lord the king and you. Wherefore, in the ardent desire to recall you both to your former concord, we have come to the conclusion that at the present time it would be of advantage to you both that an adjournment of the whole question should be granted. To this end, a truce running from now to some appointed date should be made between you, and nothing should be done by either party against the other or his interests to violate the terms of this agreement. This, we repeat, we consider will be of advantage to you, and we desire you to inform us whether or no you will agree to it." The archbishop replied, "I do not reject peace and concord. Nevertheless I think I see the true purport of this peace you offer. But, lest some of you should think that I put greater trust in my own understanding than in that of others, I agree to accept what you and the lord king think fit to determine, under God, for the maintenance of the peace of the realm, saving always the reverence and obedience I owe to the lord Urban, the pontiff of the apostolic see." They approved his statement and referred it to the king. So a truce was granted until the Octave of Pentecost,[1] and it was decreed on the king's oath that in the meantime everything belonging to both parties should be unmolested. The king added, "If the conclusion of a perfect peace has not extinguished the present conflict between us before this date, when the truce has expired the case shall be brought before us again and shall be determined in all respects the same as it stands this day." So matters were left. Having obtained the king's permission, Anselm returned to his see, foreknowing that this truce or patched-up peace served but to veil in an empty and transient fashion the hatred and tyranny he would suffer in the near future: which in brief was afterwards apparent. Indeed, after a few days had elapsed, the monk Baldwin,[2] Anselm's chief confidant, and two of his clerks, were expelled from the kingdom by the king because of the dispute described above. By this act he struck a grievous and fearful blow at the archbishop. What need to refer to his chamberlain, arrested in his chamber before his very eyes, and to other

[1] 20 May 1095. [2] See above, p. 655.

servants of his condemned by unjust verdicts, plundered or afflicted by innumerable evils? And all these things were wrought by this king of "constant faith" against the archbishop between the day the truce was granted and that appointed for the conclusion of peace. So the church of Canterbury endured at that time so fierce a storm in the persons of its tenants, that almost all of them agreed that it would be better to be without a shepherd at all, as in former days, than to have such a shepherd as this. . . .

Book III

In[1] the second year after our return from Rome to Lyons and in the third of our exile, there came to Anselm, who was then on the third day of a visit to the monastery of Casa Dei,[2] two monks, one from Canterbury and the other from Le Bec, announcing the death of King William. At first stunned to silence at the news, the archbishop then burst into a flood of tears. We who were witnesses of the scene were deeply affected by it. But he, his voice choked with sobs, avowed that, if he could have so ordered it, by the truth which a servant of God ought not to transgress, he would sooner have chosen to die himself than that the king should do so.

After we had arrived back in Lyons, behold! there came a second messenger from the monks of Canterbury bearing a letter in which they besought him earnestly on behalf of the mother-church of England, now that the tyrant was dead, to be good enough to return and comfort his sons without delay. Having taken counsel from the venerable Hugh, the bishop of Lyons mentioned above, Anselm set out on the journey back to England, to the grief of the bishop and all the people of the city who would have prevented his going by every possible means, had it not been contrary to reason. For indeed they saw themselves bereft of great consolation through his departure. For several days he was pursued from village to village by a band of men and women, who tried to run after him, uttering sighs and groans of desolation. We had not yet reached Cluny when yet another messenger arrived post-haste from the new king of England[3] and the magnates of the realm, reproaching Anselm for his delay in returning. The whole land awaited his arrival in awed expectation and all the business of the realm had been postponed for his consideration and determination. The messenger had brought with him a letter[4] from the king explaining his verbal message in greater detail and testifying by its contents to the king's wishes and entreaties. It requested the archbishop to come with all speed, and promised that the king himself and his kingdom should be subject to Anselm's guidance and governance. These considerations and others of a similar nature, more than I can relate, constrained us to hasten our journey home.

So by a favourable crossing we braved the perils of the deep and anchored at Dover on 23 September,[5] where we found the whole land rejoicing with great joy at Anselm's coming. For indeed the hope of a new resurrection, as it were, sprung up in the mind of every man, each promising himself liberation from the late oppression

[1] Rolls Series edition, p. 118.
[2] Casa Dei (*Chaise Dieu*, "God's House"), near Brioude in Auvergne.
[3] Henry I, 1100–1135.
[4] The text of this letter is given on p. 673.
[5] 1100.

and misfortune and the opening of the age of prosperity for which he yearned. This hope was greatly encouraged by the fact that Henry, who had recently succeeded his dead brother on the throne, had pledged himself on the day of his coronation[1] to preserve good and holy laws for all his people, to forbid and overthrow throughout his dominion all the oppression and wickedness, both in ecclesiastical and secular affairs, which had taken place under his brother, and, after confirming all these promises on oath and embodying them in a charter[2] guaranteed under his seal, had ordered it to be promulgated throughout the realm. Nevertheless, the presence of their common father, the archbishop, now greatly strengthened this hope in men's minds, for they knew his constancy and integrity, and confidently expected that in the near future he would introduce and execute measures for the reform of the state of religion which had in many respects fallen into decay since the death of Archbishop Lanfranc of venerated memory.

A few days after his return Anselm came to the king at Salisbury and received a warm welcome from him. Anselm accepted his excuse for not waiting for his blessing before taking the royal title to himself, although he knew it was the prerogative of the archbishop to sanction it. The latter was then asked to do homage to the king according to the custom of the kingdom and to receive investiture of the archbishopric at his hands. He replied that he neither could nor would by any means consent to this; when they asked the reason why, he forthwith declared unto them openly what he had assented to in respect of this and certain other matters in the Roman council,[3] adding these remarks: "If the lord king is willing to accept these decrees and to hold fast to them, all will be well between us and a lasting peace established. But if not, I do not see that I can either conscientiously or usefully remain in England, especially since, in the event of his bestowing bishoprics or abbeys, I must needs wholly separate myself from communion both with him and those who have received them from him. For I have not returned to live in England in order that he may refuse to obey the pope. Wherefore I beg him to make known his decision, that I may learn where I stand." At these words the king was sore dismayed. Certainly it seemed to him a grievous thing to lose the investiture of churches and the homage of prelates, but it was a no less serious matter to suffer Anselm to depart while he himself was not yet firmly established on the throne. In the one case he appeared likely to lose, as it were, half his kingdom; in the other he feared lest Anselm should make overtures to his brother, Robert, who had just returned to Normandy from Jerusalem,[4] and that, having brought him into subjection to the apostolic see, which could very easily be done, he would then make him king of England. Accordingly, from the arguments advanced on both sides it was agreed to postpone the question until the following Easter, so that both parties might send envoys to Rome to get the papal decrees modified to suit the ancient custom of the realm. In the meantime the churches in England were to remain in their present state, and Anselm was to be reinstated in all the lands which

[1] 5 August 1100. [2] The "Coronation Charter" of Henry I (see above, No. 19).

[3] The council of the Vatican, April 1099. Anselm considered himself bound by the decrees forbidding lay investiture and payment of homage by ecclesiastics passed by the council, since he had been present in person. He would not therefore renew to Henry I the fealty he had already given to William II without question.

[4] Where he had taken part in the First Crusade; he reached home in September 1100.

the deceased monarch had filched from the church of Canterbury. Thus, if the pope could not be moved from his recent judgment, the whole question would revert to the position in which it now stood. Although Anselm realized and openly proclaimed that this proposal was ridiculous and could serve no useful purpose, nevertheless, in order not to arouse suspicion against himself in the minds of the new monarch or the magnates with regard to the possible transference of the crown or any other matter, he allowed himself to be overcome by their entreaties. He agreed to what they wanted and returned to his diocese in peace. . . .[1] So[2] when we had come to court,[3] the king, following the advice of his brother, the duke, and his partisans, who were inflamed against Anselm with bitter hatred because of the duke's failure to obtain the crown,[4] demanded that the archbishop should either become his 'man' and consecrate those to whom he had promised bishoprics and abbeys in accordance with the custom of his predecessors, or quit the realm instantly and without delay. To this demand the archbishop replied, "I have already mentioned how I was present at the Roman council and what was enjoined upon me there by the see of St. Peter. If then I myself were to incur excommunication for some cause for which I stood as champion in this kingdom, to whom, I ask you, could I afterwards appeal, when I had been excommunicated by my own judgment? The envoys, charged with the task of obtaining a modification of this decree, have returned with their mission unfulfilled. To suggest that I should become a transgressor of those very ordinances which I cannot break with safety and honour, does not seem to me to be sound advice." "What is that to me?" said the king: "I will not lose the customs of my predecessors, nor suffer in my realm any man who is not mine." Said the archbishop, "I follow the trend of your words and I am perturbed thereat. Nevertheless, for the time being I will not obey your command and quit the country, but I will go back to my church; and in pursuing what I consider to be the right course of action I will take note of any violence any man may try to work against me or mine." Many things were done after this manner with regard to this affair, but the upshot of them all was as follows. The bishops and magnates of the realm gave voice to the same opinions as they were wont to do in the previous reign, and vied with each other in showing obedience in everything to the royal will; or rather they persisted obstinately in their determination that the king should not become subject to the obedience of the pope. Accordingly Anselm returned to his diocese, endeavouring earnestly to do God's pleasure in everything and bewailing the oppression of the churches in England with heartfelt contrition. . . .

[The dispute continued, and on 27 April 1103 Anselm left England with the king's approval in order to go to Rome to ascertain whether a compromise was in any way possible. After much correspondence and protracted negotiations, which are recorded by Eadmer at great length, arrangements for a settlement were achieved in 1106. Anselm by this time had returned to the abbey of Le Bec-Hellouin.]

---

[1] The joint embassy to Rome effected nothing. Pope Paschal sent back a letter to the king containing a peremptory refusal of the compromise suggested. The letter is printed in the Rolls Series edition, pp. 128–131.

[2] Rolls Series edition, p. 131. [3] 1101.

[4] A reference to Duke Robert's bid for the crown made earlier in 1101, supported by a section of the Anglo-Norman baronage. Anselm had been largely instrumental in retaining the crown for Henry in this crisis.

Book IV

. . . When[1] William[2] reached the king in England[3] and reported to him what had transpired in his negotiations with the pope, the king, delighted at what he heard, forthwith requested Anselm through the said William to return to his see. A few days later William repaired to us, and finding Anselm sick was greatly disturbed. For by this time he had the freedom of the Church much at heart and took the utmost pains to effect Anselm's restoration to his see in peace and honour. Fearing then lest the archbishop's love of the place[4] and the brethren, no less than the bodily infirmity under which he was labouring, might deter him from making the journey to England, William strove by every means in his power, acting both on his own initiative and through us who were with him, to get Anselm to move from the place and to set out on the desired journey. Thus, by proffering entreaties on behalf of his lord, the king of the English, he appealed to the archbishop to return with all speed to the country so long desolate through his absence. He asserted and solemnly promised that the king would show the utmost regard to Anselm's wishes in all his future commands, and that he would no longer dissent from the decree of the Roman Church. Moreover, he added, "I therefore beg you to brook no delay in your coming, lest some worldly wind blow up from an adverse quarter to change the king's disposition." At these words the archbishop gave thanks to God for his wonderful gift, took leave of the monks among whom we had so long dwelt in great charity and honour, and setting out for England reached Jumièges. There he suffered a renewal of the sickness he had experienced at Le Bec, and he could not leave the place. For this cause he sent messengers to England to inform the king of the reason which prevented his return. The latter was exceedingly distressed and grieved at these tidings, swearing by Almighty God that he would endure the loss of everything more easily than the death of Anselm. With the swift return of the messengers the king begged the archbishop to spare himself and enjoy rest and quiet in every way. He also placed at his disposal everything within his jurisdiction in Normandy, ordered proper provision to be made for the archbishop and his followers, and announced that he would be crossing to Normandy in the near future. This Anselm gratefully accepted and remained at Jumièges about a month. His illness having abated, he then returned to Le Bec, judging it would be more appropriate and honourable if he were there before the arrival of the royal visitor was expected. There, while everyone was rejoicing with wonderful excitement at his return, behold! a deplorable calamity shattered and destroyed that joy. For so serious a malady again seized hold of Anselm, that we anticipated nothing but death would ensue from it. Bishops and abbots streamed in from the countryside and all who would have been concerned with his funeral. But Almighty God of his goodness restored him to health contrary to universal expectation and made many glad thereof with great joy.

[1] Rolls Series edition, p. 181.

[2] William Warelwast, later bishop of Exeter, who by mutual consent had gone to Rome in order to promote the reconciliation. As will appear below (Nos. 109–112), he had been successful in his object.

[3] 1106.

[4] The abbey of Le Bec-Hellouin.

So on the Feast of the Assumption of the Blessed Virgin Mary[1] the king came to Bec, and after Anselm had celebrated a solemn Mass, the king and he conferred together. At last everything which had drawn them in opposite directions was settled in peace and concord. The churches in England, which King William, brother of King Henry, had first placed under taxation, as I have related above in detail, the king restored to Anselm free from this impost and promised that during his lifetime he would take nothing from them while they were without a shepherd. But as for the money which, as we have said, he had exacted from the clergy, he pledged himself to make reparation as follows. Those who had not yet paid their quota should give nothing, and those who had given for three years should possess all their goods freely and in peace and quiet. But everything taken from the archbishopric during Anselm's exile by the king's command, he promised by surety to restore when he had returned to England.

These and other matters, which the case demanded, having been settled between them, Anselm resumed his journey to England, and fortified by divine protection landed safe and sound with all his companions at Dover. With what joy, pleasure and good expectations his arrival in England was welcomed, may be in my estimation to some extent inferred from a consideration of the evils abounding there before his return, which we have briefly touched upon. Wherefore I pass over in silence the joy shown by men of diverse age and rank in order to refer briefly to that of the queen, whom neither worldly cares nor any pomp of earthly glory could restrain from going before the archbishop, as he passed through various places, and monks or canons came to meet him in the customary manner. Ahead of them went the queen with kindly forethought to prepare his lodgings with suitable provisions. . . .[2]

. . . The[3] magnates of the realm having been gathered together at the king's court at Eastertide,[4] a hitch occurred in the accommodation which the king had been minded to make with the Church. This was caused by the arrival in France of Pope Paschal, who had previously instructed the king and the archbishop to dispatch the aforesaid William and Baldwin to him at the council he was about to hold at Troyes.[5] Supposing that on the return of the envoys some new concessions would be offered to him, the king adjourned the whole business until the Feast of Pentecost, so that on their report he might ascertain the pope's wishes and arrange matters more securely. . . .

Accordingly[6] on 1 August[7] an assembly of bishops, abbots and lay magnates of the realm was held at London in the king's palace, and for three whole days the matter of the investitures of churches was fully discussed between the king and the bishops, Anselm being absent. Some of them urged that the king should perform them after the custom of his father and brother, and not according to the command

[1] 15 August 1106.

[2] After a successful campaign in Normandy, crowned with the decisive victory of Tinchebrai (28 September 1106), the king returned to England. (See above, No. 9.)

[3] Rolls Series edition, p. 184.

[4] 14 April 1107.

[5] The first canon of the council of Troyes repeats the condemnation of lay investitures which had been pronounced at the Roman synod and endorses the penalties which had there been imposed upon recalcitrant ecclesiastics.

[6] Rolls Series edition, p. 186.

[7] 1107.

of the pope. For the latter, while standing firm on the decision which had been promulgated thereon, had made a concession in respect of the homage which Pope Urban had forbidden equally with investitures, and by this had obtained the king's consent on the point of investitures, as may be inferred from the letter transcribed above.[1] Thereupon, in Anselm's presence, while the assembled multitude stood by, the king granted and decreed that from that time forth for evermore no one should be invested in England with bishopric or abbey by the gift of staff or ring, either by the king or the hand of any layman; Anselm also making the concession that no one elected to a prelacy should be refused consecration on account of homage done to the king. These matters having been thus settled, fathers-in-God were appointed by the king, on the advice of Anselm and the magnates of the realm, in almost all the churches in England which had been long widowed of their pastors, and this without any investiture of pastoral staff or ring. Certain prelates were also appointed by the king on the same occasion to take charge of certain of the churches of Normandy which were likewise destitute of pastors. . . .

108. Letter from Henry I to Archbishop Anselm (? September 1100)

This letter, written by Henry I soon after the death of William Rufus, is an attempt to excuse his hasty seizure of the crown, to the detriment of the claims of his elder brother, Robert, duke of Normandy, and the precipitate character of his coronation. In view of Anselm's exile on the Continent and the extreme age and failing health of Thomas, archbishop of York, the ceremony had been performed by Maurice, bishop of London, in contravention of all precedent. Hence the apologetic tone of the letter which is printed in W. Stubbs, *Select Charters* (ed. 1913), p. 120.

Henry (by the grace of God), king of the English, to his most reverend father-in-God, Anselm, bishop [*sic*] of Canterbury, greeting and token of all friendship. Be it known to you, dearest father, that my brother, King William, is dead and that, with God's approval, I have been elected by the clergy and people of England and, albeit unwillingly, already crowned king in your absence. In concert with the people of the whole realm of England, I entreat you as a father to come as quickly as possible and to give counsel to me, your son, and this same people, whose souls have been committed to your care. I commend myself and all the people of this realm to your counsel and that of those who ought to advise me, together with yourself. I beg you not to be displeased that I have accepted the royal title without your blessing; for, had it been possible, I would sooner have received it from you than from any other. But the need was urgent because enemies would have risen up against me and the people I have to govern, and in consequence my barons and people were unwilling to delay the ceremony longer. So I have taken the opportunity to receive consecration from your suffragans. I would indeed have sent you money from my Treasury by some of my servants, but on account of my brother's death the whole world round about the realm of England is so disturbed that they could by no means reach you in safety. Wherefore I advise and command you not to come through Normandy but by way of Wissant, and I will have my barons meet you at Dover with money to receive you, and, God willing, you shall find the money sufficient to pay your expenses. Speed then your coming, father, that our mother-church of Canterbury so long disturbed and desolate may not sustain further ruin of souls through you. Witness: Gerard the

[1] See Rolls Series edition, pp. 178–179.

bishop;[1] William,[2] bishop-elect of Winchester; William Warelwast;[3] Henry the earl;[4] Robert, son of Haimo; Haimo the steward;[5] and others my liegemen, both bishops and barons. Farewell.

109. Letter from Archbishop Anselm to Henry I (1105)

This letter, the text of which is given in Eadmer, *Historia Novorum* (ed. M. Rule, Rolls Series, 1884), p. 175, relates to the negotiations for a reconciliation between the king and the exiled archbishop (see above, p. 671). It and the letters which immediately follow (Nos. 110–112) are part of a larger correspondence. In this correspondence there is also a letter from Paschal II, dated 22 April 1106, giving Anselm leave to release from excommunication all who had come under sentence for breaking the canons about homage and investiture. The way was thus laid open for the archbishop's return to England, and for him to re-establish communion with the offending bishops.

To his dearest lord, Henry, by the grace of God king of the English, Anselm, archbishop of Canterbury, offers faithful prayers and loyal service. It is my duty not to keep silence if I learn that you do anything inexpedient for your soul, lest (which God avert) he be wroth with you if you do what is displeasing to him, and with me by reason of my silence. I learn that your highness is taking vengeance on the clergy of England and is imposing a fine upon them because they have not kept the canon of the council I held at London with your permission, together with other bishops and ecclesiastics. This has hitherto been unheard of, and it is an action without precedent in the Church of God on the part of any monarch or other prince. For, according to God's law, the punishment of a fault of this kind pertains only to each individual bishop within his diocese or, if the bishops themselves be negligent in this, to the archbishop and primate. I therefore entreat you, as my dearest lord, whose soul I cherish more than the life of my own body, and I counsel you, as one truly loyal both to your body and your soul, not to run counter to the custom of the Church in so grave a sin. Desist therefrom altogether, if you have already begun to do so. For I tell you that, having obtained money by these means–I can maintain silence only to the peril of my soul–you ought to be much afraid lest the outlay of it bring less profit to your wordly interests than the disorder it will afterwards create. Finally, you know that in Normandy you received me back in your peace and put me again in possession of my archbishopric, and you recognize that the responsibility for punishing this heinous offence belongs to the office of archbishop, seeing that I am bishop by virtue of my spiritual charge and not by virtue of my worldly possessions. May Almighty God so direct your heart according to his will both in this and other acts, that after this life he may bring you into his glory. Amen.

110. Letter from Henry I to Archbishop Anselm (1106)

This letter is in answer to the preceding document. Printed: Eadmer, *Historia Novorum* (ed. M. Rule, Rolls Series, 1884), p. 176.

Henry, by the grace of God king of the English, to Anselm, archbishop of Canterbury, greeting. Your letter with your seal affixed was delivered to me at Tonbridge on St. George's Day.[6] I marvel much at the message you have sent me, because what I have done, I believe I have done on your behalf. On the day of our

[1] Bishop of Hereford and subsequently archbishop of York, see below, p. 675.
[2] William Giffard consecrated by Anselm.
[3] Later bishop of Exeter, for whom see above, p. 671.
[4] Henry of Beaumont, earl of Warwick, for whom see Table 12.
[5] Sheriff of Kent.
[6] 23 April.

Lord's Ascension[1] I will have my barons gathered with me, and by their advice I will conveniently make answer to you of such a kind that when I speak with you I do not think you will accuse me of perjury. Whatever else may happen, be it known to you that your flock in all their lands have remained in peace, no matter what they have done.

111. Letter from Archbishop Anselm to Henry I (1106)

A continuation of the correspondence exemplified in Nos. 109 and 110. Printed: Eadmer, *Historia Novorum* (ed. M. Rule, Rolls Series, 1884), p. 176.

To his dearest lord, Henry, by the grace of God king of the English, Anselm, archbishop of Canterbury, loyal service and faithful prayers. I give thanks to God and your highness that in your letter you promise to make favourable answer to me concerning the clergy of England for whom I made entreaty in my letter, and I beseech the Lord, whose counsel abides to all eternity, that he may inspire you to reply and to act as may please him. In that case the true lovers of your soul will be led to rejoice. I have moreover read in your letter that what you have done in this affair you believe to have been done on my behalf. You must know, however, that this is not so, seeing that if it were so I should be acting against God. Wherefore I pray with great and loyal affection that no one may advise you to proceed in this design. Farewell.

112. Letter from Henry I to Archbishop Anselm (1106)

A continuation of the correspondence exemplified in Nos. 109–111. Printed: Eadmer, *Historia Novorum* (ed. M. Rule, Rolls Series, 1884), p. 177.

Henry, king of the English, to Anselm, archbishop of Canterbury, greeting and friendship. Concerning the matter of the clergy, you may know that I have acted with all seemliness as I consider I ought to have done. Be it known to you also that within a short time I purpose to cross overseas; and after I have had speech with you, if I have offended in anything, I will amend it with your advice and with that of Almighty God. Witness: Waldric the chancellor. At Marlborough.

113. Select passages from the *Tractatus Eboracenses*

The passages here presented are taken from a series of tractates printed by Heinrich Böhmer in 1897 and 1899 under the title of *Tractatus Eboracenses* (see Bibliography above, p. 591). The tractates, thirty in number, appear to have been written over a long period, the extreme limits of which are 1080–1104. Böhmer attributed them to a canon of Rouen, who later took service under Gerard, archbishop of York, but, despite much research on the problem in recent years, the author remains anonymous, and it is by no means certain that the tractates are all the work of the same man, as Böhmer contended (see Z. N. Brooke, *English Church and the Papacy* (1931), pp. 157–160). In the latest investigation of the subject G. H. Williams (*The Norman Anonymous of A.D. 1100*, Harvard U.P., 1951) agrees with Böhmer that, with one exception, the tractates are the product of a single author, but claims that he was a Norman ecclesiastic of the church of Rouen. The passages here selected are of particular interest as illustrating the high notions held by the author concerning the royal prerogative in ecclesiastical affairs. The passages are taken from Tractate 24a, "On the Consecration of Prelates and Kings", printed in *Mon. Germ. Hist., Libelli de Lite*, vol. III (ed. H. Böhmer), pp. 663–679, Tractate 28, "On the Roman Pope" (*ibid.*, pp. 684–685) and Tractate 30, printed by Böhmer in an appendix to *Kirche und Staat in England und in der Normandie im XI und XII Jahrhundert* (1899), pp. 482–483. This work, and those of Brooke and Williams, cited above, should be consulted for further information on the problems which arise from consideration of the character and authorship of the tractates.

[1] Ascension Day, 1106, fell on 3 May.

(*a*) *Extracts from Tractate 24a, "On the Consecration of Prelates and Kings"* (Mon. Germ. Hist., Lib. de Lite, *vol. III, pp.* 663–679)

By divine authority and the institution of the holy fathers kings are consecrated in God's Church before the sacred altar and are anointed with holy oil and sacred benediction to exercise the ruling power over Christians, the Lord's people, "a chosen generation, an holy nation, a peculiar people",[1] the holy Church of God. For what indeed is God's Church other than the congregation of faithful Christians dwelling together in one bond of faith, hope and charity within God's house? For the governance of the Church kings receive power at their coronation,[2] to rule and confirm her in justice and judgment and to order her affairs according to the discipline of the Christian law. Thus they reign over the Church, which is the kingdom of God; they reign together with Christ in order to rule, protect and defend her. For to reign is to rule one's subjects well and to serve God in fear. To this same end are the bishops also instituted and consecrated with holy oil and sacred benediction, that they in their turn may govern the Church in accordance with the teaching handed down to them by God. For this cause the blessed Pope Gelasius wrote thus, "There are two orders by which this world is chiefly governed, the priestly authority and the royal power." . . .[3] Notwithstanding, if the king has so great a dominion over the bodies of Christians, will he not also have dominion over God's sacred temple? . . . If this be so, it is plain that the king has dominion over those who obtain the priestly office. The king ought, therefore, not to be excluded from the governance of the Church, that is, the Christian people, because the kingdom would then be separated from the Church and destroyed. . . .

King and priest are both anointed with holy oil; they receive the same Holy Spirit of sanctification and the same virtue of benediction; they have a common name in Christ and a common interest, to whose merits they owe their name. . . .

King and priest have the same grace and certain privileges in common, but they have also their own peculiar and diverse offices. For although they may appear to have the power to rule in common, yet this power is to be exercised in one way by the priest and in another way by the king, and grace is accorded to each for the fulfilment of his office. . . .

No one ought by right to take precedence of the king, on whom is bestowed so many and great blessings, who is consecrated with so many and great sacraments and dedicated to God, because no one receives greater or better blessings or is consecrated and dedicated to God with greater or higher sacraments, not even with the same or like sacraments, and in this respect the king is unique. Wherefore he is not to be considered a mere layman, for he is the Lord's anointed[4] and by adoption and grace made like unto God; he is the supreme ruler, the chief shepherd, master, defender and instructor of holy Church, lord over his brethren and worthy to be worshipped by all men as chief 'bishop' and supreme ruler. Nor is he to be spoken of as inferior to

[1] I Peter ii. 9.

[2] In other passages the author makes considerable use of the coronation rite to enforce his arguments.

[3] *Duo sunt quibus hic mundus principaliter regitur; sacerdotalis auctoritas et regalis potestas;* the opening sentence of the rescript of Pope Gelasius I issued in 492, which became the classic definition of the respective jurisdictions of Church and State in the early Middle Ages.

[4] *Christus Domini.*

the bishop, because the latter consecrates him, since it often happens that superiors are consecrated by their inferiors, just as the pope is consecrated by the cardinals and the metropolitan by his suffragans. This is done because they are not the authors of the consecration, but the ministers. God is the author of the sacrament, the bishops merely officiate as his agents. . . .

(*b*) *Extracts from Tractate* 28, "*On the Roman Pope*" (Mon. Germ. Hist., Lib. de Lite, *vol. III, pp.* 684–685)

But, laying aside these matters, let us pass to another wherein they [the popes] act to the grievous detriment of the whole Church, namely inasmuch as they strive to deprive the royal power of the rule and governance of all the churches, despite the dictum of the blessed Pope Gelasius, "There are two orders by which this world is chiefly governed, the priestly authority and the royal power."[1] By 'the world' he means the Christian people, that is, the holy Church as yet sojourning in the world, and this Church is chiefly ruled by the sacerdotal authority and the royal power. Whence it follows that both are rightly recognized as having lordship over the Church, because both are the chief rulers in her. For she could not be governed properly and well by the one without the other, but has need of both for this purpose. The authority of the priest is necessary for this reason, to absolve and teach us, to guard us carefully against our unseen enemies, and to offer propitiation and sacrifice for the sins of the people. But the regal power is ordained by God to this end, to protect and guard the Church, and indeed the priestly authority itself, from evil and wicked men, and to fight manfully in her defence against the enemies that are seen. . . .

Wherefore it is a great and divine gift and a heavenly 'investiture' that the king should reign together with Christ and dispose of temporal matters in Christ's kingdom, that the power of life and death has been bestowed upon him, and that a sword has been put into his hand, not so much for actual use but for intimidation. . . . This is indeed a sublime and glorious 'investiture', wherewith God has invested emperor or king, that he may have power from heaven granted him over all men, to succour those who seek good, to make the road to heaven broader for them, to make the earthly kingdom the servant of the heavenly, and that Christ may commit his priests into his hand and grant him dominion over them. Whoever then strives to deprive kings of this 'investiture' is striving to act contrary to the ordinance and decree of God. It is indeed only just that the same hand to whose governance priests are by God committed, should bestow a portion of this investiture upon them. I mean, of course, investiture of temporalities, of secular lordship over the people and of worldly goods, not investiture of the priestly office and of sacerdotal grace. For I have never heard the term 'investiture' applied to the latter. Moreover, when the king confers the investiture of temporalities, he does so not as a mere layman, but as the Lord's anointed,[2] since by divine grace the Lord Christ reigns jointly with him; Christ is the natural lord, and because kings reign together with Christ, he and they both, at one and the same time, bestow the privileges and carry out the measures pertaining to his kingdom. . . .

[1] See above, p. 676.

[2] *Christus Domini.*

(c) *Extract from Tractate* 30, "*On Charity and Obedience*" (*H. Böhmer*, Kirche und Staat, *pp.* 482–483)

But is not this supreme arrogance, nay rather, sheer madness, to assume a power of lordship where Christ took upon him the form of a servant?[1] . . . Wherefore, if thou be a member of Christ, thou shouldst also take on thee the form of a servant and desire not to be ministered unto, but to minister.[2] Sit not in the judgment-seat, where Christ never sat; refuse to give judgment in the place where he would be judged. For if thou sayest thou dost dwell in Christ, thou shouldst walk in his ways. He himself spake, "My kingdom is not of this world."[3] If then his kingdom is not of this world, a kingdom which is of this world is not Christ's. Whosoever seeks to govern a kingdom of this world, seeks to become a prince and a judge, and will have no portion in Christ's kingdom or be numbered among his disciples. . . . But thou, O man, who seekest after a princedom in this world, desirest not to become as the younger or as he that serveth but to exercise lordship like the kings of the Gentiles and to be called benefactor like they that exercise authority upon them.[4] So then thou art not Christ's disciple nor a member of him, but a member and disciple of the devil.

(b) CHURCH AND STATE IN THE REIGN OF STEPHEN

114. John of Salisbury: "The Papal History" (*Historia Pontificalis*)

Although the *Historia Pontificalis* of John of Salisbury has come down to us in an incomplete form covering only the years 1148 to 1152, it is nevertheless one of the principal sources for the history of Anglo-papal relations in the reign of Stephen. It supplements the information on ecclesiastical affairs at this time given by William of Malmesbury (see above, No. 8, pp. 298–303) and by Gervase of Canterbury. The *Historia Pontificalis* is a continuation of the chronicle of Sigebert of Gembloux, and records the stirring events of the pontificate of Eugenius III, events of which John is now known to have been an eyewitness, for R. L. Poole has proved that from 1148 to 1153 he was employed as a clerk in the papal chancery. He was present in the papal retinue at the council of Rheims in 1148, and his work gives the best account of the business there transacted. From the papal chancery at Rome John passed, after the death of Eugenius in 1153, straight to the archiepiscopal chancery at Canterbury as clerk or secretary to Archbishop Theobald. This to a great extent explains the prominent position given to the latter in the parts of the work dealing with English politics. Other noteworthy features in the extracts here presented are the accounts of the disputes between King Stephen and the archbishop, between the archbishop and the monks of St. Augustine's, Canterbury, and of the intrigues and ambitions of that enigmatic figure in the politics of the reign, Henry of Blois, the king's brother, bishop of Winchester and apostolic legate in England.

The exact date of the composition of the *Historia Pontificalis* is still undetermined. From internal evidence it was plainly not completed before 1164 at the earliest, but R. L. Poole was of the opinion that much of it was written some years earlier. It seems never to have been finally revised. It has survived in a unique MS. in the town library at Bern and was first published in 1868 by W. Arndt in the *Monumenta Germaniae Historica*, vol. xx, pp. 525 *et seq.*, as the work of an anonymous author. In 1873 Giesebrecht[5] claimed that it was written by John of Salisbury, and subsequently R. Pauli[6] and R. L. Poole, working on internal evidence, have endorsed this verdict.

The definitive edition of the work is that of R. L. Poole (Oxford, 1927), which contains a valuable preface and appendices. Reference may also be made to the same writer's *Studies in Chronology and History* (Oxford, 1934), to C. C. J. Webb, *John of Salisbury* (London, 1932) pp. 126–136, and to G. W. Greenaway, *Arnold of Brescia* (Cambridge, 1931), pp. 207–208.

---

[1] Philippians ii. 7. [2] Mark x. 45. [3] John xviii. 36.
[4] Luke xxii.
[5] *Sitzungsberichte der Königliche Akademie der Wissenschaften* (1873), pp. 123–154, reprinted under the title of *Arnold of Brescia* (Munich, 1873).
[6] *Zeitschrift für Kirchenrecht*, vol. XVI (1881), pp. 265–287.

Extracts from the Historia Pontificalis *of John of Salisbury illustrating relations between Church and State in England in the reign of Stephen*

... The[1] aforesaid king of the English[2] had aroused the anger of the lord pope[3] through his refusal to allow John Paparo, cardinal-deacon and legate to Ireland, to pass through England on his way to the province assigned to him;[4] through his detention of the bishops and abbots of England who had been summoned to the council,[5] and through his exclusion of the archbishop of York[6] from his see. The king not only failed to make amends after due warning, but added misdeed to misdeed and injury to injury. He had, it is true, sent three of his bishops–Robert of Hereford,[7] William of Norwich[8] and Hilary of Chichester[9]–to the council to excuse the absence of the archbishop.[10] But it was believed at the time, and afterwards verified by events, that this had been contrived for the damage and ruin of the archbishop, and as much by the king and queen, and by their counsel, as by certain of the bishops. The archbishop, however, had his suspicions and took refuge in flight. For snares had been set for him on every side, and the king himself had come to Canterbury so that he might more easily deprive the archbishop of every means of escaping from the country.[11] But the latter, "knowing that to obey is better than sacrifice",[12] and trusting in God's mercy, entered into a fishing-boat which he had hired in a hidden creek, remotely concealed from the haunts of men. The boat held no more than thirteen people and was almost wholly lacking in the necessary provisions; so he crossed the Channel more like a shipwrecked mariner than a passenger on a vessel.[13] Moreover, with the king's permission, he had sent on before him certain of his clerks on the pretext of making his excuses in the council. On his unexpected arrival, therefore, he was welcomed by everyone with the highest honours and as a man most intimate with the king. For, when in the final session of the council the candles had been lit and the lord pope rose up to launch a sentence of excommunication against the king on account of the misdeeds related above, and the prelates and great men, who had come there and were promising to make amends, could obtain no further postponement, the archbishop of

[1] Chap. II, p. 6.
[2] Stephen.
[3] Eugenius III, 1145–1153.
[4] Here John of Salisbury seems to be confusing two different legations, that of St. Malachy, archbishop of Armagh and primate of Ireland, who was prevented from passing through England on his way to Rome *from* Ireland in 1148, and that of his successor in the legateship, John Paparo, cardinal-deacon of St. Adrian, who was present at the council of Rheims and was refused a safe-conduct by Stephen through England on his way *to* Ireland some time between May and December 1150. The cardinal thereupon returned to Rome, and his mission was postponed for a year; on these points, see R. L. Poole's edition of the *Historia Pontificalis*, p. 6, n.
[5] Council of Rheims held in March 1148.
[6] Henry Murdac, abbot of Fountains, consecrated archbishop of York, 7 December 1147; see also below, p. 685.
[7] Robert of Bethune, bishop of Hereford, 1131–1148; he fell ill on the third day of the council of Rheims and died on 16 April 1148.
[8] William 'de Turbe', bishop of Norwich, 1146–1174.
[9] Hilary, bishop of Chichester, 1147–1169, one of the great administrative English bishops of the twelfth century and well known at the papal *curia*; see also below, pp. 709, 710, 716, 718, 723, 727, 731, 737, 783.
[10] Theobald, archbishop of Canterbury, 1139–1161.
[11] The king had the seaports closely guarded to prevent the archbishop from leaving the country; see Gervase of Canterbury (Rolls Series edition), vol. I, p. 134.
[12] I Samuel xv. 22.
[13] *non tam nauigio quam quasi naufragio transfretauit.*

Canterbury most charitably begged that the sentence might be stayed, and he alone of them all, as the pope himself publicly testified, was judged worthy to obtain a hearing. Stunned and astounded at the archbishop's boundless generosity, after a little thought and a few sighs, the pope addressed them as follows: "Behold! brethren, a man who in our own day has fulfilled the Gospel precepts, who is wont to love his enemies and ceaseth not to pray for his persecutors. Therefore, although this king has properly incurred our wrath and that of God's Church, we cannot but approve such charity manifested by one whose wishes we are compelled to respect. At his intercession we now suspend sentence and grant the king a delay of three months for making reparation. But if by that time he has not done so, an even greater condemnation will be visited upon his head and upon his realm. . . ."

Ever[1] prompt to punish disobedience, as the apostle commands,[2] the pope suspended by name the bishop of Winchester[3] and the archbishops of Mainz and Cologne, besides all who had not come to the council when summoned.[4] But the bishop of Winchester, through his brother, Count Theobald,[5] and other influential persons, at length obtained a relaxation of the sentence for six months, during which time he was to seek audience of the pope.[6] The others remained for a long time under suspension and the archbishop of Mainz was finally deposed. So the council was dissolved, but the more important members were kept back to finish off certain matters. The archbishop of Canterbury, who had deserved much thanks from the pope, was permitted to absolve those who had been suspended or hold them under sentence according to his pleasure. . . .

When[7] the prelates who had been detained for this purpose had been dismissed to their own sees, the lord pope took his journey to Italy, committing the case of the English bishops to Theobald, archbishop of Canterbury.[8] While the latter was occupied therewith, there came to him messengers from the king, Richard of Lucé,[9] William Martel[10] and others–men who were bound by ties of loyalty to the archbishop –bidding him depart from the realm in all haste, because he had presumed to attend the council in face of the king's prohibition. His goods were confiscated and he was banished a second time for his obedience to the apostolic see. For he had once before been exiled for this cause, when at the urgent request of Henry, bishop of Winchester, who then enjoyed the office of legate in England, he had welcomed the empress[11] along with the other bishops. But although the king and his counsellors were the

[1] Chap. IV, p. 11.

[2] Cf. II Corinthians x. 6.

[3] Henry of Blois, brother of King Stephen, consecrated bishop of Winchester, 17 May 1129. After the death of William of Corbeil in 1136 he aspired to the archbishopric of Canterbury, and henceforward viewed Theobald as a rival who had thwarted his ecclesiastical promotion. In compensation for his disappointment he was invested with legatine powers in England by Innocent II; see R. L. Poole, Preface to *Historia Pontificalis*, pp. liii *et seq*.

[4] Among them were the bishops of Durham, Bath and Exeter; see Poole, *op. cit.*, p. lii.

[5] Theobald, count of Champagne.

[6] He duly visited Rome either in 1148 or 1149; see Poole, *op. cit.*, p. lvi.

[7] Chap. XV, p. 41.

[8] This was not by virtue of legatine authority, which seems not to have been conferred upon Theobald until some time after September 1148; see Poole, *op. cit.*, p. lv, n. 1.

[9] Later justiciar of England under Henry II; see below, p. 750.

[10] Steward of King Stephen.

[11] Refers to the archbishop's presence at the election of the empress, Maud, in April 1141

archbishop's most bitter enemies, neither in this second banishment nor in the first were any of his friends or faithful servants banished or driven into exile, not even those who preferred to share their master's fate rather than remain in their native land. The archbishop alone suffered the hardships and injuries of exile: his friends were free to visit him and return to their country at will and, had they so wished, to afford him consolation and relieve his necessities. But, in common with the lot of all who suffer deprivation, he found few who remained faithful to him and often experienced the truth of the proverb that "to choose men without faith is to be unhappy in one's choice of friends".[1] In the meantime he dwelt at St. Omer, beloved by all for his honesty of character and from respect for his rank, but chiefly because he was mild of speech and devoted to the poor, and seemed to be a unique example of kindliness and generosity. . . .

. . . Envoys[2] from the archbishop of Canterbury came upon the pope at Brescia[3] and, after pleading their cause before him, easily contrived to return with their wishes fulfilled. But, so far as they dared, the cardinals Octavian[4] and Guy of Crema[5] opposed them, boasting of their kinship with the king of the English by reason of the fact that his grandmother was a Lombard.[6] Guido 'de Summa',[7] however, was more temperate in his partiality for the bishop of Winchester; but truth and the apostolic faith prevailed. The pope wrote to all the bishops of England, both jointly and individually, bidding them warn the king to put aside every occasion of delay, to restore to the archbishop everything of which he had been despoiled and to make proper satisfaction for his wrongs. Unless the king complied with these injunctions and obeyed, the pope ordered the bishops, incontinently and rejecting any appeal, to place his kingdom under interdict and to inform him that the lord pope would proceed to excommunicate him by name on the following Michaelmas. He wrote also to the bishops and lay magnates of France, requesting them to give aid to the archbishop as opportunity afforded. Besides this he ordered all men in the province of Canterbury to pay implicit obedience to their archbishop and to appear at his summons just as though he were present in his see.

But almost all the bishops who were in the king's power were turned aside from the archbishop like a deceitful bow,[8] and the clergy preferred tranquillity to obedience. For some took to flight so that no orders could be given in their absence; others offered in excuse the danger to themselves and their friends, the loss to the Church and a justifiable fear of schism breaking out. Indeed the first of all to fall into the sin of disobedience were the Londoners, who had recourse to an appeal, despite the fact that this had been expressly forbidden in the papal letter. . . . The see of Canterbury alone obeyed the interdict, with the exception, however, of the monastery of St. Augustine's, where the monks ventured to celebrate the divine offices. The archbishop

[1] Lucan, *Pharsalia*, VIII, 535

[2] Chap. XVIII, p. 44.

[3] Where Eugenius sojourned from 15 July to 8 September 1148.

[4] Cardinal-deacon of St. Nicholas, legate to Germany in 1152 and in 1159 the anti-pope Victor IV in opposition to Alexander III. He died at Lucca on 20 April 1164.

[5] Cardinal-deacon of St. Mary in Porticu, an active supporter of the anti-pope Victor IV and succeeded him as Paschal III. For the many other cardinals named Guido, see R. L. Poole, *op. cit.*, pp. xv–xvi.

[6] For a discussion of the truth of this statement, see R. L. Poole, *op. cit.*, Appendix IV.

[7] Cardinal-priest of St. Lawrence, bishop of Ostia, 1149; see below, p. 684.

[8] Psalms lxxviii. 58.

did not leave this temerity unpunished, but excommunicated the authors of this presumptuous act in person, Sylvester, the prior, who afterwards became abbot,[1] and William, the sacristan, who is now prior, together with their accomplices. The abbot, Hugh, was ordered to break off relations with those who had been excommunicated. He obeyed in all humility, recalling to mind the obedience he owed to the archbishop by reason of his profession. For this he publicly avowed, and bore witness to it in his letter to the lord pope, remaining in the Isle of Thanet and avoiding intercourse with the excommunicates until the case was settled. Both sides repeatedly sent envoys to Rome, but the archbishop prevailed. For the lord pope confirmed the sentence of anathema issued against the monks and authorized the archbishop to absolve them after they had made amends. They were commanded to desist from performing the divine offices for as long a period as they had dared to celebrate them since the interdict had been in force.

In[2] the meantime Gilbert,[3] abbot of Gloucester, was elected bishop of Hereford with the advice and assent of the archbishop of Canterbury. This was highly pleasing on personal grounds to the Norman duke who is now king,[4] in whose power the election to the bishopric then resided,[5] but he would not give his consent or bestow the *regalia* until the bishop-elect had bound himself by solemn oath to do homage to him within a month of his consecration and had undertaken not to do homage to King Stephen, whom the entire English Church acknowledged by a decree of the Roman Church. For although the lay magnates were divided in their allegiance to the rival princes,[6] the Church was united. When, however, the bishop-elect applied to the archbishop for consecration, the bishops who had been summoned and were attending for this purpose, namely Robert of London,[7] Jocelyn of Salisbury[8] and Hilary of Chichester,[9] were enjoined on the authority of the lord pope to co-operate with the archbishop in the consecration of their brother. But they refused to obey, on the pretext of their allegiance to King Stephen and on the ground that it was against the ancient customs that any man should be consecrated outside the kingdom, especially without the king's assent and in the case of one who had not paid homage to him. The archbishop, notwithstanding, proceeded to the consecration in the church of St. Omer, in the presence and with the co-operation of Nicholas, bishop of Cambrai, Miles of Térouanne and other French bishops in accordance with the papal

[1] See below, p. 686.
[2] Chap. XIX, p. 47.
[3] Gilbert Foliot, formerly prior of Cluny and abbot of St. Peter's, Gloucester since 1139. He was translated from Hereford to London in 1163 and became one of the most redoubtable opponents of Thomas Becket; see below, pp. 711, 718, 723, 726 *et sqq.*, 748, 750, 758.
[4] Henry of Anjou, the future Henry II. John of Salisbury is in error in giving him the title of duke of Normandy, for the duchy was not handed over to him by his father, Geoffrey, until 1150. It is possible that the words *qui modo rex est* are a later interpolation and that the passage really refers to Geoffrey. On this point, see J. H. Round, *Eng. Hist. Rev.*, vol. v (1890), p. 749, n. 13, and R. L. Poole, *op. cit.*, p. 47, n.
[5] The forces of the empress, Maud, Henry's mother, were then holding the west midlands and the Welsh border, including the city of Hereford.
[6] Stephen and Maud.
[7] Robert 'de Sigillo', appointed bishop of London by the empress, Maud, in 1141. He was driven from his capital by the Londoners and joined Maud at Oxford the same year; for the circumstances of his death, see below, p. 686.
[8] Bishop of Salisbury, 1142–1148.
[9] See above, p. 679.

mandate. At the reading of the Gospel this prophecy was found:[1] "Sleepest thou? couldst thou not watch with me one hour?"[2] Some were of the opinion that this was truly fulfilled, when the bishop on his return to England paid homage to King Stephen contrary to the pledge by which he was bound to the duke. With the authority of the archbishop he planned to retain his abbacy together with the bishopric, but the monks, forestalling his design, caused Hamelin[3], the present abbot, to be hastily consecrated to the office by Simon, bishop of Worcester. The duke, moreover, having learnt how the bishop of Hereford had proffered homage to the king by a solemn oath, charged him before the archbishop with breach of faith, both by letter and through envoys, and swore that he would never accept as bishop one who showed neither fear nor shame in acting contrary to the faith which he had publicly and personally pledged. The archbishop, however, now with threats and now with flattery, appeased the duke, persuading him that it was not lawful for a bishop to cause a schism in the Church by withdrawing allegiance from one whom the Roman Church acknowledged as king.

King Stephen,[4] nevertheless, persisted in his evil course, relying on the advice of certain bishops and on the hope he entertained of winning the favour of some of the cardinals, whom he perceived could be seduced to any kind of baseness by the rumour of a mouldy purse. Meanwhile the bishops, whom the archbishop had summoned, put forward as an excuse for their disobedience their inability to quit the realm without the king's leave. The Roman Church again and again postponed giving the archbishop the aid she had promised.

Wherefore, on the advice of prudent counsellors, the archbishop returned to England[5] and was received with great reverence and piety by Earl Hugh Bigot,[6] with whom he lodged in his castle of Framlingham. Thither he summoned the bishops to meet him, and there he dealt with their cases individually and executed his office with all severity until peace was restored, reparation made for lands that had been confiscated and new charters drawn up concerning the privileges and dignities to be observed in the Church. This done, he returned to his own diocese. . . .

. . . With[7] the return of the envoys of the archbishop and of the monks of St. Augustine's, peace now reigned in the church of Canterbury. Sylvester the prior, and William the sacristan, who had been excommunicated,[8] were compelled to present themselves before the archbishop, armed with a papal letter, and to confess their fault and promise satisfaction in order to obtain absolution. They were absolved at Northfleet, having first been scourged at the church door in accordance with canonical discipline. This penance was laid upon them; the monks who had chanted to the grief of the Church while closed under the interdict, were forbidden to celebrate

[1] The *prognosticum* or the first words discovered when the book of the Gospels was laid on the elected prelate's shoulders.

[2] Mark xiv. 37.

[3] Sub-prior of the abbey, elected abbot 26 September 1148.

[4] Chap. XX, p. 49.

[5] He set sail from Gravelines and landed at Gosford in Suffolk, a port now submerged by the encroachment of the sea, some time after 5 September 1148; cf. Gervase of Canterbury, *op. cit.*, vol. I, pp. 135–136.

[6] Steward of Henry I, created earl of Norfolk by Stephen, deserted to the empress at Oxford after Stephen's defeat at Lincoln.

[7] Chap. XXII, p. 51.

[8] See above, p. 682.

the divine offices in the great church, which they had profaned. And because they had transgressed the sentence of the lord pope for a hundred and ninety days,[1] they were suspended from celebrating the divine offices in the chapel of the abbey for a like number of days. But this favour the archbishop of his clemency accorded them, that they should be allowed to hear Mass elsewhere. So they erected an altar in the chapter-house, where, as often as their brother-monks were chanting their office, they were able to console themselves by celebrating the divine mysteries in grief and shame. Thus their laughter was changed to mourning, and the sorrow of those who had remained obedient was turned into joy. . . .

Theobald,[2] archbishop of Canterbury, had relaxed the suspension of the bishops and abbots of England,[3] with the exception of that of Henry of Winchester, who had set out for Rome to make satisfaction in his own person. Graciously received there, he laboured with the help of Guido 'de Summa',[4] bishop of Ostia, Gregory of St. Angelo and other friends, who afterwards admitted the fact, to contrive that the *pallium* might be bestowed upon him and that he might be made archbishop of the west of England and apostolic legate in the kingdom,[5] or at least that his diocese might be exempted from the jurisdiction of Canterbury. Although he left no stone unturned to accomplish his ends, he was firmly repulsed. Finally he begged to be personally vindicated. But the lord pope turned a deaf ear to all his requests, partly because he suspected him of evil intentions and referred to him as the bane of all England, and partly because he had recognized the justice of the cause of the church of Canterbury. The bishop was also credited with having stirred up his brother, the king, against the Church. The latter, however–as his deeds openly showed–was acting neither by his advice nor that of any other prudent counsellor. Meanwhile the king was vexing the Church with fresh disturbances.[6] When this was reported to the pope while the bishop was present, the latter remarked, "I am glad I am not there now, or I should be blamed for this trouble." The pope smiled and delivered himself of the following anecdote: "The devil and his dam were engaged in friendly conversation, and while she, to check her son's misconduct, was scolding and upbraiding him for the wickedness of his ways, a storm arose and a great number of ships were sunk before their very eyes. 'Behold!' said the devil, 'if I had been there, you would have laid this mischief also to my account.' Said she, 'Even if you were not there at the time, it is evident that you have trailed your tail across beforehand.'" Then, applying the saying to the bishop, the pope addressed him, "See to it, brother, that you do not trail your tail in the English sea." When the bishop perceived that he could obtain nothing except his absolution, he received permission to return home, bought some ancient statues in Rome and had them sent to Winchester. Wherefore,

[1] Probably a copyist's error from the original MS.; the correct figure should be 180 days; see R. L. Poole, *op. cit.*, p. xlix.

[2] Chap. XL, p. 80.

[3] The bishops of Worcester, Bath, Exeter and Chichester were reconciled with the archbishop before 11 November 1148; see Gervase of Canterbury, *op. cit.*, vol. I, p. 138.

[4] See above, p. 681.

[5] Here John is confusing Henry's two journeys to Rome, the first in 1148 and the second in 1151. It was on the latter occasion that he mooted his scheme for the creation of a separate archbishopric for the west country; see R. L. Poole, *op. cit.*, p. lvi and footnote.

[6] A reference to King Stephen's attempt early in 1152 to coerce Archbishop Theobald and the bishops into crowning his son, Eustace. See also below, p. 685.

when a certain grammarian[1] saw him, as he stood conspicuous among the others in the *curia* for his long beard and philosophic gravity, purchasing idols wrought by the subtle and laborious, if unintentional, error of the pagans, he thus made game of him:

"Damasippus acts like a madman in buying up old statues."[2]

Having heard the counsel the bishop had given when asked for his advice, the same man also aimed another shaft at him, saying,

> "Damasippus, may the powers divine
> For this sage counsel of thine
> Grant thee a barber."[3]

... The bishop gave few presents, and to few people, and returned home by sea on account of the perils lurking for him in Tuscany, Lombardy and Burgundy. Traversing Spain as far as St. James of Compostella, he at last reached home[4] in safety and riches. ...

... Henry,[5] archbishop of York,[6] made his peace with Stephen, king of the English, and promised to do his utmost to get the pope to crown Eustace, the king's son. But this could not be done unless the king obtained pardon from the pope.[7] For a complaint had often been made against him on the ground of his usurpation of the throne, which he had seized contrary to the oath he had sworn to King Henry.[8] For he had sworn fealty to the Empress Maud, the said king's daughter, and had promised that after her father's death he would help her to acquire and maintain England and Normandy against all comers. Ulgerius, the venerable bishop of Angers,[9] laid the empress's complaint before Pope Innocent,[10] accusing the king of perjury and illegal usurpation of the throne. On the other side stood envoys sent by the king, Roger, bishop of Chester,[11] Lovel, clerk to William, archbishop of Canterbury[12] of happy memory, and, as advocate for their cause, Arnulf, archdeacon of Séez, afterwards bishop of Lisieux. ...[13]

... Pope Innocent would not endure to hear further argument between the two advocates, nor would he give a decision or adjourn the case to a later date. Against the advice of certain of the cardinals, however, especially that of Guido, cardinal-priest of St. Mark's, he accepted presents from King Stephen and in a private letter confirmed him in his possession of the kingdom of England and the duchy of Normandy. ...

Later, when the aforesaid Cardinal Guido had become pope as Celestine[14] by

[1] Perhaps a thin disguise for John himself.

[2] Horace, *Satires*, II, 3, 64.

[3] Horace, *Satires*, II, 3, 16–17.

[4] Not till after September 1152.

[5] Chap. XLII, p. 85.

[6] Henry Murdac, see above, p. 679.

[7] For his action in preventing Archbishop Theobald from attending the council of Rheims.

[8] Henry I. Mention of the archbishop of York's mission to Rome leads John of Salisbury into a digression on the proceedings at Rome relating to Stephen's claim to the throne which took place before Innocent II in the Lateran Council of 1139. See R. L. Poole, *op. cit.*, Appendix VI.

[9] Bishop of Angers, 1125–1148.

[10] Innocent II, 1130–1143.

[11] Roger Clinton, bishop of Chester, 1129–1148. He died on the Second Crusade and was buried at Antioch.

[12] William of Corbeil, Theobald's predecessor as archbishop of Canterbury.

[13] The trusted counsellor and agent of Henry II and opponent of Thomas Becket.

[14] Celestine II, 1143, 1144.

favour of the empress, he wrote to the lord Theobald, archbishop of Canterbury, forbidding any change to be made in respect of the crown of England, since the case was under litigation and any transference was prohibited by law. His successors, Popes Lucius[1] and Eugenius, renewed this prohibition, and so it came to pass that the aforesaid archbishop of York was unable to obtain the advancement of Eustace.

On[2] the death of Hugh, abbot of St. Augustine's, Canterbury, he was succeeded by Sylvester, prior of the said church.[3] But many suspected that his election was tainted with simony, from the fact that the king accepted five hundred marks in return for allowing the monks, on the death of the abbot, freedom to elect whom they would and the right to dispose of the goods of the vacant church at will. Since it was the prior who had made this bargain, had paid the money and forthwith been elected, suspicion was aroused. Nevertheless, as there was no one who could publicly accuse him of the crime–for it was unsafe to do so, seeing the king himself and the chief men of his household were involved–the archbishop of Canterbury confirmed the election.[4] But a dispute arose concerning the place of consecration by reason of certain privileges ordaining that the abbot of the house should receive consecration in his own abbey and not be dragged off to another. These privileges, however, were regarded as suspect, both because they were not drawn up in the form practised by the Roman Church, and because, when the documents and the seals were compared,[5] they were found not to be those of the popes whose names they bore. Besides, the monks had not hitherto made use of this privilege, for it was admitted that the other abbots of St. Augustine's had received consecration in the churches of the archbishop. The dispute dragged on for nearly a year and was finally referred to Pope Eugenius. . . .[6]

On[7] the death of Robert, bishop of London, whom many suspected had been poisoned, Pope Eugenius ordered the clergy of the city to elect within three months a man honest, learned and adorned with the religious habit. But they, fearing that their autonomy would be impugned, sent to the Roman Church and obtained in a papal letter this interpretation of the new clause, namely that not only monks and canons-regular, but also those who are commonly called secular clerks might be regarded as *adorned with the religious habit*; on the ground that when a man was tonsured as a clerk, at the moment the words of benediction were uttered over him he immediately assumed the habit of holy religion. Nevertheless, there were some in the *curia* itself who argued that this interpretation was absurd and that the form of the earlier mandate was superfluous, unless perchance the pope feared that the Londoners were planning to choose a layman for bishop. The king, indeed, would not concede them freedom of election until they had paid him five hundred pounds, following the example of the monks of St. Augustine's. When this sum had been

[1] Lucius II, 1144–1145. [2] Chap. XLIII, p. 89. [3] See above, pp. 682, 683.

[4] In obedience to a papal mandate dated 20 January 1152; see R. L. Poole, *op. cit.*, pp. l–li.

[5] *i.e.* with genuine documents. A remarkable instance of John's critical faculty as an expert in the forms and methods of the papal chancery; see Poole, *op. cit.*, p. li.

[6] Theobald consecrated Sylvester abbot on 28 August 1152, apparently under protest, for the matter was not allowed to drop, and after a further appeal to Rome in the papacy of Anastasius IV, it was decided in the council of Northampton in July 1157 that the abbot should make profession of obedience to the archbishop; see Poole, *op. cit.*, p. lii.

[7] Chap. XLV, p. 90.

handed over, Richard, archdeacon of the said church,[1] was elected, who is known to have discharged the said debt, not without suspicion of simony; for at that time many men cloaked the evil of simony under the pretext of winning freedom.

King Stephen and Maud, his wife, founded a monastery at Faversham in Kent, and Clarembald. . . .[2]

(c) MATERIAL RELATING TO THE ESTABLISHMENT OF THE CISTERCIAN ORDER IN ENGLAND

115. The "Charter of Love" (*Carta Caritatis*) (? 1117)

The *Carta Caritatis* is the fundamental constitution of the Cistercian Order. It was the work of Stephen Harding, the second abbot of Cîteaux, an Englishman who was one of the original monks who seceded from the Benedictine community at Molesme in order to found the abbey of Cîteaux in 1098. The actual date of the *Carta Caritatis* is difficult to determine, but it was certainly issued during Stephen's abbacy and was probably put into its final shape about the year 1117, since Morimond, the last of the daughter-houses of Cîteaux, founded in 1116, is frequently mentioned in the text together with the other three. Papal confirmation of the "Charter" was obtained from Calixtus II in a bull dated 23 December 1119. The first general chapter of the Order, as created by the "Charter", was held in 1120, and thereafter met annually, thus becoming a permanent part of the Cistercian constitution, as envisaged in the "Charter". The *Carta Caritatis* thus described the Cistercian Order, and in doing so laid down a full and finished plan for its future governance. In place of the extreme centralization characteristic of the Cluniac Order it established for the Cistercians a system of 'federal' government based on the power of the four greater abbots. In every house of the Order the powers of visitation and ultimate discipline and control are vested not in the abbot of Cîteaux, the titular head of the whole Order, but in the abbot of the mother-house from which the house was founded. The abbot of Cîteaux is himself a 'limited' monarch, subject to visitation, veto, correction and, in the last resort, to deposition by the corporate action of the abbots of its four daughter-houses and the general chapter of the Order. The ecclesiastical authority of the bishop of the diocese is also implicitly safeguarded,[3] and this would appear to be an innovation in twelfth-century monasticism. Uniformity of custom, ceremonial and discipline is prescribed for all Cistercian houses, the primary object being to maintain the Rule of St. Benedict in its entirety and pristine purity; considerable stress is laid on this in the "Charter". The Latin text is printed in Migne, *Patrologia Latina*, vol. CLXVI, col. 1377–1584, and in the older collections of Cistercian statutes. The most recent edition, used for this version, is that of Dom. J.-M. Canivez, *Statuta Capitulorum Generalium Ordinis Cisterciensis* (Bibliothèque de la Revue d'Histoire Ecclésiastique, Louvain, 1933), vol. I, pp. xxvi–xxxi. A précis of the document is given in W. A. P. Mason, "The Beginnings of the Cistercian Order", *Trans. R. Hist. Soc.*, New Series, vol. XIX (1905), pp. 169–207.

THE CHARTER OF LOVE

Before the Cistercian abbeys began to flourish, the lord abbot, Stephen, and his monks ordained that abbeys were on no account to be established in the diocese of any bishop prior to his ratification and confirmation of the decree drawn up in writing between the abbey of Cîteaux and its daughter-houses, in order to avoid occasion of offence between the bishop and the monks. In this decree, therefore, the aforesaid brethren, guarding against possible dangers to their mutual peace, have made clear and established and handed down to later generations in what manner and by what agreement, nay rather, with what *love* the monks of their Order, though separated in body in abbeys in divers parts of the world, might be knit together inseparably in spirit. Moreover, they were of opinion that this decree should be called the "Charter of Love", because it casts off the burden of all exactions, pursues love alone and promotes the welfare of souls in things human and divine.

[1] Richard 'de Belmeis', archdeacon of Middlesex, nephew of an earlier bishop of the same name. He was consecrated bishop of London on 28 September 1152 and died on 4 May 1162.

[2] The MS. of the *Historia Pontificalis* breaks off at this point.

[3] *Carta Caritatis*, prefatory clause.

I. Inasmuch as we are known to be servants of the One True King, Lord and Master, albeit unprofitable, we therefore make no claim for worldly advantage or temporal gain on our abbots and brother monks, whom in divers places devotion to God shall call through us, the most wretched of men, to live under regular discipline. For, in our desire for their profit and that of all sons of holy Church, we are not disposed to lay any burden upon them or to effect anything calculated to diminish their substance, lest in striving to grow rich at their expense, we may not escape the sin of avarice, which is declared by the apostle to be servitude to idols.[1]

II. Nevertheless we desire for love's sake[2] to retain the cure of their souls, so that if they shall essay to swerve from their sacred purpose and the observance of the holy Rule–which God forbid–they may through our solicitude return to righteousness of life.

III. We will therefore and command them to observe the Rule of St. Benedict in all things as it is observed in the new monastery.[3] Let the monks put no other interpretation upon the holy Rule but what the holy fathers, our predecessors, namely the monks of the new minster, have understood and maintained; and as we today understand and uphold it, so let them do also.

IV. And inasmuch as we receive in our cloister all the monks of their houses who come to us, and they likewise receive ours in theirs, so it seems good to us and in accordance with our will that they should maintain the customary ceremonial, chants[4] and all books necessary for the canonical offices, both by day and by night, and for the Mass, after the form of the customs and books of the new minster, so that there be no discord in our worship, but that we may all dwell in one love and under one rule and with like customs.[5]

V. No church or person of our Order shall presume to solicit from anyone a privilege contrary to the common customs of the Order, or in any wise retain it, if it has been granted.

VI. When the abbot of the new minster shall come on a visitation to one of these houses, let the abbot of the place recognize the church of the new minster as his mother-church and give place to him in all the precincts of the monastery, and let the visiting abbot take the place of the abbot of that house, so long as he remains there.

VII. Except that he shall not take his meals in the guest-room,[6] but in the refectory with the brethren, that discipline may be preserved, unless the abbot of the house be absent. Likewise let it be done in the case of all abbots of our Order who may chance to come on a visit. But if several shall come at the same time, and the abbot of the house be absent, let the abbot senior in rank take his meals in the guest-room.[6] An exception shall also be made that the abbot of the house shall, even when a greater abbot is present, bless his own novices after the regular term of probation.

VIII. But let the abbot of the new minster be careful not to presume in any wise to conduct or order the affairs of the house he is visiting, or meddle in them, against the will of the abbot or the brethren.

IX. But if he learn that the precepts of the Rule or of our Order are transgressed

[1] Colossians iii. 5.
[2] *gratia caritatis.*
[3] *i.e.* Cîteaux, called at first the "new minster".
[4] *cantum.*
[5] *una caritate, una regula, similibusque vivamus moribus.*
[6] *hospicio.*

in the said house, let him be diligent to correct the brethren lovingly, and with the advice and in the presence of the abbot. Even if the abbot be absent, he shall nevertheless correct what he has found wrong therein.

X. Once a year let the abbot of the mother-church[1] visit all the houses of his foundation either in person or through one of his co-abbots. And if he shall visit the brethren more often, let them the more rejoice.

XI. Moreover, let the abbey of Cîteaux be visited by the four primary abbots, namely of La Ferté, Pontigny, Clairvaux and Morimond, together in person on such a day as they may choose, except that appointed for the holding of the annual chapter, unless perchance one of them be prevented by grievous sickness.

XII. When any abbot of our Order shall come to the new minster, let fitting reverence be shown to him; let him occupy the abbot's stall and take his meals in the guest-room if the abbot be absent. But if the abbot be present, let him do none of these things, but let him dine in the refectory. Let the prior of the abbey take charge of its affairs.

XIII. Between abbeys having no direct relationship with each other, this shall be the rule. Let every abbot give place to his co-abbot within the precincts of his monastery, that the saying may be fulfilled, "in honour preferring one another". If two or more abbots shall come to the monastery, the superior in rank shall take precedence of the others. But let them all take their meals together in the refectory, except the abbot of the house, as stated above. But whenever they meet on other occasions, they shall maintain their rank in accordance with the seniority of their abbeys, so that he whose church is of older foundation, shall take precedence of the others. Whenever they take their seats together, let each humble himself before the others.

XIV. But when any of our churches has by God's grace so increased that it is able to establish a new house, let the two houses maintain the same relationship[2] between them as obtains between us and our brethren,[3] except that they shall not hold an annual chapter among themselves.

XV. But all the abbots of our Order shall without fail attend each year the general chapter at Cîteaux, with the sole exception of those detained by bodily infirmity. The latter, however, ought to appoint a suitable delegate, by whom the reason for their absence may be reported to the chapter. An exception may also be made for those who dwell in distant lands; let them attend at the intervals appointed for them in the chapter.[4] But if, and when, on any other occasion any abbot shall presume to absent himself from our general chapter, let him crave pardon for his fault at the chapter held in the following year; let his absence not be passed over without serious attention being paid to it.

XVI. In this general chapter let the abbots take measures for the salvation of their souls, and if anything in the observance of the holy Rule or of the Order ought to be amended or supplemented, let them ordain it and re-establish the bond of peace and charity among themselves.

[1] *i.e.* Cîteaux. [2] *diffinitionem.* [3] *confratres.*

[4] The intervals were later fixed as follows: abbots from Spanish houses were to attend every other year, those from Ireland, Scotland, Portugal and Sicily every fourth year, and those from Syria and Palestine every seventh year.

XVII. But if any abbot be found remiss in keeping the Rule, or too intent upon worldly affairs or in any way corrupt or wicked, let him be charged with the offence in the chapter, albeit in all charity. Let the accused crave pardon and perform the penance laid on him for his fault. Such a charge, however, may not be brought except by an abbot.

XVIII. If perchance any dispute shall arise between certain abbots, or an offence be charged against one of them so grave as to merit suspension or deposition, the decision of the chapter shall be observed without question.[1]

XIX. But if, by reason of a difference of opinion, the case shall result in discord, the judgment of the abbot of Cîteaux and of those of sounder and more appropriate counsel shall be inflexibly upheld, precaution being taken that none of those personally involved in the case shall take part in the judgment.

XX. Should any church fall into extreme poverty, let the abbot of that house take pains to inform the whole chapter of the fact. Thereupon the abbots, one and all inflamed with an ardent fire of love, shall hasten to relieve that church from its poverty, so far as they are able, out of the resources bestowed upon them by God.

XXI. If any house of our Order become bereft of its abbot, let the abbot of the house from which it sprung, take every care for its governance, until a new abbot shall be elected. Moreover, on the day appointed for the election, let the abbots of the daughter-houses of that house be summoned, and let them and the monks of that house elect an abbot with the advice and assent of the abbot of the mother-house.

XXII. When the house of Cîteaux, the mother of us all, shall be bereft of its abbot, let the four primary abbots, namely those of La Ferté, Pontigny, Clairvaux and Morimond, make provision for it, and let the responsibility for the abbey rest upon them, until a new abbot be elected and appointed.

XXIII. A day having been fixed and named for the election of an abbot of Cîteaux, let a summons be conveyed with at least fifteen days' notice to the abbots of the houses sprung from Cîteaux and to such others as the aforesaid abbots and the monks of Cîteaux shall deem suitable and, being assembled in the name of the Lord, let the abbots and the monks of Cîteaux elect an abbot.

XXIV. It is permissible for any monk to be raised to the office of abbot of the mother-church of our Order, not only those of her daughter-churches, but also, in case of necessity for their abbots to be free to do so. But no member of another Order may be elected abbot, even as it is not permissible for one of us to be appointed to another monastery which is not of our Order.

XXV. Should any abbot beg leave of his father, the abbot of the house from which his own has sprung, to be relieved of the burden of his office on the pretext of his incapacity or through faint-heartedness,[2] let the father-abbot have a care lest he assent to his request too readily and without a reasonable cause and urgent need. But if the necessity be very great, let the father-abbot do nothing in the matter of his own initiative, but let him summon certain other abbots of our Order and by their advice act in the way they have agreed upon.

XXVI. If any abbot become notorious for contempt of the holy Rule or as a

[1] *sine retractatione.* [2] *pro inutilitate seu pusillanimitate sua.*

transgressor[1] of the Order or an accessory to the faults of the brethren committed to his charge, let the abbot of the mother-church, either in person or through his prior, or in whatever way is more convenient, exhort him on four occasions to mend his ways. But if he will neither suffer correction nor yield of his own accord, let a sufficient number of the abbots of our congregation be gathered together, and let them remove the transgressor of the holy Rule from his office; after which another more worthy of it may be elected by the monks of that church with the advice and goodwill of the greater abbot and in co-operation with the abbots and those who are related to it, as stated above.

XXVII. But if–which God forbid–the deposed abbot or his monks shall be contumacious and rebellious, and will not acquiesce in the sentence, let them be subject to excommunication by the abbot of the mother-church and his co-abbots, and thereafter coerced by him according as he thinks fit and is able.

XXVIII. Arising out of this, should any one of those so condemned come to himself again and desire to arise from the death of the soul and return to his mother, let him be received as a penitent son. For except for this occasion, which should always be avoided as far as possible, let no abbot retain a monk belonging to any other abbot of our Order without his assent; also let none bring his monks to dwell in the house of any other without his permission.

XXIX. In like manner if–which God forbid–the abbots of our Order shall discover that our mother-church of Cîteaux is becoming lukewarm in its sacred purpose,[2] or is departing from the observance of the holy Rule, let them admonish the abbot of that house four times through the four primary abbots, namely those of La Ferté, Pontigny, Clairvaux and Morimond, in the name of the other abbots of the Order, to amend his life and take pains to amend that of others, and let them diligently fulfil in his case the remaining precepts prescribed for the other abbots, when they are intolerant of correction. But if he will not yield of his own accord, they may neither depose him nor condemn him as contumacious, until they come to depose him from his office as an unprofitable steward, either in the general chapter or–if perchance it be already known that the chapter is not due for summons–in another assembly specially convened for the abbots of the daughter-houses of Cîteaux and some of the others; whereupon both the said abbots and the monks of Cîteaux shall take care to elect a suitable abbot in his place. But if the former abbot and the monks of Cîteaux shall contumaciously resist, let them not forbear to strike them with the sword of excommunication.

XXX. Should any such transgressor afterwards come to his senses and, in the desire to save his soul, take refuge in one of our four primary churches, whether at La Ferté, or Pontigny, or Clairvaux, or Morimond, let him be received as an inmate and co-partner[3] in the abbey in accordance with the Rule, until such time as he be justly reconciled with his own church, whereupon he may be restored thither. In the meantime the annual chapter of the abbots shall not be held at Cîteaux, but wheresoever the above-named four abbots shall previously have appointed.

[1] *praevaricator.*
[2] *in sancto proposito languescere.*
[3] *sicut domesticus et coheres.*

116. Narrative of the coming of the Cistercians to England and of the foundation of the abbey of Rievaulx

This narrative occurs in a fifteenth-century copy of a Fountains manuscript, but it is probable that it derives directly from a lost chronicle of the thirteenth century. It thus represents early Cistercian tradition at first-hand. It is here included as showing the manner in which the Cistercian discipline was brought to England, which received it directly from Cîteaux (see above, p. 66). The narrative is printed in W. Dugdale, *Monasticon Anglicanum*, vol. v, p. 292, and in *Memorials of Fountains Abbey* (ed. J. R. Walbran, Surtees Soc., 1863), vol. I, pp. 3-4.

During the reign in England of the illustrious King Henry, son of William, nicknamed the bastard, the land was kept in peace before his face. Churches were erected in many places, monasteries were built, and in the absence of wars religion spread. There flourished in that time of happy memory, blessed Bernard, abbot of Clairvaux, a man of splendour, a strenuous worker at the business of God, one who was notable in his holiness and famous in his teaching, being glorious also in the miracles which he wrought. His greatest care was for divine worship and for the salvation of souls. He strove, moreover, to increase his community, giving glory to God with his lips and himself being glorified in his Name. He was the spiritual father of many monks, and he caused not a few monasteries to be built. He sent the soldiers of his army to conquer distant lands, and thus he won notable victories over the old enemy, seizing plunder which he could restore to his King. This man, then, moved by divine inspiration, desired to plant an offshoot of good hope from the noble vine of Clairvaux. He therefore sent a chapter of monks to England, hoping to obtain fruit there as well as in so many other lands. There still exists the letter which he wrote to the king, saying that he wished to seize plunder for his heavenly Lord out of the lands of the king [of England], adding that he had sent valiant soldiers from his army who would not be slow to capture what they wanted. In this manner he concluded his entreaty. And this is what was done. His men were received with honour by the king and the kingdom, and they established new fortifications in the province of York. They constructed the abbey which is called Rievaulx, which was the first plantation of the Cistercian Order in the province of Yorkshire. Those who were sent were holy men, being monks who glorified God in the practice of poverty. They dwelt in peace with all men, although they warred with their own bodies and with the old enemy. They showed forth the discipline of Clairvaux whence they came, and by works of piety they spread the sweet savour of their mother-abbey, as it were, a strong perfume from their own house. The story spread everywhere that men of outstanding holiness and perfect religion had come from a far land; that they had converse with angels in their dwelling; and that by their virtues they had glorified the monastic name. Many therefore were moved to emulate them by joining this company whose hearts had been touched by God. Thus very soon they grew into a great company. . . .

117. Benefactions to the Cistercian abbey of Rievaulx

This list of benefactions to Rievaulx Abbey was drawn up later in the Middle Ages, but there is no reason to doubt its authenticity. Indeed many of the grants here recorded are independently vouched for by the contemporary charters which conferred them. The list is important as showing the very rapid growth of the Cistercian abbeys in England, and the enthusiasm which the Cistercian movement inspired. Most, if not all, of these grants were made between 1131 and 1189. Printed: W. Dugdale, *Monasticon Anglicanum*, vol. v, p. 281; *Cartularium Rievallense* (ed. J. C. Atkinson, Surtees Soc., 1889), pp. 260-262.

These are the perpetual possessions of Rievaulx which were given to us in the following manner:

In the beginning 9 carucates of land were given to the blessed Bernard, abbot of Clairvaux, to wit, 'Grif' and 'Tilleston' in order there to build the abbey in the year 1131. Then, after some years, Odo of Boltby gave to the lord abbot, William, Hesketh with its appurtenances.

In 1145 Walter Espec[1] gave us Bilsdale with its appurtenances. Stephen 'de Mainil' gave us Stainton with its appurtenances. Gervase likewise, together with Benedict, his son, and Hugh 'de Tuit' gave us the meadow of 'Rokesbergh'. Odo 'de Nes' gave us the meadow of Waterholm. In the time of the lord abbot, Ailred, Gilbert of Ghent gave us the grange of Hunmanby with its appurtenances.

In 1152 William,[2] bishop of Durham, gave us the grange of Crosby with its appurtenances. Besides this, Hugh,[3] bishop of Durham, gave us Cotton with all its appurtenances. In the second year after that, Roger of Mowbray gave us Welburn with its appurtenances. Ralph Beler gave us the whole of 'Hoveton'.

In the year of the Incarnation of our Lord 1158 King Henry II gave us the waste land round Pickering in exchange for Stainton, which Walter of Ghent gave us to build an abbey there. Robert 'de Lasceles' gave us 1 carucate of land in Morton with its appurtenances. Walter Engelram gave us 5 bovates of land with their appurtenances in Welbury. Walter, son of Ivo, gave us half a carucate in Folkton with its appurtenances. Torfin of Allerston gave us 1 carucate of land in Allerston with its appurtenances. Walter Engelram gave us 30 acres of land in Heslerton, and pasture for 1000 sheep.[4] Peter 'de Tresc' gave us pasture in Arden. Hugh Malebestie gave us 'Oswaldesenges'. Jordan 'de Bussai' gave us half a carucate of land in Bolton. Richard Cumin gave us 1 carucate of land and half a carucate in Staincroft. Adam, son of Peter, gave us 'Rumblesmor' and forges in Stainborough and in Shitlington. Copsi of Tunstall gave us a house in Bolton with a toft. Ralph 'de Novavilla' gave 1 carucate of land in Rigton. In the time of the lord abbot, Silvanus, William, the son of Theobald, gave us 16 acres of land in Folkton. Henry of Willerby, and Alard, his son, gave us 4½ acres of meadow. Torphin of Allerston gave us 12 perches of arable land and 10 perches of meadow. And 10 bovates were quitclaimed to us in 'Hoveton' and 5 acres. The nuns of Welburn gave us 2 bovates of land. Among our forges there were given to us 70 acres and half an acre. Archarius of Tunstall gave us the grange of Bolton with its appurtenances. Everard 'de Ros' gave us the assart of Helmsley and the common pasture of Pockley. Robert of Sproxton, and Simon, his son, gave us land and pasture for 200 sheep in the fields of Sproxton. William of Amundaville gave us 1 acre of land in the fields of Trafford, next to the fishpond of Newsom. All these things did Bernard of Bailleul give us: the land of Teesdale with its appurtenances, with pasture for 60 mares with their foals of two years old, and for six score beasts, and for 12 cows and 2 bulls with their forage; and the land of Westerdale with its appurtenances, and pasture for six score beasts, and the fishpond of Newhouse. Jordan

[1] He took part in the battle of the Standard.
[2] William of Sainte-Barbe, bishop of Durham, 1143–1152.
[3] Hugh of Le Puiset, bishop of Durham, 1153–1195.
[4] Note throughout the prominence given to sheep-farming.

Payn gave us the grange of Broughton with its appurtenances, and the rest of the freemen of that village joined in the gift. Richard, son of Thurstan, and Robert, his son, and Richard Losth gave us the fishpond of Normanby and 43 acres of land and pasture for 100 sheep and for 8 horses or oxen, and for the baggage beasts that may be necessary. John, the son of John Vinitor, gave us the house and land of Beverley 'in Flammangaria'. Robert of Skirlaugh gave us land in the garden of William, son of Leuric, in Beverley, measuring 60 feet in length and 30 in breadth, in order to build a house there. William of 'Etun' gave us 9 acres and 1 perch of meadow in Layerthorp near York.

118. William of Malmesbury: Essay on the Cistercian Order contained in the "Deeds of the Kings of the English"

An interesting account as indicating contemporary opinion in England on the Cistercians. Printed: *W. Malmesburiensis Gesta Regum Anglorum* (ed. W. Stubbs, Rolls Series), vol. II (1889), p. 380. Translated by J. A. Giles, *William of Malmesbury's Chronicle* (1847), p. 347.

In his time[1] began the Cistercian Order, which is now both believed and asserted to be "the surest road to heaven".[2] To speak of this does not seem irrelevant to the work I have undertaken, since it redounds to the glory of England to have produced the distinguished man who was the author and promoter of that rule. To us he belonged, and in our schools he passed the earlier part of his life. Wherefore, if we are not envious, we shall embrace his good qualities the more kindly in proportion as we know them more intimately. And, moreover, I am anxious to extol his praise, because it is a mark of an ingenuous mind to approve that virtue in others, the absence of which you regret in yourself. He was named Harding and born in England of no very illustrious parents. From his early years he was a monk at Sherborne; but when secular desires had captivated his youth, he grew disgusted with the monastic garb, and went first to Scotland and afterwards to France. Here, after some years' exercise in the liberal arts, he became awakened to the love of God. For, when in manlier years he had put away childish things, he went to Rome with a clerk who shared his studies. Neither the length and difficulty of the journey, nor the scantiness of their means of subsistence by the way prevented them, as they went and returned, from singing daily the whole psalter. Indeed the mind of this celebrated man was already meditating the design which soon after, by the grace of God, he attempted to put into execution. For, returning into Burgundy, he became a monk at Molesme, a new and magnificent monastery. Here he readily admitted the first elements of the Rule, as he had formerly seen them; but when additional matters were proposed for his observance, such as he had neither read in the Rule nor seen elsewhere, he began, modestly and as became a monk, to ask the reason of them, saying: "By reason the supreme Creator has made all things; by reason he governs all things; by reason the fabric of the world revolves; by reason even the planets move; by reason the elements are directed; and by reason and by due regulation our nature ought to conduct itself. But since through sloth it too often departs from reason, many laws were formerly enacted for her use; and latterly a divine Rule has been promulgated by St. Benedict to bring

[1] *i.e.* the time of William Rufus.

[2] Juvenal, *Satires*, I, 38.

back the deviations of nature to reason. In this, though some things are contained the design of which I cannot fathom, yet I deem it necessary to yield to authority. And though reason and the authority of the holy writers may seem at variance, yet still they are one and the same. For since God hath created and restored nothing without reason, how can I believe that the holy fathers, no doubt strict followers of God, could command anything but what was reasonable, as if we ought to give credit to their bare authority. See then that you bring reason, or at least authority, for what you devise; although no great credit should be given to what is merely supported by human reason, because it may be combated with arguments equally forcible. Therefore from that Rule which, equally supported by reason and authority, appears as if dictated by the spirit of all just persons, produce precedents, which if you fail to do, in vain shall you profess his Rule, with whose regulations you disdain to comply."

Sentiments of this kind, spreading as usual from one to another, justly moved the hearts of such as feared God, "lest by any means they should run, or had run in vain".[1] The subject then being canvassed in frequent chapters, they ended by bringing over the abbot[2] himself to the opinion that all superfluous matters should be passed by, and merely the essence of the Rule be scrutinized. Two of the brethren therefore of equal piety and learning were elected, who by vicarious examination were to inquire into the intention of the founder's Rule; and when they had discovered it, to propound it to the rest. The abbot diligently endeavoured to induce the whole convent to give their assent, but, as it is difficult to eradicate from men's minds what has early taken root, since they reluctantly relinquish the first notions they have imbibed, almost the whole of them refused to accept the new customs, because they were attached to the old. Eighteen only, among whom was Harding, otherwise called Stephen, stubbornly persevered in their holy determination and, together with their abbot, left the monastery, declaring that the purity of the Rule could not be preserved in a place where riches and gluttony warred against even the heart that was well inclined. They came therefore to Cîteaux; a place formerly densely covered with woods but now so translucent from the abundant piety of its monks that it is not undeservedly esteemed to know God himself. Here, by the favour of the archbishop of Vienne, who is now pope,[3] they entered on a labour worthy to be remembered and venerated to the end of time.

Certainly many of their regulations seem severe, and more particularly these: they wear nothing made with furs or linen, nor even that finely spun linen garment, which we call *staminium*;[4] neither breeches, unless when sent on a journey, which at their return they wash and restore. They have two tunics with cowls, but no additional garment in winter, though, if they think fit, in summer they may lighten their garb. They sleep clad and girded, and never after matins return to their beds: but they so order the time of matins that it shall be light ere the lauds begin; so intent are they on their Rule that they think no jot nor tittle of it should be disregarded. Directly after lauds they sing the prime, after which they go out to work for stated hours. They complete whatever labour or service they have to perform by day without any other

[1] Galatians ii. 2. [2] Robert, abbot of Molesme.
[3] Calixtus II, 1119–1124: an indication of the time at which the *Gesta Regum* was written.
[4] An upper garment of wool.

light. No one is ever absent from the daily offices nor from compline, except the sick. After compline the cellarer and hospitaller wait upon the guests, yet observing the strictest silence. The abbot allows himself no indulgence beyond the others, and is everywhere present, everywhere attending to his flock, except that he does not eat with the rest, because his table is with the strangers and the poor. Nevertheless, wherever he may be, he is equally sparing of food and speech; for never more than two dishes are served either to him or to his company; lard and meat never but to the sick. From 13 September until Easter they do not take more than one meal a day,[1] except on Sunday, making no allowance for any other festival. They never leave the cloister but for the purpose of labour, nor do they ever speak, either there or elsewhere, save only to the abbot or prior. They continue unwearied in the canonical hours, making no addition to them except the vigils for the dead. They use in the divine office the Ambrosian chants and hymns, so far as they were able to learn them at Milan.[2] While they bestow care on the stranger and the sick, they inflict intolerable mortifications on their own bodies for the salvation of their souls.

At first the abbot both encountered these privations with great eagerness himself and compelled the rest of the brethren to do the same. In process of time, however, the man repented; he had been delicately brought up and could not well endure such daily abstinence. The monks, whom he had left behind at Molesme, hearing of this either by messages or by letters, drew him back to their monastery on the ground of his obedience to the pope, for such was their pretext. Thus they compelled him to a measure to which he was already well disposed.[3] For, as if worn out by the pertinacity of their entreaties, he left the narrow confines of poverty and sought again his former magnificence. All who had gone thither with him returned with him from Cîteaux, save eight. These latter, few in number but great in virtue, appointed Alberic, one of their party, to be abbot, and Stephen prior. The former, surviving no more than eight years, was by the will of heaven happily called away. Thereupon, doubtless by God's appointment, Stephen, though absent at the time, was elected abbot, being the original author of the whole scheme, the especial and celebrated ornament of our times. Sixteen abbeys which he has already completed, and seven which he has begun, are sufficient testimony to his abundant merit. Thus by the resounding trumpet of God he directs the people around him, both by word and deed, to heaven, acting fully up to his own precepts, affable in speech, pleasant in demeanour and with a mind always rejoicing in the Lord. Hence, openly, that noble joy of countenance; hence, secretly, that compunction coming from above. For, despising this state of a sojourner, he constantly yearns for a heavenly country. For these reasons he is beloved by all; for God graciously imparts to the minds of other men a love for the man he loves. Wherefore the inhabitant of that country counts himself happy if

[1] This was in conformity with the primitive custom of St. Benedict's monks at Monte Cassino; see Dom E. C. Butler, *Camb. Med. Hist.*, vol. I (1911), p. 538.

[2] The Ambrosian rite of the church of Milan was but one of the many known and practised in the Western Church from the fourth to the eighth century. In the time of Charlemagne it became superseded by the Roman rite in most churches in the West, but continued to survive in Milan and the other churches of Lombardy, where it was jealously guarded as a symbol of independence from Rome.

[3] This statement appears without justification. There is no evidence that Robert returned to Molesme of his own free will; he was recalled in 1098 by express mandate of the pope, as stated in the text.

through his hands he can transmit his wealth to God. He receives much indeed, but expends little on his own wants and those of his flock. The rest he distributes to the poor or employs it immediately on the building of monasteries; for the purse of Stephen is the public treasury of the indigent. A proof of his abstinence is that you see nothing there, as in other monasteries, gleaming with gold, blazing with jewels or glittering with silver. For as a Gentile says, "Of what use is gold to a saint?" We think our holy vessels to be lacking in something, unless the ponderous metal be eclipsed by precious stones; by the flame of the topaz, the violet of the amethyst or the green shade of the emerald; unless the vestments of the priests sparkle with gold; and unless the walls glisten with multi-coloured paintings and throw the reflection of the sun's rays upon the ceiling. These men, however, placing those things second which mortals foolishly esteem first, give all their diligence to improve their morals, and love pure minds more than glittering vestments; knowing that the best recompense for well-doing is to enjoy a clear conscience. Moreover, if at any time the laudable kindness of the abbot either desires, or feigns a desire to modify aught from the strict letter of the Rule, they are ready to oppose such indulgence, saying, that they have no long time to live, nor shall they continue to exist for as long a time as they have already done; that they hope to remain steadfast in their purpose to the end, and to be an example to their successors, who will transgress if they should give way. And indeed through human weakness, the perpetual law of which is that nothing attained, even by the greatest labour, can long remain unchanged, it will be so. But to sum up all the things which are or can be said of them, the Cistercians at the present day are a model for all monks, a mirror for the diligent, a spur to the indolent.

C. THE CHURCH IN ENGLAND 1154–1189

THE dominant theme in the history of the Church in England during this period is the long and dramatic struggle between Henry II and Thomas Becket culminating in the murder of the archbishop in Canterbury Cathedral on 29 December 1170. The relations between Henry II and the papacy in respect of Ireland also demand attention. And thirdly it is fortunate that various aspects of the medieval ecclesiastical polity were discussed at this time by so distinguished a writer as John of Salisbury.

(*a*) THOMAS BECKET AND HENRY II

The sources for the history of Thomas Becket are extremely voluminous and of unequal value. Since therefore it has here been necessary (for reason of space) to make a somewhat drastic selection from among them, it will be convenient at this place to note the general scope of this abundant testimony, and also to observe its varied character.

The Rolls Series edition of *Materials for the History of Thomas Becket, Archbishop of Canterbury* (ed. J. C. Robertson and J. B. Sheppard, 1875–1885) contains a great accumulation of material written in Latin about the archbishop by his contemporaries and writers of the next generation. This collection superseded that made by J. A. Giles (*Sanctus Thomas Cantuariensis*, 8 vols., London, 1845–1846). It comprises seven volumes of which vols. I–IV are mainly devoted to contemporary biographies of the archbishop, and vols. V–VII to the extensive contemporary correspondence which relates to him. The texts printed in this major work of scholarship are for the most part accurate and good, but much still remains to be done in respect of the dating of many of the documents. Forthcoming editions of the letters of Gilbert Foliot and John of Salisbury may be expected to do much to elucidate these questions.

In addition to the materials printed in Robertson's collection the chief contemporary chroniclers devote considerable space in their general histories to Thomas Becket's career, the principal sources in this respect being Gerald of Wales, William of Newburgh, Ralph 'de Diceto', Roger of Howden, and Gervase of Canterbury. Further biographical information may be obtained from certain foreign writers whose work will be noted below.

Among the earliest of the *Lives* of Thomas Becket in point of time was that written in French verse by *Garnier of Pont-Ste-Maxence*. He began this in the second year after the saint's martyrdom and finished it sometime between 1174 and 1175. He had seen Thomas in the flesh when as chancellor he took part in the continental campaign of Henry II of 1159–1160. After the martyrdom Garnier visited Canterbury, questioned those most intimate with the archbishop and also gleaned additional information from his sister, Mary, abbess of Barking. His sources were therefore reliable and he seems to have taken great pains to be accurate in his facts and to present a truthful portrait of Thomas and his work. He often corrected his writing when fresh information came to hand. By quaint, vivid touches it often adds to the knowledge derived from the Latin biographers. His poem is written in rhyming stanzas of five lines each and runs to 5,835 lines. It is an important source for the student of the

French language in the twelfth century. The most recent edition is that of E. Walberg (1922).

The eight Latin *Lives* are those by William fitz Stephen, Edward Grim, Herbert of Bosham, 'Roger of Pontigny', John of Salisbury, whose short account was supplemented by Alan of Tewkesbury, the so-called Anonymous of Lambeth, and William of Canterbury. To these should be added the *Passion of St. Thomas*, prefixed to the collection of the saint's miracles made by Benedict of Peterborough. All these biographies are strictly contemporary, with the possible exception of the Lambeth Anonymous, about whose work the opinions of scholars are divided. Many of the biographers were intimate with the archbishop at some period or other of his career. Comparison between them entails questions of great complexity which may best be studied in E. Walberg, *La tradition hagiographique de Saint Thomas Becket avant la fin du XII siècle* (Paris, 1929).

William fitz Stephen. From first to last he is an authority of the highest value and may perhaps be regarded as the best and most satisfying of the biographers. In his Prologue he sets down the character and circumstances of his relations with the archbishop. Strangely enough his *Life* is not mentioned by any other biographer and formed no part of the composite *Life* produced in 1220 and known as the *Quadrilogus*, but the internal evidence of its veracity is very strong. It was not made public until after the death of Henry II, by which time the last of the other *Lives* had been completed. It would appear that fitz Stephen was not very favourably regarded by the stricter partisans of the archbishop, possibly because, as he himself admits, he made his peace with Henry II soon after the martyrdom and subsequently rose high in the king's favour, being made sheriff of Gloucester and an itinerant justice. His *Life* is thin and meagre on the middle part of Becket's career, since he did not accompany his master into exile. On the other hand, he supplies some valuable data on what was happening in England at the time. His narrative is lively and interesting; he shows a sincere esteem and admiration for the archbishop's character as a stalwart champion of the Church, a dear friend and honoured master, and not least as a fellow-citizen of London.

Edward Grim was not one of the Canterbury monks, as was formerly supposed, but a secular clerk born at Cambridge. He had no previous acquaintance with the archbishop, but was a visitor come to Canterbury to see him on his return from exile. His presence at the martyrdom was thus fortuitous. The fact that he stood by the archbishop to the last, and received a blow from the sword of one of the knights which nearly severed his arm, constitutes his claim to enduring fame. Grim ever afterwards regarded Thomas with deep reverence and affection, and took the utmost pains to procure from the lips of the saint's companions an accurate record of his life. Grim's *Life* was probably written between 1171 and 1172. He himself was dead by 1187, a fact recorded by some of the other biographers.

Herbert of Bosham is the most voluminous of the biographers. He seems to have known little of Becket's early life, but became acquainted with him at least as early as his tenure of the chancellorship. From that point he accompanied his master in all his vicissitudes until a few days before the martyrdom, when he was sent by the archbishop overseas. He was therefore not an eyewitness of the tragedy in Canterbury Cathedral. His *Life* shows him to have been a bold, violent man, always prodigal in advice to the archbishop, and invariably inciting him to take the sternest measures against his enemies. After the martyrdom he seems to have resided abroad, devoting himself to the enrichment of the hagiography of the saint, his late master. He records many details of remarkable interest, writes with sympathy and zeal for the archbishop's cause, but is given to moralizing and to inserting long speeches into the mouths of the archbishop, of himself and others, probably of his own composition. Even contemporaries complained of his prolixity and egoism. He did not begin to compose his *Life* until most of the other biographies had been completed, and his work was finished in 1186 or 1187.

A *Life* of Becket has been ascribed to Roger, a monk of Pontigny, who is known to have acted as the archbishop's personal servant during his sojourn in that abbey. This identification was accepted by Freeman[1] but rejected by Robertson, who prints it in his collection under the title of 'Anonymous I'. The *Life* certainly emanates from Pontigny and may perhaps be tentatively regarded as the work of Roger. The writer has surprisingly little to say about Becket's sojourn there, but this may be explained by the circumstance that the author wrote primarily for the edification of the monks, and did not trouble to enlarge on matters that were familiar to them. It is much fuller and more valuable for the period of the exile which followed the archbishop's departure from Pontigny. It also presents a fairly full account of the saint's earlier years, probably derived from the mouth of the archbishop himself. The *Life* was composed about the year 1176. It has affinities with the French *Life* of Garnier, from whom many details and expressions are copied. It is cited below as *Roger of Pontigny*.

The short *Life* by *John of Salisbury* is little more than an essay on the character and policy of Becket cast in biographical form. Its brevity is regretted alike by John's contemporaries and by modern scholars. It should be remembered, however, that an admirable commentary on the stirring events of Thomas's career is to be found in John's correspondence.

John's *Life* was supplemented by *Alan of Tewkesbury*, a former canon of Benevento, who returned to England in 1174, became a monk of Christ Church, Canterbury, and prior there in 1179. In 1189 he was elected abbot of Tewkesbury, where he died in 1202. He was therefore not personally acquainted with St. Thomas but, as a monk of Canterbury, he had good opportunities of acquiring trustworthy information, which he used to good purpose. His supplement was composed between 1176 and 1180 and covers the period from the council of Clarendon in January 1164 to the conference of Montmirail in January 1169.

The *Anonymous of Lambeth* ('Anonymous II' in Robertson's edition) is a *Life* preserved in a unique MS. in Lambeth Palace Library. It is by no means certain that it is a contemporary work, although the author speaks in his preface of having witnessed the martyrdom. If it is contemporary, it may be regarded as of some value, since, to quote Freeman,[2] "it is written in a tone of unusually independent criticism and has fewer coincidences with other *Lives* than any one in the series. It states the case for Henry and against Thomas with great fullness and fairness."

Last of the Latin biographies are the works of the two Canterbury monks. *William of Canterbury* first became a monk of Christ Church during the archbishop's exile and was invested with his habit and ordained deacon by Thomas on his return. He was present at the martyrdom and afterwards appears to have held an official position in connexion with the martyr's tomb and the entertainment of the pilgrims who visited it. Hence he was in a good position to make a collection of the miracles

[1] Freeman, 'St. Thomas of Canterbury', reprinted in *Historical Essays*, 1st Series (London, 1871, and later editions), p. 90.
[2] *ibid.*, p. 93.

wrought there. This he presented to the king. Later he wrote a *Life* of the saint, which embodies the picture of Thomas as the head and champion of the monks of Christ Church, who by his martyrdom had conferred such signal fame upon the abbey.

The *Passion of St. Thomas* by *Benedict, abbot of Peterborough*, was completed in 1171 or 1172. It therefore stands first in chronological order among original sources. At this time Benedict was a monk of Christ Church; in 1175 he became prior, and in 1177 he was elected abbot of Peterborough. He died in 1193.

There remain to be considered two later compilations which either embody, or are based on, earlier material. The first of these is the *Quadrilogus* or Quadripartite History, begun in 1198–1199 and reshaped by Roger of Croyland in 1212–1213, who augmented the original version by including part of the Becket correspondence. This second edition was presented to Archbishop Stephen Langton on the occasion of the Translation of St. Thomas in 1220. The *Quadrilogus* is a digest of the material made available in the *Lives* of *four* authors mentioned above (hence the name given to the work), namely John of Salisbury, Alan of Tewkesbury, William of Canterbury and Herbert of Bosham. It is still useful for purposes of comparison, but as a source it has now been largely superseded by the recovery and publication of the original *Lives* from which it was compiled, and also of those by other authors not included, Edward Grim, William fitz Stephen and 'Roger of Pontigny'. It is the earlier version of the *Quadrilogus* which is printed in Robertson, *op. cit.*, vol. IV, pp. 269–430.

The second compilation is that of the *Icelandic Thomas Saga*, a composite work constructed from authentic records of the archbishop's history and translated from Latin into the Icelandic tongue. It is based mainly on the account of Benedict of Peterborough and a late twelfth-century *Life* by *Robert of Cricklade*, prior of St. Frideswide, Oxford, no longer extant. In its completed fourteenth-century form the saga contains some interesting descriptions of the saint's personality and character, though it adds hardly anything to our knowledge of the facts of his life. It is also interesting as illustrating how the fame of the martyred archbishop spread to the most distant lands. In fact it secured for him in Iceland a popularity which eclipsed that of every other Christian saint. The saga is printed, together with a translation, in the Rolls Series under the title *Thomas Saga Erkibyskups*, edited by E. Magnússon (2 vols., 1875–1883).

So far as the main story of the archbishop's life is concerned, the measure of agreement between the narratives is remarkable and impressive. Nevertheless, there is much discrepancy and contradiction on points of detail. On the other hand, there is often a minute or verbal agreement between two or more writers, which suggests that they copied from each other or from a common source. Occasionally differences occur in respect of the sequence of events or the identity of the speakers in the various councils, conferences or conversations recorded. But the common ground between them is far greater than the discrepancies.

The contemporary chroniclers mentioned above[1] provide useful correctives or supplementation to the biographies. They are especially of service in helping to establish a more exact chronology of the events which took place in England during the archbishop's exile, where the biographers are often either silent altogether or make erroneous statements.

William of Newburgh, wrote Freeman,[2] "is chiefly remarkable for the manly and

[1] See above, p. 103.

[2] Freeman, *op. cit.*, p. 94; for Newburgh's narrative, see above, pp. 331–333, 336–339.

independent tone with which he treats the whole controversy, doing full justice to the originally honest motives of both the king and the primate, but not scrupling to deal severe censure on particular actions of both". Ralph 'de Diceto' supplies some important facts not found in the biographies and a more or less correct chronological arrangement. His attitude generally is that of a moderate partisan of the king. The *Gesta Regis Henrici Secundi* does not begin until 1170, the year of Becket's martyrdom, and gives only a short and mainly second-hand account of this cardinal event. Roger of Howden and Gervase of Canterbury were both younger contemporaries, largely dependent on the biographies. Gervase, however, as a Canterbury monk and possibly an eyewitness of the murder, had access to good sources of information.

Finally in this survey of materials come the letters and State-papers contained in Robertson's last three volumes. It would be almost impossible to exaggerate the importance of the Becket correspondence, both as a source of factual information and as providing in many cases insight into the minds of the writers and of their correspondents. Moreover, only through them can the student of the period get a true idea of the ramifications of the controversy between king and primate and its repercussions throughout Europe. More especially is this the case in respect of the difficulties and embarrassment caused to Pope Alexander III and the papal *curia* during Becket's long exile on the Continent.

The translations of the majority of the pieces given below are independent, but mention must be made of two works which have afforded guidance in this respect to the editors. These are *The Life and Letters of Thomas Becket* by J. A. Giles (2 vols., London, 1846), and W. H. Hutton, *St. Thomas of Canterbury from Contemporary Biographers and other Chroniclers* (2nd ed., London, 1899).

Most of the original authorities cited above relate to all phases of Becket's stormy career. In view of the complexity of the testimony (and its bulk) it has here, however, been deemed advisable to group the material under four sub-headings relating respectively to: (i) Thomas Becket's chancellorship and his election as archbishop; (ii) his disputes with Henry II between 1162 and November 1164; (iii) the period of his exile, November 1164–1170; and (iv) his murder and its sequel.

(i) *Thomas Becket as chancellor and archbishop*

119. William fitz Stephen on Thomas Becket as chancellor and archbishop

Printed: J. C. Robertson and J. B. Sheppard, *Materials for the History of Thomas Becket, Archbishop of Canterbury*, vol. III (1878), p. 1.

To the glory of Almighty God and in perpetual memory of the blessed Thomas, and to the profit and edification of all who read and hear it, I, William fitz Stephen, have undertaken to write the life and passion of the said Thomas, the good archbishop and martyr. I was the fellow-citizen of my lord, his chaplain and a member of his household, called by his mouth to share his cares. I was his remembrancer[1] in his chancery; in chapel, when he celebrated, I was subdeacon; when he sat to hear causes, I was the reader of the letters and documents put forward and, at his command, sometimes the advocate[2] in certain causes. I was present with him at the council of Northampton,[3] where matters of great moment were debated; I was a witness of his

[1] *dictator*. [2] *patronus*. [3] See below, No. 129.

passion at Canterbury, and many other things which are here written I saw with my eyes and heard with my ears; others I learnt from the relation of those who were cognizant of them. . . .[1]

. . . The Lord knew and predestined the blessed Thomas before ever he issued from the womb, and revealed to his mother what manner of man he would be. For during pregnancy she saw in a dream that she carried in her womb the whole church of Canterbury. As soon as the child saw the light of day, the midwife lifted him up in her arms, saying, "I have raised from the ground a future archbishop." Whilst he was still a babe lying in his cradle, his mother dreamed that she rebuked the nurse for not putting a coverlet over him. The nurse replied, "Nay, my lady, he has the best of coverlets." "Show it to me," said her mistress. The nurse brought it and showed it her, but when she tried to unfold it, she could not do so and said to the mother, "It is too large for me to spread over the bed." Whereupon the mother answered, "Come into the hall and unfold it there." The nurse tried hard to do so but failed and said, "I simply cannot unfold the whole of it here." The astonished mother then said, "Go out into the market-place, which is now empty, and no doubt you will succeed in unfolding it there." But neither could the nurse do so there, whereupon she exclaimed, "The coverlet is so large that I cannot find the end of it; methinks all England would be too small for it to cover."[2]

Thomas, then, was born in lawful wedlock and of honourable parents, his father being Gilbert, sometime sheriff of London, and his mother Matilda. Both were citizens of London, of the middle class, not making money by usury nor engaged in business, but living respectably on their income.[3]

That his father received some divine intimation concerning his future we may learn from this. The father commended him while still a child to Robert, prior of the canons of Merton,[4] to be educated in their religious house. One day the father came to see his son. When the boy was brought into the presence of the prior and his father, the latter fell prone before him worshipping him. Indignantly the prior exclaimed, "O crazy old man, what doest thou? Dost fall at thy son's feet? The honour thou doest to him, he should rather do to thee." To whom the father answered in secret, "My lord, I know what I do: that boy will be great in the sight of the Lord."

So Thomas spent his years of infancy, boyhood, and adolescence in simplicity in his father's house and the schools of the city. When he was grown to manhood he studied at Paris, and on his return took part in the affairs of the city of London, being

[1] Here follows William fitz Stephen's famous description of the city of London, which is given in the present work below, No. 281.

[2] An anecdote typical of the legends which afterwards grew up round the birth and boyhood of Thomas.

[3] Thomas was born on 21 December 1118, and was so named after the apostle commemorated on that day. Gilbert, his father, was certainly of Norman birth and, according to the *Anonymous of Lambeth* (Robertson, *op. cit.*, vol. IV (1879), p. 81), a native of Rouen. His mother, who is named *Roesa* (Rose) by the *Anonymous of Lambeth*, is stated to have been born at Caen. Both parents of Thomas were therefore Norman, sprung from the burgher class; there is no evidence to support the contention of Lord Lyttelton (*Life of Henry II* (1777 ed.), vol. II, p. 310) and H. Thierry, *History of the Norman Conquest of England* (Everyman ed., vol. II, p. 59) that Gilbert was of Saxon race. The assertion that Thomas's mother was a noble Saracen lady, though repeated by Giles (*Life and Letters of Thomas Becket*, vol. I (1846), pp. 10–22), is now recognized as mere legend.

[4] In Surrey. Prior Robert attended Thomas in his last hours at Canterbury; see below, pp. 766, n. 2, 769, n. 4.

made clerk and accountant to the sheriffs.[1] In this employment he conducted himself in a manner worthy of all praise, and acquired such a knowledge of the world that in after-life he had no difficulty in managing with caution and prudence the common interests of the Church in England and the public affairs of the kingdom, which he dispatched in a grand and efficient style. . . .

As his years and virtues increased, he entered the household of Theobald, archbishop of Canterbury of blessed memory, having been brought to his notice by two brethren of Bologna, Baldwin the archdeacon, and Master Eustace,[2] frequently his father's guests and well acquainted with the archbishop. Thus he became the more intimate with him because the said Gilbert used to converse with the lord archbishop concerning their neighbourhood and their kinsfolk, the latter being by origin a Norman of knightly birth from the neighbouring town of Thierceville. Through the introductions of these men and of his father the archbishop numbered Thomas among his flock, and thereafter found him valiant and worthy. He came first to the archbishop's court at the town of Harrow with only a single squire, Ralph of London. . . . In the archbishop's court there were some great and extremely learned clerks, many of whom the archbishop afterwards promoted to bishoprics in England, and one of them, Roger of Pont-l'Evêque, to the archbishopric of York.[3] In comparison with these men Thomas was not so well learned, but he was greatly superior to them in character and strove to direct his mind to goodness and wisdom, so that, while still inferior to them in learning, he might appear the more acceptable and conspicuous by his virtues; later indeed he became a most accomplished scholar. . . .[4] Soon, perceiving his diligence, the archbishop on several occasions sent him to Rome on business for the Church of England, where, with God's help, he conducted himself prudently and was received in high favour by the pope and the holy Roman Church.

Thomas was handsome and pleasing of countenance, tall of stature, with a prominent and slightly aquiline nose, nimble and active in his movements, gifted with eloquence of speech and an acute intelligence, high-spirited, ever pursuing the path of highest virtue, amiable to all men, compassionate towards the poor and the oppressed, resisting the proud, zealous for the promotion of his fellows, not from any insincerity, but out of pure courtesy and kindness,[5] and aiming to secure the respect of all good men. He was liberal and witty, ever on his guard against deceiving men or being deceived by them, at once a prudent child of this world and destined to become a child of light.[6]

[1] *Vicecomitum clericus et rationalis effectus;* this would seem to be identical with the service in the household of Osbern, a man eminent in the city of London, mentioned in the *Lives* of Edward Grim, 'Roger of Pontigny' and Garnier.

[2] Both Baldwin and Eustace were eminent 'civilians' then on a mission to the archbishop of Canterbury.

[3] In 1147.

[4] The short passage here omitted refers to the spite and jealousy shown by Roger against Thomas; cf. 'Roger of Pontigny', *Materials for the History of Thomas Becket*, vol. IV (1879), p. 9.

[5] *non ficte sed officiose.*

[6] This character sketch may be compared with the tradition of the young Thomas preserved in the Icelandic saga (Trans. E. Magnússon, Rolls Series, vol. I, p. 29): "He was now two and twenty years of age, slim of growth and pale of hue, dark of hair with a long nose and straightly featured face; blithe of countenance was he, keen of thought, winning and lovable in all conversation, frank of speech in his discourse, but slightly stuttering in his talk, so keen of discernment that he could always make difficult questions plain after a wise manner. Of such wondrously strong memory was he that whatsoever he had heard of sentence and law-awards he could cite it at any time he chose to give it forth."

His first preferment he had at the gift of John, bishop of Worcester,[1] namely the church of St. Mary-le-Strand. Afterwards, on the presentation of the archbishop, he obtained the church of Otford.[2] Yet later he held a prebend at St. Paul's in London and another at Lincoln. Then, after leave to sojourn abroad had been given him by his lord, the archbishop, he studied law for a year at Bologna[3] and afterwards at Auxerre. In process of time, and as a result of his virtues, the archbishop ordained him deacon and made him archdeacon of Canterbury,[4] which is the highest and most dignified office in the Church of the English after those of the bishops and abbots, and was worth to him a hundred pounds of silver.

After Henry II, king of the English, had been crowned at the hands of the said archbishop, through the good offices and recommendation of the latter[5] and at the instigation of the noble Henry, bishop of Winchester,[6] Thomas was made chancellor in preference to all others. Being a man of diligence and industry, revolving great matters in his mind and experienced in many and great affairs, he so discharged the onerous duties and obligations of the office to the praise of God and the well-being of the whole realm, that it may be regarded as doubtful whether he served the king with greater distinction and efficiency or to greater advantage in peace or in war.

The chancellor of England has so exalted a dignity that he is accounted next after the king in the realm.[7] He has the custody of the royal seal, and seals his own orders with the obverse thereof; he is in charge of the order and arrangement of the king's chapel; he takes into his keeping all vacant archbishoprics, bishoprics, abbeys and baronies that fall into the king's hands; he takes his seat in all the king's councils and may enter there even when not summoned. Everything is signed by his clerk, who bears the king's seal, and everything is ordered by the advice of the chancellor; so that if, by God's grace, the virtues of his life should procure it for him, he may himself be made an archbishop or bishop before his death if he so please. . . .

In his consecration [as archbishop] he [Thomas Becket] was anointed with the visible unction of God's mercy. Putting off the secular man, he now put on Jesus Christ. He vacated the secular duties of the chancellorship[8] and was at pains to fulfil the functions of a good archbishop. To this end he kept a strict watch over his mind. His speech was grave and to the edification of his hearers; his works were those of mercy and piety; his decisions in conformity with justice and equity. Clad in a

[1] John of Pagham, bishop of Worcester, 1151–1158.

[2] In Kent.

[3] Where Gratian, the learned canonist, was then lecturing. It was customary for archdeacons to study civil and canon law abroad; cf. W. Stubbs, *Lectures on Medieval and Modern History* (1886), pp. 302–303.

[4] In succession to his enemy, Roger of Pont-l'Evêque.

[5] For Archbishop Theobald's motive in urging the appointment of Becket as chancellor, see 'Roger of Pontigny', *Materials for the History of Thomas Becket*, vol. IV (1879), p. 11: "It seemed to him [the archbishop] that if he could make Thomas a partner of the king's counsels, there might ensue therefrom the utmost peace and tranquillity for the English Church. For he knew him to be a man of high character and prudence, possessing zeal for God according to his lights and striving with all his heart to preserve the freedom of the Church." A similar interpretation is given by John of Salisbury, *ibid.*, vol. II (1876), p. 304.

[6] See above, Nos. 8, 10, 114, for his earlier career.

[7] See above, No. 30. This description of the chancellorship is of great interest, but it may be suspected that the author exaggerated the importance of the office at this time.

[8] Thomas resigned the chancellorship almost immediately upon his consecration as archbishop; much to the disappointment and chagrin of the king, who had intended he should retain his secular office.

hair-shirt of the roughest kind, which reached to his knees and swarmed with vermin, he mortified his flesh with the sparest diet, and his accustomed drink was water used for cooking of hay. He was always, however, the first to taste the wine before giving it to those who sat at table with him; he ate some of the meat that was placed before him, but chiefly fed on bread. Yet all things are pure to the pure, and it is the appetite, not the food, which is to blame. He often exposed his naked back to the lash of discipline. Immediately over his hair-shirt he wore the habit of a monk, as being abbot of the monks of Canterbury;[1] above this he wore the garb of a canon[2] so as to conform to the custom of clerks. But the stole, the emblem of the sweet yoke of Christ, was ever day and night around his neck. His outward visage was like to that of ordinary men, but within all was different. In this he took as his pattern St. Sebastian and St. Cecilia, the former of whom under cover of a warrior's cloak conducted himself as a soldier of Christ, whilst the latter, mortifying the flesh with sackcloth, appeared outwardly adorned with vesture of gold. In food and clothing alike he endeavoured to be more devout than he appeared. Intent on prayer, he strove to reconcile, and in some measure to unite his soul to the Holy Spirit, his Creator. Constituted, as it were, a mediator between God and man, in his prayers he commended men to God, while in his preaching he interpreted God to men. He was diligent in reading the Scriptures and had a learned man to instruct him in its sacred pages. Sometimes after dinner he would converse with his fellows, hearing them and asking them questions.[3] He chose devout men for his companions at table, and virtuous and learned men for his clerks. Likewise he had a select household, devoted to showing hospitality and respect to all good men. In almsgiving he was most liberal, sometimes sending four or five marks to hospitals and poorhouses, at other times meat and provisions. . . .

Furthermore, he entertained in his house the outcast and the needy; he clothed many against the severity of winter. At Canterbury he received many of them in person, sitting in the cloisters like one of his monks, studying some large volume; afterwards he would go and visit the monks who were sick, in order to learn their wants and fulfil their desires. He was the consoler of the oppressed, the husband of the widow, the friend of orphans. He was, besides, humble and amiable to the gentle, but stern to the proud. Against the injustice and insolence of the mighty he was strong like the lofty tower in Damascus, nor did the letters or entreaties of the king himself in favour of any man avail aught with him, if they were contrary to justice.

The purity of his life was now perfect, seeing that even as chancellor he had not exceeded the bounds of chastity and honour. He was like a second Moses, continually entering and issuing from the tabernacle of the Lord, entering it at the accepted time to contemplate God and issuing therefrom to perform some pious action for his neighbours. Like another Jacob at one time he was united to the fruitful Leah, at another he clung to the embraces of the fairer Rachel. He was like one of the angels

[1] *i.e.* Christ Church.

[2] In his youth at the abbey of Merton, Thomas had first assumed the habit of the Augustinian canons, but there is no record of his ever having been professed as a monk. During his exile at Pontigny he also assumed the Cistercian cowl; see below, p. 740.

[3] Luke ii. 46.

of God on the ladder, whose top reached to heaven, now descending to relieve the necessities of men, now ascending to gaze upon the divine Majesty and heavenly splendour. Holding himself aloof from earthly and transitory things, he strove with all his might to gain the things of heaven. He was occupied with the virtues which both sanctify this present life and win for us the life eternal. The queen of his life was reason, which governed his covetous desires and evil impulses as a mistress rules her maidens. Under her guidance he was led on to virtue, which cherishes itself and spurns everything opposed to it: deriving its origin from itself, it returns to itself again, and embracing all within itself, seeks nothing elsewhere. He possessed four species of virtue: prudence, which gave him discernment in the recognition of things, in the estimate of character and the judgment of time and place, in the avoidance of evil men and in the choice of good; justice, whereby he was zealous to preserve to God and his neighbour what he possessed himself; fortitude, which vindicates a man in adversity and protects him from the pain of present evils and the fear of those to come; temperance, which did not allow him to pass the bounds of moderation in prosperity, which restrained him from all licentiousness and covetousness of this world's goods and unwonted indulgence in dissipation. . . .

This blessed state of life Archbishop Thomas consistently cultivated; in all his actions he displayed constancy, sublimity, gravity and honesty. All things he referred to the test of wisdom; to govern himself, to stand by the judgment of wisdom, not of the crowd; not to fear the snares of fortune; to show himself fenced and fortified and impregnable against adversity; to believe himself born not for himself, but for all who needed his help, especially his own church, whose rule he had undertaken; to contemplate the divine even in the midst of earth; to imitate Jesus Christ, who was born and came down to suffer for mankind; to love him dearly and to keep his commands, and to win salvation for his own soul and those committed to his charge. Whence it came to pass that he found favour in God's sight and secure fame among men. All good men consented to his praise, judging well of him with uncorrupt lips. This it is which rightly responds to virtue, as the echo answers to the voice and the image corresponds to its model. Since glory is the companion of those who live well, so it is not to be sought by them, neither is it to be rejected, but to be ascribed to God. The apostle saith, "For though I would desire to glory, I shall not be a fool; for I will say the truth."[1] Thomas feared this glory and rejected it, lest perchance pride should steal in, remembering it is written, "However just you be, you can never be secure." There is also another vain and false glory, which the proud and vain, rich men and hypocrites, seek, a specious likeness of true glory, but with no solid virtue to commend it. To the eye indeed it appears like unto it, but it is not so in reality. As the righteous fear the glory of true praise, so do evil men court this false glory; or, even if they have done righteously, by seeking to win for it praise or reward, they lose thereby both the title and the merit of virtue.

The glorious Archbishop Thomas, contrary to the expectation of the king and all men, so utterly abandoned the world and so suddenly experienced that conversion, which is the finger of God, that all men marvelled thereat.

[1] II Corinthians xii. 6.

120. Herbert of Bosham on the appointment of Thomas Becket as archbishop

Printed: *Materials for the History of Thomas Becket*, vol. III, p. 180.

After these things, while our Thomas far outshone all others at the king's court in renown and in the king's favour, and had already taken charge of the chief business of the State, Theobald, archbishop of Canterbury, a man of transparent sanctity and true religion, who had served both as chariot and charioteer for our Thomas, who also had ruled the church of Canterbury well and wisely for two-and-twenty years and was now an old man and full of days, went the appointed way of all flesh.[1] When news of this reached the king and the courtiers, straightway all mer indulged in conjecture; some whispered and others openly affirmed that the chancellor was destined to become the successor to the dead archbishop; the people also proclaimed the same thing. But the king wholly dissembled his intention, save that the archbishopric was handed over to the care and custody of the chancellor, as was customary in the case of vacant bishoprics and abbacies. The chancellor, however, who from certain forebodings and conjectures already had an inkling of the king's purpose, kept silence about the matter, even as the king concealed his intentions. But when the king was absent from the realm overseas and the chancellor with him, he arranged to send him back to England on account of the frequent incursions of the Welsh and certain other affairs of State. And because the latter were many and of great moment, and no other servant of his was fitted for so responsible a task, he gave the mission to the chancellor. Having received his instructions some days earlier, on the eve of his departure Thomas came to court at the castle of Falaise in Normandy to pay his respects to the king before starting out on his journey. Calling him aside, the king spake to him privately, saying, "You do not yet fully comprehend the reason for your mission." And he added, "It is my intention that you should become archbishop of Canterbury." To whom the chancellor replied, looking down and pointing with a smile at the gay attire he was wearing, "How religious, how saintly, is the man whom you would appoint to that holy see and over so renowned and pious a body of monks.[2] I know of a truth that, should God so dispose it, you would speedily turn your face away from me, and the love which is now so great between us would be changed into the most bitter hatred. I know indeed that you would make many demands–for already you presume overmuch in ecclesiastical affairs–which I could never bear with equanimity. And so the envious would find occasion to stir up endless strife between us."[3]

[1] 18 April 1161.

[2] The abbey of Christ Church.

[3] Cf. John of Salisbury (*Materials for the History of Thomas Becket*, vol. II (1876), p. 305): "Being a man of great experience and well accustomed to measure the future, he weighed carefully the dangers of so great a charge, for by long familiarity he had learned what the burden and the honour of that office really were. For he had grown to know the character of the king and the wickedness and obstinacy of his officials, and how effective was the malice of informers at court. From these considerations he rightly drew the conclusion that, if he accepted the post offered to him, he would lose either the favour of God or that of the king. For he could not cleave to God and obey the royal will, or give precedence to the laws of the saints without making an enemy of the king."

121. 'Roger of Pontigny' on the election of Thomas Becket as archbishop

Printed: *Materials for the History of Thomas Becket*, vol. IV, p. 14.

About the same time, on the death of Theobald, archbishop of Canterbury, the king designed to make Thomas his successor, for he judged him to be most worthy of so great an honour and trusted that he would be fully prepared to do his will and consult his interests in everything. For Thomas had made a point of showing great severity towards the persons and interests of ecclesiastics in order by this means to remove all mark of suspicion from himself and, under cover thereof, to meet more easily the king's wishes, of which he had intimate knowledge. The king, therefore, believed that his design against the Church could be most effectively carried out through Thomas, whom indeed he had found by experience was most loyal to him in everything and well disposed to his wishes. Accordingly he took the irrevocable decision to promote him archbishop of Canterbury.

The king therefore sent two bishops[1] [to Canterbury], accompanied by a certain trusty magnate of his named Richard of Lucé, giving them letters of mandate to convene the chapter of Canterbury for the election of an archbishop. Arriving at Canterbury, they entered the chapter-house, and having first expatiated at great length on the generosity and condescension of the king, they charged Richard of Lucé with the delivery of the royal mandate, who thereupon addressed the assembly as follows: "Since the lord bishops have signified their pleasure that I should declare unto you the king's wishes, be it known of a truth to all of you, that our lord, the king, as you have already heard from the bishops, is most zealous in everything which concerns the things of God and displays the utmost devotion towards holy Church, especially towards this church of Canterbury, which he recognizes in all humility, loyalty and filial affection as his particular mother in the Lord. Wherefore, that she be not in any way oppressed or thrown into disorder by remaining long bereft of a shepherd, be it known to you that the king accords you full freedom of election, provided, however, that you choose a man worthy of so great an office and equal to the burden thereof. For it is not unknown to you that our lord, the king, is wont to endeavour nothing in such a matter save what he believes to be well-pleasing to God and profitable to his Church. For the rest, then, it is incumbent on you, and wholly expedient, to elect one under whose protection you may rejoice before God and men. For if king and archbishop be joined together in the bond of affection and cherish each other in all friendship, there is no doubt that the times will be happy and the Church will preserve her estate in joy and tranquillity. But if, which God forbid, things should turn out otherwise, the dangers and confusion, the labours and tumults, and, in the end, the loss of property and the peril to souls which may result therefrom, are not, I imagine, hidden from your reverences."

When Richard had made an end of speaking and the bishops had declared their approval, the prior of Canterbury[2] first gave thanks to God and then with due

[1] According to Gervase of Canterbury (ed. W. Stubbs, Rolls Series, vol. I, p. 169) the royal commissioners were Hilary, bishop of Chichester, Bartholomew, bishop of Exeter, Walter, bishop of Rochester, Walter, abbot of Battle, and his brother, the justiciar, Richard of Lucé.

[2] Named Guibert, according to Gervase of Canterbury, *loc. cit., ante*.

reverence expressed his deep gratitude to the king for his kindness and solicitude on their behalf. And so, with the permission of the bishops, he summoned to him certain of the older and wiser monks and retired with them. But after they had been in session together to consider the message they had received, they came to the conclusion that nothing could be decided without the advice of Richard of Lucé and the bishops, who were fully acquainted with the king's wishes, on which the whole question of the election must depend. Accordingly they now called in the royal commissioners, namely Bartholomew, bishop of Exeter, Hilary, bishop of Chichester, and Richard.[1] And when the latter had entered and discussed the proposed election with the monks at some length, they all, both monks and bishops, with one voice and one mind elected the chancellor to be the shepherd and bishop of their souls. The monks indeed had for some time hesitated over the election, not because they failed to recognize that Thomas was a virtuous man, but because he did not wear the habit of religion;[2] for up to that time the church of Canterbury had almost always had for pastors men who wore the religious habit and observed the monastic rule. For St. Augustine, the monk sent by the blessed and apostolic Pope Gregory, who first preached the faith of Christ to the English people, settled and established the church of Canterbury and many others in these parts under regular and monastic discipline, and this custom had hitherto been more carefully observed in the church of Canterbury than elsewhere, especially in the choice of an archbishop. Nevertheless, when the monks came to set this feature which they disliked in the character of their choice against the other virtues and graces which shone so brightly in him, they unanimously elected him with one heart and will.

The bishops, therefore, whom the king had sent for this purpose, appointed a day for the prior and monks of Canterbury to meet them in London, in order that whatever remained necessary to complete the formalities of the election might be publicly performed before all the bishops and abbots of the realm and in the presence of the young king.[3] For the king, his father, had now given over his kingdom to him and, as stated above, had caused the homage and fealty of the realm to be paid to him at the hand of his chancellor. The king had also written to him about the election to the archbishopric of Canterbury, signifying that whatever might be done in that matter in his son's presence, he would himself consent to, confirm and ratify for all time. Accordingly, the aforesaid bishops, by virtue of the king's mandate, summoned all the bishops and abbots of the realm, together with the priors of the conventual churches, the earls and magnates and all the king's officers of State to assemble in London on the appointed day. When that day came and they were all gathered together, the prior of Canterbury reverently manifested, in the presence and hearing of all the bishops, the form of election which had taken place at Canterbury with the

[1] See above, p. 675, n. 1.

[2] Thomas being a secular clerk, Edward Grim gives the subsequent dispute between the monks and the archbishop on this point: "When the monks began to murmur that, contrary to custom, he came to the choir in the garb of a secular priest, one of his household, reproving him, declared that there had stood before him a man of terrible countenance, who commanded him in threatening words, 'Go, tell the chancellor (from indignation he did not use the name of archbishop) that he change his habit without delay, for if he refuse to do so, I will go against him all the days of his life.'" (*Materials for the History of Thomas Becket*, vol. II (1876), p. 368.)

[3] The younger Henry.

king's consent and by his mandate before the three bishops whom he had dispatched for that very purpose; affirming that by the inspiration of the Holy Spirit Thomas, the chancellor of the realm, had been unanimously and canonically elected archbishop. The bishops also, who had been sent by the king and had witnessed the election at Canterbury, were warm in their commendation both of the form of the election and of the person of the elect, whereupon all present gave their assent and with one accord raised their voices to God in thanksgiving.

Only Gilbert Foliot, bishop of London,[1] opposed and murmured against the election, but when he saw that the others were unanimous in their assent and that of his own malice he could effect nothing, he likewise gave his consent. He was a man advanced in years, of considerable learning, and a monk by profession, who by repute had himself long since aspired to the archbishopric. After this the bishops in a body drew near to the young king to beg his consent and favour to the election; with great joy he praised their action and gave his favour and assent. Moreover, the great officers of State (to whom the king had also written on the subject) hailed the election with great joy and devotion. But Henry, bishop of Winchester, famous no less for his lineage than for his prudence and piety, thus addressed the young king: "The lord chancellor, our archbishop-elect, has now for a long time enjoyed the highest place in the household of the king, your father, and in the whole realm, which he has entirely under his governance, nor has anything been done in the kingdom during his time save at his command. We demand therefore that he shall be handed over to us and God's Church free and absolved from all ties and service to the court, and from all suits, accusations or any other charges, and that from this hour and henceforward he may be at liberty and leisure to pursue freely the service of God. For we know full well that the king, your father, has delegated his authority to you in this matter, and will gladly ratify whatever you shall do therein." The young king willingly accepted this petition and released Thomas freely and absolutely from all secular obligations[2] in accordance with the bishop of Winchester's request. But Thomas himself, from the first moment that his promotion was mooted, opposed it by every means in his power; knowing full well that it was impossible for him to serve two masters at once, whose wills were so much at variance, and that whoever was made archbishop of Canterbury would be sure soon to offend either God or the king. Nevertheless, God had ordained otherwise, and Henry of Pisa, cardinal-priest and legate of the apostolic see, and a monk of the Cistercian Order, encouraged and urged him by every means to undertake the office. So finally his election was completed in the way we have briefly described.

On the day fixed for the consecration the bishops assembled at Canterbury and with them an immense number of abbots, monks and clergy of the land, desirous of being present at the consecration of the archbishop and of hearing his first Mass and receiving his blessing. Thomas also arrived, attended by a large body of monks and other religious personages. The bishops went out to meet him, together with the

[1] This is an error; Gilbert was at this time still bishop of Hereford; he was translated to London in March 1163.

[2] This release from all obligations to the king was instanced by Thomas when cited later at Northampton; see below, p. 730.

monks and clergy and a vast concourse of the people, acclaiming him with heartfelt joy and high honour; so great was their devotion and exultation that it cannot be expressed in words. But Thomas paid no heed to these manifestations, but advanced on foot with great humility and contrition, the tears flowing from his eyes, as he thought less of the honour vouchsafed to him than of the burden imposed on him. So he was ordained and consecrated archbishop[1] at the hands of the venerable Henry, bishop of Winchester. . . . It was in the eighth year of the king's reign that Thomas was consecrated archbishop of Canterbury.

* * *

(ii) *The disputes between Henry II and Thomas Becket* (1162–*November* 1164)

These disputes began with arguments respecting payment of the sheriff's aid, and the matter was debated at the council of Woodstock (July 1163). There followed the much more serious disagreement respecting jurisdiction over "criminous clerks". This was outlined in the case of Philip 'de Brois' (No. 123), and further argued at the council of Westminster (October 1163) (No. 124). It remained unsettled and reappeared in the heated discussions at the council of Clarendon (January 1164), where the issue broadened into a controversy respecting the whole question of the relations between the spiritual and temporal authorities. The Constitutions of Clarendon (1164) (No. 126) are of cardinal importance on this matter, and the magnitude of the issues involved, together with the rising temper of the disputants, was displayed in the debates at the council of Northampton (October 1164) (No. 129). Thomas Becket went into exile immediately afterwards.

122. William fitz Stephen on the beginning of the disputes between Henry II and Thomas Becket

Printed: *Materials for the History of Thomas Becket*, vol. III, p. 41.

The ancient enemy was envious of so erect a pillar in the Church of the Lord, of so bright a candle on God's candlestick. The enemy sowed tares. First he took from the archbishop the king's goodwill, inasmuch as the latter regarded it as an affront that the man whom he had first made chancellor and then archbishop should now withdraw from his obedience[2] and withstand him in many things. The king's courtiers, seeking to win his favour and itching to gain his ear, defamed the archbishop and hated him without a cause. This was the first occasion of hostility against him. There were joined to the king and the courtiers in this strife many bishops, for fear of losing their land and goods. The archbishop was deprived of their counsel and aid. The indignation of the king and of the nobility of the realm was increased by the archbishop's attempt to recover from Roger of Clare, the earl,[3] the castle of Tonbridge and the whole honour, formerly alienated from the church of Canterbury; because according to law his predecessors and the patrons[4] of the church were permitted to

[1] 2 June 1162. He was ordained priest by Walter, bishop of Rochester, the previous day; his consecration took place on Trinity Sunday, a festival instituted by Thomas to mark the day, the observance of which was extended to the whole Western Church by Pope John XXII in the fourteenth century. The claim of Roger, archbishop of York, to the right of participating in the ceremony was disallowed on the ground that he had not yet professed obedience to the see of Canterbury.

[2] A reference to Thomas's resignation of the chancellorship; see above, p. 705.

[3] See Table 11.

[4] *oeconomis ecclesiae.*

care for and increase the estate, but not to diminish or alienate it. Moreover, almost all the nobility of England were kin to the said earl, and his sister was more beautiful than any lady in the land, and the king had at one time passionately loved her. Nevertheless the archbishop had previously obtained leave from the king to reclaim for the church of Canterbury the property wrongfully alienated by his predecessors or usurped by laymen. Likewise the church of Eynsford had been bestowed by the archbishop on a certain clerk named Laurence, for he had the right to present to vacant churches on the estates of his barons and of the monks of Canterbury. The lord of the township, William of Eynsford,[1] objecting, expelled Laurence's men; the archbishop then excommunicated him. The king straightway wrote to the archbishop that he should absolve him. The archbishop replied that it was not the king's place to give order either to absolve or excommunicate any man. The king contended that it pertained to his royal prerogative that no one who held of him in chief should be excommunicated, without his being consulted.[2] At length to pacify the king, who was by now hotly enraged against him and would hold no converse with him except through envoys, the archbishop absolved William. And of him said the king at Windsor, "Now for this I owe him no thanks." Moreover, some time before, that is, in the time of Archbishop Theobald, the king had conceived a design against the clergy of England as a body, having been provoked by the insolence of certain clerks. . . .[3]

123. Edward Grim: The council of Woodstock (July 1163), and the case of Philip 'de Brois'

The dispute here described concerned the payment of certain customary dues for which the sheriffs under Henry II were accustomed to make a composition to the Exchequer. The exact nature of the payment remains somewhat uncertain. The older view that it was Danegeld has been challenged by J. H. Round (*Feudal England* (1895), pp. 498–502), who suggested that the payment in question was the *auxilium vicecomitis*, the sheriff's aid, which the king now wished to incorporate into the finances of the Exchequer. Becket's challenge to the king on this question raised up many enemies against him, and the council of Woodstock may be said to have witnessed the formation of two distinct parties in England supporting respectively the king and the archbishop. Printed: *Materials for the History of Thomas Becket*, vol. II, p. 373.

While the king was tarrying at his manor of Woodstock in the company of the archbishop and the great men of the realm, among other matters the question was raised concerning a certain custom which obtained in England. Two shillings from each hide were given to the king's officials who, in the capacity of sheriffs, guarded the shires. This sum the king wished to have enrolled in the treasury and added to his own revenue; whom the archbishop resisted to his face, saying that it ought not to be exacted as revenue. "Nor will we", said he, "give it as revenue, my lord king, saving your pleasure. But if the sheriffs and officials or servants of the shires shall provide us with good service and maintain our vassals by their arms, we will by no means be remiss in contributing to their aid." The king, however, took the

[1] He held seven knights' fees.

[2] This is given by Eadmer, *Historia Novorum* (Rolls Series, 1884), p. 6, as one of the customs enforced by William the Conqueror; it was afterwards embodied in the Constitutions of Clarendon; see below, No. 126.

[3] Here follows an account of the complaints made at Scarborough concerning the exactions of archdeacons and rural deans, who could not be brought to trial in the king's courts by reason of their claim to benefit of clergy.

archbishop's answer amiss and said, "By the eyes of God, it shall be given as revenue and inscribed in the king's scroll; nor is it seemly for you to gainsay me, when no one would vex your men against your will." The archbishop, foreseeing the issue and being on his guard lest by his sufferance a custom should be introduced whereby posterity should be harmed, replied, "By the reverence of those eyes by which you have sworn, my lord king, not a penny shall be given from all my land or from the jurisdiction of the Church." The king was silent, repulsed by the archbishop's bold objection, but his indignation was not allayed; for in the meantime his fury was surreptitiously turned from secular matters, which seemed to cause little difficulty to the archbishop, against the clergy, and his rage was directed against the ministers of the Church, whose injuries would especially redound upon the head of the archbishop. . . .

A new method of attack was resorted to against a clerk named Philip 'de Brois'[1] by the revival of a charge that had long been forgotten. He had been accused of the murder of a certain knight, but when the case had been brought before the bishop of Lincoln, he cleared himself by ecclesiastical law. The case thus disposed of, he was claimed as a free man by his kinsfolk. But one of the king's officers,[2] to whose province the affair belonged, desiring from an ancient grudge he bore him to compass his ruin, reopened the case and again charged him with homicide. But the clerk, being of high birth, was overwhelmed with grief and indignation and attacked the sheriff with abuse. When the sheriff had reported this outrage to the king, the latter, so it is believed, delighted at the opportunity of venting his spleen against a clerk, poured forth upon Philip the vials of his wrath. When the complaint against this clerk had been raised in the presence of the archbishop, the king protested that full justice should be done both in respect of the homicide and of the outrage against the sheriff, and that the acquittal should not stand. But the archbishop received the clerk into his court and placed him under the protection of the Church, that he might there answer for himself and reply to the charge. Bishops and other persons of both orders[3] were accordingly sent by the king to judge the clerk. He denied the charge of homicide, asserting that he ought not to be compelled to make a further answer to it, and that there was no legal justification for trying the case over again, seeing it had been terminated by the solemn purgation and buried by the peace he had made with his adversaries. "I confess", he said, "that overcome by bitterness I have abused the king's officer, but I promise full reparation for my outrage; only let not the penalty exceed the bounds of reason." "And we", they said, "decree that your prebend shall remain under the king's hand for two years, and your possessions and all your income shall be distributed at his will and pleasure to the poor." The judges added that he was to stand naked before the sheriff, just as a layman might, and to offer him his arms for the injury he had done him and live in subjection to him. The clerk complied with this judgment, glad to have escaped the sentence of death, with which the king threatened him. The king, on the other hand, wishing to condemn the man to death, complained that an injury had been done to himself and to the

[1] According to William fitz Stephen he was a canon of Bedford.
[2] *i.e.* the sheriff.
[3] *i.e.* both clerks and laymen.

prejudice of his court. He complained also that the bishops had shown respect of the clerk's person on account of the archbishop, and had not judged according to equity; and he added, "By the eyes of God you shall swear to me that you judged a just judgment and did not spare the man because he was a clerk."

124. Herbert of Bosham: The council of Westminster (October 1163)

The dispute respecting jurisdiction over "criminous clerks" reached a new stage in the debates at the council of Westminster. Printed: *Materials for the History of Thomas Becket*, vol. IV, p. 299.

Having explained the cause of the summons, the king instantly demanded that clerks seized or convicted of great crimes should be deprived of the protection of the Church and handed over to his officers, adding that they would be more prone to do evil unless after spiritual penalty they were subjected to corporal punishment, and that those who were not restrained from such outrages by the thought of their sacred orders would trouble little at the loss of them; moreover, the more worthy they were than others of the privilege of clergy, so much the greater was their guilt; wherefore they should be coerced by sterner penalties whenever they were detected in crime. Accordingly the king, relying on the advice of certain individuals who made a show of their learning and skill in both branches of the law,[1] incontinently demanded that such guilty clerks should speedily be deprived of their orders and handed over to the civil court; which procedure was sanctioned not only by human law, but also by the canonical authority of the divine law; whence also, concerning such, it is frequently found in the canons: "Let him be handed over to the court." From this those who were apparently prepared to put their learning at the king's service in order to curry favour with him, argued that such clerks should in no wise be exiled or sent into a monastery, but rather, as the canons ordain, they ought "to be handed over to the court", and this they interpreted to mean to be delivered to the secular arm to be punished.

To these arguments brought forward by the king and his advisers, the archbishop, having taken counsel with the bishops of his province and his learned prelates, made an excellent and convincing answer at some length in a plea for the liberty of the clergy in accordance with the canonical rule of the ancient fathers. At the close of his speech he begged the royal clemency with great earnestness not to introduce into his kingdom a new discipline contrary to the decrees of the holy fathers under a new king, Christ, and a new law of Christ by a new and strange kind of Lord. And this he humbly and repeatedly begged for himself and for the stability of the realm, interposing again and again that he neither could nor ought to endure it.

Nothing moved by this plea, but rather the more excited as he saw the archbishop and the bishops opposing him and, as he surmised, so unanimous and firm, the king then demanded whether they would observe his royal customs.[2] Whereupon the archbishop, after consultation with his brethren, said that he and they would observe them, *saving their order*. And the bishops each made the same answer one after the

[1] *i.e.* both the civil and the canon law.

[2] William of Canterbury states that the king also added that, since these customs had been observed by the archbishops and bishops in the time of his grandfather, he was not disposed to acquiesce in their condemnation now: *Materials for the History of Thomas Becket*, vol. I (1875), p. 13.

other when questioned individually by the king. But one of them, Hilary, bishop of Chichester, hearing that the king was highly enraged on account of the almost unanimous opinion they gave, without consulting the archbishop and his brother bishops, altered the formula, promising to observe the royal customs *in good faith*; and this, I believe, he really did with good intent, to allay the king's wrath. But the king was in no way softened thereby and spurned his good intentions with contumely. Turning to the archbishop and the bishops, after having received the same answer from them all, he declared that they had formed a firm and united front against him, that poison lurked in the phrase "*saving their order*" and that it was a mere sophistry. Wherefore he demanded that they should absolutely and without qualification promise to observe the royal customs. To this the archbishop replied that they had sworn fealty to him in life and limb and earthly honour *saving their order*, that in the term *earthly honour* were comprehended the royal customs, and that they would by no means bind themselves in another form to observe them, but only in that to which they had previously sworn. When the day was already far advanced, the king, who had been in an ill temper the whole day, suddenly and without bidding farewell to the prelates departed from the hall in ire and indignation. The bishops, equally perturbed by the day's proceedings, likewise departed and retired to their lodgings. As they withdrew, the bishop mentioned above was fiercely reproached by the archbishop for presuming to alter the formula of their common response without consulting him and his brother bishops.

On the morrow the king demanded and obtained restitution of the castles and honours which the archbishop had held in custody from him in the time of his chancellorship; and without exchanging greetings with the prelates, or rather completely ignoring them, he returned to London secretly and before daybreak. This indeed gave rise to great wrath and indignation.

125. 'Roger of Pontigny' on the discussions following the council of Westminster (October 1163)

Printed: *Materials for the History of Thomas Becket*, vol. IV, p. 27.

For the present the king was frustrated in his purpose, but not long afterwards, while he was staying at Northampton, he summoned the archbishop, wishing to try his constancy, whether perchance he might bend him to his will. When the archbishop had drawn nigh to the town and informed the king of his arrival, the latter–I know not with what cunning design–sent certain persons to meet him. "The king", they said, "has occupied the town with many men, and now you are come with a very great multitude; there is no room to hold you both, wherefore the king commands you to await him here. Here he will come to speak with you." And when the archbishop had turned aside into a field, forthwith and without delay the king appeared. Hastening to meet him the archbishop sought to anticipate his coming with the salutation of honour due to him. But when, because of the neighing and rearing of the high-spirited horses on which they were riding, they could not come nigh each other, they both changed their mounts and withdrew together apart. The king then addressed the archbishop thus, "Have I not raised you from a poor and lowly station to the pinnacle of honour and rank. It seemed but a small thing to me unless I made you father of the kingdom and even preferred you to myself. How comes it then that so many benefits, so many proofs of my love for you, well known to all, have so soon been obliterated from your mind, that you are now not only ungrateful, but oppose me in everything?" The archbishop replied, "Far be it from me, my lord. I am not unmindful of the favours which, not you alone, but God who dispenseth all things hath condescended to confer on me through you: wherefore, far be it from me to show myself ungrateful or to act contrary to your will in anything, so long as it accordeth with the will of God. Your highness knows how faithful I have been to you, from whom I look but for an earthly reward. How much more then must we do faithful and true service to Almighty God from whom we have received temporal, and hope for eternal benefits! You are indeed my liege lord, but he is both your Lord and mine, to ignore whose will in order to obey yours would be expedient neither for you nor for me. For in the dread Judgment Day we shall both be judged as servants of One Lord, wherein neither of us can answer for the other, and each of us, all excuses being of none avail, will be rewarded according to his deeds. For temporal lords should be obeyed, yet not against God, as saith St. Peter, 'We ought to obey God rather than men.'"[1] To this the king replied, "I don't want a sermon from you; are you not the son of one of my villeins?" "In truth", answered the archbishop, "I am not 'sprung from royal ancestors';[2] neither was St. Peter, prince of the apostles, on whom the Lord deigned to confer the keys of the kingdom of heaven and the primacy of the whole Church." "True," said the king, "but he died for his Lord." But the venerable prelate replied, "And I will die for my Lord when the time comes." Then said the king, "You trust too much to the ladder you have mounted by." And the archbishop answered, "I trust and rely upon God, for 'cursed is the man that putteth his hope in man'.[3] Nevertheless, whatever you may say and I answer, as of old so now, I am ready for your honour and good pleasure, *saving my order*. But on those things which concern your honour and the salvation of your soul you ought rather to have consulted me, whom you have so oft found faithful and useful in counsel, rather than those who, under a specious regard for your honour, have kindled this flame of envy and strive to take vengeance on me who have done them no harm. You will not deny, I think, that before I received holy orders I was ever loyal to you; how much more then ought you to believe me faithful in all things since I have been raised to the priesthood?" After the archbishop had concluded by speaking many wholesome words full of love and faith, the king still vehemently insisted that he should utterly abandon the expression *saving our order*. As he could by no means obtain this concession, for the archbishop persisted obstinately in his opinion, they took leave of each other.

At this time Arnulf, bishop of Lisieux, who was out of favour with the king, crossed the sea[4] on a visit to England, desirous of finding some means of making his peace with him. And because he flattered the king in everything and said what was

[1] Acts v. 29.
[2] *atavis edite regibus*, Horace, *Odes*, I, 1.
[3] Jeremiah, xvii. 5.
[4] From Normandy.

agreeable to him, he did not scruple also to give the king advice aimed against the archbishop. For he said to the king, "The dispute between you and the archbishop is a difficult one and may not easily be brought to a conclusion. It is impossible to force the archbishop to submit to you so long as his suffragans continue unanimous and of the same opinion as himself. Wherefore, even if you cannot detach all of them from him, you may at least by some means or other endeavour to draw some of them over to your side, and once this has been accomplished, the remainder will not easily maintain their firm opposition. For, with the bishops espousing your cause, if the archbishop alone should decide to persist obstinately in his opinion, he will not only fail to stand his ground, but may also easily incur sentence of suspension at the initiative of the bishops."[1] Accordingly, schooled by this advice, the king summoned to his side at Gloucester those he deemed to be the more pliable among the bishops, namely Roger, archbishop of York, and the bishop of Lincoln,[2] upon whom he so worked that they signified their willingness to confirm his customs, while he in his turn promised to exact from them nothing which would contravene the privileges of their order. So these two submitted and solemnly engaged to do his pleasure. Not long afterwards the king won over Hilary, bishop of Chichester, to his party. . . .

126. The Constitutions of Clarendon (January 1164)

Following the abortive interview with the king at Northampton, the archbishop received letters from the pope and cardinals, advising him to submit to the king's demand for the legal surrender of "criminous clerks". Many of the bishops joined in this plea, and Thomas consented so to do. Accordingly the king summoned a council to meet at Clarendon in order that a solemn and public assent might be given. Exactly what transpired when the council met in January 1164 is not clear. The debates, which stretched over three or four days, were certainly heated. In the earlier sessions the archbishops and bishops appear to have given a verbal promise to observe the "royal customs" in general terms. On the second, or possibly the third day, the king commanded that a formal statement embodying the customs of his grandfather should be drawn up and should receive the assent of all present. The resultant document embodied the Constitutions of Clarendon printed below. It has been many times edited and translated. Particular reference may be made to Gervase of Canterbury (Rolls Series), vol. I (1879), p. 178; and W. Stubbs, *Select Charters* (ed. 1913), p. 163.

In the year 1164 from our Lord's Incarnation, being the fourth of the pontificate of Alexander,[3] and the tenth of Henry II, most illustrious king of the English, in the presence of the said king was made this record and declaration of a certain part of the customs, liberties and privileges of his ancestors, that is, of King Henry, his grandfather, and of other things which ought to be observed and maintained in the realm. And by reason of the dissensions and discords which had arisen between the clergy and the justices of the lord king[4] and the barons of the realm concerning the customs and privileges of the realm, this declaration was made in the presence of the archbishops, bishops and clergy, and of the earls, barons and magnates of the realm. And

[1] Edward Grim (*Materials for the History of Thomas Becket*, vol. II (1876), p. 377) and William of Canterbury (*ibid.*, vol. I (1875), p. 14) confirm this story of the intrigue of Arnulf of Lisieux, and their accounts are similar in substance to that of Roger. The unscrupulous bishop still continued to pose as a friend, well-wisher and counsellor to Thomas; see his letter written to the archbishop in March 1165 given below, No. 135.

[2] Robert 'de Chesney' 1148–1166; Edward Grim (*loc. cit.*, *ante*) substitutes the bishop of London, and this is the more probable, for Gilbert Foliot, but recently translated from Hereford, was by now the archbishop's most determined opponent.

[3] Alexander III.

[4] The "criminous clerks" controversy.

these same customs were acknowledged by the archbishops and bishops, and the earls, barons, nobles and elders[1] of the realm. Thomas, archbishop of Canterbury; and Roger, archbishop of York; Gilbert, bishop of London; Henry, bishop of Winchester; Nigel, bishop of Ely; William, bishop of Norwich; Robert, bishop of Lincoln; Hilary, bishop of Chichester; Jocelyn, bishop of Salisbury; Richard, bishop of Chester; Bartholomew, bishop of Exeter; Robert, bishop of Hereford; David, bishop of St. David's; and Roger, bishop-elect of Worcester; agreed to, and by word of mouth steadfastly promised on the word of truth to the lord king and his heirs, that these customs should be kept and observed in good faith and without evil intent. There were present: Robert, earl of Leicester;[2] Reginald, earl of Cornwall; Conan, count of Brittany; John, count of Eu; Roger of Clare, the earl;[3] Geoffrey of Manneville, the earl;[4] Hugh, earl of Chester; William,[5] earl of Arundel; Earl Patrick;[6] William of Ferrières, the earl;[7] Richard of Lucé; Reginald of Saint-Valery; Roger Bigot; Reginald 'de Warenne'; Richer of Laigle;[8] William of Briouze; Richard 'de Camville'; Nigel 'de Moubrai'; Simon 'de Beauchamp'; Humphrey 'de Bohun'; Matthew of Hereford; Walter of Mayenne; Manasser Bissett the steward; William Malet; William of Courcy; Robert of Dunstaville; Jocelyn 'de Balliol'; William 'de Lanvalis'; William 'de Chesney'; Geoffrey 'de Ver'; William of Hastings; Hugh of Morville; Alan 'de Neville'; Simon fitz Peter; William Maudit the chamberlain; John Maudit; John the marshal; Peter 'de Mara'; and many other magnates and nobles of the realm, both clerks and laymen.

Now of the acknowledged customs and privileges of the realm a certain part is contained in the present document, of which part these are the heads:

1. If a dispute shall arise between laymen, or between clerks and laymen, or between clerks, concerning advowson and presentation[9] to churches, let it be treated and concluded in the court of the lord king.[10]

2. Churches within the fief of the lord king cannot be granted in perpetuity without his consent and concession.[11]

3. Clerks cited and accused of any matter shall, when summoned by the king's justice, come before the king's court to answer there concerning matters which shall seem to the king's court to be answerable there, and before the ecclesiastical court for what shall seem to be answerable there, but in such a way that the justice of the king

[1] *antiquiores*.
[2] Robert of Beaumont. See Table 12.
[3] Earl of Hertford.
[4] Earl of Essex.
[5] William of Aubigny.
[6] Earl of Salisbury.
[7] Earl of Derby.
[8] He was Becket's patron as a young man, and was responsible for introducing him to the court of Archbishop Theobald.
[9] The *Jus praesentationis* or right of patronage; the Church claimed that suits arising out of disputes concerning this right pertained to the *cure of souls*, while the king regarded them as questions of *real property*, which he was bound to protect. There is no doubt that in Stephen's reign such suits were heard in ecclesiastical courts. The king regarded this as usurpation and claimed in this clause to be restoring an older right and custom of his predecessors.
[10] The *curia regis*.
[11] *i.e.* churches on the king's estates must not be alienated. The object of this clause was to preserve the feudal services, and to this Becket raised no objection.

shall send to the court of holy Church to see how the case is there tried. And if the clerk be convicted or shall confess, the Church ought no longer to protect him.[1]

4. It is not lawful for archbishops, bishops and beneficed clergy[2] of the realm to depart from the kingdom without the lord king's leave. And if they do so depart, they shall, if the king so please, give security that neither in going, nor in tarrying, nor in returning will they contrive evil or injury against the king or the kingdom.[3]

5. Excommunicates ought not to give pledges of security for future good behaviour[4] nor take oaths, but only to give sufficient pledge of security to abide by the judgment of the Church in order to obtain absolution.

6. Laymen ought not to be accused save by accredited and lawful accusers and witnesses in the presence of the bishop, in such wise, however, that the archdeacon may not lose his right nor anything due to him thereby. And if the accused persons be such that no one either wishes or dares to prefer a charge against them, the sheriff, when requested by the bishop, shall cause twelve lawful men of the neighbourhood or township to swear before the bishop that they will manifest the truth of the matter to the best of their knowledge.[5]

7. No one who holds of the king in chief nor any of the officers of his demesne shall be excommunicated, nor the lands of any one of them placed under interdict, unless application shall first be made to the lord king, if he be in the realm, or to his chief justice, if he be abroad, that right may be done him; in such wise that matters pertaining to the royal court shall be concluded there, and matters pertaining to the ecclesiastical court shall be sent thither to be dealt with.[6]

8. With regard to appeals, if they should arise, they should proceed from the archdeacon to the bishop, and from the bishop to the archbishop. And if the archbishop should fail to do justice, the case must finally be brought to the lord king, in order that by his command the dispute may be determined in the archbishop's court, in such wise that it may proceed no further without the assent of the lord king.[7]

9. If a dispute shall arise between a clerk and a layman, or between a layman and

[1] The interpretation of this clause now usually accepted is that of F. W. Maitland in his *Roman Canon Law in the Church of England*, Essay VI: "Henry II and the Criminous Clerks" (1898), pp. 132–147. A clerk accused of a grave offence, murder and the like, is to answer before the king's justice for the breach of the king's peace committed by the felony. Then he is to be sent on to the ecclesiastical court to answer there, as a clerk, to the homicide, in which court the trial will take place (*res ibi tractabitur*). If convicted by this spiritual tribunal, he will be degraded, and the Church "ought no longer to protect him". He is then to be brought back to the king's court, now no longer a clerk but a mere layman, to be sentenced without further trial to the penalties appropriate to a layman, death or mutilation. The object of sending a royal officer to witness the proceedings in the ecclesiastical court is to prevent the possibility of the offender's escape. In this view purely ecclesiastical offences were not in question, there was no dispute between king and primate as to the competence of either tribunal, and the king was certainly not proposing that a clerk accused of crime should be tried in a temporal court, which would have been a gross contradiction of the canon law, to which incidentally the king appealed in support of his claim. Hence the support which the king received from the English bishops generally at the council of Clarendon in this matter on the ground that the king's demand was not unreasonable.

[2] *personis*.

[3] The clause is designed to restrict the relations between the English clergy and Rome, and should be taken in conjunction with clause 8, dealing with appeals.

[4] *ad remanens*; the clause is directed towards obtaining just treatment for excommunicates.

[5] *secundum conscientiam suam*; the sworn inquest is here applied in the form of the accusing jury.

[6] Reaffirms and safeguards the separation of the two jurisdictions by William I; see above, No. 79.

[7] *i.e.* no appeals may proceed to Rome without the king's consent. This clause aroused bitter opposition and was abandoned after the king's surrender at Avranches in 1172; see below, No. 156.

a clerk, in respect of any holding which the clerk desires to treat as free alms,[1] but the layman as lay fee,[2] it shall be determined by the recognition of twelve lawful men through the deliberation, and in the presence of the king's chief justice, *whether*[3] the holding pertains to free alms or to lay fee. And if it be judged to pertain to free alms, the plea shall be heard in the ecclesiastical court; but if to lay fee, it shall be heard in the king's court, unless both of them shall claim from the same bishop or baron. But if each of them appeal concerning this fief to the same bishop or baron, the plea shall be heard in the latter's court, in such wise that he who was originally in possession shall not lose possession by reason of the recognition that has been made, until the matter has been settled by the plea.

10. If any one of a city or castle or borough or demesne manor of the lord king be cited by archdeacon or bishop for any offence for which he is obliged to make answer to them, and he refuse to give satisfaction at their citations, it is highly proper to place him under interdict; but he ought not to be excommunicated until application has been made to the chief officer of the lord king in that town, in order that it may be adjudged meet for him to make satisfaction. But if the king's officer fail to act in this, he himself shall be at the mercy of the lord king, and thereafter the bishop shall be allowed to coerce the accused by ecclesiastical justice.

11. Archbishops, bishops and all beneficed clergy of the realm,[4] who hold of the king in chief, have their possessions from the lord king by barony and are answerable for them to the king's justices and officers; they observe and perform all royal rights and customs and, like other barons, ought to be present at the judgments of the king's court together with the barons,[5] until a case shall arise of judgment concerning mutilation or death.[6]

12. When an archbishopric or bishopric is vacant, or any abbey or priory of the king's demesne, it ought to be in his own hand, and he shall receive from it all revenues and profits[7] as part of his demesne. And when the time has come to provide for the church, the lord king ought to summon[8] the more important of the beneficed clergy of the church, and the election ought to take place in the lord king's chapel with the assent of the lord king and the advice of the clergy of the realm whom he shall summon for this purpose. And the clerk elected shall there do homage and fealty to the lord king as his liege lord for his life and limbs and his earthly honour, saving his order, before he is consecrated.[9]

13. If any of the magnates of the realm should forcibly prevent[10] an archbishop or bishop or archdeacon from doing justice to himself or to his people, the lord king ought

[1] The purely ecclesiastical tenure of 'frankalmoign'.

[2] *i.e.* by the ordinary feudal tenures.

[3] The assize *Utrum*; a procedure invented by Henry II to deal with disputes regarding the form of tenure. The jury or sworn inquest procedure is here employed to ascertain a question of fact; see above, No. 58, p. 474.

[4] *universae personae regni.*

[5] Ecclesiastical tenants-in-chief of the crown are to hold by ordinary feudal tenures and are to be bound by feudal law and custom. To this Becket raised no objection.

[6] By canon law no ecclesiastic could be present at, or take part in, "shedding of blood"; hence they are to be allowed to retire from the *curia regis* when sentences of this nature are pronounced.

[7] *omnes reditus et exitus.*

[8] *mandare.*

[9] The clause places on record the tacit compromise regarding investitures reached by Henry I and Anselm in 1107; see above, p. 673.

[10] *defortiaverit.*

to bring him to justice. And if perchance anyone should forcibly dispossess[1] the lord king of his right, the archbishops, bishops and archdeacons ought to bring him to justice, so that he may make satisfaction to the lord king.

14. The chattels of those who are under forfeiture to the king may not be retained by any church or cemetery against the king's justice, because they belong to the king, whether they be found within the churches or without.[2]

15. Pleas of debt due under pledge of faith, or even without pledge of faith, are to lie in the justice of the king.[3]

16. Sons of villeins ought not to be ordained without the consent of the lord on whose land they are known to have been born.[4]

This record of the aforesaid customs and privileges of the crown was drawn up by the archbishops, bishops, earls, barons, nobles and elders of the realm at Clarendon on the fourth day previous to the Purification of the Blessed Virgin Mary[5] in the presence of the lord, Henry,[6] and of his father the lord king. There are, moreover, many other great customs and privileges pertaining to holy Mother-Church and to the lord king and his barons of the realm which are not contained in this document. Let them be safe for holy Church and for our lord the king and his heirs and the barons of the realm. And let them be inviolably observed for ever and ever.

127. Herbert of Bosham on the Constitutions of Clarendon

Despite his verbal promise Thomas Becket objected to the detailed concessions embodied in the Constitutions of Clarendon. He therefore at first refused his assent to them. Considerable pressure was thereupon brought to bear upon him both by the bishops and the lay magnates. Finally, still reluctant but overcome by threats and entreaties, he agreed to pledge his word to the observance of the "customs". Herbert of Bosham's comment on these events is given in *Materials for the History of Thomas Becket*, vol. IV, p. 305.

When the customs had been written down in the form of a chirograph, the king demanded from the archbishop and his suffragans that for greater safety and security they should append their seals thereto. But the archbishop, though exceeding sorrowful, disguised his real feelings, being unwilling further to vex the king. With some caution he did not utterly refuse, but asked that the question should be deferred for the present. Even if they were prepared to do so, he added, a short delay was fitting on account of the gravity of the business, since according to the Book of Wisdom no weighty matter should be decided without counsel; then, after deliberation, the bishops and he might more fittingly be asked to do so on another occasion. Nevertheless he accepted the documents containing the said customs with forethought and prudence, that he might have, as it were, his cause with him in writing. The archbishop of York received the second part of the chirograph, and the king kept the third to be deposited in the royal archives. So the archbishop departed from court and set out for Winchester.

[1] *defortiaverit*.

[2] A clause asserting the king's rights in respect of movable property left by those who had been condemned for treason or felony and had fled the country: such possessions were often stored within ecclesiastical precincts.

[3] *i.e.* within the king's jurisdiction.

[4] A clause aimed at preventing the loss of villein services to the lords.

[5] 29 January 1164.

[6] Afterwards "the young king".

128. Alan of Tewkesbury on events following the council of Clarendon

Printed: *Materials for the History of Thomas Becket*, vol. IV, p. 305.

And as he went there arose by the way a murmuring among his household; some put forward the usual argument that the matter had to be so dealt with on account of the urgency of the time; others were indignant that the Church's guarantee of freedom should have been extinguished at the consent of one man. Among these latter there stood forth one who said, "The civil power disturbs everything. Iniquity rages against Christ himself. The synagogue of Satan profanes the sanctuary of God. Princes did sit and gather themselves together against the Lord's Anointed. No man is safe who loveth equity. In the world's judgment they alone are wise and to be respected who obey the prince to the uttermost. This tempest has shaken even the pillars of the Church, and when the shepherd has fled the sheep lie scattered before the wolf. From henceforth what will be the place of innocence, who will stand against the adversary or who will triumph in the battle when the leader is vanquished?" Thus murmured he who bore the cross before the archbishop.[1] The rest were silent in perplexity. And he, taking up his parable, added more boldly, "What virtue is left to him who has betrayed his conscience and his reputation?" "To what purpose are these words of thine, my son?" said the archbishop. "To thee they refer," he answered, "who hast today wholly betrayed both thy conscience and thy fame, and having left to posterity an example hateful to God and contrary to honour, thou hast now stretched forth thy hands to observe impious customs and hast joined with the wicked servants of Satan to the confusion of the Church's freedom." At this the archbishop groaned and said with sighs, "I repent and am so aghast at my transgression that I judge myself from henceforth unworthy as a priest to approach him whose Church I have thus basely sold.[2] I will sit silent in grief until the 'day-spring from on high hath visited me',[3] and until I thus become worthy to be absolved by God and the lord pope."

129. William fitz Stephen: The council of Northampton (October 1164)

In the nine months' interval between the close of the council of Clarendon and the opening of that of Northampton the tension between king and primate steadily mounted, and both sides were guilty of discourtesy and illegalities. The archbishop made two abortive attempts to escape by sea to the Continent without the king's permission to leave the country. This was an infringement of the Constitutions of Clarendon to which Thomas had sworn. The king affected to take no notice of this, and for a while acted with studious moderation, his real objective being to prevail upon Thomas to resign the archbishopric. He could now feel strong in the support of a majority of the hierarchy, Roger of York, Gilbert of London, Jocelyn of Salisbury and Hilary of Chichester being his staunch adherents. The king then determined to bring the dispute with the primate to an issue at a council summoned to meet at Northampton. Thomas was accordingly cited to appear before the king to answer purely secular charges before his peers. To this end the archbishop did not receive the customary individual summons appropriate to his rank, but his attendance was ordered by a writ addressed to the sheriff of Kent.[4] Besides being designed to humiliate the primate, the action constituted a flagrant illegality. The king, no less than Thomas, had now put himself gravely in the wrong.

---

[1] Alexander Llewelyn.

[2] William of Canterbury (*Materials for the History of Thomas Becket*, vol. I, p. 24) is more explicit and says that Becket did penance for his transgression in sackcloth and ashes, besides suspending himself, as here stated, from saying Mass. A letter from the pope (*ibid.*, vol. V, p. 88) subsequently ordered him to resume his priestly functions.

[3] *Benedictus*, verse 11.

[4] See below, p. 724.

The best and fullest account of the momentous events which took place in the council of Northampton is from the pen of William fitz Stephen, who was an eyewitness of the debates.[1] His narrative has therefore been selected for presentation here, together with occasional supplementation from other sources. The original is printed in *Materials for the History of Thomas Becket*, vol. III, p. 49.

The king decreed that another general council should be held at Northampton on Tuesday, 6 October, being the Octave of St. Michael. On the day appointed we came to Northampton. The archbishop did not see the king that day because he went hawking along every river and stream as he came, and was late in entering the town. Next morning, when Mass and the canonical hours had been said, the archbishop went to court in the royal castle.[2] Having been admitted to the antechamber, he sat down to await the king, who was then hearing Mass, at whose coming he rose with reverence and showed a firm and placid countenance in readiness for the favour of a kiss, according to the English custom, if the king should offer it. But he was not admitted to the kiss.

The archbishop began by speaking of the case of William of Courcy who had occupied one of his lodgings, and he asked the king to order him to vacate possession. The king gave the order. Next the archbishop intimated that he had come to meet the summons taken out against him by John the marshal. This John demanded from the archbishop a piece of land which was part of the archiepiscopal township of Pagham. And when several days had been set aside for the hearing of the suit, he had come to the archbishop's court with a writ from the king. When he could obtain no advantage there, being supported by no right, he contended, as the law then permitted, that a defect existed in the archbishop's court; but he used for taking the oath a book of tropes,[3] which he produced from under his cloak, though the judges of the archbishop's court declared that he ought not to have brought such a book with him nor used it to such purpose. Having returned to the king, he obtained a summons citing the archbishop to answer him in the king's court, the day fixed for the hearing of the suit being the Feast of the Exaltation of the Holy Cross.[4] The archbishop, however, did not appear on that day, but sent to the king four knights with letters from himself and the sheriff of Kent, bearing witness both to the wrong done by John and the inconclusive nature of his evidence. But to what profit? The king, being angry that the archbishop had not come in person to answer the citation and to prove his allegation, evil entreated his messengers with anger and threats for bringing a false, hollow and useless excuse in answer to a summons to the *curia regis*, and would scarcely let them depart, even when they had given sureties. And at the instance of the said John he fixed another day for the case to be heard (that is, the first day of the council),[5] and sent out his letter to the sheriff of Kent[6] summoning the archbishop. For he would not then, nor for a long time before, write to him in person, because he would not give him the customary word of greeting. Nor had the archbishop any other summons to the council, legal in form and directed to him in person, according to ancient custom.[7]

[1] See above, p. 702.
[2] Wednesday, 7 October.
[3] *i.e.* a book containing the versicles commonly sung before the *Introit* at Mass.
[4] 14 September 1164.
[5] Of Northampton.
[6] Hugh of Dover, sheriff of Kent, Christmas 1160–Easter 1168.
[7] The bishops and greater abbots were summoned by special writs addressed to them personally, like the lay magnates, as tenants-in-chief of the crown, the lesser nobles collectively through writs issued to the sheriffs.

The archbishop, I say, announced that he had come at the king's command concerning the case of John; to which the king replied that John was engaged on his service in London, but would arrive on the morrow, and then he himself would take cognizance of their suit. For this John sat with the treasurers and other receivers of revenue and public money in London at the quadrangular table commonly called the Exchequer from its use of coloured counters, but rather is it the table of the king's 'blanched' coins, where also pleas of the crown are heard.[1] On that day nothing further was transacted between the king and the archbishop, but the king told him to go to his lodging and return to court for his suit on the morrow, and he did so.

On the second day,[2] when the bishops, earls and all the barons of England, as well as many of Normandy, had taken their seats – except the bishop of Rochester,[3] who had not yet arrived, and one other, who was absent – the archbishop was accused of contempt of the crown because, although, as related above,[4] he had been summoned by the king at the suit of John, he had neither come nor given a valid excuse. The archbishop's defence was not accepted, when he declared the wrongs committed by John and maintained the validity and integrity of the jurisdiction of his own court in this matter. The king demanded judgment and the archbishop's defence was wholly rejected. It seemed to all that, considering the respect due to the king and the oath of liege homage which the archbishop had taken, and the maintenance of his lord's earthly honour, to which he had sworn, he had little defence or excuse; because, when summoned by the king, he had neither come nor pleaded sickness or imperative business in respect of his ecclesiastical office. They therefore declared that he should be condemned to forfeit all his goods and movables at the king's mercy.

A diversity of opinion then arose between the bishops and the lay magnates concerning the pronouncement of sentence, each party trying to impose this duty upon the other, while excusing themselves. The barons said, "You, the bishops, ought to pronounce sentence; this is not our province, for we are laymen. You are ecclesiastics like him, fellow-priests and brother-bishops with him." To this one of the bishops retorted, "Nay rather, it is your office, not ours; for this is a secular judgment, not an ecclesiastical. We sit here, not as bishops, but as barons. You and we are equally barons here. In vain you rely upon our order for an argument, for if now you have regard for our ordination you ought likewise to do so in the archbishop's case. Because we are bishops, we cannot presume to judge one who is both our archbishop and our lord." What followed? The king, having listened to this argument concerning the pronouncement of sentence, was moved to anger, and soon put an end to the dispute. At his command the bishop of Winchester, though very unwillingly, finally pronounced the sentence.[5]

The archbishop, because it was not lawful to gainsay the sentence and the declaration of the king's court of England, submitted by the advice of the bishops; and bail

[1] See above, No. 70.
[2] Thursday, 8 October.
[3] Walter, bishop of Rochester, 1148–1182.
[4] See above, p. 724.
[5] Herbert of Bosham adds this comment (*Materials for the History of Thomas Becket*, vol. IV (1879), p. 312): "When the archbishop heard that judgment had been passed upon him, he said 'Even if I were to remain silent at such a sentence, future ages will not do so. For this is a new form of judgment, perhaps in accordance with the new canons recently promulgated at Clarendon. From time immemorial such a thing has never been known as this, that an archbishop of Canterbury should be tried in the court of the king of the English

being granted him (as the custom is at court) to make satisfaction in respect of the judgment that had been pronounced, all the bishops stood surety for him, with the exception of Gilbert of London, who refused when asked to be security for him; which peculiarity made him conspicuous.

Later on the same day the archbishop was sued for 300 pounds which he had received as keeper of the castles of Eye and Berkhamsted. Having previously refused to answer the suit on the ground that he had not been cited therein, the archbishop said, not, however, in formal pleading, that he had used this money and much more besides to defray the expenses of repairing the Tower of London and the castles in question, as it was plain to see. The king denied that this had been done on his authority and demanded that judgment should be given. Whereupon the archbishop agreed for the king's sake to restore this money, since he was wholly unwilling that a mere question of money should occasion a quarrel between them. He therefore put forward as sureties certain laymen, the earl of Gloucester, William of Eynsford and a third person, all of whom were vassals of his.

On the third day[1] the archbishop was interrogated by messengers [from the king] concerning a loan of 500 marks in connexion with the war of Toulouse and another 500 marks borrowed from a certain Jew on the king's security. He was next arraigned by action of wardship[2] for all the proceeds of the archbishopric while vacant, and of other bishoprics and abbacies vacant during his chancellorship;[3] and he was ordered to give an account of all these to the king. The archbishop replied that for this he had not been summoned, nor was he prepared for it. Furthermore, if he were charged at the proper time and place, he would render the satisfaction due by right to his lord, the king. The king thereupon demanded the safeguard of sureties from him. He answered that on this matter he ought to take the advice of his suffragans and his clergy. The king stuck to his point, and the archbishop retired. From that day forth the barons and the knights no longer came to see him in his lodging, for they had well understood the mind of the king.

On the fourth day[4] came all the ecclesiastics to the lord archbishop's lodging. He had separate conversations with the bishops and the abbots, and took counsel on the matter with each in turn. By the advice of the noble Henry, bishop of Winchester, who had consecrated him[5] and now promised him substantial aid, an attempt was made to discover if the king could be pacified with money. The archbishop offered him 2000 marks, but the king refused it. There were certain of the clergy who told the archbishop that on account of his office he was bound to protect the Church, to pay heed to his own person and dignity, and to honour the king in all things, saving the reverence due to God and the honour of the Church; he need fear no opposition,

on such a charge. It is contrary to custom on account of the dignity of the Church and of the authority of his person, and also because the archbishop is the spiritual father of the king and of all men in the kingdom. Wherefore he ought to be reverenced by all.' But he complained more of the judgment of his brother-bishops than of the judgment of the lay magnates, declaring that it was truly a judicial innovation that an archbishop should be judged by his suffragans, and a father by his sons."

[1] Friday, 9 October.

[2] *actione tutelae.*

[3] The sum probably amounted to about 30,000 marks.

[4] Saturday, 10 October.

[5] See above, p. 712.

since no crime or infamy could be laid to his charge. He had been given to the church of Canterbury free of the chancellorship and from every secular suit of the king, just as any vacant abbey would not elect and receive as abbot a monk of another house unless he were sent to it freed from all obedience to his abbot. But others, who were more in touch with the secret mind and ear of the king, showed a far different opinion, and said, "Our lord the king is grievously angry with him. From certain indications we interpret his mind to be this, that the lord archbishop should in everything, and above all by resigning the archbishopric, throw himself utterly on the king's mercy." Among them Hilary of Chichester, who was more inclined to the king's party, said to him, "Would that you could cease to be archbishop and remain plain Thomas." And on another occasion he said concerning him, "Every plant which my heavenly Father hath not planted, shall be rooted up",[1] as though he meant that it was the king's declared will which had procured his election. Concerning this prelate the archbishop afterwards in his exile said to one who was with him, "And he among my brethren occupied the place of the traitor Judas." And afterwards, before the archbishop's recall and reconciliation with the king, as though smitten by God, he died.[2] This same bishop of Chichester, speaking for himself and certain of his accomplices, said, "From your companionship and familiarity at his board as chancellor you must know the king better than we do. There is no doubt that he will be more easily convinced by you, whether you contend with him or yield to him. In the chancellorship, both in peace and war, you did your duty by him honourably and well, and though not unenvied you won the praise of men. Those who then envied you, now inflame the king against you. Who could stand surety for so great a reckoning or for so uncertain a sum? The king is reported to have said that the two of you could no longer remain together in England, he as king and you as archbishop. It were safer to leave everything to his mercy, lest perchance (which God forbid) he detain you without sureties on a charge of embezzlement of the moneys you received from him as chancellor and auditor of accounts, or lay hands upon you; whence would accrue sorrow to the English Church and shame to the realm." But another said, "Far be it from the archbishop to consider the safety of his person and dishonour the church of Canterbury, which chose him for her own. Not so did any of his predecessors, although they in their days suffered persecution. Besides, although he might be able perhaps for a time to avert the seizure by the king of the archiepiscopal see, townships and such-like, and so preserve the Church's rights, yet he could by no means do so with his office." Thus those who were consulted gave diverse opinions, some advising one thing, others the contrary.

The fifth day,[3] which was Sunday, was wholly employed in consultations. Scarce could one find a breathing-space. The archbishop departed not from his lodging.

On the sixth day[4] a sudden weakness seized him, so that he could not go to court. His reins trembled with cold and pain, and it was necessary to apply warm pillows to his side. When the king heard this, he sent all his earls and many of his barons to demand an answer,[5] now that the archbishop had taken counsel, as to whether he

[1] Matthew xv. 13. [2] 16 July 1169. [3] Sunday, 11 October. [4] Monday, 12 October.

[5] The king apparently suspected the archbishop's indisposition was feigned as an excuse for not attending the session of the council; cf. D. Knowles, *Episcopal Colleagues of Thomas Becket*, p. 167.

would offer security for the revenues of vacant churches received during his chancellorship and would stand to judgment thereon in the king's court. The archbishop replied through the bishops, that if his bodily infirmity would allow, he would come to court the next day and perform his duty.

On the morrow[1] he celebrated at the altar of St. Stephen, the first martyr, the Mass, "Princes also did sit and speak against me."[2] Straightway informers, spying on him for the king, told him how this Mass had been sung, maliciously interpreting it that the archbishop had celebrated that Mass for himself, like another Stephen, against the king and his wicked persecutors.

Afterwards he went to the court. On the way he said to Alexander,[3] his cross-bearer, who preceded him, "I had done better to have come in my vestments." For he had proposed to go barefoot, vested and carrying his cross into the king's presence in supplication to him for the peace of the Church. But his clerks dissuaded him from this design, and did not dream that he would carry his cross himself. Having entered the hall of the castle and dismounted from his horse, he took the cross which Alexander the Welshman[3] had carried in front of him on the way. There met him at the gate of the hall Gilbert, bishop of London, to whom said Hugh of Nunant, archdeacon of Lisieux, who had accompanied the archbishop and was a member of his household, "My lord bishop of London, why do you suffer him to carry his cross?" The bishop answered, "My good man, he was always a fool and always will be." Everyone made way for the archbishop. He entered the council chamber and took his accustomed seat, the bishops sitting with him, the bishop of London next to him. All present were astonished, and the eyes of all were turned upon him. The bishop of London advised him to hand over his cross to one of his clerks, and said that he looked as though he were prepared to disturb the whole realm. "You hold in your hands the cross," he said; "if now the king should gird on his sword, behold! a king bravely adorned and an archbishop likewise." Said the archbishop, "If it were possible, it should be mine to carry it always in mine own hands; but now I know what I do, for it is to preserve the peace of God for my own person and the Church of the English. Say what you will. If you were here in my place, you would feel otherwise. But if my lord the king should, as you say, now take the sword, that surely would not be a sign of peace." Perchance the archbishop remembered in what straits he had been at Clarendon when, with tears in their eyes, the king's envoys had come to him.

Then all the bishops were summoned to the king and remained within for some time. With them was Roger, archbishop of York, who had been the last to come to court in order to make a more distinguished entry and not to appear to be of the king's counsel. He had his own cross carried before him, albeit outside his province, as though "threatening blow for blow".[4] He had been forbidden by the lord pope in letters dispatched to him to have his cross borne before him in the province of Canterbury; but, on receipt of this prohibition, he lodged an appeal on a plea of false

[1] Tuesday, 13 October.

[2] The words of the *Introit* of the Mass for St. Stephen's Day, 26 December. To use this Mass on another day was liturgically peculiar, if not irregular. Gilbert Foliot subsequently denounced it to the pope as an act of sorcery, designed to procure the archbishop protection.

[3] See above, No. 128.

[4] *pila minantia pilis*, Lucan, *Pharsalia*, I, 7.

allegations on the part of the archbishop of Canterbury, and thereby considered himself safe. No wonder that grief and groaning and contrition of heart beset the archbishop; for it had been told him that on that day he would either be made a prisoner by some sentence or other, or, if he escaped this, he would be slain by a conspiracy of wicked men formed against him, as though without the king's knowledge. Meanwhile, as they sat silent, Herbert,[1] his master in Holy Scripture, said privately to the archbishop, "My lord, if they lay impious hands on you, you may launch a sentence of excommunication against them on the spot, so that the spirit may be saved in the day of the Lord." To whom William fitz Stephen, who was sitting at the archbishop's feet, said in a little louder tone so that the archbishop might hear, "Far be it from him: not so did God's holy apostles and martyrs when they were seized and lifted up on high; rather, should this occur, let him pray for them and forgive them, and possess his soul in patience. For if it should come to pass that he suffer for the cause of justice and the freedom of the Church, by God's providence his soul will be at rest and his memory blessed. If he should pronounce sentence against them, it would appear to all men that from anger and impatience he had done his utmost to avenge himself. And without doubt he would be acting contrary to the canons." . . .[2]

The archbishop listened to these remarks and pondered them in his heart. A little while after, the same William fitz Stephen–desirous of speaking with the archbishop and being forbidden to do so by one of the king's marshals, who stood beside him with his rod and said that no one was to speak to him–after a short space looked at the archbishop and, raising his eyes and moving his lips, made a sign to him that he should gaze upon the Cross and on the image of the Crucified which he held, and spend his time in prayer. The archbishop well understood the sign and did so, taking comfort in God. Many years afterwards, when the archbishop was an exile in France at St. Benedict's house on the Loire,[3] he met the said William, who was then on his way to the pope, and reminded him of this among other memories of his distresses. . . .[4]

Then[5] the bishops, as they talked within with the king, told him that, when they had come to the archbishop that day, they had been reprimanded by him because they had, together with the barons, recently treated him in a hostile manner and judged him with unjust severity and in an unheard-of fashion, since for a single absence he should not have been adjudged contumacious or condemned at the king's mercy to the forfeiture of all his movables. For by this means the church of Canterbury might be ruined, if the king saw fit to harden his heart unmercifully against him, and a similar captious judgment might in a like case be given against the bishops and barons themselves. Then [the archbishop maintained] that it was laid down that in every shire a fixed sum of money should be paid by those condemned to pecuniary forfeiture at the king's mercy. In London it was fixed at 100 shillings. In Kent, which through its

[1] Herbert of Bosham.

[2] The passage omitted contains citations from Gregory the Great and Gratian in justification of William's assertion.

[3] The monastery of Fleury.

[4] The lengthy passage here omitted contains an apostrophe to the king on the subject of clerical immunities. William fitz Stephen argues that the archbishop was not bound by reason of his temporalities to stand to judgment in the royal court, since, at the time of his election, he was given free to the Church, and as archbishop was subject to the jurisdiction of the pope alone. This argument he fortifies with precedents.

[5] *Materials for the History of Thomas Becket*, vol. III, p. 62.

proximity to the sea has to ward off pirates from the English coast and claims the right to strike the first blow in war against a foreign enemy, and where, since the burden is the greater, the greater is the freedom, there a fine of 40 shillings is fixed for those in such wise condemned. Wherefore he, having his residence and see in Kent, ought at least to have been judged and fined by the law of Kent. Furthermore, the bishops said, on that very day, within ten days of the sentence being passed, the archbishop had summoned them to the lord pope, and had forbidden them on the pope's authority to judge him in future on any secular charge brought against him in respect of the time prior to his appointment as archbishop.

Then the king was wroth and sent to him his earls and many of his barons to inquire of him whether he was indeed responsible for this appeal and prohibition; especially in view of the fact that he was the king's liegeman and bound to him by the common oath and the particular covenant made at Clarendon[1] in word of truth that he would preserve the royal privileges in good faith, lawfully and without guile. Among them was one that the bishops should take part in all the king's trials, save only in judgments involving shedding of blood.[2] They were also to ask him if he would give pledges for rendering an account of his chancellorship and stand therein to the judgment of the king's court. Whereupon he, gazing upon the image of the Crucified, steadfast in mind and countenance, and remaining seated in order to preserve the dignity of an archbishop, delivered an address after this manner, clearly and smoothly, without stumbling over a single word:

"Men and brethren, earls and barons of the lord king, I am indeed bound to the king, our liege lord, by homage, fealty and oath; but the oath of a priest hath justice and equity for its fellows to a peculiar degree. In honour and fealty to the lord king am I bound in all due and devoted submission[3] to offer him for God's sake obedience in all things, saving my obedience to God, my ecclesiastical rank and my personal honour as archbishop. I decline this suit since I received my summons neither to render accounts nor for any other cause save only for the cause of John;[4] neither am I bound to answer or to hear judgment at the suit of another. I confess and recall that I received many commissions and dignities from the lord king, wherein I served him faithfully both here and overseas, and also, after I had joyfully expended all my own revenues, I became bound on his behalf as a debtor for a considerable sum of money. Furthermore, when, by divine permission and the favour of the lord king, I was elected archbishop and awaited consecration, I was dismissed by the king and given free to the church of Canterbury, quit and loosed from every secular suit of the king, although now he angrily denies it: but this many of you well know, and all the ecclesiastics of the realm. And you who know the truth of this I pray, beseech and adjure to bring this to the king's notice, against whom it were not safe, even if it were lawful, to produce witnesses; nor indeed will there be any need, for I will not litigate in this affair. After my consecration I set myself to sustain the honour and responsibility I had assumed with all my strength, and to be of some service to the Church of God over

[1] See above, p. 719.
[2] Constitutions of Clarendon, clause 11; see above, No. 126.
[3] *tam devota quam debita subjectione.*
[4] *i.e.* John the marshal; see above, p. 724.

which I was placed. If it is not given me to make any progress or achieve any profit through the blasts of adversity, I impute this not to the lord king nor to any other man, but chiefly to my own sins. God is able to give the increase of grace to whom and when he will.

"I cannot give sureties for rendering an account. I have already bound all the bishops and friends of mine who could help me here; neither should I be compelled thereto, for it has not been so judged against me. Nor am I being impleaded concerning this account, for I was not summoned for that cause nor for any other suit, save that of John the marshal. But as to the prohibition and appeal which the bishops have this day alleged against me, I remember indeed that I did say to my brother-bishops that they had condemned me for a single absence, and not for contumacy, with undue severity and contrary to custom and age-long precedent. For this I have appealed against them and forbidden them, while this appeal is pending, to judge me again in any secular suit arising from the time prior to my assumption of the archiepiscopal dignity. I still appeal, and I place both my person and the church of Canterbury under the protection of God and the lord pope." He ended his speech, and some of the magnates returned in silence to the king, pondering and weighing his words. Others said, "Behold, we have heard the blasphemy proceeding out of his mouth." . . .[1]

The king, having received the archbishop's answer, approached the bishops, commanding and conjuring them by the homage and fealty due to him and sworn by them, to join the barons in pronouncing sentence upon the archbishop. They began to excuse themselves by citing the archbishop's prohibition. The king was not satisfied, asserting that this single prohibition would not hold in face of what had been determined and sworn at Clarendon. The bishops, on the other hand, represented to the king that the archbishop might lay a heavy hand upon them if they did not obey his prohibition and respect his appeal; they urged that they desired and felt obliged for the king's good and the welfare of the kingdom to agree to the prohibition. When at length they had succeeded in persuading the king, they returned to the archbishop. Robert of Lincoln[2] was weeping, and some of the others could scarce restrain their tears. Then the bishop of Chichester spoke thus, "My lord archbishop, saving your favour, we have much to complain of against you. You have gravely injured us, your bishops. You have shut us up in a trap by your prohibition, you have placed us, as it were, between the hammer and the anvil; for if we disobey, we are ensnared in the bonds of disobedience; if we obey, we infringe the constitution and trespass against the king. For recently, when we were assembled together with you at Clarendon, we were required by our lord the king to observe his royal dignities and, lest perchance we should be in any doubt, he showed us in writing the royal customs[3] of which he spoke. At length we pledged our assent and promised to observe them, you in the first place, and we, your suffragans, afterwards at your command. When, furthermore, the lord king exacted an oath from us as security and required the impression of our seals, we told him that our oath as priests, sworn to him in the word of truth, to observe his royal privileges in good faith, lawfully and without

[1] Cf. Matthew xxvi. 65. William fitz Stephen then states that other barons spoke threateningly in the archbishop's ears of the vengeance of past kings on recalcitrant ecclesiastics.

[2] One of the king's party; see above, No. 125, p. 718. [3] The Constitutions of Clarendon; see above, No. 126.

guile, ought to suffice. The lord king was persuaded and agreed. You now compel us to act contrary to this, forbidding us to take part in the trial,[1] as he requires of us. From this grievance and whatsoever further injury you may add to it, we appeal to the lord pope and for the present obey your prohibition."

The archbishop made answer, "I hear what you say, and if it please God I will meet your appeal. But at Clarendon no concession was made by me, or by you through me, except *saving the honour of the Church*. For, as you yourselves affirm, we made there these three reservations, *in good faith, lawfully and without guile*, whereby these privileges are saved to our churches, since we have them by canon law.[2] For whatsoever is contrary to the faith we owe to the Church and to the laws of God cannot be observed 'in good faith' and 'lawfully'. Besides, it is not to the dignity of a Christian king that the liberty of the Church, which he has sworn to defend, shall perish. Moreover, these same articles, which you call the royal privileges, the lord king has transmitted to the pope for confirmation, but they have been sent back rejected rather than approved. He has given us an example for our learning that we should also do likewise, being ready with the Roman Church to receive what he receives and to reject what he rejects. Besides, if we fell at Clarendon (for the flesh is weak) we ought to take fresh courage and strive in the strength of the Holy Spirit against the ancient enemy. . . . If, under covenant in the word of truth, we there yielded or swore what was unjust, you well know that an unlawful oath is not binding."

Then the bishops returned to the king and, having been excused by him from judging the archbishop, they took their seats apart from the barons; nevertheless the king demanded judgment concerning the archbishop from the earls and barons. Certain sheriffs and barons of the second rank, men full of years, were also summoned to take part in the judgment. After some little delay the magnates returned to the archbishop. Robert, earl of Leicester,[3] who in age and rank excelled the others, tried to depute the pronouncement of sentence to certain others, but when they refused, he began to recapitulate the business enacted at Clarendon point by point. . . .[4] and signified to the archbishop that he must hear the sentence. But the archbishop could endure no more and said, "What is this which you would do? Have you come to judge me? You have no right to do so. Judgment is a sentence given after trial. This day I have said nothing in the way of pleading. For no suit have I been summoned hither save only at the suit of John,[5] who has not come to prove his charge. With respect to this you cannot give sentence. Such as I am, I am your father; you are magnates of the household, lay powers, secular personages. I will not hear your judgment." The magnates then retired. After a short interval the archbishop arose and, bearing his cross, made for the door, which had all day been securely fastened, but now opened as though of its own accord. A certain man pursued him, slandering him as he went forth, calling him a perjurer; another cried out that he fled like a

[1] No. 126, clause 11. [2] *e jure pontificio*.

[3] Robert of Beaumont; he had shared the justiciarship with Richard of Lucé; several biographers mention Richard, earl of Cornwall, as having also taken part in the proceedings; see Edward Grim, *Materials for the History of Thomas Becket*, vol. II, p. 397; 'Roger of Pontigny', *ibid.*, vol. IV, pp. 50–51; William of Canterbury, *ibid.*, vol. I, p. 39; cf. Roger of Howden, *Chronica* (Rolls Series), vol. I, p. 231.

[4] *articulatim*. [5] John the marshal; see above, pp. 724, 725.

traitor and carried the king's sentence with him.[1] In the hall, which was full of servants, he stumbled over a bundle of faggots, but did not fall. He came to the gate where were his horses. Mounting his steed, he took with him Master Herbert, who could not secure his own horse so quickly on account of the crowd thronging him,[2] and carried him to his lodging at the monastery of St. Andrew. O how great was the martyrdom he bore in spirit that day! But he returned the happier from the examination of the council, since he had been deemed worthy there to suffer shame for the Name of Jesus.

After praying before the altar, he laid down his cross near the shrine of the Blessed Virgin Mary. There he sat with his followers around him. Then said William fitz Stephen to him, "This has indeed been a bitter day for us"; to whom the archbishop made answer, "The Last Day will be even more bitter." And a little while after, exhorting his followers, he said to them, "Let each one of you keep silence and remain in peace; let no word of bitterness proceed out of your mouth. Make no response to them who speak evil of you, but let them go on railing. It is the mark of a higher nature to suffer injury, and of a lower to inflict it. As they are lords of their own tongues, so let us be masters of our ears. It is not I who am reviled, but the man who recognizes in himself the evil spoken against him."

The king, having become aware of the archbishop's departure and of the abuse hurled at him by the courtiers, at the entreaty of Robert of Melun,[3] bishop of Hereford, or possibly prompted by some other person before Robert had arrived, gave orders for it to be proclaimed in the streets by the crier that no man should injure the archbishop with insults or reproaches, or in any wise or at any time molest him or any of his men. The archbishop dined late that night in the company of his followers, as he was wont to do. After supper all his knights there present, having renewed their homage to him, received permission to withdraw and took leave of him with tears. Afterwards he sent three bishops, Walter of Rochester,[4] his chaplain, and two others, whom he had consecrated, Robert of Hereford and Roger of Worcester,[5] to the king to ask his permission to depart next day and to obtain from him a safe-conduct for the journey. The bishops found the king in a cheerful mood, but he deferred his answer to the next day. When the envoys brought back this reply, the archbishop feared that the king's delay in answering boded some future ill to him.

* * *

[1] Cf. the account here given of the archbishop's flight from the council with those of other biographers. William of Canterbury (*Materials for the History of Thomas Becket*, vol. I, p. 39) gives the names of those who shouted after him as Rannulf 'de Broc' and Earl Hamelin, the king's illegitimate brother. He also states that Thomas retorted with violent language, calling Hamelin "varlet and bastard" and reminding Rannulf that one of his kinsmen had been hanged. Edward Grim (*op. cit.*, p. 399) declares that he made no reply. Herbert of Bosham (*Materials*, vol. III, p. 310) gives this version: "He turned a stern countenance on those who derided him, and answered that, if his priestly orders did not prevent him, he would defend himself with arms against their charges of perjury and treason. And so we departed from the council. This is the disciple which testifieth of these things and both saw them and wrote them; he was at this moment the only one outside the inner door, following the archbishop as he bore his cross, until we entered the hall." 'Roger of Pontigny' (*op. cit.*, p. 52) gives this version of the archbishop's reply to his assailants: "If I were a knight, I would prove thee a liar with my own hand."

[2] Herbert of Bosham (*loc. cit.*, *ante*) states that the archbishop could scarcely control his horse and carry his cross for the multitude that thronged him and begged his blessing.

[3] Bishop of Hereford, 1163–1167, successor of Gilbert Foliot in that see. He had had a distinguished career abroad as a scholar and teacher, and was the friend and master of John of Salisbury.

[4] Bishop of Rochester, 1148–1182.

[5] Bishop of Worcester, 1164–1179.

(iii) *Material relating to the dispute between Henry II and Thomas Becket during the period of the archbishop's exile (November* 1164–*November* 1170)

Thomas Becket was in exile from November 1164 to November 1170, and the documents which here follow supply evidence of the actions taken by the various parties to the dispute during that period and of certain of the opinions expressed by them. The measures taken by Henry II against the supporters of the archbishop in England appear, for instance, in Nos. 133, 134; while the French king's concern with the controversy can be seen in Nos. 130, 131. The main drama, however, was played out by the English king, the archbishop and the pope. Both Henry II and Becket had immediately appealed to Alexander III, and their negotiations with him are displayed in Nos. 131, 132. The correspondence between the pope and Becket (*e.g.* Nos. 136, 137) shows how the pope was at first disposed to adopt a mediating attitude and counselled restraint to the archbishop, but in the spring of 1166 his policy hardened towards the king. In April 1166 Becket received the legatine commission from the pope, and in June he pronounced sentence of excommunication at Vézelay against many of his opponents in England (No. 139). No. 140 gives the reply of the bishops and clergy of England to his censures. Between 1167 and 1170 Alexander sought to settle the dispute by appointing four successive commissions for this purpose. As a result of these negotiations several conferences were held in France, of which the most important were that at Montmirail on 6 January 1169 and that at Montmartre on 18 November 1169 (No. 144). At both of these conferences there were present Becket himself and the kings of England and France. A new phase in the controversy opened in June 1170 when Henry II had his son, Henry, crowned by the archbishop of York in Becket's absence (No. 145). This had the effect of alienating from Henry II not only the pope, but also the French king, and partly from fear for the safety of his continental dominions the English king now began to show himself disposed to compromise. Henry II and Thomas Becket were, in consequence, formally reconciled at Fréteval on 22 July 1170 (No. 146). In December of that year Becket returned to England and was restored to his archbishopric.

130. Letter of Henry II to Louis VII, king of France (October 1164)

On the night of 13 October 1164 the archbishop fled from Northampton, and after remaining in hiding for some weeks he crossed the Channel on 2 November and proceeded at once to the Cistercian monastery of Clair-Marais near St. Omer. He then went to the monastery of St. Bertin. The following letter was written by the king very soon after the archbishop's flight. It is printed in *Materials for the History of Thomas Becket*, vol. v, p. 134.

To his lord and friend, Louis, illustrious king of the French, H[enry], king of the English, duke of the Normans and of the men of Aquitaine, and count of the Angevins, greeting and love. Be it known to you that Thomas, who was archbishop of Canterbury, has been publicly judged in my court by full council of the barons of my realm as a wicked and perjured traitor against me, and under the manifest name of traitor has wrongfully departed, as my messengers will tell you more fully. Wherefore I earnestly beg you not to permit a man guilty of such infamous crimes and treasons, or his men, to remain in your realm. Let not this great enemy of mine, so it please you, have any counsel or aid from you and yours, even as I would not give any such help myself to your enemies in my realm, nor would I allow it to be given.

Rather, if it please you, help me to take vengeance on my great enemy for this insult, and seek my honour, even as you would wish me to do for you if there were need of it. Witness Robert,[1] earl of Leicester. At Northampton.[2]

131. Herbert of Bosham's account of negotiations with the pope (October–November 1164)

It will be noted that the author himself took part in these negotiations. Printed: *Materials for the History of Thomas Becket*, vol. III, p. 332.

Leaving the archbishop in the monastery of St. Bertin at St. Omer, let us pursue first the itinerary and acts of the king's envoys. On the day following their arrival at St. Omer they continued their journey for three or four days and then found Louis,[3] king of the French, of pious memory, at his royal castle of Compiègne. After paying their respects to him, they presented a letter from the king of the English,[4] the form of which was like unto that of the one addressed to the count of Flanders–that is to say, that Thomas, *formerly archbishop of Canterbury*, had fled from his kingdom like a traitor; wherefore the king begged Louis as his lord not to admit the archbishop into his land. But when the king of the French heard at the beginning of the letter, "Thomas, formerly archbishop", straightway he was seized of a mighty zeal, as a most devoted son of the Church, and deeply moved at that saying. . . . Then the king asked again and again who had deposed the archbishop, and added, "Of a truth, like the king of the English, I also am a king, but I have no power to depose even the least of the clerks of my realm." As the envoys were unable to give a discreet answer to the king's question, they could not obtain the answer they wished to their request.

But the disciple who wrote these things and a certain other of the archbishop's company, wary and learned, by the counsel and command of the archbishop, followed the steps of the envoys without their knowledge, in such a way that they were always a day's journey ahead of us. And this indeed was done diligently and by instruction, so that we might with greater caution and certainty search out their words and investigate their activities. And when we had come to the most Christian king of the French, from whom the envoys had departed the previous day, as soon as we could gain access to him, we greeted him humbly and devoutly in the name of the archbishop, of whom the king had thought highly from the time he was chancellor on account of his greatness, his honesty and devotion to duty. And because we were previously unknown to him, he asked us repeatedly, as was his wont, whether we were of the archbishop's household and family; the which, when he knew, he admitted us to the kiss and graciously listened to us. And when we had, according to the command of our lord, the archbishop, opened to him our woeful history, our labours and perils, the king's compassion was strongly aroused, and he deigned to reveal to us how and in what terms the king [of England] had written to him against the archbishop, and how he had answered him. And he added, "Your lord, the king of

[1] Robert of Beaumont. See Table 12.
[2] The letter was evidently written before the council of Northampton broke up on 20 October.
[3] Louis VII.
[4] See above, No. 130.

the English, before he dealt so harshly and cruelly with one who has been so great a friend of his and so great an archbishop, ought to have remembered that verse, "Be ye angry and sin not."[1] Whereupon my companion and fellow-messenger answered humorously, "My lord, perchance he would have remembered it, if he had heard it as often as we do in the canonical hours"; at this the king smiled. On the morrow, before we departed, having taken counsel with his vassals, who were there present with him, he promised peace and security to the archbishop within his realm in answer to the petition brought by us: moreover, he added that it was an ancient prerogative of the crown of France that exiles, especially ecclesiastics, should enjoy peace and security within his kingdom and find protection from the injuries of their persecutors. . . .

So, secure in the enjoyment of the king's peace, that most Christian monarch, in joy and exultation, gave us permission to depart. Nevertheless we did not return to the archbishop immediately, neither did we report the result of our interview to him, because we were hoping to repair to him before long; but, as we had been ordered, we hastened to seek the lord pope and came to Sens whither the king's envoys had arrived the day before. On the same day at even we had an audience with the lord pope, and saluted him as father and lord in the name of the archbishop with fitting devotion and humility. We told him we were but two who had escaped from the house of Rechab,[2] and had come to the feet of his holiness to tell him that his son, Joseph, was yet alive[3] but ruled no longer in the land of Egypt, but rather was oppressed by the Egyptians and wellnigh destroyed. He listened with fatherly compassion as we told him of his son, the archbishop's hardships, difficulties and griefs, of his perils in that fight with beasts at Northampton, perils among false brethren, perils in his flight, perils in the way, perils in the sea and even in the harbour, his labour, poverty and distress, and his change of dress and name in order to avoid the snares of the enemy. And when he heard these things, the father of all fathers was moved with compassion towards his son and could not restrain his paternal affection, but wept and said to us, "Your lord yet liveth in the flesh, as ye say, yet while still living he can claim the privilege of martyrdom." And because it was now very late and we were wearied with our journey, he dismissed us quickly to our lodging after giving us his apostolic benediction.

132. Alan of Tewkesbury's account of negotiations with the pope (November 1164)

Printed: *Materials for the History of Thomas Becket*, vol. IV, p. 337.

On the morrow[4] when the lord pope held a consistory in session with the cardinals, a public audience was proclaimed, and the archbishop's envoys[5] also attended in order to see the issue of the affair. The king's envoys on the other side arose, and their leader and standard-bearer, the bishop of London,[6] opened the debate after this manner: "Father," he said, "to you the Catholic Church looks with care

[1] Ephesians iv. 26.
[2] I Chronicles ii. 55.
[3] Genesis xlv. 26.
[4] 26 November 1164.
[5] Herbert of Bosham and his companion; see above, No. 131.
[6] Gilbert Foliot.

and anxiety that the wise may be nurtured by your wisdom for an example of conduct, and that fools may be rebuked and corrected by apostolic authority that they may learn wisdom. But your apostolic wisdom will never account him wise who trusts in his own wisdom and endeavours to disturb the concord of his brethren, the peace of the Church and the devotion of a king. Of late there has arisen in England a dissension between the king and the priesthood on a minor and unimportant matter, which might easily have been resolved if a discreet moderation had been shown. But my lord of Canterbury, following his own individual opinion and not acting on our advice, has pushed the matter to extremes, not considering the evil of the times or what harm might arise from such hostility, and has thus laid a trap both for himself and his brethren. Had we given our consent to his proposals, matters would have become worse. But because we would not be led astray by him, as indeed we ought not, he has tried to throw the blame for his own rashness on the lord king, on us and indeed on the whole realm. Wherefore, in order to cast infamy upon us, his brethren, he has taken to flight, although no violence has been used or even a threat uttered against him–as it is written, 'The wicked fleeth when no man pursueth.'" Here the pope interrupted him, "Spare, brother", and the bishop replied, "My lord, I will spare him." But the pope answered, "I say not, brother, that you should spare him, but yourself." At this rebuke the Lord so confused the mind of the bishop that he could utter no more.

Then the fluent Hilary, bishop of Chichester, took up the debate, trusting rather in his own eloquence than in justice and truth, as afterwards appeared. "Father and lord," said he, "it is the part of your holiness to restore peace and concord whenever, through wrongdoing, ruin has been brought on the whole world, lest the boundless presumption of one man should cause the destruction of many and create schism in the Catholic Church. To this my lord of Canterbury paid too little heed when he forsook the mature counsel of others and took counsel only with himself, so bringing hardship and distress upon the king and the realm, the clergy and the people. And, indeed, for a man in a position of such great authority to act thus was neither fitting nor right."[1] . . . And when they heard this master of grammar thus leap *from port to port*[2] they were all dissolved in laughter. And one of them burst out with, "Ill hast thou reached *port* at last." Whereat the Lord made the bishop to look so foolish that he became forthwith speechless.

But the archbishop of York,[3] observing the downfall of earlier speakers, took care to moderate the vehemence of his attack. "Father," said he, "to none are the character and purpose of the archbishop of Canterbury better known than to me. For I have known the temper of his mind from the first, that he cannot easily be turned from an opinion he has once formed. Wherefore it is easier to believe that this obstinacy proceeds, as of old, from levity. And I see no other way of correcting him, but that your discretion should lay a heavy hand upon him. I think I have said enough to a man of understanding."

[1] *non decuit, nec oportuit, nec aliquando oportuebat:* "thus", continues Alan, "he grammatized by using the word *oportuebat*", *i.e.* an *impersonal* verb as a *personal* one.

[2] *de portu in portum*, a pun on the words *oportuit* and *oportuebat*.

[3] Roger of Pont l'Evêque; see above, pp. 331, 357–359, 704, 718, 719, 723, 728.

Then followed the bishop of Exeter.[1] "Father," he said, "it is not meet for me to dwell long on this matter. This suit can never be determined in the absence of the archbishop of Canterbury. We therefore ask for legates who may hear this suit between the king and the archbishop and decide it." Then he held his peace, and after him none of the bishops added anything further. Perceiving this the earl of Arundel,[2] standing in his rank among the host of knights, craved a hearing. And when silence had been called, "My lord," said he, "we unlearned men are wholly ignorant of what the bishops have said.[3] It behoves us therefore to explain, as well as we can, why we have been sent. It was not that we should be contentious or insult anyone, especially in the presence of so great a personage, to whose will and authority the whole world rightly bows; but we are come without question for this purpose, that in your presence and that of the whole Roman *curia* we may lay before you the love and devotion which our lord the king has ever borne and still bears towards you. By whom, do I say? By the greatest and noblest of his subjects in all his lands–that is, by the archbishops, bishops, earls and barons. Greater than these the king cannot find in his dominions, and if he had, he would have sent them to bear witness to his reverence for you and the holy Roman Church. To this we may add that you yourself, father, in the early days of your pontificate, made full proof of the fidelity and devotion of the king in the way in which he placed himself and all that he had entirely at your service: to be sure, there is not within the unity of the Catholic Church, over which you bear rule in Christ, one more faithful, so we believe, or more devoted to God, or more anxious to preserve peace in his realm. Nevertheless, the lord archbishop is equally instructed in his rank and order, and prudent and discreet in the things which concern him; although, as it appears to some, a little too impetuous. Were it not for this present dispute between the king and the archbishop, the secular power and the priesthood would rejoice together in peace and concord under a good prince and the best of pastors. This then is our entreaty, that your grace will take careful heed for the removal of this dissension and the restoration of peace and love." Thus elegantly spoke the earl, but in his own tongue, so that his discretion and moderation were greatly commended by all.

To this speech the lord pope circumspectly replied, "We know, son earl, and recollect with what great devotion the king of England conferred many and rich benefits upon us, the which we desire, when opportunity occurs, to repay as far as we are able with God's aid. Since you have asked for legates, you shall have them." Having kissed the pope's foot they then withdrew, believing that they had won their case, for they cherished hope that the cardinals might be corrupted. Accordingly, after consultation the bishop of London returned and inquired of the lord pope with what authority the cardinals would come. "With due authority," replied the pope. "But", said the bishop, "we ask that they be empowered to determine the case without appeal." "That", said the pope, "is my privilege, which I will not give to another; and, of a truth, when he[4] is to be judged, he shall be judged by us, for it were against

[1] Bartholomew, bishop of Exeter, 1162–1184, friend and correspondent of John of Salisbury.
[2] William of Aubigny.
[3] Because they had spoken in Latin.
[4] Archbishop Thomas.

all reason to send him back to England to be judged by his adversaries and among his enemies." Then our opponents, their hopes frustrated when they heard this, departed in indignation to inform the king of the answer they had received.

[On the fourth day of the council, 29 November 1164, Thomas himself arrived at Sens. He had an audience of the pope after the withdrawal of the king's envoys, gave a full exposition of his case against Henry, and produced the Constitutions of Clarendon for the pope's inspection. On the following day he formally resigned his archbishopric into the pope's hands. Alan of Tewkesbury gives this version of his address to the council on this occasion (*op. cit.*, pp. 342–343).]

"Fathers and lords, every man ought to speak the truth at all times, and much more before God and your persons. Wherefore I willingly confess with sighs and groans that these distresses have befallen the English Church through my wretched fault. I climbed up into the fold of Christ, not through him who is the door,[1] as one summoned by canonical election, but I was forcibly intruded by the secular power. And albeit I have accepted this burden unwillingly, nevertheless it was the will of man and not the will of God which induced me to do so. What wonder then if it has brought me to misfortune? Yet, had I renounced the jurisdiction of episcopal authority conferred upon me at the threat of the king, as my brother-bishops urged me to do, it would have constituted an evil precedent, dangerous to the interests of princes and the will of the Catholic Church. I therefore delayed to do so until I should appear before you. But, recognizing that my appointment was far from canonical and dreading lest the issue become even worse for me, realizing also that my strength is unequal to the burden and fearing lest I should involve in my own ruin the flock to which, such as I am, I was given as shepherd, I now resign into your hands, father, the archbishopric of Canterbury."[2] So saying he wept and sobbed, and brought tears to the eyes of the lord pope and all there present.

[The pope and the cardinals then retired to consider the new situation created by the archbishop's dramatic and unexpected action. There was a division of opinion among them as to the propriety of accepting his proffered resignation of his see. One party was inclined to view it as affording a means of effecting a compromise with the king, who was known to favour this solution. But the pope, supported by an influential body among the cardinals, was opposed to the idea. "It is expedient", he said, "that this man should be restored to office even against his will, for he is fighting the battle of us all, and should therefore receive our succour to the utmost of our power."[3] The narrative then continues (*op. cit.*, pp. 344–346).]

Accordingly the archbishop was recalled, together with his followers, and the lord pope communicated to him his decision. "Now at last, brother," said he, "it is plain to us from your resignation what zeal you have shown, and still show, for the house of the Lord, with how clear a conscience you have stood like a wall against the adversary, and how pure a confession you have witnessed from the time you were first made archbishop; these things can and ought to wipe away all stain of guilt. You may now safely receive anew from our hands the cure of the episcopal office, pending your effectual restoration to it in its entirety. And deservedly so, for we know you to be a man tried and proved in manifold temptations, far-sighted and prudent, beloved of God and men, and loyal in everything to us and the holy Roman Church. As you have been made an inseparable partner of our trials, so also, with God's help,

[1] Cf. John x. 1, 2.

[2] William of Canterbury (*Materials for the History of Thomas Becket*, vol. I, p. 46) adds that he took from his finger his episcopal ring and gave it to the pope.

[3] Alan of Tewkesbury, *op. cit.*, p. 344.

we will not fail you, so long as life remains in this our body. But, in order that you, who have hitherto lived in affluence and luxury, may learn in future what you ought to be, the comforter of the poor–a lesson which can only be learnt from poverty herself, the mother of religion–we have decided to commend you to the poor of Christ, I mean to the abbot of Pontigny"[1]–for he was there present at the pope's request–"to be trained by him and his monks; not, I say, to fare sumptuously but in simplicity, as befits an exile and the athlete of Christ. Among them you must for a time abide, with but few companions and those who are indispensable, while the rest of them are dispersed among friends; until the day of consolation approaches and peace descends upon us from on high. Meanwhile be strong and of a good courage, and manfully resist the disturbers of peace."

Having thus received the papal benediction, the lord archbishop of Canterbury entered the abbey of Pontigny[2] with a few of his closest friends, the remainder of his household having been bestowed elsewhere as decreed. There he deemed himself unworthy to have received the pastoral charge from the pope's hand unless he also received the habit of religion. For in his episcopal see he had to rule monks as his first-born sons, and he had learnt that from the first foundation of the church of Canterbury the archbishops had nearly all been monks, nor according to the histories of olden times had there ever been a schism in the kingdom or a translation of office save when the archbishop had been a secular priest. Accordingly messengers were dispatched to the pope, who sent back to him a monastic habit, which he himself had blessed, made of thick and coarse woollen cloth. Wherefore he commanded the messengers, "Tell the archbishop of Canterbury that we have sent him a habit, such as we have, not such as we would." The abbot of Pontigny vested the archbishop with the habit in private, with only a few persons present. Now there was also standing by one of the archbishop's companions (he[3] who had before put the question to him at Clarendon, "Who can retain his virtue when he has lost conscience and reputation?"). When he saw that in that habit the hood was disproportionately small, he said in all seriousness, "Whether it be *regular* or not, I do not know, but it is manifest that the lord pope has not well joined the hood to the cowl." The archbishop smiled and said, "It was done on purpose, lest you should mock me again, as you did the other day." "How and when was that?" said he. "The day before yesterday," replied the archbishop, "when I was putting on the sacred vestments for Mass, and I seemed to be stuffed out with the girdle, and you asked why I was so swollen out behind. So, if a large hood hung from my shoulders and appeared to form a protuberance there, you would doubtless mock at me for a hunchback.[4] For which reason this was carefully provided for me to prevent such insults." In fact he wore a hair-shirt from his neck to his knees, unknown even to his nearest friends; and when he was girt closely its stiffness made it stick out and he appeared stout, whereas he was lean, though jovial in countenance.

[1] The Cistercian abbey, one of the four daughter-houses of Cîteaux; see above, No. 115.

[2] 30 November 1164. Thomas remained an inmate of the abbey until May 1166. According to Herbert of Bosham (*Materials for the History of Thomas Becket*, vol. III, p. 357) the archbishop chose this place of retreat.

[3] Alexander Llewelyn, the archbishop's cross-bearer; see above, No. 128.

[4] *gibbosum*.

133. Writ of Henry II addressed to the bishops of England (December 1164)

The king sequestrates the see of Canterbury. This and No. 134 indicate the consequent administrative action. Printed: *Materials for the History of Thomas Becket*, vol. v, p. 151.

You know with what malice Thomas, archbishop of Canterbury, has acted towards me and my kingdom, and how basely he has fled. I therefore command you that his clerks, who were with him after his flight, and the other clerks, who have disparaged my honour and the honour of the realm, shall not receive any of the revenues which they have within your bishopric except by my order. Witness: Richard of Lucé. At Marlborough.

134. Writ of Henry II addressed to the sheriffs of England (December 1164)

Printed: *Materials for the History of Thomas Becket*, vol. v, p. 152.

I command you that, if any clerk or layman in your bailiwick shall have appealed to the court of Rome, you shall take him and keep him in custody until you learn my wishes; and that you shall receive into my hand[1] all the revenues and possessions of the archbishop's clerks, as Rannulf 'de Broc' and others of my servants shall direct you. And the fathers and mothers, brothers and sisters, nephews and nieces of all the clerks who are with the archbishop shall be put under safe pledges, together with their chattels, until you shall learn my will in the matter. And this writ you shall bring with you when you have been summoned.

135. Letter from Arnulf, bishop of Lisieux, to Thomas Becket (March 1165)

This letter was written after the Constitutions of Clarendon. It is printed in F. Barlow, *Letters of Arnulf of Lisieus* (R. Hist. Soc., 1939), pp. 69-88.

You have to deal with one[2] whose astuteness is dreaded by those at a distance, whose power is feared by those close at hand, and whose severity is felt by those who are subject to him; whom continuous success and good fortune have rendered so sensitive that every act of disobedience is rewarded by an outrage; whom it is as easy to provoke as it is difficult to placate; who does not encourage rashness by impunity, but whose vengeance is instant and summary. He will sometimes show himself amenable to humility and patience, but will never submit to compulsion; whatever he does openly must appear to have sprung from his own will and not from weakness. He is more covetous of glory than of gain, which fact might be deemed commendable in a prince, if virtue and truth, not vanity and the honeyed flattery of courtiers, provided the substance of that glory. He is a great, indeed the greatest of monarchs, for he has no superior of whom he stands in awe, nor subject who may resist him. His innate ferocity has not been tamed by injuries inflicted upon him by foreigners from abroad, but all who have had occasion to contend against him have preferred to conclude precarious treaties of an empty peace rather than run the risk of a trial of strength with one pre-eminent in the abundance of his riches, the number of his forces and the strength of his power.

[1] *i.e.* to the Exchequer; see No. 70.

[2] Henry II.

136. Letter from Pope Alexander III to Thomas Becket (June 1165)

Written from Clermont, it annuls the sentence passed against the archbishop at the council of Northampton. The letter is printed in *Materials for the History of Thomas Becket*, vol. v, p. 178.

That the less cannot judge the greater, and especially him to whom he is known to be subject by right of prelacy and is held bound by the chain of obedience, is declared by laws both human and divine, and is set forth with particular clarity in the statutes of the holy fathers. Accordingly we, whose province it is to correct errors of judgment and to amend those things which, if not corrected, would leave a pernicious example to posterity, and, having pondered these matters with anxious care, and considering that through the fault of one man the Church ought not to sustain hurt or loss, we adjudge the sentence presumptuously passed against you by the bishops and barons of England on the ground that you did not obey the king's first summons –in which sentence the said bishops and barons adjudged a forfeiture of all your movables contrary both to the form of law and ecclesiastical custom, especially since you have no movables save the goods of your church–to be utterly void, and we quash the same by apostolic authority, ordering that for the future it shall have no force, and avail nothing to bring prejudice or hurt hereafter to you or your successors or to the church committed to your governance.

137. Letter from Pope Alexander III to Thomas Becket (? June 1165)

In this letter, written from Clermont, the pope counselled moderation to the archbishop and ordered him to withhold any projected measures against the king or the realm until Easter 1166. Printed: *Materials for the History of Thomas Becket*, vol. v, p. 179.

Since the days are evil and many things must be endured through the nature of the times, we beg you to be discreet, and we warn, advise and exhort you to show yourself wary, prudent and circumspect in all your actions for your own sake and that of the Church.[1] Do nothing hastily or precipitately, but act with gravity and deliberation by every means at your disposal, with a view to recovering the favour and goodwill of the illustrious king of the English, so far as is consistent with the liberty of the Church and the dignity of your office. Forbear with the king until the following Easter, and study to avoid taking any measures against him or his realm until the prescribed date. For by then God will vouchsafe better days, and both you and we may safely proceed further in this matter.

[1] A letter from Master Hervey, Becket's clerk at the papal *curia*, throws further light on the motives actuating the pope at this time in his counsels of moderation. The Becket dispute was already having serious repercussions on the general political situation in Europe. At a council held by the Emperor Frederick I in May 1165 the election of the anti-pope, Paschal III, was confirmed, and the archbishop of Cologne asserted that the English bishops had declared their willingness to desert the cause of Alexander III. John of Oxford and Richard of Ilchester were present at the council as envoys of Henry II and took an oath of allegiance on behalf of the king and the barons to the anti-pope. This oath was later retracted on orders from the king, who was unwilling to commit himself so far at this stage. The action of the English delegation was probably designed to cause embarrassment and to serve as a warning to Alexander that he could not afford to make an enemy of the king by a whole-hearted championship of Becket's cause. Whether or no this was intended, it certainly had this effect. Hervey's letter to the archbishop (*Materials for the History of Thomas Becket*, vol. v, pp. 180–181) describes the pope as being unwilling to commit himself to support Becket.

138. Letter from Thomas Becket to Henry II (May 1166)

This is the third of three successive letters addressed to the king by the archbishop during the year 1166 in ascending magnitude of severity. Thomas seems by now to have been prepared to go to extremities against the king. The letter is printed in *Materials for the History of Thomas Becket*, vol. v, p. 278.

These are the words of the archbishop of Canterbury to the king of the English.[1] With desire I have desired to see your face and to speak with you; greatly for my own sake, but even more for yours. For my sake, that when you saw my face you might recall to mind the services I rendered faithfully and devotedly to the best of my conscience when I was under your obedience–so help me God in the Last Judgment, when we shall all stand before his judgment seat to receive according to the deeds we have done in the body, whether good or evil–and that so you might be moved to pity me, who am forced to beg my bread among strangers; yet, thanks be to God, I have abundant victuals for my sustenance. And I have much consolation, as saith the apostle, "All that will live godly in Christ Jesus shall suffer persecution,"[2] and the prophet, "Yet saw I never the righteous forsaken, nor his seed begging their bread."[3] For your sake (I desire to see you) for three reasons, because you are my lord, because you are my king, and because you are my spiritual son. In that you are my lord, I owe and offer you my counsel and service, such as a bishop owes to his lord according to the honour of God and holy Church. In that you are my king, I am bound to you in reverence and regard; in that you are my son, I am bound by reason of my office to chasten and correct you. . . . Christ founded the Church and purchased her liberty with His Blood, undergoing the scourging and spitting, the nails and the anguish of death, leaving us an example that we should follow in his steps. Whence also saith the apostle, "If we suffer, we shall also reign with him; if we be dead with him, we shall also live with him."[4]

For the Church of God consists of two orders, clergy and people. Among the clergy are apostles, apostolic men, bishops and other doctors of the Church, to whom is committed the care and governance of the Church, who have to treat and perform ecclesiastical business, that the whole may redound to the saving of souls. Wherefore to St. Peter it was said, and in Peter to the other rulers of the Church, and not to kings or princes, "Thou art Peter, and upon this rock will I build my Church, and the gates of hell shall not prevail against it."[5]

Among the people are kings, princes, dukes, earls and other powers who perform secular business, that the whole may conduce to the peace and unity of the Church. And since it is certain that kings receive their power from the Church, not the latter hers from them but from Christ, so, if I may speak with your pardon, you have not the power to give orders to bishops, nor to absolve or excommunicate anyone, nor to drag clerks before secular tribunals, nor to judge concerning churches or tithes, to forbid bishops to adjudge causes concerning breach of faith or oath, and many other

[1] The English bishops complained of the way the primate had omitted all heading and salutation in writing to the king; see below, No. 140.

[2] II Timothy iii. 12.

[3] Psalms xxxvii. 25.

[4] II Timothy ii. 11, 12.

[5] Matthew xvi. 18.

things of this kind which are written among those customs of yours which you call ancient. . . .[1]

Let my lord, therefore, if it please him, listen to the counsel of his subject, to the warnings of his bishop, and to the chastisement of his father. And first let him for the future abstain from all communion with schismatics. It is known almost to the whole world with what devotion and honour you formerly received our lord the pope and what attachment you showed to the Church of Rome, and also what respect and deference were shown you by them in return. Forbear then, my lord, if you value your soul's salvation, to deprive that Church of her right or to work further injustice against her. Rather do you permit the Church in your realm to enjoy all the liberties she is known to enjoy in other realms. Be mindful also of the promise which you made and placed in writing on the altar at Westminster when you were crowned and anointed king by my predecessor, the promise to preserve to the Church her liberties.[2] Restore then to the church of Canterbury, from which you received your promotion and coronation, the rank and status it held in the time of your predecessors and mine, together with all its possessions, townships, castles and farms, and whatsoever else has been taken by violence either from myself or from my dependants, whether laymen or clerks. And further, if it so please you, permit us to return freely and in peace and in all security to our see, there to perform the duties of our office as we ought, and right commands. And we are ready faithfully and devotedly to serve you as our dearest lord and king with all our strength in whatsoever we are able, saving the honour of God and the Roman Church, and saving also our order. Otherwise you may know for certain that you will experience the divine severity and vengeance.

139. Excommunications pronounced by Thomas, archbishop of Canterbury, at Vézelay (Whit-Sunday, 12 June 1166) as described by John of Salisbury

Extract from a letter written by John of Salisbury to Bartholomew, bishop of Exeter, printed in *Materials for the History of Thomas Becket*, vol. v, p. 382.

On the day after Ascension Day[3] [the archbishop] hastened to Vézelay, intending on the Day of Pentecost to pronounce anathema on the king and his followers. . . . But after he had been informed of the king's illness[4] by a messenger from the king of the French, he forbore to pass sentence on the king, just as I myself had earlier advised, telling him that otherwise he would soon regret it. John of Oxford,[5] however, he publicly excommunicated by the authority of the pope,[6] because–I quote the archbishop's own words–"he had fallen into a damnable heresy in taking a sacrilegious oath to the emperor and holding communication with the schismatic archbishop of Cologne,[7] and usurping for himself the deanery of the church of Salisbury against the express mandate of the pope". These reasons he

[1] The customs of the realm embodied in the Constitutions of Clarendon (No. 126).
[2] The coronation oath.
[3] 3 June 1166.
[4] Henry II had been unable to attend a conference prearranged with Louis VII of France.
[5] See above, p. 742.
[6] By virtue of the legatine authority recently granted to him.
[7] Reginald, archbishop of Cologne, a supporter of the anti-pope, Paschal III. The reference is to the negotiations with the emperor, Frederick I, undertaken by Henry II in May 1165; see above, p. 742.

alleged from the pulpit in the hearing of the whole congregation of divers nations who had flocked to Vézelay on the day of the festival. Likewise in the same place, alleging various and just occasions, he also excommunicated Richard, archdeacon of Poitiers,[1] Richard of Lucé, Jocelyn 'de Balliol', Rannulf 'de Broc', Hugh of St. Clare and Thomas, son of Bernard,[2] together with all who should in future stretch forth their hands against the possessions and goods of the church of Canterbury, or misuse them or in any way interfere with those for whose necessities they have been set apart.

140. The reply of the bishops and clergy of England to the censures of the archbishop of Canterbury (June 1166)

The letter to the archbishop of Canterbury here presented is the second of the two letters dispatched by the bishops and hierarchy of England in answer to the archbishop's condemnation of them at Vézelay. In the earlier letter the whole course of the dispute between the king and the primate is traced out and the blame squarely laid upon the shoulders of the archbishop. Protest is made against the Vézelay proceedings as being invalid and uncanonical, and an appeal against them is lodged with the pope. The second letter is given below; it is printed in *Materials for the History of Thomas Becket*, vol. v, p. 408.

THE CLERGY OF ENGLAND TO THOMAS, ARCHBISHOP OF CANTERBURY

To their venerable father and lord, Thomas, by the grace of God archbishop of Canterbury, the suffragan bishops of the same church and beneficed clergy established in divers places throughout their dioceses, due subjection and obedience. Whatever disturbances, father, your unexpected departure to so great a distance has produced among us, we had hoped they would have been dispelled by God's grace and your own humility and prudence, and turned again to the brightness of former peace. It was some consolation to us after your departure to hear it reported on all sides that in your exile abroad you were indulging in no vain imaginings and harbouring no plots against our lord the king and his realm, but were bearing with modesty the yoke of poverty you had voluntarily taken upon you.[3] It was alleged that your attention was being given to study and prayer, and to redeem with fasting, vigils and mourning the time which you had lost, and that by these spiritual occupations you were climbing the road of accumulated merits to the height of blessed perfection. We rejoiced that by such studies you were zealously pursuing the way to the renewal of peace and all its blessings, and hoped that you might by these means evoke grace from on high into the heart of our lord the king, that so his royal mercy might relax his anger against you and forget in his heart the injuries brought about through your departure. Your friends and well-wishers found access to the king freely so long as these reports were heard of you, and he received with kindness the petitions that were made to restore you to his favour. But now we have learnt from certain persons, and we recall it to mind with some anxiety, that you have sent him a letter of denunciation, in which you omit the usual salutation,[4] and employ neither counsel nor petition to obtain his favour, but that your words and sentiments are alike unfriendly, and you

[1] Richard of Ilchester.
[2] Ralph 'de Diceto' adds the name of Alan 'de Neville'. The sentences were duly confirmed by the pope, *Materials for the History of Thomas Becket*, vol. v, p. 392.
[3] A satirical reference to Becket's sojourn at Pontigny.
[4] See above, No. 138.

threaten, with expressions of the sharpest severity, to launch an interdict and anathema against him. Should this sentence be as rigidly executed as it has been harshly pronounced, so far from hoping to restore tranquillity after our late turmoils, we fear lest they be kindled into a flame provoking a lasting and inexorable hatred. Sacred prudence looks to the end of things and is ever careful to conclude with success what has been commenced in wisdom. Let your discretion, we pray you, recoil from the course on which you are set, and consider whether you can ever obtain the desired end by this means. We have already fallen from the great hope of peace we had conceived and are plunged into the abyss of despair. The sword has again been drawn and the battle engaged, nor can we any longer find grounds for interceding on your behalf. In charity, therefore, we write this counsel to you as to a father, not to add toil to toil, and injury to injury, but to cease these threats, to study patience and humility, to commit your cause to the divine mercy and to the compassionate consideration of our lord the king, and by such conduct you may heap coals of fire upon the heads of many. By this means charity will be enkindled, and by God's grace and the counsels of good men, piety alone will obtain what threats have failed to accomplish. It is better to be praised for voluntary poverty than to be marked in public by all men with the stamp of ingratitude towards your benefactor. The minds of all men are strongly impressed with the favours which our lord the king conferred upon you, the honours to which he raised you from so lowly an estate, and the familiar intercourse to which he admitted you, so that all his dominions, from the northern ocean to the Pyrenees, were subject to your administration, and the world looked upon all as happy who obtained favour in your sight. That your renown might not be shaken by the storms to which all human affairs are exposed, the king wished to anchor you fast in the things which belong to God and his Church. Thus, against the advice of his mother and amid the disapprobation of the whole kingdom, while the Church too, so far as it was able, mourned and murmured at the act, he used every means in his power to raise you to your present rank, hoping that thereby he might henceforth reign in peace and security, rejoicing in your aid and advice. If then he has found an axe that smites, where he looked for safety, what, think you, will the whole world say of you? Will they not bear in mind this unheard-of way of requiting favours received? Spare your good fame, we entreat, have respect to your own glory; and study rather to vanquish by your humility him who is your master, by your charity him who is your son. If our warnings cannot move you, yet the love and fidelity of the supreme pontiff and of the holy Roman Church ought at least to have power to move you. There ought to be little difficulty in inducing you to attempt nothing calculated to increase the difficulties of your holy mother, the Church, already so severely straitened; nothing whereby the disobedience of many may be aggravated by the loss of the remainder who still continue in their obedience. Suppose that by your means and by your exasperation our lord the king (which God forbid!), with so many nations and kingdoms which God has given him, should desert our lord the pope and refuse for the future to follow him, because perchance he may not aid him against you. You know what entreaties, what gifts and promises have been used to induce him to do so. As yet, however, he has stood firm as a rock and magnanimously trodden underfoot all that the world can offer. One thing, however, remains to be feared, lest his own anger prompt him to do that for which treasures or wealth and all that is valued among men have been offered in vain. If all this should happen through you, it will be yours to lament, and the fountain of your tears may ever flow, for it will be out of your power, out of reason, to dry them up. Take counsel, then, in time, if it so please your highness, counsel that may benefit the cause of our lord the pope and the holy Roman Church, and may also be of use to yourself in every way, if it be followed. Perchance those about you are wise in their own conceits, and will not allow you to advance along this road. They encourage you to try what you can do against our lord the king and exercise your power and prerogative against him and his. This power is to be feared by one that is in error, but greatly to be dreaded by one unwilling to make satisfaction. We do not assert that our lord the king has never erred, but we do say and assert with confidence that he has always been prepared to make recompense to God. He has been made king by the Lord to provide in everything for the peace of his subjects. It is to preserve this peace to the churches and peoples committed to his charge that he wishes and requires the dignities vouchsafed to his predecessors to be maintained and secured to himself. If on this point any dispute has arisen between you and him, and the supreme pontiff with fatherly piety has admonished him through our venerable brethren, the bishops of London and Hereford, he has not raised his head aloft into the clouds, but in every matter wherein either the Church or any ecclesiastic has shown himself aggrieved, the king has always answered humbly and mildly that he has never coveted that which belongs to others, but that he will submit to the judgment of the clergy of his realm, and he has always shown himself ready to fulfil what he has thus promised. Obedience is sweet to him when he is warned to correct what he has done amiss to God. Nor does he limit this to mere satisfaction in word, but is ready to give whatever justice may demand. Inasmuch then as he is ready to do and give all that is required, and neither in the slightest particular shuns the judgment of the Church in aught that concerns the Church, nor shows the least disposition to withdraw his neck from the yoke of Christ; by what justice, by what law or canon can you assail him with an interdict, or (God forbid it!) cut him off by the spiritual axe from Christian fellowship? It is praiseworthy in a king not to be carried away by passion, but to be ruled by prudence and discretion. Wherefore it is the common petition of us all that you will not by precipitate measures scatter and destroy, but provide with paternal solicitude that the sheep committed to your charge may enjoy life, peace and security.

We are all moved by what has been lately enacted – some think preposterously – against our brother, the bishop of Salisbury,[1] and his dean,[2] against whom you have launched sentence of suspension and deprivation, and condemned before inquiry had been made into their fault, following, as it seems to us, the heat of anger rather than the course of justice. This is a new mode of giving judgment, unknown hitherto, as we hope, to the laws and canons, to pass sentence first and afterwards to hear the cause. That you may not attempt to exercise or extend this prerogative against our lord the king and his kingdom, against us and the churches and parishes committed to our charge, to the injury of the lord pope, the disgrace and detriment of the holy

[1] Jocelyn 'de Bohun'.
[2] John of Oxford; see above, No. 139.

Roman Church and to the no small increase in our own confusion, we stand upon the remedy of an appeal against you. And whereas we have already appealed directly to our lord the pope before the face of the Church against the sentence which we feared; we do now also appeal a second time to the same in writing, and we fix as the term for the appeal the day of our Lord's Ascension, praying with all possible devotion that you will adopt more salutary counsel and spare this expense and toil to both of us, and so shape your cause that a remedy may be found for it. Father, we bid you farewell in the Lord.

141. Letter from Gilbert Foliot to Thomas Becket (1166)

The letter, from which this passage is extracted, is an apology for the conduct of the bishops and clergy of England in answer to the charges made against them by the archbishop in a letter written earlier in that same year. It rehearses the origin and progress of the dispute between king and primate from its first beginnings, and gives the story of the councils of Clarendon and Northampton from the standpoint of the king. It is printed in *Materials for the History of Thomas Becket*, vol. v, p. 521.

Let us recall to mind what took place at Clarendon, where for three whole days the sole object was to obtain from us [the bishops] a promise to observe unconditionally the customs and privileges of the realm. We stood by you then, because we thought you were standing courageously in the Spirit of the Lord. We stood immovable and undismayed. We stood firm, to the ruin of our fortunes, ready to suffer bodily torment or exile, or, if God so willed, even the sword. What man ever succeeded in getting more unanimous support than you did on that occasion? We were all shut up in one chamber, and on the third day the princes and nobles of the realm, waxing hot in their wrath, burst into the chamber where we sat, muttering and clamouring, threw off their cloaks and shook their fists at us, exclaiming, "Attend all ye who set at naught the statutes of the realm and heed not the king's commands. These hands, these arms, yea, even our bodies are not our own, but belong to our lord the king, and they are ready at his nod to avenge every wrong done to him and to work his will, whatever it may be. No matter what he may command, it will be most just in our eyes since it proceeds from his will alone. Take fresh counsel then, and bend your minds to his command, that you may avert the danger while yet there is time." What followed upon this? Did anyone flee or turn tail? Was anyone broken in spirit? Your letter reproaches us with having turned our backs in the day of battle, with having neither gone up against the adversary nor placed ourselves as a wall of defence before the house of the Lord. Let God judge between us; let him judge in whose cause we would not bend before the threats of princes; let him judge who it was that fled, and who was a deserter in the battle. For assuredly it was not that noble and most constant champion of God's cause, Henry of Winchester, nor Nigel of Ely, nor Robert of Lincoln, nor Hilary of Chichester, nor Jocelyn of Salisbury, nor Bartholomew of Exeter, nor Richard of Chester, nor Roger of Worcester, nor Robert of Hereford, nor Gilbert of London. All these lacked not courage, but there was none found to strike them; they accounted temporal things as dross and exposed themselves and their possessions fearlessly for Christ and his Church. Let the truth then be told, let the light of day be shed on what then occurred in the presence of us all. It was the leader of our chivalry who turned his back, the captain of our camp who fled; our lord of Canterbury himself abandoned the society of his brethren and forsook our common counsel, and making his own decision, returned to us after a space and uttered these words: "It is the Lord's will that I should forswear myself; for the present I submit and incur perjury, to do penance for it later as best I may." At hearing these words we stood thunderstruck, clinging to each other with mutual astonishment and groaning in spirit at the fall of one whom we had judged to be a champion of virtue and constancy. There is no such thing as yea-and-nay with the Lord, nor did we anticipate that his disciple was so easily to be moved. When the head is faint, the other members of the body become faint also and straightway suffer from the same weakness. Our archbishop himself acquiesced in the king's royal prerogative and the ancient customs of the realm, and in their being recorded in writing; and when he had himself sworn unconditionally to our lord the king "in the word of truth" to observe them for the future, he constrained us by force to bind ourselves by a similar pledge of obedience. . . .

142. Letter from Thomas Becket to William of Pavia (November or December 1167)

Late in 1166 Alexander III had appointed William of Pavia[1] and Otto of Ostia[2] as legates to try to settle the case between the king and the archbishop. This letter shows Becket's reaction to the legation. He seeks to identify his cause with that of the papacy, and places the responsibility for the issue of events on the pope and the legates. Printed: *Materials for the History of Thomas Becket*, vol. VI, p. 296.

To his revered lord and father, William, by the grace of God, cardinal-priest of the holy Roman Church, Thomas, by the same grace humble minister of the church of Canterbury and wretched exile, greeting. May you so act as to live in the Lord. I did not think I was to be put up for sale, or that you would make profit out of my blood and win from the price of iniquity a name and reputation for yourself. You would have taken pains to promote a very different issue of events, if you had not been perilously forgetful of your status, and if you had not weighed the spoils of fortune in a different balance from mine. You were perhaps encouraged to do so by the contemplation of my present lot, but while you beheld my misfortunes, you should have hoped for my greater felicity hereafter. The vicissitudes of this life are ever changeable, and as it is easy to fall from success and prosperity, so also the opposite is equally possible. I cannot believe you to be ignorant, although you have as yet had no personal experience of it, that nothing is so firmly established that it does not involve danger, and that the contrary is also true. I write thus that you may in future carefully weigh these sudden changes of fortune; mark them well and, when you have done so, exercise forbearance. The ship of Peter ought not to have been exposed to such hazards; although she cannot be crushed, she may often be shaken; she cannot sink, but will float again, however the waves may toss her. If then you would be a true disciple and good seaman of that true fisherman and best of pilots,[3] as you have often experienced the benefit of the fair wind of prosperity, so also you

[1] Cardinal-priest of St. Peter ad Vincula.
[2] Cardinal-deacon of St. Nicholas.
[3] St. Peter.

should in every danger oppose a firm courage to the gathering storm. If you have been glad to receive peace at his hand, will you not also patiently bear adversity, which perhaps will endure but for a moment? Even so your master, the prince of the apostles, not by yielding to princes nor by dispensing peace to the wicked, but by resisting them, won for himself by martyrdom a name on earth and glory in the heavens. Thus has the Church grown in strength, when it was believed she was extinguished. In short, this is what I desire for you; so to act here that you may live happily in the Lord. Farewell, that so I may fare better.

143. A list of persons excommunicated by Thomas Becket during the year 1169

This list, printed in *Materials for the History of Thomas Becket*, vol. VI, pp. 601–602, was evidently compiled after Ascension Day, 29 May 1169, since it includes the names of persons whom the archbishop had merely threatened with excommunication on that day.

These are the names of those excommunicated by the lord archbishop of Canterbury:

Gilbert, bishop of London.
Jocelyn, bishop of Salisbury.
Geoffrey Ridel, archdeacon of Canterbury.
Richard of Ilchester, archdeacon of Poitiers.
Nigel 'de Sackville'.
Richard 'de Hastings', nephew of Richard 'de Hastings'.
Letard, nephew of Archbishop Theobald.
Robert 'de Broc'.
Robert, brother of William of Eynsford.
Robert, vicar of Geoffrey, archdeacon of Canterbury.
The incumbent of the church of Chart.
The incumbent of the church of Helles.
Richard of Lucé.[1]
Hugh of St. Clare.[2]
Thomas, son of Bernard.
Rannulf 'de Broc'.
William of Ashford.
Robert, the butler of Archbishop Theobald.
Alan of Ratling.
William of Le Bec.
The tenant of the land of Mundeham, of the manor of Pagham, which the king confiscated from the church of Canterbury on account of John the marshal,[3] if it be held by any man other than the king.
The tenant of the land of Lese, of the manor of Otford, which was held by William of Eynsford, if it be held by any man other than the king.
John Comyn.[4]

[1] Justiciar of England; see above, p. 680.
[2] Hugh Bigot, earl of Norfolk.
[3] See above, pp. 724 *et sqq.*
[4] Afterwards archbishop of Dublin.

Guy Rufus who holds, like those aforesaid, is to restore whatsoever he received from the revenues of the treasurer of Lisieux to the archbishop of Canterbury.

These are they who hold ecclesiastical and lay possessions of the church and of the archbishop of Canterbury, which he wills and demands should be restored to him and his men in their entirety. From the bishop of London he demands restitution of whatsoever he has received from the revenues of his clergy. And if there are others who have received possessions, whether ecclesiastical or lay, from the king's hand or by his bequest, belonging to the church of Canterbury, they are excommunicate, until they shall restore these same possessions and everything obtained therefrom to the church of Canterbury and the lord archbishop. In addition, the following have also been excommunicated by the said archbishop: Wimar, who was clerk to Earl Hugh, Adam of Charing, and William Giffard.

144. The conference at Montmartre (18 November 1169) as described by Herbert of Bosham

At this conference, where were present the kings of France and England, the archbishops of Canterbury and Rouen, and the legate, Vivian, a settlement of the outstanding differences between king and primate was all but reached. Alarmed by reports that Becket had threatened to launch an interdict on England, Henry II made sweeping concessions, virtually yielding everything. He promised to withdraw all obnoxious customs and usages[1] and to guarantee full freedom to the Church in matters of appeals and visitations. In return Becket agreed to omit the saving clause and to return immediately to England. Even the vexed question of the confiscated ecclesiastical property and revenues was satisfactorily settled. At this point the archbishop overreached himself: he demanded to be admitted to the kiss of peace. The king refused on pretext of a vow, and the meeting broke up with nothing tangible gained. The failure of the conference is described by Herbert of Bosham. Printed: *Materials for the History of Thomas Becket*, vol. III, p. 449.

Thus, it seemed, and we all hoped, that after so many and various storms we were on the point of entering harbour, when the archbishop, through the mediators, demanded some guarantee of the peace offered to him, not, as he added, because he suspected any treachery on the king's part, but because he entertained suspicions about the king's vassals, on account of the enmity they had so long shown towards him. He particularly wished for some outward sign or token of peace to be passed between them. Now, being a prudent man, he had some days before the meeting consulted the lord pope as to what guarantee he should require, if perchance the king should permit him after so long variance to be reconciled and to return to his church. To this inquiry the pope replied that as a priest he ought not to exact a pledge or an oath from the king as security. To this he added that the cause the archbishop was advocating was the cause of justice and of the Church, and that, if peace was to be made, it must be at one and the same time the peace of the Church and the peace of justice. For the Church, whether in peace or without peace, it was precious to yield one's life, and for the archbishop more precious than for others. None of the ordinary guarantees was therefore to be required of a priest in such a case, declared the pope in his reply. . . . He therefore wrote to the archbishop that if it were God's will that peace should be restored between him and the king, he might be content with the

[1] Though not expressly mentioned, the Constitutions of Clarendon might be regarded as included.

kiss of peace without demanding any temporal guarantee.[1] For the kiss of peace should of itself suffice for a priest maintaining the cause of justice, and unless any other security were spontaneously offered, it ought not to be exacted.

The archbishop, fortified by this advice, after everything had been arranged with much difficulty and labour, followed the pope's counsel, and desired that the king should bestow upon him the kiss of peace as a token of amity and concord between them, saying that after such great enmity he would be content with that alone. But when this was reported to the king through the French king and the other mediators, he answered that he would gladly have done so, if he had not in his wrath previously sworn in public never to grant the archbishop the kiss of peace, even if he should at some future time be minded to make peace with him and restore him to favour. For no other reason would he now refuse it, certainly not because he retained in his heart any anger or grudge against the archbishop, but solely because he had sworn this oath.

The king of the French and the majority of the mediators, when they heard this, suspected that beneath the honeyed speeches which had previously passed between them they had imbibed some hidden poison. So they returned in haste to the archbishop, who was awaiting them in the chapel of the Martyrdom, and reported the king's answer. And because they were timid men, and now entertained suspicions of everything, they neither persuaded nor dissuaded him as to his course of action, but contented themselves with delivering the king's answer word for word, as he had spoken it.

Now the archbishop was one of the most wary of men by reason of his great experience, and as soon as he heard the king's answer, he and his followers became suspicious. The first words he cautiously uttered showed that he foresaw the future. He did not stop to take advice as to his response, but answered decisively and absolutely that he would not for the present make peace with the king, unless, in accordance with the advice of the pope, it were ratified by the kiss of peace. This decisive answer broke up the conference just as night was drawing nigh, and the kings had a long journey before them to Mantes, about twelve leagues distant from Paris, where their quarters had been prepared.

The king of the English, who was weary after his full day and now had a long night's journey before him, repeatedly cursed the archbishop on the way, recapitulating and reckoning up the labours, annoyances and distresses which he had caused him.

After the kings had departed, we immediately repaired to a house called the Temple, belonging to the Templars, just outside Paris, where we had our lodging. As we were leaving the chapel of the Martyrdom, in which, as we have said, the peace negotiations had been conducted that day, one of our company came up to the archbishop and said, "This day the peace of the Church has been discussed in the chapel of the Martyrdom, and it is my belief that only through your martyrdom will the Church ever obtain peace." The archbishop, turning round, answered him laconically, "Would to God she might be delivered, even by my blood!"

[1] The kiss of peace was commonly employed to mark the final confirmation of an agreement; it was regarded as a pledge of security to the parties, though there were cases where it did not secure a rebel from punishment at the hands of his lord. Becket was reminded of the experience of Robert 'de Silian', a subject of the count of Flanders, who was subsequently seized and thrown into a dungeon.

145. Account of the coronation of the young King Henry (June 1170), by William fitz Stephen

The coronation of his son may be considered a cardinal blunder on Henry's part. It alienated the pope and his legates, and gave Thomas the opportunity of appearing in the rôle of a prelate who had suffered yet further outrage through a tyrant king. It seems that the papal rescript, forbidding the coronation unless the archbishop of Canterbury conducted the ceremony, was never delivered. The king crossed to England, and the coronation took place, in spite of letters from the pope and Becket forbidding the archbishop of York to usurp the rights of the church of Canterbury. William fitz Stephen's narrative is printed in *Materials for the History of Thomas Becket*, vol. III, pp. 103 *et seq.*

The king caused the ports to be very strictly watched. Meanwhile he returned to England[1] and suddenly caused his son, Henry, to be crowned in London,[2] the above-mentioned Roger, archbishop of York, performing the act, against the desire and opinion of almost everyone in the kingdom.[3] The archbishop of Canterbury had with foresight bent his eyes on this event, and had obtained letters from the lord pope, which were delivered to the archbishop of York and the bishop of London on the Saturday of the week of the coronation, forbidding them or any of the English bishops to lay hands on the prince to crown him in the absence of the archbishop of Canterbury, who had not been recalled for this purpose, because this coronation ought to belong to the church of Canterbury. Nevertheless, he was crowned on the day before the Feast of SS. Vitus and Modestus. Immediately afterwards the king recrossed the Channel.[4]

Now before these events, when he was making preparations for the coronation, he informed the bishop of Worcester of his design when they were both overseas, and ordered him to return home and take his place with the bishops, few of whom were then in England, at the coronation of his kinsman.[5] But the king did not make it clear to him that he wished his son to be crowned by the archbishop of York. The bishop, hoping for better times, agreed, and came to the seaport of Dieppe. The king had already sailed for England. The queen,[6] who had stayed behind in Normandy, and Richard of Le Hommet, justiciar of Normandy, sent letters to the bishop of Worcester at the said port, forbidding him to cross the Channel. They also sent other letters to the *prévôt* and the owners of transports forbidding them to convey the bishop over, or to allow him to be conveyed. For they had sure intelligence that the bishop would never permit the young prince to be crowned at the hands of the archbishop of York within the province of Canterbury, while the archbishop of Canterbury, whose prerogative it was to crown kings, was still alive. Thus being forbidden to cross, the bishop remained in Normandy.

After the coronation the king immediately returned to Normandy, as stated above. The bishop of Worcester met him three miles outside Falaise. The king showed himself enraged with him and at once broke forth into words of contumely, saying,

[1] 3 March 1170, after four years' absence from England.

[2] 14 June 1170.

[3] Four English bishops assisted at the ceremony: Hugh of Durham, Gilbert of London, Jocelyn of Salisbury and Walter of Rochester. The Norman bishops present were Henry of Bayeux and Giles of Evreux.

[4] *circa* 24 June.

[5] The bishop was Roger, son of Robert, earl of Gloucester, half-brother of the Empress Maud, mother of Henry II. He held the see of Worcester from 1164 to 1179.

[6] Eleanor of Aquitaine, formerly wife of Louis VII of France; see above, Nos. 12, 15.

"Now it is plain that you are a traitor. I myself ordered you to be present at my son's coronation and named the day for you. You refused to come; whereby you have clearly shown that you love neither me nor my son's advancement. The truth of the matter is that you favour my enemy[1] and hate me and mine; but the revenues of your bishopric shall remain to you no longer. I will snatch them out of your hands, since you have proved yourself unworthy either of bishopric or benefice. Truly never were you the son of good Earl Robert, my uncle, who brought us both up in his castle and had us taught there the rudiments of good conduct and learning." The bishop, secure in his innocence, told the king simply and discreetly what had happened, how he had come to the port and how he had received letters ordering him not to cross the Channel. The king did not believe him and replied in great anger, "The queen is in the castle of Falaise and Richard of Le Hommet is perhaps also there or will be on the morrow; do you name them as the instigators of this?" "Not the queen," answered the bishop, "lest perchance out of fear and respect for you she suppress the truth and your anger burn more hotly against me; or if she should confess it to be true, then you might rage madly and rudely against that noble lady. The matter does not seem to me of sufficient importance for her to suffer one harsh word from you about it. But I had rather this happened than that I should have been present at the coronation, which was unjust and contrary to God's will, not through any fault of him who was crowned, but through the presumption of the man who crowned him. . . .[2] Why do you threaten to deprive me of the benefices of my bishopric? I am expelled or not expelled, as you please: they are yours, if you are not satisfied with what you receive, without doubt unjustly and to the peril of your soul, from the archbishopric and the six vacant bishoprics, besides numerous abbeys, and with confiscating to secular uses the alms of your forefathers, the pious kings, and the patrimony of Jesus Christ."

These things and others like unto them were spoken in the hearing of all the king's retinue who were riding with him, and a certain knight of Aquitaine, who did not know the bishop, said to his companions, "And who is this who speaks thus?" He was told that it was a bishop. He replied, "It is lucky for the king that he is a priest; if he were a knight, he would not leave the king two acres of land." Another, desirous of pleasing the king, bitterly reviled the bishop. The king heard it, turned on him angrily and abused him in vile language, saying among other things, "Do you think, you rascal, that if I say what I choose to my bishop and kinsman, either you or any other man may dishonour him with your tongue or threaten him? I can hardly keep my hands from your eyes: neither you nor the others may say one word against the bishop." They came to their lodgings. After dinner the king and the bishop talked amicably in private together concerning a reconciliation with the archbishop.

146. The reconciliation between Henry II and Thomas Becket at Fréteval (22 July 1170) as described by Herbert of Bosham

The passage of the legates, Rotrou, archbishop of Rouen, and Bernard, bishop of Nevers, appointed to the fourth commission by Alexander III, to Normandy was delayed until the beginning of June 1170. They had an interview with Becket at Sens on 16 July[3] and succeeded in persuading him to attend a conference of the kings of France and England arranged for that month. After this

[1] Becket. [2] The archbishop of York; see above, p. 753.

[3] R. W. Eyton, *Court, Household and Itinerary of King Henry II* (1878), p. 140.

events moved rapidly, though the final reconciliation at Fréteval seems to have taken most people by surprise. Henry was, however, considerably alarmed by this time. The coronation of his son, the younger Henry, without his bride, Margaret, daughter of Louis VII, had enraged and alienated Louis, while it was known that the legates were authorized to lay Henry's continental dominions under interdict,[1] if he refused to make peace and reconcile himself with the archbishop. In such a case the whole Angevin empire would be seriously threatened by the French king. In these circumstances Henry showed himself willing to grant all that was demanded of him.[2] The account of the reconciliation given below is from Herbert of Bosham. Printed: *Materials for the History of Thomas Becket*, vol. III, pp. 465-467.

The king, therefore, seeing matters reduced to this extremity, promised to make peace without fail. Accordingly we were summoned to attend a meeting due to take place between the two kings and did so. On the third day of the conference, after the conclusion of the parley between the kings and the withdrawal of the most Christian king of the French, the question of our peace was immediately considered through the mediation of certain magnates[3] whom the French king had appointed for that purpose. He himself neither could nor would take part in the negotiations. But why should I multiply words? There peace was made between us, and the kiss, which had before in the other conference[4] been sought but denied, was now neither demanded by the archbishop nor offered or refused by the king. No mention was there made of it, but the king granted us peace and security publicly in the presence of the prelates and lay magnates there assembled. As regards the royal customs and the property, both movable and immovable, which had been taken from us, the same form of peace was now observed and conceded to us as we have described above at the previous conference between the kings,[4] where the refusal to bestow the kiss of peace had been the sole obstacle to our reconciliation. And now Christ's doughty champion,[5] eager for peace and not afraid of death, did not demand the kiss, lest this should be an impediment to peace, but prudently and consciously accepted the terms as they were offered, influenced by his love of peace rather than by fear of death. Peace was concluded on the Feast of St. Mary Magdalene,[6] hard by the scene of the parley between the two kings on the previous day, that is to say, on the borders of Chartraine and Maine, between the two castles of Viefui and Fréteval, in a verdant meadow which, as we learnt long afterwards, was from ancient times called by the inhabitants "Traitors' Field".

The king and the archbishop then turned their horses aside and rode together towards a level place, talking to one another in private. Among other things the archbishop craved the king's permission to punish by ecclesiastical censure his own suffragans for the injury they had inflicted on him and the church of Canterbury in concert with the archbishop of York by crowning the king's son, Henry. To this the king assented, and the archbishop, in gratitude for this concession, forthwith dismounted from his horse and in the sight of all there present humbly prostrated himself

[1] They had delivered to the king a letter of warning from the pope at the end of June; R. W. Eyton, *loc. cit.*, *ante*.

[2] According to William fitz Stephen (*Materials for the History of Thomas Becket*, vol. III, p. 106) one of the king's courtiers remarked to the king, "Why do you persist in keeping the archbishop abroad? It would be better to have him in England than out of it?" This consideration seems to have carried some weight with Henry.

[3] William, archbishop of Sens, was the chief mediator, and deserves most of the credit for the successful outcome of the meeting.

[4] Montmartre; see above, No. 144.

[5] *fortis Christi athleta.*

[6] 22 July.

at the king's feet. But as he was about to remount his horse, the king held the stirrup for him,[1] while all the bystanders gazed in astonishment, not knowing the cause, until the archbishop related it privately to his followers as they were returning. Then indeed you might have seen the thoughts of many hearts revealed, especially among the courtiers, some of whom rejoiced while others were downcast and put to confusion, because up till then they had vomited the venom of sedition and discord. Others, however, were neither dejected nor bewildered, for they suspected some insincerity in these proceedings[2] and anticipated that in the end the peace would engender discord, sorrow and lamentation. And in this they were not deceived, as the sequence of events was to show.

147. Writ of Henry II announcing his reconciliation with the archbishop (15 October 1170)

This writ addressed to the young king, Henry, who was acting as regent for his father in England, is an official notification of the agreement made at Fréteval. It is attested by one of the legates appointed by the pope to bring about the settlement. Printed: R. W. Eyton, *Court, Household and Itinerary of King Henry II* (1878), p. 146.

Henry, king of England, to his son, Henry the king, greeting. Know that Thomas, archbishop of Canterbury, has made peace with me according to my will. I therefore command that he and all his men shall have peace. You are to ensure that the archbishop and all his men who left England for his sake shall have all their possessions as they had them three months before the archbishop withdrew from England. Moreover, you will cause to come before you the senior and more important knights of the honour of Saltwood, and by their oath you will cause recognition[3] to be made of what is held there in fee from the archbishopric of Canterbury; and what the recognition shall declare to be in the fief of the archbishop you will cause him to have. Witness: Rotrou,[4] archbishop of Rouen. At Chinon.

* * *

(iv) *The murder of Thomas Becket and its sequel (December 1170–February 1173)*

The dramatic sequence of events is made clear in the vivid narratives which follow. They are separately introduced.

148. The return of Thomas Becket to Canterbury (1 December 1170) as described by William fitz Stephen

On 24 November, Becket reached Wissant. On 31 November he dispatched letters suspending the archbishop of York, and excommunicating afresh the bishops of London and Salisbury, whose absolution from the previous sentence had been conditional. These letters were delivered to the

[1] This is confirmed by the letter written by the archbishop to the pope, giving his own version of the proceedings at Fréteval. The letter continues: "What more?" said the king; "My lord archbishop, let us restore again our old affection, let each of us show the other what good he can, and forget altogether the former hatred." *Materials for the History of Thomas Becket*, vol. VII, p. 332.

[2] Towards the end of the proceedings Arnulf of Lisieux suggested that, since the king had restored Becket to favour, the latter should absolve all whom he had excommunicated. The archbishop, suspecting a trap, declined to do this in every case and without satisfaction being made; *ibid.*, p. 335.

[3] An interesting example of the use of the sworn inquest.

[4] Rotrou, archbishop of Rouen, 1165–1183.

censured prelates as they were leaving to join the king in Normandy. On 1 December, Becket landed at Sandwich and at once proceeded to Canterbury. This account of his triumphal progress is printed in *Materials for the Life of Thomas Becket*, vol. III, p. 119.

It became known in the church and city of Canterbury that the lord archbishop had landed. Then all the people rejoiced from the greatest down to the most humble. They decorated the cathedral; they clad themselves in silk and precious garments; they made ready a public banquet for many guests and prepared ample bedding for them. The archbishop was received in solemn procession. The church resounded with hymns and organ-music, the hall with fanfares of trumpets, and the city with loud rejoicings on every side. The archbishop preached a most edifying sermon, taking for his text: "Here we have no continuing city, but we seek one to come."[1] The two archdeacons, Geoffrey Ridel of Canterbury[2] and Richard of Poitiers,[3] the king's familiar counsellors, whom, however, the archbishop had promoted to their present eminence, and who were also his vassals, had already arrived in Kent on their way to the king overseas. But when they heard of the archbishop's arrival at Canterbury, they straightway turned their horses and made for a port farther to the west. This flight of theirs was taken by several persons for an evil omen.

149. The return of Thomas Becket to Canterbury (1 December 1170) as described by Herbert of Bosham

Printed: *Materials for the History of Thomas Becket*, vol. III, p. 478.

On the morrow[4] the archbishop left the port where he had landed, which was about six miles distant from Canterbury. As he set out for the city he was welcomed by the poor of the land as a victim sent from heaven, yea, even as an angel of God, with joy and thanksgiving. But why do I say with joy? Rather–if one can use such a term–Christ's poor received him with the victor's laurels and as the Lord's anointed. So wherever the archbishop passed, a swarm of poor folk, small and great, young and old, flocked to meet him, some prostrating themselves in the way before him, others tearing off their garments and strewing them in the way, crying aloud, again and again, "Blessed is he that cometh in the name of the Lord."[5] Likewise the parish priests with their flocks went out to meet him in procession with their crosses, saluting their father and begging his blessing, reiterating that oft-repeated cry: "Blessed is he that cometh in the name of the Lord." But to what end? You would certainly have said, had you seen it, that the Lord was a second time approaching his Passion, and that, amidst the rejoicings of children and the poor, he, who died once at Jerusalem for the salvation of the whole world, was now again ready to die a second time at Canterbury for the English Church. And though the road was short, yet amidst the thronging and pressing crowds he could scarce reach Canterbury that day, where he was welcomed with the sound of trumpets and organs, with psalms and hymns and spiritual songs by the poor of Christ, his children, and by his holy

[1] Hebrews xiii. 14.
[2] See above, No. 143.
[3] Richard of Ilchester; see above, No. 143.
[4] William fitz Stephen gives 1 December for Becket's landing at Sandwich; Herbert of Bosham 3 December.
[5] Matthew xxi. 9.

monastery with the devotion and reverence due to its father. Then, at his first coming into the cathedral you might have seen the face of this man, which some saw and noted with astonishment, for it seemed as though his heart aflame burned in his very countenance. . . .

Then the archbishop, standing up in his episcopal throne, admitted each of his brethren to the kiss of peace, with much weeping and lamentation on all sides. And as he stood there, the disciple who wrote these things[1] came up to him and said, "My lord, it matters not to us now when you depart out of this world, since today in you Christ's spouse, the Church, has conquered, nay rather, Christ himself conquers, Christ reigns, Christ rules." And the archbishop looked on him that said these things, yet answered he nothing. So, when all the ceremonies solemnly performed in the cathedral that day were ended, the archbishop retired to his palace, pondering on the events of that joyful yet solemn day.

150. The events leading up to the murder of Thomas Becket (December 1170) as described by William fitz Stephen

Early in December, Roger, archbishop of York, Gilbert, bishop of London, and Jocelyn, bishop of Salisbury, joined the king in Normandy and brought him the news that they had once again been excommunicated by the archbishop (see above, p. 756). After hearing their story, and during the discussions which followed, the king in great anger uttered the fatal words which were the direct cause of the murder of the archbishop. The four knights, who were to kill the archbishop, left the king on 26 December. They arrived at Saltwood Castle in Kent, belonging to the 'de Broc' family, who were among Becket's bitterest enemies. On Christmas Day Becket had preached his famous sermon at High Mass in the cathedral. The following narrative is printed in *Materials for the History of Thomas Becket*, vol. III, pp. 127 *et seq.*

The archbishop of York and the bishops of London and Salisbury, accompanied by the archdeacon of Poitiers[2]–the archdeacon of Canterbury,[3] having been delayed by stormy seas, had not yet caught up with them–were on their way to the court of the king overseas. By chance they met the king, who was going to visit the archbishop of Tyre. They related the story of the excommunication and suspension of the bishops, which, however, so it was reported, he already knew. They laid all the blame on the archbishop of Canterbury: they charged him with treason, they accused him in his absence when he was defenceless, fearing lest he should be summoned to a hearing. . . . Their evil accusations were doubled by falsehood. It was reported to the king that the archbishop was careering about the kingdom at the head of a strong force of armed men. The king asked the bishops for their advice. The archbishop of York replied, "Seek advice from your barons and your knights; it is not for us to say what should be done." At length one of them said, "My lord, while Thomas lives, you will not have peace or quiet or see good days." At this such fury, bitterness and passion against the archbishop took possession of the king, that they appeared on his countenance and in his gestures.[4] Perceiving his emotion and eager to win his

[1] Cf. above, p. 735.

[2] Richard of Ilchester; see above, Nos. 143, 148.

[3] Geoffrey Ridel; see above, Nos. 143, 148.

[4] Edward Grim, in describing the scene, thus records the king's words: "I have nourished and promoted in my realm idle and wretched knaves, faithless to their lord, whom they suffer to be mocked thus shamefully by a low-born clerk." (*Materials for the History of Thomas Becket*, vol. II, p. 429; cf. Herbert of Bosham, *ibid.*, vol. III, p. 487.)

favour, four knights of his household, Reginald fitz Urse, William 'de Traci', Hugh of Morville and Richard Brito, having sworn, so it was said, to encompass the death of the archbishop, quitted the court. . . .

The four knights, Reginald fitz Urse and his fellows, who had sailed from different ports, by the guidance of the devil, the old enemy of all good men, met at the same hour in England at the castle of Saltwood belonging to the family of 'de Broc'. Ere this, however, the blessed archbishop had received most sure tidings of the imminent arrival of his murderers. Finding great consolation in the Lord, he played the man and put on the whole armour of God, that he might be able to stand in the day of the Lord;[1] but, so far as he could, he kept the matter secret, lest a tumult should arise at this festive season. . . .[2]

On Christmas Eve he read the lesson from the Gospel, "the book of the generation",[3] and celebrated the midnight Mass. Before the High Mass on Christmas Day, which he also celebrated, he preached a splendid sermon to the people, taking for his subject a text on which he was wont to ponder, namely "on earth peace to men of good will".[4] And when he made mention of the holy fathers of the church of Canterbury who were therein confessors, he said that they already had one archbishop, who was a martyr, St. Alphege, and it was possible that in a short time they would have yet another. And because of the shameful injury inflicted on the horse of a certain poor peasant of his in the service of the church of Canterbury by cutting off its tail, he bound Robert 'de Broc'[5] with a sentence of excommunication, as he had previously threatened him by messengers, while inviting him to make reparation. But he, being contumacious, had returned answer by a certain knight, David of Romney, that if the archbishop excommunicated him, he would act like an excommunicate. Also, those who had violently taken possession of his two churches of Harrow and Throwley and had not admitted his officers, he involved in the same sentence.

On St. Stephen's Day[6] he again celebrated at the High Mass and on the next day, the Feast of St. John, Apostle and Evangelist, he sent secretly to France two of his clerks, Master Herbert[7] and Alexander the Welshman,[8] his cross-bearer. A third, Gilbert 'de Glanville', he dispatched to the lord pope; two others, Richard, his chaplain, and John Planeta, he sent to the bishop of Norwich[9] to absolve provisionally certain priests of the land of Earl Hugh[10] who, being excommunicate, had presumed to celebrate the divine offices. But the priests were first to give a pledge that they would visit the lord pope within a year, or send two of their number to represent them all, for the purpose of obtaining pardon and penance from the pope in person.

[1] Cf. Ephesians vi. 11, 13.

[2] After the flight of the four knights had been discovered, the king issued a warrant for Becket's arrest and gave orders to stop the knights, whose purpose was suspected. There is no doubt, as Edward Grim says, that the king was at the time wholly ignorant of their flight.

[3] The opening words of the Gospel of St. Matthew.

[4] Luke ii. 14 (Vulgate).

[5] This outrage was actually the work of John 'de Broc', Robert's nephew, but the elder members of the family had also perpetrated other crimes since the archbishop's return to England: Robert himself had waylaid a train of packhorses, while Rannulf had plundered one of his ships.

[6] 26 December 1170.

[7] Herbert of Bosham.

[8] Alexander Llewelyn; see above, pp. 723, 728, 740.

[9] William 'de Turbe', bishop of Norwich, 1146–1174.

[10] Hugh Bigot, earl of Norfolk.

151. The events leading up to the murder of Thomas Becket (December 1170) as described by Herbert of Bosham

This account may in some sense be regarded as a continuation of No. 149. It is printed in *Materials for the History of Thomas Becket*, vol. III, p. 484.

On the day of our Lord's Nativity, which was, if I mistake not, about the twenty-seventh[1] day after our arrival in England, the archbishop ascended the pulpit and preached to the people. At the end of his sermon he predicted that the time of his departure drew nigh, and that shortly he would be taken from them. And when he said these things concerning his departure, verily, tears rather than words burst from him. Likewise the hearts of his hearers were beyond measure moved with grief and contrition, so that you might have seen and heard in every corner of the church weeping and lamentation and the people murmuring among themselves, "Father, why dost thou desert us so soon, and to whom dost thou leave us so desolate?" For these were no wolves but sheep who knew the voice of their shepherd and grieved when they heard that he would so soon leave this world, although they knew not when nor where nor in what way this should come to pass. . . . Truly, had you witnessed these things, you would have said that you heard with your ears and saw with your eyes that beast of the prophet's vision whose face was that of a lion and of a man.[2] The service ended, the archbishop, who had shown himself so devout at the Lord's Table that day, afterwards made merry, as was his wont, at the table of this world. Moreover, as it was the Feast of the Nativity, although a Friday, he partook of meat as on other days, thereby demonstrating that on such a festival it was more religious to eat than to abstain. . . .

On the morrow of the Nativity, that is, on the Feast of the Blessed Martyr Stephen, he called apart the disciple who wrote these things,[3] saying, "I have arranged to send thee to our lord the king of the French, to our venerable brother, the archbishop of Sens, and to other princes of the land to tell them what thou hast seen and heard concerning this peace, how that for us it is a peace which is no peace, but rather turmoil and confusion." To whom the disciple, unable to restrain his tears, answered, "Holy father, why hast thou done this? Why act in this way? I know for certain that I shall see thee in the flesh no more. I had determined to stay faithfully at thy side; verily, as it seems to me, thou seekest to deprive of the fruit of thy consummation, one who has hitherto continued with thee in thy temptations;[4] nor shall I be, as now I see, a companion of thy glory, who have been partner in thy pain."

Then said the archbishop amid a flood of tears, "Not so, my son, not so; thou shalt not be deprived of the fruit, if thou fulfil the command of thy father and follow his counsel. Nevertheless what thou sayest and bewailest is indeed true, that thou shalt see me in the flesh no more. Yet I will that thou depart, especially since the king holds thee in greater suspicion, where the cause of the Church is at stake, than the others."[5]

[1] This is wrong, even according to Herbert's own reckoning; see above, p. 757. Actually it was the twenty-fourth.

[2] Revelations iv. 7.

[3] See above, pp. 735, 758.

[4] Cf. Luke xxii. 28.

[5] This remark perhaps gives a clue to the archbishop's real reason for sending Herbert away, namely to remove from his counsels at this critical juncture in his affairs the man who was recognized to be the strongest advocate of extreme measures.

So, on the third day after Christmas, being the Feast of St. John the Evangelist, in the darkness of the night, because I feared to be waylaid, with lamentation and many tears, again and again begging and receiving his blessing, I took leave of my father, whom, as he himself had foretold, I never again saw in the flesh nor shall see. Yet, and with this I end[1] my history, I pray with my whole heart, with all my soul and all my strength, that him whom I shall not see again in time, I may be worthy to see in eternity, and may be made partner of his crown, as I was his comrade in the battle.

152. Narrative of the murder of Thomas Becket (29 December 1170) by Edward Grim

All the contemporary biographers of Becket, with the exception of Alan of Tewkesbury, whose work is a mere supplement to the *Life* of John of Salisbury, include in their narratives accounts of the martyrdom. Of these five were written, wholly or in part, from ocular testimony, namely those by Edward Grim, William fitz Stephen, John of Salisbury, whose account is on the same meagre scale as the earlier part of his *Life*, and those by the two monks, William of Canterbury, and Benedict, later abbot of Peterborough, whose *Passion of St. Thomas* survives only in fragments. Herbert of Bosham gives, as usual, a lengthy and prolix account, but he was absent from England at the time of the murder. So also was 'Roger of Pontigny', although his narrative is vivid, dramatic and extremely well-informed. The account of the 'Lambeth Anonymous' is so inaccurate as to be almost worthless, although the writer expressly states in his preface that he was an eyewitness of the event.

Of these various narratives the two best are those of William fitz Stephen and Edward Grim, both of whom are known to have stood by the archbishop to the last. That of Benedict of Peterborough is also highly circumstantial, but he did not actually witness the tragedy for, as he sorrowfully admits, he had earlier fled along with John of Salisbury and the other clerks.

Edward Grim may be regarded as the most detached and impartial witness, since he was a stranger only lately come to Canterbury for the purpose of seeing the archbishop, and his presence there was thus accidental. All the incidents he records are confirmed by the other writers, though they naturally add other details not to be found in his work. Grim's account is therefore to be preferred and is the one selected for presentation here. It is supplemented in places by extracts from William fitz Stephen and Benedict. It should be noted that, while considerable differences on points of detail exist in the various narratives, there is substantial agreement among them as to the basic facts and the sequence of events. A detailed comparative analysis of all the accounts is to be found in E. A. Abbott, *St. Thomas of Canterbury, his Death and Miracles*, vol. I (London, 1898). The Latin text of Grim's narrative is printed in *Materials for the History of Thomas Becket*, vol. II, pp. 430–438.

So then the aforesaid men,[2] no knights forsooth but miserable wretches, as soon as they landed, summoned the king's officials, whom the archbishop had already excommunicated, and by falsely proclaiming that they were acting with the king's approval and in his name, they got together a band of knights and their followers.[3] For they were easily persuaded to this crime by the knights' statement that they had come to settle the affair by order of the king. They then collected in a body, ready for any impious deed, and on the fifth day after the Nativity of Christ,[4] that is, on the morrow of the Feast of the Holy Innocents, they gathered together against the innocent. The hour of dinner being over,[5] the saint had already withdrawn with some of

[1] The *Life* does not end here; a further book describes the martyrdom of the archbishop, though Herbert, due to his absence on the Continent, was not an eyewitness. This book may have been added later, though this is unlikely. It is more probable that the reading "cum *historiae hujus finem*" is due to a copyist's error and that *sub* or *ante* is the correct word (*Materials for the History of Thomas Becket*, vol. III, p. 486, n. 1.)

[2] The four knights, Reginald fitz Urse, William 'de Traci', Hugh of Morville and Richard Brito, who had set out from the king's court in Normandy; see above, p. 759.

[3] The band consisted mainly of members of the 'de Broc' family and their retainers from Saltwood Castle, where the knights had lodged.

[4] 26 December 1170.

[5] The knights arrived at Canterbury about three o'clock in the afternoon.

his household into an inner chamber to transact some business, leaving the crowd awaiting his return in the hall without. The four knights with one attendant[1] forced their way in. They were received with respect as servants of the king and well known to the archbishop's household; and those who had waited on the archbishop, being now themselves at dinner, invited them to share their table. They scorned the offer, thirsting rather for blood than for food. By their order the archbishop was informed that four men had arrived who wished to speak with him on behalf of the king. On his giving consent, they were permitted to enter. For a long time they sat in silence and neither saluted the archbishop nor spoke to him.[2] Nor did the man of wise counsel salute them immediately they came in, in order that, according to the Scriptures, "By thy words shalt thou be justified", he might discover their intentions from their questions. After a while, however, he turned to them and, carefully scanning the face of each, he greeted them in a friendly manner; but the unhappy wretches, who had made a pact with death, straightway answered his greeting with curses and ironically prayed that God might help him. At these words of bitterness and malice the man of God flushed deeply, for he now realized that they had come to work him injury. Whereupon fitz Urse, who seemed to be their leader and more prepared for the crime than the others, breathing fury, broke out in these words: "We have somewhat to say to thee by the king's command; say if thou wilt that we tell it here before all."[3] But the archbishop knew what they were about to say and answered, "These things should not be spoken in private or in the chamber, but in public." Now these wretches so burned for the slaughter of the archbishop that if the door-keeper had not called back the clerks–for the archbishop had ordered them all to withdraw–they would have killed him with the shaft of his cross which stood by, as they afterwards confessed. When those who had gone out returned, he, who had before reviled the archbishop, again addressed him saying, "When the king made peace with you and all disputes were settled, he sent you back to your own see, as you requested; but you, in contrary fashion, adding insult to injury, have broken the peace, and in your pride have wrought evil in yourself against your lord. For those, by whose ministry the king's son was crowned and invested with the honours of sovereignty, you with obstinate pride have condemned with sentence of suspension.[4] You have also bound with the chain of anathema those servants of the king by whose counsel and prudence the business of the kingdom is transacted.[5] From this it is manifest that you would take away the crown from the king's son if you had the power. But now the plots and schemes you have hatched in order to carry out your designs against your lord the king are known to all men. Say therefore whether you are prepared to come into the king's presence and make answer to these charges." The archbishop replied, "Never was it my wish, as God is my witness, to take away the crown from

[1] An archer named Rannulf, according to 'Roger of Pontigny', *Materials for the History of Thomas Becket*, vol. IV, p. 70.

[2] Sufficiently accounted for by the fact that Thomas was engaged in discussing business with his monks; see 'Roger of Pontigny', *ibid.*

[3] Hereabouts the prudent John of Salisbury intervened with, "My lord, let us discuss this in private." (William fitz Stephen, *Materials for the History of Thomas Becket*, vol. III, p. 134.)

[4] Roger, archbishop of York, and the bishops of London and Salisbury.

[5] See the list of those excommunicated by Becket given above, No. 143.

my lord the king's son or to diminish his power; rather would I wish him three crowns and help him to obtain the greatest realms of the earth, so it be with right and equity. But it is unjust that my lord the king should be offended because my people accompany me through the towns and cities and come out to meet me, when for seven years now they have been deprived through my exile of the consolation of my presence. Even now I am ready to satisfy my lord wherever he pleases, if in anything I have done amiss; but he has forbidden me with threats to enter any of his cities and towns, or even villages. Moreover, it was not by me, but by the lord pope that the prelates were suspended from office." "It was through you", said the infuriated knights, "that they were suspended; do you absolve them?" "I do not deny", he answered, "that it was done through me, but it is beyond my power and utterly incompatible with my dignity to absolve those whom the lord pope has bound. Let them go to him, on whom redounds the injury and contempt they have shown towards me and their mother, the Church of Christ at Canterbury."

"Well then," said these butchers, "this is the king's command, that you depart with all your men from the kingdom and the lands which own his dominion; for from this day forth there can be no peace betwixt him and you or any of yours, for you have broken the peace." To this the archbishop answered, "Cease your threats and still your brawling. I put my trust in the King of Heaven who for his own suffered on the Cross; for from this day forth no one shall see the sea between me and my church. I have not come back to flee again; here shall he who wants me find me. It is not fitting for the king to issue such commands; sufficient are the insults received by me and mine from the king's servants, without further threats." "Such were the king's commands," they replied, "and we will make them good, for whereas you ought to have shown respect to the king's majesty and submitted your vengeance to his judgment, you have followed the impulse of your passion and basely thrust out from the Church his ministers and servants." At these words Christ's champion,[1] rising in fervour of spirit against his accusers, exclaimed, "Whoever shall presume to violate the decrees of the holy Roman see or the laws of Christ's Church, and shall refuse to come of his own accord and make satisfaction, whosoever he be, I will not spare him, nor will I delay to inflict ecclesiastical censures upon the delinquent."[2]

Confounded by these words, the knights sprang to their feet, for they could no longer bear the firmness of his answers. Coming close up to him they said, "We declare to you that you have spoken in peril of your head." "Are you then come to slay me?" said he. "I have committed my cause to the great Judge of all mankind; wherefore I am not moved by threats, nor are your swords more ready to strike than is my soul for martyrdom. Go, seek him who would fly from you; me you will find foot to foot in the battle of the Lord." As they retired amidst tumult and insults, he who was fitly surnamed 'the bear'[3] brutishly cried out, "In the king's name we command you, both clerks and monks, to seize and hold that man, lest he escape by

[1] *athleta Christi.*

[2] In William fitz Stephen's account (*op. cit.*, p. 135) Thomas added, "Besides all this, considering the tie between us, I am the more surprised that you dare to threaten the archbishop in his own palace." This remark is an allusion to the fealty sworn to him by three of the knights when he was chancellor.

[3] Reginald fitz Urse.

flight ere the king take full justice on his body." As they departed with these words, the man of God followed them to the door and cried out after them, "Here, here will you find me"; putting his hand on his neck, as though marking beforehand the place where they were to strike.[1]

The archbishop then returned to the place where he had before been seated, consoled his clerks and exhorted them not to fear;[2] and, so it seemed to us who were present, he sat there waiting as unperturbed, although his death alone was sought, as if they had come to invite him to a wedding. Ere long back came the murderers in full armour, with swords, axes and hatchets, and other implements suitable for the crime on which their minds were set. Finding the doors barred and unopened at their knocking, they turned aside by a private path through an orchard till they came to a wooden partition, which they cut and hacked and finally broke down. Terrified by the noise and uproar, almost all the clerks and the servants were scattered hither and thither like sheep before wolves. Those who remained cried out to the archbishop to flee to the church; but he, mindful of his former promise that he would not through fear of death flee from those who kill the body, rejected flight. For in such case it were not meet to flee from city to city, but rather to set an example to those subject to him, so that every one of them should choose to die by the sword rather than see the divine law set at naught and the sacred canons subverted. Moreover, he who had long since yearned for martyrdom, now saw that the occasion to embrace it had seemingly arrived, and dreaded lest it should be deferred or even altogether lost, if he took refuge in the church. But the monks still pressed him, saying that it was not becoming for him to absent himself from vespers, which were at that very moment being said in the church. He lingered for a while motionless in that less sacred spot,[3] deliberately awaiting that happy hour of consummation which he had craved with many sighs and sought with such devotion; for he feared lest, as has been said, reverence for the sanctity of the sacred building might deter even the impious from their purpose and cheat him of his heart's desire. For, being confident that after martyrdom he would pass from this vale of misery, he is reported to have said in the hearing of many after his return from exile, "You have here a martyr, Alphege, beloved of God and a true

[1] William fitz Stephen (*op. cit.*, pp. 135-136) describes in greater detail what occurred at this juncture. On their way out the knights seized and carried off with them William, son of Nigel, and Ralph Morin, two of the archbishop's knights. They removed the porter and stationed Simon 'de Croil', one of their supporters, in his place. The gate was shut and only the wicket left open. Meanwhile fitz Urse and his fellows donned their armour in the porch of the hall, the former seizing an axe from a carpenter who was repairing some steps there.

[2] Benedict records at this point a remarkable conversation between the archbishop and John of Salisbury, in which the latter rebuked the saint for his intransigent attitude in general and his tactless treatment of the knights in particular. His narrative runs, "The man of God returned to his seat and complained to those about him of the king's message and the abusive language of his minions. One of his clerks, Master John of Salisbury, a man of much learning, great eloquence and profound wisdom, and what is greater than these, one steadfast in the fear and love of God, returned this answer to his complaints: 'My lord, it is a remarkable thing that you will take advice from no one. What need was there in a man of your rank to rise up and exasperate those wicked men still further, and to follow them out to the door? Would it not have been better to have taken counsel with your followers here present, and vouchsafed them a softer answer? For their malice seeks only how to do their worst against you and, by provoking you to anger, to catch you out in your words.' But the saint, who longed for death, as for the enjoyment of peace and rest in the defence of righteousness and the liberty of the Church, replied, 'My counsel is now all taken. I know well enough what I ought to do.' 'Pray God', said Master John, 'that it may turn out well.'" 'Roger of Pontigny' (*op. cit.*, p. 74) also records the incident.

[3] *i.e.* the palace.

saint; the divine compassion will provide you with yet another; he will not tarry."[1] O pure and trustful was the conscience of that good shepherd, who in defending the cause of his flock would not delay the hour of his own death, when it was in his power to do so, nor shun the executioner, that the fury of the wolves, satiated with the blood of the shepherd, might spare the sheep. But when he would not be persuaded by argument or entreaties to take refuge in the church, the monks seized hold of him in spite of his resistance, and pulled, dragged and pushed him; without heeding his opposition and his clamour to let him go, they brought him as far as the church.[2] But the door, which led to the monks' cloister, had been carefully barred several days before, and as the murderers were already pressing on their heels, all hope of escape seemed removed. But one of them, running forward, seized hold of the bolt, and to the great surprise of them all, drew it out with as much ease as if it had been merely glued to the door.

After the monks had retreated within the precincts of the church, the four knights came following hard on their heels with rapid strides. They were accompanied by a certain subdeacon called Hugh, armed with malice like their own, appropriately named Mauclerc,[3] being one who showed no reverence either to God or his saints, as he proved by his subsequent action. As soon as the archbishop entered the monastic buildings, the monks ceased the vespers,[4] which they had already begun to offer to God, and ran to meet him, glorifying God for that they saw their father alive and unharmed, when they had heard he was dead. They also hastened to ward off the foe from the slaughter of their shepherd by fastening the bolts of the folding doors giving access to the church. But Christ's doughty champion[5] turned to them and ordered

[1] According to William fitz Stephen these words were uttered by the archbishop in his Christmas Day sermon in the cathedral. It is possible that Grim, who had but lately come to Canterbury, had not heard the sermon; this would explain the vagueness of his reference.

[2] William fitz Stephen's narrative is at this point even more graphic and circumstantial: "He [the archbishop] ordered the cross of the Lord to be borne before him. It was borne by a certain clerk of his named Henry of Auxerre. [The archbishop's usual cross-bearer, Alexander Llewelyn, had been sent abroad on a mission a few days earlier; see above, p. 759.] When we had reached the monks' cloister, the monks wished to shut the door fast behind him. But he was displeased and would not allow it. He walked on behind them, last of all, at a slow pace, driving all before him, as a good shepherd doth his sheep. For indeed fear was so banished from him by the love of God, that there was no trace of it either in his gesture or in his gait. It was as far off from all his outward appearance as it was from the innermost citadel of his mind. Once indeed he cast his eye backward over his right shoulder, perchance in case he might see the king's men following his footsteps, perchance lest some one should bolt the door behind him" (*op. cit.*, p. 138). The discrepancy between the two accounts should be noted. While Edward Grim, in company with 'Roger of Pontigny' (*op. cit.*, p. 75), states that the archbishop was compelled by force to seek the shelter of the church, William fitz Stephen, supported in this instance by Herbert of Bosham (*op. cit.*, p. 496) (who, however, was not an eyewitness of the scene), gives the impression of an orderly and more or less dignified procession having taken place. This is but one of the many discrepancies in points of detail among the biographers recording the dramatic events of the day.

[3] *Malus clericus*, evil clerk.

[4] This is corroborated by William fitz Stephen. William of Canterbury suggests that some of the monks remained to complete the office, and this may not be inconsistent with Edward Grim's subsequent remark; see p. 766. William fitz Stephen supplies further details concerning the archbishop's entry into the cathedral: "He was proceeding to the altar higher up the church, where he was wont to say private Masses and his canonical hours, and had already ascended four steps, when lo! at the cloister door, through which we had come [from the palace], there came up first Reginald fitz Urse, clad in hauberk and with drawn sword, shouting, 'Hither now to me, king's men!' A moment later he was joined by his three companions likewise clad in hauberks, head and body in full armour, all but their eyes, and with naked swords. They were followed by several others, besides, without hauberks, but armed, their retainers and friends, and some from the city of Canterbury, whom they had compelled to come along with them."

[5] *athleta mirabilis.*

the doors to be thrown open, saying, "It is not meet to make a fortress of the house of prayer, the Church of Christ, which, even if it be not closed, affords sufficient protection to its children; by suffering rather than by fighting shall we triumph over the enemy; for we are come to suffer, not to resist." Straightway these sacrilegious men, with drawn swords, entered the house of peace and reconciliation, causing no little horror to those present by the mere sight of them and the clash of their armour. All the onlookers were in tumult and consternation, for by this time those who had been singing vespers[1] had rushed up to the scene of death.[2]

In a spirit of mad fury the knights called out, "Where is Thomas Becket, traitor to the king and the realm?" When he returned no answer, they cried out the more loudly and insistently, "Where is the archbishop?" At this quite undaunted, as it is written, "The righteous shall be bold as a lion and without fear", he descended from the steps, whither he had been dragged by the monks through their fear of the knights, and in a perfectly clear voice answered, "Lo! here am I, no traitor to the king, but a priest. What do you seek from me?" And whereas he had already told them that he had no fear of them, he now added, "Behold, I am ready to suffer in His Name who redeemed me by His Blood. Far be it from me to flee from your swords, or to depart from righteousness." Having thus said, he turned aside to the right, under a pillar, having on one side the altar of the blessed Mother of God, Mary ever-Virgin, on the other, that of the holy confessor, Benedict, by whose example and prayers, having crucified the world and its lusts, he endured whatsoever the murderers did to him with such constancy of soul, as if he were no longer in the flesh. The murderers pursued him. "Absolve", they cried, "and restore to communion those whom you have excommunicated, and the functions of their office to the others who have been suspended." He answered, "There has been no satisfaction made, and I will not absolve them." "Then you shall die this instant", they cried, "and receive your desert." "I, too," said he, "am ready to die for my Lord, that in my blood the Church may obtain peace and liberty; but in the name of Almighty God I forbid you to harm any of my men, whether clerk or lay." Thus did the noble martyr provide piously for his followers, and prudently for himself, in that no one standing near should be hurt nor the innocent oppressed, lest any serious mishap befalling any that stood by him should dim the lustre of his glory as his soul sped up to Christ. Most fitting was it that the soldier-martyr should follow in the footsteps of his Captain and Saviour, who, when the wicked sought to take him, said, "If ye seek me, let these go their way."[3]

Then they made a rush at him and laid sacrilegious hands upon him, pulling and

[1] See above, p. 765, n. 4.

[2] *ad lethale spectaculum.*

William fitz Stephen adds this comment on what took place at this juncture (*op. cit.*, vol. III, p. 139): "Just as he was in the act of descending from the altar steps towards the door to prevent it being closed, John of Salisbury and his other clerks (all except Robert the canon, William fitz Stephen and Edward Grim who had newly come to him) sought shelter and forsook him, making it their only care to place themselves in safety, some at various altars, others in hiding-places. And indeed, had he wished, the archbishop might easily have turned aside and saved himself by flight. For both time and place offered an opportunity of escaping without being found. It was evening, the longest night was approaching, and the crypt was near at hand where there were many dark and winding passages. There was also another door through which he might have climbed by a spiral staircase to the arched chambers in the roof of the church. Perchance he might not have been discovered, or in the meantime some diversion might have occurred. But none of these ways of escape would he take."

[3] John xviii. 8.

dragging him roughly and violently, endeavouring to get him outside the walls of the church and there slay him, or bind him and carry him off prisoner, as they afterwards confessed was their intention. But as he could not easily be moved from the pillar, one of them seized hold of him and clung to him more closely. The archbishop shook him off vigorously, calling him a pandar[1] and saying, "Touch me not, Reginald; you owe me fealty and obedience; you are acting like a madman, you and your accomplices." All aflame with a terrible fury at this rebuff, the knight brandished his sword against that consecrated head. "Neither faith", he cried, "nor obedience do I owe you against my fealty to my lord the king." Then the unconquered martyr understood that the hour was approaching that should release him from the miseries of this mortal life, and that the crown of immortality prepared for him and promised by the Lord was already nigh at hand. Whereupon, inclining his head as one in prayer and joining his hands together and uplifting them, he commended his cause and that of the Church to God and St. Mary and the blessed martyr, St. Denys.[2] Scarce had he uttered the words than the wicked knight, fearing lest he should be rescued by the people and escape alive, leapt suddenly upon him and wounded the sacrificial lamb of God in the head, cutting off the top of the crown which the unction of the sacred chrism had dedicated to God, and by the same stroke he almost cut off the arm of him who tells the story.[3] For he, when all the others, both monks and clerks had fled, steadfastly stood by the saintly archbishop and held his arms around him, till the one he opposed to the blow was almost severed. Behold the simplicity of the dove, the wisdom of the serpent in this martyr who presented his body to the strikers that he might preserve his head, that is to say, his soul and the Church, unharmed, nor would he take any forethought or employ any stratagem against those who slay the body whereby he might escape. O worthy shepherd, who gave himself so boldly to the wolves, in order that his flock might not be torn to pieces! Because he had cast away the world, the world in seeking to crush him unconsciously exalted him.

Next he received a second blow on the head, but still he stood firm and immovable.[4] At the third blow he fell on his knees and elbows, offering himself a living sacrifice and saying in a low voice, "For the Name of Jesus and the protection of the Church I am ready to embrace death."[5] But the third knight[6] inflicted a terrible wound as he lay prostrate. By this stroke the sword was dashed against the pavement and the crown of his head, which was large, was separated from the head in such a way that

[1] *lenonem*.

[2] This invocation is corroborated by William of Canterbury, John of Salisbury and William fitz Stephen, who adds the name of St. Alphege to the list of saints.

[3] Grim's wound is attested by nearly all the other biographers, but there is some doubt as to the accuracy of his account of the episode, in respect of the knight who struck the blow. 'Roger of Pontigny' agrees with Grim that it was fitz Urse; William of Canterbury says that fitz Urse struck the first blow at the archbishop, but that 'de Traci' wounded one of the monks whom he identified with John of Salisbury, who is known for certain to have already fled! William fitz Stephen is definite that the blow came from 'de Traci'. Such discrepancies in the authorities are probably the natural result of the confusion created by the knights' assault; see on the point, E. A. Abbott, *St. Thomas of Canterbury, his Death and Miracles*, vol. I (1898), pp. 139–140.

[4] This was possibly the blow struck by 'de Traci'; William fitz Stephen describes how the archbishop stood wiping off with his arm the blood that streamed from his head, giving thanks to God the while, saying, "Into thy hands, O Lord, I commend my spirit" (Psalms xxxi. 6, used in the office of Compline).

[5] The archbishop's last recorded utterance; this was the second blow, according to William fitz Stephen (*loc. cit., ante*), who says the archbishop fell flat on his face.

[6] Richard Brito, as William fitz Stephen categorically states.

the blood white with the brain and the brain no less red from the blood, dyed the floor of the cathedral with the white of the lily and the red of the rose, the colours of the Virgin and Mother and of the life and death of the martyr and confessor. The fourth knight[1] warded off any who sought to intervene, so that the others might with greater freedom and licence[2] perpetrate the crime. But the fifth–no knight he, but that same clerk who had entered with the knights[3]–that a fifth blow[4] might not be wanting to the martyr who in other things had imitated Christ, placed his foot on the neck of the holy priest and precious martyr and, horrible to relate, scattered the brains and blood about the pavement, crying out to the others, "Let us away, knights; this fellow will rise no more."[5]

In all his sufferings the illustrious martyr displayed an incredible steadfastness. Neither with hand nor robe, as is the manner of human frailty, did he oppose the fatal stroke. Nor when smitten did he utter a single word, neither cry nor groan, nor any sound indicative of pain. But he held motionless the head which he had bent to meet the uplifted sword until, bespattered with blood and brains, as though in an attitude of prayer, his body lay prone on the pavement, while his soul rested in Abraham's bosom.

153. Description of the scene after the murder of Thomas Becket as given by Benedict of Peterborough

Before they rode away from Canterbury the knights sacked the archbishop's palace. Meanwhile the alarm had been given, and the townsfolk came pouring in to view the body. Night was now approaching, for the murder had taken place about four o'clock in the afternoon. At last the monks succeeded in clearing the church of the crowd, and the doors were closed. They then took up the body in preparation for burial. Printed: *Materials for the History of Thomas Becket*, vol. II, p. 15.

While the body still lay on the pavement, some of them[6] smeared their eyes with blood. Others brought bottles and carried off secretly as much of it as they could. Others cut off shreds of clothing and dipped them in the blood. At a later time no one was thought happy who had not carried off something from the precious treasure of the martyr's body. And indeed with everything in such a state of confusion and tumult, each man could do as he pleased. Some of the blood left over was carefully and cleanly collected and poured into a clean vessel and treasured up in the church. The archbishop's pallium and outer vesture, stained with blood, were with indiscreet piety given to the poor to pray for his soul, and happy would it have been for them, if they had not with inconsiderate haste sold them for a paltry sum of money.[7]

Thus the night passed in lamentation and mourning, groans and sighs; not a ray of gladness shed its light upon the sad scene, and when the day dawned it brought with it the prospect of yet greater evil. . . .[8] The monks, fearing lest the corpse should be

[1] Hugh of Morville. [2] *liberius ac licentius.* [3] Hugh Mauclerc; see above, p. 765.

[4] An allusion to the five wounds of Christ.

[5] Mauclerc's part in the murder is attested by the other biographers, but his parting cry to the knights only by 'Roger of Pontigny', and that in the version, "Let us go, for the traitor is dead."

[6] The townsfolk of Canterbury.

[7] According to 'Roger of Pontigny' the monks placed the body before the high altar for the night and maintained a watch around it. William fitz Stephen says that the body lay for a time unguarded.

[8] The author then states that Robert 'de Broc' came threatening to drag the corpse out and tear it in pieces, unless the monks disposed of it speedily and secretly.

shamefully abused and so precious a treasure be taken from them, prepared to bury it with all speed. They therefore had no time to wash and embalm the body, according to the custom of the church of Canterbury.[1] And this, we believe, was occasioned not so much by the malice of men as by the providence of God. For what need had he of less precious perfumes whom the Lord had caused to be anointed with his own blood? They therefore stripped him of his outer garments to put on him his pontifical vestments; in so doing they discovered that the body was covered in a hair-shirt, no less painful from its stiffness than from other causes[2] and–a circumstance of which we have neither read nor heard of an example in the case of any other saint–they found the body covered in sackcloth, even from the thighs down to the knees, beneath the cowl and robe of the Cistercian habit.[3] At this sight the monks gazed at one another, astounded at this proof of a hidden piety greater than would have been credited the archbishop, and at this second cause of sorrow, they multiplied their tears.[4] How could such a man have been suspected of covetousness or treachery? Could he ever have set his thoughts upon an earthly kingdom, who had thus preferred sackcloth above all worldly pleasures? Was he not betrayed by, rather than a traitor to his king, who would neither yield to his betrayers, those sons of perdition, nor, as he could have done, resist them? . . .[5]

Such was the passion of God's doughty champion, Thomas, archbishop of Canterbury, primate of all England and legate of the apostolic see, which took place in the year of our Lord's Incarnation 1170 and the fifty-third of his age, on Tuesday, 29 December, at about five o'clock in the afternoon, so that on the fifth day after the Lord's Nativity in this world of woe his servant might be born to glory and stand in the presence of the same Jesus Christ, our Lord, to whom with the Father and the Holy Spirit be honour, glory, virtue, power and dominion, world without end. Amen.

[1] Herbert of Bosham says that the body *was* washed, but this is flatly contradicted by all the biographers who were eyewitnesses.

[2] All the under-garments were discovered to be full of lice, so that, as Grim puts it, "anyone would have thought that the martyrdom of the day was less grievous than that which these small enemies continually inflicted".

[3] First adopted by the archbishop at Pontigny; see above, p. 740.

[4] The discovery of the hair-shirt caused a great sensation among the monks and the archbishop's intimate followers. Benedict's narrative may be compared with that of William fitz Stephen: "Brother Robert, a priest and canon of the religious house at Merton, an honourable man, who had been the archbishop's chaplain and constant companion since the day of his ordination, and was also his confessor, among other things showed the monks what no one had hitherto been aware of, that the archbishop was clad in a hair-shirt. Thrusting his hand into his bosom, he disclosed the hair-shirt next his skin and underneath the habit of a monk. . . . Then the monks, in an ecstasy of spiritual joy, raised their hearts and hands to heaven, glorifying God. Their sorrow was turned into joy, their lamentations into paeans of praise. Having seen with their own eyes his twofold martyrdom, the voluntary one of his life and the violent one of his death, they prostrated themselves on the ground, they kissed his hands and feet, they invoked him as a saint and proclaimed him God's holy martyr. All ran to view, clad in sackcloth, him whom as chancellor they had beheld vestured in purple and satin."

[5] William fitz Stephen completes the story of the archbishop's interment: "When everything pertaining to the burial had been performed and settled, no Mass having been said because the cathedral had been desecrated by the entry of the armed men, the sacred remains of the archbishop were interred in a new marble tomb in the crypt between two altars (dedicated to St. John the Baptist and St. Augustine respectively) amid many tears and great lamentation." Here, in the crypt, the body remained until 7 July 1220, when it was translated to the shrine constructed for it in the chapel at the east end of the cathedral, immediately behind the high altar. This solemn event took place in the reign of Henry III and the primacy of Archbishop Stephen Langton.

154. Letter from Arnulf, bishop of Lisieux, to Pope Alexander III written after the murder of Thomas Becket (1171 and probably in January of that year)

Henry II was at Argentan when the news of the murder of the archbishop reached him on 1 January 1171. The ensuing letter describes the consternation at court. Printed: F. Barlow, *Letters of Arnulf of Lisieux* (R. Hist. Soc., 1939), p. 122.

To his beloved lord and father, Alexander, by the grace of God supreme pontiff of the Catholic Church, Arnulf, humble minister of the church of Lisieux, greeting and due obedience with all devotion. While we were assembled in council with our lord the king and supposed we were about to discuss important business relating to the Church and the realm, the sudden news about the archbishop of Canterbury plunged us all into the deepest distress, so that in a moment our complacency was turned to stupefaction and our deliberations into mourning. We learnt on the unimpeachable authority of some who had just come over from England, that certain enemies of the archbishop, provoked, so they said, by frequent causes of exasperation to anger and madness, have suddenly set upon him and–I can hardly write without tears–have assaulted his person and put him to a cruel death. This bad news has at last come to the king's ears, for such a deed could not be hidden from him whose particular duty it is to avenge the archbishop's death with the authority of his power and with the sword. At the first words of the messenger the king burst into loud lamentation and exchanged his royal robes for sackcloth and ashes, acting more like a friend than the sovereign of the deceased. At times he fell into a stupor, after which he would again utter groans and cries louder and more bitter than before. For three whole days he remained shut up in his chamber, and would neither take food nor admit any to comfort him, till it seemed from his excessive grief that he had obstinately made up his mind to contrive his own death. The state of affairs was lamentable and the reason for our grief and anxiety was now changed. First we had to lament the death of the archbishop, now, as a consequence, we began to despair of the life of the king, and so by the death of the one we believed in our misery that we should be losing both. Moreover, when his friends, and especially the bishops, complained that he seemed determined not to return to his senses, he answered that he feared that the perpetrators of the crime and their accomplices, counting upon his old enmity with the archbishop, had promised themselves impunity on that account. Although he might have incurred fresh hostility through his recent injuries and frequent taunts at the archbishop, he thought it likely that his good name and reputation would be smirched by the slander of his enemies that the crime had been committed with his knowledge. But he called Almighty God to witness that he had neither willed this impious deed nor known that it had been committed, nor had contrived it by guile, unless it be his fault that men believed he was not yet fully reconciled with the archbishop. On this head he submits himself entirely to the judgment of the Church, and will humbly abide by her decision, whatever it may be. So then, after taking counsel, he calmed down and acquiesced in the advice that he should have recourse to the wisdom and authority of the apostolic see, which proclaims the Christian faith in the spirit of wisdom and in the fullness of power, and before which he may labour to prove his innocence by lawful and canonical means.

We therefore entreat you, according to the spirit of counsel and courage which God has bestowed on you, to recompense the authors of this outrage with the severity proportionate to the heinousness of their crime, but to vindicate the king's innocence with your apostolic piety and to preserve the integrity of his status.

May Almighty God preserve your person in safety to rule the Church for many years to come!

155. Report from Henry II's envoy at the papal court (April or May 1171)

Richard of Ilchester, the recipient of this report, was at the papal court at Tusculanum engaged in endeavouring to obtain absolution from his sentence, when the news of Becket's martyrdom arrived about 4 February 1170. As he remained there three months, the letter from the king's agent here presented must be of subsequent date. It describes the shock caused by the sad tidings at the papal court, the grief of the pope and his confirmation of the interdict which the archbishop of Sens, as papal legate, had launched against the continental dominions of Henry II. It also describes the negotiations carried on by the king's successive embassies to Rome and the pope's refusal to accept any solution but that of unconditional surrender on the part of the king. It is printed in *Materials for the History of Thomas Becket*, vol. VII, pp. 475–478.

Who were the first envoys the king sent, who the second, what both embassies came for, and in what manner they left the court, I will relate as briefly as I can. The first envoys were John Comyn[1] and Master David,[2] and their object was to obtain absolution and remission for the bishops.[3] But John Comyn came to court first, about fifteen days before Master David,[4] and after great pressure on his part and a promise to pay five hundred marks, he was admitted to a hearing. He was supported by some clerks of the archbishop of York and an agent of the bishop of Durham, who spoke much in extenuation of the bishops. And I verily believe they would have brought back absolution, if the news of the archbishop's death had not supervened and darkened everything. So shocked was the lord pope at the news, that for eight days he refused to discuss it even with his own people and issued a general order that no Englishman should have access to him. All negotiations were at once suspended.

The second embassy consisted of the bishops of Worcester[5] and Evreux,[6] the abbot of La Valasse, the archdeacons of Salisbury and Lisieux, Lord Robert of Newburgh, Richard Barre,[7] Master Henry Pichun[7] and a certain Templar. They were sent to defend the king against the charge that he had either ordered or desired the archbishop's death. They did not deny, however, that he had given cause for the murder by uttering words which had afforded the murderers a pretext for slaying the archbishop. This second group of envoys did not arrive at the *curia* together, but the archdeacons of Salisbury and Lisieux, the abbot, Master Henry and Richard Barre came before the others.[8] They were not admitted to the lord pope nor given a hearing. Then, at the entreaty of certain cardinals, the abbot and the archdeacon of Lisieux were received by him.[9]

[1] See above, No. 143. He arrived *circa* 13 January 1170.
[2] A canon of St. Paul's and an agent of Gilbert Foliot.
[3] *i.e.* from the sentence of excommunication and suspension served on them by Becket's agents, 1 December 1170; see above, p. 756.
[4] David arrived *circa* 30 January.
[5] See above, pp. 753, 754.
[6] Gilles de la Perche.
[7] These were agents of the king well known at the court of Rome.
[8] *circa* 20 March.
[9] Presumably as not being Englishmen.

Maundy Thursday[1] drew nigh, and it was generally said in the *curia* that the lord pope would that day pass sentence of excommunication against the king and his realm. Terror-stricken the envoys therefore intimated to the lord pope through the mediation of certain cardinals that they had received orders from their lord the king to swear that he would abide by the pope's mandate, and this he would also swear in his own person. So, on the Thursday about the ninth hour both the messengers of the king and those of the bishops were summoned, and the former, namely the abbot of La Valasse, the two archdeacons, Henry and Richard Barre, swore in full consistory that the king would abide by the pope's mandate and would himself take an oath to this effect. The envoys of the archbishop of York and of the bishops of London and Salisbury likewise swore that their masters would stand by his decision, and would pledge themselves on oath thereto. But from the envoy of the bishop of Durham, who was also present, no such oath was exacted or invited. On the same day the pope issued a general excommunication against the murderers of the archbishop, all who had given them counsel, countenance or aid and all who should receive them or give them shelter on their lands.

After Easter came the bishops of Worcester and Evreux; I know not whether they were called upon to take the oath, but this at least I know, they did not swear. When they had been fifteen days or rather more at court, they were summoned to receive an answer: for they were in accord with the others, as well in excusing the king as in the accusations made against him, as I have before stated. Whilst they were expecting a favourable issue, the lord pope confirmed both the sentence of interdict, which the archbishop of Sens[2] had pronounced against the king's continental domains, and the sentence of excommunication and suspension which had been passed on the bishops. He ordered also that the king should refrain from entering a church and added that he would send legates to see whether the king was truly humbled. At last, after much pressure from the envoys and through the mediation of certain cardinals, and also, it is said, by handing over a large sum of money, it was decided that the lord pope should write to the archbishop of Bourges[3] to the effect that, if he should not hear within a month after the arrival of the envoys in Normandy that the legates had crossed the Alps, he might then absolve the bishops of London and Salisbury from their excommunication, having first administered an oath both to them and to the others remaining under suspension, that they would abide by the mandate of the lord pope; the bishop of Durham, who enjoyed in this matter a special prerogative, was exempted. For his envoy had already brought back his release, although he had only been able to procure it with great difficulty and after considerable delay. So the envoys of the lord king returned from the *curia* with nothing more to show. I do not believe that even the cardinals know who are to be the legates or when they are to start. However, you need not now fear, I think, that an interdict will be laid on England, provided the king will obey the legates. The lord pope has also written to the king, exhorting him to humility; but they had great difficulty in getting him to do so.

[1] 25 March.

[2] See above, p. 771.

[3] Stephen de la Chapelle, formerly bishop of Meaux.

156. Account by an anonymous writer of the submission of Henry II to the papal legates at Avranches (May 1172)

This document relates the king's negotiations with the legates, Theodwin and Albert, and the terms of Henry II's reconciliation at Avranches. The king's oath of abjuration, and the absolution which followed, were both re-enacted on 28 September 1172 at the synod of Avranches following the second coronation of the young king, Henry.[1] Printed: *Materials for the History of Thomas Becket*, vol. VII, p. 513.

The first meeting between the lord king and the legates took place at "Gorram" on the Tuesday before Rogationtide,[2] and there the kiss of peace was mutually bestowed. On the morrow they came to Savigny, where the archbishop of Rouen and many bishops and lay magnates were assembled. After protracted negotiations for peace, due to the king's utter refusal to pledge himself to accept their mandate, he departed from them in high dudgeon, saying, "I shall return to Ireland[3] where I have many things to attend to. As for you, you may go in peace in my land wherever you please, and exercise your legatine powers as you have been instructed." And so he took leave of them.

Then the cardinals, after deliberating privately together, summoned the bishop of Lisieux, the archdeacon of Poitiers and the archdeacon of Salisbury, and by their mediation the king and the cardinals met at Avranches on the following Friday.[4] There it was agreed between them that the king should willingly accept and assent to whatever proposal the cardinals might make to him. But because he wished his son[5] to be present, in order that he might also give his assent to what his father should promise, the termination of the affair was postponed until the following Sunday,[6] which was the Sunday before the Lord's Ascension. On that day in public audience the king, laying his hand upon the sacred Gospels, swore that he had neither ordered nor willed the murder of the archbishop of Canterbury, and that when he heard thereof, he had rather grieved than rejoiced. He also added of his own accord that he grieved more for this deed than ever he had done for the death of his father or mother. He swore also that he would carry out to the letter whatever penance or reparation the cardinals should impose on him. For he admitted before them all that he had been the cause of the archbishop's death, and that what had been done was for his sake; not that he himself had ordered it, but that his friends and retainers, seeing his flushed face and flashing eyes, knowing also his sorrow of heart and hearing the words of complaint against the archbishop, which oft-times fell from his lips, made ready, without his knowledge, to avenge his wrongs. On this account, he affirmed, he would now submit to everything the legates might order, with all humility and devotion.

Upon this the legates bound him to provide two hundred knights for the whole year at his own expense, that is to say, at the rate of three hundred gold pieces for each knight, to fight against the infidel in the Holy Land under the command of the Templars.

Secondly, to abrogate in their entirety the perverse statutes of Clarendon[7] and all

[1] *Gesta Regis Henrici Secundi* (ed. W. Stubbs, Rolls Series), vol. I (1867), p. 30, n. 8.
[2] 16 May 1172.
[3] Where he had been from October 1171 to April 1172. See above, p. 342 and below, Nos. 159–162.
[4] 19 May 1172.
[5] The young King Henry.
[6] 21 May.
[7] See above, No. 126.

evil customs which had been introduced into God's churches during his reign.[1] Moreover, such evil customs as were in existence before his time were to be restricted in accordance with the mandate of the lord pope and the counsel of religious men.

Thirdly, to make full restitution to the church of Canterbury of all its lands and other possessions as it held them in the year before the archbishop fell foul of the king, and to reinstate fully in their possessions all who had offended him by espousing the cause of the archbishop, and to restore them to peace and favour.

Fourthly, if necessary and the lord pope should so order him, to go to Spain to liberate that land from the infidel.

In addition they secretly imposed on him fasting and almsgiving and certain other things which never came to the knowledge of the public.

The king cheerfully assented to all these demands, saying, "My lord legates, I am entirely in your hands; rest assured I am prepared to obey your command. I will go to Jerusalem or Rome or St. James,[2] or anywhere else, if you order me." All those present, observing his humility and devotion, could scarcely restrain their tears.

Matters having been thus settled,[3] the legates, in order that nothing might be left undone, led the king of his own accord out of the church, and there on his knees, but without removing his clothes or receiving stripes, he was absolved and led back into the church.

Moreover, in order that some of the subjects of the French king might be informed how matters had progressed, the legates decided that the archbishop of Tours and his suffragans should be asked to meet the king and the legates at Caen on the Tuesday following Ascension Day.[4] The king's oath was confirmed by his son, the young king, who swore to observe on his part the conditions agreed upon. He also gave a pledge that if the king, his father, should be prevented by death or any other cause from fulfilling his penance, he would himself perform it for him.

157. Bull of Pope Alexander III, dated 12 March 1173, announcing the canonization of St. Thomas on 21 February 1173

The fame and popularity of the martyred archbishop with both clergy and people, coupled with the miracles of healing wrought at his tomb, facilitated the Church's official recognition of his claim to sanctification unusually soon after death. Alexander's bull is the official intimation of Thomas's canonization at Rome and, as such, is properly addressed to the monks of Christ Church, Canterbury, of whom the late archbishop had been the head. Printed: *Materials for the History of Thomas Becket*, vol. VII, p. 545.

Alexander, the bishop, servant of the servants of God, to his beloved sons, the prior and monks of the church of Canterbury, greeting and apostolic benediction. The whole body of the faithful should rejoice at the marvels wrought by that saintly

[1] Since it was argued by the king and his counsellors that the customs embodied in the Constitutions of Clarendon were the ancient customs of the realm, and that few new ones had been introduced in his reign, this prohibition by itself meant very little.

[2] Of Compostella, the famous centre of pilgrimage in Spain.

[3] Though by the terms of this surrender Henry had made important concessions, he still retained the substance of his power over the Church. While the *privilegium fori* and "benefit of clergy" remained unimpaired until the time of Henry VIII, and appeals to Rome in ecclesiastical causes remained unrestricted, on the other hand the king retained his jurisdiction in suits of patronage and over all Church lands not held in free alms.

[4] 30 May. At Caen the king reiterated publicly the professions he had made at Avranches.

and reverend man, Thomas, your archbishop. But still greater joy and exultation should fill the hearts of you, who have again and again witnessed his miracles, and whose church is especially honoured by the presence of his most sacred body. Having therefore duly considered the glorious merits by which his life was so highly distinguished, the public fame of his miracles and the testimony given to them by our beloved sons, Albert, cardinal-priest of St. Laurence, and Theodwin, cardinal-priest of St. Vitalis, legates of the apostolic see,[1] and by many other persons; having, moreover, full confidence in that testimony, and having also taken counsel with our brethren in the presence of a large number of clergy and laity, we have on Ash Wednesday last[2] solemnly canonized the aforesaid archbishop and ordained that he should be numbered in the roll of saintly martyrs. We command you and the whole body of the faithful in England by our apostolic authority to observe his feast every year on the day on which he closed his life by his glorious passion[3] with fitting reverence. Since therefore it is meet and highly expedient for you that his sacred body should be buried with the reverence and honour due to it, we command you by this our apostolic rescript to hold a solemn procession on some high feast-day when the clergy and people are met together, to inter his body devoutly and reverently behind the altar, or to place it in a chest, elevated above the altar, whichever be more convenient, and by devout supplication to God to obtain his intercession for the salvation of the faithful and the peace of the universal Church. Given at Segni, 12 March [1173].

158. The penance of Henry II at Canterbury (12 July 1174) as described by Gervase of Canterbury

More than two years elapsed between the king's surrender at Avranches and his celebrated act of penance at the martyred archbishop's tomb. All this time he had been detained abroad by the revolt of his continental feudatories in support of the young King Henry.[4] The following narrative of the dramatic scene at Canterbury is taken from the chronicle of Gervase of Canterbury. It should be compared with the account given by William of Newburgh in his *Historia Rerum Anglicarum* printed earlier in this volume.[5] The Latin text of Gervase is printed in the Rolls Series (ed. W. Stubbs, London, 1879), vol. I, pp. 248–249.

So then, the king returned to England at the beginning of July [1174].[6] Taught by good advice he postponed dealing with nearly every matter of State, and immediately on landing set out with a penitent heart to the tomb of St. Thomas at Canterbury. Accordingly on Saturday, 12 July he left the church of St. Dunstan, which is sited a good distance outside the city, and walked barefoot and clad in a woollen smock all the way to the martyr's tomb. There he lay prostrate for a great while and in devout humility, and of his own free will was scourged by all the bishops and abbots there present and each individual monk of the church of Canterbury.[7] There he remained, constant in prayer before the holy martyr all that day and night. He neither took food nor went out to relieve nature, but, as he had come, so he remained, and would not permit a rug or anything of the kind to be provided for him. After

[1] See above, p. 773. [2] 21 February 1173.
[3] 29 December.
[4] For the feudal rebellion of 1173–1174, see above, No. 12, pp. 342–356.
[5] See above, p. 351.
[6] He landed at Southampton 8 July 1174.
[7] *i.e.* the monks of Christ Church.

lauds[1] he made a tour of the altars in the choir of the church and the bodies of the saints interred there, and then returned to the tomb of St. Thomas in the crypt. At dawn on Sunday he heard Mass. Last of all he drank of the water [from the well] of the holy martyr and was honoured with the gift of a phial [of the martyr's blood?]. So he departed from Canterbury rejoicing, reaching London on the Sunday. But on the very day[2] he left Canterbury, William, king of Scots, having dispatched his troops on a foray, was left to conduct the siege of Alnwick with only a few of his knights; whereupon the army of York arrived at the scene unexpectedly. The king, supposing his enemies to be his own men returning with their spoils, suddenly found himself surrounded and taken prisoner. The remainder of his force was either slain or put to flight.[3]

(*b*) HENRY II, THE POPE AND IRELAND

159. The Bull *Laudabiliter*

The text of this privilege, alleged to have been granted by Pope Adrian IV to Henry II, is given by Gerald of Wales in his *Expugnatio Hibernica* (*Opera*, Rolls Series, vol. v, p. 316), and also by Ralph 'de Diceto' (*Ymagines Historiarum*, Rolls Series, vol. I, p. 300). According to Gerald the original document was preserved at Westminster in his time, but Ralph 'de Diceto' may have taken his text direct from Gerald. A heated controversy has raged as to whether the document is genuine or not. Among the more recent contributions to this discussion may be mentioned K. Norgate, "The Bull Laudabiliter" in *Eng. Hist. Rev.*, vol. VIII, pp. 13–52, where the authenticity of the privilege is defended, and J. H. Round, *Commune of London and Other Studies*, pp. 171–200, where it is impugned. G. H. Orpen, *Ireland under the Normans* (1911), vol. I, pp. 287–318; 399, 400) reviews the controversy at length and supports the authenticity of the document, and there is a further discussion by Charles Bémont in *Mélanges . . . offerts à Ferdinand Lot* (1925), pp. 41–55. The main question of the papal attitude towards Henry II's conquest of Ireland is, however, hardly affected by this controversy, since it can be adequately illustrated without reference to *Laudabiliter*. Thus John of Salisbury, when referring to an incident that occurred in Rome before 1160, and perhaps in 1155, tells in his *Metalogicon* (see below, No. 171) the story of how the pope sent Henry II an emerald ring in token of his bestowal of Ireland on that king. More important, however, is the evidence of certain letters of Pope Alexander III (see below, Nos. 160, 161, 162), which are generally recognized as genuine. In short, whether *Laudabiliter* is, or is not, an authentic document, there seems little doubt that the papacy supported Henry II in Ireland. The Latin text of *Laudabiliter* is given in the works cited above. An excellent translation which has been used as the basis of the version which follows is in G. H. Orpen, *op. cit.*, vol. I, pp. 294–297.

Adrian the bishop, servant of the servants of God, to his most dearly beloved son in Christ, the illustrious king of the English, greeting and apostolic benediction. Laudably and profitably does your magnificence contemplate extending your glorious name on earth and laying up a reward of eternal happiness in heaven, inasmuch as you endeavour like a Catholic prince to enlarge the boundaries of the Church, to expound the truth of the Christian faith to ignorant and barbarous peoples, and to root out the weeds of vice from the Lord's field; and for the better execution of this, you seek the advice and favour of the apostolic see. In which work the more lofty the counsel and the greater the discretion with which you proceed, so much the more do we trust that by God's help your progress may be fortunate therein; in that those things, which have their beginning in ardent faith and love of religion, are wont always to attain to a good issue and termination.

There is certainly no doubt, as your excellency doth also acknowledge, that

[1] Commonly sung or said at midnight or soon after.
[2] Sunday, 13 July.
[3] Cf. William of Newburgh, above, No. 12, pp. 349, 350.

Ireland and all other islands which Christ, the Sun of Righteousness has illumined, and which have received the doctrines of the Christian faith, belong to the jurisdiction of St. Peter and the holy Roman Church. Wherefore so much the more willingly do we implant in them the faith and sow the seed pleasing to God, since, we perceive, by examining our conscience, that this will be required of us.

You have, indeed, indicated to us, dearest son in Christ, that you desire to enter into the island of Ireland for the purpose of subjecting its people to the laws and of rooting out from it the weeds of vice, and that you are willing to pay a yearly tribute to blessed Peter of one penny from every house, and to preserve the rights of the churches of that land whole and unimpaired. We, therefore, seconding with due favour your pious and praiseworthy desire, and granting our generous assent to your petition, are well pleased to agree that, for the extension of the boundaries of the Church, for the restraint of vice, for the correction of morals and for the implanting of virtues, and for the increase of the Christian religion, you may enter that island and perform there the things that have regard to the honour of God and the salvation of that land. And may the people of that land receive you with honour, and reverence you as their lord, saving indeed the rights of the churches to remain whole and unimpaired, and to St. Peter and the holy Roman Church annual payment of one penny from each house. If, therefore, you deem fit to complete in effect what you have conceived in your mind, strive to imbue that nation with good morals; and may you so act both for yourself and through those whom you recognize from their faith, their words and their life to be well qualified for this task, that the Church there may be adorned, the Christian religion implanted and made to grow, and the things which pertain to the honour of God and the salvation of souls may be so ordered, that you may deserve to obtain from God the crown of everlasting reward and on earth a name glorious throughout the ages.

160. Letter of Pope Alexander III addressed to the prelates of Ireland, and relating to Henry II's conquest of that country (most probably 1172)

This letter and the letters which follow (Nos. 161, 162) are of the highest interest as illustrating the papal attitude towards Henry II's Irish enterprise. It will be noted also that they are to be placed in the period immediately following the murder of Thomas Becket and the king's subsequent reconciliation with the Church. These letters are generally accepted as genuine, and they are fully discussed in J. H. Round, *Commune of London and Other Studies* (1899), pp. 185–190, and in G. H. Orpen, *Ireland under the Normans* (1911), vol. I, pp. 301–306. This letter is printed in *Liber Niger Scaccarii* (ed. T. Hearne, 1728), vol. I, pp. 42–44.

Alexander the bishop, servant of the servants of God, to his venerable brethren: Christian, bishop of Lismore, legate of the apostolic see; Gilbert, archbishop of Armagh, Donat, archbishop of Cashel; Laurence, archbishop of Dublin; Catholicus, archbishop of Tuam; and all their suffragans: greeting and apostolic benediction. Through your letters, and through the reliable report of others, it has come to the notice of the apostolic see how great are the enormities of vice into which the people of Ireland are lapsed,[1] and how they have departed from the fear of God and the established practice of the Christian faith, so that souls have been placed in peril. We have further learnt from your letters that Henry, the noble king of the English, our

[1] *quantis vitiorum enormitatibus gens Hibernica sit infecta.*

dearest son in Christ, moved by inspiration from God and summoning all his strength, has subjugated this barbarous and uncouth race which is ignorant of divine law; and that through his power those forbidden things which used to be practised in your land now begin to diminish. We have been filled with great joy about this, and have rendered abundant thanks to him who gave the aforesaid king so great and so triumphant a victory. And we earnestly pray that through the vigilance and care of the king, and by your co-operation with him, this undisciplined and untamed people may in every way be led to respect the divine law and the practice of the Christian faith, and that thereby you and all the men of the Church may be brought to rejoice in honour and peace. In order that this work, so well begun, may continue, it is fitting that you should show it favour and support. Therefore we order and command, through this apostolic writing, that you zealously and strongly assist the aforesaid king (who is a man of majesty and a devoted son of the Church) to maintain and keep that land; and that, so far as is consistent with your order and office, you help him in extirpating the foulness of such abominable practices.[1] If any king, prince, or other man in that land, violating the oath of fealty which he has properly sworn to the aforesaid king, shall rashly go against him, and thereafter basely refuse to accept your admonition as he ought, you are, without excuse or delay, to strike him with the censure of the Church, relying in so doing upon the apostolic authority. This Catholic and most Christian king has heard us in respect of tithes and other rights of the Church, and in restoring to you and to all men those things which pertain to the liberty of the Church. Therefore, executing our mandate with zeal and steadfastness, you must resolutely guard those things which pertain to his royal dignity and, as far as lies in your power, make others respect it also. Given at Tusculum, 20 September.

161. Letter of Pope Alexander III addressed to the lay nobles of Ireland, concerning Henry II's conquest of that country (most probably 1172)

This letter should be read in connexion with Nos. 160 and 162. It is printed in *Liber Niger Scaccarii* (ed. T. Hearne, 1728), vol. I, pp. 47–48.

Alexander the bishop, servant of the servants of God, to our dear sons, the noble kings and princes of Ireland, greeting and apostolic benediction. Public report and reliable information has reached us that you have taken for your king and lord our dearest son in Christ, Henry, the noble king of the English, and that you have sworn fealty to him. Our heart has been filled with joy at this news since, through the power of that king, a greater peace and tranquillity will, with the help of God, be made to prevail in your land; and the Irish race, which has fallen so far through the enormity and foulness of its vices, will thus become more readily accustomed to the practice of Christian worship, and will better submit to the discipline of Christian faith. Thus, in so far as of your own free will you have submitted to that powerful and majestic king who is a devoted son of the Church, you have acted for your own good and in a manner worthy of praise. And there is good hope that no little benefit may accrue to you and the Church, and to all the people of your land. We therefore strictly admonish your excellencies, and we command that

[1] *ad extirpandam inde tantae abominationis spurcitiam.*

you keep firm and unbroken the fealty which you have, with a sacred oath, sworn to this great king. By so doing, you will be able always to deserve his bountiful favour through showing him submission in humility and quietness; and we on our part will for this have cause duly to commend your prudence. Given at Tusculum, 20 September.

162. Letter of Pope Alexander III addressed to Henry II concerning that king's conquest of Ireland (most probably 1172)

This remarkable letter should be read in connexion with Nos. 160 and 161. It is printed in *Liber Niger Scaccarii* (ed. T. Hearne, 1728), vol. I, pp. 44–47.

Alexander the bishop, servant of the servants of God, to his dearest son in Christ, Henry, the noble king of the English, greeting and apostolic benediction. By public report and by reliable private testimony we have had welcome news concerning that people of Ireland which without fear of God has wandered unbridled through the paths of vice and, abjuring the practice of the Christian faith, has torn itself with internecine slaughter; we have had news, indeed, concerning that kingdom which, as we have heard, the Roman princes, lords of the world, left unsubdued in their own time; and now we have learnt that you, a pious and majestic prince, have wonderfully and mightily triumphed, and by the favour of God, by whose inspiration we are assured you acted, you have extended over that barbarous and uncouth people the plenitude of your peace. We forbear to mention for the present the other enormities and vices which this race so wantonly follows through neglect of the practice of Christian religion, about which our venerable brothers Christian, bishop of Lismore, legate of the apostolic see, and the archbishops and bishops of the land have informed us in their letters; and our dear son, R[alph], archdeacon of Llandaff, a prudent and discreet man, and one devoted to your royal interests, who has seen these things with the eye of faith, has revealed to us matters which perchance have come more fully to the notice of your majesty: the men of this race (it is said) have intercourse with their stepmothers, and do not blush to get them with child; men, likewise, degrade themselves with their sisters-in-law while their brothers are still alive; and many have intercourse with the daughters of mothers they have deserted. Further, all of them eat flesh during Lent; they do not pay tithes; and they do not reverence, as they should, either the churches of God or those ecclesiastical persons who serve them. Therefore, when we heard from these archbishops and bishops, and in fuller detail from the aforesaid archdeacon, that you had assembled a stupendous force by sea and land in order to subject this people to your rule, and to extirpate the foulness of their abominations, we were duly thankful. And we made fervent thanksgiving also to him from whom all good proceeds, and who is pleased to favour in the way of salvation the pious acts and purposes of the faithful. We besought Almighty God with prayers and offerings that, through the power of your majesty, the forbidden things which were done in that land might now begin to be discontinued; that the seeds of virtue might be planted in place of the weeds of vice; and that, with the aid of God, this people might through you be brought to abjure the foulness of their sins, and to submit themselves to the discipline of Christian practice. Thus might you deserve an imperishable crown of eternal glory, and this race be brought to salvation. We therefore beg your royal excellency–nay, as you value the remission of your sins, we exhort you in the Lord–to continue in that which you have so laudably begun. We bid you to strengthen and renew your purpose to bring back this people to the worship of Christ and by your power to keep them in it. In this way, even as you have undertaken this great work (as we believe) for the remission of your sins, so also in perfecting it shall you be made worthy to receive an eternal crown. And since (as in the excellence of your majesty) the Roman Church has fuller rights of jurisdiction over islands than it has over main lands,[1] we, trusting in your fervent devotion, now hope that you will not only maintain the rights of that Church but also increase them. We therefore ask and admonish your majesty that, where no such privileges are specified, you will confer them. We enjoin that throughout this land you will zealously safeguard the rights of blessed Peter, and if these have lapsed, we request your majesty to restore them. If you do this, we shall owe copious thanks to your royal highness, and you, on your part, will be seen to have offered to God the first-fruits of your glory and your triumph. Given at Tusculum, 20 September.

* * *

(c) SELECT "EPISCOPAL ACTS"

The texts which here follow (Nos. 163–169) are representative of a class of documents to which too little attention has as yet been given, and to which the title *Acta Episcoporum* has been assigned. They reflect the administrative activities of a medieval bishop, and are thus of particular value for the study of the Church on its secular side. They became more frequent in the time of Henry II, and the examples here given are therefore inserted at this place, but, as will be seen, many of them are of earlier date, and may in this respect be compared with the notable act of Bishop Wulfstan preserved above (No. 85). The nature of such texts and the circumstances of their production are admirably discussed in F. M. Stenton, "Acta Episcoporum" (*Camb. Hist. Journal*, vol. III, 1929) and in C. R. Cheney, *English Bishops' Chanceries, 1100–1250* (Manchester, 1950).

163. Charter of William of Corbeil, archbishop of Canterbury, confirming the restoration of the church of Calk to the canons of Calk Priory (1130–1136)

Printed in C. R. Cheney, *English Bishops' Chanceries, 1100–1250* (1950), Appendix III, no. 1, p. 150.

William, by the grace of God, archbishop of Canterbury and legate of the apostolic see, to Roger, by the same grace bishop of Chester,[2] to Rannulf, earl of Chester,[3] and to all the faithful of the holy Church of God throughout England, greeting and God's benediction. Be it known to the piety of all men that, in our presence and in that of the archbishops of York and Rouen and of other bishops attending the council held at London in the time of King Henry[4] on the Sunday when "I am the Good Shepherd" is sung,[5] William, abbot of Chester, has restored to the canons of Calk their church of Calk, and has renounced and promised to surrender or make good all their possessions which have been appropriated by him

[1] A reference to the apocryphal "Donation of Constantine". See also below, No. 171, p. 796.
[2] Roger 'de Clinton', bishop of Lichfield, Chester and Coventry, 1129–1148.
[3] Rannulf 'de Gernon'. [4] Henry I.
[5] The opening words of the Gospel for the Second Sunday after Easter.

or by his men, and also to give back to them the charter which they had from the earl respecting them, and which they had lost through the said abbot. Wherefore I will and firmly command that the said church shall from henceforth remain free and immune for the needs of the aforesaid canons in their service to God. I also beg you all out of love to God and ourself to fortify the said church by your counsel and help. Farewell.

164. Charter of William Warelwast, bishop of Exeter, confirming a concord made between the monks of St. Pancras and Robert fitz Martin in respect of the chapel of Combe Martin, Devon (14 June 1133)

This document is of particular interest as illustrating the judicial function of the diocesan synod in the early twelfth century. The parties to the suit are brought to make a formal agreement by the bishop, presiding in his cathedral over a synod of his diocese, and without reference to either the king or the pope. It is printed in F. M. Stenton, "Acta Episcoporum" (*Camb. Hist. Journal*, vol. III, 1929, pp. 9–10).

William, by the grace of God bishop of Exeter, to all clerks and laymen belonging to his diocese,[1] both present and future, greeting and God's benediction. I make known to you all that the monks of St. Pancras and Robert fitz Martin, in my presence and in a synod held in our church of St. Peter,[2] have brought to an end, and made an agreement concerning the controversy and suit which had arisen between them in respect of the chapel of Combe in these terms. The monks have withdrawn their claim to the chapel and wholly renounced it in favour of Robert fitz Martin, in return for the gift and concession to the monks by the said Robert of two acres of land in his manor of Combe worth 3 shillings a year; the monks are to obtain and possess this in 'frankalmoign' wholly free and absolute for ever, to wit, as quittance and for the liberty of his chapel of Combe, and also for the salvation of his soul and that of his wife, Maud, and for the souls of his ancestors and his heirs. In order that the aforesaid concord may remain truly ratified and inviolate for ever, I have endorsed and confirmed it by charter and by my seal, by my authority and the counsel of our whole church. Witnesses, my archdeacons, William, Odo and Ernald, together with Ernald, archdeacon of Salisbury, Harold, archdeacon of Bath, William, prior of Taunton, Hilary, clerk to the bishop of Winchester, and many other clerks and lay witnesses; Aldred, son of Joel, Osmund, steward of the bishop of Salisbury; Hubert, steward of Baldwin of Reviers;[3] Robert 'Daco'; Richard of Holloway; Richard fitz Ralph; Philip 'de Beri'; Richard 'de Pontcardun' and many other laymen. The aforesaid concord was made in my presence and in that of the afore-mentioned persons, and witnessed by our synod in the new church of St. Peter on Wednesday, 14 June, in the year of our Lord's Incarnation 1133. . . . Farewell.

165. Grant by John 'de Chesney' to the canons of Rudham with confirmation thereof by William 'de Turbe', bishop of Norwich (19 May 1148)

Printed in C. R. Cheney, *English Bishops' Chanceries, 1100–1250* (1950), p. 153.

To William, by the grace of God bishop of Norwich, and to his lord, William 'de Warenne' the earl, and to all the sons of holy Church, both present and future, John 'de Chesney' greeting. Be it known to you that I have granted to God

[1] *parochie.*

[2] Exeter Cathedral; mention of the "new church" later in the document throws light on the date of the building of the Norman cathedral by William Warelwast.

[3] Earl of Devon.

and St. Mary and to the canons of Rudham two churches of that village with everything pertaining to them and, in addition, all the secular property held by Bruno and William, the priests, to wit, the land which my grandfather, Ralph 'de Chesney', and William, his son and my uncle, and I made free of all customs and dues and gave in ecclesiastical possession. . . .

And in order that the said canons may hold all the aforesaid lands inviolate and in honour and peace by perpetual right, for the souls of my grandfather, Ralph 'de Chesney', and of his wife, and for the souls of my father and mother and of William 'de Chesney', my uncle, of Roger and their sisters, and of Waleran 'de Rocesforde', and the souls of all my relatives, and for my soul and that of my wife, and those of my brothers and sisters, I corroborate and confirm this gift both by the testimony of this present instrument and by affixing my seal, saving the service due to the earl.

Of this gift the following are witnesses: Reginald 'de Warenne'; Ralph of Wiveton; Ralph, son of Osmund and Sibyl, wife of the lord John; Peter 'de Chesney' and Matthew, his brother; Nicholas the clerk and Godwine, his brother; Scul, and William, his brother; Ralph, priest of Saxthorpe; and Master William Maurinus; William the priest; Nicholas of Stanhoe; Wace the deacon; Geoffrey of West Rudham; Ralph Avis; Nicholas the clerk of Barsham; Walter the clerk; Albert; Rigolf; Warin; and Robert of Croft.

This covenant was renewed in the presence of the lord William, bishop of Norwich, at Thorney on the eve of the Ascension of our Lord, being St. Dunstan's Day, John 'de Chesney' himself being present. Of this gift and its renewal the following are witnesses: William, archdeacon of Norwich; Turold the chaplain; Ralph of Snoring; Ernald the chaplain; Adam 'de Calna'; Ralph, clerk of Saxlingham; John the steward; Peter the constable; William 'de Backetuna'; Arthur; Adam, son of John the steward; and William, son of Ralph.

166. Charter of Robert 'de Chesney', bishop of Lincoln, concerning the rights of the church of St. Peter at Northampton (1155–1158)

This instrument, to which No. 168 is consequent, is here printed as representative of a large and important class of documents to which Sir Frank Stenton has given the name *Acta Episcoporum*. Most of these still remain unprinted, but in due course they may be made to throw much new light upon the organization of practice of the twelfth-century church in England. The matter here under discussion is the disputed rights of a 'mother-church' over a chapel founded within its original 'parish'–particularly in respect of fees for baptisms and burials. This charter has been printed and fully discussed by F. M. Stenton in "Acta Episcoporum" (*Camb. Hist. Journal*, vol. III (1929), p. 4).

Robert, by the grace of God bishop of Lincoln, to all the sons of holy Mother-Church greeting. Let all those present and to come, whom this letter shall reach, know that by the order of our lord, Henry, king of England, we have caused diligent inquiry to be made whether the church of Thorpe is a baptismal church in itself or whether it belongs to some other church. By the testimony of many witnesses, both clerk and lay, we have ascertained that it belongs to the church of St. Peter of Northampton as a member to its head and as a daughter to her mother. We have heard, moreover, many of the parishioners say that they have brought their babes to the aforesaid church of St. Peter for baptism, and that there also they have buried their dead. We therefore bear witness to what we have heard from so many, and we confirm it with the authority of our seal. These are the witnesses: William, archdeacon of Northampton; David, archdeacon of Buckingham; Master Thomas; Geoffrey Crassus; Laurence the clerk.

167. Charter of Thomas Becket, archbishop of Canterbury, concerning the amends promised to Ramsey Abbey by Geoffrey 'de Mandeville' for his father's misdeeds (6 April 1163)

Printed in C. R. Cheney, *English Bishops' Chanceries, 1100–1250* (1950), p. 154.

Thomas, by the grace of God humble minister of the church of Canterbury, to all the faithful of holy Mother-Church greeting. It is public knowledge that Geoffrey 'de Mandeville' inflicted many injuries on the abbey of Ramsey in the time of hostilities.[1] On this account and from a desire to make amends for his father, Earl Geoffrey, his son, has made a covenant with Abbot William and the monks of Ramsey to this effect. For the next three years the aforesaid earl will pay to the monks annually 100 shillings, half the amount at Michaelmas and half at Easter; and before the end of the third year Earl Geoffrey will assign to the abbey of Ramsey revenue of 100 shillings in lands or churches at a suitable and convenient place. This he has promised to do, pledging his faith as a Christian in our hand, in the presence of our venerable brother, Hilary, bishop of Chichester, and sitting with us our clerks, Robert, archdeacon of Oxford, John of Tilbury, Robert of Belfou, Stephen of Eckton, and William of Leicester. This covenant was made at Windsor in the year of our Lord's Incarnation 1163 on the first Saturday after the Octave of Easter.

168. Charter of Robert 'de Chesney', bishop of Lincoln, concerning the rights of the church of St. Peter at Northampton (before 1166)

This instrument is of particular interest because it throws light on ecclesiastical privilege in respect of the procedure of trial by ordeal in the twelfth century. The supervision of the Church was an essential part of a valid procedure. The document is to be dated before 1166, the year when the Assize of Clarendon introduced major changes in the administration of criminal jurisdiction. It is printed in F. M. Stenton, "Acta Episcoporum" (*Camb. Hist. Journal*, vol. III (1929), p. 12).

Robert, by the grace of God bishop of Lincoln, to William, archdeacon of Northampton, to the dean[2] [*sic*] and the justice[3] greeting. We have learnt that it is the privilege of the church of the blessed Peter at Northampton that no one who is to be brought to the ordeal for any judgment ought to clear himself within the said town or within the area subject to its jurisdiction except through the aforesaid church, and in such a way that he shall first keep vigil and offer prayer in the said church before taking the ordeal. Wherefore we command you that no one shall presume to diminish or infringe the privilege of this same church. If anyone shall attempt to act contrary to this, let him know that, inasmuch as we ought to be debtors in justice to all men, we shall not be remiss in meting out justice against him.

[1] The civil war between Stephen and Maud.
[2] Probably the rural dean of Northampton.
[3] Presumably the local justice for Northamptonshire.

169. Charter of William 'de Turbe', bishop of Norwich, in favour of the canons and clerks of St. Martin-le-Grand, London (1146–1174)

Printed in C. R. Cheney, *English Bishops' Chanceries, 1100–1250* (1950), p. 155.

William, by the grace of God bishop of Norwich, to all archdeacons, deans, priests and to the whole clergy and people of his diocese greeting. Be it known to you that we have granted to the canons of the blessed Martin in London and to their clerks licence to preach in our churches and parishes in aid of the building of their church. Wherefore we wish you to know that to those who give support to them by their alms we remit forty days' penance. Farewell.

(*d*) THE CHRISTIAN COMMONWEALTH

170. Select passages from the *Policraticus* of John of Salisbury

The passages printed below are from the *Policraticus* of John of Salisbury, his longest and most ambitious work. In Dr. Clement Webb's critical edition the text fills two quarto volumes of nearly 800 pages (*Joannis Saresberiensis Episcopi Carnotensis Policraticus sive De Nugis Curialium et Vestigiis Philosophorum*, Oxford, 1909). The greater part of the work was written between 1159 and 1160 when John was living at Canterbury as clerk or secretary to Archbishop Theobald. It was finally revised during John's exile abroad in 1164. The title is most properly to be rendered *The Statesman's Book*; the sub-title–*The Courtier's Toys and the Footsteps of Philosophers*–indicates John's view of the two things indispensable for success in politics, a knowledge of the conventions and obligations of public life and an acquaintance with the teachings of ancient philosophy, without which he holds that true statesmanship is impossible of attainment. But the *Policraticus* is by no means a planned book or an orderly political treatise. Rather is it in the words of R. L. Poole "an encyclopaedia of the cultivated thought of the middle of the twelfth century". Reminiscences of his personal experiences or those of his friends, anecdotes of the great personages of his own day, accounts of his dealings with officials at the royal court and the papal *curia* are continually employed "to point a moral or adorn the tale".

For John's general position as a writer and exponent of the twelfth-century hierarchical doctrine of the State the following works may be consulted: C. Schaarschmidt, *Joannes Saresberiensis nach Leben und Studien, Schriften und Philosophie* (Leipzig, 1862); P. Gennrich, *Die Staats- und Kirchenlehre Johanns von Salisbury* (Gotha, 1894); R. L. Poole, *Illustrations of the History of Medieval Thought and Learning* (2nd ed., London, 1922), *Studies in Chronology and History* (Oxford, 1934); A. J. and R. W. Carlyle, *History of Mediaeval Political Theory*, vols. III and IV (London, 1922); E. F. Jacob, "John of Salisbury and the Policraticus" in F. J. C. Hearnshaw (ed.), *Social and Political Ideas of some Great Mediaeval Thinkers* (London, 1923); and C. C. J. Webb, *John of Salisbury* (London, 1932).

(i)

[The body-politic compared with the physical organism. The image is here derived from the treatise known as the *Institutio Traiani* which John ascribes to Plutarch, though it is patently of later date.]

The[1] nature of the State, according to Plutarch, and what takes the place therein of the soul and the members of the body.

Headings of the same political construction follow in the little book entitled *The Institutes of Trajan*, which I have in part thought fit to make use of in this present work. But this I have done by reproducing its views in outline rather than by using its actual words.

First of all it is laid down that the prince should judge everything for himself and diligently consider what place he occupies in the whole body-politic. Moreover, in Plutarch's view, the State is a kind of organism, whose life is a gift of God, controlled

[1] Book V, chap. II; *Ioannis Saresberiensis . . . Policraticus* (ed. C. C. J. Webb), vol. I, p. 282.

by the motions of divine equity and ruled by the governing force of reason. But the powers which establish and implant in us the practices of religion and hand down to us the ceremonies of God–I may not speak of the gods, as Plutarch doth–in the body-politic take the place of the soul. Those, indeed, who preside over the practice of religious duties, ought to be upheld and reverenced as being the soul of the body. For who doubts that the ministers of God's holiness are his vicars? Furthermore, like as the soul hath the pre-eminence over the whole body, so also those whom God calls to be officials of religion are set over the whole body. . . . The prince, indeed, in the State occupies the position of the head, being subject to the one true God and his representatives on earth, like as in the human body the head is both animated and ruled by the spirit. The senate takes the place of the heart, whence spring the impulses to good and evil deeds. The judges and provincial governors appropriate the functions of the eyes, ears and tongue, the officials and soldiers correspond to the hands, the courtiers to the sides, the treasurers and financial experts[1]–I am not referring to those put in charge of prisons,[2] but to the custodians of private interests–represent the stomach and intestines. These, if they become clogged through excessive indulgence of appetite and remain stubbornly constipated, engender manifold and incurable disorders and bring ruin upon the whole body. The husbandmen correspond to the feet, ever cleaving to the ground, for which the foresight of the head is the more necessary as they find occasion for stumbling, when they tread the earth in obedience to the dictates of the body. Wherefore they should properly be well shod, for they support the weight of the whole body, keep it erect and enable it to move. Take away the support of the feet from a healthy body and it will be unable to walk in its own strength, but will either crawl on its hands, shamefully, helplessly and with great difficulty, or be propelled with the assistance of the animal creation. . . .

(ii)

[The function of the secular arm.]

The[3] sacred history of the Gospel bears witness that two swords suffice for the Christian empire;[4] the others all belong to those who come out with swords and staves to take Christ captive,[5] and desire to blot out His name. What kind of soldiers are they who, despite their oaths, do not conform to the law, but think that the glory of their warfare consists in showing contempt for the priesthood, in disparaging the authority of the Church, in expanding man's empire in such a way as to contract the dominion of Christ, in singing their own praises and flattering and exalting themselves by false proclamations, aping the famous warrior amidst the derision of their hearers? The courage of such men is most evident when they wound the clergy, the defenceless soldiery, either with weapons or with their tongues. What then is the true function of the professional soldier? To protect the Church, to fight against treachery, to reverence the priesthood, to ward off injuries from the poor, to ensure peace throughout

[1] *quaestores et commentarienses.*

[2] John means that by his use of the classical term *quaestor* he is not referring to the criminal jurisdiction exercised by the ancient Roman magistrates of that name, but to the duties of a medieval financial official.

[3] Book VI, chap. VIII, *Iohannis Saresberiensis . . . Policraticus* (ed. C. C. J. Webb), vol. II, pp. 22, 23.

[4] Luke xxii. 38. Cf. St. Bernard, *De Consideratione*, Lib. IV, cap. 3. Migne, *Patrologia Latina*, vol. CLXXXII, col. 776; *ibid.*, col. 463.

[5] Luke xxii. 52.

the provinces and (as taught by a true understanding of the Sacrament) to shed his blood and, if need be, to lay down his life for his brethren. "Let the praises of God be in their mouth and a two-edged sword in their hands, to be avenged of the heathen and to rebuke the people, to bind their kings in chains and their nobles with links of iron."[1] But to what end? That they may become the slaves of passion, vanity and avarice, or their own lusts? By no means; but rather that they may execute thereby the decrees of the judges; wherein each man follows not his own judgment but that of the angels of God and of men from the dictates of equity and the public weal. I say to execute the decrees for, as it is the office of the judges to pronounce sentence, in like manner also it is the duty of these men to execute it: as it is written, "Such honour have all his saints."[2] For the soldiers who do these things are just as much saints and loyal to their prince in proportion as they preserve the faith of God; and they promote the glory of their virtue more effectively inasmuch as they faithfully seek in everything the glory of God. . . .

(iii)

[On Tyrants and Tyrannicide.]

[Here is outlined a distinction between the tyrant and the legitimate prince. The importance of John's famous justification of tyrannicide may be exaggerated, for there is no indication that he expected his advice to be put into practice. Here may be an echo of republican sentiment derived by John from his reading of classical authors.]

That[3] it is lawful to flatter one whom it is also lawful to slay; and that the tyrant is a public enemy.

. . . In profane letters[4] there is contained a warning that life should be carried on in one way with a friend and in the opposite way with a tyrant. One should certainly not indulge in servile flattery of a friend, but it is permissible to soothe the ears of a tyrant. For it is permissible to flatter one whom it is lawful to slay. Moreover, not only is it lawful to slay the tyrant, but it is likewise just and equitable to do so.[5] For he that takes the sword deserves to perish by the sword.[6] But taking the sword is to be understood of him who seizes it for his own fell purpose, not of him who receives power to wield it from the Lord. He that receives power from God complies with the laws and is the servant of right and justice. But he who seizes power oppresses the rights of men and subordinates the laws to his own will. Therefore the law is justly armed against the man who would disarm the laws, and the authority of the State strikes heavily against him who strives to weaken its power. And though there are many treasonable offences, none is more serious than this which is practised against the body of the laws themselves. Tyranny therefore is not only a public crime, but, if it be possible, it is an even greater one. For if treason admits the accusations of all men, how much more does the crime of suppressing the laws which should govern the rulers themselves? Assuredly no man takes private vengeance upon a public enemy, but whoso does not bring an accusation against him fails in his duty towards himself and towards the whole body-politic. . . .

[1] Psalms cxlix. 6–8. [2] Psalms cxlix. 9.

[3] Book III, chap. XV; *Iohannis Saresberiensis . . . Policraticus* (ed. C. C. J. Webb), vol. I, p. 232.

[4] Cicero, *De Amicitia*, XXIV, 89.

[5] All means of tyrannicide, says John in another passage, are lawful save that of poison, which has ever been abhorrent to Englishmen; *Policraticus*, Book VIII, chap. XX, p. 378; chap. XIX, p. 372.

[6] Matthew xxvi. 52.

Wherein[1] the tyrant differs from the prince, and of the tyranny of priests.

The distinction between the prince and the tyrant has been stated above, when we were turning over the pages of Plutarch's *Institutes of Trajan*.[2] Similarly the functions of the prince and the members of the body-politic have been carefully explained. From this may easily and briefly be set down what should be said on the opposite side about the tyrant.

The tyrant then, as the philosophers have depicted him, is one who oppresses the people by violent and despotic rule, even as the prince governs by the laws. Moreover, the law is the gift of God, the model of equity, the pattern of justice, the image of the divine will, the guardian of security, the force unifying and consolidating the people, the rule of conduct for officials, the exclusion and extermination of vices, the penalty for violence and all wrongdoing. The law may be assailed either by force or by cunning; it may be, as it were, ravaged by the cruelty of the lion or lured into the lair of the dragon. By whatever means this occurs, it is clear that divine grace is attacked and that God is in some measure provoked to battle. The prince fights for the laws and the liberty of the people; the tyrant reckons that naught has been accomplished unless he has made the laws of none effect and enticed the people into servitude. The prince bears the stamp of divinity, while the tyrant's image is that of a perverted strength and satanic wickedness, in that he copies Lucifer who forsook virtue and strove to place his seat in the north part of heaven and become like unto the most High. . . .[3]

As the image of the deity the prince is worthy of love, reverence and worship; the tyrant, being the image of wickedness, for the most part merits assassination. The tyrant has his roots in iniquity, and from a poisoned root a tree brings forth evil and deadly fruits and should be felled with the axe. For if wickedness and injustice, the destroyer of love, had not engendered the tyrant, his people had enjoyed firm peace and perpetual tranquillity, and no one would have contemplated the extension of its territories. . . . Kings indeed are not the only ones to practise tyranny. . . . For many are found in the ranks of the clergy who act thus from overweening ambition and avail themselves of every artifice to play the tyrant under cover of their office. For the ungodly State also has head and members and strives, as it were, by civil institutions to conform to the pattern of the lawful State. Its head, the tyrant, is the devil's image; heretical, schismatic and sacrilegious priests and, to employ Plutarch's term, the officers of religion,[4] who impugn God's law, represent the soul; evil counsellors or, so to speak, a senate of iniquity represent the heart; the eyes, ears, tongue and hands, when unarmed, are represented by the judges and their laws, unjust officials; when armed the hands are the violent soldiery whom Cicero designates robbers; the feet are those who in their lowlier transactions act contrary to the precepts of the Lord and lawful institutions. All these similes can indeed be very easily comprehended from what has been written above. But the clergy should not be angry with me if I admit that tyrants can also be found in their ranks. . . .

[1] Book VIII, chap. XVII; *Iohannis Saresberiensis . . . Policraticus* (ed. C. C. J. Webb), vol. II, pp. 345 *et seq.*

[2] See above, p. 786.

[3] Cf. Isaiah xiv. 12–14.

[4] *praefecti religionis.*

. . . Despite[1] the Lord's interdiction the house of prayer has become a house of merchandise, and the temple built on him as corner-stone is turned into a cave of robbers.[2] For the Church is verily given over to pillage, some laying open hands on her possessions, others acquiring them by secret usurpation; and in a case where there are no possessions to be alienated the church itself is seized. For it is very rare to find a man who will gird his sword upon his thigh[3] to restrain the presumption of ambition. The ambitious man devises many different stratagems in order to take the Church by storm when there is none to defend her. One man, trusting in his noble birth or in the weight of his authority, bursts headlong into the holy places, and if perchance he be repulsed at the door, he is not afraid to undermine the walls or the threshold. For he will stir up rebellion against Moses, offer strange fire in the Lord's temple and defile the vessels of the sanctuary.[4] Another, trusting in the multitude of his riches,[5] enters in with Simon Magus as his guide and finds none therein to bid him and his money depart to perdition.[6] Another fears to approach Peter openly with gifts, but creeps into the Church's lap secretly and adulterously, like Jupiter entering through the roof and stealing into Danae in a shower of gold. Another sidles up obsequiously, as if with no thought of offering a gift, or as though his complaisance matched the extent of his present, whereas in reality there is no greater gift offered than when a man devotes himself to the service of his fellows.

. . . On[7] the other side are ranged many who by no means conceal their purpose, but by blowing their own trumpet,[8] as we say, mock at the tardiness in their ambition shown by those whom we have considered above, which they liken to that of soldiers who dare not openly acknowledge the decorations they have won in war. Of these former–impure as they are, and unwilling to amend their own way of life and ignorant how to instruct that of others–it is said that they break into the Holy of Holies with unclean feet and bear in their polluted hands the shewbread of the Lord[9] and the Flesh of the Immaculate Lamb consumed by the fire of his Passion on the Cross. Albeit unworthy to approach the outer doors, yet they incontinently thrust themselves into the priesthood, rush into the sanctuary[10] and, repulsing others, take possession of the sacred altars in such wise that Holy Orders would now appear to have been instituted, not for the purpose of offering a pattern and example to the laity, but to afford an opportunity to live in plenty and security. It might be supposed that the priesthood is not an office subject to the stern judgment of God but some administrative post secure and above dispute. . . .

The majority of them feel themselves secured by a papal privilege or a royal mandate from the need to conform to the decrees of the judges or to execute justice or to subject themselves to the law of God. I do not blame the leniency of the apostolic see for this, but I do not consider that such indulgence is expedient for the Church. We read of none such in existence among that glorious band of Christ's followers, although there was strife among them as to which of them should be the greater.[11]

[1] An earlier development of the same theme: Book VII, chap. XVII; *Iohannis Saresberiensis . . . Policraticus* (ed. C. C. J. Webb), vol. II, p. 162.
[2] Cf. Matthew xxi. 13; John ii. 16.
[3] Psalms xlv. 4.
[4] Cf. Leviticus x. 1.
[5] Psalms lii. 8.
[6] See Acts viii. 18.
[7] Book VII, chap. XIX; *Iohannis Saresberiensis . . . Policraticus* (ed. C. C. J. Webb), vol. II, p. 169.
[8] *insignia praeconantes.*
[9] Exodus xxv. 30; cf. I Samuel xxi. 6.
[10] *tribunal.*
[11] Luke xxii. 24.

We have no mention of any dispensation of this kind having been made by the apostles, although we have read that Paul and Barnabas parted from each other.[1] We believe there is no ground for opposition in that celestial city which is our mother above, nor ought there to be here on earth, except when the most urgent reason demands it. For in these matters–if I may speak with the leave of the mob and of those who favour this abuse–I will write as I feel, lest I abate anything of the truth or what is worthy of credit. I declare then my firm belief that those who, carried away by their own pride, seek dispensations[2] of this kind, would, if it were possible, shake off the yoke of Christ and his Divine Father. Nay! I go even further and say that to the best of their ability they are casting off and wilfully breaking the ordinance of God. . . . This gives rise to a grave scandal in religion and the Christian faith, because the priesthood and the ministry are undertaken more from the motive of ambition and to curry favour than from merit. So run they all, but when they have reached the goal, one receiveth the prize,[3] namely he that hath proved himself swifter than others in the race of ambition and hath even outrun Peter[4] and every other disciple of Christ. For such a one has attained his ambition and forestalled the utmost speed of a rapid summons. . . .

(iv)

[The dangers and difficulties besetting the pope.]

. . . I recollect[5] how once I set out for Apulia for the purpose of visiting the lord pope, Adrian IV,[6] who had admitted me into intimate friendship with him.[7] I stayed with him nearly three months at Benevento.[8] After the manner of friends we had frequent conversations together on a variety of topics. On one occasion he bade me tell him frankly and in confidence what men were saying about him and the Roman Church. I replied with complete sincerity, and made known to him the grievances of which I had heard tell in the various provinces of the Church. For it was asserted by many that the Roman Church, the mother of all the churches, was treating her sons more like a stepmother than a true mother.[9] Scribes and Pharisees, they were saying, sit in her seat, binding heavy burdens and grievous to be borne on men's shoulders, which they would not touch with one of their fingers.[10] The Roman prelates lord it over the clergy instead of serving as a pattern to a flock treading the straight and narrow path which leadeth to eternal life.[11] They amass costly furniture, loading their tables with gold and silver, and even stint themselves from the motive of avarice. Seldom or never is a poor man invited to feast with them, and even when he is, it is their vain-glory which brings him thither rather than the spirit of Christ. They disturb the churches, provoke litigation, set clergy and people against each other and show not the slightest sympathy with the distress and misery of the afflicted. They revel in the

[1] Acts xv. 39.
[2] *emancipationes.*
[3] I Corinthians ix. 24.
[4] John xx. 4.
[5] Book VI, chap. XXIV; *Iohannis Saresberiensis . . . Policraticus* (ed. C. C. J. Webb), vol. II, pp. 67–73.
[6] Nicholas Breakspear, the only English pope, styled Adrian IV, 1154–1159. (See above, pp. 326, 327.)
[7] John had probably made the acquaintance of the future pope at least as early as 1146 or 1148 when resident in the papal *curia* under Eugenius III. His intimacy with his fellow-countryman assumed political importance with Nicholas's election as pope.
[8] Adrian IV was resident at Benevento from November 1155 to July 1156.
[9] *se non tam matrem exhibet aliis quam novercam.*
[10] Cf. Matthew xxiii. 2, 4; Luke xi. 46.
[11] Cf. Matthew vii. 14.

spoils of the churches and count all gain as godliness.[1] They dispense justice, not according to truth, but for money. Today everything has its price and tomorrow nothing will be obtainable without paying for it. They frequently inflict injuries and copy the demons in that they are said only to cease from doing harm when they have gained some profit; exception may be made of a few who properly fulfil the name and office of shepherd. Even the pope himself has become grievous and wellnigh insupportable to all men. Further, they all complain, that while the churches built by the piety of their fathers are tottering and crumbling into ruins and altars are forsaken, the pope has erected palaces[2] and dwells therein clad, not only in purple, but also in gold. The palaces of priests shine in splendour, while the Church of Christ is defiled at their hands. They pillage and despoil the provinces as if they were intent on restoring the treasury of Croesus. But the Most High hath dealt justly with them, seeing that they in their turn have been given over to pillage at the hands of others, often the vilest of men. It is my opinion too that so long as they wander out of the way,[3] the scourge of the Lord will never leave them. For the mouth of the Lord hath spoken it: they shall be judged with the judgment wherewith they have judged, and with what measure they mete it shall be measured to them again.[4] For the Ancient of days knoweth not a lie. "This, father, is what the people are saying, since you wish me to make known their views to you." "And what do you yourself think?" asked the pope. "Troubles beset me on every side," I replied: "I fear to incur the charges of falsehood and flattery, if I were the only one to contradict the people. On the other hand, if I do not do so, I dread being found guilty of treason and judged worthy of death for having, as it were, stretched forth my mouth unto heaven.[5] Nevertheless, since Guido Dens, the cardinal-priest of St. Pudentiana,[6] has publicly borne witness to this, I do not presume in any way to contradict him. For he has stated that the Roman Church, being the source of double-dealing and the instigator of avarice, is the head and root of all evil. Nor did he utter this remark in some obscure corner, but proclaimed it openly to his fellow-cardinals in a session presided over by the saintly Pope Eugenius and held at Ferentino,[7] when he was wroth with me personally without a cause and impugned my innocence.[8] Yet one thing I boldly acknowledge, and to it my conscience bears witness, that I have nowhere found more upright clerks, nor any who more detest avarice, than in the Roman Church. Who does not marvel at the integrity and contempt for money shown by Bernard of Rennes, the cardinal-deacon of SS. Cosmas and Damian?[9] The man is not yet born from whom he would accept gifts. Indeed, when on one occasion he was urged to do so, he withdrew from communion with his brethren, being guided by a higher law. Who is not amazed at the bishop of Palestrina[10] who, fearing the pricks of conscience, abstained from

[1] I Timothy vi. 5.

[2] A reference to the palaces constructed by Eugenius III and Anastasius IV adjacent to the sites of ancient churches in Rome.

[3] *dum sic in inuio errauerint*; cf. Psalms cvii. 40.

[4] Matthew vii. 2.

[5] Psalms lxxiii. 9.

[6] For his identity, see R. L. Poole, *Historia Pontificalis*, pp. xiv–xvii.

[7] Eugenius III resided at Ferentino from 23 November 1150 to 22 June 1151. John gives an account of the business transacted at the council here mentioned in the *Historia Pontificalis*, chap. XXXV.

[8] Presumably in connexion with some episode in the affairs of the English Church, which figured largely on the agenda.

[9] An earlier reference is made to him in the *Policraticus*, Book V, chap. XV; see below, p. 794.

[10] Guarino of Bologna.

participation in the goods common to all the cardinals? Such moderation, such seriousness of purpose is characteristic of many more, so that they are not inferior to Fabricius, whom they in every way excel, having learned the true road of salvation. Since then you earnestly importune and command me–and one certainly must not lie to the Holy Spirit–I admit that in this case your order must be carried out, although not every pope is to be imitated in his works. For he who dissents from your teaching is either a heretic or a schismatic; but by God's mercy there are some who do not imitate the works of all of you. Thus the sins of a few popes have left stains on upright men and brought disgrace on the universal Church, and in my opinion the reason why they die at such frequent intervals is lest they should corrupt the whole Church. But the good popes are sometimes also carried off lest they be turned to evil, and because corrupt Rome is found unworthy of them in God's sight. Do you therefore, who now occupy the papal chair, seek out and cultivate the meek and them that despise vainglory and wealth. But I fear that so long as you persist in following your own will, you will continue to hear unpalatable truths from your indiscreet friend. Why is it, father, that you dissect the lives of others and so seldom examine your own? All men speak well of you, call you father and lord of all and pour down upon your head the balm of sinners.[1] If then you be a father, why do you expect presents and rewards from your children? If a lord, why do you not strike terror into your Romans, curb their audacity and bring them back to their fealty?[2] But you wish to preserve the city for the Church by means of presents? Did Pope Sylvester acquire it by such means?[3] Father, you have altogether wandered out of the way and are off the beaten track.[4] The city must be preserved by the same gifts whereby it was obtained. 'Freely ye have received, freely give.'[5] Justice is the queen of virtues and blushes to be exchanged for money.[6] If she is partial in the future, at least let it be for naught:[7] let not her that is incorruptible be prostituted for money, for she remains for ever pure and undefiled. While you oppress others, you yourself are yet more grievously oppressed."

The pope laughed and congratulated me on having spoken so freely. He bade me inform him without delay whenever any unfavourable opinion concerning him came to my ears. And after he had said many things in answer to me, some in his own favour and others against himself, he propounded to me this fable. "Once upon a time", said he, "the other members of the body conspired against the stomach on the ground that it weakened and impoverished all their activities by its gluttony. The eye was not satisfied merely with seeing or the ear with hearing,[8] the hands rested from their labours, the feet became numb from lack of exercise, and even the tongue restrained itself and suitably observed the occasions for speech and silence. In brief, all the members of the body watched over the public interests. Amidst so much solicitude and labour on the part of all of them, the belly alone remained idle; and when every function had been distributed as the manifold activities of the body required, of its own lust it devoured and consumed everything. What was the result?

[1] *oleum peccatoris, i.e.* flattery; cf. Psalms cxl. 5 (Vulgate).
[2] *ad fidem*, an allusion to the rebel citizens of the Roman Republic led by Arnold of Brescia.
[3] An allusion to the "Donation of Constantine"; see above, p. 780, below, p. 796.
[4] *in inuio, pater, es et non in uia*; cf. Psalms cxlvii. 40.
[5] Matthew x. 8.
[6] Cicero, *De Officiis*, III, 6, 28.
[7] *Si gratiosa futura est, sit gratuita.*
[8] Ecclesiastes i. 8.

The others agreed to cease work and subdue this idler, this public enemy, by undertaking a strict fast. Thus a whole day passed, and was followed by another even more tedious. The third day was so disastrous that it saw the collapse of nearly all of them. Under pressure of events, therefore, the brethren again met together to discuss their own health and the state of the public enemy. But when they were all gathered together, behold! the eyes were grown languid, the feet were unable to support the weight of the body, the arms had become stiff, and even the tongue was lifeless and had lost its taste, and would not venture to speak for the common cause. So everything was left to the counsel of the heart, and after due deliberation the brain disclosed that the organ, which had earlier been denounced as a public enemy, was responsible for these ills. Because for this reason all tribute had been withheld from it, and it in return (that is to say, the public treasurer[1]) had deprived all the members of nourishment. And because none can fight without wages, when these are not forthcoming the soldier becomes weak and dispirited. But the blame could not be laid on the treasurer, who could hardly disburse to others what he had not received himself. It is far safer to provide him with the means of distribution than that all the members should suffer hunger through his store being depleted. So it was done accordingly. On the advice of the brain the belly was refilled, the limbs revived their strength and peace was restored to all. So the stomach, although it is greedy and covetous of gain, was absolved from blame, because it craves food, not indeed for itself, but for the sake of other parts of the body, which cannot be maintained in health while it remains empty. So it is, brother," the pope added, "in the body-politic, if you apply the fable correctly. Here, although high office is the more sought after, a man accumulates them, not for himself, but for others. For if the stomach be empty, there is nothing to impart strength to the members; for the stomach in the body and the ruler in the State have the same office. . . . Judge not harshly then of us and the secular princes, but have regard to the common interest." . . .

. . . Speaking[2] from my own knowledge, the pope's office is at all times full of hardship, and in the present state of affairs his condition is most wretched. If he is the slave of avarice, that is death to him; if he is not, he will not escape the hands and tongues of the Romans. For, unless he has the means wherewith to stop their mouths and bind their hands, he must shut his eyes, harden his ears and steel his heart to endure insults, infamy and sacrilege. There are three things above all others which subvert the judgment of the wise: love of gifts, repect of persons and a too credulous disposition. For no man can be swayed by these considerations and at the same time dispense justice. The pope must perforce be immune from them, if he is to curb the excesses of all men as he should. If he hates gifts, who will confer benefits on an unwilling person? But what shall he bestow who has himself received nothing? Or, if he makes no presents, how else will he appease the Romans? If their persons are unacceptable to him, how will he endure their presence? For he is scarcely able to ponder a priestly problem alone in his chamber without being forced to admit them to all his counsels. What of the presents and rewards he is compelled to condemn as simony? If he follows after these things, does he not condemn himself out of his own

[1] *publicus dispensator.*
[2] Book VIII, chap. XXIII; *Iohannis Saresberiensis . . . Policraticus* (ed. C. C. J. Webb), vol. II, p. 408.

mouth? If very little freedom is allowed to the supreme power, nevertheless he that presides over the laws is subject to no man and should be more closely guarded from that which is unlawful. Therefore the greater the prerogative of the pope, the less the licence permitted to him. What is more onerous than the care of all the churches? The apostolic commission has been handed on to their successors, and plainly part of that commission is covered by what the apostle writes to the Corinthians: "Who is weak, and I am not weak? who is offended and I burn not?"[1] Even if you will not turn the pages of the whole epistle, let him who contends for the primacy take this passage as an example, and, I reckon, he will soon give place. Besides, in the present state of the Church whoever is pope must needs be *a servant of servants*, not, of course, in a purely honorific sense, as some people believe, but in a very real one, inasmuch as he must serve the servants of God, even if it be against his will. For the Persons of the Blessed Trinity each serve and dispense God's mercy and justice. Angels and men, whether they be good or evil, all serve, and even the devil, the prince of this world. So too the Romans serve God, and the tyrants whom the Roman pontiff must needs serve, if he is not to become an ex-pontiff or an ex-Roman.[2]

Who then can be in any doubt that the pope is the *servant of servants*? I invoke the testimony of Pope Adrian, whose pontificate may God make prosperous, that no one is to be more pitied than the pope, and no one in a more wretched condition. Even if no other troubles befall him, he must soon break down through overwork. For Pope Adrian confessed to me that he had found such great misery in the papal chair that by comparison with his present woes all the bitterness of his past life seemed now to him sheer delight. The papal throne, he declared, was stuffed with thorns, and the apostolic mantle laced with very sharp prickles and so heavy as to crush and bruise the stoutest shoulders. Mitre and crown might well seem bright and shining, for they are made of fire. He would rather never have left his native soil in England,[3] or have remained for ever in obscurity in the cloister of St. Rufus,[4] than have undertaken so great a burden, but that he dared not disobey the divine command. While he is still alive, ask him and give credence to his experience.[5] He also repeatedly told me that in each step he had taken in office, from the time he was a clerk in the cloister up to his accession to the papal throne, he had never found that a higher position had brought any addition to the peace and happiness he had enjoyed in a lowlier station. Moreover, he said to me–I quote his actual words (for he would condescend in my presence to keep nothing hidden from me)–"The Lord hath even laid me between the anvil and the hammer; may it now please him to support with his own right arm the burden he has laid upon me, for I am too weak to bear it." Does not the man who struggles for such misery deserve to gain it? However rich he be when elected to the papal office, the next day he will be a pauper and under obligation to a host of creditors. What then can he expect, who is not elected to the office, but thrust into it contrary to the will of Christ expressed in his members through blind ambition, and not without

[1] II Corinthians xi. 28, 29.
[2] *i.e.* suffer deposition or go into exile.
[3] For the pre-papal career of Adrian IV, see above, pp. 326, 327.
[4] At Avignon, see above, p. 326.
[5] *Dum superest, ipsum interroga, et crede experto*. This gives a clear indication that this section of the *Policraticus* was written before 1159.

cruel effusion of a brother's blood?[1] This in sooth is to be the successor of Romulus in his fratricide rather than of Peter, to whom was committed the custody of the sheepfold.

(v)

[On papal legates.]

Pope[2] Eugenius,[3] whom you yourself[4] have met, and whose memory should be cherished while his holiness is to be imitated, would never accept a gift from any suitor whose cause was pending. So when a certain prior of limited resources, immediately after his arrival in Rome and before his suit had been heard, offered the pope a golden mark with semblance of great piety, the latter exclaimed, "You have not yet entered the house, and would you corrupt the master of it already?";[5] for the saintly pope regarded whatever was offered while a suit was pending as corruption.

Bernard [of Rennes], a monk of Clairvaux and cardinal-deacon of SS. Cosmas and Damian,[6] during his residence at Rome lived in his high station in complete simplicity and kept his hands clean from bribes, so that the man is yet unborn from whom he deigned to accept gold and silver.[7] Need I mention Cardinal Martin,[8] who, contrary to the prevailing custom, returned from his legation[9] a poor man? Being compelled by most pressing need to accept from the bishop of Florence[10] a horse for his attendant, he restored it to the donor upon learning that at the time the gift was made he had a case due for hearing in the court of Rome. This story of him has been fully told by St. Bernard, abbot of Clairvaux, who knew him intimately, in the book he has written for the instruction of Pope Eugenius entitled *De Contemplatione* or *De Consideratione*.[11] I need barely mention the venerable Geoffrey of Chartres[12] who, when legate in Aquitaine, refused all presents offered to him by the provincials, save gifts of food and drink, and these he accepted only with the utmost reluctance. Everything else offered in the way of presents or money he used to despise as dross. St. Bernard tells[13] how he refused to accept a sturgeon as a gift from a certain devout clerk in his legatine jurisdiction and would not absolve the donor from an act of impropriety until he had named a price for the fish. . . .

. . . The[14] name and office of a bishop are venerable if his duties are performed with a solicitude equal to the ambition with which they are sometimes sought after. Bishops may be loved as fathers, feared as lords and revered as saints, if they refrain from extortion, put out of their minds whatever issues from calumny and count all

[1] Possibly an allusion to the schism of 1130 between Innocent II and the anti-pope Anacletus, though the passage may have been added subsequently in the author's revision of the work in 1164 and may therefore also be taken as his reflection on the schism between Alexander III and Victor IV in 1159.

[2] Book V, chap. XV; *Iohannis Saresberiensis . . . Policraticus* (ed. C. C. J. Webb), vol. I, p. 347.

[3] Eugenius III, 1145–1153.

[4] Thomas Becket, then chancellor of England, to whom the whole work is addressed.

[5] John of Salisbury in other writings gives many instances of alleged bribery and corruption at the papal court.

[6] A pupil of St. Bernard of Clairvaux; he was promoted cardinal by Eugenius III in 1150 and died in 1154.

[7] See also p. 790 above.

[8] Cardinal-priest of St. Stephen. He was promoted to this office by Innocent II (*circa* 1130) and died in 1144.

[9] To Denmark in 1134.

[10] Godfrey 'de Contalbertis', bishop of Florence, 1113–1142.

[11] *De Consideratione* IV, cap. 5; Migne, *Patrologia Latina*, vol. CLXXXII, cols. 782–783.

[12] Bishop of Chartres, 1116–1148.

[13] *De Consideratione* (*loc. cit.*, *ante*).

[14] Book V, chap. XVI *Iohannis Saresberiensis . . . Policraticus* (ed. C. C. J. Webb), vol. I, p. 354.

gain as less than godliness.[1] Otherwise they banish reverence and love from themselves if they solicit honours, covet money and either make false accusations themselves or favour those of others. Indeed, I cannot imagine how they who claim as their due at least two-thirds of the profits from every false charge can escape all stigma of disgrace and punishment. For they either appropriate the whole sum for themselves, or yield merely the third part as a fine to the archdeacons and other officers (not to call them as the people do, ministers of iniquity).

Nor do the legates of the apostolic see keep their hands clean from all bribes, but they sometimes run amok[2] in the provincial churches as if Satan had gone forth from the presence of the Lord to scourge the Church.[3] They shake the corners of the house in order to cast down to the ground the sons and daughters of him who on the Cross had compassion on their fainting and grief-stricken souls. They agitate and disturb the land in such a way that they appear to be afflicted with the very ills they are called upon to heal. In this, however, I speak not of all, but of those who serve their own ends in contempt of their Father's will. For it is plain that in every office of the Lord's house some are left that others may be taken.[4] In all of them I myself have seen deans[5] or archdeacons, bishops or legates, labouring with such devotion in the Lord's harvest-field, that by virtue of their faith and rectitude of conduct they would seem to have been placed in charge of their Father's vineyard wisely and to great profit. . . .

171. John of Salisbury's review of the state of the Church in 1159, in the concluding chapter of his *Metalogicon*

Printed: *Joannis Saresberiensis Episcopi Carnotensis Metalogicon* (ed. C. C. J. Webb Oxford, 1929), p. 216. The translation is, with a few minor alterations, that of Dr. Webb in his *John of Salisbury*, p. 95.

So much for these things. It is time rather for weeping than for writing; and I am taught by the evidence of my own eyes that the whole world is made subject to vanity. We looked for peace, and lo! the war-cloud which hangs over Toulouse[6] is drawing English and French troops to the spot from every quarter; and the kings,[7] whom we once saw united in the closest bonds of friendship, are now obstinately set on one another's destruction. Moreover, the death of our lord, Pope Adrian,[8] which has dismayed all Christian peoples and nations, has brought especially bitter grief to our country of England, whereof he was a native.[9] He is to be lamented by all good men, but by no one more than myself, whom, though he had a mother and a brother living, he loved with a more intimate affection than he bestowed on them. Alike in public and in private he made no secret of the fact that no one was so dear to him as I; and he had come to think so much of me that he never missed an opportunity of gladly opening his inner thoughts to me. While he was pope, he took pleasure in

[1] Cf. I Timothy vi. 5. [2] *debaccantur.* [3] Cf. Job ii. 7. [4] Cf. Matthew xxiv. 40, 41.

[5] *i.e.* rural deans, who often assisted the archdeacons in fiscal and administrative work.

[6] The war of Toulouse: Henry II besieged the town from July to September 1159. Thomas Becket, the chancellor, to whom John dedicated the *Metalogicon*, was there present. The siege was finally raised on 26 September.

[7] Henry II and Louis VII, king of France.

[8] Adrian IV died 31 August 1159. [9] See above, No. 12, p. 326.

inviting me to his table and in making me, against my will, eat from his plate and drink from his cup. It was at my request that he granted to the illustrious king of the English, Henry II, the hereditary possession of Ireland, as his letter[1] bears witness to the present day; for all islands are reputed to belong by a long-established right to the Church of Rome by the Donation of Constantine,[2] who instituted and endowed it. Moreover, he sent to the king through me a golden ring, adorned with a fine emerald, in token of his investiture with the government of Ireland; and this ring is still by the king's command preserved in the public treasury.[3] Were I to enumerate all the virtues of the late pope, this topic alone would fill a large volume. But a greater disaster to us all even than his death is the schism in the Church,[4] which for our sins has befallen us upon the removal from our midst of this great father in God. Satan hath sought to sift her as wheat,[5] and by the ministry of a second Judas,[6] is sowing on every side the seeds of bitterness and scandal. Thence have sprung wars which are worse than civil, being wars between brother priests. Now is the judgment of this world,[7] and it is to be feared that the ruin of the ambitious traitor may involve along with him a third part of the stars of heaven.[8] Woe to that man by whom the offence cometh; certainly it had been better if he had not been born.[9] I am setting forth the causes of public sorrow; and yet I am afflicted with one no less grave which touches me. For my father and master–and yours also[10]–Theobald, archbishop of Canterbury, has fallen sick, so that one cannot tell what one ought to hope or fear. He can no longer manage his own affairs as he used to do; and he has imposed on me a hard task, nay, an intolerable burden, in the care of all ecclesiastical business. Therefore is my spirit vexed on every side and the torments I endure are beyond my powers of description. But in all these I have one resource left to me, namely to pray to the God made Man, the Son of the spotless Virgin, who while He is, as it were, asleep in the boat,[11] must be aroused by the prayers of the faithful to still the storm which threatens His Church with shipwreck and in His mercy to deliver my lord, as He knows to be most expedient for him and for us, from all infirmity of mind and body. May He, I say, by whom kings reign and princes exercise lordship, set over His universal Church a fit pastor and one pleasing in His sight; may He defend our kings and princes from all adversity and cause them to preserve the flock committed to their charge to the honour and glory of His name. I pray also those who read or hear me to intercede for me, poor empty wretch that I am, with the Virgin's Son, who is the Way, the Truth and the Life, that He may remove from me the darkness of ignorance and the love of vanity, may pour upon me the light of the knowledge of himself and may make me a diligent seeker after truth and no less a lover and worshipper of it when found.

[1] The bull *Laudabiliter*; see above, No. 159.

[2] *ibid.*: all islands *in the Mediterranean* were declared subject to the jurisdiction of the pope; this provision had been extended in the course of the centuries to cover all islands.

[3] See above, No. 159.

[4] The schism between Alexander III and Victor IV which broke out in 1159 after the death of Adrian IV; see above, pp. 681, 947.

[5] Luke xxii. 31.

[6] Presumably a reference to the anti-pope, Cardinal Octavian, set up as Victor IV by the emperor, Frederick Barbarossa.

[7] John xii. 31.

[8] Revelations xii. 4; here John is probably referring to the defection of the German Church to the cause of the anti-pope.

[9] Matthew xviii. 7; xxvi. 24.

[10] Addressing Thomas, the chancellor.

[11] Cf. Mark iv. 36.

Part IV
LAND AND PEOPLE

LAND AND PEOPLE

Introduction

EVIDENCE respecting the social history of England between 1042 and 1189 has here been arranged according to a fourfold plan. In the first place, there are presented texts relating to the agrarian structure of England at this time, the conditions of peasant status and service, and the essential social units of village and manor. Secondly, an attempt has here been made to represent the evidence of Domesday Book, a unique text and the product of a unique occasion. Thirdly, there is here set out some of the more important testimony relating to the origins and organization of Anglo-Norman feudalism, the feudal structure of England being exhibited in feodaries, in charters, in the *cartae* of knight-service drawn up in 1166, and in the legal treatise known as 'Glanville'. Fourthly, there will be found evidence concerning the towns of England and their inhabitants in this period.

A topical arrangement of this nature can, however, only be made illuminating if the general nature of this mass of evidence be clearly appreciated. Apart from unique texts such as Domesday Book and the *cartae* of knight-service which need individual consideration, the student of English social history in this age must chiefly rely upon two types of document which, together, illustrate all aspects of this subject. These are, on the one hand, surveys and statements of services; and, on the other hand, charters. They share, moreover, one common characteristic. Both possess in the first instance a local application, and only secondarily are they to be considered as having a general significance. They must therefore always be studied with due regard for their particular origins, and in relation to the localities to which they more especially refer.

The surveys and statements of peasant services which survive from this period of English history, though difficult to interpret, are sufficient to provide a picture of manorial economy at this time. Among them not the least interesting is the Anglo-Saxon record of "The Rights and Ranks of People" (*Rectitudines Singularum Personarum*). This probably derives from the time of Edward the Confessor, and is of particular importance as affording a means whereby the agrarian conditions existing in England before the Norman Conquest may be compared with those revealed in the surveys drawn up in the twelfth century; for instance, for the abbeys of Peterborough, Burton and Ramsey, or for the bishop of Durham. Perhaps the two chief facts which will be revealed from a study of these records will be the great local variations in English agrarian structure in this period, and also the essential continuity of English peasant life throughout this age.

Of more general importance than the surveys are the charters which illuminate every aspect of this age, and which in particular illustrate its feudal and tenurial history. A charter may be described broadly as a deed couched in the form of a letter giving notice that an important transaction – usually a grant of land or privilege – has taken place. Very many such charters dating from this period are, moreover, still in existence. Sometimes the actual deed has itself most fortunately been preserved, but more often the surviving text of the charter is a copy contained either in one of the great cartularies compiled in the religious houses of England during the Middle Ages or in the later enrolments of the royal administration. By such means a multitude of English charters has survived from the period 1042–1189, and their importance to the student of history can scarcely be over emphasized. Feudal society, it has been justly observed, can best be studied in the feudal charter.

The royal charters of this age can be classified as pertaining to two distinct types, both of which were issued with regularity in the time of Edward the Confessor. The former of these is the charter proper, or, as it may more conveniently be termed, the *diploma*. This is a long and very formal document describing at length a grant of land or privilege with all possible solemnity of style and language. It is normally written in Latin, and indicates the reasons for the gift and its nature. It has a formal prologue, often a detailed description of the land bestowed, very frequently an anathema directed against anyone who might interfere with the grant, and always a long list of witnesses whose names are usually appended after crosses which symbolize their solemn participation in the act. This type of instrument is of ancient origin, being the outcome of Germanic custom adapted by ecclesiastical practice. In fairly frequent use in the time of Edward the Confessor it began to disappear after the Norman Conquest. Solemn *diplomata*, however, exist from the early Norman period (see No. 77), though when they occur they must always be regarded with some suspicion. They are the survivals of older custom, and of a legal instrument which by the end of the eleventh century was in England passing out of use.

The writing-office of Edward the Confessor, however, also issued another and very different type of document to which the name *writ* is given. This was a letter, usually very short, and most frequently addressed by the king personally to his officials in the shire to which it was sent. It announced tersely that some transaction had taken place, or else gave orders that some administrative action should be taken. The Old English writ (*e.g.* Nos. 182, 186) is unique among the legal documents of eleventh-century Europe in being written in the vernacular; and in marked contrast to the *diploma* it is characterized by a certain informality. It has no preamble, little solemnity of language, and no witnesses. The efficient brevity of such instruments was ideally adapted to express the terse orders of the Norman monarchy in the period after 1066, and it is therefore perhaps not surprising to find the writs of William I following in a continuous sequence on those of Edward the Confessor. Even the use of the Saxon vernacular was not immediately discarded, but fairly soon the Anglo-Norman writ came to be couched in Latin, the primitive form being, however, at first retained without any change. The writ was in fact the most important diplomatic form of the period, and it proved also to be the most prolific in development. It grew. With Henry I a dating clause of place began to be common, and later a general address is to be found which gradually came to be expressed with an elaboration of formulae. At the same time witnesses made their appearance, at first one or two, and then very many. Out of the primitive writ there was thus developed in time a hybrid type of document to which the name *writ-charter* has been applied, and the more formal instruments of the Anglo-Norman and Anglo-Angevin kings such as the "Coronation Charter" of Henry I (No. 19) are of this pattern. Alongside of them, however, the primitive writ in all its pristine brevity continued to be used as the routine expression of royal administration.

The development of private charters during this period was inevitably less regular, but it followed, with modifications, the changing practice of the royal Chancery. The old *diploma* style continued during the earlier decades of this epoch to influence the form of many charters, particularly those of ecclesiastics, but in general the private charters of this age were of the writ-charter type or related to it. The normal feudal charter of the twelfth century will open with an address; it will continue with the words of grant; it will probably record the consent of interested parties; it will make some description of the land or privilege bestowed; it will close with a list of witnesses; and it will very probably be authenticated by a seal. But private charters throughout this period are very miscellaneous in form, and sometimes they lack precision. Thus a private charter composed before the thirteenth century will usually be undated, and even the list of witnesses is not invariably to be taken as evidence that the men mentioned therein were actually present when the charter was authenticated. In general, however, it is this lack of formal uniformity in the private charters of the twelfth century which adds to their value as evidence. The twelfth-century draughtmanship of private charters was frequently defective and not seldom ambiguous, but with its unexpected variations of phrase and method it produced documents of greater value as evidence than those which were couched in the common form of a later age. It is therefore particularly fortunate that so many of these deeds have survived, ranging from the acts of the most important magnates of the land down to the small grants by free peasants whose status even in the reign of Henry II was sufficiently assured, particularly in the Danelaw, for them thus to record their gifts.

To utilize the charter as a source of history it is very necessary to appreciate its legal quality. It will be noted that these documents are usually couched in the past tense, and this in itself is an indication of their function. They are evidential not dispositive, that is to say, they do not in themselves constitute the legal act but are testimony that the legal act has taken place. The transaction itself was normally made by oral declaration before witnesses, and it was legally valid even if no written record of it was subsequently made. In the case of gifts it was the common practice for there to be a ceremony of donation, the grantor offering, for instance, a sod of the land bestowed, or perhaps making a symbolic presentation of some precious object such as a dagger to the grantee (*e.g.* No. 239). Such an act was the veritable gift, and the charter was designed not to take its place, but to provide written testimony which might prove more permanent than that of mortal witnesses. This consideration has also an important bearing on the difficult question of the authenticity of charters. The forged charter is a harassing feature of the documentary material of the age. But the men, and more especially the monks, who concocted these spurious instruments apparently made some distinction between the fabrication of a charter designed to record a true gift of which no contemporary record had been made, and the forgery of a charter which is false not only as to its alleged date but also as to the facts which it records. The point of morals involved need not here be debated. But it deserves emphasis that a forged charter is by no means devoid of value to the historical student. It throws light upon the motives of the men who perpetrated the forgery, and it may even provide the sole written testimony of some earlier transaction which in truth took place.

It is, however, the authentic charter which, of course, is of paramount interest to the historian, and there is scarcely an aspect of English history between 1042 and 1189 which is not in some measure to be illustrated by these instruments. They may, moreover, be supplemented by other official and semi-official records. Thus alongside the private charters of this age should be considered those interesting Anglo-Saxon 'wills' (see Nos. 181, 183, 184, 187–189) which were not strictly wills in the modern sense of the term, but are the records of irrevocable contracts *inter vivos* designed to take effect after the death of one or more of the contracting parties. Similarly, since charters were mainly, though not exclusively, the product of the aristocracy, their usefulness as testimony respecting the lower ranks of society is restricted. A relatively small number of free peasants might use the charter to ratify their gifts, but these were a small minority, and alongside them lived the vast bulk of the peasant population whose unfree status prohibited their use of such an instrument.

SELECT BIBLIOGRAPHY

of the Social and Economic History of England between 1042 and 1189

I. ORIGINAL SOURCES

The narrative sources of English history (see above, pp. 103–105) and the records relating to government and administration in Church and State (see above, pp. 395, 396 and pp. 589–592) can all be used to illustrate social and economic history. The following texts, however, more specifically relate to this subject.

(*a*) DOMESDAY BOOK

The sole and indispensable printed edition of Domesday Book as a whole is that which was issued by the Record Commission (2 vols., London, 1783). This great edition, which was the anonymous work of Abraham Farley, reproduces the whole of Domesday Book in record type. Vol. II is the "Little Domesday" which deals with Essex, Norfolk, and Suffolk; vol. I covers the rest of the survey; the foliation corresponds with the foliation of the original. To this edition there were added two supplementary volumes under the editorship of Henry Ellis (vols. III and IV, London, 1816). Vol. IV of this supplement contains various surveys which in this bibliography will be considered separately. Vol. III contains Ellis's indexes to Domesday Book itself, which were subsequently reprinted (2 vols., London, 1833). These indexes are still of high value, though that of the tenants in the time of Edward the Confessor has been superseded by O. von Feilitzen, *The Pre-Conquest Personal Names of Domesday Book* (Uppsala, 1937). A photographic facsimile of the whole of Domesday Book was published by the Ordnance Survey Office, Southampton, between 1861 and 1864.

The accounts given by Domesday Book of various counties have often been separately edited, and many of these are accompanied by translations. Among them may be specially mentioned: *The Devonshire Domesday and Geld Inquest* (2 vols., Devonshire Assoc., Plymouth, 1884, 1892), L. B. Larking, *The Domesday Book of Kent with translation and appendix* (London, 1869), and W. H. Jones *Domesday for Wiltshire* (Bath, 1865). J. Tait, *Domesday Survey of Cheshire* (Chetham Soc., 1916), is an admirable edition, and C. W. Foster and T. Longley, *The Lincolnshire Domesday and the Lindsey Survey* (Lincoln Rec. Soc., 1924), is a translation of the highest value accompanied by important critical notes.

Translations of Domesday Book (by counties) are being included in the *Victoria History of the Counties of England*. These translations are admirable in themselves, and are preceded by introductions which are often (as in the case of Essex, Huntingdonshire and Worcestershire) of the highest value.

Surveys which were, or have been considered to have been, compiled as a result of the Domesday Inquisition have been printed in the following works: N. E. S. A. Hamilton, *Inquisitio Comitatus Cantabrigiensis, subjicitur Inquisitio Eliensis* (1876); A. Ballard, *An eleventh-century Inquisition of St. Augustine's, Canterbury* (Brit. Acad., 1920); D. C. Douglas, *Feudal Documents from the Abbey of Bury St. Edmunds* (Brit. Acad., 1932), pp. 1–44; D. C. Douglas, *Domesday Monachorum of Christ Church, Canterbury* (London, 1944). The "Exon Domesday" is included in vol. IV of the Record Commission edition of Domesday Book, and is partially contained in *The Devonshire Domesday and Geld Inquest* (2 vols., Plymouth, 1884, 1892) and in W. H. Jones, *Domesday for Wiltshire*, cited above. Abridgements and copies of Domesday Book were made for particular counties in the twelfth and thirteenth centuries, and some of these are of especial interest, as is shown by V. H. Galbraith, *The Hereford Domesday* (Pipe Roll Soc., New

Series, vol. xxv, 1950). For discussion as to the relation of these texts to Domesday Book, and for books relating to the criticism of Domesday Book, and the evidence which it supplies, see under "Modern Works" below (pp. 810, 811).

(b) SURVEYS AND STATEMENTS OF SERVICES

Some of the surviving surveys relating to this period are represented in this book (see below, Nos. 172–180). The *Rectitudines Singularum Personarum* appears below (No. 172) in translation; the best edition of the original is in F. Liebermann, *Die Gesetze der Angelsachsen*, vol. I (1898), pp. 444–453. Among other documents of this nature coming from the time of Edward the Confessor must be mentioned the fragments of surveys from the abbey of Bury St. Edmunds (see below, No. 175), the text of which is edited in *Eng. Hist. Rev.*, vol. XLIII (1928), and in A. J. Robertson, *Anglo-Saxon Charters* (Cambridge, 1939), pp. 193 *et sqq.* Notable among surveys from the twelfth century, some of which are discussed in J. H. Round, *Feudal England*, pp. 147–224, are: the *Lindsey Survey* (1115–1118) which was edited by W. Greenstreet in 1884, and which is admirably translated in C. W. Foster and T. Longley, *The Lincolnshire Domesday and the Lindsey Survey* (Lincoln Rec. Soc., 1924); and a Northamptonshire survey of approximately the same date which was translated by J. H. Round for the *Victoria County History* of that county (vol. I, pp. 357–389). Nearly contemporary with these are the surveys made at Burton Abbey (see below, No. 176), the best edition of which is by G. C. O. Bridgeman (William Salt Archaeol. Soc., 1936), and in the reign of Henry I there were also made certain notable surveys of the lands of Peterborough Abbey (see below, No. 177) which were printed by T. Stapleton as an appendix to his *Chronicon Petroburgense* (Camden Soc., 1849). Among manorial surveys of the reign of Henry II may be mentioned the descriptions of manors at that time made for the abbot of Ramsey and printed in vol. III of the *Cartularium Monasterii de Rameseia* (3 vols., Rolls Series, 1893), and the survey of the manors of the Templars in England which was edited by B. A. Lees in *Records of the Templars in England in the twelfth century* (Brit. Acad., 1935). In 1124 Earl David, later to be king of Scotland, ordered to be drawn up a survey of the lands of the see of Glasgow in Cumbria (see above, No. 54, and A. C. Lawrie, *Early Scottish Charters prior to 1153*, Glasgow 1905, pp. 44–47). But the most extensive survey of manors in the north of England dating from this period is the *Boldon Book* which was compiled in 1183. It is discussed below, p. 834: the best edition is by W. Greenwell (Surtees Soc., 1852), and the best translation is that by G. T. Lapsley with a fine introduction in the *Victoria County History: Durham*, vol. I (1905), pp. 327–351.

(c) CHARTERS

(i) *General Collections*

The most important single collection of charters in respect of this period is the great *Monasticon Anglicanum* compiled in the seventeenth century by William Dugdale and others, and sumptuously reissued in the nineteenth century (W. Dugdale, *Monasticon Anglicanum*, new ed., 6 vols. in 8, London, 1817–1830; reprinted 1846). J. M. Kemble, *Codex Diplomaticus aevi Saxonici* (6 vols., London, 1839–1848), contains many charters relating to the reign of Edward the Confessor, and the Anglo-Saxon documents among them can be most conveniently studied in *Anglo-Saxon Charters* edited with translation and notes by A. J. Robertson (Cambridge, 1939). D. Whitelock, *Anglo-Saxon Wills* (Cambridge, 1930), is likewise important both for the texts and also for the translations it contains. The interest of A. C. Lawrie, *Early Scottish Charters prior to 1153* (Glasgow, 1905), is indicated by its title, and very many documents of high importance are included in H. E. Salter, *Facsimiles of Early Charters in Oxford Muniment Rooms* (Oxford, 1929). Of equal service is G. F. Warner and H. J. Ellis, *Facsimiles of Royal and Other Charters in the British Museum* (vol. I, William I–Richard I, London, 1903), whilst *Sir Christopher Hatton's Book of Seals* (ed. L. C. Loyd and D. M. Stenton, Oxford, 1950) is a magnificent collection of charters, a large number of which relate to the period 1066–1189. The continental material can best be approached through the medium of J. H. Round's *Calendar of Documents preserved in France, illustrative of the History of Great Britain and Ireland* (vol. I, A.D. 918–1206, London, 1899). Texts relating to English history will be found in A. du Monstier, *Neustria Pia* (Rouen, 1663); in vols. XII–XVI and vol. XXIII of the *Recueil des Historiens des Gaules et de la France*; and more particularly in vol. XI of *Gallia Christiana* which is devoted to Normandy. The fundamental importance of L. Delisle and E. Berger, *Recueil des Actes de Henri II concernant les provinces françaises et les affaires de France* (4 vols. and atlas of plates, Paris, 1909–1927), is warranted by the names of its editors. T. Madox, *Formulare Anglicanum, or a Collection of Ancient Charters* (London, 1702), is almost as valuable as when it was first issued. Other smaller collections may also be mentioned as having a general significance. H. W. C. Davis, *Regesta Regum Anglo-Normannorum* (vol. I, 1066–1100, Oxford, 1913), which needs considerable correction, provides a convenient introduction to the acts of the Conqueror and Rufus; some of the more important charters of the mid-twelfth century are published in J. H. Round, *Geoffrey de Mandeville* (London, 1892); in the same writer's *Ancient Charters royal and private prior to A.D. 1200* (Pipe Roll Soc., 1888); and in W. de G. Birch, "A Fasciculus of the Charters of Mathildis, empress of the Romans" (*Journal Brit. Archaeol. Assoc.*, 1875). There is a valuable appendix of forty-eight feudal charters of general importance in F. M. Stenton, *English Feudalism* (Oxford, 1932). The calendars issued by the Public Record Office, and in particular the *Calendar of Charter Rolls* (6 vols., London, 1903–1927), contain the texts of many documents relating to this period, and a useful topographical index to some of this material is the *Index to the Charters and Rolls in the British Museum* (ed. H. J. Ellis and F. B. Bickley, 2 vols., London, 1900, 1912) which, however, does not touch the cartulary texts.

(ii) *Particular Collections* (*England*)

A charter, being issued for a definite and restricted purpose, has naturally in the first place a particular application. Similarly, a cartulary compiled by some religious corporation will usually contain only such documents as relate in the first instance to the interests of its compiler. In consequence the printed texts of charters relating to the history of England between 1042 and 1189 are very widely scattered. The purpose of the list that follows is limited to an attempt to indicate some of the principal books wherein the feudal charters of the period can be studied, and the works here cited are arranged under the regions, churches or families to which the charters contained therein more particularly relate. The list of course is in no sense exhaustive.

Abingdon. *Chronicon Monasterii de Abingdon*, ed. J. Stevenson (2 vols., Rolls Series, 1858).

Alsop. *Alsop and other Charters transcribed and translated* (Derbyshire Archaeol. and Nat. Hist. Soc., February 1886).

Bath. *Two Chartularies of the Priory of St. Peter of Bath*, ed. W. Hunt (Somerset Rec. Soc., 1893). (Contains the text of some important charters not printed elsewhere.)

Battle Abbey. *Chronicon Monasterii de Bello* (London, 1846). (Charters in appendix.)

Boarstall. *The Boarstall Cartulary*, ed. H. E. Salter (Oxford, 1930).

Bridlington. *Chartulary of the Priory of Bridlington*, ed. W. T. Lancaster (Leeds, 1912).

Brinkburn. *Chartulary of Brinkburn Priory*, ed. W. Page (Surtees Soc., 1893).

Bristol. *Bristol Charters, 1155–1373* (ed. N. D. Harding, Bristol Record Soc., 1930).

Bury St. Edmunds, abbey of. *Feudal Documents from the Abbey of Bury St. Edmunds*, ed. D. C. Douglas (Brit. Acad., 1932).

Bury St. Edmunds, abbey of. *The Pinchbeck Register*, ed. Lord F. Hervey (2 vols., Brighton, 1925).

Canterbury. *The Domesday Monachorum of Christ Church, Canterbury*, ed. D. C. Douglas (London, 1944).

Colchester. *Cartularium Monasterii Sancti Iohannis Baptistae de Colecestria*, ed. S. A. Moore (2 vols., Roxburghe Club, London, 1897).

Colne. *Cartularium Prioratus de Colne*, ed. J. L. Fisher (Colchester, 1946).

Danelaw. *Documents illustrative of the Social and Economic History of the Danelaw*, ed. F. M. Stenton (Brit. Acad., 1920).

Danelaw. *The Free Peasantry of the Northern Danelaw*, by F. M. Stenton (Lund, 1926). (Contains many charters.)

Darley Abbey. *The Cartulary of Darley Abbey*, ed. R. R. Darlington (2 vols., Kendal, 1945).
Derbyshire. *Descriptive Catalogue of Derbyshire Charters*, ed. I. H. Jeayes (London, 1906).
Dieulacres Abbey. *Chartulary of Dieulacres Abbey*, ed. G. Wrottesley (London, 1906).
Dunstable. *A Digest of the Charters preserved in the Cartulary of Dunstable*, ed. G. H. Fowler (2 vols., Beds. Hist. Soc., 1926).
East Anglia. *The Social Structure of Medieval East Anglia*, by D. C. Douglas (Oxford, 1927). (Appendix of 65 charters.)
Ely. *The History . . . of the . . . Cathedral Church of Ely*, by James Bentham (2nd ed., Norwich, 1812). (Important appendix of charters.)
Exeter. *Monasticon Dioecesis Exoniensis*, by George Oliver (Exeter, 1846).
Glamorgan. *Cartae et alia Munimenta quae ad Dominium de Glamorgancia pertinent*, ed. G. T. Clark (6 vols., Cardiff, 1910).
Glastonbury. *The Great Chartulary of Glastonbury*, ed. A. Watkin (Somerset Rec. Soc., 1944).
Gloucester, abbey of. *Historia et Cartularium Monasterii S. Petri Gloucestriae*, ed. W. H. Hart (3 vols. Rolls Series, 1863–1867).
Gresley, family of. *Descriptive Catalogue of the Charters and Muniments of the Gresley Family*, by I. H. Jeayes (London, 1895).
Guisborough, priory of. *Cartularium Prioratus de Gyseburne*, ed. W. Brown (2 vols., Surtees Soc., 1889, 1891).
Gournay. *The Record of the House of Gournay*, by D. Gurney (2 vols., London, 1845, 1848). (Contains many charters, some of which were collected for the author by L. Delisle.)
Kirkstall Abbey. *The Coucher Book of Kirkstall Abbey* (3 vols., Thoresby Soc., 1896–1904).
Lancashire. *Lancashire Pipe Rolls and Early Lancashire Charters*, ed. W. Farrer (Liverpool, 1902).
Lewes. *The Chartulary of the Priory of St. Pancras at Lewes*. Sussex portion, ed. L. F. Salzmann (2 vols., Sussex Rec. Soc., 1932, 1934). Cambridgeshire portion, ed. J. H. Bullock and W. M. Palmer (Cambridge, 1938). Yorkshire portion, ed. C. T. Clay (Yorks. Archaeol. Soc. Journal, 1933).
Lincoln. *The Registrum Antiquissimum of the Cathedral Church of Lincoln*, ed. C. W. Foster and K. Major (5 vols. and in progress, Lincoln Rec. Soc., 1930). (Perhaps the most important of all the printed cartularies for this period.)
Lincolnshire. *Transcripts of Charters relating to Gilbertine Houses*, ed. F. M. Stenton (Lincoln Rec. Soc., 1922). (Important introduction by the editor.)
London. *Early Charters of the Cathedral Church of St. Paul*, ed. M. Gibbs (R. Hist. Soc., 1939).
London. *Gilbert Crispin, Abbot of Westminster*, by J. Armitage Robinson (Cambridge, 1911). (Important appendix of Westminster charters.)
London. *The History of Westminster Abbey by John Flete*, ed. J. Armitage Robinson (Cambridge, 1909). (Appendix of charters.)
Newminster. *Chartularium Abbathiae de Novo Monasterio*, ed. J. T. Fowler (Surtees Soc., 1878).
Northamptonshire. *Facsimiles of Early Charters in Northamptonshire Collections* (Northants. Rec. Soc., vol. IV, 1930).
Oxford. *The Cartulary of the Monastery of St. Frideswide at Oxford*, ed. S. R. Wigram (2 vols., Oxford Hist. Soc., 1895, 1896).
Percy. *The Percy Chartulary* (ed. M. T. Martin, Surtees Soc., 1911).
Pontefract. *The Chartulary of St. John of Pontefract*, ed. R. Holmes (2 vols., Yorks. Archaeol. Soc., 1899, 1902).
Ramsey Abbey. *Cartularium Monasterii de Rameseia*, ed. W. H. Hart and P. A. Lyons (3 vols., Rolls Series, 1884–1893).
Richmond (Yorks.). *Registrum Honoris de Richmond*, ed. R. Gale (London, 1722).
Rievaulx. *Cartularium Abbathiae de Rievalle*, ed. J. C. Atkinson (Surtees Soc., 1889).
Rippingale. *Early Land Charters of Rippingale*, ed. G. H. Fowler (Associated Architectural and Archaeological Societies, vol. XLI, pt. ii, 1933; vol. XLIII, 1935).
Robertsbridge. *Calendar of Charters . . . relating to the Abbey of Robertsbridge, preserved at Penshurst* (London, 1873).

Rochester. *Registrum Roffense, or a Collection of Ancient Records, Charters, etc. . . .*, ed. J. Thorpe (London, 1769).

Rochester. *Textus Roffensis*, ed. T. Hearne (Oxford, 1720). (This collection, which has proved invaluable to Anglo-Saxon scholars, also contains a large number of important deeds relating to the Anglo-Norman period.)

Sallay-in-Craven. *The Chartulary of . . . St. Mary in Craven*, ed. J. McNulty (2 vols., Yorks. Archaeol. Soc., 1933, 1934).

Selby. *Coucher Book of Selby*, ed. J. T. Fowler (2 vols., Yorks. Archaeol. Soc., 1891, 1893).

Sele. *The Chartulary of the Priory of St. Peter at Sele*, ed. L. F. Salzmann (Cambridge, 1923).

Shirley, family of. *Stemmata Shirleiana*, by E. P. Shirley (London, 1873). (Important appendix of charters.)

Turvey. *Early Records of Turvey and its Neighbourhood*, ed. G. H. Fowler (Beds. Hist. Rec. Soc., 1927).

Wardon, Old. *Cartulary of the Abbey of Old Wardon*, ed. G. H. Fowler (Beds. Hist. Rec. Soc., 1930).

Whitby. *Cartularium Abbathiae de Whiteby*, ed. J. C. Atkinson (2 vols., Surtees Soc., 1879, 1881).

Yorkshire. *Early Yorkshire Charters* (8 vols. and index vol.; vols. I–III, ed. W. Farrer, Edinburgh, 1914–1916; index to vols. I–III, by C. T. Clay, Yorks. Archaeol. Soc., 1942; vols. IV and V, Honour of Richmond, ed. C. T. Clay, Yorks. Archaeol. Soc., 1938; vol. VI, Paynel Fee, ed. C. T. Clay, Yorks. Archaeol. Soc., 1939; vol. VII, Honour of Skipton, ed. C. T. Clay, Yorks. Archaeol. Soc., 1947; vol. VIII, The Honour of Warenne, ed. C. T. Clay, Yorks. Archaeol. Soc., 1949). This great work, which is still in progress, is indispensable for the study of English twelfth-century charters.

(iii) *Particular Collections (France)*

Very many French cartularies and collections of charters, particularly of course those from Normandy, contain documents relating either directly to English history at this period or to persons who were responsible for the government of England at this time. A few of them, out of a large number, are here cited. They are listed below both for their individual importance and also as representing what is perhaps the least worked source of the history of England in the Anglo-Norman age.

Angers. *Cartulaire de l'abbaye de Saint-Aubin d'Angers*, ed. Bertrand de Broussillon (3 vols., Paris, 1903).

Bayeux. *Antiquus cartularius ecclesiae Baiocensis (Livre Noir)*, ed. V. Bourrienne (2 vols., Soc. Hist. Norm., Rouen, 1902–1903).

Beaumont-le-Roger. *Cartulaire de l'église de la Sainte-Trinité de Beaumont-le-Roger*, ed. E. Deville (Paris, 1911).

Bec, Le. *Histoire de l'abbaye du Bec*, by A. A. Porée (2 vols., Evreux, 1901). (Includes texts of charters.)

Bival. *Documents et courte notice sur l'abbaye de Bival*, ed. J. Malicorne (Rouen, 1897).

Bolbec. *Chronicon Valassense*, ed. F. Sommenil (Rouen, 1868).

Boscherville. *Essai historique et descriptif sur l'église et l'abbaye de Saint-Georges-de-Boscherville*, by A. Deville (Rouen, 1827). (Contains texts of charters.)

Briquebec. *Cartulaire de Saint-Ymer-en-Auge*, ed. C. Bréard (Soc. Hist. Norm., Rouen, 1908).

Brittany. *Histoire de Bretagne*, by G. A. Lobineau (2 vols., Paris, 1707). (The second volume contains the *preuves* and includes many charters, particularly some relating to the honour of Richmond (Yorks.).)

Caen. *Analyse d'un ancien cartulaire de l'abbaye de Saint-Étienne de Caen*, by E. Deville (Evreux, 1905).

Channel Islands. *Cartulaire des Îles Normandes. Recueil de documents concernant l'histoire de ces Îles* (Jersey, 1918–1924).

Chartres. *Cartulaire de Notre-Dame de Chartres*, ed. E. de Lepinois and L. Merlet (3 vols., Chartres, 1861–1865). (This is the cathedral cartulary.)

Chartres. *Cartulaire . . . de Saint-Père de Chartres*, ed. B. E. C. Guérard (2 vols., Paris, 1840). (Perhaps the most important of all the northern French cartularies. It contains some texts relating to England.)

Cluny. *Charters and Records among the Archives of the Ancient Abbey of Cluny*, ed. Sir. G. F. Duckett (2 vols., Lewes, 1888).

Craon, family of. *La Maison de Craon, 1050–1480. Étude historique accompagné du cartulaire de Craon*, ed. Bertrand de Broussillon (2 vols., Paris, 1893).

Eure. *Mémoires et notes pour servir à l'histoire du département de l'Eure*, by A. Le Prévost (3 vols., Evreux, 1862–1869). (Highly important: contains the texts of many charters relating to England not published elsewhere.)

Grestain. *L'Abbaye de Notre-Dame de Grestain*, by C. Bréard (Rouen, 1904). (Includes the text of two important confirmation charters of Richard I referring to earlier conditions.)

Harcourt, family of. *Histoire généalogique de la Maison de Harcourt*, by G. A. de la Roque (4 vols., Paris, 1662). (Vols. III and IV contain a number of charters and extracts from cartularies.)

Jumièges. *Chartes de l'abbaye de Jumièges*, ed. J. J. Vernier (2 vols., Soc. Hist. Norm., Rouen, 1916).

Laval. *La Maison de Laval (1020–1605). Étude historique accompagné du cartulaire de Laval et de Vitré*, ed. Bertrand de Broussillon (5 vols., Paris, 1895–1903).

Le Mans. *Cartulaire de Saint-Victeur au Mans*, ed. Bertrand de Broussillon (Paris, 1905).

Le Mans. *Cartulaire de Saint-Vincent du Mans*, ed. R. Charles and Menjot d'Elbenne (2 vols., Le Mans, 1886, 1913).

Longueville. *Chartes du Prieuré de Longueville*, ed. P. Le Cacheux (Soc. Hist. Norm., Rouen, 1934). (This should be used in connexion with *Newington-Longueville Charters*, ed. H. E. Salter (Oxfordshire Rec. Soc., 1921).)

Louviers. *Cartulaire de Louviers*, ed. Th. Bonnin (5 vols., Evreux, 1870–1883). (This is a *cartulaire factice*, that is to say a collection of documents assembled by the editor.)

Meulan. *Recueil des chartes de Saint-Nicaise de Meulan*, ed. E. Houth (Pontoise, 1924).

Normandy. *Les Archives de Normandie et de la Seine-Inférieure: Recueil de Facsimiles*, by P. Chevreux and J. Vernier (2 vols., Rouen, 1911).

Normandy. *Études sur les privilèges d'exemption . . . des abbayes normandes*, by J.-F. Lemarignier (Paris, 1937). (Charters in appendix.)

Normandy. *Les anciennes abbayes de Normandie*, by Lechaudé-d'Anisy (2 vols., Caen, 1838). (Abstracts of numerous charters.)

Normandy. *Norman Institutions*, by C. H. Haskins (Cambridge, Mass., 1918). (Appendix of charters.)

Normandy. *Le Duc de Normandie et sa Cour*, by L. Valin (Paris, 1910). (Appendix of charters.)

Normandy. *Recueil de Facsimiles de Chartes Normandes*, ed. J. J. Vernier (Rouen, 1919).

Philip I, King. *Recueil des Actes de Philippe I, roi de France*, ed. M. Prou (Paris, 1908).

Ponthieu. *Recueil des Actes des Comtes de Ponthieu*, ed. C. Brunel (Paris, 1930).

Pontoise. *Cartulaire de l'abbaye de Saint-Martin de Pontoise*, ed. J. Depoin (2 vols., Pontoise, 1895–1909).

Rouen. *Histoire de l'abbaye de Saint-Amand de Rouen*, by M. J. Le Cacheux (Caen, 1937). (Charters in appendix.)

Rouen. *Histoire du prieuré du Mont-aux-Malades lès Rouen et correspondance du prieur avec Saint-Thomas de Cantorbéry*, ed. P. Langlois (Rouen, 1851).

Rouen. *Histoire du prieuré de Saint-Lô de Rouen*, by L. Boistard de Glanville (2 vols., Rouen, 1890, 1891). (Charters in appendix.)

Rouen. *Histoire de l'abbaye royale de Saint-Ouen de Rouen*, by F. Pommeraye (Rouen, 1672). (Texts of numerous charters.)

Rouen. *Chartularium Monasterii Sanctae Trinitatis de Monte Rothomagi*, ed. A. Deville. (This is pp. 402–487 of the *Cartulaire . . . de Saint-Bertin* (Paris, 1841). It is the most important of the early Norman cartularies and contains much information respecting the personalities responsible for the Norman Conquest.)

Saint-Pierre-sur-Dive. *Les Diplômes de Henri I, roi d'Angleterre, pour l'abbaye de Saint-Pierre-sur-Dive*, ed. R. N. Sauvage (Soc. Hist. Norm., Mélanges Série 12, Rouen, 1933).

Saint-Sauveur-le-Vicomte. *Histoire du Château et des Sires de Saint-Sauveur-le-Vicomte suivie de pièces justificatives*, by Léopold Delisle (Valognes, 1867).

Saint-Wandrille. *Études critiques sur l'abbaye de Saint-Wandrille*, by F. Lot (Paris, 1913). (Contains a highly important collection of charters.)

Saumur. *Chartes normandes de l'abbaye de Saint-Florent*, ed. P. Marchegay (Caen, 1880).

Solesmes. *Cartulaire des abbayes de Saint-Pierre de la Couture et de Saint-Pierre de Solesmes* (Le Mans, 1881).

Tancarville. *Histoire du château et des sires de Tancarville*, by A. Deville (Rouen, 1834).

Tiron. *Cartulaire de l'abbaye . . . de Tiron*, ed. L. Merlet (2 vols., Chartres, 1882–1885).

Troarn. *L'abbaye de Saint-Martin de Troarn*, by R. N. Sauvage (Caen, 1911). (Numerous charters relating especially to the family of Montgomery.)

(iv) *Works dealing with the criticism of charters*

The most famous of the older works dealing generally with the criticism of charters are J. Mabillon, *De Re Diplomatica* (Paris, 1681; supplement, 1704), and the *Nouveau Traité de Diplomatique* (6 vols., Paris, 1750–1764); and both are still of great value. Among later studies may be cited A. Giry, *Manuel de Diplomatique* (Paris, 1894). For most students of English history the best approach to charter criticism will be by means of F. M. Stenton's introduction to *Transcripts of Charters relating to Gilbertine Houses* (Lincoln Rec. Soc., 1922), and by means of an article by W. H. Stevenson (*Eng. Hist. Rev.*, vol. XI, 1896). For the earlier part of the period reference should be made to F. E. Harmer's admirable *Anglo-Saxon Writs* (Manchester, 1952). The critical comments in T. Madox, *Formulare Anglicanum* (1702) are usually excellent. Reference on particular points may be made to R. L. Poole, "The Dates of Henry II's Charters" (*Eng. Hist. Rev.*, vol. XXIII, 1908), and to V. H. Galbraith, "Monastic Foundation Charters of the Eleventh and Twelfth Centuries" (*Camb. Hist. Journal*, vol. IV, 1934). C. R. Cheney, *English Bishops' Chanceries, 1100–1250* (Manchester, 1950), is an admirable work which is indispensable for the study of the subject with which it deals: it may be read in connexion with F. M. Stenton, "Acta Episcoporum" (*Camb. Hist. Journal*, vol. III, 1929).

II. MODERN WORKS

(*a*) MODERN WORKS RELATING GENERALLY TO SOCIAL AND ECONOMIC HISTORY IN THIS PERIOD

Social and economic history in this period cannot be separated. The opening chapters of E. Lipson, *Economic History of England* (vol. I, 7th ed., 1937) gives a good introduction to both, and the connexion between them is further illustrated in various chapters of the *Cambridge Economic History*, vol. I (ed. J. H. Clapham and E. Power, Cambridge, 1941).

The relation between the agrarian structure of England at this time and the ranks of society is well brought out in F. W. Maitland, *Domesday Book and Beyond* (Cambridge, 1897). This fascinating book sets out the chief problems of this subject and, although the author's solutions to some of them have not proved acceptable (see *Eng. Hist. Rev.*, vol. XII, 1897), his treatment remains as stimulating as when it first appeared. A modern analysis is A. L. Poole, *Obligations of Society in the Twelfth and Thirteenth Centuries* (Oxford, 1946), and the significance of the same writer's "Livestock Prices in the Twelfth Century" (*Eng. Hist. Rev.*, vol. LV, 1940) is indicated by its title. M. Postan, "The Chronology of Labour Services" (*Trans. R. Hist. Soc.*, 4th Series, vol. XX, 1937), deals with much of the evidence relating to this period, and much further information may be derived from the introductions to the various editions of surveys cited above, pp. 803, 804.

The basis of many later studies on this subject is to be found in the works of Sir Paul

Vinogradoff, a bibliography of which is included in *The Collected Papers of Paul Vinogradoff*, ed. H. A. L. Fisher (vol. II, Oxford, 1928, pp. 479–499). P. Vinogradoff, *English Society in the Eleventh Century* (Oxford, 1908), is an exhaustive treatment of the subject, and the latter sections of the same writer's more generalized *Growth of the Manor* (London, 1911) also refer to this period. But of all Vinogradoff's books, *Villainage in England* (Oxford, 1892) is probably the most valuable, and its introductory chapter contains a critical account of previous controversial literature on this subject. Vinogradoff's influence is to be discerned in several books devoted to particular localities, among which may be mentioned F. M. Stenton, *Types of Manorial Structure in the Northern Danelaw* (Oxford, 1910), and D. C. Douglas, *Social Structure of Medieval East Anglia* (Oxford, 1927). Other local studies are J. E. A. Jolliffe, "Northumbrian Institutions" (*Eng. Hist. Rev.*, vol. XLI, 1926), and E. B. Demarest, "Inter Ripam et Mersam" (*ibid.*, vol. XXXVIII, 1923). But of all such studies of individual provinces the most important is the introduction to F. M. Stenton, *Documents illustrative of the Social and Economic History of the Danelaw* (Brit. Acad., 1920) which may be supplemented by the same author's *The Free Peasantry of the Northern Danelaw* (Lund, 1926). All recent studies have tended to demonstrate the regional variations in English social structure at this time. H. S. Bennett, *Life on the English Manor* (Cambridge, 1937), contains sources of information relative to this period.

The study of English agrarian society in the eleventh and twelfth centuries must take full account of the field systems operating in England. Much of this work must therefore be comparative, and in this sense students of English history are heavily indebted to A. Meitzen, *Siedlung und Agrarwesen der Westgermanen und Ostgermanen, der Kelten, Römer, Finnen, und Slawen* (3 vols. and atlas, Berlin, 1896). H. L. Gray, *English Field Systems* (Cambridge, Mass., 1915), describes the chief variations in England, and a full discussion of the dependence of this system upon the exigences of co-operative husbandry is in C. S. and C. S. Orwin, *The Open Fields* (Oxford, 1938).

(*b*) DOMESDAY BOOK

All work on the social and economic history of England in this period is based to a greater or lesser degree upon Domesday Book. It remains, however, to add certain books and articles which are more specifically devoted to that record. The beginning of the modern study of Domesday Book is to be found in the remarkable essay of J. H. Round, "Domesday Book", which forms the opening section of his *Feudal England* (London, 1895), and other important accounts are in the concluding chapter of F. M. Stenton, *William the Conqueror* (London, 1928), and by W. J. Corbett in the *Cambridge Medieval History*, vol. V, pp. 506–516. A. Ballard, *The Domesday Inquest* (London, 1906) is a lucid and informative description, and the second edition of this book (1923) includes "a Bibliography of Matter relating to Domesday Book published between the years 1906 and 1923".

Among the older works upon Domesday Book, R. Kelham, *Domesday Book illustrated* (London, 1788) is more than a curiosity, and of substantial value are the works of R. W. Eyton: *A Key to Domesday exemplified by an Analysis and Digest of the Dorset Survey* (London, 1878); *Domesday Studies: Analysis and Digest of the Somerset Survey* (2 vols., London, 1880); and *Domesday Studies: Analysis and Digest of the Staffordshire Survey* (London, 1881). Sir Henry Ellis, *General Introduction to Domesday Book* (2 vols., London, 1833) is useful for the indexes contained therein, though some of these need correction, and G. H. Fowler, *Bedfordshire in 1086: an analysis and synthesis of Domesday Book* (Beds. Hist. Rec. Soc., 4th Series, vol. XI, 1927) is of general importance. Finally, the essays of A. S. Ellis on the Domesday tenants-in-chief which appeared in the *Yorkshire Archaeological Journal* (vol. IV, 1875, 1877), and in the *Transactions of the Bristol and Gloucestershire Archaeological Society* (vol. IV, 1880) are widely informative.

Some of the problems relating to the conduct and results of the Domesday Inquisition of 1086 are set out below (pp. 847–851). Among the works which may be consulted on this controversial theme in addition to those cited above are: W. H. Stevenson, "A Contemporary Description of the Domesday Survey" (*Eng. Hist. Rev.*, vol. XXII (1907)), F. H. Baring, "The Exeter Domesday" (*ibid.*, vol. XXVII (1912)), A. Ballard, *An Eleventh-Century Inquisition of St.*

Augustine's, Canterbury (Brit. Acad., 1920), D. C. Douglas, *Feudal Documents from the Abbey of Bury St. Edmunds* (Brit. Acad., 1932), and the same writer's "The Domesday Survey" (*History*, vol. XXI (1936)). The most important recent treatment of this theme is V. H. Galbraith, "The Making of Domesday Book" (*Eng. Hist. Rev.*, vol. LVII (1943)). It may be read in connexion with D. C. Douglas, *Domesday Monachorum of Christ Church, Canterbury* (London, 1944).

(*c*) ANGLO-NORMAN FEUDALISM

All modern studies of Anglo-Norman feudalism owe much to the seventeenth-century scholars whose work has been noted in the general introduction to this volume (see above, pp. 3–6). In particular, W. Dugdale, *Baronage of England* (2 vols., London, 1675, 1676) still retains much of its original importance. Among modern books, F. M. Stenton, *English Feudalism, 1066–1166* (Oxford, 1932) is fundamental, as are also the works of J. H. Round cited above (pp. 88, 89). L. C. Loyd, *The Origins of some Anglo-Norman families* (Harleian Soc., vol. CIII, 1951) has an importance far greater than its title would suggest, and being the posthumous production of one who was probably the greatest feudal scholar of his generation, its influence on future studies is likely to be enduring and pervasive. Most of the works cited above as relating to Domesday Book are concerned to a greater or lesser extent with this theme, and C. H. Haskins, *Norman Institutions* (Cambridge, Mass., 1918) contains much information of primary importance to the student of English feudal history.

There are a large number of more specialized studies: H. M. Chew, *The English Ecclesiastical Tenants-in-Chief* (Oxford, 1932), G. B. Adams, "Anglo-Saxon Feudalism" (*Amer. Hist. Rev.*, vol. VII (1901)), C. Stephenson, "The Origin and Significance of Feudalism" (*ibid.*, vol. XLVI (1941)), C. Stephenson, "Feudalism and its antecedents in England" (*ibid.*, vol. XLVIII (1943)), D. C. Douglas, "The Norman Conquest and English Feudalism" (*Econ. Hist. Rev.*, vol. LX (1938)), W. O. Ault, *Private Jurisdiction in England* (Yale U.P., 1923), R. R. Reid, "Baronage and Thegnage" (*Eng. Hist. Rev.*, vol. XXX (1915)). S. Painter, *Studies in the History of the English Feudal Barony* (Johns Hopkins U.P., 1943), contains some useful statistical information, and the importance of the reign of Henry II in the modification of English feudal structure is brought out in the literature respecting *The Red Book of the Exchequer* and the *cartae* of knight-service contained therein (see above, p. 395, and below, pp. 903–906).

An important feature of recent research into feudal conditions has been the study of particular honours and fiefs. Among such works are W. Farrer, *Honours and Knights Fees* (3 vols., London, 1923, 1924; Manchester, 1925), W. Farrer, *Feudal Cambridgeshire* (Cambridge, 1920), Sir George Sitwell, *Barons of Pulford* (Scarborough, 1889), and the work of G. H. Fowler published by the Bedfordshire Historical Record Society. The value of this work depends upon the accurate identification of persons and places and their interrelation, and this in turn depends to a large extent upon the notable indexes which have been published in modern times. Among these the most important are those of J. H. Round's *Calendar of Documents preserved in France* (London, 1889), C. T. Clay's index to vols. I–III of *Early Yorkshire Charters* (1942), and most particularly the index to the official edition of the *Book of Fees* (1931) which by itself fills up the whole of a large quarto volume, and is a model of exact scholarship.

A comparison of English and continental feudalism can perhaps best be made by reference to M. Bloch, *La Société féodale* (2 vols., Paris, 1939, 1940), a notable and stimulating book. C. Petit-Dutaillis, *La Monarchie féodale en France et en Angleterre du Xe au XIIIe siècle* (Paris, 1923), and F. L. Ganshof, *Qu'est-ce que la Féodalité?* (Brussels, 1947), are also valuable in this respect.

(*d*) THE ENGLISH BOROUGHS, 1042–1189

The indispensable work on English municipal history in this period is J. Tait, *The Medieval English Borough* (Manchester, 1936). This book, whose appearance marked the end of a stage in the study of the English towns in the Middle Ages, was in one sense a reply to the important work of Professor Carl Stephenson, who in a series of influential publications has endeavoured to interpret the English development in the light of the continental evolution as depicted by

Pirenne and others. The more important of Stephenson's works on this theme are *Borough and Town* (Cambridge, Mass., 1933), "The Origin of the English Town" (*Amer. Hist. Rev.*, vol. XXXII, 1926), and "The Anglo-Saxon Borough" (*Eng. Hist. Rev.*, vol. XLV, 1930). The distinction of these essays has been generally admired, but the views which they sustain have not escaped criticism (see *Eng. Hist. Rev.*, vol. XLVII, 1933). The reader must be left to form his own judgment upon the controversies they have engendered.

The publications of Tait and Stephenson have relegated to a position of secondary importance earlier works on the history of the English boroughs of this period. Excellent summaries of that work will be found in J. Tait, *op. cit.*, chap. XII, and by R. R. Darlington in *History*, (vol. XXIII, 1938). It is necessary therefore only to cite here a few of the more influential books there discussed: F. W. Maitland, *Township and Borough* (Cambridge, 1898), F. Pollock and F. W. Maitland, *History of English Law*, vol. I, pp. 634–688 (Cambridge, 1898), C. Gross, *Gild Merchant* (Oxford, 1890), A. Ballard, *Domesday Boroughs* (London, 1904), Mary Bateson's articles on the "Laws of Breteuil" in *Eng. Hist. Rev.*, vols. XV–XVII, 1900–1902, and in Hemmeon, *Burgage Tenure in Medieval England* (Manchester, 1914), R. H. Gretton, *The Burford Records* (Oxford, 1920), may also be mentioned as an excellent study of a smaller borough; K. M. E. Murray, *Constitutional History of the Cinque Ports* (Manchester, 1935), has a special interest; and F. M. Stenton, *Norman London* (London, 1934), is a model of compression and lucidity. The best introduction to the borough charters of this period is A. Ballard, *British Borough Charters*, vol. I (London, 1913), and much information is to be found in the commentaries on such charters appended to the editions of the charters of particular towns. Most of these will be mentioned at headings of the documents printed in this book on pp. 962–974.

A. ENGLISH AGRARIAN SOCIETY, 1042–1189

(a) SURVEYS AND STATEMENTS OF SERVICE

172. Rights and Ranks of People: *Rectitudines Singularum Personarum*[1]

The 'mysterious document' known as *Rectitudines Singularum Personarum* exists in two versions: the one in Anglo-Saxon, the other in an inaccurate Latin translation made early in the twelfth century. The original should most probably be placed in the half-century preceding the Norman Conquest, and it may therefore fairly be regarded as a description of agrarian conditions in the time of Edward the Confessor, made by one familiar with the management of a great estate. The fullness of the description, and the wide range of social ranks discussed, make this a unique text for the period with which it deals, but it is most difficult to interpret on points of detail. Not the least prominent of its features is its insistence on the variety of regional traditions and their importance: the status of a peasant might in large measure depend upon local custom. The chief interest of this text lies in its value as evidence of the 'growth of the manor'. For this reason much discussion has taken place respecting it. Here it will be sufficient to note that many of the characteristics of later manorial organization are to be discerned in this document: for example, the separation of demesne-land and tenant-land; the distinction between week-work and boon-work; and the mingling of free and servile elements in the status of the peasantry. The best text of *Rectitudines Singularum Personarum* is in F. Liebermann, *Die Gesetze der Angelsachsen*, vol. I (1898), pp. 444–453. Among the works in which this document has been discussed may be mentioned F. Seebohm, *English Village Community* (ed. 1915), pp. 129–147; F. W. Maitland, *Domesday Book and Beyond* (ed. 1921), pp. 328, 329; P. Vinogradoff, *The Growth of the Manor* (ed. 1920), pp. 231–235.

Thegn's Law. The law of the thegn is that he be entitled to his book-right,[2] and that he shall contribute three things in respect of his land: armed service, and the repairing of fortresses and work on bridges.[3] Also in respect of many estates, further service arises on the king's order such as service connected with the deer fence at the king's residence, and equipping a guard ship, and guarding the coast, and guarding the lord, and military watch, almsgiving and church dues and many other various things.

Geneat's Right.[4] Geneat-right is various according to what is fixed in respect of the estate: in some he must pay rent and contribute a pasturage swine a year, ride and perform carrying service and furnish means of carriage, work and entertain his lord, reap and mow, cut deer hedges and keep up places from which deer may be shot, build and fence the lord's house, bring strangers to the village, pay church dues and alms money, act as guard to his lord, take care of the horses, and carry messages far and near wheresoever he is directed.

Cottar's-Right.[5] The cottar's right is according to the custom of the estate: in some he must work for his lord each Monday throughout the year, or 3 days each week at harvest-time. . . . He does not make land payment.[6] He should have 5 acres: more if

[1] The editors are deeply indebted to Miss S. I. Tucker for her translation of this tract.

[2] Land protected by charter. On book-right, see P. Vinogradoff, in *Eng. Hist. Rev.*, vol. VIII (1895), pp. 1–17; G. J. Turner, in *Essays in honour of James Tait* (1933), pp. 357–386.

[3] The ancient *trinoda necessitas.*

[4] *Geneat:* the original meaning of the word is courtier or companion. By the middle of the eleventh century some kind of service was implied. *Geneat* is translated in the Latin version as *villanus*, but his position does not correspond with that occupied by the typical villein of later surveys (see Nos. 176–179). Here he appears as primarily a riding servant, acting perhaps as a bailiff on a large estate. He was a man of some standing. His agricultural work is limited and is confined to boon-works at harvest-time, etc.

[5] The cottar's holding of approximately 5 acres was to be characteristic of the later manorial economy (see below, No. 176). Sometimes these men were later described as *lundinarii*, "Monday-men".

[6] *landgafol.*

it be the custom on the estate; and it is too little if it ever be less; because his work must be frequent. Let him give his hearth-penny[1] on Ascension Day even as each freeman ought to do. Let him also perform services on his lord's demesne-land[2] if he is ordered, by keeping watch on the sea-coast and working at the king's deer fence and such things according to his condition. Let him pay his church dues at Martinmas.

Boor's-Right. The boor's[3] duties are various, in some places heavy and in others light. On some estates the custom is that he must perform week-work for 2 days in each week of the year[4] as he is directed, and 3 days from the Feast of the Purification to Easter. If he perform carrying service he need not work while his horse is out. At Michaelmas he must pay 10 pence for *gafol*,[5] and at Martinmas 23 sesters of barley, and 2 hens, and at Easter a young sheep or 2 pence. And he must lie from Martinmas to Easter at his lord's fold as often as it falls to his lot; and from the time when ploughing is first done until Martinmas he must each week plough 1 acre, and himself present the seed in the lord's barn. Also [he must plough] 3 acres as boon-work,[6] and 2 for pasturage. If he needs more grass, let him earn it as he may be permitted. Let him plough 3 acres as his tribute land[7] and sow it from his own barn, and pay his hearth-penny.[8] And every pair of boors must maintain 1 hunting dog, and each boor must give 6 loaves to the herdsman of the lord's swine when he drives his herd to the mast-pasture. On the same land to which the customs apply a farmer ought to be given for his occupation of the land 2 oxen, 1 cow, 6 sheep and 7 acres sown on his rood of land. After[9] that year let him perform all the dues that fall to him, and let him be given tools for his work and utensils for his house. When death befalls him let the lord take charge of what he leaves.

The estate-law is fixed on each estate: at some places, as I have said, it is heavier, at some places, also, lighter, because not all customs about estates are alike. On some estates a boor must pay tribute in honey, on some in food, on some in ale. Let him who has the shire[10] always know what are the ancient arrangements about the estate and what is the custom of the district.

About the bee-keeper. A bee-keeper if he hold a swarm which is subject to payment must pay what is appointed on that estate. Amongst us it is appointed that he should give 5 sesters of honey as tax: in some estates a greater tax is due. Also at certain times he must be ready for many sorts of work at his lord's pleasure besides boon-work and the cutting of corn when ordered and the mowing of meadows. And if he will be provided with land he must be provided with a horse so as to give it to supply his lord with a beast of burden or to go with his horse himself, whichever he is directed.

[1] Peter's Pence, see above, No. 82.

[2] 'Inland'. In the Burton Cartulary (see No. 176) 'inland' is contrasted with 'warland': 'warland' being at once the land occupied by the tenants and also the land assessed to the king's geld.

[3] *Gebur*. Compare his service with those of the later villein. On the conclusions to be drawn from this comparison contrast F. Seebohm, *op. cit.*, p. 139, and P. Vinogradoff, *Growth of the Manor*, p. 234.

[4] One of the chief characteristics of villein tenure: so many days' work each week for the benefit of the lord.

[5] Perhaps 'rent' or 'tribute' would be a suitable translation.

[6] Special services at special times of the year.

[7] *gafol-erðe:* probably the lord's land scattered in the strips of the open fields to be cultivated by the peasantry for the lord's benefit.

[8] By contrast to the above a characteristic of freedom.

[9] Or 'during'.

[10] Possibly the sheriff, but not necessarily so. The steward of a great lord might be so described.

And many things must a man of such condition do: I cannot recount them all now. When death befalls him let his lord take charge of what he leaves unless there should be anything free.

A swine-herd at pay[1] ought to pay for his animals that are to be slaughtered according to the amount fixed on the estate. On many estates it is fixed that he pay every year 15 swine for killing, 10 old and 5 young. Let him have himself whatever he raises beyond that. On many estates a more severe due is incumbent on the swine-herd. Let each swine-herd take care that after the slaughter of his swine he prepare them properly and singe them: then he will be well entitled to the perquisites. Also he must be – as I said before about the bee-keeper – always ready for every sort of work, and provided with a horse at the lord's need.

A slave swine-herd and a slave bee-keeper after death are liable to one and the same law.

A herdsman slave belonging to his lord who keeps the demesne herd ought to have a young pig kept in a sty, and his perquisites when he has prepared the bacon, and also the dues that belong to a slave.

About men's provisioning. Every slave ought to have as provisions 12 pounds of good corn and 2 carcasses of sheep and 1 good cow for food[2] and the right of cutting wood according to the custom of the estate.

About women's provisioning. For a female slave 8 pounds of corn for food, 1 sheep or 3 pence for winter food, 1 sester of beans for lenten food, whey in summer or 1 penny.

All slaves belonging to the estate ought to have food at Christmas and Easter, a strip of land for ploughing and a "harvest-handful" besides their dues.

About retainers. A retainer[3] ought to have the use of 2 acres, 1 sown and 1 not sown. Let him sow the latter himself. And he is entitled to his food and shoes and gloves.

About the sower. A sower ought to have a seedlip full of every kind of seed when he has properly sown every seed throughout the space of a year.

About the ox-herd. The ox-herd must pasture 2 oxen or more with the lord's herd on the common pasture with the cognizance of the overseer. Let him earn thereby shoes and gloves for himself. And his cow for food must go with the lord's oxen.

About the cow-herd. A cow-herd ought to have an old cow's milk for a week after she has newly calved, and the beestings of a young cow for a fortnight. His cow for food is to go with the lord's cow.

About the shepherd. A shepherd's due is that he should have 12 nights' dung at Christmas, and 1 lamb from the year's young ones, 1 bell-wether's fleece, and the milk of his flock for a week after the equinox, and a bowl-full of whey or buttermilk all summer.

About the goat-herd. A goat-herd ought to have the milk of his herd after

[1] *gafolswane.*

[2] Note that it is only the food of the slave that is indicated. His obligations are probably regarded as unlimited subject only to the custom of the estate.

[3] Clearly a privileged person on the estate.

Martinmas, and before that his portion of whey, and 1 kid a year old, if he looks after his herd properly.

About the cheese-maker. 100 cheeses pertain to the cheese-maker, and it behoves her to make butter for the lord's table out of the whey pressed out from the cheese; and let her have all the buttermilk except the shepherd's portion.[1]

About the keeper of the granary. The granary-keeper ought to have the corn spilt at the barn door at harvest-time if his overseer grant it to him, and if he deserves it.

About the beadle. The beadle ought to be more free from work because of his office, since he is bound to be always ready. Also he ought to have some bit of land for his labour.

About the woodward. Every tree blown down by the wind ought to go to the woodward.

It[2] is proper that the hayward should be rewarded for his labour in those parts which lie near the pasture; because if he has neglected his work he can expect . . . (if) he has been granted such a piece of land it must be nearest the pasture by custom; because, if out of laziness he neglects his lord's land his own will not be protected if it is provided in this way. If he makes properly secure what he has to guard he will be well entitled to his reward.

The customs of estates are various, as I have said before. Nor do we apply these regulations we have described to all districts. But we declare what the custom is where it is known to us. If we learn better, we will eagerly delight in what we learn and maintain it according to the custom of the district in which we then live.

Wherefore one must delight among the people to learn laws if one does not oneself wish to lose honour on the estate.

There are many common rights: in some districts are due winter provisions, Easter provisions, a harvest feast for reaping the corn, a drinking feast for ploughing, reward for haymaking, food for making the rick, at wood-carrying a log from each load, at corn-carrying food on completion of the rick, and many things which I cannot recount.

This, however, is a memorandum of people's provisions. And all these I have enumerated before.

173. Statement (in Anglo-Saxon) of services rendered at Hurstbourne Priors, Hampshire (? *circa* 1050)

Of uncertain date but usually attributed to the same period as *Rectitudines Singularum Personarum* and the Tidenham survey (see below, No. 174) with which this document should be compared. Printed, translated and annotated by A. J. Robertson, *Anglo-Saxon Charters* (1939), pp. 207, 454.

Here are recorded the dues which the peasants must render at Hurstbourne. First from every hide they must render 40 pence at the autumnal equinox, and 6 church 'mittan'[3] of ale and 3 sesters of wheat for bread, and they must plough 3 acres in their own time, and sow them with their own seed, and bring it to the barn in

[1] This entry presents certain difficulties. The process of butter-making here described seems impossible. The cheese-maker is definitely a woman.

[2] This entry is defective and obscure. The meaning seems to be that the land of the hayward should be so situated as to suffer first from straying beasts if he has neglected his duties.

[3] According to one account the 'mittan' contained 8 bushels.

their own time, and give 3 pounds of barley as rent, and mow half an acre of meadow as rent in their own time, and make it into a rick, and supply 4 fothers of split wood as rent, made into a stack in their own time, and supply 16 poles of fencing as rent likewise in their own time, and at Easter they shall give 2 ewes with 2 lambs–and we reckon 2 young sheep to a full-grown sheep–and they must wash the sheep and shear them in their own time, and work as they are bidden every week except three–one at midwinter, the second at Easter, the third at the Rogation Days.

174. Survey of an estate at Tidenham, Gloucestershire (? *circa* 1060)

Valuable as a statement of labour services at an early date. Tidenham was granted to the abbot of Bath in 956, and was leased to Archbishop Stigand at some date between 1061 and 1065. It is possible that this text is connected with the latter transaction, but the date of its compilation is uncertain. Liebermann was inclined to place the date about 1050 in view of its similarities with *Rectitudines Singularum Personarum* (see No. 172) with which it should be compared. The survey is discussed in F. Seebohm, *English Village Community*, p. 149, who assigns it, wrongly as it seems, to an earlier period. It is also discussed in F. W. Maitland, *Domesday Book and Beyond*, p. 330. The document is printed, translated and annotated in A. J. Robertson, *Anglo-Saxon Charters*, pp. 205, 451.

In Tidenham there are 30 hides made up of 9 hides of demesne-land[1] and 21 hides of land occupied[2] [by the tenants]. At Stroat there are 12 hides, including 27 yardlands of rent-paying land and 30 basket weirs on the Severn. At Milton 5 hides, including 14 yardlands of rent-paying land,[3] 14 basket weirs on the Severn and 2 hackle weirs on the Wye. At 'Kingston' there are 5 hides, including 13 yardlands of rent-paying land, and 1 hide above the dyke is now rent-paying land also, and what is there outside the enclosed land is still partly in demesne, partly let for rent to the Welsh sailors. At 'Kingston' there are 21 basket weirs on the Severn and 12 on the Wye. At Bishton there are 3 hides and 15 basket weirs on the Wye. In Landcaut there are 3 hides and 2 hackle weirs on the Wye and 9 basket weirs. Throughout the whole estate 12 pence is due from every yardland and 4 pence as alms. At every weir within the 30 hides every alternate fish belongs to the lord of the manor, and every rare fish which is of value–sturgeon or porpoise, herring or sea fish–and no one has the right of selling any fish for money when the lord is on the estate without informing him about it. From Tidenham much labour is due. The *geneat*[4] must labour either on the estate or off the estate, whichever he is bidden, and ride and furnish carrying service and supply transport and drive herds and do many other things. The boor[5] must do what is due from him–he must plough half an acre as week-work and himself fetch the seed from the lord's barn, and a whole acre for church dues[6] from his own barn. For weir building he must supply 40 larger rods? or a fother of small rods, or he shall build 8 yokes for 3 ebb tides, supply 15 poles of field fencing or dig 5, fence and dig 1 pole of the manor-house hedge, reap 1½ acres, and mow half an acre, and work at other kinds of work, always in proportion to the work. He shall give 6 pence after

[1] *ix inlandes;* see above, p. 814 n.2.
[2] *gesettes landes:* possibly but not certainly here equated with *gafollandes.*
[3] *gafollandes.*
[4] Compare these services with those described in *Rectitudines Singularum Personarum*, see above, No. 172.
[5] *gebur.*
[6] Church scot which in *Rectitudines Singularum Personarum* is not mentioned in connexion with the boor.

Easter and half a sester of honey, at Lammas 6 sesters of malt, at Martinmas[1] a ball of good net yarn. On the same estate it is the rule that he who has 7 swine shall give 3 and thereafter always the tenth, and in spite of this pay for the right of having mast when there is mast.

175. Fragments (mainly in Anglo-Saxon) of surveys from the abbey of Bury St. Edmunds (dating from period 1045–1098)

The text which follows is not a unity. The Saxon portion at the beginning dates from the time of Abbot Leofstan (1045–1065), the latter part comes mainly from the time of Abbot Baldwin (1065–1098). The text is of interest for many reasons. The emphasis on food-rents in the time of Abbot Leofstan is noteworthy. The most important information given by the text relates to the problem of the early history of the hundred. The 'hundreds' mentioned in the text as existing in the Marshland district of Norfolk are not the Domesday hundreds but small units which are probably to be equated with the small Lincolnshire hundreds of 12 carucates (for which see F. M. Stenton, *Danelaw Documents*, p. lxiii) and which are perhaps to be related to the 'leets' frequently mentioned in the East Anglian Domesday (see D. C. Douglas, *Medieval East Anglia*, (1927), pp. 138–144;191–202; *Feudal Documents from the Abbey of Bury St. Edmunds*, pp. clx–clxiii). The division of these hundreds into 'manlots' is also notable, since the 'manlot' (man's share) was apparently a Danish division of land which is mentioned in other texts both from England and Normandy and may be an allocation of land consequent upon the Scandinavian invasions. Its size was apparently usually of about 12 acres. The text is printed and discussed by D. C. Douglas in *Eng. Hist. Rev.*, vol. XLIII (1928), pp. 376–383. It is also printed, translated and annotated in A. J. Robertson, *Anglo-Saxon Documents*, pp. 193, 440.

Here is stated the agreement that Ætheric has made with the abbot at Newton, namely 3 bushels of malt and half a bushel of wheat, 1 ox for slaughtering, 5 sheep, 10 flitches of bacon and 1000 loaves to be ready on 4 September. Abbot Leofstan adds this additional contribution to the old food-rent: namely 1 bushel of malt and 300 loaves and 6 flitches of bacon and another 6 to complete it, and 10 cheeses, and Brihtric the prior[2] the same amount, and Leofstan the same amount, except for the 10 cheeses, and Thurstan relish for 300 loaves, and 2 ores[3] to the kitchen and Brihtric 16 pence.

In Islington[4] hundred St. Edmund has 27 manlots.[5]
In Spellow[6] hundred, 45 manlots.[5]
In 'In' hundred, 10 manlots.[5]
In 'Fuwelege' hundred, 7½ manlots.[5]
In 'Ærnehogo' hundred, 25 manlots.[5]
In Clenchwarton[4] hundred, 7½ manlots.[5]
In Lynn[4] hundred, 5 manlots.[5]

[1] 11 November.

[2] Or perhaps 'priest': the contraction is 'pr'.

[3] The Danish *ora* of 16 pence (which appears later in this document may here be implied), if the reckoning of 16 pence is meant to be the equivalent of half of the "2 ores". On the other hand, an *ora* of 20 pence may here be implied.

[4] Not Domesday hundreds. Islington, Clenchwarton and Lynn are neighbouring places in Marshland, Norfolk.

[5] The 'manlot' appears in a tenth-century Nottinghamshire charter, in a Norman charter of the early eleventh century, in two twelfth-century Lincolnshire charters, and in an East Anglian extent of the thirteenth century. In all these cases it has been held to indicate land-sharing arrangements deriving from the Scandinavian settlements. (On this term, see further: D. C. Douglas, *Medieval East Anglia* (1927), pp. 50–58; *Rise of Normandy* (1949), p. 6.)

[6] The name "Spellow" is applied at the present day to six fields lying between Islington and Clenchwarton.

From Athulf's[1] Sutton to the old 'Walbeck',[2] from Watlington[3] north to the sea St. Edmund has a share of the land with his neighbours.[4] May the noble name of our Lord the Saviour Christ be honoured for ever to all eternity. He formed the glorious company of angels for his own honour, and likewise fashioned the winsome countenance of men after his own image, bestowing abundantly upon them the gifts of heaven and earth. In these days he has given and granted to King Edward the fair island of Britain,[5] as he did of yore to his kinsmen, one of whom was by name the noble and honourable St. Edmund who now dwells in heaven with Christ himself. The good and honourable King Edward has now entrusted his kinsman's monastery at Bedericesworth[6] to Abbot Leofstan[7] to take charge of everything there both inside and out, and he has found this much there, namely 10 books[8] inside the church, consisting of 4 gospel books and 1 missal and 1 epistle book, and 1 psalter and 1 good book of homilies and 1 capitulary and the *life* of St. Edmund. In the treasure house he has found 12 chasubles and 9 cantor's copes and 4 vestments and 7 stoles and 33 cloaks and 9 altar cloths and 15 ornamented super-humerals and 25 albs and 7 seat-covers and 13 wall curtains and 3 dorsals and 2 movable curtains and 5 chalices and 3 offertory cloths and 7 corporals and 2 censers and 3 marble stones bound with metal and 4 screens and 14 crosses. Blacere has 1 winter lectionary. Brihtric has 1 Mass vestment, a chalice and a paten, 1 missal and a winter lectionary and a summer book. Siferth has 1 Mass vestment and 1 missal and Leofstan 1 manual; Ætheric 1 missal and a capitulary; Thurstan 1 psalter. Oscytel has 1 Mass vestment and 1 missal and 1 *Ad te levavi*. At Bury St. Edmunds there are 16 hides of arable land,[9] 6 hides in demesne and the remaining 10 hides held by men in return for services.[10] Worlingworth supplies a month's food-rent along with the berewick of Soham; Palgrave a month's food-rent along with Thorpe; Redgrave a month's food-rent; Rickinghall a month's food-rent along with Stoke and Brockford; Barton a month's food-rent; Rougham a month's food-rent; Elmswell a month's food-rent along with Woolpit and Groton; Cockfield a month's food-rent along with Chelsworth; Whepstead a month's food-rent along with Bradfield; Horringer a month's food-rent along with Risby; Lackford a month's food-rent along with Herringswell; Runcton a month's food-rent along with Culford and Fornham. There are 30 books here, all in Abbot Leofstan's possession.[11] Pakenham supplies one month's food-rent along with Stanton.

[1] Perhaps Long Sutton in South Lincolnshire.

[2] Is it possible that this is related to the present names of Walpole and Walsoken in Marshland?

[3] This is Watlington a few miles south of King's Lynn.

[4] *ah Sce Eadmund landes dæle mid his landemacan.*

[5] Note reference to Edward the Confessor as still alive.

[6] The old name of Bury St. Edmunds.

[7] Does this suggest that this inventory was taken when Leofstan was appointed as abbot in 1045? If so, it would give an early date for the commencing part of the survey.

[8] This list is discussed by M. R. James, *On the Abbey of Bury St. Edmunds* (1895), pp. 5, 6. He calls it "the earliest thing that can in any sense be called a Catalogue" of the books belonging to the abbey. None of the volumes here mentioned can, however, be identified with books known later to have belonged to the library of the monastery which later contained more than 2000 volumes.

[9] *xvi hida eordes landes*. The appearance of hides here is very notable. In Domesday there are no hides in East Anglia, the assessment being made by carucates, which in turn are here absent. It is doubtful whether the Domesday assessment of East Anglia or of the Danelaw was of high antiquity.

[10] *manna earningaland*. On this term, see D. C. Douglas, *Eng. Hist. Rev.*, vol. XLIII (1928), p. 378. The division into demesne- and tenant-land is notable.

[11] This sentence is probably misplaced.

Here is[1] recorded what was found at Egmere after Cole left it, namely 7 oxen and 8 cows and 4 grazing bullocks and 2 inferior horses and 115 sheep including both full grown and young ones, and 160 acres sown and 1 flitch of bacon and 1 pig and 24 cheeses.

Here[2] is recorded what Abbot Baldwin has granted to his brethren as a charitable gift, namely the rent of 2 mills at Lackford, half a pound from the one and 12 ores from the other. We shall have the half-pound at the Nativity of St. Mary and 6 ores at the festival of St. Dionysius and 6 ores at the festival of St. Nicholas, and 2 fat pigs shall likewise be produced to supply lard or else 3 ores.

This is the charitable gift which Abbot Baldwin has granted to his brethren for the soul of Edward the good king, namely half a pound to supply fish at his anniversary on condition that they remember him the more often in their prayers, and half a pound on the anniversary of my coming here to the monastery, that is 19 August. And this pound shall continue to be given at my anniversary by the grace of God and St. Edmund whoever succeeds here. The money shall be due from Ixworth which belongs to Pakenham. At Abbot Ufi's anniversary we shall have half a pound for fish and 40 pence for mead and 2 measures of wheat, and that shall be due from Lackford.

At[3] the anniversary of the burial of King William[4] the lord abbot, Baldwin, has appointed that every year on the same day 10 shillings shall be given as a charitable gift, and on the day of the death of his queen, namely Maud, he has decreed that the same amount, namely 10 shillings, shall be paid to us in addition as a perpetual obligation. And in order that it may be established whence this money, namely 20 shillings, shall be paid every year for the sake of the brethren, the same lord abbot has decreed in full chapter in the presence of all, that it should be paid from the manor of Warkton which the said King William gave to St. Edmund for the soul of the aforesaid queen,[5] since the abbot judges it proper that the brethren should enjoy something better as food on the anniversaries of those whose names they do not hesitate to repeat in their prayers before God frequently and, so to say, without intermission. At the anniversary of the burial of King Edward the above-mentioned abbot has appointed 10 shillings as a charitable gift for his brethren that they may remember his soul with greater devotion. I, Abbot Baldwin, likewise appoint for perpetual observation by whoever comes after me as abbot that 10 shillings shall be given on my behalf on the anniversary of my coming as abbot, namely on 19 August. These 20 shillings[6] shall be given from Ixworth which belongs to Pakenham. On the anniversary of Abbot Ufi the brethren shall have 10 shillings as a charitable gift, and 3 shillings and 4 pence for mead and 2 measures of wheat. And these shall be given from Lackford. This is the charitable gift which Abbot Baldwin has appointed for the Nativity of St. Mary,[7] namely 10 shillings, and 8 shillings at the festival of

[1] This sentence seems to be wholly detached from the general contents. An interlinear Latin translation is given in the MS.

[2] This paragraph and the next record gifts by Abbot Baldwin who succeeded Abbot Leofstan. They and what follows are therefore later in date than the beginning of the document.

[3] What follows is in Latin.

[4] William I died 9 September 1087, and if this note implies that he was already dead, this section of the record must be placed between that date and January 1098.

[5] Maud died 2 November 1083, and this section of the record is certainly subsequent to this.

[6] *i.e.* the 10 shillings for King Edward's and Baldwin's anniversaries.

[7] 8 September.

St. Dionysius[1] and 4 shillings at the festival of St. Nicholas,[2] and in addition 2 fat or pigs 4 shillings for lard. The whole of this shall be given from 2 mills at Lackford of which one shall render 10 shillings and the other 16 shillings.

This[3] is St. Edmund's food-rent from Barton, namely 4 measures of malt, including both mash and grist, half a measure of wheat, 1 bullock, 2 pigs, 4 geese, 20 hens. From Rougham the same amount, and from Redgrave the same. From Pakenham and from Stanton the same amount. From Elmswell and from Woolpit and from Groton the same. From Herringswell and from Coney Weston the same amount. From Palgrave and from Thorpe the same amount. From Horringer and from Risby the same amount. From Cockfield and from Chelsworth the same amount. From Whepstead and from Bradfield the same amount. From Worlingworth and from Soham the same amount. From Runcton and from Culford and from Fornham the same amount. From Brockford and from Rickinghall the same amount. From Tivetshall 1 measure of malt including mash and grist, and 1 'lepene' of wheat and the quarter of a bullock and half a pig and 1 goose and 5 hens.

176. Twelfth-century surveys from Burton Abbey

In the cartulary of the abbey of Burton-on-Trent are two early surveys which are assigned by the compiler of that cartulary respectively to the time of Abbot Nigel (*i.e.* 1094–1114), and to the first year of Abbot Geoffrey (*i.e.* 1114). Neither of these dates can be accepted without reservation, and it seems certain that the latter of these surveys was prior in date to the former (see J. H. Round, in *Eng. Hist. Rev.*, vol. xx (1905)). It would be safe to date the earlier of these two surveys at 1114–1118 and the later at about 1126. Two parallel surveys of this very early date obviously provide information of the highest value and they have been used in many investigations of the social condition of England in the period immediately subsequent to Domesday. The surveys themselves were admirably re-edited in 1916 by G. C. O. Bridgeman for the William Salt Archaeological Society with an extensive commentary to which the reader is here referred for information on points of detail. The material which here follows concerns the manors of Burton, Branston and Stretton.

(i) *Account of the manors of Burton, Branston and Stretton given in the earlier of the Burton Surveys*

[This survey is sometimes known as Survey 'B' which may be dated 1114–1118.]

In Burton there is 'inland'[4] for 2 ploughs. There are 2 ploughs with 16 oxen. Besides these there are 4 other oxen for carting lime and 4 for carting wood; and there is 1 brood mare in addition to the brood mares which were there in the time of Abbot Nigel:[5] these between the mares and the foals then numbered 70. There are 3 Spanish asses;[6] 19 cows; 1 bull; 8 calves; 2 beasts for food; 128 pigs.

The land of the men is assessed at 1½ hides. The villeins are Fredebert; Edward; Adelon; Alwin; Leviet; Uctebrand; Eluric; Edric. Each one of these holds 2 bovates[7] and works [for the lord] for 2 days each week. He must find a horse each year for the journey to the abbot's court or pay 3 pence. He must go for salt once, and for fish once, or give 2 pence for each carrying service. He must cart 1 cartload of wood. He

[1] 9 October. [2] 6 December.

[3] What follows is in Anglo-Saxon and is of uncertain date, possibly representing conditions in Abbot Baldwin's time.

[4] Probably used here to indicate land exempted from the king's geld. It is normally here the lord's demesne, and is to be contrasted with 'warland' which here "bears the double implication of land in the occupation of the dependent peasantry, and land rated to the king's geld" (F. M. Stenton, *Types of Manorial Structure in the Northern Danelaw*, 1910, pp. 10, 11).

[5] 1094–1114. [6] *asini hispani.* [7] The typical villein holding.

must pay 2 hens at Christmas, and make 1 sester of malt and give pannage.[1] He must plough twice in the year, and besides this half an acre in Lent. From Pentecost to the Feast of All Saints he must send his beasts into the lord's fold.[2] [ ][3] he must find 1 man in August to reap. And anyone who between Pentecost and August goes to the wood for a cartload of timber must pay 2 pence.

Rauechetus holds 1 bovate and works for 1 day a week for the lord and goes where he is sent.

Alwin likewise.

The monks' man likewise.

The cottars are Godric; Aluric; another Godric; Seietus; Leviet; Bristold; Ulviet; Lefldea; Alvena; Doune; William the cobbler. Each one has a croft, and works for 1 day.[4] There are 2 monks' ox-herds who each hold 1 bovate.

The rent-paying tenants[5] are these:

William of 'Sobehalle' holds 2 bovates for 2 shillings and must go wherever he is sent, either with the abbot or without the abbot.

The chief ox-herd (?)[6] holds 2 bovates for 2 shillings and 6 pence, and twice a year he must lend his plough; and thrice in August he must reap, twice with 1 man and the third time with all his household, with the lord providing their food; and the wife of Aldeon shall reap for 1 day.

Stevinulf holds 2 bovates for 3 shillings.

Uctebrand likewise must lend his cart for carting the demesne hay.

Aluric the cook, Aluric the baker, and Ulwin the mason each hold 2 bovates for 2 shillings and must perform the same customs.

Lepsi the baker, Alsi the cook, Ulsi the gardener,[7] and Godric the carpenter each hold 1 bovate for 12 pence, and owe the same customs.

Wardbois holds 2 bovates and 3 acres of meadow for his rent, that is to say, for 2 shillings.

Edeva, the sister of Bruning, holds 1 croft and 1 acre of 'inland' on which she lives.

Hardwin holds 1 acre for 1 'vano' and 1 'cana'.

Richard, son of Godit, holds 1 house.

Gilbert holds 1 dwelling for 16 pence.

Cacerel holds 1 house for 6 pence.

Acelin holds 1 dwelling for 12 pence.

Recelbert[8] holds 4 acres of 'inland' and his dwelling on them, and he has half the revenue of the parish altar except the candles which he does not have, but which are found for him for his ministry; and he has 2 sheaves of the tithe of the demesne ploughs; and in Burton and Branston and in Stapenhill and in Winshill

[1] The payment for permission to turn swine into the wood for mast.

[2] Foldsoke, valuable for the manure.

[3] Meaning obscure.

[4] Cf. No. 172.

[5] *censarii*; on this class, see P. Vinogradoff, *Villainage in England*, p. 186.

[6] *tintor*.

[7] 'gardiner'.

[8] Clearly the parish priest, and his endowment is of great interest, in particular the division of the tithe between the abbey and the parish priest.

he has 1 thrave from everyone and a tithe of their cattle, and the ration of 1 monk in the court.

Gilbert has 1 dwelling for 16 pence.

Godwin 1 dwelling for 12 pence.

William 1 dwelling for 12 pence.

The mother of Steinulf 1 dwelling for 12 pence.

Acelin 1 dwelling for 12 pence.

The mother of Richard the monk lives on the 'inland'.

Aluric holds a dwelling for 12 pence.

Fromund holds a dwelling for 12 pence.

Lepsi holds 2 mills for 50 shillings for 4 years from the Feast of All Saints in the first year of Abbot Geoffrey; and he must grind freely the corn and malt of the demesne and give such fishes as are caught; and he must restore the mills as well as they were when he took them and with new millstones if such be needed.

Alured holds a dwelling for 16 pence.

Walt holds a dwelling for 6 pence.

Widsi holds a dwelling and 1 acre for 12 pence and, since this is of the 'inland', he ought to pay geld to the abbot,[1] and he owes the other customs.

Godwin holds 1 dwelling for the work of 4 weeks, to wit, 2 in the summer and 2 in Lent.

Durand holds a dwelling for 14 pence.[2]

In Branston there is half a hide of 'inland' which can be ploughed by 3 ploughs. Now there are 2 with 16 oxen; 1 mare; 24 cows; 1 bull; 14 calves; 7 beasts for food. The land of the men is assessed at 1½ hides.

The villeins are: Ulsi; Siric; Uluric; Alwin; Edwin; Bront; Osbern; Redwi. Each of them holds 2 bovates and owes all the customs which are performed by the villeins of Burton except that in Lent these plough half an acre more than those (in Burton); that is to say they plough 1 acre in Lent, while those at Burton plough half an acre. But these do not give 2 pence for their carts going to the wood, as the villeins in Burton do. Godric and Edric, the ox-herds, each have 2 bovates; Osbern the ox-herd has 1 bovate. Toli holds 1 bovate for 15 pence. Godric Colebras holds 2 bovates for 3 shillings.

The rent-paying tenants[3] are these:

William of Tatenhill holds 2 bovates for 2 shillings.

Alured the pilgrim holds 2 bovates for 2 shillings.

Ulwin holds 2 bovates for 3 shillings, and he must perform the same customs as those performed by the rent-paying tenants at Burton.

Orm holds 8 bovates of the 'warland' and has 7 men holding under him, each one of whom holds 1 bovate and the seventh 2 bovates.[4] The same Orm holds 24 acres of 'inland' and 16 acres of meadow. He must go to the pleas, and to courts of the shire and the wapentake, and on expeditions[5] and wherever he may be sent, either with the abbot or without the abbot; and he owes 4 boon-works at the

[1] See above, p. 821 n.4. [2] MS. adds *summa est xl.* [3] *censarii.*

[4] This holding shows the interesting development of the subletting of tenant-land.

[5] *exercitus.*

court, and 2 at the wood, and he goes to the hunts when he is ordered, and twice a year he lends his plough and thrice in August he reaps with all his men.

Tracemusca holds 2 bovates for 2 shillings.

Godwine the blond holds 2 bovates for 3 shillings.

The land of Alured is waste. He holds 2 bovates for 2 *oras*.[1]

Aschetil Wardbois has 2 bovates of 'inland' for 2 shillings and for his service. In the wood are 3 charcoal furnaces in demesne.[2]

In Stretton there is as much 'inland' as can be served by 3 ploughs. Now there are 2 with 16 oxen. A mare and a foal.

The land of the men is assessed to the geld at 1½ hides.

The villeins are: Leuric the reeve; Algar, his son; Alveva; Raura; Alward; Godwine; Levenot; Meriet; Baldwin; Ernesius; Ordric; Edwin; another Levenot; Lewin Wite; Walter the ox-herd; Ailwi; Elric; Eilmund Smith.

Each of these men holds 2 bovates and works [for the lord] 2 days in each week, and owes all the customs which the villeins of Burton owe except that they plough a whole acre in Lent.

The rent-payers[3] are these:

Ulnod the mason holds 2 bovates of 'warland' and 2 of 'inland' for 6 shillings.

Ailward holds 2 bovates for 3 shillings and he owes 2 boon-works at the court and 2 at the wood, and twice a year he must offer his plough, and three times in August he must reap with his household.

Edric 'de Fonte' holds 2 bovates of 'warland', and 3 acres of land and 3 acres of meadow in the 'inland', and he owes 2 boon-works at the court and 2 at the wood, and he must offer his plough twice and reap thrice.

William Gamel holds 5 bovates of 'warland', and 9 acres of land and 3 acres of meadow in the 'inland', and he owes 5 boon-works at the court and 5 at the wood and the rest of the customs.

Hugh 'le Sele' holds 3 bovates for 6 shillings and 4 pence and owes 4 boon-works at the court and 4 at the wood and the aforesaid customs.

The son of Algar holds 1 bovate of 'warland' and pays the king's geld.

Edric holds 3 bovates of 'inland' for 10 shillings and owes to the abbot the king's geld in respect of the 'inland', and he owes also 4 boon-works at the court and at the wood with the aforesaid customs.

Steinchete the man of Orm of Okeover holds 4 bovates of 'warland' and 2 bovates of 'inland' and owes 4 boon-works at the court and the rest of the aforesaid customs.

Edwin holds 2 mills for 25 shillings and a salmon. This is what he shall pay for 3 years and afterwards he shall hold it for 30 shillings.

8 bovates of land are waste and 4 dwellings. Of these Aschetil of the castle holds 2 bovates for 2 shillings.

4 ox-herds are in Stretton, Lewin Wite, Walter, Ailwi, Elric, and one in Wetmore, by name Leuric; each holds 2 bovates and 4 acres sown in return for

[1] The *ora*, a Scandinavian reckoning of money, usually of 16 pence. The meaning of this entry is doubtful.
[2] MS. adds *summa est*. [3] *censarii*.

their service, and their wives work for 1 day in the week. They must return the sown acres if their oxen are lacking.

Eilmund the smith holds 2 bovates for 16 pence.

Brand holds 2 bovates for 22 pence.

Tovi the deaf holds 1 dwelling and 1 acre of meadow and 1 acre of arable land for 12 pence.

Algar holds 2 bovates for 2 shillings.

Big Hugh holds 6 bovates for 8 shillings.

Edric the forester holds 2 bovates in Horninglow for 3 shillings.

(ii) *Account given of Burton, Branston and Stretton in the later of the Burton Surveys*

[This survey, sometimes known as Survey 'A', is later in date than Survey 'B' printed above. It may be assigned to the years 1116–1128 and should probably be placed in or about the year 1126. It is thus nearly contemporary with the Peterborough Survey (see below, No. 177).]

In Burton there is 'inland' for 2 ploughs on the demesne. The land of the men is assessed at 1½ hides. On the 'warland' are 15 bovates held by work and 15 by pay,[1] that is to say between the two, 30 bovates. Among those who hold by work are 2 ox-herds holding 2 bovates, that is, each one holds 1 bovate. And Rauechetus holds 1 bovate. 6 villeins hold the remainder of these bovates–that is to say 12 bovates–each one holding 2 bovates. Besides this, another 2 ox-herds each hold by work 6 acres of 'inland'.

Aluric Salverius,[2] the cottar, holds 1 dwelling and works for 1 day.
William the cobbler holds a dwelling and works 1 day.
Bristold holds 1 dwelling and works 1 day.
Lewin Fiton holds 1 dwelling and works 1 day.
Godric with the beard holds 1 dwelling and works for 1 day.
Another Godric holds 1 dwelling and works for 1 day.
Ulviet holds 1 dwelling and works for 1 day.
Wulfric the carpenter holds 1 dwelling and works for 1 day.
Hardwin holds 1 dwelling for 1 'vano' and 1 'cana'.
Lewi holds 1 dwelling and works for 1 day.
These are those who hold at pay:[3]

Wardbois holds 2 bovates for 2 shillings.
Ailric holds 2 bovates for 2 shillings.
Gladewin holds 2 bovates for 36 shillings.
Steynulf holds 2 bovates for 3 shillings.
Aluric holds 2 bovates and 1 croft and 1 dwelling for 3 shillings.
Uctebrand holds 2 bovates for 2 shillings.

[1] *ad malam.*

[2] These are the typical cottars' holdings, each of which owes 1 day's ploughing work in the fields for the lord. It will be noted that many of these tenants practise a trade.

[3] *ad malam:* the meaning here seems to be clearly "for pay" corresponding to the *censarii* of the earlier survey.

Lepsi holds 1 bovate for 12 pence.
Alsi holds 1 bovate for 12 pence.
Godric the carpenter holds 1 bovate for 12 pence.
Terric holds 1 dwelling.
Odard holds 1 dwelling for 16 pence.
Droet holds 1 dwelling for 16 pence.
William the cook holds 1 dwelling for 18 pence.
Gilbert holds 1 dwelling for 16 pence.
Aluric holds 1 dwelling for 16 pence.
Acelin holds 1 dwelling and 1 acre of land for 12 pence.
Ælmer holds 1 dwelling for 18 pence.
Godwine holds 1 dwelling for 12 pence.
Leflet holds 1 dwelling for 12 pence.
Cacerel holds 1 dwelling for 6 pence.
Frawin holds 1 dwelling for 16 pence.
Lepsi holds 3 mills for 31 shillings. The sum of this is .[1]

Besides this Ulsi holds in Shobnall 1 dwelling and 3 acres of land and 1 acre of meadow for 12 pence.

Ingelram in Burton holds 1 dwelling for 12 pence.

Aluric holds in Burton 4 acres of land and in Wetmore 7 acres of the 'inland' and 1 acre of meadow for 18 pence.

Ælmer and Herl and Semer each hold in Shobnall a dwelling and 3 acres of land and 1 acre of meadow for 12 pence.

Wardbois has in Burton 6 acres of 'inland' for 18 pence.

Godwine holds 1 bovate for 18 pence which before was held by the son of Rauechet.

Alfred holds 1 dwelling and 5 acres of 'inland' and 1 acre of meadow for 12 pence.

Ernwi the gardener holds a dwelling and a croft for 12 pence.
Heort holds 1 dwelling for 12 pence.
Ailward Copro holds 1 dwelling for 12 pence.
Ernwi the huntsman holds 1 dwelling by work.
Big Hugh holds 1 dwelling for 12 pence.
Rannulf holds 1 dwelling for 12 pence.
Ælmer, the son of Allic, holds 4 acres of 'inland' in Shobnall for 12 pence.

In Branston is as much 'inland' as is sufficient for the 2 ploughs on the demesne. The land of the men is assessed at $1\frac{1}{2}$ hides. In the 'warland' are 11 bovates held by work and 15 bovates held by pay, that is to say, 26 bovates in all. Of the bovates held by work, Osbern the ox-herd has 1. The rest, that is to say, 10 bovates, are held by 5 villeins, and each villein has 2 bovates. Besides this, Brunning the reeve holds 2 bovates of the 'inland' by work, and he pays his geld to the abbot.

Gildenehele the cottar has a dwelling on the 'inland' and works for 1 day.

Edwin the ox-herd has 1 dwelling on the 'inland'.

[1] Blank in MS.

Wallevus has 14 acres of the 'inland' and 1½ acres of meadow for 18 pence, and this is outside the farm.

Besides this Orm holds 8 bovates of 'warland' and 4 bovates of 'inland'.

These are those who hold by pay:[1]

Godwine the blond holds 2 bovates of 'warland' and 1 acre of 'inland' for 3 shillings.

Tracemusca holds 2 bovates of 'warland' and 4 acres of arable and 1 acre of meadow on the 'inland' for 3 shillings.

Ulsi holds 2 bovates of 'warland' and an acre of 'inland' for 3 shillings.

Ulwin holds 2 bovates of 'warland' and 1 croft for 3 shillings.

Calebras holds 2 bovates for 3 shillings.

Alured holds 2 bovates for 32 pence.

William of Tatenhill holds 2 bovates for 2 shillings.

Aschetill holds 1 bovate for 18 pence.

Toli holds 1 bovate of 'inland' for 15 pence.

Wardebois holds 1 bovate of 'inland' without a croft for 12 pence.

The sum is 23 shillings and 5 pence.

In the wood are 3 charcoal furnaces in the demesne. And Robert of Ferrières[2] holds part of the wood belonging to Branston for 20 shillings. And for a watersluice in 'Eginton', including 34 feet of dry land which by agreement ought to belong to us, he restored to our demesne after the death of Arfast, Tichnall which he used to hold from us for 10 shillings.

Edwin the monk holds the land of this manor at 'farm' for 100 shillings a year, except the wood and the hedges and except the land which used to belong to Tracemusca, all of which the abbot has in his own hand. Now Herbert holds the land which used to belong to Tracemusca, that is 2 bovates, for 3 shillings. And the land which was Orm's three of his sons hold in like manner. Uviet has 2 bovates for 2 shillings, and he owes the customs of the other rent-paying tenants. Raven and Leysing have the rest of the 'warland', that is 6 bovates, and 4 bovates of 'inland' for 8 [shillings] a year, and they must go to the hundred court of Offlow,[3] and besides this they perform all the customs of the other rent-paying tenants.

In Stretton is as much 'inland' as will suffice for the 2 very strong ploughs on the demesne.

The land of the men defends itself for 1½ hides.

In the 'warland' are 32 bovates held by work, and between the 'warland' and the 'inland' 32 bovates held at rent, making in all 64 bovates. Of the bovates held by work, Leuric the reeve holds 2 bovates; Eilmund Smith 2 bovates; Orm Halesoen 2 bovates; and 4 ox-herds 8 bovates. 9 villeins hold the remaining 18 bovates, that is to say each villein holds 2 bovates.

Robert has 1 dwelling on the 'inland', and his wife works for 1 day.

[1] *ad malam.*

[2] Robert of Ferrières-St. Hilaire, third son of Henry of Ferrières, the Domesday tenant-in-chief. He later became first earl of Derby.

[3] Cf. below. pp. 831, 832, 845.

Concerning the bovates which are held at pay:[1]

William holds 5 bovates of 'warland', and 9 acres of 'inland', and 3 acres of meadow, and a certain pear orchard for 8 shillings.

Andrew holds 4 bovates of 'warland' and 2 of 'inland' which Orm held and in addition another 2 bovates of 'warland', that is to say 8 bovates in all for 8 shillings.

Gilbert holds 2 bovates of 'warland' and 2 of 'inland' for 6 shillings.

Hugh 'le Sele' holds 3 bovates of 'warland' and 23 acres with 4 acres of meadow of 'inland' for 6 shillings.

Edric, son of Algar, holds 2 bovates of 'warland' and 4 of 'inland', and for these 4 he pays geld to the abbot.

Edric 'de Fonte' holds 2 bovates of 'warland' and 6 acres of 'inland' for 3 shillings.

Osbern holds 2 bovates of 'warland' for 3 shillings.

Tovi holds a dwelling and a croft and 1 acre of land and 1 acre of meadow of 'inland' for 12 pence.

Edwin holds a mill for 20 shillings.

Ordric, son of Algar, holds 2 bovates for 3 shillings; formerly Raven held these by work.

Besides this, William holds 2 acres of 'warland', that is the land, Merget,[2] and 2 bovates of 'inland' by the service of his body.

Also Eilmund Smith holds 2 bovates of 'inland' for 3 shillings; these were formerly held by an ox-herd.

Also Raven, son of Leuric, holds 2 acres of 'inland' for 3 shillings and he must pay geld to the abbot.

Also Algar holds 2 bovates of 'warland' by work.

These last-named 4 bovates were previously held by Gilbert.

The afore-mentioned 2 bovates which Eilmund holds lack a croft and a meadow.

Also Alwi the cottar has 1 dwelling and a croft on the 'inland', and 1 acre of meadow, and he works for 1 day in the week.

Orm the smith has a dwelling and a croft of 'warland' in Horninglow, and an acre of meadow, for 12 pence or for 2 ploughing services; this was previously held by Ailwin by work.

Also in Stretton Edwin the miller holds the land which Gamel held for 4 shillings.

Ernwi holds by work 1 bovate which formerly William the cook held by rent.

Soen holds 2½ acres of 'inland' for 4 pence, and also 8 acres, that is 1 bovate, for 12 pence.

Algar holds a dwelling and a croft and an acre, and 1 acre of meadow in the 'inland' by work; Tovi formerly held it for 12 pence.

Ailwin Halsoen holds 4 acres of land and 1 acre of meadow in the 'inland' for 12 pence; so long as Halsoen held it, it was held by work.

[1] *ad malam.* [2] Or perhaps "the land of Margaret".

177. Surveys of certain manors belonging to the abbey of Peterborough (1125–1128)

These surveys are taken from the "Black Book" of Peterborough which was compiled as an account of all the abbot's possessions some time in the years 1125–1128, during which time Henry I had possession of the temporalities of the monastery. The clerk who drew it up seems to have been familiar with the terms used in the royal Exchequer, and to have had some knowledge not only of conditions in his own time, but also of those in the time of Edward the Confessor (see F. M. Stenton, *Types of Manorial Structure in the Northern Danelaw* (1910), p. 6). The "Black Book" is of great value as an early description of the manorial economy, and as such it may be compared with the more generalized statements of *Rectitudines Singularum Personarum* (No. 172). It has been used in most discussions of early manorial history. It is printed as an appendix to T. Stapleton, *Chronicon Petroburgense* (Camden Soc., 1849), and what follows is the account of a few typical manors taken from this record.

This is the description of the manors of the abbey of Peterborough as Walter the archdeacon received them and possessed them in the hand of the king.

In Kettering are 10 hides for the king's geld. And of these 10 hides 40 villeins hold 40 virgates. And these men plough in the spring from each virgate 4 acres for the work of the lord. And besides this they provide ploughs for the work of the lord four times in the winter, and three times in the spring and once in the summer. And these men have 22 ploughs with which they work. And all these men work for the lord 3 days in each week. And besides this they render each year from each virgate by custom 2 shillings and 3 halfpence. And all the men render 50 hens and 640 eggs. And besides this, Ailric holds 13 acres with 2 acres of meadow, and pays for them 16 pence. And there is a mill with a miller and it pays 20 shillings. And 8 cottars each of whom has 5 acres and they work (for the lord) 1 day each week, and twice a year they make malt. And each one of them gives 1 penny for a he-goat (if he has one) and 1 halfpenny for a nanny-goat. And there is a shepherd and a swine-herd who holds 8 acres. And in the court of the demesne there are 4 ploughs with 32 oxen, and 12 cows with 10 calves, 2 beasts for food, 3 draught horses, 300 sheep, 50 pigs, and 16 shillings' worth of the surplus hay from the meadow. The church of Kettering belongs to the altar of the abbey of Peterborough. And for the love of St. Peter it renders 4 rams and 2 cows or 5 shillings. . . .

In Pilsgate there are 3 hides for the king's geld. And 3 villeins hold 1 hide and 1 virgate. And these have 2 ploughs with which they plough for the lord 8 acres for the winter sowing and 8 acres for the spring sowing; and they work 3 days each week for the lord. And there is 1 bordar and 2 ox-herds holding land by service. And there is 1 shepherd. And there are 44 sokemen. And all these together with the villeins pay 44 shillings a year. And all these sokemen have 8 ploughs and with them they plough for the lord three times a year. And each one of them reaps in August half an acre of the lord's corn, and they give boon-work twice in August. And each one harrows 1 day in spring. And there is a mill which pays 4 shillings. And in the court of the demesne there is 1 plough with 8 oxen, and 1 boar and 2 calves and 1 horse for harrowing and 2 foals. And 180 sheep and 20 pigs. On the Feast of St. Peter[1] [is paid] 6 sheep or 1 cow and 5 ells of cloth.

In Thorpe Achurch are 2 hides and 1 virgate for the king's geld. And there are 12 full villeins and each one of them holds 11 acres and works (for the lord) 3 days each week. And 6 half-villeins who perform the same in proportion to their holdings.

[1] 29 June.

And all of these make a customary payment of 10 shillings. And besides this they pay for love of St. Peter 5 'multones', and 10 ells of cloth,[1] and 10 baskets and 200 loaves. And all these men plough 16½ acres for the lord's work. And there are 6 bordars who pay 7 shillings. And all these pay each year 22 skepfuls of oats in return for dead wood and 22 loaves and 64 hens and 160 eggs. And one sokeman is there who performs service with a horse. And William, son of Ansered, holds a fourth part of 3 yardlands by knight-service. And William, son of Odard the cook, holds a fourth part of 3 yardlands by service in the abbot's kitchen. And the men of this William perform work for the court, that is to say, they provide their ploughs for the lord twice a year. And on the land of this William there are 4 full villeins who reap half an acre in August. And Godric holds a fourth part of 3 yardlands, and for that he and his horse do the abbot's service, providing their own food. And this Godric has 3 villeins and each one of them reaps half an acre for the abbot in August, and with their ploughs they perform two boon-works. In the court of the demesne there are 2 ploughs with 16 oxen, and 3 cows and 8 beasts for food and 1 draught horse and 8 pigs.

In Collingham[2] there are 4 carucates and 1 bovate less a fifth part of 1 bovate for the king's geld. And there are 20 villeins who hold 1½ carucates. Each one of these works[3] for the lord throughout the year 1 day in each week. And in August he performs 3 boon-works. And all these men bring 60 cartloads of wood to the lord's court, and they also dig and provide 20 cartloads of turves, or 20 cartloads of thatch. And they must harrow throughout the winter. And each year they pay 4 pounds of rent. And there are 50 sokemen who hold 2½ carucates of land. And each one of these must work by custom each year for 6 days at the deer hedge. And in August each shall work 3 days. And all these have 14 ploughs and with them they shall work for the lord four times in Lent. And they plough 48 acres, and harrow, and reap in August. And the aforesaid sokemen pay 12 pounds each year. And in the court of the demesne are 2 ploughs with 16 oxen, and 4 cows and calves and 1 beast for food and 160 sheep and 12 pigs. . . .

178. Survey of the manor of Stukeley, Hunts., made for the abbot of Ramsey in the time of Henry I

A short survey of interest as showing the varieties of tenure in a Huntingdonshire village in the time of Henry I and Henry II. Printed: *Cartularium Monasterii de Rameseia* (Rolls Series, 1893), vol. III, p. 274.

At Stukeley are 7 hides.

The village rendered 7 pounds in the time of King Henry.[4] It had then this equipment: 3 ploughs with 30 oxen were then at the court, and each of the oxen was worth 3 shillings. There were then 3 horses,[5] each worth 3 shillings; 100 sheep; and 2 horses for harrowing.

These were the freemen who were enfeoffed in those days:

Jocelyn of Stukeley held 2 hides and 1 virgate. He followed the county and the hundred and the pleas of the abbot.

[1] *lineo panno.*

[2] This is Collingham, Notts., and the assessments are in carucates and bovates, not hides and virgates, as is the case in Domesday Book.

[3] Note the lighter duties of the villeins, characteristic of peasant concessions in the Danelaw.

[4] Henry I.

[5] *caballi* not *equi*. Compare the valuation at Elton; see below, No. 179.

Robert the knight held 1½ hides and performed the same service.

Fulk of 'Lisures' held 1 hide for which he likewise followed the pleas of the abbot. He also held 2½ virgates in Ripton. In those days these pertained to Stukeley, but now they are not there. One of them used to pay 5 shillings and the rest were held by work.

2 hides and 1 virgate, that is to say, 9 virgates, were then held by work and not by pay. And this is the service which each (holder of a) virgate then performed and now still performs:

From Michaelmas to the beginning of August he works 2 days in each week and ploughs on a third, except at Christmas and Easter and Pentecost. And from the beginning of August until Michaelmas he works the whole week except on Saturdays. He gives 4 hens at Christmas.

To the church there belonged in those days half a virgate quit of service, and it still so belongs.

Henry Lenveise now holds 1 rood.

The house of Henry the archdeacon is on the abbot's demesne.

Thomas, son of Henry, holds 1 virgate which formerly was held by work. Now he gives for it 4 shillings. In the time of Abbot Walter[1] it only paid 2 shillings.

Four cottars dwell on the demesne, and they work every Monday, and 2 days in each week during August.

Adam, son of Henry the archdeacon, now holds this village for 8 pounds and with 2 ploughs.[2]

179. Survey of the manor of Elton, Hunts., made for the abbot of Ramsey in the time of Henry II

Interesting, not only as being itself an early survey, but also for its copious references to conditions in the time of Henry I. Comparison may here therefore be made in this respect between the earlier and the latter half of the twelfth century. Printed in *Cartularium Monasterii de Rameseia* (Rolls Series, 1893), vol. III, p. 257.

At Elton there were in the time of King Henry,[3] and still are,[4] 10½ hides, each containing 5 virgates. And in those days it rendered full payment in all things, and 10 pounds to the treasury of the abbot. It had this equipment: 5 ploughs each of 8 oxen, and each worth 40 pence; 10 cows and 1 bull of his price; 160 sheep; 2 horses for harrowing; and 100 pigs.

Of the free fees Reiner, son of Ædnoth, in the time of King Henry had 3 free virgates for which he followed the county and the hundred.[5]

Thuri the priest had 2 virgates and he followed the county and the hundred. And he had also 10 acres and a toft worth 8 pence adjoining the church.

Edward, the father of Jordan, had 1½ virgates. And he followed the county and

[1] Abbot of Ramsey, 1133–1160.

[2] That is to say he farms it for the abbot at a rent of 8 pounds.

[3] Henry I.

[4] When the survey was taken, *i.e.* in the time of Henry II.

[5] The duty of attending the courts of shire and hundred. This burden had at an early date after the Conquest been attached to particular holdings. On the importance of this class of 'hundredors', see P. Vinogradoff, *Villainage in England*, pp. 188–194, and F. W. Maitland, in *Eng. Hist. Rev.*, vol. III (1888), pp. 417 *et sqq*.

the hundred. And he ploughed half an acre every Friday. And he harrowed. He also gave 2 shillings a year for rent and 13 pence as 'heusire'.[1] This land Jordan, his son, now holds for the same service except that he pays 12 pence more.

Blundel, the grandfather of Gilbert, had 1½ virgates by the same service. And Gilbert, his grandson, now holds the same land in the same manner. The aforesaid Blundel also had then another 1½ virgates for which he paid 7 shillings and this his son, Richard, now holds in the same manner.

Gilbert the reeve then held and now holds 1 virgate in like manner by payment of 6 shillings and by ploughing 6 acres. He holds also another virgate for 7 shillings.[2]

Thorold the priest held 1 virgate for 6 shillings and was free from all work and service. And Rainald, the brother of Robert the clerk, now holds this land in the same manner and is free.

Gisla the widow had then, and still has, 1 virgate for 6 shillings and by ploughing 6 acres.

The mill with 1 virgate and with 6½ acres used formerly to give 40 shillings. And he who farmed the village had then his provision from it.

Alan Ruffus has 2 crofts for 4 shillings by the grant of Abbot Walter;[3] and 1 virgate which was held by a certain man named Dac for 4 shillings.

In the days of King Henry[4] there were in this village 35 virgates held by work,[5] and on the demesne were the holdings of 8 ox-herds and 1 swine-herd and 1 shepherd.[6] Now, however, there are no more than 28½ virgates held by work.

And this is the work and the service of [the holder of] 1 virgate:

> From Michaelmas to the beginning of August he works for 2 days in each week and ploughs for a third, except at Christmas and Easter and Pentecost. And from the beginning of August to the Nativity of St. Mary[7] he works for 3 days each week. And from the Nativity of St. Mary until Michaelmas he works every day except Saturday. In winter he ploughs half an acre, and sows it with his own seed; and he harrows and reaps this, and also another half-acre in August.[8] And he performs carrying services at his own expense. And he makes 2 mitts[9] of malt from the lord's corn and the sixth part of 1 'milla'. He makes payments for rights on the common; and he pays 13 pence as 'heusire'. He pays also 4 pence at Michaelmas, and 1 halfpenny for wool. And he shall go errands: if he goes outside the county he shall be quit of his week's work except for ploughing. And in August he gives 1 carrying service of timber, and 1 work at fencing and he performs 2 carrying services of corn in August. And each 5 virgates give 4 pence for fish, and each 2 virgates give 1 cart of thatch, and they make the thatch. When the winnower comes there, all shall go to the court and thresh the corn from day to day

[1] Probably house payment.
[2] It is noteworthy that in the time of Henry I the suit to the shire court from Elton seems to have been discharged by the reeve, the priest and four best men of the village.
[3] Abbot of Ramsey, 1160; became abbot of Cluny, 1177.
[4] Henry I.
[5] *ad opus.*
[6] Cf. *Rectitudines Singularum Personarum* (above, No. 172).
[7] 8 September.
[8] Note the variation of week-work during the seasons and its increase at harvest-time.
[9] Possibly 8 bushels.

until the 'farm' is made up. And if there is such hard frost in winter that he cannot plough, then he shall work on Fridays instead of ploughing. And when the farmer calls for boon-works in August he shall come to them with his whole household, and he shall then be fed by the farmer.

After the death of King Henry, Ralph of 'Asekirche' received from Abbot Walter[1] at a rent of 6 shillings 1 virgate which previously had been held by work.

Richard, son of Rainald, has 2 virgates which Thuri the priest held.

Franceis holds 1 virgate for 6 shillings and by ploughing 6 acres.

Geoffrey of Walsoken holds 1 virgate for 6 shillings and by ploughing 6 acres.

Gilbert of Newton holds 1 virgate for 6 shillings and by ploughing 6 acres.

Gilbert of 'Loituna' holds 1 virgate and 1 toft for 6 shillings, and he ploughs every Friday. And he harrows. He also holds 1 rood for 4 pence.

Godwine the white holds 1 virgate for 5 shillings and by ploughing 3 acres.

This is the equipment in the court of Elton: 4 ploughs with 24 oxen and 8 horses[2] and 10 cows. Each ox and horse is worth 4 shillings; each cow is worth 40 pence. 160 sheep; 26 pigs of more than a year old; and 24 piglets; 16 cocks at work. With this equipment it now renders the full 'farm', and 10 pounds in money; with the mill which gives 100 shillings.

A certain William has half an acre for 2 pence.

Master Ralph has an acre of the demesne.

The men of Elton give 17 pence for a croft.

And this is the sum of the payment of Elton: 6 pounds, besides the 28½ virgates which are held by work.

Robert, brother of Thurkil, holds an acre of land for 16 pence.

Of 13 acrelands the six better pay 18 shillings, and each of the others gives 20 pence.

There are 2 tofts which Ketelburn and the widows hold for 18 pence.

Walter pays 15 pence for a toft.

A certain widow, 6 pence.

Thomas, 12 pence.

Hestida, 12 pence.

Ralph, 12 pence.

Roger, 18 pence.

Hurri, 12 pence.

Hured, 12 pence.

Ailsueda, 12 pence.

Robert, 12 pence.

Geoffrey the cobbler, 12 pence.

Siwald, 12 pence.

The other Thomas, 12 pence.

Edward holds 12 acres *in lanssetagio*[3] for 9 pence and 1 halfpenny.

Geoffrey holds 12 acres *in lanssetagio* for 9 pence and 1 halfpenny; and 12 acres of demesne for 2 pence; and his sheep for 8 pence.

[1] Abbot of Ramsey, 1133–1160.

[2] Compare this with the ploughs at the time of Henry I.

[3] Literally land-settlement; here apparently used to imply tenant-land.

180. Select surveys from the "Boldon Book" (1183)

In 1183 there was drawn up, by order of Hugh le Puiset, bishop of Durham, a record designed to assist the administration of the vast estates of the bishopric of Durham. This record is traditionally known as the "Boldon Book" because the services rendered at Boldon are very often referred to elsewhere in the record as a standard. The main interest of the record lies in the contrast it indicates between the agrarian economy of the north and south of England. In particular there may here be noted the existence of large estates often comprising several villages (see below, p. 835) which sometimes share a single demesne. This record also frequently reflects an economy based primarily on pastoral pursuits. The Boldon Book has been used in most discussions of the agrarian history of England in the twelfth century, and particular reference should perhaps be made to R. Reid, "Baronage and Thegnage", *Eng. Hist. Rev.*, vol. XXXV, p. 161; and also to J. E. A. Jolliffe, "Northumbrian Tenures", *ibid.*, vol. XLI, p. 1. But the fullest discussion of the Boldon Book and its testimony is that made by G. T. Lapsley; it is to be found in *Victoria County History: Durham*, vol. I (1905), pp. 259–317. The Boldon Book was printed by H. Ellis in his supplementary volume to the Record Commission edition of Domesday Book (vol. IV, 1816), but the best edition of the Latin text is by W. Greenwell (Surtees Soc., 1852). An admirable translation of the whole record (which has been followed in the extracts here printed) was made by G. T. Lapsley and is contained in *Victoria County History: Durham*, vol I (1905), pp. 327–351.

In the eleven hundred and eighty-third year of our Lord's Incarnation, at the Feast of St. Cuthbert in Lent, Lord Hugh, bishop of Durham, caused to be described in the presence of himself and his court all the returns of his whole bishopric, and its assizes and customs as they then were and as they had been aforetime. . . .

In Boldon there are 22 villeins, every one of whom holds 2 bovates of land of 30 acres and renders 2 shillings and 6 pence of scotpenny and the half of a scot-chalder of oats and 16 pence of averpenny and 5 wagonloads of wood and 2 hens and 10 eggs, and works throughout the whole year 3 days in the week except Easter and Whitsun-week and 13 days at Christmastide, and in his works he does in the autumn 4 boon-days at reaping with his entire household, except the housewife, and they reap, moreover, 3 roods of the standing crop of oats and he ploughs 3 roods of oat-stubble and harrows it. Every plough of the villeins, also, ploughs 2 acres and harrows, and then they have once a dole from the bishop and for that week they are quit of work, but when they make the great boon-days they have a dole. And in their works they harrow when it is necessary and they carry loads, and when they have carried them every man has a loaf of bread; and they mow one day at Houghton in their work until the evening, and then they have a dole. And every two villeins build one booth for the fair of St. Cuthbert. And when they are building lodges and carrying loads of wood they are quit of all other works. There are 12 cottars there, every one of whom holds 12 acres, and they work through the whole year 2 days in the week, except at the three feasts aforenamed, and they render 12 hens and 60 eggs.

Robert holds 2 bovates of 36 acres and renders half a mark.

The pinder holds 12 acres and he has a thrave of corn from every plough, and he renders 40 hens and 500 eggs.

The mill renders 5½ marks.

The villeins in their work in each year ought to make, if need be, a house 40 feet in length and 15 feet in breadth, and when they make it every man is quit of 4 pence of averpenny. The whole village renders 17 shillings of cornage[1] and 1 milch cow.

[1] The *cornage* payments which are so often mentioned in this record have been widely discussed. J. H. Round (*Commune of London* (1899), pp. 278–288) showed that these payments were not derived from castle-guard as had been sometimes supposed; G. T. Lapsley ("Cornage and Drengage", *Amer. Hist. Rev.*,

The demesne is at 'farm' with stock of 4 ploughs and 4 harrows and tenders for 2 ploughs, 16 chalders of wheat and 16 chalders of oats and 8 chalders of barley, and for the other 2 ploughs 10 marks. . . .

In Quarringtonshire, namely in North Sherburn and Shadforth and Cassop, there are 51 villeins and every man holds, renders and works as they do at Boldon. Also in North Sherburn, Ulkill holds 2 bovates for 40 pence of rent and goes on the bishop's errands. And Thomas of Shadforth holds 2 bovates for 40 pence of rent and goes on the bishop's errands. In Cassop, William of Kent holds 4 bovates for half a mark and goes on the bishop's errands. In South Sherburn, Christian the mason holds 40 acres which the bishop gave him from the moor for 5 shillings and 2 bovates which used to belong to Arkill for 14 pence, but of these he shall be quit while he is in the service of the bishop as mason. Watling with Sama, his wife, holds 4 bovates and renders half a mark. Also 5 firmars who hold there every man 12 acres and each one renders 2 shillings and 1 hen and 20 eggs, and does 4 boon-days in the autumn, and for every one of their ploughs they plough 1 acre. Also there are 10 cottars there, every man of whom holds 6 acres, and they work from Lammas Day to Martinmas 2 days in the week, and from Martinmas to Lammas Day 1 day in the week. The smith holds 12 acres there for making the iron gear of the ploughs. The pinder of Quarringtonshire holds 20 acres and renders 120 hens and 1000 eggs. The demesne of Sherburn is at 'farm' with a stock of 2 ploughs and 2 harrows and renders 6 pounds. The demesne of Quarrington has 4 ploughs, and the sheep with the pasture are in the hand of the bishop. The reeve holds 1 bovate there for his service. The smith holds 12 acres for his service.

Quarringtonshire renders 75 shillings of cornage and 3 milch cows. . . .

* * *

(*b*) SELECT CHARTERS AND 'WILLS' ILLUSTRATING ENGLISH AGRARIAN SOCIETY BETWEEN 1042 AND 1189

The documents which here follow illustrate varieties of land tenure during this period, but they do not include texts which relate more specifically to the establishment of the Anglo-Norman feudal aristocracy. These will be found below (Nos. 235–267). The documents here following will be found of especial value for the condition of the thegn in the time of Edward the Confessor, and for the history of non-military tenures of land after the Conquest. They illustrate, though usually incidentally, the village, the manor and the soke as agrarian units. The very numerous charters made by free peasants, or witnessed by them in the latter part of the twelfth century, can only be sparsely illustrated in a volume of this nature, and the examples given of them (Nos. 195–197) deserve attention as representative of a large and important class of documents. It is, moreover, a cardinal feature of the documentary history of this period that such charters come in greatest abundance from East Anglia and the Danelaw, that is to say, from those regions where Domesday Book describes a peasant society more generally free in status than that to the south and west.

vol. IX (1904), pp. 670 *et sqq.*) in a learned and exhaustive article contended that this due originated in payments made to lords for rights of pasture; N. Neilson (*Customary Rents* (1910), pp. 120–121) suggests that cornage was originally "simply a form of the geld which in the north, in localities where pasture was common and agriculture less common, happened to be levied on the number of animals possessed by the individual or by the vill, instead of on the unit of land".

181. The 'will' (in Anglo-Saxon) of Ælfric Modercope (*circa* 1043)

This text should be compared with that which immediately follows it. Ælfric had commended himself to the abbots of Bury St. Edmunds and Ely. These two abbots now benefit by his 'will'. Printed, translated and annotated by D. Whitelock, *Anglo-Saxon Wills* (1930), pp. 74, 185.

This is the will which Ælfric made before he went across the sea. First to St. Edmund's, Loddon, woodland, open land and fen, with as full rights as ever I owned it; and I grant the estate at Bergh to St. Etheldreda's[1] with all the rights with which I acquired it, both woodland and open land; and Barton to St. Benedict's at Holme, with as full rights as those with which I owned it. And I grant to Ramsey 6 marks of silver, and that my brother, Godric, is to pay. And I grant 'Thurwineholm' with Loddon and 'Fuglholm' with Bergh. And the sheep are to be divided into two parts, half for Loddon and half for Bergh. And for my heriot bequeath 1 mark of gold, and Godric, my brother, is to pay it. And I bequeath to Bishop Ælfric my tent and my bed-clothing, the best that I had out on my journey with me. And Bishop Ælfric, Tofi the proud,[2] and Thrym are to be executors of this will, especially in order that no one may alter it. And if anyone wishes to alter it, may God Almighty turn his face from him on the Day of Judgment.

182. Writ (in Anglo-Saxon) of Edward the Confessor granting permission that Ælfric Modercope should commend himself to the abbots of Bury St. Edmunds and Ely (*circa* 1048)

An excellent example of commendation, that is to say, of the voluntary submission by one man to another in return for protection. Commendation normally implied service or gifts from the commended man. Estates were bequeathed by Ælfric to both Bury St. Edmunds and to Ely. This text illustrates further how commendation could be divided, as is frequently stated in the East Anglian Domesday Book. It also suggests that Ælfric had previously been a man of the king, but was free (in the Domesday phrase) to "go with his land where he would". Text printed and translated in B. Thorpe, *Diplomatarium Anglicum* (1865), p. 416.

I, King Edward, greet Bishop Aylmer and Earl Ælfgar and all my thegns in Suffolk and in Norfolk, friendly. And I give you to know that I will, and that it is my full grant, that Ælfric Modercope may put himself under the two abbots, at St. Edmund's and at St. Etheldreda's, by God's leave and mine.

183. A bequest (in Anglo-Saxon) by Thurstan, son of Wine (1042–1043)

Interesting for the tenure from Christ Church, Canterbury, which it creates, for the manumission clause and for the list of witnesses. Facsimile in *Facsimiles of Anglo-Saxon MSS.* (Ordnance Survey, 1878), part v, no. 25, and (of another copy) in E. A. Bond, *Facsimiles of Ancient Charters in the British Museum*, part iv, no. 33. Text printed, translated and annotated in D. Whitelock, *Anglo-Saxon Wills* (1930), pp. 79, 189.

Here in this document it is made known that Thurstan grants the estate at Wimbish, for his soul and for Leofwaru's and for Æthelgyth's to Christ Church, for the sustenance of the community after Thurstan's death and after Æthelgyth's; but each year, as long as we live, a pound shall be paid as a sufficient proof of the reversionary right. And the community at Christ Church is to pay to the community of

[1] Ely.

[2] He married Gytha, the daughter of Osgod Clapa; see above (No. 2, p. 204).

St. Augustine's, whichever they prefer, 12 pounds 'by tale', or 2 hides. These are the witnesses of this bequest: King Edward and the Lady Ælfgifu[1] and Archbishop Eadsige and Archbishop Ælfric, and Earl Godwine,[2] and Earl Leofric[3] and Ælfgar, the earl's son,[4] and Ælfweard, bishop of London, and Ælfwine, bishop of Winchester, and Stigand the priest, and Eadwold the priest, and Leofcild the sheriff, and Osulf Fila and Ufic and Ælfwine, son of Wulfred, and Ælfric, son of Wihtgar,[5] and all the thegns in Essex.[6] And their men are to be free after the death of both of them. And after their death no one is to have authority on that estate except the community at Christ Church, and those are to inherit whom they know to be entitled. There are three of these documents: one is at Christ Church; the second at St. Augustine's; and the third with the testators themselves.

184. The 'will' (in Anglo-Saxon) of Thurstan, son of Wine (1043–1045)

Interesting as describing the possessions of an important thegn in the time of Edward the Confessor, and in illustrating varieties of tenure. The description of the heriot is also notable, and the list of witnesses is remarkable. Printed, translated and annotated in D. Whitelock, *Anglo-Saxon Wills* (1930), pp. 81, 192.

In our Lord's name I, Thurstan, son of Wine,[7] make known to all men how I grant the things which God has lent to me for as long as it shall be his will. That is I grant the estate at Wimbish to Christ Church for my soul and Leofwaru's and Æthelgyth's; the men are to be free and 12 pounds 'by tale' is to be paid by Christ Church to St. Augustine's. And I grant to St. Edmund's the estate at Harlow, except the half-hide which Ælfwine had at Ealing Bridge, and except the homestead which Ælfgar occupies and the spur of land which belongs to it; and all the men are to be free. And I grant the estate at the north hall at Shouldham to St. Edmund's after the death of both of us; and the men are to be free. And I grant to Ely the estate at Wetheringsett except the land that Æthelric has. He is to hold that freely for his life and his wife's, and after the death of both of them it is to go to the village church, and the men are to be free. And I grant the estate at Knapwell to Ely, except the land which Ordheah and the monk, Æthelric, hold; and the men are to be free. And I grant the estate at Weston to Æthelswith, and after her death to Ely, except the land which Sæwine holds in return for service, which is to go to the village church; and the men are to be free. And I grant half the estate at the middle hall at Shouldham to St. Benedict's at Ramsey and half to St. Benedict's at Holme, as it belongs there after the death of both of us; and the men are to be free. And I grant to my royal lord as heriot 2 marks of gold and 2 horses with trappings, and a helmet and a coat of mail and a sword and 2 shields and 2 spears.[8] And I desire that the estate at 'Bidicheseye' shall be sold, and

[1] The queen mother, mother of Cnut.
[2] Earl of Wessex.
[3] Earl of Mercia.
[4] Son of Leofric; father of Edwin and Morcar.
[5] A notable East Anglian landowner.
[6] This has the appearance of a witan held in Essex.
[7] See above, No. 183.
[8] A heavy heriot applicable to an important king's thegn. The heriot, which must be distinguished from the relief, probably took its origin in the return at death of the arms given by a lord to his man.

that 2 marks of gold shall be taken from that estate for the king's heriot; and Earl Harold[1] is to receive half a mark of gold, and Bishop Stigand half a mark of gold, and my partner[2] 1 mark of gold; and 1 mark of gold is to be given to his child, Thorth's brother, and 1 mark of gold to his child. And what is left over the heirs are to distribute for the sake of his soul in his partner's witness except that the outermost mill is to go to St. Æthelburga's at Barking. And it is my wish that Ulfketel's and my partnership shall hold good on the terms to which we have agreed: namely that the estate at Borough is to go to whichever of us shall live the longer–except half a hide at Westley and a hide at Dullingham which I grant to my servant, Viking–and Ulfketel has laid down on his side 4 marks. And I grant to my wife, Æthelgyth, everything which I have in Norfolk as I gave it her before as a marriage payment and in accordance with our contract; and the estate at Pentlow and at Ashdon except the land at Bromley which is to go to the village church after the death of us both. And I grant to Æthelgyth the estate at Henham except half a hide which is to go to the church. And I grant to the priest, Ælfwig, and to my chaplain, Thurstan, and to my chaplain, Ordheah, that they shall have the estate at Kedington after our death. And I grant to Merewine and his wife and their children the estate at Dunmow except half a hide which is to go to the church, and a homestead. And to my servants I grant the wood at Ongar except the deer enclosure and the stud which I have there. These are the witnesses in Norfolk: Earl Harold[3] and Bishop Stigand, and Osgod Clapa,[4] and Godwine and Wulfgeat and Edwin and Osbeorn and Ulf and Gouti; and in Suffolk: Leofstan the dean[5] and all the community of Bury St. Edmunds, and Eadric, and Ælfric and Ulfketel and Leofmær; and in Cambridgeshire: Abbot Leofsige and all the community at Ely; and Abbot Ælfwine and all the community at Ramsey, and Ælfwine and Ulfketel Cild, and Osgod Sweyn and Ordgar and the other Ordgar; and in Essex: Ælfgar, son of the earl,[6] and Leofcild and Osulf Fila and Wulfwine and Sendi and Leofric the seneschal.[7] He who wishes to alter this will, unless it be I myself, may God destroy him now and on the Day of Judgment. Amen. There are three of these documents: one shall go to St. Edmund's, and one to Ely, and one shall be in my own household.

And Thurstan and Æthelgyth and Askil grant to Æthelswith the estate at Henham after their death; and after the death of all of them the estate is to go to St. Etheldreda's for her own soul and for Thurstan's and for Æthelgyth's and for Leofwaru's and for Askil's except the 2 hides which Æthelmær Parl has, and except the 1 hide which Wulfmær had, and 1 yardland which Lustwine had. And I grant to Thurgot, my servant, a half-hide which Ælfstan occupies at Ongar, and to Merewine a half-hide and the little enclosure near 'Meredene', and to Sweyn half a hide; and they may obtain what is left over by agreement with us both, if we are willing to allow them.

[1] Harold was earl of East Anglia before he succeeded his father as earl of Wessex in 1053 (see above, No. 1, pp. 130, 131). This is perhaps the earliest documentary reference to him as earl.

[2] Partner in the sense of one who holds goods in common with another. The reference is probably here to Ulfketel, to whom the text later alludes.

[3] Earl of East Anglia until 1053.

[4] See the Anglo-Saxon Chronicle, above, No. 1, pp. 114, 117, 132.

[5] Probably the Leofstan who later became abbot of Bury St. Edmunds.

[6] Son of Earl Leofric of Mercia.

[7] Many of these witnesses will be found in the Anglo-Saxon Chronicle (No. 1).

185. Lease of land (in Anglo-Saxon) by Aldred, bishop of Worcester, to Wulfgeat (1046–1053, and probably 1051–1052)

A lease for three lives to a thegn in return for service. This text is printed, translated and annotated in A. J. Robertson, *Anglo-Saxon Charters*, pp. 209, 456.

✠ Here it is declared in this document that Bishop Aldred[1] has granted to Wulfgeat a certain piece of land, namely 1½ hides in the manor called Ditchford, to be held and enjoyed for three lives, and after their time the estate shall return once more to the disposal of him who is in control of the bishopric of Worcester at the time. And they shall always be submissive and obedient and acknowledge the lordship of whoever is bishop at that time, and if they are guilty of any defection they shall forfeit the property.[2] The witnesses of this are all the community at Worcester and the community at Evesham and the community at Pershore and Earl Leofric[3] and Earl Odda[4] and Ælfric, his brother, and Brihtric, son of Ælfgar, and Owine and Wagen and Æthelric, the bishop's brother, and Ceolwine and Atser and Esbearn and Ordwig and Æthelstan the fat and Ælfweard of Longdon, and all the leading thegns in Worcestershire, both Danish and English.[5] And at the king's summons the holder shall discharge the obligations on these 1½ hides at the rate of one for three lives.

186. Writ (in Anglo-Saxon) of Edward the Confessor concerning a housecarl (1045–1058)

Housecarls were essentially the members of a standing bodyguard of a magnate, usually the king, but they might as here be endowed with land. On them, see F. M. Stenton, *English Feudalism* (1932), pp. 119–121. The text which follows is printed and translated in B. Thorpe, *Diplomatarium Anglicum* (1865), p. 414.

I, King Edward, greet Bishop Alfwold and Earl Harold and Alfred the sheriff and all my thegns in Dorsetshire, friendly. And I give you to know that Urk my housecarl may have his strand, all in front of his own land, over all well and freely, up from sea and out on sea, and all that is driven to his strand by my full command.

187 'Will' (in Anglo-Saxon) of the Lady Wulfgyth (1042–1053; probably 1046)

The interest of this charter derives very largely from its relation to the documents which follow it in this series. These documents illustrate the history of a family of thegnly rank in the period immediately prior to the Norman Conquest. Wulfgyth, the maker of this will, was the mother of Ketel the thegn (see below, No. 189), and Ketel was the nephew of Edwin the thegn (see below, No. 188). Both Ketel and Edwin appear in Domesday Book as having held land in East Anglia in the time of Edward the Confessor. After the Norman Conquest some of their land passed into the possession of the abbey of St. Benet of Holme, and in the case of one estate its tenurial history can be watched in the subsequent period. These documents (Nos. 188–191) provide, in short, remarkable evidence of

[1] Bishop of Worcester in 1046, subsequently archbishop of York.
[2] These obligations should be compared and contrasted with tenure by knight's-service (see below, pp. 894, 895).
[3] Earl of Mercia.
[4] For Earl Odda, see the Anglo-Saxon Chronicle (above, No. 1, pp. 125, 126, 135).
[5] The reference and the precedence given to Danish thegns in a Worcestershire document is very notable.

tenurial practice on a particular estate during the period of the Conquest. They are discussed in this sense in D. C. Douglas, *Feudal Documents from the Abbey of Bury St. Edmunds* (1932), pp. cxii–cxvii. This document is printed, translated and annotated in D. Whitelock, *Anglo-Saxon Wills* (1930), pp. 85, 197.

Here in this document it is made known how Wulfgyth grants after her death the things which Almighty God has allowed her to enjoy in life. First to my lord his due heriot.[1] And I grant the estate at Stisted, with the witness of God and my friends, to Christ Church[2] for the sustenance of the monks in the community, on condition that my sons, Ælfketel and Ketel, may have the use of the estate for their lifetime; and afterwards the estate is to go to Christ Church without controversy, for my soul and for my lord, Ælfwine's, and for the souls of all my children: and after their lifetime half the men are to be free. And I grant to the church at Stisted, besides what I granted during my life, Eldemes land and in addition so much that in all there shall be after my death 50 acres of woodland and of open land. And I grant to my sons, Ælfketel and Ketel,[3] the estates at Walsingham and at Carleton and at Harling; and I grant to my two daughters, Gode and Bote, Saxlingham and Somerleyton. And to the church at Somerleyton 16 acres of land and 1 acre of meadow. And to my daughter, Ealdgyth, I grant the estates at Chadacre and at Ashford, and the wood which I attached to the latter. And I grant Fritton to Earl Godwine and Earl Harold. And I grant to Christ's altar at Christ Church a little gold crucifix and a seat-cover. And I grant to St. Edmund's two ornamented horns. And I grant to St. Etheldreda's[4] a woollen gown. And I grant to St. Osyth's[5] half a pound of money, and that my children shall give. And I grant to St. Augustine's[6] one dorsal.[7] And he who shall detract from my will which I have now declared in the witness of God, may he be deprived of joy on this earth, and may the Almighty Lord who created and made all creatures exclude him from the fellowship of all saints on the Day of Judgment, and may he be delivered into the abyss of hell to Satan the devil and all his accursed companions and there suffer with God's adversaries, without end, and never trouble my heirs. Of this King Edward and many others are witnesses.

188. 'Will' (in Anglo-Saxon) of Edwin the thegn (shortly before 1066)

Edwin was the brother or the brother-in-law of the Lady Wulfgyth, being the uncle of her son, Ketel. This 'will' should be compared with the texts immediately preceding and following it in this series. Edwin's tenurial agreement with his brother and his nephew is notable. The text is printed, translated and annotated in D. Whitelock, *Anglo-Saxon Wills* (1930), pp. 87, 199.

In the Lord's name I, Edwin, make known how I grant the things which Almighty God has lent me in this life. That is, that I grant the estate at Algarsthorpe to St. Edmund's except 10 acres which I give to the church there. And Leofric is to have the 3 acres which he occupies. And I grant the estate at Little Melton to St. Benedict's and 10 acres to the church.[8] And I grant to St. Etheldreda's the estate at Bergh south

[1] This is the only known instance of a heriot in the will of a woman.
[2] At Canterbury.
[3] See below, No. 190.
[4] At Ely.
[5] Essex.
[6] At Canterbury.
[7] An ornamental cloth hung usually at the back of the altar.
[8] St. Benet of Holme. It is this estate at Little Melton which is particularly to be noted in the texts which follow.

of King's Street except the northern enclosure at 'Appelsco'. And half the turfpit is to belong to Apton, and a way to it 2 rods broad. And 10 acres south of the street to Bergh church. And 10 acres north of the street to Apton church, and 4 acres to Holverstone church, and 4 acres to Blyford church, and 10 acres to Sparham church. And all my men are to be free everywhere after my time. This is the free property[1] which Edwin has granted to Christ and St. Mary and all Christ's saints for the redemption of his soul and the forgiveness of his sins. And this is the agreement which the two brothers, Wulfric and Edwin, made between them about the two estates, Thorpe and Little Melton: that is, that whichever of them shall live the longer is to have both the estates; and after the death of both of them, the estate at Melton is to go to St. Benedict's for the souls of them both: and Ketel is to succeed to the estate at Thorpe after the death of them both on such terms as are set forth here: namely that Ketel is to pay each year to St. Edmund's 2 pounds–that is the rent of the estate–and one Mass shall be said every day for the souls of both of them. And after Ketel's death the estate is to go to St. Edmund's without controversy; and that at Melton to the church which Thurward owned; and the land which Edwin, Ecgferth's son, had free to the church; and 8 acres from the estate at Thorpe to Ashwell church; and 8 acres from the estate at Wreningham to the old church, and 2 acres to Fundenhall church, and 2 to Nayland church. There are three of these documents. One is at St. Edmund's; the second at St. Benedict's at Holme; and the third Edwin himself has.

189. 'Will' (in Anglo-Saxon) of Ketel the thegn (1052–January 1066)

Ketel was the nephew of Edwin the thegn who made the preceding 'will'. He is once described in Domesday Book as thegn of King Edward and once as a thegn of Archbishop Stigand–the latter statement being borne out in this 'will'. This document is notable for many reasons: the description of the heriot, the family arrangements here made, and the reference to the estate at Little Melton. It will be noted also that this 'will' is made on the occasion of Ketel's making a pilgrimage to Rome. The text is printed, translated and annotated in D. Whitelock, *Anglo-Saxon Wills* (1930), pp. 89, 201.

Here in this document is Ketel's will: namely that I grant Stisted[2] to Christ Church after my time for the sake of my father's soul and for Sæflæd's.[3] And it is my will that all my men shall be free and that my reeve, Mann, shall occupy the free land which I have given over into his possession, for ever during his life; and after his death the estate is to go with the other. And I grant to the church the land which Wihtric had in his possession, and Leofwine and Siric and Goding to where the fence reaches Leofric's hedge; and I enjoin that no one shall refuse him egress. And I desire that all the men to whom I grant freedom shall have all things which are in their possession except the land. And I grant to Archbishop Stigand, my lord, the estate at Harling just as it stands, except that the men shall be free, and that I grant 10 acres to the church. And if I do not come back again, I grant to him as my heriot a helmet and a coat of mail, and a horse with harness, with a sword and a spear.[4] And I desire that

[1] Probably in the sense that Edwin is free to dispose of this property as he wishes without making agreement with other members of his family.

[2] See above, p. 840.

[3] Was she Ketel's wife?

[4] This seems to be the heriot of a median thegn as described in Cnut's second code.

in accordance with the agreement Edwin and Wulfric shall after my time succeed to everything that is mine everywhere in that village, except so much as I grant to the church; namely the land let for services which my man, Ælfwold, holds; and he is to occupy the other during his lifetime. And afterwards all the land which comes into his possession is to go with the other to the church. If Edwin, my uncle,[1] will maintain the partnership with me and my Uncle Wulfric with regard to the estate at Little Melton, if we outlive him we are to succeed to the estate at Thorpe on condition that, after the death of both of us, the estate at Melton shall go to St. Benedict's at Holme for our ancestors' souls and for our own souls: and the estate at Thorpe to Bury St. Edmunds. And this is the agreement between me and my sister, Bote: if I end my life before her, she is to succeed to the estate at Ketteringham and a mark of gold or the equivalent: and if I outlive her, then I shall have the land at Somerleyton. And my sister, Gode, and I have made a similar agreement: if she survive me, she is to take possession of the estate at Walsingham except 10 acres which are to go to the church: and if I live longer than she, then I shall have the estate at Preston. And I grant to my brother, Godric, the estate at Hainford just as it stands in my possession, and Coggeshall. And for the land at Stratton he shall give Ælfwig my servant 2 pounds. And I and my stepdaughter, Ælfgifu, have made an agreement about the estate at Onehouse that whichever of us shall live the longer is to have as much land as the two of us have there. And if death befall us both on the way to Rome, the estate is to go to Bury St. Edmunds for me and for Sæflæd and for Ælfgifu, but the men are all to be free.[2] And I grant to Earl Harold after my time the half estate at 'Moran' as fully and completely as I rightfully acquired it with my wife in the witness of God and of many men: and I have since neither lost it by lawsuit nor have I forfeited it. And I beseech you by the Lord who created you and all creatures that if I do not come back, you will never let it be possessed after my time by my enemies who wrongfully occupy it and make use of it to my continual injury.[3] And I grant the estate at Frating according to the agreement which you yourself and Archbishop Stigand, my lord, have made. And I grant to Ælfric, my priest and relation, the estate at Rushford. And if anyone be so foolish as to wish to detract from my will, may God and all his saints destroy him at the Day of Judgment.

190. Charter of Godric the steward relating to Little Melton, Norfolk (1101–1116)

Edwin the thegn and his family (see Nos. 188, 189) seem to have lost their estates at the Norman Conquest, and the estate at Little Melton passed into the hands of Godric the steward. The connexion of the former holders with the abbey of St. Benet of Holme, however, survived. In Domesday Book (vol. II, fol. 204b) there is the following notice: "Land of Godric the steward . . . Edwin the thegn held Little Melton in the time of King Edward from St. Benedict in such manner that he had granted it to the abbot after his death." This confirms the evidence of the wills, and the charter which follows is the agreement made between Godric and the abbey in respect of this land. It is thus of exceptional interest as displaying a continuity of tenure throughout the period of the Norman

[1] See No. 188.

[2] These complicated contracts within the family are interesting as indicating the variations of tenure in the thegnly class in the time of Edward the Confessor. Nothing in the nature of organized military tenure is here to be observed. For the people concerned in them, see above, pp. 839, 841.

[3] Notable as indicating conditions in the time of Edward the Confessor, and the value to a man of powerful support.

Conquest, and it shows that in some cases one of the new landowners could succeed one of his Saxon predecessors in a mesne non-military tenure on much the same terms as had prevailed in the time of Edward the Confessor. Printed: D. C. Douglas, *Medieval East Anglia* (1927), p. 244.

Godric the steward and his wife, Ingreda, have given to the church of Christ and of St. Benedict and to the monks of Holme the land of Little Middleton for their souls after their death. Ralph, the son of Godric, has taken up the same land of Melton which is to be held as long as he lives for a rent each year of 10 shillings for the table of the brothers of the church of St. Benedict. Lesceline, the wife of the same Ralph, has given a curtain to the church of St. Benedict on the understanding that if she survives Ralph she may have the same land of Little Melton by the same service by which Ralph holds it during his life. But if Ralph shall have an heir from a betrothed woman this heir of the same Ralph shall hold the same land of Melton by paying for it each year 40 shillings to the table of the monks. But if he have not such an heir, then after the death of both of them[1] the same land of Melton with all the revenue which they have exacted from it shall be quit and free to St. Benedict, to God, and to the monks of Holme.[2] This agreement I, Abbot Richer, have made and granted with the common consent of the brothers in chapter. Witness: Ralph the prior; the monks, Aky, Wulfric, Godwine and Gyomar; Herman the steward; Mainard the knight; Master Bernard; Ralph, the nephew of the abbot; Siric; Jocelyn; William the priest; Lisewy, nephew of Ralph; William of Hereford; and others. Whoever shall presume to break this agreement, let him be struck by the authority of God the Father Almighty, and of Holy Mary the Virgin, and of St. Benedict and of all the saints of God and of the holy canons, and by the perpetual curse of our mystery. Amen.

191. Confirmation of the tenure of Little Melton to Ralph, son of Godric the steward, by Abbot Anselm of St. Benet of Holme (1133–1140)

A continuation of the tenure described in the preceding documents. Printed: D. C. Douglas, *Medieval East Anglia* (1927), p. 246.

Be it known to all present and to come that I, Anselm, by the grace of God abbot of St. Benet of Holme, have with the counsel of the brothers of this same church granted to Ralph, the son of Godric, the land of Little Melton which his father, Godric the steward,[3] together with his wife, Ingreda, gave to St. Benedict. This land is to be had and held by the same Ralph on the terms which were defined and confirmed in the privileges in common chapter and in the presence of Abbot Richer; to wit, that so long as he lives he shall give 10 shillings a year for the food of the monks, and that after his death the true heir of Ralph shall give 40 shillings each year to the monks. If, however, he does not have an heir, the same land of Melton shall remain quit and free to God and St. Benedict and the monks of Holme. These were the witnesses of this transaction: Hubert, son of the same Godric; Ralph 'Kriketot'; Alan of Heckingham; William, son of Asketil; William, priest of Reedham; and others.

[1] *i.e.* Ralph and Lesceline who were, as it seems, childless.

[2] These contracts, it will be noted, are of the same character as those made by Edwin and Ketel who formerly held the land.

[3] See No. 190.

192. Charter of Geoffrey Boterel respecting Nettlestead, Suffolk (1139)

This document is of interest as showing the circumstances in which a charter might be promulgated, and the various parties which, in a feudal society, might need to be associated even with a small benefaction. This family of Boterel were military tenants of the earls of Richmond (see below, No. 261). This instrument is printed in D. C. Douglas, *Medieval East Anglia* (1927), p. 231.

Geoffrey Boterel to Baldwin his steward of Nettlestead[1] greeting. I, together with my wife and sons, have given a mark of silver to the monks of St. Melaine[2] dwelling at Hatfield Regis for the sake of my soul and for the souls of my wife and sons and of my predecessors and successors, and you are without any contradiction to render this sum to their monastery every year so long as you are my agent.[3] I and my wife, Vigolenta, and my sons, William and Peter, will, moreover, and order that all those who shall succeed you in the office you now hold, shall duly pay the said mark of which I speak to the aforesaid monks every year on the Feast of St. Michael. We further will and order that this little charter shall be read in the church before the whole parish in order that all the parishioners may be witness of this my gift, and that the monks may have it from now on freely and without hindrance. Among[4] the barons of Count Alan,[5] Aymeri and Geoffrey 'Aldroeni' heard this ordered by us in the year of the Incarnation of our Lord 1139.

193. Grant by Peter Boterel to the monks of St. Melaine of a peasant in Nettlestead, Suffolk (1153–1164)

The peasant in question appears to have been reeve of Nettlestead. He also appears to have been a 'hundredor' (see above, p. 831 n.5). And the village of Nettlestead was called to witness the transaction. This charter is printed in D. C. Douglas, *Medieval East Anglia* (1927), p. 232.

To William,[6] by the grace of God, bishop of Norwich, and to Walkelin the archdeacon, and to Count Conan[7] his lord, and to all sons of holy Church, Peter Boterel[8] gives greeting. Know that for the souls of my father, my mother, and my ancestors, and for my own soul, I have given and granted to the church of St. Melaine of Rennes, Godwine, reeve[9] of Nettlestead, and his heirs with all that they hold from me. This I have given in perpetual alms, quit and free from all service and exaction and custom, and free also from all the dues which come to me from it. Let it be wholly removed from my power except so far as concerns the service of the king and of the count.[10] I grant also that the same Godwine and his heirs shall continue to have in my village of Nettlestead the same rights of common which he previously held in wood, in plain, in pastures, in waters, in ways, in paths, and in all things.[11] Furthermore I give and grant to the same church 12 acres of my demesne in 'sorland'[12] quit and free alike from my service and from the service of the king and count. And if Godwine or any of his heirs shall be impleaded for any failure of the services due to

[1] *prefecto suo.*
[2] St. Melaine of Rennes. The earls of Richmond were counts of Brittany.
[3] *rerum mearum procurator.*
[4] This last clause is in different ink.
[5] Alan III, earl of Richmond, died 1146.
[6] Bishop of Norwich, 1146–1174.
[7] A count of Brittany and earl of Richmond.
[8] Son of Geoffrey Boterel, see No. 192.
[9] *prepositum.*
[10] These are Peter's overlords. Their rights are reserved.
[11] The holding is to continue to share in the co-operative husbandry of the village.
[12] Meaning uncertain.

me, he shall be judged in respect of this by the monks in the court of the monks of the aforesaid church. The same Godwine and his heirs shall not be compelled by me or by my servants to go to the hundreds or shires,[1] but having made his wonted payment they may remain at home in peace. I wish, moreover, that the aforesaid church may hold this gift from me and my heirs, freely and for ever in peace. The witnesses of this transaction are: Maud, my wife, who joined with me in this gift and herself granted it; Adam, the priest of the same village; Arnold 'medicus'; Richard the priest; William, priest of 'Pileberge'; Rannulf the tailor; Godric, his son; Godric 'de fonte'; William, son of Lifrum; Roger the reeve; Peter of 'Chalgrafe'; Andrew, son of Arnold; Geoffrey, priest of Blakenham;[2] Robert of Willisham;[3] and the whole village[4] of Nettlestead.

194. Charter of Reginald 'de Craci' confirming land to Bullington Priory (1150–1160)

Interesting in particular for the attestation of Redbourne hundred. Redbourne hundred was one of the small hundreds characteristic of the Danelaw and assessed to the geld in Domesday Book at 12 carucates. Printed: F. M. Stenton, *Danelaw Charters*, p. 61.

To all the faithful of Christ Reginald 'de Craci' greeting. Be it known to you all that for my salvation, and for the salvation of all my ancestors, I have granted and by the present charter confirmed to God and to blessed Mary and to the nuns of Bullington and to their brethren, both clerks and laymen, in pure and perpetual alms, whatever my father, Walter 'de Craci' gave them, as his charters bear witness. And I and my heirs after me will warrant this alms against all men. Witness: Gregory the priest; Robert Wascelin; Robert 'de Cauce'; Peter the deacon; Robert the clerk; Alexander, his son; William, son of Ralph; William . . . and the hundred of Redbourne.

195. Charter of Ketel Dumping in favour of Lincoln Cathedral (1176)

This charter is important as showing the manner in which a free peasant might be able by charter to dispose of his land. He terms his land "free", and in his charter there is no mention of his over-lord who was a count of Brittany. His grant seems to have been subject only to the consent of his own heir. There were many men like Ketel Dumping in the Danelaw at the time of Henry II. Printed and discussed in F. M. Stenton, *The Danes in England* (1927), p. 25.

To all the sons of holy Mother Church, present and to come, Ketel Dumping gives greeting. Know all of you that I have given to God and St. Mary 5 acres of my free land, and that I have offered them with my son, Odo, at the altar of St. Mary in pure and perpetual alms. And the said Odo will hold the aforesaid 5 acres from God and from St. Mary by hereditary right by paying 12 pence a year on Whit-Tuesday to the canons of St. Mary. And in order that in the future this gift may not be annulled, I have confirmed it by this my present charter, and fortified it with the witness of my seal. This gift was made in the week of Pentecost in the year of the Incarnation of our Lord 1176.

[1] *i.e.* to attend the courts of shire and hundred; see above, pp. 827, 831, 832.

[2] 'Blacheham': Blakenham is within three miles of Nettlestead.

[3] 'Wilasham': Willisham is within four miles of Nettlestead.

[4] *villata.* The attestation by the village is of interest. Nettlestead in the time of Domesday was divided up among several lords. On the importance of this clause, see D. C. Douglas, *Medieval East Anglia* (1927), pp. 161–164.

196. Charter of Ralph, son of Stephen of Holland, Lincs., to Kirkstead Abbey of land in Snelland, Lincs. (before 1187)

Interesting as illustrating the conditions of peasant tenure and the organization of the village in the Danelaw. Printed: F. M. Stenton, *Danelaw Charters*, p. 160.

To all the sons of holy Church, present and to come, Ralph, son of Stephen of Holland, greeting. Know that I have granted and given, and by this charter confirmed, to God and the church of St. Mary of Kirkstead and the monks of that place in perpetual alms 1 toft in the village of Snelland on which the monks, if they so wish, may freely erect buildings; that is to say, from the toft of Richard Haribrun as it is bounded by the ditch up to the toft of Ralph the clerk between the road and the water-duct. And I give whatever in the marsh pertains to my fee on the far side of the said water-duct to the west and the south as far as the arable whereby the toft which I have given them may be enlarged so that they include in it whatever towards the said water-duct belongs to me. And let them do with it whatever they wish to their own profit and convenience. Besides this I have given them in the fields of the aforesaid village of Snelland 1 bovate of arable land of 20 acres measured by a perch of 18 feet,[1] to wit, 10 acres in each part of the village with as much meadow as pertains to each holding of 20 acres,[2] and with pasture sufficient for 100 sheep reckoned by the 'long hundred'.[3] And in order that the said monks may have and hold all these things freely and honourably and quit from all secular service and custom and exaction, I and my heirs will warrant and acquit them for the use of the monks from all things and all services towards all men in perpetuity. And that all this may be firmly held, I, Ralph, have pledged my faith in the hand[4] of Walter, chaplain of Holy Trinity. Witness: William, priest of Wellingore; Godric, son-in-law of Beorn; Alan, son of Romfar;[5] Ingulf the mercer; Simon, son of Thocca; Richard, nephew of Adam; John 'de Ballio'; Helton, son of John the dean; Robert, son of Sortebrand; Richard, son of Jacob; Ralph the clerk; Alan, son of Robert; Walter of Arras.

197. Charter of Walter, son of Ulmar, in favour of Lewes Priory and concerning land at Sherburne, Norfolk (late twelfth century)

Interesting as an example of the charter of a free peasant, and also for the attestation of the soke. The territorial soke, mainly characteristic of the Danelaw and East Anglia, was an agrarian unit often of large extent, held together by the contributions of a tribute-paying peasantry and with a court of its own. Printed: D. C. Douglas, *Medieval East Anglia* (1927), p. 236.[6]

Let all present and to come know that I, Walter, son of Ulmar of Sherburne, have sold and relinquished to the lord prior of Lewes and to the chapter for 5 shillings the rent of 3 pence a year which Geoffrey paid to me for those lands, to wit, for 2½ roods within the road at 'Fering' and for 2½ roods at 'Brechamgate' and for 3½ roods at 'Fole', and for 1 rood at Sudbriche. This sale I made in the presence of the [court of the] soke of Heacham. Witness the soke and many others.

[1] Note that the measures of land vary from village to village.

[2] A two-field system of agriculture is clearly here implied, and meadow and pasture is reckoned as being appurtenant to the arable.

[3] The 'long hundred' of 120.

[4] *affidavi in manu.*

[5] The Rome-farer or pilgrim.

[6] The MS. reference there given should be amended to "P.R.O. Ancient Deeds A. 15568".

B. THE DOMESDAY SURVEY

AT Christmas 1085, William the Conqueror, holding his court at Gloucester, ordered that a special survey should be made of his kingdom, and during the next year, that is 1086, he

> sent his men all over England into every shire and caused them to ascertain how many hundred hides were in the shires or what of land and of cattle the king himself owned in this country or what dues he ought to receive every year from the shires. Also he caused them to write down how much land belonged to his archbishops and his suffragan bishops and his abbots and his earls; what and how much in land and in cattle each man possessed who was an occupier of land in England, and how much money it was worth. So very narrowly did he cause the survey to be made that there was not a single hide or rood of land, nor even was there an ox or a cow or a pig left that was not set down in his writing. And afterwards all these writings were brought to him.[1]

The commissioners who thus went through the shires of England received sworn verdicts concerning these things from selected jurors. The verdicts were recorded territorially, that is to say, village by village, and hundred by hundred. Subsequently this material was summarized and rearranged upon a feudal plan, that is to say, according to the holdings in each shire of the king's tenants-in-chief. It is this re-arranged digest which is contained in the two volumes officially known as Domesday Book. They were originally kept in the king's Treasury at Winchester, and they are now preserved in the Public Record Office in London. The material which here follows illustrates The Domesday Inquisition and its results. It is arranged as follows:

(*a*) Early evidence relating to the making of Domesday Book.
(*b*) Material from Domesday Book itself: firstly, the complete description of a single county, namely Huntingdonshire; and, secondly, passages selected for their special interest from both volumes of Domesday Book.
(*c*) Material from other records which were the direct products of the Domesday Inquisition. The texts which are here exemplified are:

- (*i*) The Cambridgeshire Survey.
- (*ii*) The Ely Inquest.
- (*iii*) The "Exon Domesday".
- (*iv*) The Domesday Monachorum of Christ Church, Canterbury.
- (*v*) The Feudal Book of Abbot Baldwin of Bury St. Edmunds.

The relation of these texts to each other, and to Domesday Book, is a matter of great complexity. A distinction must in the first instance be drawn between the two volumes of Domesday Book itself. Volume II, which contains the account of Essex, Norfolk and Suffolk, is far less compressed than volume I; its leaves are smaller in size and its handwriting is arranged in one column instead of two; its workmanship is inferior and its character is distinct.

The other surveys mentioned above are all related to Domesday Book whose statistics and phraseology they very generally reproduce. Each of them must be judged separately, but they appear to possess three common characteristics: (i) they omit

[1] Anglo-Saxon Chronicle (above, No. 1, p. 161).

certain material contained in Domesday Book; (ii) they add information which is not to be found in Domesday Book; and (iii) they differ from Domesday Book (in greater or lesser degree) in arrangement. In the Cambridgeshire Survey the material is arranged territorially, not feudally, and this survey, together with the Ely Inquest, gives also the names of the Domesday jurors in the hundreds with which it is concerned. For these reasons, it has seemed impossible to account at once for the differences between these surveys and Domesday Book, and at the same time to explain their close connexion with it, except by postulating a common source–the returns made to the Domesday commissioners. Some, or all, of these surveys were independently compiled from the Domesday returns.

The later stages in the making of Domesday Book are less clear. It has been suggested that the returns (made territorially) were sent to Winchester, and that, there, as the result of work, the duration of which is uncertain, they were in due course digested into the two volumes of Domesday Book. On the other hand, it has been suggested that this rearrangement took place at local centres where the material was regrouped under the holdings of the tenants-in-chief, so that it was a record of baronial tenures within each shire which was at last forwarded to Winchester. Sometimes, it is further suggested, local 'books' were compiled out of the returns, such as perhaps the Ely Inquest or the Domesday Monachorum, or records of wider areas, such as perhaps the "Exon Domesday" or volume II of Domesday Book. All these theories have certain difficulties to overcome. The reader must be left to form his own judgment from the evidence. A full discussion of these questions will be found in J. H. Round, *Feudal England* (1895), pp. 1–146; F. M. Stenton, *William the Conqueror* (1908), pp. 465–501; V. R. Galbraith in *Eng. Hist. Rev.*, vol. LVII (1942), pp. 161–171; D. C. Douglas, *Domesday Monachorum of Christ Church, Canterbury* (1944), pp. 16–33.

Domesday Book describes the whole of England south of the Tees and the Westmorland fells. The character of that description and its scope may be best discerned from the prologue to the Ely Inquest, which states that the jurors were asked in each instance by the commissioners:

> the name of the manor; who held it in the time of King Edward; who holds it now; how many hides there are; how many ploughs in demesne and how many belonging to the men; how many villeins; how many cottars; how many slaves; how many freemen; how many sokemen; how much woodland; how much meadow; how much pasture; how many mills; how many fisheries; how much has been added to, or taken away from, the estate; what it used to be worth altogether; what it is worth now; and how much each freeman and sokeman has. All this to be recorded thrice: to wit, as it was in the time of King Edward; as it was when King William gave the estate; and as it is now.[1]

In general, Domesday Book reflects very faithfully the answers to these questions, and they provide the key to its interpretation. It is necessary to remind the reader that Domesday Book was compiled, not to solve the problems of later students of history, but to supply William the Conqueror with specific information.

The dominant theme in these questions was financial. The primary purpose of Domesday Book was to provide the king with an exact record of the local contributions to the king's geld–or Danegeld–"the one great direct tax levied over the whole of England". In this sense Domesday Book must be compared with the Northamptonshire Geld Roll,[2] and with the account of the Geld Inquest taken in 1084. A normal

[1] No. 215. [2] No. 61.

entry in Domesday Book begins with the statement of the liability of the estate to geld, and this estimate is given in accordance with a system of assessment derived from the Old English State. Thus, when a manor in Domesday Book is assessed at so many 'hides' (each usually divided into 4 virgates), or at so many 'carucates' (each usually divided into 8 bovates), this gives no information about actual acreage, but merely states the amount of tax to be paid from that particular manor when a general geld is laid upon the shire as a whole. The arbitrary nature of this assessment is further indicated by the prevalence throughout the south and west of England of assessments arranged in multiples of 5 hides. The fiscal purpose of the Domesday Inquisition must always be borne in mind. It affects the interpretation of every entry in Domesday Book.

The Domesday Survey had also a further purpose. The annals in the Anglo-Saxon Chronicle 'E' for 1085 and 1086 show that the inquiry was made at a time of crisis.[1] In the summer of 1085 the king, being in Normandy, heard of a threatened invasion from Scandinavia. He therefore hurried back to England with a large force, and very shortly afterwards held his Christmas court at Gloucester where the Domesday Survey was planned. In August 1086, moved by the same sense of urgency, he held the moot at Salisbury, where he took a special oath of allegiance from many of his magnates just at the time when the Domesday commissioners were carrying out their work through England. At such a time it may well be assumed that military necessities, and the needs of defence, made it advisable for the king to obtain more precise information as to how the land of England had been allocated among his greater followers. Many of the early accounts of the survey stress the feudal information which the inquiry was meant to supply, and the results are apparent in Domesday Book itself. It is true that Domesday Book gives little information about feudal organization as such, and unlike any normal feodary, it omits to indicate the amounts of knight-service owed. In these respects it must be compared and contrasted with, for instance, the description of the Canterbury barony in 1096,[2] and with the *cartae* of knight-service taken in 1166.[3] But on the other hand, unlike previous geld inquests, Domesday Book is arranged within each shire according to fiefs. It assumes throughout the existence of the newly established feudal order, and indicates its resources.

Finally, Domesday Book must be considered as in one sense the product of a great judicial inquiry, and related to the earlier litigation of the Conqueror's reign.[4] In many districts a continuous process of litigation led up to the Domesday Inquest, and the Domesday commissioners, who had themselves often, like Geoffrey of Coutances, conducted the previous trials by the same method of the sworn inquest, were frequently in 1086 dealing with matters which were still in dispute. William the Conqueror regarded himself as the legitimate successor of the Confessor. He therefore not only wished for a complete record of English conditions before his coming, but he also desired to legalize the great changes which the Conquest had caused. Domesday Book bears unmistakable traces of being connected with the controversies respecting ownership and possession which had marked the two previous decades. Individual entries often describe and attempt to reconcile contested claims, and the accounts of Yorkshire, Lincolnshire, and, in particular, Huntingdonshire,[5] record the *clamores* or disputes which came up for settlement at the time of the Domesday Inquisition.

Domesday Book may therefore usefully be compared with many other documents contained in this volume. But if it is to be regarded as in a sense a geld inquest, a feudal

[1] No. 1. [2] No. 222. [3] Nos. 224–234. [4] Nos. 50, 51. [5] No. 205.

record, and a judicial statement, its special character must never be forgotten. It is a record without parallel. It is not simply a geld book, for it is unlike all other geld books. It is not simply a feodary, for it is unlike all other feodaries. It is not simply the outcome of a great judicial eyre, for its scope was much wider. It was the unique product of a unique occasion. The events of 1085 gave urgency to the desire of a great king to obtain the fullest possible information about the kingdom he had won. The result was Domesday Book, which embodied the description of a recently conquered country, and recorded the changes which that conquest had caused.

It is the wide scope of Domesday Book which makes it of such exceptional importance as a source for English social history. The incidental testimony it supplies can only be appreciated after long and careful study. One feature of that evidence must, however, immediately be noted. A cardinal fact revealed by Domesday Book is the great variety in English social structure. Care must therefore always be taken not to utilize without proper caution information derived from one shire to illustrate the history of another. Huntingdonshire has here been chosen as a typical Domesday description,[1] but the passages which follow from other parts of Domesday Book give some indication of how the accounts varied. One broad distinction may at once be mentioned. Lincolnshire,[2] Nottinghamshire, Leicestershire, Derbyshire and Yorkshire are assessed in terms of 'carucates', not of 'hides', and this descriptive method, together with the social structure it reveals, reflects the influence of widespread Scandinavian settlements in these regions. The larger proportion of the peasantry enjoying an exceptional degree of freedom in these districts is also significant. In Norfolk and Suffolk, also, the peasantry seem to possess a greater degree of freedom than elsewhere owing to the fact that this area was more loosely organized under manorial lordship; and in these counties the liability to tax was exceptionally expressed, not in geld carucates, but by stating the number of pence paid by each property when one pound of geld was payable by the hundred. The description of Kent is made unique by the employment in the county of the 'suling'–perhaps a double hide–as the unit of assessment.

The classification of the peasantry in Domesday Book raises problems which admit no brief solution. Domesday Book speaks of five main classes of peasants: freemen, sokemen, villeins, bordars, slaves. Broadly speaking, these terms represent a descending scale of freedom. The freemen and sokemen were normally bound to their lords by payment of money rents, and by some jurisdictional dependence. The villein is the typical peasant under bondage, subject to labour services and servile payments, but possessed of his share in the open fields of his village. The bordar may usually be regarded as a cottager possessed of a small holding. The slave was the chattel of his lord. This classification was not, however, applied in Domesday with any consistent accuracy. The Domesday commissioners were describing an alien society in alien terms, and each description of a manor must be interpreted individually in relation to its context. Further information respecting the Domesday peasantry may be obtained from F. W. Maitland, *Domesday Book and Beyond* (1897), Essay I; and from P. Vinogradoff, *Growth of the Manor* (ed. 1920), pp. 332–365.

In the translations which follow, an attempt has been made to give actuality to the evidence from Domesday Book by giving each place-name wherever possible in its modern form, and by adopting in most cases a uniform spelling for personal names. For the sake of brevity the symbol *T.R.E.* (*Tempore regis Edwardi*) has been retained

[1] Below, No. 205. [2] No. 211.

to indicate conditions in the reign of Edward the Confessor. The punctuation has been modernized. Much of Domesday terminology must remain technical even in translation, and its interpretation demands long study. But the material here displayed represents some essential features of the most important statistical record ever compiled in any medieval kingdom.

(a) EVIDENCE RELATING TO THE MAKING OF DOMESDAY BOOK

The best descriptions of the making of Domesday Book are contained: (i) in the Anglo-Saxon Chronicle 'E' (see above, p. 161), and (ii) in the prologues to the Ely and Bury St. Edmunds surveys printed below (Nos. 215, 217). These accounts should, however, be supplemented by the material which here immediately follows.

198. Note added by Robert Losinga, bishop of Hereford, 1079–1095, to the chronicle of Marianus Scotus

Printed by W. H. Stevenson, in *Eng. Hist Rev.*, vol. XXII (1907), p. 74, and in the later editions of W. Stubbs, *Select Charters*.

In the twentieth year of his reign by order of William, king of the English, there was made a survey[1] of the whole of England, that is to say, of the lands of the several provinces of England, and of the possessions of each and all of the magnates. This was done in respect of ploughland and habitations, and of men both bond and free, both those who dwelt in cottages, and those who had their homes and their share in the fields; and in respect of ploughs and horses and other animals; and in respect of the services and payments due from all men in the whole land. Other investigators followed the first; and men were sent into provinces which they did not know, and where they were themselves unknown, in order that they might be given the opportunity of checking the first survey and, if necessary, of denouncing its authors as guilty to the king. And the land was vexed with much violence arising from the collection of the royal taxes.

199. Charter of William I to Westminster Abbey, dated by reference to the Domesday Inquisition

Printed (from the original) in T. Madox, *Formulare Anglicanum* (1702), p. 238, and in J. Armitage Robinson, *Gilbert Crispin* (1911), p. 29.

William, king of the English, to Ralph the sheriff, and all his ministers in Surrey, greeting. Know that for the salvation of my soul I give to God and to St. Peter of Westminster and to Abbot Gilbert 8 hides in the manor of Pyrford which are in my demesne within the forest of Windsor, to be always quit and free from scot and from all my customary rights and from the payment of money which in English is called geld. Witness: William, bishop of Durham; and Ivo 'Taillebosc'. After the survey of the whole of England.[2]

[1] *descriptio.* [2] *Post descriptionem totius Anglie.*

200. Writ of William II concerning property of the abbey of St. Benet of Holme (1094–1095 or 1099–1100, and probably during the earlier period)

The importance of this writ lies in the fact that it refers to certain *brevia* which may have been the original returns made at the Domesday Inquisition. The passages from Domesday here printed with the writ indicate the particular returns to which appeal may have been made. It has been further suggested that if the appeal was in fact made to these returns (and not to Domesday Book which was digested out of them) then Domesday Book itself had not been completed at the time when this writ was issued. The matter has been much discussed, for instance, in *Victoria County History: Norfolk*, vol. II, p. 3; D. C. Douglas, *Feudal Documents from the Abbey of Bury St. Edmunds* (1932), p. lxviii; D. C. Douglas, *Domesday Monachorum of Christ Church, Canterbury* (1944), p. 24; V. H. Galbraith, in *Eng. Hist Rev.*, vol. LVII (1942), p. 61. The text is printed in *Norfolk Record Society*, vol. II, p. 6, and in *Monasticon Anglicanum*, vol. III, p. 86.

William, king of the English, to H. the earl, and Jocelyn the reeve, greeting. I order you to give possession to the abbey of St. Benet and to Rannulf the monk of 100 acres of land and 6 acres of meadow and 4 men; and in Burgh St. Margaret 30 acres and 3 bordars, even as St. Benet possessed them on the day on which my father was alive and dead. Know also that this land was enrolled in my writs which are in my Treasury at Winchester[1] as belonging to the church of St. Benet. And my writs bear witness of this concerning the 100 acres of land, the 6 acres of meadow and the 4 men in Winterton,[2] and the 30 acres and 3 bordars in Burgh St. Margaret.[3] Witness the bishop of Durham and W. the chancellor.

201. Record of a plea relating to the abbey of Abingdon (either between July 1108 and May 1109, or between August 1111 and the summer of 1113)

Judgment is given in favour of Abbot Faritius of Abingdon. This record is mainly important as containing what is at present the earliest known reference to the completed Domesday Book. This record has been extensively discussed, notably in J. H. Round, *Feudal England* (1895), pp. 142–146, in D. C. Douglas, *Domesday Monachorum of Christ Church, Canterbury* (1944), p. 24, and elsewhere. Printed: J. Stevenson, *Chronicon Monasterii de Abingdon* (1858), vol. II, pp. 115–116.

The men of the hundred of 'Peritune' strove to subject a manor of this church called Lewknor to their jurisdiction. But this abbot[4] showed that the claim was unjust, stating his case in the castle of Winchester before Roger, bishop of Salisbury, Robert, bishop of Lincoln, Richard, bishop of London, and many barons of the king. Wherefore by judgment of the king's judges he secured that this manor ought not to be subjected in anything to any other hundred but its own. But because the king was then in Normandy, the queen who was then present confirmed this with her seal as follows:

Maud, queen of England, to Robert, bishop of Lincoln, and Thomas of St. John, and all the barons, both French and English, of Oxfordshire, greeting. Know that Faritius, abbot of Abingdon, in the court of my lord, and in my court, at Winchester, in the Treasury before Roger, bishop of Salisbury, and Robert, bishop of Lincoln, and Richard, bishop of London, and William of Courcy, and Adam of Port-en-Bessin, and Thurstan the chaplain, and Walter of Gloucester, and Herbert the chamberlain, and William 'd'Oilly' and Geoffrey, son of Herbert,

[1] *Et sciatis quod ista terra inbreviata fuit in meis brevibus ad opus ecclesiae sancti Benedicti qui sunt in thesauro meo Wyntoniae.*

[2] Domesday Book, vol. II, fol. 216: "St. Benet holds Winterton . . . and there is 1 sokeman with 100 acres . . . [and there are] 6 acres of meadow . . . [and] 4 free men."

[3] *ibid.*, vol. II, fol. 217: "In Burgh St. Margaret, St. Benet holds 30 acres and 4 acres of meadow and 3 bordars."

[4] Faritius, abbot of Abingdon.

and William of Anisy, and Ralph Basset, and Geoffrey of Manneville, and Geoffrey Ridel and Walter, archdeacon of Oxford, proved by the Book of the Treasury[1] that Lewknor, his manor, owes no duties whatever to the hundred of 'Peritune'. All its obligations lie in the hundred of Lewknor in which hundred the church of Abingdon holds 17 hides.

202. Account of the Domesday Inquisition given by an annalist of Worcester early in the twelfth century

Printed: F. Liebermann, *ngedruckte Uanglo-normannische Geschichtsquellen* (1879), p. 21.

A.D. 1086. William, king of the English, sent through all the provinces of England, and caused it to be inquired how many hides were held in the whole of England, and how much the king had in lands and cattle and livestock in each province, and what customary dues each year. This he caused to be done in respect of the lands and dues both of all churches and of all his barons. He inquired what these were worth, and how much they then rendered, and how much they were able to render in the time of King Edward. And so thoroughly was all this carried out that there did not remain in the whole of England a single hide or a virgate of land or an ox or a cow or a pig which was not written in that return.[2] And all the writings of all these things were brought back to the king. And the king ordered that all should be written in one volume, and that that volume should be placed in his Treasury at Winchester and kept there.[3]

203. Account of the Domesday Inquisition given before 1118 by 'Florence of Worcester'

Printed in *Chronicon ex Chronicis*, ed. B. Thorpe (1848), vol. II, p. 18.

King William caused all England to be surveyed:[4] how much each of his barons possessed; and how many enfeoffed knights; and how many ploughs, villeins, animals, and livestock, each one possessed in all his kingdom from the greatest to the least; and what dues each estate was able to render. And as a consequence the land was vexed with much violence.

204. Account of the Domesday Inquisition given by Henry of Huntingdon

Printed in Henry of Huntingdon, *Historia Anglorum*, ed. T. Arnold (1879), p. 211.

This most powerful king sent his justices through every shire, that is to say, every province of England, and caused an inquiry to be made by sworn inquest how many hides (that is to say, ploughlands each sufficient for one plough in the year) there were in each village, and what livestock. He also made inquiry what each city, castle, township, village, marsh and wood was wont to render each year. All these writings in records[5] were brought to the king, and they are preserved in the Treasury to this day.

[1] *per Librum de Thesauro disratiocinavit.* [2] *in breviatione illa.*

[3] *Omnesque scripture omnium harum rerum representate sunt regi. Qui precepit ut omnes scriberentur in uno volumen et poneretur volumen illud in thesauro suo Wintonie et servaretur ibi.*

[4] *fecit describi omnem Angliam.* [5] *Haec omnia in cartis scripta.*

(b) DOMESDAY BOOK

205. The survey of Huntingdonshire in Domesday Book

The account of Huntingdonshire in Domesday Book occupies folios 203–208 in volume 1 of Domesday Book. It is printed in the Record Commission's edition (1783). A translation was made in 1864, and another was executed in 1926 by F. M. Stenton for the *Victoria County History: Huntingdonshire*, vol. 1, pp. 337–355. The passages which follow are based on Professor Stenton's translation. The account of Huntingdonshire, though comparatively short, illustrates very well the main features of Domesday Book. Attention may be drawn to the account of the borough, and to the arrangement of the land of the shire under the holdings of the tenants-in-chief. The appendix of 'claims' is of especial importance. The general purposes of the Domesday Survey (see above, pp. 848, 849) explains the general form of the Huntingdonshire Domesday. A typical entry in this account will be found to contain five elements:

(1) The manor is assessed at so many hides to the geld. These 'hides' are units of assessment, and are not here used as agrarian measures. For instance, the statement that Bottlebridge is assessed at 5 hides to the geld gives no information about the acreage of Bottlebridge, but merely states that when geld is levied upon the shire Bottlebridge pays according to an assessment of 5 hides. The prevalence of the 5-hide unit and its multiples will be noted, and very often scattered entries relating to the same village will be found when added together to amount to the same unit or its multiples.

(2) A statement that there is land for so many 'ploughs'. This indicates the amount of arable measured according to the amount of land capable of being ploughed each year by a plough team of 8 oxen.

(3) A statement as to the number of ploughs on the demesne of the manor, and the number of ploughs possessed by the peasantry, the latter being classified according to their grades – freemen, sokemen, villeins, bordars, slaves (for which see above, p. 850).

(4) Miscellaneous information relating to pasture, meadows, churches, pannage for swine, etc.

(5) A statement as to the value of the manor in the time of the Confessor, in 1066, and in 1086.

Each individual manor must be studied individually, but further information respecting this text may be found in Professor Stenton's work cited above. The essential preliminary to understanding the Huntingdonshire Domesday is to bear in mind that the 'hide' is used chiefly as a unit of assessment to the geld, and that the 'plough' is employed to measure the amount of arable land in any estate.

HUNTINGDONSHIRE

In the borough of Huntingdon there are 4 quarters.

In 2 quarters there were *T.R.E.*, and are now, 116 burgesses rendering all customs and the king's geld, and under them there are 100 bordars who help them to pay the geld. Of these burgesses St. Benedict of Ramsey had 10 with sake and soke and every custom except that they paid geld *T.R.E.* Eustace took them away wrongfully from the abbey and they are, with the others, in the king's hand. Ulf Fenisc had 18 burgesses, now Gilbert of Ghent has them with sake and soke except for the king's geld.

The abbot of Ely has 1 toft with sake and soke except for the king's geld.

The bishop of Lincoln had in the site of the castle a messuage with sake and soke which has now disappeared.

Earl Siward had a messuage with a house with sake and soke, quit from all custom, which the Countess Judith has now.

In the site of the castle there were 20 messuages assessed to all customs, and rendering yearly 16 shillings and 8 pence to the king's 'farm'. These do not exist now.

In addition to these, there were and are 60 waste messuages within these quarters. These gave and give their customs. And in addition to these there are 8 waste messuages which *T.R.E.* were fully occupied. These gave all customs.

In the other 2 quarters there were and are 140 burgesses, less half a house, assessed to all customs and the king's geld, and these had 80 haws for which they gave and give all customs. Of these St. Benedict of Ramsey had 22 burgesses *T.R.E.* Two of these were quit of all customs, and 30 rendered 10 pence yearly each. All other customs belonged to the abbot, apart from the king's geld.

In these quarters Aluric the sheriff *T.R.E.* had 1 messuage which King William afterwards granted to his wife and sons. Eustace has it now, and the poor man, with his mother, is claiming it. In these 2 quarters there were and are 44 waste messuages which gave and give their customs. And in these 2 quarters Borred and Turchil *T.R.E.* had 1 church with 2 hides of land and 22 burgesses with houses belonging to the same church with sake and soke; Eustace has all this now. Wherefore these men claim the king's mercy; nevertheless these 22 burgesses give every custom to the king.

Geoffrey the bishop has 1 church and 1 house from the aforesaid which Eustace took away from St. Benedict, and the same saint is still claiming them.

In this borough Gos and Hunef had 16 houses *T.R.E.* with sake and soke and toll and team. The Countess Judith has them now.

The borough of Huntingdon used to defend itself towards the king's geld for 50 hides as the fourth part of Hurstingstone hundred, but now it does not so pay geld in that hundred, after the king set a geld of money on the borough. From this whole borough 10 pounds came out *T.R.E.* by way of 'Landgable' of which the earl had the third part, and the king two-thirds. Of this rent 16 shillings and 8 pence, divided between the earl and the king, now remain upon 20 messuages where the castle is. In addition to these payments the king had 20 pounds and the earl 10 pounds from the 'farm' of the borough more or less according as each could make disposition of his part. One mill rendered 40 shillings to the king and 20 shillings to the earl. To this borough there belong 2 ploughlands and 40 acres of land and 10 acres of meadow, of which the king with two parts, and the earl with the third part, divide the rent. The burgesses cultivate this land and take it on lease through the servants of the king and the earl. Within the aforesaid rent there are 3 fishermen rendering 3 shillings. In this borough there were 3 moneyers paying 40 shillings between the king and the earl, but now they are not there. *T.R.E.* it rendered 30 pounds; now the same.

In Hurstingstone hundred demesne ploughlands are quit of the king's geld. Villeins and sokemen pay geld according to the hides written in the return, apart from Broughton where the abbot of Ramsey pays geld for 1 hide with the others.

Here are noted those holding lands in Huntingdonshire

1. King William
2. The bishop of Lincoln.
3. The bishop of Coutances.
4. The abbey of Ely.
5. The abbey of Crowland.
6. The abbey of Ramsey.
7. The abbey of Thorney.
8. The abbey of Peterborough.
9. Count Eustace.
10. The count of Eu.
11. Earl Hugh.
12. Walter Giffard.
13. William of Warenne.
14. Hugh of Bolbec.
15. Eudo, son of Hubert.
16. Sweyn of Essex.
17. Roger of Ivry.
18. Arnulf of Hesdins.
19. Eustace the sheriff.
20. The Countess Judith.

21. Gilbert of Ghent.
22. Aubrey 'de Vere'.
23. William, son of Ansculf.
24. Rannulf, the brother of Ilger.
25. Robert Fafiton.
26. William 'Ingania'.
27. Ralph, son of Osmund.
28. Rohais, the wife of Richard.
29. The king's thegns.

1. *The land of the king*

Hurstingstone hundred

A manor. In Hartford King Edward had 15 hides assessed to the geld. There is land for 17 ploughs. Rannulf the brother of Ilger keeps it now. There are 4 ploughs now on the demesne; and 30 villeins and 3 bordars have 8 ploughs. There is a priest; 2 churches; 2 mills rendering 4 pounds; and 40 acres of meadow. Woodland for pannage, 1 league in length and half a league in breadth. *T.R.E.* it was worth 24 pounds; now 15 pounds.

Normancross hundred

A manor. In Bottlebridge King Edward had 5 hides assessed to the geld. There is land for 8 ploughs. The king has 1 plough now on the demesne; and 15 villeins have 5 ploughs. There is a priest and a church; 60 acres of meadow and 12 acres of woodland for pannage in Northamptonshire. *T.R.E.* it was worth 100 shillings; now 8 pounds. Rannulf keeps it.

In this manor belonging to the king, and in other manors, the enclosure of the abbot of Thorney is doing harm to 300 acres of meadow.

In Stilton the king's sokemen of Normancross have 3 virgates of land assessed to the geld. There is land for 2 ploughs, and there are 5 ploughing oxen.

In Orton the king has soke over 3½ hides of land in the land of the abbot of Peterborough which was Godwine's.

Toseland hundred

A manor. In Gransden Earl Alfgar had 8 hides of land assessed to the geld. There is land for 15 ploughs. There are 7 ploughs now on the demesne; and 24 villeins and 8 bordars have 8 ploughs. There is a priest and a church; 50 acres of meadow; 12 acres of underwood. From the pasture come 5 shillings and 4 pence. *T.R.E.* it was worth 40 pounds; now 30 pounds. Rannulf keeps it.

Leightonstone hundred

A manor. In Alconbury, and in Gidding, which is an outlying estate, there were 10 hides assessed to the geld. There is land for 20 ploughs. There are now 5 ploughs belonging to the hall on 2 hides of this land; and 35 villeins have 13 ploughs there; 80 acres of meadow. *T.R.E.* it was worth 12 pounds; now the same. Rannulf, the brother of Ilger, keeps it.

A manor. In Keyston King Edward had 4 hides of land assessed to the geld. There is land for 12 ploughs. There are 2 ploughs now on the demesne; and 24 villeins and 8 bordars have 10 ploughs; 86 acres of meadow. Scattered woodland for pannage

5 furlongs in length and 1½ furlongs in breadth. *T.R.E.* it was worth 10 pounds; now the same. Rannulf, the brother of Ilger, keeps it.

A manor. In Brampton King Edward had 15 hides assessed to the geld. There is land for 15 ploughs. There are 3 ploughs now on the demesne; and 36 villeins and 2 bordars have 14 ploughs. There is a church and a priest; 100 acres of meadow. Woodland for pannage half a league in length and 2 furlongs in breadth. Two mills rendering 100 shillings. *T.R.E.* it was worth 20 pounds; now the same. Rannulf, the brother of Ilger, keeps it.

Soke.[1] In Graffham there are 5 hides assessed to the geld. There is land for 8 ploughs. The soke is in Leightonstone hundred. There 7 sokemen and 17 villeins have 6 ploughs now and 6 acres of meadow. Woodland for pannage 1 league in length and 1 league in breadth. *T.R.E.* it was worth 5 pounds; now 10 shillings less.

A manor. In Godmanchester King Edward had 14 hides assessed to the geld. There is land for 57 ploughs. There are 2 ploughs now on the king's demesne on 2 hides of this land; and 80 villeins and 16 bordars have 24 ploughs. There is a priest and a church; 3 mills rendering 100 shillings; 160 acres of meadow; and 50 acres of woodland for pannage. From the pasture come 20 shillings. From the meadows come 70 shillings. *T.R.E.* it was worth 40 pounds; now it is worth the same 'by tale'.

2. *The land of the bishop of Lincoln*

Toseland hundred

A manor. In 'Cotes' the bishop of Lincoln had 2 hides assessed to the geld. There is land for 3 ploughs. There are 2 ploughs now on the demesne; and 3 villeins have 2 oxen; 20 acres of meadow. *T.R.E.* it was worth 40 shillings; now the same. Thurstan holds it of the bishop.

A manor. In Staughton the bishop of Lincoln had 6 hides assessed to the geld. There is land for 15 ploughs. There are 2½ ploughs on the demesne; and 16 villeins and 4 bordars have 8 ploughs. There is a priest and a church; 24 acres of meadow; 100 acres of underwood. *T.R.E.* it was worth 10 pounds; now the same. Eustace holds it of the bishop. The abbot of Ramsey claims this manor against the bishop.

A manor. In Diddington the bishop of Lincoln had 2½ hides assessed to the geld. There is land for 2 ploughs. There are now 2 ploughs on the demesne and 5 villeins have 2 ploughs. A church, and 18 acres of meadow. Woodland for pannage half a league in length and half in breadth. *T.R.E.* it was worth 60 shillings; now 70 shillings. William holds it of the bishop.

A manor. In Buckden the bishop of Lincoln had 20 hides assessed to the geld. There is land for 20 ploughs. There are now 5 ploughs on the demesne; and 37 villeins and 20 bordars have 14 ploughs. There is a church and a priest; 1 mill worth 30 shillings; 84 acres of meadow. Woodland for pannage 1 league in length and 1 league in breadth. *T.R.E.* it was worth 20 pounds; now 16 pounds and 10 shillings.

[1] This term prefixed to estates in this survey indicates "a group of tenements–united to some manor by the ties of rent, the homage of the peasant landholders, and in most cases their suit of court to the manorial centre".

Normancross hundred

A manor. In Denton Godric had 5 hides assessed to the geld. There is land for 2 ploughs. There is 1 plough on the demesne; and 10 villeins and 2 bordars have 5 ploughs. There is a church and a priest; 24 acres of meadow and 24 acres of underwood. *T.R.E.* it was worth 100 shillings; now 4 pounds. Thurstan holds it of the bishop.

A manor. In Orton Leuric had 3 hides and 1 virgate of land assessed to the geld. There is land for 2 ploughs and 1 ox. There is now 1 plough on the demesne; and 2 villeins and 9 acres of meadow. *T.R.E.* it was worth 20 shillings; now 10 shillings. John holds it of the bishop. The king claims the soke of this land.

A manor. In Stilton Tovi had 2 hides assessed to the geld. There is land for 2 ploughs and 7 oxen. There is now 1 plough on the demesne; and 6 villeins have 3 ploughs; 16 acres of meadow and 5 acres of underwood. *T.R.E.* it was worth 40 shillings; now the same. John holds it of the bishop. This land was given to Bishop Wulfwig *T.R.E.*

Leightonstone hundred

A manor. In Leighton Bromswold Turchil the Dane had 15 hides assessed to the geld. There is land for 17 ploughs. There are now 6 ploughs on the demesne; and 33 villeins and 3 bordars have 10 ploughs. One mill rendering 3 shillings; 3 knights hold 3 hides less 1 virgate of this land: they have 3 ploughs and 3 villeins with half a plough. There are 30 acres of meadow and 10 acres of underwood. *T.R.E.* the bishop's demesne was worth 20 pounds and it is worth the same now. The land of the knights is worth 60 shillings. Earl Waltheof gave this manor in alms to St. Mary of Lincoln.

In Pertenhall Alwin had 1 virgate of land assessed to the geld. There is land for half a plough. This land is situated in Bedfordshire but renders geld and service in Huntingdonshire. The king's servants claim this land for his use. *T.R.E.* it was worth 5 shillings; now the same. William holds it of Bishop Remigius and ploughs it with his own demesne.

3. *The land of the bishop of Coutances*

In Hargrave Semar had 1 virgate of land assessed to the geld. There is land for 2 oxen. The soke belongs to Leightonstone hundred. The same man himself holds it of the bishop of Coutances and ploughs there with 2 oxen and has 2 acres of meadow. *T.R.E.* it was worth 5 shillings; now the same.

4. *The land of the abbey of Ely*[1]

Hurstingstone hundred

A manor. In Colne the abbey of Ely had 6 hides assessed to the geld. There is land for 6 ploughs and in demesne the abbey has land for 2 ploughs apart from the 6 hides. There are now 2 ploughs on the demesne, and 13 villeins and 5 bordars have 5 ploughs; 10 acres of meadow. Woodland for pannage 1 league in length and half a league in breadth; marsh of the same extent. *T.R.E.* it was worth 6 pounds; now 100 shillings.

[1] See below, No. 215.

A manor. In Bluntisham the abbey of Ely had 6½ hides assessed to the geld. There is land for 8 ploughs, and, apart from these hides, the abbey has land for 2 ploughs in demesne. There are now 2 ploughs on the demesne; and 10 villeins and 3 bordars have 3 ploughs. There is a priest and a church; 20 acres of meadow. Woodland for pannage 1 league in length and 4 furlongs in breadth. *T.R.E.* it was worth 100 shillings; now the same.

A manor. In Somersham the abbey of Ely had 8 hides assessed to the geld. There is land for 12 ploughs, and, apart from these hides, the abbey has land for 2 ploughs in demesne. There are now 2 ploughs on the demesne; and 32 villeins and 9 bordars have 9 ploughs. There are 3 fisheries rendering 8 shillings, and 20 acres of meadow. Woodland for pannage 1 league in length and 7 furlongs in breadth. *T.R.E.* it was worth 7 pounds; now 8 pounds.

A manor. In Spaldwick the abbey of Ely had 15 hides assessed to the geld. There is land for 15 ploughs. There are now 4 ploughs on the demesne on 5 hides of this land; and 50 villeins and 10 bordars have 25 ploughs. There is 1 mill rendering 2 shillings; and 160 acres of meadow; and 60 acres of woodland for pannage. *T.R.E.* it was worth 16 pounds; now 22 pounds.

A manor. In Little Catworth, outlying estate of Spaldwick, there are 4 hides assessed to the geld. Land for 4 ploughs; 7 villeins have 2 ploughs there now.

5. *The land of the abbey of Crowland*

A manor. In Morborne the abbey of Crowland has 5 hides assessed to the geld. There is land for 9 ploughs. There are now 2 ploughs on the demesne on 1 hide of this land; and 16 villeins and 3 bordars have 7 ploughs. There is a church and a priest; 40 acres of meadow; 1 acre of underwood. *T.R.E.* it was worth 100 shillings; now the same.

In Thurning there are 1½ hides assessed to the geld. There is land for 1½ ploughs. The soke belongs to the king's manor of Alconbury. Eustace holds it now from the abbot of Crowland, and had 1 plough there and 1 villein with half a plough and 6 acres of meadow. *T.R.E.* it was worth 20 shillings; now the same.

6. *The land of St. Benedict of Ramsey*

[This is similarly described as lying in Stukeley; Abbot's Ripton; Broughton; Wistow; Upwood; Holywell; St. Ives; Houghton; Wyton; Warboys; Sawtry; Elton; Lutton; Yelling; Hemingford Abbots; Offord; Dillington; Gidding; Bythorn; Bringtin; Old Weston; Ellington.]

7. *The land of St. Mary of Thorney*

[This is similarly described as lying in Yaxley; Stanground; Woodstone; Haddon; Water Newton; Sibson; Stibbington.]

8. *The land of St. Peter of Peterborough*

[This is similarly described as lying at Fletton; Alwalton; Orton Waterville.]

9. *The land of Count Eustace*[1]

[This is similarly described as lying at Glatton; Chesterton; Sibson.]

[1] Eustace of Boulogne.

10. *The land of the count of Eu*[1]

[This is similarly described as lying at Buckworth.]

11. *The land of Earl Hugh*[2]

[This is similarly described as lying in Upton; Coppingford.]

12. *The land of Walter Giffard*

[This is similarly described as lying at Folksworth.]

13. *The land of William of Warenne*

[This is similarly described as lying at Kimbolton; Keysoe; Catworth.]

14. *The land of Hugh of Bolbec*

[This is similarly described as lying at Wood Walton.]

15. *The land of Eudo, son of Hubert*

[This is similarly described as lying at Hamerton.]

16. *The land of Sweyn of Essex*

[This is similarly described as lying at Waresley.]

17. *The land of Roger of Ivry*

[This is similarly described as lying at Covington.]

18. *The land of Arnulf of Hesdins*

[This is similarly described as lying in Offord Cluny.]

19. *The land of Eustace the sheriff*

[This is similarly described as lying in Sawtry; Caldecot; Washingley; Orton Longueville; Stilton; Chesterton; Bottlebridge; Swineshead; Catworth; Hargrave; Gidding; Winwick; Thurning; Luddington; Weston; Wooley; Hemingford; Offord; Waresley; Hail Weston; Southoe; Perry; Catworth.]

20. *The land of the Countess Judith*[3]

[This is similarly described as lying in Conington; Sawtry; Stukeley; Molesworth; 'Cotes'; Eynesbury; Offord; Diddington; Paxton.]

21. *The land of Gilbert of Ghent*

[This is similarly described as lying in Fen Stanton.]

22. *The land of Aubrey 'de Vere'*

[This is similarly described as lying in Yelling; Hemingford.]

23. *The land of William, son of Ansculf*

[This is similarly described as lying in Waresley.]

24. *The land of Rannulf, brother of Ilger*

[This is similarly described as lying in Everton.]

[1] Robert, count of Eu, son of William, count of Eu.
[2] Hugh, *vicomte* of Avranches, and earl of Chester.
[3] Niece of William the Conqueror. She became countess of Huntingdon on marrying Waltheof, who was executed in 1076.

25. *The land of Robert Fafiton*

[This is similarly described as lying in Hail Weston; Southhoe.]

26. *The land of William 'Ingania'*

[This is similarly described as lying in Gidding.]

27. *The land of Ralph, son of Osmund*

[This is similarly described as lying in Hemingford.]

28. *The land of Rohais, wife of Richard fitz Gilbert*[1]

Toseland hundred

A manor. In Eynesbury Robert, son of Wimarc, had 15 hides assessed to the geld. There is land for 27 ploughs. Rohais, the wife of Richard, has 7 ploughs on the demesne there now. In the same place St. Neot has from her 3 ploughs on the demesne, and in the same village 19 villeins and 5 bordars have 7 ploughs. There is 1 mill worth 23 shillings, and 1 fishery which is valued with the manor; 65½ acres of meadow. *T.R.E.* it was worth 24 pounds; now it is worth 21 pounds apart from that which is assigned to the food of the monks, which is valued at 4 pounds. William 'Brito' holds 2 hides and 1 virgate of this land from Rohais and has half a plough on the demesne; and 3 villeins and 4 bordars have 1 plough. It is worth 30 shillings.

29. *The land of the king's thegns*

A manor. In Washingley, Chetelebert had 2½ hides assessed to the geld. There is land for 4 ploughs. He himself holds from the king and has 1 plough there; and 10 villeins have 4 ploughs. There is a church and a priest; 12 acres of meadow. Woodland for pannage 7 furlongs in length and 10½ furlongs in breadth. *T.R.E.* it was worth 10 shillings; now the same.

Leightonstone hundred

In Keysoe Alwine had 1 virgate of land assessed to the geld with sake and soke. There is land for 2 oxen. It belongs to Bedfordshire, but gives geld in Huntingdonshire. He himself holds now of the king and has 1 villein there with 2 oxen in a plough. *T.R.E.* it was worth 16 pence; now the same.

A manor. In Catworth Avic had 3 hides assessed to the geld. There is land for 4 ploughs. Eric holds it now of the king. And the same man has under the king 1 hide assessed to the geld. There is land for 1 plough. He has 2 villeins there, and 6 acres of meadow. *T.R.E.* it was worth 40 shillings; now 20 shillings.

In Brampton Elric has 1 hide and 1 virgate of land assessed to the geld. There is land for 10 oxen. There are 3 bordars and 1 plough. It is worth 30 shillings.

A manor. In Wooley Golde and Uluric, his son, had 3 hides assessed to the geld. There is land for 6 ploughs. They themselves now have it from the king. There is 1 plough on the demesne; and 14 villeins have 5 ploughs; 20 acres of meadow. *T.R.E.* it was worth 60 shillings; now the same.

[1] See Table 11.

In Sawtry Alwine had half a carucate assessed to the geld. There is land for 6 oxen. His wife holds it now of the king, and has 1 plough there and 2 acres. *T.R.E.* it was worth 10 shillings; now the same.

[*Claims*]

The jurors of Huntingdon say that the church of St. Mary of the borough and the land which is annexed to it belonged to the church of Thorney, but the abbot gave it in pledge to the burgesses. Moreover, King Edward gave it to Vitalis and Bernard, his priests, and they sold it to Hugh, chamberlain to King Edward. Moreover, Hugh sold it to two priests of Huntingdon, and in respect of this they have the seal of King Edward. Eustace has it now without livery, without writ, and without seisin.

Eustace took away wrongfully the house of Leveve and gave it to Oger of London.

They bear witness that the land of Hunef and Gos was under the hand of King Edward on the day when he was alive and dead and that they held of him and not of the earl. But the jurors say that they heard that King William was said to have given it to Waltheof.

Touching the 5 hides of Broughton the jurors say that it was the land of sokemen *T.R.E.*, but that the same king gave the land and the soke over the men to St. Benedict of Ramsey in return for a service which Abbot Alwin did for him in Saxony, and ever afterwards the saint had it.

The shire bears witness that the land of Bricmer 'Belehorne' was 'reeveland' *T.R.E.* and belonged to the king's 'farm'.

They bear witness that the land of Alwin the priest was to the abbot. . . .[1]

They bear witness that Aluric's land of Yelling and Hemingford belonged to St. Benedict and that it was granted to Aluric for the term of his life on the condition that after his death it ought to return to the church, and 'Bocstede' with it. But this same Aluric was killed in the battle of Hastings, and the abbot took back his lands and held them until Aubrey 'de Vere' deprived him of possession.

Touching 2 hides which Ralph, son of Osmund, holds in Hemingford, they say that one of them belonged to the demesne of the church of Ramsey in King Edward's day, and that Ralph holds it against the abbot's will. Touching the other hide, they say that Godric held it from the abbot, but when the abbot was in Denmark, Osmund, Ralph's father, seized it from Sawin the fowler, to whom the abbot had given it for love of the king.

Touching Summerlede they say that he held his land from Turulf who gave it to him, and afterwards from the sons of Turulf, and they had sake and soke over him.

The jurors say that the land of Wulwine Chit of Weston was a manor by itself, and did not belong to Kimbolton, but that nevertheless he was a man of Earl Harold.

Touching a hide and a half of land which was Ælget's, the jurors say that this Ælget held them from Earl Tosti with sake and soke and afterwards of Waltheof.

Godric the priest likewise held 1 hide of land from Earl Waltheof *T.R.E.*, and Eustace holds it now.

[1] The missing words are *et utrunque fuisse terram presbiter et prefecti*: these seem untranslatable.

They say that the land of Godwine of Weston in no way belonged to Saxi, Fafiton's predecessor.

The men of the shire bear witness that King Edward gave Swineshead to Earl Siward with sake and soke, and so Earl Harold had it, except that the men paid geld in the hundred, and performed military service with them.

Touching the land of Fursa, the soke was the king's. King Edward had soke over 1 virgate of land of Alwin Deule in Pertenhall.

The jurors say that the hide of land which Wulwine Chit had in Catworth was in the king's soke and that Earl Harold did not have it.

In Little Catworth the same Wulwine had 1 hide over which King Edward always had sake and soke. But Wulwine could give and sell the land to whom he wished. But the men of the countess say that the king gave the land to Earl Waltheof.

The shire bears witness that the third part of half a hide which lies in Easton and pays geld in Bedfordshire belongs to the abbot of Ely's manor of Spaldwick. The abbot of Ely thus held it *T.R.E.*, and for five years after the coming of King William. Eustace seized this land wrongfully from the church, and kept it.

The jurors say that Keystone was and is of the 'farm' of King Edward, and although Aluric the sheriff resided in that village, he nevertheless always paid the king's 'farm' therefrom, and his sons after him, until Eustace took the sheriffdom. They have never seen or heard of a seal of King Edward that he put it outside his 'farm'.

Alwold and his brother claim that Eustace took away their land from them, and the men of the shire deny that they have ever seen a seal, or seen anyone who gave Eustace seisin of it.

On the day when King Edward was alive and dead, Gidding was an outlying estate of Alconbury in the king's 'farm'.

The men of the shire bear witness that Buckworth was an outlying estate of Paxton *T.R.E.*

They say that 36 hides of land in Brampton which Richard 'Ingania' claims to belong to the forest were of the king's demesne 'farm', and did not belong to the forest.

They say that Graffham was and is the king's sokeland, and that they have not seen the writ, or anyone who gave legal possession of this to Eustace.

Touching 6 hides in Conington they said they had heard that these formerly belonged to the church of Thorney, and that they were granted to Turchill on condition that after [his] death they ought to return to the church with the other 3 hides in the same village. The jurors said that they had heard this, but they had not seen evidence of it, nor were they present when the arrangement was made.

Touching the land of Tosti of Sawtry, they say that Eric, his brother, bequeathed it to the church of Ramsey after his death and after the death of his brother and sister.

Touching Fletton the jurors say that *T.R.E.* the whole belonged to the church of Peterborough, and so it should.

Touching Leuric's land the jurors say that it was in the king's soke, but Bishop Remigius shows the writ of King Edward by which he gave Leuric with all his land to the bishopric of Lincoln with sake and soke.

206. Domesday Book, vol. I, fols. 4 and 4b: The Knights of Lanfranc

Domesday Book normally alludes to the holdings of knights only incidentally as they occur on the estates of the king's tenants-in-chief. In the description of Kent, however, a separate section is exceptionally allotted to the estates of the knights of the archbishop of Canterbury in that county. It should be compared with the description of the barony of the archbishop given below in No. 222. This is printed in the edition (1783) of the Record Commission. A translation is in the *Victoria County History: Kent*, vol. III (1932), p. 213.

LAND OF THE ARCHBISHOP OF CANTERBURY

Land of his knights

In Axton hundred

Ansgot holds Farningham from the archbishop. It is assessed at 1 suling. There is land for .[1] In the demesne there are 2 ploughs, and 13 villeins with 5 bordars have 3½ ploughs. There are 6 acres of meadow, and woodland for 20 pigs, and of this same woodland Richard of Tonbridge holds as much again in his lowy. *T.R.E.* this manor was worth 7 pounds; now 11 pounds. Of this the monks of Canterbury have 4 pounds to provide for their clothing.

Ralph, son of Unspac, holds Eynsford from the archbishop. It is assessed at 6 sulings. There is land for .[1] In the demesne there are 5 ploughs, and 29 villeins with 9 bordars have 15 ploughs. There are 2 churches and 9 slaves, and 2 mills worth 43 shillings and 29 acres of meadow. Woodland for 20 pigs. *T.R.E.* it was worth 16 pounds; now 20. Of this manor Richard of Tonbridge holds as much woodland as can sustain 20 pigs, and 1 mill worth 5 shillings and 1 fish-pond in his lowy.

Mauger holds from the archbishop 3 yokes in Orpington, and it was assessed for as much apart from Orpington. Now it is assessed for 2 yokes within Orpington, and for a third yoke apart from Orpington. There is land for .[1] In the demesne there is 1 plough; and 4 villeins with 1 bordar and 4 slaves have half a plough; 3 acres of meadow, and woodland for 11 pigs. *T.R.E.* it was worth 40 shillings; when received, 20 shillings; now 50 shillings.

Haimo the sheriff holds Brasted from the archbishop. It is assessed at 1½ sulings. There is land for 10 ploughs. In the demesne there are 2 ploughs; and 34 villeins with 16 bordars have 12 ploughs. There is a church; 15 slaves; and 2 mills worth 24 shillings; woodland for 80 pigs; and 9 shillings and 6 pence from herbage. *T.R.E.* it was worth 10 pounds; when received the same; now 17 pounds. Alnod the abbot held this manor from the archbishop.

The count of Eu holds Ulcombe from the archbishop. It is assessed at 2½ sulings *T.R.E.*, and is now assessed at 2 sulings. There is land for 9 ploughs. In the demesne are 2 ploughs; and 23 villeins with 7 bordars have 7 ploughs. There is a church; a mill worth 4 shillings; 8 acres of meadow; woodland for 80 pigs. In all it was worth *T.R.E.* 10 pounds; when received 8 pounds; now 11 pounds. Alfer held this manor from the archbishop.

In Eyhorne hundred

Ralph, the son of Turold, holds Boughton from the archbishop. It is assessed at half a suling and it is included in the 6 sulings of Hollingbourne. There is land for 1½

[1] A space is left for the number of ploughs.

ploughs. In the demesne is 1 plough; and 3 villeins with 2 bordars have 1 plough. There is a church; 2 acres of meadow; and woodland for 16 pigs. In all it is worth, and always was worth, 40 shillings.

In Faversham hundred

Richard, a man of the archbishop, holds Leaveland from him. It is assessed for 1 suling. There is land for .[1] In the demesne is 1 plough, and 2 villeins with 1 bordar have 1 plough. Woodland for 5 pigs. *T.R.E.* and afterwards it was worth 30 shillings. Now 20 shillings.

In Boughton-under-Blean hundred

The same Richard holds Graveney from the archbishop. It is assessed at 1 suling. There is land for .[1] In the demesne is 1 plough; and 8 villeins with 10 bordars have 2 ploughs. There are 5 slaves; 10 acres of meadow; and 4 salt-pans worth 4 shillings. *T.R.E.* and afterwards it was worth 100 shillings; now 6 pounds. Out of this the monks of Canterbury have 20 shillings.

In Calehill hundred

Godfrey the steward holds Lenham from the archbishop. It is assessed for 2 sulings. There is land for .[1] In the demesne are 2 ploughs, and 15 villeins with 2 bordars have 4 ploughs. There are 4 slaves; 6 acres of meadow; 1 mill worth 7 shillings; and woodland for 10 pigs. In all it was worth 8 pounds, but it renders 12 pounds and 10 shillings.

In Teynham hundred

The same Godfrey holds from the archbishop, in Sheppey, half a suling. There is land for .[1] In the demesne is 1 plough with 2 bordars and 4 slaves. *T.R.E.* and afterwards it was worth 30 shillings; now 4 pounds, but it renders 100 shillings.

In Eastry hundred

Osbern, the son of Letard, holds 1 yoke from the archbishop in Buckland, and there he has in demesne 1 plough; and it is worth 10 shillings.

William Folet holds Tilmanstone from the archbishop. It was assessed at 1 suling. In the demesne there are 2 ploughs and 5 bordars. Once it was worth 20 shillings. Now 30 shillings.

William Folet holds Finglesham from the archbishop. It is assessed at half a suling. There he has 6 villeins with 1½ ploughs. The same William holds Statenborough from the archbishop. It was assessed at half a suling. There he has 12 villeins with 1½ ploughs. These lands *T.R.E.* were worth 40 shillings. When the archbishop received them, 10 shillings. Now 30 shillings.

In Heane hundred

Hugh of Montfort-sur-Risle holds Saltwood from the archbishop. It was assessed at 7 sulings, *T.R.E.*, and now it is assessed at 3 sulings. There is land for 15 ploughs. In

[1] Space left for the number of ploughs.

the demesne there are 2 ploughs; and 33 villeins with 12 bordars have 9½ ploughs. There is a church; 2 slaves; 9 mills worth 20 shillings; 33 acres of meadow; woodland for 80 pigs. To this manor belong 225 burgesses in Hythe. The borough and the manor together were *T.R.E.* worth 16 pounds; when received 8 pounds. Now it is altogether worth 29 pounds, 6 shillings, and 4 pence.

In Street hundred

William of Adisham holds Berwick from the archbishop, for a manor. It is assessed at half a suling. There is land for 3 ploughs. In demesne there are 2 ploughs, and 9 villeins with 9 bordars have 1½ ploughs. There are 18 acres of meadow, and woodland for 20 pigs. *T.R.E.* it was worth 60 shillings, and afterwards 20 shillings. Now it is worth 7 pounds, but it renders 11 pounds.

In Langport hundred

Robert of Romney holds Langport from the archbishop. It is assessed for 1½ sulings. There is land for 6 ploughs. In demesne are 2 ploughs, and 29 villeins with 9 bordars have 9 ploughs. There are 7 salt-pans worth 8 shillings and 9 pence. To this manor belong 21 burgesses who are in Romney. From these the archbishop has the three forfeitures: theft, breach of the peace, and public violence. The king, however, has all their service, and they themselves have all customs and the other forfeitures in return for their sea-service. They are in the hand of the king. *T.R.E.* and afterwards it was worth 10 pounds; now 16 pounds.

207. Domesday Book, vol. 1, fol. 56: The Customs of Berkshire

Printed in the Record Commission's edition of Domesday Book (1783) and in W. Stubbs, *Select Charters*. Translated in *Victoria County History: Berkshire*, vol. 1, p. 326.

When in the time of King Edward a general geld was given, each hide throughout the whole of Berkshire used to give 3 pence and 1 halfpenny before Christmas, and as much again at Pentecost.

If the king was sending out an army anywhere, only one soldier[1] went out from each 5 hides, and for his provision or pay 4 shillings for 2 months was given him from each hide. The money, however, was not sent to the king but given to the soldiers. If anyone summoned to serve in an expedition failed to do so, he forfeited all his land to the king. If anyone secured a substitute and that substitute failed to serve, the lord of the substitute was fined 50 shillings.

When a thegn, or a demesne warrior of the king,[2] was dying he sent all his weapons to the king as a 'relief',[3] and 1 horse saddled and 1 horse unsaddled. If he possessed hounds or falcons, these were offered to the king for his acceptance if he wished to have them.

If anyone slew a man who was under the protection of the king's peace, his person and his possessions were forfeit to the king. If anyone broke into a town by night, he paid 100 shillings to the king and not to the sheriff. If anyone summoned to drive deer for the king's hunting failed to do so, he paid 50 shillings to the king.

[1] *miles.* [2] *Tainus vel miles regis dominicus.* [3] *pro relevamento.*

208. Domesday Book, vol. 1, fol. 154: The customs of Oxford and Oxfordshire

Printed in the edition of Domesday Book (1783) by the Record Commission and in W. Stubbs, *Select Charters*. A translation is in the *Victoria County History: Oxfordshire*, vol. 1, p. 401.

The shire of Oxford pays a 'farm' of three nights. It thus pays 150 pounds. As an increase to this it pays 25 pounds by weight. There comes from the borough 20 pounds by weight. From the mint there are 20 pounds in pennies which are reckoned at 20 to the ounce; 4 shillings are paid for weapons; 100 shillings 'by tale' are paid in respect of the queen's gift; 10 pounds are paid in respect of a hawk; 20 shillings in respect of a sumpter horse; 23 pennies reckoned at 20 to the ounce in respect of hounds; 6 sesters of honey and 15 pennies in respect of customary dues.

From the land of Earl Edwin in Oxfordshire and Warwickshire the king has 100 pounds and 100 shillings.

Anyone breaking the king's peace given under his hand and seal to the extent of committing homicide shall be at the king's mercy in respect of his life and members. That is if he be captured. And if he cannot be captured, he shall be considered as an outlaw, and anyone who kills him shall have all his possessions.

The king shall take the possessions of any stranger who has elected to live in Oxford and who dies in possession of a house in that town, and without any kinsfolk.

The king shall take 100 shillings from anyone who breaks into the court or house of another so that he inflicts death or injury upon him by assault.

The king shall likewise take 100 shillings from any man who having been summoned for military service fails to discharge that service.

The king shall be entitled to the body and the possessions of any man who kills another within his own court or house excepting always the dower of his wife, if he has a wife who has received a dower.

209. Domesday Book, vol. 1, fol. 262b: Account of the city of Chester

Printed in the Record Commission's edition of Domesday Book, in W. Stubbs, *Select Charters*, and in J. Tait, *The Domesday Survey of Cheshire* (Chetham Soc., 1916). The last-named work contains an excellent translation, upon which the version which follows is directly based.

The city of Chester paid geld *T.R.E.* for 50 hides. There are 3½ hides which are outside the city, that is 1½ hides beyond the bridge, and 2 hides in Newton and Redcliff and in the bishop's borough: these paid geld with the city.

There were in the city *T.R.E.* 431 houses which paid geld, and besides these the bishop had 56 houses which paid geld. This city then paid 10½ marks of silver. Two-thirds went to the king, and one-third to the earl.

These were the laws which were there observed:

If the peace given by the king with his own hand, or by his writ, or by his messenger was broken by anyone, the king received a fine of 100 shillings. But if the same peace of the king given by the earl at his command was broken, the earl had the third penny of the 100 shillings which were given in fine for this offence. If, however, the same peace, given by the king's reeve, or by the earl's servant, was broken, a fine of 40 shillings was paid, and the earl had the third penny.

If any freeman, breaking the king's peace which had been given, killed a man in a house, all his land and chattels were forfeit to the king, and he became an outlaw. The earl exacted the same penalty, but only when his own man incurred this forfeiture. Nobody, however, could give back peace to any outlaw except by the will of the king.

A man who shed blood from the morning of Monday to noon on Saturday paid a fine of 10 shillings. But from noon on Saturday until the morning of Monday 20 shillings was the amount of the fine for bloodshed. A like 20 shillings was paid as a fine by the man who shed blood in the 12 days of Nativity, on Candlemas Day, on the first day of Easter, and the first day of Pentecost, on Ascension Day, on the day of the Assumption or of the Nativity of Holy Mary, and on the day of the Feast of All Saints.

He who killed a man on these holy days paid a fine of 4 pounds; but on other days 40 shillings. So too he who committed 'hamfare'[1] or 'forsteal'[2] on these feast days and on Sunday paid 4 pounds; on other days 40 shillings.

He who incurred 'hengwite'[3] in the city paid 10 shillings; but a reeve of the king or earl incurring this forfeiture paid a fine of 20 shillings.

He who was guilty of robbery[4] or theft, or assaulted a woman in a house, paid a fine of 40 shillings.

If a widow had unlawful intercourse with any man, she paid a fine of 20 shillings; a young girl paid 10 shillings for this offence.

A man who seized the land of another in the city and could not prove it to be his, paid a fine of 40 shillings. He who made the claim paid a like fine if he could not prove the land to be his by right.

He who wished to take up his land or the land of his kinsman gave 10 shillings, and if he could not or would not pay this, the reeve took his land into the king's hand.

He who did not pay his 'gafol' at the term when it was due paid 10 shillings as a fine.

If fire broke out in the city, the man from whose house it came paid a fine of 3 ounces of pennies, and to his next-door neighbour he gave 2 shillings.

Two-thirds of all these forfeitures were the king's and one-third the earl's.

If ships arrived at the port of the city, or departed therefrom without the permission of the king, the king and the earl had 40 shillings from each man who was on the ships.

If a ship came against the king's peace, and despite his prohibition, the king and the earl had the ship, and the men, and all that was in the ship.

But if the ship came in the king's peace, and with his leave, then those on board might sell what they had undisturbed. When it left, however, the king and the earl took 4 pence from each last. If the king's reeve ordered those who had martens' pelts not to sell to anyone until the king had seen them and been given an opportunity of buying, then he who neglected to do this paid a fine of 40 shillings.

[1] Breaking into a house to commit a robbery.
[2] Probably, here, violence in the streets.
[3] Probably failure to raise the hue and cry after a thief.
[4] 'reulach'.

A man or a woman caught giving false measure in the city paid a fine of 4 shillings. Likewise the maker of bad beer was either set in the cucking-stool,[1] or paid 4 shillings to the reeves. The officers of the king and the earl took this forfeiture in the city in whosoever's land it arose, whether the bishop's or that of any other man. In like manner did they take toll, and anyone who delayed paying it beyond three nights paid a fine of 40 shillings.

There were in this city *T.R.E.* 7 moneyers who, when the coinage was changed, paid 7 pounds to the king and earl over and above the 'farm'.

There were then 12 'judges' of the city[2] and these were taken from the men of the king and the bishop and the earl. If any of them absented himself from the hundred court on the day of its session without proper excuse, he paid a fine of 10 shillings to the king and the earl.

For the repair of the city wall the reeve was wont to call up one man from each hide in the county. The lord of any man who failed to come paid a fine of 40 shillings to the king and the earl. This forfeiture was not included in the 'farm'.

This city then rendered a 'farm' of 45 pounds and 3 'timbres' of martens' pelts. A third of this was the earl's and two-thirds the king's.

When Earl Hugh received it, it was not worth more than 30 pounds for it was greatly wasted; there were 205 houses less than there had been *T.R.E.* There are now the same number as he found there.

Mundret held the city from the earl for 70 pounds and 1 mark of gold. The same Mundret had at 'farm' for 50 pounds and 1 mark of gold all the earl's pleas in the shire court, and in the hundred courts, except Englefield.

The land on which the church of St. Peter stands, which Robert of Rhuddlan claimed as thegn-land, never belonged to a manor outside the city, and this was proved by witness of the county. It belongs to the borough and always paid dues to the king and the earl like the lands of the other burgesses.

210. Domesday Book, vol. I, fols. 172 and 268: Salt-making in Domesday Book

These passages from Domesday Book are printed in the Record Commission's edition. The former is translated in the *Victoria County History: Worcestershire*, vol. I, p. 286. Of the latter there is an excellent translation, which is here reproduced, in J. Tait, *Domesday Survey of Cheshire* (1916), p. 219. Before modern methods were invented salt was obtained in England by evaporating brine in sheds called 'salterns', and the presence of these is frequently noted in Domesday Book as being part of the wealth of a manor. In a few places, however, such as Droitwich, the industry was more highly developed; and in one part of Cheshire the making of salt was of such importance that it created a "little industrial enclave in the midst of an agricultural district". Further information about salt-making in the time of Domesday may be obtained by reference to Tait, *op. cit.*, pp. 39-43, and to J. H. Round, in *Victoria County History: Worcestershire*, vol. I, p. 235.

In Wich[3] King Edward had 11 houses, and the same King Edward had his share in 5 brine-pits. In one brine-pit which is called 'Upewic' there are 54 salterns and 2 'hocci', and these together pay 6 shillings and 8 pence. In another brine-pit called 'Helperic' there are 17 salterns. In a third brine-pit called 'Midelwic' there are 12

[1] *in cathedra stercoris.*

[2] Cf. the Lincoln entry, below, No. 211, p. 872.

[3] *i.e.* Droitwich.

salterns, and two-thirds of a 'hoccus', and these together pay 6 shillings and 8 pence. In 5 other brine-pits there are 15 salterns. In respect of all these King Edward used to receive a 'farm' of 52 pounds. In these brine-pits Earl Edwin used to have 51½ salterns, and from the 'hocci' he used to have 6 shillings and 8 pence. All this used to pay 24 pounds for 'farm'. Now King William has in demesne both what King Edward and what Earl Edwin used to have. In respect of this the sheriff pays 65 pounds by weight and 2 'mits' of salt while he has the wood; and he says that unless he had the wood he could not possibly pay.

There was *T.R.E.* in Nantwich hundred a 'Wich'[1] in which there was a brine-pit for making salt, and there were 8 salterns so divided between the king and Earl Edwin that of all the issues and renders of the salterns the king had two-thirds and the earl one-third. But apart from these the earl had a saltern of his own which belonged to the manor of Acton. From this saltern the earl had sufficient salt for his house throughout the year. If, however, any was sold from that source the king had 2 pence of the toll and the earl the third penny.

In the same 'Wich' a number of men of the country had [2] salterns, from which there was the following custom. From the Ascension of our Lord to the Feast of St. Martin[3] anyone having a saltern might carry home free of toll his own salt; but if he sold any of it either there or elsewhere in the county of Cheshire, he paid toll to the king and the earl. After the Feast of St. Martin[3] anyone who carried salt away from there, whether his own or salt that he had purchased, paid toll. This, however, did not apply to the aforesaid saltern belonging to the earl since this had its own custom.

All these 8 salterns of the king and the earl, on the Friday in each week in which they were employed in boiling salt, rendered 16 boilings, of which 15 made 1 horse-load of salt. The salterns of the other men did not give these boilings on Fridays between the Ascension of our Lord and the Feast of St. Martin;[3] but from the Feast of St. Martin to the Ascension of our Lord they all gave boiling custom like the salterns of the king and the earl. All these salterns, both those that were and those that were not in demesne, were surrounded on one side by a certain stream, and on the other by a certain ditch. A man incurring a forfeiture within this boundary could make amends by a fine of 2 shillings or 30 boilings of salt. This did not include homicide, or such cases of theft as involved the penalty of death; these offences, if committed here, were amended as in the rest of the shire.

If a man went from the aforesaid precinct of the salterns to any part of the county without having paid his toll, and was convicted of this offence, he had to come back and pay it, and also to make amends there by a fine of 40 shillings, if he was a freeman, and 4 shillings if he was not free. But if he went to some other shire leaving his toll unpaid, he had to pay the fine in the place where it was demanded.

The 'Wich' paid 21 pounds in 'farm' *T.R.E.*, including all the pleas of this hundred. When Earl Hugh received it, it was waste except for only 1 saltern. William

[1] Nantwich. [2] Blank in MS. [3] 11 November.

Malbank now holds the said 'Wich' from the earl with all customs pertaining to it, and the whole of the hundred which is valued at 40 shillings, of which sum 30 shillings are charged upon the land of the said William; and the remaining 10 shillings are charged upon the land of the bishop and upon the lands of Richard of Vernon and Gilbert 'de Venables', which they hold in the same hundred. The 'Wich' is let at 'farm' for 10 pounds.

In Middlewich hundred there was another 'Wich'[1] shared between the king and the earl. There were no demesne salterns, but the same laws and customs were in force there as have been mentioned in connexion with the previous 'Wich', and the king and the earl similarly took their shares of the issues. This 'Wich' was let at 'farm' for 8 pounds, and the hundred in which it lay for 40 shillings. The king took two-thirds and the earl one-third. It was waste when Earl Hugh received it. Now the earl holds it himself, and it is let at 'farm' for 25 shillings and 2 cartloads of salt. The hundred is worth 40 shillings.

A man who carried away from these two 'Wiches' salt which he had bought, paid 4 pence in toll if he had 4 oxen or more in his cart; if 2 oxen he paid 2 pence, provided there were 2 horseloads of salt.

A man from any other hundred paid 2 pence for a horseload; but a man from the same hundred only a halfpenny for a horseload. Anyone who so loaded his cart that the axle broke within a league of either 'Wich' paid 2 shillings to the king's officer, or the earl's, if he could be overtaken within a league. Similarly he who so loaded his horse as to break its back, paid 2 shillings if overtaken within a league; beyond that he paid nothing.

A man who made 2 horseloads of salt out of one paid a fine of 40 shillings if the officer could overtake him. If he was not found, he did not pay the fine through any other person.

Men on foot from another hundred buying salt there paid 2 pence for 8 men's loads; men of the same hundred paid a penny for 8 loads.

In the same hundred of Middlewich there was a third 'Wich' which was called Northwich, and it was let to 'farm' for 8 pounds. There were the same laws and customs as prevailed in the other 'Wiches', and the king and the earl similarly divided the receipts.

None of the thegns who had salterns in this 'Wich' gave boilings of salt on Fridays in any part of the year.

A man who brought a cart with 2 or more oxen from another shire paid 4 pence in toll. A man from the same shire paid 2 pence for his cart within three nights of his return home. If the third night passed without payment having been made, he paid a fine of 40 shillings. A man from another shire paid a penny for a horseload; a man from the same shire paid a *minuta* within the third night.

If a man living in the same hundred carted salt about the shire in order to sell it, he paid a penny for each cart as often as he loaded it. If he carried salt on a horse in order to sell it, he paid a penny at the Feast of St. Martin. Anyone who failed to pay then was fined 40 shillings. All the other customs in these 'Wiches' are the same. This one was waste when Earl Hugh received it; now it is worth 35 shillings.

[1] Middlewich.

211. Domesday Book, vol. 1, fols. 336, 336b, 337: Passages from the survey of Lincolnshire

Printed in the edition by the Record Commission. An excellent critical translation (upon which the version which follows is directly based) will be found in C. W. Foster and T. Longley, *The Lincolnshire Domesday and the Lindsey Survey* (Lincoln Rec. Soc., 1924). This volume also contains an admirable introduction by F. M. Stenton indicating the general character of the Domesday description of this shire. The passages here printed include the description of the borough of Lincoln; the important statement of those who held jurisdictional rights in the shire in the time of King Edward; and part of the description of the king's land.

In the city of Lincoln there were *T.R.E.* 970 inhabited messuages. This number is reckoned according to the English method by which 100 counts for 120. In the same city there were 12 lawmen,[1] that is, men having sake and soke. These were Hardecnut; Suartin, son of Grimbold; Ulf, son of Sortebrand, who had toll and team; Walraven; Alwold; Brictric; Guret; Ulbert; Godric, the son of Eddeve; Siward the priest; Lewine the priest; and Aldene the priest. Now there are as many there having sake and soke in like manner: (i) Suartinc in place of his father, Hardecnut; (ii) Suartinc; (iii) Sortebrand in place of his father, Ulf; (iv) Agemund in place of his father, Walraven; (v) Alwold; (vi) Godwine, the son of Brictric; (vii) Norman Crassus in place of Guret; (viii) Ulbert, brother of Ulf, who is still living; (ix) Peter of Valognes in place of Godric, son of Eddeve; (x) Ulnod the priest in place of Siward the priest; (xi) Buruolt in place of his father, Lewine, who is now a monk; (xii) Ledwin, the son of Ravene, in the place of Aldene the priest.

Tochi, son of Outi, had in the city 30 messuages besides his hall and 2½ churches. And he had his hall quit of all custom. And with respect to 30 other messuages he had the rights of letting; and in addition to this he had from each messuage 1 penny, that is 'landgable'. Over these 30 messuages the king used to have toll and forfeiture, as the burgesses made oath. But Ulviet the priest gainsays their sworn testimony, and offers himself to prove by the ordeal of fire that it is not as they say. Geoffrey Alselin holds this hall, and his nephew, Ralph. Bishop Remigius holds the aforesaid 30 messuages in respect of the church of St. Mary, so that Geoffrey Alselin has nothing therein either by way of exchange or other render. The same Geoffrey has 1 messuage outside the wall and from this he has 'landgable' even as Tochi had.

Ralph Paynel has 1 messuage which was Merlsweyn's quit of all custom.

Ernuin the priest has 1 messuage which was Earl Morcar's with sake and soke; and he holds it of the king in the same way as Morcar had it, as he himself says.

Gilbert of Ghent has 1 messuage which was Ulf's with sake and soke; and another messuage from which he used to have 1 penny; and yet another messuage, which was Siward's, quit of all custom.

Earl Hugh has 1 messuage which was Earl Harold's with sake and soke and 2 messuages from which he has 'landgable'.

Roger of Bully has 1 messuage which was Sweyn's, the son of Suaue, with sake and soke.

The Countess Judith has 1 messuage which was Stori's without sake and soke; and Ivo 'Taillebosc' claims this through the burgesses. Bishop Remigius has 1 little manor

[1] Cf. the account of Chester, above, No. 209.

with 1 carucate of land near the city of Lincoln with sake and soke and with toll and team over it; and likewise over 3 messuages and over 2 churches; and likewise over 78 messuages except for the king's geld which they give with the burgesses. Of these messuages 20 are waste. Of the 3 messuages mentioned here, 1 is quit of all obligations, but 2 pay geld with the burgesses.

In the fields of Lincoln outside the city there are 12½ carucates of land, beside the carucate of the bishop of the city. Of this land the king and the earl have 8 carucates in demesne. Of these King William gave 1 carucate to a certain Ulchel for a ship which he bought from him. But he who sold the ship is dead, and no one has this carucate of land except by grant from the king. In addition to these 8 carucates the king and the earl have 231 acres of arable land which is 'inland'[1] and 100 acres of meadow.

Of the rest of the land, that is 4½ carucates, Ulf had *T.R.E.* 1 carucate; now his son, Sortebrand, has it.

Siward the priest and Outi had another carucate *T.R.E.* and 6 acres of land which Ulviet the priest holds. Now Alfnod has a moiety of this carucate, and Norman, the son of Siward the priest, has the other moiety. But Unlof the priest invaded this aforesaid moiety of this land, and Siward the priest's wife, while it was in the possession of the king on account of a fine of 40 shillings which the king himself had laid upon Siward the priest.

Peter of Valognes has the third carucate which *T.R.E.* Godric had. The fourth carucate belonged to the church of All Saints *T.R.E.* and 12 tofts and 4 crofts. Godric, son of Gareuine, had this church, and the church's land, and whatever belonged to it; but on his becoming a monk the abbot of Peterborough obtained it. But all the burgesses say that he has it unjustly, because neither Gareuine nor his son, Godric, nor anyone else could give it outside the city, or outside their own kindred, except by grant of the king. This church and what belongs to it, Ernuin the priest claims by inheritance from his kinsman, Godric.

St. Mary of Lincoln, in which the bishopric now is, had and has the remaining half carucate of land.

The churches of Lincoln and the burgesses had among them 36 crofts in Lincoln excepting the 12½ carucates of land which are enumerated above.

Of the aforesaid messuages which were inhabited *T.R.E.* there are now waste 200 by English reckoning, that is to say 240; and by the same computation 760 are now inhabited.

Those written below have not paid the king's geld as they ought:

The land of St. Mary's on which Tedbert lives in the High Street has not paid geld; nor has the bishop's land situated at St. Lawrence's paid geld in respect of 1 house.

The abbot of Peterborough has not paid geld in respect of 1 house and 3 tofts.

Earl Hugh has not paid geld in respect of any of his land; nor has Thorold of Greetwell nor Losuard nor Chetelbert. Hugh, son of Baldric, has not paid geld in

[1] See above, No. 176, p. 821, n. 4.

respect of 2 tofts, nor Geoffrey Alselin likewise in respect of 2 tofts. Nor has Gilbert paid geld in respect of 3 houses. Nor has Peter of Valognes in respect of his house; nor has the Countess Judith in respect of her house; nor has Ralph Paynel in respect of 1 house; nor has Ralph of Bapaume in respect of his house; nor has Ertald in respect of his house.

The house in respect of which the abbot of Peterborough has not, so they say, paid geld, Norman Crassus claims as belonging to the king's fief, for Godred his predecessor had it in pledge for 3½ marks of silver.

Colsweyn has in the city of Lincoln 4 tofts of his nephew Cole's land; and outside the city he has 36 houses and 2 churches to which nothing belongs, which he built on the waste land which the king gave him, and which was never before built upon. Now the king has all the customs from them.

Alfred, the nephew of Thorold, has 3 tofts from Sybi's land, which the king gave him, in which he has all customs except the king's geld in respect of minting.

The abbot of Ely has half a messuage of land from Edstan's land.

Hugh, son of Baldric, has 2 tofts which the king gave him.

Of the aforesaid waste messuages 166 were destroyed on account of the castle. The remaining 74 are waste outside the castle boundary, not because of the oppression of the sheriffs and officers, but by reason of misfortune and poverty, and the ravage of fires. *T.R.E.* the city of Lincoln used to render to the king 20 pounds and to the earl 10 pounds. Now it renders 100 pounds 'by tale' between the king and the earl. The mint, however, renders 75 pounds.

The county of Lincoln

The customs of the king and the earl in South Lincoln render 28 pounds.

In the North Riding the customs of the king and the earl render 24 pounds.

In the West Riding the customs of the king and the earl render 12 pounds.

In the South Riding the customs of the king and the earl render 15 pounds.

The king's peace

If the peace given by the king's hand, or by his seal, be broken, let a fine be paid by 18 hundreds. Each hundred pays 8 pounds; 12 hundreds pay the fine to the king, and 6 to the earl. If anyone for any crime shall have been outlawed by the king and by the earl and by the men of the shrievalty, no one but the king can give him peace. . . .

Here are written those who had sake and soke and toll and team in Lincolnshire

Bishop of Lincoln.
Queen Edith.
Abbot of Peterborough.
Abbot of Ramsey.
Abbot of Crowland.
Earl Harold.
Earl Morcar.
Earl Waltheof.
Earl Ralph.
Ulf Fenisc.
Merlsweyn.
Turgot.
Tochi, son of Outi.
Stori.
Ralph the staller.
Siward Barn.

Harold the staller.
Fyach.
Rolf, son of Sceldeware.
Godric, son of Torvert.
Achi, son of Siward, and Wilac, his brother, in respect of their father's land.
Lewine, son of Alwine.
Azer, son of Sualeva.
Ailric, son of Marfete.
Outi, son of Azer.
Adestan, son of Godran.
Tori, son of Rold.
Toli, son of Alsi.
Azer, son of Burg.
Wulward Wite.
Ulf.
Haminc.
Bardi.
Sweyn, son of Suaue.

The king's land

In Aswardhurn wapentake

A manor. In Kirkby Earl Morcar had 5 carucates assessed to the geld. There is land for 4 ploughs. Now the king has there 1 plough in demesne, and there are 14 sokemen with 2 ploughs, and 5 villeins and 5 bordars with 1 plough. There is half a church there. *T.R.E.* it was worth 4 pounds; now 8 pounds by weight and assay.

A berewick.[1] Evedon belongs to the aforesaid manor, and it is assessed at 10 bovates. There is land for 1 plough; 2 sokemen and 2 villeins have 1 plough. There is a mill worth 5 shillings and 4 pence, and the site of 1 mill, and 6 acres of meadow.

To the same manor belongs this sokeland:

Ewerby Thorpe, 1 carucate.
Howell, $2\frac{1}{2}$ bovates.
Heckington, 1 bovate.
Quarrington, 1 bovate. . . .

A manor. In South Kyme Earl Morcar had 4 carucates and 2 bovates of land assessed to the geld. There is land for 2 ploughs. Now the king has half a plough there in demesne, and 12 villeins and 3 bordars have 2 ploughs. There are 2 churches there, and 1 priest, and 2 acres of meadow, and 6 fish-ponds worth 4 shillings. There is, throughout this estate, 210 acres, and 700 acres of marsh. *T.R.E.* it was worth 40 shillings; now 60 shillings by weight and assay.

A manor. In Boothby Graffoe Earl Morcar had 8 carucates of land assessed to the geld. There is land for 9 ploughs. The king has 2 ploughs there in demesne, and 20 villeins and 2 bordars have 4 ploughs, and 11 sokemen on 3 carucates of land have 3 ploughs. There is a church and a priest; 1 carucate of land belongs to the church. There is 1 mill worth 3 shillings; and 120 acres of meadow. *T.R.E.* it was worth 20 pounds; now likewise 20 pounds by weight.

A manor. In Wellingore Earl Morcar had 18 carucates of land assessed to the geld. There is land for the same number of ploughs. Now the king has 2 ploughs there in demesne, and 7 villeins and 7 bordars have 1 plough, and 28 sokemen have 7 ploughs. There is a church and a priest with 2 carucates and 2 bovates of the same land. The

[1] An outlying estate, or grange.

church belongs to the church of St. Peter of Lincoln; 129 acres of meadow, and other 14 acres belonging to the church. *T.R.E.* it was worth 30 pounds; now 15 pounds by weight.

A manor. In Coleby Siward had 7 carucates of land assessed to the geld. There is land for the same number of ploughs. Now the king has 1 plough in demesne; and 5 villeins and 6 bordars have 1 plough; and 10 sokemen have 2 ploughs and 30 acres of meadow. *T.R.E.* it was worth 4 pounds. King William, however, assigned this land to Washingborough, and it is valued there. There is a priest and a church here with 1 bovate of this land.

Soke and berewick. In the same Coleby are 12 carucates of land assessed to the geld. There is land for the same number of ploughs. Of these 1 carucate is 'inland' in Washingborough; but 11 are sokeland. Ralph the staller had this land. Now the king has 14 sokemen and 7 villeins there with 8 ploughs; 60 acres of meadow. This is valued with Washingborough.

In Grantham Queen Edith had 12 carucates assessed to the geld. There is no arable land there outside the village. No one had sake or soke there except Elsuid the nun, who gave it to the abbey of Peterborough, and now Colegrim has this with sake and soke. Queen Edith had a hall and 2 ploughs in demesne, and land for 3 ploughs exempt from geld. There were 111 burgesses, and 77 tofts of the sokemen of the thegns. Now the king has a like number. Ivo found there 1 plough, which is still there, and 72 bordars. There is a church with 8 tofts; and 4 mills worth 12 shillings; and 8 acres of meadow exempt from geld. Of the aforesaid tofts the bishop of Durham claims 7 tofts which Ernuin the priest has, and the hundred bears testimony in the bishop's favour. *T.R.E.* all Grantham was sokeland, rendering 52 pounds; now it renders 100 pounds by weight. The church was farmed at 8 pounds; now it is farmed at 10 pounds; but it is only worth 100 shillings.

Soke and berewick. In Great Gonerby there are 7 carucates of land assessed to the geld. There is land for 9 ploughs; 3 carucates are 'inland', and 4 are sokeland belonging to Grantham. Now the king has 1 plough there in demesne; and 21 sokemen and 1 villein and 1 bordar have 6 ploughs; 105 acres of meadow.

Soke and berewick. In Harlaxton there are 12 carucates of land assessed to the geld. There is land for 16 ploughs; 9 carucates and sokeland, and 3 belong to the hall of Grantham. Now the king has 10 villeins and 2 bordars there with 2 ploughs, and 58 sokemen have 14 ploughs; 2 mills worth 2 shillings; 60 acres of meadow; 60 acres of underwood.

Soke. In South Stoke and North Stoke there are 9 carucates of land assessed to the geld. There is land for 12 ploughs. Now the king has 1 plough there in demesne; and 16 villeins have 3 ploughs; and 10 sokemen have 2 ploughs; 2 mills worth 20 shillings and 4 pence. Meadow 9 furlongs in length and 3 in breadth, and 20 acres.

Soke. In 'Nongtone' there are 3 carucates and 5½ bovates assessed to the geld. There is land for the corresponding number of ploughs. It is sokeland belonging to Grantham. The king has 13 sokemen and 6 villeins there with 4 ploughs; 1 mill worth 13 shillings and 4 pence; 3 acres of meadow.

Manor and soke. In Great Ponton Queen Edith had 12 carucates assessed to the geld. There is land for 10 ploughs. Now this land is sokeland belonging to Grantham.

There are now 10 villeins, 3 bordars and 12 sokemen and half a plough. Ivo found the same there. There is underwood 8 furlongs in length and 3 in breadth.

To Grantham belongs this sokeland:

Somerby, 2 carucates and 2 bovates.
Sapperton, 5 carucates.
Braceby, 5 carucates.
Welby, 8 carucates.
Belton, 5 carucates.
Harrowby, 4 carucates.
Dunsthorpe, 2 carucates.
Londonthorpe, 5 carucates and 6 bovates.
Barkston, 8 carucates.
Denton, 10 carucates.

Altogether 55 carucates assessed to the geld. There is land for 60 ploughs. The land is all in Aswardhurn wapentake.

In Somerby the king has 2½ carucates and 2 bovates and 8 sokemen with 2½ ploughs.

In Sapperton and Braceby there are 24 sokemen and 5 villeins and 2 bordars with 9 ploughs; 140 acres of meadow; 46 acres of woodland for pannage; 64 acres of underwood. And 1 church.

In Welby there are 37 sokemen and 7 villeins and 4 bordars with 10 ploughs; 160 acres of meadow; 150 acres of underwood; and a church with a priest.

In Belton there are 18 sokemen and 14 villeins with 4 ploughs and 68 acres of meadow.

In Harrowby there are 16 sokemen with 4 ploughs; 34 acres of meadow.

In Dunsthorpe there are 5 villeins and 1 bordar and 8 sokemen with 2 ploughs; 20 acres of meadow.

In Londonthorpe there are 21 sokemen and 6 villeins with 5 ploughs; 44 acres of meadow; 1 mill worth 10 shillings.

In Barkston there are 35 sokemen and 10 bordars with 6 ploughs; 70 acres of meadow; 2 mills which Turved, son of Ulved, had. Their soke belongs to Grantham.

In Denton there are 80 acres of meadow.

In Skillington there is sokeland of Grantham assessed to the geld at 3 carucates. There is land for 3 ploughs; 14 villeins and 2 bordars and 1 sokeman have 3 ploughs there; 10 acres of meadow; 140 acres of underwood. It is valued with Grantham....

212. Domesday Book, vol. II, fol. 210: Lands of the abbey of Bury St. Edmunds in Henstead hundred, Norfolk

Volume II of Domesday Book, containing the description of Essex, Norfolk and Suffolk, differs from volume I both in scope and character (see J. H. Round, *Feudal England* (1895), pp. 139–142, and cf. V. R. Galbraith in *Eng. Hist. Rev.*, vol. LVII (1942), p. 161). As far, at least, as Norfolk and Suffolk are concerned it also describes a society which seems to be less rigidly organized under manorial lordship (see D. C. Douglas, *Social Structure of Medieval East Anglia*). The number of relatively free peasants holding estates of irregular size is large, and their holdings are usually described separately from the manors to which they are attached. The following passage printed in the Record Commission's edition of Domesday Book (1783) and translated in *Victoria County History: Norfolk*, vol. II, p. 131, is intended to illustrate the descriptive method of volume II of Domesday Book. Reference may also be made to the account of Pakenham (Suffolk) printed below (No. 217).

Land of the abbot of St. Edmund

Henstead hundred

Caister now and then is held by St. Edmund for a manor and for 3 carucates. Then as now there are 10 villeins and 7 bordars, and there are 2 ploughs on the demesne and 4 ploughs belonging to the men. There are 6 acres of meadow and half a mill. Now 3 rounceys, 5 beasts, 30 pigs, 40 sheep.

Four sokemen hold 25 acres of land by the king's grant with all custom, and they belong to this manor as the hundred testifies. It was then worth 40 shillings; now 100 shillings. It is 6 furlongs in length and 4 in breadth. It renders 16 pence in geld, and several hold there. To the church belong 11 acres worth 16 pence.

Brooke was held by Earl Gyrth *T.R.E.*, and King William when he first came to St. Edmund's gave it to the abbey of St. Edmund to be held as 4 carucates. There were then 33 villeins; now 38. Then as now 3 slaves. Now 3 ploughs on the demesne, and 6 ploughs belonging to the men. Woodland for 30 pigs; 9 acres of meadow. Now 5 rounceys, 14 beasts, 40 pigs. Now 65 sheep and 20 goats.

There are 40 sokemen with 1½ carucates, and then as now 9 ploughs among them.

In Shotesham 16 freemen, Gyrth's men under commendation, have 1 carucate belonging to Brooke, and under them are 7 bordars; 4 acres of meadow and 3 ploughs. And the fourth part of a church. Of this Berengar holds 20 acres.

In Howe was 1 freeman of Gyrth belonging to Brooke. He had 1 carucate which Berengar now holds. Then as now 5 villeins and 6 bordars and 2 ploughs on the demesne. Then as afterwards 3 ploughs belonging to the men; now 2. Woodland for 40 pigs. To the church belong 15 acres worth 2 shillings.

In Poringland there was 1 freeman of Gyrth under commendation, and he belonged to Brooke. He held 30 acres and there was 1 bordar with half an acre. Then as now 1 plough.

Over all these freemen King Edward had sake and soke, and afterwards Gyrth took it by force. But King William gave with the manor sake and soke over all Gyrth's freemen, just as he himself had it. This the monks claim. Then and afterwards it was worth 10 pounds; now 15.

Brooke is 1 league and 4 furlongs in length, and 1 league in breadth, and gives 17 pence of geld. Others hold there.

213. Domesday Book, vol. II, fol. 450: Colophon to volume II of Domesday Book

In the year one thousand and eighty-six from the Incarnation of our Lord, and in the twentieth year of the reign of William there was made this survey[1] not only through these three counties,[2] but also through others.

[1] For parallel uses of the word *descriptio* in this sense, see above, Nos. 198, 199.

[2] *i.e.* Norfolk, Suffolk and Essex, which are the subject of volume II.

(*c*) SURVEYS CONNECTED WITH DOMESDAY BOOK

214. Description of part of the hundred of Staploe, Cambs., as given in the Cambridgeshire Survey (*Inquisitio Comitatus Cantabrigiensis*)

This survey which was made as a result of the Domesday Inquisition describes thirteen out of the sixteen hundreds of Cambridgeshire. Its relationship to Domesday Book is indicated above (pp. 847, 848), and it has been exhaustively discussed in J. H. Round, *Feudal England* (1895), pp. 1–146, by V. H. Galbraith in *Eng. Hist. Rev.*, vol. LVII (1942), pp. 161–171, and elsewhere. Two of the most important features of this survey may especially be noted: (i) at the beginning of each hundred (save one) the names of the Domesday jurors are given; and (ii) the material is arranged territorially (*i.e.* hundred by hundred) instead of (as in Domesday Book) under the holdings of the tenants-in-chief. Both these features appear in the section of the survey printed below, where it has been placed in juxtaposition with the corresponding entries in Domesday Book. The *Inquisitio Comitatus Cantabrigiensis* was edited by N. E. S. A. Hamilton in 1876, and a translation is given in the *Victoria County History: Cambridgeshire*, vol. I (1938), pp. 400–427.

CAMBRIDGESHIRE SURVEY

In Cambridgeshire. In Staploe hundred the following gave sworn evidence: Nicholas of Kennett; Hugh of 'Heselinges'; William of Chippenham; Warin of Soham; Robert of Fordham; Ormar of Badlingham; Alan of Burwell; Aluric of Snailwell; Picot the sheriff; and all the Frenchman and Englishmen.[1] In this hundred Nicholas holds Kennett from William of Warenne. It was assessed at 3½ hides *T.R.E.*; now at 2½ hides. There is land for 10 ploughs. There are 5 ploughs for the demesne and 5 for the villeins. There are 6 villeins, 1 priest and 12 slaves. There is also a mill, but it pays nothing. There is meadow for 2 ploughs. The livestock on the demesne are 8 beasts; 480 sheep; 10 pigs; 4 rounceys. There is pasture for the livestock of the village. In all it is worth 12 pounds; when he received it, 9 pounds; *T.R.E.* 12 pounds. 'Thobillus', a thegn of King Edward, held this manor; and in this manor there was a certain sokeman named Godric who was his man, and he could dispose of his land without the leave of his lord. *T.R.E.* 1 virgate of the same land always provided carrying service or made a customary payment of 57 pence yearly.

DOMESDAY BOOK

[Domesday Book, vol. I, fol. 196b]

Kennett, a manor, was assessed *T.R.E.* at 3½ hides: now at 3½ hides. There is land for 10 ploughs. Nicol holds it from William. There are 5 ploughs on the demesne, and 7 villeins with 5 bordars have 5 ploughs. There are 12 slaves; 1 mill which pays nothing; meadow for 2 ploughs, and pasture for the beasts of the village. In all it is worth 12 pounds; when he received it, it was worth 9 pounds; *T.R.E.* 12 pounds. Tochil, a thegn of King Edward, held this manor *T.R.E.* and 1 sokeman had 1 virgate under him. The sokeman performed carrying service or paid 8 pence, but he could give and sell his land.

[1] The Domesday Jurors.

CAMBRIDGESHIRE SURVEY

Staploe hundred

In this hundred Ormar holds Badlingham from Count Alan. It was assessed at 3½ hides (and 6 ploughs) *T.R.E.* Now it is assessed at 2½ hides. There is land for 6 ploughs; 2 ploughs are on the demesne and 4 are for the villeins. There are 9 villeins and 6 bordars, 6 slaves and 2 mills. One mill renders 2 shillings and the other serves the demesne. Meadow for 2 ploughs. There is pasture for the livestock of the village. There are 2 beasts, 60 sheep, 20 pigs and 2 rounceys. In all it is worth 60 shillings, and when he received it, 60 shillings; *T.R.E.* 100 shillings. *T.R.E.* Ormar, a man of Ediva, held this manor and could give it where he wished.

DOMESDAY BOOK

[Domesday Book, vol. I, fol. 195b]

Ordmær holds Badlingham from the count. It was assessed *T.R.E.* for 3½ hides, and now it is assessed at 2½ hides. There is land for 6 ploughs; 2 ploughs are on the demesne, and 9 villeins with 6 bordars have 4 ploughs. There are 6 slaves and 2 mills, one of which pays 6 shillings, and the other of which serves the demesne. There is meadow for 2 ploughs and pasture for the beasts of the village. In all it is, and was, worth 60 shillings; *T.R.E.* 100 shillings. Ordmær held this manor under Edeva and could dispose of it as he wished.

In this hundred Geoffrey of Manneville holds Chippenham. *T.R.E.* there were 10 hides and these hides were assessed at only 5. The sheriff of this shire had these hides assessed *T.R.E.* at only 5. There is land for 17 ploughs, 3 in the demesne and 14 for the villeins. There are 29 villeins, 13 bordars, 6 slaves. There is meadow for 3 ploughs, and there is pasture for the livestock of the village, 14 beasts, 9 pigs, 285 sheep, 3 rounceys; 1 mill. A fishery provides 1500 eels. In all it is worth 20 pounds; when he received it, 16 pounds; *T.R.E.* 12 pounds. Orgar the sheriff held this manor *T.R.E.* and was afterwards the man of Esgar the staller on the day on which King Edward was alive and dead. Of the aforesaid 10 hides, 5 provided contributions to King Edward's 'farm'; 2 sokemen held 2 hides *T.R.E.* and they could dispose of their land as they wished. But each of them was obliged by custom to pay 8 pence or to provide a horse for the service of King Edward. And if they failed in this they made amends in Fordham. And Orgar the sheriff himself had 3 hides and could give them to whom he would. This same Orgar gave this

[Domesday Book, vol. I, fol. 197a]

Chippenham, a manor, was assessed *T.R.E.* at 10 hides, but a certain sheriff by permission of the king reduced this assessment to 5 hides because the 'farm' oppressed him, so that now it is assessed at 5 hides. There is land for 17 ploughs. Geoffrey holds it from the king. In the demesne there are 3 hides, and 3 ploughs are there; 19 villeins with 13 bordars have 14 ploughs. There are 6 slaves. There is meadow for 3 ploughs and pasture for the beasts of the village. From the fishery there are 1500 eels. In all it is worth 20 pounds. When he received it, it was worth 16 pounds; *T.R.E.* 12 pounds. Orgar, sheriff of King Edward, held this manor, and afterwards he was the man of Asgar the staller; 5 hides of this land contributed to King Edward's 'farm'; 2 sokemen had 3 hides from the king, and could dispose of their land as they wished. Each one paid 8 pence, or supplied a horse in the king's service. If they failed in this duty they made amends at Fordham. Orgar the sheriff had himself 3 hides of this land, and could give it to anyone he wished. Orgar pawned this land for 7 marks of gold and 2 ounces, as

CAMBRIDGESHIRE SURVEY

land in pledge for 7 marks of gold and 2 ounces as the men of Geoffrey say. But the men of the hundred have seen neither a writ nor a messenger of the king, nor do they produce any evidence of this.

In this hundred, Hugh of Port-en-Bessin holds Snailwell. It was assessed for 5 hides *T.R.E.* and now is assessed as part of the fief of the bishop of Bayeux. There is land for 10 ploughs: 2 are on the demesne, and there might be a third; 8 are for the villeins. There are 8 villeins, 3 bordars, 7 sokemen, 4 mills worth 14 shillings and 4 pence. Meadow for 2 ploughs. There is wood for fencing to the extent of 2 cartloads from the king's demesne wood at Cheveley. The live-stock on the demesne is 100 sheep, 56 pigs, and 1 rouncey. In all it is worth 14 pounds, when he received it 12 pounds. *T.R.E.* 15 pounds. Stigand the arch-bishop held this manor *T.R.E.* And in this manor there were 6 sokemen who were the men of this archbishop. They could give their land to whom they wished, but the archbishop possessed their soke. This manor pertained to the church of St. Etheldreda [of Ely] *T.R.E.* and to the demesne 'farm' of the monks, but Abbot Leofsi lent it to Archbishop Stigand. And now Abbot Simeon re-claims it in virtue of the rights of his predecessors, as the men of the hundred testify. . . .

DOMESDAY BOOK

Geoffrey's men say, but the men of the hundred have neither seen a writ nor any messenger of the king concerning this matter, and they produce no evidence respecting it.

[Domesday Book, vol. I, fol. 199b]

Hugh holds Snailwell of the fief of the bishop of Bayeux. It was always assessed at 5 hides. There is land for 10 ploughs, 2 of which are on the demesne and there might be a third. There are 6 sokemen, 8 villeins, 3 bordars and 3 slaves. There are 4 mills worth 14 shillings and 4 pence, meadow for 2 ploughs, wood for fencing with 2 carts from the king's wood at Cheveley. In all it is worth 14 pounds; when he received it, it was worth 12 pounds; *T.R.E.* 15 pounds. Archbishop Stigand held this manor on the day on which King Edward was alive and dead, and there were always 6 sokemen here who were the men of the same arch-bishop. They could leave without his permission and give or sell their land, but soke over them remained to the arch bishop. This manor *T.R.E.* pertained to the demesne of the church of Ely, contri-buting to its demesne levy, but the abbot of that time pledged it to the archbishop as the men of the hundred bear witness. Abbot Simeon now reclaims it by reason of the right of his predecessors.

215. The Ely Inquest (*Inquisitio Eliensis*): Prologue and select passages

The Ely Inquest is not, like the Cambridgeshire Survey, an account of a whole county. It concerns merely the estates owned or claimed by the abbey of Ely, but it describes these as they lay in six shires: Cambridgeshire, Hertfordshire, Norfolk, Suffolk, Essex and Huntingdonshire. It was drawn up in connexion with the Domesday Inquisition, of which it gives a full description, together with a list of jurors in the hundreds of Cambridgeshire and Hertfordshire. These should be compared with the similar list supplied by the Cambridgeshire Survey, since this comparison elucidates the relation of both surveys to the Domesday Inquisition (No. 214). The Ely Inquest is independent (at least as far as Cambridgeshire and Hertfordshire are concerned) of the completed Domesday Book. The text was printed by H. Ellis in the *Additamenta* to Domesday, being volume IV (1816) of the Record Commission's edition of Domesday Book. The best edition is in N. E. S. A. Hamilton,

Inquisitio Comitatus Cantabrigiensis (1876). The Ely Inquest is exhaustively discussed in J. H. Round, *Feudal England* (1895), pp. 1–146. The passages printed below illustrate the character of this record.

Here follows the inquiry concerning lands which the king's barons made according to the oath of the sheriff of the shire and of all the barons and their Frenchmen, and of the whole hundred court–the priest, reeve and 6 villeins from each village. They inquired what the manor was called; who held it in the time of King Edward; who holds it now; how many hides there are; how many ploughs in demesne and how many belonging to the men; how many villeins; how many cottars; how many slaves; how many freemen; how many sokemen; how much woodland; how much meadow; how much pasture; how many mills; how many fisheries; how much has been added to, or taken away from, the estate; what it used to be worth altogether; what it is worth now; and how much each freeman and sokeman had and has. All this to be recorded thrice: to wit, as it was in the time of King Edward, as it was when King William gave the estate, and as it is now. And it was also noted whether more could be taken from the estate than is now being taken.

In Staploe hundred these men gave sworn evidence:[1] Nicholas of Kennet; William of Chippenham, the man of Geoffrey; Hugh 'de Heselinge'; Warin of Soham; Robert the Englishman of Fordham; Ordmar of Badlingham; Alan of Burwell; Alfric of Snailwell.

(These men gave sworn evidence.)

In Cheveley hundred the following gave sworn evidence:[1] Richard, the reeve of this hundred; Edward, the man of Aubrey of Ver; Ralph 'de Hotot'; William 'de Mara'; Stanhard of Silverley; Frawin of Kirthling; Charles of Cheveley; Ulmar, the man of 'Wighen'.

In Staine hundred the following men gave sworn evidence: Aleran; Roger, the man of Walter Giffard; Richard, the reeve of this hundred; Farman, the housecarl of Swaffham; Leofwin; Harold, the man of Hardwin 'de Scalers'; Alfric of Wilbraham; and all other Frenchmen and Englishmen of this hundred.

In Armingford hundred the following gave sworn evidence: Walter; Humphrey 'de Anslevilla'; Hugh Petwolt; Richard of Morden; Colsweyn; Ailmar, his son; Turulf; Alfwin Odesune; and all other Frenchmen and Englishmen of this hundred.

In Thriplow hundred the following gave sworn evidence: Ralph, the reeve of this hundred; William of Cailly; Ralph of Barrington; Theobald, the man of Hardwin; Stanhard of Hauxton; Godric of Fowlmere; Alfric of Thriplow; Sigar the steward; and all other Frenchmen and Englishmen of the hundred.

In Radfield hundred the following gave sworn evidence: Manfrid; David of Balsham; William, the man of Walter; Ralph 'de Cluneia'; Adestan of Weston Colville; Grim of West Wratting; Algar of Dullingham; Pinna of Balsham; and all other Frenchmen and Englishmen of this hundred.

In Flendish hundred the following gave sworn evidence: Robert of Histon; Osmund the small; Fulcold, the man of the abbot of Ely; Baldwin the cook; Edwin the priest; Wulfric of Teversham; Silac; Godwin of Fulbourn.

In Whittlesford hundred the following gave sworn evidence: Ansketill 'de Herolfvilla'; Payn, the steward of Hardwin; Gerard of Lorraine; Hervey of Sawston;

[1] *juraverunt.*

Lemar of Whittlesford; Lefo of Duxford; Leofric, son of Grim; Lemar of Hinxton.

In Wetherley hundred the following gave sworn evidence: Sefrid, the reeve of the hundred; Ralph 'de Bans'; Fulk, the man of the sheriff; Rumold, the man of Count Eustace; Saward of Harlton; Turbert of Orwell; Brixcet of Barton; Almar Blacsune; and all other Frenchmen and Englishmen of this hundred.

In [Long]stow hundred the following gave sworn evidence: William, the man of Picot the sheriff; Tehel, the reeve of the abbot of Ely; Warin the priest; Guy, the man of the abbot of Ramsey; Godric of Croxton; Alfric, the reeve of Eudes; Wulfwig of Hatley; Almar Cilt; and all other Frenchmen and Englishmen of this hundred.

In Papworth hundred the following men gave sworn evidence: Richard, the man of Hardwin; Ralph 'de Felegeres'; Albert, the man of the abbot of Ramsey; Thehard, the man of the abbot of Ely; Leofwine 'Gricus'; Osbert, the man of Gilbert of Ghent; Bricstan, the man of Gilbert of Ghent; Godwine the priest; and all other Frenchman and Englishmen of this hundred.

In Northstowe hundred the following gave sworn evidence: Walter of 'Cleis'; Roger, son of Morin; Hugh 'Farsit'; Robert, son of Warin; Godlive; Azor; Godmar of Girton; Waluric of Girton; and all other Frenchmen and Englishmen of this hundred.

In Chesterton hundred the following gave sworn evidence: Roger of Childerley; Giffard of Dry Drayton; Gilbert of Histon; Sturmid of Cottenham; Bruning of Chesterton; Almar of Cottenham; 'Ledmarus' of Dry Drayton; Erni of Childerley; and all other Frenchmen and Englishmen of this hundred.

In the two hundreds of Ely which meet at Witchford the following men gave sworn evidence: Rainald of Downham; Geoffrey, the reeve of these hundreds; Tancred of Sutton; Osmund of Stretham; Gilbert of Lindon; Geoffrey, the constable of the abbot; Robert the chamberlain; Bernard 'de Monte'; Huna of Ely; Alfric Wordepund; Alfric Serdere; Osmund of Witcham; Alnod of Sutton; Ledmar of Witchford; Leodman the priest; Alfuin of 'Haningetuna'.

Hertford

In Edwinstree hundred the following gave sworn evidence: Ralph Baiard; Riculf, the man of the bishop of London; Rodri, the man of the bishop; Huart 'de Noderes'; Godwin of Hormead; Lexius, the man of the abbess of Chatteris; Siric, the man of Count Eustace; Siward of Hormead; and all other Frenchmen and Englishmen of this hundred.

In the double hundred of Broadwater the following gave sworn evidence: Letard, the man of the abbot; Gosbert of Beauvais; William of Latchworth; Liuet, the man of G. 'de Brec'; Ralph of Sheephall; Humphrey of Knebworth; Geoffrey of Chisfield; Geoffrey of 'Westbroc'; Alward of Mardleybury; Haldene; Thorkill of Digsvell; Alric of 'Winwoodeslaio'; Alfwin of 'Weslaio'; Alfric of Weston; Alward Framward; Alward of Munden; and all other Frenchmen and Englishmen of these two hundreds.

In Odsey hundred the following gave sworn evidence: Hugh, man of the bishop of Bayeux; Fulk, the man of Goisfrid of Beauvais; Germund of St. Ouen; Alfwin of Rushden; Boia, the man of the bishop; Wulfsi of Kelshall; Albert 'de Samsona'; Wigar of Horwell; and all other Frenchmen and Englishmen of this hundred.

In the county of Cambridge

In Staploe hundred. Snailwell was assessed in the time of King Edward for 5 hides; and there is now land for 10 ploughs; 2 ploughs are in the demesne and 1 could be added; and there are 8 villein ploughs; 8 villeins; 3 cottars; 3 slaves; a mill worth 4 [pounds] and 14 shillings; meadow for 2 ploughs. In the wood of Cheveley they have by customary right 2 carts [*c.*] for fencing; 111 sheep; 16 pigs; 1 rouncey. It is worth 14 pounds; when he received it, 12 pounds; *T.R.E.* 15 pounds. In the same village are 6 sokemen, who are men of the abbot [of Ely]. They could give or sell their land as they wished, but soke over them always belongs to the abbot. This manor pertained to the church of St. Etheldreda of Ely *T.R.E.* and contributed to the demesne 'farm' of the monks. But Abbot Leofsi pledged it to Stigand the archbishop, and now Abbot Simeon reclaims it by the right of his predecessors, as the men of the hundred witness.

In Soham the abbot of Ely holds half a hide. There is land for 2 ploughs: 1 on the demesne and 1 for the villeins. There are 3 villeins and 10 cottars. There is meadow for 2 ploughs, and pasture for the beasts of the village. In this village one boat fishes in the mere by customary right. 3 pigs. It is now worth 30 shillings; when he received it, 20 shillings; *T.R.E.* 30 shillings. This land always pertained to the church in demesne. . . .

The following concerns the borough of Cambridge. It was assessed *T.R.E.* for 1 hundred:

In the first ward of Cambridge the abbot of Ely has 2 messuages.
In the second ward which is called Bridgeward. . . .
In the third ward 2 messuages, 1 of which is empty.
In the fourth ward 1 messuage and 1 church is situated, and 2 empty dwellings.
In the fifth ward 1 messuage is not empty.
In the sixth ward. . . .
In the seventh ward. . . .
In the eighth ward. . . .
In the ninth ward 1 empty messuage.
In the tenth ward 3 plots are not empty, and besides there is 1 empty plot.

In Cambridgeshire the abbot reclaims the fourth penny as his charters witness, and as the men of the shire testify. . . .

In Huntingdonshire[1]

In Spaldwick the abbot of Ely has 1 manor assessed at 15 hides to the geld among the manor and the outlying estates of Stowe, Easton, 'Bercheham'; 15 ploughs can plough this land. The lord had 4 ploughs in demesne, and there were 42 villeins and 8 bordars in thegn-land outside the geld. Now the abbot of Ely has there 4 ploughs; 7 beasts; 30 pigs; 120 sheep; 1 rouncey; 4 beehives; and 1 mill worth 2 shillings. There are 50 villeins and 10 bordars. Among them all there are 25 ploughs and 160 acres of meadow; 60 acres of woodland for pannage. It was worth *T.R.E.* with all

[1] What follows should be compared with the account given of these manors in Domesday Book. See above, No. 250, pp. 858, 859.

its appurtenances 16 pounds; and now it is worth 22 pounds. The whole is 3 leagues long and 2 leagues broad.

In Catworth Abbot Thurstan had 4 hides assessed to the geld. This is an outlying estate of Spaldwick. And there were 8 villeins with 8 ploughs. Now the abbot of Ely has it. And there are 7 villeins with 2 ploughs. And this is valued in Spaldwick.

In Colne Abbot Thurstan had a manor assessed at 6 hides to the geld and 6 ploughlands for ploughing. And there were 19 villeins and 5 bordars with 8 ploughs. The same abbot had land for 2 ploughs apart from the 6 hides. Now Abbot Simeon has it. And 1 villein has 2 ploughs. There are 30 sheep, 45 pigs, 13 villeins and 5 bordars with 5 ploughs. Now the abbot himself has 2 ploughs, and 30 sheep and 45 pigs, and 13 villeins and 5 bordars with 5 ploughs; and 10 acres of meadow. Wood for pannage 1 league long and half a league broad. A marsh 1 league long and half a league broad. The whole 2 leagues long and 1 league broad. *T.R.E.* it was worth 6 pounds; now 5 pounds.

In Bluntisham Abbot Thurstan had a manor assessed at 6½ hides to the geld. There were 8 ploughlands for ploughing. And 20 villeins and 6 bordars with 7 ploughs. The abbot himself had land for 2 ploughs apart from the aforesaid hides. And now Abbot Simeon finds there 2 ploughs and 12 beasts and 60 sheep and 30 pigs. And 10 villeins and 3 bordars have 3 ploughs. Now the abbot himself has 2 ploughs; 12 beasts; 60 sheep; 45 pigs; 1 church and 1 priest; 20 acres of meadow. Woodland for pannage 1 league long and 4 furlongs in breadth. The whole 2 leagues long, 1 league in breadth. It was worth *T.R.E.* 5 pounds; now 5 pounds.

Somersham. Abbot Thurstan had a manor assessed at 8 hides to the geld; 12 ploughlands for ploughing. And 28 villeins and 9 bordars with 16 ploughs. The abbot himself had land for 2 ploughs outside the aforesaid hides. Abbot Simeon finds there 2 ploughs and 12 beasts and 90 sheep and 40 pigs and 13 bordars with 20 ploughs, and 3 fish-ponds worth 8 shillings and 20 acres of meadow. Woodland for pannage 1 league long and 7 furlongs broad. The whole 3 leagues long and 1 league broad. It was worth *T.R.E.* 7 pounds; now 8 pounds.

216. Description of some of the lands held by the abbot of Tavistock in Devon contained in the "Exon Domesday"

The "Exon Domesday" is "a pretty full digest of the original returns for Somerset, nearly all Devon and Cornwall, each fief of importance having a separate booklet or quire; also for nearly half Dorset, and one manor of Wiltshire – the rest have no doubt been lost before the MS. was bound together about 1400". The "Exon Domesday" is printed in the *Additamenta* to Domesday Book, being volume III (1816) of the Record Commission's edition. The portion relating to Devon is printed in translation in the *Victoria County History: Devonshire*, vol. I, and the portion relating to Somerset in the *Victoria County History: Somerset*, vol. I. A rearranged translation putting the text into juxtaposition with Domesday Book will be found in *The Devonshire Domesday and Geld Inquest* (1884–1892), edited for the Devonshire Association. The close connexion of this text with Domesday Book will be apparent to its readers. The "Exon Domesday" has, however, many features peculiar to itself. Its workmanship is inferior to that of Domesday Book; in the spelling of place-names it reflects local pronunciation; it contains a mass of detailed information not to be found in Domesday Book; and it omits both the preliminary list of tenants-in-chief, and also the names of the hundreds. It has been held to be a "first draft of the rearranged returns". Whether Domesday Book for these counties was digested independently from the returns, or whether it was taken either from the "Exon Domesday" or from some recension thereof has been disputed, but opinion now tends to the latter view, and the reader can find the matter more fully discussed in the introduction to the "Domesday Survey" in the *Victory County History: Devonshire*, vol. I; by

V. H. Galbraith in *Eng. Hist. Rev.*, vol. LVII (1942), and vol. LXV (1950); by R. Welldon Finn, *ibid.*, vol. LXVI (1951); and by H. P. R. Finberg, *Tavistock Abbey* (1951). It may be noted further that the "Exon Domesday" contains for Devon, Cornwall and Somerset a section relating to *terrae occupatae*, lands entered upon, which deals with the unauthorized acquisition of territory after the Conquest; and this finds no place in the account given by Domesday Book for these counties. The passages printed below have been placed in juxtaposition with the corresponding entries in Domesday Book in order that the relation between the two texts may be appraised.

EXON DOMESDAY

Lands of the abbot of Tavistock in Devonshire

The abbot of Tavistock has a manor called Tavistock. *T.R.E.* it paid geld for 3½ hides; 40 ploughs can till this. The abbot has there half a hide and 5 ploughs in demesne; and the villeins have 1½ hides and 14 ploughs. There the abbot has 17 villeins; 20 bordars; 12 slaves; 1 rouncey; 26 beasts; 12 pigs; 200 sheep; 30 goats; 1 mill for the service of the abbey; woodland 2 leagues long and 1 league broad; 16 acres of meadow; pasture 10 furlongs long and the same in breadth.

Of these 3½ hides 6 knights hold 1½ hides which 4 thegns held *T.R.E.* of the abbot without being able to separate themselves from the church.

Of this Ermenald has half a virgate. He has 1 plough, and his villeins have 1 plough, 7 beasts and 40 sheep.

Of this Ralph has half a virgate, 1 villein; 3 cotsets; and they have half a plough.

Hugh has half a hide, a third of a virgate and 1 ferling and has 2 ploughs in demesne. He has there 1 villein; 6 bordars; 2 slaves; and they have 7 ploughing oxen. Hugh has there 10 beasts; 12 pigs; 60 sheep.

Robert has 1 virgate and 2 ferlings, 1½ ploughs in demesne; and the villeins have 1½ ploughs. Robert has there 3 villeins; 6 bordars; 2 slaves; 12 beasts; 60 sheep; 20 goats.

Ralph 'de Tilio' has three-quarters of a virgate and 1 plough; 1 villein and 4 bordars have 2 oxen; 7 beasts; 30 sheep; 10 goats.

Geoffrey has 1 ferling and he has

DOMESDAY BOOK

Land of the church of Tavistock

The church of Tavistock holds the manor of Tavistock. *T.R.E.* it paid geld for 3½ hides. There is land for 40 ploughs. In demesne there are 5 ploughs and 12 slaves; and 17 villeins, and 20 bordars with 14 ploughs. There is a mill for the service of the court and 16 acres of meadow. Pasture 10 furlongs long and the same in breadth. Woodland 2 leagues long and 1 league broad. Of the land of this manor Ermenald holds half a virgate. Ralph holds the same. Another Ralph holds three-quarters of a virgate. Robert holds 1 virgate and 2 ferlings. Geoffrey 1 ferling. Hugh holds half a hide and a third of a virgate and 1 ferling. These lands were held from the abbot by 4 thegns *T.R.E.*, and the thegns could not be separated from the church. There are in demesne 6½ ploughs and 4 slaves; and 6 villeins, 17 bordars and 3 cotsets with 4 ploughs. The whole is worth to the abbot 12 pounds; to the knights 100 shillings. Formerly it was worth altogether 22 pounds.

EXON DOMESDAY	DOMESDAY BOOK
there 1 plough; 1 bordar; 6 beasts; 30 sheep. This manor is worth to the abbot 12 pounds a year; to the knights 100 shillings. When the abbot and the knights received it, it was worth 14 pounds and 8 pounds respectively.	
The abbot of Tavistock has a manor called Milton which *T.R.E.* paid geld for half a hide; 15 ploughs can till this. The abbot has there 1 virgate and 5 ploughs in demesne; the villeins have 1 virgate and 10 ploughs. The abbot has there 14 villeins; 12 bordars; 12 slaves; 22 beasts; 12 pigs; 170 sheep; 30 goats; 10 acres of woodland; 20 acres of meadow; 400 acres of pasture. It is worth 8 pounds, and was worth 4 pounds when the abbot received it.	The church itself holds Milton. *T.R.E.* it paid geld for half a hide. There is land for 15 ploughs. In demesne are 5 ploughs and 12 slaves; and 14 villeins and 12 bordars have 10 ploughs; 20 acres of meadow; 400 acres of pasture; 10 acres of woodland. Formerly it was worth 4 pounds; now 8 pounds.
Along with this manor the abbot holds 2 manors which, *T.R.E.*, 2 thegns held in parage, one called Leigh and the other Liddaton; and they paid geld for half a hide; 15 ploughs can till this. Of this the abbot has 1 ferling and 1 plough in demesne, and the villeins have 1 virgate, 3 ferlings and 4 ploughs. There the abbot has 4 villeins; 3 slaves; 5 bordars; 4 beasts; 30 sheep. They are worth 60 shillings a year; when the abbot received them, 30 shillings.	With this manor the abbot holds 2 lands, Leigh and Liddaton. *T.R.E.* these were held by 2 thegns as 2 manors, and they paid geld for half a hide. There is land for 15 ploughs. In demesne are 1 plough and 3 slaves; and 4 villeins and 5 bordars have 4 ploughs. Formerly it was worth 30 shillings; now 60 shillings.
The abbot has a manor called Liddaton which *T.R.E.* paid geld for half a hide; 3 ploughs can till this. Geoffrey holds it from the abbot, and it is part of the abbot's demesne. Of this Geoffrey has half a virgate and 1 plough in demesne, and the villeins half a virgate and 2 ploughs. There Geoffrey has 5 villeins; 2 bordars; 3 slaves; 24 beasts; 10 pigs; 100 sheep; 50 goats; 12 acres of woodland; 10 acres of meadow; 80 acres of pasture. Now worth 30 shillings a year; when the abbot received it, it was worth 20 shillings.	Geoffrey holds Liddaton from the abbot. *T.R.E.* it paid geld for half a hide. There is land for 3 ploughs. [They are there with] 5 villeins; 2 bordars; 3 slaves; 10 acres of meadow; 80 acres of pasture; 12 acres of woodland. Formerly it was worth 20 shillings; now 30 shillings.
The abbot has a manor called Hatherleigh which *T.R.E.* paid geld for 3 hides;	The church itself holds Hatherleigh. *T.R.E.* it paid geld for 3 hides. There is

EXON DOMESDAY

30 ploughs can till this. Of this the abbot has half a hide in demesne and 3 ploughs; and the villeins have 1½ hides and 10 ploughs.

Nigel, a French knight, had half a virgate all but half a ferling. Here Nigel has 1 plough in demesne, and the villeins have 1 plough. He has there 5 cotsets; 1 slave; 6 beasts; 4 pigs; 40 sheep.

Walter has half a hide and half a virgate and 1 plough on the demesne; and the villeins have half a hide, 4 ploughs and 12 beasts. On it Walter has 10 pigs; 50 sheep; 1 mill paying 6 pence yearly; 7 villeins; 2 bordars; 1 slave. Geoffrey has half a virgate and half a ferling. On it he has 1 plough, and the villeins have another. Also 4 villeins; 1 slave; 1 cow; 5 goats.

Ralph has half a virgate and 1 plough; 1 villein; 4 bordars; 7 beasts; 3 pigs; 12 sheep; 6 goats.

Of this manor the abbot has 26 villeins; 6 cotsets; 6 slaves; 15 beasts; 4 pigs; 44 sheep; 24 goats; woodland 2½ leagues in length and half a league in breadth; 100 acres of meadow; pasture 3 leagues in length and half a league in breadth. This manor is yearly worth to the abbot 10 pounds; and to the knights 60 shillings. When the abbot received it, it was worth 4 pounds, and when the abbot received the land of the knights it was worth 40 shillings.

The abbot has a manor called Thornbury which *T.R.E.* paid geld for 1 hide; 10 ploughs can till this. Ralph holds it from the abbot. Of this Ralph holds 1 virgate and 2 ploughs in demesne; and the villeins have 3 virgates and 4 ploughs. Ralph has there 10 villeins; 6 bordars; 3 slaves; 14 beasts; 15 pigs; 50 sheep; 30 goats; 20 acres of woodland; 100 acres of meadow; 120 acres of pasture.

On the day on which King William sent his barons to inquire about the lands of England, the abbot of Tavistock was

DOMESDAY BOOK

land for 30 ploughs. In demesne are 3 ploughs and 6 slaves; and 26 villeins and 6 cotsets have 10 ploughs; 100 acres of meadow. Pasture 3 leagues in length and half a league in breadth. Out of this land Nigel holds half a virgate less half a ferling. Walter 3 virgates. Geoffrey half a virgate and half a ferling. Ralph half a virgate. There are in demesne 4 ploughs and 3 slaves; and 12 villeins; 4 bordars and 5 cotsets have 6 ploughs. There is a mill on Geoffrey's land paying 6 pence. This manor is worth to the abbot 10 pounds. To the knights 3 pounds. Formerly it was worth, altogether, 9 pounds.

Ralph holds Thornbury from the abbot. *T.R.E.* it paid geld for 1 hide. There is land for 10 ploughs. In demesne are 2 ploughs and 3 slaves; and 10 villeins and 6 bordars have 4 ploughs; 100 acres of meadow; 120 acres of pasture; 20 acres of woodland. It is worth 3 pounds.

[No corresponding entry in Domesday Book]

EXON DOMESDAY	DOMESDAY BOOK
possessed of a manor called Werrington, and his predecessor before him had possessed this. But by the king's barons, he was dispossessed of this because, according to the testimony of the English, it did not belong to the abbey in the time of King Edward.[1]	
The abbot has a manor called Ham which paid geld for 2 hides; 20 ploughs can till this. Of this the abbot has 1 virgate and 2 ploughs in demesne; and the villeins have 1 hide, 3 virgates and 15 ploughs. The abbot has there 21 villeins; 6 bordars; 4 slaves; 6 beasts; 4 pigs; 118 sheep; 2 acres of woodland; 6 acres of meadow; 60 acres of pasture. The manor pays 100 shillings a year; when the abbot received it, it was worth 60 shillings.	The church itself holds Ham. *T.R.E.* it paid geld for 2 hides. There is land for 20 ploughs and 4 slaves; and 21 villeins and 6 bordars have 15 ploughs; 6 acres of meadow; 60 acres of pasture; 2 acres of woodland. Formerly it was worth 60 shillings; now 100 shillings.

217. The Feudal Book of Baldwin, abbot of Bury St. Edmunds

The prologue to this record relates it directly to the Domesday Inquisition. The record itself is divided into three distinct parts. The first part contains a portion of the material included in Domesday Book, vol. II. This material is arranged in a different order, and there is a little additional information given, although the statistics are much abbreviated. The second part of this record is a regrouping of certain of the estates of the abbot according to the holding of its feudal tenants. This also in the main reproduces selected statistics from Domesday Book, but again there is some additional information. The third section of this record is a list of peasant holdings and rents. The relationship of the three parts of the Feudal Book to Domesday is somewhat doubtful. Part i may be, like the *Inquisitio Eliensis*, an independent summary of the Domesday returns, or it may be a summarized and rearranged copy made from Domesday Book itself. Part iii has been considered as a list of the names and holdings of the free peasants who in the second volume of Domesday are mentioned in composite statements separately from the manors to which they are attached; but this section of the Feudal Book has also been considered as a distinct survey made some time in the reign of Henry I. The whole record is printed and discussed in D. C. Douglas, *Feudal Documents from the Abbey of Bury St. Edmunds* (1932). Reference should also be made to V. H. Galbraith, *Eng. Hist. Rev.*, vol. LXVII (1942), p. 161. Here follow passages from all three parts of this text.

(i)

In Suffolk

These are the manors which St. Edmund had in his demesne. And these are the lands of his men which they held also at the time when, by the order of King William, there was made a survey[2] of the whole of England according to the sworn evidence which was then given by almost all the inhabitants of the land, whereby each one gave a true verdict when questioned about his own land and substance, and about the land and substance of his neighbours. These things the saint and his men held on the day on which the aforesaid king was alive and dead. . . .

[1] *De mansione que vocatur Olwritona erat saisitus abbas Tavistochensis ea die qua rex Willelmus misit barones suos ad inquirendas terras Anglie, et antecessor suus ante eum fuerat inde saisitus; et per barones regis inde desaisitus fuit propter hoc quod testati sunt Angli quod ad abbatiam non pertinuit ea die qua rex Edwardus vivus et mortuus fuit.*
[2] *descriptio.*

In Long Melford the abbot holds 12 carucates of land and 17 villeins and 30 bordars and 2 sokemen with 80 acres of land. . . .

[Domesday Book, vol. II, fol. 359]

At Long Melford St. Edmund held 12 carucates of land for a manor. Out of this land Walter holds 40 acres from the abbot. There were always 37 villeins; then 25 bordars, now 10 . . . and 2 sokemen with 80 acres of land. . . .

In Pakenham the abbot holds 7 carucates of land, and 44 villeins and 23 bordars; and 31 sokemen have 2 carucates of land; and 3 freemen have 30 acres of land. There, also, 1 freeman who has 1 carucate of land asked the abbot to lend him half a carucate of land on this agreement that all his land, wherever it may be, shall remain in the possession of the saint after his death. Now, of this land 1 carucate belongs to the demesne[1] of Pakenham, and there are 5 bordars.

[Domesday Book, vol. II, fol. 361]

At Pakenham St. Edmund held 7 carucates of land for a manor. There were always 44 villeins and 23 bordars. Then 3 ploughs in demesne; now 4. Always 23 ploughs for the men. Then 6 slaves; now 9; 26 acres of meadow. Wood for 100 pigs. Then 2 mills; now 1; 3 rounceys, and 48 beasts and 65 pigs and 190 sheep and now 8 beehives. And 31 freemen and 1 bordar have 2 carucates of land. There were always among them 11 ploughs and 3 acres of meadow. All these belong to St. Edmund with soke and all custom and fold-soke. In the same village 3 freemen with 30 acres of land. Always 1 plough. Wood for 4 pigs. These can give and sell their land as they wish, but the soke over them, and their commendation, remain to the saint. In the same village 1 freeman who has 1 carucate of land asked the abbot to lend him half a carucate of land on this agreement that all his land wherever it was should remain in the possession of the saint after his death. Now 1 carucate of this land is in the demesne of Pakenham.[2] And there is 1 plough and 5 bordars and 2 slaves, and 1 winter mill. And the saint always had over him soke and his commendation. A church is in this village with 30 acres of land delivered in alms. Then Pakenham with its appurtenances was worth 10 pounds; now 25 pounds. It is 16 furlongs in length and 1 league in breadth and it pays 13 pence and 1 halfpenny to the geld.

At Livermere the abbot holds 23 freemen with 3 carucates of land. There Edric of Laxfield had 1 freeman whose wife belonged to St. Edmund. King William took his land and gave it to Werno 'de Peiz'. But when Werno became a monk, the aforesaid king returned the land which had formerly held to St. Edmund and to

[Domesday Book, vol. II, fol. 363b]

In Livermere. . . . This land the king accepted from the abbot and gave it to Werno 'de Peiz'. Afterwards, becoming a monk, he returned the land.

[1] *allam.*

[2] *dominium.*

the lord abbot, Baldwin.[1]

. . .

(At Ixworth Thorpe)	[Domesday Book, vol. II, fol. 367b]
. . . This land the lord abbot, Baldwin, redeemed[3] from the barons of the king, to wit, William the bishop, Ingelric the priest, and Ralph the staller. . . .	At Ixworth Thorpe. . . . This land the abbot pledged[2] against the barons of the king, to wit, William the bishop, Engelric and Ralph the staller for 100 shillings.

(ii)

These are the lands of the enfeoffed men of St. Edmund and of Abbot Baldwin, as they are written above with the others. Now they will be written out afresh so that anyone wishing to know how much each one holds will easily be able to discover it.

Richard holds of the saint at Middleton 1 carucate of land and 3 villeins and 2 bordars and 2 salt-pans and 1 sokeman with 5 acres of land.

At Harling he holds 1 carucate, 4 villeins and 3 bordars.

At Wendling he holds 1 carucate, 2 villeins, 6 bordars, and 1 sokeman with 12 acres.

At Tibenham he holds 2 carucates, 6 villeins and 9 bordars.

Roger Bigot holds of the saint at Buckenham 1 carucate, 8 bordars, and 9 freemen with 60 acres.

At Starston he holds 2 carucates and 2 villeins.

At Bressingham he holds 1 carucate, 1 villein, 4 bordars, and 1 sokeman with $1\frac{1}{2}$ acres.

At Waldringfield he holds $1\frac{1}{2}$ carucates and 8 bordars. . . .

[A description of the holdings of thirty-four other feudal tenants of Bury St. Edmunds follows.]

(iii)

In Thedwestry hundred. At Barton

Ailric Brenebec holds 10 acres and gives 9 pence.

Godwy Haiwart, 12 acres and gives 12 pence.

Wistric Oftun, 7 acres and gives 5 pence and 1 halfpenny.

Godwy the smith, 7 acres and gives 5 pence.

Cenric Cres, 4 acres and gives 4 pence.

Godwy, the son of Grimbold, 7 acres and gives 5 pence and 1 halfpenny.

Aluric Godhand, 3 acres and gives 3 pence.

Hardman, 3 acres and gives 3 pence.

Syric, 4 acres and gives 4 pence.

Ailward, son of Godwin, 41 acres and gives 41 pence.

Ædric Hopehevene, 6 acres and gives 6 pence.

[1] Writ of William I (of date 1066–1072) to Bury St. Edmunds (printed in J. H. Round, *Feudal England*, p. 429): "William, king of the English, to Egelmar the bishop and William Malet greeting. Be it known to you all, my faithful vassals, that I have granted to St. Edmund the service of Livermere which Werno has hitherto held from me. And the daughter of Werno during her life held it from Abbot Baldwin."

[2] *invadiavit.* [3] *redemit.*

Goding, son of Godwine, 12 acres and gives 11 pence and 1 halfpenny.

Boio, 2 acres and gives 2 pence.

Godwine, son of Theda, 10 acres and gives 9 pence.

Stannard and Ælric, his brother, 7½ acres and give 7 pence and 1 halfpenny.

Hardwin, 4 acres and gives 4 pence.

Lefwi bastard, 3 acres and gives 3 pence.

Godwine Hert, 6 acres and gives 5 pence and 1 halfpenny.

Lefstan Frost, 4 acres and gives 4 pence.

Leveve the widow, 4 acres and gives 4 pence.

Lefwine, brother of Tovi, 4½ acres and in another part 10 acres, and gives 14 pence and 1 halfpenny.

Godric and Brihtwy, 4 acres and give 4 pence and 1 halfpenny.

Alwin Dod, 9 acres and gives 9 pence.

Edric Ingerefe, 7 acres and gives 7 pence.

Godwine, nephew of Alwin, 9 acres and 9 pence.

Lefstan, son of Brihtric, 6 acres and gives 6 pence.

Ulfchetel, 3 acres and gives 3 pence.

Baldwin, 3 acres and gives 3 pence.

Bruning, 3 acres and gives 3 pence.

Æluric the swine-herd, 1 acre and gives 1 penny.

Lefstan, son of Bruning, 3 acres and gives 3 pence.

Ælfget, son of Sedemode, 8 acres and gives 8 pence.

Godwine, son of Ulfget, 24 acres and gives 26 pence.

Orgar, 30 acres and gives 32 pence.

Ælwin, son of Becca, 12 acres and gives 12 pence.

Godwy, son of Boia, 20 acres and gives 20 pence.

Ædwy Mus, 4 acres and gives 4 pence.

Ailric, son of Luta, 3 acres and gives 3 pence and 1 halfpenny.

Godric, son of Brune, 3 acres and gives 3 pence.

Lefstan, son of Scule, 16 acres and gives 16 pence.

Godwy 'Coccesune', 1 acre and gives 1 penny.

Ordric, nephew of Wihtric, 5 acres and gives 5 pence.

Wihtric Heiward, 6 acres and gives 6 pence.

Wulwin Stettel, 27 acres and gives 27 pence.

Alwin Horsthein, 81 acres and gives 7 shillings and 1 penny.

Wulwin, stepson of 'Brune', 3 acres and gives 2 pence and 1 halfpenny.

Odric Tederi, 3 acres and 3 pence.

Godwy Gott, 6 acres and pays 6 pence.

Oswald, 19 acres and gives 19 pence.

Godmod, 5 acres and gives 5 pence.

Godwy, son of Thurstan, 5 acres and gives 5 pence.

'Godlef Crepunder Huitel', 3 roods and gives 1 halfpenny.

Brun, son of Becca, 5 acres and gives 5 pence.

Thurstan, son of Godwine 'Betere', 3½ acres and gives 3 pence and 1 halfpenny.

Aluric, son of Godric, 46 acres and gives 46 pence.

Fulcard, 15 acres and gives 16 pence.
Ailwin 'Candela', 4½ acres and gives 4 pence and 1 halfpenny.
Oslac, 3 acres and gives 3 pence.
Ælric, son of Osfrid, 2 acres and gives 2 pence.
Ælwin Prisun, 1½ acres and gives 1 penny and 1 halfpenny.
Robert, 19 acres and gives 9 pence.
There are 5 carucates here and they render 40 oras and 10 measures of corn.[1]

[1] This record of Barton should be compared with Domesday Book, vol. II, fol. 361b: "St. Edmund held Barton *T.R.E.* for a manor, and for 5 carucates. . . . *And there were 70 freemen with 5 carucates of land*. . . . Over all these men the saint had jurisdiction and every custom, and they pertained to his fold."

C. ANGLO-NORMAN FEUDALISM

PERHAPS the most important consequence of the Norman Conquest was the establishment of a new aristocracy holding its lands by military service and knit together, and to the king, by a new scheme of feudal tenure. The character of this revolution, and its importance in the social and constitutional history of England have been discussed elsewhere in this book (see above, pp. 21–28). Here the evidence relating to Anglo-Norman feudalism will be set out in four sections. The first will contain testimony relating to the establishment of tenure by knight-service in the time of William the Conqueror. The second will contain selections from the *Cartae Baronum* which were drawn up at the command of Henry II in 1166 and which supply the chief evidence of the composition and extent of the English honours. The third will contain a number of charters illustrating the operation and implications of military feudalism in England during this period. And the fourth will comprise a statement of feudal law as applied to English conditions given in the legal treatise known as 'Glanville'.

(*a*) THE INTRODUCTION OF TENURE BY KNIGHT-SERVICE INTO ENGLAND DURING THE REIGN OF WILLIAM THE CONQUEROR

The starting-point in the history of Anglo-Norman feudalism was the imposition by William the Conqueror of quotas of knights arbitrarily fixed by the king as due from his tenants-in-chief, both lay and ecclesiastical, in return for the lands they held from him. These quotas of service owed (*servitia debita*) were fixed by the will of the king, and bore no constant relation to the amount of land held by the tenant-in-chief. The type of tenure which was set up as a result of their imposition was new to England.[1]

As a consequence of their having to provide a stipulated number of knights for the king's service, the tenants-in-chief in due course enfeoffed knights on their own estates. The imposition of the *servitium debitum* on the tenant-in-chief by the king, and the enfeoffment of knights by the tenant-in-chief were thus connected, but the two processes must none the less be kept distinct. The number of knights which the tenant-in-chief might enfeoff and the persons he might select for such endowment were normally, though not invariably, left to the discretion of the tenant-in-chief himself. The king was primarily concerned with the *servitium debitum*, that is to say, with the number of equipped knights he might compel the tenant-in-chief to produce for the royal service.

The *servitium debitum* was the basis of the whole arrangement. Its amount in each case was fixed by a bargain between the king and the tenant-in-chief; of this original bargain no record seems to have survived in any particular instance. Matthew Paris, however, writing in the thirteenth century, refers to the imposition of the *servitia debita* on the lands of the Church. In a remarkable passage placed in his annal for 1070[2] he states:

> King William following most evil advice took spoils of gold and silver from all the monasteries of the English, and to the great scandal of holy Church did not even spare the sacred

[1] See J. H. Round, *Feudal England* (1895), pp. 225–317.

[2] *Historia Anglorum* (ed. F. Madden, Rolls Series, 1866), vol. I, pp. 12–13.

vessels and ornaments . Also, all the bishoprics and abbacies which held baronies and which up to this time had been free from all secular service he ordered to come under military servitude. He caused to be set down in his rolls according to his pleasure how many knights he wished each bishopric and abbacy to produce in time of war for himself and his successors. And placing the records of this servitude of the Church in the Treasury, he exiled from the kingdom many ecclesiastical persons who were reluctant to submit to this most evil decree.

This is a later tradition, and the description is introduced by Matthew Paris to illustrate an ecclesiastical grievance; but the documents printed below indicate that Matthew Paris was correct both as to the method by which knight-service was introduced into England, and as to the period at which this took place. The writ to the bishop of Evesham (No. 218) shows that the system, which was unknown in Anglo-Saxon England, was already in operation before 1077, and, as it seems, in 1072. The records from Canterbury show the early enfeoffments which were made on a great ecclesiastical barony. The narrative from Abingdon describes how the tenurial change was brought about. This testimony, which may be reinforced by that of several of the feudal charters printed below, indicates that military feudalism, which was already known in Normandy, was introduced into England after, and shortly after, the Norman Conquest.

218. Summons to the feudal host (probably in 1072)

This writ which must have been issued before 16 February 1077, and which should most probably be assigned to the year 1072,[1] is of cardinal importance as illustrating the establishment of tenure by knight-service very shortly after the Norman Conquest. It instructs the abbot of Evesham to supervise the feudal levy in the districts over which he is set. It also bids him, as himself a tenant by knight-service, to appear with the five knights which he owed for his barony. The significance of this document is discussed in J. H. Round, *Feudal England*, where the Latin text is printed (p. 304). It is also printed in the later editions of W. Stubbs, *Select Charters*.

William, king of the English, to Æthelwig, abbot of Evesham, greeting. I order you to summon all those who are subject to your administration and jurisdiction that they bring before me at Clarendon on the Octave of Pentecost all the knights they owe me duly equipped. You, also, on that day, shall come to me, and bring with you fully equipped those 5 knights which you owe me in respect of your abbacy.[2] Witness Eudo the steward. At Winchester.

219. An early enfeoffment of a knight by Gilbert, abbot of Westminster (in, or shortly after, 1083)

The dating clause given in the first sentence creates some difficulties, and it is very possible that it formed no part of the original charter. Even if the charter be dated a few years after 1083, it remains a very early record of an enfeoffment. Printed: J. Armitage Robinson, *Gilbert Crispin* (1911), p. 38.

In the year of the Incarnation of our Lord, one thousand and eighty-three. We Gilbert, the abbot, and the convent of Westminster have given to William Baynard a certain farm[3] in the township[4] of Westminster, by name 'Totenhala' to house him, and to be held by him for the whole of his life by the service of 1 knight. This is to be held by him with all things that pertain to it, as well and freely as ever Wulfric the thegn surnamed 'Bordewayte' held it from the church. Therefore William shall

[1] For other references to the feudal levy in that year, see below, p. 902.
[2] The *servitium debitum* of the abbot of Evesham was in fact 5 knights (see below, p. 905).
[3] *berwicum*.
[4] *villa*.

himself have the customs and the liberties which we have in the same, always excepting the aids which we shall receive from our knights, as is done on the other lands of the church, and always excepting the tithes of this land which are assigned to our house in alms. We have granted these things to be held by him because of the love and service he has shown to our church; but on the condition that after his death the aforesaid land may remain bound to our church and quit of obligations. And in respect of this, the aforesaid William has pledged us that he will neither sell this land nor place it in pawn nor alienate it to anyone to the loss of our church. Witness: Robert the prior; William and Herbert, monks; Ralph Bainard; Herluin, brother of Gunzo; and many others.

220. An early enfeoffment on the land of the abbey of Bury St. Edmunds (1066–1087)

This important text is only preserved in confused copies made in the fourteenth century. The translation therefore must in places be regarded as tentative, and should be compared with the Latin version, which is printed in D. C. Douglas, *Feudal Documents from the Abbey of Bury St. Edmunds* (1932), p. 151, and fully discussed on pp. lxxxix–xciii of that book. The references to homage, to the former holders of the land in question, and to the military and other duties attached to the tenancy are all notable, as is also the date to which the document must be assigned.

Be it known to all of you that Peter, a knight of King William, will become the feudal man of St. Edmund and of Baldwin the abbot, by performing the ceremony of homage.[1] He will do this by permission of the king[2] and with the consent of the monks, and in return for the service which will here be stated, saving always the fealty which he owes to the king, the fief having been freely received except for the six royal forfeitures. Peter promises[3] that he will serve on behalf of the abbot within the kingdom with 3 or 4 knights at their own expense if he has been previously summoned by the king and the abbot to take part in the earlier or later levies of the king's host.[4] If he is bidden to plead on the abbot's behalf at any place within the kingdom, they shall likewise bear their own expense. But if the abbot shall take him anywhere else, then the expense of his service shall be borne by the abbot. Besides this, he shall equip a knight for service without or within the kingdom where and when the abbot shall require to have this knight as his own retainer. This is the description of the fee. The land of Edric the blind[5] with 14 freemen and as many peasants; Wulfmær the priest and his land with 3 freemen; Thorkill with his wife and land; and Guthred and his land; Grimbald the priest; Leofstan; Gunnulf; Osfrith; Acwuf; Wlfgive; Leofgeat; Wlfgife; Lufe;[6] Wlfricus; Tonhardus; Thurstan; Oslac; Thurstan 'Cati'; Thurstan 'Rumpe'; Godwine the priest; Glupus with the

[1] *manibus iunctis*. The reference is to the ceremony of homage whereby the man joins his hands together and places them between the hands of his lord. On homage generally, see below, No. 268, pp. 937–940.

[2] The interest of the king in a subinfeudation is noteworthy.

[3] The careful description of Peter's obligations suggests that knight's tenure has as yet not been clearly defined. It will be noted further that no mention is made in the text of hereditary right.

[4] Translation doubtful.

[5] Edric the blind was apparently Edric of Laxfield, and he and many of the following men can be discovered in Domesday Book as landholders in Suffolk in the time of Edward the Confessor. By comparison with Domesday Book this text therefore provides evidence of the manner in which a particular fief was constructed.

[6] Possibly a repetition of the two previous names.

following 7 freemen who are his neighbours: Thurkeda; Brother; Brunstan; Wulfmær; Godgive; Deorun; Stubhart. All these and their lands are free. Witnesses on behalf of the abbot:[1] Robert Blunt; Frodo; Robert 'de Vals'; Arnulf; Fulcher; Burgard; Jocelyn. Witnesses on behalf of Peter: Rannulf; Richard; Herdwin; Philip; Ralph 'fachiez'; William, son of Robert; Thorold 'papilio'.

221. A grant of land to be held by military service made by Robert Losinga, bishop of Hereford (1085)

This document creates a tenancy for life at Holm Lacy, Herefordshire, to be held by military service from the bishop of Hereford. It is important as evidence of the early imposition of knight-service in England, and also for the terms on which this land is to be held. It is important also in respect of the notable people who were concerned in this transaction. The document itself is printed and discussed by V. H. Galbraith in *Eng. Hist. Rev.*, vol. XLIV (1929), pp. 353 *et sqq.*

This privilege Robert, bishop of the church of Hereford, ordered to be recorded as agreed between him and Roger, son of Walter, concerning certain land which is called 'Hamme',[2] and those things which pertain to it. This land belongs to the church of Holy Mary, the Mother of God, and of St. Ethelbert the martyr; and previously the said bishop held this land as his own demesne and for the sustenance of the church. This land the aforesaid knight,[3] to wit, Roger, asked from the bishop through his friends, and he offered money in respect of it. But the bishop, by the counsel of his vassals,[4] gave him this same land in return for a promise that he would serve the bishop with 2 knights as his father did whenever the need arose. This also was part of the contract: that the men of the bishop belonging to King's Hampton and Hereford, and to the estates pertaining thereto, should be at liberty to take timber from the wood for the use of the bishop as often as it should be needed for fuel or for repairing houses; and the pigs of these manors should feed in the same wood. This refers to the men belonging to the bishop. And this contract further enjoins that if Roger becomes a monk, or dies, neither his mother nor his wife nor his sons nor his brothers nor any of his kinsfolk shall have rights in the aforesaid land, but let the bishop receive whatever in the estate may be to the profit of holy Church, and his men shall receive the same without any contradiction whatsoever. This instrument was executed in the year of the Incarnation of our Lord 1085, it being the eighth Indiction. The following were witnesses to this matter: Earl Roger,[5] and his son, Hugh,[6] and his other son, Everard,[7] and the countess[8] and the sheriff, Warin;[9] Osbert, son of Richard; Drew, son of Pons; Gerard of Tournay-sur-Dive; William 'Malbedan'; Gilbert, Earl Roger's constable. Of the men of the bishop there were these: Gerald, his brother; Humphrey the archdeacon; Ansfrid the priest; William; Leofwine; Alfweard; Sæwulf; Alwine. And there were these laymen from among

[1] These men can also be found in Domesday Book as the honorial barons of the abbey established after the Norman Conquest. They are here in the capacity of witnesses in the honour court of the abbot.
[2] Holme Lacy.
[3] *miles.*
[4] The court of the bishop's honour.
[5] Roger II of Montgomery, first earl of Shrewsbury.
[6] Hugh, Roger's son by his first wife, Mabel of Bellême.
[7] Everard, Roger's son by his second wife. Adelaide 'de Puiset'.
[8] Adelaide 'de Puiset'.
[9] A honorial baron of Roger of Montgomery in Shropshire in 1086.

the men of the bishop: Udo; Athalard; Franco; Arnulf; Tetbald; Robert; Gozo; Osbert; Peter; Richard the butler. Of the men of Earl Roger there were these clerks: Ralph; Geoffrey; Odo; Gerold. And there were these laymen of Earl Roger: Walter; Heribert 'de Furcis'; Richard of Stanton; Herman 'de Drewis'; Robert of Boscherville; Richard of Ectot; William of Evreux; Ralph of Le Saussey; Nicholas; Godmund.[1] The aforesaid Roger holds other land devoted to the sustenance of the bishop, to wit, at Onibury, on these conditions. As long as he lives he shall give each year on St. Martin's Day 20 shillings, and after his death, or if he becomes a monk, the land shall be returned without question to the bishop in the same condition as it is now. On this matter the following were witnesses: Ansfrid of Cormeilles; Edric of Wenlock; another Edric, to wit, the steward; and all the aforesaid except Earl Roger and his household.

222. The barony of the archbishop of Canterbury (December 1093–October 1096)

This is a very early description of a feudal honour in England. The numbers which follow the names represent knight-service in terms of the knight's fee and its fractions. This document is printed in D. C. Douglas, *Domesday Monachorum of Christ Church, Canterbury* (1944), p. 105, and it is fully discussed in the course of that work. Translations appear in *Victoria County History: Kent*, vol. III, p. 269, and in D. Jerrold, *Introduction to the History of England* (1949), p. 573.

Concerning the knights of the archbishop

The bishop of Rochester, 10.
Haimo the sheriff, 6.
Hugh of Montfort-sur-Risle,[2] 4.
Gilbert, son of Richard,[3] 4.
Robert, son of Wazo, 6.
William, son of Ralph, 7½.
The count of Eu, 4.
William of Briouze,[4] 1.
Godfrey of Thannington, 3.
Lambert of Romney, 3.
Vitalis, 3.
Godfrey of Malling, 3.
Bainard, 2.
William Peverel, 2.
Wimund of Leaveland, 1.
Ralph 'guiz', 1.
William Folet, 2.
Anquetil of Rots,[5] 1½.
William of Adisham, 1.
Godfrey the archer, 1.
Ralph of Eastry, 1.
Wibert, 1.
Arnold, 1.
Herengod, 1.
Niel of Monville,[6] 1.
Roger the butler, 1.
William, son of Hermerfred, 1.
Richard of the Marsh, 1.
Geoffrey of Rots, 1.
Talbot, 1.
Biset, 1.
Restwold, 1.
Osbern, 1.
Rodulf of Bec, 1.
Hugh of Port-en-Bessin, 2.
Wulfsige of Croydon, 1.
Geoffrey 'de Munbro'; 1.
Buselin of Dives,[7] 1.
Niel of Whiteacre, ½.
Æthelwine, son of Brihtmær,[8] 1.

[1] The attestations reveal the composition of two great baronial households.
[2] 'de Mundford'.
[3] His father was Richard 'fitz Gilbert', son of Gilbert of Brionne, the count.
[4] 'de Brausa'. [5] 'de Ros'. [6] 'de Mundevilla'.
[7] 'de Diva'. [8] See Nos. 278, 279.

Robert, son of Godbert, 1.
Ulf and Heribert, 1.
William of Pagham, 1.
Ralph 'de Ferno' and William 'Pollex', 1.
Osbern the butler, ½.
Reiner, ½.
Robert Leofgyth,[1] ½.
Robert of Hardres, ½.
Robert 'Brutin', ½.
William of Wrotham, ½.
Withard, ½.
William of Ifield, ½.
William of Detling, ½.
Deorman,[2] ½.
Osbern Pasforir, ¼.
Albold, ¼.
Ordgar, ¼.
Mauger, ¼.
Peter of Burstow, ¼.
Wulfnoth[3] of Barham, ¼.
William of Meopham, ¼.
Walter of Ricarville, ¼.
Osmelin, ¼.
Salomon, son of the archdeacon, ½.

223. The abbey of Abingdon and its tenants at the time of the Norman Conquest

The text which follows is taken from the Abingdon Chronicle (*Chronicon Monasterii de Abingdon*, ed. J. Stevenson (Rolls Series), vol. I, p. 482; vol. II, pp. 1 *et sqq*.). It is derived from two manuscripts, the one of the early thirteenth century and the other of about half a century later. The latter can be regarded as a revised edition of the former. The narrative is interesting as recording the Abingdon tradition of what took place on the estates of the abbey at the time of the Norman Conquest, and it is particularly valuable for its reference to the imposition of knight-service. This text should be compared with the evidence printed below in No. 226. Further discussion of this text is contained in J. H. Round, *Feudal England* (1895), p. 299; D. C. Douglas in *Eng. Hist. Rev.*, vol. XLIV (1929), pp. 618–625.

Abbot Ordric who had returned to his own monastery, after having devotedly served the Prince of the Apostles, and who had afterwards honourably governed the abbey committed to his charge, died after a long illness on the Feast of St. Vincent.[4] Then two men were promoted: Earl Harold became king of England; and Ealdred who had been in charge of the abbey's external property became abbot of the monks at Abingdon.

At the next Eastertide[5] an unusual star, called a comet, appeared during a whole week, and this was taken to be an omen of great and untoward misfortune. Nor was this opinion falsified, for, in the month of September, the king of Norway who bore the same name as the king of England, to wit, Harold, arrived in England and sought to gain the kingdom for himself as booty. He had the support of Earl Tosti, the brother of Harold, our king. King Harold, however, meeting them outside the walls of York destroyed both of them in battle with their followers.

Scarcely was this victory won, when Harold learnt from a messenger that William, count of Normandy, was threatening him, being prepared to offer him battle at Hastings unless the kingdom was speedily yielded. William alleged that he had the better right to rule in England because Edward, the late king, had solemnly bequeathed the kingdom to him on the grounds of their kinship. Harold treated this message with scorn; placing too much confidence in his own strength, he advanced against the count with less than proper caution. Having been taunted as the weaker, he thought

[1] Liuegit.
[2] Dirman. See No. 277, p. 953.
[3] Wulnoth.
[4] 22 January 1066.
[5] 16 April 1066.

himself the stronger, and so, rushing into battle, he perished, together with all his companions.

William[1] obtained the crown of England. Some submitted to him and swore fealty, but not a few departed into exile, hoping that they might find for themselves homes in other lands. Abbot Ealdred at first joined the former of these parties and swore fealty to the king. But when many, including the mother of the slain king, changed over and joined the latter party, the abbot also left England taking with him among others a priest named Blacheman. This priest, as has earlier been mentioned in connexion with Abbot Ordric, was a man of the church of Abingdon and held from the monastery Sandford and Chilton and Leverton. When he left England, everything which he possessed was taken into the hands of the king since he was held to be a renegade, and it was with the greatest difficulty that the abbot secured the restoration of his lands to the church.

As the abbot was successful in this instance, so also in other cases where lands had been alienated from the church he might perhaps have vindicated his right if he had not to his own loss and to the loss of the church incurred the enmity of the king. Of this we shall learn more later. A certain rich man, Turchill by name, with the witness and consent of Earl Harold, had performed homage to the church and to Abbot Ordric for his land which was called Kingston. For then a freeman was allowed so to act that the lordship of the aforesaid village might ever after pertain to the church. When this man fell in the famous battle [of Hastings] Henry of Ferrières seized his land for himself despite the protests of the abbot, and despite the fact that the lordship of this land had been vested in the church a long time before this battle. A similar usurpation took place at Fyfield. There, a certain Godric, who was sheriff, had held from the church on a lease for three lives, on the understanding that whatever mischance might befall the tenants, the church should suffer no loss therefrom. But when Godric likewise was killed in the same battle, Henry of Ferrières added this village also to his possessions.

In these days not only was the abbey thus robbed of its estates, but the ornaments of the sanctuary itself were stolen. An order came that the most precious of these should be sent to the queen. The abbot and the monks took counsel what should be done in this matter, and planned to send to the queen certain ornaments. But she declined those which were offered and demanded more precious treasures. Wherefore the abbot and monks, oppressed by fear of their new rulers from overseas, decided that their orders must in some measure be obeyed. To meet the wishes of the queen they therefore made a compromise, and sent a chasuble wonderfully embroidered throughout with gold and the best ceremonial cope, and an alb with a stole, and a gospel book decorated with gold and precious gems.

Meanwhile many plots were hatched in the kingdom of England by those who resented the unaccustomed yoke of a foreign rule. Some of them hid in woods and islands, living like outlaws and plundering and attacking those who came their way. Others besought the Danes to come to England. And when the Danes came in answer to this call, they in their turn plundered the land and laid it waste by fire, and took away

[1] The six ensuing paragraphs occur only in the earlier MS.

many into captivity. But they were not strong enough to wage a pitched battle or to subdue the kingdom, and so with their task unaccomplished they returned to their own land.

Men of all ranks and classes took part in these attempts. Æthelwine, bishop of Durham, for instance, was found amongst those who were taken prisoner, and having been brought to Abingdon he ended his days there in captivity. The men of the abbey of Abingdon, although they ought to have sustained the cause of King William, listened to the opposite advice and went armed to join a gathering of the enemies of the king. Being intercepted on their journey, they were captured and imprisoned and grievously punished. For this reason the king was incensed against their lord, that is to say, Abbot Ealdred, also named Brichwin, who was therefore thrown into prison immediately in Wallingford Castle. After being kept for some time in that place, he was at length taken thence and given into the charge of Walkelin, bishop of Winchester, with whom he remained for the rest of his life.

At this time, owing to the changed state of the kingdom, many treasures were deposited in the monastery of Abingdon in the hope that, being protected by the custody of the abbey, they might escape plunder. But when the officers of the court obtained knowledge of this through informers, everything that had been secretly sent, and everything that was found so stored, was taken away. Besides this, whatever was found in the treasure chests of the monks was removed. Thus much of what had been contributed for the honour and use of the church was removed, gold and silver, vestments, books and vessels. No respect was paid to the threshold of the holy places, and no pity was shown to the afflicted monks. Outside, with a similar lack of respect, the villages were widely devastated. How much of the property of the abbey was lost at this time it would be hard to reckon. In these acts Froger, then sheriff of Berkshire, was prominent. But God the Judge later punished this mighty man who persecuted the humble, for the royal justice deprived him of the office which he had turned into a tyranny, and he spent the remainder of his life in brutish want despised by all. In his misery he shows to all how much better it is to foster than to rob the place specially protected by the Queen of Heaven, and the house hallowed by the memory of those holy men who founded and sustained it. . . .

While the lord abbot, Ealdred, was in captivity, as has been said, Athelhelm was raised to the place of abbot by the express order of King William. He was a monk from the monastery of Jumièges which is in Normandy, and from there he brought letters of this kind to the primates of the kingdom of England. . . .

Charter of King William respecting this church:

> William, king of the English, to Lanfranc the archbishop, and Robert 'd'Oilly' and Roger 'de Pistri' and all his other liegemen in the whole of England, greeting. Know that I have granted to St. Mary of Abingdon and to Athelhelm, abbot of that house, all the customs of their lands which pertain to the aforesaid church, wherever it holds them, in borough or outside borough, according as this same Abbot Athelhelm shall be able to prove them by writ or by charter to have been held by St. Mary of Abingdon and by his predecessor through the grant of King Edward.

When this writ was read in the shire court of Berkshire, it brought much benefit to the abbot and the church. For the king's officials were in those days wont to inflict much injury on the men occupying the scattered estates of the church, exacting from them many obligations of different kinds, all of which were sufficiently grievous. But when the aforesaid royal orders had been proclaimed, and when the rights given to the church by King Edward's charter had been publicly recognized by the same shire court which had witnessed that charter, then these officials suffered a rebuff which was of great advantage to the church. . . .

. . . At the beginning of his abbacy [Abbot Athelhelm] deemed it necessary never to go about without an armed retinue, for in the midst of the conspiracies which broke out almost daily against the king and the kingdom, he felt compelled to take measures for his own protection. Then castles were built at Wallingford and Oxford and Windsor and other places for the safety of the realm, and the king ordered this abbey to provide guards in Windsor. For this purpose soldiers who had come to England from overseas were considered to be the most suitable. In the midst of such upheavals the lord abbot, Athelhelm, securely protected the place committed to his charge with an armed force of knights. For this purpose he first used stipendiary knights.[1] But after the disturbances had died down, it was noted in the annals[2] by the king's command what knights should be demanded from bishoprics and abbacies for the defence of the realm when the need arose.[3] Abbot Athelhelm, therefore, having retained the lands which had aforetime been given to the church afterwards allotted the manors of those who would hold them from the church, and in each case he declared what would be the obligations involved in its tenure.[4] These estates had previously been held by men called thegns[5] who had been killed in the battle of Hastings. . . .

. . . Malcolm, king of Scots, at this time refused to submit to King William.[6] An army was therefore raised and placed under the command of Robert, eldest son of the king, who was sent to Scotland on behalf of the king. With him were many of the magnates of England, including Abbot Athelhelm. They were instructed to offer peace or war: peace if submission were promised; otherwise war. Then King Malcolm coming to Lothian with his troops chose to treat rather than to fight. Accordingly he gave hostages in surety that the principality of Scotland should be subjected to the kingdom of England. On the completion of this pact, the son of the king with his army hastened joyfully to his father. And in recompense for their achievement, he and those who were with him received such rewards as were suitable to their several ranks.

Also the army was sent against the Welsh, and in this expedition also almost all the knights of the abbey were ordered to join, but this time the abbot remained at home. When the king's plans in this expedition had been fulfilled he went to Normandy. . . .

Then a report spread through England that the Danes were preparing a fleet wherewith to invade the country. Wherefore stipendiary knights[7] were collected from

[1] 'Household knights' not enfeoffed with land. [2] *Cum iam regis edicto in annalibus annotaretur.*

[3] The imposition of feudal tenure upon the prelacies of the land is noted as having taken place during the Conqueror's reign.

[4] The actual enfeoffments by the tenant-in-chief follow the imposition by the king on the tenant-in-chief of the *servitium debitum* (see above, pp. 894, 895, and below, pp. 903, 904).

[5] Note distinction between the new enfeoffed knights and the Anglo-Saxon thegns (see above, pp. 24–26).

[6] This may refer to the events of 1072.

[7] *militibus quos solidarios vocant:* to be distinguished from those knights who had already been enfeoffed.

all quarters, and the king ordered that provision should be made for them wherever they were, including the bishoprics and abbacies, until it should be known for certain whether the invasion would in fact take place. Nearly a year elapsed, and still no Danish invasion could be predicted with certainty; and so the stipendiary knights (who were paid by the king) were allowed to return to their own homes.

Thus the causes of strife and unrest in England were diminished, and the blessings of peace were enjoyed. Wherefore the abbot, turning his mind from secular affairs, studied the needs of the church. He supervised the instruction in letters of those who were under his care, and watched over their practice of the religious life. He also added to the ornaments of the church, and sought to arrange for the future good conduct of its affairs. Besides all this, he made plans to rebuild the church from its foundations, and set aside money which might be sufficient for that purpose. He died suddenly in the midst of these activities on 10 September.[1]

* * *

(*b*) THE *CARTAE BARONUM* OF 1166, BEING THE RETURNS MADE BY HIS TENANTS-IN-CHIEF TO KING HENRY II IN RESPECT OF AN INQUIRY INSTITUTED BY HIM AS TO THE KNIGHTS ENFEOFFED ON THEIR HONOURS

Early in 1166 King Henry II gave orders through the sheriffs to all his tenants-in-chief that before the first Sunday of Lent they should send him returns answering the following questions:

(i) How many knights were enfeoffed on your estates "by the old enfeoffment" – that is to say, at the time of the death of Henry I?

(ii) How many have been enfeoffed "by the new enfeoffment" – that is to say, since 1135?

(iii) How many knights are "on your demesne" (*super dominium*) – that is to say, how many knights, if any, are required in addition to those you have enfeoffed in order to make up the amount of knight-service you owe to the king?

(iv) What are the names of your knights?

It will be noted that all these questions (whose scope is exactly indicated in the return of the archbishop of York printed below) refer not to the *servitium debitum*[2] the quota of knights owed by the tenant-in-chief for the king's service – but to the actual enfeoffments which the tenants-in-chief had made, or had failed to make, upon their lands.[3] This distinction must always be borne in mind in studying these records, and it is clear that in any particular case the tenant-in-chief might in fact have enfeoffed either the requisite number of knights for the king's service,[4] or more,[5] or less,[6] than that amount.

It was in the last eventuality that the third question became of importance. If the tenant-in-chief had not enfeoffed sufficient knights to perform the service he owed to the king, then the balance was described as being chargeable on his demesne – *super dominium*.[7] When, therefore, a return states that so many knights are "on the demesne",

[1] 1084. [2] The *servitia debita* are given on pp. 904–906.
[3] Expressly stated in return of bishop of Exeter (No. 225).
[4] See return of abbot of Evesham (No. 228).
[5] See return of archbishop of York (No. 224).
[6] See return of Walter of Ancourt (No. 230).
[7] Cf. J. H. Round, *Feudal England*, p. 241.

it does not mean that these knights were actually established on the demesne, but merely that the lord had to provide this number of knights in addition to his enfeoffed knights in order to fulfil his obligations to the king.

It is probable that this distinction between the *servitium debitum* and the actual enfeoffments also explains the main motive of the royal inquiry. The purpose of the king may have been to provide a new feudal assessment. If the tenant-in-chief had enfeoffed more than the necessary number of knights, his *servitium debitum* might be raised to correspond with the actualities on his honour. If less than the required number of knights had been enfeoffed, then the *servitium debitum* could be retained as the basis of his assessment. The new assessment might therefore be made to work "in no case to the advantage of the tenant, but in many to the advantage of the crown".[1]

The king may also in 1166 have had a political motive in instituting this inquiry. He was in that year about to leave England for a considerable time, and the return of the archbishop of York (No. 224) suggests that "he wished to assure himself that the knights enfeoffed by his tenants had done allegiance to him before his departure". [2]

Few of the tenants-in-chief seem to have failed to make a return, and these records therefore supply an exhaustive survey of English military feudalism in 1166. In their totality they indicate, not only that each honour must be considered as a separate unit reflecting the results of an individual development, but also that "the establishment of knight-service upon a territorial basis belongs in the main to the time before the death of Henry I". "On most honours the fees of the new enfeoffment form an insignificant addition to those which had been created before 1135."[3]

The returns which have been printed below have been selected to give an indication of the character of these indispensable records, and to show the chief varieties in the returns. As will be seen, they include both large honours and small, and the holdings of both laymen and ecclesiastics. They also show some honours where enfeoffments have been made in excess of the *servitium debitum*, and others where the enfeoffments are insufficient to discharge the knight-service due to the king.[4]

The *Cartae Baronum* are among the most important records for the study of Anglo-Norman feudalism. They provide in particular evidence, not only of the number of knights enfeoffed in 1166 and before 1135, but also of the *servitia debita* which in the vast majority of cases had been fixed by William the Conqueror and had subsequently remained unchanged. This testimony as to the *servitia debita* may be set out in tabular form, but it must be emphasized that the figures which follow[5] indicate in each case *not* the number of knights which had been enfeoffed by the tenant-in-chief, but the *servitium debitum* of the tenant-in-chief as expressed in the number of knights he was required to produce for the king's service:

THE *SERVITIA DEBITA*

(*a*) *Bishoprics*

Canterbury	60	Norwich	40
Winchester	60	Ely	40
Lincoln	60	Salisbury	32
Worcester[6]	60	Bath	20

[1] Cf. J. H. Round, *op. cit.*, pp. 242–243.
[2] Cf. F. M. Stenton, *English Feudalism*, p. 157; D. M. Stenton in *Camb. Med. Hist.*, vol. v, p. 390.
[3] Cf. F. M. Stenton, *op. cit.*, p. 138.
[4] This type of honour was apparently common in the Danelaw.
[5] They are taken from Round, *op. cit.*, pp. 249–256.
[6] Later 50.

York[1]	20	Hereford	15
London	20	Durham	10
Exeter[2]	$17\frac{1}{2}$	Chichester	2
Chester	15		

(*b*) *Abbeys*

Peterborough	60	Wilton	5
Glastonbury	60	Ramsey	4
Bury St. Edmunds[3]	40	Chertsey	3
Abingdon[4]	30	St. Benet of Holme	3
Hyde	20	Cerne	3
St. Augustine's	15	Pershore	3
Westminster	15 (?)	Malmesbury	3
Tavistock	15 (?)	Winchcombe	2
Coventry	10	Middleton	2
Shaftesbury	10	Sherborne	2
St. Albans	6	Michelney	1
Evesham[5]	5	Abbotsbury	1

(*c*) *Greater lay tenants-in-chief* (*where ascertainable*)

Robert, 'son of the king'[6]	100	William, son of Robert	30
Earl of Derby (Ferrières)[7]	80 or 60	William 'de Tracy'	30
Honour of Totness	75	Robert of Valognes	30
Honour of Tickhill	60	Maurice 'de Craon'	30
Robert of Stafford	60	William of Aubigny	30
Count of Eu	60	Bernard Balliol	30
Earl Warenne	60	Roger of Arundel	30
Lacy of Pontefract	60	Walter of Mayenne	30 (?)
Roger 'of Mowbray'	60	Robert of Aubigny	25
Earl of Essex	60	Robert, son of Hugh	25
Honour of Richmond (Yorks.)	50	Alfred of Lincoln	25
Gervase Paynell	50	Ralph Hanselin	25
Reginald of St Valery	50	William of Briouze	25
Walter of Ancourt[8]	40	Oliver 'de Tracy'	25
Earl of Salisbury	40	Gerard of Limesy	25
William of Montfiquet	40	Walter Waleran	20
Payn of Montdoubleau	40	Richard 'de Hay'	20
William of Roumare	40 (?)	Honour of Holderness	20
Hubert of Ryes	35	William of Windsor	20
Hubert, son of Ralph	30	Hugh of Bayeux	20
Walter 'de Wahulle'	30	William 'de Vesci'	20

[1] See No. 224.
[2] See No. 225.
[3] See No. 227.
[4] See No. 226.
[5] See Nos. 218, 228.
[6] Illegitimate son of Henry I by Edith, probably daughter of Forn Sigalfson, lord of Greystoke.
[7] See No. 209.
[8] See No. 230.

Daniel of Crevecourt	20	Richard of Rames	10
Thomas 'de Arcy'	20	Roger 'de Buron'	10
Hugh of Dover	15	Richard of Cormeilles	10
Walter Bret	15	Roger of Kentwell	10
Baderon of Monmouth	15	William Trussebut	10
Richard of Reviers,[1] the earl	15	Nigel of Louvetot	10
Adam 'de Brus'	15	Manasser Arsic	10
Haimo, son of Meinfelin	15	Richard 'de Montacute'	10
Osbert, son of Hugh	15	Wandrille of Courcelles	10
Gilbert of Picquigny	15	Walter of Bolbec	10
Geoffrey Ridel	15	Robert of Hastings	10
Robert Foliot	15	Lambert of Etocquigny[2]	10
Robert 'de Choques'	15	Drogo 'de Montacute'	10
Robert 'de Caux'	15	William of Rames	10
William Paynell	15	William of Helléan[3]	10

Such were the *servitia debita* imposed upon the greater baronies of England[4] as the result of the introduction during the reign of William the Conqueror of knight-service into England.

All studies of Anglo-Norman feudalism, and especially all accounts of particular English fiefs in this period, must to a large extent be based upon the *Cartae Baronum*. It is not surprising therefore that the literature concerning this source is very extensive. The best introduction to their use is contained in Round's classic essay "The Introduction of Knight-Service into England" printed in *Feudal England* (1895), pp. 225 *et sqq.* Reference should also be made to F. M. Stenton, *English Feudalism* (1932), pp. 136–139. The returns themselves are printed in full in *Liber Niger Scaccarii*, ed. T. Hearne (1728), vol. I, pp. 49–340, and in *The Red Book of the Exchequer*, ed. H. Hall (Rolls Series, 1886), pp. 186–445.

224. Return (*carta*) of Roger, archbishop of York[5]

To his dearest lord, Henry, by the grace of God, king of the English, duke of the Normans and of the men of Aquitaine, count of the Angevins, his man Roger, by the same grace, archbishop of York, and legate of the apostolic see, gives greeting. Your dignity has ordered all your liegemen, both clerks and lay, who hold of you in chief in Yorkshire to send to you, by letters carrying their seals outside, answers to the following questions: how many knights does each possess by the old enfeoffment of the time of the king, your grandfather, that is to say, in the year and on the day in which that king was alive and dead; and how many knights has he of the new enfeoffment, that is to say, enfeoffed after the death of your grandfather of good memory; and how many knights are on the demesne[6] of each? And there is also be to included

[1] The name became anglicized as Redvers. He was earl of Devon.

[2] See below, p. 915.

[3] Helléan in Brittany. In English this name is represented in Helion's Bumpstead (Essex).

[4] No attempt has been made to tabulate baronies owing a service of less than 10 knights.

[5] *Liber Niger Scaccarii*, vol. I, p. 303; *The Red Book of the Exchequer*, p. 412. This return supplies the best evidence of the scope of the whole inquiry. The *servitium debitum* of the archbishop in 1166 was 20 knights, and it will be noted that many more knights had been enfeoffed than were required by the king.

[6] *super dominium*; for the meaning of this term, see above, p. 903.

in the return the names of all those, both of the old and new enfeoffments, because you wish to know if there are any who have not yet done you allegiance and whose names are not written in your roll, so that they may do you allegiance before the first Sunday in Lent. Wherefore I, being one of those subjected in all things to your orders, have made as thorough an investigation in my holding as the short time permitted, and in this return I am declaring all these things to you as my lord.

Know therefore, in the first place, my lord, that there is no knight's fee on the demesne of the archbishopric of York, since we have sufficient enfeoffed knights to discharge all the service which we owe you, and which our predecessors have performed. We have indeed more knights enfeoffed than are necessary for that service as you may learn from what follows. For our predecessors enfeoffed more knights than they owed to the king, and they did this, not for the necessities of the royal service, but because they wished to provide for their relatives and servants.

Here follow the names of those who were enfeoffed in the time of King Henry:[1]

William, count of Aumale, holds a fee of 3 knights.
Henry of Lassy, 2 knights.
Roger of Montbrai [Mowbray], a quarter of a knight's fee.
Herbert, son of Herbert, 3 knights.
Gilbert, son of Nigel, 2 knights.
Payn 'de Landa', 3 knights.
Mauger, son of Hugh, 1 knight.
Richard, son of Hugh, 1 knight.
William of Bellewe, 1 knight.
Robert Morin, 2 knights.
Gilbert, son of Herbert, 2 knights.
Hugh 'de Muschamp', 2 knights.
Walter of Ancourt, 2 knights.
Robert Mansel, 1 knight.
Robert, son of Wiard, half a knight's fee.
Peter 'de Perintone', half a knight's fee.
Hugh of Vesly, 4 knights.
William Cokerel, 1 knight.
Thomas of Everingham, 2½ knights' fees.
Simon Wahart, 1 knight.
Ralph 'de Nowewica', half a knight's fee.
Robert Poer, half a knight's fee.
Walter of Denton, half a knight's fee.
Robert, son of Hugh, a quarter of a knight's fee.
William of Lubbenham, half a knight's fee.
Alexander of Newby, 4 parts of half a knight's fee.
Herbert of Markington, a quarter of a knight's fee.
Peter 'de Belingee', 1 knight.
Oliver the Angevin, 1 knight.

[1] Henry I.

William 'de Pantone', 1 knight.
Thomas, son of Aubert, a quarter of a knight's fee.
Alice of Molescroft, a quarter of a knight's fee.
Thomas, son of Hervey, 1 knight.
Benedict of Sculcoates, the eighth part of a knight's fee.
Bernard of Cottingham, a quarter of a knight's fee.
Leofred, a thirteenth of a knight's fee.
John of Meaux, an eighth of a knight's fee.
Ivo, a quarter of a knight's fee.
Serlo of Poole, a third of a knight's fee.

After the death of King Henry there were enfeoffed:

Peter the butler, with half a knight's fee.
Peter the chamberlain, with the twentieth part of a knight's fee.
Geoffrey of Burton, with a twelfth of a knight's fee.
Gervase of Bretton, with a third of a knight's fee.

And since, my lord, I claim from some of these men more service than they are now performing, whereas others are keeping back services which are said to be due, not to themselves, but to the table and the demesne of the archbishop, I humbly beg that this my return may not be allowed to do harm to me or to my successors by preventing the Church from recovering or preserving its legal rights. Farewell, my lord.

And besides the aforesaid knights:

Thurstan 'de Lechamtone' [holds] half a knight's fee.
Gilbert 'de Miners', a third of a knight's fee.
Werri 'de Marinis', a third of a knight's fee.
William of Escures, a half of a knight's fee.
William Pallefrei, 1 knight.
William of Bellewe and Richard 'de Crochetone' hold a quarter of a knight's fee.

225. Return (*carta*) of the bishop of Exeter[1]

To his revered lord, Henry, by the grace of God, the illustrious king of the English, etc. Bartholomew, by the grace of God styled bishop of Exeter, greeting and faithful service. You have commanded me that I should inform you by my sealed and open writ not how much service I owe you,[2] but how many knights there are enfeoffed on my land from the enfeoffment of the time of King Henry, your grandfather, and how many knights have been enfeoffed since his death, and how many knights there are on my demesne.[3] Wherefore I send you a true record of these things in so far as my diligent inquiry has been able to discover it.

Robert, son of the king,[4] holds from me 3 knights' fees.
William 'de Tracy', 1 knight's fee.

[1] *Liber Niger Scaccarii*, vol. 1, p. 115; *The Red Book of the Exchequer*, p. 248; the *servitium debitum* of the bishop of Exeter was of 17½ knights' fees.
[2] *i.e.* not the *servitium debitum* but the details of actual enfeoffments; see above, p. 903.
[3] *super dominium;* for the technical meaning of this term, see above, p. 903.
[4] Robert, bastard son of Henry I.

Eustace 'de Jou', 3 knights' fees.
Cecilia 'de Beuz', 3 knights' fees.
Richard of Raddon, 2 knights' fees.
William 'de Boterellis', 1 knight's fee.
Alexander of Colebrooke, 2 knights' fees.
Osbert 'de Wadetone', 1 knight's fee.
Osbert of Bicton, 1 knight's fee.
Alan 'de Furnellis', 1 knight's fee.
William, son of John, 1 knight's fee.
William Hay, 1 knight's fee.
Ralph 'de Roke', 1 knight's fee.
Ralph, son of Stephen, 1 knight's fee.
William 'de Egloshail', 1 knight's fee.

Henry of La Pommeraye holds 1 knight's fee in Cornwall, and half a knight's fee in Devon. He denies the duty of service in respect of this half knight's fee. But it is owing from him.

Roger, son of Etard, half a knight's fee.
Stephen 'de Stantora', half a knight's fee.
Roger 'de Lanovatora', half a knight's fee.
Roger 'de Campello', half a knight's fee.
Geoffrey 'de Torkaringa', half a knight's fee.
Payn, son of Reinfrid, 1 knight's fee except for a fifth part.
Adam 'de Landechei' holds the fifth part.
Edil of Northcott and his lady cousin hold a quarter of a knight's fee.
The prior of Plympton, a quarter of a knight's fee.

Joel of St. Winnow holds half a knight's fee but claims that it should belong to his demesne.

Osbert 'de Crugalain', half a knight's fee.
Baldwin of Penare, a quarter of a knight's fee.
Jordan of Trecarrel, half a knight's fee.
Peter 'de Lameil', half a knight's fee.

Robert 'de Venmene', two-thirds of a knight's fee. Margaret holds the other third

Richard, son of Osulph, half a knight's fee.
John 'de Talumpna', half a knight's fee.
Jordan 'de Menestre', half a knight's fee.
Edward 'de Wotolta', half a knight's fee.

All the aforesaid were enfeoffed in the time of King Henry.

Ralph 'de Stanga' holds a third of a knight's fee of the new enfeoffment.
John Bernard, the son of Bernard, holds a quarter of a knight's fee.
Ivo and Osbert of Eu hold a quarter of a knight's fee.
William, son of Wimund, holds a twelfth of a knight's fee.

Roger, son of Roger 'Larcevesque', holds half a knight's fee but claims that it ought to belong to his demesne.

And besides all these, as I have heard from many, the earl of Gloucester and

Earl Hugh and the earl 'of Clare' ought to hold from the bishop of Exeter; but they do no service, nor do they admit that they should.

Gilbert Marshall holds 1 knight's fee from the bishop of Exeter.

226. Return (*carta*) of the abbot of Abingdon[1]

These are the names of the knights who hold of the church of Abingdon by the old enfeoffment:

Jordan of Sandford, 4 knights.

Seacourt, 2 knights.

Vincent, 1 knight.

Reginald of St. Valery, 1 knight.

William of Lea, 2 knights.

Raer 'de Alra', 1 knight.

Hugh, son of Berner, 1½ knights' fees.

John of Tubney, 1 knight.

John of St. Helens, 3 knights.

Gilbert 'de Columbariis', 2 knights.

Hugh of Buckland,[2] 1 knight.

Herbert, son of Herbert, 1 knight.

William of Bradley, half a knight's fee.

Bohemund 'de Leges', 3 knights with 2 hides which Humphrey 'de Bohun' takes away.

Henry of Pusey, 1 knight.

Roger of Cherbourg, half a knight's fee.

Gilbert, son of John, half a knight's fee.

Payn, son of Henry, and Roger of Hille, 1 knight; but William Giffard takes away a third of a knight's fee from the fief of Hille.

Thurstan, son of Simon, half a knight's fee.

Geoffrey, son of William, 1 knight.

Roger, son of Heming, 1 knight.

Baldwin 'de Flagesflore', 1 knight.

Ralph of Pont de l'Arche, half a knight's fee.

William of Wheatley, half a knight's fee.

Richard 'de Caumund' and Richard Gernun and Robert, the son of the steward, and Geoffrey of Sandford and William Grim and Reginald of Goosey and Peter 'de Aldebiry' and Henry of Lockinge and Geoffrey of Fervaques do the service of a knight and half the service of a knight.

The sum of the knights of the old enfeoffment is 33. There is no knight of the new enfeoffment. And no knight is on the demesne.[3]

[1] *Liber Niger Scaccarii*, vol. I, p. 181; *The Red Book of the Exchequer*, p. 305. This return should be compared with the narrative printed above (No. 223). The *servitium debitum* of the abbot of Abingdon was 30 knights.

[2] See below, No. 232.

[3] *super dominium;* for the technical meaning of this term, see above, p. 903.

227. Return (*carta*) of the honour of St. Edmund[1]

These are the knights of the honour of St. Edmund of the old enfeoffment, that is to say, of the time of King Henry:

William of Hastings, 5 knights.
William Blunt, 1 knight.
Peter of Brockley, 1 knight.
Hugh of Brent Eleigh, 2 knights.
Gilbert, son of Ralph, 3 knights.
Robert Revel, half a knight.
Robert of Languetot, 3 knights.
Adam of Horringer, half a knight's fee.
William 'de Bokeham', half a knight's fee.
Richard 'de Anisi', half a knight's fee.
Earl Aubrey,[2] a fee of 5 knights and half a knight's fee.
Simon of Ixworth, 2 knights.
Haimo Pecche, 2 knights.
Robert of Valognes, 1 knight.
Henry of Livermere, two parts of a knight's fee.
Gilbert of Thurston, the third part of a knight's fee.
Fulk, the son of William, 2 knights.
Robert of Saxham, 1 knight.
William 'de Hou', 2 knights.
Gilbert of St. Clare, two parts of 1 knight's fee.
Richard of Wyken, the third part of a knight's fee.
John of Loddon, 1 knight.
William, son of Golbod, 1 knight.
Robert of Cockfield, a knight's fee and half a knight's fee.
Walter 'de Lindeseia', 1 knight.
Earl Hugh, 3 knights.
William of Bardwell, 2 knights.
William 'de Taidene', half a knight's fee.
Norman of Risby, half a knight's fee.
Anselm of Throndeston, 1 knight.
Raymond Bigot, 1 knight.
Ralph of Hawstead, 1 knight.
Adam of Whelnetham, three-quarters of a knight's fee.
Wibert, a quarter of a knight's fee.
William of Le Quesnay, 1 knight.
Rannulf 'de Glanville', 1 knight.
Alexander of Wordwell, a quarter of a knight's fee.
Stephen of Brockdish, a quarter of a knight's fee.

[1] *Liber Niger Scaccarii*, vol. I, p. 281; *The Red Book of the Exchequer*, p. 392. This return should be compared with Nos. 217 and 220. The *servitium debitum* of the abbey of Bury St. Edmunds was 40 knights.
[2] Aubrey 'de Vere' III, earl of Oxford.

Humphrey of Barningham is the only knight of the new enfeoffment, and he holds a quarter of a knight's fee.

This is the sum of the knights of the church of St. Edmund, to wit, $52\frac{3}{4}$ knights' fees. But the church owes the service of no more than 40.[1] And of these Earl Hugh[2] retains and discharges a guard of 3 knights in the castle of Norwich.

228. Return (*carta*) of the abbey of Evesham[3]

The service of knights from the abbey of Evesham:

Rannulf 'de Coctone' does the full service of 1 knight with horses and arms, and the abbot shall pay his expenses so long as he is in the service of the king.

Rannulf 'de Kinewartone' likewise.

Richard of Weston and Richard 'de Piplumtone' likewise.

Bertram and Payn Travers likewise.

William 'de Bello Campo' half the service of a knight at the expense of the abbot.

The aforesaid are of the old enfeoffment.

Richard, son of Maurice of Amberley, half the service of a knight at the expense of the abbot, and he alone is of the new enfeoffment.

229. Return (*carta*) of William of Ferrières, the earl[4]

To Henry, king of the English, his dearest lord, Earl William of Ferrières, sends greeting. I give you to know that in the time of King Henry your grandfather:

Henry, son of Sawald, held 5 knights' fees; Fulcher, his brother, held 4 knights' fees; and now Sawald, the heir of both of them, holds these same 9 knights' fees.

William, son of Nigel, held 4 knights' fees, and Robert, his son, holds the same fees.

Richard of Courson held 4 knights' fees, and Robert, his son, holds the same.

Walter of Montgomery held 4 knights' fees.

Robert of Bacquepuits, 3 knights' fees.

Henry of Boscherville held 3 knights' fees which John, his son, now holds.

Robert, son of Walkelin, held 2 knights' fees; now Robert, his son, holds them.

Robert 'de Dum' held 2 knights' fees; now Jacob, his son, holds them.

Ralph Little held 2 knights' fees; now Reginald of Gresley holds them.

Robert of Louvetot held 2 knights' fees; now William Pantulf holds them for the service of 1 knight.

[1] The *servitium debitum*; see above, p. 905.

[2] Hugh Bigot, earl of Norfolk.

[3] *Liber Niger Scaccarii*, vol. I, p. 175; *The Red Book of the Exchequer*, p. 301. The *servitium debitum* of the abbey of Evesham was for 5 knights. See writ printed above (No. 218).

[4] *Liber Niger Scaccarii*, vol. I, p. 218; *The Red Book of the Exchequer*, p. 336. William of Ferrières (dép. Eure, arr. Bernay, cont. Broglie) was in 1166 earl of Derby. The English form of the name is Ferrers. In this return the *servitium debitum* of the honour is stated as being of 60 knights. Other records suggest it was 80 knights. In either case the honour was over-enfeoffed.

Henry of Chambrais[1] held 1 knight's fee.

William 'de Seyle' held 2 knights' fees; now Ralph, his son, holds them.

Geoffrey the chamberlain held 2 knights' fees; of these Robert, son of Ralph, now holds one, and Peter 'de Goldintone' the other.

Ivo of Harcourt and William, son of Walkelin, held 3 knights' fees; and now the heir of Geoffrey Marmion holds them.

Richard 'de Fifhide' held 2 knights' fees.

William of Boscherville held 3 knights' fees; of these Ralph, his son, holds one, and Odo, son of John, another; the third my father gave to the Hospital.

Geoffrey 'de Tiretey' held 1 knight's fee which now the White Monks hold by the gift of Maurice, his son.

Hubert of Courson held 3 knights' fees; of these Stephen, his nephew, holds two, while the third has been given to the Temple.

William, son of Oto, held 1 knight's fee which the White Monks of Thame now hold.

Payn of Newton held half a knight's fee, and it was given to the White Monks of Combermere.

Robert of Chartres held 1 knight's fee, and Henry 'de Cuningestone' held 1 knight's fee. Both of these William of Hastings now holds.

John 'de Turbelvulle' held 1 knight's fee, and now Henry 'Hossatus' holds this.

William 'de Trusselay' held 1 knight's fee which Robert, his son, now holds.

Atrop Hastenge held 1 knight's fee.

I will now name the knights which my grandfather[2] enfeoffed:

Nicholas of Brailsford held 1 knight's fee which Henry, his son, now holds.

William, son of Herbert, held 1 knight's fee.

William of St. Quentin held half a knight's fee.

David of Stanton held half a knight's fee.

Ernald of Le Bec held half a knight's fee.

Adam, son of Swann, held half a knight's fee which his heir now holds.

Walter of Le Bec held 1 knight's fee which William of Le Quesnay now holds.

Hugh, son of Richard, held 1 knight's fee.

Roger 'de Graindone' held 1 knight's fee.

Robert 'of Aubigny' held 1 knight's fee.

Ralph, son of William, held half a knight's fee which Humphrey 'de Tolka' now holds.

There was half a knight's fee pertaining to 'Stepla', which Maurice holds.

Landry held 1 knight's fee which Jordan, his son, now holds.

All these my grandfather enfeoffed out of his demesne.

The earl, my father,[3] enfeoffed the following from his demesne:

Humphrey 'de Tolka' holds 1 knight's fee.

Geoffrey 'de Bruencurt' holds 1 knight's fee.

[1] Now Broglie.

[2] Henry II of Ferrières, created earl of Derby by King Stephen in 1138.

[3] Robert of Ferrières, second earl of Derby, died before 1160.

Geoffrey 'Salvagius' holds half a knight's fee.
Robert 'de Pirario' holds half a knight's fee.
William Giffard holds half a knight's fee.
Maurice 'de Tiretey' holds half a knight's fee.
Adam the sheriff of Berkshire holds half a knight's fee.
William 'de Tolka' holds a quarter of a knight's fee.
Hugh Gobio holds a third part of a knight's fee.
Walter 'de Sumerville' holds a quarter of a knight's fee.
William of Ferrières holds a manor from the demesne of his father, and for that he performs the service of 4 knights.

These 9 knights' fees with the third of a knight's fee, my father gave from his demesne.

'Baggerugge' belongs to my 60 knights.[1] I render you service for it, and 'Meinfeninius' holds it from me for as much as shall please you. I have been dispossessed of 'Cruc' without judgment, and this is a fee of 1 knight.

This is the sum of the knights of the old and new enfeoffments: 69⅓ knights' fees.

230. Return (*carta*) of Walter of Ancourt[2]

Of the enfeoffment of Walter of Ancourt:
Payn of St. Mary holds 5½ knights' fees.
William of Bellewe, half a knight's fee.
Ralph of Ancourt, 3 knights' fees.
Robert, son of Walter, 3 knights' fees.
Hugh 'de Haveringe', 4 knights' fees.
Geoffrey of Stainton and Thomas of Rolleston, 4 knights' fees.
Elias of Fallencourt,[3] 1 knight's fee.
Ralph 'de Haia', 1 knight's fee.
William of Colleville, 1 knight's fee.
Maurice and Henry, 1 knight's fee.

All these hold of the old enfeoffment.

Of the new enfeoffment:
Gervase 'de Heriz' holds 1 knight's fee.
Guy 'de Russedale' and Fulk of Aunay, 1 knight's fee.
Ralph of Ancourt, 1 knight's fee.
Philip 'de Kime' and Eustace 'de Berchectane', 1 knight's fee.
Ralph of Vatierville[4] and Ralph of Graincourt, half a knight's fee.
Elias of Fallencourt,[3] half a knight's fee.

And on the demesne there are 11 knights.

[1] A reference to the *servitium debitum* which is elsewhere reckoned as of 80 knights.

[2] *Liber Niger Scaccarii*, vol. 1, p. 268; *The Red Book of the Exchequer* p. 380. The name which appears in many forms, (*e.g.* Aincurt, Daincurt) represents Ancourt (dép. Seine-Inférieure, arr. Dieppe, cont. Offranville). The *servitium debitum* of this honour was 40 knights, and the chief interest of this return is in showing an honour which was heavily under-enfeoffed. No less than 11 knights are "on the demesne".

[3] 'Fanucurt'. Fallencourt is some 18 miles from Ancourt.

[4] Walterivilla. Vatierville is some 7 miles from Fallencourt.

231. Return (*carta*) of Lambert of Etocquigny[1]

To his revered lord, Henry, king of the English, Lambert of Etocquigny, greeting. Know that I hold from you by your favour 16 carucates of land and 2 bovates by the service of 10 knights. In these 10 carucates of land I have 5 knights enfeoffed by the old enfeoffment:

Richard 'de Haia' holds 1 knight's fee; and he withheld the service which he owes to you and to me from the day of your coronation up to now, except that he paid me 2 marks.

Odo 'de Cranesbi' holds 1 knight's fee.

Thomas, son of William, holds 1 knight's fee.

Roger 'de Millers' holds 2 knights' fees.

And from my demesne I provide the balance of the service I owe you, to wit, that of 5 knights. And from that demesne I have given Robert 'de Portemort' three-quarters of 1 knight's fee. Therefore I pray you that you will send me your judgment concerning Richard 'de Haia' who holds back the service of his fee, because I cannot obtain that service except by your order. This is the total service in the aforesaid 16 carucates of land. Farewell.

232. Return (*carta*) of Hugh of Buckland[2]

Hugh of Buckland holds a fee of 1 knight of the old enfeoffment from the time of King Henry, and from that fee after the death of King Henry he enfeoffed 1 knight and half a knight.

And William, son of Ernald, holds 1 knight's fee. Richard, son of William, holds with him the other part, so that after the death of King Henry together they perform the service of 1½ knights' fees.

233. Return (*carta*) of Gerard Giffard[3]

I Gerard Giffard have no knight enfeoffed by the old enfeoffment from the time of King Henry, the grandfather of the king, nor of the new enfeoffment after his death, but from my demesne I discharge the service of 1 knight to the lord king.

234. Return (*carta*) of William of London[4]

To his dearest lord, Henry, by the grace of God, king of the English, William of London, greeting. Know that I have no knight enfeoffed either by the old enfeoffment or the new, but I am bound to discharge the obligations of my fee by the service of my own body.

[1] *Liber Niger Scaccarii*, vol. 1, p. 273; *The Red Book of the Exchequer*, p. 385. Lambert's *servitium debitum* was 10 knights. This barony was under-enfeoffed: 5 knights were "on the demesne". Lambert 'de Scotenni' took his name from Etocquigny, a hamlet of St. Martin-le-Gaillard.

[2] *Liber Niger Scaccarii*, vol. 1, p. 183; *The Red Book of the Exchequer*, p. 307. A typical small honour. Hugh of Buckland was not only a tenant-in-chief but a sub-tenant of the abbey of Abingdon by knight-service. See above, p. 910.

[3] *Liber Niger Scaccarii*, vol. 1, p. 114; *The Red Book of the Exchequer*, p. 247.

[4] *Liber Niger Scaccarii*, vol. 1, p. 113; *The Red Book of the Exchequer*, p. 246. The simplest form of tenure-in-chief—a man discharging his military service in person or by deputy.

(c) SELECT FEUDAL CHARTERS

The essential record for the study of feudalism is the feudal charter, and every charter in this book which may be dated between 1066 and 1189 is in some sense to be regarded as a feudal charter. The texts which follow in this place have been selected to illustrate particular aspects of Anglo-Norman feudalism in its origins and its development. They are arranged in a rough chronological order, and the particular relevance of each text is separately indicated. For the general development of the charter in England during this period, see above, pp. 801, 802.

235. Charter of Roger of Clères[1] in favour of St. Ouen of Rouen (*circa* 1066)

This important charter is evidence of the existence and the conditions of feudal tenure in Normandy before the Norman Conquest (cf. D. C. Douglas, *The Rise of Normandy* (1947), pp. 19, 20). The family of Clères were feudal under-tenants of the family of Tosny at least from the middle of the eleventh century until the last quarter of the twelfth century, and both families possessed land, not only in Normandy, but also in England. This charter passed before, but only shortly before, the Norman Conquest, is particularly notable for the reference to the consent of Ralph of Tosny in the grant of his vassal. It is also notable for the allusion at this date to the feudal 'incident' of 'relief'. The association of Duke William with the benefactions is also significant. The text is printed in A. Le Prevost, *Mémoires . . . pour servir à l'histoire du département de l'Eure*, vol. III (1869), p. 467.

✠ We wish it to be known to all the faithful of holy Church, both present and to come, that I, Roger of Clères, have given to the church of St. Peter and St. Ouen and to the monks, all my land of Blainville with its appurtenances, and the land of Crevon, and of St. Arnoul-sur-Ri and of St. Aignan-sur-Ri and all the churches and tithes of the same villages for the sake of my soul and the souls of my predecessors. And the gift has been made with the consent of my lord, William, duke of the Normans. Nor have I kept back anything from this land except the 'reliefs' of the vassals[2] and one guard[3] a year. Also, for love of the life of heaven I have given myself to the Church.[4] And my lord, Duke William himself, for his soul's sake and for the souls of his predecessors has granted all his customs in the same villages to God and to the aforesaid church. This gift has also been granted by my lord, Ralph of Tosny.[5] These were the witnesses of this transaction: Robert of Tosny and his brothers; Osbern of Cailli; Roger of Varneville the butler; Berengar Spina; Mauger of Venables; Robert the steward; Gilbert of Grugni; Gilbert Folenfant of Ormesnil. And the men and the holders of free estates of the same honour[6] were also witnesses: Robert, priest of 'Bleduinvilla'; Alger of Houlmesnil; Ralph Folenfant; William Agollant, and Robert, his brother; Ralph, son of Gotmund, and Gilbert, his brother; Azo of Salmonville; Ralph, son of 'Antuardus'; Restolph, priest of St. Arnoul; Gunfred of l'Epinai; Theodoric of Les Marettes; Osbern the knight; Roger of Capendu; Hugh of Gruchy. Let anyone who shall dispute this grant, watch lest he fall under an eternal curse, even as did Dathan and Abiron whom the earth swallowed up.

✠ The sign of William, duke of the Normans.
✠ The sign of Robert, count of Eu.[7]

[1] Dép. Seine-Inférieure, arr. Rouen. [2] *vavassoribus*. [3] *custodem*. [4] He has become a monk.
[5] Ralph II of Tosny (dép. Eure, arr. Louviers, cont. Gaillon) was present at Hastings.
[6] Note feudal use of the term at this early date.
[7] A grandson of Richard I, duke of Normandy; he acquired large estates in England, and survived until after 1086.

✠ The sign of William the steward, son of Osbern.[1]
✠ The sign of Ralph of Tosny.
✠ The sign of Roger of Clères.
✠ The sign of Gerald the steward.
✠ The sign of Ralph the chamberlain.
✠ The sign of Osbern of Cailli.
✠ The sign of Berengar Spina.

236. Notification of a grant made by Roger, son of Thorold, to Holy Trinity, Rouen (probably in 1066)

The probable allusion to the campaign of 1066 is interesting, as is also the reference at this time to Roger's knight. This instrument is printed in *Chartularium Monasterii Sanctae Trinitatis de Monte Rothomagi*, ed. A. Deville. This is an appendix to the *Cartulaire . . . de St. Bertin* (*Documents Inédits*, Paris, 1841). The charter occurs on p. 453.

Roger, the son of Thorold, being about to put to sea with Count William, gave in allodial tenure to the monks of Holy Trinity, Rouen, three yokes of land in Sotteville for the sake of his soul, but being overtaken by death on that same voyage,[2] he could not confirm this gift, and therefore his knight, by name William Trenchfoil, most readily grants the same benefice in his stead. To this William, king of the English, assents.

✠ The sign of William the king.
✠ The sign of William Trenchfoil.
✠ The sign of Bernard the forester.
Witness: Richard; Osbern; Roger Poncon.

237. Notification of a grant made by Roger of Montgomery to Holy Trinity, Rouen (1066)

One of the few references in a contemporary document to the invasion of 1066. This instrument is printed in *Chartularium Monasterii Sanctae Trinitatis de Monte Rothomagi*, ed. A. Deville. This is an appendix to the *Cartulaire . . . de St. Bertin* (*Documents Inédits*, Paris, 1841) and this charter is at p. 442.

Let it be known to all the liegemen of Christ that in the year of the Incarnation of our Lord 1066 when William, duke of the Normans, was about to set out across the sea with a fleet, a certain noble man named Roger of Montgomery,[3] in the presence of the said duke, completely released his claim on the land of Holy Trinity which is called Giverville to Abbot Rainer and his monks, so that from that hour this same land might never again be molested by any claim from him or his heirs, but might remain, hereditarily, free and quiet in the possession of Holy Trinity and the monks. This was done with the assent and with the confirmation of William, the illustrious prince of the Normans.

[1] William fitz Osbern, later earl of Hereford; died 1071. For his Norman career, and that of his father, see D. C. Douglas, *Eng. Hist. Rev.*, vol. LIX (1944), p. 62.

[2] *in eadem navigatione morte preventus*. Does this imply that he was killed at Hastings?

[3] Roger II of Montgomery, later first earl of Shrewsbury, did not himself go on the English expedition in 1066, but remained that year in Normandy with the duchess.

✠ The sign of the same [Duke William].
✠ The sign of Roger of Montgomery.
✠ The sign of William, son of Osbern.[1]
✠ The sign of Gerold the seneschal.
✠ The sign of Rodulph the chamberlain.
✠ The sign of Hugh the butler.[2]
Witnesses: Richard the seneschal; Bernard the cook; Ansfrid, son of Athla.

238. Writ (in Anglo-Saxon) of William I to the abbot of Bury St. Edmunds respecting the tenants of the abbey, and particularly those who had fallen in battle fighting against the king (1066–1070)

This document refers to the fighting at and after Hastings and concerns especially the estates of the greater tenants of an East Anglian monastery who had been slain in the course of that fighting. It is printed with a translation in H. W. C. Davis, *Regesta Regum Anglo-Normannorum*, p. 119, and in D. C. Douglas, *Feudal Documents from the Abbey of Bury St. Edmunds* (1932), p. 47.

I, William the king, give friendly greeting to Æthelmær the bishop and Ralph the earl and to all my thegns in Suffolk and in Norfolk. I give you to know that I will that Abbot Baldwin hand to me all the land which those men held who belonged to St. Edmund's soke and who stood in battle against me and there were slain. And I will that those men be now the abbot's men, who were previously held by his predecessor, even as their predecessors were. And I will not allow anyone to take from him anything that I have given him.

239. Charter of William I to Holy Trinity, Rouen, granting land in England to that monastery (1069)

A very early example of the grant of land in England to a Norman monastery. This instrument is interesting also for the reference to William fitz Osbern as steward and for the illuminating description of the ceremony of gift. It will be noted that in 1069 the conquest of England was not yet fully complete. This charter is printed in *Chartularium Monasterii Sanctae Trinitatis de Monte Rothomagi*, ed. A Deville. This is an appendix to the *Cartulaire . . . de St. Bertin* (*Documents Inédits*, Paris, 1841) and this charter is at p. 455.

By the bounteous grace of Christ, the King of kings who rules everything with a pious government, William, duke of the Normans, having acquired the kingdom of England, when he was in the royal township which in English is called 'Gueritho',[3] by the counsel and request of his liegeman William, son of Osbern the steward, who was chief of the palace, and in the presence of Abbot Rainer and the two monks, Nicholas and William, gave to Holy Trinity of the Mount in perpetual heredity the land which in English is called 'Hermodesodes' with the church and all its appurtenances, to wit, in fields and meadows and pastures and mills and waters and marshes and woods and with the rest of the neighbourhood of this village. This gift was made by the presentation of a dagger, and when the king gave it to the abbot, he pretended to stab the abbot's hand.[4] "Thus", he jestingly exclaimed, "ought land to be bestowed." With this clear sign therefore, and with the testimony of the many

[1] William fitz Osbern, later earl of Hereford.
[2] Hugh 'd'Ivry', who in 1086 possessed estates in England.
[3] A variant reading is Guenth(onia). Winchester may thus be plausibly suggested, and the king was in fact at Winchester at Easter, 1069.
[4] Note the reference to the ceremony of gift.

nobles who stood by the king's side, was this gift made in the year of the Incarnation of our Lord 1069.

✠ The sign of William the king.
✠ The sign of Maud the queen.
✠ The sign of William, son of Osbern.
✠ The sign of William, bishop of London.
✠ The sign of Geoffrey, bishop of Coutances.
✠ The sign of Robert, son of Guimar.
✠ The sign of Richard, son of Thurstan Goz.[1]
✠ The sign of Herfast (then chaplain afterwards bishop).[2]
✠ The sign of Hugh of Sierville.

240. Charter (in Latin and Anglo-Saxon) by Odo, bishop of Bayeux and earl of Kent, announcing an exchange between him and the monastery of Christ Church, Canterbury (1071–1082)

This charter is interesting because of its bilingual form, and because it forms a commentary upon the disputes between Odo and Lanfranc in Kent between the Norman Conquest and the Domesday Survey (see above, No. 50). The charter has been printed with a facsimile and with critical comments in *Sir Christopher Hatton's Book of Seals*, ed. L. C. Loyd and D. M. Stenton (1950), p. 301.

Odo, bishop of Bayeux to Lanfranc the archbishop and Haimo the sheriff, and to all the liegemen of the king in Canterbury, greeting.[3] Be it known to all of you that I, Odo, bishop of Bayeux and earl of Kent, hand over to our mother-church of Canterbury, which was built in honour of the Holy Trinity, these four denns of land, to wit, Losenham, 'Adalardendena', 'Blacecota' and Acton, to be possessed by Archbishop Lanfranc and all his successors for their perpetual use. I do this for the redemption of my lord, William, king of the English, and for my own salvation and for the salvation of those whose redemption it is especially incumbent on me to procure. I do it also in exchange for 25 acres of land which are contained within my park of Wickham.[4]

241. Grant by Gilbert fitz Richard of Clare to the abbey of Bury St. Edmunds of two freemen of Westley, Suffolk, the grant being witnessed, as it seems, by the honour courts of Gilbert and of the abbot (1090–1098)

Printed: D. C. Douglas, *Feudal Documents from the Abbey of Bury St. Edmunds* (1932), p. 152.

Be it known to all Christians, French and English, that I, Gilbert of Clare, the son of Lord Richard,[5] give and grant to Christ and to St. Edmund and his monks for the soul of my father and for the souls of my relatives and for my own soul, two

[1] 'Tursteingoz'. Richard, *vicomte* of the Avranchin, was the son of Thurstan Goz, and the father of Hugh, earl of Chester.

[2] The description was clearly added to the copy. Herfast was chaplain to William from before 1059. In 1070 he became bishop of Elmham. See above, No. 91.

[3] *omnibus Cantuariensibus regis fidelibus.* The Anglo-Saxon version has "all the king's thegns of Kent"–an important variation, and one which has an important bearing upon the establishment of feudalism in England (see above, pp. 24–26). This, and other features of this charter, suggest to the present editors that it most probably passed early within the period indicated by the dating limits.

[4] Later Wickhambreux.

[5] Richard fitz Gilbert of Tonbridge, son of Count Gilbert of Brionne.

freemen Wulfwine[1] and Wulfmær[2] of Westley, with their land and its appurtenances for service in the work of the monastery of the said Holy Martyr. I make this grant on the condition that they shall never be given to any other man, clerk or layman, and that no other custom be imposed upon them other than those which were wont to be imposed on him who used to hold them under me. Let them perform for the monks in the work of the monastery what they were wont to perform for Rainald, the son of Ivo, who joins with me in this gift and grant of them to St. Edmund. Always excepting the 'scot' of the king which they shall pay with their neighbours in the hundred when this runs throughout England. And let anyone who may break this gift be cursed by my prayer and wish before God. And of this my men are witness: the lady, my mother, Rohais;[3] Rainald, the son of Ivo, who holds them of me; Geoffrey 'de Bech'; Gyrulph, my chaplain; 'Maskerellus'; Arnulf 'de Brie' Richard Peket; Picot 'de Friardel'; Richard, my butler; Robert, the keeper of my bedchamber;[4] Gilbert 'de Brunevilla'. These are witnesses from among the men of Abbot Baldwin:[5] Fulcher[6] of Mesnières and his son, Gilbert; Arnulf the woodman;[7] Ralph, the abbot's proctor; Ailbold, the abbot's priest; Wulfweard of Wangford;[6] Hugh Strabo; Hubert of Melford.

242. Writ of Henry I enforcing the feudal service owed by Jocelyn 'de la Rivière' to the abbey of Abingdon (1101–1102)

This charter is important as illustrating the early descent of a mesne military tenancy from its first institution on the lands of a great ecclesiastical house. Its significance can only be appreciated in the light of passages from the *Chronicon Monasterii de Abingdon* (Rolls Series, 1852). Among the original enfeoffments made by Abbot Athelhelm of Abingdon (see above, p. 902) was that of Walter 'de la Rivière' at Beedon for the service of 2½ knights. Subsequently, however, as the *Chronicon* narrates (vol. II, p. 23): "A certain knight called Walter 'de la Rivière' holding the land which is called Beedon died at this time leaving a young son of the same name. Whereupon Jocelyn, the uncle of this boy, sought to acquire the fee for himself and began a plea to this end in the king's court which was then being held at Beckley. But Abbot Rainald, leading the boy by the hand and opposing this plea, frustrated this attempt. Whereupon Jocelyn changing his demand asked that the fee should remain in his hand until the boy came of age, on condition that he pledged his faith that in the meantime he would plot no harm against the boy to his own advantage, and that he would in his place perform the service of 3 knights for this land in the accustomed manner. What he asked was granted, and he pledged his faith to the abbot that he would fully perform the service he had promised. Nevertheless the boy when he grew up could not be admitted to his possessions, which had been pledged to him by public proof, without various objections being made thereto."

It will be noted that these arrangements were made in the time of Abbot Rainald, *i.e.* between 1084 and 1097, and that their effect was to raise the service of this estate from that of 2½ knights (as established in the time of Abbot Athelhelm, 1072–1084) to 3 knights. But the dispute was not yet over. In 1101, the *Chronicon* remarks (vol. II, p. 129): "Abbot Faritius successfully claimed against Jocelyn 'de la Rivière' the service of 1 knight. For Jocelyn had said that he owed no more than the service of 2 knights for the fee which he held from the church, and the abbot and his men said that he owed the service of 3 knights. But at length he gave pledges and service and right to the abbot, and confirmed, and in every way conceded, that he owed, and would henceforth perform the service of 3 knights. This was done in the chamber at Abingdon before Abbot Faritius with the witness of many."

The ensuing charter (printed in the *Chronicon*, vol. II, p. 92) relates to this last dispute, and at the same time refers the establishment of knight-service at Abingdon to the time of Abbot Athelhelm.

---

[1] Wlwinum.

[2] Wlmarum.

[3] Roaydis. She was wife of Richard fitz Gilbert and daughter of the elder Walter Giffard. See Table 11.

[4] *cubicularium*.

[5] Abbot, 1065–1098.

[6] Occur in Domesday Book

[7] Obviously a nickname.

Henry, king of the English, to Jocelyn 'de la Rivière', greeting. I order you to perform to Faritius, abbot of Abingdon, such service for the fee which you hold from him and from the abbey, as your brothers performed to his predecessor, Athelhelm. And if you do not do this the abbot will constrain you at the expense of your fief. Witness: Robert, son of Haimo. Issued by William 'de la Rochelle' at London.

243. Writ of Henry I concerning the service of castle-guard from the tenants by knight-service of the abbey of Abingdon (1100–1117, and most probably at the beginning of this period)

This instrument is important as illustrating the obligation of castle-guard as part of knight-service almost from its earliest institution. It should be compared with the narrative from Abingdon printed in No. 223. The institution is here, as will be seen, explicitly referred to the time of Abbot Rainald (1084–1097), and there can be little doubt that it goes back to the establishment of knights' fees on the Abingdon lands. The charter is printed in *Chronicon Monasterii de Abingdon* (Rolls Series), vol. II, p. 90.

Henry, king of the English, to all the barons[1] of the abbey of Abingdon, greeting. I will and I firmly order you to perform my guard of Windsor as you were wont to do in the time of Abbot Rainald, and in the time of my brother, and as Abbot Faritius commands you. See that you are obedient to him. It displeases me much that you do not obey his order as you ought to do. Witness: Urse of Abbetot. At Wallingford.

244. Grant by Henry I to Miles of Gloucester of Sibyl, daughter of Bernard of Neufmarché, with her marriage portion and with all the possessions of her father and mother (10 April–29 May 1121)

This charter is of exceptional interest as evidence of feudal practice. It testifies to a notable marriage settlement, and should in this respect be compared with No. 245. It further illustrates many of the conditions of feudal tenure, and its references to fealty and to liege homage are particularly notable. It is printed in J. H. Round, *Ancient Charters* (Pipe Roll Soc., vol. x, 1888), p. 8.

Henry, king of the English, to his archbishops, bishops, abbots, earls, sheriffs, and all his barons and liegemen, both French and English, of the whole of England and Wales, greeting. Know that I have given and firmly granted to Miles of Gloucester,[2] Sibyl, daughter of Bernard of Neufmarché,[3] with all the land of Bernard her father and of her mother after their death, or if they should wish it during their life, with this marriage portion: Talgarth, and the forest of Ystradyw, and the castle of Hay, and all the land of Bren' as far as the boundary of the land of Richard, son of Pons, that is to say, as far as Cantref Bychan and Much Cowarne, a certain village in England, and also the fee and the service of Roger of Baskerville, and the fee and service of William Revell, and the service of Robert 'de Turberville', and the fee and service of Picard. And I will and command that all the tenants of the aforesaid marriage portion shall likewise do their liege homage[4] to him saving their fealty to me as their lord. And all the tenants of the aforesaid land of Bernard shall likewise do their liege homage[4] to him as their lord, saving their fealty to me and to Bernard so long as he shall wish to

[1] Honorial barons of the abbey of Abingdon.
[2] Sheriff of Gloucestershire.
[3] Son of Geoffrey of Neufmarché. Geoffrey was active in Normandy as early as 1050, and Bernard married a daughter of Osbern, son of Richard Scrob. Bernard's son, Philip, died without heirs.
[4] On liege homage, see Nos. 57, 268.

hold that land. And this I give and grant to him in return for the payment which Bernard gave me, and at the request of Bernard himself and of his wife, and of his barons.[1] And I will and firmly order that he shall hold this as well and honourably and quietly and freely as ever Bernard held it. Witness: Roger, bishop of Salisbury; and Robert, bishop of Lincoln; and Rannulf the chancellor; and Robert, the king's son;[2] and William of Tancarville; and Nigel of Aubigny; and Payn, son of John; and Geoffrey, son of Payn; and Geoffrey 'de Clinton'; and Ralph Basset; and William of Aubigné 'Brito'. At Winchester between Easter and Pentecost in the same year as that in which the king took to wife the daughter of the duke of Louvain.[3]

245. Charter of Henry I concerning the feudal arrangements to be made on the occasion of Richard Basset's marriage with the daughter of Geoffrey Ridel (1120–1123)

This charter is printed, translated and fully discussed in F. M. Stenton, *English Feudalism* (1932), pp. 33–35, 258. In it the king is disposing of the inheritance of his justice, Geoffrey Ridel, who was drowned in the White Ship in 1120. To understand the arrangements here described, it is necessary to remember that Richard Basset was the son of Ralph Basset, and that Geoffrey Ridel had married Geva, the daughter of Hugh I, earl of Chester. This charter, adds Professor Stenton (*op. cit.*, p. 34), "illustrates more than one detail of feudal custom, notably the significance of knighthood as a sign that a military tenant has come of age, the practice by which the king would occasionally increase a baron's honour by a grant of knights already enfeoffed on the royal demesne, and the care with which members of the higher baronage regarded the interests of those connected with them by family relationship. But for general history the details of this arrangement are less interesting than the composition of the body which the king took into counsel in this matter. . . . It would be a mistake to regard this body as showing the normal composition of the king's court. . . . But it certainly illustrates the various elements which could combine at any time to form that court and its meeting shows the care with which the king moved in matters interesting his greater barons."

Henry, king of the English, greets the bishop of Lincoln and Earl David and the earl of Leicester and Earl Rannulf of Chester and all the barons and lords of whom Geoffrey Ridel held lands, and all the sheriffs within whose jurisdiction he held them. Know that I have given to Richard Basset the daughter of Geoffrey Ridel to wife, and the custody of Geoffrey Ridel's land until Robert Ridel can be made a knight and marry the granddaughter of Ralph Basset, namely the daughter of one of his daughters. Thereupon the aforesaid Richard shall have 20 librates of land of my fee in demesne, in marriage with his wife, and 4 enfeoffed knights, and if Robert shall die without heir by his wife, I grant to Richard Basset and the heir whom he shall have by the daughter of the aforesaid Geoffrey, the whole land of Geoffrey Ridel, of whomsoever he held it. And if the daughters of Geoffrey Ridel shall not be married during the life of Robert their brother, or while under the wardship of Richard Basset, he shall provide for them according to my advice and discretion. And this gift and compact have been made at the request and with the advice of Rannulf, earl of Chester, and William, his brother, and Nigel of Aubigny and [Robert Ridel's] other kin and Geva, his mother, and Geoffrey, the earl's chancellor, and Simon, dean of Lincoln, and William, son of Rannulf, and Thomas of St. John and Geoffrey 'de Clinton' and Payn, son of John, and William of Aubigny and Humphrey 'de Bohun'

[1] The honorial barons of Bernard of Neufmarché.
[2] Robert, illegitimate son of Henry I, later to be earl of Gloucester, for whom see also above, pp. 201–203, 306–308.
[3] Adela.

and Robert Musard and Robert Basset and Osmund Basset and Thurstan Basset and William, constable of Earl Rannulf of Chester, and Ralph, the son of Norman, and Hugh Maubanc. At Woodstock.

246. Charter of Henry I respecting the barony of the bishop of Ely (1127)

This important charter offers evidence of the institution of military feudalism in England in the time of William the Conqueror, and it indicates the conditions in which the great ecclesiastical baronies were then established. The text is printed in James Bentham, *History and Antiquities . . . of the Church of Ely* (ed. 1781), Appendix, p. 19.

Henry, king of the English, to his archbishops, bishops, abbots, earls, etc., greeting. Know that I wish and grant and order that all those barons and vavassors who hold such lands, as my charter of the Treasury of Winchester witnesses to have been sworn to, have belonged, in the time of my father, to the fee of the church of Ely,[1] shall acknowledge them and shall hold them of the aforesaid church and of the bishop of Ely, now and in perpetuity by performing for them to the church military service in accordance with their tenures, and in accordance with the service which was decreed for these lands. In this manner shall the barons and vavassors holding these lands be quit towards me and towards their other lords of as much service as they are obliged to perform for their lands to the aforesaid bishop and church according to the decreed military service. And I will and order that the bishop and the church shall hold them well and honourably and in peace and quiet with sake and soke, toll and team and infangentheof, and with all other customs and quittances with which they will quietly and honourably hold their other fee. And those who hold the aforesaid lands shall perform service for them to the bishop when the bishop performs his other service from the church. Witness: Roger, bishop of Salisbury; and Geoffrey the chancellor; and Robert of the Seal;[2] and William of Tancarville; and William of Aubigny, the butler; and Ralph Basset; and Geoffrey 'de Clinton'. At Eling,[3] at the time of my crossing.[4]

247. Charter of Henry I respecting the payment of scutage from the barony of the bishop of Ely (1127)

This charter is evidence for the payment of scutage or shield money in the time of King Henry I, and of the connexion of that payment with the institution of tenure by knight-service. It is printed and discussed in J. H. Round, *Feudal England* (1895), p. 260, and it is also printed in J. Bentham, *History and Antiquities of the . . . Church of Ely* (ed. 1781), Appendix, p. 20.

Henry, king of the English, to the archbishops, bishops, earls, etc., greeting. Know that I have pardoned to the church of St. Etheldreda of Ely for the love of God and for the souls of my father and mother and for the redemption of my sins, and at the request of Hervey, bishop of the same church, 40 pounds out of those 100 pounds which the aforesaid church was wont to give for scutage when scutage ran throughout my land of England. The church shall now therefore and in perpetuity pay no more

[1] *ut omnes illi barones et vavassores qui terras illas tenent quas carta mea Wintonie de thesauro meo testatur fuisse juratas tempore patris mei ad feudum ecclesie de Ely.*

[2] 'de Sigillo', the keeper of the king's seal. See No. 70, pp. 501, 529.

[3] Eling in Hampshire. The king was on his way to the coast and on 26 August 1127 he set sail for Normandy, possibly from Portsmouth.

[4] *in transitu meo.*

than 60 pounds when scutage[1] is levied on the land, and of the aforesaid [40] pounds let the same church be for ever quit. Witness: Roger, bishop of Salisbury, and Geoffrey, my chancellor, and Robert of the Seal[2] and William of Tancarville, and William of Aubigny, the butler, and Ralph Basset and Geoffrey 'de Clinton', and William of Pont de l'Arche. At Eling[3] at the time of my crossing the sea.

248. Charter of Henry I confirming an enfeoffment made on the lands of the abbey of Ramsey (1114–1130)

Printed in *Cartularium Monasterii de Rameseia* (Rolls Series, 1884), vol. I, p. 248

Henry, king of the English, to the bishop of Lincoln and to the sheriff and to all his barons and liegemen of Bedfordshire greeting. Know that Reginald, abbot of Ramsey, has granted to Simon 'de Beauchamp' the land of Holywell on the condition that Simon must in return for this land do the service of 1 knight to the church of Ramsey fully and in everything. Witness: Ralph Basset and Geoffrey 'de Clinton', at Westminster.

249. Charter of William of Anisy[4] granting a fief to his son with the consent of the court of the honour (? 1120–1140)

This important charter illustrates many features of English feudal society. It concerns a grant by a military tenant to one of his sons who was not his heir, and its chief interest lies in the detailed description of the procedure involved. In particular, the action of the honorial court, which is apparently essential to the transaction, and which is here fully displayed, deserves note. It will be further observed that the grantee becomes the immediate tenant of the chief lord; that the land concerned was "of acquisition" not inheritance, and therefore more readily alienable; and that the assent of the heir is treated as necessary. This charter is printed, dated and fully annotated as No. 301 of *Sir Christopher Hatton's Book of Seals*, ed. L. C. Loyd and D. M. Stenton (Oxford, 1950).

William of Anisy to all his men, both French and English, greeting. Know that I have given and granted my land at Sherfield which is of my acquisition[5] with all its appurtenances, to wit, 30 shillings at Lockerley, and the land of Embley, to my son, Richard of Anisy, and to his heirs freely. It is to be held in wood and plain and pasture from my lord, Henry of Port-en-Bessin,[6] and from his heirs. This grant has been made with the counsel and will of William of Anisy, my heir. And I have returned that fee to my lord, Henry of Port-en-Bessin, by the counsel of my friends and peers,[7] and with the assent of William of Anisy, my heir. And my lord, Henry of Port-en-Bessin, has himself put my son, Richard of Anisy, into possession of the same fee, and has received his homage by the same service that I rendered, to wit, the

[1] *scutagiam*. For a full discussion of the various implications of this word at this period, see J. H. Round, *op. cit.*, pp. 262 *et sqq*.

[2] See above, p. 923, n 2. [3] See above, p. 923, n.3.

[4] Calvados (arr. Caen, cant. Creully), 17 miles from Port-en-Bessin. The whole charter offers a singularly clear illustration of the manner in which a local Norman connexion made up an English honour.

[5] *de acato*. The distinction between lands of acquisition and lands of inheritance is brought out in the succession of Norman magnates in England, where it was customary for the Norman lands, *i.e.* the lands of inheritance, to go to the eldest son and the lands of acquisition, *i.e.* the English lands, to go to the second son.

[6] Calvados (arr. Bayeux, cant. Ryes).

[7] Here is the honour court. On peers of a fee, see p. 939 and Nos. 250, 253.

service of 1 knight.[1] And the same Richard has acquitted me of the 11 pounds of the service of the same fee which was formerly rendered to my lord, Henry of Port-en-Bessin. These are the witnesses:[2] William of Port-en-Bessin; John of Port-en-Bessin; Reginald of Port-en-Bessin; Henry of Port-en-Bessin; Ralph of Port-en-Bessin; Roger of Escures,[3] and Matthew, his son; Robert 'de Heriet' and Alfred and Henry, his sons; Henry of Brébeuf,[4] and Hugh, his son; Hugh of Arundel; and William of Arundel; Hugh 'de Burhun'; Geoffrey 'de Barnevile'; John of Hastings; Ralph of Dummer; Robert of Dummer; 'Ervicus de Basli'; Ralph 'de Basli'; Rannulf of Anisy; Ivo of Anisy; William, son of Roger; Nicholas and John, his sons; Andrew and Samson; Cresp the butler, and Robert, his son; Wire the parker and his sons; Robert Sor; Richard 'de Dene'; Robert 'de Manerio' and Jordan, his nephew; Robert Brun; and many others. At Basing.[5]

250. Charter of Anselm, abbot of Bury St. Edmunds, granting land in Suffolk to Adam of Cockfield, his military tenant (1121–1148)

This charter is of interest in that it shows the manner in which a tenure by knight-service was constructed in order to be adequate to the service which it owed. It is also important as providing early evidence for the conception of peerage, and for the organization of a feudal honour. The court of the honour consisted of the knights who were the 'peers' of the fee. The Latin text of this charter is printed in *Chronica Jocelini de Brakelonda*, ed. J. G. Rokewode (Camden Soc., 1840), p. 140, and in D. C. Douglas, *Feudal Documents from the Abbey of Bury St. Edmunds* (1932), p. 121.

Anselm, by the grace of God, abbot of the church of St. Edmund, to all his successors, and to all the men of the same church, both French and English, present and to come, greeting. I bid you to know that I, with the consent of the whole chapter, have granted to Adam of Cockfield and to his heirs that he should now hold in heredity and by the service of 1 knight the land in Cockfield and in Lindsey with all that pertains to it, to wit, the land which his father held on the day on which he was alive and dead. And the men of St. Edmund swore and witnessed that Leofmær,[6] his father, held it on the day on which he was alive and dead, and they attested this in the presence of the lord, Talbot, the prior and in the presence of the monks, Eadnoth and Sired and Wulfric and Ording and Jocelyn and Wulfweard the clerk, and Roger the weak, and Osbern of Melton and Almær of Whatfield. And that he may be able the better to perform the service of 1 knight from the aforesaid estates I have with the consent of the chapter added to them for an increment 5 solidates of land and 4 denariates of land, to wit, the service from the land of Ailstan of Lindsey, and the service from the land of his grandfather, Wulfric of Groton. And I wish and order that he and his heir may hold it well and as peaceably and honourably and freely as do his peers, that is to say, the knights of the abbey. And these are the witnesses: Wulfweard the steward; William, son of 'Ansgeb'; Salomon the clerk; Wulfric the priest; and others.

[1] The land is returned to the chief lord, who regrants it to the new tenant.
[2] These are the members of the honorial court.
[3] Calvados (arr. Bayeux, cant. Ryes), a mile and a half from Port-en-Bessin.
[4] Calvados (arr. Caen, cant. Evrecy).
[5] The *caput* of Henry of Port-en-Bessin's English honour.
[6] Lemmerum.

251. An agreement between several holders of fiefs (1124–1130)

This document illustrates the type of dispute which might arise in connexion with intermixed tenures and the numerous parties which might be involved in such cases. The use of a sworn fact-finding jury of twelve is also notable. The Latin text is printed in *Cartularium Monasterii de Rameseia* (Rolls Series, 1884, vol. I, p. 143).

Let all the faithful of holy Church know that Robert Foliot and Payn and Elias, his brothers, have quitclaimed God and St. Benedict and the abbot of Ramsey in the claim concerning the boundaries of Cranfield and Crawley as the men of the three lordships who were called to judge that claim have attested them: four, that is to say, from among the men of the abbot at Cranfield, Edwin, Siward, Leofwine and Theodoric; four from among the men of Walter of Bolbec at Crawley, Aluric, Seman, Godric and Norman; four from among the men of Simon 'de Beauchamp' and of Mahald, his mother, John Smith, Godmer, Leofric and Sæwi. Further, we have held it useful for us to note that the settlement of these disputes and of the claim respecting these boundaries between the abbot of Ramsey and the aforesaid Robert Foliot and his brothers is made by the order of Henry, king of England, and by the order of David, king of Scots, who is head of this land under the king of England, and by the order of the bishop of Salisbury who was justiciar of the whole of England, and with the consent of William of Houghton of whose fee this land was. These are the witnesses: Hugh, son of Richard; Robert 'de Broi'; Ralph 'de Borohard'; Ebroin; Hugh Hayrun; Robert, son of Brian; Hugh 'de Faldhou'; Ordric; Alan; Hugh, son of Harlewin; Robert, son of Anschetil; and others. Whoever shall violate this agreement or take anything here or elsewhere from the land of St. Benedict, may he be excommunicate by the authority of God, the Omnipotent Father, Son, and Holy Spirit, and of Holy Mary ever-Virgin, and of all the chosen of God, and let him be eternally exiled from their communion. *Fiat. Fiat.* Amen. Amen.

252. Charter of Henry I granting to Aubrey 'de Vere' the master-chamberlainship of all England (July 1133)

This charter should be read in connexion with the "Establishment of the King's Household" (above, No. 30) with which document it is roughly contemporary. It will be noted that Normandy is not concerned in the grant, the chamberlainship of Normandy and formerly for a time of England also being in the possession of the family of Tancarville. The reference to Robert Malet is to a former holder of the English office alone, and the allusion here is to a man who was prominent in the Domesday Survey. This charter, together with all matters relating to this office, is discussed at length by G. H. White in *Complete Peerage*, vol. x, Appendix F. It is printed with further comments in *Sir Christopher Hatton's Book of Seals*, ed. L. C. Loyd and D. M. Stenton (1950), pp. 25, 26.

Henry, king of the English, to his archbishops, bishops, abbots, earls, justiciars, barons, sheriffs, and to all his liegemen established in England, greeting. Be it known to all of you that I have given and granted to Aubrey 'de Vere' and to his heirs after him, to be held from me and my heirs, the master-chamberlainship of all England, and he is to hold this in fee and heredity. Wherefore I will and firmly order that he and his heir shall hold this in hereditary right with all the dignities, liberties and emoluments pertaining to it as well and as freely and as honourably as Robert Malet or any other before or after him held it. He shall hold it with the liveries and allowances of my court which pertain to the office of the chamberlainship. Witness: Roger, bishop of Salisbury; and Geoffrey, bishop of Durham, the chancellor; and Nigel, bishop of Ely; and Robert 'of the Seal'; and Robert, earl of Gloucester; and Brian, son of the count; and Robert 'de Vere', the constable; and Humphrey 'de Bohun'; and Hugh Bigot; and William of Aubigné 'Brito'; and Richard Basset; and William of Pont de l'Arche. At Fareham[1] at the time of the king's crossing.

253. Charter of Walter of Bolbec enfeoffing the abbot of Ramsey with two knights' fees (1133–1160)

This enfeoffment of a great ecclesiastical lord as a tenant by knight-service is of special interest, not only for itself, but as illustrating many of the conditions of knight-service and its implications. The references to feudal litigation, and to the payment of relief, deserve special note, as also does the allusion to the "peers of the fee". The Latin text is printed in *Cartularium Monasterii de Rameseia* (Rolls Series, 1884), vol. I, p. 153.

Be it known to all men both living and to come that Walter of Bolbec has given to Walter, abbot of Ramsey, and to the rest of the abbots who shall follow in that office the land of Walton to be held of him and his heirs by the service of 2 knights in all services which are performed by his peers of the same fee except the ward of New Castle. This also is agreed: if Abbot Walter dies or changes his life, the monks will pay 10 marks of silver as relief for this land and shall hold it and do service to Walter of Bolbec or his heir until the new abbot comes, and the new abbot shall pay the same relief for the land and shall do the service. Further, if the monks are unwilling to pay this relief, then Walter of Bolbec or his heir shall hold it until the new abbot comes, and the new abbot shall then pay the same relief of 10 marks of silver which the monks would have given had they wished. And Abbot Walter gave assurance of this agreement by establishing 2 knights in his place, namely Hoverwinus and Henry of Whiston. And if either of them should die the abbot is to establish another knight in his place at the choice of Walter of Bolbec or of his heir. And if a new abbot comes he shall again make the lord, Walter of Bolbec, or his heir secure in this agreement by establishing two other knights (if he shall wish to have others) at the choice of Walter of Bolbec or his heir. And if the abbot defaults in any matter towards lord Walter so that Walter wishes to sue him, the abbot shall come into his court and shall do him right as for a lay fee.[2] And this, I mean, in Bedfordshire or Buckinghamshire and not elsewhere. And if the abbot fails to come, Walter of Bolbec or his heir may fine him as for a lay fee. And if the lord, Walter of Bolbec, shall hold a plea in his court and shall desire the abbot to attend, the abbot shall come, if he can, or send worthy representatives from his men in the aforesaid shires, and this by the usual summons and without dispute. And if anyone should come and make claims in respect of the said land so that the lord Walter must pass judgment, then the lord Walter will bear himself towards the abbot as to his man. And if such a one was to prove his right to that land, then he should hold the same from Abbot Walter and his successors without any exchange of land or repetition of the payment which the lord may give to this abbot or his successors; and the abbot shall hold it from Walter of Bolbec and his heirs. And this

[1] Fareham is near Portsmouth from which the king was to cross to France on 2 or 3 August.

[2] The point being that in respect of this fee the abbot is not entitled to claim his special jurisdictional privileges.

pact was granted by the lord, Walter of Bolbec, and 'Heleinius', his wife, and Hugh, his son, to Abbot Walter and to all succeeding abbots. And in this pact there was associated Aubreye who was the heir to this land, and she granted it as her inheritance to Abbot Walter and his successors with the gift of the lord. Of this grant, which that writ describes, the witnesses are: Robert of Amfreville and Eustace, son of John, and Walter Espec and Simon 'de Beauchamp' and Walkelin 'Mamot'. And these are the witnesses on the parts of Walter of Bolbec and of Abbot Walter: Ralph, son of William, and Robert, his son, and Robert 'de Gray', and many others, both of the homage of Walter and of the tenants of the abbey.

254. Grant by Ording, abbot of Bury St. Edmunds, to Aubrey, count of Guines, of two military tenancies to be held from the abbey (*circa* 1140)

Important as showing the early feudal organization of the honour of Bury St. Edmunds, and also for the personalities concerned in the transaction. It is printed with a facsimile in *Facsimiles of Royal and Other Charters in the British Museum* (ed. G. F. Warner and H. J. Ellis, 1903), No. 18; also in J. H. Round, *Geoffrey de Mandeville* (1892), p. 189.

Ording, by the grace of God, abbot of the church of St. Edmund to all his men and his friends and his liegemen, both French and English, greeting. Know that I have granted to Aubrey, count of Guines,[1] with the consent of the whole chapter, all the fee and the service which his uncle, Robert 'de Vere' holds from the honour of St. Edmund, by the service of $1\frac{1}{2}$ knights; and also the whole fee and service which Alan, son of Frodo,[2] holds of the honour of St. Edmund for the service of 3 knights and for the payment each Easter of 100 shillings at my chamber.[3] All these things I concede to him and to his heirs to be held in fee and in heredity from the church of St. Edmund and from my successors. Wherefore I will and firmly order that the same Aubrey, count of Guines, and his heirs by hereditary right shall hold all the aforesaid things from the church of St. Edmund well and honourably, for the service we have stated above. And these are the witnesses on my part: William the prior; Ralph the sacrist; Jocelyn and Odo, monks; Maurice the steward; Gilbert Blund; Adam of Cockfield; Ralph of Loddon; William, son of Ailbricht; Elias of Melford, and Geoffrey, his brother. Witnesses on the part of the count: Geoffrey 'de Vere'; Robert, son of Humphrey; Robert, son of Eilred; Warin fitz Gerold;[4] Hugh 'de Ginga'; Aubrey of the chapel; Ralph, son of Adam, and Warin, his brother; Ralph of Guines; Geoffrey, son of Humphrey; Geoffrey Arsic; Robert of Cockfield; Ralph Carbuneal and Hugh, his son; and many others.

255. Charter of Stephen creating Geoffrey 'de Mandeville' earl of Essex (June–December 1140)

This is perhaps the earliest extant charter of creation. The career of Geoffrey 'de Mandeville' who by supporting in turn the king and the empress, was able to exact an increasing number of

[1] Aubrey III 'de Vere' became count of Guines in or about 1139, and was to become the first earl of Oxford in 1142. 'Vere' represents Ver (dép. Manche, arr. Coutances, can't. Gavray).

[2] Frodo was brother of Abbot Baldwin, 1065–1098, and appears in Domesday Book as a tenant of the abbey.

[3] *camera*, probably implying treasury.

[4] Warin fitz Gerold (died 1160–1161) was one of the chamberlains of the Exchequer.

concessions from both has been taken as typical of the politics of the civil war. Printed with facsimile in *Facsimiles of Royal and Other Charters in the British Museum* (ed. G. F. Warner and H. J. Ellis, 1903), No. 21. Printed and discussed in J. H. Round, *Geoffrey de Mandeville* (1892), p. 51.

Stephen, king of the English, to his archbishops, bishops, abbots, earls, justices, barons, sheriffs, and to all his servants and liegemen, both French and English, of the whole of England, greeting. Know that I have made Geoffrey 'de Mandeville' earl of the county of Essex in heredity.[1] Wherefore I will and grant and firmly order that he and his heirs after him shall hold by hereditary right from me and my heirs well and in peace, and quietly and honourably, even as my other earls of my land well and freely and honourably hold the counties of which they are earls; with all dignities and liberties and customs with which the other earls aforesaid worthily and freely hold. Witness: William of Ypres, and Henry of Essex, and John, son of Robert fitz Walter, and Robert of Neufbourg, and Mainfen' Brit' and Turgis of Avranches and William of St. Clare and William 'de Dammartin', and Richard, son of Urse, and William of Eu, and Richard, son of Osbert, and Ralph 'de Wiret', and 'Eglinus', and William, son of Aluric, and William, son of Ernald. At Westminster.

256. The marriage settlement executed by Roger, earl of Warwick, on the occasion of the marriage of his daughter, Agnes, to Geoffrey 'de Clinton', sometime chamberlain to Henry I (1123–1153)

This charter is interesting for many reasons. It affords an early illustration of a great lay honour, it provides much genealogical information, it indicates the importance of marriage alliances to the structure of Anglo-Norman feudalism, and it affords one of the rare illustrations of castle-guard among the services which a knight might be called upon to render in the time of the Norman kings. The grant of the county is also very notable. The instrument was printed by J. H. Round in "A Great Marriage Settlement" (*Ancestor*, vol. XI (1904), p. 153) and is there discussed by him. Reference may also be made to F. M. Stenton, *English Feudalism* (1932), p. 209.

Roger, earl of Warwick, to all his barons and his faithful friends, both present and to come, greeting. Know that I have given Agnes, my daughter, in marriage to Geoffrey the chamberlain, with the counsel of the king and of the bishop of Winchester and of Earl 'de Warenne'[2] and of Robert, my brother, and of my other brothers and of my men; and with her I have given 10 knights for service out of the 17 which he holds from me in fee, that these 10 knights may be quit and free of all service which pertains [to me] and may perform their guards at [the castle of] Brandon. Besides this I have given the service of Henry, son of Voster. And if the king shall take a common aid from all his kingdom, Geoffrey shall contribute as much as falls on 10 knights. And if the king shall go on a military expedition within England, then these 10 knights shall go with him at my cost.[3] But if I shall have pardon or quittance or abatement of service from the king, then Geoffrey shall have such pardon or quittance or abatement of service in respect of these 10 knights. And if I exact an aid from my knights, Geoffrey may exact the same if he wishes. And besides this I grant to Geoffrey and his heir to hold the county of Warwick from me and from my heirs in the same manner as I hold and may hold it from the king. These are the witnesses.[4] On my

[1] *Sciatis me fecisse comitem de Gaufrido de Magnavilla de Comitatu Essexe hereditarie.*

[2] 'de Warr'. The text of this charter is somewhat corrupt, and the possibility must not be excluded of confusion between War(wick) and War(enne). The earl 'de Warenne' is the brother-in-law of the earl of Warwick.

[3] *ad castrum meum* (!), the word mistranscribed appears to be *costum*.

[4] The witnesses are identified by Round.

part: the earl 'de Warenne';[1] Robert, my brother, and Geoffrey and Henry; Siward, son of Turi; Hastecill 'de Haruc'; Hugh, son of Richard; Thurstan 'de Munst'; Walter, son of Hugh; Henry Drap; William Giffard; Hugh Abidon. On the part of Geoffrey: William 'de Clinton'; William, son of Ralph; Hugh 'de Clinton' and Maurice, his brother; Richard Turn; Robert, son of Geoffrey, and Elias, his brother; Stephen, son of Ralph, and Richard, his brother; Roger 'de Frevilla'; Ralph 'de Martinmast'; 'Mig.' of Northampton; Payn of Barford; William, son of Odo; Ralph of Drayton.

257. Treaty between the earls of Chester and Leicester effected towards the close of the civil war in the reign of King Stephen (1148–1153)

This document is printed, translated and fully discussed in F. M. Stenton, *English Feudalism* (1932), pp. 249–255, 285–288. It is also considered by J. H. Round in *Geoffrey de Mandeville* (1892), p. 380, who sees in it "the intervention, if not the arbitration of the Church". Concerning this document, Professor Stenton remarks: "It would be hard to find another document which illustrates so clearly the tendencies of a feudal state emancipated from royal control. . . . In reality, the treaty represents the restoration of order by the only means effective in a land where the royal power had fallen into temporary abeyance. . . . The re-establishment of an effective feudal monarchy was inevitable when the earls of Chester and Leicester made their treaty, and the earl of Leicester himself was destined to become its chief minister."

This is the agreement between Rannulf, earl of Chester[2] and Robert, earl of Leicester,[3] and the final peace and concord which was granted and arranged by them before Robert II, bishop of Lincoln, and their own men; on behalf of the earl of Chester, Richard of Louvetot, William, son of Nigel, and Rannulf the sheriff; on the part of the earl of Leicester, Ernald 'de Bosco', Geoffrey Abbas and Reginald 'de Bordineio'; namely, that Earl Rannulf has given and granted to Robert, earl of Leicester, the castle of Mountsorrel to hold to him and his heirs, hereditarily, and as the charter of Earl Rannulf bears witness, so that the earl of Leicester ought to receive Earl Rannulf and his following in the borough and baileys of Mountsorrel, as in his fee, to make war on whomsoever he wishes, and so that the earl of Leicester may not attack Earl Rannulf therefrom for anything, and if it shall be necessary for Earl Rannulf, the earl of Leicester will receive him personally in the demesne castle of Mountsorrel, and so that the earl of Leicester will keep faith with Earl Rannulf saving the faith due to his liege lord. And if it shall be necessary for the earl of Leicester to attack the earl of Chester with his liege lord, he may not bring with him more than twenty knights, and if the earl of Leicester or those twenty knights shall take anything from the goods of the earl of Chester, he will return the whole. Neither the earl of Leicester's liege lord, nor any other may attack the earl of Chester or his men from the earl of Leicester's castles or his land. And the earl of Leicester may not for any cause or chance lay snares for the person of the earl of Chester unless he has defied him fifteen days before. And the earl of Leicester ought to help the earl of Chester against all men except the earl of Leicester's liege lord and Earl Simon.[4] He may help Earl Simon in this way: if Earl Rannulf attacks Earl Simon and refuses to make amends

[1] "Waren".
[2] Rannulf II 'de Gernon', earl of Chester from about 1129 to 1153.
[3] Robert 'le Bossu', earl of Leicester from 1118 to 1168.
[4] Simon II 'de St. Liz', an adherent of King Stephen and recognized by him as earl of Northampton in 1138. He died in 1153.

at the request of the earl of Leicester, then the earl of Leicester may help him, but if Earl Simon attacks the earl of Chester and refuses to make amends at the request of the earl of Leicester, then he may not help him. And the earl of Leicester ought to guard the lands and goods of the earl of Chester which are in the power of the earl of Leicester without ill will. And the earl of Leicester has promised Earl Rannulf that he will destroy the castle of Ravenstone unless Earl Rannulf shall allow that it may remain, and so that if anyone wishes to hold that castle against the earl of Leicester, Earl Rannulf will help him to destroy that castle without guile. And if Earl Rannulf makes a claim upon William of Aunay, the earl of Leicester will have him to right in his court so long as William shall remain the earl of Leicester's man and hold of him, so that if William or his men shall have withdrawn from the earl of Leicester's fealty on account of the destruction of his castle, or because he refuses to do right in the earl of Leicester's court, neither William nor his men shall be received into the power of the earl of Chester to work ill against the earl of Leicester. In this agreement the castle of Whitwick remains to the earl of Leicester fortified with his other castles.

On the other hand, Earl Rannulf will keep faith with the earl of Leicester saving the faith of his liege lord, and if it shall be necessary for the earl of Chester to attack the earl of Leicester with his liege lord he may not bring with him more than twenty knights. And if the earl of Chester or those twenty knights shall take anything of the goods of the earl of Leicester he will return the whole, and neither the earl of Chester's liege lord nor any other may attack the earl of Leicester or his men from the earl of Chester's castles or from his land. And the earl of Chester may not for any cause or chance lay snares for the person of the earl of Leicester unless he has defied him fifteen days before. And the earl of Chester ought to help the earl of Leicester against all men except the earl of Chester's liege lord and Earl Robert of Ferrières.[1] He may help Earl Robert in this way: if the earl of Leicester attacks Earl [Robert] of Ferrières and refuses to make amends at the request of the earl of Chester, then the earl of Chester may help him, but if Earl Robert of Ferrières attacks the earl of Leicester and refuses to make amends at the request of the earl of Chester, then the earl of Chester shall not help him. And the earl of Chester ought to guard the lands and goods of the earl of Leicester which are in the power of the earl of Chester without ill will. And the earl of Chester has promised the earl of Leicester that if anyone wishes to hold the castle of Ravenstone against the earl of Leicester, Earl Rannulf will aid him to destroy that castle without guile. Neither the earl of Chester nor the earl of Leicester ought to build any new castle between Hinckley and Coventry, nor between Hinckley and Hartshill, nor between Coventry and Donington, nor between Donington and Leicester, nor at Gotham nor at Kinoulton, nor nearer [to Leicester], nor between Kinoulton and Belvoir, nor between Belvoir and Oakham, nor between Oakham and Rockingham, nor nearer [to Leicester], except with the common consent of both. And if anyone shall build a castle in the aforesaid places, or within the aforesaid limits, each shall aid the other without any ill will until the castle shall be destroyed.

[1] Robert II of Ferrières, earl of Derby from 1139. He died before 1160.

And each earl, namely of Chester and of Leicester, has pledged his faith in the hand of Robert II, bishop of Lincoln,[1] to hold this agreement as it is contained in this charter, and they have set the bishop as their security for this agreement, on his Christianity, so that if anyone departs from this agreement and refuses to make amends within fifteen days after he has been requested to do so, without ill will, then the bishop of Lincoln and the bishop of Chester shall each give up the two pledges whom they have received as security for the observance of these agreements, to him namely who shall keep these aforesaid agreements.

258. Charter of Henry II respecting the rights of the church of St. Peter at Northampton (1155–1158)

Interesting as illustrating the interconnexion between royal and ecclesiastical justice in the reign of Henry II. It should be compared with No. 166. Printed by F. M. Stenton in *Camb. Hist. Journal*, vol. III, pt. 1 (1929), p. 4.

Henry, king of the English, duke of the Normans and of the men of Aquitaine and count of the Angevins, to Robert, bishop of Lincoln, and W., archdeacon of Northampton, greeting. I order you that you cause the church of St. Peter in Northampton to hold in peace the chapel of Thorpe, if that village can be proved to have pertained to the aforesaid church in the time of King Henry, my grandfather, and to have then belonged to its parish. I am unwilling to allow any change to remain which has been wrongly made from my demesne by another since the time of King Henry, my grandfather. Witness: Warin fitz Gerold the chamberlain. At Worcester.

259. Charter by Robert, earl of Leicester, acknowledging the conditions under which he holds a fee of one knight from the bishop of Lincoln (1160–1163)

An excellent description of feudal tenure. Printed: *Registrum Antiquissimum of the Cathedral Church of Lincoln*, vol. II, No. 313 (Lincoln Rec. Soc., vol. XXVIII, p. 5).

Robert, earl of Leicester, to all his men, both French and English, greeting. Know that I hold in the manor of Knighton 10 librates of land from the bishop and from the church of Lincoln. This I hold in heredity for myself and my heirs in return for our homage and by the service of 1 knight. If, moreover, any one of us fails to do or to observe the homage, the bishop of Lincoln will compel him through that land according to the judgment of his court and the statute of the realm. These are the witnesses: Roger, archbishop of York; Gilbert, bishop of Hereford; Laurence, abbot of Westminster; Gilbert of Sempringham; William Burdet; Ivo of Harcourt; Robert the butler; Geoffrey the abbot; Ernald 'de bosco'; Andrew Revel; Richard 'de Taurai'; Ralph Basset; Hugh Burdet; Walter of Ancourt; Walter 'de Amundevilla'; Gilbert 'de Nevil'; Simon, son of William; William of Colleville; Hugh Bardulf.

[1] Robert 'de Chesney', bishop of Lincoln, 1148–1166.

260. Notification that Herbert 'de Castello' was present when Robert 'de Mare' enfeoffed Robert's brother (*circa* 1166)

This charter describes an enfeoffment, and shows a lord confirming that enfeoffment by one of his tenants by declaring that he was present when the enfeoffment was made. Printed: F. M. Stenton, *Facsimiles of Early Charters in Northamptonshire Collections* (Northants. Rec. Soc., 1930), p. 83.

Be it known to all present and to come that I, Herbert 'de Castello', was in the place in which Robert 'de Mare' gave Uffington to John 'de Mare', his brother, in fee and heredity with all its appurtenances to be held by him and his heirs. He took his homage, and also a mewed falcon in recognition that [John] owed half a knight's service. Now at the petition of Robert 'de Mare', I, Herbert, confirm and grant this gift by this my charter. Witness: Robert 'de Giros'; William 'des Boterels'; Robert Chrestien and Hettrop Chrestien and Henry Chrestien; Ricard 'de Linlee'; William 'de Bulardone'; and Robert of Bold; and Herlewin of Dudmaston; and Robert, son of Louon.

261. Charter of Conan of Brittany, earl of Richmond, respecting property at East Witton, Yorks., and concerning the fee of his knight, Reginald Boterel (1158–1171)

The notion that a knight must be assured of a definite provision is of interest, as is also the statement of the terms of service. This instrument is printed by C. T. Clay in *Early Yorkshire Charters*, vol. IV (1935), p. 51.

Conan, duke of Brittany and earl of Richmond, to his steward and his chamberlain and to all his barons and to all his servants and to all his men, both French and English, greeting. You are all to know, both present and to come, that I have granted, given and by this my charter confirmed to Reginald Boterel, my knight, in augmentation of his provision, the whole village of East Witton with the advowson of the church and with the mill of that village and with all its appurtenances, to be held of me and my heirs by him and his heirs in fee and heredity for three-quarters of the service of one knight, in wood and plain, in forests and waters, in meadows and fields, in tofts and crofts, and in all pastures and in all places pertaining to that village. Wherefore I firmly order you that he shall have and hold the aforesaid village freely and quit of all custom with sake and soke and toll and team and infangtheof. Excluded from this grant are all the lands, tenements and possessions previously given and granted in perpetuity by me to God and to blessed Mary and to my monks at Jervaulx; these possessions have in my charters been defined in height and depth, above and below ground, and nothing is here retained from them to me or my heirs, or to Richard and his heirs either in the lands or pastures or estates of the said monks who are to hold them with all their appurtenances for ever. These are the witnesses: Alan the constable; Eudo, son of Eudo; Derian the summoner; William 'de Coynerris'; Henry Bertram; William the summoner; William Brohulle; Ralph the chamberlain; Geoffrey, son of Boniface. At Quimper.

262. Charter of Roger of Valognes in favour of Binham Priory (*circa* 1145)

This charter is printed, translated and discussed in F. M. Stenton, *English Feudalism* (1932), pp. 37–40, 259. It is of interest in indicating the formalities of a feudal grant, in showing that a fee of six knights was held to be an adequate endowment for a man of substance and position, and in supplying evidence of the early establishment in England of the later rule that in default of sons a fee should be divided among the daughters as co-heiresses.

Roger of Valognes greets all his friends and men, French and English. It is generally known to many that Walter of Valognes, my kinsman, before he became a monk, gave Barney with the land of Thursford and with all the things that are there and belong thereto, within wood and without, for his soul's health and mine, and for the soul's health of all our kin, living and dead, to the church of the blessed Mary of Binham, to remain for ever for the use of the monks who serve and shall serve God there, with the assent and in the presence of Rohais, his wife, before the abbot of St. Albans and before clerks and knights. We know also that Agnes, his daughter, with the same Walter, her father, has placed the aforesaid land upon the altar with a knife before all who were standing around, Agnes namely, who was Walter's heir in respect of this land of Barney, according to the appointed law[1] that where there is no son the daughters divide their father's land by the spindles, nor can the elder take from the younger her half of the inheritance without violence and injury. Now I myself, Roger of Valognes, moved by the love of God, and of the blessed and glorious Virgin Mary, mother of our Lord Jesus Christ, have granted that this gift should be made, and do now confirm it thus made, at the request and prayer of the aforesaid Walter, for the third of the service of one knight only, for the soul of my father[2] who first gave Barney to the church of Binham, and commanded Walter that this should be done, and for the soul of my mother, and for the souls' health of myself, my wife, Agnes, and my sons who are of one mind with me in this, and grant the same themselves, and for the common salvation of all our kin alive and dead. Moreover, I have done this at the advice and with the approval of many wise men, moved especially by the exhortation, the request, and the counsel of the lord Theobald, archbishop of Canterbury[3] and primate of all England, who showed me by most reasonable and unanswerable arguments, that a noble gentleman who has the fee of six knights should give, not only the third part of a knight's land to God and holy Church for the soul's sake of himself and his kin, but the whole of a knight's land, or more than that, adding also that if this man's heir should try to take away the alms which is interposed as a bridge between his father and paradise, by which his father may be able to pass over, the heir, so far as he may be, is disinheriting his father from the kingdom of heaven, and therefore should not obtain the inheritance which remains, since he who has killed his father has proved himself no son. All this the archbishop by careful argument has impressed upon us, and therefore let Walter's aforesaid gift of Barney remain firm for ever with all its appurtenances to the church of blessed Mary of Binham, as freely, well and honourably as Walter best held it in my father's time and mine. As to him therefore who shall desire to take away this alms from the church of Binham, let him have his lot with Dathan and Abiron and Judas the traitor in the depth of hell. As for

[1] *statutum decretum.* [2] Peter of Valognes, the Domesday tenant-in-chief.
[3] Archbishop of Canterbury, 1139–1161.

him, however, who shall confirm it to the church, support, and maintain it, may his soul be in the lot of the elect and enjoy eternal life. Amen. And these are the witnesses: Agnes of Valognes; Fulk of Montpincon; Geoffrey the priest of 'Herefordingberia'; Ralph, son of Robert; Ralph, son of Turgis; Gilbert, son of William 'de Roinges'; Geoffrey the chaplain; Robert of Valognes; Winemar; Geoffrey 'de Manavilla'; Simon, son of William; Robert, son of Ralph.

263. Charter of Walter of Ancourt in favour of his military tenant, Elias of Fallencourt (*circa* 1155)

This charter which is printed, translated and discussed in F. M. Stenton, *English Feudalism* (1932), pp. 106, 272, should be compared with the return made to the king by Walter of Ancourt in 1166 (see above, No. 230). It shows the wide distribution of the estates of an important mesne tenant by knight-service, and also the jurisdictional rights which he possessed. These are expressed in Anglo-Saxon formulae, and the reference to Gerard, the father of Elias suggests that they pertained to the fee from the time of its orginal grant.

Walter of Ancourt[1] to all, etc. Know that I have restored to Elias of Fallencourt the whole land which Gerard of Fallencourt, his father, held of me, namely the fee of 1 knight in Hickling and Kinoulton, and the fee of 1 knight in Burnby, and 4 carucates of land in Scopwick and 1 carucate of land in Granby as half a knight's fee in exchange for the land which he had in Timberland, to hold to him and his heirs of me and my heirs, and as ever his father best and most freely held of me in wood and plain, in fields, in meadows, in waters, in mills, in paths, in all places, with all free customs, with soke and sake and toll and team and infangtheof. Witness: Robert, etc.

264. Writ of Rannulf, earl of Chester, concerning his military tenants at Bisley (1129–1141)

This writ is interesting for its date and for its reference to *vavassores* (see also p. 923). The meaning of this term is discussed with reference to this document in F. M. Stenton, *English Feudalism* (1932), pp. 20–21, 257. At this early date the term was in England often applied merely to denote vassalage in a general sense, and in this case the *vavassores* seem to have included knights among them. At a later date the term *vavassor* was sometimes applied, according to Norman usage, particularly to lesser military tenants – to those who served with an equipment less elaborate than that of the knight. Printed: Stenton, *op. cit.*, p. 257.

R[annulf],[2] earl of Chester, to Richard of Vains[3] and to the rest of his vavassors of Bisley, greeting. I order you to perform your service to Milo the constable as willingly and as well as ever you did. Farewell.

265. Charter of Malcolm IV, king of Scots, in favour of Warden Abbey, Beds. (1157–1159)

Interesting as illustrating the history of the kings of Scotland as earls of Huntingdon (see above, pp. 42, 48). Printed with critical comments in *Sir Christopher Hatton's Book of Seals*, ed. L. C. Loyd and D. M. Stenton (1950), p. 306.

Malcolm, king of Scots, to the bishops, abbots, earls, sheriffs, barons, officers, and to all men of account in all his kingdom and in the honour of Huntingdon, both clercis and laymen, greeting. Know all of you, both present and to come, that I have

[1] 'Deyncurt'. [2] Rannulf 'de Gernon', earl of Chester.
[3] 'de Veim'; Vains is within 2 miles of Avranches, of which Earl Rannulf was *vicomte*.

given and granted, and by this my charter confirmed to God and St. Mary and to the monks of the Cistercian Order which are of Warden Abbey[1] in perpetual alms to construct their abbey, for the salvation of my soul and of the souls of my predecessors and successors, all Sawtry with all that pertains to it in wood and plain, in meadows and waters, in pastures and marshes and in all other things, even as David, the king, my grandfather, of good memory held it, and as Henry, king of England, restored it to me with my other rights in Huntingdon.[2] Wherefore I will and firmly order that the aforesaid monks shall have and hold it from me and from my heirs as my own proper alms well and in peace, and honourably and quietly and free from all temporal obligations and service as the other monks of this Order in my kingdom have and hold their alms. These are the witnesses: Herbert, bishop of Glasgow; Waltheof, abbot of Melrose; Ernald, abbot of Roxburgh; Osbert, abbot of Jedburgh; Walter the chancellor; Adam the chaplain of Roxburgh; Nicolas the clerk; William, my brother;[3] Walter, son of Alan; Richard of Morville;[4] Rannulf 'de Sulis'; William of Morville; William 'de Sumervilla'; Liulf, son of 'Maccus'; Orm, son of Elaf; David Olifard; Robert 'Freb'; David 'de Boevilla'; H. 'de Perci'. At Roxburgh.

266. Charter of Queen Eleanor, wife of Henry II, respecting the knight-service owed to the abbey of Abingdon (1156–1164)

Illustrates the direct concern of the king in the proper performance of knight-service on the baronies of his tenants-in-chief. Printed: *Chronicon Monasterii de Abingdon* (Rolls Series, 1858), vol. II, p. 225.

Eleanor, queen of England, duchess of Normandy and Aquitaine, and countess of Anjou, to the knights and men who hold lands and tenures of the abbey of Abingdon, greeting. I order that justly and without delay you do full service to Walkelin, abbot of Abingdon, as your predecessors did to his predecessors in the time of King Henry, the grandfather of the lord king. And if you do not do this, the justice of the king and my own justice will cause it to be done. Witness: Jocelyn 'de Balliol'. At Winchester. By writ of the king from over the sea.

267. Charter of Henry II granting Meath to Hugh of Lassy (1172)

The grant of this immense territory to Hugh of Lassy was an important event in the history of the Normans in Ireland, and it was one of the factors which rendered inevitable future conflicts in the island. Perhaps the king wished to set up a counterpoise in Ireland to the power of Strongbow in Leinster. The lack of limitations to Hugh of Lassy's power as here granted is notable, and the king's action was both remarkable and exceptional. Printed: G. H. Orpen, *Ireland under the Normans*, vol. I, pp. 285, 286.

Henry, king of England, and duke of Normandy and Aquitaine, and count of Anjou, to his archbishops, bishops, abbots, earls, barons, justiciars, servants, and to his liegemen, French, English and Irish, in all his lands, greeting. Know that I have given and granted and by this my charter confirmed to Hugh of Lassy for his service the land of Meath with all its appurtenances to be held by him and his heirs for the service of 50 knights. This shall be held and possessed from me and from my heirs

[1] *qui sunt de domo de Sartis.*
[2] Malcolm was confirmed in the earldom by Henry II in 1157.
[3] Afterwards William the Lion, king of Scots. (See Table 16.)
[4] Dép. Manche, arr. Valognes, cant. Bricquebec.

as fully as Murrough O'Melaghlin ever held it, or anyone before or after his time. And by way of increment to this grant I give to him all the fiefs around Dublin which came to him or shall come to him in discharging my service in my city of Dublin. Wherefore I will and firmly order that the said Hugh and his heirs after him shall have and hold the aforesaid land and all the liberties and free customs which I have or can have there for the stipulated service. He shall hold it from me and my heirs well and in peace, freely and quietly and honourably, in wood and plain, in meadows and pastures, in waters and mills, in fish-ponds and pools, in fisheries and warrens, in ways and paths, and in seaports, and in all other places and with all other things pertaining to it and with all the liberties which I have there, or which I can give to him. And I have confirmed this with this my charter. Witnesses: Earl Richard, son of Gilbert; William of Briouze; William of Aubigny; Reginald 'de Cortenay'; Hugh 'de Gundevilla'; William, son of Aldelin the steward; Hugh of Cressy; William of Estouteville; Ralph 'de Aya'; Reginald of Pavilly; Ralph of Verdun; William of Jarpenville; Robert of Rouellé. At Wexford.

(*d*) THE CONDITIONS AND INCIDENTS OF FEUDAL TENURE AS DESCRIBED IN THE LEGAL TREATISE KNOWN AS 'GLANVILLE'

268. 'Glanville': "Concerning the laws and customs of the kingdom of England." Select passages bearing on tenure by knight-service

On the character and authorship of this treatise which was compiled towards the end of the reign of Henry II, see above, No. 58. The treatise is of great value in providing a contemporary description of the law regulating military tenure, and many of the practices it describes were, as is shown in the charters printed above, of still higher antiquity. Of particular interest is the discussion of the "feudal incidents". The holder of land by knight-service, whether he held immediately from the king, or from some other lord, was liable to certain obligations which are usually described as the "feudal incidents". The chief of these "incidents" were: (*a*) *aids*, that is to say, the payments due by the tenant to the lord on the lord being in need of pecuniary assistance; (*b*) the *relief* that is to say, the payment due from the heir to an hereditary fief on taking over his estate on the death of his predecessor; (*c*) the claim of the lord to take into his own hands the estate of a deceased tenant until the relief was paid: this was known as *primer seisin*; (*d*) the right of the lord to *wardship* over the person and land of a male heir under age; (*e*) the right of the lord to dispose of his female ward in *marriage*; (*f*) the right of the lord in certain circumstances to take back the land of the tenant into his own hands: in this case the land was said to *escheat* to the lord. The regulation of these "incidents" was a matter of considerable dispute, and during the period 1066–1189, the general tendency in this matter was towards an increased definition of the liabilities which sometimes operated to the advantage of the tenant and sometimes to the advantage of the lord. The description supplied below offers the fullest extant discussion of these incidents, but it should be compared with earlier references to the incidents in the charters, and particularly perhaps with the "Coronation Charter" of Henry I (see above, No. 19). Since the "feudal incidents" provided a large part of the revenue of every lord, including the king, their regulation was a matter not only of social, but also of constitutional importance. At a later date *Magna Carta* was to be much concerned with their definition.

BOOK IX. *Chap. I.* It remains to continue upon the subject of performing homage[1] and receiving reliefs. Upon the death of the father or any other ancestor, the lord of the fee is bound from the first to receive the homage of the true heir,[2] whether the

[1] Homage was the ceremonial act by which a feudal tenant became the man of his lord (cf. *e.g.* No. 220). This constituted between them a *quasi*-religious bond. In addition to homage the man had to swear fealty to the lord.

[2] Since the taking of homage was a recognition of heirship it was important for the lord not to accept homage from anyone without careful investigation.

heir has attained full age or not, provided always that he be male. For females cannot by law perform any homage, although, generally speaking, they are wont to do fealty to their lords. But if they are married their husbands ought to do homage to their lords for their fee; if, I mean, homage be due in respect of such fees. If, however, the heir be male and a minor, the lord of the fee is not entitled by law to the wardship[1] of the heir or of his holding until he has received the homage of the heir; because it is a general principle that no one can exact from an heir, whether he is of age or not, any service, whether a relief or otherwise, until he has received the homage of the heir in respect of that holding for which the service is claimed. But[2] a person may perform homage to several lords on account of different fees, but of these homages one should be the chief and should be liege homage,[3] and this must be performed to the lord from whom the person performing homage holds his chief tenement. Homage ought to be done in this manner, namely, that he who performs it shall so become the man of his lord that he shall bear faith to him for the tenement in respect of which he performs homage, and shall preserve the earthly honour of his lord in all things save the faith due to the king and to his heirs. From this it is evident that a vassal cannot injure his lord without breaking the faith involved in homage, unless perhaps in his own defence, or unless on the order of the king he joins the king's army when it goes against his lord. Generally speaking, the law holds that no one can, without breaking the faith implied in homage, do anything which tends to deprive his lord of his inheritance, or do anything to the dishonour of his body. If then a tenant has, in respect of several fees, done homage to different lords who afterwards make war upon each other, and the chief lord[4] should command the tenant to go in person with him against another of his lords, he ought to obey this command saving, however, the service due to the other lord in respect of the fee held from him. From what has been said it therefore follows that if a tenant should do anything contributing to the disinheritance of his lord, and should be convicted of it, he and his heirs shall according to the law lose for ever the fee held of this lord.[5] The same consequence will follow if

[1] On wardship, see further below, p. 940.

[2] *Potest autem quis plura homagia diversis dominis facere de feodis diversorum dominorum. Sed unum eorum oportet esse praecipuum et cum ligeantia factum, illi scilicet domino faciendum a quo tenet suum capitale tenementum is qui homagium facere debet.*

[3] The closest bond of homage, which overrode all other obligations. Cf. the *Leges Henrici Primi* (above, No. 57) which also emphasizes the importance of liege homage. It should be noted that every tenant-in-chief owed liege homage to the king since it was from the king that he held his chief tenement, his *caput honoris*. On the subject of *ligius* and *ligeancia*, see further F. M. Stenton, *English Feudalism* (1932), esp. pp. 29–31.

[4] *capitalis dominus*; see n.2 above.

[5] This is the escheat (see above, p. 937). A fee might escheat to the lord for many reasons and for many crimes, but the most common cause of an escheat was lack of heirs. On escheats 'Glanville' further remarks (Book VII, chap. XVII):

> The ultimate heir of any person is his lord. When therefore a man dies without leaving a certain heir . . . the lords of the fee may, and indeed usually do, take the vacant inheritance into their hands and retain them as escheats, whoever such lord may be, whether the king or any other person. . . . Besides this, if a female heir, in the wardship of her lord, be guilty of incontinence, her inheritance shall escheat to her lord on account of her crime. And if any person be convicted of felony or confess his guilt in court, he shall be deprived by the law of the realm of his inheritance and his land shall remain with his lord as an escheat. It is to be observed that if anyone holds of the king in chief, then as well as his land, all his movables and chattels, in whosoever possession they may be, shall be taken into the king's use, and the heirs shall be for ever debarred from recovering them. If an outlaw or one convicted of felony hold of any person other than the king, then also all his movables shall belong to the king, whilst his lands shall remain in the king's hands for one year and then, after this time, shall revert to the right lord, to whom the fee belongs, the houses, however, being thrown down and the trees rooted up. And, generally

the tenant lays violent hands on his lord to hurt him, or puts him to shame, and this be lawfully proved in court against the tenant. But it may be asked whether anyone can be compelled to defend himself against the lord in the lord's court against such charges; and whether his lord can, by the judgment of his own court, distrain the tenant so to do, without the precept of the king or of his justices or without the king's writ or that of his chief justice. The law indeed permits a lord by the judgment of his court to summon and distrain one who has paid him homage to appear in court, and unless such a one can purge himself against the charge of his lord by three persons, or as many as the court shall decide, he shall be amerced to the lord to the extent of the whole fee that he holds from this lord. It may also be inquired whether a lord can distrain one who has paid him homage to appear in his court to answer for a service which the lord claims has not been rendered, or of which some part has been withheld. The answer is that the lord may by law well do so, and this even without the precept of the king or his justices. And in such a controversy the lord and the man who has paid him homage may submit their dispute to the duel, or to the Grand Assize[1] by means of one of the tenant's peers[2] who duly witnesses to the fact that he has seen the tenant himself or his ancestors perform such service for the fee to the lord or his ancestors, and is prepared to prove the fact. And if the tenant be convicted of this charge, he shall by law be disinherited of the whole fee which he holds of his lord. If, however, anyone is unable to constrain his tenants, it then becomes necessary to have recourse to the [king's] court. Every free male person may perform homage, whether of full age or otherwise, whether clerk or layman. But consecrated bishops are not accustomed to perform homage to the king even for their baronies; but merely fealty accompanied by an oath. But bishops-elect are wont to do homage previous to their consecration.

Chap. II. Homage is only due for lands, free tenements, services, and dues, either of money or in kind, which have been precisely determined. Only in respect of demesne should homage be rendered to no one except to the king. Yet homage ought not always to be performed for every kind of land. Thus it is not due for land in dower or for a marriage portion freely bestowed, nor from the fee of younger sisters holding from the eldest, within the third descent on both sides; nor is it due from a fee given in frankalmoign, nor for any tenement given in any way as a marriage portion, so far as concerns the person of the husband of the woman to whom the property belongs as her marriage portion.

Chap. III. Homage may, however, be done to any free person whether male or female, whether of full age or otherwise, and whether clerk or lay. But it should be understood that if a person has done homage for a tenement to a woman who afterwards marries, then he shall be compelled to repeat it to her husband for the same tenement. If, however, anyone has by agreement made in court recovered a tenement against another who had previously paid a relief for it to the chief lord, it may be

speaking, whenever a person has done or said anything in court for which he has been by the judgment of the court disinherited, his inheritance is wont to return as an escheat to the lord of the fee of whom it is held.

[1] See above, No. 58.

[2] On "peers of a fee", see above, Nos. 250, 253.

questioned whether the person so recovering the tenement ought to pay any further relief for it.

Chap. IV. There ought to be a reciprocal obligation of fidelity between lordship and homage. Nor does the tenant owe more to his lord in respect of homage than the lord owes to the tenant on account of lordship, reverence alone excepted.[1] Hence if one person gives to another any land in return for service and homage, which land is afterwards recovered against the tenant by a third party, the lord shall be bound to warrant such land to him or to return him an adequate equivalent. It is otherwise, however, in the case of a man who holds a fee from another as his inheritance and in this character has done homage, because in this instance although he lose his land the lord shall not be bound to give him an equivalent. In the case we have previously mentioned of the death of the father or ancestor leaving an heir who is a minor, the lord of the fee has no right to the wardship of the heir or of his inheritance unless he has first received the homage of the heir. But after homage has been received, the heir with his inheritance shall remain, as mentioned earlier, in the wardship of his lord until he has attained full age.[2] Having at last arrived at such age and received restitution of

[1] *Mutua quidem debet esse dominii et homagii fidelitatis connexio, ita quod quantum homo debet domino ex homagio, tantum illi debet dominus ex dominio praeter solam reverentiam.* This is the very essence of feudal doctrine–the notion of reciprocal rights and duties reinforced by the obligation of reverence towards the lord. Just as the tenant could forfeit his fee to the lord if he broke his contract, so also could the lord forfeit the allegiance of his men if he abused his rights. The *diffidatio* or formal renunciation of faith by the vassals of a lord who has abused his position was a legal remedy in feudal law.

[2] This is the incident of wardship which elsewhere is more fully described by 'Glanville' (Book VII, chap. IX):

> Some heirs are evidently of age, some as clearly not of full age, whilst of others it may be doubted whether they are of full age or not. The first class may immediately on the death of their ancestors hold themselves in possession of their inheritance, although their lords, may take the fee together with the heir into their hands. This, however, ought to be done with such moderation as not to cause any dispossession to the heirs who may, should it be necessary, resist any violence from their lords, provided they are prepared to pay the due reliefs and services.

This is a reference to *primer seisin* (on which see below, p. 942), that is to say, the claim of the lord to take possession of the estate on the death of its holder until relief has been paid by the heir. Concerning wardship 'Glanville' continues:

> But if it be evident that the heir is under age, and he hold by military service, he is considered to be in the wardship of his lord until he attains full age. The full age of an heir, if the son of a knight, or of one holding by military service, is when he has completed his twenty-first year. But if the heir be the son of a sokeman, he is esteemed to have reached full age when he has completed his fifteenth year. If he is the son of a burgess, he is understood to have attained full age when he has discretion to count money and measure cloth and in like manner to manage his father's other concerns. In so extensive a sense have lords the custody of the sons and heirs of their men and of their fees that they exercise, for example, absolute control in presenting to churches in their wardship, in giving females in marriage and in regulating other matters in such a way as if they were their own. The law does not, however, permit the lords to make any absolute disposition of the inheritance. And the lord must in the meantime maintain the heir in a manner suitable to his dignity and to the extent of his inheritance. He must discharge the debts of the deceased so far as the estate and the length of wardship will admit. Lords are bound by law in this sense to pay the debts of the ancestors of their tenants under ward. The lords may also manage the concerns of the heir and prosecute all suits for the recovery of his rights, provided no exception be taken on account of the minor's age. But the lord is not bound to answer for the heir in a question of disputed ownership or possession, except only when one minor has the wardship of another after the decease of his father. Should the latter minor, upon attaining full age, be refused his inheritance, he may have the assize of *Mort d'Ancestor* [see above, p. 473] nor shall the recognition in such case cease on account of the minority of the lord. If a minor be accused of any felony, then he shall be attached by safe pledges. Yet while he continues under age, he shall not be compelled to answer the charge. Those persons who have wardship are bound to restore the inheritance in good condition and discharged from debts in proportion to the duration of the wardship and the extent of the inheritance.

This interesting account of feudal wardship should be compared with that given in the "Coronation Charter" of Henry I (No. 19).

his inheritance, he shall by reason of his having been in ward be exempt from the payment of relief. But a female heir, whether she has attained full age or not, shall remain in the wardship of her lord until with his consent she is married.[1] If, however, she was below age when the lord received her into wardship, then upon her marriage the inheritance shall be quit from the relief so far as it concerns herself and her husband. But if she was of full age at that time, although she may continue for a space in the wardship of her lord before she is married, her husband shall pay a relief. When, however, the relief has been once paid by the husband of a woman, it shall exempt both the husband and the wife during their several lives from the payment of another relief for the inheritance, because neither the woman, nor her second husband should he survive her ought again to pay relief for the same land. But when a male heir is left of full age, and known to be such, he shall hold his inheritance as we have noted above, even though his lord be unwilling, provided that he offers to his lord, as he ought, in the presence of worthy persons, his homage and a reasonable relief. According to the custom of the realm a reasonable relief for a knight's fee is said to be 100 shillings,[2] whilst that of land held in socage is said to be one year's value. But as to baronies, nothing definite is fixed, because barons holding of the king in chief are wont to pay their reliefs to the king according to his will and pleasure.[3] The same rule applies to serjeanties. If, however, the lord will neither receive the homage nor a reasonable relief from the heir, then the latter should keep the relief in safety and frequently offer it to his lord by the hands of reputable persons. If the lord will even so not receive it, then the heir shall make complaint to the king or to his justices; and he shall receive the following writ:

Chap. V.

The king to the sheriff greeting. Order *N.* that justly and without delay he receive the homage and the reasonable relief of *R.* concerning the free tenement which he holds in such-and-such a village, and that he claims to hold of him. And if he fails to do this, summon him by good summoners to attend before me or my justices on such-and-such a day to show why he has not done it. And you shall have there the summoners, etc.

Chap. VI. As to the procedure to be followed in case the lord should not obey this summons, and the means by which he shall be distrained to appear in court, they may be collected from the former part of this treatise. When at last he appears in court he will either acknowledge that the tenant is the right heir, or deny that he is the heir, or express doubt on this point. If he acknowledges him to be the right heir, he will then either deny that the tenant has offered him homage and reasonable relief or he will admit it. If he confess both the one and the other, then he shall either accept forthwith the tenant's homage and reasonable relief, or he shall appoint a suitable day for doing

[1] The feudal incident of right over the *marriage* of wards. Compare this with the "Coronation Charter" of Henry I (No. 19). The burden seems to have increased.

[2] This attempt to fix the amount of relief is to be contrasted with the vague terms of Henry I's charter. But it may be doubted whether so high a sum as 100 shillings ever represented the average relief of a knight's fee in England.

[3] The king retains the right to make with each of his tenants-in-chief the best individual bargain he can, but the charter of Henry I had insisted that the relief paid must be just and reasonable, and *Magna Carta* was to impose specific restrictions on the king in this matter.

this. And provided that he admits the tenant to be the heir, the same course should be adopted even if he denies that the tenant has offered him homage and relief. But if in clear terms he denies the tenant to be the heir, then the latter, if out of possession, may claim against his lord an assize of *Mort d'Ancestor.*[1] Should the tenant, however, be in possession, he may retain it and patiently wait until the lord is pleased to accept his homage, because no one is bound to pay relief to his lord before the lord has received his homage for the fee for which homage is due. But if the lord doubts whether the person offering homage is the right heir or not, being for example, unknown as such to the lord himself or even to the neighbourhood, then the lord of the fee may take the land into his own hands, and retain it until the matter be fully elucidated. This, moreover, is the course which the king usually adopts in the case of all baronies held of him in chief. For upon the death of a baron holding in chief, the king immediately retains the barony in his own hands until the heir has given security for the relief,[2] even though the heir be of full age. But for a reasonable cause lords may sometimes postpone receiving homage and relief for their fees. Suppose, for example, another person than the one who asserts himself to be the heir claims a right to the inheritance: then while this suit is pending homage ought not to be received nor a relief given. Or, if the lord think that he has himself a right to hold the inheritance as part of his own demesne, and if in such case he should by means of the king's writ or that of his justices, sue the person in possession: then the tenant may put himself upon the Grand Assize.[3]. . .

Chap. VIII. After it has been settled between the lord and the heir of the tenant concerning the giving and receiving of a reasonable relief, the heir may exact reasonable aids[4] in respect of this from his own men. This, however, must be done with moderation in accordance with the number and resources of their fees lest they should be too much oppressed or should lose their contenement.[5] But nothing certain is fixed concerning the giving and exacting of aids of this kind except that the conditions we have noted must be always observed. There are also other cases in which a lord can exact from his men similar aids, always observing the prescribed form: as when his son and heir is made a knight, and when he gives his eldest daughter in marriage. But whether lords can exact aids to maintain private war[6] is doubtful. The opinion which prevails is that they cannot lawfully distrain their tenants for such a purpose except in so far as the tenants agree. But with respect to the payment of reasonable aids, lords may of their own right, without the king's precept or that of his justices, but by the judgment of their own court, distrain their tenants by such of their chattels as may be found within their fees or if necessary by their fees themselves; provided always that the tenants are dealt with according to the judgment of the lord's court and consistently with its reasonable custom. If therefore a lord may thus distrain his tenants to pay such reasonable aids, much stronger is the argument that he may lawfully distrain in the same manner for a relief, or for any other service necessarily due to him in

[1] See above, No. 58, p. 473.
[2] *primer seisin.* See above, pp. 937, 938.
[3] See above, No. 58, pp. 466 *et sqq.*
[4] See above, p. 937.
[5] *contenementum*: is the property necessary to enable a man to maintain his position.
[6] *werram.*

respect of the fee. If, however, a lord is unable by judgment to compel his tenant to render his due and customary services, then recourse must be had to the king or to his chief justice, and he shall obtain the following writ:

Chap. IX.

> The king to the sheriff greeting. I order you to compel *N.* justly and without delay to render to *R.* the due and customary services which he ought to render in respect of the tenement he holds of him in such-and-such a village, as can be reasonably shown to be due to the lord, lest complaint be made again in respect of default of justice. Witness, etc.

Chap. X. When the plea proceeds by virtue of this writ, the plaintiff shall in the shire court and before the sheriff demand his dues, whether they consist of reliefs or other things, according to the custom of the shire court. And if the plaintiff shall prove his case, then the tenant shall render the reasonable relief to his lord, and shall in addition be amerced to the sheriff, it being a recognized principle that the amercement which results from any suit dealt with and decided in the shire court belongs to the sheriff. The amount of such amercement has, it is true, been determined by no general assize, but is regulated by the custom of the different shires, in one shire more, in another less.

D. SELECT DOCUMENTS RELATING TO THE HISTORY OF ENGLISH TOWNS

THE documents which here follow have been arranged in two sections, the former relating to London, and the latter to other English towns. They should be studied in connexion with other texts in this volume and more particularly in connexion with the accounts of English boroughs given in Domesday Book (see Nos. 208, 209).

Most of these documents are grants of privilege and most of the distinctive burghal privileges are illustrated in them. The more important of these privileges may perhaps be classified as follows:

(i) Tenurial privileges–and in particular the limitation of the services due from burgesses in respect of their holdings, together with special devices designed to ensure security of tenure.

(ii) Jurisdictional privileges–notable among which are exemptions from the courts of shire and hundred, and from trial by battle. There are also special judicial procedures indicated for use in mercantile litigation.

(iii) Mercantile privileges–relating in particular to markets and fairs, to exemption from customs and tolls. The establishment of merchant and craft gilds should be noted in this connexion.

(iv) Financial privileges–of which the chief is the *firma burgi*, the right of the burgesses to 'farm' their own borough, raising the revenue themselves and paying an annual fixed sum to the king. In cases where this privilege was obtained the borough became financially as well as jurisdictionally independent of the sheriff of the shire.

Every borough, recognized as such, possessed some of these privileges; very few, if any, had all; and their several circumstances were widely different. Generalizations about English boroughs in this period are therefore dangerous, since each town needs to be specially studied in relation to its particular environment.

(*a*) DOCUMENTS RELATING TO LONDON IN THE PERIOD 1042–1189

The texts here printed have been selected to illustrate in the first place the privileges granted or confirmed to the Londoners by William I and Henry I, and the partial development of a civic constitution following on the charter bestowed by the latter king. These documents might seem to reveal a desire on the part of the Londoners rather to develop inherited privileges than to establish for themselves a centralized administration. A further development in this latter direction was, however, to come with the establishment of the 'commune' in 1191. The variations of administration existing in London at this time may be watched in the history of the different jurisdictions or 'sokes' which continued in this period, and in particular in the texts relating to the *cnihtengild*. These texts also reveal some of the chief city families at this time, and they throw some light upon the history of the London churches and of the Tower of London. The series closes with William fitz Stephen's panegyric of London in the time of Henry II.

269. Writ (in Anglo-Saxon) of William I to the city of London (1066–1075)

A cardinal text in the history of London. Recognizes London as a borough, and grants to the burgesses special privileges in respect of the inheritance of land. Printed: F. Liebermann, *Die Gesetze der Angelsachsen*, vol. I (1903), p. 486; W. Stubbs, *Select Charters* (ed. 1913), p. 97; facsimile in R. R. Sharpe, *London and the Kingdom* (1894), vol. I.

William the king greets William,[1] bishop of London, and Gosfrith the portreeve, and all the burgesses of London friendly. I give you to know that I will that you be worthy of all the laws you were worthy of in the time of King Edward. And I will that every child shall be his father's heir after his father's day. And I will not suffer any man to do you wrong. God preserve you.

270. Charter of Henry I in favour of the citizens of London (Michaelmas 1130–August 1133)

This charter recognizes and confirms the privileges of the city of London. These privileges fall, it will be seen, in the main, into the two categories of judicial and mercantile. The most important clause in the charter is the grant to the citizens of the right to 'farm' their own borough. The city, it will be noted, was seeking to emancipate itself from the shire, and the authority of the sheriff, financially as well as judicially. London was to lose this right to Geoffrey 'de Mandeville' a few years later (see above, No. 45), but it was subsequently regained, and the same claim was in due course successfully made by most of the greater boroughs of England. It is for this reason that the present charter may be said to represent a landmark in the history of English municipal self-government. As such it has been widely and frequently discussed. Particular reference may be made to J. H. Round, *Geoffrey de Mandeville* (1892), pp. 347–373, and to J. Tait, *Medieval English Borough*, pp. 154–161. The charter is printed in F. Liebermann, *Die Gesetze der Angelsachsen*, vol. I, p. 524, and in W. Stubbs, *Select Charters* (ed. 1913), p. 129.

Henry, by the grace of God, king of the English, to the archbishop of Canterbury, and to the bishops and abbots, and earls and barons and justices and sheriffs, and to all his liegemen, both French and English, of the whole of England, greeting. Know that I have granted to my citizens of London that they shall hold Middlesex at 'farm' for 300 pounds 'by tale' for themselves and their heirs from me and my heirs,[2] so that the citizens shall appoint as sheriff from themselves whomsoever they may choose, and shall appoint from among themselves as justice whomsoever they choose to look after the pleas of my crown and the pleadings which arise in connexion with them. No other shall be justice over the same men of London. And the citizens shall not plead outside the walls of the city in respect of any plea; and they shall be quit of scot and of Danegeld and the murder-fine.[3] Nor shall any of them be compelled to offer trial by battle.[4] And if any one of the citizens shall be impleaded in respect of the pleas of the crown, let him prove himself to be a man of London by an oath which shall be judged in the city. Let no one be billeted within the walls of the city, either of my household, or by the force of anyone else. And let all the men of London and their property be quit and free from toll and passage and lestage and from all other customs throughout all England and at the seaports. And let the churches and barons and citizens hold and have well and in peace their sokes,[5] with all their customs, so that those who dwell in these sokes shall pay no customs except to him who possesses the

[1] Bishop of London, 1051–1075.
[2] The *firma burgi*.
[3] See above, p. 543.
[4] See above pp. 464–466.
[5] On the sokes within London, see below, pp. 948, 951.

soke, or to the steward whom he has placed there. And a man of London shall not be fined at mercy[1] except according to his 'were',[2] that is to say, up to 100 shillings: this applies to an offence which can be punished by a fine. And there shall no longer be 'miskenning'[3] in the hustings court,[4] nor in the folk-moot, nor in other pleas within the city. And the hustings court shall sit once a week, to wit, on Monday. I will cause my citizens to have their lands and pledges and debts within the city and outside it. And in respect of the lands about which they make claim to me, I will do them right according to the law of the city. And if anyone has taken toll or custom from the citizens of London, then the citizens of London may take from the borough or village where toll or custom has been levied as much as the man of London gave for toll, and more also may be taken for a penalty. And let all debtors to the citizens of London discharge their debts, or prove in London that they do not owe them; and if they refuse either to pay, or to come and make such proof, then the citizens to whom the debts are due may take pledges within the city either from the borough or from the village or from the county in which the debtor lives. And the citizens shall have their hunting chases, as well and fully as had their predecessors, to wit, in Chiltern and Middlesex and Surrey. Witness: the bishop of Winchester; Robert, son of Richer; Hugh Bigot; Alfred of Totnes; William of Aubigny; Hubert the king's chamberlain; William of Montfiquet; Hagulf 'de Tani'; John Belet; Robery, son of Siward. Given at Westminster.

271. Charter of Henry II in favour of London (1155)

This charter should be studied in close connexion with that of Henry I for London (No. 270). It will be seen by means of detailed comparison that this charter, which has sometimes been regarded as a mere confirmation, in reality, gives less privileges than those awarded to the city by Henry I. The matter is fully and admirably discussed in J. H. Round, *Geoffrey de Mandeville* (1892), pp. 367–371. Printed: *Munimenta Gildhallae* (Rolls Series, 1859–1862), vol. II, p. 29; and from a better text in W. Page, *London* (1923), p. 277.

Henry, king of the English, and duke of the Normans and of the men of Aquitaine, count of the Angevins, to the archbishops, bishops, abbots, earls, barons, justiciars, sheriffs, and all his servants and liegemen of England, both French and English, greeting. Know that I have granted to my citizens of London that none of them shall plead outside the walls of the city of London, except respecting holdings outside the city, and in respect of my moneyers and my servants. I have also granted to them quittance from the murder-fine both within the city and in the Portsoken;[5] and that none of them shall be tried by battle; and that in respect of pleas of the crown they may make their proof according to the ancient custom of the city; and that within the walls no one shall be forcibly billeted, or by the assignment of the marshal. I have

[1] *non judicetur in misericordia pecuniae*, *i.e.* fined at discretion, and to an unlimited amount.

[2] The 'were' or blood price derives from Anglo-Saxon tribal custom. The 'were' of the London citizen, as here described, was slightly higher than that of the Anglo-Saxon *ceorl*, but far below that of the thegn. See *Munimenta Gildhallae* (Rolls Series, 1859–1862), vol. II, p. 33.

[3] 'miskenning' was verbal error in reciting the formal oaths protesting innocence. This entailed loss of the case. The reference shows that the ancient proofs by compurgation and by oath helpers were still used in London in the time of Henry I.

[4] Apparently at this time a smaller assembly than the folk-moot.

[5] For the Portsoken outside the walls, which was possessed by the *cnihtengild*, see below, p. 948.

also granted that all the citizens of London shall be quit of toll and lestage through all England and in every harbour; and that no one of them shall be fined at discretion except according to the law of the city which they had in the time of King Henry, my grandfather. And in no plea in the city shall there be 'miskenning',[1] nor shall the hustings court be held more than once a week. I grant further that they shall have their lands and pledges and debts whoever owes them; and that right shall be done them according to the law of the city respecting their lands and tenures within the city; and that pleas respecting all their debts contracted in London, and respecting pledges there taken, shall be held in London. And if anyone in all England shall take toll or custom from the men of London, and shall refuse them satisfaction, then shall the sheriff of London take a surety respecting it within London. I also grant to them that they shall have their chases wherever they had them in the time of King Henry, my grandfather. Further,[2] in respect of payments made by the city, I grant that they shall be quit of 'brudtolle'[3] and of 'childwyte'[4] and of 'jeresgieve'[5] and of 'scotale',[6] so that neither my sheriff of London nor any other bailiff shall exact 'scotale'. The aforesaid customs I grant them, and all other liberties and free customs as well as ever they had them in the time of King Henry, my grandfather. Wherefore I will, and firmly order that they and their heirs shall have and hold them by hereditary right from me and my heirs. Witness: Theobald, archbishop of Canterbury; Richard, bishop of London; Philip, bishop of Bayeux; Arnulf, bishop of Lisieux; Thomas the chancellor; Robert of Neufbourg; Richard of St. Valery; Walkelin Maminot; Richard of Lucé; Warin fitz Gerold; Manasser Biset; Loc' 'de Baillolio'. At Westminster.

272. Charter of Henry II in favour of the gild of weavers in London (1154–1162)

Interesting as early evidence for the existence of a craft gild. It will be noted that this gild is referred to the time of Henry I. A note in the MS. states that this charter was annulled by John. Printed: *Munimenta Gildhallae* (Rolls Series, 1859-1862), vol. II, p. 33.

Henry, by the grace of God, king of England, duke of Normandy and Aquitaine, count of Anjou,[7] to the bishops, justiciars, sheriffs, barons, and all his servants and liegemen of London, greeting. Know that I have granted to the weavers of London to have their gild in London with all the liberties and customs which they had in the time of King Henry, my grandfather. Let no one carry on this occupation unless by their permission, and unless he belong to their gild, within the city or in Southwark or in the other places pertaining to London, other than those who were wont to do so in the time of King Henry, my grandfather. Wherefore I will, and firmly order that they shall everywhere legally carry on their business, and that they shall have all the aforesaid things as well and peacefully and freely and honourably and entirely as ever they

[1] See above, p. 946 n.3.
[2] This is the only clause added in this charter to the grants of Henry I, though considerable concessions are omitted.
[3] Perhaps 'breadwite' the fine for breaking the assize of bread.
[4] Fine exacted on a man for the incontinence of his daughter resulting in a bastard birth.
[5] This is probably the same as 'yaresilver' a payment for the repair of weirs and dams.
[6] Here probably used in the sense of payments exacted for enforced beer drinking of which the sheriff took the profits. See N. Neilson, *Customary Rents* (1910), p. 150.
[7] Title as given in the copy.

had them in the time of King Henry, my grandfather; provided always that for this privilege they pay me each year 2 marks of gold at Michaelmas. And I forbid anyone to do them injury or insult in respect of this on pain of 10 pounds forfeiture. Witness: Thomas of Canterbury; Warin fitz Gerold. At Winchester.

273. Writ (in Anglo-Saxon) of Edward the Confessor respecting the jurisdiction of the *cnihtengild* of London (June 1042–July 1044)

Among the most interesting, and the most mysterious, of the early institutions of London is the English *cnihtengild* whose existence before the Norman Conquest is illustrated in the present charter. The *cnihtengild* was an association of prominent citizens which, being possessed of the 'portsoken', exercised one of the most important of the private jurisdictions (sokes) characteristic of eleventh-century London (see W. Page, *London* (1923), pp. 127–158). The soke of the *cnihtengild* extended over a district lying outside the walls from Aldgate to the Thames. The history of this gild, whose rights and property subsequently passed into the hands of Holy Trinity, Aldgate (see below, No. 277), is interesting not only for itself but for the evidence it affords of many of the earliest known London families. It has been discussed in this sense, for instance, in H. C. Coote, "The English Gild of Knights and their Socn" (*Trans. London and Middlesex Archaeol. Soc.*, vol. v, 1881), and by J. H. Round, *Geoffrey de Mandeville*, pp. 347–373, and *Commune of London*, pp. 97–124. The present document is printed in Coote, *op. cit.*, p. 481, and in F. E. Harmer, *Anglo-Saxon Writs* (1952), p. 234.

I, Edward the king, greet Ælfweard the bishop and Wulfgar, my port-reeve, and all the burgesses of London friendly. And I give you to know that I will that my men in the English gild of *cnihts* shall have their jurisdiction over their men within the city and without. And I will that they have the good laws which they had in the days of King Edgar and of my father and of Cnut. And I will also increase their privileges, and I will not allow any man to wrong them. Let them be all at peace. God keep you all.

274. Writ of William II in favour of the *cnihtengild* of London (1087–1100)

To be compared with the preceding document. Printed in translation in *Monasticon Anglicanum*, vol. VI, p. 156; *Trans. London and Middlesex Archaeol. Soc.*, vol. V (1881), p. 488.

William, king of the English, to Maurice the bishop,[1] and Geoffrey 'de Mandeville'[2] and R. Delpare[3] and to his liegemen of London, greeting. Know that I have granted to the men of the *cnihtengild* their gild and the land which belongs to it, with all customs as they were held in the time of King Edward and of my father. Witness: Hugh of Buckland.

275. Charter of Henry I in favour of the *cnihtengild* of London (1100–1107)

To be compared with the preceding document. Printed in translation in *Trans. London and Middlesex Archaeol. Soc.*, vol. V (1881), p. 488; *Monasticon Anglicanum*, vol. VI, p. 156.

Henry, king of the English, to Maurice the bishop, and to the sheriff of London and to all his barons and his liegemen of London, both French and English, greeting. Know that I have granted to the men of the *cnihtengild* their gild and the land which belongs to it with all customs as well as they held it in the time of King Edward and of my father, and as my brother granted it to them by his writ and seal. And I forbid anyone to do them injury in respect of this on pain of forfeiture. Witness: Robert of Montfort-sur-Risle; Roger Bigot; Hugh of Buckland. At Westminster.

[1] Bishop of London, 1086–1107. [2] Sometime sheriff of London.
[3] Possibly a mistranscription. The text of this charter is not satisfactory.

276. Charter of Henry I in favour of Holy Trinity, Aldgate, and in particular granting to this priory the jurisdiction formerly possessed by the English *cnihtengild* in London (1121–1122)

To be compared with the preceding and following documents of this series. Printed in translation in *Monasticon Anglicanum*, vol. VI, p. 157.

Henry, by the grace of God, king of the English, to the archbishops, bishops, abbots, earls, barons, sheriffs and to all his servants and liegemen, greeting. Know that I have granted and by this present charter confirmed the canonry of the canons regular of Holy Trinity in London which Maud the queen, my wife, there founded, to be for ever established and free from all ecclesiastical subjection. The said canons may stop up the way which is between their church and the city wall. I have also granted to the same canons for my own soul and for the soul of Maud, my wife, 25 pounds 'blanch' a year for ever in pure and perpetual alms, out of the revenues of the same Queen Maud at Exeter, which the said Queen Maud with my consent gave them during her life; so that whoever shall be sheriff in Devonshire shall pay this to the aforesaid canons at Easter and at Michaelmas in London as regularly as they were ever paid. I have also given to the said canons the gate of Aldgate with the jurisdiction belonging to the same. And I have granted to the same canons that they have the jurisdiction of the English *cnihtengild* with the lands and with all the liberties belonging to the same jurisdiction within and without the city of London. And I will, and strictly order that the aforesaid canons and their men shall have and hold all their lands and possessions and their fees and alms, both things ecclesiastical and things and possessions that are secular, with all liberties and free customs and quittances, in woods and plains, in meadows and pastures, in waters and mills, in roads and paths, in lakes and ponds, in marshes and fisheries, in granges and underwoods, within the city and without, within the borough and without, with sake and soke, toll and team, and infangtheof. And I have granted that the same canons and their men be for ever free and quit from all gelds and scots and dues and assessments, and of all aids to the sheriff and his servants, and from attendance at the courts of shire, hundred, leet and hustings, and from all pleas and suits. They shall also be quit and free from hidage, scutage, musters and expeditions, from armed service and from castle-guard, from the upkeep of parks, bridges, warrens, walls and enclosures, and from all carrying services, cart, packhorse or ships. They shall likewise be free of duty at royal dwellings, and from all secular service and payments. I have also granted that the aforesaid canons and their men shall be quit of toll in all markets and fairs, and on the roads, bridges and harbours, and throughout all my kingdom. And men who hold from the aforesaid canons, whether they be within the city of London or outside it, shall not plead anywhere except in the court of the canons where they are to plead. And I forbid under pain of forfeiture that they should be impleaded on account of any tenement which they hold in this manner except before me or before my justice. And inasmuch as all their lands and possessions, and the lands and possessions of their men are in my keeping and under my protection, let no man wrong them contrary to this my charter. Witness: Rannulf the chancellor; Geoffrey 'de Clinton'; Ralph Basset. At Northampton.

277. Narrative respecting the foundation of the Augustinian priory of Holy Trinity, Aldgate, and concerning the manner in which this priory became possessed of the jurisdiction of the London *cnihtengild*

Foundation narratives need to be approached with caution as sources of history, but this is of especial interest to the history of London. It affords the fullest evidence extant respecting the personalities of the leading citizens of Anglo-Norman London. It has been discussed in this respect by H. C. Coote in *Trans. London and Middlesex Archaeol. Soc.*, vol. v (1881), pp. 477 *et sqq.*; more particularly in J. H. Round, *Geoffrey de Mandeville* (1892), pp. 304–311, and in *Commune of London* (1899), pp. 97–124; also in D. C. Douglas, *Domesday Monachorum of Christ Church, Canterbury*, pp. 58–63. Reference should also be made to F. M. Stenton, *Norman London* (1934). The text which follows is derived partly from H. C. Coote, *op. cit.*, pp. 477, 478, and partly from J. H. Round, *Commune of London*, pp. 99–102.

In the year of the Incarnation of our Lord 1108, and in the eighth year of the reign of the glorious King Henry, there was founded the church of the Holy Trinity within Aldgate by the venerable Queen Maud, wife of the aforesaid king; and by the advice of Anselm, the holy archbishop, the said church was given to Norman, the first canon prior in the whole of England. By him the whole of England was adorned by the Rule of St. Augustine and clothed in the habit of the canons, and when the brothers had there assembled, there arose day and night an ever-increasing volume of praise so that the whole city delighted in the sight of the brothers. For this reason, in the year of the Incarnation of our Lord 1125, certain burgesses of London, from that old descent of noble English knights,[1] coming together in the chapter of Christ Church,[2] which is situate within the walls of the city next to the gate which is called Aldgate, gave to this same church and the canons who there served God all the land and jurisdiction which is in English described as belonging to the English *cnihtengild*, and which stretches from outside the wall of the city by the same gate as far as the river Thames. The names of the burgesses who did this were Ralph, son of Algod;[3] Wulward 'le Doverisshe'; Ordgar 'le Prude'; Edward Upcornhill;[4] Blackstan and Ailwin, his cousin; Ailwin and Robert, his brother, the sons of

[1] *quidam burgenses Londoniae ex illa antiqua nobilium militum progenie.* The word *militum* should not of course be taken here in the technical Norman sense. It is here clearly a translation of the Old English word *cniht*, a retainer. See further on this, F. M. Stenton, *English Feudalism*, p. 134.

[2] The alternative dedication of Holy Trinity.

[3] Ralph, son of Algod, was in charge of one of the wards of the city about 1130 (see below, p. 953) and is possibly to be identified with a contemporary canon of St. Paul's of the same name.

[4] Edward of Cornhill married Godeleve, daughter of Edward of Southwark, and his daughter married Gervase, son of Roger, afterwards known as Gervase of Cornhill, and the founder of an important city family. The connexions of this man, established by J. H. Round (*Geoffrey de Mandeville*, pp. 307, 308), illustrate some of the personalities of Norman London, and the connexion between English and Normans therein:

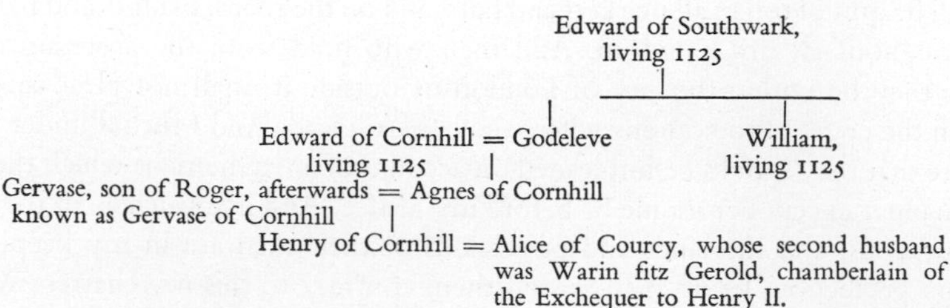

Leofstan;[1] Leofstan the goldsmith and Wyzo, his son;[2] Hugh, son of Wulfgar;[3] Algar Fecusenne; Ordgar, son of Deorman;[4] Osbert Drenchwyn; Adelard Hornewitesune. They made their gift, I say, and became members of the fraternity and sharers in the benefits of that place by the hand of Norman the prior who received them and their predecessors into the society on the text of the Holy Gospel.[5] And that this gift should remain firm and unbroken they offered on the altar the charter of St. Edward which they had,[6] together with their other charters. And then in the church of St. Botulph, which was built upon their land and might be said to be its head, they put Norman the prior into possession.[7] All these things were done in the presence of these witnesses: Bernard, prior of Dunstable; John, prior of 'Landa';[8] Geoffrey 'de Clinton' the chamberlain, and Peter his chaplain; Nicholas 'Cunand'; William the clerk; Edward, son of Alfward; Hugh, son of Ralph (his steward and chaplain); Edward of Southwark and William, his son; Lenegar the priest; Eylwyn, son of Sired; Haco the deacon;[9] Algar the priest; Aschetil; and many others, both clerks and laymen, both French and English. Therefore the aforesaid donors sent one of themselves, to wit Ordgar 'le Prude', to King Henry asking that he would permit and confirm their gift. The king gladly granted the aforesaid jurisdiction and the land to this church, free and quit as alms should be, from all service; and he confirmed this with his charter.[10] . . .

[Later there was a dispute respecting land in "East Smithfield" which lay within the soke of the *cnihtengild*, where Geoffrey 'de Mandeville' as Constable of the Tower and his agents, particularly Aschvil, had encroached to make a vineyard. The matter in due course came to trial. The narrative proceeds.]

In the second year of the reign of King Stephen, at a time when the king was at Westminster, Prior Norman appeared before him in the presence of Maud, the king's wife, Algar, bishop of Coutances, Roger, who was then chancellor, Arnulf, archdeacon of Séez, William Martel the steward, Robert of Courcy, Aubrey of Ver, Geoffrey 'de Mandeville', Hugh Bigot, Adam 'de Balnai', Andrew Buchuinte,[11] and many other burgesses of London. The prior came before the court and carefully showed with what force and injury that part of the land had been separated from the rest, and in the presence of the king he asked Aschvil by what right he held that part, and what claim he could make for it. But he replied that he made no claim. "I held it",[12] he said. Then the king in a loud voice ordered Andrew his justiciar and the rest

[1] Æthelwine (Ailwin) appears as a witness in several contemporary charters, and Robert accounts to the Exchequer in 1130 for the weavers' gild.

[2] Wyzo, son of Leofstan, owed the Exchequer in 1130 half a mark of gold in respect of the land and the office of his father.

[3] In charge of a ward of the city about 1130. See below, p. 953.

[4] On him, see D. C. Douglas, *op. cit.*, pp. 62–63.

[5] This does not of course mean that they became monks.

[6] See above, No. 273.

[7] Formal livery of seisin.

[8] The text is at this point corrupt.

[9] See below, p. 953.

[10] See above, No. 276.

[11] A highly important man. He was at one time justiciar of London, and may have been the first justiciar elected under the terms of Henry I's charter (see above, No. 276). One of his sons, named John, made Gervase of Cornhill his heir. Andrew Buchuinte, who was probably of Italian origin, was the founder of a great city family (see J. H. Round, *Commune of London*, pp. 110–113).

[12] He decides to stand on possession alone.

of the barons who were present, and instructed them and others by his writ, that they should appoint a definite day on which they might carefully consider the business, so that after examination it might appear what was the situation about this land in the time of the holy King Edward.[1] And if the prior could show that that part of the land belonged by this right to the church, then he should be placed in possession of it forthwith. This was therefore done. On the appointed day there met about this land on the one part the prior with his advisers, and on the other part Andrew Buchuinte and many other of the greatest and best men of London. The matter was examined from the time of holy King Edward down to the day of the plea, and it was found and shown that that part ought to go with the rest, and the whole likewise. And this was proved by the witness of many, and by the oath of twenty-one men whose names were these: Ordgar the monk, nicknamed 'le Prude'; Ailwin, son of 'Radumf'; Estmund; Alfruc Cherch; Briccred; Cucherd; Wulfred; Semer Batum; Alsi; Berman; Wulfsi the smith; Alfwin Hallen; Leuesune the smith; Wulwin abbot; Alfwin the clerk; Alfgar the brother of Gerald; Wulfric the butcher; Elfret Cugel; Wulfric; Edric Modheusune; Godwin Balle;[2] and many others were prepared to swear, but these were judged sufficient. In this manner and with this reason and justice was the whole of that land and jurisdiction adjudged to the aforesaid church. And this King Stephen confirmed to the aforesaid church by the following charter:[3]

> Stephen, king of the English, to the bishop of London, and to the justiciars, sheriffs, barons, and all his servants and liegemen, French and English, of London, greeting. Know that for the soul of King Henry and for my salvation and for the salvation of Maud the queen, my wife, and of Eustace, my son, and of my other boys, I have restored and granted to God and the church of Holy Trinity, London, and to the canons regular there serving God, their land of Smithfield in perpetuity which Earl Geoffrey had taken to make a vineyard. Wherefore I will, and firmly order, that they shall have and hold this land as well, peacefully, freely, quietly and honourably as they hold their other lands and as King Henry granted it to them and confirmed it by his charter. Witness: Maud the queen; Thomas the chaplain; William of Ypres; Richard of Lucé. At London.

Also, Geoffrey, earl of Essex and the chief constable of the Tower, renounced all claim on the aforesaid land as appears in the following charter:[4]

> Geoffrey, earl of Essex, to the bishop of London and to all the faithful of holy Church greeting. Know that I have restored to Christ Church, London, and to the brothers serving there, their mills next the Tower and the whole land outside which used to belong to the English *cnihtengild* with Smithfield and the men and all the other things appertaining to it. I also give back to them the half-hide at Bromley[5] in land and meadows and pastures and with all other things and liberties

[1] The king orders an action respecting not possession but ownership.

[2] Some of these names are clearly corrupt.

[3] The following charter has been arbitrarily introduced. It cannot be as early as 1137 and should be assigned to the years 1140–1144.

[4] This charter is also introduced arbitrarily, and it has been suggested (J. H. Round, *Commune of London*, p. 100) that it was in fact issued by the notorious earl on his death-bed. If so the attestations of the two doctors give a grim actuality to the document.

[5] Bremlega; the identification is not certain but it is probably Bromley, Essex.

and customs as William, son of Guy, gave it to them when he assumed the robe of the canons. And I will, and firmly order, that they should hold the aforesaid lands from me and my heirs freely and quietly and quit from all claim and secular service, so that neither my heirs nor any of my men after me for ever shall be allowed to do them any injury or insult respecting this. Witness: Rohais the countess, my wife; Gregory, my steward; Payn of the Temple; Warin fitz Gerold; Ralph of Criquetot; Geoffrey 'de Querendun'; Ernulf the doctor; Iwodus the doctor. And I also grant them for ever 1 mark of silver from the service of Edward 'de Seligeford' with the testimony of the aforesaid witnesses and of William, archdeacon of London.

All these things were done in the second year of King Stephen in the presence of the following who stood by and heard and saw: Ralph, son of Algod;[1] Ralph, chancellor of St. Paul's; Haco the dean; William Travers; Gilbert the priest; Lungus the priest; Wimund the priest; Joseph the priest; Geoffrey the priest; John the priest; Hubert the priest; Aluric the priest; Richard the priest; Jacob the clerk; Gervase the clerk; William the clerk; Andrew Buchuinte;[1] Stephen Bukerel;[2] William the chamberlain; Ralph, son of Andrew; Lawrence Buchuinte; Thierry, son of Deorman;[3] John Buchuinte; Stephen Bukerel; Gilbert Becket;[4] Gervase, son of Agnes; Hugh, son of Ulgar; Eustace, nephew of Fulcred; Walkelin; Robert, son of Ralph with his brothers, Richard and David; Ailward the smith; Edmund Ward the alderman; Edward, son of Simon; Edgar Fulone; Edward; Robert, son of But'; Alfege; Ailwin; Godwine; Ralph Godesune and Algar, his son, and Edmund, his brother; Huneman; Suethin; Edward Her'; Godwine Bredhers; Hereward; Gerald Rufus; Sexi Forfot; Godwine Oxefot; John, son of Edwin; Saward; Sired; and many others.

278. Grant (in Anglo-Saxon) by Brihtmær of Gracechurch, London, to Christ Church, Canterbury (*circa* 1054)

Brihtmær is the "earliest named alderman of London known to us" and his family is also notable, as will be seen in the succeeding documents. One of the sons here mentioned was a knight of the honour of Canterbury in 1093–1096 (see above, No. 222). This document is printed, translated and annotated in A. J. Robertson, *Anglo-Saxon Charters*, pp. 217, 468.

Here is declared in this document the agreement which Brihtmær of Gracechurch[5] has made with Archbishop Stigand and with Godric the dean and with all the community of Christ Church, Canterbury. He has granted to Christ to be held by Christ Church after his death and that of Eadgifu, his wife, and after the death of his children, Eadmær[6] and Æthelwine,[7] the homestead which he occupies and the church

[1] See above, pp. 930, 931.
[2] The Bukerels, who were also probably of Italian origin, later became a great city family.
[3] Another London connexion of the highest interest. Thierry was the son of Deorman of London who is recorded in Domesday Book as having held land in Middlesex before the Norman Conquest. Deorman of London became in time a knight of the honour of the archbishop of Canterbury, and was apparently alive in 1093. It seems also that Thierry, son of Deorman, married a member of the great Norman family of Clare. On these men see J. H. Round, *Commune of London*, p. 106; D. C. Douglas, *Domesday Monachorum of Christ Church, Canterbury* (1944), pp. 62–63.
[4] The father of the archbishop.
[5] Gerschereche. The name survives in Gracechurch Street, London.
[6] Was he Eadmer 'the one-handed'? See below, No. 279.
[7] See above, No. 222.

of All Hallows[1] with all the endowments which they have bestowed upon it, for the redemption of their souls, on these terms, that the community shall see to it that the service which belongs to the church neither ceases nor falls off in view of the endowments of the church. The witnesses of this are Leofstan, the town reeve, and the bishop, and Æthelwine 'Stikehare' and many other thegns both within the city and without.

279. The agreement between Gundulf, bishop of Rochester and Eadmer 'the one-handed', a burgess of London (1077–1087)

Important as evidence for the building of the Tower of London, and the most important testimony of the part played by Bishop Gundulf in that work. Interesting also as illustrating the history of the civic family of Brihtmær of Gracechurch. Printed in T. Hearne, *Textus Roffensis* (1720), p. 212.

When the same Gundulf[2] by the command of King William the Great was supervising the great work of the Tower of London, and while he was a guest with Eadmer himself, the same Eadmer began at that time to ask the bishop that he would grant him the society of the church over which he ruled, to wit, the church of St. Andrew. This the bishop freely granted him. And [Eadmer] granted to St. Andrew and to the brothers there serving God half the fishery which is called New Weir so long as he lived. And after his death he granted to them the whole. And he further granted to them after his death all his land which he had in London and his houses on this understanding, that he and his wife should be brought to Rochester and there buried, and that each year the anniversary of their death should be observed. These are the witnesses of this transaction: the two sons of Brihtmær, Æthelwine[3] and Ordgar; Ralph, the clerk of the bishop; and Godfrey the fat; and many others.

280. A list of London properties belonging to Christ Church, Canterbury (*circa* 1100)

Of particular interest in the history of the churches of London. The earliest known mention of many of these is contained in this document, which also makes the earliest known reference to London Stone and to Eastcheap. The text is printed with a summarized translation, and admirably discussed by B. W. Kissan in "An early list of London properties" (*Trans. London and Middlesex Archaeol. Soc.*, New Series, vol. VIII, pp. 57–69).

These are the lands and the houses in the city of London which belong by right to the church of Canterbury and are in its possession.

The church of Blessed Mary[4] with the lands and houses and churches pertaining to it, which Living the priest gave when he became a monk at Canterbury. The rent owed from his church each year is 40 pounds.

The church which Godwine named Bac, the clerk[5] when he became a monk in the church of Canterbury. This pays every year 7 shillings on the Feast of St. Alphege.[6]

[1] Perhaps All Hallows, Lombard Street.

[2] Bishop of Rochester, 1077–1108.

[3] See also No. 222.

[4] The earliest reference as yet known to the church of St. Mary le Bow (see B. W. Kissan, *Trans. London and Middlesex Archaeol. Soc.*, New Series, vol. VII, pp. 436 *et sqq.*).

[5] The earliest known reference to the church of St. Dionis Backchurch.

[6] 19 April.

The church of St. Benedict or St. Pancras,[1] which Lifric the priest gave when he became a monk in the church of Canterbury. This pays 1 ounce of gold at Pentecost.

The church of St. Michael[2] which Æthelweard[3] the priest gave. This pays 5 shillings.

The church of St. Dunstan the Confessor,[4] and also the other church of St. Alphege with the lands and houses pertaining to the same, which Andrew the clerk gave when he became a monk at Canterbury. These pay each year 35 shillings.

The church of St. Peter the Apostle[5] with all its appurtenances which Brihtmær,[5] senator of the city of London, once possessed, and which he granted to Christ Church, Canterbury, after his own death and after the death of his sons to be held by the monastery in hereditary right. In witness of this Æthelwine,[6] who alone among his sons survives, pays each year 2 shillings.

The church of St. Werburga the Virgin[7] which Gumbert possessed with the adjoining house. This pays 1 ounce of gold.

The land also of Ceatermund which each year pays 10 shillings or half a *modium* of wine.

The land which Brungares Lave gave. This pays 6 shillings and 4 pence on the Feast of St. Alphege.[8]

The land which Bernard has in Eastcheap,[9] which the lord Abel and Henry, his nephew, granted to Christ Church. This pays 14 shillings.

The land of Æthelmær the smith owes 2 shillings on the Feast of St. Alphege.[8]

The lands which Sired the priest gave when, leaving the world behind, he became a monk in the church of Canterbury. These lands with the houses he granted to Siward the clerk, his son, on the understanding that Siward should hold them so long as he lived and that by way of recognition he should pay each year 10 shillings to Christ Church.

Half the church which is called 'Berkinges'[10] which Ælfwine, the son of Farman, gave to the church of Canterbury. This Gundulf, bishop of Rochester,[11] holds at the agreed rent.

Land with a house, and an underground house, 'Valdebona', which Edric Bolt's son gave. Walkelin, bishop of Winchester,[12] held this inclosed in his court, and it was wont to pay, as long as Walkelin lived, each year an agreed rent to Christ Church, with the consent of Lanfranc.

[1] The church of St. Pancras, Soper Lane. No other record seems to exist of the alternative dedication to St. Benedict.

[2] Either St. Michael, Paternoster, or St. Michael, Crooked Lane.

[3] Elwardus.

[4] St. Dunstan in the East.

[5] From the connexion with Brihtmær it seems possible that this is All Hallows, Lombard Street. The dedication, however, raises difficulties.

[6] For Brihtmær and his son, Æthelwine, who became a knight of the Canterbury honour, see above, No. 278. It has been suggested that 'senator' here can only mean alderman.

[7] This seems to be the earliest mention of St. Werburgh's.

[8] 19 April

[9] *Terra quam Bernardus habet in eastceape.*

[10] This is All Hallows, Barking.

[11] Bishop of Rochester, 1077–1108. He was still alive at the time of the survey.

[12] Died 3 January 1098.

The land which Alfgar the priest gave pays every year to Christ Church 8 shillings, and it is situated in the street opposite Radel's wharf next the land of Sperling the moneyer.

Ælfwine, a layman, gave to Christ Church, Canterbury, a wharf which is situated by the bank of the river Thames. This pays 10 pounds.

Eadwaker at London Stone[1] gave his land with houses to Christ Church on the understanding that so long as he lives he shall pay 2 shillings by way of recognition on the Nativity of St. Mary,[2] and that after his death his relatives shall likewise every year pay 2 shillings.

The land which Alfred, son of Picot, gave pays 5 shillings.

Eadgifu gave two estates of which the one pays 16 shillings and the other pays according to this arrangement: . . .[3] and Leveve gives 1 penny on the Nativity of St. Mary,[2] and after her death all the land. And the anchoress of St. Margaret[4] shall pay 4 pence every year on the Feast of St. John the Baptist,[5] and after her death the aforesaid land shall pay 32 pence.

Æthelwine of Benfleet gave to Christ Church one messuage in Southwark. From this, so long as he and his daughter shall live, Christ Church shall have 4 shillings for recognition at Michaelmas. After their death Christ Church shall do with the messuage what it wills.

Ælfwine, the son of Stephen, has now given to Christ Church two messuages in London, of which one pays 6 shillings at Pentecost, and the other 30 pence.

Witness: Waldsi; Wulfsi; Godwine; Osmer; Geoffrey.

281. William fitz Stephen: Description of the city of London (1170–1183)

This rhetorical description of the city of London in the time of Henry II is given as a preamble to William fitz Stephen's *Life of Thomas Becket* to which reference has so often been made above. It has been many times translated, and attention may in particular be called to the excellent translation by H. E. Butler which is printed as an appendix to F. M. Stenton, *Norman London* (1934). The Latin text which is here followed is that given in *Materials for the History of Thomas Becket* (Rolls Series), vol. III, pp. 2–13.

A DESCRIPTION OF THE MOST NOBLE CITY OF LONDON

Among the noble and celebrated cities of the world that of London, the capital of the kingdom of the English, is one which extends its glory farther than all the others and sends its wealth and merchandise more widely into distant lands. Higher than all the rest does it lift its head. It is happy in the healthiness of its air; in its observance of Christian practice; in the strength of its fortifications; in its natural situation; in the honour of its citizens; and in the modesty of its matrons. It is cheerful in its sports, and the fruitful mother of noble men. Let us look into these things in turn.

If the mildness of the climate of this place softens the character of its inhabitants, it does not make them corrupt in following Venus, but rather prevents them from being fierce and bestial, making them liberal and kind.

[1] *Eadwaker æt Lundene stane.*
[2] 8 September.
[3] The text is here broken and corrupt.
[4] Possibly the reference here is to the church of St. Margaret Pattens.
[5] 29 August.

In the church of St. Paul there is the episcopal seat. Once it was metropolitan, and some think it will again become so, if the citizens return to the island, unless perhaps the archiepiscopal title of the blessed martyr, Thomas, and the presence of his body preserves that dignity for ever at Canterbury where it is at present. But as St. Thomas has made both cities illustrious, London by his rising and Canterbury by his setting, each can claim advantage of the other with justice in respect of that saint. As regards the practice of Christian worship, there are in London and its suburbs thirteen greater conventual churches and, besides these, one hundred and twenty-six lesser parish churches.

It has on the east the Palatine castle,[1] very great and strong: the keep and walls rise from very deep foundations and are fixed with a mortar tempered by the blood of animals. On the west there are two castles very strongly fortified, and from these there runs a high and massive wall with seven double gates and with towers along the north at regular intervals. London was once also walled and turreted on the south, but the mighty Thames, so full of fish, has with the sea's ebb and flow washed against, loosened, and thrown down those walls in the course of time. Upstream to the west there is the royal palace[2] which is conspicuous above the river, a building incomparable in its ramparts and bulwarks. It is about two miles from the city and joined thereto by a populous suburb.

Everywhere outside the houses of those living in the suburbs, and adjacent to them, are the spacious and beautiful gardens of the citizens, and these are planted with trees. Also there are on the north side pastures and pleasant meadow lands through which flow streams wherein the turning of mill-wheels makes a cheerful sound. Very near lies a great forest with woodland pastures in which there are the lairs of wild animals: stags, fallow deer, wild boars and bulls. The tilled lands of the city are not of barren gravel, but fat Asian plains that yield luxuriant crops and fill the tillers' barns with the sheaves of Ceres.

There are also outside London on the north side excellent suburban wells with sweet, wholesome and clear water that flows rippling over the bright stones. Among these are Holywell, Clerkenwell and St. Clement's Well, which are all famous. These are frequented by great numbers and much visited by the students from the schools and by the young men of the city, when they go out for fresh air on summer evenings. Good indeed is this city when it has a good lord!

The city is honoured by her men, glorious in its arms, and so populous that during the terrible wars of King Stephen's reign the men going forth from it to battle were reckoned as twenty thousand armed horsemen and sixty thousand foot-soldiers, all equipped for war. The citizens of London are regarded as conspicuous above all others for their polished manners, for their dress and for the good tables which they keep. The inhabitants of other towns are called citizens, but those of London are called barons. And with them a solemn pledge is sufficient to end every dispute.

The matrons of this city are very Sabines.

In London the three principal churches (that is to say, the episcopal church of

[1] The Tower of London.
[2] The Palace of Westminster.

St. Paul, the church of the Holy Trinity, and the church of St. Martin) have famous schools by special privilege and by virtue of their ancient dignity. But through the favour of some magnate, or through the presence of teachers who are notable or famous in philosophy, there are also other schools. On feast-days the masters hold meetings for their pupils in the church whose festival it is. The scholars dispute, some with oratory and some with argument; some recite enthymemes; others excel in using perfect syllogisms. Some dispute for ostentation like wrestlers with opponent; others argue in order to establish the truth in its perfection. Sophists who speak paradoxes are praised for their torrent of words, whilst others seek to overthrow their opponents by using fallacious arguments. Now and then orators use rhetoric for persuasion, being careful to omit nothing essential to their art. Boys of different schools strive against each other in verses, or contend about the principles of grammar and the rules governing past and future tenses. Others use epigrams, rhythm and metre in the old trival banter; they pull their comrades to pieces with "Fescennine Licence": mentioning no names, they dart abuse and gibes, and mock the faults of their comrades and sometimes even those of their elders, using Socratic salt and biting harder even than the tooth of Theon in daring dithyrambics. Their hearers, ready to enjoy the joke, wrinkle up their noses as they guffaw in applause.

Of the ordering of the city

Those engaged in business of various kinds, sellers of merchandise, hirers of labour, are distributed every morning into their several localities according to their trade. Besides, there is in London on the river bank among the wines for sale in ships and in the cellars of the vintners a public cook-shop. There daily you may find food according to the season, dishes of meat, roast, fried and boiled, large and small fish, coarser meats for the poor and more delicate for the rich, such as venison and big and small birds. If any of the citizens should unexpectedly receive visitors, weary from their journey, who would fain not wait until fresh food is bought and cooked, or until the servants have brought bread or water for washing, they hasten to the river bank and there find all they need. However great the multitude of soldiers and travellers entering the city, or preparing to go out of it, at any hour of the day or night–that these may not fast too long, and those may not go out supperless–they turn aside thither, if they please, where every man can refresh himself in his own way. Those who would cater for themselves fastidiously need not search to find sturgeon or the bird of Africa or the Ionian godwit. For this is a public kitchen, very convenient to the city, and part of its amenities. Hence the dictum in the Gorgias of Plato that the art of cookery is an imitation of medicine and flatters a quarter of civic life.

Immediately outside one of the gates there is a field which is smooth[1] both in fact and in name. On every sixth day of the week, unless it be a major feast-day, there takes place there a famous exhibition of fine horses for sale. Earls, barons and knights, who are in the town, and many citizens come out to see or to buy. It is pleasant to see the high-stepping palfreys with their gleaming coats, as they go through their paces, putting down their feet alternately on one side together. Next, one can see the horses

[1] Smithfield.

suitable for esquires, moving faster though less smoothly, lifting and setting down, at is were, the opposite fore and hind feet: here are colts of fine breed, but not yet accustomed to the bit, stepping high with jaunty tread; there are the sumpter-horses, powerful and spirited; and after them there are the war-horses, costly, elegant of form, noble of stature, with ears quickly tremulous, necks raised and large haunches. As these show their paces, the buyers first try those of gentler gait, then those of quicker pace whereby the fore and hind feet move in pairs together. When a race is about to begin among such chargers that are so powerful to carry and so swift to run, a shout is raised, and orders are given that the inferior animals should be led apart. Three jockeys who mount these flying steeds (or at times two, as may be agreed) prepare themselves for the contest; skilled in managing them, they curb their untamed mouths with bitted bridles. To get a good start in the race is their chief concern. Their mounts also enter into the spirit of the contest as they are able; their limbs tremble, and so imaptient are they of delay that they cannot keep still. When the signal is given, they stretch their limbs to the uttermost, and dash down the course with courageous speed. The riders, covetous of applause and ardent for victory, plunge their spurs into the loose-reined horses, and urge them forward with their shouts and their whips. You would agree with Heraclitus that all things are in motion! You would know Zeno to be completely wrong when he said that there was no motion and no goal to be reached!

By themselves in another part of the field stand the goods of the countryfolk: implements of husbandry, swine with long flanks, cows with full udders, oxen of immense size, and woolly sheep. There also stand the mares fit for plough, some big with foal, and others with brisk young colts closely following them.

To this city from every nation under heaven merchants delight to bring their trade by sea. The Arabian sends gold; the Sabaean spice and incense. The Scythian brings arms, and from the rich, fat lands of Babylon comes oil of palms. The Nile sends precious stones; the men of Norway and Russia, furs and sables; nor is China absent with purple silk. The Gauls come with their wines.

London, as historians have shown, is a much older city than Rome, for though it derives from the same Trojan ancestors, it was founded by Brutus before Rome was founded by Romulus and Remus. Wherefore they still have the same laws from their common origin. This city is like Rome divided into wards; it has annual sheriffs instead of consuls; it has its senatorial order and lower magistrates; it has drains and aqueducts in its streets; it has its appointed places for the hearing of cases deliberative, demonstrative and judicial; it has its several courts, and its separate assemblies on appointed days.

I do not think there is a city with a better record for church-going, doing honour to God's ordinances, keeping feast-days, giving alms and hospitality to strangers, confirming betrothals, contracting marriages, celebrating weddings, providing feasts, entertaining guests, and also, it may be added, in care for funerals and for the burial of the dead. The only plagues of London are the immoderate drinking of fools and the frequency of fires.

To this it may be added that almost all the bishops, abbots and magnates of England are in a sense citizens and freemen of London, having their own splendid town-houses. In them they live, and spend largely, when they are summoned to great councils by the king or by their metropolitan, or drawn thither by their private affairs.

Of the sports of London

We now come to speak of the sports of the city, for it is not fitting that a city should be merely useful and serious-minded, unless it be also pleasant and cheerful. For this cause on the seals of the supreme pontiff, down to the time of the last Pope Leo,[1] on one side of the lead was engraved the figure of Peter the fisherman and above him a key, as it were, held out to him from heaven by the hand of God, and around it was inscribed the verse, "For me didst thou leave the ship, receive now the key." And on the other side was engraved a city with the inscription "Golden Rome". Moreover, it was said in honour of Augustus Caesar and Rome, "It rains all night, games usher in the day; Caesar, thou dost divide dominion with Jove." Instead of shows in the theatre and stage-plays, London provides plays of a more sacred character, wherein are presented the miracles worked by saintly confessors or the sufferings which made illustrious the constancy of martyrs. Furthermore, every year on the day called Carnival – to begin with the sports of boys (for we were all boys once) – scholars from the different schools bring fighting-cocks to their masters, and the whole morning is set apart to watch their cocks do battle in the schools, for the boys are given a holiday that day. After dinner all the young men of the town go out into the fields in the suburbs to play ball. The scholars of the various schools have their own ball, and almost all the followers of each occupation have theirs also. The seniors and the fathers and the wealthy magnates of the city come on horseback to watch the contests of the younger generation, and in their turn recover their lost youth: the motions of their natural heat seem to be stirred in them at the mere sight of such strenuous activity and by their participation in the joys of unbridled youth.

Every Sunday in Lent after dinner a fresh swarm of young men goes forth into the fields on war-horses, steeds foremost in the contest, each of which is skilled and schooled to run in circles. From the gates there sallies forth a host of laymen, sons of the citizens, equipped with lances and shields, the younger ones with spears forked at the top, but with the steel point removed. They make a pretence at war, carry out field-exercises and indulge in mimic combats. Thither too come many courtiers, when the king is in town, and from the households of bishops, earls and barons come youths and adolescents, not yet girt with the belt of knighthood, for the pleasure of engaging in combat with one another. Each is inflamed with the hope of victory. The fiery steeds neigh with tremulous limbs and champ their bits; impatient of delay they cannot stand still. When at last their trampling hooves ring on the ground in rapid flight, their boy riders divide their ranks; some pursue those immediately in front of them, but fail to catch up with them; others overtake their fellows, force them to dismount and fly past them.

At the Easter festival they play at a kind of naval warfare. A shield is firmly bound to a tree in mid-stream, and a small boat, swiftly impelled by many an oar and the current of the river, carries on the stern a youth armed with a lance with which

[1] Leo IX, 1048–1054.

to strike the shield. If he breaks the lance by striking the shield, and yet keeps his footing, he has achieved his aim and gratified his wish, but if he strikes the shield firmly and the lance remains unbroken, he is thrown overboard into the flowing river, and the boat, impelled by its own motion, rushes past him. There are, however, two other boats moored, one on each side of the target, with several youths on board to seize hold of the striker who has been engulfed by the stream, as soon as he comes into view or when he rises on the crest of the wave for the second time. On the bridge and the terraces fronting the river stand the spectators, ready to laugh their fill.

On feast-days throughout the summer the young men indulge in the sports of archery, running, jumping, wrestling, slinging the stone, hurling the javelin beyond a mark and fighting with sword and buckler. Cytherea leads the dance of maidens, and until the moon rises, the earth is shaken with flying feet.

In winter on almost every feast-day before dinner either foaming boars, armed with lightning tusks, fight for their lives "to save their bacon", or stout bulls with butting horns, or huge bears do battle with the hounds let loose upon them. When the great marsh that washes the north wall of the city is frozen over, swarms of young men issue forth to play games on the ice. Some, gaining speed in their run, with feet set well apart, slide sideways over a vast expanse of ice. Others make seats out of a large lump of ice, and whilst one sits thereon, others with linked hands run before and drag him along behind them. So swift is their sliding motion that sometimes their feet slip, and they all fall on their faces. Others, more skilled at winter sports, put on their feet the shin-bones of animals, binding them firmly round their ankles, and, holding poles shod with iron in their hands, which they strike from time to time against the ice, they are propelled swift as a bird in flight or a bolt shot from an engine of war. Sometimes, by mutual consent, two of them run against each other in this way from a great distance, and, lifting their poles, each tilts against the other. Either one or both fall, not without some bodily injury, for, as they fall, they are carried along a great way beyond each other by the impetus of their run, and wherever the ice comes in contact with their heads, it scrapes off the skin utterly. Often a leg or an arm is broken, if the victim falls with it underneath him; but theirs is an age greedy of glory, youth yearns for victory, and exercises itself in mock combats in order to carry itself more bravely in real battles.

Many of the citizens take pleasure in sporting with birds of the air, with hawks, falcons and such-like, and with hounds that hunt their prey in the woods. The citizens have the rights of the chase in Middlesex, Hertfordshire, all the Chiltern country, and in Kent as far as the river Cray. The Londoners, who were then known as Trinobantes, drove back Julius Caesar, whose delight it was to wade through paths steeped in blood. Whence Lucan writes: "To the Britons whom he had sought he turned his back in flight."

The city of London has given birth to several men who have subdued many realms and even the Roman empire to their dominion, and also many another whose valour has raised him to the gods as lord of the world, as was promised to Brutus by the oracle of Apollo: "Brutus, beyond Gaul, beneath the setting sun, there lies an isle washed by the waves of ocean. Thither direct thy course, for there shall be thy seat for ever. This shall be to thy sons a second Troy. Here from thy stem shall kings arise, and the whole world shall be subject unto them."

Afterwards in Christian times this city produced that noble emperor Constantine, son of the empress Helena, who bestowed the city of Rome and all the imperial insignia on God and St. Peter and on Sylvester, the Roman pope,[1] to whom he dispensed the office of a groom, no longer rejoicing to be called emperor but rather the defender of the holy Roman Church; and, lest the peace of the lord pope should be disturbed by the uproar of secular strife occasioned by his presence, he himself altogether abandoned the city which he had bestowed upon the lord pope, and built for himself the city of Byzantium. And in modern times also London has given birth to illustrious and noble monarchs, the empress Maud, King "Henry III",[2] and the blessed Archbishop Thomas, that glorious martyr of Christ, than whom she bore no purer saint nor one more dear to all good men throughout the Latin world.

* * *

(*b*) REPRESENTATIVE DOCUMENTS ILLUSTRATING THE HISTORY OF ENGLISH TOWNS, OTHER THAN LONDON, IN THE PERIOD 1042–1189

The texts which follow are arranged in alphabetical order in respect of the towns to which they relate. They must be regarded merely as representative of a very large class of documents, and as illustrating the variations of burghal privilege. The different quarters from which these privileges were granted will be noted, for not all boroughs received their charters in the first instance from the king. Not the least interesting feature of these texts is the evidence they supply of the wide variations in privilege and practice in different towns. It will be noted that the privileged status of one town was frequently taken as the model for that of another, but no town can be considered apart from the local conditions which modified its individual history.

282. Charter of Thurstan, archbishop of York, in favour of Beverley (1124–1133, and probably *circa* 1130)

This is one of the earliest town charters extant. It is interesting, not only in relation to Beverley, but as evidence for the privileges which Henry I had conferred upon York. Printed: W. Farrer, *Early Yorkshire Charters*, vol. I (1914), p. 90; W. Stubbs, *Select Charters* (ed. 1913), p. 131.

Thurstan, by the grace of God, archbishop of York, to all the faithful of Christ both present and to come, greeting, and God's blessing and his own. Be it known to you that I have given and granted and with the counsel of the chapter of York and of Beverley, and by the counsel of my barons, confirmed by this my charter to the men of Beverley all their liberties by the same laws by which the men of York have them in their city. Let it, moreover, not be concealed from you that our lord, King Henry, has granted to us of his own goodwill the authority to do this, and has confirmed by his charter our statutes and laws according to the form of the laws of the burgesses of York, saving the dignity and honour of God and of St. John and of ourselves and our canons; he did this that he might exalt and promote the honour of the alms of his predecessors. I will that my burgesses of Beverley shall have their hans house with all free customs which I give and grant them in order that they may there

[1] A reference to the Donation of Constantine.

[2] The "young King Henry", son of Henry II.

administer their statutes to the honour of God and of St. John, and of the canons, and to the good government of the whole town, with the same law of liberty as the men of York have in their hans house. I grant also to them the toll for ever for 18 marks yearly, except on the three feasts on which the toll belongs to us and to our canons, to wit, the Feast of St. John the Confessor in May,[1] and the Feast of the Translation of St. John,[2] and the Feast of the Nativity of St. John the Baptist;[3] moreover, on these three feasts I have granted that all the burgesses of Beverley shall be free and quit of all toll. Also by witness of this charter I grant to the same burgesses free ingress and egress, that is to say, within the town and without, in plain and wood and marsh, in ways and paths, and in other places except meadows and fields, as well freely and largely as anyone could grant and confirm it. And know that they shall be free and quit of all toll throughout the whole of Yorkshire, even as are the men of York. And I will that anyone who shall undo this shall be accursed, as the custom of the same church of St. John asserts, and as it is decreed in the church of St. John. Witness: Geoffrey Murdac; Nigel Fossard; Alan of Percy; Walter Spec; Eustace, son of John; Thomas the reeve; Thurstan the archdeacon; Herbert the canon; William, son of Tole; William of Bayeux; in the presence of the whole household[4] of the archbishop, both clerk and lay, in York.

283. Charter of Henry I in favour of Beverley (1124–1133)

Confirms Thurstan's charter printed above, and makes specific mention of the gild-merchant and of free burgage. Printed: W. Farrer, *Early Yorkshire Charters* (1914), vol. I, p. 92.

Henry, king of the English, to the archbishops, bishops, justiciars, sheriffs and all his liegemen, greeting. Know that I have granted and given and by this my charter confirmed to the men of Beverley free burgage according to the free laws and customs of the burgesses of York, and also their gild-merchant with its pleas and toll, and with all its free customs and liberties in all things, as Thurstan the archbishop gave it to them and confirmed it in his charter, within Beverley and without, in wood, in plain, in marshes and elsewhere. And I will that they shall be quit of toll throughout the whole of Yorkshire, even as are the men of York. Witness: Geoffrey the chancellor; Robert, son of the count of Meulan. At Woodstock.

284. Charter of Henry II in favour of Bristol (1155)

Printed and translated by N. D. Harding, *Bristol Charters* (Bristol Rec. Soc.), vol. I, pp. 2–3.

Henry, king of England and duke of Normandy and Aquitaine, and count of Anjou,[5] to the archbishops, bishops, abbots, earls, barons, justiciars and sheriffs, and to all the men of his land, greeting. Know that I have granted to my burgesses of Bristol that they should be quit of toll and passage and every custom throughout the whole of my land of England, Normandy and Wales wherever they or their goods shall come. Wherefore I will and firmly command that they should have all their liberties and quittances and free customs fully and honourably as my free and faithful men, and that they may be free of toll and passage and every other custom. And on

[1] 7 May. [2] 25 October. [3] 24 June. [4] *familia*. [5] Title as in copy.

penalty of a forfeiture of 10 pounds I forbid anyone to disturb them in this against the command expressed in this charter. Witnesses: Thomas the chancellor;[1] William, the king's brother; Reginald, earl of Cornwall; Roger, earl of Hereford; Patrick, earl of Salisbury; Richard of Le Hommet the constable; Warin fitz Gerold the chamberlain; Walter of Hereford; John the marshal. At Salisbury.

285. Charter of John, count of Mortain (subsequently King John), in favour of Bristol (probably in, or after, 1189)[2]

This confirms and describes in detail the privileges of Bristol in the reign of Henry II. It should therefore be read in connexion with No. 284. Printed and translated by N. D. Harding, *Bristol Charters* (Bristol Rec. Soc.), vol. I, p. 8.

John, count of Mortain, to all men and to his friends, French and English, Welsh and Irish, present and to come, greeting. Know that I have granted and by this present charter confirmed to my burgesses of Bristol dwelling within the walls and without the walls, up to the boundaries of the town, to wit, between Sandbrook and Bewell and Brightneebridge and the spring in the road next Aldebury by Knowle, all their liberties and free customs as well, freely and fully as ever they had them in my time, or in the time of my predecessors. The liberties thus granted to them are these. That no burgess of Bristol shall plead outside the walls of the town concerning any plea except those relating to holdings which do not pertain to the hundred of the town. And they shall be quit of the murder-fine within the boundaries of the town. And no burgess shall be forced to submit to trial by battle unless he be accused concerning the death of a stranger not belonging to the town who has been killed within the town. And no one shall take a dwelling within the walls by assize, or by livery of the marshals, against the will of the burgesses. And they shall be quit of toll and lastage and passage and pontage and of all other customs throughout all my land and power. And none shall be judged to be 'in mercy' as to his money except according to the law of the hundred, to wit, by forfeiture of 40 shillings. And the hundred court shall be held only once a week. And in no plea shall any be able to sue by 'miskenning'.[3] And they shall have their lands and their tenures and their pledges and their debts as is proper throughout all my land whoever be their debtors. And right shall be done to them, according to the custom of the town, concerning all lands and tenures which are within the town. And pleas shall be held within the town, according to its custom, concerning debts and pledges which have been contracted in Bristol. And if anyone from any part of my land shall take toll of the men of Bristol, and after having been required to restore it shall fail to do so, then the reeve of Bristol shall take a distress at Bristol in respect of it, and shall continue to distrain until it be restored. And no merchant from outside the town shall buy within the town hides or corn or wool from any stranger but only from the burgesses. And no stranger shall keep a tavern except on shipboard, nor shall he sell cloths for cutting except in the fair. And no stranger shall tarry in the town with his wares beyond the space of forty days in

[1] Thomas Becket.

[2] The date raises difficulties. The charter has been assigned to 1188, but it is not certain that John was styled count of Mortain before the coronation of Richard I in 1189 (see *Complete Peerage*, vol. IX, p. 423), so, unless the title is here a later interpolation, the document may be presumed probably to have passed in or after that year.

[3] See above, p. 946, n. 3.

order to sell his goods. And no burgess shall be attached or distrained anywhere in my land for any debt except he himself be debtor or pledge. And they shall be permitted to marry, and to give their sons and daughters and widows in marriage without licence from their lords. And none of their lords shall have the wardship of their sons, daughters or widows, or be permitted to bestow these in marriage because of lands which the burgesses may hold outside the town; their lords shall only have custody of such holdings as are of their fiefs until such time as the wards are of age. And no one shall take 'tine' in the town except for the use of the lord count, and that only according to the custom of the town. And they shall be able to grind their corn wherever they wish. And they shall have all their legitimate gilds as well as they had them in the time of Robert and William, his son, earls of Gloucester.[1] And no burgess shall be compelled against his will to repledge anyone although he be dwelling on his own land. I have granted also to them all their holdings within the walls and outside the walls, as far as the aforesaid boundaries, in messuages, in gardens, in buildings by the waterside, and everywhere in the town to hold in free burgage: that is to say, by payment of landgable which they shall pay within the walls. I have granted also that everyone of them shall be allowed to erect or improve buildings anywhere on the waterfront or elsewhere, provided this be done without damage to the borough and the town. And they shall be allowed at their pleasure to build on any land or empty spaces which they have and hold within the aforesaid boundaries. Wherefore I will and firmly command that my aforesaid burgesses of Bristol and their heirs shall have and hold all their aforesaid liberties and free customs as are written down above, from me and my heirs as well and fully as ever they had them at any time they have been in operation. Let them have them well, and in peace, and honourably, and let them be immune from any impediment or molestation which anyone may put upon them. Witness: Stephen Ridel my chancellor; William 'de Wenneval'; Roger 'de Planis'; Roger of Neufbourg; Maurice of Berkeley; Robert, his brother; Haimo of Valognes; Simon 'de Marisco'; Gilbert Bass'; William of Falaise; Master Benedict; Master Peter; and many others. At Bristol.

286. Charter of Robert, son of Haimo, in favour of Burford (1088–1107)

Interesting for its very early reference to a gild-merchant, and as illustrating the formation of a small borough by a lord in his own interests. The surviving copy of this charter is very defective, but in the light of later confirmations it is possible to discern with confidence the wording of its operative clauses. Printed: R. H. Gretton, *Burford Records* (1920), pp. 10, 301.

Robert, son of Haimo, to all his men and friends, greeting. . . . Further I grant that each of the [burgesses of Burford] shall be able to sell or place in pledge a house, land, or any property, and may make his heir his son, daughter or wife or any other person without asking permission of his lord. And let them have the gild and customs which the burgesses of Oxford have in the gild-merchant. And all those who wish to come to the market, may come and buy in the market whatever they wish, but not wool or hides unless they be men of the said town.

[1] It was in his capacity of earl of Gloucester that John issued this charter. He married Isabel, heiress of that earldom, 29 August 1189.

287. Charter of Anselm, abbot of Bury St. Edmunds declaring the customs of the borough of Bury St. Edmunds (1121–1138)

An important charter revealing at an early date in some detail the customs of a borough on ecclesiastical land. Boroughs of this type were in many respects a class apart. For instance, they rarely acquired the right often gained by royal boroughs to elect freely their own officers or to control their own court. Bury St. Edmunds was already a fairly fully developed community at the time of the issue of this charter, and it will be noted that its customs are here referred back to the time of Edward the Confessor. This charter is further of interest in view of the struggle between the abbey and the borough which developed at Bury St. Edmunds at a later date. It is discussed in M. D. Lobel, *The Borough of Bury St. Edmunds* (1935), p. 10, and is printed with a commentary by J. H. Round in *Amer. Hist. Rev.*, vol. II, p. 688. It is printed from an earlier text also in D. C. Douglas, *Feudal Documents from the Abbey of Bury St. Edmunds* (1932), p. 114.

Anselm, by the grace of God abbot of St. Edmunds, to all his barons[1] and men, French and English, and to all their successors, greeting. I give you to know that these are the customs which the burgesses of St. Edmund have proved in my court and in my presence that they had in the time of King Edward and in the time of King William and his sons, William and Henry, and in the time of my predecessors, to wit, Abbot Baldwin[2] and other abbots, and which I have granted and confirmed by the consent of the whole chapter of St. Edmund. The custom is therefore for them to find eight men a year for the four guards to guard the town by night, and on the Feast of St. Edmund[3] sixteen men for the four gates, two men by day for each gate and the same number by night, and likewise for twelve days at Christmas. They also find five gate-keepers throughout the year at the four gates. The fifth gate is the east gate and is in the hand of the abbot. If need arises, the sacrist shall provide building material for the repair of the gates and the burgesses shall work it. But if the moat which surrounds the town needs to be repaired, the burgesses shall join with the knights and free sokemen in this work only if the knights of the abbey and free sokemen perform this labour, because this work does not devolve upon the burgesses more than upon the knights. Whoever has houses on burgage land in the town of St. Edmund shall give to the reeve for each house a halfpenny at the two terms of Pentecost and Martinmas. They shall not, furthermore, need to go outside the town of St. Edmund to the hundred court or to the shire court, nor shall they be impleaded in any plea except at their portmoot. If any of the burgesses have land in the town of St. Edmund or his patrimony, or if any one of them buys or acquires land legally in the town or in the market, and holds it for a year and a day without a claim, and can prove this by the testimony of the burgesses, he need not afterwards reply to any claimant subsequently coming against him; and this land he may sell to whom he will within the fee of St. Edmund without any licence from the reeve, his wife or sons or any of his relatives, provided always that necessity compels him to take this course, and provided also that he has no son or other near relative who is able and willing to give him as much as he can secure from another. If anyone lends his money to another within or without the town, and shall not be able to receive it back at the appointed term, and this shall be formally recognized in the same town, he may take distress for it; but if he has a pledge for that debt and hold it for a year and a day, and the debtor is unwilling either to admit the debt or to redeem the pledge, and this is proved, he shall sell the pledge

[1] The honorial barons of the abbey.
[2] Baldwin was abbot of Bury St. Edmunds from 1065 to 1097 or 1098. For him, see also above, Nos. 175, 217.
[3] 20 November.

for as much as he can in the presence of good witnesses and therefrom take his money. If there is any balance he shall return it to the debtor. But if there is not enough to pay him, he shall take distress again for what is lacking. If anyone has acquired land in the same town which was of burgage tenure, he shall perform such custom as that land was wont to perform, no matter who he may be. And these are the witnesses: Talbot the prior; Sired; Ædnoth; Ording; Jocelyn; Hervey the sacrist; Adam the steward; Wulward the clerk; Gilbert, son of Fulcher; William, son of Albold; Ralph of Loddon; Gilbert of Loddon; Richard of Loddon; Roger of Gissing; Ralph of Buckenham; Hugh 'de Kersing'; Robert of Hawstead; Ailbric 'de Capeles'; Ailmer of Whitfield; Leofmær of Barningham; Berard, his nephew; Brian; Osward; William, son of Peter; Rainald the lion; Ralph the constable; Osbern the butler; Geoffrey of Melford; John 'de Valle'; Robert Malet.

288. Charter of Henry II to Cambridge (1161–1189; perhaps 1185)

Grants the *firma burgi* to the burgesses of Cambridge. Printed: F. W. Maitland and M. Bateson, *Cambridge Borough Charters* (1911), p. 3; W. Stubbs, *Select Charters* (ed. 1913), p. 196.

Henry, by the grace of God, king of England and duke of Normandy and count of Anjou,[1] to the justices, sheriffs, and to all his servants and liegemen, greeting. Know that I have delivered my town of Cambridge to my burgesses at Cambridge to be held by them at 'farm' from me in chief by the same 'farm' which the sheriffs were wont to pay me, so that the burgesses shall henceforward answer for it at my Exchequer. Wherefore I order that you keep the aforesaid burgesses and all their possessions, and maintain them, as you would my own possessions, lest anyone should do them any injury or hindrance or harm. For I wish that they shall answer for this to no one except to me and to my Exchequer. Witness: Roger, son of Reinfrid at Quévilly.

289. Charter of Henry II to Dublin (1171–1172)

For the circumstances in which this very remarkable charter was given, see above, pp. 47, 341. It should be compared with No. 284 above. It has been much discussed, and the reader may be referred in the first instance to G. H. Orpen, *Ireland under the Normans*, vol. I (1911), p. 268. Printed: *Historical and Municipal Documents of Ireland* (Rolls Series, 1870), p. 1.

Henry, king of the English, duke of the Normans and of the men of Aquitaine, count of Anjou, to his archbishops, bishops, abbots, earls, barons, justiciars, sheriffs, servants, and to his liegemen, French, English and Irish, of all his land, greeting. Know that I have given and granted to my men of Bristol my city of Dublin to inhabit. Wherefore I will, and firmly order, that these should inhabit and hold it from me and from my heirs, freely and quietly, fully and wholly, and honourably, with all the liberties and free customs which the men of Bristol have at Bristol and throughout my land. Witness: William of Briouze; Reginald 'de Courtenay'; Hugh 'de Gundvilla'; William, son of Aldhelm; Rannulf 'de Glanville'; Hugh 'de Cressy'; Reginald 'de Paulli'. At Dublin.

[1] Title as in MS.

290. Charter of Henry II in favour of Gloucester (1155–1166)

Relates the privileges of Gloucester to those of London and Winchester. Printed: *Calendar of Charter Rolls*, vol. III (1908), p. 200.

Henry, king of the English and duke of the Normans, count of the Angevins, to all archbishops, bishops, abbots, earls, barons, justices, sheriffs, and to all his liegemen of the whole of England, both French and English, greeting. Know that I have granted and confirmed to my burgesses of Gloucester the same customs and liberties throughout all my land in respect of toll and all other things, as well as ever the citizens of London and Winchester had them in the time of King Henry, my grandfather. Wherefore I will, and firmly order, that my aforesaid burgesses shall have all those liberties, and free customs and full quittances, and that no one in respect of these shall cause them injury, or loss, or molestation. Witness: Reginald, earl of Cornwall; Manasser Biset the steward; Warin fitz Gerold the chamberlain; Hugh of Longchamp. At Westminster.

291. Charter of Henry II in favour of Hastings (1154–1158)

Interesting as illustrating the special history of the Cinque Ports (Hastings, Sandwich, Dover, Romney, Hythe). Hastings was the chief of these ports and before 1206 is the only one of them which is known to have had 'barons'–as here described. These ports made important contributions to the navy, and in return had special privileges. This charter should be compared in this sense with Nos. 284, 285. Printed: *Calendar of Charter Rolls*, vol. III (1908), p. 221.

Henry, king of the English and duke of the Normans and of the men of Aquitaine, count of the Angevins, to the archbishops, bishops, earls, barons, and all his liegemen of England, Normandy, Aquitaine and Anjou, greeting. Know that I grant to my barons of Hastings[1] their honours in my court, and their liberties and quittances of toll and lestage and passage and rivage and 'sponsage', and all wreck and resale, and freedom from all customs throughout the whole of my land wherever they may come. And let them have strand and den at Yarmouth. And I order that they shall there take care of my peace and justice with my reeve. And I give them treasure trove in sea and land. Let them be quit of all things as my freemen. And let no one disturb them or their property on penalty of 10 pounds forfeiture. And in return for these liberties they shall provide for me each year twenty ships for fifteen days at their own cost; and if further service is needed, they shall have full payment. Witness: Thomas the chancellor;[2] Reginald, earl of Cornwall; Walkelin Maminot. At Westminster.

292. Charter of Robert, count of Meulan, to the merchants of Leicester (1103–1118)

Interesting for its early reference to a gild-merchant. Printed: M. Bateson, *Records of the Borough of Leicester* (1899), vol. I, p. I.

Robert, count of Meulan, to Ralph the butler, and all his barons, both French and English, of all his land of England, greeting. Know that I have granted to all my merchants of Leicester their gild-merchant with all the customs by which they held it in the time of King William and King William, his son, and which they now hold in the time of King Henry. Witness: Robert, son of Alcitil.

[1] On the barons of Hastings and later of the Cinque Ports, see J. Tait, *Medieval English Borough* (1936) and the authorities there cited. [2] Thomas Becket.

293. Writ of Henry I in favour of Leicester (1118–1135)

Printed: M. Bateson, *Records of the Borough of Leicester* (1899), vol. I, p. I.

Henry, king of England, to Restold the sheriff and to his servants of Oxford, greeting. I order that the men of Robert, earl of Leicester, shall be quit at Oxford by such customs as they performed in the time of Robert, count of Meulan. You may demand no other customs from them. Witness: Nicholas of Aubigny. At Redbridge.

294. Writ of Henry II in favour of Lincoln (1154–1158)

An important writ, granting to the citizens of Lincoln the right to 'farm' their borough. Printed: *Calendar of Charter Rolls*, vol. III (1908), p. 312.

Henry, king of the English, and duke of the Normans and of the men of Aquitaine, count of the Angevins, to his justices and his sheriffs of Lincolnshire, greeting. Know that I have delivered my city of Lincoln to the citizens of this same city at that 'farm' at which it was wont to be in the time of King Henry, my grandfather, with all customs and liberties belonging to that city within borough and without. Witness: Earl Reginald[1] and Warin fitz Gerold. Given at Stamford.

295. Charter of Henry II to Lincoln (*circa* 1157)

This charter generally describing the municipal customs of Lincoln and having particular reference to the gild-merchant should be compared with the account given of Lincoln in Domesday Book (see above, No. 211). Printed: *Hist. MSS. Comm. 14th Rep.*, Appendix VII; W. Stubbs, *Select Charters* (ed. 1913), p. 197.

Henry, by the grace of God, etc., to the bishop of Lincoln, and to the justices, sheriffs, barons, servants and all his liegemen, both French and English, of Lincoln, greeting. Know that I have granted to my citizens of Lincoln all their liberties and customs and laws which they had in the time of Edward and William and Henry, kings of England. And I have granted them their gild-merchant, comprising men of the city and other merchants of the shire,[2] as well and freely as they had it in the time of our aforesaid predecessors, kings of England. And all the men who live within the four divisions of the city and attend the market, shall stand in relation to gelds and customs and the assizes of the city as well as ever they stood in the time of Edward, William and Henry, kings of England. I grant also that if anyone shall buy any land within the city by the burgage tenure of Lincoln, and shall hold it for a year and a day without dispute, and if he who bought it can show that he who claims it has made no claim during that period, although resident in England, then let him who bought it hold it well and in peace and without a plea. I also confirm to them that if anyone has lived in Lincoln for a year and a day without dispute from any claimant, and has paid the customs, and if the citizens can show by the laws and customs of the city that the claimant has remained in England during that period and has made no claim, then let

[1] Earl of Cornwall, one of Henry I's numerous bastards.

[2] A phrase of interest in that it has been suggested that the merchant-gild comprised the burgesses who held the borough at 'farm', and that it was therefore indistinguishable from the ruling body in the city. Here it seems that the gild was larger than the burgess body. On the other hand, it is possible that these merchants from the shire were only subordinate members of the gild. Nevertheless this passage needs to be considered in connexion with the early constitutional history of the English boroughs.

the defendant remain in peace in my city of Lincoln as my citizen, without [having to defend his] right. Witness: Philip, bishop of Bayeux; Arnulf, bishop of Lisieux; Thomas the chancellor;[1] Earl Reginald; Richard of Le Hommet, constable; Henry of Essex, constable. At Nottingham.

296. Writ of Henry II in favour of the gild-merchant of Lincoln (1154–1160)

This writ, which should be compared with the document immediately preceding, is interesting, not only in relation to the gild-merchant but also for its reference to the cloth industry. Printed: *Calendar of Charter Rolls*, vol. III (1908), p. 7.

Henry, king of the English, and duke of the Normans and of the men of Aquitaine, count of the Angevins, to the bishop of Lincoln and to the justice and sheriff and the barons of Lincoln and of Lincolnshire, greeting. I order that no merchant who is a stranger and from outside shall be resident in Lincoln for the purpose of dyeing his cloths or of selling by retail, except those who are in the gild, and who contribute to the customs of the town, and who pay my geld with the inhabitants as they were wont to do in the time of King Henry. Witness: Reginald, earl of Cornwall; Henry of Essex, the constable; Richard of Le Hommet.

297. Writ of Henry II enforcing the right of the reeves of Lincoln to toll from Norse merchants visiting Grimsby (1155–1175)

A significant allusion to the mercantile connexions between the Danelaw and Scandinavia in the twelfth century. Printed: *Calendar of Charter Rolls*, vol. III (1908), p. 7.

Henry, king of the English, and duke of the Normans and of the men of Aquitaine, count of the Angevins, to all the Norsemen who come to the port of Grimsby or to other ports of Lincolnshire, greeting. I order you to pay to my reeves of Lincoln all the rights and customs which you were wont to pay to the reeves of Lincoln in the time of King Henry, my grandfather. And I forbid any one of you to retain their toll or any other custom unjustly, on a penalty of 10 pounds forfeiture. Witness: William, son of John. At Worcester.

298. The customs of Newcastle-upon-Tyne in the time of Henry I

This record was drawn up in the reign of Henry II to record what were the customs of Newcastle-upon-Tyne in the time of his grandfather. It would be hard to find a more elaborate or detailed description of English burghal custom at this period. It will be noted that these customs refer mainly to legal and mercantile privileges, and are not in the main concerned with organization. This record exists in two versions, one of which is printed in *Acts of Parliament of Scotland* (1844), vol. I, p. 33, and also in W. Stubbs, *Select Charters* (ed. 1913), p. 133; and the other is printed in the *Percy Cartulary* (ed. M. T. Martin, Surtees Soc., 1911), p. 333.

These are the laws and customs which the burgesses of Newcastle-upon-Tyne had in the time of Henry, king of England, and which they still have by right:

The burgesses may distrain foreigners within their market and without, and within their houses and without, and within their borough and without, and they may do this without the permission of the reeve, unless the courts are being held within the borough, or unless they are in the field on army service, or are doing

[1] Thomas Becket.

castle-guard. But a burgess may not distrain on another burgess without the permission of the reeve.

If a burgess shall lend anything in the borough to someone dwelling outside, the debtor shall pay back the debt if he admit it, or otherwise do right in the court of the borough.

Pleas which arise in the borough shall there be held and concluded except those which belong to the king's crown.

If a burgess shall be sued in respect of any plaint he shall not plead outside the borough except for defect of court; nor need he answer, except at a stated time and place, unless he has already made a foolish answer, or unless the case concerns matters pertaining to the crown.

If a ship comes to the Tyne and wishes to unload, it shall be permitted to the burgesses to purchase what they please. And if a dispute arises between a burgess and a merchant, it shall be settled before the third tide.

Whatever merchandise a ship brings by sea must be brought to the land; except salt and herring which must be sold on board ship.

If anyone has held land in burgage for a year and a day justly and without challenge, he need not answer any claimant, unless the claimant is outside the kingdom of England, or unless he be a boy not having the power of pleading.

If a burgess have a son in his house and at his table, his son shall have the same liberty as his father.

If a villein come to reside in the borough, and shall remain as a burgess in the borough for a year and a day, he shall thereafter always remain there, unless there was a previous agreement between him and his lord for him to remain there for a certain time.

If a burgess sues anyone concerning anything, he cannot force the burgess to trial by battle, but the burgess must defend himself by his oath, except in a charge of treason when the burgess must defend himself by battle. Nor shall a burgess offer battle against a villein unless he has first quitted his burgage.

No merchant except a burgess can buy wool or hides or other merchandise outside the town, nor shall he buy them within the town except from burgesses.

If a burgess incurs forfeiture he shall give 6 oras to the reeve.

In the borough there is no 'merchet' nor 'heriot' nor 'bloodwite'[1] nor 'stengesdint'.[2]

Any burgess may have his own oven and handmill if he wishes, saving always the rights of the king's oven.

If a woman incur a forfeiture concerning bread or ale, none shall concern himself with it except the reeve. If she offend twice she shall be punished by the forfeiture. If she offend thrice justice shall take its course.

No one except a burgess may buy cloth for dyeing or make or cut it.

A burgess can give or sell his land as he wishes, and go where he will, freely and quietly unless his claim to the land is challenged.

[1] The fine imposed for drawing blood.

[2] A fine for striking another.

299. Charter of Henry II in favour of Nottingham (1154–1189; perhaps 1157)

The privileges of Nottingham are here described in some detail and are referred back to the time of Henry I. The references to the cloth industry are particularly notable. Printed: W. H. Stevenson, *Nottinghamshire Charters*, p. 2; W. Stubbs, *Select Charters* (ed. 1913), p. 198.

Henry, king of the English, etc. Know that I have granted, and by this my charter confirmed, to the burgesses of Nottingham all those free customs which they had in the time of King Henry, our grandfather; to wit, toll, and team and infangtheof,[1] and the right of levying dues from Thurmaston to Newark, and from all those crossing the Trent, as fully as in the borough of Nottingham, and from the other part from the brook beyond Rempstone up to the water of Radford 'in Nort'. Also the men of Nottinghamshire and of Derbyshire ought to come to the borough of Nottingham on Friday and Saturday with carts and sumpter beasts. Nor may anyone within ten leagues of Nottingham work coloured cloth except in the borough. And if anyone from elsewhere lives for a year and a day in the borough of Nottingham, in time of peace, and without dispute, then no one afterwards except the king shall have rights over him. And any burgess who buys the land of his neighbour and possesses it for a year and a day without any claim by the relatives of the seller, the same relatives being in England, shall afterwards possess it in quiet. Nor need any answer be made to the reeve of the borough of Nottingham, if he makes claim against any burgess, unless another burgess be the accuser in the case. And let everyone living in the borough, no matter to whose fee he belongs, join in paying the tallages and the forfeitures of the borough. And no one who comes to Nottingham market between Friday evening and Saturday evening shall be put in pledge except in respect of the king's 'farm'. And the river Trent ought to be free from travellers as far as a perch extends from each part of the stream of water. Wherefore I will and order that the aforesaid burgesses shall have and hold the aforesaid customs well and in peace, freely and quietly, and honourably, and fully, and entirely, even as they had them in the time of King Henry, my grandfather. Witness, etc.

300. Charter of Henry II to Oxford (1155–1162)

Interesting especially for its reference to the gild-merchant and more particularly as indicating the close connexion between the privileges of Oxford and those of London. Printed: W. Stubbs, *Select Charters* (ed. 1913), p. 198.

Henry, by the grace of God, king of England, duke of Normandy and Aquitaine,[2] etc. Know that I have granted and confirmed to my citizens of Oxford their liberties, customs, laws, and quittances which they had in the time of King Henry, my grandfather, and in particular the gild-merchant with all its liberties and customs in lands and woods and pastures and other things; and especially that no one who is not of that gild-merchant may act as merchant in the city or the suburbs save as was allowed in the time of King Henry, my grandfather. Further, I have granted and confirmed to them that they shall be quit of toll and passage and of all custom throughout England and Normandy, by land and water, and by the seashore, 'by land and by strand'. And let them have all their other customs and liberties and laws

[1] 'infangentheof', that is jurisdiction over thieves apprehended within the limits of the privileged territory. [2] Title as in copy.

which they have in common with my citizens of London. And let them serve me at my feast with those of my butlery, and in common with them let them transact their business within London and outside it, and in all places. And if there is doubt or dispute about any judgment respecting what they ought to do, let them send messengers about it to London, and what the Londoners judge about it, they shall have firmly and with assurance. And they shall not plead nor be impleaded about anything outside the city of Oxford, but in any plea whatsoever they shall make their proof according to the laws and customs of the citizens of London and not otherwise; because they and the citizens of London are of one and the same law and custom and liberty. Wherefore I will, etc., that they have and hold their aforesaid liberties, laws, customs and tenures freely and in peace, etc., with sake and soke, toll and team and infangtheof, and with all other liberties and customs and quittances as well as ever they had them in the time of King Henry, my grandfather; and as my citizens of London have them. Witness: Thomas the chancellor;[1] Reginald, earl of Cornwall; Hugh, earl of Norfolk,[2] etc.

301. Charter of Henry II in favour of the corvesars and cordwainers of Oxford (*circa* 1175)

References to a craft gild are rare at this period. A parallel instance is Henry II's charter to the London weavers (No. 272). Printed: *Calendar of Charter Rolls*, vol. II (1906), p. 34.

Henry, by the grace of God, king of the English, and duke of the Normans and of the men of Aquitaine, count of the Angevins, to the archbishops, bishops, abbots, earls, barons, justiciars, sheriffs, and all his servants and liegemen, French and English, of the whole of England, greeting. Know that I have granted and by the present charter confirmed to the corvesars[3] of Oxford all the liberties and customs which they had in the time of King Henry, my grandfather, and confirming that they should have their gild as they then had it, so that nobody not a member of that gild shall carry on their trade in the town of Oxford. I grant also that the cordwainers[4] who may come later into the town of Oxford shall have the same liberties and customs which the corvesars have, and ought to have. For this concession and confirmation the corvesars and the cordwainers must pay me every year one ounce of gold. Witness: Geoffrey and Roger, the king's chaplains; Richard Brito; Ralph, son of Stephen the chamberlain; Richard Ruffus. At Woodstock.

302. Charter of Henry II recognizing the gild-merchant of Winchester (7 July–29 September 1155, or early in 1158)

A gild-merchant might exist without royal concession, but a confirmation such as this was valuable, the more especially when as here it included an exemption from toll, etc. Printed: W. Stubbs, *Select Charters* (ed. 1913), p. 196, and (from the original) in J. S. Furley, *Winchester Records* (1923), p. 178.

Henry, king of the English and duke of the Normans and of the men of Aquitaine, count of the Angevins, to the archbishops, bishops, abbots, earls, sheriffs, and to all his liegemen, both French and English, and to his servants throughout the whole of

[1] Thomas Becket. [2] Hugh Bigot. [3] *corvesarii*. [4] *corduanarii*.

England and in every seaport, greeting. I order that my citizens of Winchester belonging to the merchant gild shall, together with all their possessions, be quit of all toll and passage and customs; and let no one disturb them about this, nor do them injury or insult, on pain of forfeiture to me. Witness: Thomas the chancellor;[1] Earl Reginald;[2] the earl of Gloucester; Richard of Le Hommet the constable; Warin fitz Gerold the chamberlain; William, son of Haimo; Jocelyn 'de Bailliol'. At Salisbury.

303. Charter of Henry II in favour of Winchester (7 July–29 September 1155, or early in 1158)

Printed: J. S. Furley, *Winchester Records* (1923), p. 178.

Henry, king of the English, and duke of the Normans and of the men of Aquitaine, count of the Angevins, to the archbishops, bishops, abbots, earls, barons, justiciars, sheriffs, and all his liegemen, both French and English, greeting. Know that I have granted to my citizens of Winchester all the liberties which they had in the time of King Henry, my grandfather. And I order that they have and hold all their purchases and pledges and their tenements according to the custom of the city as freely, quietly and honourably as ever they did in the time of King Henry. And if other customs have unjustly grown up in the war[3] let them be suppressed. And whoever shall come into the city with his merchandise, from any place whatsoever, whether he be a stranger or not, shall come, tarry and depart protected by my peace, having paid the just dues. Let no one unjustly disturb them in respect of this my charter. And I will and order that the aforesaid citizens shall justly have my firm peace. Witness: Thomas the chancellor;[1] William, the king's brother;[4] Reginald, earl of Cornwall; Richard of Le Hommet the constable; Warin fitz Gerold the chamberlain; William, son of Haimo; Jocelyn 'de Bailliol'; John the marshal. At Salisbury.

[1] Thomas Becket.
[2] Earl of Cornwall.
[3] *guerra*, the civil war of Stephen's reign.
[4] Third son of Geoffrey and Maud, died 1164.

Appendices

I. CHART CHRONOLOGY OF REIGNING PRINCES, 1042–1189

	ENGLAND[1]	NORMANDY[2]	ANJOU[3]	FRANCE[4]	FLANDERS[5]	SCOTLAND[6]	EMPERORS	POPES	
		William (succeeded 1035)	Geoffrey II (succeeded 1040)	Henry I (succeeded 1031)	Baldwin V (succeeded 1035)	Macbeth (succeeded 1040)	Henry III (succeeded 1039)	Benedict IX (succeeded 1033)	
1042	Edward								1042
1043									1043
1044								(Sylvester–anti-pope)	1044
1045								Gregory VI	1045
1046								Clement II	1046
1047									1047
1048								Damasus II Leo IX	1048
1049									1049
1050									1050
1051									1051
1052									1052
1053									1053
1054								Victor II	1054
1055									1055
1056							Henry IV		1056
1057								Stephen IX	1057
1058						Malcolm Canmore		Benedict X	1058
1059								Nicholas II	1059
1060			Geoffrey III Fulk IV, 'Rechin'	Philip I					1060
1061								Alexander II	1061
1062			[Geoffrey III is imprisoned by Fulk in 1066, and afterwards takes no effective part in the government of Anjou]						1062
1063									1063
1064									1064
1065									1065
1066	Harold William I								1066
1067					Baldwin VI				1067
1068									1068
1069									1069
1070					Arnulf III				1070
1071					Robert I				1071

[1] See Tables 1, 3, 4, 5, 6, 7.
[2] See Tables 2, 4, 5, 6.
[3] See Table 5.
[4] See Table 17.
[5] See Table 18.
[6] See Table 16.

	ENGLAND	NORMANDY	ANJOU	FRANCE	FLANDERS	SCOTLAND	EMPERORS	POPES	
1072									1072
1073								Gregory VII	1073
1074									1074
1075									1075
1076									1076
1077									1077
1078									1078
1079									1079
1080								[Clement: anti-	1080
1081								pope]	1081
1082									1082
1083									1083
1084									1084
1085									1085
1086								Victor III	1086
1087	William II	Robert II						Urban II	1087
1088									1088
1089									1089
1090									1090
1091									1091
1092									1092
1093					Robert II	Duncan II			1093
1094						Donald Bain			1094
1095									1095
1096		[William II]							1096
1097									1097
1098			[About this time			Edgar			1098
1099			Geoffrey IV be-					Paschal II	1099
1100	Henry I	Robert II	gins to dispute						1100
1101			Anjou with his						1101
1102			father Fulk IV.					[Albert: anti-	1102
1103			Geoffrey IV					pope]	1103
1104			dies in 1106]						1104
1105								[Sylvester: anti-	1105
1106		Henry I					Henry V	pope]	1106
1107						Alexander I			1107
1108				Louis VI					1108
1109			Fulk V						1109
1110									1110
1111					Baldwin VII				1111

	ENGLAND	NORMANDY	ANJOU	FRANCE	FLANDERS	SCOTLAND	EMPERORS	POPES	
1112									1112
1113									1113
1114									1114
1115									1115
1116									1116
1117									1117
1118								Gelasius II [Gregory: anti-pope]	1118
1119					Charles 'the good'			Calixtus II	1119
1120									1120
1121								(Celestine: anti-pope)	1121
1122									1122
1123									1123
1124						David I		Honorius II	1124
1125							Lothair II		1125
1126									1126
1127					William 'Clito'				1127
1128					Thierry (of Alsace)				1128
1129			Geoffrey V (Plantagenet)						1129
1130								Innocent II	1130
1131								[Anacletus: anti-pope]	1131
1132									1132
1133									1133
1134									1134
1135	Stephen	Stephen							1135
1136		[Geoffrey of Anjou claimant]							1136
1137				Louis VII					1137
1138							Conrad III	[Victor: anti-pope]	1138
1139									1139
1140									1140
1141									1141
1142									1142
1143								Celestine II	1143
1144								Lucius II	1144
1145								Eugenius III	1145
1146									1146
1147									1147
1148									1148
1149									1149

	ENGLAND	NORMANDY	ANJOU	FRANCE	FLANDERS	SCOTLAND	EMPERORS	POPES	
1150		Henry of Anjou later Henry II							1150
1151			Henry of Anjou later Henry II						1151
1152							Frederick I [Barbarossa]		1152
1153						Malcolm IV		Anastasius IV	1153
1154	Henry II							Hadrian IV	1154
1155									1155
1156									1156
1157									1157
1158									1158
1159								Alexander III	1159
1160								[Victor: anti-pope]	1160
1161									1161
1162									1162
1163									1163
1164								[Paschal: anti-pope]	1164
1165						William I "the Lion" [died 1214]			1165
1166									1166
1167									1167
1168					Philip of Alsace [died 1191]			[Calixtus: anti-pope]	1168
1169									1169
1170									1170
1171									1171
1172									1172
1173									1173
1174									1174
1175									1175
1176									1176
1177									1177
1178									1178
1179									1179
1180				Philip II (Augustus) [died 1223]					1180
1181								Lucius III	1181
1182									1182
1183									1183
1184									1184
1185								Urban III	1185
1186									1186
1187								Gregory VIII	1187
1188								Clement III [died 1191]	1188
1189									1189

II. TABLES: EIGHTEEN SELECT CHART PEDIGREES ILLUSTRATIVE OF ENGLISH HISTORY BETWEEN 1042 AND 1189

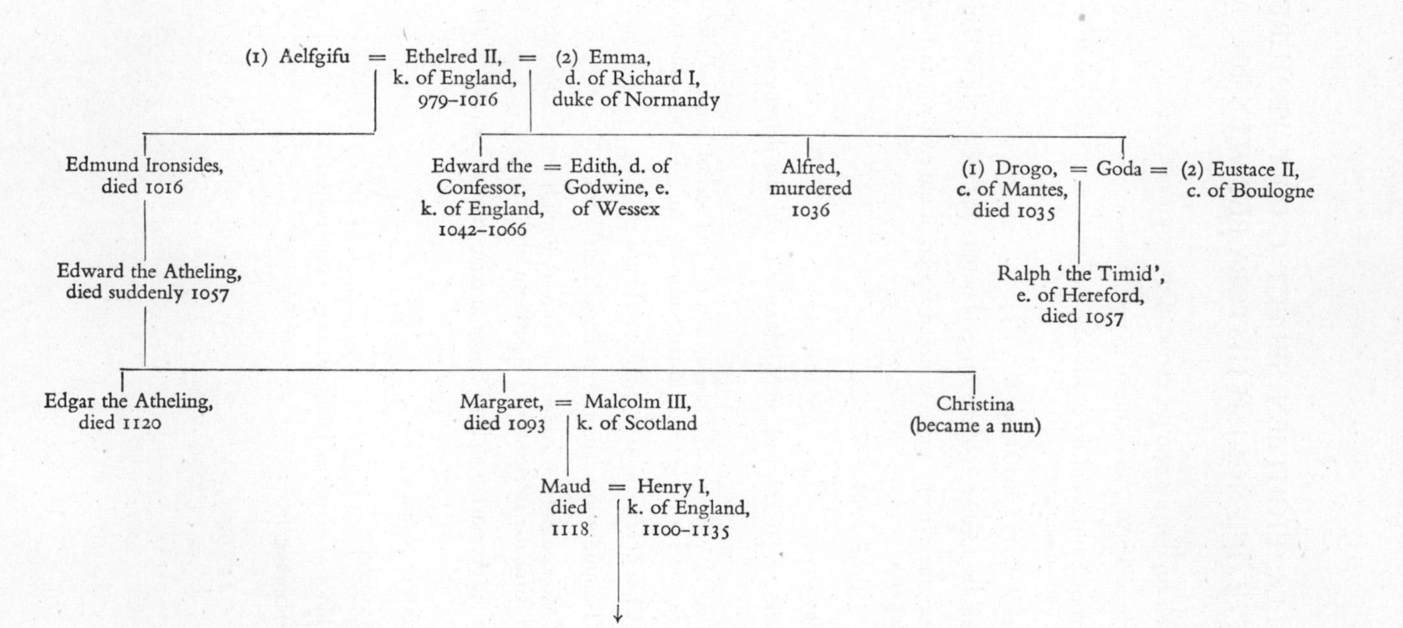

Table 1. The Old English royal dynasty in the period of the Norman Conquest.

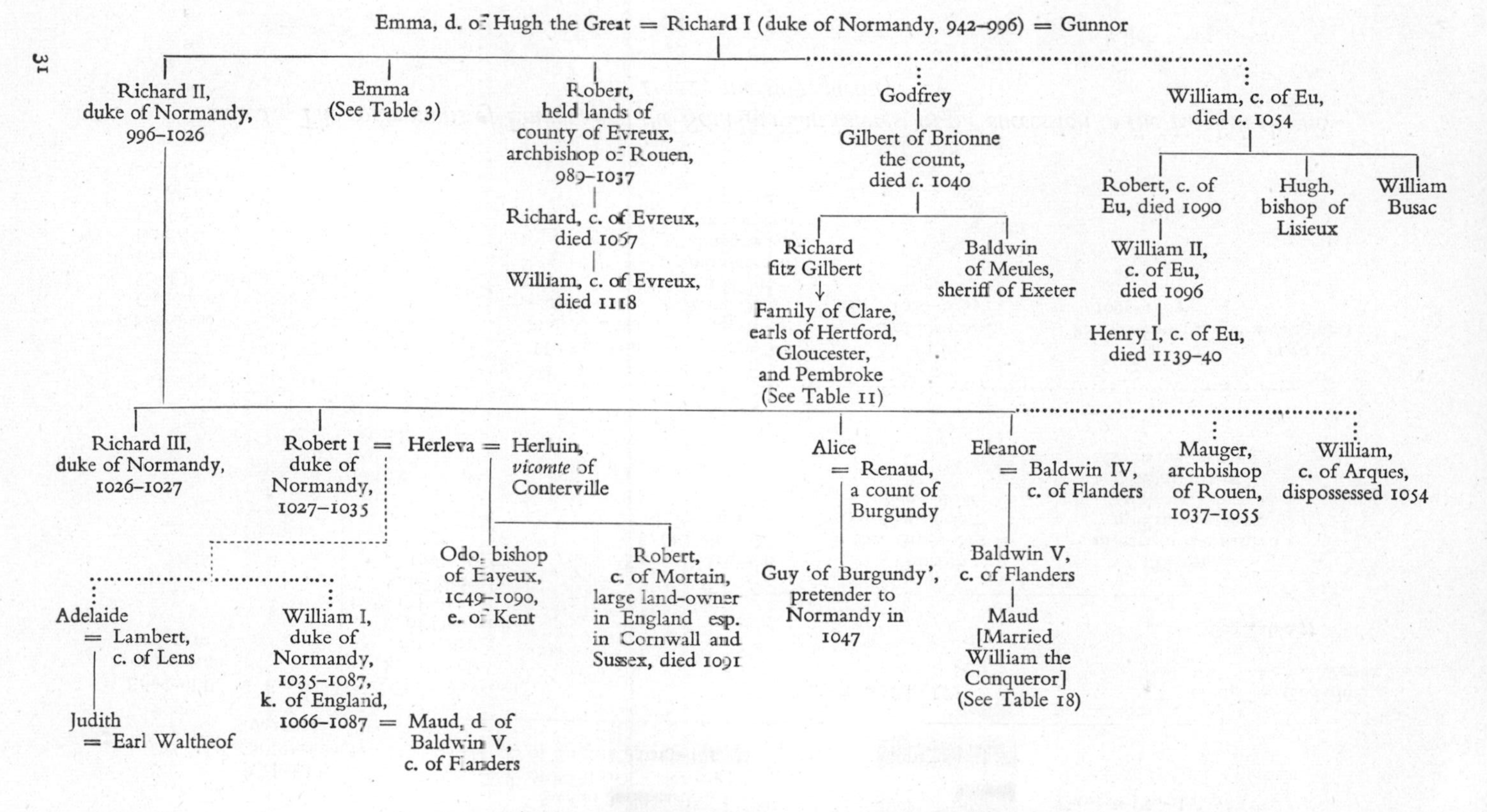

Table 2. The Norman ducal dynasty and some of its connexions.

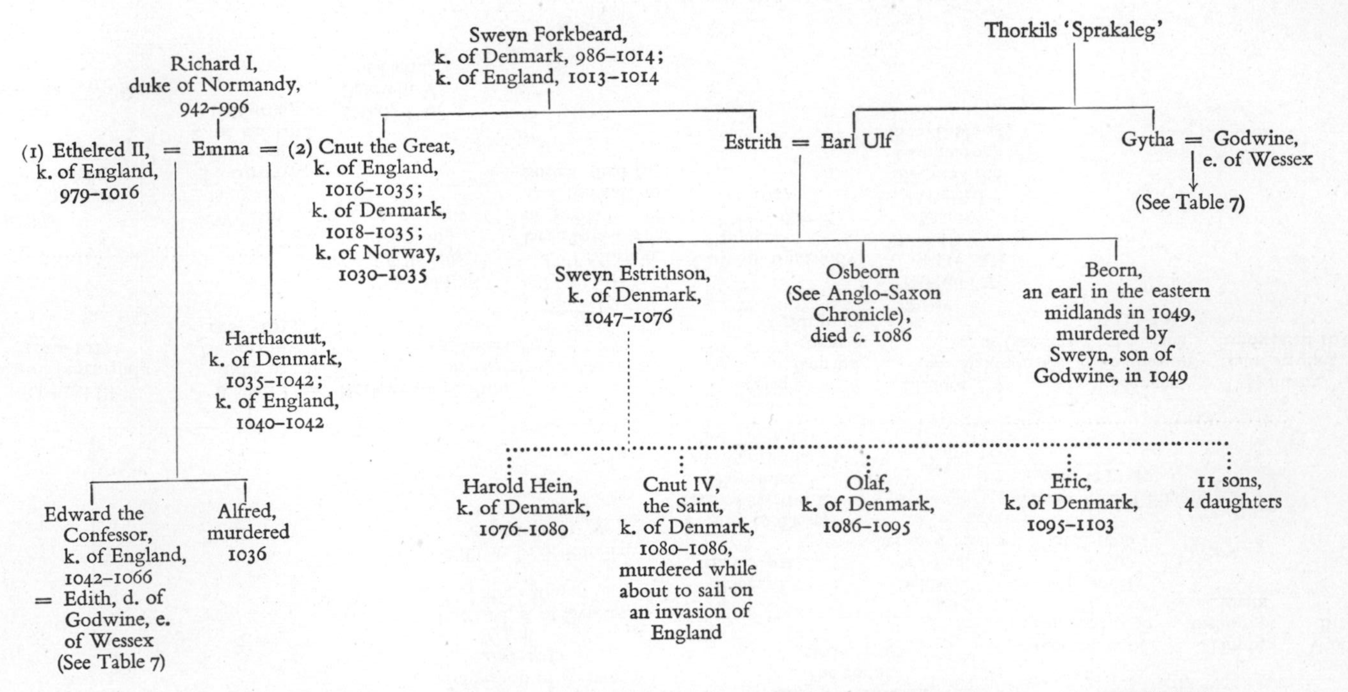

Table 3. The connexions of Emma, and the Scandinavian interest in the succession to the English throne in 1042, and subsequently.

William I = Maud, d. of Baldwin V, c. of Flanders

Robert II, duke of Normandy = Sibyl, of Conversano
- William 'Clito'

Richard died *s. p.*

William II, k. of England

Henry I, k. of England = (1) Maud, niece of Edgar Atheling (2) Adela, d. of Geoffrey VII, c. of Louvain

Agatha betrothed to Harold II of England

Adeliza, a nun

Constance = Alan Fergant, duke of Brittany

Adela = Stephen I, c. of Blois (See Table 6)

Cecilia, abbess of Caen

Children of Henry I (legitimate):

William, died 1120 = Maud, d. of Fulk V of Anjou

(1) Henry V, emperor = Maud
(2) Geoffrey V, c. of Anjou

Children of Henry I (illegitimate):

Robert of Caen, in 1122 e. of Gloucester

Richard, died 1120 (mother: Ansfride)

Rainald of Dunsterville, e. of Cornwall in 1141 (mother: Sibyl Corbet)

Robert, 'the king's son', a great tenant-in-chief, owing 100 knights in 1166 (mother: Edith, d. of Forn)

Gilbert

William 'de Tracy'

Henry (mother: Nesta, d. of Rhys ap Tudor)

Fulk, monk of Abingdon (mother: Ansfride)

Maud = Rotrou, c. of Perche, died 1120 (mother: Edith)

Maud = Conan III, d. of Brittany

Juliana = Eustace 'de Pacy' (mother: ? Ansfride)

? wife of William of Montmirail

Constance = Roscellin 'de Beaumont'

Alice = Matthew 'de Montmoreau'

Isabel (mother = Isabel, d. of Robert 'de Beaumont', first e. of Leicester)

Sibyl = Alexander I, k. of Scotland

Maud, abbess of Montivilliers

Gundred

Rohais = Henry 'de la Poncerat'

Table 4. The children of William I and Henry I.

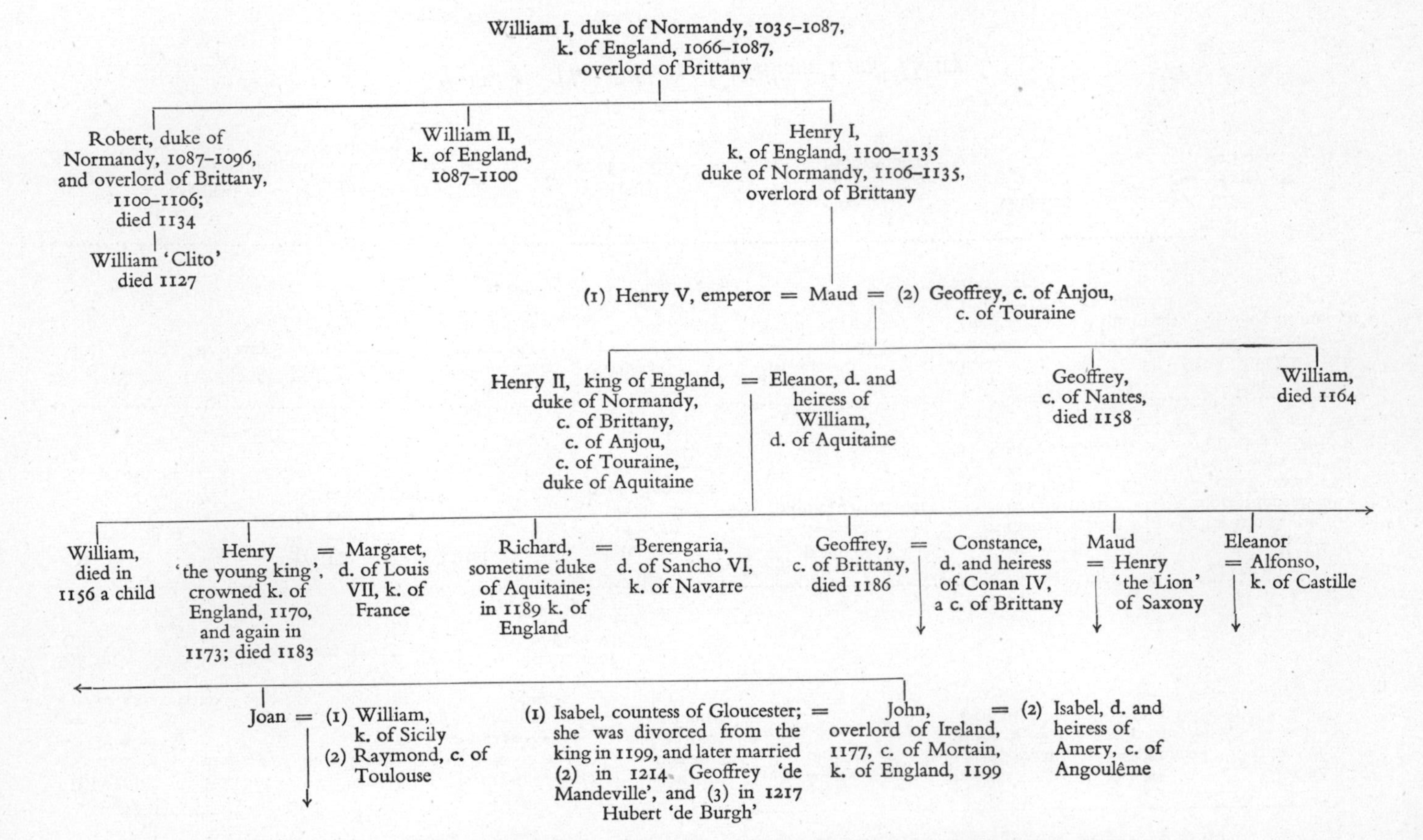

Table 5. Chart illustrating the formation of the Angevin empire and the family of Henry II.

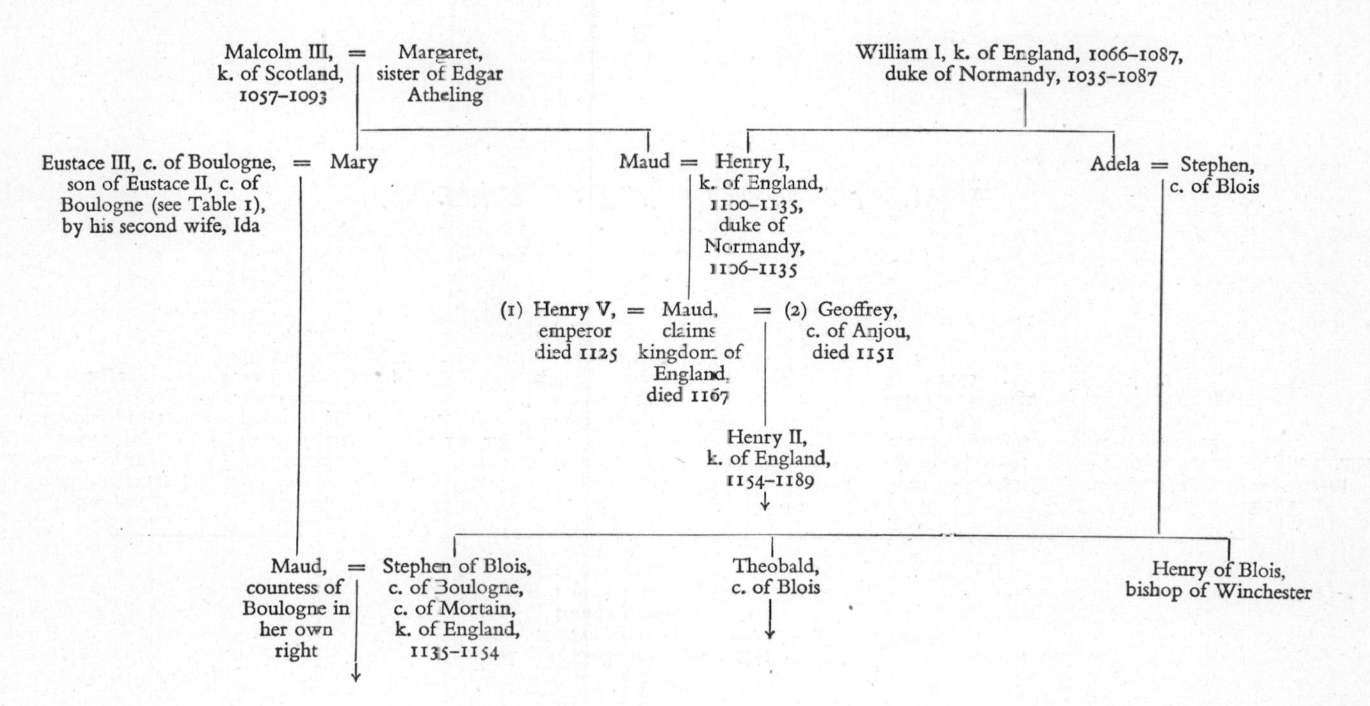

Table 6. Chart to illustrate the dynastic and continental aspects of the civil war in England during the reign of Stephen.

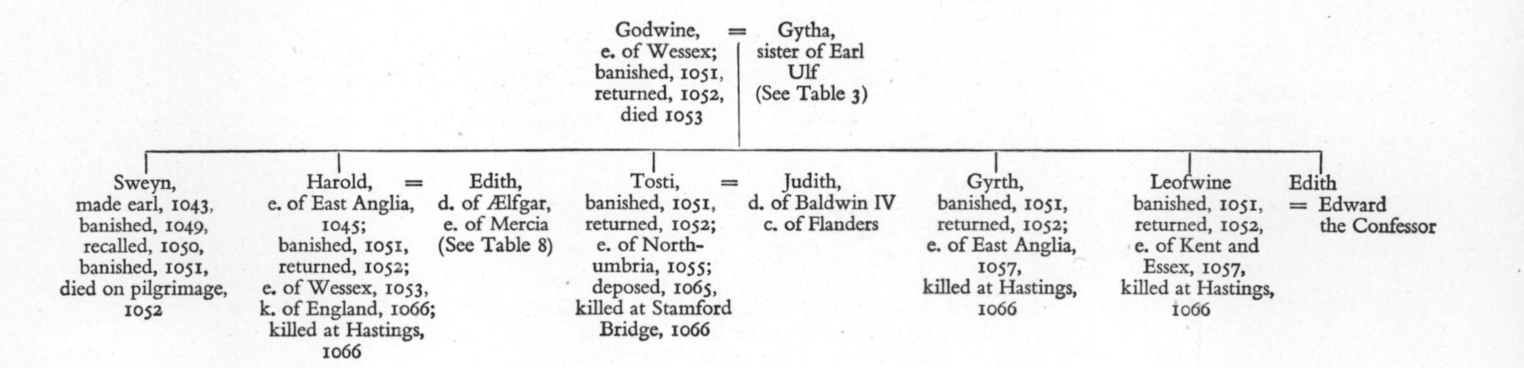

Table 7. The family of Godwine, earl of Wessex.

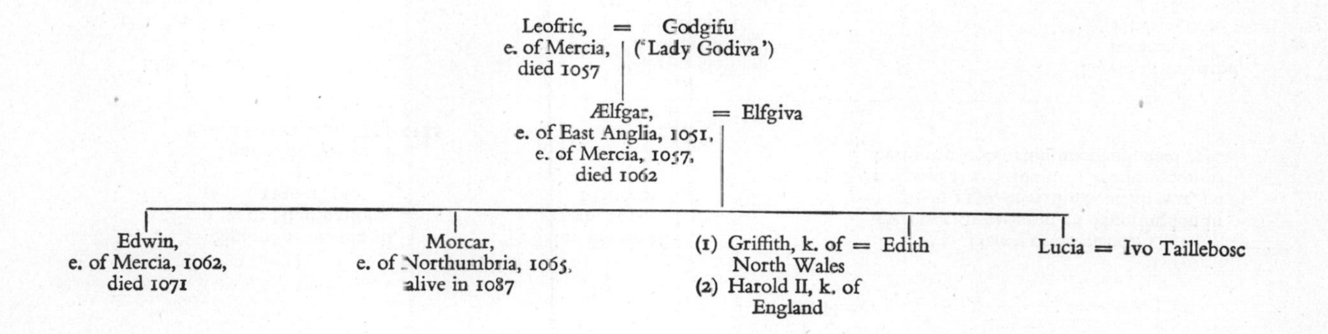

Table 8. The earls of Mercia.

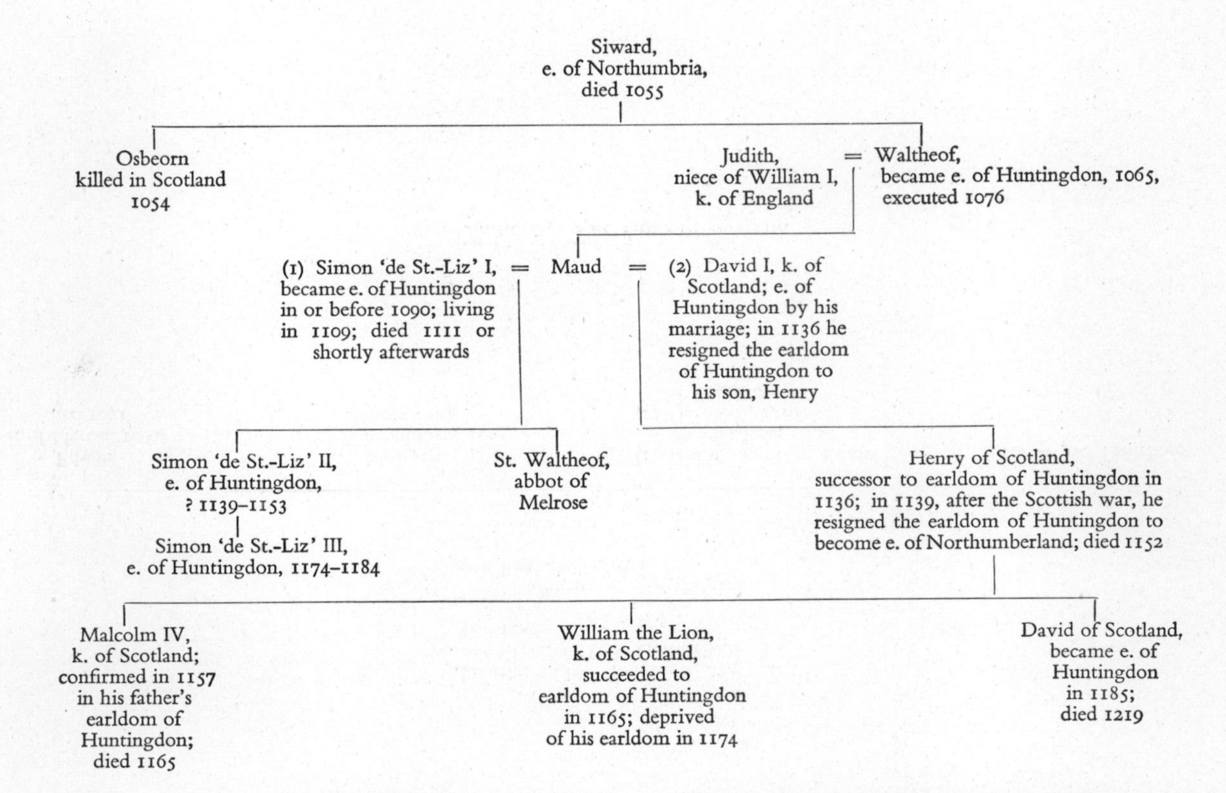

Table 9. Some descendants of Siward, earl of Northumbria, and the descent of the earldom of Huntingdon.

[The interest of the Scottish royal house will be noted, and also the manner in which the succession fluctuated between the two branches.]

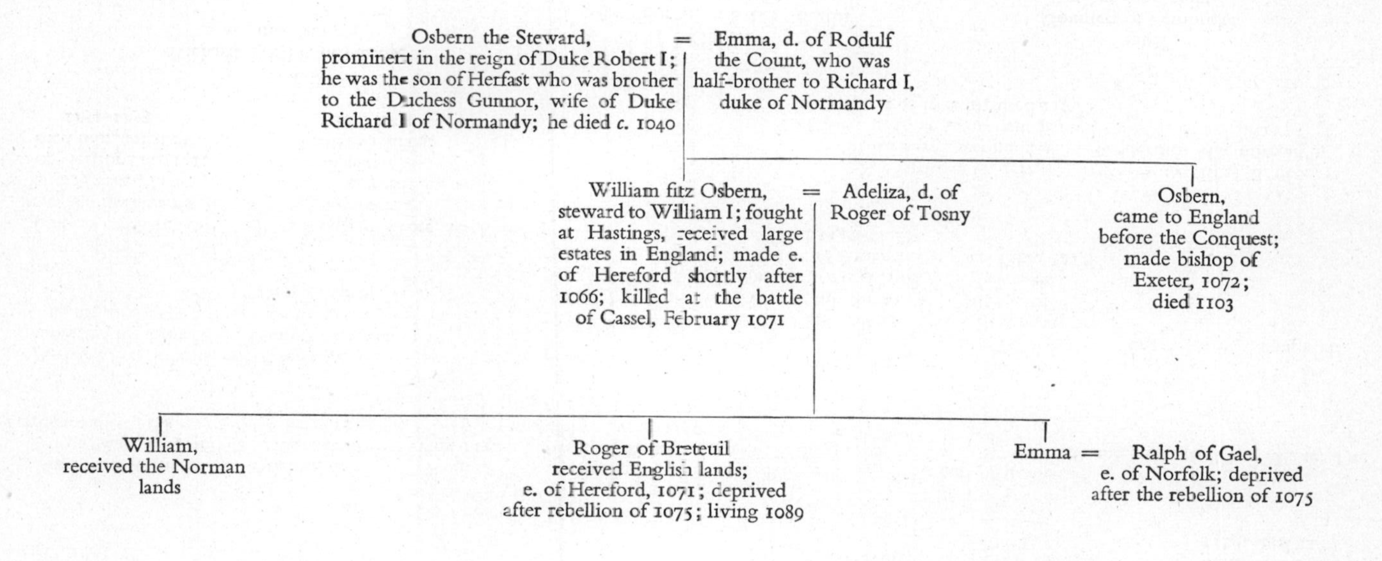

Table 10. Some connexions of William fitz Osbern, steward and earl of Hereford, to illustrate the history of the Conqueror's reign, and in particular the Anglo-Saxon Chronicle for 1075.

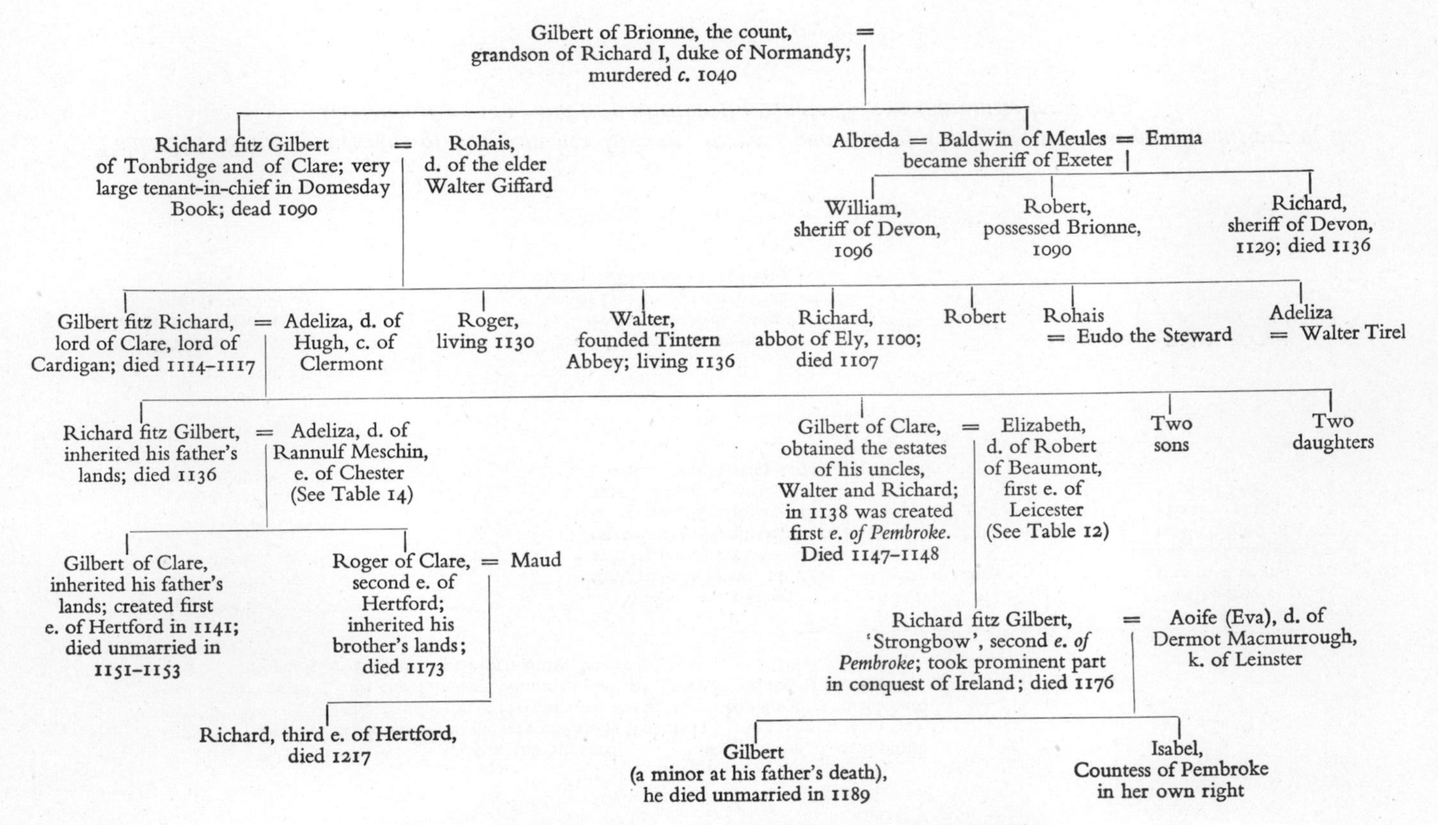

Table 11. The family of Clare in relation to its English earldoms.

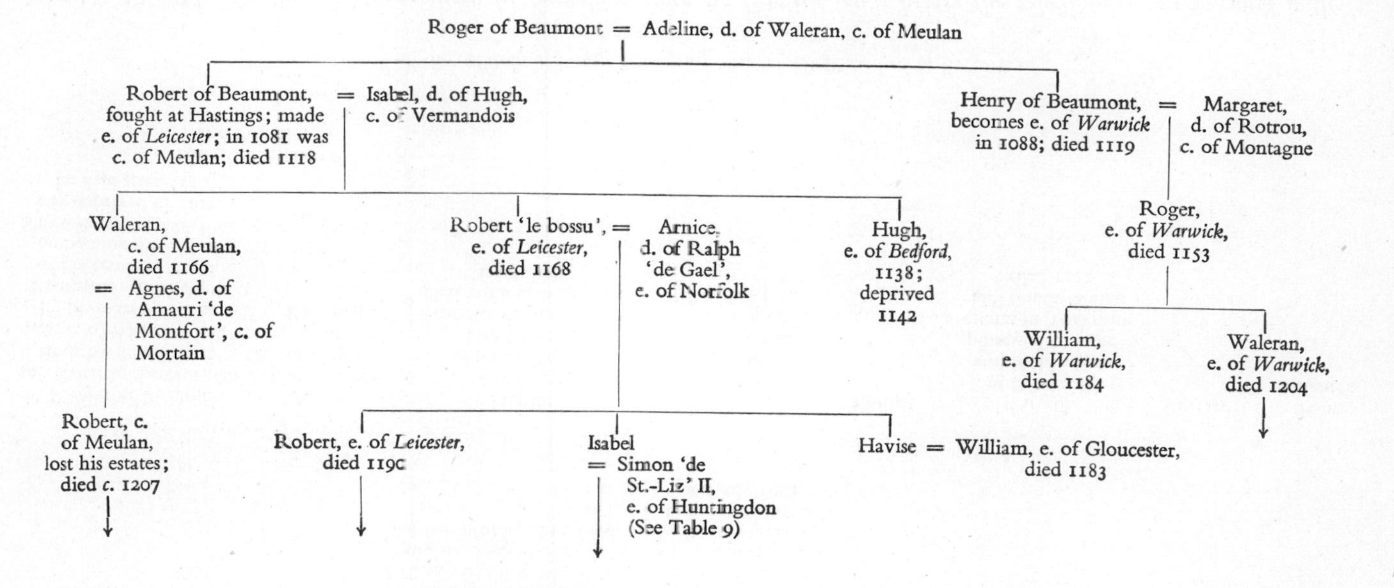

Table 12. The family of Beaumont in relation to its English earldoms.

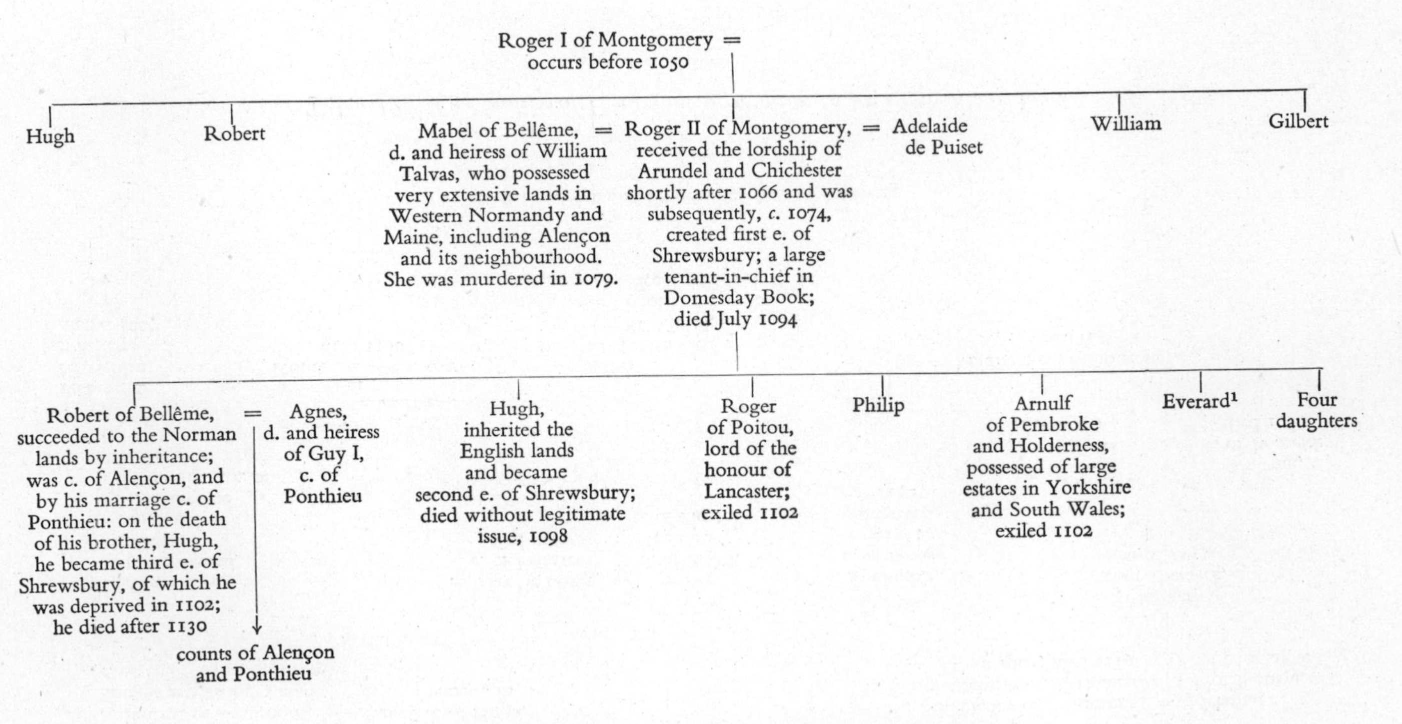

[1] All the children of Roger II were by Mabel of Bellême except Everard.

Table 13. The family of Montgomery in connexion with its English lands before the rebellion of 1102, and with particular reference to the earldom of Shrewsbury.

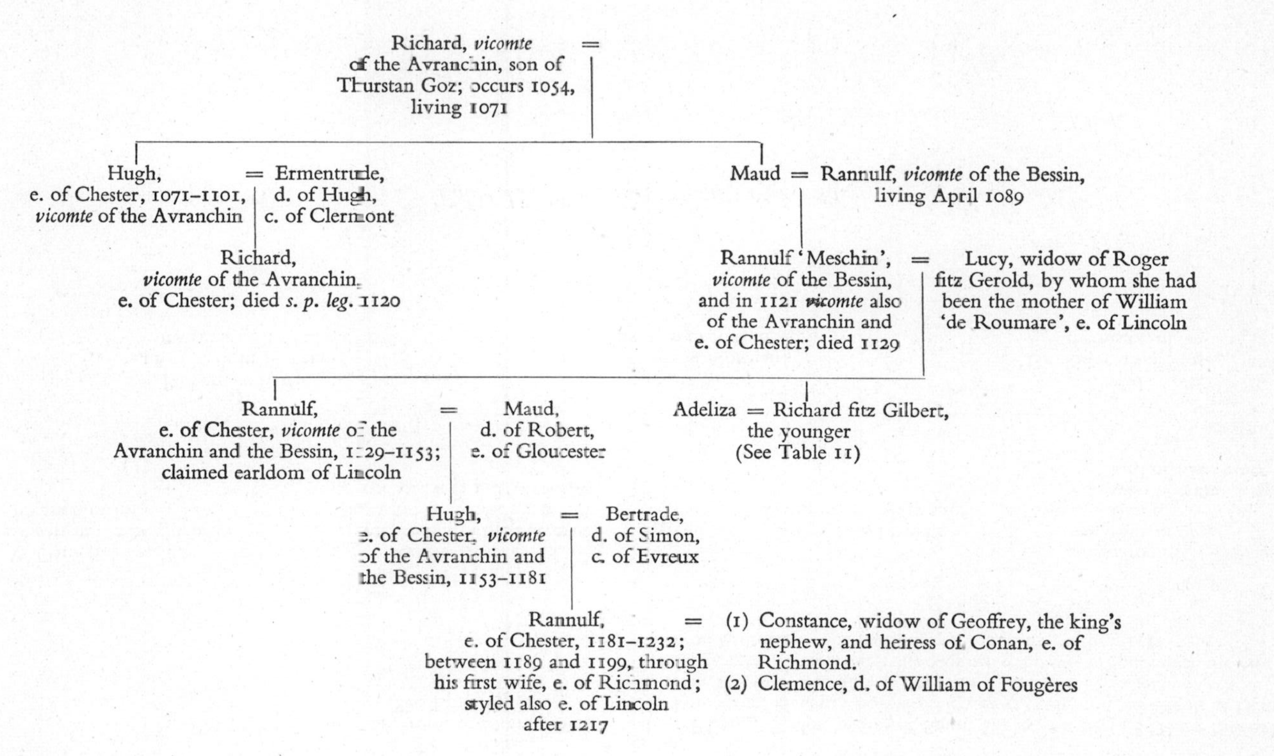

Table 14. The vicomtes of the Avranchin and the Bessin in relation to the descent of the earldom of Chester.

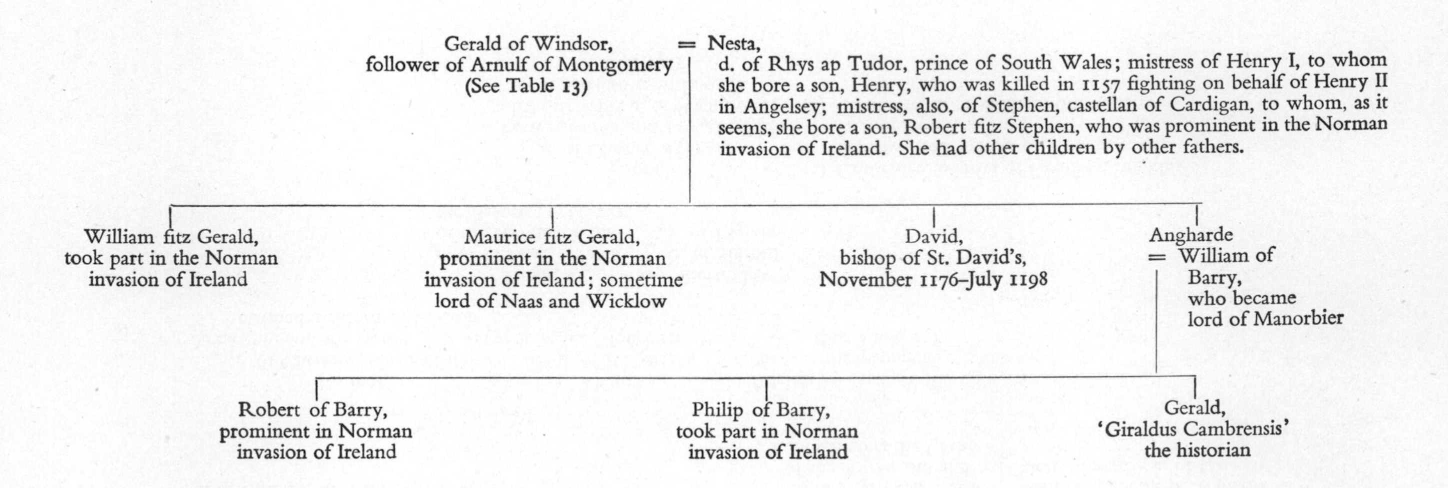

Table 15. Some descendants of Nesta.

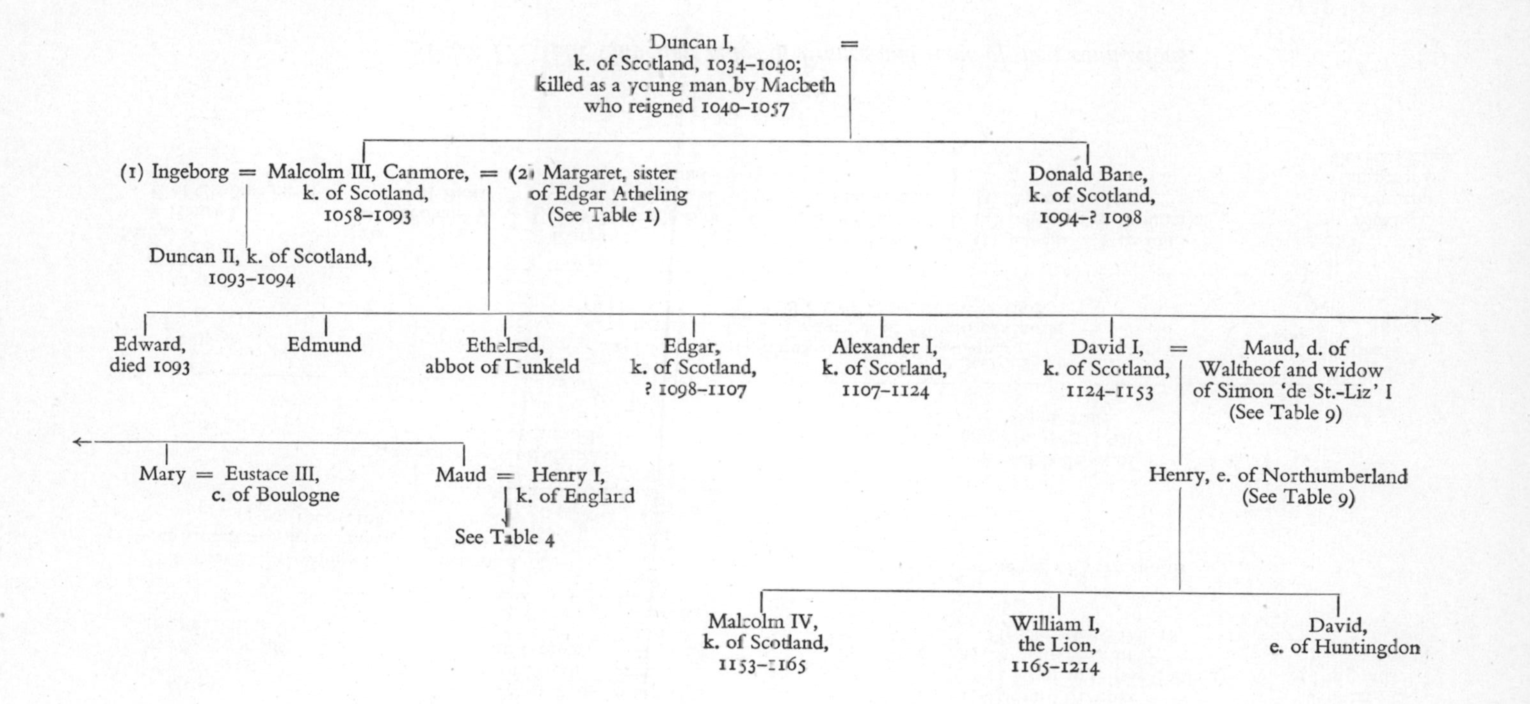

Table 16. *The kings of Scotland.*

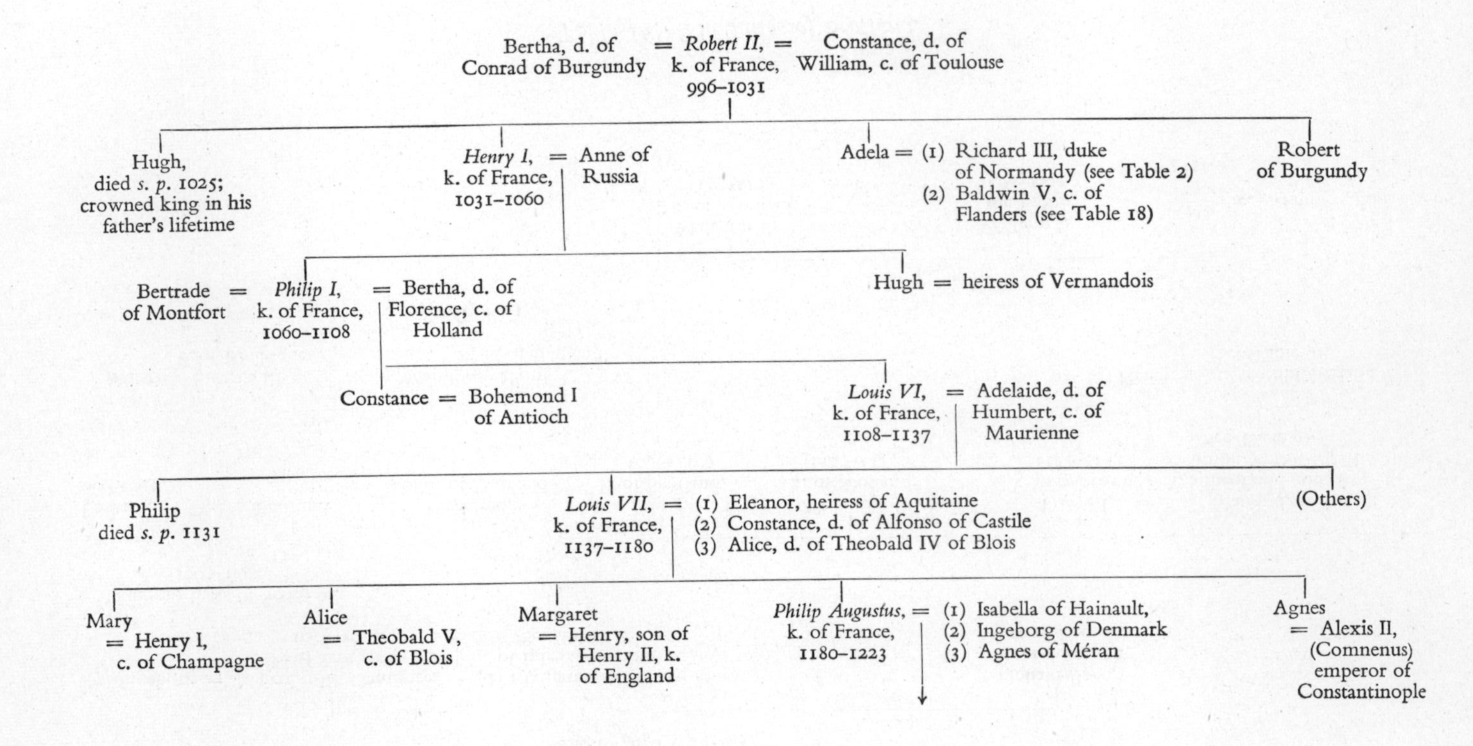

Table 17. The Capetian kings of France and some of their connexions.

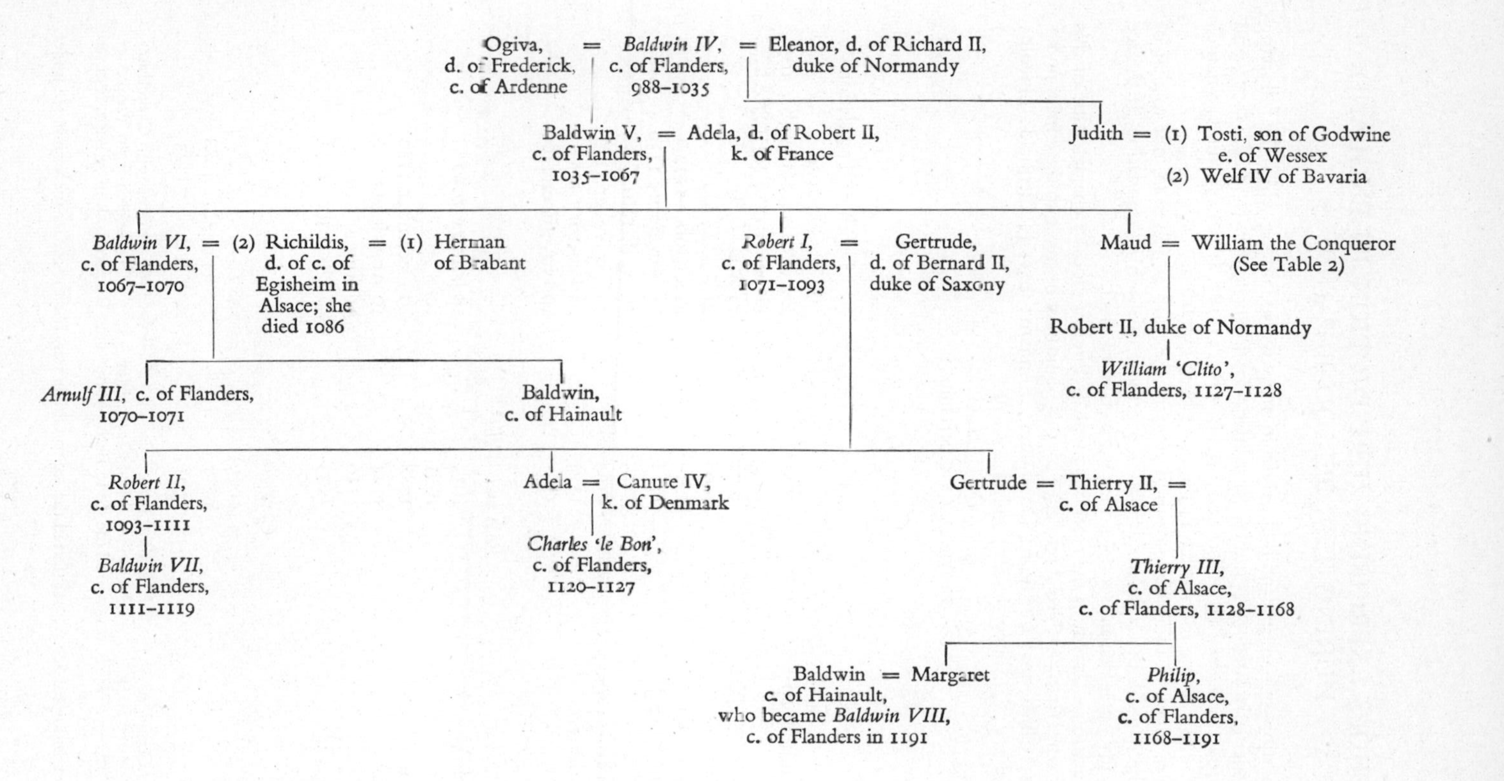

Table 18. The counts of Flanders.

III. BISHOPS EXERCISING JURISDICTION IN ENGLAND DURING THE PERIOD 1042–1189

The episcopal succession in England is displayed in many works, among which the following may here be particularly cited: W. Stubbs, *Registrum Sacrum Anglicanum* (2nd ed., 1897), and *Handbook of British Chronology* (R. Hist. Soc., 1939), pp. 132–187. It is from the last-named work that the synopsis which follows has in the main been extracted.

The dates here given in the middle column refer to the year of accession, not to that of consecration. The dates in the right-hand column are those of death or translation. If the see was vacated for any other reason, special notice is given of the fact.

Particular attention is drawn to the rearrangement of English dioceses characteristic of this period (see above, pp. 64–65). Special reference on this point may be made to the entries under Bath and Wells; Chichester; Crediton; Dorchester; Elmham; Exeter; Lichfield; Lincoln; Norwich; Ramsbury; Salisbury; Selsey; and Sherborne.

PROVINCE OF CANTERBURY

Canterbury

	Accession	Death or Translation
Eadsige	1038	29 October 1050
Robert (of Jumièges)	1051[1]	Expelled 14 September 1052[2]
Stigand	1052[3]	Deposed 11 April 1070[4]
Lanfranc	1070	24 May 1089
Anselm	1093	21 April 1109
Ralph 'd'Escures'	1114[5]	20 October 1122
William (of Corbeil)	1123	21 November 1136
Theobald	1139	18 April 1161
Thomas Becket	1162	29 December 1170
Richard (of Dover)	1174	16 February 1184
Baldwin	1185[6]	19 November 1190

Bath and Wells[7]

Duduc (Wells)	1033	18 January 1060
Giso (Wells)	1061	1088
John 'of Tours'	1088	29 December 1122
Godfrey	1123	16 August 1135
Robert	1136	31 August 1166
Reginald	1174	26 December 1191

Chichester[8]

Stigand	(1075)	1087
Gosfrid	1087	25 September 1088
Ralph Luffa	1091	24 December 1123

[1] Translated from London. [2] He died 1070. [3] He held Winchester with Canterbury.
[4] He died 22 February 1072. [5] Translated from Rochester. [6] Translated from Worcester.
[7] In 1090 John, bishop of Wells, transferred the see to Bath. About 1140 Robert, bishop of Bath, restored Wells.
[8] In 1075 Stigand, bishop of Selsey, transferred the see to Chichester. For the earlier succession, see under 'Selsey'.

	Accession	Death or Translation
Seffrid I	1125	Deprived 1145
Hilary	1147	19 July 1169
John	1174	26 April 1180
Seffrid II	1180	17 March 1204

Crediton

Lyfing[1]	1027	1046
Leofric[2]	1046	(1050)[2]

Dorchester[3]

Eadnoth II	1034	1049
Ulf	1050	Expelled 14 September 1052
Wulfwig	1053	1067
Remigius	1067	(1072)[4]

Elmham

Grimketel[5]	1043	Ejected 1043
Stigand	1043[6]	1047[7]
Æthelmær	1047	Deposed 1070
Herfast[8]	1070	? 1085
William	1086	1091[9]

Ely

Hervey[10]	1109[11]	30 August 1131
Nigel	1133	30 May 1169
Geoffrey Ridel	1174	21 August 1189

Exeter

Leofric	(1050)[12]	10 February 1072
Osbern	1072	1103
William Warelwast	1107	27 September 1137
Robert Chichester	1138	28 March 1155
Robert Warelwast	1155	22 March 1160
Bartholomew	1162	15 December 1184
John the Chanter	1186	1 June 1191

Hereford

Athelstan	?	10 February 1056
Leofgar	1056	16 June 1056
Aldred[13]	1056	1060[14]

[1] Lyfing was "bishop of Cornwall" (see above, p. 113), and also, after 1041, of Worcester.

[2] Leofric was also "bishop of Cornwall". He transferred the see of Crediton to Exeter in 1050. For the later succession, see under 'Exeter'.

[3] Oxfordshire.

[4] In 1072 Remigius transferred the see to Lincoln.

[5] Grimketel apparently held the sees of Selsey and Elmham together.

[6] Stigand had been elected in 1042, but was deposed before he had been consecrated.

[7] Translated to Winchester.

[8] Herfast removed the see to Thetford in 1075.

[9] After this the see was removed to Norwich, and the succession may be studied under that head.

[10] Translated from Bangor.

[11] The see of Ely was established in this year.

[12] Removed see from Crediton (*q.v.*) to Exeter in this year.

[13] From 1056 to 1060 he held Hereford with Worcester.

[14] Translated to York.

	Accession	Death or Translation
Walter	1061	1079
Robert Losinga	1079	26 June 1095
Gerard	1096	1101[1]
Reinhelm	1107	27 October 1115
Geoffrey 'de Clive'	1115	3 February 1120
Richard 'de capella'	1121	15 August 1127
Robert of Bethune	1131	16 April 1148
Gilbert Foliot	1148	1163[2]
Robert of Melun	1163	27 February 1167
Robert Foliot	1174	9 May 1186
William 'de Vere'	1186	24 December 1198

Lichfield, Chester and Coventry[3]

Wulfsige	1039	October 1053
Leofwine	1053	1067
Peter	1072	1085
Robert 'de Limesey'	1086	1 September 1117
Robert Peche	1121	22 August 1127
Roger 'de Clinton'	1129	16 April 1148
Walter Durdent	1149	7 December 1160
Richard Peche	1161	6 October 1182
Gerard 'la Pucelle'	1183	13 January 1184
Hugh Nonant	1188	27 March 1198

Lincoln

Remigius	(1072)[4]	7 May 1092
Robert Bloet	1094	10 January 1123
Alexander	1123	20 February 1148
Robert 'de Chesney'	1148	27 December 1166
Walter of Coutances	1183[5]	1184[6]
Hugh of Avalon	1186	16 November 1200

London

Ælfweard	1035	25 July 1044
Robert (of Jumièges)	1044	1051[7]
William	1051	1075
Hugh (of Orival)	1075	12 January 1085
Maurice	1086	26 September 1107
Richard 'of Beaumais' I	1108	16 January 1127
Gilbert 'the Universal'	1128	10 August 1134
Robert 'de Sigillo'	1141	1151
Richard 'of Beaumais' II	1152	4 May 1162
Gilbert Foliot	1163[8]	18 February 1187

[1] Translated to York. [2] Translated to London.

[3] Wulfsige and Leofwine were bishops of Lichfield. Peter took some steps to remove the see to Chester. Robert of Limesey, being bishop of Lichfield, removed his see to Coventry. All three titles were employed on occasion, but the normal style after 1102 was 'of Coventry'.

[4] Remigius in this year removed his see to Lincoln from Dorchester.

[5] Between 1173 and 1182 Geoffrey, natural son of King Henry II, was bishop-elect of Lincoln, but he is not usually recognized as forming part of the succession.

[6] Translated to Rouen. [7] Translated to Canterbury.

[8] Translated from Hereford.

	Accession	Death or Translation
	Norwich[1]	
Herbert Losinga	1091	22 July 1119
Everard of Montgomery	1121	Deprived 1145[2]
William 'de Turbe'	1146	17 January 1174
John (of Oxford)	1175	2 June 1200
	Ramsbury	
Beorhtweald	?	22 April 1045
Herman	1045	Resigned 1055. Subsequently re-established and continued to 1058[3]
	Rochester	
Godwine II	Before 1047	In or before 1058
Siward	1058	1075
Ernost	1076	15 July 1076
Gundulf	1077	7 March 1108
Ralph 'd'Escures'	1108	1114[4]
Ernulf	1115	15 March 1124
John	1125	22 June 1137
Ascelin	1142	24 January 1148
Walter	1148	26 July 1182
Waleran	1182	29 August 1184
Gilbert Glanville	1185	24 June 1214
	Salisbury[5]	
Osmund	1078	3 December 1099
Osmer	?	?
Roger	1107	4 or 11 December 1139
Jocelyn 'de Bohun'	1142	18 November 1184
	Selsey	
Grimketel[6]	1039	1047
Heca	1047	1057
Æthelric II	1058	Deprived May 1070
Stigand	1070	(1075)[7]
	Sherborne	
Ælfweald II	1045	1058
Herman[8]	1058	20 February 1078[9]

[1] For the earlier succession, see under Elmham.

[2] He died 15 October 1150.

[3] In 1058 Herman being bishop of Ramsbury was translated to Sherborne, but he joined the see of Ramsbury to that of Sherborne. For the succession, see under 'Sherborne' and 'Salisbury'.

[4] Translated to Canterbury.

[5] The see was removed in 1078 to Salisbury from Sherborne to which the see of Ramsbury had previously been joined. For the earlier succession see under 'Ramsbury' and 'Sherborne'.

[6] He also held the see of Elmham.

[7] The see was removed to Chichester in 1075. For further succession, see under 'Chichester'.

[8] Herman was bishop of Ramsbury when he obtained the see of Sherborne, and he combined the two sees.

[9] In 1078 the see was removed to Salisbury. The further succession can be studied under that head.

	Accession	Death or Translation
	Winchester	
Ælfwine	1032	29 August 1047
Stigand[1]	1047	Translated to Canterbury *q.v.*, but retained Winchester. Deprived 1070
Ælfsige III	?	?
Walkelin	1070	3 January 1098
William Giffard	1107	25 January 1129
Henry of Blois	1129	9 August 1171
Richard (of Ilchester)	1174	22 December 1188
	Worcester	
Lyfing[2]	1041	23 March 1046
Aldred	1047	1062[3]
Wulfstan II	1062	18 January 1095
Samson	1096	5 May 1112
Theulf	1115	20 October 1123
Simon	1125	20 March 1150
John (of Pagham)	1151	31 March 1158
Alfred	1158	31 July 1160
Roger (of Gloucester)	1164	9 August 1179
Baldwin	1180	1185[4]
William Northall	1186	3 May 1190
	PROVINCE OF YORK	
	York	
Ælfric Puttoc	? 1041[5]	22 January 1051
Cynesige	1051	22 January 1060
Aldred	1061[6]	11 September 1069
Thomas I	1070	18 November 1100
Gerard	1101	21 May 1108
Thomas II	1109	24 February 1114
Thurstan	1119	5 February 1140
William 'fitz Herbert'	1143	Deprived 1147
Henry Murdac	1147	14 October 1153
William 'fitz Herbert'	1153	8 June 1154
Roger of Pont l'Evêque	1154	26 November 1181[7]
	Carlisle[8]	
Adelulf	1133	1157

[1] See also under 'Canterbury' and 'Elmham'. He died 22 February 1072.

[2] See also under 'Crediton'.

[3] He was translated to York in 1061 and for a time held both York and Worcester. He was compelled to relinquish the latter in 1062.

[4] Translated to Canterbury.

[5] He had been archbishop from 1023. He was deprived (?) 1041 in favour of Æthelric, who was deprived in 1042. Ælfric Puttoc seems, however, to have been restored in 1041.

[6] Until 1062 he held York with Worcester, but in that year he was deprived of Worcester and subsequently only held York.

[7] Geoffrey, illegitimate son of Henry II, who was bishop-elect of Lincoln, 1173–1186 (see above, p. 1002), was archbishop-elect of York in 1189. He succeeded to the see of York in 1191.

[8] The see of Carlisle, created as a result of the acquisition of Cumbria by the Norman kings, received no bishop between 1157 and 1219. In 1203 it was placed in the hands of an administrator.

	Accession	Death or Translation
	Durham	
Æthelric	1042	Resigned 1056[1]
Æthelwine	1056	Deprived 1071[2]
Walcher	1071	14 May 1080
William of Saint-Calais	1081	1 January 1096
Rannulf Flambard	1099	5 September 1128
Geoffrey Rufus	1133	6 May 1140
William of Sainte-Barbe	1143	24 November 1152
Hugh of Le Puiset	1153	3 March 1195

[1] He died 15 October 1072.
[2] It is probable that he died in 1071.

IV. EASTER TABLE FOR THE PERIOD 1042–1189

In the texts contained in this volume many events are dated by reference to Easter, or by reference to feasts of the Church whose incidence is dependent upon that of Easter. In nearly every case when this has occurred the day of the month has been indicated. But in view of the language of many documents it may be convenient to display the dates at which Easter fell during this period; and it may also be noted for reference that:

Septuagesima falls *9 weeks before* Easter,
Sexagesima falls *8 weeks before* Easter,
Quinquagesima falls *7 weeks before* Easter,
Quadragesima falls *6 weeks before* Easter,
Ascension Day falls *39 days after* Easter,
Whitsunday falls *7 weeks after* Easter.

The Leap Years in this period are all those years whose last two digits are divisible by 4, and also the year 1100.

Dates of Easter

1042	April 11	1075	April 5	1108	April 5
1043	April 3	1076	March 27	1109	April 25
1044	April 22	1077	April 16	1110	April 10
1045	April 7	1078	April 8	1111	April 2
1046	March 30	1079	March 24	1112	April 21
1047	April 19	1080	April 12	1113	April 6
1048	April 3	1081	April 4	1114	March 29
1049	March 26	1082	April 24	1115	April 18
1050	April 15	1083	April 9	1116	April 2
1051	March 31	1084	March 31	1117	March 25
1052	April 19	1085	April 20	1118	April 14
1053	April 11	1086	April 5	1119	March 30
1054	April 3	1087	March 28	1120	April 18
1055	April 16	1088	April 16	1121	April 10
1056	April 7	1089	April 1	1122	March 26
1057	March 30	1090	April 21	1123	April 15
1058	April 19	1091	April 13	1124	April 6
1059	April 4	1092	March 28	1125	March 29
1060	March 26	1093	April 17	1126	April 11
1061	April 15	1094	April 9	1127	April 3
1062	March 31	1095	March 25	1128	April 22
1063	April 20	1096	April 13	1129	April 14
1064	April 11	1097	April 5	1130	March 30
1065	March 27	1098	March 28	1131	April 19
1066	April 16	1099	April 10	1132	April 10
1067	April 8	1100	April 1	1133	March 26
1068	March 23	1101	April 21	1134	April 15
1069	April 12	1102	April 6	1135	April 7
1070	April 4	1103	March 29	1136	March 22
1071	April 24	1104	April 17	1137	April 11
1072	April 8	1105	April 9	1138	April 3
1073	March 31	1106	March 25	1139	April 23
1074	April 20	1107	April 14	1140	April 7

Year	Easter	Year	Easter	Year	Easter
1141	March 30	1158	April 20	1175	April 13
1142	April 19	1159	April 12	1176	April 4
1143	April 4	1160	March 27	1177	April 24
1144	March 26	1161	April 16	1178	April 9
1145	April 15	1162	April 8	1179	April 1
1146	March 31	1163	March 24	1180	April 20
1147	April 20	1164	April 12	1181	April 5
1148	April 11	1165	April 4	1182	March 28
1149	April 3	1166	April 24	1183	April 17
1150	April 16	1167	April 9	1184	April 1
1151	April 8	1168	March 31	1185	April 21
1152	March 30	1169	April 20	1186	April 13
1153	April 19	1170	April 5	1187	March 29
1154	April 4	1171	March 28	1188	April 17
1155	March 27	1172	April 16	1189	April 9
1156	April 15	1173	April 8		
1157	March 31	1174	March 24		

INDEX TO TEXTS

The figures refer to the numbered documents. In the few cases when, for the sake of clarity, it has been found necessary to add a page reference, this has been placed within parentheses.